STRATEGY

AN INTERNATIONAL PERSPECTIVE

To Pam and Liz
and
Leen and Anneke
Family matters

SIXTH EDITION

STRATEGY

AN INTERNATIONAL PERSPECTIVE

The first four editions of *Strategy: Process, Content and Context* were co-authored by Bob de Wit and Ron Meyer. The fifth and sixth editions were authored by Bob de Wit.

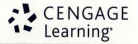
CENGAGE
Learning·

Australia • Brazil • Mexico • Singapore • United Kingdom • United States

**Strategy: An International Perspective,
6th Edition**
Bob de Wit

Publisher: Annabel Ainscow

Commissioning Editor: Jenny Grene

Content Project Manager: Melissa Beavis

Manufacturing Manager: Eyvett Davis

Marketing Manager: Vicky Pavlicic

Typesetter: Lumina Datamatics

Cover design: Jeroen Brinkhuis

Text design: Lumina Datamatics

© 2017, Cengage Learning EMEA

While the publisher has taken all reasonable care in the preparation of this book, the publisher makes no representation, express or implied, with regard to the accuracy of the information contained in this book and cannot accept any legal responsibility or liability for any errors or omissions from the book or the consequences thereof.

Products and services that are referred to in this book may be either trademarks and/or registered trademarks of their respective owners. The publishers and author/s make no claim to these trademarks. The publisher does not endorse, and accepts no responsibility or liability for, incorrect or defamatory content contained in hyperlinked material.

All the URLs in this book are correct at the time of going to press; however the Publisher accepts no responsibility for the content and continued availability of third party websites.

For product information and technology assistance,
contact **emea.info@cengage.com**.

For permission to use material from this text or product,
and for permission queries,
email **emea.permissions@cengage.com**.

British Library Cataloguing-in-Publication Data
A catalogue record for this book is available from the British Library.

ISBN: 978-1-4737-2515-7

Cengage Learning EMEA
Cheriton House, North Way, Andover, Hampshire, SP10 5BE
United Kingdom

Cengage Learning products are represented in Canada by Nelson Education Ltd.

For your lifelong learning solutions, visit **www.cengage.co.uk**

Purchase your next print book or e-book at
www.cengagebrain.com

Printed in Croatia by Zrinski d.d.
Print Number: 01   Print Year: 2017

BRIEF CONTENTS

CONTENTS

SECTION

I

STRATEGY   1

SECTION V

CASES   653

LIST OF EXHIBITS

ACKNOWLEDGEMENTS

The meaning of life is not to be discovered only after death in some hidden, mysterious realm; on the contrary, it can be found by eating the succulent fruit of the Tree of Life and by living in the here and now as fully and creatively as we can.

Paul Winter Kurtz (1925–2012); American sceptic and secular humanist

Only one professor should have been nominated as role model for students; only one colleague as university professor benchmark; only one human as friend exemplar; one man as perfect husband and father. He is the one who understood the meaning of life in full by eating the succulent fruit of the Tree of Life and by living in the here and now. I worked with him in our early university career, and again many years later. This man contributed to the previous edition of this book, with the intention of cooperating in many more editions. Tragically, on 15 June 2015, while cycling up the Col du Galibier in the French Alps, enjoying life to the full, my colleague and friend Gep Eisenloeffel suffered a stroke and passed away in the arms of his wife, Nienke. I miss him dearly still, and my thoughts remain with Nienke and their daughter Katrien.

Life continued of course, and apart from an empty heart I also had an empty diary. During the summer of 2015 I had planned to start work with Gep on the next edition of this book, especially on the international perspective sections. Katrien very kindly donated Gep's library to our brilliant student from Leiden University, Wester Wagenaar, who had also contributed to the previous edition. Wester picked up the work, and although not yet as experienced as Gep, he has done a marvellous job.

As in previous editions, this sixth edition brings together the work of great people in the management field, chiefly from the field of strategy. I thank them for creating new knowledge and insights, for their inspiration and hard work, and for developing the management field to where it is today. Writing this book would not have been possible without the current academic knowledge base and the authors of many phenomenal papers. I also apologize for not being able to include all of the excellent contributions: as the architect of this edition I read many excellent papers, but since there is a limitation to a book's size I could select only a few. It was simply not possible to include all the great papers and, therefore, several tough and (sometimes) personal choices had to be made.

I would like to thank the professors who select the book as the basis of class discussions, to help students develop their strategic mind. As in previous editions, many improvements to this sixth edition are based on the feedback of professors who have used earlier editions in their classrooms. I am grateful for their valuable insights, and for sharing their experiences. Many thanks also to other academic colleagues: the anonymous reviewers of the manuscript and particularly Paul Knott, who has been so kind to update his great Fonterra short case again.

I would also like to thank all of my colleagues at *Nyenrode Business University*, including management, support staff and faculty, and particularly my strategy department colleagues: Jeroen van der Velden for updating the short case on 3M, Claudia Janssen for providing recent insights on the short case on TomTom, and Jeroen Brinkhuis. Jeroen has helped develop the book's navigation tool, *Tree of Strategy,* and has then spent many hours designing the book cover on the basis of the Tree of Strategy.

Developing this edition has also been an enormous effort of my *Strategy Works* team members, and particularly (in alphabetical order) Adriaan de Bruijn, Alexandra Fulea, Christien van Rijs, Jasper de Vries and Roel Meijers. I am extremely proud and grateful to be a member of this tremendous team. Special thanks are due to our research associate, Sander Wisman. Sander has spent numerous hours – beyond duty and often working throughout the night until sunrise – reading and pre-selecting the growing number of publications and cases in the strategy field, and also co-developing short cases and illustrations. Not only has Sander been very committed, he has also proved to be a safe pair of hands, which with hindsight is not surprising as his main interest and thesis topic for his Leiden University study is cyber security.

Leiden University is also Wester Wagenaar's alma mater. While finishing his Japanese Studies degree, Wester had already contributed to the previous edition of this book, by co-developing short cases and illustrations, just before he moved to Nagasaki to finish his thesis. Wester then studied in Sweden, Germany and Japan for his Master's in *Euroculture: Society, Politics and Culture in a Global Context*. While in Uppsala, Sweden, our cooperation on this book resumed. This was in itself not surprising as it had been previously planned, however the timing and magnitude of his contribution to this edition was not anticipated. Gep Eisenloeffel's untimely death in June 2015 was unexpected and extremely tragic, but it forged the beginning of an intellectual cooperation with Wester. Although my expectations of Wester's academic talents were already high, he has exceeded them by far. His academic performances are at peak professional standards – easily matching those of experienced academics – which combined with his phenomenal linguistic capabilities have significantly contributed to what I consider to be the best edition of this book. Apart from the already mentioned international perspective sections, Wester has co-authored 16 short cases and illustrations.

I would also like to thank the Cengage Learning team I have worked with on this new edition. In particular, I thank Andrew Ashwin for trusting me to develop the new editions, and Jennifer Grene for doing an incredible job in managing this great project. Also I will not forget the man who got us started over 20 years ago, our first editor, David Godden. Thank you all.

Finally, and most importantly, I would like to thank my family: my wife Pamela, my daughter Liz, my father Leen and his partner Anneke. Thank you so much. I promise that in the immediate future I will be eating the succulent fruit of the Tree of Life and be living in the here and now as fully and creatively as I can.

AUTHOR BIOGRAPHY:

Bob de Wit is Professor of Strategic Leadership at Nyenrode Business University, The Netherlands. He is also founder and director of Strategy Works and Strategy Academy in Rotterdam. Bob is a member of the *Journal of Change Management* Advisory Board, and a reviewer for the Strategic Management Society conference. His mission is to combine academic rigour and practical relevance.

Bob holds a bachelor's degree in Psychology from Utrecht University, an MBA at the Interdisciplinary Institute Bedrijfskunde in Delft, and a PhD degree in Management Science from Erasmus University, Rotterdam. After graduation he became a professor in Strategic Management at the Rotterdam School of Management, Erasmus University, teaching Strategy in MSc programmes and the international MBA programme. In 1996 he started working at the Maastricht School of Management, a market leader in management education in non-Western countries. Since then, Bob has taught in over 40 countries on all continents. Bob has served as the Chairman of Interest Group 'The Practice of Strategy' of the Strategic Management Society, and the Dutch Society for Strategic Decision Making (VSB), and has been a member of the Academic Council of the *Ecole Nationale des Ponts et Chaussees* in Paris.

Bob passionately loves his wife Pamela and daughter Liz.

PREFACE

*Not only is there an art in knowing a thing,
but also a certain art in teaching it.*

Cicero (106–43 BC); Roman orator and statesman

What is a good strategy for teaching and learning about the topic of strategy? Judging by the similarity of the strategic management textbooks currently available, there seems to be a general consensus among business professors on the best approach to this task. It is not an exaggeration to say that strategic management education is dominated by a strong *industry recipe* (Spender, 1989). Almost all textbooks share the following characteristics:

- *Few differing perspectives.* Only a limited number of perspectives and theories are presented, often as accepted knowledge, from which prescriptions can easily be derived.

- *Step-by-step structure.* A step-by-step strategic planning approach is used as the books' basic structure, to decompose strategy-making into a number of simple sequential activities.

- *No primary material.* The key academic articles and books on strategy are reworked into the textbook authors' own words to create consistent and easily digestible pieces of text.

- *Domestic orientation.* Despite fancy subtitles referring to globalization, the choice of perspectives, theories, examples and cases are heavily biased towards the textbook authors' own domestic context.

It is interesting to speculate on the causes of this isomorphism in the 'strategic management education' industry. Institutionalists would probably point to the need for legitimacy, which leads textbook authors to conform to widely accepted practices and to avoid major innovations (e.g. Abrahamson, 1996; Powell and DiMaggio, 1991). Social psychologists would likely suggest that over the years shared cognitive structures have developed within the strategic management community, which makes the prevailing educational paradigm difficult to challenge (e.g. Smircich and Stubbart, 1985; Walsh, 1995). Theorists taking a new institutional economics perspective would probably interpret the uniformity of strategic management textbooks as a form of lock-in, caused by the large investments already made by publishers and business professors based on a shared educational 'standard' (e.g. Arthur, 1996; David, 1994). Whatever the reason, it is striking that the character of strategic management textbooks has not significantly changed since the founding of the field.

But what would strategy education look like if educational orthodoxy was actively challenged and the industry rules broken? How might strategy be taught if the current constraints were thrown aside and the teaching process was boldly reinvented? In short, what would happen if some strategic thinking was applied to the teaching of strategy?

During the last 20 years, we have constantly asked ourselves these questions. Our conclusion is that all four of the above features of current strategic management textbooks greatly inhibit the development of independent strategic thinkers and therefore urgently need to be changed. It is for this reason that we decided to create a book ourselves, with the following characteristics:

- *Multiple strategy perspectives.* A broad range of differing, and often opposite, perspectives and theories are presented, reflecting the richness of current debate among academics and practitioners in the field of strategic management.
- *Issue-based structure.* An issue-based book structure is used, with each chapter focusing on a key strategic issue, which is discussed from a variety of angles, leaving readers to draw their own conclusions.
- *Original readings.* A large number of original articles and book chapters are included, to offer readers a first-hand account of the ideas and theories of influential strategy thinkers.
- *International orientation.* A strong international orientation is at the core of this book, as reflected in the choice of topics, theories, readings, examples and cases.

In the following paragraphs the rationale behind the choice for these characteristics is explained. Following this discussion, the structure of the book and the ways in which it can be employed is further clarified.

USING MULTIPLE STRATEGY PERSPECTIVES

Learning without thought is labour lost; thought without learning is perilous.
Confucius (551–479 BC); Chinese teacher, editor, politician and philosopher

What should students learn on a strategic management or business policy course? It seems an obvious question to start with, especially for professors who teach about objective setting. Yet, in practice, the large majority of strategic management textbooks do not make their teaching objectives explicit. These books implicitly assume that the type of teaching objectives and teaching methods needed for a strategic management course do not radically differ from any other subject - basically, strategy can be taught in the same way as accounting or baking cookies. Their approach is based on the following teaching objectives:

- *Knowledge.* To get the student to clearly understand and memorize all of the major 'ingredients'.
- *Skills.* To develop the student's ability to follow the detailed 'recipes'.
- *Attitude.* To instill a disciplined frame of mind, whereby the student automatically attempts to approach all issues by following established procedures.

This is an important way of teaching – it is how all of us were taught to read and write, do arithmetic and drive a car. This type of teaching can be referred to as *instructional*, because students are told what to know and do. The instructor is the authority who has all of the necessary knowledge and skills, and it is his/her role to transfer these to the students. Thus, the educational emphasis is on communicating know-how and ensuring that students are able to repeat what they have heard. Students are not encouraged to question the knowledge they receive – on the contrary, it is the intention of instructional teaching to get students to absorb an accepted body of knowledge and to follow established recipes. The student should *accept, absorb* and *apply.*

However, while instructing students on a subject and programming their behaviour that might be useful in such areas as mathematics, cooking and karate, we believe it is not a very good way of teaching strategy. In our opinion, a strategic management professor should have a different set of teaching objectives:

- *Knowledge.* To encourage the understanding of the many, often conflicting, schools of thought and to facilitate developing insight into the assumptions, possibilities and limitations of each set of theories.
- *Skills.* To develop the student's ability to define strategic issues, to critically reflect on existing theories, to creatively combine or develop conceptual models where necessary and to flexibly employ theories where useful.
- *Attitude.* To instill a critical, analytical, flexible and creative mindset that challenges organizational, industry and national paradigms and problem-solving recipes.

In other words, strategy professors should want to achieve the opposite of instructors – not to instill recipes, but rather to encourage students to dissect and challenge recipes. Strategic thinking is in its very essence questioning, challenging, unconventional and innovative. These aspects of strategic thinking cannot be transferred through instruction. A critical, analytical, flexible and creative state of mind must be developed by practising these very qualities. Hence, a learning situation must encourage students to be critical, must challenge them to be analytical, must force them to be mentally flexible and must demand creativity and unconventional thinking. Students cannot be instructed to be strategists, but must learn the art of strategy by thinking and acting for themselves – they must *discuss, deliberate* and *do*. The role of the professor is to create the circumstances for this learning. We therefore refer to this type of teaching as *facilitative*.

This teaching philosophy has led to a radical departure from traditional textbooks that focus on knowledge transfer and application skills, and that have often been written from the perspective of just one paradigm. In this book, the fundamental differences of opinion within strategic management are not ignored or smoothed over. On the contrary, an important objective of this book is to expose students to the many, often opposite, perspectives in the field of strategy. It is our experience that the challenge of comparing and reconciling rival strategy perspectives sharpens the mind of the 'apprentice' strategists. Throwing students into the midst of the central strategy debates, while simultaneously demanding that they apply their thinking to practical strategic problems, is the most likely way to enhance the qualities of creativity, flexibility, independence and analytical depth that students will need to become true strategic thinkers.

FOCUSING ON STRATEGY ISSUES

Some people are so good at learning the tricks of the trade that they never get to learn the trade.
Sam Levenson (1911–1980); American teacher and comedian

While it is the objective of this book to increase students' strategic thinking abilities by exposing them to a wide range of theories and perspectives, it is not the intention to confuse and disorient. Yet in a subject area like strategic management, in which there is a broad spectrum of different views, there is a realistic threat that students might go deaf listening to the cacophony of different opinions. The variety of ideas can easily become overwhelming and difficult to integrate.

For this reason, the many theories, models, approaches and perspectives have been clustered around eleven central strategy issues, each of which is discussed in a separate chapter. These eleven strategy issues represent the key questions with which strategists must deal in practice. Only the theorists whose ideas have a direct bearing on the issue at hand are discussed in each chapter.

The advantage of this issue-based book structure is that it is *decision-oriented* – each chapter is about a key type of strategic decision that needs to be made. Students are challenged to look at a strategic issue holistically, taking various aspects and perspectives into account, and to arrive at a proposed course of action. This type of decision-focus closely reflects what strategizing managers need to do in practice. Step-by-step books are much more *tool-oriented*, teaching students how to go through each phase of a strategic planning process and how to use each analysis framework – useful, especially for junior analysts, but unlikely to stimulate real strategic thinking and to provide insight into difficult strategic choices.

Within each chapter, the opposing perspectives on how the strategic issue should be approached are contrasted with one another by staging a virtual 'debate'. Two opposite perspectives are presented to kick off the debate and highlight areas of disagreement, after which the students (and their professors) are invited to further debate the issue and decide on the value and limitations of each point of view.

The advantage of this debate-based chapter structure is that it encourages the students' engagement and also provokes critical thinking. As students need to determine the strengths and weaknesses of each strategy perspective, they also become more adept at combining different 'lenses' to gain a fuller understanding of a problem, while becoming more skilled at balancing and mixing prescriptions to find innovative solutions to these problems. Some students will feel ill at ease at not being presented with the 'right approach' or the 'best practice', as they are used to getting in many other books. This is all the more reason to avoid giving them one – as strategizing managers the security of one truth won't get them far, so it is preferable to learn to deal with (and benefit from) a variety of opinions as soon as possible.

While the intention is not to present the 'right answer' or provide a 'grand unifying theory', the chapter offers a third view on the issue that combines elements of both perspectives. Not only leaders take elements of both perspectives into account to manage the issue at hand, increasingly also strategy theorists do. Recent works of thought leaders in the strategy field address a third way of dealing with the issue, not by choosing one of the opposite perspectives, but by providing possible routes on how to deal with opposites. This third view is meant to stimulate students' strategic thinking, to find innovative and creative resolutions to the problem, but still students must make up their own minds, depending on the context and based on the arguments placed before them.

TAKING AN INTERNATIONAL PERSPECTIVE

Be bent, and you will remain straight.
Be vacant, and you will remain full.
Be worn, and you will remain new.
Lao Tzu (6th century BC); philosopher of ancient China

This book has been explicitly developed with an international audience in mind. For students, the international orientation of this book has a number of distinct advantages:

- *Cross-cultural differences.* Although there has been relatively little cross-cultural research in the field of strategy, results so far indicate that there are significant differences in strategy styles between companies from different countries. This calls into question the habit among strategy researchers of presenting universal theories, without indicating the cultural assumptions on which their ideas have been based. It is not unlikely that strategy theories have a strong cultural bias and therefore cannot be simply transferred from one national setting to another. Much of the debate going on between strategy theorists might actually be based on such divergent cultural assumptions. In this book the issue of cross-cultural differences in strategy style is raised in each chapter, to discuss whether strategists need to adapt their theories, perspectives and approaches to the country in which they are operating.

■ *International context.* Besides adapting to a specific country, many companies are operating in a variety of countries at the same time. In this international arena they are confronted with a distinct set of issues, ranging from global integration and coordination, to localization and transnationalization. This set of issues presented by the international context is debated in depth in Chapter 12.

■ *International cases and illustrations.* To explore how the various strategy perspectives can be applied to different national contexts, it is imperative to have cases and illustrations from a wide variety of countries, spread around the world. In this book the 24 cases (12 long and 12 short cases) cover more than 20 countries and most of the cases have an international orientation. The 22 main illustrations have also been drawn from around the world. It must be noted, however, that we have had a bias towards well-known firms, as these examples are more recognizable to most global audiences.

USING ORIGINAL READINGS

Education is not filling a bucket but lighting a fire.
William Butler Yeats (1865–1939); Irish poet and dramatist

There are no better and livelier debates than when rivals put forward their own ideas as forcefully as they can. For this reason, we have chosen to structure the strategy debates by letting influential theorists speak for themselves. Instead of translating the important ideas of key writers into our own words, each chapter contains three original readings in which the theorists state their own case. These three readings can be viewed as the discussants in the debate, while our role is that of chairmen – we set the stage for the debate and introduce the various perspectives and 'speakers', but as conscientious chairmen we avoid taking a position in the debate ourselves.

The three readings in each chapter have been selected with a number of criteria in mind. As a starting point, we were looking for the articles or books that are widely judged to be classics in the field of strategy. However, to ensure the broad representation of different perspectives, we occasionally looked beyond established classics to find a challenging minority point of view. Finally, discussants are only as good as their ability to communicate to the non-initiated, and therefore we have sometimes excluded certain classics as too technical.

To keep the size of the book within acceptable limits, most readings have had to be reduced in length, while extensive footnotes and references have been dropped. At all times this editing has been guided by the principle that the author's key ideas and arguments must be preserved intact. To compensate for the loss of references in each article, a combined list of the most important references has been added to the end of each chapter.

CONTACT US

A stand can be made against invasion by an army; no stand can be made against invasion by an idea.

Victor Hugo (1802–1885); French poet, novelist and playwright

Books are old-fashioned, but based on a proven technology that is still the most appropriate under most circumstances. One drawback, however, is that a book is unidirectional, allowing us to send a message to you, but not capable of transmitting your comments, questions and suggestions back to us. This is unfortunate, as we are keen on communicating with our audience and enjoy hearing what works and doesn't work 'in the field'.

Therefore, we would like to encourage both students and professors to establish contact with us. You can do this by visiting our online support resources to check out the extra features we have for you and to leave your comments and suggestions. But you can also contact us directly by email at **b.dewit@nyenrode.nl**

REFERENCES

Abrahamson, E. (1996) 'Management Fashion', *Academy of Management Review,* 21, pp. 254–285.

Arthur, W.B. (1996) 'Increasing Returns and the New World of Business', *Harvard Business Review,* July/August, pp. 100–109.

David, P.A. (1994) 'Why are Institutions the "Carriers of History"?: Path Dependence and the Evolution of Conventions, Organizations and Institutions', *Structural Change and Economic Dynamics,* pp. 205–220.

Powell, W.W. and DiMaggio, P.P. (eds) (1991) *The New Institutionalism in Organization Analysis,* Chicago, IL: University of Chicago Press.

Smircich, L. and Stubbart, C. (1985) 'Strategic Management in an Enacted World', *Academy of Management Review,* 10, pp. 724–736.

Spender, J.C. (1989) *Industry Recipes: The Nature and Sources of Managerial Judgement,* Oxford: Basil Blackwell.

Walsh, J. (1995) 'Managerial and Organizational Cognition: Notes from a Trip Down Memory Lane', *Organization Science,* 6, pp. 280–321.

Digital Support Resources

All of our Higher Education textbooks are accompanied by a range of digital support resources. Each title's resources are carefully tailored to the specific needs of the particular book's readers. Examples of the kind of resources provided include:

- A password protected area for instructors with, for example, a testbank, PowerPoint slides and an instructor's manual.

- An open-access area for students including, for example, useful weblinks and glossary terms.

Lecturers: to discover the dedicated lecturer digital support resources accompanying this textbook please register here for access: login.cengage.com.

Students: to discover the dedicated student digital support resources accompanying this textbook, please search for **Strategy: An International Perspective** on: cengagebrain.co.uk

STRATEGY

INTRODUCTION

As conflict – difference – is here in the world, as we cannot avoid it, we should, I think, use it.

Mary Parker Follett (1868–1933); American social worker, management consultant and pioneer in organizational theory and organizational behaviour.

THE NATURE OF STRATEGY

In a book entitled *Strategy*, it seems reasonable to expect Chapter 1 to begin with a clear definition of strategy that would be employed with consistency in all subsequent chapters. An early and precise definition would help to avoid conflicting interpretations of what should be considered strategy and, by extension, what should be understood by the term 'strategic management'. However, any such sharp definition of strategy here would actually be misleading. It would suggest that there is widespread agreement among practitioners, researchers and theorists as to what strategy is. The impression would be given that the fundamental concepts in the area of strategy are generally accepted and hardly questioned. Yet, even a quick glance through current strategy literature indicates otherwise. There are strongly differing opinions on most of the key issues, and the disagreements run so deep that even a common definition of the term 'strategy' is illusive.

This is bad news for those who prefer simplicity and certainty. It means that the topic of strategy cannot be explained as a set of straightforward definitions and rules to be memorized and applied. The strongly conflicting views mean that strategy cannot be summarized into broadly agreed-on definitions, rules, matrices and flow diagrams that one must simply absorb and learn to use. If the fundamental differences of opinion are not swept aside, the consequence is that a book on strategy cannot be like an instruction manual that takes you through the steps of how something should be done. On the contrary, a strategy book should acknowledge the disagreements and encourage thinking about the value of each of the different points of view. That is the intention of this book.

The philosophy embraced here is that an understanding of the topic of strategy can only be gained by grappling with the diversity of insights presented by so many prominent thinkers and by coming to terms with the fact that there is no simple answer to the question of what strategy is. Readers who prefer the certainty of reading only one opinion, as opposed to the intellectual stimulation of being confronted with a wide variety, should read no further – there are plenty of alternatives available. Those who wish to proceed should lay aside their 'opinions of habit', and open their minds to the many other opinions presented, for in these pages there is 'knowledge in the making'.

IDENTIFYING THE STRATEGY ISSUES

If the only tool you have is a hammer, you treat everything like a nail.
Abraham Maslow (1908–1970); American psychologist

The approach taken in this book is in line with the moral of Maslow's remark. To avoid hammering strategy issues with only one theory, a variety of ways of viewing strategic questions will be presented. But there are two different ways of presenting a broad spectrum of theoretical lenses. This point can be made clear by extending Maslow's hammer-and-nail analogy. To become a good carpenter, who wisely uses a variety of tools depending on what is being crafted, an apprentice carpenter will need to learn about these different instruments. One way is for the apprentice to study the characteristics and functioning of all tools individually and only then to apply each where appropriate. However, another possibility is for the apprentice to first learn about what must be crafted, getting a feel for the materials and the problems that must be solved, and only then to turn to the study of the necessary tools. The first approach to learning can be called 'tools-driven' – understanding each tool comes first, while combining them to solve real problems comes later. The second approach to learning can be termed 'problem-driven' – understanding problems comes first, while searching for the appropriate tools is based on the type of problem.

Both options can also be used for the apprentice strategist. In a tools-driven approach to learning about strategy, all major theories would first be understood separately, to be compared or combined later when using them in practice. A logical structure for a book aiming at this mode of learning would be to allot one chapter to each of the major theories or schools of thought. The advantage of such a theory-based book structure would be that each chapter would focus on giving the reader a clear and cohesive overview of one major theory within the field of strategy. For readers with an interest in grasping the essence of each theory individually, this would probably be the ideal book format. However, the principal disadvantage of a theory-by-theory summary of the field of strategy would be that the reader would not have a clear picture of how the various theories relate to one another. The apprentice strategist would be left with important questions such as: Where do the theories agree and where do they differ? Which strategy phenomena does each theory claim to explain and which phenomena are left unaccounted for? Can various theories be successfully combined or are they based on mutually exclusive assumptions? And which strategy is right, or at least most appropriate under particular circumstances? Not knowing the answers to these questions, how could the apprentice strategist try to apply these new theoretical tools to practice?

This book is based on the assumption that the reader wants to learn to actively resolve strategic problems. Understanding the broad spectrum of theories is not an end in itself, but a means for more effective strategizing. Therefore, the problem-driven approach to learning about strategy has been adopted. In this approach, key strategy issues are first identified and then each is looked at from the perspective of the most appropriate theories. This has resulted in an issue-based book structure, in which each chapter deals with a particular set of strategy issues. In each chapter, only the theories that shed some light on the issues under discussion are brought forward and compared to one another. Of course, some theories are relevant to more than one set of issues and therefore appear in various chapters.

In total, 11 sets of strategy issues have been identified that together largely cover the field of strategic management. These 11 will be the subjects of the remaining 11 chapters of this book. How the various strategy issues have been divided into these 11 sets are explained in the following paragraphs.

Strategizing, missioning and visioning

Section I of this book addresses two important inputs for strategy: the cognitive processes of individual strategists (strategizing) and purpose as the impetus for strategy activities (missioning and visioning).

It is widely presumed that strategists are rational actors who identify, determine, evaluate, choose, translate and carry out, based on rigorous logic and extensive knowledge of all important factors. This belief has been challenged, however. Many authors have criticized the strong emphasis on rationality in these traditional views of the strategizing process. Some writers have even argued that the true nature of strategic thinking is more intuitive and creative than rational. In their opinion, strategizing is about perceiving strengths and weaknesses, envisioning opportunities and threats, and creating the future, for which imagination and judgement are more important than analysis and logic. This constitutes quite a fundamental disagreement about the cognitive processes of the strategizing leader. These issues surrounding the nature of strategic thinking will be discussed in Chapter 2 on strategizing.

Making strategy is not an end in itself, but a means for reaching particular objectives. Organizations exist to fulfil a purpose and strategies are employed to ensure that the organizational mission and vision are realized. Oddly enough, most authors write about missions and visions without any reference to the organizational purpose being pursued. It is generally assumed that all organizations exist for the same basic reasons and that this purpose is self-evident. However, in reality, there is extensive disagreement about what the current purposes of organizations are, and especially about what their purpose should be. Some people argue that it is the business of business to make money. In their view, firms are owned by shareholders and therefore should pursue shareholders' interests. And it is the primary interest of shareholders to see the value of their stocks increase. On the other hand, others believe that companies exist to serve the interests of multiple stakeholders. In their opinion, having a financial stake in a firm should not give shareholders a dominant position vis-à-vis other groups that also have an interest in what the organization does. Other stakeholders usually include employees, customers, suppliers and bankers, but could also include the local community, the broader industry and even the natural environment. These issues on the organizational purpose will be discussed in Chapter 3 on missioning and visioning.

Strategy dimensions: Content, process and context

The most fundamental distinction made in this book is between strategy content, strategy process and strategy context (see Figure 1.1). These are the three dimensions of strategy that can be recognized in every real-life strategic problem situation. They can be generally defined as follows:

- Strategy content. The combined decisions and choices that lead a company into the future are referred to as the strategy content. Stated in terms of a question, strategy content is concerned with the *what* of strategy: what is, and should be, the strategy for the company and each of its constituent units?

- Strategy process. The manner in which strategies come about is referred to as the strategy process. Stated in terms of a number of questions, strategy process is concerned with the *how, who* and *when* of strategy: how is, and should, strategy be made, analysed, dreamt-up, formulated, implemented, changed and controlled; who is involved; and when do the necessary activities take place?

- Strategy context. The set of circumstances under which both the strategy content and the strategy process are determined is referred to as the strategy context. Stated in terms of a question, strategy context is concerned with the *where* of strategy: where (that is in which firm and which environment) are the strategy process and strategy content embedded?

FIGURE 1.1   Dimensions of strategy and the organizational purpose

It cannot be emphasized enough that strategy content, process and context are not different parts of strategy, but are distinguishable dimensions. Just as it is silly to speak of the length, width and height parts of a box, one cannot speak of the three parts of strategy either. Each strategic problem situation is by its nature three-dimensional, possessing process, content and context characteristics, and only the understanding of all three dimensions will give the strategist real depth of comprehension. In particular, it must be acknowledged that the three dimensions interact (Ketchen, Thomas and McDaniel, 1996; Pettigrew and Whipp, 1991). For instance, the manner in which the strategy process is organized will have a significant impact on the resulting strategy content, while likewise, the content of the current strategy will strongly influence the way in which the strategy process will be conducted in future. If these linkages are ignored, the strategist will have a flat view instead of a three-dimensional view of strategy. A useful analytical distinction for temporarily unravelling a strategic problem situation will have turned into a permanent means for fragmenting reality.

However, it is possible to concentrate on one of the strategy dimensions if the other two are kept in mind. In fact, to have a focused discussion it is even necessary to look at one dimension at a time. The alternative is a debate in which all topics on all three dimensions would be discussed simultaneously: such a cacophony of opinions would be lively, but most likely less than fruitful. Therefore, the content–process–context distinction is cautiously used as the main structuring principle of this book, splitting the text into three major sections.

Most strategy research, by its very nature, is more atomistic than holistic, focusing on just a few variables at once. Consequently, most writings on strategy, including most of the theories discussed in this book, tend to favour just one, or at most two, strategy dimensions, which is usually complex enough given the need to remain comprehensible. In particular, the divide between strategy content and strategy process has been quite pronounced, to the extent of worrying some scholars about whether the connections between the two are being sufficiently recognized (Pettigrew, 1992). Although sharing this concern, use of the content–process–context–purpose distinction here reflects the reality of the current state of debate within the field of strategic management.

Strategy content: Business, corporate and network levels

Section II of this book will deal with the strategy content. Strategies come in all shapes and sizes, and almost all strategy writers, researchers and practitioners agree that each strategy is essentially unique. There is widespread disagreement, however, about the principles to which strategies should adhere. The debates are numerous, but there are three fundamental sets of issues around which most conflicts generally centre. These three topics can be clarified by distinguishing the level of strategy at which each is most relevant.

Strategies can be made for different groups of people or activities within an organization. The lowest level of aggregation is one person or task, while the highest level of aggregation encompasses all people or activities within an organization. The most common distinction between levels of aggregation made in the strategic management literature is between the functional, business and corporate levels (see Figure 1.2). Strategy issues at the *functional level* refer to questions regarding specific functional aspects of a company (operations strategy, marketing strategy, financial strategy, etc.). Strategy at the *business level* requires the integration of functional level strategies for a distinct set of products and/or services intended for a specific group of customers. Often companies only operate in one such business, so that this is the highest level of aggregation within the firm. However, there are also many companies that are in two or more businesses. In such companies, a multi-business or *corporate level* strategy is required, which aligns the various business level strategies.

A logical extension of the functional–business–corporate distinction is to explicitly recognize the level of aggregation higher than the individual organization. Firms often cluster together into groups of two or more collaborating organizations. This level is referred to as the multi-company or *network level*. Most multi-company groups consist of only a few parties, as is the case in strategic alliances, joint ventures and value-adding partnerships. However, networks can also have dozens, even hundreds, of participants. In some circumstances, the corporation as a whole might be a member of a group, while in other situations only a part of the firm joins forces with other organizations. In all cases, when a strategy is developed for a group of firms, this is called a network level strategy.

In line with the generally accepted boundaries of the strategic management field, this book focuses on the business, corporate and network levels of strategy, although this will often demand consideration of strategy issues at the functional level as well. In Section II, on the strategy content, the different strategy issues encountered at the different levels of strategy will be explored. And at each level of strategy, the focus will be on the fundamental differences of opinion that divide strategy theorists.

Chapter 4 deals with strategy issues at the business level. Here the fundamental debate surrounds whether firms are, and should be, primarily market-driven or resource-driven. Some authors argue that firms should be strongly externally oriented, engaged in a game of positioning vis-à-vis customers, competitors, suppliers and other parties in the environment, and should adapt the firm to the demands of the game. In other words, companies should think 'outside-in'. Yet, other authors strongly disagree, stressing the need for companies to exploit and expand their strengths. They recommend a more 'inside-out' view, whereby companies search for environments and positions that best fit with their resource base.

Chapter 5 is concerned with strategy issues at the corporate level. The fundamental debate in this chapter is whether corporations are, and should be, run as federations of autonomous business units or as highly integrated organizations. Some authors argue that corporate strategists should view themselves as investors, with financial stakes in a portfolio of business units. As a shrewd investor, the corporate centre should buy up cheap companies, divest underperforming business units, and invest its business units with the highest profit potential, independent of what industry they are in. Each business unit should be judged on its merits and given a large measure of autonomy, to be optimally responsive to the specific conditions in its industry. However, other authors are at odds with this view, pointing to the enormous potential for synergy that is left untapped. They argue that corporations should be tightly knit groupings of closely related business units that share resources and align their strategies with one another. The ensuing synergies, it is expected, will provide an important source of competitive advantage.

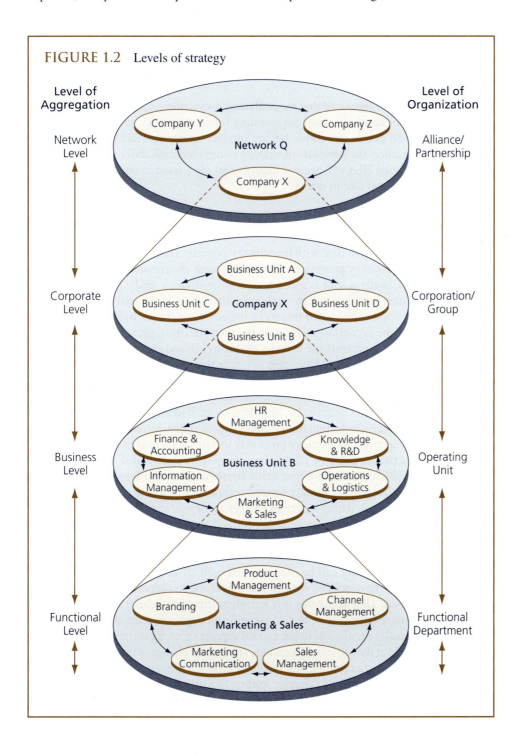

FIGURE 1.2 Levels of strategy

Chapter 6 focuses on the strategy issues at the network level. The fundamental debate in this chapter revolves around the question of whether firms should develop long-term collaborative relationships with other firms or should remain essentially independent. Some authors believe that competition between organizations is sometimes more destructive than beneficial, and argue that building up durable partnerships with other organizations can often be mutually advantageous. Participation in joint ventures, alliances and broader networks requires a higher level of inter-organizational trust and interdependence, but can pay off handsomely. It is therefore recommended to selectively engage in joint – that is, multi-company – strategy development. Other authors, however, are thoroughly sceptical about the virtues of interdependence. They prefer independence, pointing to the dangers of opportunistic partners and creeping dependence on the other. Therefore, it is recommended to avoid multi-company level strategy development and only to use alliances as a temporary measure.

Again, it must be emphasized that the analytical distinction employed here should not be interpreted as an absolute means for isolating issues. In reality, these three levels of strategy do not exist as tidy categories, but are strongly interrelated and partially overlapping. As a consequence, the three sets of strategy issues identified above are also linked to one another. In Section III it will become clear that taking a stand in one debate will affect the position that one can take in others.

Strategy process: Forming, changing and innovating

Section III of this book will deal with the strategy process. Traditionally, most textbooks have portrayed the strategy process as a basically linear progression through a number of distinct steps. Usually a split is made between the strategy analysis stage, the strategy formulation stage and the strategy implementation stage. In the analysis stage, strategists identify the opportunities and threats in the environment, as well as the strengths and weaknesses of the organization. Next, in the formulation stage, strategists determine which strategic options are available to them, evaluate each and choose one. Finally, in the implementation stage, the selected strategic option is translated into a number of concrete activities, which are then carried out.

The division of the strategy process into a number of sequential phases has drawn heavy criticism from authors who believe that in reality, no such identifiable stages exist. They dismiss the linear analysis–formulation–implementation distinction as an unwarranted simplification, arguing that the strategy process is messier, with analysis, formulation and implementation activities going on all the time, thoroughly intertwined with one another. In their view, organizations do not first make strategic plans and then execute them as intended. Rather, strategies are usually formed incrementally, as organizations think and act in small iterative steps, letting strategies emerge as they go along. This represents quite a difference of opinion on how strategies are formed within organizations. These issues surrounding the nature of strategy formation are discussed in Chapter 7.

Another major assumption of the traditional view, that strategy is made for the entire organization and everything can be radically changed all at once, has also been challenged. Many authors have pointed out that it is unrealistic to suppose that a company can be boldly redesigned. They argue that it is terribly difficult to orchestrate an overarching strategy for the entire organization that is a significant departure from the current course of action. It is virtually impossible to get various aspects of an organization all lined up to go through a change at the same time, certainly if a radical change is intended. In practice, different aspects of an organization will be under different pressures, on different timetables and have different abilities to change, leading to a differentiated approach to change. Moreover, the rate and direction of change will be seriously limited by the cultural, political and cognitive inheritance of the firm. Hence, it is argued, strategic change is usually more gradual and fragmented than radical and coordinated. The issues surrounding this difference of opinion on the nature of strategic change will be discussed in Chapter 8.

The traditional focus on improving efficiency of current products, services and business models has also been challenged. Many authors argue that companies need constant renewal by developing new products, services and business models. Although improved efficiency of the present is important in organizational processes, enhancing effectiveness of innovation processes to secure the future is what managers should be focusing on. Exploring in uncharted waters may be costly and results are not guaranteed, but in order to be able to be efficient in the future, managers need to ensure the company has a future. The issues surrounding this difference of opinion on the nature of strategic innovation are discussed in Chapter 9.

These three chapter topics – strategy formation, strategic change and strategic innovation – do not constitute entirely separate subjects. Let it be clear that they are not phases, stages or elements of the strategy process that can be understood in isolation. Strategy formation, strategic change and strategic innovation are different aspects of the strategy process, which are strongly linked and partially overlapping (see Figure 1.3). They have been selected because they are sets of issues on which there is significant debate within the field of strategy. As will become clear, having a particular opinion on one of these aspects will have a consequence for views held on all other aspects as well.

FIGURE 1.3   Aspects of the strategy process

Strategy context: Industry, organizational and international

Section IV of this book is devoted to the strategy context. Strategy researchers, writers and practitioners largely agree that every strategy context is unique. Moreover, they are almost unanimous that it is usually wise for managers to strive for a fit between the strategy process, strategy content and the specific circumstances prevalent in the strategy context. However, disagreement arises as soon as the discussion turns to the details of the alignments. Does the context determine what the strategizing manager must do, or can the manager actually shape the context? Some people argue or assume that the strategy context has a dynamic all on its own, which strategists can hardly influence, and therefore that the strategy context sets strict confines on the freedom to manoeuvre. The context is not malleable and hence the motto for the strategist is 'adapt or die'. Others believe that strategists should not be driven by the context, but have a large measure of freedom to set their own course of action. Frequently it is argued that strategizing managers can, and should, create their own circumstances, instead of being enslaved by the circumstances they find. In short, the strategy context can be determined, instead of letting it determine.

In Section IV, the difference of opinion hinges on the power of the context to determine strategy surfaces when discussing the various aspects of the strategy context. The section has been split into three chapters, each focusing on a different aspect of the strategy context. Two distinctions have been used to arrive at the division into three chapters (see Figure 1.4). The first dichotomy employed is that between the organization and its industry environment. The *industry context* is the subject of Chapter 10. In this chapter, the strategic issues revolve around the question of whether the industry circumstances set the rules to which companies must comply, or whether companies have the freedom to choose their own strategy and even change the industry conditions. The *organizational context* is dealt with in Chapter 11. Here, the key strategic issues have to do with the question of whether the organizational circumstances largely determine the strategy process and strategy content followed, or whether the strategist has a significant amount of control over the course of action adopted.

The second dichotomy employed relates to the difference between the domestic and the international strategy context. The domestic context does not raise any additional strategic issues, but the *international context* clearly does. Strategists must deal with the question of whether adaptation to the diversity of the international context is strictly required or whether companies have considerable freedom to choose their strategy process and content irrespective of the international context. The difference of opinion between writers on the international context actually goes one step further. Some authors predict that the diversity of the international context will decline over time and that companies can encourage this process. If global convergence takes place, it is argued, adaptation to the international context will become a non-issue. Other authors, however, disagree that international diversity is declining and therefore argue that the international context will remain an issue that strategists must attempt to deal with. This debate on the future of the international context is conducted in Chapter 12.

FIGURE 1.4   Aspects of the strategy context

STRUCTURING THE STRATEGY DEBATES

Where there is much desire to learn, there of necessity will be much arguing, much writing, many opinions; for opinion in good men is but knowledge in the making.

John Milton (1608–1674); English poet

Every real-life strategic problem is complex. Most of the strategic issues outlined earlier in this chapter are present in every strategic problem, making the prospect of a simple solution an illusion. Yet, even if each set of strategy issues is considered independently, it seems that strategy theorists cannot agree on the right way to approach them. On each of the topics there is widespread disagreement, indicating that no simple solution can be expected here either.

Why is it that theorists cannot agree on how to solve strategic problems? Might it be that some theorists are right, while others are just plain wrong? In that case, it would be wise for problem-solvers to select the valid theory and discard the false ones. While this might be true in some cases, it seems unlikely that false theories would stay around long enough to keep a lively debate going. Eventually, the right (i.e. unfalsified) theory would prevail and disagreements would disappear. Yet, this does not seem to be happening in the field of strategy.

Could it be that each theorist only emphasizes one aspect of an issue – only takes one cut of a multi-faceted reality? In that case, it would be wise for problem-solvers to combine the various theories that each approach the problem from a different angle. However, if this were true, one would expect the different theories to be largely complementary. Each theory would simply be a piece in the bigger puzzle of strategic management. Yet, this does not explain why there is so much disagreement, and even contradiction, within the field of strategy.

It could also be that strategy theorists start from divergent assumptions about the nature of each strategy issue and therefore logically arrive at a different perspective on how to solve strategic problems. In that case, it would be wise for problem-solvers to combine the various theories, in order to look at the problem from a number of different angles.

All three possibilities for explaining the existing theoretical disagreements should be kept open. However, entertaining the thought that divergent positions are rooted in fundamentally different assumptions about strategy issues, is by far the most fruitful to the strategist confronted with complex problems. It is too simple to hope that one can deal with the contradictory opinions within the field of strategy by discovering which strategy theories are right and which are wrong. But it is also not particularly practical to accept all divergent theories as valid depictions of different aspects of reality – if two theories suggest a different approach to the same problem, the strategist will have to sort out this contradiction. Therefore, in this book the emphasis is on surfacing the basic assumptions underlying the major theoretical perspectives on strategy, and debating whether, or under which circumstances, these assumptions are appropriate.

Assumptions about strategy tensions

At the heart of every set of strategic issues, a fundamental tension between apparent opposites can be identified. For instance, in Chapter 6 on network level strategy, the issues revolve around the fundamental tension between competition and cooperation. In Chapter 10 on the industry context, the fundamental tension between the opposites of compliance and choice lies at the centre of the subject (see Figure 1.5). Each pair of opposites creates a tension, as they seem to be inconsistent, or even incompatible, with one another; it seems as if both elements cannot be fully true at the same time. If firms are competing, they are not cooperating. If firms must comply with the industry context, they have no choice. Yet, although these opposites confront strategizing managers with conflicting pressures, somehow they must be dealt with simultaneously. Strategists are caught in a bind, trying to cope with contradictory forces at the same time.

The challenge of strategists is to wrestle with these tricky strategy tensions. All strategy theories make assumptions, explicitly or implicitly, about the nature of these tensions and devise ways in which to deal with them. However, every theorist's assumptions differ, giving rise to a wide variety of positions. In fact, many of the major disagreements within the field of strategic management are rooted in the different assumptions made about coping with these strategy tensions. For this reason, the theoretical debate in each chapter will be centred around the different perspectives on dealing with a particular strategy tension.

FIGURE 1.5   Chapter topics and strategy tensions

Section	Chapter Topic	Strategy Tension
Strategy	Introduction	
	Strategizing	Logic ←→ Intuition
	Missioning and Visioning	Profitability ←→ Responsibility
Strategy Content	Business Level Strategy	Markets ←→ Resources
	Corporate Level Strategy	Responsiveness ←→ Synergy
	Network Level Strategy	Competition ←→ Cooperation
Strategy Process	Strategy Formation	Deliberateness ←→ Emergence
	Strategic Change	Revolution ←→ Evolution
	Strategic Innovation	Exploitation ←→ Exploration
Strategy Context	Industry Context	Compliance ←→ Choice
	Organizational Context	Control ←→ Chaos
	International Context	Globalization ←→ Localization

Identifying strategy perspectives

The strategy issues in each chapter can be viewed from many perspectives. On each topic there are many different theories and hundreds of books and articles. While very interesting, a comparison or debate between all of these would probably be very chaotic, unfocused and incomprehensible. Therefore, in each chapter the debate has been condensed into its most powerful form – two diametrically opposed perspectives are confronted with one another. These two poles of each debate are not always the most widely held perspectives on the particular set of strategy issues, but they do expose the major points of contention within the topic area.

In every chapter, the two strategy perspectives selected for the debate each emphasize one side of a strategy tension over the other (see Figure 1.6). For instance, in Chapter 6 the discrete organization perspective stresses competition over cooperation, while the embedded organization perspective does the opposite. In Chapter 10, the industry dynamics perspective accentuates compliance over choice, while the industry leadership perspective does the opposite. In other words, the two perspectives represent the two extreme ways of dealing with a strategy tension, emphasizing one side or emphasizing the other.

FIGURE 1.6   Strategy topics, paradoxes and perspectives

Strategy Topics	Strategy Paradoxes	Strategy Perspectives
Introduction		
Strategizing	Logic vs. Intuition	Analytic Reasoning vs. Holistic Reasoning
Missioning and Visioning	Profitability vs. Responsibility	Shareholder Value vs. Stakeholder Value
Business Level Strategy	Markets vs. Resources	Outside-in vs. Inside-out
Corporate Level Strategy	Responsiveness vs. Synergy	Portfolio Organization vs. Integrated Organization
Network Level Strategy	Competition vs. Cooperation	Discrete Organization vs. Embedded Organization
Strategy Formation	Deliberateness vs. Emergence	Strategic Planning vs. Strategic Incrementalism
Strategic Change	Revolution vs. Evolution	Discontinuous Renewal vs. Continuous Renewal
Strategic Innovation	Exploitation vs. Exploration	Strategic Improvement vs. Radical Rejuvenation
Industry Context	Compliance vs. Choice	Industry Dynamics vs. Industry Leadership
Organizational Context	Control vs. Chaos	Organizational Leadership vs. Organizational Dynamics
International Context	Globalization vs. Localization	Global Convergence vs. International Diversity

In the first part of each chapter, the core strategic issue and the underlying strategy tension are explained. Also, the two strategy perspectives are outlined and compared. However, such a measured overview of the perspectives lacks colour, depth and vigour. Reading the summary of a debate does not do it justice – just like reading the summary of a sports match is nothing like watching a game live. Therefore, to give readers a first-hand impression of the debate, theorists representing both sides will be given an opportunity to state their own case by means of a reading. Readers will be part of a virtual debate in which the authors of the first and second readings will participate.

Strategy tensions as both/and problems

With both strategy perspectives emphasizing the importance of one side of a strategy tension over the other, how should strategists deal with these opposites? In general, there are two fundamentally different kinds of problems, 'either/or problems' and 'both/and problems', and each should be handled in different ways.

Either/or problems are for example:

- Puzzles. A puzzle is a challenging problem with an optimal solution. Think of a crossword puzzle as an example. Puzzles can be quite complex and extremely difficult to analyse, but there is a best way of solving them. For example, when facing decreasing margins or market share, managers can solve the puzzle by testing several hypotheses on the root causes of the problem.

- Dilemmas. A dilemma is a vexing problem with two possible solutions, neither of which is logically the best. Think of the famous prisoner's dilemma as an example. Dilemmas confront problem-solvers with difficult either/or choices, each with its own advantages and disadvantages, but neither clearly superior to the other. The uneasy feeling this gives the decision maker is reflected in the often-used expression 'horns of a dilemma' – neither choice is particularly comfortable. The manager is forced to make a choice in favour of either one or the other. For instance, the manager must choose between forming an alliance with firm A or its main competitor firm B, each of which has clear advantages. Which of the two the strategist judges to be the most appropriate will usually depend on the manager's preferences or the specific circumstances.

As opposed to either/or problems that can be solved by analysing and choosing, both/and problems can only be managed. Both/and problems are for example:

- Trade-offs. A trade-off is a problem situation in which there are many possible solutions, each striking a different balance between two conflicting pressures. In a trade-off, many different combinations between the two opposites can be found, each with its own pros and cons, but none of the many solutions is inherently superior to the others. Think of the trade-off between work and leisure time as an example – more of one will necessarily mean less of the other. Of course a position on the trade-off line needs to be set, but when circumstances change the position may also change. In other words, the balance is unstable and temporal.

- Paradoxes. A paradox is a situation in which two seemingly contradictory, or even mutually exclusive, factors appear to be true at the same time. A problem that is a paradox has no real solution, as there is no way to logically integrate the two opposites into an internally consistent understanding of the problem. Hence, a paradox presents the problem-solver with the difficult task of wrestling with the problem, without ever arriving at a definitive solution. For example, companies with more than one business unit need to create synergies between business units but also have to allow the businesses independence to act upon market circumstances. Comparable with trade-offs, the problem-solver can find a workable reconciliation to temporarily cope with the unsolvable paradox (see Figure 1.7).

Taking a dialectical approach

Throughout this book, the strategy tensions will be presented as strategy paradoxes. As stated earlier, the virtual debate in each chapter has been condensed into its most powerful form – two diametrically opposed perspectives are confronted with one another, each emphasizing one pole of the paradox. These two opposite positions are in fact the thesis and the antithesis of the debate, challenging the reader to search for an appropriate option to manage the two tensions. This form of debate is called 'dialectical enquiry' – by using two opposite points of view, the problem-solver attempts to arrive at a better understanding of the issue and a 'higher level resolution' that integrates elements of both the thesis and the antithesis. This approach has a number of advantages:

- Range of ideas. By presenting the two opposite poles in each debate, readers can quickly acquire an understanding of the full range of ideas on the strategy issue. While these two extreme positions do not represent the most widely-held views, they do clarify for the reader how diverse the thinking actually is on each strategy issue. This is the *book-end function* of presenting the two opposite perspectives – they 'frame' the full set of views that exist on the topic.

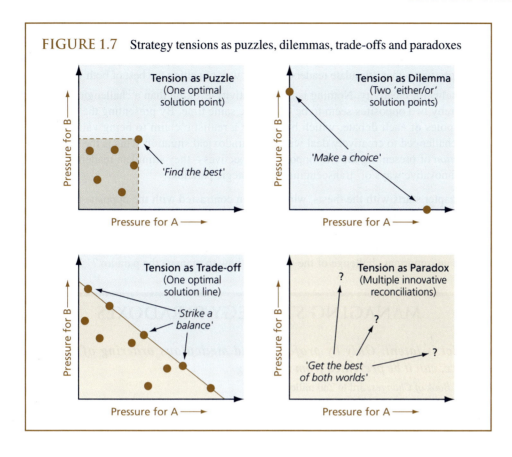

FIGURE 1.7   Strategy tensions as puzzles, dilemmas, trade-offs and paradoxes

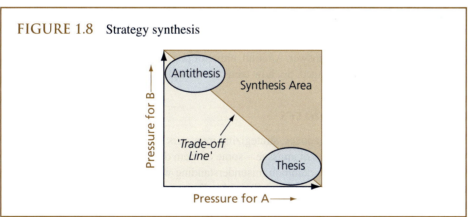

FIGURE 1.8   Strategy synthesis

- Points of contention. Usually there is not across-the-board disagreement between the various approaches to each strategy issue, but opinions tend to diverge on a number of critical points. By presenting the two opposite poles in each debate, readers can rapidly gain insight into these major points of contention. This is the *contrast function* of presenting the two opposite perspectives – they bring the key points of contention into sharper focus.

- Stimulus for bridging. As the two opposite poles in each debate are presented, readers will be struck by the fact that neither position can be easily dismissed. Both extreme strategy perspectives make a strong case for a particular approach and readers will experience difficulty in simply choosing one over the other. With each extreme position offering certain advantages, readers will feel challenged to incorporate aspects of both into a more sophisticated synthesis. This is the *integrative function* of presenting the two opposite perspectives – they stimulate readers to seek a way of getting the best of both worlds.

■ Stimulus for creativity. Nothing is more creativity-evoking than a challenging paradox whereby two opposites seem to be true at the same time. By presenting the two opposite poles of each debate, which both make a realistic claim to being valid, readers are challenged to creatively deal with this paradoxical situation. This is the *generative function* of presenting the two opposite perspectives – they stimulate readers to generate innovative ways of 'transcending' the strategic paradox.

Each chapter starts with the thesis, which is then contrasted with the opposite pole as the antithesis. The first two readings in each chapter will speak on behalf of the two-pole perspectives, while the third reading has been selected to bridge the two poles. The intention of the third reading is not to give the 'correct' outcome of the debate, however it does address an important challenge of the strategist: how to manage the paradox?

MANAGING STRATEGY PARADOXES

Conflict is latent. Only by profound and meticulous ordering of aims, in advance, can it be prevented from emerging.
I Ching, *Book of Changes*, 3rd to 2nd millennium BC

From an academic point of view, a discussion between representatives of opposite perspectives leads to a better and often new understanding of an issue, and so it contributes to the key academic objective: scientific progress. For strategizing managers, however, understanding the problem is a great beginning but not an end in itself. Much more important are the subsequent steps of making better strategic decisions and acting more effectively. And although strategists may prefer the correct academically validated solution, in the case of strategy paradoxes there is no single best answer. After all, either/or puzzles can be solved, while both/and paradoxes can 'only' be managed. So, how then can strategists manage strategy paradoxes?

Dealing with paradoxes

When faced with strategy paradoxes, strategizing managers have a range of options for dealing with the opposite elements of an issue – some of them desirable and others not so much. Not every solution will do – a common misunderstanding when there is no single solution – and there is no fixed number of options. Several options can be considered in some strategy issues, while other possibilities may be thought of in other situations. For example, separating research and development from the company's operations (the paradox of exploration and exploitation) may work, but separating the corporate objective to create multi-business synergies from business unit operations (the paradox of synergy and responsiveness) is not an option. To make things worse, the attractiveness of an option is related to the specific company context, such as the industry context and the firm's company culture. In other words, judging which option might work in a particular situation is an important capability for strategists. Yet, the literature indicates that the strategists' option menu is not infinite.

The literature in the strategy field and related disciplines (such as organizational behaviour) suggest that a limited number of options are at the strategist's disposal. In some publications the available options are specifically related to the strategic issue at hand, e.g. scholars addressing tensions related to strategic innovation, such as March (1991,

FIGURE 1.9   Managing paradoxes taxonomy

Options:	Alternative terminologies:	Discussed in Chapter:
Navigating	Temporal separation; Punctuated equilibrium	2 (Strategizing) 5 (Corporate level strategy) 6 (Network level strategy) 8 (Strategic change) 9 (Strategic innovation) 12 (International context)
Parallel processing	Spatial separation	2 (Strategizing) 4 (Business level strategy) 6 (Network level strategy) 9 (Strategic innovation)
Balancing	Yin Yang Balancing; Blending; Trade-off; Dilemma; Accepting contradictions	5 (Corporate level strategy) 7 (Strategy formation) 9 (Strategic innovation) 11 (Organizational context) 12 (International context)
Juxtaposing	Manage opposites simultaneously	4 (Business level strategy) 6 (Network level strategy) 7 (Strategy formation) 10 (Industry context) 11 (Organizational context)
Resolving	Synthesis; Resolving the paradox; Beyond trade-off; Best-of-both	3 (Missioning and visioning) 5 (Corporate level strategy) 12 (International context)
Embracing	Dialectic; Combining; Exploit the tension	2 (Strategizing) 11 (Organizational context) 12 (International context)

Reading 9.3), Tushman and O'Reilly (1996), Raisch *et al.* (2009), and Jay (2013); to missioning and visioning such as Porter and Kramer (2011, Reading 3.3); and to dynamic capabilities, such as Teece (2007, Reading 4.3). However, a growing number of publications are also addressing how paradoxes may be dealt with in general, such as Smith and Tushman (2005, Reading 1.2), Lewis (2000); Poole and Van de Ven (1989); Smith (2009); Smith and Lewis (2011) and Smith, Lewis and Tushman (2016). Taking all suggestions together, the option menu consists of six different options (see the taxonomy in Figure 1.9).

■ Navigating: The first option is to focus on one contrary demand at a time. In this case the paradox is managed over time by a series of contrary initiatives, which leads to a development path comparable with a tacking sailing boat. Hence this option is called 'navigating' (Jay, 2013). In the literature, 'tacking' is also referred to as 'punctuating'; the phase of sustaining one route is called the state of 'equilibrium'; the combination is called 'punctuated equilibrium' (Burgelman, 2002; Tushman and O'Reilly, 1996). For example, in managing the paradox of multi-business synergy and business responsiveness a company may start a corporate initiative to capture synergies between businesses (such as 'One Firm'), which is then followed by another initiative (such as 'Customer First'), aimed at improving responsiveness of the business units (discussed in Chapter 5 on corporate-level strategy).

■ Parallel processing: The second option, following Lawrence and Lorsch's (1967) seminal work, is to separate the contrary demands in different internal (departments or business units) or external (alliance partners) organizational units. Often, the differentiated demands are then integrated at a different – usually higher – organizational level (Smith *et al.*, 2016). For example, a company may separate improving existing products and developing a new generation of products in different units, because the drivers such as processes, people and rewards differ (discussed in Chapter 9 on strategic innovation). In this case, managing the paradox of exploitation (improving) and exploration (rejuvenating) takes place at the next organizational level up. The company may also outsource one side of the paradox to alliance partners (discussed in Chapter 6 on network level strategy) and then import the products or outcomes into the organization (Rothermael, 2001). For example, a firm may outsource production while internally focusing on developing new products – or the reverse. The paradox is then dealt with at higher management levels. This option has also become known as 'spatial separation' (Benner and Tushman, 2003; Duncan, 1976).

- Balancing: The third option – also referred to as dynamic equilibrium (Smith *et al.*, 2016) – is to manage opposite demands by trading off elements of the opposing demands and blending the most appropriate balance. The strategist is not searching for a (static) synthesis, but instead chooses constituting elements of each demand to create a company-specific balance that can change based on circumstances (dynamic). For example, a manager may choose to comply with some industry rules while changing others (discussed in Chapter 10 on the industry context).

- Juxtaposing: The fourth option is to simultaneously manage opposite demands on a permanent basis. The conflict between the two opposites is accepted, and the strategist will accommodate both factors at the same time. Juxtaposing requires dynamic capabilities (Teece, Pisano and Shuen, 1997) to manage the paradox on a daily or project basis. For example, companies may cooperate and compete in business networks at the same time, even with the same network partners (discussed in Chapter 6 on network-level strategy), or combine client-driven and resource-driven processes in the same units (discussed in Chapter 4 on business level strategy).

- Resolving: The fifth option is to arrive at a higher level equilibrium, by developing a new synthesis between competing demands or by exploiting the tension. Developing a novel synthesis creates a new balance between contrary elements that will sustain for some time, but will eventually be replaced by a new one. For example, companies may adopt societal demands into their mission statement, and combine the need to create shareholder value with the need to create societal value to arrive at some statement of shared value (discussed in Chapter 3 on missioning and visioning).

- Embracing: The sixth option is to embrace and actively use the tension as a source of creativity and opportunity (Beech *et al.*, 2004). The conflict between two opposites is not only accepted, but actually exploited to benefit from the innovative power of tensions. For example, a firm may assign two opposite personalities in the leadership team to combine the messy entrepreneurial process with controlled execution (discussed in Chapter 11 on the organizational context).

As organizations are complex and dynamic systems in changing environments, the attractiveness of available options may depend on the specific context (contingencies) and timing. Strategizing managers need to be able to master the variety of alternative options, actively manage strategy paradoxes and change route when needed. In other words, the list of available options above is not a passive checklist of solutions for specific issues, but instead provides a menu of available strategizing options that can be dynamically applied. It should be kept in mind, however, that being able to effectively manage strategy paradoxes is not a *goal* in itself. For strategists, this capability is a necessary *means* to managing paradoxes and creating an advantage over competitors. Ultimately, the desired outcome of managing paradoxes is to outperform competitors.

DEVELOPING AN INTERNATIONAL PERSPECTIVE

Every man takes the limits of his own field of vision for the limits of the world.

Arthur Schopenhauer (1788–1860); German philosopher

In a highly integrated world economy, in which many firms operate across national boundaries, strategy is by nature an international affair. Some theorists ignore the international arena as irrelevant, uninteresting or too complex, but most theorists, particularly those interested in strategy content, acknowledge the importance of the international context and write extensively on international competition and global strategy. In this book there has been a strong preference to include those authors who explicitly place their arguments within an international setting. Gaining an international perspective is greatly enhanced by reading works that do not take a domestic arena as their default assumption.

To further accentuate the international angle of this book, the international context has been singled out for a closer look in Chapter 12. In this chapter, the conflicting views about developments in the international context will be debated. This, too, should challenge readers to take an international perspective.

However, despite all this attention paid to the international competitive arena, internationalizing companies, cross-border strategies and global products, few authors in the strategy field explicitly question whether their own theories can be globally standardized. Most fail to wonder whether their theories are equally applicable in a variety of national settings. It is seldom asked whether they base themselves on universally valid assumptions, or if they have been severely limited by their domestic 'field of vision'. Yet, there is a very real danger that theories are based on local assumptions that are not true or appropriate in other nations – a threat that could be called 'think local, generalize global'.

Developing an international perspective requires strategists to guard against the indiscriminate export of domestically generated strategy theories across international borders. For international strategists it is important to question whether theories 'travel' as well as the companies they describe. Unfortunately, at the moment, strategizing managers have little to base themselves on. There has been only a modest amount of international comparative research carried out in the field of strategy. National differences in strategic management practices and preferences have occasionally been identified, but in general the topic has received little attention. In practice, the international validity of locally formulated strategy theories has gone largely unquestioned in international journals and forums.

Although there is still so little published material to go on, in this book readers will be encouraged to question the international limitations of strategy theories. Furthermore, they will be challenged to question whether certain strategy perspectives are more popular or appropriate in some countries than in others. To point readers in the right direction, in each chapter a subsection is presented that places the strategy topic being debated in an international perspective. In these subsections it will be argued that the strategy paradoxes identified in this book are fundamentally the same around the world, but that there might be international differences in how each paradox is coped with. Strategy perspectives and theories might be more predominant in particular countries because they are based on certain assumptions about dealing with the strategy paradoxes that are more suitable to the national context. In each 'international perspective' subsection, a number of factors are discussed that might cause national differences in strategy styles.

Using the cases

An additional way of gaining an international perspective is by trying to employ the strategy perspectives in a variety of national settings. It is especially when trying to deal with concrete strategic problems on an international stage that the limitations of each theory will become more apparent. For this reason, a large number of cases have been included in this book, from many different countries. In each case, readers are encouraged to evaluate the specific national circumstances in which the problem situation is embedded, and to question whether the national context will have an influence on the validity or appropriateness of the various strategy theories and perspectives.

The cases have been selected to cover a wide variety of countries and industries. Furthermore, they have been chosen for their fit with a particular chapter. Each of the chapters in this book has two corresponding cases, in which the paradox under discussion is prominently present. One case per chapter is relatively lengthy, and has been included in Section V of this book. The short case for each chapter has been inserted as an exhibit into the main text. In each case readers will encounter the fact that grappling with strategy paradoxes in 'practice' is just as difficult as dealing with them in 'theory'.

EXHIBIT 1.1 SHORT CASE

DISNEY: IS MAGIC BACK IN THE MOUSE HOUSE?

It is little known that the world's most famous mouse actually used to be a bunny. The main character in Walt Disney's first cartoon was a creature named 'Oswald the Lucky Rabbit', but after Disney was cheated out of his copyrights, he modified the ears and renamed him Mickey Mouse. What is more widely known is that Walt, together with his brother Roy, subsequently captured the attention of audiences around the world with Mickey as *Steamboat Willie* (1928), in the first cartoon with synchronized sound.

After some modest successes with such new characters as Goofy and Donald Duck, the business of Walt Disney Studios really started to accelerate when they moved into full-length animated films, releasing blockbusters like *Snow White and the Seven Dwarfs* (1937), *Pinocchio* (1940) and *Bambi* (1942). Soon Disney discovered the lucrative merchandising business, licensing the use of Disney characters for items such as clothing, pencils and soda-cans. On the basis of this success, Disney branched out into TV programmes, film music and live-action movie productions. In 1955, Walt's dream of creating a 'Magical Kingdom' was realized, when Disneyland was opened in Anaheim, California. After Walt's death in 1966, Roy carried on to build Disney World in Orlando, Florida, which was completed just before he passed away in 1971.

While the empire the brothers left behind carried on to entertain billions of children and adults all over the world, the creative pipeline dried up completely. After the release of Walt's last project, *Jungle Book* (1967), the Disney studios spent the 1970s looking for ways to emulate the founder's magic, but without clear results. By 1983, only 4 per cent of US moviegoers went to a Disney picture, and the 15-year drought of hit movies was being severely felt in the sales of Disney merchandise and licensing income. In the same year, the Disney Channel was launched in the US, but did not get off to a flying start. To make things worse, the crowds that initially swamped the theme parks were getting bored with Disney's dingy image and visitor numbers began to shrink, while at the same time Disney was incurring heavy costs to finish the Epcot Center at Disney World. To stem the tide, a new management team was hired in 1984, consisting of a brash young executive from Paramount Studios, Michael Eisner, who became CEO, and a level-headed operational man from Warner Brothers, Frank Wells, who took on the role of COO.

Together, the two worked just like Walt and Roy, with the passionate and outspoken Eisner driving the creative process, and the stable and diplomatic Wells getting things organized. At Paramount, Eisner had produced hit movies such as *Raiders of the Lost Ark* and *Grease*, as well as the successful television shows *Happy Days* and *Cheers*. He was known for his fanatical attention to detail, to the extent of getting involved in reading scripts and selecting costumes. At Disney, he did the same, getting deeply involved in rejuvenating the film business. On the live-action movie side, Eisner and Wells redirected Disney towards lower budget productions, using promising scripts from less established writers and recruiting actors that seemed at the end of their career. Through a new subsidiary, Touchstone Pictures, Disney also entered the attractive market for films for the teen and young adult audience. With hits such as *Good Morning Vietnam* and *Down and Out in Beverly Hills*, Disney reached a 19 per cent US box office share by 1988, causing Eisner to comment that 'nearly overnight, Disney went from nerdy outcast to leader of the popular crowd'. Later, Disney was responsible for successes such as *Pretty Woman* (1990) and *Pulp Fiction* (1994) – the latter made by Miramax, an avant-garde movie studio Disney had acquired a year before.

The animation part of the business was also revitalized, with major investments made in new animation technology and new people, in particular a new creative producer, Jeffrey Katzenberg. Eventually, this resulted in a series of very successful films: *The Little Mermaid* (1989), *Beauty and the Beast* (1991), *Aladdin* (1992) and *The Lion King* (1994). To get the new movies back in the limelight, alliances were formed with McDonald's and Coca-Cola to do promotional tie-ins. And to get spin-off merchandise flowing at greater volumes, Eisner moved beyond mere licensing, building up a global chain of Disney stores. Helped by a little luck, Disney also profited from the new home video trend that was sweeping the world. Not only could Disney release its new movies twice – first in the theatres and then on video – but it could also rerelease a steady stream of classic pictures for home audiences.

In the theme park business, the major innovation spearheaded by Eisner and Wells was to make Disneyland and Disney World more appealing to adults. In 1989 the Disney-MGM Studios theme park was opened near Disney World, as well as the Pleasure Island nightlife complex. Based on the success of Tokyo Disneyland, which was opened in 1983, Disney also built a theme park outside Paris, called Euro Disney in 1992. It turned out that while the Japanese visitors appreciated an almost replica of Disneyland in Tokyo, European tastes were very different, requiring a long period of adaptation to the local market conditions and causing Euro Disney (later renamed Disneyland Resort Paris) to suffer significant losses for a number of years.

Then, in 1994, Frank Wells was killed in a helicopter crash, Eisner had bypass heart surgery, and a period of boardroom infighting commenced, leading to the high profile departure of the studio head, Katzenberg, who later teamed up with Steven Spielberg and David Geffen to found a new independent film company, DreamWorks SKG. Other executives also left, pointing to Eisner's overbearing presence. 'People get tired of being second guessed and beaten down', a former studio executive remarked. 'When people came out of Michael's office wounded, Frank was the emergency room', another Disney insider reported to *Fortune*, but with Wells gone, no one was there to repair damaged egos and soothe hurt feelings. However, Eisner viewed the situation differently: 'I've never had a problem with anybody who was truly talented … This autonomy crap? That means you're off working alone. If you want autonomy, be a poet.'

In 1996, Eisner made his biggest move yet, acquiring Capital Cities/ABC for US$19.6 billion. This deal included the ABC Television Network (distributing to 224 affiliated stations), the ABC Radio Networks (with 3400 radio outlets) and an 80 per cent share of ESPN, a sports-oriented network, which includes various cable channels and radio stations. Ironically, Eisner had previously worked for ABC as a daytime programmer, and felt that he had a lot to add to ABC: 'I would love, every morning, to go over and spend two hours at ABC. Even though my children tell me that I am in the wrong generation and I don't get it any more, I am totally convinced that I could sit with our guys and make ABC No. 1 in two years.' But the opposite happened, as ABC quickly fell to last place, where it lingered for almost ten years.

After Katzenberg's departure, Disney's animation track record also took a turn for the worse – movies such as *Pocahontas* (1995) and *Tarzan* (1999) didn't do too badly, although soaring costs made them only mildly profitable. Other features, such as *Atlantis* (2001), *Treasure Island* (2002) and *Home on the Range* (2004) were box office fiascos. Disney's real animation successes came from their deal with Pixar, an independent studio specializing in computer-generated animations, owned by Apple CEO, Steve Jobs. Such co-productions as *Toy Story*

(1995), *Monsters Inc.* (2000) and *Finding Nemo* (2003) were hits in the cinemas and on DVD. In the area of live-action films, Katzenberg's replacement Joe Roth scrapped the policy of setting a 'financial box' within which the creatives had to operate, leading to bigger budgets, big names and big special effects – and just a few too many big disasters. Illustrative are *Pearl Harbour* (2001) and *Gangs of New York* (2002), both with immense production budgets, yet unable to live up to their promise. The result was a high market share for Disney films, but profitability hovering just above zero.

Although Eisner had taken Disney from US$1.5 billion in revenues in 1984 to US$30 billion 20 years later, a revolt broke out among shareholders, led by Walt's nephew Roy Disney and director Stanley Gold. They lambasted Eisner's perceived arrogance and inability to foster creativity, calling for his resignation. Eventually, Eisner decided to step down, and the board appointed Eisner's right-hand man and company president since 2000, Bob Iger, to the position of CEO in 2005. Although Gold called Iger 'a modest man with a lot to be modest about', the new CEO was a popular choice among 'Mouseketeers', because of his calm demeanour and team player mentality.

Iger immediately disbanded the strategic planning department at corporate headquarters in Burbank, California, which was held responsible for blocking many of the divisions' strategic initiatives. Instead, Iger gave the heads of the four divisions – Studio Entertainment (films), Parks & Resorts, Media Networks (TV & radio) and Consumer Products (merchandising) – more autonomy to make decisions, while at the same time keeping Eisner's emphasis on leveraging Disney characters across all activities. Iger also mended relationships with Stanley Gold and Roy Disney, asking the latter to join the board of directors as consultant. A surprised Gold remarked: 'He's got the company working like a team again. It's very impressive.'

Relations with Katzenberg and DreamWorks were also restored, leading to further cooperation, but most importantly Iger was able to defuse the tense relationship with Pixar's owner, Steve Jobs. As the six-year co-production agreement with Pixar was about to end, Iger needed to find some way to continue the partnership, since Pixar's films were responsible for more than half of Disney's studio profits. The solution turned out to be a classic win–win, with Disney purchasing Pixar for US$7.4 billion in Disney shares, while bringing in Steve Jobs as board member. Part of the deal was also that Pixar's president, Ed Catmull, and its top creative executive, John Lasseter, would take over Disney's struggling animation studios. Furthermore, Disney would work together more closely with Apple in making premium content available through Apple's iTunes stores.

Disney's financial results were further strengthened by a renaissance at ABC, where hit shows like *Lost, Desperate Housewives, Grey's Anatomy* and *Ugly Betty* helped catapult the network to a leading position. Significant growth was also achieved at the Disney Channel, where the traditional focus on the very young was broadened to include 'tweens', nine to 14-year-olds, offering them shows like *Hannah Montana* and *High School Musical*. Not only did these programmes attract a whole new audience, but they led to a wave of new merchandising opportunities. Although Disney once again proved to possess talent for making money by exploiting its franchises, its portfolio was still lacking those that appealed to the male tween audience.

In order to fill this gap, Disney purchased the comic-book publisher Marvel Entertainment for US$4.2 billion. Unfortunately, the barrel of the comic-book publisher was not as full as it could have been; various media competitors already had the most famous characters contracted, with Spider-Man, X-Men and the Hulk bound respectively to Sony, News Corporation and Universal. Although Disney received revenue from projects involving these characters, profiting from highly successful movies such as *Iron Man 2* (2010) and *Thor* (2011), for Disney it was only a matter of time before the contracts would run out and it acquired them exclusively. It seems well worth the wait, with *The Avengers* (2012) accumulating impressive box office results of US$1.5 billion, making it the fifth-highest grossing film of all time. In addition, Disney is making good use of the Marvel takeover; television series based on popular Marvel characters debuted on the boy-focused Disney XD channel with the creation of the Marvel Universe block.

Considering *Pirates of the Caribbean* had been the only highly leverageable movie hit Disney had for quite some years, Iger was eagerly looking for new themes around which to build the Disney synergies. He not only found this in Marvel, but also eyeballed Lucasfilm, the company responsible for such hits as

Star Wars and *Indiana Jones*. Both had a history of collaborating on attractions based on these two franchises for Disney Parks, but the cooperation only went so far. George Lucas, owner of Lucasfilm, considering his retirement, needed someone capable of handling his franchises, while ensuring enduring quality and providing the creators with a certain degree of freedom. He found this in Iger, who had previously handled the acquisition of Pixar well. For a stellar US$4.1 billion, Lucasfilm became a subsidiary of Disney. Similar to the Pixar deal, George Lucas was welcomed as a board member and future films would be co-branded with both the Disney and Lucasfilm names. Disney aims to ensure its investment was a solid business decision and *Star Wars VII: The Force Awakens* proved the company right. With box office results of a stellar US$2.7 billion, the seventh iteration in the Star Wars series turned into the third-highest grossing film of all time. With five more new Star Wars films in the pipeline, the future seems bright.

Yet, peace is not necessarily restored in the Disney galaxy, as Iger has plenty of strategic issues to deal with. One key strategic challenge for him is to continue to reap the synergies between the divisions, by taking movie characters to television, the Internet, theme parks, merchandise and Disney stores. The company now has more than ten of these 'franchises', ranging from *Mickey Mouse* to *Frozen*, *Disney Fairies* and *Pirates of the Caribbean*, that it tries to leverage, but the question is how this should be managed, without creating a complex organizational structure and reducing each division's freedom to set its own strategy. Throwing in Marvel and Lucasfilm only reinforces the need for Disney to get this right.

Another issue is internationalization, which Iger has set high on his priority list. If Disney wants to break into non-US markets in a big way, can it do so by leveraging its franchises across borders or must Disney go local, developing local movies and characters? With more or less standardized theme parks in Tokyo, Paris and Hong Kong (2005), and resorts in a variety of locations, there is much to be said for sticking to global franchises. Yet, on the other hand, emerging markets like China, Russia, India and Brazil might be too diverse to cover successfully with globally standardized wares. Shanghai Disney Resort, which opened on 16 June 2016 and is costumed to serve the taste of China, might be able to indicate what direction is best for Disney.

Disney's future in interactive media is another issue. Disney's gaming division lost US$1.4 billion between fiscal year 2008 to 2013. An overhaul was made in 2014, when one-quarter of the employees were fired, fewer games were in development and a shift was made to cater more to the mobile market. Profits entered the black again, but Disney nevertheless continued to prove overly zealous. Disney Infinity, in which plastic toys of familiar characters can be bought and used in-game, crushed its competitors in terms of sales, but still proved barely profitable. Higher inventory reserves of the figurines were met with lower unit sales volume. In other words, Disney kept releasing more of the toys that hardly left stores and proved too optimistic at times. It supposedly produced two million figures of the Hulk, while only a million of them left stores.

Probably Iger's biggest challenge, however, is to keep Disney's heart and soul fresh – its film business. With the movie industry suffering from tough times in which people buy fewer physical copies of movies, be it on DVD or Blu-ray Disc, and cinema success is limited to familiar franchises, Disney places fewer daring bets. Thus far that has proven successful, with for example Marvel's superhero movies consistently raking in hundreds of millions at the box offices worldwide. Meanwhile Pixar also plays the safe card, focusing their resources mostly on sequels, such as the upcoming *Cars 3* and *Toy Story 4*. How many of those can you churn out before it starts to bore audiences, however? By putting only cash cow eggs in one basket, Disney might not be able to guarantee quality can be preserved.

Bob Iger extended his contract to remain CEO until June 2018, making sure that he has enough time to unleash more magic in the Mouse House. He had proven to be able to do so before, a task the company and shareholders now happily entrust him with. But if Iger fails to make the right strategic decisions, the clock might strike 12 and the magic will be over.

Co-authors: Casper van der Veen and Wester Wagenaar

References: www.thewaltdisneycompany.com; www.boxofficemojo.com; Disney Annual Report 2008–2015; *ABC News*, 7 October 2011; *Bloomberg*, 1 September 2009, 1 November 2012 and 16 February 2016; *Business Week*, 5 February 2007, 9 February 2009 and 14 April 2011; *The Economist*, 26 January 2006, 17 April 2008, 3 September 2009 and 3 November 2012; *Fortune*, 23 December 2001; *Kotaku*, 12 May 2016; *Reuters*, 12 June 2014; *Sunday Times*, 20 February 2005 and 2 October 2005.

INTRODUCTION TO THE READINGS

*Unless a variety of opinions are laid before us, we have no opportunity of selection,
but are bound of necessity to adopt the particular view which may have been brought
forward. The purity of gold cannot be ascertained by a single specimen; but when
we have carefully compared it with others, we are able to fix upon the finest ore.*
Herodotus (5th century BC); Greek historian

In the following 11 chapters the readings will represent the different points of view in the
debate. The readings will 'lay the variety of opinions before us'. However, in this opening
chapter there is no central debate. Therefore, three readings have been selected that provide a stimulating introduction to the topic of strategy, or reinforce some of the arguments
made in the preceding pages. Here, each of the readings are briefly introduced and its relevance for the discussion is highlighted.

The opening reading, 'Complexity: The Nature of Real World Problems', is the first
chapter of Richard Mason and Ian Mitroff's classic book, *Challenging Strategic Planning
Assumptions*. This extract has been selected for this chapter to serve as an introduction to
the complex nature of the strategic problems addressed in this book. Mason and Mitroff's
main argument is that most strategic problems facing organizations are not 'tame' – that
is, they are not simple problems that can be separated and reduced to a few variables and
relationships, and then quickly solved. Strategic problems are usually 'wicked': strategists
are faced with situations of organized complexity in which problems are complicated and
interconnected, there is much uncertainty and ambiguity, and they must deal with opposing views and conflicting interests. Therefore, strategic problems have no clearly identifiable correct solutions, but must be tackled by debating the alternatives and selecting the
most promising option. Mason and Mitroff call on strategists to systematically doubt the
value of all available solutions and to employ dialectics – which is exactly the approach
taken in this book. In the context of this chapter, the most important message that Mason
and Mitroff have is that the variety of opinions might make things more complex, but is
also a useful resource for finding better quality solutions.

The second reading is a 2005 *Organizational Science* article by Wendy Smith and
Michael Tushman: *Managing Strategic Contradictions*. The original article combines
insights on several strategy topics in this book, such as strategic innovation, strategizing
and strategic leadership; however, its main purpose in this chapter is to discuss why strategists should engage in managing strategic contradictions. The authors, both from Harvard
Business School, represent the philosophy of this book well.

The last reading, 'Cultural Constraints in Management Theories' by Geert Hofstede, has
been selected to sow seeds of further doubt about the universal validity of strategic management theories. Hofstede is one of the most prominent cross-cultural researchers in the field of
management and is known, in particular, for his five dimensions for measuring cultural traits.
In this reading he briefly describes the major characteristics of management in Germany,
Japan, France, Holland, South-East Asia, Africa, Russia and China, contrasting them all to
the United States, to drive home his point that management practices differ from country to
country depending on the local culture. Each national style is based on cultural characteristics
that differ sharply around the world. Hofstede argues that theories are formulated within these
national cultural contexts, and thus reflect the local demands and predispositions. Therefore,
he concludes that universal management theories do not exist – each theory is culturally constrained. If Hofstede is right, this re-emphasizes the necessity to view strategic management
and strategy theories from an international perspective. Readers must judge which strategy
approach is best suited to the national circumstances with which they are confronted.

READING 1.1

Complexity: The nature of real world problems

By Richard Mason and Ian Mitroff[1]

Try a little experiment. Make a short list of the major problems or issues facing policymakers in the world today. Now take your list and arrange it as a matrix like the one in Figure 1.1.1. For each element in the matrix ask yourself the following question: Is the solution to one problem (the row problem) in any way related to the solution of the other problem (the column problem)? If the answer is yes, place a check mark at the point where the row and column intersect; otherwise leave it blank. When you have completed the process, review the matrix and count the number of blanks. Are there any?

'Not fair!' you may say. 'There were a lot of check marks in my matrix because many of these world problems are linked together.' World problems involve all nations. One would not expect to get the same result if the focus was, say, on one's company, city, family, or personal life. Really? Try it and see. Recently, several managers at a major corporation tried this little experiment as part of a strategic planning effort.

Among the issues and problem areas they identified were the following:

- Satisfy stockholder dividend and risk requirements.
- Acquire adequate funds for expansion from the capital markets.
- Ensure a stable supply of energy at reasonable prices.
- Train a corps of middle managers to assume more responsibility.
- Develop a marketing force capable of handling new product lines.

The managers found that all of these problems and issues were related to each other. Some were only related weakly, but most were related quite strongly. Repeated attempts in other contexts give the same result: *basically, every real world policy problem is related to every other real world problem.* This is an important finding. It means that every time a policymaker attempts to solve a particular policy problem he or she must consider its potential relationship with all other problems. To do this one must have both

a comprehensive set of concepts for dealing with any policy and a rich set of tools for acquiring the holistic information needed to guide policy making.

Characteristics of complexity

There are several characteristics of policy making that the foregoing little experiment is intended to illustrate:

- Any policy-making situation comprises many problems and issues.
- These problems and issues tend to be highly interrelated. Consequently, the solution to one problem requires a solution to all the other problems. At the same time, each solution creates additional dimensions to be incorporated in the solutions to other problems.
- Few, if any, problems can be isolated effectively for separate treatment.

These are the characteristics of complexity. Complexity literally means the condition of being tightly woven or entwined together. Most policymakers find that the problems they face today are complex in this sense. Moreover, almost all of today's problems seem to be getting more plentiful and complex.

There is an especially vexing aspect of complexity as it presents itself to policymakers. It is organized. As we have seen in the little experiment, there tends to be an illusive structure underlying problems that gives pattern and organization to the whole. Organization is usually considered the route to the solution of a complex problem. In reality, however, organization in complexity can become an insurmountable barrier to the solution of a problem. This is the major challenge to real world problem solving because we have very few intellectual tools for coping with 'organized complexity.'

The tools we have available seem to work best on simple problems, those that can be separated and reduced to relatively few variables and relationships. These problems of simplicity usually have a one-dimensional value system or goal structure that guides

---

[1]Source: This article was adapted from Chapter 1 of R. Mason and I. Mitroff, *Challenging Strategic Planning Assumptions*, © John Wiley & Sons, Inc. 1981. This material is used by permission of John Wiley & Sons, Inc..

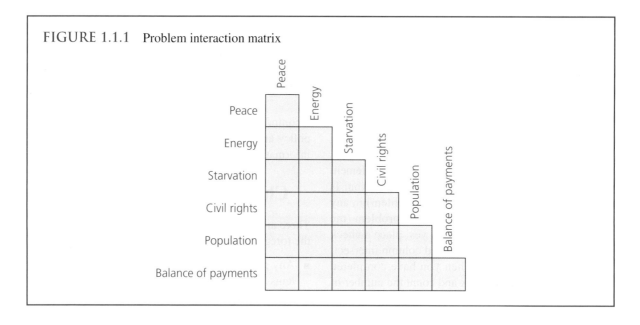

FIGURE 1.1.1 Problem interaction matrix

the solution. Three factors – separability, reducibility, and one-dimensional goal structure – mean that simple problems can be bounded, managed, and, as Horst Rittel (1972) puts it, 'tamed.'

Ironically, problems of the utmost complexity can also be tamed as long as the complexity is 'disorganized.' That is, whenever the number of variables is very large and the variables are relatively disconnected, the problem can be tamed with the elegant simplicity of statistical mechanics. For example, there is no known way of predicting how a given individual will vote on a political candidate. However, using polling procedures and statistical techniques it is possible to predict with a fair degree of confidence how an entire population of voters will vote. Similarly, it is difficult to predict whether a given customer will purchase a new product or not. However, using market research methods, a fairly good estimate can be made of a new product's potential market share.

Perhaps one of the greatest insights of the 20th century is the discovery that when a problem situation meets the condition for random sampling – many individual elements exhibiting independent, probabilistic behaviour – there is a potential statistical solution to the problem. In short, disorganized complexity can generally be tamed by statistical means.

One place where the assumption of disorganized complexity has proven invaluable in the past is in the actuarial sciences. Today, however, the insurance industry is discovering that many of the risks once assumed to be reasonably independent and hence

analysable according to standard actuarial methods are no longer so. People, organizations and facilities have become more tightly woven together over wider geographical areas. Consequently, the probabilities of death, accident, fire, or disaster on which the risks and premiums are based are no longer as straightforward as they once were. The result is that the statistical methods that applied under conditions of disorganized complexity have become less reliable as the system has become more organized.

The great difficulty with connected systems of organized complexity is that deviations in one element can be transmitted to other elements. In turn, these deviations can be magnified, modified and reverberated so that the system takes on a kind of unpredictable life of its own. Emery and Trist (1965) refer to this condition as 'environmental connectedness' and have labelled this type of environment the 'turbulent' environment.

Emery and Trist cite an interesting case to illustrate the nature of environmental connectedness and the great difficulties it presents to policymakers. In Great Britain after World War II, a large food canning company began to expand. Its main product was a canned vegetable – a staple in the English diet. As part of the expansion plan, the company decided to build a new, automated factory, requiring an investment of several million pounds sterling. For over a decade the company had enjoyed a 65 per cent market share for their product line and saw no reason for this strong market position to deteriorate. Given this large volume, the new plant offered the 'experience curve' advantages of economies to scale and made possible the long production runs required to meet the demand from the traditional market.

After ground was broken, but well before the factory was completed, a series of seemingly detached and isolated socioeconomic events occurred. These relatively insignificant events were to change the destiny of the company. Taken collectively, they rendered the factory economically obsolete and threw the corporate board of directors into a state of turmoil. The scenario of events went something like this. Due to the release of wartime controls on steel strip and tin, a number of new small firms that could economically can imported fruit sprang up. Initially, they in no way competed directly with the large vegetable canner. However, since their business was seasonal, they began to look for ways to keep their machinery and labour employed during the winter. Their answer came from a surprising source – the US quick-frozen food industry. The quick-freezing process requires a substantial degree of consistency in the crop. This consistency is very difficult to achieve. However, it turned out that large crops of the vegetable were grown in the United States and a substantial portion of US crops was unsuitable for quick freezing (a big industry in the United States) but quite suitable for canning. Furthermore, American farmers had been selling this surplus crop at a very low price for animal feed and were only too happy to make it available at an attractive price to the small canners in the United Kingdom. The canners jumped at the opportunity and imported the crop. Using off-season production capacity they began to offer a low-cost product in the large canner's market. The small canners' position was further strengthened as underdeveloped countries began to vie with the United States in an effort to become the cheapest source of supply for the crop.

These untimely events in the large canner's supply market were compounded by events in its product market. Prior to the introduction of quick-freezing, the company featured a high quality, higher price premier brand that dominated the market. This market advantage, however, was diminished by the cascading effect of several more unpredictable events. As the scenario unfolded the quick-frozen product captured the high quality strata of the market, a growing dimension due to increased affluence. The smaller canners stripped off the lower price layers of the market, aided in part by another seemingly unrelated development in retailing – the advent of supermarkets. As supermarkets and large grocery chains developed, they sought to improve their position by establishing their own in-house brand names and by buying in bulk. The small canner filled this need for the supermarket chains. Small canners could undercut the price of the manufacturer's brand product because they had low production costs and almost no marketing expenses. Soon supermarket house brands (which had accounted for less than 1 per cent of the market prior to the war) became the source of 50 per cent of the market sales. The smaller canners were the benefactors of almost all of this growth.

As a result, the company's fancy new automated factory was totally inappropriate for the current market situation. The company's management had failed to appreciate that a number of outside events were becoming connected with each other in a way that was leading up to an inevitable general change. They tried desperately to defend their traditional product lines, but, in the end, this was to no avail. After a series of financial setbacks, the company had to change its mission. It reemerged several years later with a new product mix and a new identity. Management had learned the hard way that their strategy problems were neither problems of simplicity nor problems of disorganized complexity. They were problems of organized complexity.

Many corporate policy planning and strategy issues exhibit this property of organized complexity. The vegetable canning company's automated plant decision clearly was made under conditions of organized complexity. Pricing problems also frequently display this characteristic. Recently, a large pharmaceutical firm addressed the seemingly simple problem of setting a price for its primary drug line. The company's management soon learned, however, that there was an intricate web of corporate relationships woven around this one decision. Below the surface there was a structure of complex relationships between the firm's drug pricing policy and physicians, pharmacists, patients, competitors, suppliers, the FDA and other parties. These relationships organized the complexity of the firm's pricing decision problem. Purely analytical or statistical methods were rendered inappropriate.

'Wicked' problems

Today, few of the pressing problems are truly problems of simplicity or of disorganized complexity. They are more like the problems described in the illustrative cases above and the ones we uncovered in our little experiment: problems of organized complexity. These problems simply cannot be tamed in the same way that other problems can. For this reason Rittel refers to these problems of organized complexity as 'wicked' problems. Wicked problems are not necessarily wicked in the perverse sense of being evil. Rather, they are wicked like the head of a hydra. They are an ensnarled web of tentacles. The more you attempt to tame them, the more complicated they become.

Rittel (1972) has identified several characteristic properties of wicked problems that distinguish them from tame problems. These properties are:

1 *Ability to formulate the problem*

   a Tame problems can be exhaustively formulated and written down on a piece of paper.

   b Wicked problems have no definitive formulation.

2 *Relationship between problem and solution*

   a Tame problems can be formulated separately from any notion of what their solution might be.

   b Every formulation of a wicked problem corresponds to a statement of solution and vice versa. Understanding the problem is synonymous with solving it.

3 *Testability*

   a The solution to a tame problem can be tested. Either it is correct or it is false. Mistakes and errors can be pinpointed.

   b There is no single criteria system or rule that determines whether the solution to a wicked problem is correct or false. Solutions can only be good or bad relative to one another.

4 *Finality*

   a Tame problems have closure – a clear solution and ending point. The end can be determined by means of a test.

   b There is no stopping rule for wicked problems. Like a Faustian bargain, they require eternal vigilance. There is always room for improvement. Moreover, since there is neither an immediate nor ultimate test for the solution to the problem, one never knows when one's work is done. As a result, the potential consequences of the problem are played out indefinitely.

5 *Tractability*

   a There is an exhaustive list of permissible operations that can be used to solve a tame problem.

   b There is no exhaustive, enumerable list of permissible operations to be used for solving a wicked problem.

6 *Explanatory characteristics*

   a A tame problem may be stated as a 'gap' between what 'is' and what 'ought' to be and there is a clear explanation for every gap.

   b Wicked problems have many possible explanations for the same discrepancy. Depending on which explanation one chooses, the solution takes on a different form.

7 *Level of analysis*

   a Every tame problem has an identifiable, certain, natural form; there is no need to argue about the level of the problem. The proper level of generality can be found for bounding the problem and identifying its root cause.

   b Every wicked problem can be considered as a symptom of another problem. It has no identifiable root cause; since curing symptoms does not cure problems, one is never sure the problem is being attacked at the proper level.

8 *Reproducibility*

   a A tame problem can be abstracted from the real world, and attempts can be made to solve it over and over again until the correct solution is found.

   b Each wicked problem is a one-shot operation. Once a solution is attempted, you can never undo what you have already done. There is no trial and error.

9 *Replicability*

   a The same tame problem may repeat itself many times.

   b Every wicked problem is essentially unique.

10 *Responsibility*

   a No one can be blamed for failing to solve a tame problem, although solving a tame problem may bring someone acclaim.

   b The wicked problem solver has 'no right to be wrong'. He is morally responsible for what he is doing and must share the blame when things go wrong. However, since there is no way of knowing when a wicked problem is solved, very few people are praised for grappling with them.

Characteristics of wicked problems.   Most policy planning and strategy problems are wicked problems of organized complexity. These complex wicked problems also exhibit the following characteristics:

1   Interconnectedness. Strong connections link each problem to other problems. As a result, these connections sometimes circle back to form feedback loops. 'Solutions' aimed at the problem seem inevitably to have important opportunity costs and side effects. How they work out depends on events beyond the scope of any one problem.

2   Complicatedness. Wicked problems have numerous important elements with relationships among them, including important 'feedback loops' through which a change tends to multiply itself or perhaps even cancel itself out. Generally, there are various leverage points where analysis and ideas for intervention might focus, as well as many possible approaches and plausible programmes of action. There is also a likelihood that different programmes should be combined to deal with a given problem.

3   Uncertainty. Wicked problems exist in a dynamic and largely uncertain environment, which creates a need to accept risk, perhaps incalculable risk. Contingency planning and also the flexibility to respond to unimagined and perhaps unimaginable contingencies are both necessary.

4   Ambiguity. The problem can be seen in quite different ways, depending on the viewer's personal characteristics, loyalties, past experiences, and even on accidental circumstances of involvement. There is no single 'correct view' of the problem.

5   Conflict. Because of competing claims, there is often a need to trade off 'goods' against 'bads' within the same value system. Conflicts of interest among persons or organizations with different or even antagonistic value systems are to be expected. How things will work out may depend on interaction among powerful interests that are unlikely to enter into fully cooperative arrangements.

6   Societal constraints. Social, organizational and political constraints and capabilities, as well as technological ones, are central both to the feasibility and the desirability of solutions.

These characteristics spell difficulty for the policymaker who seeks to serve a social system by changing it for the better. Policymakers must choose the means for securing improvement for the people they serve. They must design, steer and maintain a stable social system in the context of a complex environment. To do this, they require new methods of real world problem-solving to guide their policy-making activities. Otherwise, they run the risk of setting their social systems adrift.

Implications for policy making.   The wicked problems of organized complexity have two major implications for designing processes for making policy:

1   There must be a broader participation of affected parties, directly and indirectly, in the policy making process.

2   Policy making must be based on a wider spectrum of information gathered from a larger number of diverse sources.

Let us consider each of these implications in turn. The first implication indicates that policy making is increasingly becoming a political process; political in the sense that it involves individuals forming into groups to pursue common interests. Turn again to the results of the little experiment conducted at the outset of this chapter. You will find that in almost every case there are a variety of individual interests at stake in each problem area cited. Furthermore, one of the major factors creating the linkages between problem areas – organizing their complexity – is the number of diverse individual interests that cut across problem areas. Individuals are part of the problem and hence must be part of the solution.

This means that the raw material for forging solutions to wicked problems is not concentrated in a single head, but rather is widely dispersed among the various parties at stake. For any given wicked problem there is a variety of classes of expertise. Every affected party is an expert on some aspect of the problem and its solution. Furthermore, the disparate parties are bound together in a common venture. Thus some form of collective risk sharing is needed in order to deal effectively with the consequences of wicked problems. This suggests the need for a substantial degree of involvement in the policy-making process by those potentially affected by a policy in its formulation process. Effective policy is made *with*, or if adequate representation is present, *for*, but *not at* people. At least those involved should be able to voice their opinion on the relative goodness or badness of proposed solutions.

The diversity of parties at stake is related to the second implication. Since much of the necessary information for coping with wicked problems resides in the heads of several individuals, methods are needed to obtain this information from them and to communicate it to others. This means that as many of the different sources of information as possible must be identified.

The relevant information must be obtained from each and stated in an explicit manner.

Contained in the minds of each participant in a wicked problem are powerful notions as to what is, what ought to be, why things are the way they are, how they can be changed, and how to think about their complexity. This represents a much broader class of information than is commonly used to solve problems of simplicity or of disorganized complexity. Also, this participant-based information is less likely to have been stated and recorded in a communicable form. Consequently, this information must be 'objectified' – explicitly, articulated – so that the basis for each party's judgements may be exchanged with others. Objectification has the advantages of being explicit, providing a memory, controlling the delegation of judgements, and raising pertinent issues that might have been ignored otherwise. It also stimulates *doubt*.

To be in doubt about a piece of information is to withhold assent to it. Given the range of diverse information that characterizes a wicked problem, participants in the policy-making process are well advised to develop a healthy respect for the method of doubt. In dealing with problems of organized complexity one should start with Descartes' rule: 'The first precept was never to accept a thing as true until I knew it was such without a single doubt.' This does not mean that one should be a 'nay sayer' or a permanent sceptic. To do so would impede responsible action that must be taken. What it does imply is that one should withhold judgement on things until they have been tested.

All problem-solving methods presuppose some form of guarantor for the correctness of their solutions. Problems of simplicity can be tested and solutions guaranteed by means of repeated solving, just as a theorem is proven in mathematics. This is because simple problems can be stated in closed form. The solutions to problems of disorganized complexity can be guaranteed within some stated confidence interval or degree of risk because the problems are statistical in nature. However, since there are no clearly identifiable correct solutions to problems of organized complexity, neither analytic nor statistical proofs can guarantee results. For solutions to wicked problems, the method of doubt is the best guarantor available.

Dialectics and argumentation are methods of *systematizing* doubt. They entail the processes of:

1   making information and its underlying assumptions explicit;

2   raising questions and issues toward which different positions can be taken;

3   gathering evidence and building arguments for and against each position;

4   attempting to arrive at some final conclusion.

Being fundamentally an argumentative process, these four processes are inherent to policy making. For every policy decision there are always at least two alternative choices that can be made. There is an argument for and against each alternative. It is by weighing the pros and cons of each argument that an informed decision can be reached. In policy making these processes of dialectics and argumentation are inescapable.

In addition to the need for participation by a variety of parties and the existence of diverse information sources, two other characteristics of wicked problems should be noted. One is that they must be dealt with in a holistic or synthetic way as well as in an analytic way. Two processes are necessary: to subdivide a complex problem into its elements and to determine the nature of the linkages that give organization to its complexity – the task of analysis; and to understand the problem as a *whole* – the task of synthesis. A critical dimension of wicked problems of organized complexity is that they must ultimately be dealt with in their totality. This calls for holistic thinking. Analysis is only an aid toward reaching a synthesis.

A second characteristic of these problems is that there is some form of latent structure within them. They are organized to some extent. Organization is not an all or nothing phenomenon. Consequently, systems thinking and methods can be used to gain better insight into the structural aspects of wicked problems.

Quest for new methods.   The nature and implications of organized complexity suggest some new criteria for the design of real world problem-solving methods. These criteria are:

1   Participative. Since the relevant knowledge necessary to solve a complex problem and also the relevant resources necessary to implement the solution are distributed among many individuals, the methods must incorporate the active involvement of groups of people.

2   Adversarial. We believe that the best judgement on the assumptions in a complex problem is rendered in the context of opposition. Doubt is the guarantor.

3   Integrative. A unified set of assumptions and a coherent plan of action are needed to guide effective policy planning and strategy making. Participation and the adversarial process tend to differentiate and expand the knowledge base. Something else is needed to bring this diverse but relevant knowledge together in the form of a total picture.

4 Managerial mind supporting. Most problem-solving methods and computer aids focus on 'decision support systems,' that is, on systems that provide guidance for choosing a particular course of action to solve a particular decision problem. Problems of organized complexity, as we have seen, are ongoing, ill structured, and generally 'wicked.' The choice of individual courses of action is only a part of the manager's or policymaker's need. More important is the need to achieve insight into the nature of the complexity and to formulate concepts and world views for coping with it. It is the policymaker's thinking process and his or her mind that needs to be supported.

Managing strategic contradictions
By Wendy K. Smith and Michael L. Tushmann[1]

It is precisely the function of the executive to facilitate the synthesis in concrete action of the contradictory forces, to reconcile the concrete forces, instincts, interests, conditions, positions, and ideals.
(Barnard 1968, p. 21).

The paradox of administration [involves] the dual searches for certainty and flexibility.
(Thompson 1967, p. 150).

Even with Thompson's (1967) and Barnard's (1968) early admonitions, effectively managing strategic contradiction has not been at the centre of organizational analysis. While Cameron and Quinn (1988) and Poole and Van de Ven (1989) have explicitly argued that firms must build capabilities to attend to contradictions, the theoretical and empirical work on building teams and architectures to manage these tensions has remained in our field's periphery. However, contradictions abound. Firms are pressed to be both big and small, efficient and effective, and to operate in multiple time frames, as well as to be prospectors and analysers (Gavetti and Levinthal, 2000; Miles and Snow, 1978). Similarly, senior teams are pressed to search both forward and backward, to be both flexible and focused, and to both learn and unlearn (Adler *et al.*, 1999; Bunderson and Sutcliffe, 2002; Flynn and Chatman, 2001). The purpose of this paper is to encourage scholars to bring the dynamics of attending to and dealing with strategic contradiction more to the centre of organization science.

The top management team literature has been particularly silent on teams dealing with contradictions (e.g., Adner and Helfat, 2003; Finkelstein and Hambrick, 1996). This literature has focused predominantly on overcoming inertia and implementing innovation (Kaplan *et al.*, 2003; Van de Ven *et al.*, 1999). To address this question of balancing inconsistencies, we turn to the organizational literature on paradox, contradiction and conflict (Lewis, 2000; Poole and Van de Ven, 1989). This literature assumes that inconsistent and contradictory agendas coexist and can both succeed simultaneously. By shifting the perspective from choosing between contradictory agendas to embracing the contradictions, this literature provides an important lens through which to understand how to manage contradictions. Building on this literature, we argue that effectively managing contradictions is rooted in paradoxical cognition – managerial frames and processes that recognize and embrace contradiction. We explore how these frames and processes operate in the context of top management teams, and identify aspects of team design and leader behaviours to support these processes.

Top management teams and team outcomes

Top management teams balance short-term performance and long-term adaptability through resource allocation trade-offs and organizational designs decisions (Edmondson *et al.*, 2003; Eisenhardt and Zbaracki, 1992; Hambrick 1994). These strategic decisions

[1]Source: Reproduced with permission from Wendy K. Smith and Michael L. Tushman (2005) 'Managing strategic contradictions', *Organization Science*, Vol. 16(5) pp. 522–536.

require teams to negotiate between the existing product and the innovation, identifying outcomes that will ensure the performance of both agendas. Borrowing from the negotiation and conflict management literature, we define balanced strategic decisions based on two criteria: (1) their distributive nature, which we define as making balanced trade-offs over time; and (2) their integrative nature, which we define as identifying synergies (Bazerman, 1998; Lax and Sebenius, 1986; Walton and McKersie, 1965).

The distributive aspect of a decision involves the division of resources between the existing product and the innovation. Lax and Sebenius (1986) call this "claiming value," as managers identify resources for each individual product. Teams make a number of decisions in which they might preferentially support either the existing product or the innovation. These decisions are balanced when, over time, they support both products. For example, Ciba Vision's top management team balanced the ongoing demands of their conventional hard lenses even as they invested in daily disposables, extended wear and Visudyne (Tushman and O'Reilly, 1997). In allocating scarce resources, this senior team worked to balance the needs of the existing product even as they worked to develop several possible substitutes.

Decisions can also be defined by their integrative nature – the recognition of opportunities, linkages and synergies that might arise. Lax and Sebenius (1986) call this creating value, in which the negotiated value increases when teams identify creative solutions from which both parties benefit. Top management teams might be able to achieve integrative value in their decisions when they identify ways to benefit from shared resources or to benefit from shared selling in the marketplace. For example, Ciba Vision unexpectedly found that introducing soft contact lenses to the market increased the demand for their conventional lenses. Similarly, *USA Today* found that their online business could leverage the newspaper's content and accelerate readership across both platforms (Gilbert, 2005).

While organizations can excel when top management teams effectively balance strategic contradictions, structural, psychological and social psychological barriers often prevent them from doing so (Bazerman and Watkins, 2004; Van de Ven *et al.*, 1999; Virany *et al.*, 1992). Organizations benefit when structural features of the organization (tasks, skills, formal organization and culture) are internally aligned and are aligned with the firm's strategy (Chandler, 1962; Nadler and

Tushman, 1992), yet these internally congruent design features are simultaneously associated with structural and social inertia. Thus, when structure, strategies and competencies all reinforce one another, managers are psychologically more resistant to changing them (Henderson and Clark, 1991; Kaplan *et al.*, 2003; Tripsas and Gavetti, 2000). Levinthal and March (1993) suggest that managers are myopic – privileging short term over long term, close rather than far, and certainty of success over risk of failure. More broadly, Bazerman and Watkins (2004) observe that historical success is associated with a set of fundamental individual cognitive biases that drive predictable organizational (and social) pathology.

Finally, distinct from inertial forces rooting organizations and their top management teams to the past, a different impediment to balanced decision making is an individual and team drive for consistency and uncertainty reduction. If individuals privilege consistency over inconsistency, the response to these uncertainties and contradictions is to move toward reducing these inconsistencies and aligning one's own behaviours and cognitions, as well one's multiple activities and social networks, with one another (Denison *et al.*, 1995; Lewis, 2000).

This effort to preserve consistency stems from a fundamental epistemological belief of a unitary truth (Ford and Backoff, 1988; Voorhees, 1986). This belief in a unitary truth means inconsistencies cannot fundamentally coexist. There must be a contingency that mediates between inconsistent ideas. One consequence of consistency-oriented thinking is the need to solve conflicts. As this logic suggests, when two things are in conflict, one of them must be right and the other wrong. In a negotiation, this bias leads to what Bazerman (1998) calls the problem of the mythical fixed pie. By focusing on solving the conflict, negotiators focus on distributing resources between them, rather than finding cooperative means for expanding the value of resources.

However, conflicts and inconsistencies cannot be eliminated. Balancing strategic decisions requires teams to recognize and use these conflicts, rather than try to resolve them. Mary Parker Follett recognized this in her early writings. She observed, "As conflict – difference – is here in the world, as we cannot avoid it, we should, I think, use it" (Follett, 1925/1996, p. 67). Similarly, Eisenhardt *et al.* (1997) found that using conflict improves the quality of managerial strategic decision making. To make balanced strategic decisions, top management teams need to confront and overcome these structural, social psychological and psychological barriers that create tendencies for both inertia and consistency. Top management team conditions must be able to support conflict, despite inertial tendencies, and enable the coexistence of inconsistent agendas, despite forces for consistency.

Managing strategic contradictions: Paradoxical cognition

We develop a model of balancing strategic contradiction. This model takes into account challenges of inertia and consistency that reinforce the existing product and push top management teams to choose one agenda rather than to support multiple agendas. In addressing these biases, we begin with the psychological biases, and identify cognitive frames and processes that can overcome organizational pressures for inertia as well as individual preferences for consistency. We then identify structural features that might facilitate a team's ability to attend to and deal with strategic contradiction.

Cognitive biases define how managers understand a situation, seek information and make decisions (Levinthal and March, 1993; Walsh, 1995). Managers' understanding and processing of tensions and contradictions has an impact on whether they embrace the tensions and benefit from them, or are halted by the inconsistencies (Ford and Backoff, 1988; Lewis 2000; Smith and Berg, 1987). Paradoxical

cognition – paradoxical frames and cognitive processes of differentiating and integrating – enable balanced strategic decisions (see Figure 1.2.1).

Although the distinction between cognitive frames and cognitive processes is latent in the managerial cognition literature (Walsh, 1995; Weick, 1979), we make them explicit here. Cognitive frames are stable constructs that provide a lens to understand a situation. These cognitive frames, in turn, create a context for complex behavioural responses (Denison *et al.*, 1995; Walsh, 1995). Cognitive processes are behavioural routines and ways that managers use to think about and respond to information (Weick *et al.* 1999). These frames create foundations that enable a set of complex cognitive processes. Our explanation and examples of paradoxical cognition move between the individual and team levels. In the following section, we return to explore the grounding of this model at either the individual or team level in more depth.

Cognitive frames

Walsh (1995) defines a cognitive frame as "a mental template that individuals impose on an environment to give it form" (p. 281). These mental templates create a lens through which managers filter knowledge and direct action. More specifically, managerial cognitive frames drive organizational action by directing attention to particular issues (Daft and Weick, 1984; Dutton and Jackson, 1987; Kaplan, 2003), defining the leader's understanding of the issues they face (Dutton and Ashford, 1993; Gilbert, 2005), and assigning socio-emotional information to particular issues (Pinkley, 1990).

FIGURE 1.2.1   A model of managing strategic contradictions

Antecedents

Paradoxical Cognition

Team Outcomes

Organization Outcomes

Team design

Leader coaching

Cognitive frame

Paradoxical frame

Accepting the coexistence of contradictory agendas

Cognitive processing

Differentiating
Clarifying distinctions

Integrating
Shifting levels of analysis

Balancing strategic contradictions

- Distributive results
  Balanced trade-offs

- Integrative results
  Identified synergies

- Existing product performance

- Innovation performance

Balancing strategic contradiction may be associated with paradoxical frames – mental templates in which managers recognize and accept the simultaneous existence of contradictory forces. To more clearly describe paradoxical frames, we explore the nature of paradoxes more generally. Ford and Backoff (1988) define social paradox (paradoxes of thoughts, actions and beliefs, rather than paradoxes of mathematics or rhetoric) as "Some 'thing' that is constructed by individuals when oppositional tendencies are brought into recognizable proximity through reflection or interaction" (p. 89). This definition suggests that paradoxes involve aspects of both a situation (oppositional tendencies) and an actor's cognition (reflection or interaction). Specifically, a paradox is created when (1) tensions in a situation are (2) juxtaposed through actor's cognition.

Organizing inherently involves contradictions. The act of organizing creates distinctions of roles and responsibilities, which must be coordinated and integrated to achieve an overall goal. These distinctions result in contradictions within firms (Poole and Van de Ven, 1989; Weick, 1979). Organizational literature is ripe with the recognition of contradictory relations between, for example, individual and group demands, between focus and flexibility, and between autonomy and democracy (Cameron and Quinn, 1988; Flynn and Chatman, 2001; Nonaka and Toyama, 2002; Rivkin and Siggelkow, 2003). Increasingly, our literature has used the term paradox to define and describe these contradictory contexts. However, this use of paradox often obscures the role of the actor in understanding and then managing these tensions. Paradoxical frames therefore refer to an actor's cognitive juxtaposition of the opposing forces in which actors embrace rather than avoid or deny these tensions. Practitioners refer to these paradoxical frames as embracing "both/and" logic, rather than an "either/or" logic (Porras and Collins, 1997).

We can identify cognitive frames of managers through their words and actions (Huff, 1990; Kaplan, 2003; Murnighan and Conlon, 1991). For example, IBM CEO Sam Palmisano's definition of the corporate values suggests a paradoxical frame. He recently defined IBM's values as striving for both "dedication to every client's success" and "innovation that matters – for our company and for the world." The first value predominantly demands quality for today, while the second demands quality for tomorrow (Hemp and Stewart, 2004). In contrast, Goodyear's management assumed a more linear approach to innovation in the context of the radial environmental challenge. Confronted by Michelin's introduction of the radial tyre, Goodyear's

senior team initially focused on the existing product and avoided the radial challenge. When they finally introduced the radial tyre, Goodyear completely shifted from bias-ply tyres to radials (Sull et al., 1997). This strategic shift at Goodyear was associated with a fundamentally new senior team (see also Virany et al., 1992).

Recognizing and embracing contradictions leads to increased success. At an organizational level, managers of the Toyota Production System, the highly successful just-in-time manufacturing process, framed their organizational goals paradoxically – low costs and high specialization, low (or no) inventory, yet immediate access to parts (Adler et al., 1999, Eisenhardt and Westcott, 1988). The organization then built routines and processes to achieve these goals. At a team level, Murnighan and Conlon (1991) found that the performance among British string quartets was associated with members recognizing contradictions inherent in their group processes – democracy and leadership, conflict and compromise.

How might paradoxical frames increase organizational performance? First, these frames create a context that demands the articulation of distinct goals for the existing product and for the innovation. Creating clear and concise goals motivates the achievement of those goals (Latham and Locke, 1995). By defining distinct goals, managers motivate the success of both the exploitative and the exploratory products. Paradoxical frames are also associated with reduced threat and fear, which enables positive conflict. A paradoxical frame signals that managers expect both frames to succeed. This opportunistic framing helps shift the threat and competition from between the two products to how these products might benefit one another and the larger firm (Dutton and Jackson, 1987). Thus, teams that recognize the dualities and potential synergies of their challenges are associated with less anxiety and stress, and enhanced performance (Murnighan and Conlon, 1991; Smith and Berg, 1987). Similarly, clinical therapy finds that paradoxical frames, frames in which patients embrace the symptoms they want to get rid of, lead to less anxiety, less fear, and ultimately increased clinical success (Frankel, 1960; Linehan, 1993).

Cognitive processes

Paradoxical frames create a foundation for cognitive processes that can handle inconsistencies. Based on the assumption that both the existing product and innovation must succeed, managers can confront the relationship between these two products – both their differences and their similarities. Effectively managing these contradictions is associated with two distinct cognitive processes – differentiating and integrating. Whereas differentiating involves recognizing and articulating distinctions, integrating involves shifting levels of analysis to identify potential linkages. Differentiating helps overcome inertia, both by reinforcing the needs of each product and being vigilant that the innovation is not crowded out by commitments to existing strategies and processes. Integrating, in contrast, is associated with sustained attention to possible synergies between the exploitative and exploratory products. Attention to integration helps the team explicitly look for ways that the contradictory strategies can help each other. By addressing different aspects of paradoxical contexts, differentiating and integrating reinforce one another. This notion of cognitive differentiating and integrating is similar to the Van de Ven *et al.* (1999) notion of innovation processes that involve divergent as well as convergent processes.

Differentiating limits inertia by dampening cognitive commitments to the existing product. Langer's (1989) theory of mindfulness focuses on drawing novel distinctions as a core process to enable learning, creativity and effective decision making. By explicitly drawing distinctions, managers are less committed to existing categories or points of view. Rather, under these conditions, managers generate new categories and classifications. More clearly identifying and articulating the needs of both agendas allows decision makers to more effectively allocate the resources such that each agenda is allowed to evolve. Such differentiating between strategic agendas helps leaders develop the behavioural complexities such that both agendas can succeed (Denison *et al.*, 1995; Dutton and Jackson, 1987).

Cognitive differentiating also encourages managers to explore new markets, new skills and new opportunities for the innovation, unburdened by the context of the existing product. For example, newspaper managers reacted differently to the introduction of online news. In those most successful newspapers, senior managers saw online as a strategic opportunity and were able to creatively differentiate online offerings from their traditional newspaper.

This cognitive differentiation allowed these managers to build firms that excelled both in print and online. In contrast, those less successful teams saw online as a threat and, in turn, focused quickly on leveraging their existing competencies, and in turn restricting the innovation's growth (Gilbert, 2005). Differentiating helps

managers to overcome inertia as they are freed up to seek novelty and opportunity in the innovation (Dutton and Jackson, 1987).

This cognitive differentiating in top management teams generates variation along with abundant information. Such information richness helps make more effective trade-offs and strategic decisions. For example, Eisenhardt and Zbaracki (1992) found that accessing and using more information helped decision makers make decisions more rapidly. Similarly, Weick *et al.* (1999) found that in high-reliability organizations, team members are unwilling to simplify their operations. This ongoing cognitive differentiating leads to the generation of more information and, ultimately, enhanced effectiveness in responding to challenging situations.

While differentiating enables balanced decision making by reducing inertia, it can also lead to increased competition. Noticing distinctions reinforces distributive decision making at the expense of integrative decision making. These distinctions may be associated with group conflict and associated process losses (Edmondson *et al.*, 2003; Steiner, 1972). For example, Firestone's senior team's clarity about the fundamental strategic and organizational differences between radial tyres and their existing bias-ply tyres led them to underfund and undercut their development of an effective radial strategy (Sull, 1999). Similarly, at Polaroid, even with significant resources devoted to digital photography, the senior team's response to this potentially cannibalizing technology was to resist and marginalize senior team members associated with the new technology (Tripsas and Gavetti, 2000).

The potential team conflicts associated with differentiating may be offset by processes of integrating. In their analysis of integrative thinking, Suedfeld *et al.* (1992) define integrating as the "development of conceptual connections among differentiated dimensions or perspectives." Integrating involves shifting levels of analysis from the product level to the organizational level of analysis to identify possible synergies. Where cognitive differentiating at the product level builds in conflict, integrative thinking uses these conflicts to identify synergistic solutions at the organizational level. Shifting to the superordinate level (the organization) and linking to the overarching frame reinforces the cooperation between contradictory agendas and enables teams to better make trade-offs (Langer, 1989; Sherif, 1971). Recognizing conflicts associated with differentiation while also maintaining a belief that both products must succeed leads to creative, synergistic results. Rothenberg (1979) called this process Janusian thinking (after the two-faced Roman god Janus), in which holding inconsistencies simultaneously enabled creative solutions to the conflicts. Rothenberg (1979) found that genius thinking involved embracing inconsistent contradictions simultaneously. For example, at Ciba Vision, the articulation of an overarching aspiration of "Healthy Eyes for Life" as well as active senior team attention to integrative decision making created the context where the senior team was able to make a series of decisions such that both their conventional and disposable lens products flourished (Tushman and O'Reilly, 1997).

Differentiating and integrating are opposing, yet complementary, processes. These processes enable one another. Differentiating results in new categories and dimensions of the products and helps managers find synergies. In turn, as integrating reinforces the investment in each of the distinct products, it reduces the threat and competition that are obstacles to differentiating. It is the engagement in both of these cognitive processes that leads teams to be able to execute balanced decision making.

Team-centric and leader-centric models of embracing paradoxical cognition

How teams embrace paradoxical cognition depends on the locus of integration (Bunderson, 2003; Hambrick, 1994; Perlow et al., 2004). In some top management teams, integration of strategic contradiction occurs at the leader level. In other top management teams, a group of senior managers, typically the CEO/GM and his or her direct reports, share the responsibility for integrating strategic contradictions (Ancona and Nadler, 1989; Bunderson and Sutcliffe, 2003). We label these teams as leader-centric teams and team-centric teams, respectively. Following Amabile (1996), we argue that the nature of the cognitive frames and processes are similar at the individual and the group level of analysis. Where these cognitions occur primarily in the leader in leader-centric teams, they occur through social interactions within team-centric teams. The locus of strategic integration may be contingent on the team's context and the different team types are associated with contrasting antecedent conditions. Following the work of Hackman (2002) and Wageman (2001), we explore team conditions associated with team design and leader coaching. We then explore the impact of team context on the locus of strategic integration (See Figure 1.2.2).

Antecedents of leader-centric teams

In leader-centric teams, the leader integrates the contradictory agendas. Team leaders collect information about each agenda, process that information and make decisions primarily on their own. These leaders recognize the conflicts between the agendas, and they accept and manage those conflicts. These leaders may be able to most successfully embrace paradoxical cognitions and balance strategic decisions with teams that exhibit (1) distinct roles, goals and rewards; (2) a supportive integrator; (3) extensive leader-member interactions, but limited member-member interactions; and (4) leader coaching to focus on the product level and avoid conflict.

Distinct roles, goals, and rewards

Quinn (1984) and Van de Ven et al. (1999) both find that teams that successfully manage paradox involve both the roles of an advocate – one who supports a particular agenda – and the role of an integrator – one who creates connections between the disparate parts. In leader-centric teams these roles are allocated to distinct team members. The leader is the integrator and the team members are the advocates. More specifically, leader-centric teams benefit from assigning different individuals to advocate for either the existing product or the innovation. By separating these roles, team members focus on their distinct task, whether exploring or exploiting, unburdened structurally or psychologically by the contradictions associated with the other (Brown and Eisenhardt, 1997; Levinthal and March, 1993). Because the task of exploring and exploiting often requires different skills and leadership styles (Leonard-Barton, 1992; Quinn, 1984; Sutton, 2002), separating these roles allows the team leader to assign appropriate team members to these tasks.

Separating roles also helps the team leaders learn about the different needs of each product. Leaders know who to turn to when seeking information about each product. More importantly, these team members can help the leader hear and understand the needs of their particular agenda. Identifying distinct roles and decision makers for the contrasting strategic agendas may be particularly important for the exploratory product (Adler et al., 1999; Benner and Tushman, 2002). Aligning team members' responsibilities with clear goals and rewards helps motivate these managers (Hackman, 2002; Kerr, 1975; Latham and Locke,

FIGURE 1.2.2   A model of managing strategic contradictions by team type

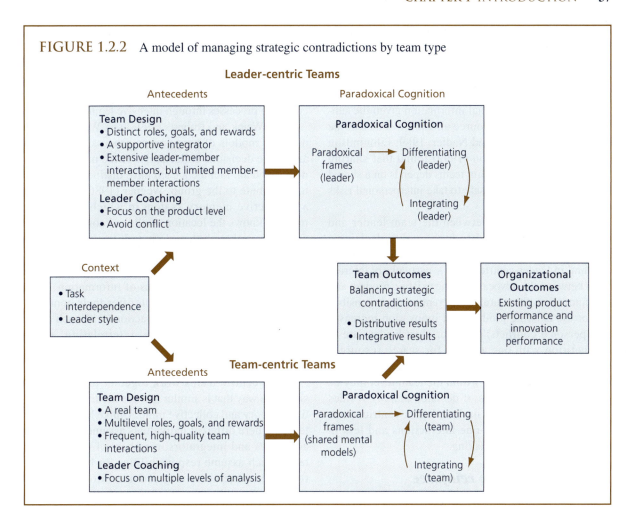

1995). Because members have distinct responsibilities for the existing product and innovation, their goals and rewards are quite distinct from one another.

Supportive integrator

In leader-centric teams, the team leader integrates the contradictory agendas. Making these trade-offs is a significant cognitive burden for team leaders (Tetlock *et al.*, 2004) and subjects the team to the leader's decision-making biases (Bazerman and Watkins, 2004). Co-leaders, trusted advisors, or a secondary team member assigned to focus on integration help offset these biases and alleviate some of the leader's cognitive burdens (Eisenhardt *et al.*, 1997). In an assessment of the roles of individuals surrounding American presidents, Porter (1980) found that someone often plays the role of a cointegrator, or "honest broker" to help collect, sort and assess information. Similarly, Heenan and Bennis (1999) found that in successful

co-leadership relationships, each of the partners offers different biases and skills to improve the quality of the leader's decisions. By providing another perspective, these supportive integrators help the team leader make balanced decisions.

High-quality leader-member interactions, but limited member-member interactions

Decision making in leader-centric teams depends on the quality of the interactions between the team members and the team leader. High-quality interactions enable the team leader to seek and process relevant decision-making information and, in turn, to make more balanced decisions (Eisenhardt *et al.*, 1997). High-quality interactions are associated with the amount of information exchanged, the amount of information revealed, and the mutual understanding between the team leader and his/ her team members. These interactions depend on the extent to which managers are willing to share potentially threatening strategic as well as tactical information with the leader (Argyris and Schon, 1978; Edmondson, 1999). Individuals within senior teams may avoid revealing crucial information given the substantial political and resource allocation stakes at the top of a firm (Ancona and Nadler, 1989; Edmondson *et al.*, 2003). Edmondson (1999) found that sharing sensitive information within teams depends on a shared belief as to whether it is safe to take interpersonal risks in team interactions.

While interactions between the team leader and team members may lead to high-quality decisions, interactions among team members may be more detrimental in leader-centric teams – particularly interactions between the advocates of the existing product and the innovation. Structurally differentiating responsibility for the existing product and innovation increases interpersonal conflicts, as the product leaders are in competition with one another for scarce resources (e.g., Deutsch, 1973; Sherif, 1971). In leader-centric teams, engaging conflict within the team level may be detrimental, as the locus of decision making resides with the leader. Leaders in these leader-centric teams engage more in one-on-one interactions and less in team strategic decision making.

Leader coaching to reinforce differentiation

In leader-centric teams, the team leader's coaching provides valuable support that reinforces team processes and team beliefs (Edmondson, 1999; Hackman, 2002; Wageman, 2001). In leader-centric teams, leaders direct and focus strategy at the team level even as they focus team members at their individual product level. Reinforcing differences between the existing product and the innovation encourages the leaders of each product to focus on their particular strategic agenda. Reinforcing the necessity of both products and exhibiting coaching behaviours consistent with the contrasting strategic agendas helps differentially motivate the performance of senior team members (Denison *et al.*, 1995).

Antecedents of team-centric teams

In team-centric teams, the teams themselves integrate the contradictory agendas. Achieving balanced decisions on team-centric teams is associated with shared mental models of paradoxical frames and collective cognitive processes. Shared paradoxical frames enable team members to build a collective understanding of the team's complex goals and a collective acknowledgment of the tensions and conflicts between their contrasting agendas (Murnighan and Conlon, 1991; Smith and Berg, 1987). These frames create a foundation for cognitive processes through intensive team interactions.

Both Weick and Roberts (1993) and Wegner (1986) describe models of how groups process information and make decisions collectively. These models recognize that team members each have distinct knowledge to contribute to the group. Wegner (1986) articulated a transactive memory system in which each group member knows the location of all the knowledge in the group, even though they do not all know the content of this knowledge. Weick and Roberts's (1993) model of collective mind suggests how team members might integrate these disparate pieces of information. They argue that team members each offer their contributions to the group through interactions with each other. Through processes of heedful interrelating, a new group-level cognition emerges that is greater than the contributions of each individual member.

Team-centric teams work together to make decisions in a way that is similar to these models of transactive memory and collective mind. Unlike leader-centric teams, where different individuals assume the roles of advocates and integrators, members of team-centric teams each assume responsibilities for both of these roles. Team members may provide information and advocate for either the existing product or the innovation. However, through processes of heedful interrelating, these team members are also responsible for integrating across their team.

Effectively embracing both intra- and interpersonal conflict is an important determinant of success for team-centric teams. Whereas leader-centric teams manage conflict by attempting to avoid it, conflict abounds on team-centric teams. Team members may experience intrapersonal conflict in their dual roles of advocates for particular products and as integrators across these products. They may also experience interpersonal conflict with other team members who are competing for scarce resources. Using this conflict to balance contradictions leads to higher quality decisions in team-centric teams. To build shared mental models and collaborative decision making, team-centric teams are associated with teams that are designed as real teams (Hackman, 2002). Further, team-centric teams exhibit (1) roles, goals and rewards at multiple levels of analysis; (2) frequent, high-quality team interactions; and (3) leader coaching to reinforce the organizational level of analysis.

Real teams

Hackman (2002) defines a real team as one with a clear sense of boundaries, an interdependent task and a clear understanding of the team's authority. A real team creates a foundation for groups of individuals to work together to achieve their collective goals. A real team allows team members to allocate clear tasks to one another, know who else has information, and work with the other members to create shared mental models and shared processes. Even as there has been a move toward increasingly using integrated teamwork among senior management, achieving teamwork is often difficult in senior teams because of the political and career issues unique to senior teams (Ancona and Nadler, 1989; Edmondson *et al.*, 2003). However, having the top management team attend to themselves as a real team helps team-centric teams deal with strategic contradiction.

Roles, goals, and rewards at multiple levels of analysis

As with leader-centric teams, team-centric teams benefit from assigning primary existing product and innovation roles to different team members and aligning these roles with product-level goals and rewards. Team members with specific product-level responsibilities focus on seeking product-specific information and ideas (Brown and Eisenhardt, 1997), even as this information is shared with the entire team (Bazerman and Watkins, 2004). These distinct responsibilities are important in overcoming inertia when teams make decisions together. When making group-level decisions, teams often prevent multiple, dissenting opinions from being expressed because team members want to quickly achieve consensus (Eisenhardt *et al.*, 1997; Nemeth and Wachtler, 1983). Often the needs of the minority opinion are not shared in group decision making. In top management teams, this minority opinion is often that of the innovation. Assigning a distinct individual to represent each agenda in team discussions encourages these opinions to be raised in team interactions.

Assigning product-level roles, goals and rewards reinforces the conflict and competition between managers of contradictory agendas. Managers of team-centric teams are able to embrace this conflict and reinforce integrative thinking by identifying a second set of roles, goals and rewards at the organizational level – dual roles, superordinate and/or opportunistic goals (Dutton and Jackson, 1987; Sherif, 1971) and common fate rewards (Tushman *et al.*, 2003). This second set

of organization-level roles, goals and rewards helps motivate team members to consider the organization's overarching and integrative strategic agenda. Creating multilevel roles, goals and rewards helps team members shift from focusing on competition to focusing on individual strategic agendas as well as the firm's overarching strategic agendas (Gilbert, 2005). Team members are asked to engage in multiple leadership roles simultaneously – both integrators as well as advocates (Quinn 1984). As Brown and Eisenhardt (1997) note, these multilevel structures and incentives provide flexibility over time, as team members shift back and forth between each of these levels.

Frequent team interactions

Weick and Roberts (1993) describe a process of integrating across distinct contributions as heedful interrelating, where team members are aware of their own and others' contributions and subordinate their own contributions for the team's benefit. Heedful interrelating involves dynamic learning processes in which team members make contributions to the team and learn from the contributions of others. Heedful interrelating depends on team members' ability to interact. The frequency of their interactions allows for more opportunity to share information with one another. As well, the quality of their interactions ensures that information is actually being shared. As with leader-centric teams, psychological safety on the team (a shared team belief that it is safe to take interpersonal risks) reinforces positive team interactions (Edmondson, 1999).

Leader coaching to facilitate integration

The behaviours of the leader in leader-centric teams reinforce the focus on differentiating products, whereas the behaviours of the leader on team-centric teams reinforce integrative behaviours. In leader-centric teams, the senior leader facilitates his/her team's interaction. These leaders encourage their team members to extend beyond their own product's focus. Team-centric leaders coach their team members to attend to both their products as well as organization-wide issues. As such, team-members in team-centric teams "wear multiple hats" (Ancona and Nadler, 1989). Such team-centric facilitation encourages team members to actively manage conflict rather than allowing it to become an obstacle in team interactions. Under what conditions do leader-centric versus team-centric teams dominate in managing strategic contradictions? It may be that task interdependence and leadership style are important contextual factors affecting the relative effectiveness of these contrasting team types. Innovation streams in which the development of the existing product and innovation are highly interdependent require increased collaborative interaction between members of the team. It may be that such tasks require increased team member interaction to attend to the uncertainty associated with such substantial task interdependence (Nadler and Tushman, 1996; Rivkin and Siggelkow, 2003; Thompson, 1967). Team-centric teams might be more able to deal with substantial interdependence than leader-centric teams. In contrast, under conditions of limited task interdependence, leader-centric teams may have sufficient information-processing capabilities to deal with the more limited coordination requirements.

A second possible moderator is the team leader's preferred leadership style. Leader-centric teams are associated with leadership that is much more authoritative, whereas team-centric teams are associated with more democratic leadership (e.g., Flynn and Chatman, 2001; Perlow et al., 2004). While team leaders may need to express multiple roles and behavioural flexibility in managing contradictory agendas (e.g., Denison et al., 1995), it may be that a leader's preferred leadership style is an important determinant of the differential effectiveness of leader-centric versus team-centric teams.

Conclusion

Competitive pressures make even more salient Thompson's (1967) and Barnard's (1968) admonitions to take contradiction and paradox seriously. We believe that the management of strategic contradiction belongs at the forefront of organizational scholarship. As such, this paper has focused on developing a set of ideas on how top management teams might deal with strategic contradiction. It may be that a root of sustained organizational performance is in the senior team's ability to successfully attend to and deal with the challenges of operating in different timeframes and strategic logics (Adler et al., 1999; Adner and Helfat, 2002; He and Wong, 2004). We argue that sustained performance occurs through attending to and dealing with strategic contradictions – short-term performance and long-term adaptability, exploration and exploitation, focus and flexibility.

The literature on organization design highlights the importance of building organizational forms that can both explore as well as exploit (e.g., Gibson and Birkinshaw, 2004; Siggelkow and Levinthal, 2003; Tushman and O'Reilly, 1997), yet even as this literature highlights the role of the senior team in creating these contradictory contexts, there is little clarity on how these teams might

deal with the challenges associated with strategic contradiction. We explore those factors that enable top management teams to achieve balanced strategic decisions in contradictory contexts. We contribute to an emerging body of literature on contradiction and paradox that explores the nature of these challenges and identifies team characteristics associated with managing them. While others have identified the roles of organizational structures, cultures and routines to manage contradictions (Adler et al., 1999; Flynn and Chatman, 2001), we argue that balancing contradiction in decision making is rooted in senior team cognitions. We argue that balanced strategic decision making in the context of contradiction is rooted in paradoxical cognition – cognitive frames and processes that allow teams to effectively embrace, rather than avoid, contradictions. We further argue that, depending on the locus of integration of the inconsistent agendas, these cognitive frames and processes occur either with the senior leader or in the interactions of the entire top management team.

Empirical exploration is necessary to systematically explore the relationships between cognitive frames, cognitive processes, locus of integration, team decisions, and organizational outcomes. Such empirical research must take into account the difficulties of assessing managerial cognition. Empirically exploring such concepts requires multiple methods involving both rich qualitative data to identify and understand the nuances of managerial cognition (Huff, 1997; Kaplan, 2003) and larger sample analysis to validate these ideas (Sundaramurthy and Lewis, 2003).

It might also be important to explore the applicability of these ideas to contradictions at different levels of analysis. While we focus on strategic contradictions between exploration and exploitation for top management teams, organizations face contradictions at multiple levels of analysis. Lorsch and Tierney (2002) and Sundaramurthy and Lewis (2003) raise questions about managing contradictory needs of multiple corporate stakeholders. Adler et al. (1999), Repenning (2002), and Tyre and Von Hippel (1997) describe contradictions between efficiency and effectiveness on the factory floor and in product development. The challenge of balancing financial and social goals has received increased attention in the organizational literature (Margolis and Walsh, 2003; Paine, 2003). It may be that managing contradiction is a window into a range of important and understudied organizational challenges (Cameron and Quinn, 1988; Poole and Van de Ven, 1989). Bringing the study of contradiction more into the centre of our field may help us rise to the challenge posed so long ago by Thompson (1967) and Barnard (1968).

Cultural constraints in management theories

By Geert Hofstede[1]

Lewis Carroll's *Alice in Wonderland* contains the famous story of Alice's croquet game with the Queen of Hearts. Alice thought she had never seen such a curious croquet ground in all her life; it was all ridges and furrows; the balls were live hedgehogs, the mallets live flamingoes, and the soldiers had to double themselves up and stand on their hands and feet to make the arches. You probably know how the story goes: Alice's flamingo mallet turns its head whenever she wants to strike with it; her hedgehog ball runs away; and the doubled-up soldier arches walk around all the time. The only rule seems to be that the Queen of Hearts always wins.

Alice's croquet playing problems are good analogies of attempts to build culture-free theories of management. Concepts available for this purpose are themselves alive with culture, having been developed within a particular cultural context. They have a tendency to guide our thinking toward our desired conclusion. As the same reasoning may also be applied to the arguments in this reading, I better tell you my conclusion before I continue – so that the rules of my game are understood. In this reading we take a trip around the world to demonstrate that there are no such things as universal management theories.

Diversity in management *practices* as we go around the world has been recognized in US management literature for more than 30 years. The term 'comparative management' has been used since the 1960s. However, it has taken much longer for the US academic community to accept that not only practices but also the validity of theories may stop at national borders, and I wonder whether even today everybody would agree with this statement.

The idea that the validity of a theory is constrained by national borders is more obvious in Europe, with all its borders, than in a huge borderless country like the US. Already in the 16th century Michel de Montaigne, a Frenchman, wrote a statement which was made famous by Blaise Pascal about a century later: '*Verite endega des Pyrenees, erreur au-dela*' – 'There are truths on this side of the Pyrenees which are falsehoods on the other'.

From Don Armado's love to Taylor's science

According to the comprehensive ten-volume *Oxford English Dictionary*, the words 'manage', 'management' and 'manager' appeared in the English language in the 16th century. The oldest recorded use of the word 'manager' is in Shakespeare's *Love's Labour's Lost*, dating from 1588, in which Don Adriano de Armado, 'a fantastical Spaniard', exclaims (Act I, Scene II. 188): 'Adieu, valour! Rust, rapier! Be still, drum! For your manager is in love; yea, he loveth.'

The linguistic origin of the word is from *Latin manus*, hand, via the Italian *maneggiare*, which is the training of horses in the *manege;* subsequently its meaning was extended to skilful handling in general, like of arms and musical instruments, as Don Armado illustrates. However, the word also became associated with the French *menage*, household, as an equivalent of 'husbandry' in its sense of the art of running a household. The theatre of present-day management contains elements of both *manege* and *menage* and different managers and cultures may use different accents.

The founder of the science of economics, the Scot Adam Smith, in his 1776 book *The Wealth of Nations*, used 'manage', 'management' (even 'bad management') and 'manager' when dealing with the process and the persons involved in operating joint stock companies. British economist John Stuart Mill (1806–1873) followed Smith in this use and clearly expressed his distrust of such hired people who were not driven by ownership. Since the 1880s the word 'management' appeared occasionally in writings by American engineers, until it was canonized as a modern science by Frederick W. Taylor in *Shop Management* in 1903 and in *The Principles of Scientific Management* in 1911.

While Smith and Mill used 'management' to describe a process and 'managers' for the persons involved, 'management' in the American sense – which has since been taken back by the British – refers not only to the process but also to the managers as a class of people. This class (1) does not own a business

[1]Source: This article was adapted from G. Hofstede, 'Cultural constraints in management theories', *Academy of Management Executive*, Vol. 7, No. 1, 1993, pp. 8–21. © Copyright 1993 by Academy of Management. Reproduced with permission of Academy of Management via Copyright Clearance Center.

but sells its skills to act on behalf of the owners and (2) does not produce personally but is indispensable for making others produce, through motivation. Members of this class carry a high status and many American boys and girls aspire to the role. In the US, the manager is a cultural hero.

Let us now turn to other parts of the world. We will look at management in its context in other successful modern economies: Germany, Japan, France, Holland and among the overseas Chinese. Then we will examine management in the much larger part of the world that is still poor, especially South-East Asia and Africa, and in the new political configurations of Eastern Europe, and Russia in particular. We will then return to the US via mainland China.

Germany

The manager is not a cultural hero in Germany. If anybody, it is the engineer who fills the hero role. Frederick Taylor's scientific management was conceived in a society of immigrants – where a large number of workers with diverse backgrounds and skills had to work together. In Germany this heterogeneity never existed.

Elements of the medieval guild system have survived in historical continuity in Germany until the present day. In particular, a very effective apprenticeship system exists both on the shop floor and in the office, which alternates practical work and classroom courses. At the end of the apprenticeship the worker receives a certificate, the *Facharbeiterbrief*, which is recognized throughout the country. About two-thirds of the German worker population holds such a certificate and a corresponding occupational pride. In fact, quite a few German company presidents have worked their way up from the ranks through an apprenticeship. In comparison, two-thirds of the worker population in Britain have no occupational qualification at all.

The highly skilled and responsible German workers do not necessarily need a manager, American-style, to 'motivate' them. They expect their boss or *Meister* to assign their tasks and to be the expert in resolving technical problems. Comparisons of similar German, British and French organizations show the Germans as having the highest rate of personnel in productive roles and the lowest both in leadership and staff roles.

Japan

The American type of manager is also missing in Japan. In the United States, the core of the enterprise is the managerial class. The core of the Japanese enterprise is the permanent worker group: workers who for all practical purposes are tenured and who aspire to lifelong employment. They are distinct from the non-permanent employees – mostly women and subcontracted teams led by gang bosses, to be laid off in slack periods. University graduates in Japan first join the permanent worker group and subsequently fill various positions, moving from line to staff as the need occurs, while being paid according to seniority rather than position. They take part in Japanese-style group consultation sessions for important decisions, which extend the decision making period but guarantee fast implementation afterwards. Japanese are to a large extent controlled by their peer group rather than by their manager.

American theories of leadership are ill-suited to the Japanese group-controlled situation. During the past two decades, the Japanese have developed their own 'PM' theory of leadership, in which P stands for performance and M for maintenance. The latter is less a concern for individual employees than for maintaining social stability. In view of the amazing success of the Japanese economy in the past 30 years, many Americans have sought the secrets of Japanese management, hoping to copy them.

France

The manager, US style, does not exist in France either. The French researcher Philippe d'Iribarne (1990) identifies three kinds of basic principles *(logiques)* of management. In the USA, the principle is the *fair contract* between employer and employee, which gives the manager considerable prerogatives, but within its limits. This is really a labour market in which the worker sells his or her labour for a price. In France, the principle is the *honour* of each class in a society which has always been and remains extremely stratified, in which superiors behave as superior beings and subordinates accept and expect this, conscious of their own lower level in the national hierarchy but also of the honour of their own class. The French do not think in terms of managers versus non-managers but in terms of *cadres* versus *non-cadres;* one becomes cadre by attending the proper schools and one remains it forever; regardless of their actual task, cadres have the privileges of a higher social class, and it is very rare for a non-cadre to cross the ranks.

The conflict between French and American theories of management became apparent at the beginning of the 20th century, in a criticism by the great French management pioneer Henri Fayol (1841–1925) of his

US colleague and contemporary Frederick W. Taylor (1856–1915). Fayol was a French engineer whose career as a *cadre superieur* culminated in the position of *President-Directeur-General* of a mining company. After his retirement he formulated his experiences in a pathbreaking text on organization: *Administration industrielle et generale*, in which he focused on the sources of authority. Taylor was an American engineer who started his career in industry as a worker and attained his academic qualifications through evening studies. From chief engineer in a steel company he became one of the first management consultants. Taylor was not really concerned with the issue of authority at all; his focus was on efficiency. He proposed to split the task of the first-line boss into eight specialisms, each exercised by a different person; an idea which eventually led to the idea of a matrix organization.

Taylor's work appeared in a French translation in 1913, and Fayol read it and showed himself generally impressed but shocked by Taylor's 'denial of the principle of the Unity of Command' in the case of the eight-boss-system. Seventy years later Andre Laurent, another of Fayol's compatriots, found that French managers in a survey reacted very strongly against a suggestion that one employee could report to two different bosses, while US managers in the same survey showed fewer misgivings. Matrix organization has never become popular in France as it has in the United States.

Holland

In my own country, Holland, or as it is officially called, the Netherlands, the study by Philippe d'Iribarne found the management principle to be a need for consensus among all parties, neither predetermined by a contractual relationship nor by class distinctions, but based on an open-ended exchange of views and a balancing of interests. In terms of the different origins of the word 'manager', the organization in Holland is more *menage* (household) while in the United States it is more *manege* (horse drill).

At my university, the University of Limburg at Maastricht, we asked both the Americans and a matched group of Dutch students to describe their ideal job after graduation, using a list of 22 job characteristics. The Americans attached significantly more importance than the Dutch to earnings, advancement, benefits, a good working relationship with their boss, and security of employment. The Dutch attached more importance to freedom to adopt their own approach to the job, being consulted by their boss in his or her

decisions, training opportunities, contributing to the success of their organization, fully using their skills and abilities, and helping others. This list confirms d'Iribarne's findings of a contractual employment relationship in the United States, based on earnings and career opportunities, against a consensual relationship in Holland. The latter has centuries old roots; the Netherlands was the first republic in Western Europe (1609–1810), and a model for the American republic. The country has been and still is governed by a careful balancing of interests in a multi-party system.

In terms of management theories, both motivation and leadership in Holland are different from what they are in the United States. Leadership in Holland presupposes modesty, as opposed to assertiveness in the United States. No US leadership theory has room for that. Working in Holland is not a constant feast, however. There is a built-in premium on mediocrity and jealousy, as well as time-consuming ritual consultations to maintain the appearance of consensus and the pretence of modesty. There is unfortunately another side to every coin.

The overseas Chinese

Among the champions of economic development in the past 30 years we find three countries mainly populated by Chinese living outside the Chinese mainland: Taiwan, Hong Kong and Singapore. Moreover, overseas Chinese play a very important role in the economies of Indonesia, Malaysia, the Philippines and Thailand, where they form an ethnic minority. If anything, the little dragons – Taiwan, Hong Kong and Singapore – have been more economically successful than Japan, moving from rags to riches and now counted among the world's wealthy industrial countries. Yet very little attention has been paid to the way in which their enterprises have been managed.

Overseas Chinese enterprises lack almost all characteristics of modern management. They tend to be small, cooperating for essential functions with other small organizations through networks based on personal relations. They are family owned, without the separation between ownership and management typical in the West, or even in Japan and Korea. They normally focus on one product or market, with growth by opportunistic diversification; in this, they are extremely flexible. Decision making is centralized in the hands of one dominant family member, but other family members may be given new ventures to try their skills on. They are low-profile and extremely cost-conscious, applying Confucian virtues of thrift and persistence.

Their size is kept small by the assumed lack of loyalty of non-family employees, who, if they are any good, will just wait and save until they can start their own family business.

Overseas Chinese prefer economic activities in which great gains can be made with little manpower, like commodity trading and real estate. They employ few professional managers, except their sons and sometimes daughters who have been sent to prestigious business schools abroad, but who upon return continue to run the family business the Chinese way.

The origin of this system, or – in the Western view – this lack of system, is found in the history of Chinese society, in which there were no formal laws, only formal networks of powerful people guided by general principles of Confucian virtue. The favours of the authorities could change daily, so nobody could be trusted except one's kinfolk – of whom, fortunately, there used to be many, in an extended family structure. The overseas Chinese way of doing business is also very well adapted to their position in the countries in which they form ethnic minorities, often envied and threatened by ethnic violence.

Overseas Chinese businesses following this unprofessional approach command a collective gross national product of some 200 to 300 billion US dollars, exceeding the GNP of Australia. There is no denying that it works.

Management transfer to poor countries

Four-fifths of the world population live in countries that are not rich but poor. After World War II and decolonization, the stated purpose of the United Nations and the World Bank has been to promote the development of all the world's countries in a war on poverty. After 40 years it looks very much like we are losing this war. If one thing has become clear, it is that the export of Western – mostly American – management practices and theories to poor countries has contributed little or nothing to their development. There has been no lack of effort and money spent for this purpose: students from poor countries have been trained in this country, and teachers and Peace Corps workers have been sent to the poor countries. If nothing else, the general lack of success in economic development of other countries should be sufficient argument to doubt the validity of Western management theories in non-Western environments.

If we examine different parts of the world, the development picture is not equally bleak, and history is often a better predictor than economic factors for what happens today. There is a broad regional pecking order, with East Asia leading. The little dragons have passed into the camp of the wealthy: then follow South-East Asia (with its overseas Chinese minorities), Latin America (in spite of the debt crisis), South Asia, and Africa always trails behind. Several African countries have only become poorer since decolonization.

Russia and China

The crumbling of the former Eastern bloc has left us with a scattering of states and would-be states for which the political and economic future is extremely uncertain. The best predictions are those based on a knowledge of history, because historical trends have taken revenge on the arrogance of the Soviet rulers who believed they could turn them around by brute power. One obvious fact is that the former bloc is extremely heterogeneous, including countries traditionally closely linked with the West by trade and travel, like the Czech Republic, Hungary, Slovenia and the Baltic states, as well as others with a Byzantine or Turkish past: some having been prosperous, others always extremely poor. Let me limit myself to the Russian republic, a huge territory with some 140 million inhabitants, mainly Russians. We know quite a bit about the Russians as their country was a world power for several hundreds of years before communism, and in the 19th century it produced some of the greatest writers in world literature. If I want to understand the Russians – including how they could so long support the Soviet regime – I tend to re-read Lev Nikolayevich Tolstoy. In his most famous novel *Anna Karenina* one of the main characters is a landowner, Levin, whom Tolstoy uses to express his own views and convictions about his people. Russian peasants used to be serfs; serfdom had been abolished in 1861, but the peasants, now tenants, remained as passive as before. Levin wanted to break this passivity by dividing the land among his peasants in exchange for a share of the crops; but the peasants only let the land deteriorate further. Here follows a quote:

[Levin] read political economy and socialistic works … but, as he had expected, found nothing in them related to his undertaking. In the political economy books – in [John Stuart] Mill, for instance, whom he studied first and with great ardour, hoping every minute to find an answer

*to the questions that were engrossing him – he
found only certain laws deduced from the state
of agriculture in Europe; but he could not for
the life of him see why these laws, which did not
apply to Russia, should be considered universal
… Political economy told him that the laws by
which Europe had developed and was developing her wealth were universal and absolute.
Socialist teaching told him that development
along those lines leads to ruin. And neither of
them offered the smallest enlightenment as to
what he, Levin, and all the Russian peasants
and landowners were to do with their millions
of hands and millions of acres, to make them as
productive as possible for the common good.*

In the summer of 1991, the Russian lands yielded a
record harvest, but a large share of it rotted in the fields
because no people were to be found for harvesting. The
passivity is still there, and not only among the peasants.
And the heirs of John Stuart Mill (whom we met before
as one of the early analysts of 'management') again present their universal recipes, which simply do not apply.

Citing Tolstoy, I implicitly suggest that management theorists cannot neglect the great literature of the
countries they want their ideas to apply to. The greatest
novel in Chinese literature is considered Cao Xueqin's
The Story of the Stone, also known as *The Dream of
the Red Chamber* which appeared around 1760. It
describes the rise and fall of two branches of an aris-
tocratic family in Beijing, who live in adjacent plots in
the capital. Their plots are joined by a magnificent garden with several pavilions in it, and the young, mostly
female members of both families are allowed to live in
them. One day the management of the garden is taken
over by a young woman, Tan-Chun, who states:

*I think we ought to pick out a few experienced
trust-worthy old women from among the ones
who work in the Garden – women who know
something about gardening already – and put
the upkeep of the Garden into their hands. We
needn't ask them to pay us rent; all we need
ask them for is an annual share of the produce.
There would be four advantages in this arrangement. In the first place, if we have people whose
sole occupation is to look after trees and flowers
and so on, the condition of the Garden will
improve gradually year after year and there will
be no more of those long periods of neglect followed by bursts of feverish activity when things
have been allowed to get out of hand. Secondly,*

*there won't be the spoiling and wastage we get
at present. Thirdly, the women themselves will
gain a little extra to add to their incomes which
will compensate them for the hard work they
put in throughout the year. And fourthly, there's
no reason why we shouldn't use the money we
should otherwise have spent on nurserymen,
rockery specialists, horticultural cleaners and so
on for other purposes.*

As the story goes on, the capitalist privatization –
because that is what it is – of the Garden is carried through, and it works. When in the 1980s Deng
Xiaoping allowed privatization in the Chinese villages,
it also worked. If we remember what Chinese entrepreneurs are able to do once they have become overseas Chinese, we shouldn't be too surprised. But what
works in China – and worked two centuries ago – does
not have to work in Russia, not in Tolstoy's days and
not today. I am not offering a solution: I only protest
against a naive universalism that knows only one recipe for development, the one supposed to have worked
in the United States.

A theory of culture in management

There is something in all countries called 'management,' but its meaning differs to a larger or smaller
extent from one country to another, and it takes
considerable historical and cultural insight into local
conditions to understand its processes, philosophies
and problems. If already the word may mean so many
different things, how can we expect one country's
theories of management to apply abroad? One should
be extremely careful in making this assumption, and
test it before considering it proven. Management is not
a phenomenon that can be isolated from other processes
taking place in a society. It interacts with what happens
in the family, at school, in politics and government. It
is obviously also related to religion and to beliefs about
science. Theories of management always had to be
interdisciplinary, but if we cross national borders they
should become more interdisciplinary than ever.

As the word culture plays such an important role in
my theory, let me give you my definition, which differs
from some other very respectable definitions. Culture
to me is *the collective programming of the mind which
distinguishes one group or category of people from
another.* In the part of my work I am referring to now,
the category of people is the nation.

Cultural differences between nations can, to some extent, be described using five bipolar dimensions. The position of a country on these dimensions allows us to make some predictions on the way their society operates, including their management processes and the kind of theories applicable to their management.

The first dimension is labelled *power distance*, and it can be defined as the degree of inequality among people which the population of a country considers as normal: from relatively equal (that is, small power distance) to extremely unequal (large power distance). All societies are unequal, but some are more unequal than others.

The second dimension is labelled *individualism*, and it is the degree to which people in a country prefer to act as individuals rather than as members of groups. The opposite of individualism can be called *collectivism*, so collectivism is low individualism. The way I use the word it has no political connotations. In collectivist societies a child learns to respect the group to which it belongs, usually the family, and to differentiate between in-group members and out-group members (that is, all other people). When children grow up they remain members of their group and they expect the group to protect them when they are in trouble. In return, they have to remain loyal to their group throughout life. In individualist societies, a child learns very early to think of itself as 'I' instead of a part of 'we'. It expects one day to have to stand on its own feet and not to get protection from its group anymore; and therefore it also does not feel a need for strong loyalty.

The third dimension is called *masculinity* and its opposite pole *femininity*. It is the degree to which tough values like assertiveness, performance, success and competition, which in nearly all societies are associated with the role of men, prevail over tender values like the quality of life, maintaining warm personal relationships, service, care for the weak and solidarity, which in nearly all societies are more associated with women's roles. Women's roles differ from men's roles in all countries, but in tough societies, the differences are larger than in tender ones.

The fourth dimension is labelled *uncertainty avoidance*, and it can be defined as the degree to which people in a country prefer structured over unstructured situations. Structured situations are those in which there are clear rules as to how one should behave. These rules can be written down, but they can also be unwritten and imposed by tradition. In countries that score high on uncertainty avoidance, people tend to show more nervous energy, while in countries that score low, people are more easy-going. A (national)

society with strong uncertainty avoidance can be called rigid; one with weak uncertainty avoidance, flexible. In countries where uncertainty avoidance is strong a feeling prevails of 'what is different, is dangerous.' In weak uncertainty avoidance societies, the feeling would rather be 'what is different, is curious.'

The fifth dimension is labelled *long-term versus short-term orientation*. On the long-term side one finds values oriented towards the future, like thrift (saving) and persistence. On the short-term side one finds values rather oriented towards the past and present, like respect for tradition and fulfilling social obligations.

Table 1.3.1 lists the scores on all five dimensions for the United States and for the other countries we just discussed. The table shows that each country has its own configuration on the five dimensions. Some of the values in the table have been estimated based on imperfect replications or personal impressions. The different dimension scores do not 'explain' all the differences in management I described earlier. To understand management in a country, one should have both knowledge of and empathy with the entire local scene. However, the scores should make us aware that people in other countries may think, feel and act very differently from us when confronted with basic problems of society.

Idiosyncrasies of American management theories

In comparison to other countries, the US culture profile presents itself as below average on power distance and uncertainty avoidance, highly individualistic, fairly masculine, and short-term oriented. The Germans show a stronger uncertainty avoidance and less extreme individualism; the Japanese are different on all dimensions, least on power distance; the French show larger power distance and uncertainty avoidance, but are less individualistic and somewhat feminine; the Dutch resemble the Americans on the first three dimensions, but score extremely feminine and relatively long-term oriented; Hong Kong Chinese combine large power distance with weak uncertainty avoidance, collectivism, and are very long-term oriented; and so on. The American culture profile is reflected in American management theories. I will just mention three elements not necessarily present in other countries: the stress on market processes, the stress on the individual, and the focus on managers rather than on workers.

TABLE 1.3.1   Culture dimension scores for ten countries

	Power distance	Individualism	Masculinity	Uncertainty avoidance	Long-term orientation
USA	40 L	91 H	62 H	46 L	29 L
Germany	35 L	67 H	66 H	65 M	31 M
Japan	54 M	46 M	95 H	92 H	80 H
France	68 H	71 H	43 M	86 H	30*L
Netherlands	38 L	80 H	14 L	53 M	44 M
Hong Kong	68 H	25 L	57 H	29 L	96 H
Indonesia	78 H	14 L	46 M	48 L	25*L
West Africa	77 H	20 L	46 M	54 M	16 L
Russia	95*H	50*M	40*L	90*H	10*L
China	80*H	20*L	50*M	60*M	118 H

*Estimated

H = top third, M = medium third, L = bottom third (among 53 countries and regions for the first four dimensions; among 23 countries for the fifth).

The stress on market processes

During the 1970s and 1980s it has become fashionable in the United States to look at organizations from a 'transaction costs' viewpoint. Economist Oliver Williamson has opposed 'hierarchies' to 'markets.' The reasoning is that human social life consists of economic transactions between individuals. We found the same in d'Iribarne's description of the US principle of the contract between employer and employee, the labour market in which the worker sells his or her labour for a price. These individuals will form hierarchical organizations when the cost of the economic transactions (such as getting information, finding out whom to trust, etc.) is lower in a hierarchy than when all transactions would take place on a free market.

From a cultural perspective the important point is that the 'market' is the point of departure or base model, and the organization is explained from market failure. A culture that produces such a theory is likely to prefer organizations that internally resemble markets to organizations that internally resemble more structured models, like those in Germany or France. The ideal principle of control in organizations in the market philosophy is competition between individuals. This philosophy fits a society that combines a not-too-large power distance with a not-too-strong uncertainty avoidance and individualism; besides the USA, it will fit all other Anglo countries.

The stress on the individual

I find this constantly in the design of research projects and hypotheses; also in the fact that in the US psychology is clearly a more respectable discipline in management circles than sociology. Culture, however, is a collective phenomenon. Although we may get our information about culture from individuals, we have to interpret it at the level of collectivities. There are snags here known as the 'ecological fallacy' and the 'reverse ecological fallacy'. None of the US college textbooks on methodology I know deal sufficiently with the problem of multilevel analysis.

A striking example is found in the otherwise excellent book *Organizational Culture and Leadership* by Edgar H. Schein (1985). On the basis of his consulting experience he compares two large companies, nicknamed 'Action' and 'Multi'. He explains the difference in cultures between these companies by the group dynamics in their respective boardrooms. Nowhere in the book are any conclusions drawn from the fact that the first company is an American-based computer firm, and the second a Swiss-based pharmaceuticals firm. This information is not even mentioned. A stress on interactions among individuals obviously fits a culture identified as the most individualistic in the world, but it will not be so well understood by the four-fifths of the world population for whom the group prevails over the individual.

One of the conclusions of my own multilevel research has been that culture at the national level and culture at the organizational level – corporate culture – are two very different phenomena and that the use of a common term for both is confusing. If we do use the common term, we should also pay attention to the occupational and the gender level of culture. National cultures differ primarily in the fundamental, invisible values held by a majority of their members, acquired in early childhood, whereas organization cultures are a much more superficial phenomenon residing mainly in the visible practices of the organization, acquired by socialization of the new members who join as young adults. National cultures change only very slowly, if at all; organizational cultures may be consciously changed, although this isn't necessarily easy. This difference between the two types of culture is the secret of the existence of multinational corporations that employ employees with extremely different national cultural values. What keeps them together is a corporate culture based on common practices.

The stress on managers rather than workers

The core element of a work organization around the world is the people who do the work. All the rest is superstructure, and I hope to have demonstrated to you that it may take many different shapes. In the US literature on work organization, however, the core element, if not explicitly then implicitly, is considered the manager. This may well be the result of the combination of extreme individualism with fairly strong masculinity, which has turned the manager into a cultural hero

of almost mythical proportions. For example, he – not really she – is supposed to make decisions all the time. Those of you who are or have been managers must know that this is a fable. Very few management decisions are just 'made' as the myth suggests it. Managers are much more involved in maintaining networks; if anything, it is the rank-and-file worker who can really make decisions on his or her own, albeit on a relatively simple level.

Conclusion

This article started with *Alice in Wonderland*. In fact, the management theorist who ventures outside his or her own country into other parts of the world is like Alice in Wonderland. He or she will meet strange beings, customs, ways of organizing or disorganizing and theories that are clearly stupid, old-fashioned or even immoral – yet they may work, or at least they may not fail more frequently than corresponding theories do at home. Then, after the first culture shock, the traveller to Wonderland will feel enlightened, and may be able to take his or her experiences home and use them advantageously. All great ideas in science, politics and management have travelled from one country to another, and been enriched by foreign influences. The roots of American management theories are mainly in Europe: with Adam Smith, John Stuart Mill, Lev Tolstoy, Max Weber, Henri Fayol, Sigmund Freud, Kurt Lewin and many others. These theories were replanted here and they developed and bore fruit. The same may happen again. The last thing we need is a Monroe doctrine for management.

REFERENCES

Adler, P.S., Goldoftas, B. and Levine, D.I. (1999) 'Flexibility Versus Efficiency? A case study of model changeovers in the Toyota production system', *Organization Science*, 10(1), pp. 43–68.
Adner, R. and Helfat, C.E. (2003) 'Corporate effects and dynamic managerial capabilities', *Strategic Management Journal*, 24(10), pp. 1011–1025.
Amabile, T.M. (1996) *Creativity in Context*, Boulder, CO: Westview Press.
Ancona, D.G. and Nadler, D.A. (1989) 'Top Hats and Executive tales: Designing the senior team', *Sloan Management Review*, 31(1), pp. 19–28.
Argyris, C. and Schon, D. (1978) *Organizational Learning: A Theory of Action Approach*, Reading, MA: Addison Wesley.
Astley, W.G. and Van de Ven, A.H. (1983) 'Central Perspectives and Debates in Organization Theory', *Administrative Science Quarterly*, Vol. 28, pp. 245–273.
Barnard, C.I. (1968) *The Functions of the Executive*, Boston, MA: Harvard University Press, (Vol. 11).
Barrett, D. (1998) *The Paradox Process: Creative Business Solutions Where You Least Expect to Find Them*, New York: Amacom.
Bazerman, M.H. (1998) *Judgement in Managerial Decision Making* (4th edn), New York: John Wiley.
Bazerman, M.H. and Watkins, M. (2004) *Predictable Surprises*, Boston, MA: Harvard Business School Press.
Beech, N., Burns, H., de Caestecker, L., Mackintosh, R. and MacLean, D. (2004) 'Paradox as invitation to act in problematic change situations', *Human Relations*, 57, pp. 1313–1332.

Benner, M.J. and Tushman, M.L. (2002) 'Process Management and Technological Innovation: A longitudinal study of the photography and paint industries', *Administrative Science Quarterly*, 47(4), 676–707.

Benner, M.J. and Tushman, M.L. (2003) 'Exploitation, exploration, and process management: The productivity dilemma revisited', *Academy of Management Review*, 2, pp. 238–256.

Brown, S.L. and Eisenhardt, K.M. (1997) 'The Art of Continuous Change: Linking complexity theory and time-paced evolution in relentlessly shifting organizations', *Administrative Science Quarterly*, 42(1), pp. 1–34.

Bunderson, J.S. (2003) 'Team member functional background and involvement in management teams: Direct effects and the moderating role of power centralization', *Academy of Management Journal*, 46(4), pp. 458–474.

Bunderson, J.S. and Sutcliffe, K.M. (2002) 'Why some teams emphasize learning more than others: Evidence from business unit management teams', in: H. Sondak (ed.) *Towards Phenomenology of Groups and Group Membership*, Vol. 4, Oxford, UK: Elsevier Science, pp. 49–84.

Bunderson, J.S. and Sutcliffe, K.M. (2003) 'Management team learning orientation and business unit performance', *Journal of Applied Psychology*, 88(3), pp. 552–560.

Burgelman, R.A. (1983) 'Corporate Entrepreneurship and Strategic Management: Insights from a Process Study', *Management Science*, Vol. 29, No. 12, pp. 1349–1364.

Burgelman, R.A. (2002) 'Strategy as Vector and the Inertia of Coevolutionary Lock-in', *Administrative Science Quarterly*, 47, pp. 325–357.

Cameron, K.S. and Quinn, R.E. (1988) 'Organizational paradox and transformation', in: R.E. Quinn and K.S. Cameron, *Paradox and Transformation: Towards a Theory of Change in Organization and Management*, Cambridge, MA: Ballinger.

Chandler, A.D. (1962) *Strategy and Structure: Chapters in the History of the Industrial Enterprise*, Cambridge, MA: MIT Press.

D'Iribarne, P. (1990) *La Logique d'Honneur*, Paris: Editions du Seuil.

Daft, R.L. and Weick, K.E. (1984) 'Toward a model of organizations as interpretation systems', *Academy of Management Review*, 9(2), pp. 284–295.

Denison, D., Hooijberg, R. and Quinn, R.E. (1995) 'Paradox and performance: Toward a theory of behavioral complexity in managerial leadership', *Organization Science*, 6(5), pp. 524–540.

Deutsch, M. (1973) *The Resolution of Conflict*, New Haven, CT: Yale University Press.

Duncan, R.B. (1976) 'The Ambidextrous Organization: Designing Dual Structures for Innovation', in: R.H. Kilmann, L.R. Pondy and D.P. Slevin (eds), *The Management of Organizational Design*, New York: Elsevier North Holland, pp. 167–188.

Dutton, J.E. and Ashford, S.J. (1993) 'Selling issues to top management', *Academy of Management Review*, 18(3), pp. 397–428.

Dutton, J.E. and Jackson, S.E. (1987) 'Categorizing strategic issues: Links to organizational action', *Academy of Management Review*, 12(1), pp. 76–90.

Edmondson, A. (1999) 'Psychological safety and learning behavior in work teams', *Administrative Science Quarterly*, 44(2), pp. 350–383.

Edmondson, A.C., Roberto, M.A. and Watkins, M.D. (2003) 'A dynamic model of top management team effectiveness: Managing unstructured task streams', *Administrative Science Quarterly*, 14(3), pp. 297–325.

Eisenhardt, K.M. (2000) 'Paradox, Spirals, Ambivalence: The New Language of Change and Pluralism', *Academy of Management Review*, 25(4), pp. 703–705.

Eisenhardt, K.M. and Westcott, B.J. (1988) 'Paradoxical demands and the creation of excellence: The case of just-in-time manufacturing', in: R. Quinn and K. Cameron (eds) *Paradox and Transformation: Towards a Theory of Change in Organization and Management*, Cambridge, MA: Ballinger, pp. 169–194.

Eisenhardt, K.M. and Zbaracki, M.J. (1992) 'Strategic decision making', *Strategic Management Journal*, 13(S2), pp. 17–37.

Eisenhardt, K.M., Kahwajy, J.L. and Bourgeois L.J. (1997) 'Conflict and strategic choice: How top management teams disagree', *California Management Review*, 39(2), pp. 42–62.

Emery, F.E. and Trist, E.L. (1965) 'The Causal Texture of Organizational Environments', *Human Relations*, 18, pp. 21–32.

Fayol, H. (1916/1949) *General and Industrial Management*, London: Pitman.

Finkelstein, S. and Hambrick, D.C. (1996) *Strategic leadership: Top Executives and Their Effect on Organizations*, St. Paul, MN: West.

Fletcher, J.L. and Olwyler, K. (1997) *Paradoxical Thinking: How to Profit from Your Contradictions*, San Fransisco: Berrett-Koehler.

Flynn, F.J. and Chatman, J.A. (2001) 'Strong cultures and innovation: Oxymoron and opportunity?' in: C. Cooper, S. Cartwright and C. Early (eds) *International Handbook of Organizational Culture and Climate*, Chichester, England: J. Wiley, pp. 263–287.

Follett, M.P. (1925/1996) 'Constructive conflict', in: P. Graham (ed.) *Mary Parker Follett: Prophet of Management*, Boston, MA: Harvard Business School Press.

Ford, J.D. and Backoff, R.W. (1988) 'Organizational change in and out of dualities and paradox', in: R. Quinn and K. Cameron (eds) *Paradox and Transformation*, Cambridge, MA: Ballinger Publishing Company, pp. 81–121.

Frankel, V. (1960) 'Paradoxical intention', *American Journal of Psychotherapy*, 14, pp. 520–535.

Gavetti, G. and Levinthal, D. (2000) 'Looking forward and looking backward: Cognitive and experiential search', *Administrative Science Quarterly*, 45(1), pp. 113–137.

Gibson, C.B. and Birkinshaw, J. (2004) 'The antecedents, consequences, and mediating role of organizational ambidexterity', *Academy of Management Journal*, 47(2), pp. 209–226.

Gilbert, C.G. (2005) 'Unbundling the structure of inertia: Resource versus routine rigidity', *Academy of Management Journal*, 48(5), pp. 741–763.

Hackman, J.R. (2002) *Leading Teams: Setting the Stage for Great Performances*, Boston, MA: Harvard Business School Press.

Hambrick, D.C. (1994) 'Top management groups: A conceptual integration and reconsideration of the "team" label', in: B.M. Staw and L. Cummings (eds) *Research in Organizational Behavior*, Greenwich, CT: JAI Press.

He, Z.L. and Wong, P.K. (2004) 'Exploration vs. exploitation: An empirical test of the ambidexterity hypothesis', *Organization Science*, 15(4), pp. 481–494.

Heenan, D.A. and Bennis, W.G. (1999) *Co-leaders: The Power of Great Partnerships*, New York: John Wiley & Sons.

Hemp, P. and Stewart, T.A. (2004) 'Leading change when business is good: An interview with Sam Palmisano', *Harvard Business Review*, 82(12), pp. 60–71.

Henderson, R. and Clark, K. (1991) 'Architectural innovation: The reconfiguration of existing product technologies and the failure of established firms', *Administrative Science Quarterly*, 35, pp. 9–30.

Hofstede, G. (1993) 'Cultural constraints in management theories', *Academy of Management Executive*, 7(1), pp. 8–21.

Huff, A.S. (1990) *Mapping Strategic Thought*, Chichester, NY: John Wiley & Sons.

Huff, A.S. (1997) 'A current and future agenda for cognitive research in organizations', *Journal of Management Studies*, 34(6), pp. 947–952.

Jay, J. (2013) 'Navigating paradox as a mechanism of change and innovation in hybrid organizations', *Academy of Management Journal*, February, 56(1), pp. 137–159.

Johnson, B. (1996) *Polarity Management*, Amherst, MA: HRD Press Inc.

Kaplan S., Murray A. and Henderson R. (2003) 'Discontinuities and senior management: Assessing the role of recognition in pharmaceutical firm response to biotechnology', *Industrial Corporate Change*, 12(4), pp. 203–233.

Kaplan, S. (2003) 'Framing contests: Strategy-making during a technological discontinuity', working paper, Philadelphia, PA: Wharton School, University of Pennsylvania.

Kerr, S. (1975) 'On the folly of rewarding A, while hoping for B', *Academy of Management Journal*, 18(4), pp. 769–782.

Ketchen, D.J., Thomas, J.B. and McDaniel, R.R. (1996) 'Process, content and context: synergistic effects on organizational performance', *Journal of Management*, 22, pp. 231–257.

Langer, E. (1989) *Mindfulness*, Boston, MA: Addison-Wesley.

Latham, G.P. and Locke, E.A. (eds) (1995) *Goal Setting: A Motivational Technique That Works*, 2nd ed., Englewood Cliffs, NJ: Prentice Hall.

Lawrence, P.R. and Lorsch, J.W. (1967) *Organization and Environment: Managing Differentiation and Integration*, Boston, MA: Harvard University Press.

Lax, D.A. and Sebenius, J.K. (1986) *The Manager as Negotiator: Bargaining for Cooperative and Competitive Gain*, New York: Free Press.

Leonard-Barton, D. (1992) 'Core capabilities and core rigidities: A paradox in managing new product development', *Strategic Management Journal*, 13(S1), pp. 111–125.

Levinthal, D.A. and March, J.G. (1993) 'The myopia of learning', *Strategic Management Journal*, 14(S2), pp. 95–112.

Lewis, M. (2000) 'Exploring paradox: toward a more comprehensive guide', *Academy of Management Review*, 25(4), pp. 760–776.

Linehan, M. (1993) *Cognitive-Behavioral Treatment of Borderline Personality Disorder*, New York: Guilford Press.

Lorsch, J.W. and Tierney, T.J. (2002) *Aligning the Stars: How to Succeed When Professionals Drive Results*, Boston, MA: Harvard Business Press.

Margolis, J.D. and Walsh, J.P. (2003) 'Misery loves companies: Rethinking social initiatives by business', *Administrative Science Quarterly*, 48(2), pp. 268–305.

Mason, R.O. and Mitroff, I.I. (1981) *Challenging Strategic Planning Assumptions*, New York: Wiley.

Miles, R.E. and Snow, C.C., (1978) *Organizational Strategy, Structure, and Process*, New York: McGraw-Hill.

Murnighan, J.K. and Conlon, D.E. (1991) 'The dynamics of intense work groups: A study of British string quartets', *Administrative Science Quarterly*, 36, pp. 165–186.

Nadler, D.A. and Tushman, M.L. (1992) 'Designing organizations that have good fit: A framework for understanding new architectures', in: D. Nadler (ed.) *Organizational Architecture*, San Francisco, CA: Jossey-Bass.

Nadler, D.A. and Tushman, M.L. (1996) *Competing By Design: The Power of Organizational Architecture*, New York: Oxford University Press.

Nemeth, C.J. and Wachtler, J. (1983) 'Creative problem solving as a result of majority vs minority influence', *European Journal of Social Psychology*, 13(1), pp. 45–55.

Nonaka, I. and Toyama, R. (2002) 'A firm as a dialectical being: towards a dynamic theory of a firm', *Industrial and Corporate Change*, 11(5), pp. 995–1009.

Paine, L.S. (2003) *Value Shift: Why Companies Must Merge Social and Financial Imperatives to Achieve Superior Performance*, New York: McGraw-Hill.

Perlow, L.A., Gittell, J.H. and Katz, N. (2004) 'Contextualizing patterns of work group interaction: Toward a nested theory of structuration', *Organization Science*, 15(5), pp. 520–536.

Pettigrew, A. (1992) 'The character and significance of strategy process research', *Strategic Management Journal*, 13, pp. 5–16.

Pettigrew, A. and Whipp, R. (1991) *Managing Change for Competitive Success*, Oxford: Basil Blackwell.

Pinkley, R.L. (1990) 'Dimensions of conflict frame: Disputant interpretations of conflict', *Journal of Applied Psychology*, 75(2), pp. 117–126.

Poole, M.S. and Van de Ven, A.H. (1989) 'Using paradox to build management and organization theories', *Academy of Management Review*, 14(4), pp. 562–578.

Porras, J.I. and Collins, J.C. (1997) *Built to Last: Successful Habits of Visionary Companies*, New York: Harper Business.

Porter, M.E. and Kramer, M.A. (2006) 'Strategy and Society: The Link Between Competitive Advantage and Corporate Social Responsibility', Harvard Business Review, December.

Porter, M.E. and Kramer, M.A. (2011) 'Creating Shared Value: How to reinvent capitalism and unleash a wave of innovation and growth', *Harvard Business Review*, January–February, pp. 3–17.

Porter, R. (1980) *Presidential Decision Making: The Economic Policy Board*, Cambridge, UK: Cambridge University Press.

Quinn, R.E. (1984) 'Applying the competing values approach to leadership: Towards an integrative model', in: J.G. Hunt, R. Steward, C. Schriesheim and D. Hosking (eds) *Leaders and Managers: International Perspectives on Managerial Behavior and Leadership*, New York: Paragon, pp. 10–27.

Quinn, R.E. (1988) *Beyond Rational Management: Mastering the Paradoxes and Competing Demands of High Performance*, San Francisco: Jossey-Bass.

Raisch, S., Birkinshaw, J., Probst, G. and Tushman, M.L. (2009) 'Organizational ambidexterity: Balancing exploitation and exploration for sustained performance', *Organization Science*, 20(4), pp. 685–695.

Repenning, N.P. (2002) 'A simulation-based approach to understanding the dynamics of innovation implementation', *Organization Science*, 13(2), pp. 109–127.

Rittel, H. (1972) 'On the planning crisis: systems analysis of the "first and second generations"', *Bedriftsokonomen*, 8, pp. 390–396.

Rivkin, J.W. and Siggelkow, N. (2003) 'Balancing search and stability: Interdependencies among elements of organizational design', *Management Science*, 49(3), pp. 290–311.

Rothenberg, A. (1979) *The Emerging Goddess: The Creative Process in Art, Science, and Other Fields* (p. 440). Chicago, IL: University of Chicago Press.

Rothermael, F.T. (2001) 'Incumbent's advantage through exploiting complementary assets via interfirm cooperation', *Strategic Management Journal*, 22(6–7), pp. 687–699.

Rumelt, R.P. (1980) 'The Evaluation of Business Strategy', in: W.F. Glueck (ed.), *Business Policy and Strategic Management*, Third Edition, New York: McGraw-Hill.

Schein, E.H. (1985) *Organizational Culture and Leadership*, San Francisco, CA: Jossey-Bass.

Sherif, M. (1971) 'Superordinate goals in the reduction of intergroup conflict', in: B.L. Hinton and H.J. Reits (eds) *Groups and Organizations*, Belmont, CA: Wadsworth.

Siggelkow, N. and Levinthal, D.A. (2003) 'Temporarily divide to conquer: Centralized, decentralized, and reintegrated organizational approaches to exploration and adaptation', *Organization Science*, 14(6), pp. 650–669.

Smith, A. (1776) *An Inquiry into the Nature and Causes of the Wealth of Nations*, London: printed for W. Strahan and T. Cadell, in the Strand.

Smith, K.K. and Berg, D.N. (1987) *Paradoxes of Group Life*, San Francisco, CA: Jossey-Bass.

Smith, W.K. (2009), 'A dynamic approach to managing contradictions', *Industrial and Organizational Psychology: Perspectives on Science and Practice*, 2, pp. 338–343.

Smith, W.K. and Lewis, M.W. (2011) 'Toward a Theory of Paradox: A Dynamic Equilibrium Model of Organizing', *Academy of Management Review*, 36(2), pp. 381–403.

Smith, W.K. and Tushman, M.L. (2005) 'Managing strategic contradictions: A top management model for managing innovation streams', *Organization Science*, 16(5), pp. 522–536.

Smith, W.K., Lewis, M.W. and Tushman, M.L. (2016), 'Both/And Leadership', *Harvard Business Review*, May, pp. 62–70.

Steiner, I. (1972) *Group Processes and Productivity*, New York: Academic Press.

Suedfeld, P., Tetlock, T. and Streufert, S (1992), 'Conceptual/integrative complexity', in: C. Smith, J. Atkinson, D. McClelland and J. Verof (eds) *Motivation and Personality: Handbook of Thematic Content Analysis*, Cambridge, England: Cambridge University Press, pp. 393–400.

Sull, D.N. (1999) 'The dynamics of standing still: Firestone tire & rubber and the radial revolution', *Business History Review*, 73(3), pp. 430–464.

Sull, D.N., Tedlow, R.S. and Rosenbloom, R.S. (1997) 'Managerial commitments and technological change in the US tire industry', *Industrial and Corporate Change*, 6(2), pp. 461–500.

Sun Tzu (1983) *The Art of War*, New York: Delacorte Press.

Sundaramurthy, C. and Lewis, M. (2003) 'Control and collaboration: Paradoxes of governance', *Academy of Management Review*, 28(3), pp. 397–415.

Sutton, R. (2002) *Weird Ideas that Work: 11½ Practices for Promoting, Managing, and Sustaining Innovation*, New York: Free Press.

Taylor, F.W (1903) *Shop Management*, New York: Harper.

Taylor, F.W. (1911) *The Principles of Scientific Management*, New York: Harper.

Teece, D.J. (2007) 'Explicating dynamic capabilities: the nature and microfoundations of (sustainable) enterprise performance', *Strategic Management Journal*, 28(13), pp. 1319–1350.

Teece, D.J., Pisano, G. and Shuen, A. (1997) 'Dynamic Capabilities and Strategic Management', *Strategic Management Journal*, 18(7, August), pp. 509–533.

Tetlock, P.E., McGraw, A.P. and Kristel, O.V. (2004) 'Proscribed forms of social cognition: Taboo trade-offs, blocked exchanges, forbidden base rates, and heretical counterfactuals', in: N. Haslam (ed.) *Relational Models Theory: A Contemporary Overview*, Mahway, NJ: Erlbaum, pp. 247–262.

Thompson, J.D. (1967) *Organizations in Action: Social Science Bases of Administrative,* New York: McGraw-Hill.

Thurbin, P.J. (1998) *The Influential Strategist: Using the Power of Paradox in Strategic Thinking*, London: Financial Times. Tripsas, M. and Gavetti, G. (2000) 'Capabilities, cognition, and inertia: Evidence from digital imaging', *Strategic Management Journal*, 21(10–11), pp. 1147–1161.

Tushman, M.L, Smith, W., Wood, R., Westerman, G. and O'Reilly, C. (2003) *Innovation Streams and Ambidextrous Organizational Forms*, Working paper, Boston, MA: Harvard Business School.

Tushman, M.L. and O'Reilly III, C.A. (1996) 'Ambidextrous organizations: Managing evolutionary and revolutionary change', *California Management Review*, 38(4, Summer), pp. 8–30.

Tushman, M.L. and O'Reilly III, C.A. (1997) *Winning Through Innovation: A Practical Guide to Leading Organization Change and Renewal*, Boston, MA: Harvard Business School Press.

Tyre, M.J. and Von Hippel, E. (1997) 'The situated nature of adaptive learning in organizations', *Organization Science*, 8(1), pp. 71–83.

Van de Ven, A.D., Poley, D.E., Garud, R. and Venkataraman, S. (1999) *The Innovation Journey*, New York: Oxford University Press.

Virany, B., Tushman, M.L. and Romanelli, E. (1992) 'Executive succession and organization outcomes in turbulent environments: An organization learning approach', *Organization Science*, 3(1), pp. 72–91.

Voorhees, B. (1986) 'Towards Duality Theory', *General Systems Bull.*, 16(2), pp. 58–61.

Wageman, R. (2001) 'How leaders foster self-managing team effectiveness: Design choices versus hands-on coaching', *Organization Science*, 12(5), pp. 559–577.

Walsh, J.P. (1995) 'Managerial and organizational cognition: Notes from a trip down memory lane', *Organization Science*, 6(3), pp. 280–321.

Walton, R.E. and McKersie, R.B. (eds) (1965) *A Behavioral Theory of Labor Negotiations: An Analysis of a Social Interaction System*, New York: McGraw Hill.

Wegner, D. (1986) 'Transactive memory: A contemporary analysis of group mind', in: B. Mullen and G.R. Goethals (eds) *Theories of Group Behavior*, New York: Springer-Verlag, pp. 185–208.

Weick, K. (1979) *The Social Psychology of Organizing* (2nd ed.), Reading, MA: Addison-Wesley.

Weick, K.E. and Roberts, K.H. (1993) 'Collective mind in organizations: Heedful interrelating on flight decks', *Administrative Science Quarterly*, 38(3), pp. 357–381.

Weick, K.E., Sutcliffe, D. and Obstfeld, D. (1999) 'Organizing for high reliability: Processes of collective mindfulness', in: R.I. Sutton and B.M. Staw (eds) *Research in Organizational Behavior*, Stamford, CT: JAI Press, pp. 81–123.

Whittington, R. (1993) *What Is Strategy and Does It Matter?* London: Routledge.

Wing, R.L. (1988) *The Art of Strategy: A New Translation of Sun Tzu's Classic 'The Art of War'*, New York: Doubleday

STRATEGIZING

A mind all logic is like a knife all blade. It makes the hand bleed that uses it.

Rabindranath Tagore (1861–1941); Indian philosopher, poet and 1913 Nobel Prize winner in Literature

INTRODUCTION

What goes on in the mind of the strategist? A fascinating question that is easy to ask, but difficult to answer. Yet, it is a question that is important in two ways – generally and personally. Generally, knowing what goes on in the minds of managers during strategy processes is essential for understanding their choices and behaviours. Opening up the black box of the strategist's mind to see how decisions are made can help to anticipate or influence this thinking. Grasping how managers shape their strategic views and select their preferred actions can be used to develop more effective strategies. It is due to this importance of strategic thinking that a separate chapter in this book is devoted to the subject. Yet, for each reader personally, the topic of strategizing is also of key importance, as it automatically raises the questions 'what is going on in *my* mind?' and 'how strategic is *my* thinking?' Exploring the subject of strategizing triggers each person to explore their own thought processes and critically reflect on their own strategy preferences. Ideally, wondering about the mind of the strategist should inspire readers to constantly question their own assumptions, thoughts, beliefs and ideas, and to sharpen their strategic thinking as they move through the following chapters. For this reason, it seems only appropriate to start the book with this topic.

So, what goes on in the mind of the strategist? Well, a lot, but if reduced to its bare essentials it can be said that strategists are engaged in the process of dealing with *strategic problems*. Not problems in the negative sense of troublesome conditions that need to be avoided, but in the neutral sense of challenging situations that need to be resolved – a strategic problem is a set of circumstances requiring a reconsideration of the current course of action, either to profit from observed opportunities or to respond to perceived threats. To deal with these strategic problems, managers must not simply think, they must go through a *strategic reasoning process,* searching for ways to define and resolve the challenges at hand. Managers must structure their individual thinking steps into a reasoning process that will result in effective strategic behaviour. The question is how managers actually go about defining strategic problems (how do they identify and diagnose what is going on?) and how do they go about solving strategic problems (how do they generate, evaluate and decide on potential answers?). It is this issue of strategic reasoning, as a string of strategic thinking activities directed at defining and resolving strategic problems, which will be examined in further detail below.

THE ISSUE OF STRATEGIC REASONING

The mind of the strategist is a complex and fascinating apparatus that never fails to astonish and dazzle on the one hand, and disappoint and frustrate on the other. We are often surprised by the power of the human mind, but equally often stunned by its limitations. For the discussion here it is not necessary to unravel all of the mysteries surrounding the functioning of the human brain, but a short overview of the capabilities and limitations of the human mind will help us to understand the issue of strategic reasoning.

The human ability to know is referred to as 'cognition'. As strategists want to know about the strategic problems facing their organizations, they need to engage in *cognitive activities*. These cognitive activities (or strategic thinking activities) need to be structured into a strategic reasoning process. Hence, the first step towards a better understanding of what goes on in the mind of the strategist is to examine the various cognitive activities making up a strategic reasoning process. The four main cognitive activities will be discussed in the first subsection below. To be able to perform these cognitive activities, people need to command certain mental faculties. While very sophisticated, the human brain is still physically strictly limited in what it can do. These limitations to people's *cognitive abilities* will be reviewed in the second subsection. To deal with its inherent physical shortcomings, the human brain copes by building simplified models of the world, referred to as *cognitive maps*. The functioning of cognitive maps will be addressed in the third subsection.

In Figure 2.1 the relationship between these three topics is visualized, using the metaphor of a computer. The cognitive abilities of our brains can be seen as a hardware level question – what are the physical limits on our mental faculties? The cognitive maps used by our brains can be seen as an operating system level question – what type of platform/language is 'running' in our brain? The cognitive activities carried out by our brains can be seen as an application level question – what type of programme is strategic reasoning?

Cognitive activities

The strategic reasoning process consists of a number of strategic thinking elements or cognitive activities – mental tasks intended to increase the strategist's knowing. A general

FIGURE 2.1   Cognitive activities, maps and abilities

Cognitive Activities → Application Level *(Mental Reasoning)*

Cognitive Maps → Operating System Level *(Mental Models)*

Cognitive Abilities → Hardware Level *(Mental Faculties)*

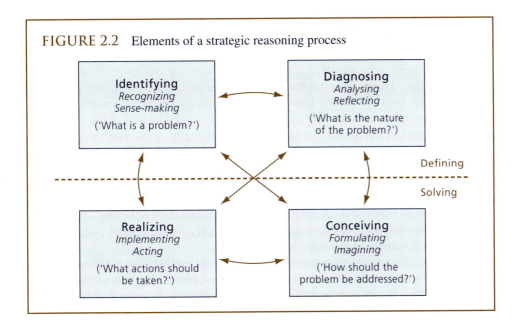

FIGURE 2.2   Elements of a strategic reasoning process

distinction can be made between cognitive activities directed towards *defining* a strategic problem, and cognitive activities directed at *solving* a strategic problem.

Each of these two major categories can be further split into two (see Figure 2.2), leading to the following general elements of a strategic reasoning process:

- Identifying. Before strategists can benefit from opportunities or to counter threats, they must be aware of these challenges and acknowledge their importance. This part of the reasoning process is also referred to as identifying, recognizing, sense-making or sensing.

- Diagnosing. To grapple with a problem, strategists must try to understand the structure of the problem and its underlying causes. This part of the reasoning process is also referred to as analysing, reflecting or shaping.

- Conceiving. To deal with a strategic problem, strategists must come up with a potential solution. If more than one solution is available, strategists must select the most promising one. This part of the reasoning process is also referred to as formulating, imagining or seizing.

- Realizing. A strategic problem is only really solved once concrete actions are undertaken that achieve results. Strategists must therefore carry out problem-solving activities and evaluate whether the consequences are positive. This part of the reasoning process is also referred to as implementing, acting or reconfiguring.

A structured approach to these four cognitive activities is to carry them out in the above order, starting with problem identification and then moving through diagnosis to conceiving solutions and finally realizing them (i.e. clockwise movement in Figure 2.2). In this approach the first step, identifying strategic problems, would require extensive external and internal scanning, thorough sifting of incoming information and the selection of priority issues. In the next reasoning step, the strategic problems recognized would have to be diagnosed by gathering more detailed data, and by further analysing and refining this information. Once the problem has been properly defined, a strategy could be formulated by evaluating the available options and deciding which solution would be best. In the final phase, realization, the strategist would need to ensure execution of the proposed solution by consciously planning and controlling implementation activities. In this case, the four elements of the strategic reasoning process could actually be labelled recognizing, analysing, formulating and implementing.

However, strategists do not always reason in this step-by-step fashion. Their thinking is often less orderly, with identifying, diagnosing, conceiving and realizing intermingled with one another – even going on at the same time. Nor are cognitive activities as straightforward as portrayed above. The identification of strategic problems is often not about objective observation, but rather subjective interpretation – by looking at the world from a particular angle, strategists see and value particular strengths, weaknesses, opportunities and threats. Such sense-making activities (Gioia and Chittipeddi, 1991; Hodgkinson and Healy, 2011; Weick, 1979) lead to attention being paid to some issues, while others do not make the strategic agenda (Dutton, 1988; Ocasio, 1997). Likewise, diagnosing strategic problems is not always a structured analytical process. Gaining a deeper understanding of strategic problems may involve explicit analysis, but also intuitive reflecting – by employing unconscious reasoning rules, strategists often quickly form a general picture of how key aspects of a strategic problem are interrelated.

Conceiving strategic solutions can be equally 'messy' and subjective. Often, strategic options are not chosen from an available repertoire of potential solutions, but they are invented. In other words, new options are often not selected, discovered or figured out, but are envisioned – strategists imagine how things could be done. Such idea generation can involve reasoning by analogy or metaphor, brainstorming or pure fantasizing. New potential solutions may come to the strategist in a flash (Eureka!) or emerge over time, but usually require a period of incubation beforehand and a period of nurturing afterwards. Furthermore, strategists often find it impossible to objectively prove which new idea would be the best solution. Therefore, the process of deciding on the solution to be pursued may involve more judgement than calculation.

Finally, it must be emphasized that action does not always come last, in the form of solution implementation. Often, strategists do not wait for a problem to be precisely defined and for a solution to be fully conceived before starting to act. On the contrary, strategists often feel they must first act – they must have experience with a problem and know that the current strategy will not be able to overcome the problem. To find a suitable solution it is often also necessary to test certain assumptions in practice and to experiment. Hence, acting regularly precedes, or goes hand-in-hand with, all other cognitive activities.

Cognitive abilities

People are not omniscient – they do not have infinite knowledge. To some extent this is due to the nature of reality – many future events are inherently unpredictable, due to factors that are uncertain or unknowable. Yet, humans are also burdened with rather imperfect cognitive abilities. The human brain is severely limited in what it can know (Simon, 1957). The limitation to humans' cognitive abilities is largely due to three factors:

■ Limited information sensing ability. Humanity's first 'handicap' is a limited information-sensing ability. While the senses – touch, smell, taste, hearing and seeing – are bombarded with stimuli, much of reality remains unobservable to humans. This is partially due to the physical inability to be everywhere, all the time, noticing everything. However, people's limited ability to register the structure of reality is also due to the inherent superficiality of the senses and the complexity of reality. The human senses cannot directly identify the way the world works and the underlying causal relationships. Only the physical consequences of the complex interactions between elements in reality can be picked up by a person's sensory system. Therefore, the mental representations of the world that individuals build up in their minds are necessarily based on circumstantial evidence.

■ Limited information processing capacity. Unfortunately, a second drawback is that humans do not have unlimited data processing abilities. Thinking through problems with many variables, complex relationships and huge amounts of data is a task that people find extremely difficult to perform. Approaching every activity in this way would totally overload a person's brain. For this reason, humans hardly ever think through a problem with full use of all available data, but necessarily make extensive use of mental shortcuts, referred to as "cognitive heuristics" (Janis, 1989). Cognitive heuristics are mental 'rules of thumb' that simplify a problem, so that it can be more quickly understood and solved. Cognitive heuristics focus a person's attention on a number of key variables that are believed to be most important, and present a number of simple decision rules to rapidly resolve an issue. The set of possible solutions to be considered is also limited in advance.

■ Limited information storage capacity. Another human cognitive shortcoming is poor memory. People have only a limited capacity for storing information. Remembering all individuals, events, dates, places and circumstances is beyond the ability of the human brain. Therefore, people must store information very selectively and organize this information in a way that it can be easily retrieved when necessary. Here again, cognitive heuristics are at play – 'rules of thumb' make the memorization process manageable in the face of severe capacity limitations. Such heuristics help to simplify complex clusters of data into manageable chunks and help to categorize, label and store this information so that it can be recalled at a later time.

To deal with these severe physical limitations, the brain has come up with more than only simple cognitive heuristics. The human mind has come to work with more holistic cognitive maps.

Cognitive maps

Knowledge that people have is stored in their minds in the form of "cognitive maps" (e.g. McCaskey, 1982; Weick and Bourgnon, 1986), also referred to as "cognitive schemata" (e.g. Anderson, 1983; Schwenk, 1988), "mental models" (e.g. Day and Lord, 1992; Knight *et al.*, 1999), "knowledge structures" (e.g. Lyles and Schwenk, 1992; Walsh, 1995) and "construed reality" (Finkelstein and Hambrick, 1996). These cognitive maps are representations in a person's mind of how the world works. A cognitive map of a certain situation reflects a person's beliefs about the importance of the issues and about the cause and effect relationships between them.

Cognitive maps are formed over time through education, experience and interaction with others. Based on the inputs of their senses, people will infer causal relationships between phenomena, making guesses about unobservable factors and resolving inconsistencies between the bits of information received. In turn, people's cognitive maps steer their senses; while cognitive maps are built on past sensory data, they will consequently direct which new information will be sought and perceived. A person's cognitive map will focus attention on particular phenomena, while blocking out other data as noise, and will quickly make clear how a situation should be perceived. In this way, a cognitive map provides an interpretive filter or perceptual screen, aiding the senses in selecting and understanding external stimuli (Starbuck and Milliken, 1988). Furthermore, cognitive maps help to direct behaviour by providing an existing repertoire of 'problem-solving' responses (also referred to as 'scripts' or 'recipes') from which an appropriate action can be derived.

In building their cognitive maps, people acquire a lot of their knowledge by means of direct experience. They learn to communicate, play an instrument, drive a vehicle and solve problems. This knowledge is added to people's cognitive maps without being explicitly articulated. In other words, knowledge gained through experiential learning is usually not codified into formal rules, principles, models or theories, but remains tacit (Nonaka, 1991; Polanyi, 1966). People formulate implicit models and draw conclusions, but do so largely unconsciously. In this way, cognitive maps evolve without people themselves being entirely aware of their own cognitive map. Hence, when people use their intuition, this is not a mystical or irrational way of reasoning, but thinking guided by the tacit knowledge they have acquired in the past (Behling and Eckel, 1991). Intuitive thinking is the opposite of analytical thinking – informal and holistic (Von Winterfeldt and Edwards, 1986). Informal means that the thinking is largely unconscious and based on experiences, variables and causal relationships not explicitly identifiable by those doing the thinking. Holistic means that the thinker does not aim at unravelling phenomena into their constituent parts, but rather maintains a more integrated view of reality.

Yet, people's cognitive maps are not developed independently, but rather in interaction with one another. People tend to construct a shared understanding of the world by interacting with each other within a group over an extended period of time. By exchanging interpretations of what they see, it is said that they *enact* a shared reality (Daft and Weick, 1984; Smircich and Stubbart, 1985). The resulting shared cognitive map is variably referred to as the group's "dominant logic" (Prahalad and Bettis, 1986), "common paradigm" (Kuhn, 1970) or "belief system" (Noorderhaven, 1995). Such a shared worldview can exist within small social units, such as a firm or a family, but also within larger units, such as an industry or a nation.

As individuals can belong to different groups, they can be influenced by different belief systems simultaneously. As members of a national culture, their cognitive maps will to a certain extent be influenced by the beliefs dominant within the nation. As employees of a company, their cognitive maps will be affected by the beliefs common within the firm and the industry as well. In the same manner, people can be impacted by the professional community to which they belong, their religious affiliation, their political party and any other groups in which they interact with others (Hambrick *et al.*, 1993; Sutcliffe and Huber, 1998). Due to the mutually inclusive nature of group membership, an individual's cognitive map will be a complex combination of elements taken from different group-level dominant logics. While these paradigms on which an individual draws can be complementary, or overlapping yet consistent, it is quite possible that inconsistencies arise (Schein, 1985; Trice and Beyer, 1993).

As shared beliefs develop over time through interaction and are passed on through socialization, they remain largely tacit. The shared cognitive map of a group is literally 'common sense' – sense shared by a common group of people. However, where members of different groups come into conflict with one another, or where an individual needs to deal with the inconsistencies brought on by multiple group memberships, beliefs can become more articulated (Glynn, 2000). Different behaviours, based on different cognitive maps, will often lead to the identification and codification of beliefs, either to protect them or to engage in debate with people with other views. As paradigms become more articulated, they also become more mobile, making it possible to transfer ideas to people without direct interaction.

The downside of cognitive maps is that they exhibit a high level of rigidity. People are generally not inclined to change their minds. Once people's cognitive maps have formed and they have a grip on reality, they become resistant to signals that challenge their conceptions. As McCaskey (1982) remarks, the mind "strives mightily to bring order, simplicity, consistency and stability to the world it encounters", and is therefore reluctant to welcome the ambiguity presented by contradicting data. People tend to significantly overestimate the value of information that confirms their cognitive map, underestimate dis-confirming information, and they actively seek out evidence that supports their current beliefs (Schwenk, 1984). Once an interpretive filter is in place, seeing is not believing, but *believing is seeing*. People might have the impression that they are constantly learning, but they are largely learning within the bounds of a paradigm. When an individual's map is supported by similar beliefs shared within a firm, industry or country, the ability to question key aspects of a paradigm will usually be rather limited. Not only does the individual have no 'intellectual sounding board' for teasing out new ideas, but deviation from the dominant logic might also have adverse social and political ramifications within the group (e.g. Aldrich and Fiol, 1994; DiMaggio and Powell, 1983). Not for nothing the old proverb is: "old ideas never change; they eventually die out" (Kuhn, 1970).

For strategists, cognitive rigidity is particularly worrying. Strategists should be at the forefront of market developments, identifying changing circumstances and new opportunities before their competitors do. Strategizing is by its very nature focused on understanding and shaping the future, and therefore strategists must have the ability to challenge current beliefs and to change their own mind. They must be able to come up with innovative, yet feasible new strategies that will fit with the unfolding reality. This places extraordinary cognitive demands on strategists – they must be able to overcome the limitations of their own cognitive maps and develop a new understanding.

THE PARADOX OF LOGIC AND INTUITION

Albert Einstein called the intuitive or metaphoric mind a sacred gift. He added that the rational mind was a faithful servant. It is paradoxical that in the context of modern life we have begun to worship the servant and defile the divine.
Bob Samples (1933–2012); independent scholar, artist and author

Many management theorists have noted that the opposites of logic and intuition create a tension for managers (e.g. Hodgkinson and Healey, 2011, Reading 2.3; Sadler-Smith, 2004). While some researchers make a strong case for more formal analysis (e.g. Isenberg, 1984; Schoemaker and Russo, 1993; Teece, 2007, Reading 2.1), there is a broad understanding that managers need to employ both logical and intuitive thinking, even if they are each other's opposites.

The extensive use of intuitive judgement among managers is understood by most as necessary and beneficial. A manager's intuition is built up through years of experience and contains a vast quantity of tacit knowledge that can only superficially be tapped by formal analysis. Intuition, therefore, can give a richer assessment of qualitative information. Moreover, intuitive thinking is faster (Kahneman, 2011) and better at capturing the big picture than logical thinking. And very practically, intuition is needed to cut corners in the large numbers of data and the contradicting information. Management would grind to a halt, overloaded by the sheer complexity of the analyses that would need to be carried out. Such a situation of rationality gone rampant is referred to as 'paralysis by analysis' (Langley, 1995; Lenz and Lyles, 1985).

However, it is equally clear to most that human intuition is efficient, but often also unreliable and imprecise. It helps people to intuitively jump to conclusions without thorough analysis, which increases speed, but also increases the risk of drawing faulty conclusions. The main danger of intuition is that it is inherently biased, as it focuses attention on only a few variables and interprets them in a particular way, even when this is not appropriate (e.g. Bazerman, 1990; Tversky and Kahneman, 1986). For this reason, many academics urge practitioners to bolster their intuitive judgements with more explicit rational analysis. Especially in the case of strategic decisions, more time and energy should be made available to avoid falling prey to common cognitive biases. Otherwise the ultimate result might be a 'corporate gravestone' with the epitaph "*extinct by instinct*" (Langley, 1995).

For strategists a fundamental question is how they can avoid getting stuck with an outdated cognitive map. How can they avoid the danger of building up a flawed picture of their industry, their markets and themselves? As strategists must be acutely aware of the unfolding opportunities and threats in the environment, and the evolving strengths and weaknesses of the organization, they must be able to constantly re-evaluate their views.

On the one hand, this requires rigorous *logical thinking*. All the key assumptions on which a strategist's cognitive map are based need to be reviewed and tested against developments in the firm and its environment. On the other hand, strategists must have the ability to engage in *intuitive thinking*. To be able to 'feel' new opportunities and strengths, strategists must be able to think beyond their current mental models. Both demands on strategists will now be reviewed in more detail.

The demand for logical thinking

It is clear that if the strategizing managers base their strategic decisions only on heavily biased cognitive maps, unconsciously built up through past experiences, this will lead to very poor results. Strategists need to have the ability to critically reflect on the assumptions they hold, to check whether they are based on actual fact, or on organizational folklore and industry recipes. They must be capable of making their tacit beliefs more explicit, so that the validity of these mental models can be evaluated and further refined. In short, to be successful strategists, managers need to escape the confines of their own cognitive maps – and those of other stakeholders engaged in the strategy process.

Assessing the validity of a cognitive map requires strong logical thinking. Logical thinking can be characterized as conscious and rigorous, based on formal rules. When employing logic, each step in an argumentation follows from the previous one, based on valid principles. In other words, a logical thinker will draw a conclusion only if it is arrived at by a sound succession of arguments.

Logical thinking can be applied to all four cognitive activities outlined in Figure 2.2. When identifying and diagnosing a strategic problem, logical thinking can help to avoid the emotional interpretations that so often colour people's understanding of environmental opportunities and threats, and organizational strengths and weaknesses. Logical thinking can also expose a person's bullish or bearish bias and can be instrumental in discarding old 'theories' of how the firm and its environment function. By analysing the empirical facts and rigorously testing the hypotheses on which the firm's shared cognitive map has been built, the strategist can prevent building a false model of reality.

When conceiving and realizing a strategic solution, logical thinking can help to avoid the danger of following outdated habits and routines. Routines are programmed courses of action that originally were deliberately conceived, but have been subsequently internalized and are used automatically (March and Simon, 1993). Habits are programmed courses of action that have developed unconsciously. By explicitly formulating strategic options and subjecting them to formal evaluation, the strategist can break away from such established behaviour and develop new approaches to gaining and retaining competitive advantage. Moreover, logical thinking can aid in making a distinction between fantasy and feasibility. Sound logic can serve to weed out strategic options that are flights of fancy, by analysing the factors that will determine success or failure.

The demand for intuitive thinking

Intuitive thinking is the opposite of logical thinking. As described above, when employing logic, a thinker bases each step in a train of thought on the previous steps, following formal rules of valid thinking – also coined "cold cognition" (Bernheim and Rangel, 2004). However, the intuitive thinker does not follow formal steps in a decision-making process, but instead pursues an informal and holistic judgement process. While judging the situation at hand, the intuitive thinker includes multiple inputs, relates the inputs to the unconsciously stored large quantities of information to detect and understand the inputs, and employs his/her emotions ('feeling in our marrow') for judging situations – also dubbed "hot cognition" (Bernheim and Rangel, 2004).

While connecting a diversity of unconsciously stored information, intuitive thinking is quite fast – especially when compared with logical thinking (e.g. Kahneman, 2003). New insights pop up when handling a "mass of experience or a complex of abstractions in a flash" (Barnard, 1938). And intuitive responses – within seconds or less – are often correct (March and Simon, 1993).

In intuitive thinking a person opens up the unconscious part of the brain – where most of the learnings and experiences are being accumulated. The power of using the unconsciously stored information is that it connects many variables to another into a whole, without a sound explanation of why a correlation is assumed. Without deliberate intent large numbers of inputs are combined and an understanding boils up as a new insight. When this insight appears to 'make sense', the search for supporting evidence gets started. Often logic is used afterwards to justify an understanding that was actually generated by intuitive means.

If a pattern of incidents indicates that there is reason to believe that 'something is going on' which may affect at least some elements of the mental map, common thinking will be challenged. If the intuitive thinker develops a 'gut feeling' in which direction the solution might be, the new idea will be brought forward, even when it challenges orthodoxy and current thinking.

When identifying and diagnosing strategic problems, intuitive thinking is often needed. Old cognitive maps usually have a very compelling logic, locking people into old patterns of thinking. These old cognitive maps are usually tried and tested, and have become immune to external signals that they are no longer fitting. Thinking within the boundaries of a shared cognitive map is generally accepted and people tend to proceed rationally – that is, they try to escape from logical inconsistencies by including dissonant signs in the current thinking. Challenging a cognitive map's fundamental assumptions, however, cannot be done in a way that is logically consistent with the map itself. Contradicting a paradigm is illogical from the point of view of those who accept the paradigm. Therefore, changing a rigid and subjective cognitive map, rooted in a shared paradigm, requires strategists that are not captured by common logic and that recognize patterns in a number of seemingly unrelated incidents. Strategic thinkers need to be willing and able to detect signs that may challenge orthodoxy and make leaps of imagination which – although not logically justified – are needed to generate fresh ways of looking at old and new problems.

The same is true when conceiving and realizing strategic solutions. New strategies are not analysed into existence, but need to be generated. Patterns of loosely connected signs need novel solutions that do not follow from the dominant logic, but are the unexpected answers that emerge when the grip of the dominant logic is loosened.

Unfortunately, the conclusion must be that logical thinking and intuitive thinking are not only opposites, but that they are partially incompatible as well. They are based on methods that are at odds with one another. Strategizing managers would probably love to be fully logical and fully intuitive at the same time, but both require such a different mindset and range of cognitive skills that in practice it is very difficult to achieve both simultaneously. The demand for logic and intuition is not only contradictory for each individual, but also within teams, departments and the overall firm: while strategizing groups would like to be fully capable of logical and intuitive thinking, finding ways of incorporating both forms of strategic thinking into a workable strategy process is extremely challenging. Commonly, opposing styles lead to opposing people, and therefore a blend between the two is not that simple. It is for this reason that we speak of the 'paradox of logic and intuition' – the two demands on managers seem to be contradictory, yet both are required at the same time.

EXHIBIT 2.1   SHORT CASE

SAMSUNG: COSMOPOLITANS ON THE HAN RIVER

The South Korean economy expanded from near zero to more than a trillion US dollars between the 1960s and 2016. This achievement, which became known as the Miracle on the Han River, was made possible with a few national champions. One of these was Samsung.

From its humble beginnings as a small trading firm, Samsung has become the largest of South Korea's chaebols – family business conglomerates – with subsidiaries in electronics, chemicals, insurance, ships, advertising, construction, hospitality, and more. Now the company enjoys recognition and market presence around the globe.

Samsung – literally meaning the "three stars": large, strong and lasting forever – has strong Japanese roots. South Korea was a Japanese colony when Samsung started, and being educated in Japan, founder Byung-chul Lee was highly influenced by the Japanese way of doing business, with its focus on continuous improvement, a hierarchical labour model, unrelated diversification, dependency on the internal capital market, long-term relationships with stakeholders, seniority-based promotions and limited recruitment.

In the aftermath of ending Japanese rule in 1945 and the Korean War in 1953, South Korea's economic situation was in terrible shape. Personal conversations with South Korea's first president Syngman Rhee strengthened Byung-chul's belief that he was not just building a company: he was 'engaging in business for national service' – to help create a stronger nation through business prosperity, or "saeobboguk" in Korean. This is illustrated by Samsung's business philosophy – in 1973 it coined the 'Samsung Spirit' – which refers to "the principle of engaging in business for national service", "man and talent first", and "pursuit of logic and reality".

When Kun-hee Lee, Byung-chul's son, took over the reins of Samsung in 1987, he was responsible for a decisive moment in Samsung Electronics' success, when the company established a position in the white goods business. Kun-hee Lee had heard of recent developments in semiconductors and decided to personally investigate the situation in Japan. His conclusion after his investigation was that semiconductors were promising enormous opportunities for high-tech products. With a firm position in white goods, the new developments could provide Samsung Electronics with the growth Lee was looking for. He also realized something else: Samsung would be forced to compete in markets dominated by non-Koreans, with new challenges and different competitive rules ahead. Lee was also convinced that Samsung Electronics should not move cautiously, just following the leading Japanese companies Sony and Matsushita. Instead, the company should try to claim a leadership role and become an innovative and entrepreneurial industry shaper. But to achieve this, the company's current slow seniority-based HR and focus on operational excellence was not going to take Samsung to the top. Lee needed a fresh look on things, which he derived from Western thinking.

Lee launched the 'New Management Initiative' in 1993, based on introducing the Western way of doing business into the company. He famously said: "change everything except your wife and kids," indicating the far-reaching attempts to reform the organizational culture of the company. For example, employee promotion became merit-based instead of seniority-based. Lee particularly focused on the Western best practices, such as strategy formation, talent management and innovation. Lee understood that a cold turkey method wouldn't do the job as it would certainly result in heavy resistance. He therefore decided to slowly inject the best practices into the company. But how do you get analysis-based practices into an Eastern firm with holistic DNA? Lee decided to let Western outsiders into his company, equipped with MBAs and a strong knowhow of the Western ways of doing business. This slowly but surely opened up the traditional Korean business mentality. In addition, he sent insiders out to the Western world, to personally experience the Western way of doing business and take Western best practices back into the South Korean context.

These practices were slowly introduced into Samsung. For example, the merit-based compensation system started with a small differential, increasing annually until it reached 50 per cent. Lee also acquired companies that could help him in entering markets. For example, in 1995 Samsung

Electronics acquired a 40 per cent stake in AST Research, a United States based personal computer maker. Long-term strategic plans were created that would enable Samsung to go beyond supplying simple technology to creating high-tech products, and would finally result in Samsung Electronics becoming a 'three starred chef' in product and process innovation.

During 1997 and 1998 the industry was hit by a dramatic dip in demand and prices for memory chips. While most competitors became nervous about short-term results, and reduced capital spending and production capacity, Samsung Electronics kept to their strategic long-term planning and continued investing and strengthening its memory chip production operations. When the bust cycle turned into boom again, Samsung was one of the few companies with sufficient manufacturing capacity to reap the benefits. Since 2004, the operating profit of the electronics subsidiary of Samsung has consistently exceeded the sum of Japan's five major electronic firms annual operating profits. Samsung has showcased itself to be the world's largest memory chip manufacturer and the world market leader in LCD screens, monitors, microwave ovens and mobile phones. By 2014 the entire Samsung Electronics had reached an astonishing US$196 trillion of revenue, while employing over 319 thousand people around the world.

The unique combination of Eastern and Western ways of thinking has made Samsung Electronics the company it is today, but will this combination prove to be as successful in the long term? And how can Lee avoid getting stuck in the middle, being neither a company successful at doing business in an 'Asian way' nor a firm pursuing the 'Western road'? Holistic thinking helped to create the Samsung chaebol. Analytical thinking helped to enter the non-Korean dominated high-tech electronic markets. And the unique Samsung 'holistic analytical thinking combination' has made Samsung Electronics the market leader in many fields and the South Korean champion on the Han River. Employees are not Koreans or Westerners but cosmopolitans who feel at home all over the globe. How can Lee successfully manage logic and intuition to make Samsung Electronics live up to what it stands for: 'large, strong and lasting forever'?

Co-authors: Jeroen Brinkhuis and Wester Wagenaar

Sources: www.samsung.com; Samsung Electronic Annual Report 2014; *Far Eastern Economic Review*, 14 September 2002; *Harvard Business Review*, July-August 2011; Haour and Cho, IMD Business Case, 2000; *The Korea Herald*, 16 January 2009; *The Korean Times*, 2 February 2010.

PERSPECTIVES ON STRATEGIZING

Irrationally held truths may be more harmful than reasoned errors.

T.H. Huxley (1825–1895), English biologist

While the need for both logical and intuitive thinking is clear, this does place strategists in a rather awkward position of needing to bring two partially contradictory thinking systems, also known as System 1 and System 2 (Kahneman, 2011; see also Dane and Pratt, 2007, Reading 2.2), together in one strategic reasoning process. Logical thinking helps to make the strategic reasoning process rigorous, consistent and precise, instead of haphazard, ad hoc and general. Intuitive thinking, on the other hand, helps to make the strategic reasoning process comprehensive, flexible and fast, instead of fragmentary, rigid and slow.

In finding a balance between these opposite forms of thinking, the main question is whether the strategic reasoning process should actually be a predominantly rational affair, or a much more intuitive process. Is strategizing largely a rational activity, requiring logical thinking to be the dominant modus operandi, with occasional bits of gut feeling needed here and there to generate new ideas? Or is strategizing largely an intuitive activity, requiring integrative thinking as the standard operating procedure, with occasional bits of logical analysis needed here and there to weed out unfeasible ideas?

The answer to this question should be found in the strategic management literature. Yet, upon closer inspection, the opinions outlined in both the academic and popular literature show that views vary widely among researchers and managers alike. A wide spectrum of differing perspectives can be recognized, each giving their own angle on how strategic thinking should use logic and intuition – sometimes explicitly mentioning the need for both, but more commonly making implicit assumptions about the role of logic and intuition in strategy processes.

As was outlined in Chapter 1, it is not the intention here to summarize all of the 'schools of thought' on the topic of strategic thinking. Instead, only the two opposite points of view will be presented in this section. These two poles in the debate form the input for a good debate – a clear-cut thesis and antithesis in a process of dialectical enquiry.

At one end of the spectrum, there are those who argue – or just assume – that strategizing should be a predominantly conscious analytic process, requiring logic to be the main form of thinking in use. This point of view is referred to as the 'analytic reasoning perspective'. At the other pole, there are those who argue that strategizing is mainly an unconscious holistic process, requiring intuition as the leading thinking style. This point of view will be referred to as the 'holistic reasoning perspective'.

The analytic reasoning perspective

 Strategists employing the analytic reasoning perspective argue that strategic reasoning is predominantly a 'logical activity' (Andrews, 1987; Teece, 2007, Reading 2.1). To deal with strategic problems the strategist must first consciously and thoroughly analyse the problem situation. Data must be gathered on all developments external to the organization, and this data must be processed to pinpoint the opportunities and threats in the organization's environment. Furthermore, the organization itself must be appraised, to uncover its strengths and weaknesses and to establish which resources are available. Once the problem has been defined, a number of alternative strategies can be identified by matching external opportunities to internal strengths. Then, the strategic options must be extensively screened, by evaluating them on a number of criteria, such as internal consistency, external consonance, competitive advantage, organizational feasibility, potential return and risks. The best strategy can be selected by comparing the scores of all options and determining the level of risk the strategist is willing to take. The chosen strategy can subsequently be implemented.

This type of intellectual effort requires well-developed analytical skills. Strategists must be able to rigorously, consistently and objectively comb through huge amounts of data, interpreting and combining findings to arrive at a rich picture of the current problem situation. Possible solutions require critical appraisal and all possible contingencies must be logically thought through. Advocates of the analytic reasoning perspective argue that such reasoning strongly resembles the problem-solving approach of chess grandmasters (Simon, 1987). They also thoroughly assess their competitive position, sift through a variety of options and calculate which course of action brings the best chances of success. Therefore, the reasoning processes of chess grandmasters can be used as an analogy for what goes on in the mind of the strategist.

While depicted here as a purely step-by-step process of recognition, analysis, formulation and implementation, proponents of the analytic reasoning perspective note that in reality strategists often have to backtrack and redo some of these steps, as new information becomes available or chosen strategies do not work out. Strategists attempt to be as comprehensive, consistent and rigorous as possible in their analyses and calculations, but of course they cannot know everything and their conclusions are not always perfect: even with the most advanced forecasting techniques, not all developments can be foreseen; even with state of the art market research, some trends can be missed; even with cutting edge test marketing, scenario analyses, competitive simulations and net present value calculations, some selected strategies can turn out to be failures. Strategists are not all knowing, and do make mistakes – their rationality is limited by incomplete information and imperfect cognitive abilities. Yet, strategists try to be as rational as possible. Simon (1957) refers to this as 'bounded rationality' – 'people act intentionally rational, but only limitedly so'.

The (bounded) rational strategist must sometimes improvise to make up for a lack of information, but will try to do this as logically as possible. Inferences and speculation will always be based on the facts as known. By articulating assumptions and explicitly stating the facts and arguments on which conclusions have been based, problem definitions and solutions can be debated within the firm to confirm that they have been arrived at using sound reasoning. This strongly resembles the scientific method, in that hypotheses are formulated and tested as a means for obtaining new knowledge. Only by this consistent alignment of mental models with empirical reality can the strategist avoid the danger of becoming stuck with an outdated cognitive map.

Of course, creativity techniques can be beneficial for escaping from an outdated mental frame. Whether it is by means of brainstorming, six thinking caps or action art, creative thinking can spark some unconventional thoughts. Even a rational scientist like Newton has remarked that 'no great discovery was ever made without a bold guess'. But this is usually where the usefulness of creativity ends, and to which it should be limited. To be able to sift the sane from the zany, logic is needed. To make sense of the multitude of new ideas the logical thinker must analyse and evaluate them.

The alternative to this rational approach, it is often pointed out, is to be irrational and illogical, which surely cannot be a desirable alternative for the strategist. Non-rational reasoning comes in a variety of forms. For instance, people's thinking can be guided by their emotions. Feelings such as love, hate, guilt, regret, pride, anxiety, frustration and embarrassment can all cloud the strategist's understanding of a problem situation and the possible solutions. Adherents of the analytic reasoning perspective do not dispute the importance of emotions – the purpose of an organization is often based on 'personal values, aspirations and ideals', while the motivation to implement strategies is also rooted in human emotions. However, the actual determination of the optimal strategy is a 'rational undertaking' *par excellence* (Andrews, 1987).

Neither is intuitive thinking an appealing alternative for strategists. Of course, intuition can often be useful: decision rules based on extensive experience ('frozen knowledge') are often correct (even if they have been arrived at unconsciously) and they save time and effort. For example, Simon argues that even chess grandmasters make many decisions intuitively, based on tacit rules of thumb, formulated through years of experience. Yet, intuitive judgements must be viewed with great suspicion, as they are difficult to verify and infamously unreliable (e.g. Hogarth, 1980; Schwenk, 1984). Where possible, intuitive thinking should be made explicit – the strategist's cognitive map should be captured on paper (e.g. Anthony *et al.*, 1993; Eden, 1989), so that the reasoning of the strategist can be checked for logical inconsistencies.

In conclusion, advocates of the analytic reasoning perspective argue that emotions and intuition have a small place in the strategic reasoning process, and that logical thinking should be the dominant ingredient. It could be said that the analytic reasoning process of the strategist strongly resembles that of the scientist. The scientific methods of research, analysis, theorizing and falsification are all directly applicable to the process of strategic reasoning – so much so, that the scientific method can be used as the benchmark for strategy development processes. Consequently, the best preparation for effective strategic reasoning would be to be trained in the scientific tradition.

EXHIBIT 2.2 THE ANALYTIC REASONING PERSPECTIVE

BERKSHIRE HATHAWAY: NOT OUTSIDE THE BOX

At the peak of the dotcom boom in September 1999, few people were derided as much as Warren Buffett (1930), chairman of the insurance and investment conglomerate Berkshire Hathaway. Buffett – admiringly nicknamed the Sage of Omaha – had gained a phenomenal reputation as an investor during the 1980s and 1990s, but to most it was clear that he hadn't grasped the opportunities presented by the Internet. The grand old man might have been the guru of the old economy, but he simply did not understand the new rules of the information age. He was considered a pitiful example of a once brilliant mind that had not been able to make the leap beyond conventional beliefs and comprehend the 'new paradigm'. The investment strategy of Berkshire Hathaway was deemed hopelessly outdated. When almost all funds were rushing into new economy shares, the investment portfolio of Berkshire consisted of companies like Coca-Cola, Walt Disney, Gillette and The Washington Post. The shares of Berkshire traded at the lowest level in years.

The person least perturbed by this new, dubious status was Buffett himself. In his 1999 annual 'Letter to the Berkshire Hathaway Shareholders', he displayed an untouched faith in the fundamentals that had made him one of the richest people in the world: "If we have a strength, it is in recognizing when we are operating well within our circle of competence and when we are approaching the perimeter. ... we just stick with what we understand. If we stray, we will have done so inadvertently, not because we got restless and substituted hope for rationality." He refused to invest in Internet stocks, which he considered "chain letters", in which early participants get rich at the expense of later ones. As the dotcom bubble eventually burst, Buffett was more than exonerated.

This famous episode was neither Buffet's first provocative stance against lemming behaviour, nor his last. Following his personal mantra that "when other investors are greedy be fearful, but when other investors are fearful be greedy", Buffett has always stuck to his analysis and gone against the grain. For instance, during the stock market frenzy of 1969 he was widely ridiculed for not participating in the party. To his shareholders he wrote: "I am out of step with present conditions. When the game is no longer played your way, it is only human to say the new approach is all wrong, bound to lead to trouble, and so on. On one point, however, I am clear. I will not abandon a previous approach whose logic I understand (although I find it difficult to apply) even though it may mean foregoing large, and apparently easy, profits to embrace an approach which I don't fully understand, have not practised successfully, and which possibly could lead to substantial permanent loss of capital."

Forty years later, during the worst stock market crash since the Great Depression, Warren Buffett was again held to be a fool. With Berkshire Hathaway having lost up to US$25 billion of market value within the span of a year, he was arguing that the time was right to boldly buy: "I don't like to opine on the stock market, and again I emphasize that I have no idea what the market will do in the short term. Nevertheless, I'll follow the lead of a restaurant that opened in an empty bank building and then advertised: 'Put your mouth where your money was.' Today my money and my mouth both say equities." True to his words, Buffett invested US$5 billion in Goldman Sachs in September 2008, as panic about the American financial system was breaking out all around him. In his 2008 shareholder report, he frankly admitted that he had done "some dumb things in investments", but that overall he was satisfied with the new additions to his portfolio: "Whether we're talking about socks or stocks, I like buying quality merchandise when it is marked down."

When valuing companies, Buffet's approach has always been based on a thorough analysis of company fundamentals, "to separate investment from speculation". Ultimately, share prices will reflect these fundamentals and therefore nothing can substitute for a meticulous diagnosis of the sustainability of the competitive advantage of a firm. As Buffet puts it: "I try to buy stock in businesses that are so wonderful that an idiot can run them. Because sooner or later, one will." Following this logic, he stays away from investing in ill-understood businesses and in fast-changing industries, "in which the long-term winners are hard to identify". And when he invests, he keeps his shareholdings for years, or even decades. "Risk", he states, "comes from not knowing what you're doing."

His emphasis on rational reasoning and not following the wisdom of crowds ('a public opinion poll is no substitute for thought'), does not mean that he takes a liking to those who pretend to be scientific and rational ('beware of geeks bearing formulas'). He warns of professionals and academicians talking of efficient markets, dynamic hedging and betas: "Their interest in such matters is understandable, since techniques shrouded in mystery clearly have value to the purveyor of investment advice. After all, what witch doctor has ever achieved fame and fortune by simply advising 'Take two aspirins'?"

While still going strong at his advanced age, many commentators have warned that Berkshire Hathaway is vulnerable due to its dependence on its elderly chairman. Buffet's response so far has been totally in character: "I've reluctantly discarded the notion of my continuing to manage the portfolio after my death – abandoning my hope to give new meaning to the term 'thinking outside the box'."

Co-author: Martijn Rademakers

Sources: www.berkshirehathaway.com; *The Economist*, 15 March 2001; 18 December 2008; *The Sunday Times*, 1 March 2009; *The New York Times*, 16 October 2008, 1 March 2009.

The holistic reasoning perspective

 Strategists taking a holistic reasoning perspective are strongly at odds with the unassailable position given to logic in the analytic reasoning perspective. They agree that logic is important, but emphasize the "wicked" (Mason and Mitroff, 1981; Reading 1.1; Rittel, 1972), "ill-defined" (Claxton, 1998; Hayashi, 2001) or "unstructured" (Shapiro and Spence, 1997) nature of strategic problems. It is argued that strategic problems cannot be rationally and objectively defined, but that they are open to interpretation from a limitless variety of angles. The same is true for the possible solutions – there is no fixed set of problem solutions from which the strategist must select the best one. Defining and solving strategic problems, it is believed, is fundamentally a judgement activity. As such, strategic reasoning has very little in common with the thought processes of the aforementioned chess grandmaster, as was presumed by the rationalists. Playing chess is a 'tame', well-defined and structured problem. The problem definition is clear and all options are known. In the average game of chess, consisting of 40 moves, 10 120 possibilities have to be considered (Simon, 1972). This makes it a difficult game for humans to play, because of their limited computational capacities. Chess grandmasters are better at making these calculations than other people and are particularly good at computational short cuts – recognizing which things to figure out and which not. However, even the best chess grandmasters have been beaten at the game by IBM's Deep Blue, a highly logical computer with a superior number crunching capability. For the poor chess grandmaster, the rules of the game are fixed and there is little room for redefining the problem or introducing innovative approaches.

Engaging in business strategy is an entirely different matter. Strategic problems are wicked. Problem definitions are highly subjective and there are no fixed sets of solutions. It is therefore impossible to 'identify' the problem and 'calculate' an optimal solution. Opportunities and threats do not exist, waiting for the analyst to discover them. A strategist understands that a situation can be 'viewed' as an opportunity and 'believes' that certain factors can be threatening if not approached properly. Neither can strengths and weaknesses be objectively determined – a strategist can employ a company characteristic as a strength, but can also turn a unique company quality into a weakness by a lack of vision. Hence, doing a SWOT analysis (strengths, weaknesses, opportunities and threats) actually has little to do with logical analysis, but in reality is nothing less than an interpretation of a problem situation. Likewise, it is a fallacy to believe that strategic options follow more or less logically from the characteristics of the firm and its environment. Strategic options are not 'deduced from the facts' or selected from a 22 matrix, but are dreamt up. Strategists must be able to use their intuition to imagine previously unknown solutions. If more than one strategic option emerges from the mind of the strategist, these cannot be simply scored and ranked to choose the optimal one. Some analyses can be done, but as the development of many factors is susceptible to fundamental uncertainty, ultimately the strategist will have to intuitively judge which vision for the future has the best chance of being created in reality.

Even when a thorough analytic reasoning would be helpful, there is often just not enough time to complete a full analysis. Strategists need to trust the reflexes of the unconscious mind that combines all sort of unrelated signs into a new and comprehending pattern, in order to think and act fast. Holistic thinking is very intense work, as strategists must leave the intellectual safety of analysing and planning processes, guided by little else than their intuition. They must be willing to operate without the security of analysing, testing, arguing, challenging, doubting and living among the rubble of demolished certainties, without having proof and new certainties to give them shelter. To proponents of the holistic reasoning perspective, it is essential for strategists to give leeway to the tacit knowing and feelings of the unconscious mind and arrive at the right judgement.

Proponents of the holistic reasoning perspective stress that logic is often more a hindrance than a help. The heavy emphasis placed on rationality can actually frustrate the main objective of strategic reasoning – to generate a novel understanding, based on intuitive judgement of a multitude of factors and the inputs of all senses (seeing, hearing, feeling) and sources (clients, reports, employees, news channels). Analysis can be a useful tool, but rigidly following formal rules and using logic to redefine deviating signs into confirmations of the common, does not tear up outdated cognitive maps. For this reason, proponents of the holistic reasoning perspective argue that strategists should avoid the false certainty projected by rational approaches to strategic reasoning, but should nurture intuition as their primary cognitive asset. To reinvent the future, intuitive thinking should be the driving force, with creativity as a supporting means. As such, strategic reasoning closely resembles the frame-breaking behaviour common in the arts. In fields such as painting, music, motion pictures, dancing and architecture, artists are propelled by the drive to challenge convention and to seek out innovative approaches.

In conclusion, advocates of the holistic reasoning perspective argue that the essence of strategic reasoning is the ability to trust their senses, generate new and unique ways of understanding, and think and act fast. Openness to intuition can be activated by using metaphors, contradictions and paradoxes, and consequently the best preparation for strategic reasoning might actually be to get trained in the artistic tradition of iconoclastic intuition and mental flexibility.

EXHIBIT 2.3   THE HOLISTIC REASONING PERSPECTIVE

Q & A WITH RICHARD BRANSON

He has conquered the most impossible adventure challenges; built over 400 companies by shaking up complacent industries; is on a mission to bring space travel to the man on the street and is committed to building world-class African entrepreneurs.

We stalked Richard Branson on a recent trip to the Johannesburg-based Branson Centre of Entrepreneurship and talked intuition vs brainpower and the implausibility of British Airways condoms.

GQ: You and others have said that businesses need to do good in order to stay relevant and in business. Do you think it's easy to get caught out when you are not?

RB: I think the public is no fool and sees through companies that have a corporate-responsibility office at the back of the building and pretend it's at the front of the building. If you are going to do good, it's got to be absolutely genuine. Having said that, I'd rather people tried something than nothing at all.

GQ: The message from many entrepreneurs is to persevere and everything will work out. You have had both experiences – where you have abandoned certain ventures and in other instances hung in there and eventually made money. Is it a gut thing, knowing which way to go?

RB: It is perhaps one of the reasons having mentors is important – someone who can sit young entrepreneurs down and give them advice when they encounter situations like that. I have in the past been known to go on too long with companies because companies are, in the end, people and you don't want to close a company down and have to lose people. I suspect you really do know when the chances of being able to pull a plane out of a nosedive sound realistic or if the course is too much. Having one or two people you can trust to go to in those situations [is important] because sometimes you get too close to the situation and the people and cannot make a dispassionate decision.

GQ: Your first business was a magazine. Given the climate we are in, if you were to launch a magazine today, what kind of magazine would it be?

RB: I love physical magazines, but I suspect it would have to be an Internet-based magazine. We recently launched a magazine called *Project* on the Internet, which is quite bold and brave because an Internet-only magazine, or on an iPad, has never really existed before. People have kind of been putting *Wired* magazine on the Internet as well as the bookstores, and therefore the advertising market wasn't there for it. But having said that, *Project* has stuck in there and the advertising is coming. I do think there is a good future for advertisers in that space; it can be so much more imaginative than on a flat page.

GQ: You're pretty much a 'gut' man. Can you identify any brain decisions in your career?

RB: Intuition based on experience is perhaps slightly more useful than pure gut. It is the intuition of flying on other people's airlines and finding that the experience was not that good, feeling you can improve on that, and then starting an airline. It's that kind of intuition that works. The intuition that makes you think that if I want to go into space, there are millions of other people like me who would like to go into space. So if we could get the price down to what was affordable then there would be a market and then therefore, screw it, let's go find an engineer who can build a spaceship company. As far as using brainpower, that comes later: finding someone who can build a spaceship and maybe finding someone with the brainpower to mop up after you when your intuition was getting ahead of you.

GQ: You have successfully 'Virginised' many industries and brands. If there was a formula for creating successful brand extensions, what would that be?

RB: Most businesses are focused on one sector. I love challenges and have been able to take Virgin forward into a lot of areas. We have been able to build a reputation that makes going to those businesses that much easier. If you were building another brand to do the same thing, you need a name that can work internationally, that works on any product. British Airways condoms wouldn't work particularly well. Anyway, nothing named British Airways would work that well [laughs]. A brand like Apple, you could stretch that brand, but others you wouldn't. So it is worth keeping in mind the international nature of the brand name.

GQ: You are involved in hundreds of businesses and are in partnership with many. How do young empire-building entrepreneurs learn salient things such as how much to take on themselves, when to get partners or when to employ people?

RB: People spend far too long clinging on and not delegating and dealing with the bigger picture. As early on in the business – as soon as you can afford it – as possible, you should find somebody better than yourself to run the business so you can push the company forward and make sure the business survives and thrives. It means you can have more time for your family and your friends and have a more decent life. I could not have grown 400 companies if I hadn't learned the art of delegation at a very young age.

Sources: Siphiwe Mpye, GQ Digital Edition, www.gq.co.za/report/636702.html. Reproduced by permission of Condé Nast Independent Magazines and Siphiwe Mpye.

MANAGING THE PARADOX OF LOGIC AND INTUITION

Men like the opinions to which they have become accustomed from youth; this prevents them from finding the truth, for they cling to the opinions of habit.

Moses Maimonides (1135–1204); Egyptian physician and philosopher

Opinions differ sharply about whether the rational or the intuitive reasoning perspective is more valuable for understanding strategic thinking. Although they are opposites and partially contradictory, both perspectives might reveal crucial aspects of strategic thinking that need to be combined to achieve superior results. Of course, the tension is not so pressing for investment managers and art painters, but most strategizing managers struggle with managing the tension. See Table 2.1 for the main differences.

So, how can strategizing managers manage the paradox of logic and intuition? With the taxonomy of the first chapter in mind (Figure 1.9), the following options have been suggested by scholars in the management sciences.

Navigating

Applying logic and intuition at the same time is complex because it requires different thinking modes and procedures. To deal with these contrasting needs, some authors have suggested "build in mental time-outs" (e.g. Sadler-Smith, 2010) in daily routines to allow creative ideas to incubate. This kind of 'creativity' is accepted by analytical thinkers as a useful contribution to a largely rational process, while intuitive thinkers categorize creativity as an inherent part of the intuitive and holistic thinking mode. When the leadership team separates formal analytic from informal intuitive processes in time, such teams engage in 'temporal separation' – navigating the paradox.

TABLE 2.1   Analytic reasoning versus holistic reasoning perspective

	Analytic reasoning perspective	*Holistic reasoning perspective*
Emphasis on	Logic over creativity	Intuition over logic
Dominant cognitive style	Analytic	Holistic
Thinking follows	Formal, fixed rules	Informal, variable rules
Nature of thinking	Deductive and computational	Inductive and imaginative
Mode of thinking	Structured	Unstructured
Direction of thinking	Vertical	Lateral
System at work	Conscious, reflective	Unconscious, reflexive
Problem solving seen as	Analysing activities	Sensemaking activities
Value placed on	Cold cognition	Hot cognition
Assumption about reality	Objective, (partially) knowable	Subjective, (partially) creatable
Thinking hindered by	Incomplete information	Adherence to current cognitive map
Strategizing speed	Slow	Fast
Strategizing based on	Calculation	Judgement
Metaphor	Strategy as science	Strategy as art

Parallel processing

Not all organizational activities need the same levels of logic and intuition, as the nature of the problems differs throughout the firm. For example, increasing production efficiency is a complex yet tame problem that mainly benefits from analytic reasoning, while new business development is more of a wicked problem that leans towards holistic reasoning. By organizing the company's activities in separate units or departments, strategizing managers also allocate people with the required competencies and different thinking styles separately. As a consequence, logical and intuitive thinking are processed in parallel throughout the organization.

Embracing

Strategists can deliberately bring analytic and holistic thinkers together in one team, so as to mix 'individuals with analytical and intuitive cognitive styles' (Hodgkinson and Clarke, 2007). The intention is not to resolve the tension between logic and intuition, but to capture the advantages of both by bringing together people with different educational backgrounds, thinking styles and also – as in the case of Samsung (Exhibit 2.1) – cultural backgrounds. Of course, applying different thinking styles in one team is likely to create tensions between team members. Such tensions, however, often actually lead to unexpected solutions and innovations. The option is demanding for the strategizing managers in the team and therefore often requires specific capabilities, such as integrative thinking (Martin, 2007) and complexity maturity (discussed in Chapter 11).

STRATEGIC THINKING IN INTERNATIONAL PERSPECTIVE

Co-authors: Gep Eisenloeffel and Wester Wagenaar

When I look carefully I see the nazuna blooming
By the hedge.
Matsuo Bashō (松尾 芭蕉 (1644–1694) born Matsuo Kinsaku (松尾 金作),
Japanese poet and greatest master of haiku

Flower in the crannied wall,
I pluck you out of the crannies,
I hold you here, root and all, in my hand,
Little flower – but if I could understand
What you are, root and all, and all in all,
I should know what God and man is.
Alfred Tennyson, 1st Baron Tennyson (1809–1892)
Poet Laureate of Great Britain and Ireland

The question that must be added to the debate on the mind of the strategist is whether there are discernable international differences in approaches to strategic thinking. Are there specific national or regional preferences between the analytic and the holistic reasoning perspective or are inclinations towards logical or intuitive thinking solely dependent on individual dispositions? Are the differing views spread randomly across the globe or are views on strategic reasoning similar around the world? As a stimulus to the debate, a number of factors will be brought forward that highlight differences in how various regions tackle the paradox between logic and intuition. These are structured into three different levels that influence an inclination towards one of the two sides: the societal, the industry and the personal level.

On the societal level

When it comes to regional preferences to engage in intuitive or analytical reasoning, scholars tend to pit West against East: the US and West-European countries favour reason, while China, Korea and Japan emphasize the normative value of intuition over rule-based reasoning (Nisbett *et al.*, 2001; Wonder and Blake, 1992). This is echoed by cross-cultural studies which indicate the preference of Western participants to base decisions on the conscious use of formal, decontextualized rules, more so than do East-Asian participants (Norenzayan *et al.*, 2002). In a more practical sense, this difference manifests itself in the way arguments are built up. Where much of the world shapes an argument logically by either putting principles first (France, Spain) or putting applications first (US), Asia is arguably a different case. According to Erin Meyer (2014), Westerners follow a 'specific approach' to build up an argument, while Asians follow a more holistic route.

Historical narratives also emphasize a regional division in preferences. The story usually starts in ancient Greece, taking us through the Age of Reason and on to rationalism and the prestige it enjoyed during the eighteenth, nineteenth and twentieth centuries. Richard Brooks (2012) argues in his book *The Social Animal* that 'the tradition of rationalism in the West tells the story of human history as the story of the logical, conscious mind. It sees human history as the contest between reason and instinct. In the end, reason triumphs over emotion. Science gradually replaces myth. Logic wins out over passion'.

This is no different in the field of strategy. As Henry Mintzberg *et al.* (1998) point out in their book *Strategy Safari*, from its inception, pioneering scholars in the strategy field, such as Chandler (1962), Ansoff (1965), and Porter (1980), were strongly influenced by the rationalist analytic approach. Strategizing was embedded in the tradition of rationality, including the tools and techniques, with problems divided into discrete parts and solved on the basis of reliable facts and figures. Conscious cognition (*sensing*) was valued over the unconscious (*intuition*), rational reasoning over holistic reasoning. This general preference of scholars in the field of strategy can also be generalized to managers in the US. Hampden-Turner and Trompenaars (2000) for example, found that over 70 per cent of managers in the US score highest on Introvert (versus Extrovert), Sensing (as opposed to Intuition), Thinking (instead of Feeling), and Judging (contrary to Perceiving) on the Meyers-Briggs Type Indicator.

Assumptions of the analytic rationalist approach have been criticized by a number of scholars, but there has been a general perception that logic and reason prevail over intuition in the West. Therefore, intuition has traditionally been downplayed or denigrated in Western societies (e.g. Gladwell, 2007; Lieberman, 2000). The Western view was most notably challenged in the 1980s by Japanese alternatives to management practices. For example, Richard T. Pascale, co-author of *The Art of Japanese Management* (1981), criticized the Western perception on strategizing, considering the rational analytic approach to be "myopic and an oversimplification of reality." It is only relatively recently that the value of intuition has truly started to enjoy appreciation in English literature on management (e.g. Dane and Pratt, 2007).

On the industry level

While individual dispositions and societies have an influence on an inclination towards either logic or intuition, this is also the case for certain industries. Regardless of where you are, some business sectors tend to demand either one and there are some where a clear preference for one of the two thinking styles can be noticed. In the biotechnology industry thinking holistically plays a major role. Here strategists tend to encourage scientists to act on promising leads by interpreting data and problems from as many angles as possible – a fine recipe for more than just following formula (Hodgkinson *et al.*, 2009, p. 278). A similar preference can be observed in the creative sector, where designers and developers are often emboldened to think outside of the box. The opposite, where logic is encouraged, can also be true: accountants generally favour the analytical reasoning perspective over the holistic reasoning perspective. The middle ground is usually occupied by entrepreneurs, people who have been found to adequately balance the intuitive and the deliberate (Groves *et al.*, 2008).

To the strategist

Psychologists tend to agree that the human mind operates through a dual process structure. Behaviour is jointly influenced by both the slow, deliberately controlled system and the fast, intuitively automatic system (Kahneman, 2011; Mukherjee, 2010; Pachur and Spaar, 2015, p. 303). Every individual has a natural inclination towards either one of them (Nisbett *et al.*, 2001, p. 291) and these differences between individual dispositions are referred to as decision styles. A 'decisional fit' occurs when the way in which a decision is made matches the preferred decision style of the decision-maker. He or she will then perceive the decision as more favourable and will feel less regret in cases of potential negative outcomes (Betsch and Kunz, 2008).

There are a variety of reasons why one style of strategizing might be overly present in one individual and less so in another, with the most prominent being the role played by the environment. When a strategist enters an environment where his preferable thinking style gets penalized, this provides unpleasant experiences. The general result is avoiding situations in which the opposite thinking style is required, which brings about a positive feedback loop of these biases.

Still, individual preferences should not be exaggerated. The world does not hold two types of strategists, one who relies solely on intuition and the other purely on logic. Instead, we see a continuum of decision-making styles where the two combine. Which of them has the preference is likely to depend on the nature of the problem (Simon, 1987, p. 61). Someone's general tendency does not manifest itself in every decision, because decision styles are not 'chronic'; they are dependent upon situations and domains (Pachur and Spaar, 2015). Therefore, the preference for one of the two frameworks depends on the experience and proficiency for a specific problem. For example, expertise in a domain tends to often lead to a desire for intuition (Kahneman, 2011) and a manager's attitude towards risk can vary considerably depending on whether it is a recreational or an investment risk (Hanoch, Johnson and Wilke, 2006).

INTRODUCTION TO THE READINGS

Those who judge by their feelings do not understand reasoning, for they wish to get an insight into a matter at a glance, and are not accustomed to look for principles. Contrarily, others, who are accustomed to argue from principles, do not understand the things of the heart, seeking for principles and not being able to see at a glance.
Blaise Pascal (1623–1662); French scientist and philosopher

So, how should managers engage in strategic reasoning processes and how should they encourage fruitful strategic reasoning within their organizations? Should strategizing managers primarily take an analytic or holistic reasoning perspective? Should strategists train themselves to follow procedural rationality – rigorously analysing problems using scientific methods and calculating the optimal course of action? Or should strategists unleash the unconscious and make judgements based on intuition?

In the strategic management literature the debate has not yet offered a clear-cut answer to the question of which strategic reasoning approach is the optimal one. At the centre of the strategic reasoning issue is the paradox of logic and intuition. Many points of view have been put forward on how to reconcile these opposing demands, but as circumstances differ, individual strategists have to find their own way of dealing with the topic of strategizing.

To help strategists come to grips with the variety of perspectives on this issue, three readings have been selected that each shed their own light on the issue. As outlined in Chapter 1, the first two readings will be representative of the two poles in this debate (see Table 2.1). The third reading addresses a more integrative style of strategizing.

Selecting the first reading to represent the analytical reasoning perspective was not very difficult. In a 2007 *Strategic Management Journal* article, 'Explicating Dynamic Capabilities: The nature and microfoundations of (sustainable) enterprise performance', David Teece explains the microeconomics of the dynamic capabilities perspective, which currently enjoys the attention of most strategy scholars. While in Chapter 4 on business level strategy the contents of this perspective will be discussed, this chapter addresses the microfoundations of dynamic capabilities thinking.

The microfoundations of the dynamic capabilities view are in line with many – but not all – important scholars in the strategy field, as Teece points out. True to the rational reasoning perspective, Teece argues that "sensing, seizing and reconfiguring" should be conducted consciously, explicitly and rationally. In his view, strategic reasoning is a "logical activity".

The second reading in this chapter is the 2007 *Academy of Management Review* article 'Exploring Intuition and its Role in Managerial Decision Making' by Erik Dane and Michael G. Pratt. Their definition of intuition ("affectively charged judgments that arise through rapid, non-conscious and holistic associations", p. 40) has become widely accepted by scholars in organizational behaviour. The article is probably the best scientifically developed overview on what intellective scientists are not supposed to do: make judgemental intuitive decisions. The authors incorporate the role of domain knowledge, implicit and explicit learning, and task characteristics on intuition effectiveness in managerial decisions. They also explore the applications of intuition on managerial decision making.

The third reading is a 2011 *Strategic Management Journal* article, 'Psychological foundations of dynamic capabilities: Reflexion and reflection in strategic management' by Gerard P. Hodgkinson and Mark P. Healey. The authors build on Teece's 'sensing, seizing and reconfiguring' distinction, but they challenge his microfoundations and incorporate the academic knowledge in neuroscience and psychology on intuition in managerial decision making (as explicated in Dane and Pratt's article). They argue that a strategist's thought processes are basically intuitive and reflexive rather than rational and reflective. In their view, strategies originate in insights that are beyond the reach of conscious analysis. They do not dismiss logic as unnecessary, but note that it is insufficient for arriving at innovative strategies and for getting organizational members' buy-in.

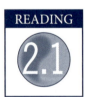

Explicating dynamic capabilities: The nature and microfoundations of (sustainable) enterprise performance

By David J. Teece[1]

Dynamic capabilities can be disaggregated into the capacity (1) to sense and shape opportunities and threats, (2) to seize opportunities, and (3) to maintain competitiveness through enhancing, combining, protecting, and, when necessary, reconfiguring the business enterprise's intangible and tangible assets. Dynamic capabilities include difficult-to-replicate enterprise capabilities required to adapt to changing customer and technological opportunities. They also embrace the enterprise's capacity to shape the ecosystem it occupies, develop new products and processes, and design and implement viable business models.

Sensing (and shaping) opportunities and threats

Nature of the capability

In fast-paced, globally competitive environments, consumer needs, technological opportunities and competitor activity are constantly in a state of flux. Opportunities open up for both newcomers and incumbents, putting the profit streams of incumbent enterprises at risk. As discussed in Teece, Pisano and Shuen (1997, Reading 4.3), some emerging marketplace trajectories are easily recognized. In microelectronics this might include miniaturization, greater chip density, and compression and digitization in information and communication technology. However, most emerging trajectories are hard to discern. Sensing (and shaping) new opportunities is very much a scanning, creation, learning and interpretive activity. Investment in research and related activities is usually a necessary complement to this activity.

Opportunities get detected by the enterprise because of two classes of factors. First, as stressed by Kirzner (1973), entrepreneurs can have differential access to existing information. Second, new information and new knowledge (exogenous or endogenous) can create opportunities, as emphasized by Schumpeter (1934). Kirzner stressed how the entrepreneurial function recognizes any disequilibrium and takes advantage of it. The Kirznerian view is that entrepreneurship is the mechanism by which the economy moves back toward equilibrium. Schumpeter, on the other hand, stressed upsetting the equilibrium. As Baumol (2006: 4) notes, 'The job of Schumpeter's entrepreneur is to destroy all equilibria, while Kirzner's works to restore them. This is the mechanism underlying continuous industrial evolution and revolution.' Equilibrium is rarely if ever achieved (Shane, 2003). Both forces are relevant in today's economy.

Microfoundations

The literature on entrepreneurship emphasizes that opportunity discovery and creation can originate from the cognitive and creative ('right brain') capacities of individual(s). However, discovery can also be grounded in organizational processes, such as research and development activity. The ability to create and/or sense opportunities is clearly not uniformly distributed amongst individuals or enterprises. Opportunity creation and/or discovery by individuals require both access to information and the ability to recognize, sense and shape developments. The ability to recognize opportunities depends in part on the individual's capabilities and extant knowledge (or the knowledge and learning capacities of the organization to which the individual belongs), particularly about user needs in relationship to existing as well as novel solutions. This requires specific knowledge, creative activity, the ability to understand user/customer decision making, and practical wisdom (Nonaka and Toyama, 2007). It involves interpreting available information in whatever form it appears – a chart, a picture, a conversation at a trade show, news of scientific and technological breakthroughs, or the angst expressed by a frustrated customer. One must accumulate and then filter information from professional and social contacts to create a conjecture or a hypothesis about the likely evolution of technologies, customer needs and marketplace responses. This task involves scanning and monitoring internal and external technological developments and assessing customer needs, expressed and latent. It involves learning, interpretation and creative activity.

While certain individuals in the enterprise may have the necessary cognitive and creative skills, the more desirable approach is to embed scanning, interpretative and creative processes inside the enterprise itself. The enterprise will be vulnerable if the sensing, creative and learning functions are left to the cognitive traits of a few individuals. Organizational processes can be put in place inside the enterprise to garner new technical information, tap developments in exogenous science, monitor customer needs and competitor activity, and shape new products and processes opportunities. Information must be filtered, and must flow to those capable of making sense of it. Internal argument and discussion about changing market and technological reality can be both inductive and deductive. Hypothesis development, hypothesis 'testing' and synthesis about the meaning of information obtained via search are critical functions, and must be performed by the top management team. The rigorous assembly of data, facts and anecdotes can help test beliefs. Once a synthesis of the evidence is achieved, recurrent synthesis and updating can be embedded in business processes designed by middle management and/or the planning unit in the business organization (Casson, 1997). If enterprises fail to engage in such activities, they won't be able to assess market and technological developments and spot opportunities. As a consequence, they will likely miss opportunities visible to others.

As noted in Teece, Pisano and Shuen (1997), more decentralized organizations with greater local autonomy are less likely to be blindsided by market and technological developments. Because of the problem of information decay as information moves up (and down) a hierarchy, businesses must devise mechanisms and procedures to keep management informed. Bill Hewlett and David Packard developed 'management by walking about' (Packard, 1995) as a mechanism to prevent top management at Hewlett-Packard from becoming isolated from what was going on at lower levels in the enterprise, and outside the enterprise as well. In other organizations (e.g., professional services) the management ranks can be filled by leading professionals who remain involved with professional work. This protects them from the hazards of managerial isolation.

The search activities that are relevant to 'sensing' include information about what's going on in the business ecosystem. With respect to technologies, R&D activity can itself be thought of as a form of 'search' for new products and processes. However, R&D is too often usually a manifestation of 'local' search. 'Local' search is only one component of relevant search. In fast-paced environments, with a large percentage of new product introductions coming from external sources, search/exploration activity should not just be local. Enterprises must search the core as well as the periphery of their business ecosystem. Search must embrace potential collaborators – customers, suppliers, complementors – that are active in innovative activity.

Customers are sometimes amongst the first to perceive the potential for applying new technology. Visionary members of customer organizations are often able to anticipate the potential for new technology and possibly even begin rudimentary development activities. Moreover, if the suppliers of new technology do not succeed in properly understanding user/customer needs, it is unlikely that new products they might develop will be successful. Indeed, one of the most consistent findings from empirical research is the probability that an innovation will be successful commercially is highly correlated with the developers' understanding of user/customer needs (Freeman, 1974). Electronic computing and the Internet itself can rightly be viewed as having a significant component of user-led innovations. Business enterprises that are alert and sense the opportunity are often able to leverage customer-led efforts into new products and services, as the users themselves are frequently ill-prepared to carry initial prototypes further forward.

Suppliers can also be drivers of innovation important in the final product. Innovation in microprocessor and DRAMs is a classic case. This upstream or 'component' innovation has impacted competition and competitive outcomes in personal computers, cellular telephony and consumer electronics more generally. Failure to 'design in' new technology/components in a timely fashion will lead to failure; conversely, success can sometimes be achieved by continuous rapid 'design in.' Indeed, continuous and rapid design around new technology/components developed elsewhere can itself be a source of durable competitive advantage. Put differently, with rapid innovation by component suppliers, downstream competitive success can flow from the ability of enterprises to continuously tap into such (external) innovation ahead of the competition. External search and acquisition of technology have been going on for decades, but as Chesbrough (2003) explains, 'Open Innovation' is now a mandate for enterprise success.

The concept and practice of open innovation underscore the importance of broad-based external search and subsequent integration involving customers, suppliers and complementors. Establishing linkages between corporations and universities assists broad-based search, as university programmes are usually unshackled from the near at hand. Indeed, a recent study of patenting in the optical disc industry (Rosenkopf and Nerkar, 2001) seems to suggest that exploration that is more confined generates lower impacts, and that the impact of exploration is highest when exploration spans organizational (but not technological) boundaries. However, it is not just a matter of searching for external inventions/innovations that represent new possibilities. Frequently it is a matter of combining complementary innovations so as to create a solution to a customer problem. The systemic nature (Teece, 2000) of many innovations compounds the need for external search.

Sensing opportunities and threats can also be facilitated if the enterprise and/or the entrepreneur explicitly or implicitly employ some kind of analytical framework, as this can help highlight what is important. Within the dynamic capabilities framework, the 'environmental' context recognized for analytical purposes is not that of the industry, but that of the business 'ecosystem' – the community of organizations, institutions and individuals that impact the enterprise and the enterprise's customers and supplies. The relevant community therefore includes complementors, suppliers, regulatory authorities, standard-setting bodies, the judiciary, and educational and research institutions.

It is a framework that recognizes that innovation and its supporting infrastructure have major impacts on competition.

Even when utilizing the ecosystem as the organizing paradigm for assessing developments in the business environment, the full import of particular facts, statistics and developments is rarely obvious. Accordingly, the evaluative and inferential skill possessed by an organization and its management is important. Indeed, much of the information gathered and communicated inside the enterprise has minimal decision relevance. Even if relevant, it often arrives too late. Management must find methods and procedures to peer through the fog of uncertainty and gain insight. This involves gathering and filtering technological, market and competitive information from both inside and outside the enterprise, making sense of it and figuring out implications for action. However, because attention is a scarce resource inside the enterprise (Cyert and March, 1963), management must carefully allocate resources to search and discovery. The enterprise's articulated strategy can become a filter so that attention is not diverted to every opportunity and threat that 'successful' search reveals. Likewise, scenario planning can collapse likely situations into a small number of scenarios that can facilitate cognition, and then action, once uncertainty is resolved.

Seizing opportunities

Nature of the capability

Once a new (technological or market) opportunity is sensed, it must be addressed through new products, processes, or services. This almost always requires investments in development and commercialization activity. Multiple (competing) investment paths are possible, at least early on. The quintessential example is the automobile industry, where in the early days, different engine technologies – steam, electric and gasoline – each had their champions. Once a dominant design begins to emerge, strategic choices become much more limited.

Addressing opportunities involves maintaining and improving technological competencies and complementary assets and then, when the opportunity is ripe, investing heavily in the particular technologies and designs most likely to achieve marketplace acceptance. When network externalities are present, early entry and commitment are necessary. The presence of increasing returns means that if one network gets ahead, it tends to stay ahead. Getting ahead may require significant upfront investments. Customers will not want an enterprise's products if there are strong network effects and the installed base of users is relatively small. Accordingly, one needs to strategize around investment decisions, getting the timing right, building on increasing return advantages, and leveraging products and services from one application to another. The capacity to make high-quality, unbiased but interrelated investment decisions in the context of network externalities, innovation and change is as rare as decision-making errors and biases are ubiquitous.

However, the issue that the enterprise faces is not just when, where and how much to invest. The enterprise must also select or create a particular business model that defines its commercialization strategy and investment priorities. Indeed, there is considerable evidence that business success depends as much on organizational innovation, e.g., design of business models, as it does on the selection of physical technology. This is true at the enterprise level as well as at the economy-wide level (Nelson, 2005). Indeed, the invention and implementation of business models and associated enterprise boundary choices involve issues as fundamental to business success as the development and adoption of the physical technologies themselves. Business models implicate processes and incentives; their alignment with the physical technology is a much overlooked component of strategic management. The understanding of the institutional/organizational design issues is typically more limited than the understanding of the technologies themselves. This ignorance affords considerable scope for mistakes around the proper design of business models and the institutional structures needed to support innovation in both the private and public sectors.

In theory, one could imagine transactions between entities that scout out and/or develop opportunities, and those that endeavour to execute upon them. In reality, the two functions cannot be cleanly separated, and the activities must be integrated inside a single enterprise, where new insights about markets – particularly those that challenge the conventional wisdom – will likely encounter negative responses. The promoters/visionaries must somehow defeat the naysayers, transform internal views, and facilitate necessary investment. Some level of managerial consensus will be necessary to allow investment decisions to be made. Investment will likely involve committing financial resources behind an informed conjecture about the technological and marketplace future. However, managers of established product lines in large organizations can sometimes have sufficient decision-making authority to starve the new business of financial capital. This posture can be buttressed by capital budgeting techniques that more comfortably support investments for which future cash flow can be confidently projected. In short, the new can lose out to the established unless management is sensitive to the presence of certain biases in accepted investment decision processes. An important class of dynamic capabilities emerges around a manager's ability to override certain 'dysfunctional' features of established decision rules and resource allocation processes.

It helps to begin by recognizing that decision-making processes in hierarchically organized enterprises involve bureaucratic features that are useful for many purposes, but they nevertheless may muzzle innovation proclivities. In particular, a formal expenditure process involving submissions and approvals is characteristic of 'well-managed' companies. Decision making is likely to have a committee structure, with top management requiring reports and written justifications for significant decisions. Moreover, approvals may need to be sought from outside the organizational unit in which the expenditure is to take place. While this may ensure a matching up of expenditures to opportunities across a wider range of economic activity, it unquestionably slows decision making and tends to reinforce the status quo. Committee decision-making structures almost always tend toward balancing and compromise. But innovation is often ill-served by such structures, as the new and the radical will almost always appear threatening to some constituents. Strong leaders can frequently overcome such tendencies, but such leaders are not always present. One consequence is a 'programme persistence bias.' Its corollary is various forms of 'anti-innovation bias,' including the 'anti-cannibalization' basis. Programme persistence refers to the funding of programmes beyond what can be sustained on the merits, and follows from the presence or influence of programme advocates in the resource allocation process. This proclivity almost automatically has the countervailing effect of reducing funds available to new initiatives.

One should not be surprised, therefore, if an enterprise senses a business opportunity but fails to invest. In particular, incumbent enterprises tend to eschew radical competency-destroying innovation in favour of more incremental competency-enhancing improvements. The existence of layer upon layer of standard procedures, established capabilities, complementary assets and/or administrative routines can exacerbate decision-making biases against innovation. Incumbent enterprises, relying on (path-dependent) routines,

assets and strategies developed to cope with existing technologies, are handicapped in making and/or adopting radical, competency-destroying, noncumulative innovation (Nelson and Winter, 1982; Tushman and Anderson, 1986; Henderson and Clark, 1990). This is true whether the competence is external to the firm or internal to the firm.

Evidence also shows that decision makers discount outcomes that are merely probable in comparison with outcomes that are certain. This has been called the certainty effect (Kahneman and Lovallo, 1993). It contributes to excessive risk aversion when choices involve possible losses. Further, to simplify choices between alternatives, individuals generally evaluate options in isolation. Viewing each alternative as unique leads decision makers to undervalue possibilities for risk pooling. This approach to decision making may produce inconsistent preferences and decision biases (timid choices) that lead to outcomes that block innovation (Kahneman and Tversky, 1979; Kahneman and Lovallo, 1993). An opposing bias to loss/risk aversion is excessive optimism. This leads to investment in low or negative return projects. As a result, entry decisions often fail.

The existence of established assets and routines exacerbates problems of excessive risk aversion. Specifically, both the isolation effect and the certainty effect can be intensified by the existence of established assets, causing incumbent enterprises to become comparably more risk averse than new entrants. In terms of innovative activity, this excessive risk aversion leads to biased decision making and limits the probability that incumbent enterprises will explore risky radical innovations. In short, success in one period leads to the establishment of 'valid' processes, procedures and incentives to manage the existing business. This can have the unintended effect of handicapping the new business. The proficiency with which such biases are overcome and a new opportunity is embraced is likely to depend importantly on the quality of the enterprise's routines, decision rules, strategies, and leadership around evaluating new investment opportunities. Business historians (e.g., Chandler, 1990a; Lazonick, 2005) and others have reminded us that over the long run the ability of enterprises to commit financing and invest astutely around new technologies is critical to enterprise performance.

Managers need to make unbiased judgments under uncertainty around not just future demand and competitive responses associated with multiple growth trajectories, but also around the pay-offs from making interrelated investments in intangible assets. In the world of tangible assets, this can sometimes be precisely modelled; not so for the world of co-specialized intangibles. In essence, the organizational challenge appears to be that in environments experiencing rapid change, activities are not fully decomposable. Cross-functional activities and associated investments must take place concurrently, rather than sequentially, if enterprises are to cut time-to-market for new products and processes. Managerial judgments (decision-making skills) take on great significance in such contexts. This was also true during prior centuries, as Alfred Chandler's (1990a, 1990b) analysis of successful enterprises from the 1870s through the 1960s makes apparent. No matter how much analytical work is done, tacit investment skills are of great importance. Chandler further argues that success in the late-nineteenth and much of the twentieth century came to those enterprises that pursued his 'three-pronged' strategy: (1) early and large-scale investments behind new technologies; (2) investment in product-specific marketing, distribution and purchasing networks; and (3) recruiting and organizing the managers needed to supervise and coordinate functional activities. The first and second elements require commitment to investments where irreversibilities and co-specialization are identified. While the nature of required investments may have changed in recent decades (less decomposable/more interrelated), investment decision skills remain important.

Microfoundations

Selecting product architectures and business models.
The design and performance specification of products, and the business model employed, all help define the manner by which the enterprise delivers value to customers, entices customers to pay for value, and converts those payments to profit. They reflect management's hypothesis about what customers want and how an enterprise can best meet those needs, and get paid for doing so. They embrace: (1) which technologies and features are to be embedded in the product and service; (2) how the revenue and cost structure of a business is to be 'designed' and if necessary 'redesigned' to meet customer needs; (3) the way in which technologies are to be assembled; (4) the identity of market segments to be targeted; and (5) the mechanisms and manner by which value is to be captured. The function of a business model is to 'articulate' the value proposition, select the appropriate technologies and features, identify targeted market segments, define the structure of the value chain, and estimate the cost structure and profit potential (Chesbrough and Rosenbloom,

2002: 533–534). In short, a business model is a plan for the organizational and financial 'architecture' of a business. This model makes assumptions about the behaviour of revenues and costs, and likely customer and competitor behaviour. It outlines the contours of the solution required to earn a profit, if a profit is available to be earned. Once adopted it defines the way the enterprise 'goes to market.' Success requires that business models be astutely crafted. Otherwise, technological innovation will not result in commercial success for the innovating enterprise. Generally there is a plethora of business models that can be designed and employed, but some will be better adapted to the ecosystem than others. Selecting, adjusting and/or improving the business model is a complex art.

Designing good business models is in part 'art.' However, the chances of success are greater if enterprises (1) analyse multiple alternatives; (2) have a deep understanding of user needs; (3) analyse the value chain thoroughly so as to understand just how to deliver what the customer wants in a cost-effective and timely fashion; and (4) adopt a neutrality or relative efficiency perspective to outsourcing decisions. Useful tools include market research and transaction cost economics. Chesbrough and Rosenbloom (2002) suggest that established enterprises often have blinders with respect to alternative business models and that this prevails even if the technology is spun off into a separate organization, where other (path-dependent constraints) are less likely to exist. In short, designing the business correctly, and figuring out what John Seeley Brown refers to as the 'architecture of the revenues' (and costs), involve processes critical to the formation and success of new and existing businesses. No amount of good governance and leadership is likely to lead to success if the wrong business model is in place. Good business models achieve advantageous cost structures and generate value propositions acceptable to customers. They will enable innovators to capture a large enough portion of the (social) value generated by innovation to permit the enterprise at least to earn its cost of capital.

Avoiding bias, delusion, deception and hubris.
As noted, proclivities toward decision errors are not uncommon in managerial decision making, particularly in large organizations. Investment decision errors already identified include excessive optimism, loss aversion, isolation errors, strategic deception and programme persistence. As Nelson and Winter (2002: 29) note, organizational decision processes often display features that seem to defy basic principles of

rationality and sometimes border on the bizarre. These errors can be especially damaging in fast-paced environments with path dependencies and network effects, as there is less opportunity to recover from mistakes. When investments are small and made frequently, there are many opportunities to learn from mistakes. Since large investments are usually occasional, major investment decisions are likely to be (potentially) more vulnerable to error.

Fortunately, biases can be recognized ahead of time. Enterprises can bring discipline to bear to purge bias, delusion, deception and hubris. However, the development of disciplines to do so is still in its infancy. The implementation of procedures to overcome decision-making biases in enterprise settings is, accordingly, not yet a well-distributed skill, and may not be for decades to come. Accordingly, competitive advantage can be gained by early adopters of techniques to overcome decision biases and errors.

Overcoming biases almost always requires a cognitively sophisticated and disciplined approach to decision making. Being alert to the incentives of the decision makers and to possible information asymmetries is a case in point. Obtaining an 'outside view' through the review of external data can help eliminate bias. Testing for errors in logic is also essential. Management also needs to create an environment where the individuals involved in making the decision, at both the management and board level, feel free to offer their honest opinions, and look at objective (historical) data in order to escape from closed thinking. Incentives must also be designed to create neutrality when assessing investments in the old and the new.

Considerable progress in combating biases has been made. Advisors call upon managers to adopt radical, non-formulaic strategies in order to overcome the inertias that inhibit breakthrough innovation (Davidow and Malone, 1992; Handy, 1990). Specifically, corrective strategies encourage change through two basic mechanisms: (1) designing organizational structures, incentives and routines, to catalyse and reward creative action; and (2) developing routines to enable the continual shedding of established assets and routines that no longer yield value. Strategies that provide structures, incentives and processes to catalyse and reward creative action serve to attenuate problems of excessive risk aversion. For example, strategies that call on the enterprise to 'cut overheads' and 'increase divisional authority' can be interpreted as efforts to reduce the number of management layers of the enterprise and to push decision making down to lower levels to minimize the inherent isolation errors associated with multilevel, hierarchical decision-making processes. These recommendations can be viewed as organizational processes and strategic mechanisms to mitigate decision-making biases.

Perhaps most importantly, executives must acknowledge the interaction effect between owning established assets and decision-making biases. Many recommended strategies (such as cannibalizing profitable product lines and licensing your most advanced technology) call for the shedding of established capabilities, complementary assets and/or administrative routines to reduce the intensity of decision-making biases. By jettisoning 'dead' or dying assets, the enterprise is no longer shackled with an asset base that can be a crutch and provide a false sense of security, and sustain groups inside the enterprise that persist in torpedoing new initiatives. In abandoning dead or dying assets, the enterprise frees itself of certain routines, constraints and opportunities for undesirable protective action inside the enterprise.

Sources of the 'anti-cannibalization' bias can also be attacked. Self-serving behaviour inside the enterprise to 'protect' incumbent constituencies undergirds this bias. Flawed investment frameworks may also contribute. Entry into a market by an enterprise with a new and superior technology will cause rapid depreciation of the economic value of an incumbent's plant and equipment. However, the incumbent may well make business decisions based on examining accounting profits that reflect depreciation rates specified by accepted accounting standards. If decision makers confuse depreciation calculated according to generally accepted accounting principles (GAAP) with real economic depreciation, and conclude that the existing business is still profitable when, in fact, it is not, then the business enterprise may eschew profit-enhancing cannibalization of its own products. To guard against this bias, investment decision makers and incumbents must use accounting data cautiously. In particular, they must also consider the opportunity cost associated with not cannibalizing their own products. Capital-budgeting procedures implicitly biased against projects with long-term horizons must be jettisoned or used cautiously. That is not to say that incumbents need to invest on the same schedule as new entrants. As Teece (1986) and Mitchell (1991) demonstrate, incumbents need not be the first movers. Superior positioning in complementary assets may enable incumbents to let the new entrants do the prospecting; investing later once market and technological risk has diminished.

There is an obvious role for leadership in making quality decisions, communicating goals, values and expectations, while also motivating employees and other constituencies. Organizational identification (and commitment, which is the corollary) can dramatically augment enterprise performance, although it is doubtful it can override completely misaligned incentives. Nevertheless, group loyalty is a 'powerful altruistic force' that conditions employee goals and the cognitive models they form of their situation (Simon, 1993: 160). Top management through its action and its communication has a critical role to play in garnering loyalty and commitment and achieving adherence to innovation and efficiency as important goals.

Since there is already an extensive literature on culture, commitment and leadership, these issues are not discussed further. However, it would be a significant oversight in a summary statement of the dynamic capabilities framework to ignore them completely. Their full integration into the framework is left to others. However, it is recognized that to the extent such properties are not ubiquitously distributed amongst business enterprises, they can be a very important source of superior performance.

Managing threats and reconfiguration

Nature

The successful identification and calibration of technological and market opportunities, the judicious selection of technologies and product attributes, the design of business models, and the commitment of (financial) resources to investment opportunities can lead to enterprise growth and profitability. Profitable growth will lead to the augmentation of enterprise-level resources and assets. Success will cause the enterprise to evolve in a path-dependent way. A key to sustained profitable growth is the ability to recombine and to reconfigure assets and organizational structures as the enterprise grows, and as markets and technologies change, as they surely will. Reconfiguration is needed to maintain evolutionary fitness and, if necessary, to try and escape from unfavourable path dependencies. In short, success will breed some level of routine, as this is necessary for operational efficiency. Routines help sustain continuity until there is a shift in the environment. Changing routines is costly, so change will not be (and should not be) embraced instantaneously. Departure from routines will lead to heightened anxiety within the organization, unless the culture is shaped to accept high levels of internal change. If innovation is incremental, routines

and structures can probably be adapted gradually or in (semi-continuous) steps. When it is radical, possibly because it is science-based, then there will be a mandate to completely revamp the organization and create an entirely new 'break out' structure (Teece, 2000) within which an entirely different set of structures and procedures is established.

As discussed earlier, the 'anti-cannibalization' bias is a particular manifestation of incentive and structural problems that can thwart innovation in established enterprises. Incumbent enterprises possessing fixed assets may further tend to limit their new investments to innovations that are 'close-in' to the existing asset base. They tend to narrowly focus search activities to exploit established technological and organizational assets. This effect makes it difficult for these enterprises to see potential radical innovations. In addition, incumbent enterprises tend to frame new problems in a manner consistent with the enterprise's current knowledge base, assets, and/or established problem-solving heuristics and established business model. This second effect means that managers may not successfully address opportunities or potential innovations even when they do recognize them. Managers face and must overcome at least two constraints – cognitive limitations and framing biases – arising from established assets (Teece, 2000).

As the enterprise grows, it has more assets to manage and to protect against malfeasance and mismanagement. Shirking, free riding, the strategic manipulation of information, and internal complacency are all issues that established enterprises will confront continuously. As discussed earlier, over time successful enterprises will develop hierarchies and rules and procedures (routines) that begin to constrain certain interactions and behaviours unnecessarily. Except in very stable environments, such rules and procedures are likely to require constant revamping if superior performance is to be sustained. It is not uncommon to find that a once functional routine becomes dysfunctional, providing inertia and other rigidities that stand in the way of improved performance (Leonard-Barton, 1995; Rumelt, 1995). As a result, less well-resourced enterprises (sometimes established enterprises that have divested certain assets, sometimes new entrants) end up winning in the marketplace.

Traditional management approaches endorse strong hierarchies with at least three levels of management: top, middle and lower. Control is exerted at the top and cascades down through multiple levels. Employees tend to end up beholden to the management and CEO, and not the customer. The existence of independent profit centres can lead to internal boundaries that stand in the way of providing integrated solutions that benefit customers. With centralized structures, strategic decisions made at the top tend to become isolated from marketplace realities. Customer care is relegated to employees who are lower down in the organization. In short, the systems and rules needed to manage many layers of organization tend to create structural rigidities and perversities that in turn handicap customer and technological responsiveness. To sustain dynamic capabilities, decentralization must be favoured because it brings top management closer to new technologies, the customer and the market.

Top management leadership skills are required to sustain dynamic capabilities. An important managerial function is achieving semi-continuous asset orchestration and corporate renewal, including the redesign of routines. This is because the sustained achievement of superior profitability requires semi-continuous and/ or continuous efforts to build, maintain and adjust the complementarity of product offerings, systems, routines and structures. Inside the enterprise, the old and the new must complement. If they do not, business units must be disposed of or placed in some type of separate structure. Otherwise, work will not proceed efficiently and conflicts of one kind or another will arise. Put differently, periodic if not sustained asset orchestration – involving achieving asset alignment, co-alignment, realignment, and redeployment – is necessary to minimize internal conflict and to maximize complementarities and productive exchange inside the enterprise.

Redeployment and reconfiguration (Capron, Dussauge and Mitchell, 1998) may also involve business model redesign as well as asset-realignment activities, and the revamping of routines. Redeployment can involve transfer of non-tradeable assets to another organizational or geographic location (Teece, 1977, 1980). It may or may not involve mergers, acquisitions and divestments. Helfat and Peteraf (2003: 1006) suggest that capability redeployment takes one of two forms: the sharing of capability between the old and the new, and the geographic transfer of capability from one market to another. Both are possible, but neither is easy.

Microfoundations

Achieving decentralization and near decomposability.
Every system comprises subsystems (elements) that are to some extent interdependent and independent. However, as discussed earlier, enterprises are unlikely to be continuously responsive to customers and new technologies absent a high degree of decentralization. With decentralized decision making, different managers observe different information and control different decisions, but there is not the need for communication to a single central decision maker, and hence no comprehensive 'rollup' of information is required. Decentralization must be pursued as enterprises expand, otherwise flexibility and responsiveness will erode.

One well-documented restructuring that is widely adopted as enterprises grow is the adoption of the multidivisional form. This involves decomposition and the devolution of decision rights to quasi-independent profit centres. The abandonment of functional structures in favour of the multidivisional form has been analysed by Chandler (1962), Williamson (1975) and many others. The basic rationale of this reconfiguration was to achieve greater accountability of managerial decisions so that the recognition of opportunities and threats could proceed more thoroughly and expeditiously. With functional internal structures, day-to-day problems tend to distract management from long-run strategic issues. Studies showed that decentralization along product or market lines with independent profit centres led to performance improvements in many industries, at least during the period in which these organizational innovations were diffusing (Armour and Teece, 1978; Teece, 1980, 1981). More recent scholarship has suggested that even further decentralization and decomposition in large organizations may be beneficial (Bartlett and Ghoshal, 1993). There is also some evidence that 'modern' human resource management techniques – involving delayering, decentralization of decision rights, teamwork, flexible task responsibilities and performance-based rewards also improve performance (Jantunen, 2005).

Of course, achieving decentralization can compromise the organization's ability to achieve integration. There is little harm and much benefit from decentralization when the customer does not benefit from an integrated product offering, or when sourcing and other inputs do not benefit from integration and/or aggregation. If customer and supply considerations allow decomposability (because the required integration between units is less than within units), then management's ability to identify and implement decomposable sub-units should enhance performance. However, if firm-specific economies of scale and scope are available, they must be captured – otherwise the enterprise is tantamount to a conglomerate. This tension can be managed through a collaborative non-hierarchical management style assisted by establishing councils and other integration forums. Middle management can also play a critical role when such forums are established. They can also design and implement tight financial controls and performance-based reward systems. Since intangibles are key drivers of performance, their enhancement and protection must become a managerial priority.

Managing co-specialization. The field of strategic management and the dynamic capabilities framework recognizes that 'strategic fit' needs to be continuously achieved. However, unless the concept is operationalized it has limited utility. The key dimension of 'fit' emphasized in the dynamic capabilities framework is that of 'co-specialization.' The concept of co-specialization operationalizes at least one dimension of the otherwise rather vague concept of organizational adaptation and 'fit.' Co-specialization can be of one asset to another, or of strategy to structure, or of strategy to process. It is important to both seizing and reconfiguration. In environments of rapid change, there is a need for continuous or at least semi-continuous realignment.

However, complementary innovation and complementary assets are of great significance, particularly in industries in which innovation might be characterized as cumulative, and/or where industry 'platforms' exist or are needed. Examples of complementary innovation are ubiquitous. In the enterprise software industry, business applications can be especially valuable to users if they can somehow be integrated into a single programme, or into a tightly integrated suite. The development of gyroscopic stabilizers made imaging devices such as video cameras and binoculars easier to use by minimizing the impact of camera shake, and enhanced the product, especially when the new feature was able to be introduced at low cost. Likewise, better high-energy rechargeable batteries enable laptop computers and cellphones to operate for longer times. Situations of complementarities where there is also co-specialization between technologies, and between technologies and other parts of the value chain are common, yet until recently poorly analysed in economic analysis and in strategy formulation.

Co-specialized assets are a particular class of complementary assets where the value of an asset is a function of its use in conjunction with other particular assets. With co-specialization, joint use is value enhancing. Co-specialization results in 'thin' markets; i.e., the assets in question are idiosyncratic and cannot be readily bought and sold in a market. Capturing

co-specialization benefits may require integrated operations (Teece, 1980). Co-specialization allows differentiated product offerings or unique cost savings. The inherent 'thin' market environment surrounding specific assets means that competitors are not able to rapidly assemble the same assets by acquisition, and hence cannot offer the same products/services at competing price points.

Management's ability to identify, develop and utilize in combination specialized and co-specialized assets built or bought is an important dynamic capability, but it is not always present in enterprise settings. Special value can be created (and potentially appropriated by another party) through asset combinations, particularly when an asset owner is not cognizant of the value of its assets to another party that owns assets whose value will be enhanced through combination. This arises because the markets for co-specialized assets are necessarily thin or non-existent.

Both innovation and reconfiguration may necessitate co-specialized assets being combined by management in order for (systemic) innovation to proceed. Managers do not always succeed in doing so, sometimes because they do not sense the need or the opportunity, and sometimes because they do but they are unable to effect the integration. If the assets cannot be procured externally, they will need to be built internally.

The ability of management to identify needs and opportunities to 'invest' in co-specialized assets (through its own development or astute purchase) is fundamental to dynamic capabilities. Mere 'horse-trading' skills (which market agents possess) will not suffice to build sustainable competitive advantage, and decisions on when and how to invest – whether and when to build or buy co-specialized assets – will depend upon many factors, including transaction costs. In particular, it will depend on management's entrepreneurial capacities with respect to matching up and integrating relevant co-specialized assets.

It is apparent that co-specialization involves 'lock-in' and is a particular form of complementarity that exists when technologies and other assets need to be part of a tightly integrated system to achieve the performance that customers want. Business success in such circumstances requires the coordination of R&D investment and alliance activity. The manner and timing with which such coordination needs to be accomplished is important to success (Teece, 1986; Mitchell, 1991). Common ownership of the parts facilitates system-wide innovation and economic performance (Teece, 2000) and protects against opportunism (Williamson, 1975).

To summarize, entrepreneurs and managers can create special value by combining co-specialized assets inside the enterprise (Teece, 2007). This may require investments to create the necessary co-specialized technologies – as illustrated by Thomas Edison and the creation of electric power as a system. It is not uncommon in technology-based industries to find that certain technologies are worth more to some market participants than to others, based on the technology they already have, and their technology and product strategy.

Learning, knowledge management and corporate governance. With intangible assets being critical to enterprise success, the governance and incentive structures designed to enable learning and the generation of new knowledge become salient. There are many types of learning – including experiential, vicarious, individual and organizational – and a large literature that explores each type. Also 'sensing' requires learning about the environment and about new technological capabilities. R&D was seen as one way that the enterprise could promote such learning. However, in the context of the dynamic capability discussed in this section, the ability to integrate and combine assets including knowledge is a core skill (Kogut and Zander, 1992; Grant, 1996). The combination of know-how within the enterprise, and between the enterprise and organizations external to it (e.g., other enterprises, universities), is important.

Integrating know-how from outside as well as within the enterprise is especially important to success when 'systems' and 'networks' are present. Good incentive design and the creation of learning, knowledge-sharing and knowledge-integrating procedures are likely to be critical to business performance, and a key (micro-) foundation of dynamic capabilities (Nonaka and Takeuchi, 1995; Chesbrough, 2003). Of equal importance are monitoring and managing the 'leakage,' misappropriation, and misuse of know-how, trade secrets and other intellectual property. Of course, tacit know-how is difficult to imitate and has a certain amount of 'natural' protection. However, much know-how does leak out. Innovating business enterprises with limited experience have been known to inadvertently compromise or lose their intellectual property rights. Failure to proactively monitor and protect know-how and intellectual property is common.

The outsourcing of production and the proliferation of joint development activities likewise create requirements that enterprises develop governance procedures to monitor the transfer of technology and intellectual property. Technology transfer activities, which hitherto took place inside the enterprise, increasingly take place across enterprise boundaries. The development of governance mechanisms to assist the flow of technology, while protecting intellectual property rights from misappropriation and misuse, are foundational to dynamic capabilities in many sectors today.

There are also several other 'governance' issues relevant to dynamic capabilities. At one level there are governance and business model issues associated with an enterprise's ability to achieve asset 'combinations' and reconfiguration. As noted earlier, there is a continuous need to modify product offerings, business models, enterprise boundaries and organizational structures. Decentralized structures that facilitate near decomposability are likely to assist in achieving reconfiguration.

One class of governance issues relates to incentive alignment. The microfoundations of incentive issues are embedded in an understanding of agency and incentive design issues, also discussed earlier. Agency theory has long emphasized that the separation of ownership from control creates interest alignment problems, particularly around management compensation and the allocation of corporate perquisites. The abuse of discretion and the use of corporate assets for private purposes can incur absent appropriate accountability/oversight. These issues become more severe as an enterprise grows and the separation between ownership and management widens. Recent corporate governance scandals in the United States, Europe and Japan indicate the need for continued vigilance. However, increasing the mix of independent and 'inside' directors will not necessarily ameliorate problems associated with strategic 'malfeasance.'

There are likely to be benefits associated with participation at the board level by individuals who can calibrate whether the top management team is sufficiently 'dynamic.' The replacement of the CEO and other members of the top management team, if they demonstrate weak sensing, seizing and reconfiguration capabilities (strategic 'malfeasance'), is important to effect. That is not to say that guarding against financial malfeasance is unimportant. It will always remain as an important corporate governance function; but its significance is likely to pale next to strategic 'malfeasance,' which is harder to detect and evaluate.

A related literature in economics has stressed how poorly designed incentives can produce tensions between the actions of employees and the actions needed to achieve profitable performance. Dysfunctional behaviour, such as activity that generates influence costs, has received considerable attention (Teece, 2003). Also, through use of collective bargaining, employees in industries insulated from global competition have been able to appropriate economic surplus. Above-market wages – which characterized, and to some extent still characterize, certain enterprises in the auto, steel and airline industries in the United States – are a case in point. These conditions can extend to managerial ranks as well. Restructuring may then require the judicious use of bankruptcy laws to rewrite uncompetitive supply contracts that are the product of unrealistic collective bargaining actions in an earlier period. The ability of some enterprises to craft work specifications, attract and retain more committed talent, design reward systems, develop corporate cultures and blunt the formation of coalitions that extract quasi-rents through threatening to withhold participation, is an important managerial capacity.

The design and creation of mechanisms inside the enterprise to prevent the dissipation of rents by interest groups (both management and employees) would also appear to be very relevant to dynamic capabilities, but has not been high on the agenda of strategy researchers. One exception is Gottschalg and Zollo (2007), who point out that the capacity to continuously achieve incentive alignment is an important performance-enhancing (and rent protecting) dynamic capability.

Many of the issues discussed here have, in the past, fallen under the rubric of human resource management; a closer connection of these issues to strategic management issues would appear to be warranted. The reason is that strategic management is focused not only on how to generate rent streams, but also on how to prevent them from being dissipated or captured by various entities or groups inside and outside the enterprise. For instance, the concepts of the 'appropriability regime' and 'isolating mechanisms' were developed by strategic management scholars to help explain how rents from innovation and other sources of superior performance can be protected and guarded from dissipation by competitors and others. However, the earlier focus on markets or 'external' competition did not address internal appropriation by interest groups.

Dynamic capabilities, 'orchestration' skills and competitive advantage

The general framework advanced here sees dynamic capabilities as the foundation of enterprise-level competitive advantage in regimes of rapid (technological)

change. The framework indicates that the extent to which an enterprise develops and employs superior (non-imitable) dynamic capabilities will determine the nature and amount of intangible assets it will create and/or assemble and the level of economic profits it can earn (see Figure 2.1.1). Furthermore, the framework emphasizes that the past will impact current and future performance. However, there is much that management can do to simultaneously design processes and structures to support innovation while unshackling the enterprise from dysfunctional processes and structures designed for an earlier period.

In Teece and Pisano (1994), and Teece, Pisano and Shuen (1997), we proposed three organizational and managerial processes – coordination/integrating, learning and reconfiguring – as core elements of dynamic capabilities. These processes are a subset of the processes that support sensing, seizing and managing threats. Together they might be thought of as asset 'orchestration' processes. A key strategic function of management is to find new value-enhancing combinations inside the enterprise, and between and amongst enterprises, and with supporting institutions external to the enterprise. Because many of the most valuable assets inside the firm are knowledge related and hence non-tradeable, the coordination and integration of such assets create value that cannot be replicated in a market. This establishes a distinctive role for managers in economic theory and in the economic system. Managers seek new combinations by aligning co-specialized assets (Teece, 2007). The need to sense and seize opportunities, as well as reconfigure when change occurs, requires the allocation, reallocation, combination and recombination of resources and assets. These are the key strategic function of executives. Indeed, skills used to identify and exploit complementarities and manage co-specialization are scarce. Figuring out how to increase value from the use of the assets the enterprise owns involves knowing the fine-grained structure of the firm's asset base, and filling in the gaps necessary to provide superior customer solutions. Gap filling may involve building new assets, or acquisitions and strategic partnerships (Ettlie and Pavlou, 2006).

The dynamic capabilities framework recognizes that the business enterprise is shaped but not necessarily trapped by its past. Management can make big differences through investment choice and other decisions. Enterprises can even shape their ecosystem. In this sense, the framework is quite Chandlerian (Chandler, 1990a, 1990b). Managers really do have the potential to set technological and market trajectories, particularly early on in the development of a market

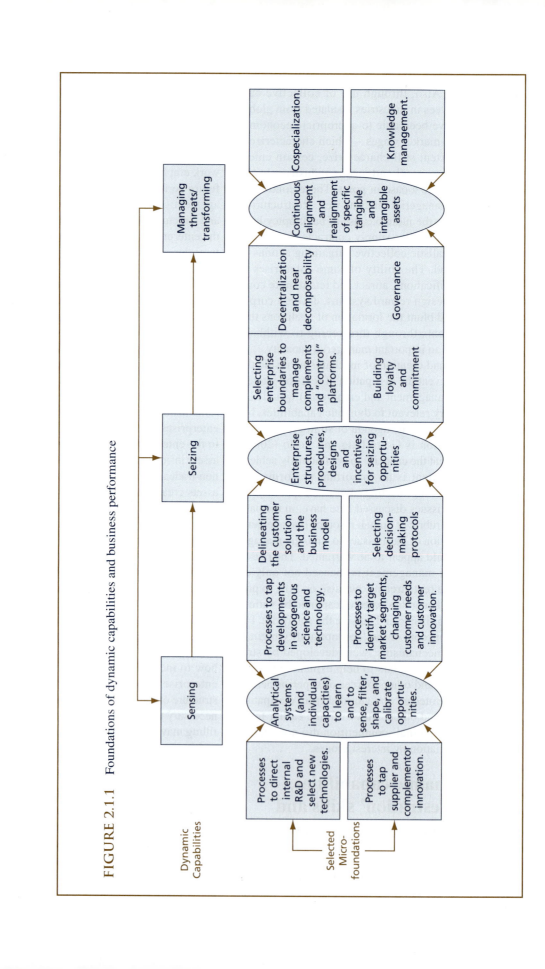

FIGURE 2.1.1 Foundations of dynamic capabilities and business performance

(David, 1992). Indeed, the enterprise and its environment frequently co-evolve. However, because of the assumed context – regimes of rapid technological change exposed to the full force of international competition – there is little room for big mistakes.

Hence, the dynamic capabilities framework is partially but not entirely in the spirit of evolutionary theorizing. The dynamic capabilities framework endeavours to capture the key variables and relationships that need to be 'manipulated' to create, protect and leverage intangible assets so as to achieve superior enterprise performance and avoid the zero-profit trap. However, building and assembling tangible and intangible assets and effecting change is seen as difficult. Long-run success is likely to require achieving necessary internal creative destruction, possibly involving spin-outs and spin-offs to help sustain superior performance. Decision biases must also be neutralized. In short, enterprises may be more like biological organisms than some economists, managers and strategy scholars are willing to admit; but they are also more malleable than some organizational ecologists are willing to recognize.

As indicated throughout this paper it is also necessary to assess the issue of the 'sustainability' or non-imitability of both assets and capabilities. This in turn depends upon a number of factors summarized adequately by the twin concepts of 'isolating mechanism' and 'appropriability regimes.' When the appropriability regime is 'tight' and the business enterprise's own isolating mechanisms are strong, differential performance can be sustained, at least for a time. Dynamic capabilities of course require the creation, integration and commercialization of a continuous stream of innovation consistent with customer needs and technological opportunities.

Note that in the dynamic capabilities framework, enterprises must employ sensing, seizing and reconfiguring mechanisms to direct their financial resources consistent with marketplace needs and imperatives. However, as a matter of pure theory, enterprises need not continuously reinvent themselves. The need to reinvent depends on events, anticipated or otherwise. If the ecosystem in which the enterprise is embedded remains stable, the need to change can be modulated accordingly. Indeed, if an enterprise controls standards, or can somehow help stabilize its own environment, then it may not need to engage in the continuous and costly exploration of radical alternatives (March, 1991). Selecting suitable business models, making the right strategic investment decisions, and pursuing incremental innovation can keep an enterprise highly competitive for a decade or so (e.g., Boeing's decision to build the 747, which 30 years later is much improved and still competitive in some configurations on some routes) if the environment is stable. Excessive internal change for the sake of it can lead to internal chaos and performance failure.

Conclusion

For open economies exposed to rapid technological change, the dynamic capabilities framework highlights organizational and (strategic) managerial competencies that can enable an enterprise to achieve competitive advantage, and then semi-continuously morph so as to maintain it. The framework integrates and synthesizes concepts and research findings from the field of strategic management, from business history, industrial economics, law and economics, the organizational sciences, innovation studies, and elsewhere.

Implicit in the dynamic capabilities framework is a recognition that relatively open regimes of free trade and investment, global dispersion in the sources of new knowledge, and the multi-invention or systemic character of such innovation have 'upped the ante' for modern management. Improving quality, controlling costs, lowering inventories and adopting best practices ('technical fitness') will no longer suffice for long-run competitive success. Nor do traditional scale economies in production always have the differentiating power they may once have had. More than scale and scope advantage are needed. Success requires the creation of new products and processes and the implementation of new organizational forms and business models, driven by an intensely entrepreneurial genre of management constantly honing the evolutionary and entrepreneurial fitness of the enterprise. Entrepreneurial managers can sense and even help shape the future, unshackle the enterprise from the past, and stay ahead by augmenting knowledge assets, protecting them with intellectual property rights, establishing new value enhancing asset combinations, and transforming organizational and, if necessary, regulatory and institutional structures. Dynamic capabilities reside in large measure with the enterprise's top management team, but are impacted by the organizational processes, systems and structures that the enterprise has created to manage its business in the past.

Maintaining dynamic capabilities thus requires entrepreneurial management. The entrepreneurial management in question is different, but related to other managerial activity. Entrepreneurship is about sensing and understanding opportunities, getting things started, and finding new and better ways of putting things together. It is about creatively coordinating the assembly of disparate and usually co-specialized elements, getting 'approvals' for non-routine activities, and sensing business opportunities. Entrepreneurial management has little to do with analysing and optimizing. It is more about sensing and seizing – figuring out the next big opportunity and how to address it.

We have come to associate the entrepreneur with the individual who starts a new business providing a new or improved product or service. Such action is clearly entrepreneurial, but the entrepreneurial management function embedded in dynamic capabilities is not confined to startup activities and to individual actors. It is a new hybrid: entrepreneurial managerial capitalism. It involves recognizing problems and trends, directing (and redirecting) resources, and reshaping organizational structures and systems so that they create and address technological opportunities while staying in alignment with customer needs. The implicit thesis advanced here is that in both large and small enterprises entrepreneurial managerial capitalism must reign supreme for enterprises to sustain financial success. Nor is entrepreneurial management merely 'intrapreneurship,' as there is a large role for the entrepreneurial manager in external activities, including shaping the ecosystem.

As discussed, there are obvious tensions and interrelationships between and amongst the three classes of capabilities identified. The managerial skills needed to sense are quite different from those needed to seize and those needed to reconfigure. All functions have a significant 'entrepreneurial' and 'right brain' component. Successful enterprises must build and utilize all three

classes of capabilities and employ them, often simultaneously. Since all three classes are unlikely to be found in individual managers, they must be somewhere represented in top management, and the principal executive officer must succeed in getting top management to operate as a team. Of course, if the principal executive officer has depth in all three classes of capabilities, the organization has a better chance of success.

The dynamic capabilities framework goes beyond traditional approaches to understanding competitive advantage in that it not only emphasizes the traits and processes needed to achieve good positioning in a favourable ecosystem, but it also endeavours to explicate new strategic considerations and the decision-making disciplines needed to ensure that opportunities, once sensed, can be seized; and how the business can be reconfigured when the market and/or the technology inevitably is transformed once again. In this sense, dynamic capabilities aspire to be a relatively parsimonious framework for explaining an extremely seminal and complicated issue: how a business enterprise and its management can first spot the opportunity to earn economic profits, make the decisions and institute the disciplines to execute on that opportunity, and then stay agile so as to continuously refresh the foundations of its early success, thereby generating economic surpluses over time. If the framework has succeeded in some small measure, then we have the beginnings of a general theory of strategic management in an open economy with innovation, outsourcing, and offshoring.

READING
2.2

Exploring intuition and its role in managerial decision making

By Erik Dane and Michael G. Pratt[1]

The human brain can be a magnificent synthesizer of disparate pieces of nebulous information, and often formal techniques and

procedures thwart this mysterious mechanism from operating efficiently
(Raiffa, 1968: 272).

A classic trade-off noted by decision theorists is that decision accuracy is often inversely related to decision speed. Consequently, there has been pressure to understand how to make high quality decisions relatively quickly (see Eisenhardt, 1989; Hitt, Keats and DeMarie, 1998; Perlow, Okhuysen and Repenning, 2002). Toward this end, in numerous articles in

the popular business press and in a steadily growing body of more scholarly literature, authors have turned to the notion of "intuition" as a means of managing this trade-off (e.g., Burke and Miller, 1999; Hayashi, 2001; Khatri and Ng, 2000). As the epigraph suggests, intuition draws on our inborn ability to synthesize information quickly and effectively – an ability that may

[1]Source: Excerpted with permission from Erik Dane and Michael G. Pratt (2007) 'Exploring intuition and its role in managerial decision making', *Academy of Management Review* 2007, Vol. 32, No. 1, 33–54.

be hindered by more formalized procedures. Within organizations, intuition has been posited to help guide a wide range of critical decisions. Research suggests that intuition may be integral to successfully completing tasks that involve high complexity and short time horizons, such as corporate planning, stock analysis, and performance appraisal (Hayashi, 2001; Isenberg, 1984; Shirley and Langan-Fox, 1996). Agor (1986) shows how managers use intuitions for strategic decisions, such as whether to invest capital in a project or whether to market controversial prescription drugs. Hayashi (2001) frames several high-profile executive-level decisions, including the development of the Dodge Viper and the prime-time launch of Who Wants to Be a Millionaire, as intuitive or "gut" decisions. Research further suggests that the need for intuition may be especially acute in organizations embedded in turbulent environments (Khatri and Ng, 2000). The effective use of intuition has even been seen as critical in differentiating successful top executives and board members from lower-level managers and dysfunctional boards (Agor, 1986; Barnard, 1938; Harper, 1989). Ralph Larsen, former chair and CEO of Johnson & Johnson, suggested:

Very often, people will do a brilliant job through the middle management levels, where it's very heavily quantitative in terms of the decision making. But then they reach senior management, where the problems get more complex and ambiguous, and we discover that their judgment or intuition is not what it should be. And when that happens, it's a problem; it's a big problem (Hayashi, 2001: 61).

We believe that there have been two major barriers to a productive discourse on the topic of intuition within the management literature. The first concerns the considerable confusion surrounding what intuition is. Although intuition has a long history in the organizational sciences (Barnard, 1938; Behling and Eckel, 1991; Isaack, 1978; Peters, Hammond, and Summers, 1974; Prietula and Simon, 1989; Simon, 1987), in the literature in this area scholars have failed to agree on what intuition is and what it does. This conceptual confusion comes, in part, from the various perspectives used to understand intuition. For example, among Western philosophers, intuition was often perceived as the most pure and immediate way of knowing (Osbeck, 2001; Wild, 1938). It represented access to divine or inborn knowledge. In the East, many Buddhists viewed intuition as a means of obtaining penetrating knowledge and as a "gateway to a wider and richer

world" (Guenther, 1958: 26). While some maintain that intuition is a mystical avenue to knowledge (e.g., Ferguson, 1999; Franquemont, 1999; Vaughan, 1979), researchers in the areas of management and psychology have explained intuition through a wide range of phenomena, including heuristics (Bazerman, 1986; Denes-Raj and Epstein, 1994; Tversky and Kahneman, 1983), expertise (Blattberg and Hoch, 1990; Prietula and Simon, 1989), and nonconscious information processing (Epstein, 1990, 1994, 2002; Kahneman, 2003; Lieberman, 2000). Thus, one purpose of this paper is to seek out sources of conceptual agreement or overlap across different disciplines and, thus, provide greater clarity about the concept of intuition. A second barrier hindering this line of inquiry is that scholars often fail to distinguish between when intuitions are used and when they are used effectively. To illustrate, evidence suggests that individuals are likely to rely on intuitive thought processes when they face extreme time pressures (De Dreu, 2003; Edland and Svenson, 1993; Kaplan, Wanshula, and Zanna, 1993; Kruglanski and Freund, 1983; Maule, Hockey, and Bdzola, 2000; Suri and Monroe, 2003). Therefore, intuition may play a significant role in the decisions of firefighters (Klein, 1998), military commanders (Kaempf, Klein, Thordsen, and Wolf, 1996), emergency room surgeons (Abernathy and Hamm, 1995), and corporate executives operating under severe time constraints (Agor, 1986; Burke and Miller, 1999; Hayashi, 2001). The mere use of intuition, however, is not a panacea for the speed-accuracy trade-off, since its use may simply facilitate speed at the expense of accuracy. Therefore, we need to better understand those conditions that foster the effective use of intuition to complement existing work on when intuition is simply most likely to be used (e.g., Ruder and Bless, 2003; Sinclair, Ashkanasy, Chattopadhyay, and Boyle, 2002; Woolhouse and Bayne, 2000). Drawing on recent advances in psychology and the decision sciences, we suggest that, under certain conditions, intuition may indeed facilitate rapid and effective decision making in organizations. Before such gains can be realized, however, we must first understand the boundary conditions that surround the concept. We begin with an exploration of what intuition is and how it is different from other related concepts, such as insight and instinct. We then consider the factors that determine when the use of intuition in decision making is most effective. Toward this end, we synthesize findings across a range of disciplines and formulate a set of propositions surrounding the effectiveness of intuitive decision making.

What intuition is: Bringing together intuitive processes and outcomes

Having both academic and nonacademic significance, "intuition," perhaps not surprisingly, has a wide range of terms associated with it, including gut feelings (Hayashi, 2001), hunches (Rowan, 1989), and mystical insights

(Vaughan, 1979; Wild, 1938). Table 2.2.1 provides a sample of definitions of intuition culled from work in psychology, philosophy, and management. One confusing aspect of past research is the tendency to call both intuitive processes and their associated products, or outcomes, "intuition." For example, Jung (1933), Westcott and Ranzoni (1963), and Raidl and Lubart (2000–2001) refer to intuition largely as a process – a way of perceiving or sorting data. Rorty (1967), in contrast, sees

TABLE 2.2.1   Definitions of intuition

Source	Definition of intuition
Jung (1933: 567–568)	That psychological function transmitting perceptions in an unconscious way
Wild (1938: 226)	An immediate awareness by the subject, of some particular entity, without such aid from the senses or from reason as would account for that awareness
Bruner (1962: 102)	The act of grasping the meaning, significance, or structure of a problem without explicit reliance on the analytic apparatus of one's craft
Westcott & Ranzoni (1963: 595)	The process of reaching a conclusion on the basis of little information, normally reached on the basis of significantly more information
Rorty (1967: 204)	Immediate apprehension
Bowers, Regehr, Balthazard, & Parker (1990: 74)	A preliminary perception of coherence (pattern, meaning, structure) that is at first not consciously represented but that nevertheless guides thought and inquiry toward a hunch or hypothesis about the nature of the coherence in question
Shirley & Langan-Fox (1996: 564)	A feeling of knowing with certitude on the basis of inadequate information and without conscious awareness of rational thinking
Simon (1996: 89)	Acts of recognition
Shapiro & Spence (1997: 64)	A nonconscious, holistic processing mode in which judgments are made with no awareness of the rules of knowledge used for inference and which can feel right, despite one's inability to articulate the reason
Burke & Miller (1999: 92)	A cognitive conclusion based on a decision maker's previous experiences and emotional inputs
Policastro (1999: 89)	A tacit form of knowledge that orients decision making in a promising direction
Lieberman (2000: 111)	The subjective experience of a mostly nonconscious process—fast, alogical, and inaccessible to consciousness—that, depending on exposure to the domain or problem space, is capable of accurately extracting probabilistic contingencies
Raidl & Lubart (2000–2001: 219)	A perceptual process, constructed through a mainly subconscious act of linking disparate elements of information
Hogarth (2001: 14)	Thoughts that are reached with little apparent effort, and typically without conscious awareness; they involve little or no conscious deliberation
Myers (2002: 128–129)	The capacity for direct, immediate knowledge prior to rational analysis
Kahneman (2003: 697)	Thoughts and preferences that come to mind quickly and without much reflection
Epstein (personal communication, 2004)	The working of the experiential system

intuition primarily as an outcome – as what one apprehends or recognizes. Others combine both process and outcome without differentiating between them. We believe that intuition is marked by a unique process and outcome; however, we also believe it is important to disentangle the two. Thus, we begin by addressing intuition as a process and positioning this process vis-a-vis the larger "dual processing" perspective that is currently favoured among decision-making theorists, especially in psychology. We then build from this perspective to identify process and outcome characteristics that historically have been central to many definitions of intuition.

Historical context: Two information processing systems

Intuition has long been viewed as involving a form of information processing that differs from rational, or analytical, processes. Distinctions between "rational" and "nonrational" human thought can be traced as far back as Aristotle (Sloman, 1996). In management research, Barnard similarly distinguished between "logical" and "nonlogical" modes of thinking, attributing intuition to the latter:

> By "logical processes" I mean conscious thinking which could be expressed in words, or other symbols, that is, reasoning. By "non-logical processes" I mean those not capable of being expressed in words or as reasoning ....This may be because the processes are unconscious, or because they are so complex and so rapid, often approaching the instantaneous, that they could not be analysed by the person within whose brain they take place (1938: 302).

More recently, psychologists have adopted a dual processing approach, arguing for two distinct types of information processing systems in human beings (e.g., Epstein, 2002; Gollwitzer and Bayer, 1999; Sloman, 1996). One information processing system, which from an evolutionary perspective is believed by some to be the older of the two systems (Epstein, 1994; Reber, 1992), involves the automatic and relatively effortless processing and learning of information (Stanovich and West, 2000). This system, which permits individuals to learn from experience and reach perceptions of knowing without conscious attention (Hogarth, 2001), has been referred to as experiential (Epstein, 1990, 1994, 2002; Epstein, Pacini, Denes-Raj, and Heier, 1996; Pacini and Epstein, 1999), automatic (Bargh, 1996; Bargh and Chartrand, 1999), tacit (Hogarth, 2001), natural (Tversky and Kahneman, 1983),

associative (Sloman, 1996), and system 1 (Kahneman, 2003; Stanovich and West, 2000). Bargh and Chartrand (1999) argue that a large portion of everyday life is determined by this first information processing system. Insofar as such processes are rapid, effortless, and often quite effective, nonconscious processes serve as "mental butlers" that conveniently manage our tendencies and preferences (Bargh and Chartrand, 1999). As we explain below, intuition is often associated with this system (e.g., Epstein, 2002, Kahneman, 2003; Sloman, 1996). The second system enables individuals to learn information deliberately, to develop ideas, and to engage in analyses in an attentive manner. This system has been referred to by various names, including rational (Epstein, 2002; Epstein et al., 1996; Pacini and Epstein, 1999), intentional (Bargh and Chartrand, 1999), deliberate (Hogarth, 2001), extensional (Tversky and Kahneman, 1983), rule based (Sloman, 1996), and system 2 (Kahneman, 2003; Stanovich and West, 2000). Rational decision-making models, which have garnered the lion's share of research on managerial decision making, utilize this system of information processing. Drawing on the conceptual foundation provided by dual processing theories, we now turn to the concept of intuition. Like other authors, we view the process of intuition as relating to the domain of the "nonconscious" information processing system (e.g., Epstein 1990, 1994, 2002; Kahneman, 2003). However, in making this case, we also stress that not all nonconscious operations are fundamental components of intuition itself. We have two primary reasons for differentiating intuition from any given nonconscious system depicted in dual processing theory. First, the nonconscious systems in dual processing theories typically involve a larger group of phenomena than are central to intuition. For example, research on the nonconscious system has often focused on learning processes. However, as we will argue, intuitive processes pertain less to learning and more to how learned information is accessed and used. We view learning as an input to intuition effectiveness, but do not see intuition as a learning process per se. Second, our focus on both processes and outcomes of intuition differentiates our work from traditional research on nonconscious systems, such as that on the experiential system, which has focused nearly exclusively on processes only. Specifically, we conceptualize intuition both by its process (which we refer to as intuiting), as well as its outcome (which we term intuitive judgments). In constructing a definition of the construct, we build on and bridge work in psychology, philosophy, and management; our focus is on those aspects of intuition that are common and central to all three. Specifically, our review of the various literature on intuition has tended to converge on four characteristics that make up the core of the construct: intuition is a (1) nonconscious process (2) involving holistic associations (3) that are produced rapidly, which (4) result in affectively charged judgments. We explore these characteristics in detail below.

Intuiting is nonconscious

One of the defining characteristics of intuitive processing is that it is nonconscious[2]—it occurs outside of conscious thought. Jung, for example, defined intuition as "that psychological function which transmits perceptions in an unconscious way" (1933: 567–568). Simple perceptions, however, are not the only type of information that is transmitted through this means. The nonconscious processing of information can occur at various levels of sophistication (Epstein, 2002; Pacini and Epstein, 1999), and intuiting can involve the processing of more complex information than perceptions. On this point, Epstein and Pacini make the following observation about the nonconscious, experiential system: At its lower reaches, it (the experiential system) is a relatively crude, albeit efficient, system for automatically, rapidly, and effortlessly processing information while placing minimal demands on cognitive resources. At higher reaches . . . the experiential system can be a source of intuitive wisdom and creativity (1999: 463). In further clarifying the connection between nonconscious processing and intuition, we reemphasize the distinction between intuitive processes and outcomes. While the outcomes of intuiting, intuitive judgments, are clearly accessible to conscious thinking, how one arrives at them is not. Hence, there is "no awareness of the rules of knowledge used for inference" during intuiting (Shapiro and Spence, 1997: 64). Similarly, Osbeck writes that intuition, from a philosophical perspective, involves direct apprehension that is "not mediated by other reasoning or representation" (2001: 123). As we discuss below, this quality differentiates intuition from insight.

Intuiting involves making holistic associations

A second characteristic of intuiting is that it involves a process in which environmental stimuli are matched with some deeply held (nonconscious) category,

pattern, or feature. Historically, this matching process has gone by numerous names, including awareness (Wild, 1938), apprehension (Rorty, 1967), recognition (Simon, 1996), and seeing (Osbeck, 1999). More recently, Raidl and Lubart described intuition as involving a process of "linking disparate elements of information" (2000–2001: 219). This linking together of elements is why many refer to intuiting as being associative (Epstein, 1994; Epstein *et al.*, 1996; Kahneman, 2003). Further, because intuiting involves recognizing features or patterns (e.g., Klein, 1998), rather than making connections through logical considerations, it has also been conceptualized as holistic (Epstein, 1990; Shapiro and Spence, 1997). As such, Bowers, Regehr, Balthazard, and Parker speak of intuition as involving a "perception of coherence (pattern, meaning, structure)" (1990: 74). In sum, since the associations in intuition refer to the recognition of patterns or structures, we refer to this aspect of intuiting as making holistic associations. Psychologists and other decision science scholars suggest that, in making holistic associations, individuals nonconsciously map stimuli onto cognitive structures or frameworks. Research has typically focused on one of two types of cognitive structures. The first and most common line of research examines the role of relatively simple cognitive structures, such as heuristics, in the formation of intuitive judgments (Bazerman, 1986; Bodenhausen, 1990; Kahneman, Slovic, and Tversky, 1982; Kahneman and Tversky, 2000; Tversky and Kahneman, 1983). As we will argue below, this line of research has often concluded that intuitive decision making is inferior to rational decision-making models. A second line of inquiry suggests that intuiting may involve the use of more complex, but still not consciously accessible, cognitive structures. For instance, drawing on the work of Agor (1989), Shirley and Langan-Fox (1996: 573) have argued that intuiting results from a process of recognition and retrieval in which large numbers – perhaps several thousands – of chunks or patterns stored in long-term memory are accessed without conscious effort. This stream of research, focusing largely on the intuitions of experts (e.g., surgeons making life-and-death decisions, chess masters engaging in competition), contends that experts possess highly sophisticated, nonconscious cognitive structures that permit rapid and accurate responses to highly demanding situations (Dreyfus and Dreyfus, 1986;

---

[2] This characteristic of intuition has been called "unconscious," "subconscious," "preconscious," and "nonconscious" (Epstein, 1994; Hogarth, 2001; Jung, 1933; Reber, 1992; Simon, 1987). However, each of these terms has a slightly different meaning (see Kihlstrom, 1987, for a review). For the sake of parsimony, we refer to what each of these terms has in common: they are nonconscious.

Klein, 1998, 2003; Prietula and Simon, 1989; Simon, 1987, 1992, 1996; Simon and Chase, 1973). Such research has tended either to favour the use of intuition over more rational models or to position intuition as a useful complement to analytical thinking. Thus, intuition is seen as a subset of the entire population of decision making approaches successfully used by experts. However, common to both the heuristic and expert decision-making perspectives is the view that individuals nonconsiously make holistic associative connections between the stimuli they encounter and their underlying cognitive structures in the process of intuiting. Making holistic associations is not only a characteristic of intuiting but also speaks to one of intuition's advantages over other decision-making approaches: our nonconscious ability to make such categorical connections is greater than our ability to mimic it consciously. As Raiffa (1968) argues in the quote that opens our paper, such ability may be undermined by our attempts to use more conscious, or rational, means of making judgments and decisions. It has even been stated that, in some instances, rational analysis may prevent people from "seeing the obvious" (Pirsig, 1974: 196). As noted above, conscious thinking appears to rely on connections made through a slow and effortful analysis (Epstein, 1990, 1994; Kihlstrom, 1987). These properties contrast sharply with the holistic and associative qualities of the experiential system. All told, it comes as little surprise that intuiting is perhaps better suited than rational methods to integrate wide-ranging stimuli into usable categories of information.

Intuiting is fast

A third characteristic of the intuition process, and the one that has seemed to spark the most interest among both managers and academics, is its speed (Bastick, 1982; Burke and Miller, 1999; Kahneman, 2003; Khatri and Ng, 2000; Myers, 2002). Although there has been some debate about whether intuiting is always fast (see Hogarth, 2001), the vast majority of researchers view intuiting as quite fast – especially when compared with the use of rational decision-making processes. The centrality of "speed" is seen in the concepts of intuition used by philosophers (see Wild, 1938, for a review). Rorty for example, views this process as involving "immediate apprehension" (1967: 74). Osbeck, in a newer review of the philosophical roots of intuition, views speed as a defining aspect of intuiting and notes that Locke and Hume viewed intuition as "the immediate perception of connection between ideas" (2001: 121). This emphasis on speed is echoed in other more recent perspectives on intuition. Researchers who view intuiting – and nonconscious information processing more generally – as an evolutionary precursor to more conscious and analytical thinking point to the advantages of having an information processing system that responds quickly to environmental stimuli (Epstein, 1994; Haidt, 2001; Reber, 1992). Kihlstrom (1987: 1447) similarly argues that processing information nonconsciously does not require attention and, thus, does not produce the same information "bottlenecks" that conscious processing does. From a managerial perspective, the speed of intuiting is not only taken for granted but is often seen as a primary motivator for developing and employing intuition at work (Agor, 1986; Burke and Miller, 1999; Khatri and Ng, 2000; Klein, 2003). Moreover, the speed characteristic of intuition has long been recognized by management theorists. Barnard proclaimed intuition to be a component of "non-logical mental processes" that are capable of handling a "mass of experience or a complex of abstractions in a flash" (1938: 305). March and Simon echo Barnard's view, asserting that one of the hallmarks of intuiting, in addition to its nonconscious nature, is its speed: The distinctive earmarks of intuition are rapid response (a matter of seconds) and inability of the respondent to report a sequence of steps leading to the result – even denial of awareness of such steps. ...what impresses observers about intuition is that responses, especially those of experts, are frequently correct even though they seem to have required almost no processing time or effort (1993: 11).

Intuiting results in affectively charged judgments

Although "intuiting" refers to a unique way of processing information, individuals often use intuition as a noun—as the product of such processing. To differentiate the process and product facets of intuition, we use the term intuitive judgment to signify intuition in its outcome state. We make reference to "judgments" rather than some other outcome state, given the strong association between intuition and problem solving. To illustrate, pioneering works in managerial problem solving (Barnard, 1938; Simon, 1987, 1996) and classic works on decision making (Kahneman et al., 1982; Tversky and Kahneman 1974, 1983) focus explicitly on how individuals use intuiting to solve problems. This problem focused treatment of intuition is echoed in the work of Policastro (1999), who holds that intuition is a type of knowledge used to orient decision making.

We further clarify intuitive judgments as "affectively charged," given that such judgments often involve emotions. Chen and Chaiken (1999: 87), for example, suggest that the presence of "cognitive feelings" may indicate that heuristic processes are operating. And, more generally, synonyms for intuition, such as "gut feelings" and "gut instincts" (Hayashi, 2001; Shapiro and Spence, 1997), as well as "feeling in our marrow" (Barnard, 1938: 306), reflect an affective component to intuitive judgments. Thus, one way that we identify a judgment as intuitive is that it is accompanied by affect. For example, Agor (1986) notes that as executives make intuitive judgments, they often experience excitement and harmony. And Shirley and Langan-Fox define intuitions as "feelings of knowing" (1996: 564). The coupling of affect and intuitive judgments has a long intellectual history. At a very basic level, these judgments may be thought of as affective because they are detached from rationality. Thus, rationality is often associated with the "head" and intuition with the "heart" – a common divide in philosophy. However, recent research suggests other possibilities. To begin with, intuitive judgments may be triggered by emotions and affect. Positive mood, for example, has been linked to an increase in the use of intuition and a decrease in more rational approaches to decision making (see Weiss and Cropanzano, 1996, for a review). Similarly, managers often view affect as an important input to intuition and describe intuitions as "affect initiated decisions" (Burke and Miller, 1999). And Hogarth argues that "emotion and affect can, therefore, be important inputs to intuitive thought in the sense that they can induce responses without corresponding awareness" (2001: 61). Moreover, emotions and affect may also play a role in the intuition process itself and, thus, result in affect-laden judgments. Epstein (1990, 1994, 2002), for example, ties emotion and intuition through the experiential information processing system described above by suggesting that all processes in the nonconscious (experiential) system are emotionally driven. Bastick makes a similar argument, suggesting that "intuitive information is accessed through appropriate feelings" (1982: 279). Epstein further argues that the cognitive frameworks in the experiential system, which he refers to as schemas, are "inductively derived from emotionally significant experiences" (1990: 170). Intriguingly, research in neuroscience has suggested a link between intuition and affect via activation of basal ganglia in the human brain (see Lieberman, 2000, for a review). This line of investigation has shown that basal ganglia are engaged through positive affective stimuli and positive emotional experience, and these same neural mechanisms play a central role in engendering the nonconscious associations that spur intuitive judgments. In essence, both intuitions and emotional appraisals appear to arise through highly similar neurological pathways. Taken together, evidence from organizational, cognitive, and neurological psychology suggests that affect and emotions are an integral component of intuitive judgments. In sum, research suggests that affect is associated both with the intuiting process and with intuition as an outcome. We therefore use the term affectively charged to denote the affective tenor of intuitive judgments, as well as to reflect how such judgments were generated (i.e., were "charged" via an affective process).

Other elements associated with intuition

Our central characteristics of intuition are based on their commonality to definitions across philosophy, psychology, and management. In addition to their commonality, they also appear to be the most "core" features. Consequently, we have excluded some additional characteristics of intuition since they appear to result from the core characteristics we suggest. To illustrate, several conceptualizations of intuition involve a feeling of certitude (Shirley and Langan-Fox, 1996) and a perception that one's intuitions are correct – despite the lack of rational analysis (Bruner, 1962; Wescott and Ranzoni, 1963). This characteristic, however, likely is due to the affective and associative properties we have discussed. As noted, Agor (1986) has argued that as executives make intuitive judgments, they often experience strong and positive emotions (e.g., excitement, harmony). Such positive feelings may, in turn, lead to an enhanced sense of confidence in an individual's own judgments (see Tiedens and Linton, 2001, for a discussion). Thus, if I feel good about a judgment, I must be right about it. In addition, the holistic, associative properties of intuition involve recognizing patterns or other linkages among disparate stimuli. Hence, philosophers have linked intuition with "seeing" or "recognizing" an answer (Osbeck, 1999, 2001). Because intuition involves "recognizing" a solution (Simon, 1996), it is likely that individuals will have more confidence in their intuition than in a "wild guess," which is often made when no solution is recognizable.[3]

---

[3] However, we should be clear that just because an individual has confidence that the solution is a good one does not mean that the individual will adopt the solution. That is, individuals may still distrust intuitive means, regardless of the veracity of the solution.

As noted earlier in the paper, we have also excluded characteristics ascribed to intuition that seem unique to a particular disciplinary domain. For example, intuition is associated with both experiential (Epstein 1990, 1994, 2002) and system 1 (Kahneman, 2003; Stanovich and West, 2000) processes in dual processing theories. Both of these processes are associated with additional characteristics (e.g., presence of "vibes," "seized by emotions," and "pleasure driven") that do not necessarily accord with the core features of intuition discussed above. Because not all of these characteristics have traditionally been associated with intuition, additional validation is needed before viewing them as core and central to the concept.

Intuition defined and delineated

To summarize, intuitions are affectively charged judgments that arise through rapid, nonconscious, and holistic associations. These characteristics not only capture what we mean by intuition but also help clarify which types of decision-making processes are intuitive and which are not. To illustrate, of all other ways of making judgments and decisions reviewed here, only the nonconscious use of heuristics and internalized patterns of information fall within what we call intuition. In contrast, we believe that rational decision making is highly dissimilar to intuition. The former involves the use of systematic procedures designed to thoroughly assess all pertinent information, evaluate costs and benefits, and, ultimately, make a decision based on conscious deliberation (see Janis and Mann, 1977, for more detail on rational decision making models). In short, it is highly analytic and relies on logical connections. Moreover, as we have discussed, rational decision making involves a completely different type of information processing system than the experiential system utilized in intuition. In brief, intuition differs from more rational models of decision making in that it is (1) nonconscious, (2) holistic, (3) associative, and (4) faster. In addition, intuition differs from other decision-making approaches that are typically viewed as "fast." For example, intuition is similar to guessing only in terms of its speed. Guessing neither involves affectively charged judgments nor requires making associations through nonconscious information processing. It also lacks the secondary outcome associated with these two characteristics of intuition: certitude. Intuition is also different from instincts and insights – terms often used synonymously with intuition in everyday speech. We follow the lead of Hogarth (2001) and Epstein (2002) in arguing that biological instincts (e.g.,

shutting one's eyes in the presence of bright light) are "hardwired" responses or autonomic reflexes to stimuli. Thus, instincts are innate capabilities that originate outside the experiential processing system. Next, insights or "sudden unexpected thoughts that solve problems" (Hogarth, 2001: 251) may involve experiential processing in the form of an "incubation period." However, unlike intuition, insight is often a lengthy process that begins with deliberate, analytical thinking that precedes the incubation period (Hogarth, 2001; Shirley and Langan-Fox, 1996). Further, when a solution is gleaned through insight, one "suddenly becomes aware of the logical relations between a problem and the answer" (Lieberman, 2000: 110; see also Sternberg and Davidson, 1995, for a more comprehensive treatment of insight). This suggests another distinction between insight and intuition: in the former one consciously becomes aware of the logical connections supporting a particular answer or solution, whereas in the latter one is unable to consciously account for the rationale underlying the judgment that has arisen.

Conditions influencing the effectiveness of intuitive decision making

Thus far, we have focused largely on the process of intuiting and how this process differs from the processes that guide other forms of decision making, such as rational analysis. We now turn our attention more fully to the products of intuiting intuitive judgments – and the conditions that explain when these judgments are most effective. In research that has focused on the effectiveness of intuitive decision making, disagreement abounds as to whether intuitive judgments lead to effective decisions. To begin with, a substantial body of research suggests that the use of intuition in decision making is generally inferior to other, more rational models (e.g., Dawes, Faust, and Meehl, 1989; Kahneman *et al.*, 1982; Meehl, 1954; Schoemaker and Russo, 1993). In contrast, a growing body of literature suggests that for certain people, under appropriate conditions, intuition may be as good as, or even superior to, other decision-making approaches (Blattberg and Hoch, 1990; Hammond, Hamm, Grassia, and Pearson, 1987; Khatri and Ng, 2000). To reconcile these divergent perspectives, we turn to an exploration of the conditions that influence whether intuition is effective as a decision-making approach. Our review suggests that two broad sets of factors influence intuition effectiveness: (1) domain knowledge factors and

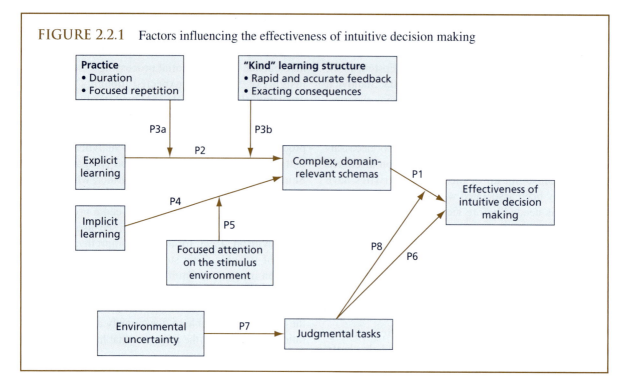

FIGURE 2.2.1   Factors influencing the effectiveness of intuitive decision making

(2) task characteristics. These factors are depicted in Figure 2.2.1. First, one of the primary differences between research on the effectiveness of intuition conducted by researchers interested in heuristics and those interested in expert decision making pertains to the relative emphasis attached to the existence and accumulation of domain knowledge. While some scholars have tended to focus primarily on heuristics and heuristic biases that affect most individuals, regardless of their domain knowledge, others have focused more extensively on expert knowledge structures and how such structures influence the quality of intuitive decision making within specific domains. We seek to integrate these bodies of work by examining how various degrees of domain knowledge, ranging from simple heuristics to sophisticated "expert" schemas, may influence the effectiveness of intuition as a decision-making approach in a given domain. We also examine how expert schemas may form via implicit and explicit learning. Second, research suggests that intuition is good in some situations but not in others. For example, research concerned with heuristic biases has focused on how the use of intuition to solve highly structured math and probability problems can lead to highly inaccurate solutions. However, as noted in our introduction, intuition may be most appropriate for "executive" decisions, which involve strategy, investment, and human resource management issues. These types of decisions

are far less structured than math problems. We discuss each set of intuition effectiveness factors below.

Domain knowledge factors: Schemas

An individual's knowledge of a domain is reflected in the schemas he or she has about that domain. We use the term schema generally to denote various cognitive structures that represent "knowledge about a concept or type of stimulus, including its attributes and the relations among those attributes" (Fiske and Taylor, 1991: 98). We suggest that a primary means for determining when intuition will be effective involves the nature of schemas employed by the intuiter. As we discuss below, schemas may be relatively simple and contain little domain knowledge (i.e., are domain independent), as in the case of heuristics (Denes-Raj and Epstein, 1994; Tversky and Kahneman, 1974). Alternatively, schemas may be complex and contain much domain knowledge, as in the case of experts' cognitive maps (Simon, 1996).

Heuristic schemas.   In a well-established body of research in psychology and the decision sciences, scholars have argued that intuition involves the use of heuristics mental shortcuts that reduce the complex tasks of assessing probabilities and predicting values to simpler judgmental operations (Tversky and Kahneman, 1974). When presented with a problem, individuals can use heuristics to draw associations among multiple stimuli, to focus on critical information, and to develop a perception of the right answer or best route by which to proceed. While heuristics are often useful for quickly assessing probabilities and making decisions in uncertain situations, they may also lead to severe and systematic errors (Tversky and Kahneman, 1974). Indeed, a large portion of decision-making literature over the past three decades has focused on heuristic-based judgmental errors. Such studies suggest that while the appeal of heuristic-based intuition is strong – and that individuals will often choose to use heuristics, even when they know it is not rational to do so (Denes-Raj and Epstein, 1994) – rational processes for problem assessment are less subject to random inconsistencies and systematic distortions (Schoemaker and Russo, 1993). We argue that heuristics and other simple cognitive frameworks are likely to lead to inaccurate intuitive judgments because they tend to be "simple" and, thus, may be inadequate to process complex environmental stimuli. This argument mirrors the bulk of research on the shortcomings of heuristics and stereotypes. It essentially takes a "requisite variety" approach that the complexity of schemas should match environmental complexity in order to be effective (see Weick, 1995). We further suggest that heuristics may be more domain independent and may be commonly applied (inappropriately) across various domains. With regard to domain independence, the relative lack of domain sensitivity diminishes the effectiveness of intuitive decision making as simple "rules of thumb" are indiscriminately applied to an inappropriately large number of problem domains. With regard to the frequency of their use, research suggests that individuals who lack adequate domain knowledge may have inflated self-assessments of their own ability to make accurate judgments (Kruger and Dunning, 1999) and, thus, may have a higher propensity to apply simple schemas across a wide variety of situations.

Expert schemas.   While the heuristic-based view of intuition has dominated research on intuition and problem solving, a growing body of research suggests that that "experts" can make highly accurate intuitive decisions (Dreyfus and Dreyfus, 1986; Klein, 1998, 2003; Prietula and Simon, 1989; Simon, 1987, 1992, 1996). We argue that the main difference between these bodies of research lies in the nature of the schemas of experts, which are (1) highly complex and (2) domain relevant. Simon and Chase's (1973) foundational article on the memory storage patterns of chess masters and grandmasters provides an early example illustrating the role of complex schemas in guiding the decisions of experts. This study revealed that chess masters are able to recognize at least 50 000 different configurations of chess pieces on sight, which are stored or "chunked" as familiar patterns in long-term memory. When presented with an arrangement of pieces on a chessboard, chess masters almost immediately recognize both the patterns of the chess pieces and the appropriate strategic moves for the given situation. Consequently, grandmasters in speed chess competitions can effectively play several games simultaneously, even when they are only allowed a few seconds per move (Simon and Chase, 1973). Broadening these findings beyond the chess domain, "expert" intuition may be aptly described as a "pattern matching" process, whereby information is encoded and chunked into patterns, stored in schemas, and then equated with environmental stimuli (Simon, 1996). As Prietula and Simon note when discussing the difference between a novice and experienced foreman:

> *In fact, the veteran does not scan the environment and process information any faster than the inexperienced foreman; rather, he (or she) has learned to grasp the meaning of certain patterns of operations and activity on the plant floor. In a sense, the foreman does not need to think about this information; he simply reacts to it* (1989: 121).

Scholars advocating for the effectiveness of expert or "mature" intuition (e.g., Baylor, 2001; Blattberg and Hoch, 1990; Burke and Miller, 1999) use the same underlying logic as Simon and his colleagues: experts have complex cognitive maps (or schemas) that trigger effective intuitive judgments. Despite the promise of these complex schemas for effective decision making, an important boundary condition applies. Because complex schemas develop in a particular domain (one's area of expertise), they are more likely to lead to effective decisions in that domain than when used in a different domain or context. Thus, complex managerial schemas may serve a manager well at the office but may lead to inaccurate intuitive judgments at home. This suggests that, for intuitions to be effective, schemas must be both complex and domain relevant:

> *Proposition 1: Individuals who can bring complex, domain-relevant schemas to bear on a problem are more likely to make effective intuitive decisions than those who employ heuristics and simpler, domain-independent schemas.*

Domain knowledge factors: Learning

In addition to research on the content of schemas, in a growing body of work, researchers are exploring how individuals come to gain the complex, domain-relevant schemas needed for effective intuition. The literature on expertise discussed above suggests that there may be a learning component to developing the schemas that underlie accurate intuitive judgments. In particular, researchers are coming to connect the formation of sophisticated cognitive structures to both explicit and implicit learning. We briefly review the general relationship between learning and the formation of complex, domain relevant schemas.

Explicit learning.   Explicit learning occurs when individuals are consciously aware that changes are accruing to their underlying knowledge bases (Lovett, 2002). Perhaps the most researched link between explicit learning and intuition has been on how experts, such as chess grandmasters, come to attain mastery over a particular domain. The general argument posited in this research is that experts deliberately develop a vast repertoire of patterns in memory that allows them to respond to contingencies in an automatic and proficient manner (Simon, 1996; Simon and Chase, 1973). Thus, we suggest a general relationship between explicit learning and intuition effectiveness:

> *Proposition 2: Explicit learning will positively influence the effectiveness of intuitive decision making through the formation of complex, domain relevant schemas.*

However, learning is heightened with certain types of practice. Research suggests three primary elements of "good" practice: duration, repetition, and feedback. First, development periods for mastery tend to be long. With respect to the relationship between practice and expert intuition in management, Khatri and Ng argue that, for managerial intuition to be effective, it "requires years of experience in problem solving and is founded upon a solid and complete grasp of the details of the business" (2000: 58). More specifically, research suggests that a ten-year period of intense preparation appears necessary for achieving expertise in a domain (Ericsson and Charness, 1994; Ericsson, Krampe, and Tesch-Römer, 1993; Simon and Chase, 1973). Additional characteristics of practice that strengthen the link between explicit learning and the development of complex, domain relevant schemas are repetition and feedback. Ericsson and colleagues, for example, argue

that it is only through "deliberate practice," involving repetition and successive refinement through concentration and immediate, accurate feedback, that an individual will develop the capacity to perform as an expert (Ericsson and Charness, 1994; Ericsson and Lehmann, 1996; Ericsson and Smith, 1991). Similarly, Hogarth (2001) argues that practice done in "kind" learning structures will facilitate effective intuition. Kind learning structures are those where feedback is both relevant and exacting. Relevant feedback is conceptualized as speedy and accurate feedback that enables the individual to learn to assign proper causal relationships among decisions, actions, and outcomes. Exacting feedback implies a significant need for precision. A brain surgeon, for example, has little room for error while operating on a patient. Exacting feedback generally leads to accurate learning because small errors can have serious consequences. In sum, we argue that individuals who want to form complex, domain-relevant schemas must engage in repetitive practice over a long period of time. They must also receive feedback about their performance that is both accurate and exacting:

> *Proposition 3a: The relationship between explicit learning and the formation of complex, domain-relevant schemas will be strengthened when individuals engage in focused, repetitive practice over long periods of time.*

> *Proposition 3b: The relationship between explicit learning and the formation of complex, domain-relevant schemas will be strengthened when individuals perform in the presence of "kind" learning structures (rapid and accurate feedback and exacting consequences).*

Implicit learning.   While explicit learning may indeed make for more advanced and effective intuitive decision making in some situations, a growing body of research suggests that it may not always be necessary for the formation of complex, domain-relevant schemas. Instead, schemas may develop through implicit learning. Implicit learning refers to the process by which one acquires – outside of one's conscious awareness – knowledge about the structure or pattern underlying a complex stimulus environment (Reber, 1989: 219; see also Lewicki, Hill, and Bizot, 1988; Reber, 1992; Reber, Walkenfeld, and Hernstadt, 1991; Seger, 1994; Stadler and Frensch, 1998). Implicit learning differs from its external counterpart in important ways. Not only are individuals unaware that such learning is occurring, but research suggests that implicit knowledge is stored in the brain differently from other types of knowledge.

To illustrate, knowledge acquired via implicit learning will be retained when an individual suffers from amnesia, even when more explicit knowledge is lost (Seger, 1994). This suggests that although explicit and implicit learning can occur simultaneously in a given context, implicit learning involves a different process of knowledge acquisition and storage. Both implicit learning and intuition have been linked to the nonconscious processing system described earlier. Just as intuition involves a nonconscious, experiential processing of information stored in memory, implicit learning refers to a similar nonconscious process of knowledge acquisition. Reber (1989) has tied implicit learning to "intuitive knowledge" and argues that it is through implicit learning that individuals come to form the complex cognitive structures necessary for intuitive judgments and decisions. In support of this claim, researchers have linked implicit learning to the acquisition of grammar rules (Reber, 1989; Reber *et al.*, 1991) and spatial processing algorithms (e.g., Lewicki *et al.*, 1988), as well as to other types of knowledge acquisition, such as covariation and puzzle learning (see Seger, 1994, for a review of implicit learning tasks). We believe that implicit learning may result in the complex, domain-relevant schemas necessary to engender the effective use of intuitive judgments in managerial decision making. To illustrate, the veteran foreman noted earlier by Prietula and Simon (1989), who "has learned to grasp the meaning of certain patterns of operations and activity on the plant floor," may have developed this proficiency not simply through explicit learning – since it is unlikely that the foreman "deliberately practiced" observing operations on the plant floor – but rather, through implicit learning as well:

> *Proposition 4: Implicit learning will positively influence the effectiveness of intuitive decision making through the formation of complex, domain relevant schemas.*

It is important to note that just as there are factors that strengthen the relationship between explicit learning and the formation of complex, domain-relevant schemas, there are also factors that strengthen the link between such schema formation and implicit learning. In particular, while implicit learning is largely automatic, there is some research that suggests that individuals may be able to "process stimuli in ways that allow implicit learning to function more effectively" (Seger, 1994: 176). Such control may be afforded by consciously paying attention to the stimuli in question (Carlson and Dulany, 1985; Nissen and Bullemer, 1987). Attention, however, is not focused on attempts to deliberately decipher cause and effects. As Reber's research has shown (Reber, 1976; Reber, Kassin, Lewis and Cantor, 1980), attention directed toward such "hypothesis testing" will lead to substandard performance. Rather, individuals should focus on stimuli as a whole. For example, while managers may be unable to consciously notice those rewards that will best motivate individuals during a time of crisis (a type of covariation learning), they may facilitate the implicit learning of these patterns by paying attention to both rewards and employees during the crisis. Thus, we build from this body of research and posit the following:

> *Proposition 5: The relationship between implicit learning and the formation of complex, domain-relevant schemas will be enhanced when individuals focus attention on the stimulus environment.*

Returning to our initial focus on speed versus accuracy, we suggest that intuitions are more likely to be effective when they tap into complex, domain-relevant schemas than when they involve heuristics. These complex, domain relevant schemas, in turn, are more likely to be developed when individuals engage in focused and repetitive practice over a long period of time, when they operate in kind learning environments, and when they focus their attention on the stimulus environment.

Task characteristic factors

In addition to factors surrounding the domain knowledge of the intuiter, evidence suggests that problem structure may also impact the effectiveness of intuitive decision making. According to Shapiro and Spence (1997), problems lie on a continuum of structuredness. At the less structured end of this continuum lie such problems as merger and acquisition decisions, new product planning, and corporate strategy formation. These unstructured problems are conducive to intuition because of the absence of well accepted decision rules for dealing with such situations. Echoing this argument, other researchers have argued that analytical strategies that work well for problems that are well defined are much less effective for ill-defined problems (Claxton, 1998; Hayashi, 2001). Intuition, as a holistically associative process, may actually help to integrate the disparate elements of an ill-defined problem into a coherent perception of how to proceed. As Shapiro and Spence (1997) further note, intuition is often more effective than analysis in enabling individuals to develop an understanding of the structure of a complex system. For this reason, intuitive judgments are said to become more effective relative to rational analysis as a problem becomes increasingly unstructured.

Intellective versus judgmental tasks. We argue that the notion of "problem structure" is captured in the distinction between intellective and judgmental tasks (Laughlin, 1980; Laughlin and Ellis, 1986; McGrath, 1984). According to Laughlin, intellective tasks involve a "definite objective criterion of success within the definitions, rules, operations, and relationships of a particular conceptual system," whereas judgmental tasks involve "political, ethical, aesthetic, or behavioral judgments for which there is no objective criterion or demonstrable solution" (1980: 128). Laughlin (1980) views the intellective/ judgmental distinction as a continuum, as opposed to a strict dichotomy. While intuition theorists have not referred specifically to intellective and judgmental tasks, research has shown that intuition may be most effective for moral judgments (Haidt, 2001), aesthetic ratings (Hammond *et al.*, 1987; Wilson and Schooler, 1991), and the like. Further, research has shown that intuition is relatively weaker than rational analysis for tasks involving definite objective criteria (MacGregor, Lichtenstein, and Slovic, 1988; McMackin and Slovic, 2000). Thus, it appears that intuitive judgments may be more effective than rational approaches to decision making on judgmental tasks, whereas the converse is true for intellective tasks. This suggests the following proposition:

Proposition 6: As the problem structure associated with a task becomes more judgmental, the effectiveness of intuitive decision making will increase.

Returning again to our discussion of speed versus accuracy, intuition is most likely to effectively manage this trade-off when it is brought to bear on judgmental tasks.

Factors influencing task characteristics: Environmental uncertainty. While we showed earlier that the domain knowledge factors concerning intuition effectiveness are rooted in a sizable body of work on explicit and implicit learning, relatively little has been said about concepts that may be linked to intuition effectiveness and task characteristics. The work that does exist suggests that the type of environment in which an organization operates may influence the effectiveness of intuitive decision making among managers (Agor, 1986; Khatri and Ng, 2000; Shapiro and Spence, 1997). In one of the few empirical studies in this area, Khatri and Ng (2000) found moderate support for their thesis that, during times of environmental uncertainty, the use of intuitive decision making among executives results in greater organizational

performance. Unfortunately, based on this study alone, it is difficult to conclude why this result was found. However, one likely possibility is that during times of environmental instability, managers have to collect and sort through a large, and often incomplete, amount of data in a short time (Khatri and Ng, 2000). That is, decision-making tasks in these environments may be non-routine. Building on this perspective, we suggest that environmental uncertainty results in a shift away from structured problems and standard operating procedures and is likely to result in a multitude of "plausible alternative solutions," rather than a single objective criterion for success. Under such conditions, decision-making scenarios may move from the intellective end of the task continuum toward the judgmental end. Thus, the positive relationship found between environmental uncertainty and the effectiveness of intuitive decision making may be mediated by the task characteristics described above:

Proposition 7: The relationship between environmental uncertainty and the effectiveness of intuition is mediated by judgmental task characteristics.

Possible relationships among effectiveness factors

In considering the two broad sets of factors that we view as determining the effectiveness of intuitive decision making, we have said little about whether there are any connections between these two sets of factors. That is, we have yet to discuss whether domain knowledge factors are in some way tied to task characteristic factors in the model we have proposed (Figure 2.2.1). While a variety of linkages may be possible, a highly likely possibility concerns linking the most effective domain knowledge characteristic – expertise – with the most desirable type of task for intuition – judgmental. As noted above, the individuals most capable of making the associations that trigger accurate intuitive judgments are those who possess complex, domain-relevant cognitive structures within a particular domain. Such individuals may be referred to as experts (Chi, Glaser, and Farr, 1988; Dreyfus and Dreyfus, 1986; Prietula and Simon, 1989; Shanteau and Stewart, 1992). In Figure 2.2.1 we identify a link between expertise and intuition effectiveness via the direct connection drawn from complex, domain-relevant schemas to the effectiveness of intuitive decision making. However, this argument raises the question of whether the relationship between schema type and intuition effectiveness is always of a similar magnitude across various types of tasks. Evidence suggests that the answer to this question is not necessarily. As we have suggested, the holistic and associative properties of intuition may help to integrate the disparate elements of an ill-defined, or judgmental, problem into a coherent perception of how to proceed. Experts may be especially well-suited to draw these holistic associations on judgmental tasks because the sophistication of their cognitive structures may permit them to integrate the components of an ill-structured problem with relative ease. Such an interaction is implied in many of the examples in the beginning of our paper. For example, the development of the Dodge Viper and the prime-time launch of *Who Wants to Be a Millionaire* both involved highly experienced executives faced with ill-structured tasks. In contrast, well-defined or intellective tasks may not call for the same extent of holistic and associative connections. As argued above, such tasks may be approached more effectively through analytical procedures. Moreover, research suggesting that the intuition of experts is ineffective has tended to examine decision making involving highly structured tasks (Bazerman, 1986; Dawes *et al.*, 1989; Kahneman *et al.*, 1982). Hence, we argue that our posited link between complex, domain-relevant schemas (as possessed by experts) and effective intuition may be stronger when experts are working on judgmental tasks. Accordingly, we suggest the following:

> *Proposition 8: The relationship between complex, domain-relevant schemas and the effectiveness of intuitive decision making is moderated by task characteristics such that as tasks become more judgmental, the strength of the relationship will increase.*

Discussion and implications

We have attempted to better delineate what intuition is[4] and when people are likely to use it well. In this effort we have synthesized a large and disparate body of research on intuition and moved the field forward through the development of several theoretical propositions. However, it is sometimes only in taking stock of what is known that it becomes clear what is not. While this review helps address many issues regarding intuition, it raises several other issues, and several additional avenues for research, as well. Our comments in this section concern the issues we feel are most critical to bear in mind when conducting further research on intuition.

Intuition "use" factors

While we have focused extensively on the factors contributing to the effectiveness of intuitive decision making, we have said little about the conditions in which individuals tend to trust in or rely on their intuitions. Intuition "use" factors are critical, because even if we can foster intuitions that are accurate (e.g., through complex, domain-relevant schema), these intuitions must be "trusted" if they are to be followed. Conversely, intuitions that develop through heuristics and more simplistic schemas may, in many circumstances, be sufficiently compelling to be used as primary inputs to decision making, despite their relative imprecision and dubious accuracy. Research on intuition suggests a variety of conditions in which we are most likely to use our intuitions rather than to invoke and rely on rational analysis. Among the most common are the presence of positive moods (e.g., Bless, Bohner, Schwarz, and Strack, 1990; Elsbach and Barr, 1999; Isen, Means, Patrick, and Nowicki, 1982; Ruder and Bless, 2003; Schwarz, Bless, and Bohner, 1991) and the role of stable individual differences in thinking style (Briggs and Myers, 1976; Pacini and Epstein, 1999; see also Jung, 1933). However, there may be other, less explored use factors that merit further attention. To illustrate, research might explore the role of the body in intuition. Bastick (1982) directly ties intuition with "body knowledge," and Agor (1986) and Hayashi (2001) link the use of intuition with specific "body cues." More generally, affective descriptions such as "gut feelings" tie changes in emotions to bodily changes. In a fascinating study, Bechara, Damasio, Tranel, and Damasio (1997) found that individuals asked to play games where the rules are not known, but which differ in terms of their level of risk, will generate skin conductance responses before engaging in high-risk games, even before they have consciously understood that the games are risky. This suggests that the body may "know" and be transmitting information outside of conscious awareness. Further, as Bodenhausen (1990) has shown, circadian variations impact the use of heuristic stereotypes such that individuals who are most alert in the morning

---

[4]We should note that we have been viewing intuition as a relatively homogenous concept. Wild (1938), however, argued for the existence of aesthetic, moral, and religious intuition. Further, he noted that intuition can arise from divine sources and from the collective unconscious – and not just from our own experientially based cognitive schemas. Future research may help to disentangle what have been perceived as different "types" of intuition (e.g., managerial versus mystical intuition).

("morning people") are more likely to rely on heuristic processing of information late in the evening, whereas "night people" exhibit the opposite pattern. While promising, research that examines the connection between the body and the use of intuition remains scant. More "macro" determinants of use, such as cultural factors, may also play a role in intuition use. For example, cultures with a low emphasis on "uncertainty avoidance" (Cyert and March, 1963; Hofstede, 2001) are willing to "take unknown risks" and are "comfortable with ambiguity and chaos" (Hofstede, 2001: 161). Because intuitive judgments are, by their very nature, difficult to justify rationally and often involve unknown levels of risk, cultures low in uncertainty avoidance may be more inclined than other cultures to favor intuitive judgments in decision making. The "masculine versus feminine" cultural distinction (Hofstede, 2001) may also account for differences in the use of intuition across cultures. In particular, feminine cultures, which emphasize the importance of feelings over logic, may be inclined to accept forms of judgment that are tied to affect and emotion. If, as we contend, intuition is tied to affect and emotions, intuitive decision making may be respected and employed in feminine cultures. Consistent with this argument, Hofstede (2001: 318) notes that managers in feminine cultures are expected to use intuition and deal with feelings. More generally, research should be done to more explicitly link intuition use factors with those factors we have identified as being integral to intuition effectiveness. For example, it may be the case that learning processes link the two models: as individuals use intuition more, they may become more effective in its use. Other factors may also be common to both intuition use and effectiveness. For example, judgmental tasks such as moral and aesthetic problems, which may be particularly conducive to intuitive problem solving, may also trigger the use of intuition (Haidt, 2001; Hammond *et al.*, 1987).

Interplay between intuition and analysis

In our attempt to differentiate intuition from other decision-making approaches, such as rational models, we did not discuss at length when and how different ways of knowing might complement each other. Researchers who advocate a dual process approach assume that these two systems of knowing work together in making decisions. In a similar vein, Simon (1987) asserts that effective managers do not have the luxury of choosing between

analysis and intuition – real expertise involves the use of both types of decision making. And Hodgkinson and Sadler-Smith (2003: 261) argue that the ability to switch between "habits of mind" and "active thinking" is the ultimate skill in today's organizations. Researchers have put forth a variety of recommendations about how to use intuitions in combination with more rational decision making. For example, Blattberg and Hoch (1990) examined the specific weightings that should be applied to rational models and intuitive judgments, respectively, in making decisions. In assessing the accuracy of brand managers' predictions of coupon redemption rates as compared to a mathematical forecasting model, they determined that a 50/50 weighted combination of model forecast and manager intuition leads to more accurate predictions than either decision-making method in isolation. Shapiro and Spence (1997) further argue that the ordering of the two types of decision making is also important. They suggest that intuition should be recorded first, followed by a more thorough analytical assessment of the problem. The degree to which rational decision making should be emphasized, however, should depend on the nature of the task (e.g., structured or unstructured). In contrast, Agor (1986) argues that many managers use intuition after engaging in rational analyses, for the purpose of synthesizing and integrating the information gathered and analysed. Unfortunately, while many provocative ideas about the interplay between rational and intuitive decision making have been suggested, empirical research in this area, particularly in the field of management, remains insufficient.

Beyond decision making

We have focused primarily on the role of intuition in decision making. However, intuition may have other positive benefits as well. To illustrate, some preliminary work suggests a link between intuition and creativity. Langer (1989: 117), for example, has suggested that creativity arises through an "intuitive experience of the world," whereas rational thinking serves only to confirm "old mindsets" and "rigid categories." Likewise, Poincaré (1969: 210) has declared that logic is the "instrument of demonstration", and intuition the "instrument of invention." However, with the exception of a few studies (e.g., Raidl and Lubart, 2000–2001), little empirical research has connected intuition to creativity. In light of the growing interest in creativity in the management sciences, unpacking how intuition ties in with creative thought may yield valuable theoretical contributions to this line of research. Next, recent appeals for additional scholarly work on business ethics (e.g., Donaldson, 2003) suggest a need for fresh perspectives on moral reasoning and ethical decision making in organizations. As noted above, Haidt (2001) has argued that moral judgments are intuitive. Thus, by better understanding how intuitive judgments are made, we might better identify the conditions under which individuals disregard their intuitions (i.e., their moral sense of ethical behavior) and engage in actions that conflict with principles of ethics in organizations.

Managerial implications

We believe that research on intuition is inherently practical. In this paper we have suggested factors that may lead managers to make good decisions quickly. Thus, organizations that wish to facilitate effective intuiting need to concentrate on promoting ongoing and deliberate practice in kind learning environments. They may also encourage managers to be mindful of their environments in order to facilitate implicit learning. By remaining alert and viewing problems from multiple perspectives, "mindful" managers may form new cognitive categories and distinctions (see Langer, 1989) that bolster the complexity and domain relevance of their schemas. Finally, we have suggested that managers should be wary of using intuitions when faced with intellective tasks. In this discussion section we have also suggested how future research might better understand the relationship between intuition effectiveness and use, thus ensuring that individuals feel comfortable "trusting their gut" when appropriate (e.g., when the individual has domain expertise and is working on a judgmental task). Moreover, we believe that better understanding of how intuition and rational analysis work together will result in an even more complete picture of decision effectiveness among managers and other organizational members. Beyond decision making, understanding how intuition plays a role in creativity and ethics seems critical to improving key organizational processes.

In addition to highlighting the promises of intuition, our research also reveals potential challenges and barriers to facilitating effective intuitions. To illustrate, one could argue that the rapid rate of change that characterizes current organizational environments makes intuitive decision making more necessary today than it has been in the past. However, it is also true that job mobility is increasing. As a result, individuals are less likely to engage in a significant degree of focused practice in a particular domain (Prietula and Simon, 1989). In our

language, this suggests that individuals may not be able to form complex, domain-relevant schemas – and, thus, must rely more often on simple schemas and heuristics. This is likely to result in the less effective use of intuitive judgments at a time when their use is increasingly critical. Accordingly, organizations that retain members for long periods of time in similar job domains may be more likely than others to provide members with sufficient conditions to develop complex, domain-relevant schemas. This suggests a need to reduce the rate of member turnover in order to foster the development of more effective intuitive decision making among members. Retention is critical if one is to keep highly specialized knowledge workers – a crucial component to competing in a "knowledge economy." Keeping experts, however, is only one challenge in utilizing experts in a knowledge economy (Matusik and Hill, 1998). Ideally, the information from experts can be captured by the organization (Hammer, Leonard, and Davenport, 2004; Osterloh and Frey, 2000). Can the complex, domain-relevant schemas of experts be transferred to automated information systems or to other individuals? While we have identified the conditions under which an individual can gain complex, domain-relevant schemas, it is not clear whether or how the content of these schemas can be transferred from one individual to another. Classic work on the transfer of expertise, however, suggests that having experts working together with novices may be critical to this issue (Collins, 1982). A related challenge for managers concerns the transferability of intuitive skills across fields and industries. Organizations, interested in acquiring individuals with expert knowledge, often hire managers and executives from other firms and agencies. While such individuals are pursued for their rich knowledge bases and decision-making abilities, our model proposes that cognitive schemas must be domain relevant to generate accurate intuitive judgments. For this reason, an individual who possesses expert intuition in one field or industry may not be as effective in making intuitive decisions in a field or industry that differs substantially from the environment in which the individual's cognitive schemas were developed. This brings to mind one of the key weaknesses ascribed to Carly Fiorina in her very public and sudden ousting from Hewlett-Packard in 2005: she did not have the right "type" of experience to succeed at HP. If true, this would suggest that her intuitive reasoning may not have been as effective as someone with more domain-relevant experience. Thus, we consider the following question. How different must context be before the cross-situational relevance of cognitive schemas is negated? While this question is, as yet, unanswered, we suggest that managers should be slow to embrace intuitive judgments made by organizational newcomers without relevant industry or occupational experience.

Conclusion

We have emphasized throughout this paper how intuition is viewed as a potential means of helping managers make both fast and accurate decisions in organizations. In this regard, we discussed how and why speed serves as one characteristic of intuition and identified factors that make intuitive judgments effective in decision making. In closing, we suggest that further research on intuition is important not only for building theory on this particular construct but also for increasing our field's

attention to nonconscious processes more generally. We have emphasized throughout this work that intuition arises through nonconscious operations. In making this point, we were informed by a growing body of literature in psychology that has shown how a large portion of cognitive thought occurs outside of consciousness (Bargh, 1996; Bargh and Chartrand, 1999; Jacoby, Lindsay, and Toth, 1992; Kihlstrom, Barnhardt, and Tataryn, 1992; Reber, 1992). Some psychologists have even referred to the 1990s as the "decade of automaticity" (Pizarro and Bloom, 2003). Yet despite bourgeoning interest in nonconscious and automatic processes among psychologists, organizational scholars have yet to focus extensively on these mechanisms and how they may influence behavior in organizations. For this reason, we hope that our treatment of intuition may help to put the "nonconscious" into organizational studies.

Psychological foundations of dynamic capabilities: Reflexion and reflection in strategic management

By Gerard P. Hodgkinson and Mark P. Healey[1]

The decision-making paradigm, as it has developed, is the product of a marriage between cognitive psychology and economics. From economics, decision theory inherited, or was socialized into, the language of preferences and beliefs and the religion of utility maximization that provides a unitary perspective for understanding all behaviour. From cognitive psychology, decision theory inherited its descriptive focus, concern with process and many specific theoretical insights. Decision theory is thus the brilliant child of equally brilliant parents. With all its cleverness, however, decision theory is somewhat crippled emotionally, and thus detached from the emotional and visceral richness of life (Loewenstein, 1996: 289).

Introduction

Since its earliest days, the field of strategic management has been preoccupied with developing rational and analytical models and theories

(e.g., Ansoff, 1965; Hofer and Schendel, 1978) to understand the nature and causes of sustainable enterprise performance (Teece, Pisano and Shuen, 1997). From Porter's (1980) analysis of competitive positioning informed by the structure-conduct-performance paradigm, to game theoretic analyses of competitive interaction (Brandenburger and Nalebuff, 1996), to the more recent evolutionary (e.g., Nelson and Winter, 1982) and resource-based (e.g., Barney, 1991; Wernerfelt, 1984) perspectives informed by Penrose's writings linking internal resources to rent generation, there is no question that the dominant perspectives in classic and contemporary strategic management emanate from the field of economics. Over the past two decades, however, a growing body of work has sought to incorporate the insights of human psychology to refine understanding of a wide variety of topics, from the evolution of competitive industry structures (Peteraf and Shanley, 1997; Porac et al., 1995) to the nature and sources of cognitive bias in strategic

[1]Source: Excerpted with permission from Gerard P. Hodgkinson and Mark P. Healey (2011) 'Psychological foundations of dynamic capabilities: Reflexion and reflection in strategic management' *Strategic Management Journal*, 32(13): 1500–1516. Copyright © John Wiley and Sons, Inc. 2011. Reproduced with permission of John Wiley and Sons, Inc..

investment decisions (Bateman and Zeithaml, 1989; Schwenk, 1984).

Reflecting the field's shift away from an analysis of the organization's external environment to a focus on its internal resources and capabilities, strategy scholars have paid increasing attention to the cognitive and behavioural processes underpinning the capabilities that promote organizational learning, adaptation and performance. This body of theory and research has accomplished much. However, this article argues that recent advances in the emerging fields of social cognitive neuroscience (Lieberman, 2007; Ochsner and Lieberman, 2001) and neuroeconomics (Brocas and Carrillo, 2008; Loewenstein, Rick and Cohen, 2008), and indeed the wider organizational sciences (Gavetti, Levinthal and Ocasio, 2007; Hodgkinson and Healey, 2008), call into question its adequacy as a foundation for future theory building and research in the strategy field. We demonstrate that the extant literature on the psychology of strategic management, like its economics-based counterpart, has emphasized the behavioural and cognitive aspects of strategy formulation and implementation at the expense of emotional and affective ones, leading to an inadequate portrayal of strategic management as a series of rational and dispassionate activities. Our analysis provides fresh insights into the origins and development of dynamic capabilities.

Teece's (2007) framework is the most comprehensive to date for analysing the psychological foundations of capabilities development. Accordingly, we utilize this framework as a basis for organizing our critique of the wider dynamic capabilities literature as a whole.

Psychological foundations of dynamic capabilities revisited

Teece (2007) posited three generic, behaviourally-based dynamic capabilities as the foundations of the evolutionary and economic fitness of the enterprise, namely: (1) sensing (and shaping) opportunities and threats; (2) seizing opportunities; and (3) reconfiguring assets and structures to maintain competitiveness. Sensing requires searching and exploring markets and technologies both local to and distant from the organization. Seizing, in contrast, necessitates making high-quality, interdependent investment decisions, such as those involved in selecting product architectures and business models. The final capability, reconfiguring, entails continuously transforming the firm in response to market and technological changes, such that it retains evolutionary fitness.

Consistent with most traditional dynamic capability formulations, the microfoundations of Teece's (2007) framework rest on an outmoded conception of the strategist as a cognitive miser. This conception stemmed from several interrelated bodies of theory and research in the cognitive sciences, not least Simon's seminal notion of bounded rationality and classical behavioural decision research, which ultimately reinforced the idea that human cognition operates in two discrete modes of information processing – one relatively automatic, the other more effortful and controlled (e.g., Schneider and Shiffrin, 1977). This core assumption has long underpinned a number of lines of inquiry in strategic management, beyond the dynamic capabilities project per se, each of which has privileged effortful forms of reasoning and dispassionate analysis as the means of overcoming cognitive bias and strategic inertia (e.g., Dutton, 1993; Hodgkinson *et al.*, 1999; Louis and Sutton, 1991; Reger and Palmer, 1996). However, contemporary social neuroscience is questioning the veracity of these earlier conceptions of dual-process theory and bounded rationality. Recent developments suggest that the biases and inertial forces that undermine sensing, seizing and transforming capabilities have emotional roots as well as cognitive ones. Building on this fundamental insight, we maintain that although the tools and processes commonly touted for engineering cognitively effortful reasoning and judgment are undoubtedly a *necessary* component of dynamic capabilities, in practice they are rarely a *sufficient* psychological mechanism for ensuring the long-term adaptability of the enterprise. Indeed, as we shall demonstrate, in some circumstances, conventional approaches for augmenting strategic cognition exacerbate the very problems they seek to alleviate.

According to a growing body of work in social cognitive neuroscience, a reflexive system underpins more automatic and basic affective forms of social cognition, such as implicit stereotyping, automatic categorization and empathizing with others, while a reflective system, a more controlled system that developed latterly in evolutionary terms, underpins higher forms of cognition, such as logical reasoning, planning and hypothetical thinking (Lieberman, 2007; Lieberman *et al.*, 2002). Within this view, the two systems operate in a dynamic interplay, reflexion variously facilitating and inhibiting the reflective processes underpinning consciously effortful reasoning and decision making (see also Bechara, Damasio and Damasio, 2000).

While acknowledging the distinction between automatic and controlled processes, neuroeconomics emphasizes the distinction between emotional and analytical processes. Bernheim and Rangel (2004), for example, view the brain as operating in either a 'cold' cognitive mode or a 'hot' emotional mode, while Loewenstein and Small (2007) similarly distinguish between 'emotional' and 'deliberative' systems. One of the key contributions of neuroeconomics has been to shed light on the conditions under which visceral feelings overcome deliberative thinking in judgment and decision making (for an overview, see Loewenstein *et al.*, 2008).

In sum, the left-brain/right-brain cognitive science underpinning Teece's (2007) analysis, which characterizes intuition and heuristic processes as primitive sources of bias, is giving way to the mounting evidence that less deliberative forms of cognition are central to skilled functioning. Rather than acting simply as a disturbance to the reflective system, to be suppressed at every opportunity, affect and emotion are integral to the very nature of cognition, infusing reasoning, learning, decision making and action (LeDoux, 2000). However, as depicted in Figure 2.3.1, the bulk of theory and research on the psychology of strategic management has hitherto focused on but one portion of the available conceptual space (i.e., the lower right-hand quadrant of the circumplex). This myopia has yielded an impoverished portrayal of dynamic capabilities.

Accordingly, the overarching goal of this article is to open up the wider conceptual space pertaining to the cognitive, affective and behavioural microfoundations of organizational adaptation (cf. Gavetti *et al.*, 2007).

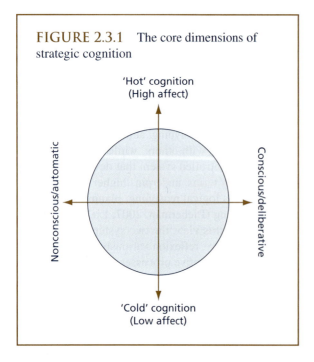

FIGURE 2.3.1   The core dimensions of strategic cognition

To this end, we explicate alternative psychological foundations for the three dynamic capabilities identified by Teece (2007) and consider the implications for theory building, research and practice.

Sensing (and shaping) opportunities and threats

The predominance of the information processing view of the firm has ensured that current conceptions of sensing capabilities are decidedly affect free (Day and Schoemaker, 2006; Gavetti and Levinthal, 2000; Prahalad, 2004; Teece, 2007; Tripsas and Gavetti, 2000). However, to the extent that affect controls attention (Compton, 2003), the moods and emotions of managers likely determine to a significant degree what the firm attends to and how it responds, to say nothing of the emotional significance of the stimuli for the individuals concerned. For instance, high anxiety might narrow attention to a subset of events, whereas an overoptimistic mood might lead to a neglect of certain signals. We postulate that affect is also crucial for effective sensing because it provides the motivation for cognitive adaptation.

Affective mechanisms of cognitive change

The ability to update decision makers' mental representations (variously labelled 'schemas,' 'mental models' and 'cognitive maps') in response to changes in the external environment is a critical sensing capability (Barr, Stimpert and Huff, 1992; Gavetti, 2005; Gavetti and Levinthal, 2000; Levinthal and March, 1993). Current conceptions of adaptive cognitive change assume that the mere effortful processing of schema inconsistent information disconfirms expectations and jolts decision makers into conscious reflection, thereby forcing them to revise their beliefs (e.g., Dutton, 1993; Hodgkinson *et al.*, 1999; Louis and Sutton, 1991; Reger and Palmer, 1996). However, recent research in neuroeconomics shows that people actively try to shield themselves from information that causes psychological discomfort, the so-called 'ostrich effect' of burying one's head in the sand (Karlsson, Loewenstein and Seppi, 2009). In keeping with this observation, studies in social cognitive neuroscience show that conflicting information is not the fundamental mechanism of belief revision, but rather how decision makers handle the affective response to that conflicting information (Lieberman, 2000; Lieberman *et al.*, 2001). Hence, the ability to recognize affective signals and utilize affect as information (Finucane *et al.*, 2000;

Slovic *et al.*, 2004) is an essential, but hitherto neglected, component of organizational sensing capabilities. By way of illustration, consider the London Stock Exchange's decision to invest in the Taurus software package to support a transactions settlement IT system (Drummond, 2001). Decision makers experienced deep unease in the early stages of the commissioning process, but unable to articulate the logical basis of their ill feelings, they chose to invest on more reasoned grounds. However, having eventually abandoned the ineffective system, at a cost of £80 million, they then expressed considerable regret at having ignored their initial misgivings. This case demonstrates that when individuals' reasoned reflective responses and visceral reflexive reactions are discordant, effective sensing requires resolution of the disequilibria.

Tensions between reflexive and reflective reactions to opportunities and threats can also occur *between* individuals and groups, as Tripsas and Gavetti's (2000) account of cognitive adaptation at Polaroid illustrates. In this case, senior executives held to a maladaptive belief in an 'instant imaging' business model that discouraged search and development efforts in the growth area of digital imaging, while managers closer to industry changes developed representations that encompassed the emerging digital landscape. Tripsas and Gavetti's (2000) view that the dissonance between the two groups resulted from differences in the industry signals they were receiving construes managers as passive victims of their informational circumstances. The logical extension of this view is that providing the two parties with the same information would have yielded consonant representations. Our analysis suggests an alternative interpretation: because the new information conflicted with executives' assumptions, they likely experienced unease at the mismatch, motivating them to neglect – if not actively reject – the painful information. In contrast, junior managers likely experienced consonance between reflexion and reflection. Put differently, the developments excited one group but troubled the other, leading, respectively, to approach and avoidance. Dissonance between individuals and groups should signal the need to re-evaluate and reconcile competing interpretations of strategic events (cf. Burgelman and Grove, 1996). At Polaroid, such reconciliation was noticeably absent, perhaps due to executives' unwillingness to lose self-esteem by relinquishing their embedded assumptions.

Our re-analysis of the Polaroid case highlights the importance of meta-cognitive capabilities – that is, the ability to develop self-awareness of, and to regulate, cognitive and emotional processes (e.g., Nelson,

1996; Ochsner *et al.*, 2002). Managers need to test the validity of their reflexive reactions to a given strategic issue; if those reactions are warranted, the firm should take whatever course of action is deemed appropriate. In cases where further analysis reveals those reflexive responses are due to managers' underlying beliefs being out of line with the overall attractiveness of the opportunity or threat in question, this likely signals the need to update the executive knowledge base. While recalibrating decision makers is often difficult, because individuals are typically unable to step outside their own framings of the problem at hand (Fischhoff, 1982), group approaches provide a potentially useful means of crosschecking affectively rooted assumptions.

Effective sensing also requires the development of a psychologically secure learning climate – one that takes account of affective signals and intuitive cognitions but also enables, where appropriate, effortful, deliberative processing. Routines that overly focus on planning for the negative consequences of events are likely to heighten negative affect and threat rigidity, and ultimately induce avoidance behaviour (Staw, Sandelands and Dutton, 1981). The converse approach of building routines that mitigate negative affect and create the psychological space for building positive affect around opportunities and threats is conducive to adaptation, because positive affect boosts responsiveness to events by broadening the scope of attention, cognition and action repertoires (Ashby, Isen and Turken, 1999; Fredrickson and Branigan, 2005). The preceding arguments suggest the following proposition:

> *Proposition 1: Organizations that rely on 'hot cognition' enhancing technologies (i.e., tools and processes aimed at mental model change underpinned by emotionally supportive mechanisms) as an aid to sensing will be significantly less likely to fall prey to cognitive blind spots and strategic inertia than organizations that rely on 'cold cognition' enhancing technologies (i.e., tools and processes aimed at mental model change in the absence of emotionally supportive mechanisms).*

To illustrate the practical implications of this proposition, consider the role of scenario planning as an aid to sensing, commonly employed to stretch actors' beliefs regarding future uncertainties (e.g., Schoemaker, 1993). Hodgkinson and Wright's (2002) case analysis illustrates the dangers of designing interventions based solely on a cold cognition logic. The goal in this case was to inculcate mental model change. However, forcing the management team to envisage threatening future scenarios in a vivid manner raised decisional stress and conflict to unacceptably high levels, leading it to adopt dysfunctional coping strategies. In contrast, Doz and Kosonen (2008) observe how organizations such as IBM and Nokia meet the need for psychological security by building a 'culture of care' when seeking to reform the beliefs of actors facing threatening changes. Practical steps include adopting routines that encourage managers to share their emotions and empathize with one another, and the use of techniques that construe strategic change in such a way that those affected do not disconnect the new requirements from enduring sources of pride.

Incorporating intuition into the sensing process

As we have indicated, strategy research has conventionally equated what Teece (2007) outlined as sensing (and shaping) capabilities with explicit, deliberative learning and elaborative formal reasoning and analysis (e.g., Porter, 1980; Zollo and Winter, 2002; for an exception, see Levinthal and Rerup, 2006). However, this view understates the advantages of non-conscious forms of cognition for navigating the social environment (Bargh and Chartrand, 1999; Bargh and Ferguson, 2000). A particular advantage of reflexive processes is their ability to cut through masses of information about trends in the business environment to reach effective judgments on opportunities and threats. As Sir Martin Sorrell, CEO of WPP recently observed, 'the reality is that leaders must, on the spur of the moment, be able to react rapidly and grasp opportunities' (Sorrell, Komisar and Mulcahy, 2010: 46).

Dane and Pratt's (2007: 40) succinct definition, 'affectively-charged judgments that arise through rapid, non-conscious and holistic associations,' renders abundantly clear why intuition is apposite to the sensing process. While the reflective (i.e., deliberative) system, restricted to the serial processing of small numbers of items, becomes overloaded when faced with complex strategic situations, intuition brings to bear large quantities of implicit knowledge in a focused manner (cf. Dutton, 1993). Moreover, in many strategic situations, executives must operate under time constraints, from the early detection and evaluation of emerging opportunities and threats, to the defence of hostile takeovers, to interventions by regulators. There is a wealth of evidence to suggest that the non-conscious pattern-matching and visceral processes at the heart of intuitive judgment (Lieberman, 2000) likely play a critical role in these circumstances (for overviews see Dane and Pratt, 2007; Hodgkinson, Langan-Fox and Sadler-Smith, 2008; Hodgkinson *et al.*, 2009; Hogarth, 2001; Klein, 2003).

Incorporating intuition into the sensing process demands a reconsideration of the role of information technologies of the sort widely advocated as an aid to organizational responsiveness (cf. Teece, 2007). Knowledge management systems, databases and expert systems designed to externalize knowledge ultimately transfer the tasks of search and sensemaking from the decision maker to the technology. This move precludes the rapid pattern-matching processes that characterize expert decision making, thus undermining true sensing. Mintzberg (1994: 299) illustrated the problems with such architectures in his analysis of elaborate strategic planning systems that 'offered no improved means to deal with the information overload of human brains; indeed, they often made matters worse…. The formal systems could certainly process more information… But they could never internalize it, comprehend it, synthesize it.' Giving due credence to reflexion in sensing requires that supporting analytical technologies be deployed in ways that exploit managers' implicit knowledge and intuitive expertise. The goal is to design search architectures to take advantage of reflexion rather than replace it with technology or effortful reasoning (Jolls, Sunstein and Thaler, 1998). Hence:

> *Proposition 2: Organizations that incorporate intuition into their repertoire of sensing capabilities will identify and respond to opportunities and threats more effectively than organizations that rely solely on analytic approaches.*

One means of incorporating intuition into the repertoire of sensing capabilities is to configure decision making units so as to possess the requisite mixture of individuals with analytical and intuitive cognitive styles (Hodgkinson and Clarke, 2007). Other prescriptions range from recognizing and rewarding those who effectively rely on expert intuition rather than fall back on established procedures (Klein, 2003), to building in 'mental time-outs' to allow creative ideas to incubate (Sadler-Smith, 2010). However, recognizing when to rely on intuition is a vital skill in itself. Kahneman and Klein (2009, 2010) suggest that intuition is appropriate for informing executive action when: (1) there is sufficient environmental regularity to learn the cues that enable the recognition of patterns and irregularities and (2) decision makers have learned those cues. The latter criterion emphasizes the domain-specific nature of intuitive expertise. For example, although a manager with 10 years experience in a particular sector might well provide valid intuitive judgments on developments within that sector, it is unlikely that the validity of those judgments would generalize to other sectors.

Seizing opportunities

It is clear from Teece's (2007) analysis that two major psychological barriers potentially undermine seizing capabilities. First, organizations must be able to evaluate sensed opportunities and threats in a progressive, forward-looking manner and, where appropriate, commit to them in a timely fashion. Second, in order to do so, they must be able to unlock dysfunctional fixations with existing strategies to mitigate or remove decisional bias, inertia and strategic persistence. As indicated in Table 2.3.1, we maintain that developing routines commensurate with the affective mechanisms underpinning decision making provides the ultimate bases for meeting both of these challenges.

Evaluating and selecting new opportunities

A well-documented tendency is for organizations to shun innovative investment choices in favour of incremental improvements in keeping with their prevailing competencies (Henderson and Clark, 1990; Nelson and Winter, 1982). Drawing on the insights of prospect theory (Kahneman and Lovallo, 1993; Kahneman and Tversky, 1979), Teece (2007) attributes this dysfunction to biases in the computational mechanisms of subjective probability assessment, centred on loss aversion and the certainty effect. From this consequentialist perspective, organizations shun innovative investment choices because their decision makers undervalue new alternatives, based on biased calculations of their likelihood of success. However, more recent evidence that valuation by feeling explains many significant economic behaviours has eroded the long-held assumption that valuation proceeds by calculation and computation alone (Kahneman, Ritov and Schkade, 1999).

Contemporary developments in the decision sciences highlight the critical influence of felt emotions on choice. Loewenstein *et al.*'s (2001) risk-as-feelings model, for example, emphasizes that people typically act based on the emotions they experience at the time of choice in reaction to their mental images of choice outcomes rather than calculations of the probability or expected utility of those outcomes. A welter of evidence demonstrates that when assessments based on affect are at odds with those based on computation, the visceral often overpowers the rational to determine behaviour (Loewenstein, 1996; Loewenstein *et al.*, 2001, 2008; Rottenstreich and Hsee, 2001). The work of Damasio and colleagues (Bechara *et al.*, 2000; Damasio, 1994) shows that the affective consequences

of potential courses of action are encoded in somatic markers, which the prefrontal cortex translates for the brain's emotion centres to guide behaviour. Mere activation of a marker provides an immediate basis for action without deliberation, although the marker's visceral information often informs subsequent deliberation. Crucially, whether instigated by cognitive appraisal or the more direct routes emphasized by Damasio (1994) and others, it is the resultant feeling states that determine overt behaviour (see also Finucane *et al.*, 2000; Sanfey *et al.*, 2003; Slovic *et al.*, 2004; Zajonc, 1980). This general point was well appreciated in Janis and Mann's (1977) classic treatise on decision making, but has been overlooked in contemporary strategy research.

The crucial implication of these developments is that harnessing, rather than suppressing, visceral reactions to strategic alternatives is critical to seizing capabilities. In cases where negative affective reactions to new opportunities outweigh the positive feelings invoked, it is unlikely that decision makers will commit fully to pursuing the developments in question – even where more dispassionate, consequentialist analyses are favourable. Because affect arises from salient imagery linked to the experience of choice outcomes, the vividness and valence of such imagery plays a vital role in determining affective valuation and subsequent approach-avoidance behaviour. By way of illustration, consider again the Tripsas and Giavetti (2000) case, in which Polaroid was contemplating a move away from its existing business model to one that prioritized alternative offerings. On one hand, the new model may have brought forth imagery associated with technological developments and rapid market growth, in turn stimulating excitement and hope; such positive emotional reactions are favourable to seizing. On the other hand, the negative mental imagery associated with potential job losses arising from the implementation of the new model might well have stimulated fear and unease. The fact that people tend to overreact emotionally to new risks (Loewenstein *et al.*, 2008) and weigh negative affect more heavily than positive affect in decision making (Ito *et al.*, 1998) compounds such affective barriers to seizing. The foregoing analysis suggests the following proposition:

Proposition 3: The greater the extent to which firms foster emotional commitment to new investment opportunities, the greater the likelihood they will seize those opportunities.

To illustrate the practical implications of this proposition consider again the role of scenario planning. In the light of the foregoing analysis, the next generation

TABLE 2.3.1   Psychological foundations of dynamic capabilities revisited

Capability	Extant psychological foundations	Indicative supporting literature(s)[†]	Revised psychological foundations	Indicative supporting literature(s)
Sensing and shaping	Opportunity discovery and creation originate from the cognitive and creative ('right brain') capacities of individuals, requiring access to information and the ability to recognize, sense, and shape developments	Entrepreneurship literature: organizational search (e.g., March and Simon, 1958; Nelson and Winter, 1982)	Identifying and creating opportunities through searching, synthesizing, and filtering information stems from the interaction between reflexive (e.g., intuition, implicit association) and reflective (e.g., explicit reasoning) cognitive and emotional capabilities	Social cognitive neuroscience research on the interaction between reflexive and reflective systems (Lieberman, 2007)
	Recognizing, scanning, and shaping depend on individuals' cognitive capabilities and extant knowledge	Knowledge-based view of the firm (e.g., Grant, 1996); organizational learning (e.g., Levinthal and March, 1993)	Recognizing, scanning, and shaping depend on the capability to harness emotion to update mental representations (e.g., dissonance recognition) and skilled utilization of intuitive processes to synthesize information and form expert judgments	Cognition and capabilities literature (Gavetti, 2005); affective processes in learning (Lieberman, 2000)
Seizing	Seizing innovative investment choices requires managers to override 'dysfunctions of decision making'	Classical behavioural decision theory (e.g., Kahneman and Tversky, 1979)	Seizing opportunities requires the fostering of appropriate emotional reactions to new directions	Neuroeconomics: immediate emotions shape choice (Loewenstein et al., 2008)
	Overcoming biases requires a cognitively sophisticated and disciplined approach to decision making	Classical behavioural decision theory (e.g., Kahneman and Tversky, 1979)	Cognitively effortful processes can exacerbate bias – alleviating bias and inertia requires both cognitive and emotional capabilities	Self-regulation (e.g., Ochsner et al., 2002) and affective routes to de-escalation of commitment (e.g., Sivanathan et al., 2008)
Reconfiguring	Top management ability to coordinate and execute strategic renewal and corporate change	Organizational structure and design and strategy and performance literatures (e.g., Bartlett and Ghoshal, 1993; Chandler, 1962)	Reconfiguration requires management of the transition and repeated redefinition of social identities by alleviating implicit bias and self-regulating emotional responses to identity threats caused by major change	Research on the neural basis of self and social identity processes (e.g., Derks et al., 2008)

[†]*Note*: The references cited in this column are taken from Teece (2007) and Teece, Pisano and Shuen (1997).

of scenario planning techniques could be adapted explicitly for building emotional as well as cognitive commitment to emerging prospects. In the context of seizing, the affect-inducing properties of scenario analysis, when skilfully deployed, could serve as a vehicle to generate and foster strong and vivid positive mental imagery pertaining to new opportunities, in turn stimulating the required visceral reactions to seize the most promising ones (Healey and Hodgkinson, 2008).

Notwithstanding the potency of building emotional commitment as a mechanism for fostering seizing, there are situations when too much emotional commitment can be problematic. Marks and Spencer's (M&S) acquisition of the Brooks Brothers retail chain for US$740 million during the late-1980s exemplifies this problem (Finkelstein, Whitehead and Campbell 2008). Despite a welter of analytical evidence that this move was inadvisable, M&S Chairman, Derek Rayner, drove through the purchase, fuelled by the overwhelming positive feelings he experienced in reaction to the long-standing imagery he associated with Brooks Brothers' exclusive clothing products. This decision was to cost more than US$1 billion, upon subsequently divesting the poorly performing acquisition for just US$225 million. More generally, this case illustrates that when visceral reactions to a low probability/utility but affect-laden alternative outweigh reasoned reactions to a high probability/utility but affect-free alternative, the primacy of the emotional reaction dictates a potentially suboptimal course of action. In all probability, seizing the opportunity in question in such circumstances is ill-advised. Finkelstein *et al.* (2008) outline various safeguards available to help organizations overcome inappropriate emotional attachments to strategic issues and courses of action. These include monitoring processes designed to identify so-called 'red-flag' situations, in which decisions are proceeding based on such attachments, and the separation of decision and governance mechanisms to counter individuals' emotional fixations.

Unlocking fixations with existing strategies

It is important to recognize that although acts of omission (i.e., the failure to pursue fruitful new avenues) can prove more costly than errors of excessive commission (i.e., the tendency to embark on new, ultimately flawed, courses of action), such omission often stems from overcommitment to existing projects (Bazerman and Watkins, 2004). In order to pursue new

opportunities, therefore, firms must often shed – or at least lessen – their commitment to existing directions (Eisenhardt and Martin, 2000; Teece, 2007; Teece *et al.*, 1997). One of the most significant biases that militates against this requirement is escalation of commitment, the tendency to 'throw good money after bad' in support of failing investments in an attempt to justify prior choices (Staw, 1976; Staw and Ross, 1987).

Hitherto, and again based on early behavioural decision research that saw biases such as framing and overconfidence as resulting from intuitive processes (e.g., Gilovich, Griffin and Kahneman, 2002), strategy scholars have generally assumed that the means for overcoming escalation of commitment and related dysfunctions is to engage decision makers in more effortful and analytical information processing (Hodgkinson *et al.*, 1999, 2002; Schwenk, 1986; Wright and Goodwin, 2002). Drawing upon this conventional line of reasoning, Teece (2007: 1333) suggests that, 'overcoming biases almost always requires a cognitively sophisticated and disciplined approach to decision making.' However, merely encouraging rational and effortful information processing *per se* can exacerbate escalation of commitment and related problems. Indeed, individuals with rational thinking styles (who favour effortful, analytical reflection) are particularly prone to escalation because they feel the pressure for vindication more intensely (Wong, Kwong and Ng, 2008). Fortunately, recent work has begun to provide mechanisms for addressing the core emotional roots of escalation and related decision biases. For example, stimulating negative affect when considering whether to reinvest in a failing course of action reduces escalation, because decision makers withdraw their commitment to avoid future regret and the anxiety associated with costs sunk in error (Ku, 2008; Wong, Yik and Kwong, 2006). Hence:

Proposition 4: The greater the strategic decision making unit's tendency to incorporate salient negative affectivity associated with extant courses of action, the lower the likelihood it will fall prey to escalation of commitment and related dysfunctional decision traps.

This analysis highlights the capacity for self regulation as an important means of overcoming dysfunctional fixations. Self-regulation involves controlling internal ego-protective goals (Lord *et al.*, 2010), which are the root cause of the desire to justify specific choices to the self and others in escalation situations. One means of implementing this requirement for self-regulation is to reflect on how new courses of action facilitate the attainment of self-esteem enhancing goals, which essentially transfers the basic drive for self-esteem protection from maintenance of the status quo to the active pursuit of new directions (Henderson, Gollwitzer and Oettinger, 2007; Zhang and Baumeister, 2006). Sivanathan *et al.* (2008) demonstrated the effectiveness of this approach in a study of de-escalation in financial decision making. Giving decision makers the opportunity to affirm their overall self-esteem and personal integrity after they had committed resources to an ineffective strategy made them less inclined to invest further because confidence in the self had alleviated the desire for self-justification that motivates escalation.

Reconfiguring assets to maintain competitiveness

Teece's (2007) explication of the psychological foundations of transforming/reconfiguring is relatively underdeveloped in comparison with his analysis of sensing and seizing, in part because strategy research on the human aspects of the latter capability has been in short supply. However, as noted by Augier and Teece (2009), one of the foremost behavioural challenges associated with the reconfiguration of the enterprise concerns managing the effects of transformation on the core identities and motivations of key individuals and groups. We extend and deepen Teece's framework by explicating how the capacity to reconfigure social identities using reflexive and reflective processes in concert is critical to successful organization transformation.

When change threatens the salient identities and associated self-concepts of managers and employees, considerable resistance can breed at all levels of the organization (Gioia, Schultz and Corley, 2000; Haslam, Eggins and Reynolds, 2003; Hogg and Terry, 2000); actors cling to and defend old directions and ways of thinking intertwined with prevailing identities, and actively resist new strategic initiatives that challenge those identities (Elsbach and Kramer, 1996; Hogg and Terry, 2000; Nag, Corley and Gioia, 2007). In this sense, the fundamental identity of the firm becomes a trap that constrains its adaptive capacity (Bouchikhi and Kimberly, 2003, 2008).

As with earlier work on overcoming dysfunctions in sensing and seizing, the bulk of theory and research concerning the problem of identity inertia during strategic change has focused on cold cognition routes to identity change. Building a common group identity that embraces the extant identities under threat (Hogg and Terry, 2000) and establishing a fluid organizational identity that facilitates adaptation (Gioia, Schultz and Corley, 2000) are the favoured solutions. However, this cold cognition logic overstates the ease of cognitive identity reconstruction and underestimates the emotional difficulties associated with identity threat and the affective processes that mediate the transition to new identities. Given that the social pain caused by identity threat activates the same neural networks as physical pain (Lieberman and Eisenberger, 2009), addressing emotional mechanisms underpinning successful identity change is critical to reconfiguring. As indicated in Table 2.3.1, the emerging evidence in social cognitive neuroscience emphasizes the importance of actors' capabilities to regulate automatic and emotional reactions to self and social identity threats, especially heightened anxiety (Scheepers and Ellemers, 2005), which affect the ability to see new directions without prejudice and embrace changes that impinge upon extant salient identities.

Since much of the bias against the people (e.g., the champions of particular strategic change initiatives) and events (e.g., restructuring to meet the challenges of new opportunities and threats) at the heart of reconfiguring stems from automatic social categorization and stereotyping processes controlled by the reflexive system (Amodio, 2008; Dovidio, Pearson and Orr, 2008), merely encouraging the conscious monitoring and adjustment of prejudices through reflective processes is an insufficient basis for overcoming them. Similar to the alleviation of escalation of commitment, the self-regulation of emotional response is a crucial mechanism for overcoming identity-based resistance to change (Amodio, 2008; Derks, Inzlicht and Kang, 2008; Klein, Rozendal and Cosmides, 2002). However, whereas self-regulation in seizing concerns top managers' ability to regulate their own feelings, self-regulation in transforming concerns the ability of managers at all levels to identify, interpret and respond to the emotions of stakeholders throughout the organization (cf. Huy, 1999, 2002). Because threats to social identities threaten, by extension, the identities and self-concepts of individuals who identify strongly with the entity in question, affirming those aspects of the salient identities unaffected by the required strategic change can help reduce the desire to cling to and defend the extant identity of the organization as a whole. In consequence, actors will be more inclined to embrace the new direction and accompanying work practices. It thus follows that:

> *Proposition 5: The greater the capacity of the organization to regulate identity-based affective responses to change, the greater the likelihood of successful strategic transformation.*

As with sensing and seizing, one of the most significant practical requirements for supporting identity transition during strategic transformation is the creation of a psychologically secure emotional climate. Practices suitable for this purpose include training and coaching in the art of emotional balancing – i.e., attending to feelings expressed during identity threatening change episodes, while building emotional commitment to identity attributes consonant with the new strategic direction (cf. Huy, 1999, 2002).

GE's recent 'ecomagination' project and the ongoing transformation of the Intel Corporation (Heath, 2010) illustrate these principles in action. In highlighting its own industry-leading green products to its employees, GE is demonstrating that it already has the people and skills needed to succeed in a world focused on sustainability. By appealing on impassioned grounds to a new direction that fits with aspects of the firm's core, the organization is easing the transition to a new identity as an innovator of sustainable solutions in a way that reassures rather than threatens. In similar vein, as PC growth slows, the Intel Corporation is transforming itself into a provider of digital platforms for health, entertainment and mobile applications by using inspiration and motivation rather than intellectual justification. One potential barrier to this project is that the senior engineers who built their careers around Intel's identity as a 'chip builder' feel directionless. Sensitized to this danger, Intel's recent national advertising campaign features star engineer Anjay Bhatt, co-inventor of the USB, walking into a canteen cheered on by adoring employees. The message is that Intel's heart already fits with the new focus on product innovation. As with GE's attempts, this approach seeks to facilitate identity transition using emotionally supportive mechanisms.

Implications

We prefaced this article with Loewenstein's (1996) provocative critique of decision theory because it resonates strongly when stepping back to gaze critically upon the behavioural microfoundations of contemporary strategic management theory. Teece's (2007) framework is not alone in privileging calculation and computation through cold, effortful processes as the primary route to organizational adaptation and performance. Like earlier work that investigated strategic issue diagnosis (Dutton and Jackson, 1987; Jackson and Dutton, 1988) and competitive positioning strategy (Hodgkinson, 1997; Peteraf and Shanley, 1997; Porac *et al.*, 1995; Reger and Palmer, 1996) from a cognitive standpoint, the dynamic capabilities project as a whole divorces cognition from emotion and affect and affords only a minimal role to automatic and non-conscious processes (see, e.g., Adner and Helfat, 2003; Alvarez and Busenitz, 2001; Amit and Schoemaker, 1993; Gavetti, 2005; Kaplan, 2008; Lane *et al.*, 2006; Tripsas and Gavetti, 2000).

Our article has demonstrated how the development and maintenance of dynamic capabilities requires firms to harness managers' reflexive *and* reflective abilities, to utilize implicit and explicit cognitive and emotional processes in harmony, to facilitate sensing, seizing and reconfiguration. In so doing, it responds to Gavetti *et al.*'s (2007) call to render theories of capabilities development and organizational adaptation consistent with what we know about human functioning from contemporary advances in the psychological sciences. The result of this endeavour is a behaviourally more plausible depiction of organizations: driven by thinking and feeling inhabitants who are fired by affect, and often as reliant on inspiration and the skilful management of emotion and intuition as on calculating cognition.

Implications for practice

Our analysis points to a need for tools and practices that will enhance sensing, seizing and transforming by augmenting the cognitive *and* affective capabilities of individuals and teams. Several commentators have recently offered behavioural prescriptions for strategic intervention which, at first glance, appear to be consistent with our analysis – for example, sharing diverse perspectives, gathering disconfirmatory evidence, discussing uncertainties, and confronting cognitive biases (for representative examples see Day and Schoemaker, 2006; Kahneman and Klein, 2009, 2010; Lovallo and Sibony, 2010). However, upon closer inspection, many of these prescriptions are predicated on a cold information processing logic. One reason executives are often reluctant to embrace practices that involve questioning their personal judgements is precisely because these practices raise, rather than assuage, emotional barriers. It is tempting, therefore, to call for a two-step approach for intervening in the strategy process – an initial emotional screening phase followed by the usual gamut of decision-aiding techniques (cf. Elsbach and Barr, 1999). However, such an arrangement runs the risk of perpetuating the error of separating reason from emotion in the strategy arena (cf. Damasio, 1994). Accordingly, we have sought to demonstrate throughout how some of the fundamental tools of strategizing, when suitably embedded in an emotionally supportive climate, can be adapted to integrate cognition and affect.

Our analysis overall signals the need for a new generation of knowledge elicitation and decision aiding techniques, predicated on hot cognition principles, for both intervention and research purposes. Rather than focusing on the mapping of strategists' conceptual knowledge per se (e.g., Eden and Ackermann, 1998; Hodgkinson, Maule and Bown, 2004; Huff, 1990), extant cognitive mapping techniques could be modified to elicit and represent feelings and affective reactions to strategic issues and choices, thereby integrating multiple modalities of thought. Such practices could be particularly valuable in helping managers make sense of how they and others react to particular problems, as an aid to sensing, seizing and transforming.

Techniques commonly used for overcoming decision traps might be similarly adapted to convert them from cold cognition to hot cognition enhancing technologies. By way of illustration, the frame analysis worksheet (Russo and Schoemaker, 1989) might be adapted to assist decision makers in comprehending the emotional tags they and others hold for a given strategic problem, as a basis for recognizing dissonant reactions to the issues at hand. The goal here would be to enhance multiple frame awareness by incorporating affective information into the exercise.

Concluding remarks

In his closing remarks, Teece (2007: 1341) observes that 'enterprises may be more like biological organisms than some economists, managers and strategy scholars are willing to admit.' Our analysis takes this biological metaphor to a new level by illuminating the ways the individuals and groups who manage these entities are governed by thoughts *and* feelings: always boundedly rational, but manifestly driven by emotion. The continued negation of this fundamental insight risks stymieing the field of strategic management from maturing in alignment with economics and psychology, the base disciplines that have hitherto provided its behavioural microfoundations.

REFERENCES

Abernathy, C.M. and Hamm, R.M. (1995) *Surgical intuition: What it is and how to get it*, Philadelphia: Hanley and Belfus.

Adner, R. and Helfat, C. (2003) 'Dynamic managerial capabilities and corporate effects', *Strategic Management Journal*, 24(10), pp. 1011–1027.

Agor, W.A. (1986) 'The logic of intuition: How top executives make important decisions'. *Organizational Dynamics*, 14(3): pp. 5–18.

Agor, W.A. (1989) *Intuition in organizations: Leading and managing productively*, Newbury Park, CA: Sage.

Ala, M. and Cordeiro, W.P. (1999) 'Can we learn management techniques from the Japanese ringi process?', *Business Forum*, 24(½), pp. 22–24.

Aldrich, H.E. and Fiol, C.M. (1994) 'Fools rush in the institutional context of industry creation', *Academy of Management Review*, 19(4), pp. 645–670.

Alvarez, S.A. and Busenitz, L.W. (2001) 'The entrepreneurship of resource-based theory', *Journal of Management*, 27, pp. 755–775.

Amit, R. and Schoemaker, P.J.H. (1993) 'Strategic assets and organization rent', *Strategic Management Journal*, 14(1), pp. 33–46.

Amodio, D.M. (2008) 'The social neuroscience of intergroup relations', *European Review of Social Psychology*, 19, pp. 1–54.

Anderson, J.R. (1983) *The Architecture of Cognition*, Cambridge, MA: Harvard University Press.

Andrews, K. (1987) *The Concept of Corporate Strategy*, Homewood: Irvin.

Ansoff, H.I. (1965) *Corporate Strategy: An Analytic Approach to Business Policy for Growth and Expansion*, New York: McGraw-Hill.

Anthony, W.P., Bennett, R.H., Maddox, E.N. and Wheatley, W.J. (1993) 'Picturing the future: Using mental imagery to enrich strategic environmental assessment', *Academy of Management Executive*, 7(2), pp. 43–56.

Armour, H. and Teece, D.J. (1978) 'Organizational structure and economic performance: a test of the multidivisional hypothesis', *Bell Journal of Economics*, 9(2), pp. 106–122.

Ashby, F.G., Isen, A.M. and Turken, U. (1999) 'A neuropsychological theory of positive affect and its influence on cognition', *Psychological Review*, 106, pp. 529–550.

Augier, M. and Teece, D.J. (2009) 'Dynamic capabilities and the role of managers in business strategy and economic performance', *Organization Science*, 20, pp. 410–421.

Bargh, J.A. (1996) 'Principles of automaticity', in: E.T. Higgins and A. Kruglanski (eds) *Social psychology: Handbook of basic principles*, New York: Guilford Press, pp. 169–183.

Bargh, J.A. and Chartrand, T.L. (1999) 'The unbearable automaticity of being'. *American Psychologist*, 54(7), pp. 462–479.

Bargh, J.A. and Ferguson, M.J. (2000) 'Beyond behaviorism: on the automaticity of higher mental processes', *Psychological Bulletin*, 126(6), pp. 925–945.

Barnard, C.I. (1938) *The functions of the executive*, Cambridge, MA: Harvard University Press.

Barney, J.B. (1991) 'Firm resources and sustained competitive advantage', *Journal of Management*, 17(1), pp. 99–120.

Barr, P.S, Stimpert, J.L. and Huff, A.S. (1992) 'Cognitive change, strategic action, and organizational renewal', *Strategic Management Journal*, 13(Summer, Special Issue), pp. 15–36.

Bartlett, C.A. and Ghoshal, S. (1993) 'Beyond the M-form: toward a managerial theory of the enterprise', *Strategic Management Journal*, 14(Winter, Special Issue), pp. 23–46.

Bastick, T. (1982) *Intuition: How we think and act*, New York: Wiley.

Bateman, T.S. and Zeithaml, C.P. (1989) 'The psychological context of strategic decisions: a model and convergent experimental findings', *Strategic Management Journal*, 10(1), pp. 59–74.

Baumol, W. (2006) 'Entrepreneurship and invention: toward restoration into microeconomic value theory'. Working paper, Ringberg Castle Presentation, Germany.

Baylor, A.L. (2001) 'A U-shaped model for the development of intuition by level of expertise', *New Ideas in Psychology*, 19: pp. 237–244.

Bazerman, M.H. (1986) *Judgment in managerial decision making*, New York: Wiley.

Bazerman, M.H. (1990) *Judgment in Managerial Decision Making* (2nd edn), New York: Wiley.

Bazerman, M.H. and Watkins, M.D. (2004) *Predictable Surprises: The Disasters You Should Have Seen Coming, and How to Avoid Them*, Boston, MA: Harvard Business School Press.

Bechara, A., Damasio, H. and Damasio, A.R. (2000) 'Emotion, decision making, and the orbitofrontal cortex', *Cerebral Cortex*, 10(3), pp. 295–307.

Bechara, A., Damasio, H., Tranel, D. and Damasio, A. R. (1997) 'Deciding advantageously before knowing the advantageous strategy', *Science*, 275, pp. 1293–1295.

Behling, O. and Eckel, N.L. (1991) 'Making Sense Out of Intuition', *Academy of Management Executive*, 5(1), pp. 46–54.

Bernheim, B.D. and Rangel, A. (2004) 'Addiction and cue triggered decision processes', *American Economic Review*, 94(5), pp. 1558–1590.

Betsch, C., and Kunz, J. J. (2008). Individual strategy preferences and decisional fit. *Journal of Behavioral Decision Making*, 21(5), 532–555.

Blattberg, R.C. and Hoch, S.J. (1990) 'Database models and managerial intuition: 50% model 50% manager', *Management Science*, 36, pp. 887–899.

Bless, H., Bohner, G., Schwarz, N. and Strack, F. (1990) 'Mood and persuasion: A cognitive response analysis', *Personality and Social Psychology Bulletin*, 16, pp. 331–345.

Bodenhausen, G.V. (1990) 'Stereotypes as judgmental heuristics: Evidence of circadian variations in discrimination', *Psychological Science*, 1, pp. 319–322.

Bossidy, L. and Charan, R. with Burck, C. (2002) *Execution: The Discipline of Getting Things Done*, New York: Crown Business.

Bouchikhi, H. and Kimberly, J.R. (2003) 'Escaping the identity trap', *Sloan Management Review*, 44(3), pp. 20–26.

Bouchikhi, H. and Kimberly, J.R. (2008) *The Soul of the Corporation: How to Manage the Identity of Your Company*, Upper Saddle River, NJ: Wharton School Publishing.

Bowers, K.S., Regehr, G., Balthazard, C. and Parker, K. (1990) 'Intuition in the context of discovery', *Cognitive Psychology*, 22, pp. 72–110.

Brandenburger, A.M. and Nalebuff, B.J. (1996) *Co-opetition*, New York: Doubleday.

Briggs, K.C. and Myers, I.B. (1976) *Myers-Briggs type indicator*, Palo Alto, CA: Consulting Psychologists Press.

Brocas, I. and Carrillo, J.D. (2008) 'The brain as a hierarchical organization', *American Economic Review*, 98(4), pp. 1312–1346.

Brooks, D. (2012) *The Social Animal*, New York: Random House.

Bruner, J.S. (1962) *On knowing*, Cambridge, MA: Harvard University Press.

Burgelman, R.A. and Grove, A.S. (1996) 'Strategic dissonance', *California Management Review*, 38, pp. 8–28.

Burke, L.A. and Miller, M.K. (1999) 'Taking the mystery out of intuitive decision making', *Academy of Management Executive*, 13(4), pp. 91–99.

Capron, L., Dussauge, P. and Mitchell, W. (1998) 'Resource redeployment following horizontal mergers and acquisitions in Europe and North America, 1988–1992', *Strategic Management Journal*, 19(7), pp. 631–661.

Carlson, R.A. and Dulany, D.E. (1985) 'Conscious attention and abstraction in concept learning', *Journal of Experimental Psychology: Learning, Memory, and Cognition*, 11, pp. 45–58.

Casson, M. (1997) *Information and Organization: A New Perspective on the Theory of the Enterprise*, New York: Oxford University Press.

Chandler, A. (1962) *Strategy and Structure: Chapters in the History of Industrial Enterprise*, Cambridge, MA: Harvard University Press.

Chandler, A. (1990a) *Scale and Scope: The Dynamics of Industrial Capitalism*, Cambridge, MA: Harvard University Press.

Chandler, A. (1990b) 'The enduring logic of industrial success', *Harvard Business Review*, 68(2), pp. 130–140.

Chen, S. and Chaiken, S. (1999) 'The heuristic-systematic model in its broader context', in: S. Chaiken and Y. Trope (eds) *Dual-process theories in social psychology*, New York: Guilford Press, pp. 73–96.

Chesbrough, H. (2003) *Open Innovation: The New Imperative for Creating and Profiting from Technology*, Boston, MA: Harvard Business School Press.

Chesbrough, H. and Rosenbloom, R.S. (2002) 'The role of the business model in capturing value from innovation: evidence from Xerox Corporation's technology', *Industrial and Corporate Change*, 11(3), pp. 529–555.

Chi, M.T.H., Glaser, R. and Farr, M.J. (1998) *The nature of expertise*, Hillsdale, NJ: Lawrence Erlbaum Associates.

Claxton, G. (1998) 'Knowing without knowing why', *Psychologist*, 11(5), pp. 217–220.

Collins, H.M. (1982) 'The replication of experiments in physics', in: B. Barnes and D. Edge (eds) *Science in context*, Cambridge, MA: MIT Press, pp. 94–116.

Compton, R.J. (2003) 'The interface between emotion and attention: a review of evidence from psychology and neuroscience', *Behavioral and Cognitive Neuroscience Reviews*, 2(2), pp. 115–129.

Cummings, S. (1993) 'Brief case: The first strategists', *Long Range Planning*, 26(3), pp. 133–135.

Cyert, R.M. and March, J.G. (1963) *A Behavioral Theory of the Firm*, Englewood Cliffs, NJ: Prentice-Hall.

Daft, R. and Weick, K. (1984) 'Toward a Model of Organizations as Interpretation Systems', *Academy of Management Review*, 9, pp. 284–295.

Damasio, A.R. (1994) *Descartes' Error: Emotion, Reason, and the Human Brain*, New York: Putnam.

Dane, E. and Pratt, M.G. (2007) 'Exploring intuition and its role in managerial decision making', *Academy of Management Review*, 32(1), pp. 33–54.

David, P. (1992) 'Heroes, herds and hysteresis in technological history: Thomas Edison and the battle of the system reconsidered', *Industrial and Corporate Change*, 1(1), pp. 129–180.

Davidow, W. and Malone, M. (1992) *The Virtual Corporation*, New York: Harper Business.

Dawes, R.M., Faust, D. and Meehl, P.E. (1989) 'Clinical versus actuarial judgment', *Science*, 31, pp. 1668–1674.

Day, D.V. and Lord, R.G. (1992) 'Expertise and problem categorization: The role of expert processing in organizational sense-making', *Journal of Management Studies*, 29, pp. 35–47.

Day, G.S. and Schoemaker, P.J.H. (2006) *Peripheral Vision: Detecting the Weak Signals That Will Make or Break Your Company*, Boston, MA: Harvard Business School Press.

De Dreu, C.K.W. (2003) 'Time pressure and closing of the mind in negotiation', *Organizational Behavior and Human Decision Processes*, 91, pp. 280–295.

Denes-Raj, V. and Epstein, S. (1994) 'Conflict between intuitive and rational processing: When people behave against their better judgment', *Journal of Personality and Social Psychology*, 66, pp. 819–829.

Derks, B., Inzlicht M. and Kang, S. (2008) 'The neuroscience of stigma and stereotype threat', *Group Processes and Intergroup Relations*, 11(2), pp. 163–181.

DiMaggio, P. and Powell, W.W. (1983) 'The iron cage revisited: Institutional isomorphism and collective rationality in organizational fields', *American Sociological Review*, 48, pp. 147–160.

Donaldson, T. (2003) Editor's comments: 'Taking ethics seriously – A mission now more possible', *Academy of Management Review*, 28, pp. 363–366.

Dovidio, J.F., Pearson, A.R. and Orr, P. (2008) 'Social psychology and neuroscience: strange bedfellows or a healthy marriage?', *Group Processes and Intergroup Relations*, 11(2), pp. 247–263.

Doz, Y.L. and Kosonen, M. (2008) *Fast Strategy: How Strategic Agility Will Help You Stay Ahead of the Game*, Harlow: Pearson.

Dreyfus, H.L. and Dreyfus, S.E. (1986) *Mind over machine: The power of human intuition and expertise in the era of the computer*, New York: Free Press.

Drummond, H. (2001) *The Art of Decision Making: Mirrors of Imagination, Masks of Fate*, Chichester: Wiley.

Dutton, J.E. (1988) 'Understanding Strategies Agenda Building and its Implications for Managing Change', in: L.R. Pondy, R.J. Boland, Jr. and H. Thomas (eds) *Managing Ambiguity and Change*, Chichester: Wiley.

Dutton, J.E. (1993) 'Interpretations on automatic: a different view of strategic issue diagnosis', *Journal of Management Studies*, 30(3), pp. 339–357.

Dutton, J.E. and Jackson, S.E. (1987) 'Categorizing strategic issues: links to organizational action', *Academy of Management Review*, 12(1), pp. 76–90.

Eden, C. (1989) 'Using Cognitive Mapping for Strategic Options Development and Analysis (SODA)', in: J. Rosenhead (ed.) *Rational Analysis in a Problematic World*, London: Wiley.

Eden, C. and Ackermann, F. (1998) *Making Strategy: The Journey of Strategic Management*, London: Sage.

Edland, A. and Svenson, O. (1993) 'Judgment and decision making under time pressure', in: O. Svenson and A.J. Maule (eds) *Time pressure and stress in human judgment and decision making*, New York: Plenum Press, pp. 27–40.

Eisenhardt, K. (1989) 'Making fast strategic decisions in high velocity environments', *Academy of Management Journal*, 32, pp. 543–576.

Eisenhardt, K. and Martin, J. (2000) 'Dynamic capabilities: what are they?', *Strategic Management Journal*, 21(October–November, Special Issue), pp. 1105–1121.

Elsbach, K.D. and Barr, P.S. (1999) 'The effects of mood on individuals' use of structured decision protocols', *Organization Science*, 10(2), pp. 181–198.

Elsbach, K.D. and Kramer, R.M. (1996) 'Members' responses to organizational identity threats: encountering and countering the *Business Week rankings*', *Administrative Science Quarterly*, 41(3), pp. 442–476.

Elster, J. (1999) *Alchemies of the Mind: Rationality and the Emotions*, Cambridge: Cambridge University Press.

Epstein, S. (1990) 'Cognitive-experiential self-theory', in: L. Pervin (ed.) *Handbook of personality: Theory and research*, New York: Guilford Press, pp. 165–192.

Epstein, S. (1994) 'Integration of the cognitive and psychodynamic unconscious', *American Psychologist*, 49, pp. 709–724.

Epstein, S. (2002) 'Cognitive-experiential self-theory of personality', in: T. Millon and M.J. Lerner (eds) *Comprehensive handbook of psychology. Volume 5: Personality and social psychology*, Hoboken, NJ: Wiley, pp. 159–184.

Epstein, S. and Pacini, R. (1999) 'Some basic issues regarding dual-process theories from the perspective of cognitive experiential self-theory', in: S. Chaiken and Y. Trope (eds) *Dual-process theories in social psychology*, New York: Guilford Press, pp. 462–482.

Epstein, S., Pacini, R., Denes-Raj, V. and Heier, H. (1996) 'Individual differences in intuitive-experiential and analytical rational thinking styles', *Journal of Personality and Social Psychology*, 71, pp. 390–405.

Ericsson, K.A. and Charness, N. (1994) 'Expert performance: Its structures and acquisition', *American Psychologist*, 49, pp. 725–747.

Ericsson, K.A. and Lehmann, A.C. (1996) 'Experts and exceptional performance: Evidence of maximal adaptation to task constraints', *Annual Review of Psychology*, 47, pp. 273–305.

Ericsson, K.A. and Smith, J. (1991) 'Prospects and limits of the empirical study of expertise: An introduction', in: K.A. Ericsson and J. Smith (eds) *Toward a general theory of expertise*, New York: Cambridge University Press, pp. 1–38.

Ericsson, K.A., Krampe, R.T. and Tesch-Römer, C. (1993) 'The role of deliberate practice in the acquisition of expert performance', *Psychological Review*, 100, pp. 363–406.

Ettlie, J.E. and Pavlou, P.A. (2006) 'Technology-based new product development partnerships', *Decision Sciences*, 37(2), pp. 117–147.

Ferguson, G. (1999) *Cracking the intuition code*, Chicago, IL: Contemporary Books.

Finkelstein, S. and Hambrick, D.C. (1996) *Strategic Leadership: Top Executives and Their Effects on Organizations*, St. Paul, MN: West.

Finkelstein, S., Whitehead, J. and Campbell, A. (2008) *Think Again: Why Good Leaders Make Bad Decisions and How to Keep it From Happening to You*, Boston, MA: Harvard Business School Press.

Finucane, M.L., Alhakami, A., Slovic, P. and Johnson, S.M. (2000) 'The affect heuristic in judgments of risks and benefits', *Journal of Behavioral Decision Making*, 13(1), pp. 1–17.

Fischhoff, B. (1982) 'Debiasing', in: D. Kahneman, P. Slovic and A. Tversky (eds) *Judgment Under Uncertainty: Heuristics and Biases*, Cambridge: Cambridge University Press, pp. 422–444.

Fiske, S.T. and Taylor, S.E. (1991) *Social cognition* (2nd edn), New York: McGraw-Hill.

Franquemont, S. (1999) *You already know what to do*, New York: Jeremy P. Tarcher/Putnam.

Fredrickson, B.L. and Branigan, C. (2005) 'Positive emotions broaden the scope of attention and thought action repertoires', *Cognition and Emotion*, 19, pp. 313–332.

Freeman, C. (1974) *The Economics of Industrial Innovation*, Harmondsworth: Penguin.

Gavetti, G. (2005) 'Cognition and hierarchy: rethinking the microfoundations of capabilities development', *Organization Science*, 16(6), pp. 599–617.

Gavetti, G. and Levinthal, D.A. (2000) 'Looking forward and looking backward: cognitive and experiential search', *Administrative Science Quarterly*, 45(1), pp. 113–137.

Gavetti, G., Levinthal, D.A. and Ocasio, W. (2007) 'Neo-Carnegie: the Carnegie School's past, present, and reconstructing for the future', *Organization Science*, 18(3), pp. 523–536.

Gilovich, T., Griffin, D. and Kahneman, D. (eds) (2002) *Heuristics and Biases: The Psychology of Intuitive Judgment*, New York: Cambridge University Press.

Gioia, D.A. and Chittipeddi, K. (1991) 'Sensemaking and Sensegiving in Strategic Change Intuition', *Strategic Management Journal*, 12, pp. 433–448.

Gioia, D.A., Schultz, M. and Corley, K.G. (2000) 'Organizational identity, image, and adaptive instability', *Academy of Management Review*, 25(1), pp. 63–81.

Gladwell, M. (2007). *Blink: The Power of Thinking Without Thinking* (1st edn), New York: Back Bay Books.

Glynn, M.A. (2000) 'When cymbals become symbols: Conflict over organizational identity within a symphony orchestra', *Organization Science*, 11(3), pp. 285–298.

Gollwitzer, P. and Bayer, U. (1999) 'Deliberative versus implemental mindsets in the control of action', in: S. Chaiken and Y. Trope (eds) *Dual-process theories in social psychology*, New York: Guilford Press, pp. 403–422.

Gottschalg, O. and Zollo M. (2007) 'Interest alignment and competitive advantage', *Academy of Management Review*, 32(2), pp. 418–437.

Grant, R.M. (1996) 'Prospering in dynamically-competitive environments: organizational capability as knowledge integration', *Organization Science*, 7(4), pp. 375–387.

Groves, K.S., Vance, C.M., Choi, D.Y. and Mendez, J.L. (2008) 'An examination of the nonlinear thinking style profile stereotype of successful entrepreneurs', *Journal of Enterprising Culture*, 16(02), 133–159.

Guenther, H.V. (1958) 'The levels of understanding in Buddhism', *Journal of the American Oriental Society*, 78, pp. 19–28.

Haidt, J. (2001) 'The emotional dog and its rational tail: A social intuitionist approach to moral judgment', *Psychological Review*, 108, pp. 814–834.

Hambrick, D.C., Geletkanycz, M.A. and Fredrickson, J.W. (1993) 'Top executive commitment to the status quo: Some tests of its determinants', *Strategic Management Journal*, 14(6), pp. 401–418.

Hamel, G. and Prahalad, C.K. (1994) *Competing for the Future*, Boston, MA: Harvard Business School Press.

Hammer, M., Leonard, D. and Davenport, T. (2004) 'Why don't we know more about knowledge?', *MIT Sloan Management Review*, 45(4), pp. 14–18.

Hammond, K.R., Hamm, R.M., Grassia, J. and Pearson, T. (1987) 'Direct comparison of the efficacy of intuitive and analytical cognition in expert judgment', *IEEE Transactions on Systems, Man, and Cybernetics*, 17, pp. 753–770.

Hampden-Turner, C. and Trompenaars, F. (2000) *Building Cross-cultural Competence: How to Create Wealth from Conflicting Values*, New Haven, CT: Yale University Press.

Handy, C. (1990) *The Age of Unreason*, Boston, MA: Harvard Business School Press.

Hanoch, Y., Johnson, J.G. and Wilke, A. (2006). 'Domain Specificity in Experimental Measures and Participant Recruitment: An Application to Risk-Taking Behavior', *Psychological Science*, 17(4), 300–304.

Harper, S.C. (1989) 'Intuition: What separates executives from managers', in: W.H. Agor (ed.) *Intuition in organizations: Leading and managing productively*, Newbury Park, CA: Sage, pp. 111–124.

Haslam, S.A., Eggins, R.A. and Reynolds, K.J. (2003) 'The ASPIRe model: actualizing social and personal identity resources to enhance organizational outcomes', *Journal of Occupational and Organizational Psychology*, 76, pp. 83–113.

Hayashi, A.M. (2001) 'When to trust your gut', *Harvard Business Review*, 79(2), pp. 59–65.

Healey, M.P. and Hodgkinson, G.P. (2008) 'Troubling futures: scenarios and scenario planning for organizational decision making', in: G.P. Hodgkinson and W.H. Starbuck (eds) *The Oxford Handbook of Organizational Decision Making*, Oxford: Oxford University Press, pp. 565–585.

Heath, C. (2010) 'Making the emotional case for change', *McKinsey Quarterly*, March, pp. 88–97.

Helfat, C. and Peteraf, M. (2003) 'The dynamic resource-based view: capability lifecycles', *Strategic Management Journal*, 24(October, Special Issue), pp. 997–1010.

Henderson, M.D., Gollwitzer, P.M. and Oettingen, G. (2007) 'Implementation intentions and disengagement from a failing course of action', *Journal of Behavioral Decision Making*, 20(1), pp. 81–102.

Henderson, R.M. and Clark, K.B. (1990) 'Architectural innovation: the reconfiguration of existing product technologies and the failure of established firms', *Administrative Science Quarterly*, 35(1), pp. 9–30.

Hitt, M.A., Keats, B. and DeMarie, S.M. (1998) 'Navigating in the new competitive landscape: Building strategic flexibility and competitive advantage in the 21st century', *Academy of Management Executive*, 12(4), pp. 22–42.

Hodgkinson, G.P. and Sadler-Smith, E. (2003) 'Complex or unitary? A critique and empirical reassessment of the Allinson-Hayes Cognitive Style Index', *Journal of Occupational and Organizational Psychology*, 76, pp. 243–268.

Hodgkinson, G.P. (1997) 'Cognitive inertia in a turbulent market: the case of U.K. residential estate agents', *Journal of Management Studies*, 34, pp. 921–945.

Hodgkinson, G.P. and Clarke, I. (2007) 'Exploring the cognitive significance of organizational strategizing: a dual process framework and research agenda', *Human Relations*, 60(1), pp. 243–255.

Hodgkinson, G.P. and Healey, M.P. (2008) 'Cognition in organizations', *Annual Review of Psychology*, 59, pp. 387-417.

Hodgkinson, G.P. and Healey, M.P. (2011) 'Psychological foundations of dynamic capabilities: Reflexion and reflection in strategic management', *Strategic Management Journal*, 32(13), pp. 1500–1516.

Hodgkinson, G.P. and Wright, G. (2002) 'Confronting strategic inertia in a top management team: learning from failure', *Organization Studies*, 23, pp. 949–977.

Hodgkinson, G.P., Bown, N.J., Maule, A.J., Glaister, K.W. and Pearman, A.D. (1999) 'Breaking the frame: an analysis of strategic cognition and decision making under uncertainty', *Strategic Management Journal*, 20(10), pp. 977–985.

Hodgkinson, G.P., Langan-Fox, J. and Sadler-Smith, E. (2008) 'Intuition: a fundamental bridging construct in the behavioral sciences', *British Journal of Psychology*, 99(1), pp. 1–27.

Hodgkinson, G.P., Maule, A.J. and Bown, N.J. (2004) 'Causal cognitive mapping in the organizational strategy field: a comparison of alternative elicitation procedures', *Organizational Research Methods*, 7(1), pp. 3–26.

Hodgkinson, G.P., Maule, A.J., Bown, N.J., Pearman, A.D. and Glaister, K.W. (2002) 'Further reflections on the elimination of framing bias in strategic decision making', *Strategic Management Journal*, 23(11), pp. 1069–1076.

Hodgkinson, G.P., Sadler-Smith, G., Burke, L.A., Claxton, G. and Sparrow, P.R. (2009) 'Intuition in organizations: implications for strategic management', *Long Range Planning*, 42, pp. 277–297.

Hofer, C.W. and Schendel, D. (1978) *Strategy Formulation: Analytical Concepts*, St. Paul, MN: West Publishing.

Hofstede, G. (2001) *Culture's consequences* (2nd edn), Thousand Oaks, CA: Sage.

Hogarth, R.M. (1980) *Judgement and Choice: The Psychology of Decision*, Chichester: Wiley.

Hogarth, R.M. (2001) *Educating Intuition*, Chicago, IL: University of Chicago Press.

Hogg, M.A. and Terry, D.J. (2000) 'Social identity and self-categorization processes in organizational contexts', *Academy of Management Review*, 25(1), pp. 121–140.

Huff, A.S. (ed.) (1990) *Mapping Strategic Thought*, Chichester: Wiley.

Huy, Q.N. (1999) 'Emotional capability, emotional intelligence, and radical change', *Academy of Management Review*, 24(2), pp. 325–345.

Huy, Q.N. (2002) 'Emotional balancing of organizational continuity and radical change: the contribution of middle managers', *Administrative Science Quarterly*, 47, pp. 31–69.

Isaack, T.S. (1978) 'Intuition: An ignored dimension of management', *Academy of Management Review*, 3, pp. 917–922.

Isen, A.M., Means, B., Patrick, R. and Nowicki, G. (1982) 'Some factors influencing decision-making strategy and risk taking', in :M.S. Clarke and S.T. Fiske (eds) *Affect and cognition*, Hillsdale, NJ: Lawrence Erlbaum Associates, pp. 243–261.

Isenberg, D.J. (1984) 'How Senior Managers Think', *Harvard Business Review*, 63 (6, November–December), pp. 81–90.

Ito, T.A., Larsen, J.T., Smith, N.K. and Cacioppo, J.T. (1998) 'Negative information weighs more heavily on the brain: the negativity bias in evaluative categorizations', *Journal of Personality and Social Psychology*, 75(4), pp. 887–900.

Jackson, S.E. and Dutton, J.E. (1988) 'Discerning threats and opportunities', *Administrative Science Quarterly*, 33(3), pp. 370–387.

Jacoby, L.L., Lindsay, D.S. and Toth, J.P. (1992) 'Unconscious influences revealed', *American Psychologist*, 47, pp. 802–809.

Janis, I.L. (1989) *Crucial Decisions: Leadership in Policymaking and Crisis Management*, New York: Free Press.

Janis, I.L. and Mann, L. (1977) *Decision Making: A Psychological Analysis of Conflict, Choice, and Commitment*, New York: Free Press.

Jantunen, A. (2005) 'New HRM practices and knowledge utilization', in: *Proceedings of the 5th International Workshop on Human Resource Management,* Seville, Spain.

Jolls, C., Sunstein, C.R. and Thaler, R. (1998) 'A behavioral approach to law and economics', *Stanford Law Review*, 50(5), pp. 1471–1550.

Jung, C. G. (1933 – First published in 1921) *Psychological types*, New York: Harcourt, Brace, and Company.

Kaempf, G.L., Klein, G., Thordsen, M.L. and Wolf, S. (1996) 'Decision making in complex naval command-and-control environments', *Human Factors*, 38, pp. 220–231.

Kagono, T.I., Nonaka, K., Sakakibira, K. and Okumara, A. (1985) *Strategic vs. Evolutionary Management*, Amsterdam: North-Holland.

Kahneman, D. (2003) 'A perspective on judgment and choice', *American Psychologist*, 58, pp. 697–720.

Kahneman, D. (2011) *Thinking, Fast and Slow*, New York: Farrar, Straus and Giroux.

Kahneman, D. and Klein, G. (2009) 'Conditions for intuitive expertise: a failure to disagree', *American Psychologist*, 64(6), pp. 515–526.

Kahneman, D. and Klein, G. (2010) 'When can you trust your gut?', *McKinsey Quarterly*, March, pp. 58–67.

Kahneman, D. and Lovallo, D. (1993) 'Timid choices and bold forecasts: a cognitive perspective on risk-taking', *Management Science*, 39(1), pp. 17–31.

Kahneman, D. and Tversky, A. (1979) 'Prospect theory: analysis of decision under risk', *Econometrica*, 47(2), pp. 263–291.

Kahneman, D. and Tversky, A. (2000) *Choices, values, and frames*, Cambridge: Cambridge University Press.

Kahneman, D., Ritov, I. and Schkade, D. (1999) 'Economic preferences or attitude expressions? An analysis of dollar responses to public issues', *Journal of Risk and Uncertainty*, 19, pp. 203–235.

Kahneman, D., Slovic, P. and Tversky, A. (1982) *Judgment under uncertainty: Heuristics and biases*, Cambridge: Cambridge University Press.

Kaplan, M.F., Wanshula, L.T. and Zanna, M.P. (1993) 'Time pressure and information integration in social judgment', in: O. Svenson and A.J. Maule (eds) *Time pressure and stress in human judgment and decision making:*, New York: Plenum Press, pp. 255–267.

Kaplan, S. (2008) 'Cognition, capabilities, and incentives: assessing firm response to the fiber-optic revolution', *Academy of Management Journal*, 51(4), pp. 672–695.

Karlsson, N., Loewenstein, G. and Seppi, D. (2009) 'The ostrich effect: selective attention to information', *Journal of Risk and Uncertainty*, 38, pp. 95–115.

Keegan, W.J. (1983) 'Strategic Market Planning: The Japanese Approach', *International Marketing Review*, 1, pp. 5–15.

Khatri, N. and Ng, H.A. (2000) 'The role of intuition in strategic decision making', *Human Relations*, 53, pp. 57–86.

Kihlstrom, J.F. (1987) 'The cognitive unconscious', *Science*, 237, pp. 1445–1452.

Kihlstrom, J.F., Barnhardt, T.M. and Tataryn, D.T. (1992) 'The psychological unconscious', *American Psychologist*, 47, pp. 788–791.

Kirzner, I. (1973) *Competition and Entrepreneurship*, Chicago, IL: University of Chicago Press.

Klein, G.A. (1998) *Sources of power: How people make decisions*, Cambridge, MA: MIT Press.

Klein, G.A. (2003) *Intuition at Work*, New York: Doubleday.

Klein, S.B., Rozendal, K. and Cosmides, L. (2002) 'A socialcognitive neuroscience analysis of the self', *Social Cognition*, 20(2), pp. 105–135.

Knight, D., Pearce, C.L., Smith, K.G., Olian, J.D., Sims, H.P, Smith, K.A. and Flood, P. (1999) 'Top Management Team Diversity, Group Process, and Strategic Consensus', *Strategic Management Journal*, 20, pp. 445–465.

Kogut, B. and Zander, U. (1992) 'Knowledge of the enterprise, combinative capabilities and the replication of technology', *Organizational Science*, 3(3), pp. 383–397.

Kruger, J. and Dunning, D. (1999) 'Unskilled and unaware of it: How difficulties in recognizing one's own incompetence lead to inflated self-assessments', *Journal of Personality and Social Psychology*, 77, pp. 1121–1134.

Kruglanski, A.W. and Freund, T. (1983) 'The freezing and unfreezing of lay-inference: Effects on impressional primacy, ethnic stereotyping, and numerical anchoring', *Journal of Experimental Social Psychology*, 19, pp. 448–468.

Ku, G. (2008) 'Learning to de-escalate: the effects of regret in escalation of commitment', *Organizational Behavior and Human Decision Processes*, 105(2), pp. 221–232.

Kuhn, T.S. (1970) *The Structure of Scientific Revolutions*, Chicago, IL: University of Chicago Press.

Lane, P.J., Koka, B.R. and Pathak, S. (2006) 'The reification of absorptive capacity: a critical review and rejuvenation of the construct', *Academy of Management Review*, 31(4), pp. 833–863.

Langer, E.J. (1989) *Mindfulness*, Reading, MA: Addison-Wesley.

Langley, A. (1995) 'Between "Paralysis by Analysis" and "Extinction by Instinct"', *Sloan Management Review*, 36(3, Spring), pp. 63–76.

Laughlin, P. (1980) 'Social combination processes of cooperative problem-solving groups on verbal intellective tasks', in: M. Fishbein (ed.) *Progress in social psychology, vol. 1*, Hillsdale, NJ: Lawrence Erlbaum Associates, pp. 127–155.

Laughlin, P.R. and Ellis, A.L. (1986) 'Demonstrability and social combination processes on mathematical intellective tasks', *Journal of Experimental Social Psychology*, 22, pp. 177–189.

Lawrence, P.R. and Lorsch, J.W. (1967) *Organization and Environment: Managing Differentiation and Integration*, Boston, MA: Harvard University Press.

Lazonick, W. (2005) 'The innovative firm', in: J. Fagerberg, D. Mowery and R.R. Nelson (eds) *The Oxford Handbook of Innovation*, New York: Oxford University Press, pp. 29–55.

LeDoux, J.E. (2000) 'Emotion circuits in the brain', *Annual Review of Neuroscience*, 23, pp. 155–184.

Lenz, R.T. and Lyles, M. (1985) 'Paralysis by Analysis: Is Your Planning System Becoming Too Rational?', *Long Range Planning*, 18(4), pp. 64–72.

Leonard-Barton, D. (1995) *Wellsprings of Knowledge-Building and Sustaining the Sources of Innovation*, Boston, MA: Harvard Business School Press.

Levinthal, D.A. and March, J.G. (1993) 'The myopia of learning', *Strategic Management Journal*, 14(4), pp. 95–112.

Levinthal, D.A. and Rerup, C. (2006) 'Crossing an apparent chasm: bridging mindful and less-mindful perspectives on organizational learning', *Organization Science*, 17, pp. 502–513.

Lewicki, P., Hill, T. and Bizot, E. (1988) 'Acquisition of procedural knowledge about a pattern of stimuli that cannot be articulated', *Cognitive Psychology*, 20, pp. 24–37.

Lieberman, M.D. (2000) 'Intuition: a social cognitive neuroscience approach', *Psychological Bulletin*, 126(1), pp. 109–137.

Lieberman, M.D. (2007) 'Social cognitive neuroscience: a review of core processes', *Annual Review of Psychology*, 58, pp. 259–289.

Lieberman, M.D. and Eisenberger, N.I. (2009) 'The pains and pleasures of social life', *Science*, 323, pp. 890–891.

Lieberman, M.D., Gaunt, R., Gilbert, D.T. and Trope, Y. (2002) 'Reflexion and reflection: a social cognitive neuroscience approach to attributional inference', in: *Advances in Experimental Social Psychology* (Vol. 34). San Diego, CA: Academic Press, pp. 199–249.

Lieberman, M.D., Ochsner, K.N., Gilbert, D.T. and Schacter, D.L. (2001) 'Do amnesics exhibit cognitive dissonance reduction? The role of explicit memory and attention in attitude change', *Psychological Science*, 12(2), pp. 135–140.

Lindblom, C.E. (1959) 'The science of "muddling through"', *Public Administration Review*, 19(2), pp. 79–88.

Loewenstein, G. (1996) 'Out of control: visceral influences on behavior', *Organizational Behavior and Human Decision Processes*, 65, pp. 272–292.

Loewenstein, G. and Small, D.A. (2007) 'The Scarecrow and the Tin Man: the vicissitudes of human sympathy and caring', *Review of General Psychology*, 11(2), pp. 112–126.

Loewenstein, G., Rick, S. and Cohen, J.D. (2008) 'Neuroeconomics', *Annual Review of Psychology*, 59, pp. 647–672.

Loewenstein, G., Weber, E.U., Hsee, C.K. and Welch, N. (2001) 'Risk as feelings', *Psychological Bulletin*, 127(2), pp. 267–286.

Lord, R.G., Diefendorff, J.M., Schmidt, A.M. and Hall, R.J. (2010) 'Self-regulation at work', *Annual Review of Psychology*, 61, pp. 543–568.

Louis, M.R. and Sutton, R.I. (1991) 'Switching cognitive gears: from habits of mind to active thinking', *Human Relations*, 44(1), pp. 55–76.

Lovallo, D. and Sibony, O. (2010) 'The case for behavioral strategy', *McKinsey Quarterly*, March, pp. 30–43.

Lovett, M.C. (2002) 'Problem solving', in: H. Pashler and D. Medin (eds) *Stevens' handbook of experimental psychology. Volume 2: Memory and cognitive processes*, New York: Wiley, pp. 317–362.

Lyles, M.A. and Schwenk, C.R. (1992) 'Top Management, Strategy and Organizational Knowledge Structures', *Journal of Management Studies*, 29, pp. 155–174.

MacGregor, D., Lichtenstein, S. and Slovic, P. (1988) 'Structuring knowledge retrieval: An analysis of decomposed quantitative judgments', *Organizational Behavior and Human Decision Processes*, 42, pp. 303–323.

Mansfield, E., Rapoport, J., Schnee, J., Wagner, S. and Hamburger, M. (1971) *Research and Innovation in the Modern Corporation*, New York: WW Norton.

March, J.G. (1991) 'Exploration and exploitation in organizational learning', *Organizational Science*, 2(1), pp. 71–87.

March, J.G. and Simon, H.A. (1993) *Organizations* (2nd edn), Cambridge, MA: Blackwell.

Martin, R. (2007) *The Opposable Mind: How Successful Leaders Win through Integrative Thinking*, Cambridge, MA: Harvard Business School Book Press.

Mason, R.O. and Mitroff, I.I. (1981) *Challenging Strategic Planning Assumptions*, New York: Wiley.

Matusik, S.F. and Hill, C.W.L. (1998) 'The utilization of contingent work, knowledge creation, and competitive advantage', *Academy of Management Review*, 23, pp. 680–697.

Maule, A.J., Hockey, G.R.J. and Bdzola, L. (2000) 'Effects of time-pressure on decision-making under uncertainty: Changes in affective state and information processing strategy', *Acta Psychologica*, 104, pp. 283–301.

McCaskey, M.B. (1982) *The Executive Challenge: Managing Change and Ambiguity*, Boston, MA: Pitman.

McGrath, J.E. (1984) *Groups: Interaction and performance*, Englewood Cliffs, NJ: Prentice-Hall.

McMackin, J. and Slovic, P. (2000) 'When does explicit justification impair decision making?', *Applied Cognitive Psychology*, 14, pp. 527–541.

Meehl, P.E. (1954) *Clinical versus statistical prediction*, Minneapolis, MN: University of Minnesota Press.

Meyer, E. (2014) *The Culture Map: Decoding how people think, lead, and get things done across cultures*, New York: Public Affairs.

Mintzberg, H. (1994) *The Rise and Fall of Strategic Planning*, New York: Free Press.

Mintzberg, H., Ahlstrand, B. and Lampel, J. (1998) *Strategy Safari: A Guided Tour through the Wilds of Strategic Management*, New York: Free Press.

Mitchell, W. (1991) 'Dual clocks: entry order influences on industry incumbent and newcomer market share and survival when specialized assets retain their value', *Strategic Management Journal*, 12(2), pp. 85–100.

Mukherjee, K. (2010). 'A dual system model of preferences under risk', *Psychological Review*, 117(1), 243.

Myers, D.G. (2002) *Intuition: Its powers and perils*, New Haven, CT: Yale University Press.

Nag, R., Corley, K.G. and Gioia, D.A. (2007) 'The intersection of organizational identity, knowledge, and practice: attempting strategic change via knowledge grafting', *Academy of Management Journal*, 50(4), pp. 821–847.

Nelson, R.R. (2005) *Technology, Institutions, and Economic Growth*, Cambridge, MA: Harvard University Press.

Nelson, R.R. and Winter, S.G. (1982) *An Evolutionary Theory of Economic Change*, Cambridge, MA: Harvard University Press.

Nelson, R.R. and Winter, S.G. (2002) 'Evolutionary theorizing in economics', *Journal of Economic Perspectives*, 16(2), pp. 23–46.

Nelson, T.O. (1996) 'Consciousness and metacognition', *American Psychologist*, 51(2), pp. 102–116.

Nisbett, R.E., Peng, K., Choi, I. and Norenzayan, A. (2001) 'Culture and systems of thought: holistic versus analytic cognition', *Psychological Review*, 108(2), 291–310.

Nissen, M.J. and Bullemer, P. (1987). 'Attentional requirements of learning: Evidence from performance measures', *Cognitive Psychology*, 19, pp. 1–32.

Nonaka, I. (1991) 'The Knowledge-Creating Company', *Harvard Business Review*, 69(6, November–December), pp. 96–104.

Nonaka, I. and Johanson, J.K. (1985) 'Japanese Management: What about "Hard" Skills?', *Academy of Management Review*, 10(2), pp. 181–191.

Nonaka, I. and Takeuchi, H. (1995) *The Knowledge Creating Company*, New York: Oxford University Press.

Nonaka, I. and Toyama, R. (2007) 'Strategic management as distributed practical wisdom (phronesis)', *Industrial and Corporate Change*, 16(3), pp. 371–394.

Noorderhaven, N.G. (1995) *Strategic Decision Making*, Wokingham: Addison-Wesley.

Norenzayan, A., Smith, E.E., Kim, B.J. and Nisbett, R.E. (2002) 'Cultural preferences for formal versus intuitive reasoning', *Cognitive Science*, 26(5), 653–684.

Ocasio, W. (1997) 'Towards an Attention-Based View of the Firm', *Strategic Management Journal*, 18(July, Special Issue), pp. 187–206.

Ochsner, K.N. and Lieberman, M.D. (2001) 'The emergence of social cognitive neuroscience', *American Psychologist*, 56(9), pp. 717–734.

Ochsner, K.N., Bunge, S.A., Gross, J.J. and Gabrieli, J.D.E. (2002) 'Rethinking feelings: an MRI study of the cognitive regulation of emotion', *Journal of Cognitive Neuroscience*, 14(8), pp. 1215–1229.

Osbeck, L.M. (1999) 'Conceptual problems in the development of a psychological notion of "intuition"', *Journal for the Theory of Social Behaviour*, 29, pp. 229–250.

Osbeck, L.M. (2001) 'Direct apprehension and social construction: Revisiting the concept of intuition', *Journal of Theoretical and Philosophical Psychology*, 21, pp. 118–131.

Osterloh, M. and Frey, B. (2000) 'Motivation, knowledge transfer, and organizational forms', *Organization Science*, 11, pp. 538–550.

Pachur, T. and Spaar, M. (2015) 'Domain-Specific Preferences for Intuition and Deliberation in Decision-making', *Journal of Applied Research in Memory and Cognition*, 4(3), 303–311.

Pacini, R. and Epstein, S. (1999) 'The relation of rational and experiential information processing styles to personality, basic beliefs, and the ratio-bias problem', *Journal of Personality and Social Psychology*, 76, pp. 972–987.

Packard, D. (1995) *The HP Way: How Bill Hewlett and I Built Our Company*, New York: HarperCollins.

Pascale, R.T. (1984) 'Perspectives on Strategy: The Real Story Behind Honda's Success', *California Management Review*, 26(3, Spring), pp. 47–72.

Pascale, R.T. and Athos, A.G. (1981) 'The Art of Japanese Management', *Business Horizons*, 24(6), pp. 83–85.

Perlow, L.A., Okhuysen, G.A. and Repenning, N.P. (2002) 'The speed trap: Exploring the relationship between decision making and temporal context', *Academy of Management Journal*, 45, pp. 931–955.

Peteraf, M. and Shanley, M. (1997) 'Getting to know you: a theory of strategic group identity', *Strategic Management Journal*, 18(Summer, Special Issue), pp. 165–186.

Peters, J.T., Hammond, K.R. and Summers, D.A. (1974) 'A note on intuitive vs. analytic thinking', *Organizational Behavior and Human Performance*, 12, pp. 125–131.

Pirsig, R.M. (1974) *Zen and the art of motorcycle maintenance: An inquiry into values*, New York: Morrow.

Pizarro, D.A. and Bloom, P. (2003) 'The intelligence of the moral intuitions: Comment on Haidt (2001)', *Psychological Review*, 110, pp. 193–196.

Poincaré, H. (1969) 'Intuition and logic mathematics', *Mathematics Teacher*, 62, pp. 205–212.

Polanyi, M. (1966) *The Tacit Dimension*, London: Routledge and Kegan Paul.

Policastro, E. (1999), 'Intuition', in: M.A. Runco and S.R. Pritzker (eds) *Encyclopedia of creativity, vol. 2*, San Diego: Academic Press, pp. 89–93.

Porac, J.F., Thomas, H., Wilson, F., Paton, D. and Kanfer, A. (1995) 'Rivalry and the industry model of Scottish knitwear producers', *Administrative Science Quarterly*, 40(2), pp. 203–227.

Porter, M.E. (1980) *Competitive Strategy: Techniques for Analyzing Industries and Competitors*, New York: Free Press.

Prahalad, C.K. (2004) 'The blinders of dominant logic', *Long Range Planning*, 37, pp. 171–179.

Prahalad, C.K. and Bettis, R.A. (1986) 'The Dominant Logic: A New Linkage between Diversity and Performance', *Strategic Management Journal*, 7(6, November–December), pp. 485–601.

Prietula, M.J. and Simon, H.A. (1989) 'The experts in your midst', *Harvard Business Review*, 67(1), pp. 120–124.

Raidl, M.H. and Lubart, T.I. (2000–2001) 'An empirical study of intuition and creativity', *Imagination, Cognition and Personality*, 20, pp. 217–230.

Raiffa, H. (1968) *Decision analysis: Introductory lectures on choices under uncertainty*, Reading, MA: Addison-Wesley.

Reber, A.S. (1976) 'Implicit learning of synthetic languages: The role of instructional set', *Journal of Experimental Psychology: Human Learning and Memory*, 2, pp. 88–94.

Reber, A.S. (1992) 'An evolutionary context for the cognitive unconscious', *Philosophical Psychology*, 5, pp. 33–51.

Reber, A.S., Walkenfeld, F.F. and Hernstadt, R. (1991) 'Implicit and explicit learning: Individual differences and IQ', *Journal of Experimental Psychology: Learning, Memory, and Cognition*, 17, pp. 888–896.

Reber, A.S. (1989) 'Implicit learning and tacit knowledge', *Journal of Experimental Psychology: General*, 118, pp. 219–235.

Reber, A.S., Kassin, S.M., Lewis, S. and Cantor, G. (1980) 'On the relationship between implicit and explicit modes in learning of complex rule structure', *Journal of Experimental Psychology: Human Learning and Memory*, 6, pp. 492–502.

Redding, S.G. (1980) 'Cognition as an Aspect of Culture and its Relationship to Management Processes: An Exploratory View of the Chinese Case', *Journal of Management Studies*, 17(May), pp. 127–148.

Reger, R.K. and Palmer, T.B. (1996) 'Managerial categorization of competitors: using old maps to navigate new environments', *Organization Science*, 7(1), pp. 22–39.

Rittel, H. (1972) 'On the Planning Crisis: Systems Analysis of the "First and Second Generations"', *Bedriftsokonomen*, 8, pp. 390–396.

Rorty, R. (1967) 'Intuition', in: P. Edwards (ed.) *Encyclopedia of philosophy*, New York: Macmillan, pp. 204–212.

Rosenkopf, L. and Nerkar, A. (2001) 'Beyond local search: boundary-spanning, exploration, and impact in the optical disk industry', *Strategic Management Journal*, 22(4), pp. 287–306.

Rottenstreich, Y. and Hsee, C.K. (2001) 'Money, kisses, and electric shocks: on the affective psychology of risk', *Psychological Science*, 12(3), pp. 185–190.

Rowan, R. (1989) 'What it is', in: W.H. Agor (ed.) *Intuition in organizations: Leading and managing productively*, Newbury Park, CA: Sage, pp. 78–88.

Ruder, M. and Bless, H. (2003) 'Mood and the reliance on the ease of retrieval heuristic', *Journal of Personality and Social Psychology*, 85, pp. 20–32.

Rumelt, R. (1995) 'Inertia and transformation', in: C. Montgomery (ed.) *Resource Based and Evolutionary Theories of the Enterprise*, Boston, MA: Kluwer Academic, pp. 101–132.

Russo, J.E. and Schoemaker, P.J.H. (1989) *Decision Traps*, New York: Doubleday.

Sadler-Smith, E. (2004) 'Cognitive style and the management of small and medium-sized enterprises', *Organization Studies*, 25(2), pp. 155–181.

Sadler-Smith, E. (2010) *The Intuitive Mind: Profiting From the Power of Your Sixth Sense*, Chichester: Wiley.

Sanfey, A.G., Rilling, J.K., Aronson, J.A., Nystrom, L.E. and Cohen, J.D. (2003) 'The neural basis of economic decision-making in the ultimatum game', *Science*, 300(5626), pp. 1755–1758.

Scheepers, D. and Ellemers, N. (2005) 'When the pressure is up: the assessment of social identity threat in low and high status groups', *Journal of Experimental Social Psychology*, 41(2), pp. 192–200.

Schein, E.H. (1985) *Organizational Culture and Leadership*, San Francisco, CA: Jossey-Bass.

Schneider, S.C. (1989) 'Strategy Formulation: The Impact of National Culture', *Organization Studies*, 10(2), pp. 149–168.

Schneider, W. and Shiffrin, R.M. (1977) 'Controlled and automatic human information processing: 1. detection, search, and attention', *Psychological Review*, 84(1), pp. 1–66.

Schoemaker, P.J.H. (1993) 'Multiple scenario development: its conceptual and behavioral foundation', *Strategic Management Journal*, 14(3), pp. 193–213.

Schoemaker, P.J.H. and Russo, J.E. (1993) 'A Pyramid of Decision Approaches', *California Management Review*, 36(1, Fall), pp. 9–32.

Schumpeter, J. (1934) *The Theory of Economic Development*, Cambridge, MA: Harvard University Press.

Schwarz, N., Bless, H. and Bohner, G. (1991) 'Mood and persuasion: Affective states influence the processing of persuasive communications', *Advances in Experimental Social Psychology*, 24, pp. 161–199.

Schwenk, C.R. (1984) 'Cognitive Simplification Processes in Strategic Decision-Making', *Strategic Management Journal*, 5(2, April–June), pp. 111–128.

Schwenk, C.R. (1986) 'Information, cognitive biases, and commitment to a course of action', *Academy of Management Review*, 11(2), pp. 298–310.

Schwenk, C.R. (1988) *The Essence of Strategic Decision Making*, Lexington, MA: Lexington Books.

Seger, C.A. (1994) 'Implicit learning', *Psychological Bulletin*, 115, pp. 163–196.

Shane, S. (2003) *A General Theory of Entrepreneurship*, Northampton, MA: Edward Elgar.

Shanteau, J. and Stewart, T.R. (1992) 'Why study expert decision making? Some historical perspectives and comments', *Organizational Behavior and Human Decision Processes*, 53, pp. 95–106.

Shapiro, S. and Spence, M.T. (1997) 'Managerial intuition: A conceptual and operational framework', *Business Horizons*, 40(1), pp. 63–68.

Shirley, D.A. and Langan-Fox, J. (1996) 'Intuition: A review of the literature', *Psychological Reports*, 79, pp. 563–584.

Simon, H.A. (1957) *Models of Man*, New York: Wiley.

Simon, H.A. (1969) *The Sciences of the Artificial*, Cambridge, MA: MIT Press.

Simon, H.A. (1972) 'Theories of Bounded Rationality', in: C. McGuire and R. Radner (eds) *Decision and Organization*, Amsterdam: North-Holland Publishing Company, pp. 161–176.

Simon, H.A. (1987) 'Making Management Decisions: The Role of Intuition and Emotion', *Academy of Management Executive*, 1(1), pp. 57–64.

Simon, H.A. (1992) 'What is an "explanation" of behavior?', *Psychological Science*, 3, pp. 150–161.

Simon, H.A. (1993) 'Altruism and economics', *American Economic Review*, 83(2), pp. 156–161.

Simon, H.A. (1996) *The sciences of the artificial* (3rd edn), Cambridge, MA: MIT Press.

Simon, H.A. and Chase, W.G. (1973) 'Skill in chess', *American Scientist*, 61, pp. 394–403.

Sinclair, M., Ashkanasy, N.M., Chattopadhyay, P. and Boyle, M.V. (2002) 'Determinants of intuitive decision-making in management: The moderating role of affect', in: N.M. Ashkanasy, W. Zerbe and C.E.J. Härtel (eds) *Managing emotions in the workplace*, Armonk, NY: M. E. Sharpe, pp. 143–163.

Sivanathan, N., Molden, D.C., Galinsky, A.D. and Ku, G. (2008) 'The promise and peril of self-affirmation in de-escalation of commitment', *Organizational Behavior and Human Decision Processes*, 107(1), pp. 1–14.

Sloman, S.A. (1996) 'The empirical case for two systems of reasoning', *Psychological Bulletin*, 119, 3–22.

Slovic, P., Finucane, M.L., Peters, E. and MacGregor, D.G. (2004) 'Risk as analysis and risk as feelings: some thoughts about affect, reason, risk, and rationality', *Risk Analysis*, 24(2), pp. 311–322.

Smircich, L. and Stubbart, C. (1985) 'Strategic Management in an Enacted World', *Academy of Management Review*, 10(4), pp. 724–736.

Sorrell, M., Komisar, R. and Mulcahy, A. (2010) 'How we do it: three executives reflect on strategic decision making', *McKinsey Quarterly*, 2, pp. 46–57.

Stadler, M.A. and Frensch, P.A. (1998) *Handbook of implicit learning*, Thousand Oaks, CA: Sage.

Stanovich, K.E. and West, R.F. (2000) 'Individual differences in reasoning: Implications for the rationality debate?', *Behavioral and Brain Sciences*, 23, pp. 645–665.

Starbuck, W. and Milliken, F. (1988) 'Challenger: Fine-Tuning the Odds Until Something Breaks', *Journal of Management Studies*, 25(4, July), 319–340.

Staw, B.M. (1976) 'Knee-deep in the big muddy: a study of escalating commitment to a chosen course of action', *Organizational Behavior and Human Performance*, 16(1), pp. 27–44.

Staw, B.M. and Ross, J. (1987) 'Behavior in escalation situations: antecedents, prototypes, and solutions', *Research in Organizational Behavior*, 9, pp. 39–78.

Staw, B.M., Sandelands, L.E. and Dutton, J.E. (1981) 'Threat rigidity effects in organizational behavior: A multilevel analysis', *Administrative Science Quarterly*, 26, pp. 501–524.

Sternberg, R.J. and Davidson, J.E. (1995) *The nature of insight*, Cambridge, MA: MIT Press.

Suri, R. and Monroe, K.B. (2003) 'The effects of time constraints on consumers' judgments of prices and products', *Journal of Consumer Research*, 30, pp. 92–104.

Sutcliffe, K.M. and Huber, G.P. (1998) 'Firm and Industry Determinants of Executive Perceptions of the Environment', *Strategic Management Journal*, 19, pp. 793–807.

Taylor, F.W. (1911) *Principles of Scientific Management*, New York, London: Harper and Brothers.

Teece, D.J. (1977) 'Technology transfer by multinational enterprises: the resource cost of transferring technological know-how', *Economic Journal*, 87(June), pp. 242–261.

Teece, D.J. (1980) 'Economies of scope and the scope of the enterprise', *Journal of Economic Behavior and Organization*, 1(3), pp. 223–247.

Teece, D.J. (1981) 'Internal organization and economic performance: an empirical analysis of the profitability of principal enterprises', *Journal of Industrial Economics*, 30(2), pp. 173–199.

Teece, D.J. (1986) 'Profiting from technological innovation', *Research Policy*, 15(6), pp. 285–305.

Teece, D.J. (2000) *Managing Intellectual Capital: Organizational, Strategic, and Policy Dimensions*, Oxford: Oxford University Press.

Teece, D.J. (2003) 'Expert talent and the design of (professional services) enterprises', *Industrial and Corporate Change*, 12(4), pp. 895–916.

Teece, D.J. (2007) 'Explicating dynamic capabilities: the nature and microfoundations of (sustainable) enterprise performance', *Strategic Management Journal*, 28(13), pp. 1319–1350.

Teece, D.J. and Pisano, G. (1994) 'The dynamic capabilities of enterprises: an introduction', *Industrial and Corporate Change*, 3(3), pp. 537–556.

Teece, D.J., Pisano, G. and Shuen, A. (1997) 'Dynamic capabilities and strategic management', *Strategic Management Journal*, 18(7), pp. 509–533.

Teece, D.J., Pisano, G. and Shuen, A. (1990a) 'Enterprise capabilities, resources and the concept of strategy'. Consortium on Competitiveness and Cooperation, Working paper CCC 90-8, Institute of Management, Innovation and Organization, University of California, Berkeley, CA.

Teece, D.J., Pisano, G. and Shuen, A. (1990b) 'Firm capabilities, resources and the concept of strategy', *Economic Analysis and Policy Working Paper EAP-38*, Institute of Management, Innovation and Organization, University of California, Berkeley, CA.

Tiedens, L. and Linton, S. (2001) 'Judgment under emotional certainty and uncertainty: The effects of specific emotions on information processing', *Journal of Personality and Social Psychology*, 81, pp. 1–16.

Trice, H.M. and Beyer, J.M. (1993) *The Cultures of Work Organizations*, Englewood Cliffs, NJ: Prentice Hall.

Tripsas, M. and Gavetti, G. (2000) 'Capabilities, cognition, and inertia: evidence from digital imaging', *Strategic Management Journal*, 21(10/11), pp. 1147–1161.

Tushman, M. and Anderson, P. (1986) 'Technological discontinuities and organizational environments', *Administration Science Quarterly*, 31, pp. 439–465.

Tversky, A. and Kahneman, D. (1974) 'Judgment under uncertainty: Heuristics and biases', *Science*, 185, pp. 1124–1131.

Tversky, A. and Kahneman, D. (1983) 'Extensional versus intuitive reasoning: The conjunction fallacy in probability judgment', *Psychological Review*, 90, pp. 293–315.

Tversky, A. and Kahneman, D. (1986) 'Rational Choice and the Framing of Decisions', *Journal of Business*, 59(4), pp. 251–278.

Vaughan, F.E. (1979) *Awakening intuition*, New York: Doubleday.

Von Winterfeldt, D. and Edwards, W. (1986) *Decision Analysis and Behavioural Research*, Cambridge: Cambridge University Press.

Walsh, J. (1995) 'Managerial and Organizational Cognition: Notes from a Trip Down Memory Lane', *Organization Science*, 6, pp. 280–321.

Weick, K. (1995) *Sensemaking in organizations*, Thousand Oaks, CA: Sage.

Weick, K.E. (1979) *The Social Psychology of Organizing*, New York: Random House.

Weick, K.E. and Bourgnon, M.G. (1986) 'Organizations as Cognitive Maps', in: H.P. Sims Jr. and D.A. Gioia (eds) *The Thinking Organization*, San Francisco, CA: Jossey-Bass.

Weiss, H.M. and Cropanzano, R. (1996) 'Affective events theory: A theoretical discussion of the structure, causes and consequences of affective experiences at work', *Research in Organizational Behavior*, 18, pp. 1–74.

Welch, J. and Byrne, J.A. (2001) *Jack: Straight from the Gut*, New York: Warner Books.

Wernerfelt, B. (1984) 'A resource-based view of the firm', *Strategic Management Journal*, 5(2), pp. 171–180.

Westcott, M.R. and Ranzoni, J.H. (1963) 'Correlates of intuitive thinking', *Psychological Reports*, 12, pp. 595–613.

Wild, K.W. (1938) *Intuition*, Cambridge: Cambridge University Press.

Williamson, O.E. (1975) *Markets and Hierarchies*, New York: Free Press.

Wilson, T.D. and Schooler, J.W. (1991) 'Thinking too much: Introspection can reduce the quality of preferences and decisions', *Journal of Personality and Social Psychology*, 60, pp. 181–192.

Wonder, J. and Blake, J. (1992) 'Creativity East and West: Intuition vs. Logic', *Journal of Creative Behavior*, 26(3), 172–185.

Wong, K.F.E., Kwong, J.Y.Y. and Ng, C.K. (2008) 'When thinking rationally increases biases: the role of rational thinking style in escalation of commitment', *Applied Psychology: An International Review*, 57(2), pp. 246–271.

Wong, K.F.E., Yik, M. and Kwong, J.Y.Y. (2006) 'Understanding the emotional aspects of escalation of commitment: the role of negative affect', *Journal of Applied Psychology*, 91(2), pp. 282–297.

Woolhouse, L.S. and Bayne, R. (2000) 'Personality and the use of intuition: Individual differences in strategy and performance on an implicit learning task', *European Journal of Personality*, 14, pp. 157–169.

Wright, G. and Goodwin, P. (2002) 'Eliminating a framing bias by using simple instructions to "think harder" and respondents with managerial experience: comment on "breaking the frame"', *Strategic Management Journal*, 23(11), pp. 1059–1067.

Zajonc, R.B. (1980) 'Preferences need no inferences', *American Psychologist*, 35, pp. 151–175.

Zhang, L.Q. and Baumeister, R.F. (2006) 'Your money or your self-esteem: threatened egotism promotes costly entrapment in losing endeavors', *Personality and Social Psychology Bulletin*, 32(7), pp. 881–893.

Zollo, M. and Winter, S.G. (2002) 'Deliberate learning and the evolution of dynamic capabilities', *Organization Science*, 13(3), pp. 339–351.

MISSIONING AND VISIONING

I prefer to be a dreamer among the humblest, with visions to be realized, than lord among those without dreams and desires.

Khalil Gibran (1886–1931); Lebanese-American artist, poet and writer

INTRODUCTION

Corporate mission is a rather elusive concept, often used to refer to the woolly platitudes on the first few pages of annual reports. To many people, mission statements are lists of lofty principles that have potential public relations value, but have little bearing on actual business, let alone impact on the process of strategy formation. Yet, while frequently employed in this superficial manner, a corporate mission can be very concrete and play an important role in determining strategic actions.

A good way to explain the term's meaning is to go back to its etymological roots. 'Mission' comes from the Latin word *mittere*, which means 'to send' (Cummings and Davies, 1994). A mission is some task, duty or purpose that 'sends someone on their way' – a motive or driver propelling someone in a certain direction. Hence, 'corporate mission' can be understood as the basic drivers sending the corporation along its way. The corporate mission consists of the fundamental principles that mobilize and propel the firm in a particular direction.

A concept that is often confused with mission is vision. Individuals or organizations have a vision if they picture a future state of affairs they wish to achieve (from the Latin *videre* – to see; Cummings and Davies, 1994). While the corporate mission outlines the fundamental principles guiding strategic choices, a strategic vision outlines the desired future at which the company hopes to arrive. In other words, vision provides a business ambition while mission provides business principles (see Figure 3.1).

Generally, a strategic vision is a type of aim that is less specific than a short-term target or longer-term objective. Vision is usually defined as a broad conception of a desirable future state, of which the details remain to be determined (e.g. Senge, 1990). As such, strategic vision can play a similar role to corporate mission, pointing the firm in a particular direction and motivating individuals to work together towards a shared end.

The corporate mission and strategic vision contribute to 'sending the firm in a particular direction' by influencing the firm's strategy. To understand how mission and vision impact strategy, three topics require closer attention. First, it is necessary to know what types of 'fundamental principles' actually make up a corporate mission. These elements of corporate mission will be described below. Second, it is important to distinguish between different envisioning processes to understand how the vision impacts strategy. Third, it needs to be examined what types of roles are played by a corporate mission and strategic vision in the strategy formation process. These functions of corporate mission and strategic vision will also be described (see Figure 3.2).

FIGURE 3.1   Corporate mission and strategic vision

FIGURE 3.2   Mission, vision and corporate governance

Besides the 'what' of corporate mission, it is equally important to explore the 'who' – who should determine a corporate mission. The implicit assumption is often that executives are the primary 'strategic actors' responsible for setting the direction of the firm. But in fact, their actions are formally monitored and controlled by the board of directors. In this way, the direction of the firm must be understood as a result of the interaction between the executives and the board of directors. As the name would imply, directors have an important influence on direction.

The activities of the board of directors are referred to as 'corporate governance' – directors govern the strategic choices and actions of the management of a firm. Due to their importance in setting the corporate mission and strategy, their input will be examined here as well. First, the various functions of corporate governance are reviewed. Then it will be examined what the different forms of corporate governance are, as this can significantly influence the mission, vision and strategy of the organization (see Figure 3.2).

Elements of a corporate mission

A corporate mission is the enduring set of fundamental principles that forms the base of a firm's identity and guides its strategic decision making. Four components can be distinguished (see Figure 3.3):

■ Organizational purpose. At the heart of the corporate mission is the purpose of an organization. Organizational purpose can be defined as the reason for which an organization exists. It can be expected that the perception managers have of their organization's purpose will give direction to the strategy process and influence the strategy content (e.g. Bartlett and Ghoshal, 1994; Campbell and Tawadey, 1990).

■ Organizational beliefs. All strategic choices ultimately include important assumptions about the nature of the environment and what the firm needs to do to be successful in its business. If people in a firm do not share the same fundamental strategic beliefs, joint decision making will be very protracted and tense – opportunities and threats will be interpreted differently and preferred solutions will be very divergent (see Chapter 2). To work swiftly and in unison, a common understanding is needed. The stronger the set of shared beliefs subscribed to by all organizational members, the easier communication and decision making will become, and the more confident and driven the group will be. While researchers refer to the organizational ideology ('system of ideas') as their 'collective cognitive map' (Axelrod, 1976), 'dominant logic' (Prahalad and Bettis, 1986) or 'team mental model' (Klimoski and Mohammed, 1994), companies themselves usually simply speak of their beliefs or philosophy.

■ Organizational values. Each person in an organization can have their own set of values, shaping what they believe to be good and just. Yet, when an organization's members share a common set of values, determining what they see as worthwhile activities, ethical behaviour and moral responsibilities, this can have a strong impact on the strategic direction (e.g. Falsey, 1989; Hoffman, 1989). Such widely embraced organizational

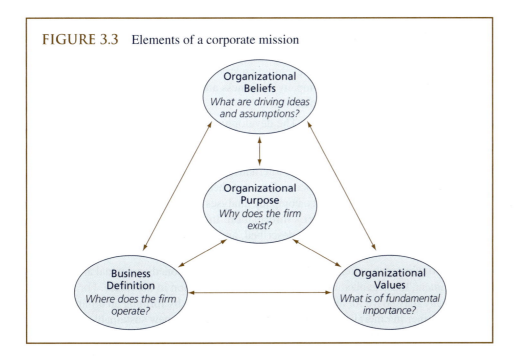

FIGURE 3.3   Elements of a corporate mission

values also contribute to a clear sense of organizational identity, attracting some individuals, while repelling others. Although it can be useful to explicitly state the values guiding the organization, to be influential they must become embodied in the organization's culture (e.g. Collins and Porras, 1996; McCoy, 1985).

■ **Business definitions.** For some firms, any business is good business, as long as they can make a reasonable return on investment. Yet, if any business is not fine, the firm will lack a sense of direction. In practice, most firms have a clearer identity, which they derive from being active in a particular line of business. For these firms, having a delimiting definition of the business they wish to be in strongly focuses the direction in which they develop. Their business definition functions as a guiding principle, helping to distinguish opportunities from diversions (e.g. Abell, 1980; Pearce, 1982). Of course, while a clear business definition can focus the organization's attention and efforts, it can likewise lead to short-sightedness and new business developments being missed (e.g. Ackoff, 1974; Levitt, 1960).

The strength of a corporate mission will depend on whether these four elements fit together and are mutually reinforcing (Campbell and Yeung, 1991). When a consistent and compelling corporate mission is formed, this can infuse the organization with a sense of mission, creating an emotional bond between organizational members and energizing them to work according to the mission.

Elements of a strategic vision

A strategic vision is the desired future state of an organization. Also termed 'strategic intent' (Hamel *et al.*, 1989) and 'envisioned future' (Collins and Porras, 1996), a strategic vision is built on four components (Figure 3.4):

■ **Envisioned contextual environment.** The many contextual factors that influence the future of the company can be roughly split into socio-cultural, economic, political/regulatory and technological factors. Although developments in the contextual environment cannot be predicted, some factors can be expected to change the company's business. For example, most companies expect an increasing economic importance of emerging countries, and believe that growing environmental awareness will lead to technological innovations. In developing a strategic vision, the contextual developments that are relevant to the company's business are described, and the future state of the contextual factors is envisioned.

■ **Envisioned industry environment.** The development of contextual factors impacts the company's industry environment: suppliers, buyers, incumbent rivals, new entrants, and substitutes and complementors. For example, competitors from emerging countries are expected to enter the industry, and alternative sources of energy are likely to replace fossil fuels in the production process. Some of these developments show up in statistics, strategic intelligence reports, company analyses and other sources of information, while others are based on insider's information. In developing a strategic vision, the relevant industry developments are described, and the future state of the industry environment is envisioned.

■ **Desired future organizational position.** Based on the envisioned contextual and industry environment, the organization describes its desired position in the future. For example, a company may strive for an industry leadership position by forming an alliance with a strong partner in emerging countries and by implementing new sustainable production technologies. The desired position reflects the company's ambitions, and is translated into long term objectives. In a strategic vision, the desired position of the company in the future is described, and the long-term objectives are formulated.

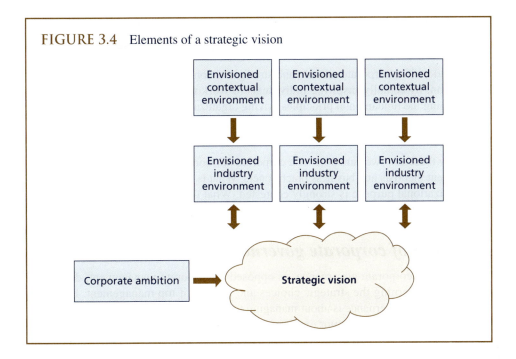

FIGURE 3.4   Elements of a strategic vision

- Time horizon. When developing a strategic vision, leaders must determine how many years ahead the future position will be envisioned. In fact, the time horizon of company visions differs significantly. For some companies 3 years is long term, while others develop visions of 30 years or longer. Many factors determine the time horizon of a company's strategic vision, including industry characteristics. For example, the upstream oil industry requires long-term thinking, as it takes dozens of years between the first exploratory drilling and oil production. Another factor is the cultural context of the company leaders (see the section 'Missioning and Visioning in International Perspective).

Functions of corporate mission and strategic vision

The corporate mission and strategic vision can be articulated by means of a mission statement and company vision, but in practice not everything that is called a mission statement and company vision meets the above criteria (e.g. Collins and Porras, 1996; David, 1989; Piercy and Morgan, 1994). Firms can, in fact, have a mission and a vision even if it has not been explicitly written down, although this does increase the chance of divergent interpretations within the organization.

In general, paying attention to the development of a consistent and compelling corporate mission and strategic vision can be valuable for three reasons. A corporate mission and strategic vision can provide:

- Direction. The corporate mission and strategic vision can point the organization in a certain direction, by defining the boundaries within which strategic choices and actions must take place. By specifying the fundamental principles on which strategies must be based, the corporate mission and strategy limit the scope of strategic options and set the organization on a particular heading (e.g. Bourgeois and Brodwin, 1983; Hax, 1990).
- Legitimization. The corporate mission and strategic vision can convey to all stakeholders inside and outside the company that the organization is pursuing valuable activities

in a proper way. By specifying the business philosophy that will guide the company, the chances can be increased that stakeholders will accept, support and trust the organization (e.g. Freeman and Gilbert, 1988; Klemm, Sanderson and Luffman, 1991).

■ Motivation. The corporate mission and strategic vision can go a step further than legitimization, by actually inspiring individuals to work together in a particular way. By specifying the fundamental principles driving organizational actions, an *esprit de corps* can evolve, with the powerful capacity to motivate people over a prolonged period of time (e.g. Campbell and Yeung, 1991; Peters and Waterman, 1982).

Especially these last two functions of a corporate mission and strategic vision divide both management theorists and business practitioners. What is seen as a legitimate and motivating organizational purpose is strongly contested. What the main factors of disagreement are is examined in a later section of this chapter.

Functions of corporate governance

The subject of corporate governance, as opposed to corporate management, deals with the issue of governing the strategic choices and actions of top management. Popularly stated, corporate governance is about managing top management – building in checks and balances to ensure that the senior executives pursue strategies that are in accordance with the corporate mission. Corporate governance encompasses all tasks and activities that are intended to supervise and steer the behaviour of top management.

In the common definition, corporate governance 'addresses the issues facing boards of directors' (Tricker, 1994: xi). In this view, corporate governance is the task of the directors and therefore attention must be paid to their roles and responsibilities (e.g. Cochran and Wartick, 1994; Keasey, Thompson and Wright, 1997). Others have argued that this definition is too narrow, and that in practice there are more forces that govern the activities of top management. In this broader view, boards of directors are only a part of the governance system. For instance, regulation by local and national authorities, as well as pressure from societal groups, can function as checks and balances, limiting top management's discretion (e.g. Demb and Neubauer, 1992; Mintzberg, 1984). Whether employing a narrow or broad definition, three important corporate governance functions can be distinguished (adapted from Tricker, 1994):

■ Forming function. The first function of corporate governance is to influence the forming of the corporate mission. The task of corporate governance is shaping, articulating and communicating the fundamental principles that will drive the organization's activities. Determining the purpose of the organization and setting priorities among claimants are part of the forming function. The board of directors can conduct this task by, for example, questioning the basis of strategic choices, influencing the business philosophy, and explicitly weighing the advantages and disadvantages of the firm's strategies for various constituents (e.g. Freeman and Reed, 1983, Reading 3.2).

■ Performance function. The second function of corporate governance is to contribute to the strategy process with the intention of improving the future performance of the corporation. The task of corporate governance is to judge strategy initiatives brought forward by top management or to actively participate in strategy development. The board of directors can conduct this task by, for example, engaging in strategy discussions, acting as a sounding board for top management and networking to secure the support of vital stakeholders (e.g. Baysinger and Hoskisson, 1990; Donaldson and Davis, 1995; Zahra and Pearce, 1989).

- Conformance function. The third function of corporate governance is to ensure corporate conformance to the stated mission and strategy. The task of corporate governance is to monitor whether the organization is undertaking activities as promised and whether performance is satisfactory. Where management is found lacking, it is a function of corporate governance to press for changes. The board of directors can conduct this task by, for example, auditing the activities of the corporation, questioning and supervising top management, determining remuneration and incentive packages, and even appointing new managers (e.g. Parkinson, 1993; Spencer, 1983).

These functions give the board of directors considerable influence in determining and realizing the corporate mission. As such, they have the ultimate power to decide on the organizational purpose. Therefore, it is not surprising that the question to whom these functions should be given is considered extremely important.

Forms of corporate governance

There is considerable disagreement on how boards of directors should be organized and run. Currently, each country has its own system of corporate governance and the international differences are large. Yet even within many countries, significant disagreements are discernible. In designing a corporate governance regime, three characteristics of boards of directors are of particular importance (adapted from Tricker, 1994):

- Board structure. Internationally, there are major differences between countries requiring a two-tier board structure (e.g. Austria, China, Germany, the Netherlands and Finland), countries with a one-tier board (e.g. Britain, Canada, Finland, Greece, India, Singapore, Spain, Sweden, Turkey, United States), and countries in which companies are free to choose (e.g. Czech Republic, Denmark, Italy, Japan, France, Slovenia and Switzerland). In a two-tier system there is a formal division of power, with a management board made up of the top executives and a distinct supervisory board made up of non-executives with the task of monitoring and steering the management board. In a one-tier (or unitary) board system, executive and non-executive (outside) directors sit together on one board (see Figure 3.5).

- Board membership. The composition of boards of directors can vary sharply from company to company and from country to country. Some differences are due to legal

FIGURE 3.5   Two- vs one-tier board structure

requirements that are not the same internationally. For instance, in Germany by law half of the membership of a supervisory board must represent labour, while the other half represents the shareholders. In French companies labour represent-atives are given observer status on the board. In China, most of the supervisory board members occupy positions in the Chinese Communist Party. In other coun-tries there are no legal imperatives, yet differences have emerged. In some cases outside (non-executive) directors from other companies are common, while in other nations fewer outsiders are involved. Even within countries, differences can be sig-nificant, especially with regard to the number, stature and independence of outside (non-executive) directors.

■   Board tasks. The tasks and authority of boards of directors also differ quite significantly between companies. In some cases boards meet infrequently and are merely asked to vote on proposals. Such boards have little formal or informal power to contradict the will of the CEO. In other companies, boards meet regularly and play a more active role in corporate governance, by formulating proposals, proactively selecting new top managers and determining objectives and incentives. Normally, the power of outside (non-executive) directors to monitor and steer a company only partly depends on their formally defined tasks and authority. To a large degree their impact is determined by how proactive they define their own role.

The question in the context of this chapter is how a board of directors should be run to ensure that the organization's mission is best achieved. What should be the structure, membership and tasks of the board of directors, to realize the ends for which the organi-zation exists?

THE ISSUE OF ORGANIZATIONAL PURPOSE

For many years there has been a lack of attention to the subject of organizational purpose in the strategic management literature. This might be due to the widespread assumption that it is obvious why business organizations exist. Some writers might have avoided the topic because it is highly value-laden and somehow outside the realm of strategic management. In recent years, however, the subject of organizational pur-pose has gained increased interest as a result of a number of developments, such as the financial crisis and the increased attention on corporate social responsibility and environmental sustainability.

Managers must constantly make choices and seek solutions based on an understand-ing of what their organization is intended to achieve. It is hardly possible to avoid taking a stance on what they judge to be the purpose of their organization. They are confronted with many different claimants who believe that the firm exists to serve their interests. Demands are placed on the firm by shareholders, employees, suppliers, customers, governments and communities, forcing managers to weigh whose interests should receive priority over others. Even when explicit demands are not voiced, man-agers must still determine who will be the main beneficiary of the value-creation activi-ties of the firm.

Determining the organizational purpose is a challenging task, not least because there are so many different views on how it should be done. In this chapter, the issue of organ-izational purpose will be explored in more detail, with the intention of uncovering the opposite perspectives on the subject of organizational purpose that lie at the heart of the divergent opinions.

THE PARADOX OF PROFITABILITY AND RESPONSIBILITY

The earth, the air, the land and the water are not an inheritance from our fore fathers, but on loan from our children. So we have to handover to them at least as it was handed over to us.

Mahatma Gandhi (1869–1948); Indian politician and lawyer

Discussions on what firms should strive to achieve are not limited to the field of strategy. Given the influential position of business organizations in society, the purpose they should serve is also discussed by theorists in the fields of economics, political science, sociology, ethics and philosophy. Since the industrial revolution and the rise of the modern corporation, the role of business organizations within the 'political economic order' has been a central theme in many of the social sciences. It has been the topic that has filled libraries of books, inspired society-changing theories and stirred deep-rooted controversies.

The enormous impact of corporations on the functioning of society has also attracted political parties, labour unions, community representatives, environmentalists, the media and the general public to the debate. All take a certain position on the role that business organizations should play within society and the duties that they ought to shoulder. Here, too, the disagreements can be heated, often spilling over from the political arena and negotiating tables into the streets.

In countries with a market economy, it is generally agreed that companies should pursue strategies that ensure economic profitability, but that they have certain social responsibilities that must be fulfilled as well. This is, however, where the consensus ends. Opinions differ sharply with regard to the relative importance of profitability and responsibility. Some people subscribe to the view that profitability is the very purpose of economic organizations and that the only social responsibility of a firm is to pursue profitability within the boundaries of the law. However, other people argue that business corporations are not only economic entities, but also social institutions, embedded in a social environment, which represents significant social responsibilities. In this view, organizations are morally obliged to behave responsibly towards society and all parties with a stake in the activities of the firm and profitability is only a means to fulfil this duty.

Most executives accept that both economic profitability and social responsibility are valuable goals to pursue. Yet, as organizational purpose, profitability and responsibility are at least partially contradictory. If managers strive towards profit maximization, shareholders might be enamoured, but this will bring executives into conflict with the optimization of benefits for other stakeholders. In other words, to a certain extent there is a tension between profitability and responsibility (e.g. Cannon, 1992; Demb and Neubauer, 1992; Drucker, 1984; Yoshimori, 1995).

The demand for economic profitability

It is clear that business organizations must be profitable to survive. Yet simple profitability, that is having higher income than costs, is not sufficient. To be an attractive investment, a company must earn a higher return on the shareholders' equity than could be realized if the money were deposited in the bank. Put differently, investors must have a financial incentive to run a commercial risk; otherwise they could just as well bring their money to the bank or buy low risk bonds.

Yet, offsetting the risk carried by investors is but a small part of the larger picture. Once a corporation has established a track record of profitability, this inspires trust among financiers. Such trust makes it much easier to raise new capital, either through borrowing (at more attractive rates) or by issuing new shares. And of course, new capital can be used to further the competitive objectives of the organization. Where companies have not been particularly profitable in the past and cannot authoritatively project an attractive level of profitability in the future, they will find it difficult or virtually impossible to find new financing. This can significantly weaken the position of the firm and undermine its long-term competitiveness.

For publicly traded corporations, strong profitability is usually reflected in higher share prices, which is not only beneficial to the shareholders at that moment, but also makes it easier to acquire other firms and to pay with shares. Moreover, a high share price is the best defence against a hostile takeover and the best negotiating chip for a friendly one. In both publicly and privately held companies, retained profits can also be an important source of funds for new investments.

In short, profitability is not only a *result*, but also a *source* of competitive power. Profitability provides a company with the financial leeway to improve its competitive position and pursue its ambitions.

The demand for societal responsibility

As economic entities engaging in formalized arrangements with employees, suppliers, buyers and government agencies, corporations have the legal responsibility to abide by the stipulations outlined in their contracts. Equally, they are bound to stay within the 'letter of the law' in each jurisdiction in which they operate. However, being good corporate citizens entails more than just staying out of court.

Companies are more than just 'economic machines' regulated by legal contracts. They are also networks of people, working together towards a common goal. And as members of a social group, people within a company need to develop a sense of 'community' if they are to function properly. One of the most basic needs is to build a level of trust among people – a feeling of security that each individual's interests will be taken into account. Trust evolves where people feel certain that others will behave in a responsible manner, instead of letting their own self-interest prevail without limitation. Once there is enough trust between people, they can engage in productive teamwork and invest in their mutual relationships.

Hence, societal responsibility – that is, acting in the interest of others, even when there is no legal imperative – lies at the basis of trust. Where there is trust, people are generally willing to commit themselves to the organization, both emotionally and practically. Emotionally, they will become involved with, and can become strongly connected to, the organization, which can lead to a sense of pride and loyalty. Practically, they will be willing to invest years acquiring firm-specific knowledge and skills, and in building a career. Such commitments make people dependent on the organization, as they will be less able and inclined to job-hop. It is therefore vital that the organization rewards such commitment by acting responsibly, even where this hurts profitability; otherwise the bond of trust can be seriously damaged.

Acting in the interest of all employees is a limited form of societal responsibility. Just as it is beneficial for trust to evolve within organizations, it is important for trust to develop between the organization and its broader environment of buyers, suppliers, governments, local communities and activist groups. Therefore, it is important that these organizations also come to trust that the organization is willing to act in a societally responsible way, even when this entails sacrificing profitability.

EXHIBIT 3.1   SHORT CASE

FONTERRA: CREAMING THE PROFITS IN DAIRY?

Fonterra is easily one of the world's top six dairy companies – quite an achievement for a firm based in the small, isolated country of New Zealand. An important part of its business is supplying bulk ingredients such as milk powder, butter and cheese to international markets. By 2013, it was the world's largest global processor and trader of milk products. It also owns valuable international brands including Anchor, Anlene and Anmum. Despite an industry downturn in 2014–2017, Fonterra's strategic position still looks attractive given that global dairy consumption is forecast to continue outstripping supply growth in India, Africa and much of Asia. On the other hand, size and prominence seldom come without controversy. Fonterra faces conflicting pressures on its strategy from the farmers who own the business and from other influential stakeholders.

Fonterra, in its present form, was founded in 2001 by a merger of the two largest farmer-owned cooperatives and the Dairy Board, which at that time held a statutory export monopoly. Since then, the dairy industry in New Zealand has continued to expand, growing production volumes from 13 billion litres of milk to 18 billion litres by 2016. This expansion has been possible because New Zealand's climate allows for a highly efficient model of milk production: the cattle graze almost exclusively on natural pasture, eliminating the expense and energy consumption of heated barns and food concentrate. As a result, milk production is not only cost efficient, but also generates lower carbon emissions than other production methods, even after accounting for shipping. The costs of producing a kilogram of milk solids in New Zealand have historically been lower than in almost any other country, although increased land prices and wider international adoption of industrial-scale dairying threaten this lowest-cost position.

In common with other dairy businesses around the world, Fonterra is a farmer-owned cooperative, with 10 700 owner–suppliers. The principle of the cooperative is that farmers own shares in proportion to the quantity of milk they supply. Fonterra's shares are not traded on any stock exchange, as non-suppliers cannot buy them, and the New Zealand government has no direct involvement with the business. The shares represent a significant financial commitment for the dairy farmers. Many of the farmers are actually highly indebted, due to the cost of land purchases and investment in irrigation, facilities and stock that many have made during the recent expansion. Indeed, to help them through lean times, in 2015 Fonterra offered its suppliers loans on favourable terms.

Fonterra's governance structure reflects its constitution as a cooperative. Not only do the farmers directly elect nine of the thirteen board members, but they also have further oversight of the board via the 35-member elected Shareholders' Council. The Shareholders' Council in turn appoints a Milk Commissioner to mediate in any disputes between Fonterra and individual shareholders. In practice, the farmers indeed have a strong influence on board behaviour. Given the trend towards fewer, larger dairy farms, this influence seems destined to increase.

Another important constraint on Fonterra's strategic freedom to manoeuvre is the reliance many of its shareholders have on dividend payments. This limits the firm's ability to fund growth and investment through retained earnings. When farmers increase the volumes of milk they supply to the cooperative, equity capital flows in and the business can use this capital to fund capacity expansion. However, this dependency on gaining supply volumes biases Fonterra's management towards processing bulk commodity products. In 2012, Fonterra's board introduced a revised capital structure that avoids redemption risk in the event that too many suppliers leave the industry or elect to supply a rival processor. Fonterra suppliers now trade Fonterra shares between them, and can sell economic rights to some of their shares to a separate fund that is open to outside investors. Farmers retain control of the business, as the outside investors do not have voting rights. However, even with the revised capital structure, the firm still has fewer options for raising capital than its larger multinational competitors.

A recurring strategic issue at Fonterra has been how, and what extent, to build businesses that add value beyond the efficient processing and trading of commodity dairy products. In 2016, its commodity-focused business generated over

▶

two-thirds of corporate revenue, despite initiatives to prioritize growth in higher-returning products. Although New Zealand's efficient dairy industry means that farmers can profit from the sale of commodities, volatile commodity prices and exchange rates undermine the value of this strategy. So too do trade barriers and farm subsidies in major markets such as the European Union and the United States.

Many of Fonterra's options to develop new sources of value creation draw on its processing and logistics expertise to manage international operations. This often involves partnership agreements with overseas suppliers and customers. The cooperative sources almost 20 per cent of its milk from outside New Zealand. From a shareholder's perspective, this can be problematic because it means that New Zealand farmers' capital helps finance ventures that, by some arguments, compete with their own milk production. The problem is compounded by the fact that many of the opportunities for Fonterra lie in fast-growing but less developed markets such as China and India. This in turn increases the risk involved in such ventures and requires more specialist skills at managing politically complex transnational relationships. Commentators have argued that the skills and preferences of Fonterra's farmer-dominated board are not closely aligned with managing multinational ventures. Furthermore, the higher levels of business risk sit uncomfortably with the financial position of many of Fonterra's owners.

One of Fonterra's international ventures was a joint venture agreement with the Sanlu dairy company in China. This arrangement came to an abrupt end in 2008 when Sanlu was struck by a milk contamination scandal that affected thousands of infants and led to the death of at least six. Because it held a 43 per cent equity stake in the business, Fonterra became embroiled in the scandal. It became clear that Fonterra's oversight of this business was weak at both board and operational levels to the extent that it either did not know about, or was unable to curtail, the contamination scandal for many months after it first came to the attention of Sanlu's management. When Sanlu went bankrupt, Fonterra had to write off over NZ$200 million of its investment in the venture. In response to these events, Fonterra took more control of its supply chain in China, including investing in several farms and managing them to its own standards. At the same time, dairy businesses in China sought the safety of New Zealand-sourced

milk. For example, Bright Dairy took a major stake in Synlait, a rival milk processor to Fonterra. This highlights the importance of New Zealand's reputation as a source of pure product: some commentators have questioned the wisdom of part-sourcing Fonterra-owned brands from elsewhere.

As well as dealing with pressures from shareholders, Fonterra must manage its relationship with other influential stakeholders. In lobbying for support, during boom times in 2012 it was not shy to point out that it contributed 26 per cent of New Zealand's export revenues. It also makes much of the economic spin-off effects of its activities, which extend beyond dairy farmers to communities, regions and cities. These spin-offs mean that the economic fortunes of the business have a major influence on those of New Zealand as a whole. However, power and importance at this level often do not engender popularity. Fonterra not only controls a very high proportion of the liquid milk supply to the domestic market, but also owns several of the major brands of cheese, butter and yoghurt. When the international commodity milk price is high, dairy prices rise for domestic consumers, which they tend to see as profiteering at their expense.

Another important area of stakeholder interest in Fonterra comes from the environmental impact of its activities. Many of these impacts come from dairy farming itself, and hence Fonterra does not directly control them, although stakeholders still consider them to be inextricably linked to Fonterra. Intensive dairying is both a major consumer of water for irrigation and potentially a polluter of water via runoff of effluent and nitrogen fertilizer. The pollution endangers local ecosystems and threatens to undermine the unusually pure municipal water supply enjoyed by domestic consumers. The high water consumption threatens these same water supplies due to over-extraction of this historically lightly-regulated resource. Fonterra has initiatives and targets to improve the industry's performance in these areas, but critics say these are still not enough. Even in 2014–2015, the industry acknowledged that almost 6 per cent of the country's dairy farms were in significant breach of standards for effluent runoff.

Perhaps the most crucial long-term stakeholder challenge for Fonterra and the dairy industry is its contribution to New Zealand's emissions of greenhouse gases. The problem arises principally from methane emissions, a by-product of cows' digestion. Methane is an especially potent greenhouse gas, such that in 2014, emissions of methane and nitrous oxide (largely from agriculture) made up 54 per cent of New Zealand's total greenhouse gas output. Because New Zealand has committed to the Kyoto Agreement, it must pay directly for above-quota emissions, triggering the government to consider the possibility that farmers should contribute to this expense.

Despite this apparently daunting set of challenges, Fonterra remains a successful, growing firm that is a leader in its industry. The decision Fonterra's board and management face if it is to sustain its performance is whether and to what degree to take into account the diverse set of stakeholder concerns. If it spends heavily to address these concerns, it risks compromising the immediate interests of its owners, hence losing their support. If it does too little, it risks undermining its operating environment (for example, by stimulating unfavourable

legislation), and hence compromising its owners' future interests. The board and management must deal with the latent conflict between competing shareholder interests. They have a delicate path to tread in resolving the tension between respecting the fundamental values perceived by many owners and keeping pace with a dynamic global industry. Quite a few issues to chew over.

Co-author: Paul Knott

Sources: www.fonterra.com; *Sunday Star Times*, September 26, 2008; *The New Zealand Farmers Weekly*, March 16, 2009; Ministry for the Environment (www.mfe.govt.nz), NZ's greenhouse gas inventory 1990–2014; Ministry of Foreign Affairs & Trade (www.mfat.govt.nz), Kyoto Protocol Part II; *New Zealand Herald*, April 14, 2013; *National Business Review*, June 10, 2013; Brook Asset Management News, October 26, 2012; Sustainable Dairying Water Accord Two Years On, (www.dairynz.co.nz).

PERSPECTIVES ON MISSIONING AND VISIONING

Perfection of means and confusion of goals seems, in my opinion, to characterize our age.

Albert Einstein (1879–1955); German-American physicist

Firms require a certain measure of economic profitability if they want to compete and survive, yet they also need to exhibit a certain amount of social responsibility if they are to retain the trust and support of key stakeholders. In itself, this creates a tension, as the two demands can be at odds with one another. Often, societally responsible behaviour costs money, which can only be partially recouped by the increased 'social dividend' it brings. But if profitability and responsibility are both seen as the ultimate purpose of business firms, the tension becomes even stronger; optimizing the one will be in conflict with maximizing the other. Emphasizing profitability means subjecting all investments to an economic rationale – societally responsible behaviour should only be undertaken if the net present value of such an investment is attractive or there is no legal way of avoiding compliance. Emphasizing responsibility means subjecting all activities to a moral or political rationale – asking who has a legitimate and pressing claim to be included as a beneficiary of the activities being undertaken – which can severely depress profitability.

Hence, it is not surprising to find that the paradox of profitability and responsibility strongly divides people across many walks of life; its relevance reaches far beyond business managers and management theorists. The main point of contention is whether firms should primarily be run for the financial benefit of the legal owners, or for the broader benefit of all parties with a significant interest in the joint endeavour. Should it be the purpose of firms to serve the interests of their shareholders or their stakeholders? Should profitability be emphasized because economic organizations belong to the providers of risk capital, or should responsibility be emphasized because organizations are joint ventures bringing together various resource providers by means of a social contract?

While there are many points of view on the 'right' organizational purpose in the strategy literature, here the two diametrically opposed positions will be identified and discussed. At the one pole are those who argue that corporations are established to serve the purposes of their owners. Generally, it is in the best interest of a corporation's shareholders to see the value of their stocks increase through the organization's pursuit of profitable business strategies. This point of view is commonly referred to as the 'shareholder value perspective'. At the other end of the spectrum are those who argue that corporations should be seen as joint ventures between shareholders, employees, banks, customers, suppliers, governments and the community. All of these parties hold a stake in the organization and therefore can expect that the corporation will undertake responsibility to develop business strategies that are in accordance with their interests and values. This point of view will be referred to as the 'stakeholder values perspective'.

The shareholder value perspective

To proponents of the shareholder value perspective it is obvious that companies belong to their owners and therefore should act in accordance with the interests of the owners. Corporations are instruments whose purpose it is to create economic value on behalf of those who invest risk-taking capital in the enterprise. This clear purpose should drive companies, regardless of whether they are privately or publicly held. According to Rappaport (1986, p. xiii): "the idea that business strategies should be judged by the economic value they create for shareholders is well accepted in the business community. After all, to suggest that companies be operated in the best interests of their owners is hardly controversial".

There is some disagreement between advocates of this perspective with regard to the best way of advancing the interests of the shareholders, particularly in publicly held companies. Many people taking this point of view argue that the well-being of the shareholders is served if the strategy of a company leads to higher share prices and/or higher dividends (e.g. Hart, 1995; Rappaport, 1986). Others are less certain of the stock markets' ability to correctly value long-term investments, such as R&D spending and capital expenditures. In their view, stock markets are excessively concerned with the short term and therefore share prices myopically overemphasize current results and heavily discount investments for the future. To avoid being pressured into short-termism, these people advocate that strategists must keep only one eye on share prices, while the other is focused on the long-term horizon (e.g. Charkham, 1994; Sykes, 1994).

According to supporters of the shareholder value perspective, one of the major challenges in large corporations is to actually get top management to pursue the shareholders' interests. Where ownership and managerial control over a company have become separated, it is often difficult to get the managers to work on behalf of the shareholders, instead of letting managers' self-interest prevail. This is known as the principal-agent problem (e.g. Eisenhardt, 1989; Jensen and Meckling, 1976) – the managers are agents, working to further the interests of their principals, the shareholders, but are tempted to serve their own interests, even when these are to the detriment of the principals. This has led to a widespread debate in the academic and business communities, especially in Britain and the United States, about the best form of corporate governance. The most important players in corporate governance are the outside, or non-executive, members on the board of directors. It is one of the tasks of these outsiders to check whether the executives are truly running the company in a way that maximizes the shareholders' wealth. For this reason, many proponents of the shareholder value perspective call for a majority of independent-minded outside directors on the board, preferably owning significant amounts of the company's stock themselves.

EXHIBIT 3.2   THE SHAREHOLDER VALUE PERSPECTIVE

MISSION STATEMENT DEAN FOODS

'The Company's primary objective is to maximize long-term stockholder value, while

adhering to the laws of the jurisdiction in which it operates and at all times observing the highest ethical standards.'

Dated: August, 2011

The emphasis placed on profitability as the fundamental purpose of firms does not mean that supporters of the shareholder value perspective are blind to the demands placed on firms by other stakeholders. On the contrary, most exponents of this view argue that it is in the interest of the shareholders to carry out a 'stakeholder analysis' and even to actively manage stakeholder relations. Knowing the force field of stakeholders constraining the freedom of the company is important information for the strategy process. It is never advisable to ignore important external claimants such as labour unions, environmental activists, bankers, governmental agencies and community groups. Few strategists would doubt that proactive engagement is preferable to 'corporate isolationism'. However, recognizing that it is expedient to pay attention to stakeholders does not mean that it is the corporation's purpose to serve them. If parties have a strong bargaining position, a firm might be forced into all types of concessions, sacrificing profitability. This has, however, little to do with any moral responsibility of the firm towards these other powers. The only duty of a company is to maximize shareholder value, within the boundaries of what is legally permissible.

The important conclusion is that in this perspective it might be in the interest of shareholders to treat stakeholders well, but that there is no moral obligation to do so. For instance, it might be a good move for a troubled company not to lay off workers if the resulting loyalty and morale improve the chances of recovery and profitability later on. In this case the decision not to fire workers is based on profit-motivated calculations, not on a sense of moral responsibility towards the employees. Generally, proponents of the shareholder value perspective argue that society is best served by this type of economic rationale. By pursuing enlightened self-interest and maintaining market-based relationships between the firm and all stakeholders, societal wealth will be maximized. Responsibility for employment, local communities, the environment, consumer welfare and social developments are not an organizational matter, but issues for individuals and governments (Friedman, 1970).

The stakeholder values perspective

Advocates of the stakeholder values perspective do not see why the supplier of one ingredient in an economic value-creation process has a stronger moral claim on the organization than the providers of other inputs. They challenge the assumption that individuals with an equity stake in a corporation have the right to demand that the entire organization works on their behalf. In the stakeholder values perspective, a company should not be seen as the instrument of shareholders, but as a coalition between various resource suppliers, with the intention of increasing their common wealth. An organization should be regarded as a joint venture in which the suppliers of equity, loans, labour, management, expertise, parts and service all participate to achieve economic success. As all groups hold a stake in the joint venture and are mutually dependent, it is argued that the purpose of the organization is to serve the interests of all parties involved (e.g. Berle and Means, 1932; Freeman and Reed, 1983, Reading 3.2).

According to endorsers of the stakeholder values perspective, shareholders have a legitimate interest in the firm's profitability. However, the emphasis shareholders place on stock price appreciation and dividends must be balanced against the legitimate demands of the other partners. These demands are not only financial, as in the case of the shareholders, but also qualitative, reflecting different values held by different groups (e.g. Clarke, 1998; Freeman, 1984). For instance, employees might place a high value on job security, occupational safety, holidays and working conditions, while a supplier of parts might prefer secure demand, joint innovation, shared risk-taking and prompt payment. Of course, balancing these interests is a challenging task, requiring an ongoing process of negotiation and compromise. The outcome will in part depend on the bargaining power of each stakeholder – how essential is its input to the economic success of the organization? However, the extent to which a stakeholder's interests are pursued will depend on the perceived legitimacy of their claim as well. For instance, employees usually have a strong moral claim because they are heavily dependent on the organization and have a relatively low mobility, while most shareholders have a spread portfolio and can 'exit the corporation with a phone call' (Stone, 1975).

In this view of organizational purpose, managers must recognize their responsibility towards all constituents (e.g. Alkhafaji, 1989; Clarkson, 1995). Maximizing shareholder value to the detriment of the other stakeholders would be unjust. Managers in the firm have a moral obligation to consider the interests and values of all joint venture partners. Managing stakeholder demands is not merely a pragmatic means of running a profitable business – serving stakeholders is an end in itself. These two interpretations of stakeholder management are often confused. Where it is primarily viewed as an approach or technique for dealing with the essential participants in the value-adding process, stakeholder management is *instrumental*. But if it is based on the fundamental notion that the organization's purpose is to serve the stakeholders, then stakeholder management is *normative* (e.g. Buono and Nichols, 1985; Donaldson and Preston, 1995).

Most proponents of the stakeholder values perspective argue that, ultimately, pursuing the joint interests of all stakeholders is not only more just, but also more effective for organizations (e.g. Jones, 1995; Solomon, 1992). Few stakeholders are filled with a sense of mission to go out and maximize shareholder value, especially if shareholders bear no responsibility for the other stakeholders' interests (e.g. Campbell and Yeung, 1991; Collins and Porras, 1994). It is difficult to work as a motivated team if it is the purpose of the organization to serve only one group's interests. Furthermore, without a stakeholder values perspective, there will be a deep-rooted lack of trust between all of the parties involved in the enterprise. Each stakeholder will assume that the others are motivated solely by self-interest and are tentatively cooperating in a calculative manner. All parties will perceive a constant risk that the others will use their power to gain a bigger slice of the pie, or even rid themselves of their 'partners'. The consequence is that all stakeholders will vigorously guard their own interests and will interact with one another as adversaries. To advocates of the stakeholder values perspective, this 'every person for themselves' model of organizations is clearly inferior to the partnership model in which sharing, trust and symbiosis are emphasized. Cooperation between stakeholders is much more effective than competition (note the link with the embedded organization perspective in Chapter 6).

Some exponents of the stakeholder values perspective argue that the narrow economic definition of stakeholders given above is too constrictive. In their view, the circle of stakeholders with a legitimate claim on the organization should be drawn more widely. Not only should the organization be responsible to the direct participants in the economic value-creation process (the 'primary stakeholders'), but also to all parties affected by the organization's activities. For example, an organization's behaviour might have an impact on local communities, governments, the environment and society in general, and therefore these groups have a stake in what the organization does as well. Most supporters of the stakeholder values perspective acknowledge that organizations have a moral responsibility towards these 'secondary stakeholders' (e.g. Carroll, 1993; Langtry, 1994). However, opinions differ whether it should actually be a part of business organizations' purpose to serve this broader body of constituents.

The implication of this view for corporate governance is that the board of directors should be able to judge whether the interests of all stakeholders are being justly balanced. This has led some advocates of the stakeholder values perspective to call for representatives of the most important stakeholder groups to be on the board (e.g. Guthrie and Turnbull, 1994). Others argue more narrowly for a stronger influence of employees on the choices made by organizations (e.g.Blair, 1995; Bucholz, 1986). Such co-determination of the corporation's strategy by management and workers can, for instance, be encouraged by establishing work councils (a type of organizational parliament or senate), as is mandatory for larger companies in most countries of the European Union. Yet others emphasize measures to strengthen corporate social responsibility in general. To improve corporate social performance, it is argued, companies should be encouraged to adopt internal policy processes that promote ethical behaviour and responsiveness to societal issues (e.g. Epstein, 1987; Wartick and Wood, 1998). Corporate responsibility should not be, to quote Ambrose Bierce's sarcastic definition, "a detachable burden easily shifted to the shoulders of God, Fate, Fortune, Luck, or one's neighbour".

EXHIBIT 3.3   THE STAKEHOLDER VALUES PERSPECTIVE

CREDO JOHNSON & JOHNSON

We believe our first responsibility is to the doctors, nurses and patients, to mothers and fathers and all others who use our products and services. In meeting their needs everything we do must be of high quality. We must constantly strive to reduce our costs in order to maintain reasonable prices. Customers' orders must be serviced promptly and accurately. Our suppliers and distributors must have an opportunity to make a fair profit.

We are responsible to our employees, the men and women who work with us throughout the world. Everyone must be considered as an individual. We must respect their dignity and recognize their merit. They must have a sense of security in their jobs. Compensation must be fair and adequate, and working conditions clean, orderly and safe. We must be mindful of ways to help our employees fulfil their family responsibilities. Employees must feel free to make suggestions and complaints. There must be equal opportunity for employment, development and advancement for those qualified. We must provide competent management, and their actions must be just and ethical.

We are responsible to the communities in which we live and work and to the world community as well. We must be good citizens – support good works and charities and bear our fair share of taxes. We must encourage civic improvements and better health and education. We must maintain in good order the property we are privileged to use, protecting the environment and natural resources.

Our final responsibility is to our stockholders. Business must make a sound profit. We must experiment with new ideas. Research must be carried on, innovative programmes developed and mistakes paid for. New equipment must be purchased, new facilities provided and new products launched. Reserves must be created to provide for adverse times. When we operate according to the principles, the stockholders should realize their fair return.

Source: Johnson & Johnson

MANAGING THE PARADOX OF PROFITABILITY AND RESPONSIBILITY

A business that makes nothing but money is a poor kind of business.

Henry Ford (1863–1947); American industrialist

So, what should be the purpose of a firm? And how should executives manage the tension between economic profitability and societal responsibility? Should managers strive to maximize shareholder value or stakeholder values? Or should executives search for a way that combines profitability and responsibility? The proponents of the shareholder value perspective are lobbying for more receptiveness to the interests of the shareholders on the part of the board, to increase top management accountability and to curb perceived executive self-enrichment at the expense of shareholders. The advocates of the stakeholder values perspective are vying for a system that would bring more receptiveness to the interests of stakeholders, to ensure that firms do not become more myopically bottom-line-oriented and short-term driven. While both sides do agree on one or two points (e.g. corporate governance is generally too weak), on the whole, the question remains of how to manage the paradox of profitability and responsibility.

Parallel processing

Managing shareholders involves different processes, departments and people from managing diverse societal stakeholders. Shareholders are managed by executive board members at shareholder conferences and other meetings with owners. In one-tier boards shareholders are also managed at board meetings – and vice versa of course. Production departments deal with environmentalists and – when outsourced to low wage countries – also with non-governmental organizations (NGOs), while finance departments are more in contact with tax authorities and other government representatives. As a consequence, shareholders and diverse stakeholders are managed in parallel – at different levels and organizational departments, by a variety of people. For example, an oil company may deal with environmental issues in a country unit's sustainability department and tax issues in another country, while shareholders are managed by the board.

TABLE 3.1   Shareholder value versus stakeholder values

	Shareholder value perspective	*Stakeholder values perspective*
Emphasis on	Profitability over responsibility	Responsibility over profitability
Organizations seen as	Instruments	Joint ventures
Organizational purpose	To serve owner	To serve all parties involved
Measure of success	Share price and dividends (shareholder value)	Satisfaction among stakeholders
Major difficulty	Getting agent to pursue principal's interests	Balancing interests of various stakeholders
Corporate governance through	Independent outside directors with shares	Stakeholder representation
Stakeholder management	Means	End
Social responsibility	Individual, not organizational matter	Both individual and organizational
Society best served by	Pursuing self-interest (economic efficiency)	Pursuing joint-interests (economic symbiosis)

Balancing

The finance function has always been prominently positioned in the corporate hierarchy of companies, usually at the board level, while diverse societal responsibilities have usually been managed at lower organizational levels. This status difference has had an effect on how societal responsibilities have been dealt with: as more of a tactical and financial issue that needs to be fixed than as a strategic tension that needs to be managed. Parallel processing has in this case been sufficient as the preferred means of managing the paradox.

However, this does not apply to all firms, while it can be argued that in recent years the need to manage the paradox of economic profitability and societal responsibility has increased in many industries. After the fall of Lehman Brothers in 2008, which marked the beginning of the credit crisis and an economic slowdown, the societal role of banks has been emphasized. The economic dependency on banks' systems has become better understood and then reduced, new regulations have been installed and governments have made system changes. Banks can no longer just strive for maximized shareholder value without significant protest from governments, regulators, societal stakeholders and clients. Also outside the banking sector, societal stakeholders have increased the pressure on companies to take responsibility for the consequences of their behaviour, such as producing in low wage countries in unsafe working conditions and – often indirectly – using child labour. Oil companies are facing increased pressure from environmental groups, NGOs and governments after a number of accidents and oil spills. The pressure of societal stakeholders on companies has grown further with the accelerated importance of social media and the use of smart phones. Stakeholders are informed better and quicker, and have more means at their disposal to pressure companies if they deem their conduct questionable.

As a result, the tension between economic profitability and societal responsibility has become more prominent and a strategic issue for company directors and sometimes corporate boards. Many companies have decided to not just react on incidents but to balance the opposing needs. Balancing has become a prime responsibility of the CEO, and in some cases a corporate sustainability officer has been appointed in order to be able to balance the tension at the directors' level or the board level.

Resolving the paradox

Balancing the paradox is finding a satisfying position in the trade-off between economic profitability and societal responsibility, resolving aims to combine both demands a higher level. For example, in 2011 the Dutch supermarket company and market leader in the Netherlands, Albert Heijn, announced a cooperative agreement with the World Wildlife Fund (WWF) with the objective of achieving full sustainability of its assortment of fish – wild caught and farmed. The agreement included packaging and worldwide production of all fish, including mussels, salmon and shrimps. After four years, 90 per cent of all Albert Heijn private label fish products have been certified by Aquaculture Stewardship Council (ASC) as environmentally responsible "with minimal negative effects on the environment and strict requirements for use of antibiotics, and respect for the local communities where they operate". Over the long term the supermarket giant has safeguarded sufficient supply of fish with the initiative and therefore its long term profitability, while in the immediate term societal stakeholders are managed.

Resolving the paradox of economic profitability and societal responsibility at a higher level has been named 'shared value' by the authors of Reading 3.3. 'Creating Shared Value', Michael Porter and Mark Kramer. They argue that "profits involving a social purpose represent a higher form of capitalism, one that creates a positive cycle of company and community prosperity", and they claim that the shared value concept moves business and society beyond trade-offs. In other words, the authors strive to resolve the paradox at a higher level to achieve a synthesis between firm profitability and societal responsibility.

MISSIONING AND VISIONING IN INTERNATIONAL PERSPECTIVE

Co-authors: Gep Eisenloeffel and Wester Wagenaar

Failure comes only when we forget our ideals and objectives and principles.
Jawaharlal Nehru (1889–1964); first prime minister of India

The debate on organizational purpose does not take place in a vacuum: institutional and cultural aspects define its context. Although a strategist can choose his or her own mission, an inclination towards following a shareholder or stakeholder perspective has little to do with individuals and more with how societies are structured. Companies have to deal with different institutional contexts in host countries while executing their mission, vision and organizational purpose. This becomes even more relevant in today's shifts in the economic power balance. It is clear that the former economic dominance of the traditional countries of *The Triad of Economic Power* (Ohmae, 1985) no longer applies and that the institutional context will vary further. As the world is not a level playing field, it is the organizational context which determines the bargaining power of the stakeholder and shareholders. It seems this situation will persist: present-day economic reality makes it unlikely that a best practice solution will be found or that globalization itself will lead to a convergence of perspectives on organizational purpose. It is therefore imperative to analyse similarities and differences in organizational purpose worldwide to better understand the international playing field.

On the societal level

When dealing with organizational purpose, institutional aspects play an import role. Porter pointed out in *The Competitive Advantage of Nations* (1990) that the sustainable competitive advantage of industries and individual companies is to a large extent based on the institutional framework within their countries – and regions – of origin. Institutional forms that have evolved over time in different national contexts have resulted in distinctive models of economic organization. This has not resulted in commonly agreed-upon categorizations however. Nevertheless, there are some conclusions to be drawn from the scholarly debate.

Albert (1993) concentrates on the differences of what he coined the Rhineland model in Germany compared with the Anglo-Saxon model of the US and (to a large extent) the UK. Peter Hall and David Soskice (2001) elaborate on this point. They stress the differences between what they call coordinated market economies (CMEs), most commonly associated with such countries as Germany, Sweden and Japan, and liberal market economies (LMEs) generally associated with the US and the UK. The main difference between the two can be found in coordination. In CMEs coordination is achieved through non-market means, investments in specific assets are preferred and banks play a prominent role. In LMEs, on the other hand, coordination follows market conditions with a preference for transferable assets (Amable, 2003; Cernat, 2004).

Many authors object to this strict dichotomy. Dicken (2015), for instance, identifies four variants of capitalism, based on differing perceptions on the proper role of the government: neo-liberal market capitalism (US, UK), social-market capitalism (Germany, Scandinavia, many other European countries), developmental capitalism (Japan, South Korea, Taiwan, India, Brazil) and authoritarian capitalism (China and Russia). Dicken shows how differences in coordination take various shapes: states operate as regulators, competitors and collaborators at the same time. In this way, states not only create the context for organizational purpose, they also fulfil the roles of shareholders and stakeholders. The more influential the state, the more active its role as shareholder and stakeholder is likely to be. Dicken's model is not the only alternative to the dichotomy of the Rhineland and the Anglo-Saxon model. Another way to categorize the diversity of systems in the world is posited by Amable. He argues for a different categorization of five types of capitalism: the market-based model (US, UK, Canada, Australia), the social-democratic model (Nordic countries), the Continental European model, the Mediterranean model and the Asian model (East Asia) (2003).

As Schneider and Barsoux (1999) point out, varieties of capitalism are not only defined by the role of governments and legislation. Media, stakeholders' and shareholders' behaviour also play an important role in shaping the context of organizational purpose. For example, concerns over ethics may be due to more aggressive journalism (or, as in the case of the US, libel suits), 'best company' rankings or greater risk of shareholder activism and consumer boycotts. Institutions are also shaped by informal rules and common knowledge acquired through history, in other words by culture.

When it comes to the influences on varieties of capitalism and organizational purpose, culture is not per se the most influential, but it is often the most neglected (Schneider and Barsoux, 1999). Nevertheless, there is a wealth of research findings (Adler and Gundersen, 2007; Hampden-Turner and Trompenaars, 2000; Hofstede, 1980; Schein, 2004; Verluyten, 2010) highlighting how cultural dimensions play an important role not in just who is responsible for formulating organizational purpose and on what grounds accountability is conducted, but on how and for whom the purpose of a company is defined. Hampden-Turner and Trompenaars (2000), for instance, show how in the United States, with its emphasis on individualism and achievement, ethical decisions are considered personal. Likewise moral judgements require individual responsibility and accountability. Universalism is an important by-product of individualism and is deeply rooted in US cultural history (Hampden-Turner and Trompenaars, 2000; Verluyten, 2010). Ethical standards in the US are considered to apply to everyone in the same way. This results in the US legalistic approach to ethics affecting organizational purpose. In more collectivist societies, however, ethical standards are applied either according to specific circumstances, strongly influenced by the nature of one's social status (ascription) as in Brazil, or to social ties (in-group versus out-group) as in China or Japan.

Traditionally, many Western business schools have preached profit maximization as the ultimate goal. This notion reflects underlying cultural assumptions like task orientation (as opposed to relationship orientation) and individualism (contrary to collectivism) (Hampden-Turner and Trompenaars, 2000). Organizations are seen as instrumental and managers as rational economic actors, driven primarily by self-interest. To contrast this approach with defining organizational purpose more to promote the well-being of society and organizations as a system of relationships, consider excerpts from the mission statement of Konosuke Matsushita, founder of Matsushita: "Profit comes in compensation for contributing to society". Matsushita did not just want to contribute to society – the end result called for nothing less than the eradication of poverty from the face of the earth (Holden, 2002).

On the industry level

Some industries are expected to have an inclination towards either the stakeholder's or shareholder's perspective on the global playing field. Regardless of where a company operates, when it comes to the financial sector, a preference towards focusing on meeting the demands of shareholders can be expected. On the other hand, when it comes to service industries, with the health care and education sectors in particular, the demand for adopting a stakeholder perspective is naturally higher. Nonetheless, the global pharmaceutical industry has largely shifted from the belief that improving the lives of patients will naturally lead to generating profits to a state in which companies prioritize satisfying the demands of shareholders (Kessel, 2014).

To the strategist

The institutional and cultural framework is an important context variable in defining company norms and values. Should a strategist impose parent company or home country norms and values in a host country environment, or should local customs, rules and regulations be adopted? On the one hand, corporate and head office efforts to insist on universal ethical principles in foreign subsidiaries are often questioned and considered as cultural imperialism or outright self-righteousness. On the other hand, however, adapting to local rules with a 'When in Rome do as the Romans' approach and presenting the company as a national champion, leads to inconsistently practicing corporate norms and values, and tensions with external stakeholders. For example, if company standards are not in line with international rules of conduct, NGOs and home country customers are likely to protest. In the words of Cor Herkströter, CEO of Shell in the mid-1990s, "stakeholders hold the *license to operate* a company".

Furthermore, the homogeneity of regulations and cultural norms within nations and of the acclaimed uniformity of organizational purpose can also be questioned (Coe, Kelly and Yeung, 2012). The regulatory and cultural framework often differs from one region to the next and even within regions. In the end this would mean that the proper unit of analysis is the firm with its specific circumstances.

INTRODUCTION TO THE READINGS

As in the previous chapter, the first two readings represent the two perspectives (see Table 3.1) to gain a sharper understanding of the breadth of opinions on this topic, while the third reading aims at bridging the two perspectives. The first reading, representing the shareholder value perspective, is from the 1976 Nobel Prize in Economic Sciences winner Milton Friedman. The title of his 1970 *The New York Times Magazine* article, 'The Social Responsibility of Business is to Increase its Profits', summarizes well the stance of the shareholder value perspective proponents in the debate. Friedman argues that "there is one, and only one, social responsibility of business – to use its resources and engage in activities designed to increase its profits so long as it stays within the rules of the game, which is to say, engages in open and free competition without deception or fraud." In the article, Friedman responds – often in sharp wordings – to a number of critics of his 1962 highly influential book *Capitalism and Freedom*. A main argument in the book is that economic freedom is both necessary and a vital means for political freedom, and that business should not be socially responsible. He argues that "if there are social responsibilities, they are the social responsibilities of individuals, not of business". The underlying view on the purpose of a business organization is that the primary purpose of corporations should be to maximize shareholder value.

The second reading (Reading 3.2) – representing the stakeholder values perspective – is also a classic – 'Stockholders and Stakeholders: A New Perspective on Corporate Governance', by Edward Freeman and David Reed. This article in *California Management Review* and Freeman's subsequent book *Strategic Management: A Stakeholder Approach* were instrumental in popularizing the stakeholder concept. In their article, Freeman and Reed challenge "the view that stockholders have a privileged place in the business enterprise". They deplore the fact that "it has long been gospel that corporations have obligations to stockholders … that are sacrosanct and inviolable". They argue that there has been a long tradition of management thinkers who believe that corporations have a broader responsibility towards stakeholders other than just the suppliers of equity financing. It is their conviction that such a definition of the corporation, as a system serving the interests of multiple stakeholders, is superior to the shareholder perspective. Their strong preference for the stakeholder concept is largely based on the pragmatic argument that, in reality, stakeholders have the power to seriously affect the continuity of the corporation. Stakeholder analysis is needed to understand the actual claims placed by constituents on the firm and to evaluate each stakeholder's power position. Stakeholder management is a practical response to the fact that corporations cannot afford to ignore or downplay the interests of the claimants. Only scarcely do Freeman and Reed hint that corporations have the moral responsibility to work on behalf of all stakeholders (which Freeman does more explicitly in some of his later works, e.g. Freeman and Gilbert, 1988; Freeman and Liedtka, 1991). In their opinion, the consequence of the stakeholder concept for corporate governance is that "there are times when stakeholders must participate in the decision-making process". However, they believe that if boards of directors adopt a stakeholder outlook and become more responsive to the demands placed on corporations, structural reforms to give stakeholders a stronger role in corporate governance will not be necessary.

So, how can strategists deal with the paradox of profitability and responsibility? While several elements of societal responsibility, such as social and environmental responsibility, have been widely discussed in academia for many years, only recently the strategy field has picked up the issue. The field was pioneered by John Elkington, with a number of publications starting in 1980. With Tom Burke, he published in 1987 *The Green Capitalists: Industry's search for environmental excellence*, in which he blended the emerging green agenda with that of business – a revolutionary idea in these years. His most influential book came in 1997: *Cannibals with Forks: The Triple Bottom Line of 21st Century Business*. In this book, Elkington asked the question whether capitalism itself was sustainable, and he introduced the concept of Triple Bottom Line – a term he had coined in 1984. Another early work in this vein is Jed Emerson's *California Management Review* article 'The Blended Value Proposition: Integrating Social and Financial Returns' (2003). He introduced the concept 'blended value', in which firms seek simultaneously to pursue profit and social and environmental objectives. 'The turning point in the debate about the emerging role and responsibility of business in society is Stuart Hart's book *Capitalism at the Crossroads* (2005)', wrote the late C.K. Prahalad, with whom Hart published his 2002 article 'The Fortune at the Bottom of the Pyramid'. Hart's book stimulated many scholars in the strategy field to reconsider the concepts of value and capitalism.

Yet, it was Michael Porter who guided the issue into the mainstream strategy field. Together with Mark Kramer, he published the 2011 *Harvard Business Review* article 'Creating Shared Value: How to reinvent capitalism and unleash a wave of innovation and growth' (Reading 3.3). The article has become highly influential in the strategy field, the corporate world and public management. The authors of this article argue that profits involving a social purpose represent a higher form of capitalism, one that creates a positive cycle of company and community prosperity. Consequently, the purpose of the organization must be redefined as shared value, not just the old-fashioned capitalists' purpose of profit. Shared value is defined as "policies and operating practices that enhance the competitiveness of a company while simultaneously advancing the economic and social conditions in the communities in which it operates". Shared value creating focuses on "identifying and expanding the connections between societal and economic progress". Porter and Kramer claim to reinvent capitalism by combining economic profitability and societal responsibility, which will drive the next wave of innovation and productivity growth in the global economy. Re-invented capitalism consists of three elements. The first element is the need to create market ecosystems, especially when selling to the poorest in developing countries. This may require firms to make partnerships with NGOs and governments. The second element is expanding their value chains to include such unconventional partners. And the third element is creating new industrial clusters.

It must be noted that the authors had explored the idea of shared value five years earlier in a 2006 *Harvard Business Review* article, 'Strategy and Society: The Link Between Competitive Advantage and Corporate Social Responsibility'. When considering the timing of both articles and their relative success, it may be argued that the idea behind shared value was in need of a good crisis.

READING 3.1

The social responsibility of business is to increase its profits

By Milton Friedman[1]

When I hear businessmen speak eloquently about the "social responsibilities of business in a free-enterprise system," I am reminded of the wonderful line about the Frenchman who discovered at the age of 70 that he had been speaking prose all his life. The businessmen believe that they are defending free enterprise when they declaim that business is not concerned "merely" with profit but also with promoting desirable "social" ends; that business has a "social conscience" and takes seriously its responsibilities for providing employment, eliminating discrimination, avoiding pollution and whatever else may be the catchwords of the contemporary crop of reformers. In fact they are – or would be if they or anyone else took them seriously – preaching pure and unadulterated socialism. Businessmen who talk this way are unwitting puppets of the intellectual forces that have been undermining the basis of a free society these past decades.

The discussions of the "social responsibilities of business" are notable for their analytical looseness and lack of rigour. What does it mean to say that "business" has responsibilities? Only people can have responsibilities. A corporation is an artificial person and in this sense may have artificial responsibilities, but "business" as a whole cannot be said to have responsibilities, even in this vague sense. The first step toward clarity in examining the doctrine of the social responsibility of business is to ask precisely what it implies for whom.

Presumably, the individuals who are to be responsible are businessmen, which means individual proprietors or corporate executives. Most of the discussion of social responsibility is directed at corporations, so in what follows I shall mostly neglect the individual proprietors and speak of corporate executives.

In a free-enterprise, private-property system, a corporate executive is an employee of the owners of the business. He has direct responsibility to his employers. That responsibility is to conduct the business in accordance with their desires, which generally will be to make as much money as possible while conforming to the basic rules of the society, both those embodied in law and those embodied in ethical custom. Of course, in some cases his employers may have a different objective. A group of persons might establish a corporation for an eleemosynary purpose – for example, a hospital or a school. The manager of such a corporation will not have money profit as his objective but the rendering of certain services.

In either case, the key point is that, in his capacity as a corporate executive, the manager is the agent of the individuals who own the corporation or establish the eleemosynary institution, and his primary responsibility is to them.

Needless to say, this does not mean that it is easy to judge how well he is performing his task. But at least the criterion of performance is straightforward, and the persons among whom a voluntary contractual arrangement exists are clearly defined.

Of course, the corporate executive is also a person in his own right. As a person, he may have many other responsibilities that he recognizes or assumes voluntarily – to his family, his conscience, his feelings of charity, his church, his clubs, his city, his country. He may feel impelled by these responsibilities to devote part of his income to causes he regards as worthy, to refuse to work for particular corporations, even to leave his job, for example, to join his country's armed forces. If we wish, we may refer to some of these responsibilities as "social responsibilities." But in these respects he is acting as a principal, not an agent; he is spending his own money or time or energy, not the money of his employers or the time or energy he has contracted to devote to their purposes. If these are "social responsibilities," they are the social responsibilities of individuals, not of business.

What does it mean to say that the corporate executive has a "social responsibility" in his capacity as businessman? If this statement is not pure rhetoric, it must mean that he is to act in some way that is not in the interest of his employers. For example, that he is to refrain from increasing the price of the product in order to contribute to the social objective of preventing inflation, even though a price increase would be in the best interests of the corporation. Or that he is to make expenditures on reducing pollution beyond the amount that is in the best interests of the corporation or that is required by law in order to contribute to the social objective of improving the environment. Or that, at the expense of corporate profits, he is to hire "hardcore" unemployed instead of better qualified available workmen to contribute to the social objective of reducing poverty.

In each of these cases, the corporate executive would be spending someone else's money for a general social interest. Insofar as his actions in accord with his "social responsibility" reduce returns to stockholders, he is spending their money. Insofar as his actions raise the price to customers, he is spending the customers' money. Insofar as his actions lower the wages of some employees, he is spending their money.

The stockholders or the customers or the employees could separately spend their own money on the particular action if they wished to do so. The executive is exercising a distinct "social responsibility," rather than serving as an agent of the stockholders or the customers or the employees, only if he spends the money in a different way than they would have spent it.

But if he does this, he is in effect imposing taxes, on the one hand, and deciding how the tax proceeds shall be spent, on the other.

This process raises political questions on two levels: principle and consequences. On the level of political principle, the imposition of taxes and the expenditure of tax proceeds are governmental functions. We have established elaborate constitutional, parliamentary and judicial provisions to control these functions, to assure that taxes are imposed so far as possible in accordance with the preferences and desires of the public – after all, "taxation without representation" was one of the battle cries of the American Revolution. We have a system of checks and balances to separate the legislative function of imposing taxes and enacting expenditures from the executive function of collecting taxes and administering expenditure programmes and from the judicial function of mediating disputes and interpreting the law.

Here the businessman – self-selected or appointed directly or indirectly by stockholders – is to be simultaneously legislator, executive and jurist. He is to decide whom to tax, by how much and for what purpose, and he is to spend the proceeds – all this guided only by general exhortations from on high to restrain inflation, improve the environment, fight poverty and so on and on.

The whole justification for permitting the corporate executive to be selected by the stockholders is that the executive is an agent serving the interests of his principal. This justification disappears when the corporate executive imposes taxes and spends the proceeds for "social" purposes. He becomes in effect a public employee, a civil servant, even though he remains in name an employee of a private enterprise. On grounds of political principle, it is intolerable that such civil servants – insofar as their actions in the name of social responsibility are real and not just window-dressing – should be selected as they are now. If they are to be civil servants, then they must be elected through a political process. If they are to impose taxes and make expenditures to foster "social" objectives, then political machinery must be set up to make the assessment of taxes and to determine through a political process the objectives to be served.

This is the basic reason why the doctrine of "social responsibility" involves the acceptance of the socialist view that political mechanisms, not market mechanisms, are the appropriate way to determine the allocation of scarce resources to alternative uses.

On the grounds of consequences, can the corporate executive in fact discharge his alleged "social responsibilities"? On the other hand, suppose he could get away with spending the stockholders' or customers' or employees' money. How is he to know how to spend it? He is told that he must contribute to fighting inflation. How is he to know what action of his will contribute to that end? He is presumably an expert in running his company – in producing a product or selling it or financing it. But nothing about his selection makes him an expert on inflation. Will his holding down the price of his product reduce inflationary pressure? Or, by leaving more spending power in the hands of his customers, simply divert it elsewhere? Or, by forcing him to produce less because of the lower price, will it simply contribute to shortages? Even if he could answer these questions, how much cost is he justified in imposing on his stockholders, customers and employees for this social purpose? What is his appropriate share and what is the appropriate share of others?

And, whether he wants to or not, can he get away with spending his stockholders', customers' or employees' money? Will not the stockholders fire him (either the present ones or those who take over when his actions in the name of social responsibility have reduced the corporation's profits and the price of its stock)? His customers and his employees can desert him for other producers and employers less scrupulous in exercising their social responsibilities.

This facet of "social responsibility" doctrine is brought into sharp relief when the doctrine is used to justify wage restraint by trade unions. The conflict of interest is naked and clear when union officials are asked to subordinate the interest of their members to some more general purpose. If the union officials try to enforce wage restraint, the consequence is likely to be wildcat strikes, rank-and-file revolts and the emergence of strong competitors for their jobs. We thus have the ironic phenomenon that union leaders – at least in the US – have objected to Government interference with the market far more consistently and courageously than have business leaders.

The difficulty of exercising "social responsibility" illustrates, of course, the great virtue of private competitive enterprise – it forces people to be responsible for their own actions and makes it difficult for them to "exploit" other people for either selfish or unselfish purposes. They can do good – but only at their own expense.

Many a reader who has followed the argument this far may be tempted to remonstrate that it is all well and good to speak of Government's having the responsibility to impose taxes and determine expenditures for such "social" purposes as controlling pollution or training the hard-core unemployed, but that the problems are too urgent to wait on the slow course of political processes, that the exercise of social responsibility by businessmen is a quicker and surer way to solve pressing current problems.

Aside from the question of fact – I share Adam Smith's skepticism about the benefits that can be expected from "those who affected to trade for the public good" – this argument must be rejected on grounds of principle. What it amounts to is an assertion that those who favour the taxes and expenditures in question have failed to persuade a majority of their fellow citizens to be of like mind and that they are seeking to attain by undemocratic procedures what they cannot attain by democratic procedures. In a free society, it is hard for "evil" people to do "evil," especially since one man's good is another's evil.

I have, for simplicity, concentrated on the special case of the corporate executive, except only for the brief digression on trade unions. But precisely the same argument applies to the newer phenomenon of calling upon stockholders to require corporations to exercise social responsibility. In most of these cases, what is in effect involved is some stockholders trying to get other stockholders (or customers or employees) to contribute against their will to "social" causes favoured by the activists. Insofar as they succeed, they are again imposing taxes and spending the proceeds.

The situation of the individual proprietor is somewhat different. If he acts to reduce the returns of his enterprise in order to exercise his "social responsibility," he is spending his own money, not someone else's. If he wishes to spend his money on such purposes, that is his right, and I cannot see that there is any objection to his doing so. In the process, he, too, may impose costs on employees and customers. However, because he is far less likely than a large corporation or union to have monopolistic power, any such side effects will tend to be minor.

Of course, in practice the doctrine of social responsibility is frequently a cloak for actions that are justified on other grounds rather than a reason for those actions.

To illustrate, it may well be in the long run interest of a corporation that is a major employer in a small community to devote resources to providing amenities to that community or to improving its government. That may make it easier to attract desirable employees, it may reduce the wage bill or lessen losses from pilferage and sabotage or have other worthwhile effects. Or it may be that, given the laws about the deductibility of corporate charitable contributions, the stockholders can contribute more to charities they favour by having the corporation make the gift than by doing it themselves, since they can in that way contribute an amount that would otherwise have been paid as corporate taxes.

In each of these – and many similar – cases, there is a strong temptation to rationalize these actions as an exercise of "social responsibility." In the present climate of opinion, with its widespread aversion to "capitalism," "profits," the "soulless corporation" and so on, this is one way for a corporation to generate goodwill as a by-product of expenditures that are entirely justified in its own self-interest.

It would be inconsistent of me to call on corporate executives to refrain from this hypocritical window-dressing because it harms the foundations of a free society. That would be to call on them to exercise a "social responsibility"! If our institutions, and the attitudes of the public make it in their self-interest to cloak their actions in this way, I cannot summon much indignation to denounce them. At the same time, I can express admiration for those individual proprietors or owners of closely held corporations, or stockholders of more broadly held corporations, who disdain such tactics as approaching fraud.

Whether blameworthy or not, the use of the cloak of social responsibility, and the nonsense spoken in its name by influential and prestigious businessmen, does clearly harm the foundations of a free society. I have been impressed time and again by the schizophrenic character of many businessmen. They are capable of being extremely farsighted and clearheaded in matters that are internal to their businesses. They are incredibly shortsighted and muddleheaded in matters that are outside their businesses but affect the possible survival of business in general. This shortsightedness is strikingly exemplified in the calls from many businessmen for wage and price guidelines or controls or income policies. There is nothing that could do more in a brief period to destroy a market system and replace it by a centrally controlled system than effective governmental control of prices and wages.

The shortsightedness is also exemplified in speeches by businessmen on social responsibility. This may gain them kudos in the short run. But it helps to strengthen the already too prevalent view that the pursuit of profits is wicked and immoral and must be curbed and controlled by external forces. Once this view is adopted, the external forces that curb the market will not be the social consciences, however highly developed, of the pontificating executives; it will be the iron fist of Government bureaucrats. Here, as with price and wage controls, businessmen seem to me to reveal a suicidal impulse.

The political principle that underlies the market mechanism is unanimity. In an ideal free market resting on private property, no individual can coerce any other, all cooperation is voluntary, all parties to such cooperation benefit or they need not participate. There are no values, no "social" responsibilities in any sense other than the shared values and responsibilities of individuals. Society is a collection of individuals and of the various groups they voluntarily form.

The political principle that underlies the political mechanism is conformity. The individual must serve a more general social interest – whether that be determined by a church or a dictator or a majority. The individual may have a vote and say in what is to be done, but if he is overruled, he must conform. It is appropriate for some to require others to contribute to a general social purpose whether they wish to or not.

Unfortunately, unanimity is not always feasible. There are some respects in which conformity appears unavoidable, so I do not see how one can avoid the use of the political mechanism altogether.

But the doctrine of "social responsibility" taken seriously would extend the scope of the political mechanism to every human activity. It does not differ in philosophy from the most explicitly collectivist doctrine. It differs only by professing to believe that collectivist ends can be attained without collectivist means. That is why, in my book *Capitalism and Freedom*, I have called it a "fundamentally subversive doctrine" in a free society, and have said that in such a society, "there is one and only one social responsibility of business – to use it resources and engage in activities designed to increase its profits so long as it stays within the rules of the game, which is to say, engages in open and free competition without deception or fraud."

Stockholders and stakeholders: A new perspective on corporate governance

By Edward Freeman and David Reed[1]

Management thought has changed dramatically in recent years. There have been, and are now underway, both conceptual and practical revolutions in the ways that management theorists and managers think about organizational life. The purpose of this article is to understand the implications of one of these shifts in world view; namely, the shift from 'stockholder' to 'stakeholder'.

The stakeholder concept

It has long been gospel that corporations have obligations to stockholders, holders of the firm's equity that are sacrosanct and inviolable. Corporate action or inaction is to be driven by attention to the needs of its stockholders, usually thought to be measured by stock price, earnings per share, or some other financial measure.

It has been argued that the proper relationship of management to its stockholders is similar to that of the fiduciary to the *cestui que trustent*, whereby the interests of the stockholders should be dutifully cared for by management. Thus, any action taken by management must ultimately be justified by whether or not it furthers the interests of the corporation and its stockholders.

There is also a long tradition of departure from the view that stockholders have a privileged place in the business enterprise. Berle and Means (1932) were worried about the 'degree of prominence entitling (the corporation) to be dealt with as a major social institution'. Chester Barnard argued that the purpose of the corporation was to serve society, and that the function of the executive was to instill this sense of moral purpose in the corporation's employees (Barnard, 1938). Public relations and corporate social action have a history too long to be catalogued here. However, a recent development calls for a more far-reaching change in the way that we look at corporate life, and that is the good currency of the idea of 'stakeholders'.

The stakeholder notion is indeed a deceptively simple one. It says that there are other groups to whom the corporation is responsible in addition to stockholders: those groups who have a stake in the actions of the corporation. The word *stakeholder*, coined in an internal memorandum at the Stanford Research Institute in 1963, refers to 'those groups without whose support the organization would cease to exist'. The list of stakeholders originally included shareowners, employees, customers, suppliers, lenders and society. Stemming from the work of Igor Ansoff and Robert Stewart (in the planning department at Lockheed) and, later, Marion Doscher and Stewart (at SRI), stakeholder analysis served and continues to serve an important function in the SRI corporate planning process.

From the original work at SRI, the historical trail diverges in a number of directions. In his now classic *Corporate Strategy: An Analytic Approach to Business Policy for Growth and Expansion*, Igor Ansoff (1965) makes limited use of the theory:

> *While as we shall see later, 'responsibilities' and 'objectives' are not synonymous, they have been made one in a 'stakeholder theory' of objectives. This theory maintains that the objectives of the firm should be derived by balancing the conflicting claims of the various 'stakeholders' in the firm: managers, workers, stockholders, suppliers, vendors.*

Ansoff goes on to reject the stakeholder theory in favour of a view which separates objectives into 'economic' and 'social' with the latter being a 'secondary modifying and constraining influence' on the former.

In the mid-1970s, researchers in systems theory, led by Russell Ackoff (1974) 'rediscovered' stakeholder analysis, or at least took Ansoff's admonition more seriously. Propounding essentially an open systems view of organizations, Ackoff argues that many social problems can be solved by the redesign of fundamental institutions with the support and interaction of stakeholders in the system.

A second trail from Ansoff's original reference is the work of William Dill, who in concert with Ackoff, sought to move the stakeholder concept from the periphery of corporate planning to a central place. In 1975 Dill argued:

> *For a long time, we have assumed that the views and the initiative of stakeholders could be dealt with as externalities to the strategic planning and management process: as data to help management shape decisions, or as legal and social constraints to limit them. We have been reluctant, though, to admit the idea that some of these outside stakeholders might seek and earn active roles with management to make decisions. The move today is from stakeholder influence towards stakeholder participation.*

Dill went on to set out a role for strategic managers as communicators with stakeholders and considered the role of adversary groups such as Nader's Raiders in the strategic process. For the most part, until Dill's paper, stakeholders had been assumed to be non-adversarial, or adversarial only in the sense of labour-management relations. By broadening the notion of stakeholder to 'people outside … who have ideas about what the economic and social performance of the enterprise should include', Dill set the stage for the use of the stakeholder concept as an umbrella for strategic management.

A related development is primarily responsible for giving the stakeholder concept a boost; namely, the increase in concern with the social involvement of business. The corporate social responsibility movement is too diverse and has spawned too many ideas, concepts and techniques to explain here. Suffice it to say that the social movements of the sixties and seventies – civil rights, the antiwar movement, consumerism, environmentalism and women's rights – served as a catalyst for rethinking the role of the business enterprise in society. From Milton Friedman to John Kenneth Galbraith, there is a diversity of arguments. However, one aspect of the corporate social responsibility debate is particularly relevant to understanding the good currency of the stakeholder concept.

In the early 1970s the Harvard Business School undertook a project on corporate social responsibility. The output of the project was voluminous, and of particular importance was the development of a pragmatic model of social responsibility called 'the corporate social responsiveness model' (Ackerman and Bauer, 1976). It essentially addressed Dill's question with respect to social issues: 'How can the corporation respond proactively to the increased pressure for positive social change?' By concentrating on responsiveness instead of responsibility, the Harvard researchers were able to link the analysis of social issues with the traditional areas of strategy and organization.

By the late 1970s the need for strategic management processes to take account of non-traditional business problems in terms of government, special interest groups, trade associations, foreign competitors, dissident shareholders, and complex issues such as employee rights, equal opportunity, environmental pollution, consumer rights, tariffs, government regulation and reindustrialization had become obvious. To begin to develop these processes, The Wharton School began, in 1977 in its Applied Research Center, a 'stakeholder project'. The objectives of the project were to put together a number of strands of thought and to develop a theory of management which enabled executives to formulate and implement corporate strategy in turbulent environments. Thus, an action research model was used whereby stakeholder theory was generated by actual cases.

To date the project has explored the implications of the stakeholder concept on three levels: as a management theory; as a process for practitioners to use in strategic management; and as an analytical framework.

At the theoretical level the implications of substituting *stakeholder* for *stockholder* needs to be explicated. The first problem at this level is the actual definition of *stakeholder*. SRI's original definition is too general and too exclusive to serve as a means of identifying those external groups who are strategically important. The concentration on generic stakeholders, such as society and customers, rather than specific social interest groups and specific customer segments produces an analysis which can only be used as a background for the planning process. Strategically useful information about the actions, objectives and motivations of specific groups, which is needed if management is to be responsive to stakeholder concerns, requires a more specific and inclusive definition.

We propose two definitions of *stakeholder:* a wide sense, which includes groups who are friendly or hostile, and a narrow sense, which captures the essence of the SRI definition, but is more specific.

- **The wide sense of stakeholder.** Any identifiable group or individual who can affect the achievement of an organization's objectives or who is affected by the achievement of an organization's objectives. (Public interest groups, protest groups, government agencies, trade associations, competitors, unions, as well as employees, customer segments, shareowners and others are stakeholders, in this sense.)

- **The narrow sense of stakeholder.** Any identifiable group or individual on which the organization is dependent for its continued survival. (Employees, customer segments, certain suppliers, key government agencies, shareowners, certain financial institutions, as well as others are all stakeholders in the narrow sense of the term.)

While executives are willing to recognize that employees, suppliers and customers have a stake in the corporation, many resist the inclusion of adversary groups. But from the standpoint of corporate strategy, *stakeholder* must be understood in the wide sense: strategies need to account for those groups who can affect the achievement of the firm's objectives. Some may feel happier with other words, such as *influencers, claimants, publics,* or *constituencies.* Semantics aside, if corporations are to formulate and implement strategies in turbulent environments, theories of strategy must have concepts, such as the wide sense of *stakeholder,* which allow the analysis of all external forces and pressures whether they are friendly or hostile. In what follows we will use *stakeholder* in the wide sense, as our primary objective is to elucidate the questions of corporate governance from the perspective of strategic management.

A second issue at the theoretical level is the generation of prescriptive propositions which explain actual cases and articulate regulative principles for future use. Thus, a *post hoc* analysis of the brewing industry and the problem of beverage container legislation, combined with a similar analysis of the regulatory environments of public utilities have led to some simple propositions which serve as a philosophical guideline for strategy formulation. For example:

- Generalize the marketing approach: understand the needs of each stakeholder, in a similar fashion to understanding customer needs, and design products, services and programmes to fulfil those needs.

- Establish negotiation processes: understand the political nature of a number of stakeholders, and the applicability of concepts and techniques of political science, such as coalition analysis, conflict management, and the use and abuse of unilateral action.

- Establish a decision philosophy that is oriented towards seizing the initiative rather than reacting to events as they occur.

- Allocate organizational resources based on the degree of importance of the environmental turbulence (the stakeholders' claims).

Other prescriptive propositions can be put forth, especially with respect to issues of corporate governance. One proposition that has been discussed is to 'involve stakeholder groups in strategic decisions', or 'invite stakeholders to participate in governance decisions'. While propositions like this may have substantial merit, we have not examined enough cases nor marshalled enough evidence to support them in an unqualified manner. There are cases where participation is appropriate. Some public utilities have been quite successful in the use of stakeholder advisory groups in matters of rate setting. However, given the breadth of our concept of stakeholder we believe that cooptation through participation is not always the correct strategic decision.

The second level of analysis is the use of stakeholder concepts in strategy formulation processes. Two processes have been used so far: the *Stakeholder Strategy Process* and the *Stakeholder Audit Process*. The Stakeholder Strategy Process is a systematic method for analysing the relative importance of stakeholders and their cooperative potential (how they can help the corporation achieve its objectives) and their competitive threat (how they can prevent the corporation from achieving its objectives). The process is one which relies on a behavioural analysis (both actual and potential) for input, and an explanatory model of stakeholder objectives and resultant strategic shifts for output. The Stakeholder Audit Process is a systematic method for identifying stakeholders and assessing the effectiveness of current organizational strategies. By itself, each process has a use in the strategic management of an organization. Each analyses the stakeholder environment from the standpoint of organizational mission and objectives and seeks to formulate strategies for meeting stakeholder needs and concerns.

The use of the stakeholder concept at the analytical level means thinking in terms which are broader than current strategic and operational problems. It implies looking at public policy questions in stakeholder terms and trying to understand how the relationships between

an organization and its stakeholders would change given the implementation of certain policies.

One analytical device depicts an organization's stakeholders on a two-dimensional grid map. The first dimension is one of 'interest' or 'stake' and ranges from an equity interest to an economic interest or marketplace stake, to an interest or stake as a 'kibitzer' or influencer. Shareowners have an equity stake; customers and suppliers have an economic stake; and single-issue groups have an influencer stake. The second dimension of a stakeholder is its power, which ranges from the formalistic or voting power of stockholders to the economic power of customers, to the political power of special interest groups. By *economic power* we mean 'the ability to influence due to marketplace decisions' and by *political power* we mean 'the ability to influence due to use of the political process'.

Figure 3.2.1 represents this stakeholder grid graphically. It is of course possible that a stakeholder has more than one kind of both stake and power, especially in light of the fact that there are stakeholders who have multiple roles. An employee may be at once shareholder, customer, employee and even kibitzer. Figure 3.2.1 represents the prevailing world view. That is, shareholders and directors have formal or voting power; customers, suppliers and employees have economic power; and government and special interest groups have political power. Moreover, management concepts and principles have evolved to treat this 'diagonal case.' Managers learn how to handle stockholders and boards via their ability to vote on certain key decisions, and conflicts are resolved by the procedures and processes written into the corporate charter or by methods which involve formal legal parameters. Strategic planners, marketers, financial analysts and operations executives base their decisions on marketplace variables, and an entire tradition of management principles is based on the economic analysis of the marketplace. Finally, public relations and public affairs managers and lobbyists learn to deal in the political arena. As long as the real world approximately fits into the diagonal, management processes may be able to deal effectively with them.

A more thoughtful examination, however, reveals that Figure 3.2.1 is either a straw man or that shifts of position have occurred. In the auto industry, for instance, one part of government has acquired economic power in terms of the imposition of import quotas or the trigger price mechanism. The Securities and Exchange Commission might be looked at as a kibitzer with formal power in terms of disclosure

FIGURE 3.2.1   "Classical" stakeholder grid

	Formal or Voting Power	Economic Power	Political Power
Equity Stake	• Stockbrokers • Directors • Minority interests		
Economic Stake		• Customers • Competitors • Suppliers • Debt holders • Foreign governments • Unions	
Influencers			• Consumer groups • Government • Nader's Raiders • Sierra Club • Trade associations

and accounting rules. Outside directors do not necessarily have an equity stake, especially those women, minorities and academics who are becoming more and more normal for the boards of large corporations. Some kibitzer groups are buying stock and acquiring an equity stake, and while they also acquire formal power, their main source of power is still political. Witness the marshalling of the political process by church groups in bringing up, at annual meetings, issues such as selling infant formula in the Third World or investing in South Africa. Unions are using their political power as well as their formal clout as managers of large portions of pension funds to influence the company. Customers are being organized by consumer advocates to exercise the voice option and to politicize the marketplace. In short, the real world looks more like Figure 3.2.2. (Of course, each organization will have its own individual grid.) Thus, a search for alternative applications of traditional management processes must begin, and new concepts and techniques are needed to understand the shifts that have occurred and to manage in the new environment.

There is a need to develop new and innovative management processes to deal with the current and future complexities of management issues. At the theoretical level, stakeholder analysis has been developed to enrich the economic approach to corporate strategy by arguing that kibitzers with political power must be included in the strategy process. At the strategic level, stakeholder analysis takes a number of groups into account and analyses their strategic impact on the corporation.

Stakeholder analysis and corporate democracy

The debate on corporate governance and, in particular, corporate democracy has recently intensified. Proposals have been put forth to make the corporation more democratic, to encourage shareholder participation and management responsiveness to shareholder needs, and to make corporations more responsive to other stakeholder needs and, hence, to encourage the participation of stakeholders in the governance process. Reforms from cumulative voting to audit committees have been suggested.

Corporate democracy has come to have at least three meanings over the years, which prescribe that corporations should be made more democratic: by increasing the role of government, either as a watchdog or by having public officials on boards of directors; by allowing citizen or public participation in the managing of its affairs via public interest directors and the like; or by encouraging or mandating the active participation of all or many of its shareholders. The analysis of the preceding section has implications for each of these levels of democratization.

The propositions of stakeholder analysis advocate a thorough understanding of a firm's stakeholders (in the wide sense) and recognize that there are times when stakeholders must participate in the decision-making process. The strategic tools and techniques of stakeholder analysis yield a method for determining the timing and degree of such participation. At the

FIGURE 3.2.2   'Real world' stakeholder grid

	Formal or Voting Power	Economic Power	Political Power
Equity Stake	• Stockbrokers • Directors • Minority interests		• Dissident stockholders
Economic Stake		• Suppliers • Debt holders • Customers • Unions	• Local governments • Foreign governments • Consumer groups • Unions
Influencers	• Government • SEC • Outside directors	• EPA/OSHA	• Nader's Raiders • Government • Trade associations

absolute minimum this implies that boards of directors must be aware of the impact of their decisions on key stakeholder groups. As stakeholders have begun to exercise more political power and as marketplace decisions become politicized, the need for awareness to grow into responsiveness has become apparent. Thus, the analytical model can be used by boards to map carefully the power and stake of each group. While it is not the proper role of the board to be involved in the implementation of tactical programmes at the operational level of the corporation, it must set the tone for how the company deals with stakeholders, both traditional marketplace ones and those who have political power. The board must decide not only whether management is managing the affairs of the corporation, but indeed, what are to count as the affairs of the corporation. This involves assessing the stake and power of each stakeholder group.

Much has been written about the failure of senior management to think strategically, competitively and globally. Some have argued that American businesspersons are 'managing [their] way to economic decline' (Hayes and Abernathy, 1980). Executives have countered the critics with complaints about the increase in the adversarial role of government and in the number of hostile external interest groups. Yet if the criteria for success for senior executives remain fixated on economic stakeholders with economic power and on short-term performance on Wall Street, the rise of such a turbulent political environment in a free and open society should come as no surprise. If the board sees itself as responsive only to the shareholder in the short term, senior management will continue to manage towards economic decline.[2] We have argued that the problem of governing the corporation in to-day's world must be viewed in terms of the entire grid of stakeholders and their power base. It is only by setting the direction for positive response and negotiation at the board level that the adversarial nature of the business-government relationship can be overcome.

If this task of stakeholder management is done properly, much of the air is let out of critics who argue that the corporation must be democratized in terms of increased direct citizen participation. Issues which involve both economic and political stakes and power bases must be addressed in an integrated fashion. No longer can public affairs, public relations and corporate philanthropy serve as adequate management tools. The sophistication of interest groups who are beginning to use formal power mechanisms, such as proxy fights, annual meetings, and the corporate charter, to focus the attention of management on the affairs of the corporation, has increased. Responsive boards will seize these opportunities to learn more about those stakeholders who have chosen the option of voice over the Wall Street Rule. As boards direct management to respond to these concerns, to negotiate with critics, to trade off certain policies in return for positive support, the pressure for mandated citizen participation will subside.

---

[2] It is arguable whether responsiveness to non-market stakeholders is in the long-term interest of the corporation. We believe that there is no need to appeal to utilitarian notions of greatest social good or altruism or social responsibility. Rather, the corporation fulfils its obligations to shareholders in the long term only through proper stakeholder management. In short we believe that enlightened self-interest gives both reasons why (personal motivation) and reasons for (social justification) taking stakeholder concerns into account. The development of this argument is, however, beyond our present scope.

Creating shared value

By Michael E. Porter and Mark R. Kramer[1]

The capitalist system is under siege. In recent years business increasingly has been viewed as a major cause of social, environmental and economic problems. Companies are widely perceived to be prospering at the expense of the broader community. Even worse, the more business has begun to embrace corporate responsibility, the more it has been blamed for society's failures. The legitimacy of business has fallen to levels not seen in recent history. This diminished trust in business leads political leaders to set policies that undermine competitiveness and sap economic growth. Business is caught in a vicious circle.

A big part of the problem lies with companies themselves, which remain trapped in an outdated approach to value creation that has emerged over the past few decades. They continue to view value creation narrowly, optimizing short-term financial performance in a bubble while missing the most important customer needs and ignoring the broader influences that determine their longer-term success. How else could companies overlook the well-being of their customers, the depletion of natural resources vital to their businesses, the viability of key suppliers, or the economic distress of the communities in which they produce and sell? How else could companies think that simply shifting activities to locations with ever lower wages was a sustainable "solution" to competitive challenges? Government and civil society have often exacerbated the problem by attempting to address social weaknesses at the expense of business. The presumed trade-offs between economic efficiency and social progress have been institutionalized in decades of policy choices.

Companies must take the lead in bringing business and society back together. The recognition is there among sophisticated business and thought leaders, and promising elements of a new model are emerging. Yet we still lack an overall framework for guiding these efforts, and most companies remain stuck in a "social responsibility" mind-set in which societal issues are at the periphery, not the core.

The solution lies in the principle of shared value, which involves creating economic value in a way that *also* creates value for society by addressing its needs and challenges. Businesses must reconnect company success with social progress. Shared value is not social responsibility, philanthropy, or even sustainability, but a new way to achieve economic success. It is not on the margin of what companies do but at the centre. We believe that it can give rise to major transformation of business thinking.

A growing number of companies known for their hard-nosed approach to business – such as GE, Google, IBM, Intel, Johnson & Johnson, Nestlé, Unilever and Wal-Mart – have already embarked on important efforts to create shared value by reconceiving the intersection between society and corporate performance. Yet our recognition of the transformative power of shared value is still in its genesis. Realizing it will require leaders and managers to develop new skills and knowledge – such as a far deeper appreciation of societal needs, a greater understanding of the true bases of company productivity, and the ability to collaborate across profit/non-profit boundaries. And government must learn how to regulate in ways that enable shared value rather than work against it.

Capitalism is an unparalleled vehicle for meeting human needs, improving efficiency, creating jobs and building wealth. But a narrow conception of capitalism has prevented business from harnessing its full potential to meet society's broader challenges. The opportunities have been there all along but have been overlooked. Businesses acting as businesses, not as charitable donors, are the most powerful force for addressing the pressing issues we face. The moment for a new conception of capitalism is now; society's needs are large and growing, while customers, employees, and a new generation of young people are asking business to step up.

The purpose of the corporation must be redefined as creating shared value, not just profit *per se*. This will drive the next wave of innovation and productivity growth in the global economy. It will also reshape capitalism and its relationship to society. Perhaps most important of all, learning how to create shared value is our best chance to legitimize business again.

Moving beyond trade-offs

Business and society have been pitted against each other for too long. That is in part because economists have legitimized the idea that to provide societal benefits, companies must temper their economic success. In neoclassical thinking, a requirement for social improvement – such as safety or hiring the disabled – imposes a constraint on the corporation. Adding a constraint to a firm that is already maximizing profits, says the theory, will inevitably raise costs and reduce those profits.

A related concept, with the same conclusion, is the notion of externalities. Externalities arise when firms create social costs that they do not have to bear, such as pollution. Thus, society must impose taxes, regulations and penalties so that firms "internalize" these externalities – a belief influencing many government policy decisions.

This perspective has also shaped the strategies of firms themselves, which have largely excluded social and environmental considerations from their economic thinking. Firms have taken the broader context in which they do business as a given and resisted regulatory standards as invariably contrary to their interests. Solving social problems has been ceded to governments and to NGOs. Corporate responsibility programmes – a reaction to external pressure – have emerged largely to improve firms' reputations and are treated as a necessary expense. Anything more is seen by many as an irresponsible use of shareholders' money. Governments, for their part, have often regulated in a way that makes shared value more difficult to achieve. Implicitly, each side has assumed that the other is an obstacle to pursuing its goals and acted accordingly.

The concept of shared value, in contrast, recognizes that societal needs, not just conventional economic needs, define markets. It also recognizes that social harms or weaknesses frequently create *internal* costs for firms – such as wasted energy or raw materials, costly accidents, and the need for remedial training to compensate for inadequacies in education. And addressing societal harms and constraints does not necessarily raise costs for firms, because they can innovate through using new technologies, operating methods and management approaches – and as a result, increase their productivity and expand their markets.

Shared value, then, is not about personal values. Nor is it about "sharing" the value already created by firms – a redistribution approach. Instead, it is about expanding the total pool of economic and social value. A good example of this difference in perspective is the fair trade movement in purchasing. Fair trade aims to increase the proportion of revenue that goes to poor farmers by paying them higher prices for the same crops. Though this may be a noble sentiment, fair trade is mostly about redistribution rather than expanding the overall amount of value created. A shared value perspective, instead, focuses on improving growing techniques and strengthening the local cluster of supporting suppliers and other institutions in order to increase farmers' efficiency, yields, product quality and sustainability. This leads to a bigger pie of revenue and profits that benefits both farmers and the companies that buy from them. Early studies of cocoa farmers in the Côte d'Ivoire, for instance, suggest that while fair trade can increase farmers' incomes by 10 per cent to 20 per cent, shared value investments can raise their incomes by more than 300 per cent. Initial investment and time may be required to implement new procurement practices and develop the supporting cluster, but the return will be greater economic value and broader strategic benefits for all participants.

The roots of shared value

At a very basic level, the competitiveness of a company and the health of the communities around it are closely intertwined. A business needs a successful community, not only to create demand for its products but also to provide critical public assets and a supportive environment. A community needs successful businesses to provide jobs and wealth creation opportunities for its citizens. This interdependence means that public policies that undermine the productivity and competitiveness of businesses are self-defeating, especially in a global economy where facilities and jobs can easily move elsewhere. NGOs and governments have not always appreciated this connection.

In the old, narrow view of capitalism, business contributes to society by making a profit, which supports employment, wages, purchases, investments and taxes. Conducting business as usual is sufficient social benefit. A firm is largely a self-contained entity, and social or community issues fall outside its proper scope. (This is the argument advanced persuasively by Milton Friedman in his critique of the whole notion of corporate social responsibility.)

This perspective has permeated management thinking for the past two decades. Firms focused on enticing consumers to buy more and more of their products. Facing growing competition and shorter-term performance pressures from shareholders, managers resorted

EXHIBIT 3.3.1   WHAT IS "SHARED VALUE"?

The concept of shared value can be defined as policies and operating practices that enhance the competitiveness of a company while simultaneously advancing the economic and social conditions in the communities in which it operates. Shared value creation focuses on identifying and expanding the connections between societal and economic progress.

The concept rests on the premise that both economic and social progress must be addressed using value principles. Value is defined as benefits relative to costs, not just benefits alone. Value creation is an idea that has long been recognized in business,

where profit is revenues earned from customers minus the costs incurred. However, businesses have rarely approached societal issues from a value perspective but have treated them as peripheral matters. This has obscured the connections between economic and social concerns.

In the social sector, thinking in value terms is even less common. Social organizations and government entities often see success solely in terms of the benefits achieved or the money expended. As governments and NGOs begin to think more in value terms, their interest in collaborating with business will inevitably grow.

---

to waves of restructuring, personnel reductions and relocation to lower-cost regions, while leveraging balance sheets to return capital to investors. The results were often commoditization, price competition, little true innovation, slow organic growth, and no clear competitive advantage.

In this kind of competition, the communities in which companies operate perceive little benefit even as profits rise. Instead, they perceive that profits come at their expense, an impression that has become even stronger in the current economic recovery, in which rising earnings have done little to offset high unemployment, local business distress and severe pressures on community services.

It was not always this way. The best companies once took on a broad range of roles in meeting the needs of workers, communities and supporting businesses. As other social institutions appeared on the scene, however, these roles fell away or were delegated. Shortening investor time horizons began to narrow thinking about appropriate investments. As the vertically integrated firm gave way to greater reliance on outside vendors, outsourcing and offshoring weakened the connection between firms and their communities. As firms moved disparate activities to more and more locations, they often lost touch with any location. Indeed, many companies no longer recognize a home – but see themselves as "global" companies.

These transformations drove major progress in economic efficiency. However, something profoundly important was lost in the process, as more fundamental opportunities for value creation were missed. The scope of strategic thinking contracted.

Strategy theory holds that to be successful, a company must create a distinctive value proposition that meets the needs of a chosen set of customers. The firm gains competitive advantage from how it configures the value chain, or the set of activities involved in creating, producing, selling, delivering and supporting its products or services. For decades businesspeople have studied positioning and the best ways to design activities and integrate them. However, companies have overlooked opportunities to meet fundamental societal needs and misunderstood how societal harms and weaknesses affect value chains. Our field of vision has simply been too narrow.

In understanding the business environment, managers have focused most of their attention on the industry, or the particular business in which the firm competes. This is because industry structure has a decisive impact on a firm's profitability. What has been missed, however, is the profound effect that location can have on productivity and innovation. Companies have failed to grasp the importance of the broader business environment surrounding their major operations.

How shared value is created

Companies can create economic value by creating societal value. There are three distinct ways to do this: by reconceiving products and markets, redefining productivity in the value chain, and building supportive industry clusters at the company's locations. Each of these is part of the virtuous circle of shared value; improving value in one area gives rise to opportunities in the others.

The concept of shared value resets the boundaries of capitalism. By better connecting companies' success with societal improvement, it opens up many ways to serve new needs, gain efficiency, create differentiation and expand markets.

The ability to create shared value applies equally to advanced economies and developing countries, though the specific opportunities will differ. The opportunities will also differ markedly across industries and companies – but every company has them. And their range and scope is far broader than has been recognized.

Reconceiving products and markets

Society's needs are huge – health, better housing, improved nutrition, help for the aging, greater financial security, less environmental damage. Arguably, they are the greatest unmet needs in the global economy. In business we have spent decades learning how to parse and manufacture demand while missing the most important demand of all. Too many companies have lost sight of that most basic of questions: Is our product good for our customers? Or for our customers' customers?

In advanced economies, demand for products and services that meet societal needs is rapidly growing. Food companies that traditionally concentrated on taste and quantity to drive more consumption are refocusing on the fundamental need for better nutrition; Intel and IBM are both devising ways to help utilities harness digital intelligence in order to economize on power usage. Wells Fargo has developed a loan of products and tools that help customers budget, manage credit, and pay down debt. Sales of GE's Ecomagination products reached $18 billion in 2009 – the size of a *Fortune* 150 company. GE now predicts that revenues of Ecomagination products will grow at twice the rate of total company revenues over the next five years.

In these and many other ways, whole new avenues for innovation open up and shared value is created. Society's gains are even greater, because businesses will often be far more effective than governments and non-profit organizations are at marketing that motivates customers to embrace products and services that create benefits, like healthier food or environmentally friendly products.

Equal or greater opportunities arise from serving disadvantaged communities and developing countries. Though societal needs are even more pressing there, these communities have not been recognized as viable markets. Today attention is riveted on India, China and, increasingly, Brazil, which offer firms the prospect of reaching billions of new customers at the bottom of the pyramid – a notion persuasively articulated by C.K. Prahalad. Yet these countries have always had huge needs, as do many developing countries.

Similar opportunities await in non-traditional communities in advanced countries. We have learned, for example, that poor urban areas are America's most underserved market; their substantial concentrated purchasing power has often been overlooked.

The societal benefits of providing appropriate products to lower-income and disadvantaged consumers can be profound, while the profits for companies can

---

EXHIBIT 3.3.2   BLURRING THE PROFIT/NON-PROFIT BOUNDARY

The concept of shared value blurs the line between for-profit and non-profit organizations. New kinds of hybrid enterprises are rapidly appearing. For example, WaterHealth International, a fast-growing for-profit, uses innovative water purification techniques to distribute clean water at minimal cost to more than one million people in rural India, Ghana and the Philippines. Its investors include not only the socially focused Acumen Fund and the International Finance Corporation of the World Bank but also Dow Chemical's venture fund. Revolution Foods, a four-year-old venture capital-backed US start-up, provides 60,000 fresh, healthful and nutritious meals to students daily – and does so at a higher gross margin than traditional competitors. Waste Concern, a hybrid profit/non-profit enterprise started in Bangladesh 15 years ago, has built the capacity to convert 700 tons of trash, collected daily from neighbourhood slums, into organic fertilizer, thereby increasing crop yields and reducing CO_2 emissions. Seeded with capital from the Lions Club and the United Nations Development Programme, the company improves health conditions while earning a substantial gross margin through fertilizer sales and carbon credits.

The blurring of the boundary between successful for-profits and non-profits is one of the strong signs that creating shared value is possible.

EXHIBIT 3.3.3   THE CONNECTION BETWEEN COMPETITIVE ADVANTAGE AND SOCIAL ISSUES

There are numerous ways in which addressing societal concerns can yield productivity benefits to a firm. Consider, for example, what happens when a firm invests in a wellness programme. Society benefits because employees and their families become healthier, and the firm minimizes employee absences and lost productivity. The graphic below depicts some areas where the connections are strongest.

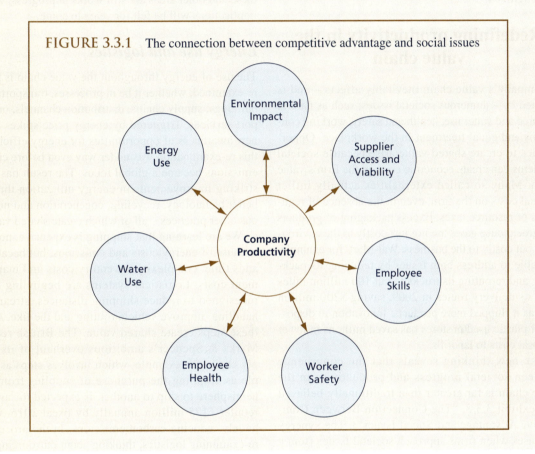

FIGURE 3.3.1   The connection between competitive advantage and social issues

be substantial. For example, low-priced cellphones that provide mobile banking services are helping the poor save money securely and transforming the ability of small farmers to produce and market their crops. In Kenya, Vodafone's M-PESA mobile banking service signed up 10 million customers in three years; the funds it handles now represent 11 per cent of that country's GDP. In India, Thomson Reuters has developed a promising monthly service for farmers who earn an average of $2,000 a year. For a fee of $5 a quarter, it provides weather and crop-pricing information and agricultural advice. The service reaches an estimated 2 million farmers, and early research indicates that it has helped increase the incomes of more than 60 per cent of them – in some cases even tripling incomes. As capitalism begins to work in poorer communities, new opportunities for economic development and social progress increase exponentially.

For a company, the starting point for creating this kind of shared value is to identify all the societal needs, benefits and harms that are, or could be embodied in the firm's products. The opportunities are not static; they change constantly as technology evolves, economies develop and societal priorities shift. An ongoing exploration of societal needs will lead companies to discover new opportunities for differentiation and repositioning in traditional markets, and to recognize the potential of new markets they previously overlooked.

Meeting needs in underserved markets often requires redesigned products or different distribution methods. These requirements can trigger fundamental innovations that also have application in traditional markets. Microfinance, for example, was invented to serve unmet financing needs in developing countries. Now it is growing rapidly in the United States, where it is filling an important gap that was unrecognized.

Redefining productivity in the value chain

A company's value chain inevitably affects – and is affected by – numerous societal issues, such as natural resource and water use, health and safety, working conditions and equal treatment in the workplace. Opportunities to create shared value arise because societal problems can create economic costs in the firm's value chain. Many so-called externalities actually inflict internal costs on the firm, even in the absence of regulation or resource taxes. Excess packaging of products and greenhouse gases are not just costly to the environment but costly to the business. Wal-Mart, for example, was able to address both issues by reducing its packaging and rerouting its trucks to cut 100 million miles from its delivery routes in 2009, saving $200 million even as it shipped more products. Innovation in disposing of plastic used in stores has saved millions in lower disposal costs to landfills.

The new thinking reveals that the congruence between societal progress and productivity in the value chain is far greater than traditionally believed (see exhibit 3.3.3, "The Connection Between Competitive Advantage and Social Issues"). The synergy increases when firms approach societal issues from a shared value perspective and invent new ways of operating to address them. So far, however, few companies have reaped the full productivity benefits in areas such as health, safety, environmental performance and employee retention and capability.

But there are unmistakable signs of change. Efforts to minimize pollution were once thought to inevitably increase business costs – and to occur only because of regulation and taxes. Today there is a growing consensus that major improvements in environmental performance can often be achieved with better technology at nominal incremental cost and can even yield net cost savings through enhanced resource utilization, process efficiency and quality.

In each of the areas in the exhibit a deeper understanding of productivity and a growing awareness of the fallacy of short-term cost reductions (which often actually lower productivity or make it unsustainable) are giving rise to new approaches. The following are some of the most important ways in which shared value thinking is transforming the value chain, which are not independent but often mutually reinforcing. Efforts in these and other areas are still works in progress, whose implications will be felt for years to come.

Energy use and logistics

The use of energy throughout the value chain is being re-examined, whether it be in processes, transportation, buildings, supply chains, distribution channels, or support services. Triggered by energy price spikes and a new awareness of opportunities for energy efficiency, this re-examination was under way even before carbon emissions became a global focus. The result has been striking improvements in energy utilization through better technology, recycling, cogeneration and numerous other practices – all of which create shared value.

We are learning that shipping is expensive, not just because of energy costs and emissions, but because it adds time, complexity, inventory costs and management costs. Logistical systems are beginning to be redesigned to reduce shipping distances, streamline handling, improve vehicle routing and the like. All of these steps create shared value. The British retailer Marks & Spencer's ambitious overhaul of its supply chain, for example, which involves steps as simple as stopping the purchase of supplies from one hemisphere to ship to another, is expected to save the retailer £175 million annually by fiscal 2016, while hugely reducing carbon emissions. In the process of re-examining logistics, thinking about outsourcing and location will also be revised (as we will discuss below).

Resource use

Heightened environmental awareness and advances in technology are catalysing new approaches in areas such as utilization of water, raw materials and packaging, as well as expanding recycling and reuse. The opportunities apply to all resources, not just those that have been identified by environmentalists. Better resource utilization – enabled by improving technology – will permeate all parts of the value chain and will spread to suppliers and channels. Landfills will fill more slowly.

For example, Coca-Cola has already reduced its worldwide water consumption by 9 per cent from a 2004 baseline – nearly halfway to its goal of a 20 per cent reduction by 2012. Dow Chemical managed to reduce consumption of fresh water at its largest production site by one billion gallons – enough water to supply nearly 40,000 people in the US for a year – resulting in savings of $4 million. The demand for water-saving technology has allowed India's Jain Irrigation, a leading global manufacturer of complete drip irrigation systems for water conservation, to achieve a 41 per cent compound annual growth rate in revenue over the past five years.

Procurement

The traditional playbook calls for companies to commoditize and exert maximum bargaining power on suppliers to drive down prices – even when purchasing from small businesses or subsistence-level farmers. More recently, firms have been rapidly outsourcing to suppliers in lower-wage locations.

Today some companies are beginning to understand that marginalized suppliers cannot remain productive or sustain, much less improve, their quality. By increasing access to inputs, sharing technology and providing financing, companies can improve supplier quality and productivity while ensuring access to growing volume. Improving productivity will often trump lower prices. As suppliers get stronger, their environmental impact often falls dramatically, which further improves their efficiency.

A good example of such new procurement thinking can be found at Nespresso, one of Nestlé's fastest-growing divisions, which has enjoyed annual growth of 30 per cent since 2000. Nespresso combines a sophisticated espresso machine with single-cup aluminum capsules containing ground coffees from around the world. Offering quality and convenience, Nespresso has expanded the market for premium coffee.

Obtaining a reliable supply of specialized coffees is extremely challenging, however. Most coffees are grown by small farmers in impoverished rural areas of Africa and Latin America, who are trapped in a cycle of low productivity, poor quality and environmental degradation that limits production volume. To address these issues, Nestlé redesigned procurement. It worked intensively with its growers, providing advice on farming practices, guaranteeing bank loans, and helping secure inputs such as plant stock, pesticides and fertilizers. Nestlé established local facilities to measure the quality of the coffee at the point of purchase, which allowed it to pay a premium for better beans directly to the growers and thus improve their incentives. Greater yield per hectare and higher production quality increased growers' incomes, and the environmental impact of farms shrank. Meanwhile, Nestlé's reliable supply of good coffee grew significantly. Shared value was created.

Embedded in the Nestlé example is a far broader insight, which is the advantage of buying from capable local suppliers. Outsourcing to other locations and countries creates transaction costs and inefficiencies that can offset lower wage and input costs. Capable local suppliers help firms avoid these costs and can reduce cycle time, increase flexibility, foster faster learning and enable innovation. Buying local includes not only local companies but also local units of national or international companies. When firms buy locally, their suppliers can get stronger, increase their profits, hire more people and pay better wages – all of which will benefit other businesses in the community. Shared value is created.

EXHIBIT 3.3.4   THE ROLE OF SOCIAL ENTREPRENEURS

Businesses are not the only players in finding profitable solutions to social problems. A whole generation of social entrepreneurs is pioneering new product concepts that meet social needs using viable business models. Because they are not locked into narrow traditional business thinking, social entrepreneurs are often well ahead of established corporations in discovering these opportunities. Social enterprises that create shared value can scale up far more rapidly than purely social programmes, which often suffer from an inability to grow and become self-sustaining.

Real social entrepreneurship should be measured by its ability to create shared value, not just social benefit.

Distribution

Companies are beginning to re-examine distribution practices from a shared value perspective. As iTunes, Kindle and Google Scholar (which offers texts of scholarly literature online) demonstrate, profitable new distribution models can also dramatically reduce paper and plastic usage. Similarly, microfinance has created a cost-efficient new model of distributing financial services to small businesses.

Opportunities for new distribution models can be even greater in non-traditional markets. For example, Hindustan Unilever is creating a new direct-to-home distribution system, run by underprivileged female entrepreneurs, in Indian villages of fewer than 2,000 people. Unilever provides microcredit and training and now has more than 45,000 entrepreneurs covering some 100,000 villages across 15 Indian states. Project Shakti, as this distribution system is called, benefits communities not only by giving women skills that often double their household income, but also by reducing the spread of communicable diseases through increased access to hygiene products. This is a good example of how the unique ability of business to market to hard-to-reach consumers can benefit society by getting life-altering products into the hands of people that need them. Project Shakti now accounts for 5 per cent of Unilever's total revenues in India and has extended the company's reach into rural areas and built its brand in media-dark regions, creating major economic value for the company.

Employee productivity

The focus on holding down wage levels, reducing benefits, and offshoring is beginning to give way to an awareness of the positive effects that a living wage, safety, wellness, training and opportunities for advancement for employees have on productivity. Many companies, for example, traditionally sought to minimize the cost of "expensive" employee health care coverage or even eliminate health coverage altogether. Today leading companies have learned that because of lost workdays and diminished employee productivity, poor health costs them more than health benefits do. Take Johnson & Johnson. By helping employees stop smoking (a two-thirds reduction in the past 15 years) and implementing numerous other wellness programmes, the company has saved $250 million on health care costs, a return of $2.71 for every dollar spent on wellness from 2002 to 2008. Moreover, Johnson & Johnson has benefited from a more present and productive workforce. If labour unions focused more on shared value too, these kinds of employee approaches would spread even faster.

Location

Business thinking has embraced the myth that location no longer matters, because logistics are inexpensive, information flows rapidly, and markets are global. The cheaper the location, then, the better. Concern about the local communities in which a company operates has faded.

That oversimplified thinking is now being challenged, partly by the rising costs of energy and carbon emissions but also by a greater recognition of the productivity cost of highly dispersed production systems and the hidden costs of distant procurement discussed earlier. Wal-Mart, for example, is increasingly sourcing produce for its food sections from local farms near its warehouses. It has discovered that the savings on transportation costs and the ability to restock in smaller quantities more than offset the lower prices of industrial farms farther away. Nestlé is establishing smaller plants closer to its markets and stepping up efforts to maximize the use of locally available materials.

The calculus of locating activities in developing countries is also changing. Olam International, a leading cashew producer, traditionally shipped its nuts from Africa to Asia for processing at facilities staffed by productive Asian workers. But by opening local processing plants and training workers in Tanzania, Mozambique, Nigeria and Côte d'Ivoire, Olam has cut processing and shipping costs by as much as 25 per cent – not to mention greatly reduced carbon emissions. In making this move, Olam also built preferred relationships with local farmers. And it has provided direct employment to 17,000 people – 95 per cent of whom are women – and indirect employment to an equal number of people in rural areas where jobs otherwise were not available.

These trends may well lead companies to remake their value chains by moving some activities closer to home and having fewer major production locations. Until now, many companies have thought that being global meant moving production to locations with the lowest labour costs and designing their supply chains to achieve the most immediate impact on expenses. In reality, the strongest international competitors will often be those that can establish deeper roots in important communities. Companies that can embrace this new locational thinking will create shared value.

As these examples illustrate, reimagining value chains from the perspective of shared value will offer significant new ways to innovate and unlock new economic value that most businesses have missed.

Enabling local cluster development

No company is self-contained. The success of every company is affected by the supporting companies and infrastructure around it. Productivity and innovation are strongly influenced by "clusters," or geographic concentrations of firms, related businesses, suppliers, service providers and logistical infrastructure in a particular field – such as IT in Silicon Valley, cut flowers in Kenya, and diamond cutting in Surat, India.

Clusters include not only businesses but institutions such as academic programmes, trade associations and standards organizations. They also draw on the broader public assets in the surrounding community, such as schools and universities, clean water, fair-competition laws, quality standards and market transparency.

Clusters are prominent in all successful and growing regional economies and play a crucial role in driving productivity, innovation and competitiveness. Capable local suppliers foster greater logistical efficiency and ease of collaboration, as we have discussed. Stronger local capabilities in such areas as training, transportation services and related industries also boost productivity. Without a supporting cluster, conversely, productivity suffers.

Deficiencies in the framework conditions surrounding the cluster also create internal costs for firms. Poor public education imposes productivity and remedial-training costs. Poor transportation infrastructure drives up the costs of logistics. Gender or racial discrimination reduces the pool of capable employees. Poverty limits the demand for products and leads to environmental degradation, unhealthy workers and high security costs. As companies have increasingly become disconnected from their communities, however, their influence in solving these problems has waned even as their costs have grown.

Firms create shared value by building clusters to improve company productivity, while addressing gaps or failures in the framework conditions surrounding the cluster. Efforts to develop or attract capable suppliers, for example, enable the procurement benefits we discussed earlier. A focus on clusters and location has been all but absent in management thinking. Cluster thinking has also been missing in many economic development initiatives, which have failed because they involved isolated interventions and overlooked critical complementary investments.

A key aspect of cluster building in developing and developed countries alike is the formation of open and transparent markets. In inefficient or monopolized markets where workers are exploited, where suppliers do not receive fair prices, and where price transparency is lacking, productivity suffers. Enabling fair and open markets, which is often best done in conjunction with partners, can allow a company to secure reliable supplies and give suppliers better incentives for quality and efficiency while also substantially improving the incomes and purchasing power of local citizens. A positive cycle of economic and social development results.

When a firm builds clusters in its key locations, it also amplifies the connection between its success and its communities' success. A firm's growth has multiplier effects, as jobs are created in supporting industries, new companies are seeded and demand for ancillary services rises. A company's efforts to improve framework conditions for the cluster spill over to other participants and the local economy. Workforce development initiatives, for example, increase the supply of skilled employees for many other firms as well.

At Nespresso, Nestlé also worked to build clusters, which made its new procurement practices far more effective. It set out to build agricultural, technical, financial and logistical firms, and capabilities in each coffee region to further support efficiency and high-quality local production. Nestlé led efforts to increase access to essential agricultural inputs such as plant stock, fertilizers and irrigation equipment; strengthen regional farmer co-ops by helping them finance shared wet-milling facilities for producing higher quality beans; and support an extension programme to advise all farmers on growing techniques. It also worked in partnership with the Rainforest Alliance, a leading international NGO, to teach farmers more sustainable practices that make production volumes more reliable. In the process, Nestlé's productivity improved.

A good example of a company working to improve framework conditions in its cluster is Yara, the world's largest mineral fertilizer company. Yara realized that the lack of logistical infrastructure in many parts of Africa was preventing farmers from gaining efficient access to fertilizers and other essential agricultural inputs, and from transporting their crops efficiently to market. Yara is tackling this problem through a $60 million investment in a programme to improve ports and roads, which is designed to create agricultural growth corridors in

Mozambique and Tanzania. The company is working on this initiative with local governments and support from the Norwegian government. In Mozambique alone, the corridor is expected to benefit more than 200,000 small farmers and create 350,000 new jobs. The improvements will help Yara grow its business but will support the whole agricultural cluster, creating huge multiplier effects.

The benefits of cluster building apply not only in emerging economies but also in advanced countries. North Carolina's Research Triangle is a notable example of public and private collaboration that has created shared value by developing clusters in such areas as information technology and life sciences. That region, which has benefited from continued investment from both the private sector and local government, has experienced huge growth in employment, incomes and company performance, and has fared better than most during the downturn.

To support cluster development in the communities in which they operate, companies need to identify gaps and deficiencies in areas such as logistics, suppliers, distribution channels, training, market organization and educational institutions. Then the task is to focus on the weaknesses that represent the greatest constraints to the company's own productivity and growth, and distinguish those areas that the company is best equipped to influence directly from those in which collaboration is more cost-effective. Here is where the shared value opportunities will be greatest. Initiatives that address cluster weaknesses that constrain companies will be much more effective than community focused corporate social responsibility programmes, which often have limited impact because they take on too many areas without focusing on value. But efforts to enhance infrastructure and institutions in a region often require collective action, as the Nestlé, Yara and Research Triangle examples show. Companies should try to enlist partners to share the cost, win support, and assemble the right skills. The most successful cluster development programmes are ones that involve collaboration within the private sector, as well as trade associations, government agencies and NGOs.

Creating shared value in practice

Not all profit is equal – an idea that has been lost in the narrow, short-term focus of financial markets and in much management thinking. Profits involving a social purpose represent a higher form of capitalism – one that will enable society to advance more rapidly while allowing companies to grow even more. The result is a positive cycle of company and community prosperity, which leads to profits that endure.

Creating shared value presumes compliance with the law and ethical standards, as well as mitigating any harm caused by the business, but goes far beyond that. The opportunity to create economic value through creating societal value will be one of the most powerful forces driving growth in the global economy. This thinking represents a new way of understanding customers, productivity and the external influences on corporate success. It highlights the immense human needs to be met, the large new markets to serve, and the internal costs of social and community deficits – as well as the competitive advantages available from addressing them. Until recently, companies have simply not approached their businesses this way.

Creating shared value will be more effective and far more sustainable than the majority of today's corporate efforts in the social arena. Companies will make real strides on the environment, for example, when they treat it as a productivity driver rather than a feel good response to external pressure. Or consider access to housing. A shared value approach would have led financial services companies to create innovative products that prudently increased access to home ownership. This was recognized by the Mexican construction company Urbi, which pioneered a mortgage financing "rent-to-own" plan. Major US banks, in contrast, promoted unsustainable financing vehicles that turned out to be socially and economically devastating, while claiming they were socially responsible because they had charitable contribution programmes.

Inevitably, the most fertile opportunities for creating shared value will be closely related to a company's particular business, and in areas most important to the business. Here a company can benefit the most economically and hence sustain its commitment over time. Here is also where a company brings the most resources to bear, and where its scale and market presence equip it to have a meaningful impact on a societal problem.

Ironically, many of the shared value pioneers have been those with more limited resources – social entrepreneurs and companies in developing countries. These outsiders have been able to see the opportunities more clearly. In the process, the distinction between for-profits and non-profits is blurring.

Shared value is defining a whole new set of best practices that all companies must embrace. It will also become an integral part of strategy. The essence of strategy is choosing a unique positioning and a distinctive value chain to deliver on it. Shared value opens up many new needs to meet, new products to offer, new customers to serve, and new ways to configure the value chain. And the competitive advantages that arise from creating shared value will often be more sustainable than conventional cost and quality improvements. The cycle of imitation and zero-sum competition can be broken.

The opportunities to create shared value are widespread and growing. Not every company will have them in every area, but our experience has been that companies discover more and more opportunities over time as their line operating units grasp this concept. It has taken a decade, but GE's Ecomagination initiative, for example, is now producing a stream of fast-growing products and services across the company.

A shared value lens can be applied to every major company decision. Could our product design incorporate greater social benefits? Are we serving all the communities that would benefit from our products? Do our processes and logistical approaches maximize efficiencies in energy and water use? Could our new plant be constructed in a way that achieves greater community impact? How are gaps in our cluster holding back our efficiency and speed of innovation? How could we enhance our community as a business location? If sites are comparable economically, at which one will the local community benefit the most? If a company can improve societal conditions, it will often improve business conditions and thereby trigger positive feedback loops.

The three avenues for creating shared value are mutually reinforcing. Enhancing the cluster, for example, will enable more local procurement and less dispersed supply chains. New products and services that meet social needs or serve overlooked markets will require new value chain choices in areas such as production, marketing and distribution. And new value chain configurations will create demand for equipment and technology that saves energy, conserves resources and supports employees.

Creating shared value will require concrete and tailored metrics for each business unit in each of the three areas. While some companies have begun to track various social impacts, few have yet tied them to their economic interests at the business level.

Shared value creation will involve new and heightened forms of collaboration. While some shared value

---

EXHIBIT 3.3.5 HOW SHARED VALUE DIFFERS FROM CORPORATE SOCIAL RESPONSIBILITY

Creating shared value (CSV) should supersede corporate social responsibility (CSR) in guiding the investments of companies in their communities. CSR programmes focus mostly on reputation and have only a limited connection to the business, making them hard to justify and maintain over the long run. In contrast, CSV is integral to a company's profitability and competitive position. It leverages the unique resources and expertise of the company to create economic value by creating social value.

In both cases, compliance with laws and ethical standards, and reducing harm from corporate activities are assumed.

CSR	CSV
Value: doing good	Value: economic and societal benefits relative to cost
Citizenship, philanthropy, sustainability	Joint company and community value creation
Discretionary or in response to external pressure	Integral to competing
Separate from profit maximization	Integral to profit maximization
Agenda is determined by external reporting and personal preferences	Agenda is company specific and internally generated
Impact limited by corporate footprint and CSR budget	Realigns the entire company budget
Example:	Example:
Fair trade purchasing	Transforming procurement to increase quality and yield

opportunities are possible for a company to seize on its own, others will benefit from insights, skills and resources that cut across profit/non-profit and private/public boundaries. Here, companies will be less successful if they attempt to tackle societal problems on their own, especially those involving cluster development. Major competitors may also need to work together on precompetitive framework conditions; something that has not been common in reputation-driven CSR initiatives. Successful collaboration will be data driven, clearly linked to defined outcomes, well connected to the goals of all stakeholders, and tracked with clear metrics.

Governments and NGOs can enable and reinforce shared value or work against it.

The next evolution in capitalism

Shared value holds the key to unlocking the next wave of business innovation and growth. It will also reconnect company success and community success in ways that have been lost in an age of narrow management approaches, short-term thinking and deepening divides among society's institutions.

Shared value focuses companies on the right kind of profits – profits that create societal benefits rather than diminish them. Capital markets will undoubtedly continue to pressure companies to generate short-term profits, and some companies will surely continue to reap profits at the expense of societal needs. But such profits will often prove to be short-lived, and far greater opportunities will be missed.

The moment for an expanded view of value creation has come. A host of factors, such as the growing social awareness of employees and citizens and the increased scarcity of natural resources, will drive unprecedented opportunities to create shared value.

We need a more sophisticated form of capitalism, one imbued with a social purpose. But that purpose should arise not out of charity but out of a deeper understanding of competition and economic value creation. This next evolution in the capitalist model recognizes new and better ways to develop products, serve markets and build productive enterprises.

Creating shared value represents a broader conception of Adam Smith's invisible hand. It opens the doors of the pin factory to a wider set of influences. It is not philanthropy, but self-interested behaviour to create economic value by creating societal value. If all companies individually pursued shared value connected to their particular businesses, society's overall interests would be served. And companies would acquire legitimacy in the eyes of the communities in which they operated,

which would allow democracy to work as governments set policies that fostered and supported business. Survival of the fittest would still prevail, but market competition would benefit society in ways we have lost.

Creating shared value represents a new approach to managing that cuts across disciplines. Because of the traditional divide between economic concerns and social ones, people in the public and private sectors have often followed very different educational and career paths. As a result, few managers have the understanding of social and environmental issues required to move beyond today's CSR approaches, and few social sector leaders have the managerial training and entrepreneurial mind-set needed to design and implement shared value models. Most business schools still teach the narrow view of capitalism, even though more and more of their graduates hunger for a greater sense of purpose and a growing number are drawn to social entrepreneurship. The results have been missed opportunity and public cynicism.

Business school curricula will need to broaden in a number of areas. For example, the efficient use and stewardship of all forms of resources will define the next-generation thinking on value chains. Customer behaviour and marketing courses will have to move beyond persuasion and demand creation to the study of deeper human needs and how to serve non-traditional customer groups. Clusters, and the broader locational influences on company productivity and innovation, will form a new core discipline in business schools; economic development will no longer be left only to public policy and economics departments. Business and government courses will examine the economic impact of societal factors on enterprises, moving beyond the effects of regulation and macroeconomics. And finance will need to rethink how capital markets can actually support true value creation in companies – their fundamental purpose – not just benefit financial market participants.

There is nothing soft about the concept of shared value. These proposed changes in business school curricula are not qualitative and do not depart from economic value creation. Instead, they represent the next stage in our understanding of markets, competition and business management.

Not all societal problems can be solved through shared value solutions. But shared value offers corporations the opportunity to utilize their skills, resources and management capability to lead social progress in ways that even the best-intentioned governmental and social sector organizations can rarely match. In the process, businesses can earn the respect of society again.

REFERENCES

Abell, D. (1980) *Defining the Business: The Starting Point of Strategic Planning*, Englewood Cliffs, NJ: Prentice Hall.

Ackermann, R.W. and Bauer, R.A. (1976) *Corporate Social Performance: The Modern Dilemma*, Reston, VA: Reston.

Ackoff, R.L. (1974) *Redesigning the Future*, New York: Wiley.

Adler, N.J. and Gundersen, A. (2007) *International Dimensions of Organizational Behavior* (5th ed.). Thomson South-Western.

Albert, M. (1993) *Capitalism Against Capitalism*, London: Whurr Publishers.

Alkhafaji, A.F. (1989) *A Stakeholder Approach to Corporate Governance: Managing a Dynamic Environment*, Westport, CT: Quorum Books.

Amable, B. (2003) *The Diversity of Modern Capitalism*, Oxford: Oxford University Press.

Ansoff, I. (1965) *Corporate Strategy: An Analytic Approach to Business Policy for Growth and Expansion*, New York: McGraw-Hill.

Axelrod, R. (1976) *The Structure of Decision: The Cognitive Maps of Political Elites*, Princeton, NJ: Princeton University Press.

Barnard, C. (1938) *The Function of the Executive*, Cambridge, MA: Harvard University Press.

Bartlett, C.A. and Ghoshal, S. (1994) 'Changing the Role of Top Management: Beyond Strategy to Purpose', *Harvard Business Review*, November–December, pp. 79–88.

Baysinger, B.D. and Hoskisson, R.E. (1990) 'The Composition of Boards of Directors and Strategic Control: Effects of Corporate Strategy', *Academy of Management Review*, 15(1, January), pp. 72–81.

Berle, A.A. and Means, G.C. (1932) *The Modern Corporation and Private Property*, New York: Transaction Publishers, McMillan.

Blair, M. (1995) *Ownership and Control: Rethinking Corporate Governance for the Twenty-First Century*, Washington: Brookings Institution.

Bourgeois, L.J. and Brodwin, D.R. (1983) 'Putting Your Strategy into Action', *Strategic Management Planning*, March–May.

Bucholz, R.A. (1986) *Business Environment and Public Policy*, Englewood Cliffs, NJ: Prentice Hall.

Buono, A.F. and Nichols, L.T. (1985) *Corporate Policy, Values and Social Responsibility*, New York: Praeger.

Campbell, A. and Tawadey, K. (1990) *Mission and Business Philosophy*, Oxford: Butterworth-Heinemann.

Campbell, A. and Yeung, S. (1991) 'Creating a Sense of Mission', *Long Range Planning*, 24(4, August), pp. 10–20.

Cannon, T. (1992) *Corporate Responsibility*, London: Pitman.

Carroll, A.B. (1993) *Business and Society: Ethics and Stakeholder Management,* (2nd edn), Cincinnati: South-Western Publishing.

Cernat, L. (2004) 'The emerging European corporate governance model: Anglo-Saxon, Continental, or still the century of diversity?', *Journal of European Public Policy*, 11(1), 147–166.

Charkham, J. (1994) *Keeping Good Company: A Study of Corporate Governance in Five Countries*, Oxford: Oxford University Press.

Clarke, T. (1998) 'The Stakeholder Corporation: A Business Philosophy for the Information Age', *Long Range Planning*, 31(2, April), pp. 182–194.

Clarkson, M.B.E. (1995) 'A Stakeholder Framework For Analyzing and Evaluating Corporate Social Performance', *Academy of Management Review*, 20(1, January), pp. 92–117.

Cochran, P.L. and Wartick, S.L. (1994) 'Corporate Governance: A Review of the Literature', in: R.I. Tricker (ed.) *International Corporate Governance: Text, Readings and Cases*, Singapore: Prentice-Hall.

Coe, N., Kelly, P. and Yeung, H.W.C. (2012. *Economic Geography: A Contemporary Introduction* (2nd edn). Wiley.

Collins, J.C. and Porras, J. (1994) *Built To Last: Successful Habits of Visionary Companies*, London: Random House.

Collins, J.C. and Porras, J. (1996) 'Building Your Company's Vision', *Harvard Business Review*, 75(5, September–October), pp. 65–77.

Cummings, S. and Davies, J. (1994) 'Mission, Vision, Fusion', *Long Range Planning*, 27(6, December), pp. 147–150.

D'Iribarne, P. (1996) 'The usefulness of an ethnographic approach to the international comparison of organizations', *International Studies of Management & Organization*, 26(4), pp. 30–47.

David, F.R. (1989) 'How Companies Define Their Mission', *Long Range Planning*, 22(1, February), pp. 90–97.

Deal, T. E. and Kennedy, A. A. (1982) *Corporate Cultures: The Rites and Rituals of Organizational Life*, New York: Addison-Wesley.

Demb, A. and Neubauer, F.F. (1992) *The Corporate Board: Confronting the Paradoxes*, Oxford: Oxford University Press.

Dicken, P. (2015). *Global Shift: Mapping the Changing Contours of the World Economy* (7th edn). New York: Guilford Press.

Dill, W.R. (1975) 'Public Participation in Corporate Planning: Strategic Management in a Kibitzer's World', *Long Range Planning*, pp. 57–63.

Donaldson, L. and Davis, J.H. (1995) 'Boards and Company Performance: Research Challenges the Conventional Wisdom', *Corporate Governance*, 2, pp. 151–160.

Donaldson, T. and Preston, L.E. (1995) 'The Stakeholder Theory of the Corporation: Concepts, Evidence, and Implications', *Academy of Management Review*, 20(1, January), pp. 65–91.

Drucker, P.F. (1984) 'The New Meaning of Corporate Social Responsibility', *California Management Review*, 26(2, Winter), pp. 53–63.

Eisenhardt, K.M. (1989) 'Agency Theory: An Assessment and Review', *Academy of Management Review*, 14(1, January), pp. 57–74.

Elkington, J. (1980) *The Ecology of Tomorrow's World*, London: Associated Press.

Elkington, J. (1997) *Cannibals with Forks: The Triple Bottom Line of 21st Century Business*, Oxford: Capstone Publishing.

Elkington, J. and Burke, T. (1987) *The Green Capitalists: Industry's Search for Environmental Excellence*, Victor Gollancz.

Emerson, J. (2003) 'The Blended Value Proposition: Integrating Social and Financial Returns', *California Management Review,* Summer.

Epstein, E.M. (1987) 'The Corporate Social Policy Process: Beyond Business Ethics, Corporate Social Responsibility, and Corporate Social Responsiveness', *California Management Review,* 29(3, Spring), pp. 99–114.

Falsey, T.A. (1989) *Corporate Philosophies and Mission Statements*, New York: Quorum Books.

Freeman, R.E. (1984) *Strategic Management: A Stakeholder Approach*, Boston, MA: Pitman/Ballinger.

Freeman, R.E. and Gilbert Jr., D.R. (1988) *Corporate Strategy and the Search for Ethics*, Englewood Cliffs, NJ: Prentice Hall.

Freeman, R.E. and Liedtka, J. (1991) 'Corporate Social Responsibility: A Critical Approach', *Business Horizons*, July–August.

Freeman, R.E. and Reed, D.L. (1983) 'Stockholders and Stakeholders: A New Perspective on Corporate Governance', *California Management Review*, 25(3, Spring), pp. 88–106.

Friedman, M. (1962) *Capitalism and Freedom*, Chicago, IL: University of Chicago Press.

Friedman, M. (1970) 'The Social Responsibility of Business is to Increase Its Profits', *The New York Times Magazine*, September 13–13.

Fukayama, F. (1992) *The End of History and the Last Man*, New York: Free Press.

Fukayama, F. (2004) *State-Building: Governance and World Order in the 21st Century*, Ithaca, NY: Cornell University Press.

Fukayama, F. (2011) *The Origins of Political Order*, London: Profile Books.

Guthrie, J. and Turnbull, S. (1994) 'Audit Committees: Is There a Role for Corporate Senates and/or Stakeholder Councils?', *Corporate Governance*, 3, pp. 78–89.

Hall, P.A. and Soskice D. (eds) (2001) *Varieties of Capitalism: The Institutional Foundations of Comparative Advantage*, New York: Oxford University Press.

Hamel, G., Doz, Y. L. and Prahalad, C. K. (1989) 'Collaborate with your competitors and win', *Harvard Business Review*, 67(1), pp. 133–139.

Hampden-Turner, C. and Trompenaars, F. (2000). *Building Cross-Cultural Competence: How to Create Wealth from Conflicting Values*, New Haven: Yale University Press.

Hart, O.D. (1995) *Firms, Contracts and Financial Structure*, Oxford: Clarendon Press.

Hax, A.C. (1990) 'Redefining the Concept of Strategy and the Strategy Formation Process', *Planning Review*, May–June, pp. 34–40.

Hayes, R. and Abernathy, W. (1980) 'Managing Our Way to Economic Decline', *Harvard Business Review*, 58(4), pp. 66–77.

Hoffman, W.M. (1989) 'The Cost of a Corporate Conscience', *Business and Society Review*, 94(Spring), pp. 46–47.

Hofstede, G. (1980) *Culture's Consequences: International Differences in Work Related Values*, Beverly Hills, CA: Sage.

Hofstede, G. (1996) 'Riding the waves of commerce: A test of Trompenaars' "model" of national culture differences', *International Journal of Intercultural Relations*, 20(2), pp. 189–198.

Holden, N.J. (2002) *Cross-Cultural Management: A Knowledge Management Perspective*, Harlow: Financial Times/Prentice Hall.

House, R.J., Hanges, P.J., Javidan, M., Dorfman, P.W. and Gupta, V. (2004) *Culture, Leadership, and Organizations*, London: Sage.

Jensen, M.C. and Meckling, W.H. (1976) 'Theory of the Firm, Managerial Behavior, Agency Costs, and Ownership Structure', *Journal of Financial Economics*, 3(4, October), pp. 305–360.

Jones, T.M. (1995) 'Instrumental Stakeholder Theory: A Synthesis of Ethics and Economics', *Academy of Management Review*, 20(2, April), pp. 404–437.

Keasey, K., Thompson, S. and Wright, M. (eds.) (1997) *Corporate Governance: Economic, Management, and Financial Issues*, Oxford: Oxford University Press.

Kessel, M. (2014) 'Restoring the pharmaceutical industry's reputation', *Nature Biotechnology*, 32(10), 983–990.

Klemm, M., Sanderson, S. and Luffman, G. (1991) 'Mission Statements', *Long Range Planning*, 24(3, June), pp. 73–78.

Klimoski, R. and Mohammed, S. (1994) 'Team Mental Model: Construct or Metaphor', *Journal of Management*, 20, pp. 403–437.

Kluckhohn, F.R. and Strodtbeck, F.L. (1961) *Variations in Value Orientations*, New York: Row, Peterson & Company.

Langtry, B. (1994) 'Stakeholders and the Moral Responsibilities of Business', *Business Ethics Quarterly*, 4, pp. 431–443.

Levitt, T. (1960) 'Marketing Myopia', *Harvard Business Review*, 38(July–August), pp. 45–56.

Lewis, R.D. (2003) *The Cultural Imperative: Global Trends in the 21st Century*, London: Nicholas Brealey Publishing.

Martin, J. (1992) *Cultures in Organizations: Three Perspectives*, Oxford University Press.

Martin, R. (2010) 'The Age of Customer Capitalism', *Harvard Business Review*, Jan–Feb, pp. 3–9.

McCoy, C.S. (1985) *Management of Values*, Cambridge, MA: Ballinger: Cambridge, MA.

Mintzberg, H. (1984) 'Who Should Control the Corporation?' *California Management Review*, 27(1, Fall), pp. 90–115.

O'Neill, J. (2001) 'Building Better Global Economic BRICs', Global Economics Paper No. 66, Goldman Sachs & Co.

Ohmae, K. (1985) *Triad Power: The Coming Shape of Global Competition*, New York: Free Press.

Pearce, J.A. (1982) 'The Company Mission as a Strategic Tool', *Sloan Management Review*, Spring, pp. 15–24.

Peters, T.J. and Waterman, R.H. (1982) *In Search of Excellence*, New York: Harper & Row.

Piercy, N.F. and Morgan, N.A. (1994) 'Mission Analysis: An Operational Approach', *Journal of General Management*, 19(3), pp. 1–16.

Porter, M.E. (1990) *The Competitive Advantage of Nations*, New York: Free Press.

Porter, M.E. and Kramer, M.A. (2006) 'Strategy and Society: The Link Between Competitive Advantage and Corporate Social Responsibility', *Harvard Business Review*, December.

Porter, M.E. and Kramer, M.A. (2011) 'Creating Shared Value: How to reinvent capitalism and unleash a wave of innovation and growth', *Harvard Business Review*, January–February, pp. 3–17.

Prahalad, C.K. and Bettis, R.A. (1986) 'The Dominant Logic: A New Linkage Between Diversity and Performance', *Strategic Management Journal,* November–December, pp. 485–601.

Prahalad, C.K. and Hart S.L. (2002) 'The Fortune ate the Bottom of the Pyramid', *Strategy+Business*, 26–26, First quarter.

Rappaport, A. (1986) *Creating Shareholder Value: The New Standard for Business Performance,* New York: Free Press.

Sarkar, J. and Sarkar, S. (2000). 'Large shareholder activism in corporate governance in developing countries: Evidence from India', *International Review of Finance*, 1(3), 161–194.

Schein, E. H. (1995) *Organizational Culture*, Frankfurt/New York: Campus Verlag.

Schein, E.H. (2004) *Organizational Culture and Leadership*, San Francisco, CA: John Wiley & Sons.

Schneider, S. and Barsoux, J-L. (1999) *Managing Across Cultures*, London: Pearson Education.

Schwartz, S.H. (1999) 'A theory of cultural values and some implications for work', *Applied Psychology*, 48(1), pp. 23–47.

Senge, P. (1990) *The Fifth Discipline: The Art and Practice of the Learning Organization*, New York: Doubleday.

Solomon, R.C. (1992) *Ethics and Excellence: Cooperation and Integrity in Business*, New York: Oxford University Press.

Spencer, A. (1983) *On the Edge of the Organization: The Role of the Outside Director*, New York: Wiley.

Stone, C.D. (1975) *Where the Law Ends*, New York: Harper & Row.

Sykes, A. (1994) 'Proposals for Internationally Competitive Corporate Governance in Britain and America', *Corporate Governance*, 2(4), pp. 187–195.

Tricker, R.I. (ed.) (1994) *International Corporate Governance: Text, Readings and Cases*, Singapore: Prentice Hall.

Verluyten, S.P. (2010) *Intercultural Skills for Business and International Relations: A Practical Introduction with Exercise*, Leuven: Acco.

Wartick, S.L. and Wood, D.J. (1998) *International Business and Society*, Oxford: Blackwell.

Weiss, J. W. (2014). *Business Ethics: A Stakeholder and Issues Management Approach* (6th edn.). San Francisco: Berrett-Koehler Publishers.

Yoshimori, M. (1995) 'Whose Company Is It? The Concept of the Corporation in Japan and the West', *Long Range Plann*ing, 28, pp. 33–45.

Zahra, S.A. and Pearce, J.A. (1989) 'Boards of Directors and Corporate Financial Performance: A Review and Integrative Model', *Journal of Management,* 15, pp. 291–334.

STRATEGY CONTENT

Every generation laughs at the old fashions but religiously follows the new.

Henry David Thoreau (1817–1862); American philosopher

The strategy content section deals with the question of what the strategy should be. What course of action should the firm follow to achieve its purpose? In determining what the strategy should be, two types of 'fit' are of central concern to managers. First, there needs to be a fit between the firm and its environment. If the two become misaligned, the firm will be unable to meet the demands of the environment and will start to underperform, which can eventually lead to bankruptcy or takeover. This type of fit is also referred to as 'external consonance'. At the same time, managers are also concerned with achieving an internal fit between the various parts of the firm. If various units become misaligned, the organization will suffer from inefficiency, conflict and poor external performance, which can also eventually lead to its demise. This type of fit is also referred to as 'internal consistency'.

As external consonance and internal consistency are prerequisites for a successful strategy, they need to be achieved for each organizational unit. Most organizations have various levels, making it necessary to ensure internal and external fit at each level of aggregation within the firm. In Figure II.1 all these possible levels within a corporation have been reduced to just three general categories, to which a fourth, supra-organizational level has been added. At each level the strategy should meet the requirements of external consonance and internal consistency:

■ Functional level strategy. For each functional area, such as marketing, operations, finance, logistics, human resources, procurement and R&D, a strategy needs to be developed. At this level, internal consistency means having an overarching functional strategy that integrates various functional sub-strategies (e.g. a marketing strategy that aligns branding, distribution, pricing, product and communication strategies). External consonance is achieved when strategy is aligned with the demands in the relevant external arena (e.g. the logistics or procurement environment).

■ Business level strategy. At the business level, an organization can only be effective if it can integrate functional level strategies into an internally consistent whole. To achieve external consonance the business unit must be aligned with the specific demands in the relevant business area.

■ Corporate level strategy. When a company operates in two or more business areas, the business level strategies need to be aligned to form an internally consistent corporate level strategy. Between business and corporate levels there can also be divisions, yet for most strategy purposes they can be approached as mini-corporations (both divisional and corporate level strategy are technically speaking 'multi-business level'). Achieving external consonance at this level of aggregation means that a corporation must be able to act as one tightly integrated unit or as many autonomous, differentiated units, depending on the demands of the relevant environment.

■ Network level strategy. When various firms work together, it sometimes is deemed necessary to align business and/or corporate level strategies to shape an internally consistent network level strategy. Such a network, or multi-company, level strategy can involve anywhere between two and thousands of companies. Here, too, the group must develop a strategy that fits with the demands in the relevant environment.

As the strategy content issues differ greatly depending on the level of aggregation under discussion, this section has been divided along the following lines. Chapter 4 focuses on business level strategy, Chapter 5 on corporate level strategy and Chapter 6 on network level strategy. The functional level strategies will not be given extensive coverage, as they are usually explored in great detail in functionally oriented books. It must be noted, however, that the aggregation levels used here are an analytical distinction and not an empirical reality that can always be found in practice – where one level stops and the other starts is more a matter of definition than of thick demarcation lines. Hence, when discussing strategy issues at any level, it is important to understand how they fit with higher and lower level strategy questions.

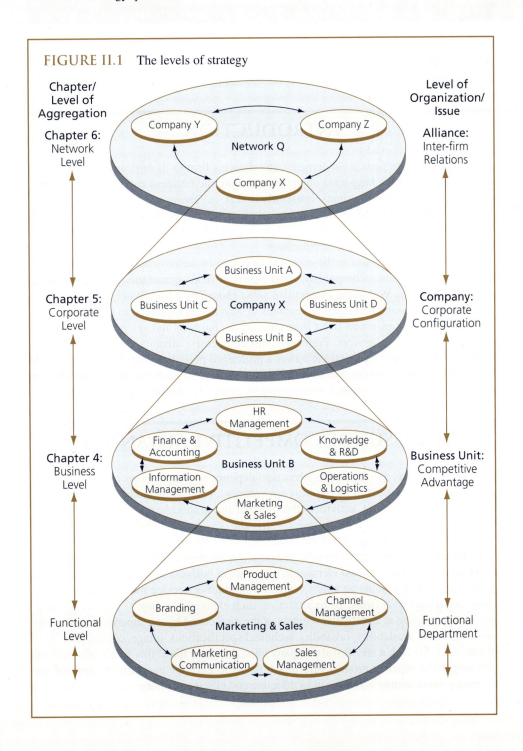

FIGURE II.1   The levels of strategy

BUSINESS LEVEL STRATEGY

Advantage is a better soldier than rashness.
William Shakespeare (1564–1616); English dramatist and poet

INTRODUCTION

Strategic management is concerned with relating a firm to its environment in order to successfully meet long-term objectives. As both the business environment and individual firms are dynamic systems, constantly in flux, achieving a fit between the two is an ongoing challenge. Managers are continuously looking for new ways to align the current, and potential, strengths and weaknesses of the organization with the current, and potential, opportunities and threats in the environment.

Part of the difficulty lies in the competitive nature of the environment. To be successful, firms need to gain a competitive advantage over rival organizations operating in the same business area. Within the competitive arena chosen by a firm, it needs to accrue sufficient power to counterbalance the demands of buyers and suppliers, to outperform rival producers, to discourage new firms from entering the business and to fend off the threat of substitute products or services. Preferably, this competitive advantage over other players in the business should be sustainable over a prolonged period of time. How firms should go about creating a (sustainable) competitive advantage in each business in which they operate is the central issue concerning managers engaged in business level strategy.

THE ISSUE OF COMPETITIVE ADVANTAGE

Whether a firm has a competitive advantage depends on the business model that it has developed to relate itself to its business environment. A business model is the configuration of resources (inputs), activities (throughput) and product/service offerings (output) intended to create value for customers – it is the way a firm conducts its business. In Figure 4.1 an overview is given of the components of a business model.

Competitive advantage can be achieved only if a business model creates superior value for buyers. Therefore, the first element in a successful business model is a superior 'value proposition'. A firm must be able to supply a product or service more closely fitted to client needs than rival firms. To be attractive, each element of a firm's 'product offering' needs to be targeted at a particular segment of the market and have a superior mix of attributes (e.g. price, availability, reliability, technical specifications, image, colour, taste, ease of use, etc.). Second, a successful company must also have the ability to actually develop and supply the superior product offering. It needs to have the capability to perform the necessary value-adding activities in an effective and efficient manner.

FIGURE 4.1   Components of a business model

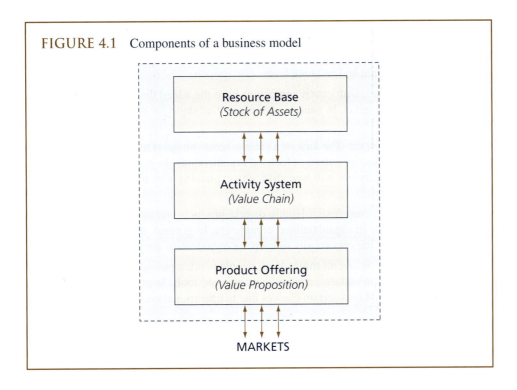

These value-adding activities, such as R&D, production, logistics, marketing and sales, are jointly referred to as a firm's value chain. The third component of a business model consists of the resource base required to perform the value-adding activities. Resources such as know-how, patents, facilities, money, brands and relationships make up the stock of assets that can be employed to create the product offering. If these firm-specific assets are distinctive and useful, they can form the basis of a superior value proposition. To create a competitive advantage, alignment must be achieved between all three elements of a business model. In the following pages all three elements will be discussed in more detail.

Product offering

At the intersection between a firm and its environment, transactions take place whereby the firm supplies goods or performs services for clients in the marketplace. It is here that the alignment of the firm and its environment is put to the test. If the products and services offered by the firm are more highly valued by customers than alternatives, a profitable transaction could take place. In other words, for sales to be achieved a firm must have a competitive value proposition – a cluster of physical goods, services or additional attributes with a superior fit to customer needs.

For the strategizing manager the key question is which products should be developed and which markets should be served. In many cases the temptation is to be everything to everybody – making a wide range of products and serving as many clients as possible. However, a number of practical constraints inhibit companies from taking such an unfocused approach to the market. Companies that do not focus on a limited set of product–market combinations run the risk of encountering a number of major problems:

- Low economies of scale. Being unfocused is expensive, because of the low economies of scale that can be achieved. In general, the less specialized the company, the lower the opportunities to organize the value chain efficiently and leverage its resource base.

- **Slow organizational learning.** Being involved in a multitude of products and markets generally slows the organization's ability to build up specific knowledge and capabilities. In general, the less specialized the company, the lower the opportunity to develop a distinctive value chain and resource base.

- **Unclear brand image.** Unfocused companies have the added disadvantage of having a fuzzy image in the market. In general, companies that stand for everything tend to stand out in nothing.

- **Unclear corporate image.** The lack of a clear external image is usually compounded by a lack of internal identity within unfocused organizations. In general, a company with highly diversified activities will have difficulty explaining why its people are employed at the same company.

- **High organizational complexity.** Highly diverse products and customers also create an exponential increase in organizational complexity. In general, the less specialized the company, the lower the opportunity to keep the organization simple and manageable.

- **Limits to flexibility.** Being all things to all people is often physically impossible due to the need to specify procedures, routines, systems and tools. In general, less specialized firms are often forced into certain choices due to operational necessity.

For these reasons, companies need to focus on a limited number of businesses and within each business on a limited group of customers and a limited set of products. This focus should not be arbitrary – the challenge for strategizing managers is to understand which businesses are (or can be made to be) structurally attractive and how their firm can gain a competitive advantage within each business, by offering specific value propositions to selected customer segments.

Determining a focus starts by looking for the 'boundaries' of a business – how can managers draw meaningful delineation lines in the environment, distinguishing one arena of competition from another, so that they can select some and ignore others? Ideally, the environment would be made up of neatly compartmentalized businesses, with clear borders separating them. In reality, however, the picture is much more messy. While there are usually certain clusters of buyers and suppliers interacting more intensely with one another, suggesting that they are operating in the same business, there are often numerous exceptions to any neat classification scheme. To explore how a business can be defined, it is first necessary to specify how a business differs from an 'industry' and a 'market'.

Delineating industries. An industry is defined as a group of firms making a similar type of product or employing a similar set of value-adding processes or resources. In other words, an industry consists of producers that are much alike – there is *supply side similarity* (Kay, 1993). The simplest way to draw an industry boundary is to use product similarity as the delineation criterion. For instance, British Airways can be said to be in the airline industry, along with many other providers of the same product, such as Singapore Airlines and Ryanair. However, an industry can also be defined on the basis of value chain similarity (e.g. consulting industry and mining industry) or resource similarity (e.g. information technology industry and oil industry).

Economic statisticians tend to favour fixed industry categories based on product similarity and therefore most figures available about industries are product–category-based, often making use of Standard Industrial Classification (SIC) codes. Strategists, on the contrary, like to challenge existing definitions of an industry, for instance by regrouping them on the basis of underlying value-adding activities or resources. Take the example of Swatch – how did it conceptualize which industry it was in? If they had focused on the physical product and the production process, then they would have been inclined to situate Swatch in the watch industry. However, Swatch also viewed its products as fashion

FIGURE 4.2   Alternative industry categorizations

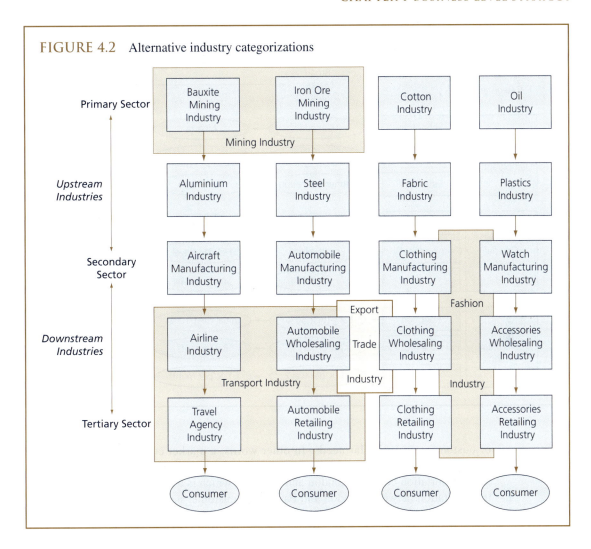

accessories, placing emphasis on the key value-adding activities of fashion design and marketing. On this basis, Swatch could just as well be categorized as a member of the fashion industry (Porac, Thomas and Baden-Fuller, 1989). For the strategizing manager, the realization that Swatch can be viewed in both ways is an important insight. As creating a competitive advantage often comes from doing things differently, rethinking the definition of an industry can be a powerful way to develop a unique product offering.

Figure 4.2 gives four examples of traditionally defined 'industry columns', which Porter (1980) draws not top-down, but left-right, using the term 'value system'. These columns start with upstream industries, which are involved in the extraction/growing of raw materials and their conversion into inputs for the manufacturing sector. Downstream industries take the output of manufacturing companies and bring them to clients, often adding a variety of services into the product mix. In practice, industry columns are not as simple as depicted in Figure 4.2, as each industry has many different industries as suppliers and usually many different industries as buyers.

A second limitation of the industry columns shown in Figure 4.2 is that they are materials-flow oriented – industry boundaries are drawn on the basis of product.

Segmenting markets.   While economists see the market as a place where supply and demand meet, in the business world a market is usually defined as a group

FIGURE 4.3   Alternative market categorizations

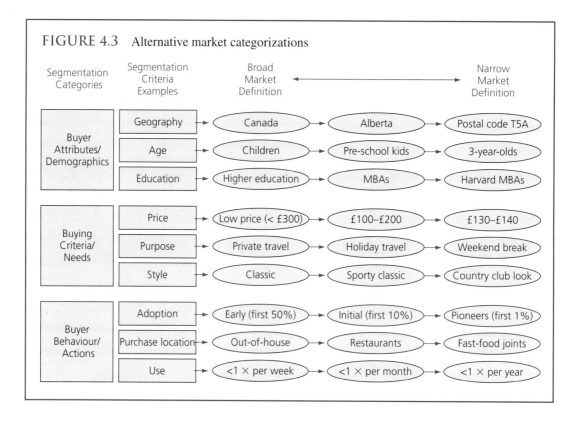

of customers with similar needs. In other words, a market consists of buyers whose demands are much alike – *demand side similarity*. For instance, there is a market for air transportation between London and Jamaica, which is a different market than for air transportation between London and Paris – the customer needs are different and therefore these products cannot be substituted for one another. But customers can substitute a British Airways London–Paris flight for one by Air France, indicating that both companies are serving the same market. Yet, this market definition (London–Paris air transport) might not be the most appropriate, if in reality many customers are willing to substitute air travel for rail travel through the Channel Tunnel, or by ferry. In this case, there is a broader London–Paris transportation market, and air transportation is a specific *market segment*. If many customers are willing to substitute physical travel by teleconferencing or other telecommunications methods, the market might need to be defined as the 'London–Paris meeting market'.

As with industries, there are many ways of defining markets, depending on which buyer characteristics are used to make a clustering. In Figure 4.3, examples of segmentation criteria are given. The first group of segmentation criteria is based on buyer attributes that are frequently thought to be important predictors of actual buying criteria and buyer behaviour. Such customer characteristics are commonly used to group potential clients because this information is objective and easily available. However, the pitfall of segmenting on the basis of buyer attributes is that the causal link between characteristics and actual needs and behaviours is often rather tenuous – not all Canadians need hockey sticks and not all three-year-olds nag their parents while shopping. In other words, the market can be segmented on the basis of any demographic characteristic (e.g. income, family composition, employment), but this might not lead to meaningful groups of customers with similar needs and buying behaviour.

Therefore, instead of using buyer attributes as *indirect* – predictive – measures of what clients probably want, segments can also be *directly* defined on the basis of buying criteria employed or buyer behaviours exhibited. The advantage is that segments can then be identified with clearly similar wishes or behaviours. The disadvantage is that it is very difficult to gather and interpret information on what specific people want and how they really act.

For strategists, one of the key challenges is to look at existing categorizations of buyers and to wonder whether a different segmentation would offer new insights and new opportunities for developing a product offering specifically tailored to their needs. As with the redefining of industry boundaries, it is often in the reconceptualization of market segments that a unique approach to the market can be found.

Defining and selecting businesses.   A business is a set of related product–market combinations. The term 'business' refers neither to a set of producers nor a group of customers, but to the domain where the two meet. In other words, a business is a competitive arena where companies offering similar products serving similar needs compete against one another for the favour of the buyers. Hence, a business is delineated in both industry and market terms (see Figure 4.4). Typically, a business is narrower than the entire industry and the set of markets served is also limited. For instance, within the airline industry the charter business is usually recognized as rather distinct. In the charter business, a subset of the airline services is offered to a number of tourist markets. Cheap flights from London to Jamaica and from London to Barcelona fall within this business, while service levels will be different than in other parts of the airline industry. It should be noted, though, that just as with industries and markets, there is no best way to define the boundaries of a business (Abell, 1980).

As stated earlier, companies cannot afford to be unfocused, operating superficially in a whole range of businesses. They must direct their efforts by focusing in two ways:

1 Selecting a limited number of businesses. The first constraint that companies need to impose on themselves is to choose a limited array of businesses within which they wish to be successful. This essential strategic challenge is referred to as the issue of corporate configuration and will be examined in more detail in Chapter 5 (multi-business level strategy). Here it suffices to say that firms need to analyse the structural characteristics of interesting businesses to be able to judge whether they are attractive enough for the firm, or can be made to be attractive. Porter presents the 'five forces analysis' as a framework for mapping the structure of industries and businesses.

2 Focusing within each selected business. Even within the limited set of businesses selected, firms need to determine what they want to be and what they want to leave aside. To be competitive, it is necessary to choose a number of distinct market segments

FIGURE 4.4   Industries, markets and businesses

and to target a few special product offerings to meet these customers' needs. As illustrated in Figure 4.1, these specific product offerings in turn need to be aligned with a focused value chain and resource base.

This act of focusing the overall business model to serve the particular needs of a targeted group of buyers, in a way that distinguishes the firm vis-à-vis rivals, is called positioning. This positioning of the firm in the business requires a clearly tailored product offering (product positioning), but also a value chain and resource base that closely fit with the demands of the specific group of customers and competitors being targeted.

Positioning within a business. Positioning is concerned with both the questions of "where to compete" and "how to compete" (Porter, 1980). Determining in which product–market combinations within a business a firm wants to be involved is referred to as the issue of competitive scope. Finding a way to beat rivals and win over customers for a product offering is the issue of competitive advantage. The two questions are tightly linked, because firms need to develop a specific advantage to be competitive within a specific product–market domain. If they try to use the same competitive advantage for too many dissimilar products and customers, they run the risk of becoming unfocused.

In selecting a competitive scope, firms can vary anywhere between being widely oriented and very tightly focused. Firms with a broad scope compete in a large number of segments within a business, with varied product offerings. Firms with a narrow scope target only one, or just a few, customer segments and have a more limited product line (see Figure 4.5). If there is a small part of the business with very specific demands, requiring a distinct approach, firms can narrowly focus on this niche as their competitive scope. In between these two extremes are firms with a segment focus and firms with a product focus, but in practice many other profiles are also possible.

In developing a competitive advantage, firms have many dimensions along which they can attempt to outdo their rivals. Some of the most important bases of competitive advantage are the following:

- Price. The most straightforward advantage a firm can have in a competitive situation is the ability to charge a lower price. All things being equal, buyers generally prefer to pay the lowest amount necessary. Hence, when purchasing a commodity product or service, most customers will be partial to the lowest priced supplier. And even when selecting among differentiated products, many customers will be inclined to buy the cheapest or at least the cheapest within a subgroup of more comparable products. For a firm wanting to compete on price, the essential point is that it should have a *low cost* product offering, value chain and resource base to match the price positioning. After all, in the long run a firm can survive at a lower price level only if it has developed a business model that can sustainably operate at a lower cost level.

- Features. Firms can also distinguish their product offerings by having different intrinsic functional characteristics rather than competing offerings. There are many ways to make a product or service different, for instance by changing its size, smell, taste, colour, functionality, compatibility, content, design or style. An ice cream manufacturer can introduce a new flavour and more chunky texture, a motorcycle producer can design a special low rider model for women, a pay TV company can develop special channels for dog owners and science fiction addicts, and a utility company can offer environmentally friendly electricity. To be able to compete on each of these product features, firms need to command different specialized resources and value chains. In some cases, they require significant technological knowledge and a technically sophisticated value chain, while in other cases design capabilities, marketing prowess or a satellite infrastructure are essential to the functioning of the business model.

FIGURE 4.5   Determining competitive scope

- **Bundling.** Another way to offer a uniquely different value proposition is to sell a package of products or services 'wrapped together'. By bundling a number of separate elements into a package, the customer can have the convenience of 'one stop shopping', while also having a family of related products or services that fit together well. So, for instance, many customers prefer to purchase their software from one supplier because this increases the chance of compatibility. In the chocolate industry, the leading manufacturer of chocolate-making machines, Rademakers, was able to gain a competitive advantage by bundling its machines with various services, such as installation, repair, spare parts and financing.

- **Quality.** When competing with others, a firm's product offering doesn't necessarily have to be fundamentally different, it can just be better. Customers generally appreciate products and services that exhibit superior performance in terms of usability, reliability and durability, and are often willing to pay a premium price for such quality. Excellent quality can be secured on many fronts, for instance through the materials used, the people involved, the manufacturing process employed, the quality assurance procedures followed or the distribution system used.

- **Availability.** The method of distribution can in itself be the main competitive edge on which a firm bases its positioning. Having a product available at the right place, at the right moment and in the right way, can be much more important to customers than features and quality. Just ask successful ice cream manufacturers – most of their revenues are from out-of-doors impulse sales, so they need to have their products available in individually wrapped portions at all locations where people have the urge to indulge. In the same way, Avon's cosmetics are not primarily sold because of their uniqueness or low price, but because of the strength of their three million sales force, who can be at the right place at the right time.

- **Image.** In the competition for customers' preference, firms can also gain an advantage by having a more appealing image than their rivals. In business-to-consumer markets this is particularly clear when looking at the impact of brands. Consumers often feel attracted to brands that project a certain image of the company or the products it sells. Brands can communicate specific values that consumers want to be associated with (Nike's 'just do it'), or can help to build trust among consumers who have too little information on which to base their product choices (GE's 'we bring good things to life'). But even in business-to-business markets, buyers often suffer from a shortage of information about the available product offerings or lack the time to research all possible suppliers. Therefore, the image of suppliers, mostly in terms of their standing ('a leading global player') and reputation ('high quality service') can be essential to be considered at all (to be 'shortlisted') and to be trusted as a business partner.

■ Relations. Good branding can give customers the impression that they know the supplier, without actually being in direct contact. Yet, having a direct relation with customers can in itself be a potent source of competitive advantage. In general, customers prefer to know their suppliers well, as this gives them more intimate knowledge of the product offering being provided. Having a relationship with a supplier can also give the customer more influence on what is offered. Besides these rational points, customers often value the personal contact, the trust and the convenience of having a longstanding relationship as well. For suppliers this means that they might acquire a competitive edge by managing their customer relationships well. To do so, however, does imply that the value chain and resource base are fit to fulfil this task.

The type of competitive advantage that a firm chooses to pursue will be influenced by what the targeted group of buyers find important. These factors of importance to potential clients are referred to as 'value drivers' – they are the elements responsible for creating value in the eyes of the customer. Which value drivers a firm will want to base its value proposition on is a matter of positioning.

According to Porter (1980) all the specific forms of competitive advantage listed above can be reduced to two broad categories, namely lower cost and differentiation. On the one hand, firms can organize their business models in such a manner that, while their products or services are largely the same as other manufacturers, their overall cost structure is lower, allowing them to compete on price. On the other hand, firms can organize their business models to supply a product or service that has distinctive qualities compared to rival offerings. According to Porter, these two forms of competitive advantage demand fundamentally different types of business models and therefore are next to impossible to combine. Firms that do try to realize both at the same time run the risk of getting 'stuck in the middle' – not being able to do either properly.

Treacy and Wiersema (1995) argue that there are three generic competitive advantages, each requiring a fundamentally different type of business model (they speak of three distinctive 'value disciplines'). They, too, warn firms to develop an internally consistent business model focused on one of these types of competitive advantage, avoiding a 'mix-and-match' approach to business strategy:

■ Operational excellence. Firms striving for operational excellence meet the buyers' need for a reliable, low cost product offering. The value chain required to provide such no-frills, standardized, staple products emphasizes a 'lean and mean' approach to production and distribution, with simple service.

■ Product leadership. Firms taking the route of product leadership meet the buyers' need for special features and advanced product performance. The value chain required to provide such differentiated, state-of-the-art products emphasizes innovation and the creative collaboration between marketing and R&D.

■ Customer intimacy. Firms deciding to focus on customer intimacy meet the buyers' need for a tailored solution to their particular problem. The value chain required to provide such a client-specific, made-to-measure offering emphasizes flexibility and empowerment of the employees close to the customer.

Other strategy researchers, however, argue that there is no such thing as generic competitive strategies that follow from two or three broad categories of competitive advantage (e.g. Baden-Fuller and Stopford, 1992). In their view, there is an endless variety of ways in which companies can develop a competitive advantage, many of which do not fit into the categories outlined by Porter or Treacy and Wiersema – in fact, finding a new type of competitive advantage might be the best way of obtaining a unique position in a business.

Value chain

To be able to actually make what it wants to sell, a firm needs to have a value chain in place. A value chain is an integrated set of value creation processes leading to the supply of product or service offerings. Whether goods are being manufactured or services are being provided, each firm needs to perform a number of activities to successfully satisfy the customers' demands. As these value-adding activities need to be coordinated and linked together, this part of the business model is also frequently referred to as the 'value chain' (Porter, 1985).

Value chains can vary widely from industry to industry. The value chain of a car manufacturer is quite distinct from that of an advertising agency. Yet even within an industry there can be significant differences. Most 'bricks and mortar' bookstores have organized their value chain differently from online book retailers like amazon.com. The value chains of most 'hub-and-spoke' airline companies hardly resemble that of 'no-frills' carriers such as Southwest in the United States and easyJet in Europe.

While these examples point to radically different value chains, even firms that subscribe to the same basic model can apply it in their own particular way. Fast-food restaurants such as McDonald's and Burger King may employ the same basic model, but their actual value chains differ in quite a few ways. The same goes for the PC manufacturers HP and Lenovo, which share a similar type of value chain, but which still differ on many fronts. 'Online mass-customization' PC manufacturer Dell, on the other hand, has a different model and consequently a more strongly differing value chain than HP and Lenovo.

Having a distinct value chain often provides the basis for a competitive advantage. A unique value chain allows a firm to offer customers a unique value proposition, by doing things better, faster, cheaper, nicer or more tailored than competing firms. Developing the firm's value chain is therefore just as strategically important as developing new products and services.

Although value chains can differ quite significantly, some attempts have been made to develop a general taxonomy of value-adding activities that could be used as an analytical framework (e.g. Day, 1990; Norman and Ramirez, 1993). By far the most influential framework is Porter's value chain, which distinguishes primary activities and support activities (see Figure 4.6). Primary activities "are the activities involved in the physical creation of the product and its sale and transfer to the buyer, as well as after-sale assistance" (Porter, 1985: 16). Support activities facilitate the primary process, by providing purchased inputs, technology, human resources and various firm-wide functions. The generic categories of primary activities identified by Porter are:

- Inbound logistics. Activities associated with receiving, storing and disseminating inputs, including material handling, warehousing, inventory control, vehicle scheduling and returns to suppliers.

- Operations. Activities associated with transforming inputs into final products, including machining, packaging, assembly, equipment maintenance, testing, printing and facility operations.

- Outbound logistics. Activities associated with collecting, storing and physically distributing products to buyers, including warehousing, material handling, delivery, order processing and scheduling.

FIGURE 4.6   The generic value chain (Porter, 1985)

- Marketing and sales. Activities associated with providing a means by which buyers can purchase the product and inducing them to do so, including advertising, promotion, sales force, quoting, channel selection, channel relations and pricing.
- Service. Activities associated with providing service to enhance or maintain the value of products, including installation, repair, training, parts supply and product adjustment.

For service industries Porter argues that the specific activities will be different, and might be performed in a different order, but can still be subdivided into these five generic categories. To ensure that the primary activities can be carried out, each firm also needs to organize four types of support activities:

- Procurement. Activities associated with the purchasing of inputs to facilitate all other activities, including vendor selection, negotiations, contracting and invoice administration.
- Technology development. Activities associated with the improvement of technologies throughout the firm, including basic research, product and process design, and procedure development.
- Human resource management. Activities associated with the management of personnel throughout the organization, including recruiting, hiring, training, development and compensation.
- Firm infrastructure. Firm infrastructure consists of all general activities that support the entire value chain, including general management, planning, finance, accounting, legal, government affairs and quality management.

The uniqueness of the value chain, and its strength as the source of competitive advantage will usually not depend on only a few specialized activities, but on the extraordinary configuration of the entire value chain. An extraordinary configuration multiplies the distinctness of a particular value chain, while often raising the barrier to imitation (Amit and Zott, 2001; Porter, 1996).

Resource base

To carry out activities and to produce goods and services, firms need resources. A firm's resource base includes all means at the disposal of the organization for the performance of value-adding activities. Other authors prefer the term 'assets', to emphasize that the resources belong to the firm (e.g. Dierickx and Cool, 1989; Itami, 1987).

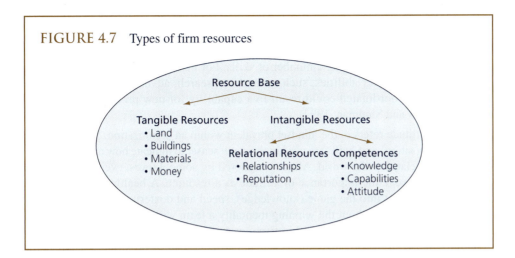

FIGURE 4.7   Types of firm resources

Under the broad umbrella of 'resource-based view of the firm', there has been much research into the importance of resources for the success and even existence of firms (e.g. Penrose, 1959; Wernerfelt, 1984; Barney, 1991, Reading 4.2). No generally accepted classification of firm resources has yet emerged in the field of strategic management, however the following major distinctions (see Figure 4.7) are commonly made:

- Tangible vs intangible resources. Tangible resources are all means available to the firm that can physically be observed (touched), such as buildings, machines, materials, land and money. Tangibles can be referred to as the 'hardware' of the organization. Intangibles, on the other hand, are the 'software' of the organization. Intangible resources cannot be touched, but are largely carried within the people in the organization. In general, tangible resources need to be purchased, while intangibles need to be developed. Therefore, tangible resources are often more readily transferable, easier to price and usually are placed on the balance sheet.

- Relational resources vs competencies. Within the category of intangible resources, relational resources and competencies can be distinguished. Relational resources are all of the means available to the firm derived from the firm's interaction with its environment (Lowendahl, 1997). The firm can cultivate specific relationships with individuals and organizations in the environment, such as buyers, suppliers, competitors and government agencies, which can be instrumental in achieving the firm's goals. As attested by the old saying, 'it's not what you know, but whom you know', relationships can often be an essential resource (see Chapter 6 for a further discussion). Besides direct relationships, a firm's reputation among other parties in the environment can also be an important resource. Competence, on the other hand, refers to the firm's fitness to perform in a particular field. A firm has a competence if it has the knowledge, capabilities and attitude needed to successfully operate in a specific area.

This description of competencies is somewhat broad and therefore difficult to employ. However, a distinction between knowledge, capability and attitude (Durand, 1996) can be used to shed more light on the nature of competencies:

- Knowledge. Knowledge can be defined as the whole of rules (know-how, know-what, know-where and know-when) and insights (know-why) that can be extracted from, and help make sense of, information. In other words, knowledge flows from, and influences, the interpretation of information (Dretske, 1981). Examples of knowledge that a firm can possess are market insight, competitive intelligence, technological expertise and understanding of political and economic developments.

- **Capability.** Capability refers to the organization's potential for carrying out a specific activity or set of activities. Sometimes the term 'skill' is used to refer to the ability to carry out a narrow (functional) task or activity, while the term 'capability' is reserved for the quality of combining a number of skills. For instance, a firm's capability base can include narrower abilities, such as market research, advertising and production skills, that if coordinated could result in a capability for new product development (Stalk, Evans and Shulman, 1992).

- **Attitude.** Attitude refers to the mindset prevalent within an organization. Sometimes the terms 'disposition' and 'will' are used in the same sense, to indicate how an organization views and relates to the world. Although ignored by some writers, every sports coach will acknowledge the importance of attitude as a resource. A healthy body (tangible resource), insight into the game (knowledge), speed and dexterity (capabilities) – all are important, but without the winning mentality a team will not get to the top. Some attitudes may change rapidly within firms, yet others may be entrenched within the cultural fabric of the organization – these in particular can be important resources for the firm. A company's attitude can, for instance, be characterized as quality-driven, internationally oriented, innovation-minded or competitively aggressive.

It must be noted that the term 'competencies' is used in many different ways, partially due to the ambiguous definition given by its early proponents (Prahalad and Hamel, 1990, Reading 5.2 in this book). It is often used as a synonym for capabilities, while Prahalad and Hamel seem to focus more on technologically oriented capabilities ('how to coordinate diverse production skills and integrate multiple streams of technologies'). Others (e.g. Durand, 1996) have suggested that a firm has a competence in a certain area, when the firm's underlying knowledge base, capabilities and attitude are all aligned. So, Honda's engine competence is built on specific knowledge, development capabilities and the right predisposition. Wal-Mart's inventory control competence depends on specific information technology knowledge, coordination capabilities and a conducive state of mind. Virgin's service competence combines customer knowledge, adaptation capabilities and a customer-oriented attitude.

As in the case of industries, markets and businesses, employing the concepts of tangible and intangible resources is quite difficult in practice. Two problems need to be overcome – resources are difficult to categorize, but worse, are often difficult to recognize. The issue of categorization is a minor one. For some resources it is unclear how they should be classified. Are human resources tangible or intangible? Problematically, both. In humans, hardware and software are intertwined – if an engineer's expertise is required, the physical person usually needs to be hired. Knowledge, capabilities and attitudes need human carriers. Sometimes it is possible to separate hardware and software by making the intangibles more tangible. This is done by 'writing the software down'. In such a manner, knowledge can be codified, for instance in a patent, a capability can be captured in a computer program and a relationship can be formalized in a contract. Sometimes intangibles become more tangible, as they become attached to physical carriers – for instance, attitude can be embodied by a person or a symbol, while reputation becomes attached to a brand.

More important is the problem of resource identification. Tangible resources, by their very nature, are relatively easy to observe. Accountants keep track of the financial resources, production managers usually know the quality of their machinery and stock levels, while the personnel department will have an overview of all people on the payroll. Intangible resources, on the other hand, are far more difficult to identify (e.g. Grant, 2002; Itami, 1987). With whom does the firm have a relationship and what is the state of this relationship? What is the firm's reputation? These relational resources are hard to pin down. Competencies are probably even more difficult to determine. How do you know what you know? Even for an individual it is a formidable task to outline areas of expertise, let alone for a more complex organization. Especially the *tacit* (non-articulated) nature of much organizational knowledge makes it difficult to identify the firm's knowledge base (Nonaka and Konno, 1998; Polanyi, 1958). The same is true for a firm's capabilities, which have developed in the form of organizational routines (Nelson and Winter, 1982). Likewise, the firm's attitudes are difficult to discern, because all people sharing the same disposition will tend to consider themselves normal and will tend to believe that their outlook is 'a matter of common sense' (see Chapter 2). Hence, firms intent on identifying their competencies find that this is not an easy task.

While an overview of the firm's resource base is important in itself, a strategizing manager will want to compare the firm's resources to other companies to determine their relative strength. In other words, are the firm's resources unique, superior to or inferior to the resources of (potential) competitors? This type of analysis is particularly difficult, as comparison requires insight into other firms' resource bases. In particular, the identification of other firms' intangible resources can be quite arduous.

Sustaining competitive advantage

A firm has a competitive advantage if it has the means to edge out rivals when vying for the favour of customers. In the previous subsections it was argued that competitive advantage is rooted in a unique business model, whereby the resource base, value chain and product–market position are all aligned to provide goods and/or services with a superior fit to customer needs.

A competitive advantage is said to be sustainable if it cannot be copied, substituted or eroded by the actions of rivals, and is not made redundant by developments in the environment (Porter, 1980). In other words, sustainability depends on two main factors, competitive defendability and environmental consonance:

- Competitive defendability. Some competitive advantages are intrinsically easier to defend than others, either because they are difficult for rivals to imitate, or because rivals find it next to impossible to find an alternative route of attack. In general, a firm's competitive advantage is more vulnerable when it is based on only a limited number of distinct elements (e.g. a different packaging technology, a different delivery system or different product colours). For rivals, imitating or substituting a few elements is comparatively easy. If, however, a firm's business model has an entirely different configuration altogether, the barriers to imitation and substitution are much higher. In such a case, it is said that a firm has a 'distinct business model'. So, for instance, in the airline industry the traditional firms have tried to imitate some parts of the low cost service of Southwest in the United States, and Ryanair and easyJet in Europe, but have been largely unsuccessful because their business model as a whole is based on a different logic. Yet, many strategists note that the best defence is not to build walls around a competitive position to 'keep the barbarians out', but to have the ability to run faster than rivals – to be able to upgrade one's resources, value chain and product offering more rapidly than competitors. In this view, a competitive advantage is sustainable due to a company's capacity to stay one step ahead of rivals, *outpacing* them in a race to stay ahead (e.g. Gilbert and Strebel, 1989; Stalk, Evans and Shulman, 1992).

- Environmental consonance. The sustainability of a firm's competitive advantage is also threatened by developments in the market. Customer needs and wants are in constant flux, distribution channels can change, government regulations can be altered, innovative technologies can be introduced and new entrants can come into the competitive arena. All of these developments can undermine the fit between the firm's competitive advantage and the environment, weakening the firm's position (Rumelt, 1980).

Yet, these two factors for sustaining competitive advantage seem to pose opposite demands on the organization. Building a distinctive business model to fend off competition would suggest that a firm should remain true to its fundamental *strengths,* especially when it comes to unique resources and activities that it has built up over a prolonged period of time. On the other hand, environmental consonance requires a firm to continually adapt its business model to the demands and new *opportunities* in the marketplace. The tension created by these opposite pressures will be discussed in the following section.

THE PARADOX OF MARKETS AND RESOURCES

Instead of being concerned that you have no office, be concerned to think how you may fit yourself for office. Instead of being concerned that you are not known, seek to be worthy of being known.
Confucius (551–479 BC); Chinese philosopher

There must be a fit between an organization and its environment. This point is often expressed in terms of the classic SWOT analysis tool, which suggests that a sound strategy should match a firm's strengths (S) and weaknesses (W) to the opportunities (O) and threats (T) encountered in the firm's environment. The key to success is *alignment* of the two sides (further discussed in Chapter 8). Yet, fitting internal strengths and weaknesses to external opportunities and threats is often frustrated by the fact that the two sides pull in opposite directions – the distinctive resource base and value chain of a firm can point in a totally different direction, as compared to the developments in their current markets. Take the example of Bally, in the 1990s the worldwide market leader in pinball machines. Their strength in the manufacturing of electromechanical games was no longer aligned with developments in the market, where young people were turning to video games developed by companies such as Nintendo, Sega and Sony. As sales of pinball machines were quickly deteriorating, it was clear that Bally had to find a new fit with the market to survive. On the one hand, this meant that there was a strong pressure on Bally to adapt to market developments, for instance by upgrading its technology to also produce video games. On the other hand, Bally felt a strong pressure to exploit its current strength in electromechanical manufacturing, instead of building a new competence base from scratch. It was not self-evident for Bally how the demands for market adaptation and resource leveraging could be met simultaneously, as they seemed to be tugging the firm in diametrically opposite directions.

This tension arising from the partially conflicting demands of market adaptation and resource leveraging is referred to as the paradox of markets and resources. In the following subsections both sides of the paradox will be examined in more detail.

The demand for market adaptation

While adaptation to the environment is a vital requirement for the success of any organization, Bally had been very slow in responding to external developments ever since the introduction of Pac-Man. Bally had not exhibited the ability to shift its product offering to follow changing customer preferences and to respond to new entrants in the gaming market. It had lost its leading position because it no longer fully understood 'the rules of the game' in its own market. As Bally drifted further and further away from developments in the market, the misalignment was threatening the survival of its business. 'Game over' was impending.

To counter this downward trend, Bally needed to identify an attractive market opportunity that it could exploit. Not a short-term sales opportunity, but a market position that could be defended against rival firms and potential new entrants over a longer period. Ideally, this market position would serve buyers willing and able to pay a premium price, and whose loyalty could be won, despite the efforts of the competition. This market position would also need to be largely immune to substitute products and should not make the firm overly dependent on strong suppliers. Once such an opportunity had been identified, it would be essential for Bally to reorganize itself to fully meet the demands of this new positioning.

Adapting to a new market position and subsequently following the many shifts in such factors as customer preferences, competitor moves, government regulations and distribution structures, can have a significant impact on a firm. It requires significant agility in changing the product offering, value chain and resource base to remain in constant alignment with the fluctuating external circumstances. For Bally, adapting to the digital technology and software environment of the current gaming industry would have had far-reaching consequences for its entire business model. Even if Bally decided to stick to electromechanical pinball machines and to target the home market of ageing pinball wizards, the company would need to make significant alterations to its business model, getting to know new distribution channels and developing new marketing competencies.

The demand for resource leveraging

Yet, for Bally it was essential to build on the resource base and value chain that it had already developed. It did not want to write off the investments it had made in building up a distinctive profile – it had taken years of acquiring and nurturing resources and fine-tuning the value chain to reach its level of expertise. Its strength in electromechanical manufacturing and the development of large 'moving parts' games was much too valuable to casually throw away just because video games were currently in fashion.

However, building a new area of competence, it was understood, should not be considered lightly. It would take a considerable amount of time, effort and money to shift the resource base and reconfigure the value chain, while there would be many risks associated with this transformation process as well. On the other hand, the danger of attempting to exploit the firm's current resources would be to excel at something of increasing irrelevance. The pinball machine might be joining the buggy whip and the vacuum tube as a museum exhibit, with a real threat that Bally too could become history.

Eventually, the solution found by Bally was to give up on pinball machines altogether and to redirect its existing resources towards a much more attractive market opportunity – slot machines. This move allowed Bally to exploit its electromechanical manufacturing capability and game-making expertise, while building a strong market position in a fast growing market. Even though Bally was able to find a synthesis, reconciling the two conflicting demands, not all companies are as successful. Neither do all managers agree on how the paradox of markets and resources can best be tackled.

EXHIBIT 4.1 SHORT CASE

YAKULT: MESSAGE IN A TINY BOTTLE

The health of the human body is heavily influenced by the food that enters it. Simply eating appropriately can get you quite far, but there seem to be more ways to decrease the risk of getting ill and improve one's body condition. The Japanese

pharmaceutical company Yakult first started with the development of functional food, successfully creating a completely new industry segment. It did so in particular by commercializing a certain probiotic milk-like beverage. That size does not matter has been well proven by these 65ml Yakult bottles; they turned out to be filled with blockbuster potential.

When Minoru Shirota finished his medical studies at Kyoto Imperial University in the 1920s, Japan was far from the economic power it is today. Unsanitary conditions caused infectious diseases, which made microorganism research a great opportunity. In his study, Shirota found that certain lactic acid bacteria were useful for improving the state of one's intestines. After he succeeded in culturing and strengthening this *Lactobacillus casei* strain, he decided to capitalize on his discovery in the form of small beverages containing the probiotic preventive medicine.

With the help of volunteers, Shirota managed to manufacture and sell his little drink to the Japanese market from 1935 onwards with the establishment of the Shirota Institute for Research on Protective Bacteria, but it was not until 1955 that he founded Yakult. Although the health condition of Japanese people drastically improved in correlation with Japan's economic rise, Shirota believed that there would still be demand for an illness-preventing beverage. Yet, there was one question that popped up in his mind: how do you sell a 65ml bottle drink to people on a daily basis?

In the hope of providing an appropriate response, the management of Yakult decided to introduce the concept of Yakult Ladies in the 1960s. These women are not your average milkmen though. In addition to home-delivering the small bottles – by bicycle, car, cart, motorbike and on foot – Yakult Ladies are also able to sell the *Lactobacilli*-fermented milk drink on the spot. The concept of women selling the preventive beverage proved to be successful: who can say no to a sweet lady carrying a few bottles of probiotic drinks? Shirota and his team quickly discovered that their special sales organization carries benefits beyond simple face-to-face marketing.

Since Yakult Ladies are recruited locally, they are able to quickly build an extensive network and thus help Yakult take root into local communities. By being locally active, by paying periodic visits to retirement homes and organizing crime prevention activities for example, Yakult's special sales women have become familiar in their close environment. As such, Yakult Ladies are able to promote Yakult's products and values more successfully.

Although Yakult makes use of special sales ladies, it primarily remains a pharmaceutical company with a focus on microorganism research. In addition to the 65ml bottles filled with lactic acid bacteria and a wide range of varieties on this beverage, Yakult also concerns itself with other types of edible nourishment. In Japan, the company sells guava leaf tea, recommended for diabetic patients anxious about their sugar intake, but also deals with vitamin and mineral drinks, in addition to vegetable, soy and fruit beverages.

By starting out with microbiological research, Yakult's R&D ends up with other projects as well, such as cosmetic products created as a result of the positive effect lactic acid bacteria has on skin. Furthermore, Yakult is occupied with pharmaceuticals. For example, the company verified that *Lactobacillus casei* YIT 9018 has an anticancer effect, which resulted in the development of *lactobacilli*-based medical drugs. Even though the company is active in over 30 other countries, the Japanese market alone is responsible for the vast majority of these sales. Furthermore, these business segments have not even come close to the level of profitability of Yakult's food and beverages, which contributed 92 per cent of Yakult's net sales in the fiscal year 2016.

These numbers illustrate the problem Yakult is facing. Whereas the company is dominant in Japan and parts of Asia, Yakult is relatively small in the rest of the world, while the competition is fierce. Outside of Japan, only the regular 65ml Yakult bottles and its Light counterpart have reached firm ground. Where the 'one Yakult bottle a day' concept has been integrated into the daily life of many Japanese, the same can hardly be said about the Western market. In particular, Yakult's entrance into the European market was accompanied with issues, since plenty of competitors had already jumped on the functional food bandwagon. In Yakult's case, the French Groupe Danone, owner of Actimel and Activia, is especially apparent.

Since the late 1980s, the European market for functional food has expanded, but most food products companies have used microorganisms in their products only to expand into the newly created market segment. That these promises of health improvement not necessarily yielded desirable results is highlighted by the European Food Safety Authority (EFSA), which provides scientific advice to the European Commission. Recent legislation demands that promises of health benefits need to be backed up by evidence. As a response to this, several companies withdrew their claims as a precaution. Danone Group did so too with its probiotic Actimel and Activia products, while the US division of the corporation even had to pay US$35 million in a lawsuit as a result of making misleading claims. Even though the functional food branch is perceived with increased scepticism, Danone retained its position largely due to expansive marketing.

But how can Yakult convince people that the positive effects claimed by its own beverages do work? Another problem is its relation with competitor Danone Group. Because the corporation signed a strategic alliance with Yakult in 2004 and became its biggest shareholder, allowing for the representation of three members on Yakult's Board, it effectively exerts influence over the Japanese firm.

The strategic alliance between Yakult and Danone Group, aimed at strengthening the global position of both companies, was terminated in 2013 due to the latter wanting to boost its stake in Yakult. The Japanese company did not regain managerial freedom, however, as Groupe Danone's members remained on its Board. Yet, the clause that ensured Yakult was represented on Danone's Board vanished. Although the corporation declared it had no intention of taking over Yakult, with its history of aggressive takeovers of competitors, Danone's loyalty concerning Yakult's independence can at the very least be called doubtful, putting the need for strategic choices on the Japanese company's even further on the front burner.

Does Yakult need to replicate its competitors in order to successfully compete in the European market? Since the image of functional food has been smudged by negative publicity, it demands a grand marketing campaign in order to alter the negative view shared by many. By putting an emphasis on the positive difference between Yakult and its competitors, the differentiation of the little beverages could be exploited.

On the other hand, one could say that you cannot put new wine in old bottles, but perhaps Yakult is able to put old wine into new containers. In Japan, Yakult has limited competition, but in Europe the situation is quite different. With Yakult's limited assortment in most countries outside of Japan, the expansion of Yakult's probiotic products abroad might be a solution. Yakult's research resulted in a wide range of innovative products, with some of them not having a direct equivalent in the portfolio of competitors, allowing for product differentiation.

Yakult might also emphasize its Yakult Ladies. There are about 80 000 Ladies operating worldwide, but it is a channel from which Europe, where the sales of beverages are limited to stores, is excluded. With Yakult Ladies accounting for 57.2 per cent of the sales of Yakult's dairy products in Japan as of 2015 and the women being able to create long-term loyalty to the company, this channel might be worthwhile to expand, not only towards Europe but also in countries where Yakult already operates.

With a limited budget and equally narrow elbowroom, Yakult's management faces a difficult decision. Due to fierce competition and the current image of functional food in Europe, the message of Yakult's probiotic products may need aggressive marketing. Alternatively, by replicating the successful business model it has in Japan, Yakult Ladies might tell the probiotics story and sell more products to help swing Yakult on top. Which route will crack the tiny bottle and release Yakult's message?

Co-author: Wester Wagenaar

Sources: www.yakult.co.jp; institute.yakult.co.jp; Yakult Annual Report 2015; Yakult Supplementary Materials for Financial Statements 2005–2016; *Bloomberg*, 15 April 2010 and 26 April 2013; *Business Week*, 25 November 2007; *Financial Times*, 27 November 2013; Heasman and Mellentin (2001); *The Wall Street Journal*, 26 April 2013.

PERSPECTIVES ON BUSINESS LEVEL STRATEGY

Always to be best, and to be distinguished above the rest.
The Iliad, Homer (8th century BC); Greek poet

Firms need to adapt themselves to market developments and need to build on the strengths of their resource bases and value chains. The main question dividing managers is 'who should be fitted to whom' – should an organization adapt itself to its environment or should it attempt to adapt the environment to itself? What should be the dominant factor driving a firm: its strengths or the opportunities? Should managers take the environment as the starting point, choose an advantageous market position and then build the resource base and value chain necessary to implement this choice? Or should managers take the organization's resource base (and possibly also its value chain) as the starting point, selecting and/ or adapting an environment to fit with these strengths?

As before, the strategic management literature comes with strongly differing views on how managers should proceed. The variety of opinions among strategy theorists is dauntingly large, posing many incompatible prescriptions. Here the two diametrically opposed positions will be identified and discussed in order to show the richness of differing opinions. On the one side of the spectrum, there are those managers who argue that the market opportunities should be leading, while implying that the organization should adapt itself to the market position envisioned. This point of view is called the 'outside-in perspective'. At the other end of the spectrum, many managers believe that competition eventually revolves around rival resource bases and that firms must focus their strategies on the development of unique resources and value chains. They argue that product–market positioning is a tactical decision that can be taken later. This view is referred to as the 'inside-out perspective'.

The outside-in perspective

 Managers with an outside-in perspective believe that firms should not be self-centred, but should continuously take their environment as the starting point when determining their strategy. Successful companies, it is argued, are externally oriented and market-driven (e.g. Day, 1990; Webster, 1994). They have their sights clearly set on developments in the marketplace and are determined to adapt to the unfolding opportunities and threats encountered. They take their cues from customers and competitors, and use these signals to determine their own game plan (Jaworski and Kohli, 1993). For these successful companies, markets are leading, resources are following.

Therefore, for the outside-in directed manager, developing strategy begins with an analysis of the environment to identify attractive market opportunities. Potential customers must be sought, whose needs can be satisfied more adequately than currently done by other firms. Once these customers have been won over and a market position has been established, the firm must consistently defend or build on this position by adapting itself to changes in the environment. Shifts in customers' demands must be met, challenges from rival firms must be countered, impending market entries by outside firms must be rebuffed and excessive pricing by suppliers must be resisted. In short, to the outside-in manager the game of strategy is about market positioning and understanding, and responding to external developments. For this reason, the outside-in perspective is sometimes also referred to as the 'positioning approach' (Mintzberg, Ahlstrand and Lampel, 1998).

Positioning is not short-term, opportunistic behaviour, but requires a strategic perspective, because superior market positions are difficult to attain. Once conquered, however, positioning can be the source of sustained profitability. Some proponents of the outside-in perspective argue that in each market a number of different positions can yield sustained profitability. For instance, Porter suggests that companies that focus on a particular niche, and companies that strongly differentiate their product offering, can achieve strong and profitable market positions, even if another company has the lowest cost position (Porter, 1980, 1985). Other authors emphasize that the position of being market leader is particularly important (e.g. Buzzell and Gale, 1987). Companies with a high market share profit more from economies of scale, benefit from risk aversion among customers, have more bargaining power towards buyers and suppliers, and can more easily flex their muscles to prevent new entrants and block competitive attacks.

Unsurprisingly, proponents of the outside-in perspective argue that insight into markets and industries is essential. Not only the general structure of markets and industries needs to be analysed, but also the specific demands, strengths, positions and intentions of all major forces need to be determined. For instance, buyers must be understood with regard to their needs, wants, perceptions, decision-making processes and bargaining chips. The same holds true for suppliers, competitors, potential market and/or industry entrants and providers of substitute products (Porter, 1980, 1985). Once a manager knows 'what makes the market tick' – sometimes referred to as the 'rules of the game' – a position can be identified within the market that could give the firm bargaining power vis-à-vis suppliers and buyers, while keeping competitors at bay. Of course, the wise manager will not only emphasize winning under the current rules with the current players, but will attempt to anticipate market and industry developments, and position the firm to benefit from these. Many outside-in advocates even advise firms to initiate market and industry changes, so that they can be the first to benefit from the altered rules of the game (this issue will be discussed further in Chapters 9 and 10).

Proponents of the outside-in perspective readily acknowledge the importance of firm resources and activities for cashing in on market opportunities the firm has identified. If the firm does not have, or is not able, to develop or obtain the necessary resources to implement a particular strategy, then specific opportunities will be unrealizable. Therefore, managers should always keep the firm's strengths and weaknesses in mind when choosing an external position, to ensure that it remains feasible. Yet, to the outside-in strategist, the firm's current resource base should not be the starting point when determining strategy, but should merely be acknowledged as a potentially limiting condition on the firm's ability to implement the best business strategy.

Actually, firms that are market-driven are often the first ones to realize that new resources and/or activities need to be developed and, therefore, are better positioned to build up a 'first mover advantage' (Lieberman and Montgomery, 1988, 1998). Where the firm does not have the ability to catch up with other firms' superior resources, it can always enter into an alliance with a leading organization, offering its partner a crack at a new market opportunity.

EXHIBIT 4.2   THE OUTSIDE-IN PERSPECTIVE

CHALLENGING CONVENTION: A RIOT IN THE GAMING INDUSTRY

Currently, Riot Gaming's multiplayer online PC game *League of Legends*, is the most played video game across the globe. With more than 100 million active monthly users it draws parallels with social networking services, such as LinkedIn or Pinterest, and its 36 million viewers of the 2015 world championship finals vastly exceed those of popular television series, such as *Game of Thrones* or *The Big Bang Theory*. Putting this big bang into practice, *League of Legends* generated US$1.6 billion revenue in fiscal year 2015, grossing more than any of its adversaries across all platforms that year. The massive influx of capital might suggest that its success stems from Riot's accumulation of financial resources into some superior hard-to-copy internal resource. Yet, the opposite holds true: *League of Legends* was developed with limited resources, under a corporate motto of prioritizing player experience over revenues. Rather than taking internal elements of the organization as a vantage point, Riot's strategic focal point is centered around, and embarks upon paths paved by understanding gamers' needs.

Although many roads lead to Rome, every road charted by Riot leads to its customers. Founded in the US in 2006, Riot dubbed the crafting process of *League of Legends* as constituting 'player-focused game development'. This customer-centric rationale was enshrined as the number one cardinal rule in the

▶

company manifesto in terms of 'Player Experience First'. This notion was similarly echoed by Brandon Beck, CEO and co-founder of Riot, who stressed the importance of impeccable alignment with its customers. As *League of Legends* was the sole game under Riot's development, this meant that synchronizing the game to the needs of the customer went hand in hand with the reconfiguring and co-evolving of the company as a whole. Needless to say, this customer-centric philosophy manifested itself as a fundamental pillar driving Riot's strategic endeavors. Yet, for a small and newly established firm to be audible through the noise of big competitors, words alone are not enough.

One way Riot sought to convert their words into action was by employing a free-to-play business model. When they published League of Legends in 2009, anyone having access to a PC could acquire the game free of charge. By adopting a 'freemium' pricing strategy, the core of the game was offered for free, while players could opt to purchase additional content such as character customizations, in-game currency and other virtual goods. This was not business as usual in gaming land though: most videogame studios easily charged customers US$60 for debut titles, while costs paired with development could rise to hundreds of millions of dollars, let alone publishing. Riot on the other hand had a starting budget of US$3 million to accomplish both. Although it might seem odd to create 'value' by offering a game free of charge, what constitutes value and what does not, is all a

matter of perspective. Creating 'superior value' might result in bigger revenues, yet this flows over in higher pricing of games, which raises costs for consumers. Instead, by offering *League of Legends* free of charge, Riot sought to enhance customer value by providing a priceless experience for gamers, literally.

Another instrument deployed by Riot to cater to its customers is its broadcasting channels, through which it airs live events and tournaments of competitive gaming for a live audience, also known as e-sports. At Riot they take the outside-in approach at word value; not only do they exclusively hire gamers at the company, they apply the same principle by offering gamers contracts to participate in competitive matches. Although the hosting of these events entails more costs than earnings through ticket sales – or price pools numbering to the millions – they contribute in creating and keeping customers. As the community evolving around League of Legends keeps growing, so does the ensuing revenue gained from sponsorships and ads. Corporate legends like Coca-Cola, Intel, Sony and many others are eager to capitalize on a myriad of business opportunities as provided by Riot. By building a loyal community of gamers, *League of Legends* has become a legend itself.

Co-author: Sander Wisman

Sources: www.riotgames.com; www.superdataresearch.com; *Bloomberg,* 15 January 2016; *The Economist,* 10 December 2011 and 25 May 2014; *Fortune,* 27 January 2016; *Harvard Business Review,* 3 June 2014, *Statista,* 2016.

The inside-out perspective

 Managers adopting an inside-out perspective believe that strategies should not be built around external opportunities, but around a company's strengths. Successful companies, it is argued, build up a strong resource base over an extended period of time, which offers them access to unfolding market opportunities in the medium and short term. For such companies, the starting point of the strategy formation process is the question of which resource base it wants to have. The fundamental strategic issue is which difficult-to-imitate competencies and exclusive assets should be acquired and/or further refined. Creating such a resource platform requires major investments and a long breath, and to a large extent will determine the culture and identity of the organization. Hence, it is of the utmost importance and should be the central tenet of a firm's strategy. Once the long-term direction for the building of the resource infrastructure has been set, attention can be turned to identifying market opportunities where these specific strengths can be exploited. To the inside-out oriented manager, the issue of market positioning is essential, as only a strong competitive position in the market will result in above-average profitability. However, market positioning must take place within the context of the broader resource-based strategy and not contradict the main thrust of the firm – selected market positions must leverage the existing resource base, not ignore it. In other words, market positioning is vital, but tactical, taking place within the boundaries set by the resource-driven strategy. For success, resources should be leading, and markets following.

Many managers taking an inside-out perspective tend to emphasize the importance of a firm's competencies over its tangible resources (physical assets). Their way of looking at strategy is referred to as the resource-based view (e.g. Wernerfelt, 1984; Barney, 1991, Reading 4.2), competence-based view (e.g. Prahalad and Hamel, 1990, Reading 5.2; Sanchez, Heene and Thomas, 1996) or capabilities-based view (e.g. Stalk, Evans and Shulman, 1992; Teece, Pisano and Shuen, 1997, Reading 4.3). These managers point out that it is especially the development of unique abilities that is such a strenuous and lengthy process, more so than the acquisition of physical resources such as production facilities and computer systems. Some companies might be able to achieve a competitive advantage based on physical assets, but usually such tangible infrastructure is easily copied or purchased. However, competencies are not readily for sale on the open market as 'plug-and-play' components, but need to be painstakingly built up by an organization through hard work and experience. Even where a company takes a short cut by buying another organization or engaging in an alliance, it takes significant time and effort to internalize the competencies in such a way that they can be put to productive use. Hence, having distinctive competencies can be a very attractive basis for competitive advantage, as rival firms generally require a long time to catch up (e.g. Collis and Montgomery, 1995; Barney, 1991, Reading 4.2).

The 'nightmare scenario' for inside-out oriented strategists is where the firm flexibly shifts from one market demand to the next, building up an eclectic collection of unrelated competencies, none of which are distinctive compared to competence-focused companies. In this scenario, a firm is fabulously market-driven, adaptively responding to shifts in the environment, but incapable of concentrating itself on forming the distinctive competence base needed for a robust competitive advantage over the longer term.

Most inside-out oriented managers also recognize the 'shadow side' of competencies – they are not only difficult to learn, but difficult to unlearn as well. The laborious task of building up competencies makes it hard to switch to new competencies, even if that is what the market demands (e.g. Christensen, 1997; Rumelt, 1996). Companies far down the route of competence specialization find themselves locked in by the choices made in the past. In the same way as few concert pianists are able (and willing) to switch to playing saxophone when they are out of a job, few companies are able and willing to scrap their competence base just because the market is taking a turn for the worse. Becoming a concert pianist not only takes years of practice but is a way of life, with a specific way of working, network and career path, making it very unattractive to make a mid-career shift towards a more marketable trade. Likewise, companies experience that their core competencies can simultaneously be their core rigidities, locking them out of new opportunities (Leonard-Barton, 1995). From an inside-out perspective, both companies and concert pianists should therefore first try to build on their unique competencies and attempt to find or create a more suitable market, instead of reactively adapting to the unpredictable whims of the current environment (see Figure 4.8).

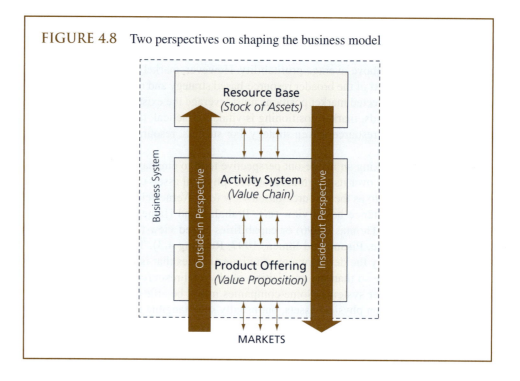

FIGURE 4.8   Two perspectives on shaping the business model

DYSON: BLOWN BY THE WIND

Who could have envisioned that the somewhat strange looking invention of the 'Ballbarrow' resulted in a number of innovating game changers in multiple markets, and made its founding father Britain's most famous engineer and a billionaire? James Dyson's revolutionary vacuum cleaners, hand-dryers, fans and heaters all changed their marketplace – and at a premium price.

It all started in 1971 with James Dyson renovating his property. The wheel of his wheelbarrow got stuck in the mud, the steel body damaged the paintwork, and the bucket got an unwanted cement coating that could not be removed. A few years later James Dyson came up with the 'Ballbarrow', a wheelbarrow with a spherical wheel and a moulded plastic bucket that solved all problems. And while everyone expected the Ballbarrow to flop, it turned into a huge success.

Frustration also triggered the idea for Dyson's next success. When he bought a Hoover vacuum cleaner, it got clogged quickly and lost suction over time. The only option was to change the filters and put in a new bag, resulting in exactly the same problems. Inspired by the way sawdust was removed at a local sawmill, he came up with the idea of using air cyclones in vacuum cleaners. Although it took Dyson more than 5 000 prototypes, his invention became a breakthrough in 1993: a cyclonic vacuum cleaner, capable of generating 100 000 G of centrifugal force (around 20 000 times greater than a roller-coaster ride), and spinning the dirt into a high-grade transparent plastic bin. That same year James Dyson started the company Dyson and opened a research centre and a factory in England.

His cyclonic vacuums conquered the world much faster than anybody could have imagined. In 2002 the average price of a vacuum in the US was about $125. In that same year, Dyson introduced its DC07 upright vacuum cleaner in the US for the astonishing price of $399. Two years later, Dyson had conquered almost 15 per cent of the 4 billion dollar US vacuum cleaner market and

40 per cent of the UK market, and it is assumed to be the current market leader in many different countries.

Profits have been rising rapidly with Dyson expanding its operations to more countries and adding new inventions to its product range. The Airblade, an innovative hand dryer that starts with a US$1199 price tag, can be seen in public lavatories worldwide. It uses a HEPA filter to get rid of bacteria in the bathroom air and it then blows a sheet of air onto your hands to scrape off water like a windshield wiper. Because it only takes about 12 seconds to dry your hands, it is not only a must-have in public toilets; it is also much more energy and cost efficient than paper towels or standard hand dryers. And then there are Dyson's cooling fans: fans without actual fans. The airflow passes over the curved outer circle of the machines, while air around it is also drawn into the airflow and amplified up to 18 times. This – according to the company – prevents the machine from 'chopping the air before it hits you' like conventional fans do, providing an uninterrupted flow of air instead. The company also invented the first LED light with an effective cooling

system, which supposedly performs at least 1.5 times as long as regular LEDs. All of these innovations have resulted in Dyson creating revenues of GB£174 billion in 2015, with more than £448 million of profit. The company now employs over 7 000 people worldwide, among which are over 2 000 engineers.

What is the secret of this company? What is the key to its success? "Our success is down to new ideas and the work of teams around the world," James Dyson said. The company relies heavily on resources, entering new markets and coming up with new products. With this perspective it is very important to keep a steady stream of new ideas. For many years now, Dyson has created the perfect conditions for innovations, resulting in the second highest number of patent applications filed in the UK in 2009, only second to Rolls-Royce. Until now, the inside-out-perspective has consistently proven to be the driver of Dyson's success.

Co-authors: Jeroen Brinkhuis and Wester Wagenaar

Sources: www.dyson.com; www.mintel.com; *The Guardian,* 26 May 2010 and 21 March 2016; *Newsweek*, 13 January 2011 and 13 August 2013; *The New Yorker*, 20 September 2010.

MANAGING THE PARADOX OF MARKETS AND RESOURCES

One does not gain much by mere cleverness.

Marquis de Vauvenargues (1715–1747); French soldier and moralist

So, how can a sustainable competitive advantage be created? Should generals create a sustainable competitive advantage by first selecting a superior position in the environment (e.g. a mountain pass) and then adapt their military resources to this position, or should generals develop armies with unique resources and then try to let the battle take place where these resources can best be employed? Should football coaches first determine how they want the game to be played on the field and then attract and train players to fit this style, or should coaches develop uniquely talented players and then adapt the team's playing style to make the best use of these resources? Should strategizing managers first understand industry dynamics and then develop resources that fit the environment? Or should they focus on developing unique and difficult-to-imitate resources and compete in industries where these resources fit best? Whether a military, sports or business strategist, an approach to creating competitive advantage must be chosen (see Table 4.1).

TABLE 4.1 Outside-in versus inside-out perspective

	Outside-in perspective	Inside-out perspective
Emphasis on	Markets over resources	Resources over markets
Orientation	Opportunity-driven (external potential)	Strength-driven (internal potential)
Starting point	Market demand and industry structure	Resource base and value chain
Fit through	Adaptation to environment	Adaptation of environment
Strategic focus	Attaining advantageous position	Attaining distinctive resources
Strategic moves	External positioning	Building resource base
Tactical moves	Acquiring necessary resources	External positioning
Competitive weapons	Bargaining power and mobility barriers	Superior resources and imitation barriers

While no consensus has yet been developed within the field of strategic management on how to manage the paradox of markets and resources, two options have been suggested by scholars. The first option is *parallel processing* and the second *juxtaposing* based on dynamic capabilities (see taxonomy in Chapter 1).

Parallel processing

In parallel processing, the company deals with the paradox of markets and resources by separating demands over different organizational units. Some organizational units focus on market demands only – such as sales managers – and others on resource leveraging – such as R&D managers. For example, the sales department analyses client demands, competitive moves and industry dynamics, and then positions the company within the industry environment, while the research and development department leverages company resources to create unique value propositions. In this case, managing the paradox of markets and resources takes place at the next organizational level up. The phenomenon of dual processing companies has also been called 'spatial separation' (see Chapter 1).

Juxtaposing

While some organizational members focus on market demands only – such as sales managers – and others on resource leveraging – such as R&D managers – strategizing managers at different organizational units or with higher hierarchical positions have to juxtapose between both demands, employing dynamic capabilities. Defined as 'the distinct skills, processes, procedures, organizational structures, decision rules and disciplines that form the basis of a company's ability to sensing, seizing and reconfiguring capabilities' (Teece, Pisano and Shuen, 1997, Reading 4.3; Teece, 2007, Reading 2.1), dynamic capabilities propel strategists to accommodate both demands at the same time.

Dynamic capabilities enable strategizing managers to manage the paradox of markets and resources by juxtaposing between the demand for market adaptation and the demand for resource leveraging. Juxtaposing is the continuous process of creating and maintaining a dynamic equilibrium in the paradox of markets and resources. The equilibrium is dynamic, because companies continuously upgrade their competencies to protect them against competitors that imitate the firms' competencies and to defend their market position. At the same time, they must also actively develop new capabilities in a changing business environment. The paradox is managed either on a project basis, or within the same organizational unit or at a higher organizational level.

BUSINESS LEVEL STRATEGY IN INTERNATIONAL PERSPECTIVE

Co-authors: Gep Eisenloeffel and Wester Wagenaar

Whoever is winning at the moment will always seem to be invincible.

George Orwell (1903–1950); English novelist

Comparative management research has not reported specific national preferences for an inside-out or an outside-in perspective thus far. This may be due to the fact that there are actually no distinct national inclinations when dealing with this paradox. Another cause may lie in the difficulty of international comparative research, or this lack of research reflects the implicit assumption that theories on strategizing are universally applicable. However, it might also be the case that the late emergence of resource-based theories – starting in the early 1980s – has not yet allowed for cross-national comparisons. Whatever the reason, the bottom line remains that little cross-cultural research has been conducted in the field of strategic management and this is especially true for specific national preferences for an inside-out or outside-in perspective.

Nevertheless, it is possible to provide a better understanding of the international playing field regarding business level strategy. Differences on the societal, industry and personal level can be held responsible for different international preferences across the world.

On the societal level

While cultural differences have not been identified yet by comparative management research, there are elements on the societal level that can have an influence on whether companies within a societal context prefer inside-out or outside-in thinking. National cultures also seem to play a role, but international comparative studies on this topic have not been carried out yet. We thus identify two factors that can influence preferences here: mobility barriers and resource mobility.

In general, industry and market positions will be of more value if there are high mobility barriers within the environment (Porter, 1980). Some of these barriers can be specifically national in origin. Government regulation, in particular can be an important source of mobility barriers. For instance, import quotas and duties, restrictive licensing systems, and fiscal regulations and subsidies, can all – knowingly or unknowingly – result in the protection of incumbent firms. Such government intervention enhances the importance of obtained positions. Other national sources of mobility barriers can be unions' resistance to change and high customer loyalty. In some economies, high mobility barriers might also be imposed by powerful groups or families. Here strategists might have a strong preference to think in terms of market positions first, because these are more difficult to obtain than the necessary resources. The opposite would be true in more dynamic economies, where market positions might easily be challenged by competitors, unless they are based on distinctive and difficult-to-imitate resources.

A second international difference might be found in the types of resources employed across countries. In nations where the dominant industries are populated by firms using relatively simple and abundant resources, market positions are far more important, since acquisition of the necessary resources is much less of an issue. If resources are not rare, are imitable and everybody has access to them, it is hard to make money from them (Peng, 2013). However, if a national economy is composed of industries using complex bundles of resources, requiring many years of painstaking development, there might be a tendency to emphasize the importance of resources over market positions.

On the industry level

Research has not been conclusive as to whether different industries have clear preferences for either an inside-out or an outside-in perspective on strategy. A general rule seems to be that primary sector industries are predominantly controlled through inside-out strategies. Companies operating in the tertiary sector, or the service industry, focus more on positioning themselves to follow the markets.

Some industries do have certain characteristics that make it more logical for them to prefer either one of the perspectives. As the emphasis of the field of marketing lies in communicating with the world outside of a company, marketers are often more familiar with the outside-in perspective. Industries with few marketers can be expected to gravitate more towards an inside-out focus. This is for instance the case for engineering and heavy industries, such as steel. Within business-to-consumer industries, however, preferences for outside-in perspectives can be expected. Here specialized product knowledge and personal networks are considered important and a focus on the environment is a logical consequence.

To the strategist

Independent of where strategists are operating or what nationality they possess, their behaviour is likely to be largely influenced and shaped by the education they received. This is especially true for a preference for inside-out or outside-in thinking and decision-making. A manager primarily schooled in marketing will likely have a preference towards an outside-in perspective. The opposite is true for a strategist with a background in HR (Wright, Snell and Jacobsen, 2004), in addition to someone proficient in the R&D side of businesses. In this case, it is expected they will make strategic decisions through an inside-out perspective, emphasizing internal strengths. Since education lays the foundation on how to perceive business and interpret the world, this is reflected in one of the basic ways to look at business, the paradox between market adaptation and resource leveraging.

Returning to the position of the strategists, for them it is important to take notice of who they are dealing with. Since there have not been any cross-cultural studies into national preferences, it is impossible for a strategist operating on the international stage to base expectations on people's nationalities. Instead, the work experience and academic background can provide an indication towards one of the two perspectives. In addition, international strategists may find their preference stem from mobility barriers or resource mobility. It is also imperative for a strategist to stay aware of his own background to realize the natural preference inherent to him. This inclination might always seem like the most logical option for him, but it is not guaranteed to be the best mode of operation.

INTRODUCTION TO THE READINGS

Drive thy business; let it not drive thee.
Benjamin Franklin (1706–1790); American writer and statesman

To help strategists to come to grips with the variety of perspectives on this issue, three readings have been selected that each shed their own light on the debate. As in previous chapters, the first two readings will be representatives of the two poles on this issue, while the aim of the third reading is to bridge the two perspectives.

Reading 4.1, *Strategy from the Outside In*, has been taken from the first chapter of George Day and Christine Moorman's 2010 book with the same title. The reading is based on three lessons that the authors claim to have taken from winning companies. The first lesson is that these companies consistently take an outside-in approach to strategy, starting from the market when designing their strategy, not the other way around. The second lesson is that they use market insights, which goes far beyond market data and information, and is based on 'deep and integrated knowledge that reveals patterns and identifies opportunities'. The third lesson is that each and every part of outside-in companies should focus on achieving, sustaining and profiting from customer value. The authors argue that there are many reasons why companies are pushed towards becoming inside-out – including the popularity of the resource-based view of the firm – but company leaders of winning companies resist these forces.

As representative of the inside-out perspective, an often-cited article by Jay Barney has been selected as a thorough introduction to the resource-based view. In Reading 4.2, 'Firm Resources and Sustained Competitive Advantage', Barney differentiates resource-based models of competitive advantage from the Porter-like environmental models. He does not dismiss externally oriented explanations of profitability, but wishes to explore the internally oriented explanation that idiosyncratic firm resources are at the base of superior performance. He sets out on this task by pinpointing the two fundamental assumptions on which the resource-based view rests – that firms have different resources *(resource heterogeneity)* and that these resources cannot be easily transferred to, or copied by, other firms *(resource immobility)*. He goes on to argue that these resources can be the basis of competitive advantage if they meet four criteria: they must be valuable and rare, while being difficult to imitate and substitute.

Reading 4.3, 'Dynamic Capabilities and Strategic Management', is an influential and already classic 1997 *Strategic Management Journal* *(SMJ)* article by David Teece, Gary Pisano and Amy Shuen. The reading addresses the issue of actively managing the paradox of markets and resources by means of dynamic capabilities, maintaining a dynamic equilibrium. Dynamic capabilities are defined as the distinct skills, processes, procedures, organizational structures, decision rules and disciplines that form the basis of a company's ability to sense, seize and reconfigure capabilities. Dynamic capabilities are difficult to develop and deploy, and are the key to competitive advantage in fast-changing business landscapes with rapid innovation.

This reading marked the beginning of the high popularity of the dynamic capabilities concept in the strategy field, and particularly within the 'resource-based view' school of thought. The importance of the dynamic capabilities concept is that it bridges the distinct and theoretically incompatible schools of thought that the outside-in and inside-out perspectives are based on. Even years before official publication as a working paper, this article inspired strategy scholars around the world. In a stream of publications, the nature of dynamic capabilities has been researched and further conceptualized, such as Kathleen Eisenhardt and Jeffrey Martin's *SMJ* article 'Dynamic capabilities: What are they?' (2000). In 2007 David Teece published another influential article in *SMJ:* 'Explicating Dynamic Capabilities: The nature and microfoundations of (sustainable) enterprise performance' (Reading 2.1 in this book). McGrath's 2013 book, provocatively entitled *The End of Competitive Advantage,* stretched the meaning of dynamic capabilities further, and underscores the importance – and confidence – of dynamic capabilities researchers.

Strategy from the outside in

By George S. Day and Christine Moorman[1]

With the wreckage of the Great Recession still smouldering and slow economic growth expected for the foreseeable future, it's not surprising to see that many companies are turning inward and hunkering down. Profits, growth and value creation seem to have become stretch goals rather than baseline expectations. Companies that were praised over the last decade for delivering shareholder value have largely fallen on hard times; buried under debt, they have no clear plan for capitalizing once customers are willing to spend again. The *Fortune* 500's top 25 at the beginning of the century included companies such as General Motors, Ford, Citigroup, Bank of America, AIG, Enron and Compaq. Measured by market value, only 8 of the 25 largest companies in the world in 2000 can claim that distinction today.

Yet a number of companies operating in the same challenging environment have gained market share, grown revenues and profits, and created more value for customers, in contrast to their competitors' intense focus on budget cutting. Indeed, there are companies that have managed market share, profit and customer value growth throughout the vertiginous boom-and-bust business cycles of the last 20 years. These companies may not have been favourite stock picks, nor have all of them topped the lists of the decade's most profitable corporations. But what they have done is found a way to build value over the long term. These are not flash-in-the-pan companies, world-beaters one year and stragglers the next. They are companies like Johnson & Johnson, Procter & Gamble, Fidelity, Cisco, Wal-Mart, Amazon, Apple, IKEA, Texas Instruments, Becton Dickinson and Tesco, among others.

These companies have been successful because they have remained true to the purpose of a business (as stated by Peter Drucker): to create and keep customers. They've kept that purpose not by focusing on shareholders and meeting quarterly numbers, by playing games with their financial statements, or by focusing just on competitive advantages. Instead, they've done it by consistently creating superior customer value – and profiting handsomely from that customer value.

We've spent years looking at these companies – and many not-so-successful ones – looking for patterns and commonalities that explain their stellar results, and we've concluded that they offer three very important lessons for any executive who wants to consistently create superior customer value and generate economic profits over the long term. There is no step-by-step formula, but there are consistencies in how these companies think, how they make strategic decisions, and, most importantly, how they operate to ensure they are maximizing the value they create and the profits they capture.

- These companies approach strategy from the outside-in rather than from the inside-out. They start

with the market when they design their strategy, not the other way around.

- They use deep market insights to inform and guide their outside-in view.

- Their outside-in strategy focuses every part of the organization on achieving, sustaining and profiting from customer value.

Two paths to strategy

The first thing that distinguishes these value- and profit-creating companies is that they drive strategy from the perspective of the market – in other words, from the *outside in*. This may sound trivial, but it is shockingly uncommon. For all the talk about "putting the customer first" and "relentlessly delivering value to customers," most management teams fail to do this. Put most simply, outside-in means standing in the customer's shoes and viewing everything the company does through the customer's eyes.

Far more common than outside-in thinking is inside-out thinking and inside-out strategy. Inside-out companies narrowly frame their strategic thinking by asking, "What can the market do for us?" rather than, "What can we do for the market?" The consequences of inside-out versus outside-in thinking can be seen in the way many business-to-business firms approach customer solutions. The inside-out view is that "solutions are bundles of products and services that help us sell more." The outside-in view is that "the purpose of a solution is to help our customers find value and make money-to our mutual benefit."

Inside-out thinking helps explain why a large database company that was looking to grow by leveraging its deep information about the companies' finances spent several million dollars to develop a product for small and medium-sized enterprises without first having in-depth conversations with potential buyers. Management, seduced by the seemingly vast potential of this market, relied on the assurances of the sales force that customers would buy. During the process, no one asked what value the company would be offering customers, or how the company's new product would offer customers more value than the status quo. Instead, managers focused on what customers could do for the company. As a result, the new product flopped and was abandoned in less than a year.

An even more costly example is Ford's unfortunate decision not to add a sliding door on the driver's side of its Windstar minivan. The extra cost of the fifth door was the major factor in this decision, but just to be sure, the designers asked a sample of buyers their opinion. Only one-third of the sample thought it was a good idea, while the rest said no or weren't sure because they couldn't envision the benefits. Meanwhile, Ford's competitors were "living with" prospective buyers at shopping malls, do-it-yourself stores and soccer fields. That fieldwork showed that the fifth door could solve a lot of problems for families and handymen. Based on these benefits to customers, Ford's competitors, including Honda, Chrysler and GM, added the door, which was an immediate hit. Ford's sales suffered so badly because of the lack of this feature that the company was forced to add it later. Doing so meant that Ford had to redesign its van to match competitors' – at an out-of-pocket cost of US$560 million (not including the opportunity cost of lost sales).

Winning from the outside in

With an outside-in mindset, top management's strategy dialogue starts with the market. The management team steps outside the boundaries and constraints of the company as it is, and looks first at its market: How and why are customers changing? What new needs do they have? What can we do to solve their problems and help them make more money? What new competitors are lurking around the corner, and how can we derail their efforts? This perspective expands the strategy dialogue and opens up a richer set of opportunities for competitive advantage and growth.

Jeff Bezos, the founder and chairman of Amazon.com, is a champion of the outside-in approach. He explained how Amazon was able to meet the needs of its customers for Web services by offering access to its cloud computing network and for a more convenient reading experience with the Kindle. He describes it as a "working backward" mentality:

> Rather than ask what we are good at and what else can we do with that skill, you ask, who are our customers? What do they need? And then you say we're going to give that to them regardless of whether we have the skills to do so, and we will learn these skills no matter how long it takes…. There is a tendency I think for executives to think that the right course of action is to stick to the knitting — stick with what you are good at. That may be a generally good rule, but the problem is the world changes out from under you if you are not constantly adding to your skill set.

The difficulties faced by Dell Computer over the last four years illustrate the need for outside-in thinking. For several decades, Dell's celebrated mastery of logistics allowed it to deliver leading edge computer hardware at prices and speeds that no rival could match. The whole organization could concentrate on assembling and shipping PCs, laptops and servers as cheaply and quickly as possible. This single-minded emphasis on efficiency made Dell the worldwide market share leader in 2005. Growth came by expanding globally and broadening the range of hardware sold through its direct-to-customer model. Everything was viewed through the prism of this business model and how to leverage it further.

But this inside-out emphasis also kept Dell from seeing and responding to a sea change in its market. More and more customers wanted to buy at retail and own products that conveyed a sense of personal style. Both Apple and Hewlett-Packard (HP) had seen the trend building and were ready to oblige. HP redesigned its machines with a focus on customer experience and distinctive value, beyond price or the latest technology. It advertised, "The Computer Is Personal Again." The market responded, and HP assumed market share leadership in 2006. Dell, on the other hand, faltered and lost sales. Nevertheless, the efficiency focus was so embedded in Dell that manufacturing executives resisted offering distinct designs, even at a premium price.

As one commentator put it, "Dell began to treat consumers and even some business customers like they were passengers on a Greyhound bus". Between 2Q 2008 and 2Q 2009, Dell's share of the US personal computer market dropped from 31.4 per cent to 26.3 per cent. On top of that, many of Dell's advantages were neutralized as HP and other competitors improved their supply-chain management and lowered costs.

Anecdotes aside, there is abundant evidence for the superiority of outside-in thinking. Much of it comes from studying the relative profit performance of market-driven companies. These firms have an inherent advantage over their more self-absorbed rivals because of their superior ability to understand markets, provide superior value over time, and attract and retain customers.

Inside-out myopia

Given both the intuitive and the data-driven appeal of outside-in strategy, why is the inside-out approach to strategy so pervasive? There are many subtle forces that converge to encourage inside-out thinking and slowly disconnect the business from its market.

Positive reinforcement

Inside-out strategic thinking ultimately relies on gaining maximum returns from existing assets – in other words, increasing efficiency. Increasing efficiency usually produces positive results. However, the quest for steady improvement in operations crowds out the question of whether the operations are worth doing in the first place! While the efficiency of the existing assets may be rising, the market is shifting, and customer value is slipping away. By the time companies that are caught in this cozy positive-feedback loop notice they are no longer delivering customer value, it's too late – competitors have seized the initiative.

Competing priorities

For most executives, there are often many stakeholders who are closer at hand than customers. Employees, boards, partners, suppliers and regulators all stand closer to executives than customers do. This proximity means that their concerns can easily become more urgent than those of customers. Meanwhile, within the organization, internal concern about resource allocation, budgeting and turf wars with other functions become the most pressing priorities.

Contemporary strategy theories

The capabilities- or resource-based view of the firm is one culprit. These ideas have inadvertently tilted the dialogue within firms toward an inside-out view. Their supporters argue that the source of a firm's defensible competitive position lies in its distinctive, hard-to-duplicate resources and capabilities. Excellent service operations, strong supply chains and superior human resource practices are advantages that are cultivated slowly over time. They are hard for competitors to copy, but they also limit the ability of the firm to adapt. In this theory, these resources exist to be used, and the task of management is to improve and fully exploit them. This is certainly a worthwhile goal to be eventually achieved. But as a starting point for strategic thinking, it myopically narrows and anchors the dialogue prematurely.

Darwin in the enterprise

A contributing factor to the lure of inside-out thinking that can't be ignored is employees' inherent drive for self-preservation. Because firms (and business units, departments and teams) are made up of human beings, they are inevitably tempted to put their own survival first. This instinct naturally accords with an inside-out view, since the outside-in view often requires a firm to reinvent itself – to employ creative destruction internally to meet ever-changing customer value expectations.

Going with the flow

Another human trait that also drives inside-out strategy is the tendency to go with the flow and behave like the others around us. Social scientists call this social norming or "groupthink" when they study social dynamics, but companies and organizations are susceptible to social norming, too. Over time, the companies in any industry or sector tend to behave in the same way and to focus on the same issues and strategies – usually inside-out ones. When these industries or sectors are truly shaken up, it is usually because a new entrant makes a breakthrough in delivering customer value that the incumbents have overlooked.

These factors and others continually push executives toward inside-out strategy. Without constant effort and vigilance, inside-out thinking comes to dominate in the firm, and outside-in strategy disappears.

Detecting inside-out thinking

The myopia of inside-out thinking is hard to detect when it becomes embedded in our mental models and shapes the way we do business. Mental models are simplifying frameworks that include prevailing assumptions, norms and even the vocabulary used to talk about customers. They help impose order and provide handy rules of thumb. The problem is that these inherent simplifications and untested ideas don't announce themselves. Table 4.1.1 illustrates some that we have encountered in our study of inside-out and outside-in thinking.

Market insight

An outside-in approach to strategy is a clear necessity. However, it will not necessarily lead to a superior customer value proposition or outstanding economic profits unless it is guided by deep market insights. This brings us to the second lesson we've gleaned from the companies we have studied: that it is not sufficient to simply view the firm from the vantage point of the market. It takes smart investments in market intelligence and an organization-wide commitment to sensing and acting on the resulting market insights.

TABLE 4.1.1   Mental models and strategy approaches

Outside-in	Inside-out
■ All decisions start with the market and opportunities for advantage	■ We'll sell to whoever will buy
■ Profits are gained through a superior value proposition and leveraging the brand and customer assets	■ Profits are gained through cost cutting and efficiency improvements. Six sigma, TQM and replicability of processes take priority
■ Customer knowledge is a valuable asset and channels are value-adding partners	■ Customer data are a control mechanism and channels are conduits
■ We know more than our competitors	■ If competitors do it, it must be good
■ No sacred cows – cannibalize yourself	■ Protect the cash flow stream
■ Customers buy the expectation of benefits	■ Customers buy performance features
■ Superior quality is defined by customers as "fitness for use"	■ Quality is conformance to internal standards
■ The best ideas come from living with customers	■ Customers don't know what they want and they can't tell you if they're asked
■ Customer loyalty is the key to profitability	■ Expanding the customer base is what matters

Within inside-out companies, market data usually reside in reports of competitors' moves, unrelated compilations of market research reports, and the occasional analysis of activity in the customer database. But data are not knowledge or insight! Valuable market insights are based on much deeper and more integrated knowledge that reveals patterns and identifies opportunities. Market insights are the difference between simply observing market trends and probing further to explain and exploit those trends.

Casella Wines saw the same trends in the wine market as its rivals did. Its deep dive underneath these trends uncovered a large non-consumption market that was turned off by the myriad of confusing choices, the haughty nature of the category, and the dense vocabulary. Its answer was the Yellow Tail brand, with a simple and fruity taste, few choices, no vintages and an endearing kangaroo symbol, which it parlayed into the most popular imported wine in the United States.

The most valuable market insights are (1) accurate reflections of reality, not just what managers want or expect to see; (2) actionable, with the potential to mobilize and inspire the entire organization to develop new strategies or improve the current strategies; (3) not seen or understood by competitors; and (4) used in novel ways to influence strategy.

When distiller Diageo applied the insight that "Men want to progress in life," the power came not from its inherent novelty, but from its application to Johnnie Walker's label (turning the man so that he is walking forward, not backward) and a mass advertising campaign that used paintings on buildings to show the walking man's progress. The campaign increased sales 50 per cent (to $5 billion) over a nine-year period.

The strategic case for market insights

The case for timely and widely shared market insights has been made persuasively by Anne Mulcahy, chairman and former CEO of Xerox Corporation and *Chief Executive Magazine's* 2008 CEO of the Year. Mulcahy believes that marketing and innovation are even more important in an era of demanding customers, information overload and economic recession. To create personalized solutions for data-intensive customers in law firms and health care, Xerox needs new learning capabilities, Mulcahy says.

In Mulcahy's view, learning about the market in which you compete starts at the top, and every senior manager has to be attuned to the voice of the customer, with marketing having overall accountability for what is learned and how it is used. To keep Xerox's management team focused on the market, its top 500 accounts are assigned to senior officers, who take responsibility for fixing customer problems. Mulcahy speaks enthusiastically about "dreaming with customers" by bringing customers into Xerox labs to identify their pain points and guide Xerox's innovation efforts.

Market-leading firms stand out in their ability to continuously sense and act on trends and events in their markets. They are better equipped to anticipate how their markets will respond to actions designed to attract and retain customers and to perceive emerging segment opportunities. In these well-educated firms, everyone from first-line sales and service people to the CEO is sensitized to listen to latent problems and opportunities. They achieve this with market-focused leadership that shapes an open-minded and inquisitive culture and a well-honed market learning capability that infuses the entire strategy development process.

Market insight is difficult for a company to master and for competitors to imitate, making it a basis for a durable competitive advantage. However, like all capabilities, it is vulnerable to creeping complacency and turning inward to focus on cost cutting, and/or an emphasis on short-term results that leads the firm to stop listening to the voice of the customer.

Intuit fell into this trap despite a history of providing superior relational value to customers that earned it the dominant share of the tax preparation market. By May 2000, its products dominated the retail market – Quicken had an 84 per cent share, QuickBooks an 87 per cent share, and TurboTax a high 60 per cent share – and had 83 per cent of the online market! Then Intuit began doing things that irritated loyal customers, such as raising the cost of customer service calls and limiting software licences to one per computer. This caused growth to flatten and made the company vulnerable to attacks from venerable competitors such as H&R Block's TaxCut and easier Web-based financial planning services, such as Mint.com, that also provided storage and better support for customers.

How market insights enable outside-in strategies

Strategically useful insights address such questions as: What are our customers' real needs? Where are competitors likely to attack? Why are valuable customers defecting, and how can we keep them? How far can we stretch our brand? What happens if we selectively cut prices? What social media should we use? Market insights that answer such questions contribute to strategy decisions in four ways.

Making fact-based decisions

Outside-in companies have a superior ability to make decisions based on accurate and up-to-date information rather than relying on gut instincts and familiar heuristics. This means the extensive use of databases that capture what is known about market structures (how are segments evolving and competitive positions changing?), market responses (what are the drivers of customer value?), and market economics (where is the firm making or losing money, and what moves will improve profitability?). The knowledge value in the data is unlocked with statistical analyses and predictive models.

Anticipating competitors' moves and countermoves

We are living in an interdependent world, where the success of strategy depends on the actions of present and potential competitors. The long-run success of the new Boeing 787 Dreamliner commercial jet depends on the way Airbus positions, prices and markets its new A350 and A380 planes. Any intelligence about potential Airbus moves has high value to Boeing, and vice versa.

Deep insights into competitors' strategies can also reveal market opportunities. Nintendo took advantage of the constraints that Sony and Microsoft imposed on themselves with their mutual emphasis on superpowerful video-game consoles that appealed to hard-core gamers. Nintendo, with the Wii console, focused on an enjoyable game experience that appealed to all demographics. Because the console didn't have the expensive digital hub features of its rivals, it was launched at half the price. Best of all, Nintendo learned that because Sony PlayStation and Microsoft's Xbox were so closely associated with hard-core gamers, neither had the consumer's permission to enter the Wii space. This meant that Wii was not likely to suffer attacks from these electronic giants.

Connecting with online and networked customers

The Internet has reshaped markets in many profound ways. Foremost is the shift in power to customers. Many information asymmetries have been wiped away, enabling consumers to ignore traditional push marketing and instead to go online to decide what to buy. This shift began with books and electronics and has steadily expanded to include most products and services. For example, currently almost 60 per cent of baby boomers, not exactly the most tech-savvy demographic, go online to supplement their doctors' advice, and many more do so to search for information about products that they want to buy. The era of the passive consumer has ended.

Proliferating media types and new distribution channels feed and are fed by increased consumer choice. The traditional three television channels and daily print newspapers have been displaced by targeted social media, online magazines, blogs and newsgroups. New media and channels are promising more points of access to customers, but at a cost of fragmented strategies that dilute the efficiency of marketing spending. Traditional communications approaches that rely on one-way broadcast of a brand message over mass media are losing their efficacy. Instead, market insight will come from engaging in two way dialogues with customers to understand what they want, and when and where they want it.

The possibilities can be imagined from Hewlett-Packard's experience with an online contest to design the skin of a new special-edition entertainment laptop. The competition was launched with a low-key announcement via the Web and MTV. But word spread virally, and eventually 8 500 entries were submitted from 112 countries. The contest site got more than 5 million hits, prompting HP to quintuple its forecast of potential sales. These and other stories of new ways to collaborate and interact with customers magnify the need for clear outside-in thinking.

Guiding growth and innovation

Firms that are armed with deep insights into their markets become adept at sensing and acting on growth opportunities ahead of their rivals. Wal-Mart found that its pharmacy customers routinely broke pills in half because they couldn't afford their full prescription. Their solution was $4 prescriptions for a limited list of popular generic medications. This offered a real benefit, especially to the uninsured, and attracted new traffic to Wal-Mart stores.

Deep market insights are essential to the pursuit of new opportunities. By 2001, Toyota (in America) understood that it's worthy, reliable brand had little appeal to Gen Y (the generation born between 1980 and 1994) – a group that it knew little about. Ethnographic and clinical research with Gen-Yers of a car-buying age uncovered key differences: these consumers were much more social, time-pressed and able to multi task with technology, and they had a preference for personalizing their possessions with accessories. Toyota designed and then tested different car concepts and mock-ups to ensure that they were in tune with the market. One small, boxy, 10S-hp model tested particularly well and became the basis of the new Scion line of cars. Toyota also learned that Gen-Yers would use

only the Internet for initial research and did not want to negotiate price. This meant that dealers offering the Scion brand had to be transparent and accept a fixed price. The ROI on these market insights was impressive. By 2006, sales had reached 175 000 units, and the median age of buyers was 31, compared to 54 for Toyota and Lexus buyers.

Designing strategy from the outside in

The third and final lesson from the companies we've examined is how they operationalize an outside-in strategy and deploy market insight to create customer value and maximize profits. Just as an outside-in perspective doesn't guarantee success without market insight, market insight and an outside-in strategy do not guarantee success without a series of intentional actions to build and reinforce customer value creation and profitability.

These actions are the major focus of this book because we find they are what really distinguish market leaders from other companies that are just muddling through. We call them the four *customer value imperatives,* because they are crucial to success. Moreover, they are imperatives for the top management of the firm. Without constant attention to these imperatives from the very top of the organization, any firm will quickly succumb to the centripetal forces pulling it toward an inside-out approach, and its position in the market will soon erode.

The four customer value imperatives

The first imperative is to *be a customer value leader* with a distinct and compelling customer value proposition. This requires the disciplined choice of where the firm will stake a claim in the market, what value it will offer its target customers, and how the organization will deliver that value.

All firms have to balance the short and the long term. A business strikes the right balance by earning superior economic profits in the short run, by maintaining its customer value leadership, and then by investing in a portfolio of innovations that will deliver results in the medium and long term. This is the second customer value imperative: *innovate new value for customers.*

Customer value and innovation benefit the firm when they are transformed into valuable customer and brand assets. The third imperative is to *capitalize on the customer as an asset.* This requires selecting and developing loyal customers, protecting them from competitive attacks, and then leveraging that customer asset by deepening and broadening relationships with customers.

Strong brands attract and retain customers and hence need to be explicitly managed. Thus, the fourth imperative is to *capitalize on the brand as an asset*. This means strengthening the brand with coherent investments, protecting it against dilution and erosion, and then leveraging it fully to capture new opportunities in both adjacent and international markets.

These imperatives build on each other, just as they build on the outside-in perspective and market insights. Different companies tend to be better at different imperatives, and companies' strengths in these imperatives also tend to vary over time. But the most profitable companies do all four better than their rivals over the long term.

Top-management focus on the four imperatives

The four customer value imperatives are the responsibility of the entire top-management team, or C-suite, and require the engagement and understanding of every part of the organization. The imperatives belong to the C-suite for four reasons.

First, as we've discussed, the pull of inside-out thinking is powerful and can knock even the best companies off course. If the senior management team is not committed to the four imperatives, then inside-out thinking will inevitably take hold, customer value will wane, and profits will erode. There is simply no way that a company can maintain an outside-in perspective if all of the C-suite has not fully bought in and committed to the four imperatives.

Second, executing on the customer value imperatives requires clear strategic choices about the allocation of resources and the capabilities to nurture. If the chief financial officer is attempting to cut working capital to the bone while the chief operations officer is attempting to deliver customer value via best-in-class inventory management, the value proposition is going to collapse. Executing on the imperatives requires every part of the firm's governance and operations to be properly aligned in the pursuit of delivering customer value – rewards and incentives, hiring strategy, risk tolerance, finance and budgeting, and sales. If any of these areas is marching to the beat of a different drummer, the firm's profits will be significantly impaired. Therefore, the C-suite doesn't just need to be familiar with the four imperatives, it needs to deeply understand them and embrace them. Ultimately, strategy is all about choices; the four imperatives crystallize these choices and provide a path toward making better decisions.

Third, these four imperatives have wide-ranging ripple effects throughout the organization. In the best companies, the imperatives resonate with all functions and at every level of the organization. Employees can readily see how their activities contribute to superior customer value. For example, the accounting group creates value when it develops flexible options based on the needs of different customer segments. The logistics/IT group enhances customer value when it works with a major account to coordinate supply chains. Service operations improve customer value by learning to anticipate and solve service problems – even before they happen!

Fourth, the imperatives are fundamental drivers of economic profit. In this reading, we'll show how each imperative contributes in direct and measurable ways to each of the components of economic profit: revenue, margins and asset utilization.

Who should be accountable for the four imperatives?

If everyone in the C-suite is responsible, then no one may be accountable in the sense of being answerable for these actions. The potential cost is lack of strategic consistency, which leads to ambiguous market positions and reactive, not proactive, decisions. Increasingly, firms are recognizing this reality and holding a specific member of the executive team accountable. Someone must be the focal point for orchestrating all the company's activities on behalf of the customer. Many entities within the company come into contact with the customer; but if no one individual is accountable, the total experience will be uneven, the brand will suffer, and customers will defect to rivals.

In many firms, this executive carries the title of chief marketing officer (CMO). But make no mistake – the key issue is the role and *not* the title. A number of the best companies we've studied do not have a CMO; another executive in the C-suite leads the firm's response to one or more of the customer value imperatives. In fact, in many companies that we've studied, the person holding the title of CMO either does not have the authority, does not have the trust of other C-suite executives, or does not have the ability to succeed in this role. The role of CMO is crucial to the success of an outside-in company, and therefore it must be earned. Executives within a marketing organization should not take it for granted that they will assume this role, nor should C-suite executives simply hand off the imperatives to the marketing function.

Firm resources and sustained competitive advantage

By Jay Barney[1]

Understanding sources of sustained competitive advantage for firms has become a major area of research in the field of strategic management. Since the 1960s, a single organizing framework has been used to structure much of this research. This framework, summarized in Figure 4.2.1, suggests that firms obtain sustained competitive advantages by implementing strategies that exploit their internal strengths, through responding to environmental opportunities, while neutralizing external threats and avoiding internal weaknesses. Most research on sources of sustained competitive advantage has focused either on isolating a firm's opportunities and threats (Porter, 1980, 1985), describing its strengths and weaknesses (Hofer and Schendel, 1978; Penrose, 1959), or analysing how these are matched to choose strategies.

Research by Porter and his colleagues (Caves and Porter, 1977; Porter, 1980, 1985) has attempted to describe the environmental conditions that favour high levels of firm performance. Porter's 'five forces model', for example, describes the attributes of an attractive industry and thus suggests that opportunities will be greater, and threats less, in these kinds of industries.

To help focus the analysis of the impact of a firm's environment on its competitive position, much of this type of strategic research has placed little emphasis on the impact of idiosyncratic firm attributes on a firm's competitive position. Implicitly, this work has adopted two simplifying assumptions. First, these environmental models of competitive advantage have assumed that firms within an industry (or firms within a strategic group) are identical in terms of the strategically relevant resources they control and the strategies they pursue. Second, these models assume that should resource heterogeneity develop in an industry or group (perhaps through new entry) that this heterogeneity will be very short lived because the resources that firms use to implement their strategies are highly mobile (i.e. they can be bought and sold in factor markets).

There is little doubt that these two assumptions have been very fruitful in clarifying our understanding of the impact of a firm's environment on performance. However, the resource-based view of competitive advantage, because it examines the link between a firm's internal characteristics and performance, obviously cannot build on these same assumptions. These assumptions effectively eliminate firm resource heterogeneity and immobility as possible sources of competitive advantage. The resource-based view of the firm substitutes two alternate assumptions in analysing

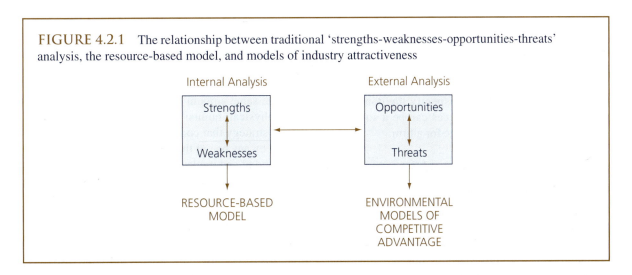

FIGURE 4.2.1   The relationship between traditional 'strengths-weaknesses-opportunities-threats' analysis, the resource-based model, and models of industry attractiveness

[1]Source: This article was adapted from J.B. Barney, 'Firm resources and sustained competitive advantage', *Journal of Management,* Vol. 17, No. 1, 1991, pp. 99–120. Copyright © 1991 by SAGE Publications Ltd.. Adapted and reprinted by Permission of SAGE Publications.

sources of competitive advantage. First, this model assumes that firms within an industry (or group) may be heterogeneous with respect to the strategic resources they control. Second, this model assumes that these resources may not be perfectly mobile across firms, and thus heterogeneity can be long lasting. The resource-based model of the firm examines the implications of these two assumptions for the analysis of sources of sustained competitive advantage.

Defining key concepts

To avoid possible confusion, three concepts that are central to the perspective developed in this reading are defined in this section. These concepts are firm resources, competitive advantage, and sustained competitive advantage.

Firm resources

In this reading, firm resources include all assets, capabilities, organizational processes, firm attributes, information, knowledge, etc. controlled by a firm that enable the firm to conceive of and implement strategies that improve its efficiency and effectiveness. In the language of traditional strategic analysis, firm resources are strengths that firms can use to conceive of and implement their strategies.

A variety of authors have generated lists of firm attributes that may enable firms to conceive of and implement value-creating strategies. For purposes of this discussion, these numerous possible firm resources can be conveniently classified into three categories: physical capital resources, human capital resources and organizational capital resources. Those attributes of a firm's physical, human and organizational capital that do enable a firm to conceive of and implement strategies that improve its efficiency and effectiveness are, for purposes of this discussion, firm resources. The purpose of this reading is to specify the conditions under which such firm resources can be a source of sustained competitive advantage for a firm.

Competitive advantage and sustained competitive advantage

A firm is said to have a competitive advantage when it is implementing a value-creating strategy not simultaneously being implemented by any current or potential competitors. It is said to have a sustained competitive advantage when it is implementing a value-creating strategy not simultaneously being implemented by any

current or potential competitors and when these other firms are unable to duplicate the benefits of this strategy. That a competitive advantage is sustained does not imply that it will 'last forever'. It only suggests that it will not be competed away through the duplication efforts of other firms. Unanticipated changes in the economic structure of an industry may make what was, at one time, a source of sustained competitive advantage, no longer valuable for a firm, and thus not a source of any competitive advantage. These structural revolutions in an industry redefine which of a firm's attributes are resources and which are not. Some of these resources, in turn, may be sources of sustained competitive advantage in the newly defined industry structure. However, what were resources in a previous industry setting may be weaknesses, or simply irrelevant, in a new industry setting. A firm enjoying a sustained competitive advantage may experience these major shifts in the structure of competition, and may see its competitive advantages nullified by such changes. However, a sustained competitive advantage is not nullified through competing firms duplicating the benefits of that competitive advantage.

Competition with homogeneous and perfectly mobile resources

Armed with these definitions, it is now possible to explore the impact of resource heterogeneity and immobility on sustained competitive advantage. This is done by examining the nature of competition when firm resources are perfectly homogeneous and mobile.

Resource homogeneity and mobility and sustained competitive advantage

Imagine an industry where firms possess exactly the same resources. This condition suggests that firms all have the same amount and kinds of strategically relevant physical, human and organizational capital. Is there a strategy that could be conceived of and implemented by any one of these firms that could not also be conceived of and implemented by all other firms in this industry? The answer to this question must be no. The conception and implementation of strategies employs various firm resources. That one firm in an industry populated by identical firms has the resources to conceive of and implement a strategy means that these other firms, because they possess the same resources, can also conceive of and implement this strategy. Because these firms all implement the same strategies, they all will improve their efficiency and effectiveness in the same way, and to the same extent. Thus, in this kind of industry, it is not possible for firms to enjoy a sustained competitive advantage.

Resource homogeneity and mobility and first-mover advantages

One objection to this conclusion concerns so-called 'first-mover advantages' (Lieberman and Montgomery, 1988). In some circumstances, the first firm in an industry to implement a strategy can obtain a sustained competitive advantage over other firms. These firms may gain access to distribution channels, develop goodwill with customers, or develop a positive reputation, all before firms that implement their strategies later. Thus, first-moving firms may obtain a sustained competitive advantage.

However, upon reflection, it seems clear that if competing firms are identical in the resources they control, it is not possible for any one firm to obtain a competitive advantage from first moving. To be a first mover by implementing a strategy before any competing firms, a particular firm must have insights about the opportunities associated with implementing a strategy that are not possessed by other firms in the industry, or by potentially entering firms (Lieberman and Montgomery, 1988). This unique firm resource (information about an opportunity) makes it possible for the better informed firm to implement its strategy before others. However, by definition, there are no unique firm resources in this kind of industry. If one firm in this type of industry is able to conceive of and implement a strategy, then all other firms will also be able to conceive of and implement that strategy, and these strategies will be conceived of and implemented in parallel, as identical firms become aware of the same opportunities and exploit that opportunity in the same way.

It is not being suggested that there can never be first-mover advantages in industries. It is being suggested that in order for there to be a first-mover advantage, firms in an industry must be heterogeneous in terms of the resources they control.

Resource homogeneity and mobility and entry/mobility barriers

A second objection to the conclusion that sustained competitive advantages cannot exist when firm resources in an industry are perfectly homogeneous and mobile concerns the existence of 'barriers to entry' (Bain, 1956), or more generally, 'mobility barriers' (Caves and Porter, 1977). The argument here is that even if firms within

an industry (group) are perfectly homogeneous, if there are strong entry or mobility barriers, these firms may be able to obtain a sustained competitive advantage vis-a-vis firms that are not in their industry (group). This sustained competitive advantage will be reflected in above normal economic performance for those firms protected by the entry or mobility barrier (Porter, 1980).

However, from another point of view, barriers to entry or mobility are only possible if current and potentially competing firms are heterogeneous in terms of the resources they control and if these resources are not perfectly mobile. The heterogeneity requirement is self-evident. For a barrier to entry or mobility to exist, firms protected by these barriers must be implementing different strategies than firms seeking to enter these protected areas of competition. Firms restricted from entry are unable to implement the same strategies as firms within the industry or group. Because the implementation of strategy requires the application of firm resources, the inability of firms seeking to enter an industry or group to implement the same strategies as firms within that industry or group suggests that firms seeking to enter must not have the same strategically relevant resources as firms within the industry or group. Thus, barriers to entry and mobility only exist when competing firms are heterogeneous in terms of the strategically relevant resources they control.

The requirement that firm resources be immobile in order for barriers to entry or mobility to exist is also clear. If firm resources are perfectly mobile, then any resource that allows some firms to implement a strategy protected by entry or mobility barriers can easily be acquired by firms seeking to enter into this industry or group. Once these resources are acquired, the strategy in question can be conceived of and implemented in the same way that other firms have conceived of and implemented their strategies. These strategies are thus not a source of sustained competitive advantage.

Again, it is not being suggested that entry or mobility barriers do not exist. However, it is being suggested that these barriers only become sources of sustained competitive advantage when firm resources are not homogeneously distributed across competing firms and when these resources are not perfectly mobile.

Firm resources and sustained competitive advantage

Thus far, it has been suggested that in order to understand sources of sustained competitive advantage, it is necessary to build a theoretical model that begins with the assumption that firm resources may be heterogeneous and immobile. Of course, not all firm resources hold the potential of sustained competitive advantages. To have this potential, a firm resource must have four attributes:

■ it must be valuable, in the sense that it exploits opportunities and/or neutralizes threats in a firm's environment;

■ it must be rare among a firm's current and potential competition;

■ it must be imperfectly imitable;

■ there cannot be strategically equivalent substitutes for this resource that are valuable but neither rare nor imperfectly imitable.

These attributes of firm resources can be thought of as empirical indicators of how heterogeneous and immobile a firm's resources are and thus how useful these resources are for generating sustained competitive advantages. Each of these attributes of a firm's resources is discussed in more detail below.

Valuable resources

Firm resources can only be a source of competitive advantage or sustained competitive advantage when they are valuable. As suggested earlier, resources are valuable when they enable a firm to conceive of or implement strategies that improve its efficiency and effectiveness. The traditional 'strengths-weaknesses-opportunities-threats' model of firm performance suggests that firms are able to improve their performance only when their strategies exploit opportunities or neutralize threats. Firm attributes may have the other characteristics that could qualify them as sources of competitive advantage (e.g. rareness, inimitability, non-substitutability), but these attributes only become resources when they exploit opportunities or neutralize threats in a firm's environment.

That firm attributes must be valuable in order to be considered resources (and thus as possible sources of sustained competitive advantage) points to an important complementarity between environmental models of competitive advantage and the resource-based model. These environmental models help isolate those firm attributes that exploit opportunities or neutralize threats, and thus specify which firm attributes can be considered as resources. The resource-based model then suggests additional characteristics that these resources must possess if they are to generate sustained competitive advantage.

Rare resources

By definition, valuable firm resources possessed by large numbers of competing or potentially competing firms cannot be sources of either a competitive advantage or a sustained competitive advantage. A firm enjoys a competitive advantage when it is implementing a value-creating strategy not simultaneously implemented by large numbers of other firms. If a particular valuable firm resource is possessed by large numbers of firms, then each of these firms have the capability of exploiting that resource in the same way, thereby implementing a common strategy that gives no one firm a competitive advantage.

The same analysis applies to bundles of valuable firm resources used to conceive of and implement strategies. Some strategies require a particular mix of physical capital, human capital and organizational capital resources to implement. One firm resource required in the implementation of almost all strategies is managerial talent (Hambrick, 1987). If this particular bundle of firm resources is not rare, then large numbers of firms will be able to conceive of and implement the strategies in question, and these strategies will not be a source of competitive advantage, even though the resources in question may be valuable.

To observe that competitive advantages (sustained or otherwise) only accrue to firms that have valuable and rare resources is not to dismiss common (i.e. not rare) firm resources as unimportant. Instead, these valuable but common firm resources can help ensure a firm's survival when they are exploited to create competitive parity in an industry. Under conditions of competitive parity, though no one firm obtains a competitive advantage, firms do increase their probability of economic survival.

How rare a valuable firm resource must be in order to have the potential for generating a competitive advantage is a difficult question. It is not difficult to see that if a firm's valuable resources are absolutely unique among a set of competing and potentially competing firms, those resources will generate at least a competitive advantage and may have the potential of generating a sustained competitive advantage. However, it may be possible for a small number of firms in an industry to possess a particular valuable resource and still generate a competitive advantage. In general, as long as the number of firms that possess a particular valuable resource (or a bundle of valuable resources) is less than the number of firms needed to generate perfect competition dynamics in an industry, that resource has the potential of generating a competitive advantage.

Imperfectly imitable resources

It is not difficult to see that valuable and rare organizational resources may be a source of competitive advantage. Indeed, firms with such resources will often be strategic innovators, for they will be able to conceive of and engage in strategies that other firms could either not conceive of, or not implement, or both, because these other firms lacked the relevant firm resources. The observation that valuable and rare organizational resources can be a source of competitive advantage is another way of describing first-mover advantages accruing to firms with resource advantages.

However, valuable and rare organizational resources can only be sources of sustained competitive advantage if firms that do not possess these resources cannot obtain them. These firm resources are imperfectly imitable. Firm resources can be imperfectly imitable for one or a combination of three reasons: (a) the ability of a firm to obtain a resource is dependent upon *unique historical conditions,* (b) the link between the resources possessed by a firm and a firm's sustained competitive advantage is *causally ambiguous,* or (c) the resource generating a firm's advantage is *socially complex.* Each of these sources of the imperfect imitability of firm resources is examined below.

Unique historical conditions and imperfectly imitable resources. Another assumption of most environmental models of firm competitive advantage, besides resource homogeneity and mobility, is that the performance of firms can be understood independently of the particular history and other idiosyncratic attributes of firms. These researchers seldom argue that firms do not vary in terms of their unique histories, but rather that these unique histories are not relevant to understanding a firm's performance (Porter, 1980).

The resource-based view of competitive advantage developed here relaxes this assumption. Indeed, this approach asserts that not only are firms intrinsically historical and social entities, but that their ability to acquire and exploit some resources depends upon their place in time and space. Once this particular unique time in history passes, firms that do not have space- and time-dependent resources cannot obtain them, and thus these resources are imperfectly imitable.

Resource-based theorists are not alone in recognizing the importance of history as a determinant of firm performance and competitive advantage. Traditional strategy researchers often cited the unique historical circumstances of a firm's founding, or the unique circumstances under which a new management team takes over

a firm, as important determinants of a firm's long-term performance. More recently, several economists (e.g. Arthur, Ermoliev and Kaniovsky, 1987; David, 1985) have developed models of firm performance that rely heavily on unique historical events as determinants of subsequent actions. Employing path-dependent models of economic performance, these authors suggest that the performance of a firm does not depend simply on the industry structure within which a firm finds itself at a particular point in time, but also on the path a firm followed through history to arrive where it is. If a firm obtains valuable and rare resources because of its unique path through history, it will be able to exploit those resources in implementing value-creating strategies that cannot be duplicated by other firms, for firms without that particular path through history cannot obtain the resources necessary to implement the strategy.

The acquisition of all the types of firm resources examined in this article can depend upon the unique historical position of a firm. A firm that locates its facilities on what turns out to be a much more valuable location than was anticipated when the location was chosen possesses an imperfectly imitable physical capital resource. A firm with scientists who are uniquely positioned to create or exploit a significant scientific breakthrough may obtain an imperfectly imitable resource from the history-dependent nature of these scientists' individual human capital. Finally, a firm with a unique and valuable organizational culture that emerged in the early stages of a firm's history may have an imperfectly imitable advantage over firms founded in another historical period, where different (and perhaps less valuable) organizational values and beliefs come to dominate.

Causal ambiguity and imperfectly imitable resources. Unlike the relationship between a firm's unique history and the imitability of its resources, the relationship between the causal ambiguity of a firm's resources and imperfect imitability has received systematic attention in the literature. In this context, causal ambiguity exists when the link between the resources controlled by a firm and a firm's sustained competitive advantage is not understood or understood only very imperfectly.

When the link between a firm's resources and its sustained competitive advantage is poorly understood, it is difficult for firms that are attempting to duplicate a successful firm's strategies through imitation of its resources to know which resources it should imitate. Imitating firms may be able to describe some of the resources controlled by a successful firm. However, under conditions of causal ambiguity, it is not clear that the resources that can be described are the same resources that generate a sustained competitive advantage, or whether that advantage reflects some other non-described firm resource. Sometimes it is difficult to understand why one firm consistently outperforms other firms. Causal ambiguity is at the heart of this difficulty. In the face of such causal ambiguity, imitating firms cannot know the actions they should take in order to duplicate the strategies of firms with a sustained competitive advantage.

To be a source of sustained competitive advantage, both the firms that possess resources that generate a competitive advantage and the firms that do not possess these resources but seek to imitate them must be faced with the same level of causal ambiguity (Lippman and Rumelt, 1982). If firms that control these resources have a better understanding of their impact on competitive advantage than firms without these resources, then firms without these resources can engage in activities to reduce their knowledge disadvantage. They can do this, for example, by hiring away well placed knowledgeable managers in a firm with a competitive advantage or by engaging in a careful systematic study of the other firm's success. Although acquiring this knowledge may take some time and effort, once knowledge of the link between a firm's resources and its ability to implement certain strategies is diffused throughout competing firms, causal ambiguity no longer exists, and thus cannot be a source of imperfect imitability. In other words, if a firm with a competitive advantage understands the link between the resources it controls and its advantages, then other firms can also learn about that link, acquire the necessary resources (assuming they are not imperfectly imitable for other reasons), and implement the relevant strategies. In such a setting, a firm's competitive advantages are not sustained because they can be duplicated.

At first, it may seem unlikely that a firm with a sustained competitive advantage will not fully understand the source of that advantage. However, given the very complex relationship between firm resources and competitive advantage, such an incomplete understanding is not implausible. The resources controlled by a firm are very complex and interdependent. Often, they are implicit, taken for granted by managers, rather than being subject to explicit analysis. Numerous resources, taken by themselves or in combination with other resources, may yield sustained competitive advantage. Although managers may have numerous hypotheses about which resources generate their firm's advantages, it is rarely possible to rigorously test these hypotheses. As long as numerous plausible explanations of the sources of sustained competitive advantage exist within a firm, the link between the resources controlled by a firm and sustained competitive advantage remains somewhat ambiguous, and thus which of a firm's resources to imitate remains uncertain.

Social complexity. A final reason that a firm's resources may be imperfectly imitable is that they may be very complex social phenomena, beyond the ability of firms to systematically manage and influence. When competitive advantages are based in such complex social phenomena, the ability of other firms to imitate these resources is significantly constrained.

A wide variety of firm resources may be socially complex. Examples include the interpersonal relations among managers in a firm, a firm's culture (Barney, 1986b), or a firm's reputation among suppliers and customers. Notice that in most of these cases it is possible to specify how these socially complex resources add value to a firm. Thus, there is little or no causal ambiguity surrounding the link between these firm resources and competitive advantage. However, understanding that, say, an organizational culture with certain attributes or quality relations among managers can improve a firm's efficiency and effectiveness does not necessarily imply that firms without these attributes can engage in systematic efforts to create them. Such social engineering may be, for the time being at least, beyond the capabilities of most firms. To the extent that socially complex firm resources are not subject to such direct management, these resources are imperfectly imitable.

Notice that complex physical technology is not included in this category of sources of imperfectly imitable. In general, physical technology, whether it takes the form of machine tools, robots in factories or complex information management systems, is by itself typically imitable. If one firm can purchase these physical tools of production and thereby implement some strategies, then other firms should also be able to purchase these physical tools, and thus such tools should not be a source of sustained competitive advantage.

On the other hand, the exploitation of physical technology in a firm often involves the use of socially complex firm resources. Several firms may all possess the same physical technology, but only one of these firms may possess the social relations, culture, traditions, etc. to fully exploit this technology in implementing strategies. If these complex social resources are not subject to imitation (and assuming they are valuable and rare and no substitutes exist), these firms may obtain a sustained competitive advantage from exploiting their physical technology more completely than other firms, even though competing firms do not vary in terms of the physical technology they possess.

Substitutability

The last requirement for a firm resource to be a source of sustained competitive advantage is that there must be no strategically equivalent valuable resources that are themselves either not rare or imitable. Two valuable firm resources (or two bundles of firm resources) are strategically equivalent when they each can be exploited separately to implement the same strategies. Suppose that one of these valuable firm resources is rare and imperfectly imitable, but the other is not. Firms with this first resource will be able to conceive of and implement certain strategies. If there were no strategically equivalent firm resources, these strategies would generate a sustained competitive advantage (because the resources used to conceive and implement them are valuable, rare and imperfectly imitable). However, that there are strategically equivalent resources suggests that other current or potentially competing firms can implement the same strategies, but in a different way, using different resources. If these alternative resources are either not rare or imitable, then numerous firms will be able to conceive of and implement the strategies in question, and those strategies will not generate a sustained competitive advantage. This will be the case even though one approach to implementing these strategies exploits valuable, rare and imperfectly imitable firm resources.

Substitutability can take at least two forms. First, though it may not be possible for a firm to imitate another firm's resources exactly, it may be able to substitute a similar resource that enables it to conceive of and implement the same strategies. For example, a firm seeking to duplicate the competitive advantages of another firm by imitating that other firm's high quality top management team will often be unable to copy that team exactly. However, it may be possible for this firm to develop its own unique top management team. Though these two teams will be different (different people, different operating practices, a different history, etc.), they may likely be strategically equivalent and thus be substitutes for one another. If different top management teams are strategically equivalent (and if these substitute teams are common or highly imitable), then a high quality top management team is not a source of sustained competitive advantage, even though a particular management team of a particular firm is valuable, rare and imperfectly imitable.

Second, very different firm resources can also be strategic substitutes. For example, managers in one firm may have a very clear vision of the future of their company because of a charismatic leader in their firm. Managers in competing firms may also have a very clear vision of the future of their companies, but this common vision may reflect these firms' systematic, company-wide strategic planning process. From the point of view of managers having a clear vision of the future of their company, the firm resource of a charismatic leader and the firm resource of a formal planning system may be strategically equivalent, and thus substitutes for one another. If large numbers of competing firms have a formal planning system that generates this common vision (or if such a formal planning is highly imitable), then firms with such a vision derived from a charismatic leader will not have a sustained competitive advantage, even though the firm resource of a charismatic leader is probably rare and imperfectly imitable.

Of course, the strategic substitutability of firm resources is always a matter of degree. It is the case, however, that substitute firm resources need not have exactly the same implications for an organization in order for those resources to be equivalent from the point of view of the strategies that firms can conceive of and implement. If enough firms have these valuable substitute resources (i.e. they are not rare), or if enough firms can acquire them (i.e. they are imitable), then none of these firms (including firms whose resources are being substituted for) can expect to obtain a sustained competitive advantage.

The framework

The relationship between resource heterogeneity and immobility; value, rareness, imitability and substitutability; and sustained competitive advantage is summarized in Figure 4.2.2. This framework can be applied in analysing the potential of a broad range of firm resources to be sources of sustained competitive advantage. These analyses not only specify the theoretical conditions under which sustained competitive advantage might exist, they also suggest specific empirical questions that need to be addressed before the relationship between a particular firm resource and sustained competitive advantage can be understood.

That the study of sources of sustained competitive advantage focuses on valuable, rare, imperfectly imitable and non-substitutable resource endowments does not suggest – as some population ecologists would

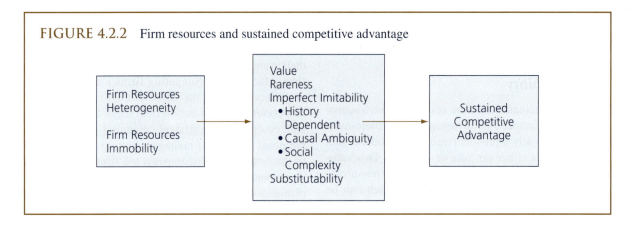

FIGURE 4.2.2 Firm resources and sustained competitive advantage

have it (e.g., Hannan and Freeman, 1977) – that managers are irrelevant in the study of such advantages. In fact, managers are important in this model, for it is managers that are able to understand and describe the economic performance potential of a firm's endowments. Without such managerial analyses, sustained competitive advantage is not likely. This is the case even though the skills needed to describe the rare, imperfectly imitable, and non-substitutable resources of a firm may themselves not be rare, imperfectly imitable, or non-substitutable.

Indeed, it may be the case that a manager or a managerial team is a firm resource that has the potential for generating sustained competitive advantages. The conditions under which this will be the case can be outlined using the framework presented in Figure 4.2.2. However, in the end, what becomes clear is that firms cannot expect to 'purchase' sustained competitive advantages on open markets. Rather, such advantages must be found in the rare, imperfectly imitable and non-substitutable resources already controlled by a firm.

READING 4.3

Dynamic capabilities and strategic management

By David J. Teece, Gary Pisano and Amy Shuen[1]

The fundamental question in the field of strategic management is how firms achieve and sustain competitive advantage. We confront this question here by developing the dynamic capabilities approach, which endeavours to analyse the sources of wealth creation and capture by firms. The development of this framework flows from a recognition by the authors that strategic theory is replete with analyses of firm-level strategies for sustaining and safeguarding extant competitive advantage, but has performed less well with respect to assisting in the understanding of how and why certain firms build competitive advantage in regimes of rapid change. Our approach is especially relevant in a Schumpeterian world of innovation-based competition, price/performance rivalry, increasing returns, and the 'creative destruction' of existing competences. The approach endeavours to explain firm-level success and failure. We are interested in both building a better theory of firm performance, as well as informing managerial practice.

In order to position our analysis in a manner that displays similarities and differences with existing approaches, we begin by briefly reviewing accepted frameworks for strategic management. We endeavour to expose implicit assumptions, and identify competitive circumstances where each paradigm might display

[1]Source: Teece, D.J., Pisano, G. and Shuen, A. (1997) 'Dynamic capabilities and strategic management', *Strategic Management Journal*, Vol. 18, No. 7, August, pp. 509–534. Copyright © John Wiley & Sons, Inc. 1997. Reproduced with permission of John Wiley & Sons, Inc..

some relative advantage as both a useful descriptive and normative theory of competitive strategy. While numerous theories have been advanced over the past two decades about the sources of competitive advantage, many cluster around just a few loosely structured frameworks or paradigms. In this paper we attempt to identify three existing paradigms and describe aspects of an emerging new paradigm that we label dynamic capabilities.

The dominant paradigm in the field during the 1980s was the competitive forces approach developed by Porter (1980). This approach, rooted in the structure-conduct-performance paradigm of industrial organization (Mason, 1949; Bain, 1959), emphasizes the actions a firm can take to create defensible positions against competitive forces. A second approach, referred to as a strategic conflict approach (e.g., Shapiro, 1989), is closely related to the first in its focus on product market imperfections, entry deterrence and strategic interaction. The strategic conflict approach uses the tools of game theory and thus implicitly views competitive outcomes as a function of the effectiveness with which firms keep their rivals off balance through strategic investments, pricing strategies, signalling and the control of information. Both the competitive forces and the strategic conflict approaches appear to share the view that rents flow from privileged product market positions.

Another distinct class of approach emphasizes building competitive advantage through capturing entrepreneurial rents stemming from fundamental firm-level efficiency advantages. These approaches have their roots in a much older discussion of corporate strengths and weaknesses; they have taken on new life as evidence suggests that firms build enduring advantages only through efficiency and effectiveness, and as developments in organizational economics and the study of technological and organizational change become applied to strategy questions. One strand of this literature, often referred to as the 'resource-based perspective,' emphasizes firm-specific capabilities and assets and the existence of isolating mechanisms as the fundamental determinants of firm performance (Penrose, 1959; Rumelt, 1984; Teece, 1984; Wernerfelt, 1984). This perspective recognizes but does not attempt to explain the nature of the isolating mechanisms that enable entrepreneurial rents and competitive advantage to be sustained.

Another component of the efficiency-based approach is developed in this paper. Rudimentary efforts are made to identify the dimensions of firm-specific capabilities that can be sources of advantage, and to explain how combinations of competences and resources can be developed, deployed and protected. We refer to this as the 'dynamic capabilities' approach in order to stress exploiting existing internal and external firm-specific competences to address changing environments. Elements of the approach can be found in Schumpeter (1942), Penrose (1959), Nelson and Winter (1982), Prahalad and Hamel (1990), Teece (1976, 1986a, 1986b, 1988) and in Hayes, Wheelwright, and Clark (1988). Because this approach emphasizes the development of management capabilities, and difficult-to-imitate combinations of organizational, functional and technological skills, it integrates and draws upon research in such areas as the management of R&D, product and process development, technology transfer, intellectual property, manufacturing, human resources and organizational learning. Because these fields are often viewed as outside the traditional boundaries of strategy, much of this research has not been incorporated into existing economic approaches to strategy issues. As a result, dynamic capabilities can be seen as an emerging and potentially integrative approach to understanding the newer sources of competitive advantage.

We suggest that the dynamic capabilities approach is promising both in terms of future research potential and as an aid to management endeavouring to gain competitive advantage in increasingly demanding environments. To illustrate the essential elements of the dynamic capabilities approach, the sections that follow compare and contrast this approach to other models of strategy. Each section highlights the strategic insights provided by each approach as well as the different competitive circumstances in which it might be most appropriate. Needless to say, these approaches are in many ways complementary and a full understanding of firm-level, competitive advantage requires an appreciation of all four approaches and more.

Models of strategy emphasizing the exploitation of market power

Competitive forces

The dominant paradigm in strategy, at least during the 1980s, was the competitive forces approach. Pioneered by Porter (1980), the competitive forces approach views the essence of competitive strategy formulation as 'relating a company to its environment... The key aspect of the firm's environment is the industry or industries in which it competes.' Industry structure strongly influences the competitive rules of the game as well as the strategies potentially available to firms.

In the competitive forces model, five industry-level forces – entry barriers, threat of substitution, bargaining power of buyers, bargaining power of suppliers, and rivalry among industry incumbents – determine the inherent profit potential of an industry or subsegment of an industry. The approach can be used to help the firm find a position in an industry from which it can best defend itself against competitive forces or influence them in its favour (Porter, 1980: 4).

This 'five-forces' framework provides a systematic way of thinking about how competitive forces work at the industry level and how these forces determine the profitability of different industries and industry segments. The competitive forces framework also contains a number of underlying assumptions about the sources of competition and the nature of the strategy process. To facilitate comparisons with other approaches, we highlight several distinctive characteristics of the framework.

Economic rents in the competitive forces framework are monopoly rents (Teece, 1984). Firms in an industry earn rents when they are somehow able to impede the competitive forces (in either factor markets or product markets) which tend to drive economic returns to zero. Available strategies are described in Porter (1980). Competitive strategies are often aimed at altering the firm's position in the industry vis-à-vis competitors and suppliers. Industry structure plays a central role in determining and limiting strategic action.

Some industries or subsectors of industries become more 'attractive' because they have structural impediments to competitive forces (e.g., entry barriers) that allow firms better opportunities for creating sustainable competitive advantages. Rents are created largely at the industry or subsector level rather than at the firm level. While there is some recognition given to firm-specific assets, differences among firms relate primarily to scale. This approach to strategy reflects its incubation inside the field of industrial organization and in particular the industrial structure school of Mason and Bain (Teece, 1984).

Strategic conflict

The publication of Carl Shapiro's 1989 article, confidently titled 'The Theory of Business Strategy,' announced the emergence of a new approach to business strategy, if not strategic management. This approach utilizes the tools of game theory to analyse the nature of competitive interaction between rival firms. The main thrust of work in this tradition is to reveal how a firm can influence the behaviour and actions of rival firms and thus the market environment. Examples of such moves are investment in capacity (Dixit, 1980), R&D (Gilbert and Newbery, 1982) and advertising (Schmalensee, 1983). To be effective, these strategic moves require irreversible commitment. The moves in question will have no effect if they can be costlessly undone. A key idea is that by manipulating the market environment, a firm may be able to increase its profits.

This literature, together with the contestability literature (Baumol, Panzar and Willig, 1982), has led to a greater appreciation of the role of sunk costs, as opposed to fixed costs, in determining competitive outcomes. Strategic moves can also be designed to influence rivals' behaviour through signalling. Strategic signalling has been examined in a number of contexts, including predatory pricing (Kreps and Wilson, 1982a, 1982b) and limit pricing (Milgrom and Roberts, 1982a, 1982b). More recent treatments have emphasized the role of commitment and reputation (e.g., Ghemawat, 1991) and the benefits of firms simultaneously pursuing competition and cooperation (Nalebuff and Brandenburger, 1995, 1996).

In many instances, game theory formalizes long-standing intuitive arguments about various types of business behaviour (e.g., predatory pricing, patent races), though in some instances it has induced a substantial change in the conventional wisdom. But by rationalizing observed behaviour by reference to suitably designed games, in explaining everything these models also explain nothing, as they do not generate testable predictions (Sutton, 1992). Many specific game-theoretic models admit multiple equilibrium, and a wide range of choice exists as to the design of the appropriate game form to be used. Unfortunately, the results often depend on the precise specification chosen. The equilibrium in models of strategic behaviour crucially depends on what one rival believes another rival will do in a particular situation. Thus the qualitative features of the results may depend on the way price competition is modelled or on the presence or absence of strategic asymmetries such as first-mover advantages. The analysis of strategic moves using game theory can be thought of as 'dynamic' in the sense that multiperiod analyses can be pursued both intuitively and formally. However, we use the term 'dynamic' in this paper in a different sense, referring to situations where there is rapid change in technology and market forces, and 'feedback' effects on firms.[2]

[2] Accordingly, both approaches are dynamic, but in very different senses.

We have a particular view of the contexts in which the strategic conflict literature is relevant to strategic management. Firms that have a tremendous cost or other competitive advantage vis-à-vis their rivals ought not be transfixed by the moves and countermoves of their rivals. Their competitive fortunes will swing more on total demand conditions, not on how competitors deploy and redeploy their competitive assets. Put differently, when there are gross asymmetries in competitive advantage between firms, the results of game-theoretic analysis are likely to be obvious and uninteresting. The stronger competitor will generally advance, even if disadvantaged by certain information asymmetries. To be sure, incumbent firms can be undone by new entrants with a dramatic cost advantage, but no 'gaming' will overturn that outcome. On the other hand, if firms' competitive positions are more delicately balanced, as with Coke and Pepsi, then strategic conflict is of interest to competitive outcomes. Needless to say, there are many such circumstances, but they are rare in industries where there is rapid technological change and fast-shifting market circumstances.

In short, where competitors do not have deep-seated competitive advantages, the moves and countermoves of competitors can often be usefully formulated in game-theoretic terms. However, we doubt that game theory can comprehensively illuminate how Chrysler should compete against Toyota and Honda, or how United Airlines can best respond to Southwest Airlines since Southwest's advantage is built on organizational attributes which United cannot readily replicate. Indeed, the entrepreneurial side of strategy – how significant new rent streams are created and protected – is largely ignored by the game-theoretic approach. Accordingly, we find that the approach, while important, is most relevant when competitors are closely matched and the population of relevant competitors and the identity of their strategic alternatives can be readily ascertained. Nevertheless, coupled with other approaches it can sometimes yield powerful insights.

However, this research has an orientation that we are concerned about in terms of the implicit framing of strategic issues. Rents, from a game-theoretic perspective, are ultimately a result of managers' intellectual ability to 'play the game.' The adage of the strategist steeped in this approach is 'do unto others before they do unto you.' We worry that fascination with strategic moves and Machiavellian tricks will distract managers from seeking to build more enduring sources of competitive advantage. The approach unfortunately ignores competition as a process involving the development, accumulation, combination and protection of unique

skills and capabilities. Since strategic interactions are what receive focal attention, the impression one might receive from this literature is that success in the marketplace is the result of sophisticated plays and counterplays, when this is generally not the case at all.

In what follows, we suggest that building a dynamic view of the business enterprise – something missing from the two approaches we have so far identified – enhances the probability of establishing an acceptable descriptive theory of strategy that can assist practitioners in the building of long-run advantage and competitive flexibility. Below, we discuss first the resource-based perspective and then an extension we call the dynamic capabilities approach.

Models of strategy emphasizing efficiency

Resource-based perspective

The resource-based approach sees firms with superior systems and structures being profitable not because they engage in strategic investments that may deter entry and raise prices above long-run costs, but because they have markedly lower costs, or offer markedly higher quality or product performance. This approach focuses on the rents accruing to the owners of scarce firm-specific resources rather than the economic profits from product market positioning. Competitive advantage lies 'upstream' of product markets and rests on the firm's idiosyncratic and difficult-to-imitate resources.

One can find the resources approach suggested by the earlier pre-analytic strategy literature. A leading text of the 1960s (Learned *et al.*, 1969) noted that

> 'the capability of an organization is its demonstrated and potential ability to accomplish against the opposition of circumstance or competition, whatever it sets out to do. Every organization has actual and potential strengths and weaknesses; it is important to try to determine what they are and to distinguish one from the other.' Thus what a firm can do is not just a function of the opportunities it confronts; it also depends on what resources the organization can muster.

Learned *et al.* proposed that the real key to a company's success or even to its future development lies in its ability to find or create 'a competence that is truly distinctive.' This literature also recognized the constraints on firm behaviour and, in particular, noted that one should not assume that management 'can rise to any occasion.' These insights do appear to keenly anticipate the resource-based approach that has since emerged, but they did not provide a theory or systematic framework for analysing business strategies. Indeed, Andrews (1987: 46) noted that much of what is intuitive in this process is yet to be identified. Unfortunately, the academic literature on capabilities stalled for a couple of decades.

New impetus has been given to the resource-based approach by recent theoretical developments in organizational economics and in the theory of strategy, as well as by a growing body of anecdotal and empirical literature that highlights the importance of firm-specific factors in explaining firm performance. Cool and Schendel (1988) have shown that there are systematic and significant performance differences among firms which belong to the same strategic group within the US pharmaceutical industry. Rumelt (1991) has shown that intraindustry differences in profits are greater than interindustry differences in profits, strongly suggesting the importance of firm-specific factors and the relative unimportance of industry effects. Jacobsen (1988) and Hansen and Wernerfelt (1989) made similar findings.

A comparison of the resource-based approach and the competitive forces approach (discussed earlier in the paper) in terms of their implications for the strategy process is revealing. From the first perspective, an entry decision looks roughly as follows: (1) pick an industry (based on its 'structural attractiveness'); (2) choose an entry strategy based on conjectures about competitors' rational strategies; (3) if not already possessed, acquire or otherwise obtain the requisite assets to compete in the market. From this perspective, the process of identifying and developing the requisite assets is not particularly problematic. The process involves nothing more than choosing rationally among a well-defined set of investment alternatives. If assets are not already owned, they can be bought. The resource-based perspective is strongly at odds with this conceptualization.

From the resource-based perspective, firms are heterogeneous with respect to their resources capabilities/endowments. Further, resource endowments are 'sticky:' at least in the short run, firms are to some degree stuck with what they have and may have to live with what they lack. This stickiness arises for three reasons. First, business development is viewed as an extremely complex process. Quite simply, firms lack the organizational capacity to develop new competences quickly (Dierickx and Cool, 1989). Secondly, some assets are simply not readily tradable, for example, tacit know-how (Teece, 1976, 1980) and reputation (Dierickx and Cool, 1989). Thus, resource endowments

cannot equilibrate through factor input markets. Finally, even when an asset can be purchased, firms may stand to gain little by doing so. As Barney (1986a) points out, unless a firm is lucky, possesses superior information, or both, the price it pays in a competitive factor market will fully capitalize the rents from the asset.

Given that in the resources perspective firms possess heterogeneous and sticky resource bundles, the entry decision process suggested by this approach is as follows: (1) identify your firm's unique resources; (2) decide in which markets those resources can earn the highest rents; and (3) decide whether the rents from those assets are most effectively utilized by (a) integrating into related market(s); (b) selling the relevant intermediate output to related firms; or (c) selling the assets themselves to a firm in related businesses (Teece, 1980, 1982).

The resource-based perspective puts both vertical integration and diversification into a new strategic light. Both can be viewed as ways of capturing rents on scarce, firm-specific assets whose services are difficult to sell in intermediate markets (Penrose, 1959; Williamson, 1975; Teece, 1980, 1982, 1986a, 1986b; Wernerfelt, 1984). Empirical work on the relationship between performance and diversification by Wernerfelt and Montgomery (1988) provides evidence for this proposition. It is evident that the resource-based perspective focuses on strategies for exploiting existing firm-specific assets.

However, the resource-based perspective also invites consideration of managerial strategies for developing new capabilities (Wernerfelt, 1984). Indeed, if control over scarce resources is the source of economic profits, then it follows that such issues as skill acquisition, the management of knowledge and know-how (Shuen, 1994), and learning become fundamental strategic issues. It is in this second dimension, encompassing skill acquisition, learning, and accumulation of organizational and intangible or 'invisible' assets (Itami and Roehl, 1987), that we believe lies the greatest potential for contributions to strategy.

The dynamic capabilities approach: Overview

The global competitive battles in high-technology industries such as semiconductors, information, services and software have demonstrated the need for an expanded paradigm to understand how competitive advantage is achieved. Well-known companies like IBM, Texas Instruments, Philips and others appear to have followed a 'resource-based strategy' of accumulating valuable technology assets, often guarded by an aggressive intellectual property stance. However, this strategy is often not enough to support a significant competitive advantage. Winners in the global marketplace have been firms that can demonstrate timely responsiveness and rapid and flexible product innovation, coupled with the management capability to effectively coordinate and redeploy internal and external competences. Not surprisingly, industry observers have remarked that companies can accumulate a large stock of valuable technology assets and still not have many useful capabilities.

We refer to this ability to achieve new forms of competitive advantage as 'dynamic capabilities' to emphasize two key aspects that were not the main focus of attention in previous strategy perspectives. The term 'dynamic' refers to the capacity to renew competences so as to achieve congruence with the changing business environment; certain innovative responses are required when time-to-market and timing are critical, the rate of technological change is rapid, and the nature of future competition and markets difficult to determine. The term 'capabilities' emphasizes the key role of strategic management in appropriately adapting, integrating and reconfiguring internal and external organizational skills, resources and functional competences to match the requirements of a changing environment.

One aspect of the strategic problem facing an innovating firm in a world of Schumpeterian competition is to identify difficult-to-imitate internal and external competences most likely to support valuable products and services. Thus, as argued by Dierickx and Cool (1989), choices about how much to spend (invest) on different possible areas are central to the firm's strategy. However, choices about domains of competence are influenced by past choices. At any given point in time, firms must follow a certain trajectory or path of competence development. This path not only defines what choices are open to the firm today, but it also puts bounds around what its internal repertoire is likely to be in the future. Thus, firms, at various points in time, make long-term, quasi-irreversible commitments to certain domains of competence.

The notion that competitive advantage requires both the exploitation of existing internal and external firm-specific capabilities, and developing new ones is partially developed in Penrose (1959), Teece (1982) and Wernerfelt (1984). However, only recently have researchers begun to focus on the specifics of how some organizations first develop firm-specific capabilities and how they renew competences to respond to shifts in the business environment. These issues are intimately tied to the firm's business processes, market positions and expansion paths. Several writers have recently offered insights and evidence on how firms can develop their capability to adapt and even capitalize on rapidly changing environments. The dynamic capabilities approach seeks to provide a coherent framework which can both integrate existing conceptual and empirical knowledge, and facilitate prescription. In doing so, it builds upon the theoretical foundations provided by Schumpeter (1934), Penrose (1959), Williamson (1975, 1985), Barney (1986a), Nelson and Winter (1982), Teece (1988), and Teece *et al.* (1994).

Toward a dynamic capabilities framework

Terminology

In order to facilitate theory development and intellectual dialogue, some acceptable definitions are desirable. We propose the following:

Factors of production.   These are 'undifferentiated' inputs available in disaggregate form in factor markets. By undifferentiated we mean that they lack a firm-specific component. Land, unskilled labour and capital are typical examples. Some factors may be available for the taking, such as public knowledge. In the language of Arrow (1996), such resources must be 'non-fugitive.' Property rights are usually well defined for factors of production.

Resources.   Resources are firm-specific assets that are difficult if not impossible to imitate. Trade secrets and certain specialized production facilities and engineering experience are examples. Such assets are difficult to transfer among firms because of transaction costs and transfer costs, and because the assets may contain tacit knowledge.

Organizational routines/competences.   When firm-specific assets are assembled in integrated clusters spanning individuals and groups so that they enable distinctive activities to be performed, these activities constitute organizational routines and processes. Examples include quality, miniaturization and systems integration. Such competences are typically viable across multiple product lines, and may extend outside the firm to embrace alliance partners.

Core competences.   We define those competences that define a firm's fundamental business as core. Core competences must accordingly be derived by looking across the range of a firm's (and its competitors') products and services. The value of core competences can be enhanced by combination with the appropriate complementary assets. The degree to which a core competence is distinctive depends on how well endowed the firm is relative to its competitors, and on how difficult it is for competitors to replicate its competences.

Dynamic capabilities.   We define dynamic capabilities as the firm's ability to integrate, build and reconfigure internal and external competences to address rapidly changing environments. Dynamic capabilities thus reflect an organization's ability to achieve new and innovative forms of competitive advantage given path dependencies and market positions (Leonard-Barton, 1992).

Products.   End products are the final goods and services produced by the firm based on utilizing the competences that it possesses. The performance (price, quality, etc.) of a firm's products relative to its competitors at any point in time will depend upon its competences (which over time depend on its capabilities).

Markets and strategic capabilities

Different approaches to strategy view sources of wealth creation and the essence of the strategic problem faced by firms differently. The competitive forces framework sees the strategic problem in terms of industry structure, entry deterrence and positioning; game-theoretic models view the strategic problem as one of interaction between rivals with certain expectations about how each other will behave; resource-based perspectives have focused on the exploitation of firm-specific assets. Each approach asks different, often complementary questions. A key step in building a conceptual framework related to dynamic capabilities is to identify the foundations upon which distinctive and difficult-to-replicate advantages can be built, maintained and enhanced.

A useful way to vector in on the strategic elements of the business enterprise is first to identify what is not strategic. To be strategic, a capability must be honed to a user need (so there is a source of revenues), unique (so that the products/services produced can be priced without too much regard to competition) and difficult to replicate (so profits will not be competed away). Accordingly, any assets or entity which are homogeneous and can be bought and sold at an established price cannot be all that strategic

(Barney, 1986a). What is it, then, about firms which undergirds competitive advantage?

To answer this, one must first make some fundamental distinctions between markets and internal organization (firms). The essence of the firm, as Coase (1937) pointed out, is that it displaces market organization. It does so in the main because inside the firms one can organize certain types of economic activity in ways one cannot using markets. This is not only because of transaction costs, as Williamson (1975, 1985) emphasized, but also because there are many types of arrangements where injecting high-powered (market like) incentives might well be quite destructive of cooperative activity and learning. Inside an organization, exchange cannot take place in the same manner that it can outside an organization, not just because it might be destructive to provide high-powered individual incentives, but because it is difficult if not impossible to tightly calibrate individual contribution to a joint effort. Hence, contrary to Arrow's (1969) view of firms as quasi markets, and the task of management to inject markets into firms, we recognize the inherent limits and possible counterproductive results of attempting to fashion firms into simply clusters of internal markets. In particular, learning and internal technology transfer may well be jeopardized.

Indeed, what is distinctive about firms is that they are domains for organizing activity in a nonmarket-like fashion. Accordingly, as we discuss what is distinctive about firms, we stress competence/capabilities which are ways of organizing and getting things done which cannot be accomplished merely by using the price system to coordinate activity. The very essence of most capabilities/competences is that they cannot be readily assembled through markets (Teece, 1982, 1986a; Zander and Kogut, 1995). If the ability to assemble competences using markets is what is meant by the firm as a nexus of contracts (Fama, 1980), then we unequivocally state that the firm about which we theorize cannot be usefully modelled as a nexus of contracts. By 'contract' we are referring to a transaction undergirded by a legal agreement, or some other arrangement which clearly spells out rights, rewards and responsibilities. Moreover, the firm as a nexus of contracts suggests a series of bilateral contracts orchestrated by a coordinator. Our view of the firm is that the organization takes place in a more multilateral fashion, with patterns of behaviour and learning being orchestrated in a much more decentralized fashion, but with a viable headquarters operation.

The key point, however, is that the properties of internal organization cannot be replicated by a portfolio of business units amalgamated just through formal contracts as many distinctive elements of internal organization simply cannot be replicated in the market. That is, entrepreneurial activity cannot lead to the immediate replication of unique organizational skills through simply entering a market and piecing the parts together overnight. Replication takes time, and the replication of best practice may be illusive. Indeed, firm capabilities need to be understood not in terms of balance sheet items, but mainly in terms of the organizational structures and managerial processes which support productive activity. By construction, the firm's balance sheet contains items that can be valued, at least at original market prices (cost). It is necessarily the case, therefore, that the balance sheet is a poor shadow of a firm's distinctive competences. That which is distinctive cannot be bought and sold short of buying the firm itself, or one or more of its subunits.

There are many dimensions of the business firm that must be understood if one is to grasp firm-level distinctive competences/capabilities. In this paper we merely identify several classes of factors that will help determine a firm's distinctive competence and dynamic capabilities. We organize these in three categories: processes, positions and paths. The essence of competences and capabilities is embedded in organizational processes of one kind or another. But the content of these processes and the opportunities they afford for developing competitive advantage at any point in time are shaped significantly by the assets the firm possesses (internal and market) and by the evolutionary path it has adopted/inherited. Hence organizational processes, shaped by the firm's asset positions and moulded by its evolutionary and co-evolutionary paths, explain the essence of the firm's dynamic capabilities and its competitive advantage.

Processes, positions and paths

We thus advance the argument that the competitive advantage of a firm lies with its managerial and organizational processes, shaped by its (specific) asset position, and the paths available to it. By managerial and organizational processes, we refer to the way things are done in the firm, or what might be referred to as its routines, or patterns of current practice and learning. By position we refer to its current specific endowments of technology, intellectual property, complementary assets, customer base and its external relations with suppliers and complementors. By paths we refer to the strategic alternatives available to the firm, and the presence or absence of increasing returns and attendant path dependencies.

Our focus throughout is on asset structures for which no ready market exists, as these are the only assets of strategic interest. A final section focuses on replication and imitation, as it is these phenomena which determine how readily a competence or capability can be cloned by competitors, and therefore distinctiveness of its competences and the durability of its advantage.

The firm's processes and positions collectively encompass its competences and capabilities. A hierarchy of competences/capabilities ought to be recognized, as some competences may be on the factory floor, some in the R&D labs, some in the executive suites, and some in the way everything is integrated. A difficult-to-replicate or difficult-to-imitate competence was defined earlier as a distinctive competence. As indicated, the key feature of distinctive competence is that there is not a market for it, except possibly through the market for business units. Hence competences and capabilities are intriguing assets, as they typically must be built because they cannot be bought.

Organizational and managerial processes

Organizational processes have three roles: coordination/integration (a static concept); learning (a dynamic concept); and reconfiguration (a transformational concept). We discuss each in turn.

Coordination/integration.   While the price system supposedly coordinates the economy, managers coordinate or integrate activity inside the firm. How efficiently and effectively internal coordination or integration is achieved is very important (Aoki, 1990). Likewise for external coordination. Increasingly, strategic advantage requires the integration of external activities and technologies. The growing literature on strategic alliances, the virtual corporation, and buyer-supplier relations and technology collaboration evidences the importance of external integration and sourcing.

There is some field-based empirical research that provides support for the notion that the way production is organized by management inside the firm is the source of differences in firms' competence in various domains. For example, Garvin's (1988) study of 18 room air-conditioning plants reveals that quality performance was not related to either capital investment or the degree of automation of the facilities. Instead, quality performance was driven by special organizational routines. These included routines for gathering and processing information, for linking customer experiences with engineering design choices, and for coordinating factories and component suppliers. The work of Clark and Fujimoto (1991) on project development in the automobile industry also illustrates the role played by coordinative routines. Their study reveals a significant degree of variation in how different firms coordinate the various activities required to bring a new model from concept to market. These differences in coordinative routines and capabilities seem to have a significant impact on such performance variables as development cost, development lead times and quality. Furthermore, Clark and Fujimoto tended to find significant firm-level differences in coordination routines and these differences seemed to have persisted for a long time. This suggests that routines related to coordination are firm-specific in nature.

Also, the notion that competence/capability is embedded in distinct ways of coordinating and combining helps to explain how and why seemingly minor technological changes can have devastating impacts on incumbent firms' abilities to compete in a market. Henderson and Clark (1990), for example, have shown that incumbents in the photolithographic equipment industry were sequentially devastated by seemingly minor innovations that, nevertheless, had major impacts on how systems had to be configured. They attribute these difficulties to the fact that systems-level or 'architectural' innovations often require new routines to integrate and coordinate engineering tasks. These findings and others suggest that productive systems display high interdependency, and that it may not be possible to change one level without changing others. This appears to be true with respect to the 'lean production' model (Womack et al., 1991) which has now transformed the Taylor or Ford model of manufacturing organization in the automobile industry. Lean production requires distinctive shop floor practices and processes as well as distinctive higher-order managerial processes. Put differently, organizational processes often display high levels of coherence, and when they do, replication may be difficult because it requires systemic changes throughout the organization and also among interorganizational linkages, which might be very hard to effectuate. Put differently, partial imitation or replication of a successful model may yield zero benefits.

The notion that there is a certain rationality or coherence to processes and systems is not quite the same concept as corporate culture, as we understand the latter. Corporate culture refers to the values and beliefs that employees hold; culture can be a de facto governance system as it mediates the behaviour of individuals and economizes on more formal administrative methods. Rationality or coherence notions are more akin to the Nelson and Winter (1982) notion of organizational routines. However, the routines concept is a little too amorphous to properly capture the congruence amongst processes and between processes and incentives that we have in mind. Consider a professional service organization like an accounting firm. If it is to have relatively high-powered incentives that reward individual performance, then it must build organizational processes that channel individual behaviour; if it has weak or low-powered incentives, it must find symbolic ways to recognize the high performers, and it must use alternative methods to build effort and enthusiasm. What one may think of as styles of organization in fact contain necessary, not discretionary, elements to achieve performance.

Recognizing the congruences and complementarities among processes, and between processes and incentives, is critical to the understanding of organizational capabilities. In particular, they can help us explain why architectural and radical innovations are so often introduced into an industry by new entrants. The incumbents develop distinctive organizational processes that cannot support the new technology, despite certain overt similarities between the old and the new. The frequent failure of incumbents to introduce new technologies can thus be seen as a consequence of the mismatch that so often exists between the set of organizational processes needed to support the conventional product/service and the requirements of the new. Radical organizational re-engineering will usually be required to support the new product, which may well do better embedded in a separate subsidiary where a new set of coherent organizational processes can be fashioned (See Abernathy and Clark, 1985).

Learning. Perhaps even more important than integration is learning. Learning is a process by which repetition and experimentation enable tasks to be performed better and quicker. It also enables new production opportunities to be identified (See Levitt and March, 1988). In the context of the firm, if not more generally, learning has several key characteristics. First, learning involves organizational as well as individual skills. While individual skills are of relevance, their value depends upon their employment, in particular organizational settings. Learning processes are intrinsically social and collective and occur not only through the imitation and emulation of individuals, as with teacher-student or master-apprentice, but also because of joint contributions to the understanding of complex problems. Learning requires common codes of communication and coordinated search procedures. Second, the organizational knowledge generated by such activity resides in new patterns of activity, in 'routines,' or a new logic of organization. As indicated earlier, routines are patterns of interactions that represent successful solutions to particular problems. These patterns of interaction are resident in group behaviour, though certain subroutines may be resident in individual behaviour. The concept of dynamic capabilities as a coordinative management process opens the door to the potential for interorganizational learning. Researchers (Doz and Shuen, 1990; Mody, 1993) have pointed out that collaborations and partnerships can be a vehicle for new organizational learning, helping firms to recognize dysfunctional routines, and preventing strategic blindspots.

Reconfiguration and transformation. In rapidly changing environments, there is obviously value in the ability to sense the need to reconfigure the firm's asset structure, and to accomplish the necessary internal and external transformation (Amit and Schoemaker, 1993; Langlois, 1994). This requires constant surveillance of markets and technologies and the willingness to adopt best practice. In this regard, benchmarking is of considerable value as an organized process for accomplishing such ends (Camp, 1989). In dynamic environments, narcissistic organizations are likely to be impaired. The capacity to reconfigure and transform is itself a learned organizational skill. The more frequently practised, the easier accomplished.

Change is costly and so firms must develop processes to minimize low pay-off change. The ability to calibrate the requirements for change and to effect the necessary adjustments would appear to depend on the ability to scan the environment, to evaluate markets and competitors, and to quickly accomplish reconfiguration and transformation ahead of competition. Decentralization and local autonomy assist these processes. Firms that have honed these capabilities are sometimes referred to as 'high-flex'.

Positions. The strategic posture of a firm is determined not only by its learning processes and by the coherence of its internal and external processes and incentives, but also by its specific assets. By specific assets we mean for example its specialized plant and equipment. These include its difficult-to-trade knowledge assets and assets complementary to them, as well as its reputational and relational assets. Such assets determine its competitive advantage at any point in time. We identify several illustrative classes.

Technological assets. While there is an emerging market for know-how (Teece, 1981), much technology does not enter it. This is either because the firm is unwilling to sell it or because of difficulties in transacting in the market for know-how (Teece, 1980). A firm's technological assets may or may not be protected by the standard instruments of intellectual property law. Either way, the ownership protection and utilization of technological assets are clearly key differentiators among firms. Likewise for complementary assets.

Complementary assets. Technological innovations require the use of certain related assets to produce and deliver new products and services. Prior commercialization activities require and enable firms to build such complementarities (Teece, 1986b). Such capabilities and assets, while necessary for the firm's established activities, may have other uses as well. These assets typically lie downstream. New products and processes either can enhance or destroy the value of such assets (Tushman, Newman and Romanelli, 1986). Thus the development of computers enhanced the value of IBM's direct sales force in office products, while disc brakes rendered useless much of the auto industry's investment in drum brakes.

Financial assets. In the short run, a firm's cash position and degree of leverage may have strategic implications. While there is nothing more tangible than cash, it cannot always be raised from external markets without the dissemination of considerable information to potential investors. Accordingly, what a firm can do in short order is often a function of its balance sheet. In the longer run, that ought not to be so, as cash flow ought to be more determinative.

Reputational assets. Firms, like individuals, have reputations. Reputations often summarize a good deal of information about firms and shape the responses of customers, suppliers and competitors. It is sometimes difficult to disentangle reputation from the firm's current asset and market position. However, in our view, reputational assets are best viewed as an intangible asset that enables firms to achieve various goals in the market. Its main value is external, since what is critical about reputation is that it is a kind of summary statistic about the firm's current assets and position, and its likely future behaviour. Because there is generally a strong asymmetry between what is known inside the firm and what is known externally, reputations may sometimes be more salient than the true state of affairs, in the sense that external actors must respond to what they know rather than what is knowable.

Structural assets. The formal and informal structure of organizations and their external linkages have an important bearing on the rate and direction of innovation, and how competences and capabilities co-evolve (Argyres, 1995; Teece, 1996). The degree of hierarchy and the level of vertical and lateral integration are elements of firm-specific structure. Distinctive governance modes can be recognized (e.g., multiproduct, integrated firms; high 'flex' firms; virtual corporations; conglomerates), and these modes support different types of innovation to a greater or lesser degree. For instance, virtual structures work well when innovation is autonomous; integrated structures work better for systemic innovations.

Institutional assets. Environments cannot be defined in terms of markets alone. While public policies are usually recognized as important in constraining what firms can do, there is a tendency, particularly by economists, to see these as acting through markets or through incentives. However, institutions themselves are a critical element of the business environment. Regulatory systems, as well as intellectual property regimes, tort laws and antitrust laws, are also part of the environment. So is the system of higher education and national culture. There are significant national differences here, which is just one of the reasons geographic location matters (Nelson, 1996). Such assets may not be entirely firm specific; firms of different national and regional origin may have quite different institutional assets to call upon because their institutional policy settings are so different.

Market (structure) assets. Product market position matters, but it is often not at all determinative of the fundamental position of the enterprise in its external environment. Part of the problem lies in defining the market in which a firm competes in a way that gives economic meaning. More importantly, market position in regimes of rapid technological change is often extremely fragile. This is in part because time moves on a different clock in such environments. Moreover, the link between market share and innovation has long been broken, if it ever existed (Teece, 1996). All of this is to suggest that product market position, while important, is too often overplayed. Strategy should be formulated with regard to the more fundamental aspects of firm performance, which we believe are rooted in competences and capabilities and shaped by positions and paths.

Organizational boundaries. An important dimension of 'position' is the location of a firm's boundaries. Put differently, the degree of integration (vertical, lateral and horizontal) is of quite some significance. Boundaries are not only significant with respect to the technological and complementary assets contained within, but also with respect to the nature of the coordination that can be achieved internally as compared to through markets. When specific assets or poorly protected intellectual capital are at issue, pure market arrangements expose the parties to recontracting hazards or appropriability hazards. In such circumstances, hierarchical control structures may work better than pure arm's-length contracts.

Paths

Path dependencies. Where a firm can go is a function of its current position and the paths ahead. Its current position is often shaped by the path it has travelled. In standard economics textbooks, firms have an infinite range of technologies from which they can choose and markets they can occupy. Changes in product or factor prices will be responded to instantaneously, with technologies moving in and out according to value maximization criteria. Only in the short run are irreversibilities recognized. Fixed costs – such as equipment and overheads – cause firms to price below fully amortized costs but never constrain future investment choices. 'Bygones are bygones.' Path dependencies are simply not recognized. This is a major limitation of microeconomic theory.

The notion of path dependencies recognizes that 'history matters.' Bygones are rarely bygones, despite the predictions of rational actor theory. Thus a firm's previous investments and its repertoire of routines (its 'history') constrain its future behaviour. This follows because learning tends to be local. That is, opportunities for learning will be 'close in' to previous activities and thus will be transaction and production specific (Teece, 1988). This is because learning is often a process of trial, feedback and evaluation. If too many parameters are changed simultaneously, the ability of firms to conduct meaningful natural quasi experiments is attenuated. If many aspects of a firm's learning environment change simultaneously, the ability to ascertain cause-effect relationships is confounded because cognitive structures will not be formed and rates of learning diminish as a result. One implication is that many investments are much longer term than is commonly thought.

The importance of path dependencies is amplified where conditions of increasing returns to adoption exist. This is a demand-side phenomenon, and it tends to make technologies and products embodying those technologies more attractive the more they are adopted. Attractiveness flows from the greater adoption of the product amongst users, which in turn enables them to become more developed and hence more useful. Increasing returns to adoption has many sources including network externalities (Katz and Shapiro, 1985), the presence of complementary assets (Teece, 1986b) and supporting infrastructure (Nelson, 1996), learning by using (Rosenberg, 1982), and scale economies in production and distribution. Competition between and amongst technologies is shaped by increasing returns. Early leads won by good luck or special circumstances (Arthur, 1983) can become amplified by increasing returns. This is not to suggest that first movers necessarily win. Because increasing returns have multiple sources, the prior positioning of firms can affect their capacity to exploit increasing returns. Thus, in Mitchell's (1989) study of medical diagnostic imaging, firms already controlling the relevant complementary assets could in theory start last and finish first.

In the presence of increasing returns, firms can compete passively, or they may compete strategically through technology-sponsoring activities.[3] The first type of competition is not unlike biological competition amongst species, although it can be sharpened by managerial activities that enhance the performance of products and processes. The reality is that companies with the best products will not always win, as chance events may cause 'lock-in' on inferior technologies (Arthur, 1983) and may even in special cases generate switching costs for consumers. However, while switching costs may favour the incumbent, in regimes of rapid technological change switching costs can become quickly swamped by switching benefits. Put differently, new products employing different standards often appear with alacrity in market environments experiencing rapid technological change, and incumbents can be readily challenged by superior products and services that yield switching benefits. Thus the degree to which switching costs cause 'lock-in' is a function of factors such as user learning, rapidity of technological change, and the amount of ferment in the competitive environment.

Technological opportunities. The concept of path dependencies is given forward meaning through the consideration of an industry's technological opportunities. It is well recognized that how far and how fast a particular area of industrial activity can proceed

is in part due to the technological opportunities that lie before it. Such opportunities are usually a lagged function of foment and diversity in basic science, and the rapidity with which new scientific breakthroughs are being made.

However, technological opportunities may not be completely exogenous to industry, not only because some firms have the capacity to engage in or at least support basic research, but also because technological opportunities are often fed by innovative activity itself. Moreover, the recognition of such opportunities is affected by the organizational structures that link the institutions engaging in basic research (primarily the university) to the business enterprise. Hence, the existence of technological opportunities can be quite firm specific.

Important for our purposes is the rate and direction in which relevant scientific frontiers are being rolled back. Firms engaging in R&D may find the path dead ahead closed off, though breakthroughs in related areas may be sufficiently close to be attractive. Likewise, if the path dead ahead is extremely attractive, there may be no incentive for firms to shift the allocation of resources away from traditional pursuits. The depth and width of technological opportunities in the neighbourhood of a firm's prior research activities thus are likely to impact a firm's options with respect to both the amount and level of R&D activity that it can justify. In addition, a firm's past experience conditions the alternatives management is able to perceive. Thus, not only do firms in the same industry face 'menus' with different costs associated with particular technological choices, they also are looking at menus containing different choices.

Assessment

The essence of a firm's competence and dynamic capabilities is presented here as being resident in the firm's organizational processes that are in turn shaped by the firm's assets (positions) and its evolutionary path. Its evolutionary path, despite managerial hubris that might suggest otherwise, is often rather narrow. What the firm can do and where it can go are thus rather constrained by its positions and paths. Its competitors are likewise constrained. Rents (profits) thus tend to flow not just from the asset structure of the firm and, as we shall see, the degree of its imitability, but also by the firm's ability to reconfigure and transform.

[3]Because of huge uncertainties, it may be extremely difficult to determine viable strategies early on. Since the rules of the game and the identity of the players will be revealed only after the market has begun to evolve, the pay-off is likely to lie with building and maintaining organizational capabilities that support flexibility.

The parameters we have identified for determining performance are quite different from those in the standard textbook theory of the firm, and in the competitive forces and strategic conflict approaches to the firm and to strategy. Moreover, the agency theoretic view of the firm as a nexus of contracts would put no weight on processes, positions and paths. While agency approaches to the firm may recognize that opportunism and shirking may limit what a firm can do, they do not recognize the opportunities and constraints imposed by processes, positions and paths.

Moreover, the firm in our conceptualization is much more than the sum of its parts – or a team tied together by contracts. Indeed, to some extent individuals can be moved in and out of organizations and, so long as the internal processes and structures remain in place, performance will not necessarily be impaired. A shift in the environment is a far more serious threat to the firm than is the loss of key individuals, as individuals can be replaced more readily than organizations can be transformed. Furthermore, the dynamic capabilities view of the firm would suggest that the behaviour and performance of particular firms may be quite hard to replicate, even if its coherence and rationality are observable. This matter and related issues involving replication and imitation are taken up in the section that follows.

Replicability and imitability of organizational processes and positions

Thus far, we have argued that the competences and capabilities (and hence competitive advantage) of a firm rest fundamentally on processes, shaped by positions and paths. However, competences can provide competitive advantage and generate rents only if they are based on a collection of routines, skills and complementary assets that are difficult to imitate. We call such competences distinctive. A particular set of routines can lose their value if they support a competence which no longer matters in the marketplace, or if they can be readily replicated or emulated by competitors. Imitation occurs when firms discover and simply copy a firm's organizational routines and procedures. Emulation occurs when firms discover alternative ways of achieving the same functionality.

Replication

To understand imitation, one must first understand replication. Replication involves transferring or redeploying competences from one concrete economic setting to another. Since productive knowledge is embodied, this cannot be accomplished by simply transmitting information. Only in those instances where all relevant knowledge is fully codified and understood can replication be collapsed into a simple problem of information transfer. Too often, the contextual dependence of original performance is poorly appreciated, so unless firms have replicated their systems of productive knowledge on many prior occasions, the act of replication is likely to be difficult (Teece, 1976). Indeed, replication and transfer are often impossible without the transfer of people, though this can be minimized if investments are made to convert tacit knowledge to codified knowledge. Often, however, this is simply not possible.

In short, competences and capabilities, and the routines upon which they rest, are normally rather difficult to replicate. Even understanding what all the relevant routines are that support a particular competence may not be transparent. Indeed, Lippman and Rumelt (1992) have argued that some sources of competitive advantage are so complex that the firm itself, let alone its competitors, does not understand them. As Nelson and Winter (1982) and Teece (1982) have explained, many organizational routines are quite tacit in nature. Imitation can also be hindered by the fact few routines are 'stand-alone'; coherence may require that a change in one set of routines in one part of the firm (e.g., production) requires changes in some other part (e.g., R&D).

Some routines and competences seem to be attributable to local or regional forces that shape firms' capabilities at early stages in their lives. Porter (1990), for example, shows that differences in local product markets, local factor markets and institutions play an important role in shaping competitive capabilities. Differences also exist within populations of firms from the same country. Various studies of the automobile industry, for example, show that not all Japanese automobile companies are top performers in terms of quality, productivity or product development (see, for example, Clark and Fujimoto, 1991). The role of firm-specific history has been highlighted as a critical factor explaining such firm-level (as opposed to regional or national-level) differences (Nelson and Winter, 1982). Replication in a different context may thus be rather difficult.

At least two types of strategic value flow from replication. One is the ability to support geographic and product line expansion. To the extent that the capabilities in question are relevant to customer needs elsewhere, replication can confer value. Another is that the ability to replicate also indicates that the firm has the foundations in place for learning and improvement. Considerable empirical evidence supports the notion that the understanding of processes, both in production and in management, is the key to process improvement. In short, an organization cannot improve that which it does not understand. Deep process understanding is often required to accomplish codification. Indeed, if knowledge is highly tacit, it indicates that underlying structures are not well understood, which limits learning because scientific and engineering principles cannot be as systematically applied. Instead, learning is confined to proceeding through trial and error, and the leverage that might otherwise come from the application of scientific theory is denied.

Imitation

Imitation is simply replication performed by a competitor. If self-replication is difficult, imitation is likely to be harder. In competitive markets, it is the ease of imitation that determines the sustainability of competitive advantage. Easy imitation implies the rapid dissipation of rents.

Factors that make replication difficult also make imitation difficult. Thus, the more tacit the firm's productive knowledge, the harder it is to replicate by the firm itself or its competitors. When the tacit component is high, imitation may well be impossible, without the hiring away of key individuals and the transfers of key organization processes. However, another set of barriers impedes imitation of certain capabilities in advanced industrial countries. This is the system of intellectual property rights, such as patents, trade secrets and trademarks, and even trade dress. Intellectual property protection is of increasing importance in the United States, as since 1982 the legal system has adopted a more pro-patent posture. Similar trends are evident outside the United States. Besides the patent system, several other factors cause there to be a difference between replication costs and imitation costs. The observability of the technology or the organization is one such important factor. Whereas vistas into product technology can be obtained through strategies such as reverse engineering, this is not the case for process technology, as a firm need not expose its process technology to the outside in order to benefit from it. Firms with product technology, on the other hand, confront the unfortunate circumstances that they must expose what they have got in order to profit from the technology. Secrets are thus more protectable if there is no

need to expose them in contexts where competitors can learn about them.

One should not, however, overestimate the overall importance of intellectual property protection; yet it presents a formidable imitation barrier in certain particular contexts. Intellectual property protection is not uniform across products, processes and technologies, and is best thought of as islands in a sea of open competition. If one is not able to place the fruits of one's investment, ingenuity or creativity on one or more of the islands, then one indeed is at sea.

We use the term appropriability regimes to describe the ease of imitation. Appropriability is a function both of the ease of replication and the efficacy of intellectual property rights as a barrier to imitation. Appropriability is strong when a technology is both inherently difficult to replicate and the intellectual property system provides legal barriers to imitation. When it is inherently easy to replicate and intellectual property protection is either unavailable or ineffectual, then appropriability is weak. Intermediate conditions also exist.

Conclusion

The four paradigms discussed above are quite different, though the first two have much in common with each other (strategizing) as do the last two (economizing). But are these paradigms complementary or competitive? According to some authors, 'the resource perspective complements the industry analysis framework' (Amit and Schoemaker, 1993: 35). While this is undoubtedly true, we think that in several important respects the perspectives are also competitive. While this should be recognized, it is not to suggest that there is only one framework that has value. Indeed, complex problems are likely to benefit from insights obtained from all of the paradigms we have identified plus more. The trick is to work out which frameworks are appropriate for the problem at hand. Slavish adherence to one class to the neglect of all others is likely to generate strategic blindspots. The tools themselves then generate strategic vulnerability. We now explore these issues further.

Efficiency vs market power

The competitive forces and strategic conflict approaches generally see profits as stemming from strategizing – that is, from limitations on competition which firms achieve through raising rivals' costs and exclusionary behaviour (Teece, 1984). The competitive forces approach in particular leads one to see concentrated industries as being attractive – market positions can be shielded behind entry barriers, and rivals costs can be raised. It also suggests that the sources of competitive advantage lie at the level of the industry, or possibly groups within an industry. In text book presentations, there is almost no attention at all devoted to discovering, creating and commercializing new sources of value.

The dynamic capabilities and resources approaches clearly have a different orientation. They see competitive advantage stemming from high-performance routines operating 'inside the firm,' shaped by processes and positions. Path dependencies (including increasing returns) and technological opportunities mark the road ahead. Because of imperfect factor markets, or more precisely the non-tradeability of 'soft' assets like values, culture and organizational experience, distinctive competences and capabilities generally cannot be acquired; they must be built. This sometimes takes years – possibly decades. In some cases, as when the competence is protected by patents, replication by a competitor is ineffectual as a means to access the technology. The capabilities approach accordingly sees definite limits on strategic options, at least in the short run. Competitive success occurs in part because of policies pursued and experience and efficiency obtained in earlier periods.

Competitive success can undoubtedly flow from both strategizing and economizing, but along with Williamson (1991) we believe that 'economizing is more fundamental than strategizing ...' or put differently, that economy is the best strategy.[4] Indeed, we suggest that, except in special circumstances, too much 'strategizing' can lead firms to underinvest in core competencies and neglect dynamic capabilities, and thus harm long-term competitiveness.

Normative implications

The field of strategic management is avowedly normative. It seeks to guide those aspects of general management that have material effects on the survival and success of the business enterprise. Unless these various approaches differ in terms of the framework and heuristics they offer management, then the discourse we have gone through is of limited immediate value. In this paper, we have already alluded to the fact that the capabilities approach tends to steer managers toward creating distinctive and

difficult-to-imitate advantages and avoiding games with customers and competitors. We now survey possible differences, recognizing that the paradigms are still in their infancy and cannot confidently support strong normative conclusions.

Unit of analysis and analytic focus

Because in the capabilities and the resources framework business opportunities flow from a firm's unique processes, strategy analysis must be situational. This is also true with the strategic conflict approach. There is no algorithm for creating wealth for the entire industry. Prescriptions they apply to industries or groups of firms at best suggest overall direction, and may indicate errors to be avoided. In contrast, the competitive forces approach is not particularly firm specific; it is industry and group specific.

Strategic change

The competitive forces and the strategic conflict approach, since they pay little attention to skills, know-how and path dependency, tend to see strategic choice occurring with relative facility. The capabilities approach sees value augmenting strategic change as being difficult and costly. Moreover, it can generally only occur incrementally. Capabilities cannot easily be bought; they must be built. From the capabilities perspective, strategy involves choosing among and committing to long-term paths or trajectories of competence development.

In this regard, we speculate that the dominance of competitive forces and the strategic conflict approaches in the United States may have something to do with observed differences in strategic approaches adopted by some US and some foreign firms. Hayes (1985) has noted that American companies tend to favour 'strategic leaps' while, in contrast, Japanese and German companies tend to favour incremental, but rapid, improvements.

Entry strategies

Here the resources and the capabilities approaches suggest that entry decisions must be made with reference to the competencies and capabilities which new entrants have, relative to the competition. Whereas the other approaches tell you little about where to look to find likely entrants, the capabilities approach identifies likely entrants. Relatedly, whereas the entry deterrence approach suggests an unconstrained search for new

---

[4]We concur with Williamson that economizing and strategizing are not mutually exclusive.

business opportunities, the capabilities approach suggests that such opportunities lie close in to one's existing business. As Richard Rumelt has explained it in conversation, 'the capabilities approach suggests that if a firm looks inside itself, and at its market environment, sooner or later it will find a business opportunity.'

Entry timing

Whereas the strategic conflict approach tells little about where to look to find likely entrants, the resources and the capabilities approach identifies likely entrants and their timing of entry. Brittain and Freeman (1980), using population ecology methodologies, argued that an organization is quick to expand when there is a significant overlap between its core capabilities and those needed to survive in a new market. Recent research (Mitchell, 1989) showed that the more industry-specialized assets or capabilities a firm possesses, the more likely it is to enter an emerging technical subfield in its industry, following a technological discontinuity. Additionally, the interaction between specialized assets such as firm-specific capabilities and rivalry had the greatest influence on entry timing.

Diversification

Related diversification – that is, diversification that builds upon or extends existing capabilities – is about the only form of diversification that a resources/capabilities framework is likely to view as meritorious (Rumelt, 1974; Teece, 1980, 1982; Teece *et al.*, 1994). Such diversification will be justifiable when the firms' traditional markets decline. The strategic conflict approach is likely to be a little more permissive; acquisitions that raise rivals' costs or enable firms to effectuate exclusive arrangements are likely to be seen as efficacious in certain circumstances.

Focus and specialization

Focus needs to be defined in terms of distinctive competencies or capability, not products. Products are the manifestation of competencies, as competencies can be moulded into a variety of products. Product market specialization and decentralization configured around product markets may cause firms to neglect the development of core competencies and dynamic capabilities, to the extent to which competencies require accessing assets across divisions.

The capabilities approach places emphasis on the internal processes that a firm utilizes, as well as how they are deployed and how they will evolve. The approach has the benefit of indicating that competitive advantage is not just a function of how one plays the game; it is also a function of the 'assets' one has to play with, and how these assets can be deployed and redeployed in a changing market.

REFERENCES

Abell, D. (1980) *Defining the Business: The Starting Point of Strategic Planning*, Englewood Cliffs, NJ: Prentice Hall.

Abernathy, W.J. and Clark, K. (1985) 'Innovation: Mapping the winds of creative destruction', *Research Policy*, 14, pp. 3–22.

Amit, R. and Schoemaker, P. (1993) 'Strategic assets and organizational rent', *Strategic Management Journal*, 14(1), pp. 33–46.

Amit, R. and Zott, C. (2001) 'Value Creation in E-business', *Strategic Management Journal*, 22, pp. 493–520.

Andrews, K. (1987) *The Concept of Corporate Strategy*, Homewood: Irvin.

Aoki, M. (1990) 'The participatory generation of information rents and the theory of the firm', in: M. Aoki, B. Gustafsson and O.E. Williamson (eds) *The Firm as a Nexus of Treaties*, London: Sage, pp. 26-52.

Argyres, N. (1995) 'Technology strategy, governance structure and interdivisional coordination', *Journal of Economic Behavior and Organization*, 28, pp. 337–358.

Arrow, K. (1969) 'The organization of economic activity: Issues pertinent to the choice of market vs. nonmarket allocation', in: *The Analysis and Evaluation of Public Expenditures: The PPB System, 1*. US Joint Economic Committee, 91st Session. US Government Printing Office, Washington DC, pp. 59–73.

Arrow, K. (1996) 'Technical information and industrial structure', *Industrial and Corporate Change*, 5(2), pp. 645–652.

Arthur, W.B. (1983) 'Competing technologies and lock-in by historical events: The dynamics of allocation under increasing returns', working paper WP-83-90, International Institute for Applied Systems Analysis, Laxenburg, Austria.

Arthur, W.B., Ermoliev, Y.M. and Kaniovsky, Y.M. (1987) 'Path Dependent Processes and the Emergence of Macro Structure', *European Journal of Operations Research*, 30, pp. 294–303.

Baden-Fuller, C. and Stopford, J.M. (1992) *Rejuvenating the Mature Business*, London: Routledge.

Bain, J. (1956) *Barriers to New Competition*, Cambridge, MA: Harvard University Press.

Bain, J. (1959) *Industrial Organization*, New York: Wiley.

Barney, J.B. (1986a) 'Strategic factor markets: Expectations, luck and business strategy', *Management Science*, 32(10), pp. 1231–1241.

Barney, J.B. (1986b) 'Organizational Culture: Can It Be a Source of Sustained Competitive Advantage?' *Academy of Management Review*, 11, pp. 656–665.

Barney, J.B. (1991) 'Firm Resources and Sustained Competitive Advantage', *Journal of Management*, 17(1), pp. 99–120.

Baumol, W., Panzar, J. and Willig, R. (1982) *Contestable Markets and the Theory of Industry Structure*, New York: Harcourt Brace Jovanovich.

Brittain, J. and Freeman, J. (1980) 'Organizational proliferation and density-dependent selection', in: J.R. Kimberly and R. Miles (eds.) *The Organizational Life Cycle*, San Francisco, CA: Jossey-Bass, pp. 291–338.

Buzzell, R.D. and Gale, B.T. (1987) *The PIMS Principles: Linking Strategy to Performance*, New York: Free Press.

Camp, R. (1989) *Benchmarking: The Search for Industry Best Practices that Lead to Superior Performance*, Milwaukee, WI: Quality Press.

Caves, R.E. and Porter, M.E. (1977) 'From Entry Barriers to Mobility Barriers: Conjectural Decisions and Contrived Deterrence to New Competition', *Quarterly Journal of Economics*, 91, pp. 24–262.

Christensen, C. (1997) *The Innovator's Dilemma*, New York: HarperBusiness.

Clark, K. and Fujimoto, T. (1991) *Product Development Performance: Strategy, Organization and Management in the World Auto Industries*, Cambridge, MA: Harvard Business School Press.

Coase, R. (1937) 'The nature of the firm', *Economica*, 4, pp. 386–405.

Collis, D.J. and Montgomery, C.A. (1995) 'Competing on Resources: Strategy in the 1990s', *Harvard Business Review*, 73(4, July–August), pp. 118–128.

Cool, K. and Schendel, D. (1988) 'Performance differences among strategic group members', *Strategic Management Journal*, 9(3), pp. 207–223.

David, P.A. (1985) 'Clio and the Economics of QWERTY', *American Economic Review Proceedings*, 75, pp. 332–337.

Day, G. and Moorman, C. (2010) *Strategy from the Outside in: Profiting from Customer Value*, McGraw-Hill Professional.

Day, G.S. (1990) *Market Driven Strategy, Processes for Creating Value*, New York: Free Press.

Dierickx, I. and Cool, K. (1989) 'Asset Stock Accumulation and Sustainability of Competitive Advantage', *Management Science*, 35(12, December), pp. 1504–1511.

Dixit, A. (1980) 'The role of investment in entry deterrence', *Economic Journal*, 90, pp. 95–106.

Doz, Y. and Shuen, A. (1990) 'From intent to outcome: A process framework for partnerships', INSEAD working paper.

Dretske, F. (1981) *Knowledge and the Flow of Information*, Cambridge, MA: MIT Press.

Duncan, R. (1976) 'The Ambidextrous Organization: Designing dual structures for innovation', in: R.H. Killman, L.R. Pondy and D. Sleven (eds) *The Management of Organization*, New York: North Holland, pp. 167–188.

Durand, T. (1996) 'Revisiting Key Dimensions of Competence', Paper presented to the SMS Conference, Phoenix.

Eisenhardt, K.M. and Martin, J.A. (2000) 'Dynamic capabilities: What are they?', *Strategic Management Journal*, 21, pp. 1105–1121.

Fama, E.F. (1980) 'Agency problems and the theory of the firm', *Journal of Political Economy*, 88, pp. 288–307.

Garvin, D. (1988) *Managing Quality*, New York: Free Press.

Ghemawat, P. (1991) *Commitment*, New York: Free Press.

Gilbert, R.J. and Newbery, D.M. (1982) 'Preemptive patenting and the persistence of monopoly', *The American Economic Review*, 72, pp. 514–526.

Gilbert, X. and Strebel, P. (1989) 'From Innovation to Outpacing', *Business Quarterly*, Summer, pp. 19–22.

Grant, R.M. (2002) *Contemporary Strategy Analysis: Concepts, Techniques, Applications* (4th edn), Oxford: Blackwell Publishers.

Hambrick, D. (1987) 'Top Management Teams: Key to Strategic Success', *California Management Review*, 30, pp. 88–108.

Hannan, M.T. and Freeman, J. (1977) 'The Population Ecology of Organizations', *American Journal of Sociology*, 82(5, March), pp. 929–964.

Hansen, G.S. and Wernerfelt, B. (1989) 'Determinants of firm performance: The relative importance of economic and organizational factors', *Strategic Management Journal*, 10(5), pp. 399–411.

Hayes, R. (1985) 'Strategic planning: Forward in reverse', *Harvard Business Review*, 63(6), pp. 111–119.

Hayes, R., Wheelwright, S. and Clark, K. (1988) *Dynamic Manufacturing: Creating the Learning Organization*, New York: Free Press.

Heasman, M. and Mellentin, J. (2001) *The Functional Foods Revolution: Healthy People, Healthy Profits?*, London: Earthscan Publications.

Henderson, R.M. and Clark, K.B. (1990) 'Architectural innovation: the reconfiguration of existing product technologies and the failure of established firms', *Administrative Science Quarterly*, 35(1), pp. 9–30.

Hofer, C. and Schendel, D. (1978) *Strategy Formulation: Analytical Concepts*, St. Paul, MN: West.

Itami, H. (1987) *Mobilizing Invisible Assets*, Cambridge, MA: Harvard University Press.

Itami, H. and Roehl, T.W. (1987) *Mobilizing Invisible Assets*, Cambridge, MA: Harvard University Press.

Jacobson, R. (1988) 'The persistence of abnormal returns', *Strategic Management Journal*, 9(5), pp. 415–430.

Jaworski, B. and Kohli, A.K. (1993) 'Market Orientation: Antecedents and Consequences', *Journal of Marketing*, 57(3, July), pp. 53–70.

Katz, M.L. and Shapiro, C. (1985) 'Network externalities, competition, and compatibility', *The American Economic Review*, 75(3), pp. 424–440.

Kay, J. (1993) *Foundations of Corporate Success: How Business Strategies Add Value*, Oxford: Oxford University Press.

Kreps, D.M. and Wilson, R. (1982a) 'Reputation and imperfect information', *Journal of Economic Theory*, 27(2), pp. 253–279.

Kreps, D.M. and Wilson, R. (1982b) 'Sequential equilibria', *Econometrica: Journal of the Econometric Society*, 50(4), pp. 863–894.

Langlois, R. (1994) 'Cognition and capabilities: Opportunities seized and missed in the history of the history of the computer industry', working paper, University of Connecticut. Presented at the conference on Technological Oversights and Foresights, Stern School of Business, New York University, 11–12 March 1994.

Learned, E., Christensen, C., Andrews, K. and Guth, W. (1969) *Business Policy: Text and Cases*, Homewood, IL: Irwin.

Leonard-Barton, D. (1992) 'Core capabilities and core rigidities: A paradox in managing new product development', *Strategic Management Journal*, 13(Summer, Special Issue), pp. 111–125.

Leonard-Barton, D. (1995) *Wellsprings of Knowledge*, Boston, MA: Harvard Business School Press.

Levitt, B. and March, J. (1988) 'Organizational learning', *Annual Review of Sociology*, 14, pp. 319–340.

Lieberman, M.B. and Montgomery, D.B. (1988) 'First Mover Advantages', *Strategic Management Journal*, 9(1, January–February), pp. 41–58.

Lieberman, M.B. and Montgomery, D.B. (1998) 'First-Mover (Dis)Advantages: Retrospective and Link with the Resource-Based View', *Strategic Management Journal*, 19(12, December), pp. 1111–1126.

Lippman, S. and Rumelt, R. (1992) 'Demand uncertainty and investment in industry-specific capital', *Industrial and Corporate Change*, 1(1), pp. 235–262.

Lowendahl, B.R. (1997) *Strategic Management of Professional Business Service Firms*, Copenhagen: Copenhagen Business School Press.

Mason, E. (1949) 'The current state of the monopoly problem in the US', *Harvard Law Review*, 62, pp. 1265–1285.

McGrath, R.G. (2013) *The End of Competitive Advantage: How to Keep Your Strategy Moving as Fast as Your Business*, Boston, MA: Harvard Business Review Press.

Milgrom, P. and Roberts, J. (1982a) 'Limit pricing and entry under incomplete information: An equilibrium analysis', *Econometrica*, 50, pp. 443–459.

Milgrom, P. and Roberts, J. (1982b) 'Predation, reputation and entry deterrence', *Journal of Economic Theory*, 27, pp. 280–312.

Miller, D., Eisenstat, R. and Foote, N. (2002) 'Strategy from the Inside-Out: Building Capability-Creating Organizations', *California Management Review*, 44(3, Spring), pp. 37–54.

Mintzberg, H., Ahlstrand, B. and Lampel, J. (1998) *Strategy Safari: A Guided Tour Through the Wilds of Strategic Management*, New York: Free Press.

Mitchell, W. (1989) 'Whether and when? Probability and timing of incumbents' entry into emerging industrial subfields', *Administrative Science Quarterly*, 34, pp. 208–230.

Mody, A. (1993) 'Learning through alliances', *Journal of Economic Behavior and Organization*, 20(2), pp. 151–170.

Nalebuff, B.J. and Brandenburger, A. (1996) *Co-opetition*, HarperCollinsBusiness.

Nalebuff, B.J. and Brandenburger, A.M. (1995) 'The right game: use game theory to shape strategy', *Harvard Business Review*, 73(4), pp. 57–71.

Nelson, R. (1996) 'The evolution of competitive or comparative advantage: A preliminary report on a study', WP-96-21, International Institute for Applied Systems Analysis, Laxemberg, Austria.

Nelson, R. and Winter, S. (1982) *An Evolutionary Theory of Economic Change*, Cambridge, MA: Harvard University Press.

Nonaka, I. and Konno, N. (1998) 'The Concept of "Ba": Building a Foundation for Knowledge Creation', *California Management Review*, 40(3, Spring), pp. 40–54.

Norman, R. and Ramirez, R. (1993) 'From Value Chain to Value Constellation: Designing Interactive Strategy', *Harvard Business Review*, July–August, pp. 65–77.

Peng, M.W. (2013) *Global Strategy* (3rd edn), Mason, OH: Cengage Learning.

Penrose, E.T. (1959) *The Theory of the Growth of the Firm*, New York: Wiley.

Polanyi, M. (1958) *Personal Knowledge*, Chicago, IL: University of Chicago Press.

Porac, J.F., Thomas, H. and Baden-Fuller, C. (1989) 'Competitive Groups as Cognitive Communities: The Case of Scottish Knitwear Manufacturers', *Journal of Management Studies*, 26, pp. 397–416.

Porter, M.E. (1980) *Competitive Strategy: Techniques for Analyzing Industries and Competitors*, New York: Free Press.

Porter, M.E. (1985) *Competitive Advantage: Creating and Sustaining Superior Performance*, New York: Free Press.

Porter, M.E. (1990) *The Competitive Advantage of Nations*, London: Macmillan.

Porter, M.E. (1996) 'What is Strategy?', *Harvard Business Review*, 74(6, November–December), pp. 61–78.

Prahalad, C.K. and Hamel, G. (1990) 'The Core Competence of the Corporation', *Harvard Business Review*, 68(3, May–June), pp. 79–91.

Rosenberg, N. (1982) *Inside the Black Box: Technology and Economics*, Cambridge, MA: Cambridge University Press.

Rumelt, R. (1991) 'How Much Does Industry Matter?', *Strategic Management Journal*, 12(3, March), pp. 167–186.

Rumelt, R.P. (1974) *Strategy, Structure, and Economic Performance*, Cambridge, MA: Harvard University Press.

Rumelt, R.P. (1980) 'The Evaluation of Business Strategy', in: W.F. Glueck (ed.) *Business Policy and Strategic Management* (3rd edn), New York: McGraw-Hill.

Rumelt, R.P. (1984) 'Towards a strategic theory of the firm', in: R.B. Lamb (ed.) *Competitive Strategic Management*, Englewood Cliffs, NJ: Prentice-Hall, pp. 556–570.

Rumelt, R.P. (1996) 'Inertia and Transformation', in: C.A. Montgomery (ed.) *Resource-based and Evolutionary Theories of the Firm: Towards a Synthesis*, Boston, MA: Kluwer Academic Publishers, pp. 101–132.

Sanchez, R., Heene, A. and Thomas, H. (eds) (1996) *Dynamics of Competence-Based Competition*, London: Elsevier.

Schmalensee, R. (1983) 'Advertising and entry deterrence: An exploratory model', *Journal of Political Economy*, 91(4), pp. 636–653.

Schumpeter, J.A. (1934) *Theory of Economic Development*, Cambridge, MA: Harvard University Press.

Schumpeter, J.A. (1942) *Capitalism, Socialism, and Democracy*, New York: Harper.

Shapiro, C. (1989) 'The theory of business strategy', *RAND Journal of Economics*, 20(1), pp. 125–137.

Shuen, A. (1994) 'Technology sourcing and learning strategies in the semiconductor industry', unpublished Ph.D. dissertation, University of California, Berkeley.

Stalk, G., Evans, P. and Schulman, L.E. (1992) 'Competing on Capabilities: The New Rules of Corporate Strategy', *Harvard Business Review*, 70(2, March–April), pp. 57–69.

Sutton, J. (1992) 'Implementing game theoretical models in industrial economics', in: A. Del Monte (ed.) *Recent Developments in the Theory of Industrial Organization*, Ann Arbor, MI: University of Michigan Press, pp. 19–33.

Teece, D.J. (1976) *The Multinational Corporation and the Resource Cost of International Technology Transfer*, Cambridge, MA: Ballinger.

Teece, D.J. (1980) 'Economics of scope and the scope of the enterprise', *Journal of Economic Behavior and Organization*, 1, pp. 223–247.

Teece, D.J. (1981) 'The market for know-how and the efficient international transfer of technology', *Annals of the Academy of Political and Social Science*, 458, pp. 81–96.

Teece, D.J. (1982) 'Towards an economic theory of the multiproduct firm', *Journal of Economic Behavior and Organization*, 3, pp. 39–63.

Teece, D.J. (1984) 'Economic analysis and strategic management', *California Management Review*, 26(3), pp. 87–110.

Teece, D.J. (1986a) 'Transaction cost economics and the multinational enterprise', *Journal of Economic Behavior and Organization*, 7, pp. 21–45.

Teece, D.J. (1986b) 'Profiting from technological innovation', *Research Policy*, 15(6), pp. 285–305.

Teece, D.J. (1988) 'Technological change and the nature of the firm', in: G. Dosi, C. Freeman, R. Nelson, G. Silverberg and L. Soete (eds) *Technical Change and Economic Policy*, New York: Pinter Publishers, pp. 256–281.

Teece, D.J. (1996) 'Firm organization, industrial structure, and technological innovation', *Journal of Economic Behavior and Organization*, 31, pp. 193–224.

Teece, D.J. (2007) 'Explicating dynamic capabilities: The nature and microfoundations of (sustainable) enterprise performance', *Strategic Management Journal*, 28, pp. 1319–1350.

Teece, D.J., Pisano, G. and Shuen, A. (1997) 'Dynamic Capabilities and Strategic Management', *Strategic Management Journal*, 18(7, August), pp. 509–533.

Teece, D.J., Rumelt, R., Dosi, G. and Winter, S. (1994) 'Understanding corporate coherence: Theory and evidence', *Journal of Economic Behavior and Organization*, 23, pp. 1–20.

Treacy, M. and Wiersema, F. (1995) *The Discipline of Market Leaders*, Reading, MA: Addison-Wesley.

Tushman, M.L., Newman, W.H. and Romanelli, E. (1986) 'Convergence and Upheaval: Managing the Unsteady Pace of Organizational Evolution', *California Management Review*, 29(1, Fall), pp. 29–44.

Webster, F. (1994) *Market Driven Management: Using the New Marketing Concept to Create a Customer-oriented Company*, New York: Wiley.

Wernerfelt, B. (1984) 'A Resource-Based View of the Firm', *Strategic Management Journal*, 5(2, April–June), pp. 171–180.

Wernerfelt, B. and Montgomery, C. (1988) 'Tobin's Q and the importance of focus in firm performance', *American Economic Review*, 78(1), pp. 246–250.

Williamson, O.E. (1975) *Markets and Hierarchies*, New York: Free Press.

Williamson, O.E. (1985) *The Economic Institutions of Capitalisms*, New York: Free Press.

Williamson, O.E. (1991) 'Strategizing, economizing, and economic organization', *Strategic Management Journal*, 12(Winter, Special Issue), pp. 75–4.

Womack, J., Jones, D. and Roos, D. (1991) *The Machine that Changed the World*, New York: Harper-Perennial.

Wright, P.M., Snell, S.A. and Jacobsen, P.H. (2004) 'Current Approaches to HR Strategies: Inside-Out Versus Outside-In', *People and Strategy*, 27(4), 36.

Zander, U. and Kogut, B. (1995) 'Knowledge and the speed of the transfer and imitation of organizational capabilities: An empirical test', *Organization Science*, 6(1), pp. 76–92.

CORPORATE LEVEL STRATEGY

We are not all capable of everything.
Virgil (70–19 BC); Roman philosopher

INTRODUCTION

As firms seek growth, they have a number of directions in which they can expand. The most direct source of increased revenue is to enlarge their market share, selling more of their current product offerings in their current market segments. Besides this growth through focused market penetration, firms can also broaden their scope by extending their product range (product development) or move into neighbouring market segments and geographic areas (market development). All of these growth options can be pursued while staying within the 'boundaries' of a single business (see Figure 5.1). However, firms can broaden their scope even further, venturing into other lines of business, thus becoming multi-business corporations. Some multi-business firms are involved in only two or three businesses, but there are numerous corporations spanning 20, 30 or more business areas.

This chapter deals with the specific strategic questions facing firms as they work on determining their multi-business scope. At this level, strategists must not only consider how to gain a competitive advantage in each line of business the firm has entered, but also which businesses they should be in at all. Corporate level strategy is about selecting an optimal set of businesses and determining how they should be integrated into the corporate whole. This issue of deciding on the best array of businesses and relating them to one another is referred to as the issue of 'corporate configuration'.

THE ISSUE OF CORPORATE CONFIGURATION

All multi-business firms have a particular configuration, either intentionally designed or as the result of emergent formation. Determining the configuration of a corporation can be disentangled into two main questions: (a) What businesses should the corporation be active in? and (b) How should this group of businesses be managed? This first question of deciding on the business areas that will be covered by the company is called the topic of 'corporate composition'. The second question, of deciding on the organizational system necessary to run the cluster of businesses, is labelled as the issue of 'corporate management'. In the following pages both questions will be explored in more detail.

Corporate composition

A multi-business firm is composed of two or more businesses. When a corporation enters yet another line of business, either by starting up new activities (internal growth) or by buying another firm (acquisition), this is called diversification. There are two general

FIGURE 5.1   Corporate growth directions

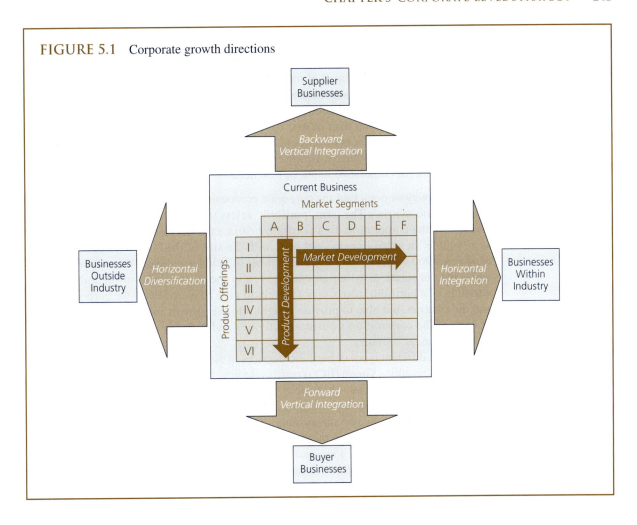

categories of diversification moves, vertical and horizontal. Vertical diversification, usually called vertical integration, is when a firm enters other businesses upstream or downstream within its own industry column (see Chapter 4) – it can strive for backward integration by getting involved in supplier businesses or it can initiate forward integration by entering the businesses of its buyers. The firm can also integrate related businesses at the same tier in the industry column – an example of such horizontal integration is when a newspaper and magazine publisher moves into educational publishing. If a firm expands outside of its current industry, the term 'integration' is no longer employed, and the step is referred to as straightforward (horizontal) diversification (see Figure 5.1).

The issue of corporate composition deals with the question of where the firm wants to have which level of involvement. Corporate level strategists must decide where to allocate resources, build up activities and try to achieve market sales. The issue of corporate composition can be further subdivided into two parts:

■ **Corporate scope.** First, the composition of the corporation depends on the business areas selected. The more 'business components' chosen, the broader the scope of the corporation. Deciding on the corporate scope is not only a matter of choosing from the diversification options depicted in Figure 5.1, but can also work in the opposite direction, as a firm can withdraw from a certain line of business, either by divesting, or closing down, its activities.

- Corporate distribution. The composition of the corporation also depends on the relative size of the activities in each business area covered. The distribution within the corporation is determined by the relative weight of each business component. Some corporations are equally active in all of their selected businesses, while other firms are more asymmetrical, placing more emphasis on just a few of their business activities. Deciding on the corporate distribution is a matter of determining which lines of business will receive more attention than others. Corporate level strategists need to decide which activities will be the focus of further growth and increased weight within the firm, allocating resources accordingly. However, they must also keep in mind that a certain balance within the corporation might be beneficial.

A common way of depicting the corporate composition is to plot all of the businesses in a 'portfolio matrix'. The term 'portfolio' refers to the set of business activities carried out by the corporation. In a portfolio matrix each business activity is represented as a 'bubble' in a two-dimensional grid, with the size of the bubble reflecting the revenue generated with that activity. The number of bubbles indicates the corporate scope, while the corporate distribution can be seen in the relative size of the bubbles. The intention of a portfolio matrix is not merely to give an overview of the corporate scope and distribution, but also to provide insight into the growth and profitability potential of each of the corporation's business activities and to judge the balance between the various business activities.

There are different types of portfolio matrices in use, the most well-known of which are the Boston Consulting Group (BCG) matrix (Hedley, 1977, see Figure 5.2 and Reading 5.1 in this book) and the General Electric (GE) business screen (Hofer and Schendel, 1978). All of these portfolio matrices are based on the same analytical format. Each business activity is mapped along two dimensions – one measuring the attractiveness of the business itself, the other measuring the strength of the corporation to compete in the business. In other words, one axis is a measure of external *opportunity,* while the other axis is a measure of internal *strength* in comparison to rival firms. The major difference between the portfolio matrices is which measures are used along the axes. The BCG matrix employs two simple variables: business growth to determine attractiveness and relative market share to reflect competitive strength. The GE business screen, on the other hand, uses composite measures: both industry attractiveness and competitive position are determined by analysing and weighing a number of different factors. Industry attractiveness will be impacted by such variables as sales growth, demand cyclicality, buyer power, supplier power, the threat of new entrants, the threat of substitutes and competitive intensity. Competitive position often reflects such factors as market share, technological know-how, brand image, customer loyalty, cost structure and distinctive competencies. Another difference between the two matrices is that in the BCG portfolio grid the bubbles represent the company's sales in a line of business, while in the GE business screen the bubbles reflect the total business size, with the pie slices indicating the firm's share of the business.

Deciding which portfolio of businesses to pursue, both in terms of corporate scope and corporate distribution, will depend on how the corporate strategist intends to create value – or as Porter (1987) puts it, how the corporate strategist wants to make "the corporate whole add up to more than the sum of its business unit parts". After all, there must be some benefit to having the various business activities together in one corporation, otherwise each business activity could just as easily (and with less overhead) be carried out by autonomous firms. This added value of having two or more business activities under one corporate umbrella is called 'multi-business synergy' and it strongly determines the corporate composition the strategist will prefer. But before turning to the topic of synergy, the counterpart of corporate composition, namely corporate management, needs to be reviewed first.

FIGURE 5.2   The BCG matrix and GE business screen

Corporate management

It has become a widespread policy to organize multi-business firms into strategic business units (SBUs). This organizational structure is often referred to as the M-form (William-son, 1975). Each strategic business unit is given the responsibility to serve the particular demands of one business area. The business units are labelled 'strategic', because each is driven by its own business level strategy.

This dominant approach to structuring multi-business firms does present managers with the issue of how to bring together the separate parts into a cohesive corporate whole. The corporation can be divided into business units with the intent of focusing each on separate business areas, but this *differentiation* must be offset by a certain degree of *integration* to be able to address common issues and realize synergies (Lawrence and Lorsch, 1967). The challenge for managers is to find the most effective and efficient forms of integration between two or more separate business units. Three key integration mechanisms can be distinguished:

- Centralization. The most straightforward form of integration is to bring resources and activities physically together into one organizational unit. In other words, where the 'division of labour' between the business units has not been applied, resources and activities will be kept together in one department. Such a centralized department can be situated at the corporate centre, but can also reside at one of the business units or at another location.

- Coordination. Even where resources, activities and product offerings have been split along business unit lines, integration can be achieved by ensuring that coordination is carried out between business units. Such orchestration of work across business unit boundaries should result in the ability to operate as if the various parts were actually one unit.

- Standardization. Integration can also be realized by standardizing resources, activities and/or product offering characteristics across business unit boundaries. By having similar resources (e.g. technologies, people), standardized activities (e.g. R&D, human resource management) and common product features (e.g. operating systems, high-tech positioning), such advantages as economies of scale and rapid competence development can be achieved without the need to physically centralize or continuously coordinate.

These three integration mechanisms are the tools available to managers to achieve a certain level of harmonization between the various parts of the corporate whole. Yet often the question is, who should take the initiative to realize integration – where in the management system is the responsibility vested to ensure that centralization, coordination and standardization are considered and carried out? If all business unit managers are looking after their own backyard, who is taking care of the joint issues and cross-business synergies? Basically there are two organizational means available to secure the effective deployment of the integration mechanisms (see Figure 5.3):

■ Control. A straightforward way to manage activities that cross the boundaries of an individual business unit is to give someone the formal power to enforce centralization, coordination and standardization. Such a division level or corporate level manager can exert control in many ways. It can be by direct supervision (telling business units what to do), but often it is indirect, by giving business units objectives that must be met and discussing initiatives. The formal authority to secure integration does not always have to be given to a manager at the corporate centre, but can be assigned to a manager within one of the business units as well. There are also various levels of authority that can be defined, ranging from full final decision-making power to 'coordinator' or 'liaison officer', who have only limited formal means at their disposal.

■ Cooperation. Centralization, coordination and standardization between business units can also be achieved without the use of hierarchical authority. Business units might be willing to cooperate because it is in their interest to do so, or because they recognize the overall corporate interests. If business units believe in the importance of certain joint activities, this can be a powerful impetus to collaborate. Corporate strategists interested in such integration by mutual adjustment will focus on creating the organizational circumstances under which such self-organization can take place (see Chapter 11 for a further discussion). For instance, they might strengthen formal and informal ties between the business units in order to enhance mutual understanding and encourage the exchange of ideas and joint initiatives. They may also support cross-business career paths and try to instil a corporation-wide culture, to facilitate the communication between business units (Eisenhardt and Galunic, 2000).

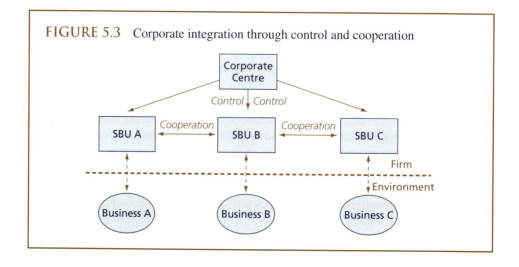

FIGURE 5.3   Corporate integration through control and cooperation

It is the task of the corporate level strategist to determine the mix of control and cooperation needed to manage the corporation. In their seminal research, Goold and Campbell (1987) distinguish three general corporate control styles, each emphasizing different levels of centralization, coordination and standardization:

■ Financial control style. In the financial control style the strategic business units are highly autonomous from the corporate centre. Few activities are centralized or standardized (except for the financial reporting system) and the corporate centre does not explicitly attempt to coordinate activities across business unit boundaries. Control is exerted by negotiating, setting and monitoring financial objectives.

■ Strategic control style. In the strategic control style the strategic business units have a closer relationship with the corporate centre. A number of central services exist, some systems and activities are standardized and the corporate centre explicitly tries to coordinate activities that reach beyond the boundaries of only one business unit. Control is exerted by negotiating, setting and monitoring strategic objectives.

■ Strategic planning style. In the strategic planning style the strategic business units have relatively little autonomy from the corporate centre. Many key activities are centralized or standardized, and the corporate centre is also heavily involved in securing cross-business coordination. Control is exerted by means of direct supervision.

Which corporate management style is adopted depends strongly on what the corporate strategist wishes to achieve. The preferred corporate management style will be determined by the type of multi-business synergies that the corporate strategist envisages, but also on the level of autonomy that the business units require. On the one hand, strategists will want to encourage integration to reap the benefits of having various business units together under one corporate roof and will therefore have a strong motivation to exert strong corporate centre control and stimulate inter-business cooperation. On the other hand, strategists will be wary of heavy-handed head office intervention, blunt centralization, rigid standardization, paralysing coordination meetings and excessive overhead. Recognizing that the business units need to be highly responsive to the specific demands of their own business area, corporate strategists will also be inclined to give business units the freedom to manoeuvre and to emphasize their own entrepreneurship. Yet, these two demands on the corporate level strategy – *multi-business synergy* and *business responsiveness* – are to a certain extent at odds with one another. How corporate strategists deal with the tension created by these conflicting demands will be examined more closely in the following section.

THE PARADOX OF RESPONSIVENESS AND SYNERGY

None ever got ahead of me except the man of one task.

Azariah Rossi (1513–1578); Italian physician

When Cor Boonstra took over as CEO of Philips Electronics in 1996, after a long career at the fast-moving consumer goods company Sara Lee, one of his first remarks to the business press was that Philips reminded him of "a plate of spaghetti" – the company's more than 60 business units were intertwined in many different ways, sharing technologies, facilities, sales forces and customers, leading to excessive complexity, abundant bureaucracy, turf wars and a lack of accountability. To Boonstra the pursuit of multi-business synergy had spiralled into an overkill of centralization, coordination and standardization, requiring direct rectification. Thus Boonstra set out to restructure Philips into, in his own words, "a plate of asparagus", with business units neatly lined up, one next to the other.

Over a period of five years he disposed of numerous business units and made sure that the others were independent enough "to hold up their own pants". The result was a loss of some valuable synergies, but a significant increase in the business units' responsiveness to the demands in their own business. Then, in 2001, Boonstra handed over the reigns to a Philips insider, Gerard Kleisterlee, who during one of his first media encounters as new CEO stated that the business units within Philips had become too insular and narrowly focused, thereby missing opportunities to capture important synergies. Therefore, he indicated that it would be his priority to get Philips to work more like a team.

What this example of Philips illustrates is that corporate level strategists constantly struggle with the balance between realizing synergies and defending business unit responsiveness. To achieve synergies, a firm must to some extent integrate the activities carried out in its various business units. The autonomy of the business units must be partially limited, in the interest of concerted action. However, integration comes with a price tag. An extra level of management is often required, more meetings, extra complexity, potential conflicts of interest, additional bureaucracy. Harmonization of operations costs money and diminishes a business unit's ability to precisely tailor its strategy to its specific business environment. Hence, for the corporate strategist the challenge is to realize more *value creation* through multi-business synergies than *value destruction* through the loss of business responsiveness (e.g. Campbell, Goold and Alexander, 1995; Prahalad and Doz, 1987).

This tension arising from the partially conflicting demands of business responsiveness and multi-business synergy is called the paradox of responsiveness and synergy. In the following subsections both sides of the paradox will be examined in more detail.

The demand for multi-business synergy

Diversification into new business areas can only be economically justified if it leads to value creation. According to Porter (1987), entering into another business (by acquisition or internal growth) can only result in increased shareholder value if three essential tests are passed:

- The attractiveness test. The business "must be structurally attractive, or capable of being made attractive". In other words, firms should only enter businesses where there is a possibility to build up a profitable competitive position (see Chapter 4). Each new business area must be judged in terms of its competitive forces and the opportunities available to the firm to sustain a competitive business model.

- The cost-of-entry test. "The cost of entry must not capitalize all the future profits". In other words, firms should only enter new businesses if it is possible to recoup the investments made. This is important for internally generated new business ventures, but even more so for external acquisitions. Many researchers argue that, on average, firms significantly overpay for acquisitions, making it next to impossible to compensate for the value given away during the purchase (e.g. Sirower, 1997).

- The better-off test. "Either the new unit must gain competitive advantage from its link with the corporation or vice versa". In other words, firms should only enter new businesses if it is possible to create significant synergies. If not, then the new unit would be better off as an independent firm or with a different parent company, and should be cut loose from the corporation.

It is this last test that reveals one of the key demands of corporate level strategy. Multi-business level firms need to be more than the sum of their parts. They need to create more added value than the extra costs of managing a more complex organization. They need to identify opportunities for synergy between business areas and manage the organization in such a way that the synergies can be realized.

But what are the sources of synergy? For quite some time, strategists have known that potential for synergy has something to do with 'relatedness' (Rumelt, 1974). Diversification moves that were unrelated (or 'conglomerate'), for example a food company's entrance into the bicycle rental business, were deemed to be less profitable, in general, than moves that were related (or 'concentric'), such as a car-maker's diversification into the car rental business (e.g. Chatterjee, 1986; Rumelt, 1982). However, the problem has been to determine the nature of 'relatedness'. Superficial signs of relatedness do not indicate that there is potential for synergy. Drilling for oil and copper mining might seem highly related (both are 'extraction businesses'), but Shell found out the hard way that they were not related, selling the acquired mining company Billiton to Gencore after they were unable to create synergy. Chemicals and pharmaceuticals seem like similar businesses (especially if pharmaceuticals are labelled 'specialty chemicals'), but ICI decided to split itself in two (into ICI and Zeneca), because it could not achieve sufficient synergy between these two business areas.

Strategy researchers have therefore attempted to pin down the exact nature of relatedness (e.g. Prahalad and Bettis, 1986; Ramanujam and Varadarajan, 1989). Following the business model framework outlined in Chapter 4, the areas of relatedness that have the potential for creating synergy can be organized into three categories (see Figure 5.4): resource relatedness, product offering relatedness and activity relatedness.

Synergy by leveraging resources.   The first area of relatedness is at the level of the businesses' resource bases. Two or more businesses are related if their resources can be productively shared between them. In principle, all types of resources can be shared, both the tangible and the intangible, although in practice some resources are easier to share than

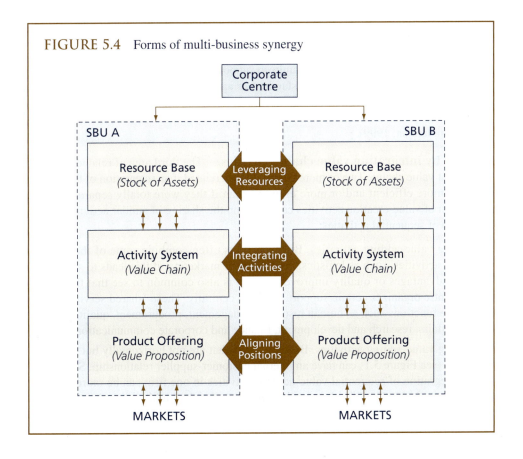

FIGURE 5.4   Forms of multi-business synergy

others – for example, it is easier to transfer money than knowledge. Such 'resource lever-aging' (Hamel and Prahalad, 1993) can be achieved by physically reallocating resources from one business area to another, or by replicating them so they can be used in a variety of businesses simultaneously:

■ Achieving resource reallocation. Instead of leaving firm resources in the business unit where they happen to be located, a corporation can create synergy by transferring resources to other business units, where better use can be made of them (Helfat and Eisenhardt, 2004). For instance, money and personnel are often shifted between business units, depending on where they are needed and the potential return is highest.

■ Achieving resource replication. While physical resources can only be used in one place at a time, intangible resources can often be copied from one business unit to another, so that the same resource can be used many times over. This happens, for example, when knowledge and capabilities are copied and reused in other business units.

Synergy by aligning positions.   A second area of relatedness is at the level of product offerings. Two or more businesses are related if they can help each other by aligning their positioning in the market. Such coordination between product-market combinations can both improve the businesses' bargaining position vis-à-vis buyers, as well as improve the businesses' competitive position vis-à-vis rival firms:

■ Improving bargaining position. Business units can improve their bargaining power vis-à-vis buyers by offering a broad package of related products or services to specific customer groups. Especially when the products being offered are complementary, share a common brand and have a comparable reputation, they will support each other in the market.

■ Improving competitive position. Coordination of product offerings within one firm can also prevent a number of business units from fighting fiercely amongst one another, which might have happened if all units were independent companies. Moreover, it is even possible for multiple business units to support each other in attacking a third party, for example by setting a common standard or aggressively pricing selected products. Similarly, business units can team up to protect each other from attacks and create barriers to entry into the industry/market (Baum and Greve, 2001; Jayachandran, Gimeno and Varadarajan, 1999).

Synergy by integrating value chain activities.   The third area of relatedness is at the level of value chains. Two or more businesses are related if an integration of their value chains is more efficient and/or more effective than if they were totally separated. Such integration of value-creation activities can focus on the sharing of similar activities or the linking up of sequential activities:

■ Sharing value-adding activities. Business units often combine some of their value-adding activities, such as logistics, production or marketing, if this leads to significant scale advantages or quality improvements. It is also common to see that the corporate centre organizes certain support activities centrally. These 'shared services' often include functions such as human resource management, procurement, quality control, legal affairs, research and development, finance and corporate communication.

■ Linking value-adding activities. Business units that are not horizontally but vertically related (see Figure 5.1) can have an internal customer-supplier relationship. Such vertical integration of sequential value-adding activities in one firm can be more efficient than operating independently where supplies need to be highly tailored to a specific type of customer demand.

Much attention in the literature has been paid to this issue of vertical integration of activities. It is also referred to as 'internalization' because firms decide to perform activities inside the firm, instead of dealing with outside suppliers and buyers. In general, companies will strive to integrate upstream or downstream activities where one or more of the following conditions are deemed important (e.g. Harrigan 1985; Mahoney, 1992):

- Operational coordination. It can be necessary for various parts of the value system to be tightly coordinated or even physically integrated, to ensure that the right components, meeting the right specifications, are available in the right quantities, at the right moment, so that high quality, low cost or timely delivery can be achieved. To realize this level of coordination it can be necessary to gain control over a number of key activities in the value system, instead of trying to get suppliers and buyers to cooperate.

- Avoidance of transaction costs. Reaching a deal with a supplier or buyer and transferring the goods or services to the required location may be accompanied by significant direct costs. These contracting costs can include the expenses of negotiations, drawing up a contract, financial transfers, packaging, distribution and insurance. Add to these the search costs required to locate and analyse potential new suppliers or buyers, as well as the policing costs, which are incurred to check whether the contract is being met according to expectations and to take actions against those parties not living up to their contractual responsibilities. If a firm vertically integrates, many of these costs can be avoided, leading to potential savings (Williamson, 1975).

- Increased bargaining power. If a firm is facing a supplier or buyer with a disproportionately high level of bargaining power (for instance, a monopolist), vertical integration can be used to weaken or neutralize such a party. By fully or partially performing the activities in-house, the firm can lessen its dependence on a strong buyer or supplier. The firm can also strive to acquire the other party, to avoid the bargaining situation altogether.

- Learning curve advantages. Where vertically linked business units work closely together, exchanging knowledge and personnel, they might also learn more quickly and more efficiently than if the business units were independent. Especially where they initiate joint R&D projects and collaborate on business process improvement efforts then significant learning curve advantages can be realized.

- Implementing system-wide changes. Besides continual operational coordination and ongoing learning, there may be a need to coordinate strategic changes throughout the value system. Switching over to new technologies, new production methods and new standards can sometimes only be implemented if there is commitment and a concerted effort in various parts of the value system. Sometimes even neighbouring value systems need to be involved in the changes. Vertical integration and horizontal diversification can give a firm the formal control needed to push through such changes.

Corporate level strategy is about determining the corporate configuration that offers the best opportunities for synergy, and implementing a corporate management system capable of realizing the intended synergies. However, what types of synergies can realistically be achieved without paying a heavier penalty in terms of integration costs? Recognizing the possible benefits of bringing together various businesses under one corporate umbrella is one thing, but developing a corporate management system that does not cost more than it yields is another. Therefore, corporate strategists need to carefully consider the potential downside of resource leveraging, activity integration and position alignment – the loss of business responsiveness.

The demand for business responsiveness

Responsiveness is defined as the ability to respond to the competitive demands of a specific business area in a timely and adequate manner. A business unit is responsive if it has the capability to tightly match its strategic behaviour to the competitive dynamics in its business. If a business unit does not focus its strategy on the conditions in its direct environment and does not organize its value-adding activities and management systems to fit with the business characteristics, it will soon be at a competitive disadvantage compared to more responsive rivals. Business responsiveness is therefore a key demand for successful corporate level strategy.

Yet, in multi-business firms the responsiveness of the business units is constantly under pressure. Various scope disadvantages limit the ability of the corporation to ensure business responsiveness. The major problems encountered by multi-business firms are the following:

- High governance costs. Coordinating activities within a firm requires managers. Layers of management, and the bureaucratic processes that might entail, can lead to escalating costs.

- Slower decision-making. Business units must usually deal with more layers of management, more meetings for coordination purposes, more participants in meetings, more conflicts of interest and more political infighting. This not only increases governance costs, but also slows down decision-making and action.

- Strategy incongruence. The resource leveraging, activity integration and position alignment envisioned in the corporate strategy can be more suited to the conditions in some businesses than to others. Consequently, some business units might need to compromise, adapting their business strategy to fit with the corporate strategy. However, such internal adaptation might lead to a misfit with the business demands.

- Dysfunctional control. The corporate centre might not have the specific business know-how needed to judge business unit strategies, activities and results. However, the corporate centre might feel the need to exert some control over business units, potentially steering them in an inappropriate direction.

- Dulled incentives. Limited autonomy combined with the aforementioned problems can have a significant negative impact on the motivation to perform optimally. This dulled incentive to be entrepreneurial and to excel can be compounded by poorly delineated responsibilities, a lack of clear accountability and the existence of 'captive' internal customers.

Together, these factors limit the business unit's drive to be responsive.

These threats make clear that multi-business firms must determine their composition and management systems in a way that enables business units to be responsive. Yet, simultaneously, corporate strategists need to strive towards the identification and realization of synergies. The question is how these two conflicting demands can be reconciled – how can corporate level strategists deal with the paradox of responsiveness and synergy?

EXHIBIT 5.1   SHORT CASE

HYUNDAI MOTOR GROUP: DRIVING APART TOGETHER?

Steel, automobiles, construction, finances, logistics, hotels, machine parts, marketing. All of these are businesses in which the Hyundai Motor Group

(HMG) is active. HMG's core philosophy is that it aims to provide innovative products able to create a better future for humanity. In other words, it allows itself to be involved in any business it pleases. This has been the way in which Hyundai was formed, and it still remains how HMG approaches industries today. Although old habits die hard, it by no means guarantees that this can be maintained in the upcoming years.

The South-Korean economy started to pick up in the 1960s in what was later called the 'miracle on the Han river', characterized by industrialization, better education, an increase in living standards and technological advancement. South Korea's developmental state model was formed principally during the authoritarian regime of Park Chung-hee, the controversial president who seized power in 1961. In order to expand the exports of South Korea, the government decided to pursue cooperation with corporations. This helped *chaebol* come into existence: giant Korean financial conglomerates run by powerful families. Hyundai became one of them.

Yet, this bright future was not apparent when the company was founded in 1947, with the poor Ju-yung Chung establishing a small construction firm. Profiting from the government's drive to rebuild the country in the wake of the Second World War (1939–1945) and the Korean War (1950–1953), his Hyundai Civil Works Company grew at a rapid pace. Chung had the luck to be at the right place at the perfect time, but fortune does not necessarily have to happen accidentally; it can also be enforced. He actively extorted his luck by entering infant industries, which is how he became involved in manufacturing and selling automobiles.

After establishing the Hyundai Motor Company (HMC) in 1967, Hyundai started with the production of cars. The newly founded company helped out Ford with car manufacturing, and after nine years Hyundai launched its own car: the Hyundai Pony, the first ever mass-produced Korean passenger automobile. This model mostly comprised of parts from overseas partners and Hyundai was still more of an automotive assembler, but there were big plans for the company's future. These were not necessarily Hyundai's however, it was the South Korean government that wanted to drastically improve the domestic automotive industry from the early 1970s onwards. The government allowed three companies to mass produce cars: Hyundai, Daewoo and Kia. In addition, it issued high protectionist tariff barriers to protect the infant industry, on the condition that the car manufacturers would utilize as many locally produced car parts as possible. Chung had hit the mark again.

Chung accumulated an assortment of companies that could benefit from one another with the steel business functioning as Hyundai's core. For example, he secured a multitude of companies concerned with manufacturing steel, developing of auto parts and producing ships. Chung also entered seemingly unconnected industries by expanding into commercial banking activities, chemicals, life insurance businesses and electronics, thus diversifying the portfolio of his company intensely. This expansionist attitude seemed to work well though: what started as a small construction firm eventually became South Korea's biggest *chaebol*. In the mid-1990s, Hyundai had 60 subsidiary companies, comprised of 200 000 employees, with total annual revenues of approximately US$90 billion. Yet, Chung's luck did not last forever.

His success started to crumble after the 1997 Asian financial crisis. At first this did not seem to impact Hyundai that much. While its *chaebol* competitors LG and Samsung backed down and reorganized, Chung continued to expand. He dropped some assets that did not add much to the corporation, but his take-overs were more abundant: he acquired Kia Motors and a 60 per cent share of chip-maker LG Semicon. He did so under the premise that the government would save the *chaebols* in case things got out of hand as South Korea could not afford such a loss. Chung guessed wrong.

Early in the crisis five major *chaebols* went bankrupt, while only a few of the largest 30 conglomerates were seen as financially stable. The impact was devastating; several thousands of Koreans lost their source of income. With the South Korean government recording a deficit of US$8.7 billion and in desperate need of a financial bailout, the International Monetary Fund gained the power to act. It decided that South Korea grew too dependent on *chaebols* and put pressure on the South Korean government, which in turn forced the family conglomerates to restructure and focus more on their core businesses. Hyundai, with debts of no less than US$10.5 billion, also coping with the death of Chung, was not spared. Since Hyundai had multiple core businesses, it was divided into a multitude of companies with the Hyundai name but without an actual corporate connection to a group. While Chung's empire crumbled, not all was lost.

Chung had played the game well. He had positioned relatives in top positions throughout his conglomerate, and even though his offspring and other family members were fighting for the lucrative parts of the former *chaebol*, the group still lived on – albeit in a disconnected way. The multiple Hyundai companies moved into more businesses and became shareholders of each other, forming complex structures. In this way, even with minority shareholdings the Chung family generally managed to maintain control.

This is illustrated well by Hyundai Motor Group, holding company for many of the Hyundai businesses. Hyundai Motor Company, de facto representative of the group, possesses some 34 per cent of Kia Motors, which holds 17 per cent of parts supplier Hyundai Mobis. In turn, Mobis owns approximately 21 per cent of HMC. Similar structures are found in the connections between HMG's other subsidiaries, such as finance, logistics and railways. Thanks to good relations with the vast network of the diverse Hyundai businesses and with shares in Hyundai Motor Company and Mobis, Mong-koo Chung, chairman and CEO of HMC and son of the late Ju-yung Chung, retains control of the Motor Group.

Yet, the holding company is not necessarily built to last. The many Hyundai affiliates are not autonomous companies but depend on each other with cross-shareholding and family-based relationships, while integrating compatible resources and activities is a real challenge with minority shareholdings. Hyundai Motor Company may capture synergies with affiliated steel companies and car parts manufacturers by boasting close relationships and leveraging activities, however these may not justify integrating the corporation.

The alternatives are contradictory though. If Chung decided to take apart the current structure of the Hyundai Motor Group and reorganize it into a vertical structure of parent and subsidiaries, this would not only cost approximately US$9.6 billion according to a research conducted in 2012, but would also result in HMG becoming a true *chaebol* all over again. This would contradict South Korea's contemporary politics, which are particularly concerned with curtailing the power of family conglomerates. Keeping HMG as it is now is risky as well, since cross-shareholdings are also perceived as a problem in South Korea's political discourse. With the third generation of Chung management dawning, it is imperative that HMG does not suffer the same fate as Hyundai did in the early 2000s.

Hyundai, which posted its ninth straight quarterly profit decline in May 2016, needs Mong-koo Chung to make decisions. Should he pick one of the alternative routes, or act upon the company's promise: new thinking, new possibilities? Whatever his choice, he will be aware of the situation that Hyundai Motor Group is not driven by only one motor.

Co-author: Wester Wagenaar

Sources: www.hyundaimotorgroup.com; www.imf.org; *Bloomberg*, 8 February 2011 and 21 December 2012; *Business Week*, 13 November 2012; *The Economist*, 4 February 1999 and 25 February 2013; Hyundai Motor Company Audit Report 2016 1Q; *The Korea Times*, 21 February 2010; Lim, Y. (2002) *Journal of East Asian Studies*, Vol. 2, No. 1; Rowley, C. and Paik, Y. (2008) *The Changing Face of South Korean Management*, London: Routledge.

PERSPECTIVES ON CORPORATE LEVEL STRATEGY

We must indeed all hang together, or, most assuredly, we shall all hang separately.

Benjamin Franklin (1706–1790); American politician, inventor and scientist

Corporations need to capture multi-business synergies and they need to ensure each business unit's responsiveness to its competitive environment. In other words, corporations need to be integrated and differentiated at the same time – emphasizing the *whole* and respecting the *part*. Striving towards synergy is a centripetal force, pulling the firm together into an integrated whole, while being responsive to business demands is a centrifugal force, pulling the firm apart into autonomous market-focused units (Ghoshal and Mintzberg, 1994). The main question dividing strategists is whether a corporation should primarily be a collection of parts or an integrated whole. Should corporations be loose federations of business units or tightly knit teams? Should corporations be business groups made up of distinctive parts, where only modest synergies can be realized and business units accorded a large measure of leeway to be responsive to their specific market conditions? Or should corporations actually be unitary organizations, with the parts serving the whole, allowing for significant synergies to be achieved, with the challenge of being responsive enough to varied business demands?

As before, the strategic management literature comes with strongly different views on how strategists should proceed. Here the two diametrically opposed positions will be identified and discussed to show the richness of differing opinions. On the one side of the spectrum, there are those strategists who believe that multi-business firms should be viewed as portfolios of autonomous business units in which the corporation has a financial stake. They argue that business responsiveness is crucial and that only a limited set of financial synergies should be pursued. This point of view is referred to as the 'portfolio organization perspective'. At the other end of the spectrum, there are strategists who believe that corporations should be tightly integrated, with a strong central core of shared resources, activities and/or product offerings keeping the firm together. They argue that corporations built up around these strong synergy opportunities can create significantly more value than is lost through limitations to responsiveness. This point of view is referred to as the 'integrated organization perspective'.

The portfolio organization perspective

In the portfolio organization perspective, responsiveness is strongly emphasized over synergy. Managers taking this perspective usually argue that each business has its own unique characteristics and demands. Firms operating in different businesses must therefore develop a specific strategy for each business and assign the responsibility for each business strategy to a separate strategic business unit. In this manner, the (strategic) business units can be highly responsive to the competitive dynamics in the business, while being a clear unit of accountability towards the corporate centre. High responsiveness, however, requires freedom from corporate centre interference and freedom from cross-business coordination. Hence, a high level of business unit autonomy is required, with the corporate centre's influence limited to arm's-length financial control.

In the portfolio organization perspective, the main reason for a number of highly autonomous business units to be in one firm is to leverage financial resources. The only synergies emphasized are financial synergies (e.g. Lubatkin and Chatterjee, 1994; Trautwein, 1990). Actually, the term 'portfolio' entered the business vocabulary via the financial sector, where it refers to an investor's collection of shareholdings in different companies, purchased to spread investment risks. Transferred to corporate strategy, the portfolio organization perspective views the corporate centre as an active investor with financial stakes in a number of stand-alone business units. The role of the centre is one of selecting a promising portfolio of businesses, keeping tight financial control and allocating available capital – redirecting flows of cash from business units where prospects are dim ('cash cows' or 'dogs'), to other business units where higher returns can be expected ('stars' or 'question marks'). The strategic objective of each business unit is, therefore, also financial in orientation – grow, hold, milk or divest, depending on the business unit's position on the portfolio grid (e.g. Hedley, 1977; Henderson, 1979;). A good corporate strategy strives for a balanced portfolio of mature cash producers and high potential ROI cash users, at an acceptable level of overall risk.

The financial synergies can be gained in a number of different ways (e.g. Chatterjee, 1986; Weston, Chung and Hoag, 1990). First, by having various businesses within one firm, the corporate centre can economize on external financing. By internally shifting funds from one business unit to another, the corporation can avoid the transaction costs and taxation associated with external capital markets. Second, the corporation can limit dependence on the whims of external capital providers, who might be less inclined to finance some ventures (e.g. new businesses or high-risk turnarounds) at acceptable levels of capital cost. Third, where the corporation does want to secure external financing, the firm's larger size, debt capacity and creditworthiness can improve its bargaining position in the financial markets. Finally, by having revenue and earning streams from two or more different businesses, the corporation can reduce its exposure to the risk of a single business. This risk balancing, or co-insurance, effect is largest where the portfolio is made up of counter-cyclical businesses. In turn, the stability and predictability of revenue and earning flows enable the corporation to plan and function more effectively and efficiently (e.g. Amit and Livnat, 1988; Seth, 1990).

The business units do not necessarily need to be 'related' in any other way than financially. In practice, the business units can be related, that is, there can be resource leveraging, activity integration and position alignment opportunities that are seized. The portfolio organization perspective does not reject the pursuit of other forms of synergy, but neither does it accommodate such efforts (Haspeslagh, 1982). Responsiveness is not compromised to achieve these synergy opportunities.

New businesses can be entered by means of internal growth, but the portfolio approach to corporate strategy is particularly well suited to diversification through acquisition. In a multibusiness firm run on portfolio principles, acquired companies are simple to integrate into the corporation, because they can be largely left as stand-alone units and only need to be linked to corporate financial reporting and control systems. Proponents of the portfolio organization perspective argue that such 'non-synergistic' acquisitions can be highly profitable (Kaplan, 1989; Long and Ravenscraft, 1993). Excess cash can be routed to more attractive investment opportunities than the corporation has internally. Moreover, the acquiring corporation can shake up the management of the acquired company and can function as a strategic sounding board for the new people. In this way, the acquirer can release the untapped value potential of underperforming stand-alone businesses (Anslinger and Copeland, 1996).

The portfolio organization perspective is particularly well-known for the analytical techniques that have been developed to support it. As was mentioned before, a large number of portfolio grids are in widespread use as graphical tools for visualizing corporate composition and for determining the position of each of the business units. These portfolio analysis tools have proven to be popular and much used (Goold and Lansdell, 1997), even among strategists who are not proponents of the portfolio organization perspective.

In conclusion, the basic assumption of the portfolio organization perspective is that business units must be responsible for their own competitive strategy. Business units are the main locus of strategic attention and the corporate centre should understand their limited ability to get involved and stimulate synergy. Corporate centres should be modest in ambition and size, taking heed of the words of the famous 'business philosopher' Groucho Marx that "the most difficult thing about business is minding your own".

EXHIBIT 5.2   THE PORTFOLIO ORGANIZATION PERSPECTIVE

CRH: BUILDING A SOLID HOUSE OF BUSINESSES

Although an unfamiliar name to most, CRH has been growing in the past 47 years from serving the small, peripheral Irish construction market to become the third largest building materials firm in the world. While the company name might not ring a bell, the brands kept by this holding surely will. Oldcastle in the United States, Ancon in the UK and Bau King in Germany are all household names that any handyman will relate to producing building materials and selling them in Do-It-Yourself stores. CRH's impressive growth in a viciously hostile environment, characterized by increased commoditization and ever decreasing cyclical demand, has been made possible by its clever acquisition strategy.

In order to overcome industry's challenges, CRH needed to gain a deep understanding of its customers in all businesses and countries in which it is active. This is challenging, as customer demands in this sector are immensely versatile across countries and products. The fact that CRH operates all over Europe and the United States, where it sells hundreds of different products, makes a centralized solution to this challenge unfeasible. Instead, CRH grew tremendously by repeatedly buying up small- to medium-sized companies, to then exploit their expert knowledge of its products and markets. CRH's headquarters only house 250 people, a relatively small number for a firm pulling in over €23 billion revenue a year, which leaves running the shop to the acquired businesses themselves.

What CRH does provide to their business units is increased efficiency by providing an experienced manager who optimizes the – often inexperienced family – company. Every year the performance of all of its business units is tested against performance and growth benchmarks. By doing so, in the words of former CEO, Myles Lee, they "earn the right to grow". Profitable units can expand rapidly due to managerial support and the financial backing CRH will continue to provide. The latter is of paramount importance since a firm the size of CRH has much more favourable credit conditions compared to the much smaller units they maintain.

CRH's approach has proven to be a formula for success. Both the small yet professional central headquarters and the visible, expert brands capitalize on their strengths to create impressive growth. CRH was clever to take this approach as opposed to one of internal growth or larger-scale acquisitions, as many small- to medium-size businesses are struggling and looking for help. Banks maintain increasingly stringent conditions for funding small firms, particularly in the case of family businesses in this sector; growth often leads to new challenges the business does not have the competencies to meet. Through acquisitions, on the other hand, CRH is able to realize its ambition to have a specialized market and product knowledge in all its markets.

Clever and innovative as its approach might be, CRH's profits had slumped in fiscal year 2013. This has to do with the fact that the pace of the construction industry is, as a rule of thumb, about half the size of the economic growth of a region. As the United States and Europe are facing either minimal or even negative growth, the building business is not exactly booming. About 90 per cent of today's demand for cement, for example, stems from emerging markets, a trend that is not expected to let up soon. These shifts in the environment prompted CRH to pursue their approach with renewed vigour, as they streamlined their portfolio through a series of divestments and investments, reallocating their capital from lower growth areas into core businesses for growth. Although these events were relatively small in scale, the cascading effects certainly were not, as they preluded the largest acquisitions ever made in the company's history.

In 2015 CRH acquired cement assets from rivals Holcim and Lafarge for €6.5 billion, which provides a foothold in the Canadian, the Brazilian, and the Philippine markets, while it solidifies CRH's position in the European market. Another large-scale acquisition followed as C.R. Laurence, a US glazing products firm, was purchased for $1.3 billion. Both acquisitions circumvent issues of stagnation and decline in US and European cement markets, as the US glazing market continues to flourish, while cement markets in other regions provide new growth opportunities. Yet challenges still remain, as these large scale acquisitions need to be properly streamlined, while cross-cultural competencies will be put to the test. Although CRH has always pursued a small- and medium-scale acquisition strategy – and still does so until this very day – it was able to act swiftly as it recognized an opportunity. As adaptation, rigour and a good read of their business environment are qualities that have led to their monumental growth in the last 47 years, it will be interesting to see how CRH's future unfolds.

Co-author: Jasper de Vries

Sources: 'CRH issues profit warning after first-half loss of €71m', *Financial Times,* August 20, 2013; 'CRH to acquire €6.5bn in cement assets from Holcim and Lafarge', *Financial Times,* February 1, 2015; CRH Annual Report, 2012–2015; CRH: Still to play its trump card, goodbody stockbrokers, 13 July 2005; CRH Strategy, www.crh.com/our-group/strategy/acquisitions, accessed 15 September, 2013.

The integrated organization perspective

 The integrated organization perspective is fundamentally at odds with the portfolio organization perspective's minimalist interpretation of corporate level strategy. To proponents of the integrated organization perspective, a multi-business firm should be more than a loose federation of businesses held together by a common investor. Actually, a corporation should be quite the opposite – a tightly knit team of business units grouped around a common core. Having various businesses together in one corporation, it is argued, can only be justified if the corporate centre has a clear conception of how strategically relevant multi-business synergies can be realized. It is not enough to capture a few operational synergies here and there – a compelling logic must lie at the heart of the corporation, creating a significant competitive advantage over rivals who operate on a business-by-business basis. The multi-business synergies generated at the core of the organization should enable the corporation to beat its competitors in a variety of business areas.

As corporate level strategists "lead from the centre" (Raynor and Bower, 2001) and develop a joint competitive strategy together with business level strategists, they must make very clear which multi-business synergies they intend to foster as the nucleus of the corporation. It is their task to determine what the core of the organization should be and to take the lead in building it. To be successful, it is necessary for them to work closely together with business level managers whose main task it is to apply the core strengths of the corporation to their specific business area. The consequence of this joint strategy development and synergy realization is that all business units are highly interdependent, requiring continual coordination.

Many different multi-business synergies can form the core of the corporation. In the strategic management literature one specific form has received a large amount of attention – the *core competence* centred corporation (Prahalad and Hamel, 1990, Reading 5.2 in this book). In such an organization a few competencies are at the heart of the corporation and are leveraged across various business units. Prahalad and Hamel's metaphor for the corporation is not an investor's portfolio, but a large tree: "The trunk and major limbs are core products, the smaller branches are business units, the leaves, flowers and fruit are end products; the root system that provides nourishment, sustenance and stability is the core competence." Business unit branches can be cut off and new ones can grow on, but all spring from the same tree. It is the corporate centre's role to nurture this tree, building up the core competencies and ensuring that the firm's competence carriers can easily be redeployed across business unit boundaries. The strategic logic behind leveraging these intangible resources is that high investments in competence development can then be spread over a number of different businesses. Moreover, by using these competencies in different business settings they can be further refined, leading to a virtuous circle of rapid learning, profiting the entire corporation. In line with the arguments of the inside-out perspective (see Chapter 4), it is pointed out that in the long run inter-firm rivalries are often won by the corporation which has been able to upgrade its competencies fastest – battles in particular markets are only skirmishes in this broader war. From this angle, building the corporation's core competencies is strategic, while engaging other corporations in specific business areas is tactical. The corporate centre is therefore at the forefront of competitive strategy, instead of the business units that are literally divisions in the overall campaign (e.g. Kono, 1999; Stalk, Evans and Schulman, 1992).

As all business units should both tap into, and contribute to, the corporation's core competencies, the business unit's autonomy is necessarily limited. Unavoidably, the responsiveness to the specific characteristics of each business does suffer from this emphasis on coordination. Yet, to advocates of the core competence model, the loss of business responsiveness is more than compensated for by the strategic benefits gained.

Besides competencies as the core of the corporation, other synergies can also be at the heart of a multi-business firm. For instance, corporations can focus on aligning a variety of product offerings for a group of 'core customers'. Many professional service firms, such as PricewaterhouseCoopers and Capgemini, are involved in a broad range of businesses, with the intention of offering an integrated package of services to their selected market segments. Another type of core is where a multi-business firm is built around shared activities. Many of the large airlines, for example, have one 'core process', flying planes, but operate in the very different businesses of passenger travel and cargo transport. Yet another central synergy can be the leveraging of the firm's 'software'. For instance, Disney is such a 'core content' corporation, letting Cinderella work hard selling Disney videos, luring families to Disney theme parks, getting kids to buy Disney merchandise and enticing people to watch the Disney Channel. Whichever synergy is placed centre stage, to the proponents of the integrated organization perspective it should not be trivial, as such minor value-creation efforts do not provide the driving motivation to keep a corporation together. The 'glue' of the corporation must be strong enough to convince all involved that they are much better off as part of the whole than on their own.

The flip side of having a tightly knit group of businesses arranged around a common core is that growth through acquisition is generally much more difficult than in the 'plug and play' set-up of a portfolio organization. To make an acquisition fit into the corporate family and to establish all of the necessary links to let the new recruits profit from, and contribute to, the core synergies, can be very challenging. Taking the previous metaphor a step further, the corporate centre will find it quite difficult to graft oak roots and elm branches onto an existing olive tree. Consequently, acquisitions will be infrequent, as the firm will prefer internal growth.

EXHIBIT 5.3   THE INTEGRATED ORGANIZATION PERSPECTIVE

THE NEW EMPEROR IN MEDIA: FOCUSED BUT NOT SMALL

The way tycoons lead their media empires is starting to change drastically. Whereas the generation of Rupert Murdoch has mainly been after wielding influence and power, their successors take a less flamboyant approach. They trade in "fruit and flower expenses", a well-known metaphor in some businesses for, in the words of News Corp CEO Robert Thomson, *relentless* cost-cutting. The shift in mindset can be observed in two main areas: increased focus on the core business and creating benefits from scale.

To effectively focus on their core business, media tycoons are shedding their non-core assets. Albeit lagging behind the same trend in other industries, this development is greatly appreciated by investors. In 2013 three major spin-offs occurred. The largest involved Rupert Murdoch's News Corporation splitting its profitable TV and film business from the declining newspaper business. This was a much

contested decision, as it was the latter with which Murdoch had built his media empire. Equally painful decisions had to be made by Time Warner, spinning off its magazine unit and Tribune divesting its newspaper business.

The main rationale behind this focus is the increasingly popular notion, held by external constituents, that TV networks, newspapers, film studios and the music business have very little benefit from sharing a parent. Some even argue that their success can be hindered by their proximity as a result of distracting management. As a result, most media empires have decided to divest the shrinking publishing business, and either focus on other more promising markets or devote more attention to their main brand. Whatever the reason, the new way of thinking is very different from what we used to see in the media business.

In addition to shedding non-core assets, a second trend in the media business is to benefit from being very large – which happens to be something quite characteristic of the media industry. In 2009,

▶

it made up over two-thirds of the S&P 500 index value, which comes down to about US$200 billion in assets. News Corp, Viacom, Disney and Time Warner deliver double the average S&P return of 6.1 per cent, with the exception of a number of years in which alternative content providers such as Netflix were feared to disrupt the pay TV business model. Combining the ever-growing scale with the newfound desire to focus activities has led to Time Warner having 80 per cent of its revenues coming from cable TV in 2013, as opposed to just 23 per cent in 2008. Viacom has made a comparable leap, leading to 90 per cent of their revenue coming from this source. This allowed both players to benefit greatly from increased efficiencies and strategic clarity.

Not everyone thinks pleasing the investors by becoming more integrated is the right way forward. Comcast bought NBCUniversal and Disney acquired Lucasfilm, which increasingly diversified their activities. Who made the right decision can only be speculated about, but the success of firms providing an alternative business model to deliver content, like Netflix and Hulu, might be a detrimental factor. For firms relying on cable TV for a predominant portion of their revenues, lack of diversification might become a liability when a real alternative to pay TV is offered.

Whatever the future might look like, investors are thrilled by the new mindset and subsequent actions. Jeff Bewkes, CEO of Time Warner, states:

> *Time Inc. will benefit from the flexibility and focus of being a stand-alone public company and will now be able to attract a more natural stockholder base.*

In addition, he mentioned that being involved in less categories provided both him and the outside world with greater strategic clarity. Although possibly difficult to accept for those who have built their fortunes in the old fashioned media, the industry will start to focus on its profitable businesses, while leaving behind the less performing counterparts. Whether consolidation is a stroke of genius or a fatal mistake can only be told in hindsight. For now, soaring share prices, continuous growth and happy shareholders make sure the end of this trend is nowhere in sight.

Co-author: Jasper de Vries

Sources: 'Time Warner to Offload Magazine Unit in Third Major Spin-off', Bloomberg, March 7, 2013; 'News Corp. Spin-off Forces Publishing Arm to Prove Growth', Bloomberg, June 29, 2013; 'Tribune to Spin Off Newspaper Business', Bloomberg, July 10, 2013; 'Breaking up is not so very hard to do', *The Economist*, June 22, 2013; 'Cutting the cord', *The Economist*, July 16, 2016.

MANAGING THE PARADOX OF RESPONSIVENESS AND SYNERGY

Consider the little mouse, how sagacious an animal it is which never entrusts its life to one hole only.

Plautus (254–184 BC); Roman playwright

So, how should the corporate configuration be determined? Should corporate strategists limit themselves to achieving financial synergies, leaving SBU managers to 'mind their own business'? Or should corporate strategists strive to build a multi-business firm around a common core, intricately weaving all business units into a highly integrated whole? As before, the strategic management literature does not offer a clear-cut answer to the question of which corporate level strategies are the most successful (see Table 5.1).

In the management field, a number of options have been put forward on how to manage the opposing demands of responsiveness and synergy. Taking the taxonomy in Chapter 1, the following options are at the strategist's disposal.

TABLE 5.1   Portfolio organization versus integrated organization perspective

	Portfolio organization perspective	Integrated organization perspective
Emphasis on	Responsiveness over synergy	Synergy over responsiveness
Conception of corporation	Collection of business shareholdings	Common core with business applications
Corporate composition	Potentially unrelated (diverse)	Tightly related (focused)
Key success factor	Business unit responsiveness	Multi-business synergy
Focal type of synergy	Cash flow optimization and risk balance	Integrating resources, activities and positions
Corporate management style	Exerting financial control	Joint strategy development
Primary task corporate centre	Capital allocation and performance control	Setting direction and managing synergies
Position of business units	Highly autonomous (independent)	Highly integrated (interdependent)
Coordination between BUs	Low, incidental	High, structural
Growth through acquisitions	Simple to accommodate	Difficult to integrate

Navigating

The common means of managing the paradox of multi-business synergy and business responsiveness is to focus on one demand at a time. Strategists in large firms are often involved in contrary company-wide initiatives. One such initiative aims at strengthening the corporation's advantage of having more than one business unit. Managers at corporate, division and business unit levels are brought together in groupings to find potential synergies within the firm. The initiatives usually have an ad hoc character, with more or less defined end dates, and jazzy names such as 'One Firm' and 'All For One'. The initiatives may include capturing and strengthening the firm's core competencies, sharing value chain activities such as establishing a shared services centre, and leadership training.

Capturing multi-business synergies usually goes at the expense of market responsiveness. As a result, the next corporate initiative will focus on the opposite side of the paradox: improving market responsiveness. Marked with flashy labels such as 'Client First' and 'Agility', strategizing managers need to find avenues to enhance speed and client orientation in the firm's markets. Examples of such initiatives are visiting key clients to find product improvements, reducing overhead and, again, leadership training. After finishing this ad hoc project, the strategizing managers will navigate the firm capturing corporate synergies by 'tacking' to the next initiative.

Balancing

After having navigated the firm to accumulated multi-business synergies or enhanced business responsiveness, the strategists have to manage the new equilibrium. During the phase 'in-between corporate initiatives', managers have to continue balancing demands for multi-business synergies and business responsiveness. SBU managers strive to achieve more business unit autonomy by enhancing responsiveness and reducing 'corporate bureaucracy', while corporate managers seek more multi-business synergies while trying to reduce SBU managers' liberty to act in the interest of separate units only. As the paradox will never be resolved, strategizing managers are destined to permanently deal with the tension.

Resolving

While dealing with the opposing demand for multi-business synergy and business responsiveness, strategizing managers notice several frictions within the firm. Most common is the friction between corporate strategists, such as the executive board members, and business unit leaders. A key factor in the game between corporate strategists, who are expected to capture synergies, and business unit managers with the main aim to strengthen the business' competitive position, is the firm's reward and compensation scheme. For example, when salaries, bonuses and promotion are related to one demand only, measured by the business unit's revenue and profit, many strategizing managers will not bother too much with corporate level initiatives. This issue is well understood, and so rewards and compensation schemes often include stimuli to capture corporate synergies.

By managing the tension, opportunities to combine the best-of-both often come across. For example, many firms have discovered the advantages of client relationship software (CRM), which not only has the potential to strengthen the firm's client relationship (at the business unit level) but also to reveal growth options for other business units. Such opportunities often manifest during a company-wide initiative to capture multi-business synergy.

The tension between multi-business synergy and business responsiveness has resulted in arguably the most effective means to combining advantages of synergy and responsiveness: the franchise. While being regarded as a modern organizational form, the franchise is by no means new. The history goes back to the 1840s when German ale brewers granted rights to a selected number of taverns to market their beer. The first person recognized as a franchiser with actual franchise contracts was Albert Singer, an American. This 'business model innovator' started distributing his Singer sewing machines across a large geographic area. The franchise became especially popular in the 'restaurant' business, with Kentucky Fried Chicken in 1930, Dunkin Donuts in 1950, Burger King in 1954 and McDonald's in 1955. Currently there are franchise formulas in many industries, including hotels, manpower companies and retail.

The most well-known franchise, McDonald's, explicates the franchise formula's strength: being close to the market while capturing synergies. McDonald's provides their franchisees with, for example, a strong brand, purchasing power, training (a Hamburger University), restaurant lay-out designs and corporate-wide values (would "Ich Bin Ein Hamburger" be an idea?). Franchisees are close to their local or niche customers with some room to adapt, and, while being agile to respond to client needs, they also capitalize on the corporate synergies.

CORPORATE LEVEL STRATEGY IN INTERNATIONAL PERSPECTIVE

Co-authors: Gep Eisenloeffel and Wester Wagenaar

The key to growth is the introduction of higher dimensions of consciousness into our awareness.

Laozi (6th–5th century BC); Chinese philosopher and founder of Taoism

Despite the high media profile of major corporations from different countries and despite researchers' fascination with large companies, little comparative research has been carried out. Yet, it does not seem unlikely that corporate strategy practices and preferences vary across national boundaries. Casual observation of the major corporations around the globe quickly shows that one cannot easily divide the world into portfolio-oriented and integration-oriented countries. In order to discuss to what extent international differences in corporate strategy perspectives exist, several factors will be put forward that might be of influence on how the paradox of responsiveness and synergy is managed in different countries.

On the national level

In the early 1980s, waves of hostile takeovers and overall poor performances in Western conglomerates led to a focus on integration. In most Western countries, most notably in the US, the belief that focused companies are better at increasing shareholder value and that diversification destroys value seems to prevail. Opportunities are generally met with a 'divisionalise or divest' approach; only if there is enough potential for shared value, is a division created. This explains why in recent history many conglomerates in the West, such as McGraw-Hill and General Electric, have been broken up into more focused, 'coherent' bodies (Ramachandran, Manikandan and Pant, 2013).

Germany is a different case, highlighting the importance of heritage. In European countries without colonies that could absorb a huge influx of capital, banks gained prominent positions by investing in promising new enterprises in their home country. Deutsche Bank for instance, founded in 1870 to facilitate foreign trade and investments, was involved in founding steel conglomerate Krupp and chemical giant Bayer. Today, it maintains over 25 per cent of the stocks in car manufacturing powerhouse Daimler-Benz. The result is strong ties between national financial institutions and industrial companies, or *das Finanzkapital* (Finance Capital), as Rudolf Hilferding, economist and former German Finance Minister, described it in 1910.

In Japan, the *keiretsu* structure, conglomerations of businesses linked by cross-shareholdings, puts a similar emphasis on banks. The *keiretsu* are an inheritance from the pre-war family-controlled *zaibatsu* institutions which proved vital in the development of Japan's modern economy (Morikawa, 1992). Unlike *zaibatsu,* the *keiretsu* is not centred around a family and either has a horizontal (or financial) or vertical (or industrial) structure (Miyashita and Russell, 1994). The horizontal *keiretsu* is set up around a Japanese bank which supports its affiliated companies with numerous financial services. Japanese law allows banks to be both creditors and equity holders, unlike most Western economies. These inter-corporate ownerships led the *keiretsu* banks to involve themselves in their partners' corporate governance and strategic decisions with greater regularity. Vertical *keiretsu* are linked through ownership of long-term equity and production activities, to suppliers, manufacturers and distributors of one industry. A vertical organizational model is further created to benefit the parent company. This model is divided into different tiers where major suppliers make up the second tier and the third and fourth tiers consist of smaller manufacturers. As a result of the 1991 crash and the subsequent 'lost decades', the lines between the individual *keiretsu* blurred and many of them merged. Since then, *keiretsu* are not as integrated as they used to be, major companies are no longer easily bailed out by their banks and the major corporations have generally adopted lower-risk profiles (Suetorsak, 2007). Nevertheless, *keiretsu* like Sumitomo Mitsui Financial Group, Mitsubishi UFJ Financial Group and Mizuho Group still make up an important part of the contemporary Japanese business landscape.

Although the *keiretsu* corporate model is unique to Japan, conglomerates with strong ties, hierarchy and loyalty between members of the inner circle or the family can be observed in many emerging markets or in societies where relational resources are highly valued. Latin America calls family conglomerates *grupos económicos*, in Turkey they are simply known as 'holding companies' and India refers to them as 'business houses'. They are also common in many (emerging) Asian economies, such as China, India, Indonesia, Malaysia and Thailand.

In Asia, South Korea's *chaebol* are among the most well-known institutions. These giant financial conglomerates are run by powerful families, traditionally supported by the South Korean government to expand domestically and internationally. Leading *chaebol* such as the Samsung Group, the LG group and the Hyundai Motor Group, are generally characterized by not sticking to one core business, but by operating in a wide range of businesses. Family conglomerates like these typically profit from various competitive advantages in their country of origin, like government assistance and protection, networks and influence in numerous industries, access to capital and exceptional market knowledge (Cavusgil, Knight *et al.*, 2014).

On the industry level

Although different preferences on corporate level strategy on the international differences are apparent, there are also some industries where one of the perspectives of the corporate level paradox is more prevalent. When laws allow it, the common investors in federations of businesses are often banks, as German and Japanese cases show. In the case of both *keiretsu* and *chaebol* banking, insurance, chemicals, manufacturing and steel are common businesses.

When it comes to vertical integration, the most well-known examples, are the do-it-all giants of the oil industry, where control 'from the source to the gas station' is common practice. The international computer industry used to be dominated by vertically integrated firms, such as IBM, but then along came Apple. In the 1970s, that company assembled a network of independent specialists which managed to manufacture machines far more efficiently. Industries are not black and white though, as Dell found a successful way to be a competitive vertically integrated company in the 1990s. Founder Michael Dell dubbed his creation 'virtual integration', assembling computers from other firm's parts, while having tight bound links between buyer and supplier.

To the strategist

Turning to the position of the strategist, the international dimension can prove quite a predicament. As shown, there are different approaches to the paradox over the world. Companies in the West still tend to swear by integration, but as the increasing competitiveness of conglomerates from Asia and Latin America highlights, the whole of multi-divisional companies does not have to be more valuable than the sum of their parts.

A strategist does not only have to deal with the paradox of responsiveness and synergy for his own enterprise, he or she also has to understand how to deal with other corporations in the international playing field. For example, when foreign companies try to enter markets dominated by family conglomerates, the many advantages enjoyed by these corporations can be overwhelming (Cavusgil *et al.*, 2014).

Strategists also have to decide whether to control as a parent or to cooperate without sharing a parent. If the essence of corporate strategy is about realizing synergies between businesses while retaining some autonomy, is it not possible for these businesses to coordinate with one another and achieve synergies without being a part of the same corporation? In other words, is it necessary to be owned and controlled by the same parent in order to leverage resources, integrate activities and align product offerings? Or could individual businesses band together and work as if they were one company – acting as a 'virtual corporation'?

INTRODUCTION TO THE READINGS

To help strategists to come to grips with the variety of perspectives on this issue, three readings have been selected that each shed their own light on the debate. As in previous chapters, the first two readings will be representative of the two poles in this debate (see Table 5.1), while the third reading will bring extra arguments into the discussion.

To open the debate on behalf of the portfolio organization perspective, Barry Hedley's article 'Strategy and the Business Portfolio' has been selected as Reading 5.1. Hedley was an early proponent of the portfolio perspective, together with other consultants from the Boston Consulting Group (BCG), such as Bruce Henderson (1979). In this article, he explains the strategic principles underlying the famed growth–share grid that is commonly known as the BCG matrix. His argument is based on the premise that a complex corporation can be viewed as a portfolio of businesses, which each have their own competitive arena to which they must be responsive. By disaggregating a corporation into its business unit components, separate strategies can be devised for each. The overarching role of the corporate level can then be defined as that of portfolio manager. The major task of the corporate headquarters is to manage the allocation of scarce financial resources over the business units, to achieve the highest returns at an acceptable level of risk. Each business unit can be given a strategic mission to grow, hold or milk, depending on their prospects compared to the businesses in the corporate portfolio. This is where portfolio analysis comes in. Hedley argues that the profit and growth potential of each business unit depends on two key variables: the growth rate of the total business and the relative market share of the business unit within its business. When these two variables are put together in a grid, this forms the BCG matrix. For the discussion in this chapter, the precise details of the BCG portfolio technique are less relevant than the basic corporate strategy perspective that Hedley advocates – running the multi-business firm as a hands-on investor.

Selecting a representative for the integrated organization perspective for Reading 5.2 was a simple choice. In 1990, the late C.K. Prahalad and Gary Hamel published an article in *Harvard Business Review* with the title 'The Core Competence of the Corporation'. This article has had a profound impact on the debate surrounding the topic of corporate level strategy, and has inspired a considerable amount of research and writing investigating resource-based synergies. In this article Hamel and Prahalad (1994) explicitly dismiss the portfolio organization perspective as a viable approach to corporate strategy. Prahalad and Hamel acknowledge that diversified corporations have a portfolio of businesses, but they do not believe that this implies the need for a portfolio organization approach in which the business units are highly autonomous. In their view, "the primacy of the SBU – an organizational dogma for a generation – is now clearly an anachronism". Drawing mainly on Japanese examples, they carry on to argue that corporations should be built around a core of shared competencies. Business units should use and help to further develop these core competencies. The consequence is that the role of corporate level management is much more far-reaching than in the portfolio organization perspective. The corporate centre must "establish objectives for competence building" and must ensure that this "strategic architecture" is carried through.

The third reading is 'Seeking Synergies' by Andrew Campbell and Michael Goold. These researchers from the Ashridge Strategic Management Centre have been responsible for a constant stream of insightful work on corporate level strategy. One of their publications has been the book *Synergy: Why Links Between Business Units Often Fail and How to Make Them Work,* from which this is the summary chapter. This reading has been selected in order to pay more attention to the issue of realizing synergies. As a large part of the debate revolves around different views on whether synergies can actually be captured or not, it is valuable to get some more input on approaches to synergy creation and a better insight into "synergy killers". Campbell and Goold give a structured and practical framework for analysing a corporation's synergy opportunities and synergy approach, followed by an analysis of the most important policies and characteristics that systematically inhibit attempts at reaping synergy advantages. In the context of this debate, it is important to note that Campbell and Goold do not necessarily side with either of the two perspectives. In their view, there are different styles of corporate strategy and different levels of synergy that can be achieved, as long as the 'parent company' develops the matching parenting capabilities and synergy parenting approach.

READING
5.1

Strategy and the business portfolio
By Barry Hedley[1]

All except the smallest and simplest companies comprise more than one business. Even when a company operates within a single broad business area, analysis normally reveals that it is, in practice, involved in a number of product-market segments which are distinct economically. These must be considered separately for purposes of strategy development.

The fundamental determinant of strategy success for each individual business segment is relative competitive position. As a result of the experience curve effect the competitor with high market share in the segment relative to competition should be able to develop the lowest cost position and hence the highest and most stable profits. This will be true regardless of changes in the economic environment. Hence relative competitive position in the appropriately defined business segment forms a simple but sound strategic goal. Almost invariably, any company which reviews its various businesses carefully in this light will discover that they occupy widely differing relative competitive positions. Some businesses will be competitively strong already, and may appear to present no strategic problem; others will be weak, and the company must face the question of whether it would be worthwhile to attempt to improve their position, making whatever investments might be required to achieve this; if this is not done, the company can only expect poor performance from the business and the best option economically will be divestment.

Even in quite small companies, the total number of possible combinations of individual business strategies can be extremely large. The difficulty of making a firm final choice on strategy for each business is normally compounded by the fact that most companies must operate within constraints established by limited resources, particularly cash resources.

The business portfolio concept

At its most basic, the importance of growth in shaping strategy choice is two-fold. First, the growth of a business is a major factor influencing the likely ease – and hence cost – of gaining market share. In low-growth businesses, any market share gained will tend to require an actual volume reduction in competitors' sales. This will be very obvious to the competitors and they are likely to fight to prevent the throughput in their plants dropping. In high-growth businesses, on the other hand, market share can be gained steadily merely by securing the largest share of the growth in the business: expanding capacity earlier than the competitors, ensuring product availability and effective selling support despite the strains imposed by the *growth,* and so forth. Meanwhile competitors may even be unaware of their share loss because their actual volume of throughput has been well maintained. Even if aware of their loss of share, the competitors may be unconcerned by it given that their plants are still well loaded. This is particularly true of competitors who do not understand the strategic importance of market share for long term profitability resulting from the experience curve effect.

An unfortunate example of this is given by the history of the British motorcycle industry. British market

[1]Source: This article was adapted from B. Hedley, 'Strategy and the business portfolio', *Long Range Planning,* February 1977, Vol. 10, No. 1, pp. 9–15, © 1977. With permission from Elsevier.

share was allowed to erode in motorcycles worldwide for more than a decade, throughout which the British factories were still fairly full: British motorcycle production volumes held up at around 80 000 units per year throughout the sixties; in sharp contrast, Japanese export volumes leapt from only about 60 000 in 1960 to 2.5 million in 1973; their total production volumes roughly tripled in the same period. The long-term effect was that while Japanese real costs were falling rapidly, British costs were not: somewhat oversimplified, this is why the British motorcycle industry faced bankruptcy in the early seventies.

The second important factor concerning growth is the opportunity it provides for investment. Growth businesses provide the ideal vehicles for investment, for ploughing cash into a business in order to see it compound and return even larger amounts of cash at a later point in time. Of course this opportunity is also a need: the faster a business grows, the more investment it will require just to maintain market share. Yet the experience curve effect means that this is essential if its profitability is not to decline over time.

Whilst these growth considerations affect the rate at which a business will use cash, the relative competitive position of the business will determine the rate at which the business will generate cash: the stronger the company's position relative to its competitors, the higher its margins should be, as a result of the experience curve effect. The simplest measure of relative competitive position is, of course, relative market share. A company's relative market share in a business can be defined as its market share in the business divided by that of the largest other competitor. Thus only the biggest competitor has a relative market share greater than one. All the other competitors should enjoy lower profitability and cash generation than the leader.

The growth–share matrix

Individual businesses can have very different financial characteristics and face different strategic options depending on how they are placed in terms of growth and relative competitive position. Businesses can basically fall into any one of four broad strategic categories, as depicted schematically in the growth–share matrix in Figure 5.1.1.

- Stars. High growth, high share – are in the upper left quadrant. Growing rapidly, they use large amounts of cash to maintain position. They are also leaders in the business, however, and should generate large amounts of cash. As a result, star businesses are frequently roughly in balance on net cash flow, and can be self-sustaining in growth terms. They represent probably the best profit growth and investment opportunities available to the company, and every effort should therefore be made to maintain and consolidate their competitive position. This will sometimes require heavy investment beyond their own generation capabilities and low margins may be essential at times to deter competition, but this is almost invariably worthwhile for the longer term: when the growth slows, as it ultimately does

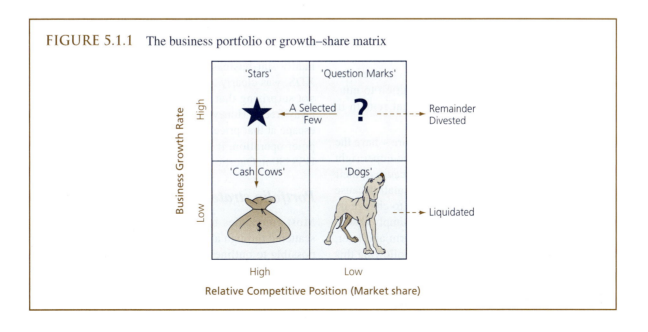

FIGURE 5.1.1   The business portfolio or growth–share matrix

in all businesses, very large cash returns will be obtained if share has been maintained so that the business drops into the lower left quadrant of the matrix, becoming a cash cow. If star businesses fail to hold share, which frequently happens if the attempt is made to net large amounts of cash from them in the short and medium term (e.g. by cutting back on investment and raising prices, creating an 'umbrella' for competitors), they will ultimately become dogs (lower right quadrant). These are certain losers.

- Cash cows. Low growth, high share – should have an entrenched superior market position and low costs. Hence profits and cash generation should be high, and because of the low growth reinvestment needs should be light. Thus large cash surpluses should be generated by these businesses. Cash cows pay the dividends and interest, provide the debt capacity, pay for the company overhead and provide the cash for investment elsewhere in the company's portfolio of businesses. They are the foundation on which the company rests.

- Dogs. Low growth, low share – represent a tremendous contrast. Their poor competitive position condemns them to poor profits. Because the growth is low, there is little potential for gaining sufficient share to achieve a viable cost position at anything approaching a reasonable cost. Unfortunately, the cash required for investment in the business just to maintain competitive position, though low, frequently exceeds that generated, especially under conditions of high inflation. The business therefore becomes a 'cash trap' likely to absorb cash perpetually unless further investment in the business is rigorously avoided. The colloquial term 'dog' describing these businesses, though undoubtedly pejorative, is thus rather apt. A company should take every precaution to minimize the proportion of its assets that remain in this category.

- Question marks. High growth, low share – have the worst cash characteristics of all. In the upper right quadrant, their cash needs are high because of their growth, but their cash generation is small because of their low share. If nothing is done to change its market share, the question mark will simply absorb large amounts of cash in the short term and later, as the growth slows, become a dog. Following this sort of strategy, the question mark is a cash loser throughout its existence. Managed this way, a question mark becomes the ultimate cash trap.

In fact there is a clear choice between only two strategy alternatives for a question mark, hence the name. Because growth is high, it should be easier and less costly to gain share here than it would be in a lower growth business. One strategy is therefore to make whatever investments are necessary to gain share, to try to fund the business to dominance so that it can become a star and, ultimately a cash cow when the business matures. This strategy will be very costly in the short term – growth rates will be even higher than if share were merely being maintained, and additional marketing and other investments will be required to make the share actually change hands – but it offers the only way of developing a sound business from the question mark over the long term. The only logical alternative is divestment. Outright sale is preferable; but if this is not possible, then a firm decision must be taken not to invest further in the business and it must be allowed simply to generate whatever cash it can while none is reinvested. The business will then decline, possibly quite rapidly if market growth is high, and will have to be shut down at some point. But it will produce cash in the short term and this is greatly preferable to the error of sinking cash into it perpetually without improving its competitive position.

These then, are the four basic categories to which businesses can belong. Some companies tend to fit almost entirely into a single quadrant. General Motors and English China Clays are examples of predominantly cash cow companies. Chrysler, by comparison, is a dog which compounded its fundamental problem of low share in its domestic US market by acquiring further mature low share competitors in other countries (e.g. Rootes which became Chrysler UK). IBM in computers, Xerox in photocopiers, BSR in low cost record autochangers, are all examples of predominantly star businesses. Xerox's computer operation, XDS, was clearly a question mark, however, and it is not surprising that Xerox recently effectively gave it away free to Honeywell, and considered itself lucky to escape at that price! When RCA closed down its computer operation, it had to sustain a write-off of about US$490m. Question marks are costly.

Portfolio strategy

Most companies have their portfolio of businesses scattered through all four quadrants of the matrix. It is possible to outline quite briefly and simply what the appropriate overall portfolio strategy for such a company should be. The first goal should be to maintain position in the cash cows, but to guard against the

CHAPTER 5 CORPORATE LEVEL STRATEGY **267**

frequent temptation to reinvest in them excessively. The cash generated by the cash cows should be used as a first priority to maintain or consolidate position in those stars which are not self-sustaining. Any surplus remaining can be used to fund a selected number of question marks to dominance. Most companies will find they have inadequate cash generation to finance market share-gaining strategies in all their question marks. Those which are not funded should be divested either by sale or liquidation over time.

Finally, virtually all companies have at least some dog businesses. There is nothing reprehensible about this, indeed on the contrary, an absence of dogs probably indicates that the company has not been sufficiently adventurous in the past. It is essential, however, that the fundamentally weak strategic position of the dog be recognized for what it is. Occasionally it is possible to restore a dog to viability by a creative business segmentation strategy, rationalizing and specializing the business into a small niche which it can dominate. If this is impossible, however, the only thing which could rescue the dog would be an increase in share taking it to a position comparable to the leading competitors in the segment. This is likely to be unreasonably costly in a mature business, and therefore the only prospect for obtaining a return from a dog is to manage it for cash, cutting off all investment in the business. Management should be particularly wary of expensive 'turn around' plans developed for a dog if these do not involve a significant change in fundamental competitive position. Without this, the dog is a sure loser. An indictment of many corporate managements is not the fact that their companies have dogs in the portfolio, but rather that these dogs are not managed according to logical strategies. The decision to liquidate a business is usually even harder to take than that of entering a new business. It is essential, however, for the long-term vitality and performance of the company overall that it be prepared to do both as the need arises.

Thus the appropriate strategy for a multi-business company involves striking a balance in the portfolio such that the cash generated by the cash cows, and by those question marks and dogs which are being liquidated, is sufficient to support the company's stars and to fund the selected question marks through to dominance. This pattern of strategies is indicated by the arrows in Figure 5.1.1. Understanding this pattern conceptually is, however, a far cry from being able to implement it in practice. What any company should do with its own specific businesses is of course a function of the precise shape of the company's portfolio, and

the particular opportunities and problems it presents. But how can a clear picture of the company's portfolio be developed?

The matrix quantified

Based on careful analysis and research it is normally possible to divide a company into its various business segments appropriately defined for purposes of strategy development. Following this critical first step, it is usually relatively straightforward to determine the overall growth rate of each individual business (i.e. the growth of the market, not the growth of the company within the market), and the company's size (in terms of turnover or assets) and relative competitive position (market share) within the business.

Armed with these data it is possible to develop a precise overall picture of the company's portfolio of businesses graphically. This can greatly facilitate the identification and resolution of the key strategic issues facing the company. It is a particularly useful approach where companies are large, comprising many separate businesses. Such complex portfolios often defy description in more conventional ways.

The nature of the graphical portfolio display is illustrated by the example in Figure 5.1.2. In this chart, growth rate and relative competitive position are plotted on continuous scales. Each circle in the display represents a single business or business segment, appropriately defined. To convey an impression of the relative significance of each business, size is indicated by the area of the circle, which can be made proportional to either turnover or assets employed. Relative competitive position is plotted on a logarithmic scale, in order to be consistent with the experience curve effect, which implies that profit margin or rate of cash generation differences between competitors will tend to be related to the ratio of their relative competitive positions (market shares). A linear axis is used for growth, for which the most generally useful measure is volume growth of the business concerned, as, in general, rates of cash use should be directly proportional to growth.

The lines dividing the portfolio into four quadrants are inevitably somewhat arbitrary. 'High growth', for example, is taken to include all businesses growing in excess of 10 per cent per annum in volume terms. Certainly, above this growth rate market share tends to become fairly fluid and can be made to change hands quite readily. In addition many companies have traditionally employed a figure of 10 per cent for their discount rate in times of low inflation, and so this

FIGURE 5.1.2   Growth rate and relative competitive position

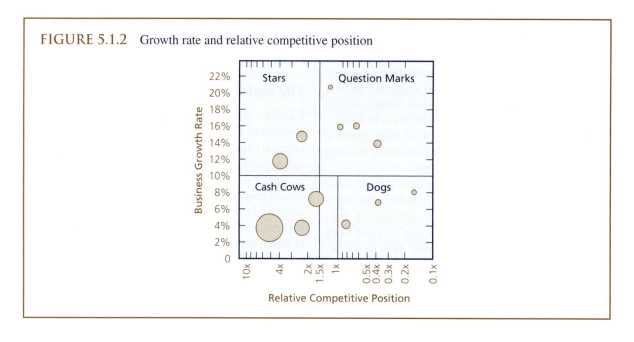

also tends to be the growth rate above which investment in market share becomes particularly attractive financially.

The line separating areas of high and low relative competitive position is set at 1.5 times. Experience in using this display has been that in high-growth businesses relative strengths of this magnitude or greater are necessary in order to ensure a sufficiently dominant position that the business will have the characteristic of a star in practice. On the other hand, in low-growth businesses acceptable cash generation characteristics are occasionally, but not always, observed at relative strengths as low as 1 times; hence the addition of a second separating line at 1 times in the low growth area, to reflect this. These lines should, of course, be taken only as approximate guides in characterizing businesses in the portfolio as dogs and question marks, cash cows and stars. In actuality, businesses cover a smooth spectrum across both axes of the matrix. There is obviously no 'magic' which transforms a star into a cash cow as its growth declines from 10.5 to 9.5 per cent. It is undeniably useful, however, to have some device for broadly indicating where the transition points occur within the matrix, and the lines suggested here have worked well in practical applications of the matrix in a large number of companies.

Portfolio approaches in practice

The company shown in Figure 5.1.2 would be a good example of a potentially well-balanced portfolio. With a firm foundation in the form of two or three substantial cash cows, this company has some well-placed stars to provide growth and to yield high cash returns in the future when they mature. The company also has some question marks, at least two of which are probably sufficiently well placed that they offer a good chance of being funded into star positions at a reasonable cost, not out of proportion to the company's resources. The company is not without dogs, but properly managed there is no reason why these should be a drain on cash.

The sound portfolio, unsoundly managed

Companies with an attractive portfolio of this kind are not rare in practice. In fact Figure 5.1.2 is a disguised version of a representation of an actual UK company analysed in the course of a Boston Consulting Group assignment. What is much rarer, however, is to find that the company has made a clear assessment of the matrix positioning and appropriate strategy for each business in the portfolio.

Ideally, one would hope that the company in Figure 5.1.2 would develop strategy along the following lines. For the stars, the key objectives should be the maintenance of market share; current profitability should be accorded a lower priority. For the cash cows, however, current profitability may well be the primary goal. Dogs would not be expected to be as profitable as the cash cows, but would be expected to yield cash. Some question marks would be set objectives in terms of increased market share; others, where gaining dominance appeared too costly, would be managed instead for cash.

The essence of the portfolio approach is therefore that strategy objectives must vary between businesses. The strategy developed for each business must fit its own matrix position and the needs and capabilities of the company's overall portfolio of businesses. In practice, however, it is much more common to find all businesses within a company being operated with a common overall goal in mind. 'Our target in this company is to grow at 10 per cent per annum and achieve a return of 10 per cent on capital.' This type of overall target is then taken to apply to every business in the company. Cash cows beat the profit target easily, though they frequently miss on growth. Nevertheless, their managements are praised and they are normally rewarded by being allowed to plough back what only too frequently amounts to an excess of cash into their 'obviously attractive' businesses. Attractive businesses, yes: but not for growth investment. Dogs on the other hand rarely meet the profit target. But how often is it accepted that it is in fact unreasonable for them ever to hit the target? On the contrary, the most common strategic mistake is that major investments are made in dogs from time to time in hopeless attempts to turn the business around without actually shifting market share. Unfortunately, only too often question marks are regarded very much as dogs, and get insufficient investment funds ever to bring them to dominance. The question marks usually do receive some investment, however, possibly even enough to maintain share. This is throwing money away into a cash trap. These businesses should either receive enough support to enable them to achieve segment dominance, or none at all.

These are some of the strategic errors which are regularly committed even by companies which have basically sound portfolios. The result is a serious sub-optimization of potential performance in which some businesses (e.g. cash cows) are not being called on to produce the full results of which they are actually capable, and resources are being mistakenly squandered on other businesses (dogs, question marks) in an attempt to make them achieve performance of which they are intrinsically incapable without a fundamental improvement in market share. Where mismanagement of this kind becomes positively dangerous, is when it is applied within the context of a basically unbalanced portfolio.

The unbalanced portfolio

The disguised example in Figure 5.1.3 is another actual company. This portfolio is seriously out of balance. As shown in Figure 5.1.3(a), the company has a very high proportion of question marks in its portfolio, and an inadequate base of cash cows. Yet at the time of investigation this company was in fact taking such cash as was being generated by its mature businesses and spreading it out amongst all the high-growth businesses, only one of which was actually receiving sufficient investment to enable it even to maintain share!

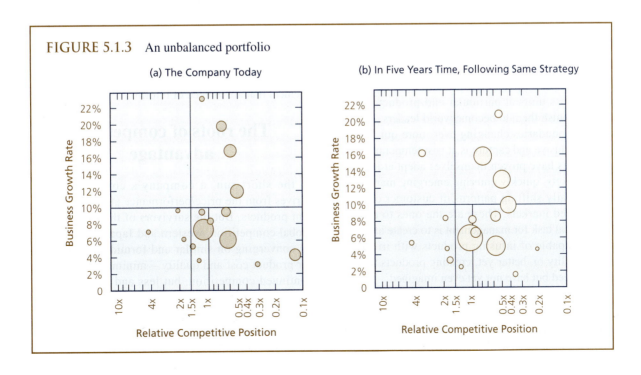

FIGURE 5.1.3   An unbalanced portfolio

Thus the overall relative competitive position of the portfolio was on average declining. At the same time, the balance in the portfolio was shifting: as shown in the projected portfolio in Figure 5.1.3(b), because of the higher relative growth of the question marks their overall weight in the portfolio was increasing, making them even harder to fund from the limited resources of the mature businesses.

If the company continued to follow the same strategy of spreading available funds between all the businesses, then the rate of decline could only increase over time leading ultimately to disaster.

This company was caught in a vicious circle of decline. To break out of the circle would require firm discipline and the strength of will to select only one or two of the question marks and finance those, whilst cutting off investment in the remainder. Obviously the choice of which should receive investment involves rather more than selection at random from the portfolio chart. It requires careful analysis of the actual nature of the businesses concerned and particularly the characteristics and behaviour of the competitors faced in those businesses. However, the nature of the strategic choice facing the company is quite clear, when viewed in portfolio terms. Without the clarity of view provided by the matrix display, which focuses on the real fundamentals of the businesses and their relationships to each other within the portfolio, it is impossible to develop strategy effectively in any multi-business company.

The core competence of the corporation

By C.K. Prahalad and Gary Hamel[1]

The most powerful way to prevail in global competition is still invisible to many companies. During the 1980s, top executives were judged on their ability to restructure, declutter and delayer their corporations. In the 1990s, they'll be judged on their ability to identify, cultivate and exploit the core competencies that make growth possible – indeed, they'll have to rethink the concept of the corporation itself.

Rethinking the corporation

Once, the diversified corporation could simply point its business units at particular end-product markets and admonish them to become world leaders. But with market boundaries changing ever more quickly, targets are elusive and capture is at best temporary. A few companies have proven themselves adept at inventing new markets, quickly entering emerging markets and dramatically shifting patterns of customer choice in established markets. These are the ones to emulate. The critical task for management is to create an organization capable of infusing products with irresistible functionality or, better yet, creating products that customers need but have not even imagined.

This is a deceptively difficult task. Ultimately, it requires radical change in the management of major companies. It means, first of all, that top managements of western companies must assume responsibility for competitive decline. Everyone knows about high interest rates, Japanese protectionism, outdated antitrust laws, obstreperous unions and impatient investors. What is harder to see, or harder to acknowledge, is how little added momentum companies actually get from political or macroeconomic 'relief'. Both the theory and practice of western management have created a drag on our forward motion. It is the principles of management that are in need of reform.

The roots of competitive advantage

In the short run, a company's competitiveness derives from the price/performance attributes of current products. But the survivors of the first wave of global competition, western and Japanese alike, are all converging on similar and formidable standards for product cost and quality – minimum hurdles for continued competition, but less and less important as sources of differential advantage. In the long run, competitiveness derives from an ability to build, at lower cost and more speedily than competitors, the core competencies that spawn unanticipated products. The real sources of advantage are to be found in management's ability to consolidate corporate-wide technologies and production skills into competencies that empower individual businesses to adapt quickly to changing opportunities.

Senior executives who claim that they cannot build core competencies, either because they feel the autonomy of business units is sacrosanct or because their feet are held to the quarterly budget fire, should think again. The problem in many western companies is not that their senior executives are any less capable than those in Japan or that Japanese companies possess greater technical capabilities. Instead, it is their adherence to a concept of the corporation that unnecessarily limits the ability of individual businesses to fully exploit the deep reservoir of technological capability that many American and European companies possess.

The diversified corporation is a large tree. The trunk and major limbs are core products, the smaller branches are business units; the leaves, flowers and fruit are end products. The root system that provides nourishment, sustenance and stability is the core competence. You can miss the strength of competitors by looking only at their end products, in the same way you miss the strength of a tree if you look only at its leaves (see Figure 5.2.1).

Core competencies are the collective learning in the organization, especially how to coordinate diverse production skills and integrate multiple streams of technologies. Consider Sony's capacity to miniaturize or Philips's optical-media expertise. The theoretical knowledge to put a radio on a chip does not in itself assure a company the skill to produce a miniature radio no bigger than a business card. To bring off this feat, Casio must harmonize know-how in miniaturization, microprocessor design, materials science and ultrathin precision casing – the same skills it applies in its miniature card calculators, pocket TVs and digital watches.

If core competence is about harmonizing streams of technology, it is also about the organization of work and the delivery of value. Among Sony's competencies is miniaturization. To bring miniaturization to its products, Sony must ensure that technologists, engineers and marketers have a shared understanding of customer needs and of technological possibilities. The force of core competence is felt as decisively in services as in manufacturing. Citicorp was ahead of others investing in an operating system that allowed it to participate in world markets 24 hours a day. Its competence in systems has provided the company with the means to differentiate itself from many financial service institutions.

Core competence is communication, involvement and a deep commitment to working across organizational boundaries. It involves many levels of people and all functions. World-class research in, for example,

FIGURE 5.2.1   Competencies as the roots of competitiveness

lasers or ceramics can take place in corporate laboratories without having an impact on any of the businesses of the company. The skills that together constitute core competence must coalesce around individuals whose efforts are not so narrowly focused that they cannot recognize the opportunities for blending their functional expertise with those of others in new and interesting ways.

Core competence does not diminish with use. Unlike physical assets, which do deteriorate over time, competencies are enhanced as they are applied and shared. But competencies still need to be nurtured and protected; knowledge fades if it is not used. Competencies are the glue that binds existing businesses. They are also the engine for new business development. Patterns of diversification and market entry may be guided by them, not just by the attractiveness of markets.

Consider 3M's competence with sticky tape. In dreaming up businesses as diverse as 'Post-it' note pads, magnetic tape, photographic film, pressure-sensitive tapes and coated abrasives, the company has brought to bear widely shared competencies in substrates, coatings and adhesives, and devised various ways to combine them. Indeed, 3M has invested consistently in them. What seems to be an extremely diversified portfolio of businesses belies a few shared core competencies.

In contrast, there are major companies that have had the potential to build core competencies but failed to do so because top management was unable to conceive of the company as anything other than a collection of discrete businesses. General Electric sold much of its consumer electronics business to Thomson of France, arguing that it was becoming increasingly difficult to maintain its competitiveness in this sector. That was undoubtedly so, but it is ironic that it sold several key businesses to competitors who were already competence leaders – Black & Decker in small electrical motors, and Thomson, which was eager to build its competence in microelectronics and had learned from the Japanese that a position in consumer electronics was vital to this challenge.

Management trapped in the strategic business unit (SBU) mind-set almost inevitably finds its individual businesses dependent on external sources for critical components, such as motors or compressors. But these are not just components. They are core products that contribute to the competitiveness of a wide range of end products. They are the physical embodiments of core competencies.

How not to think of competence

Since companies are in a race to build the competencies that determine global leadership, successful companies have stopped imagining themselves as bundles of businesses making products. Canon, Honda, Casio or NEC may seem to preside over portfolios of businesses unrelated in terms of customers, distribution channels and merchandising strategy. Indeed, they have portfolios that may seem idiosyncratic at times: NEC is the only global company to be among leaders in computing, telecommunications and semiconductors, *and* to have a thriving consumer electronics business.

But looks are deceiving. In NEC, digital technology, especially VLSI and systems integration skills, is fundamental. In the core competencies underlying them, disparate businesses become coherent. It is Honda's core competence in engines and power trains that gives it a distinctive advantage in car, motorcycle, lawn mower and generator businesses. Canon's core competencies in optics, imaging and microprocessor controls have enabled it to enter, even dominate, markets as seemingly diverse as copiers, laser printers, cameras and image scanners. Philips worked for more than 15 years to perfect its optical-media (laser disc) competence, as did JVC in building a leading position in video recording. Other examples of core competencies might include mechantronics (the ability to marry mechanical and electronic engineering), video displays, bioengineering and microelectronics. In the early stages of its competence building, Philips could not have imagined all the products that would be spawned by its optical-media competence, nor could JVC have anticipated miniature camcorders when it first began exploring videotape technologies.

Unlike the battle for global brand dominance, which is visible in the world's broadcast and print media and is aimed at building global 'share of mind', the battle to build world-class competencies is invisible to people who aren't deliberately looking for it. Top management often tracks the cost and quality of competitors' products, yet how many managers untangle the web of alliances their Japanese competitors have constructed to acquire competencies at low cost? In how many western boardrooms is there an explicit, shared understanding of the competencies the company must build for world leadership? Indeed, how many senior executives discuss the crucial distinction between competitive strategy at the level of a business and competitive strategy at the level of an entire company?

Let us be clear. Cultivating core competence does not mean outspending rivals on research and development. In 1983, when Canon surpassed Xerox in worldwide unit market share in the copier business, its R&D budget in reprographics was but a small fraction of Xerox's. Over the past 20 years, NEC has spent less on R&D as a percentage of sales than almost all of its American and European competitors.

Nor does core competence mean shared costs, as when two or more SBUs use a common facility – a plant, service facility or sales force – or share a common component. The gains of sharing may be substantial, but the search for shared costs is typically a *post hoc* effort to rationalize production across existing businesses, not a premeditated effort to build the competencies out of which the businesses themselves grow.

Building core competencies is more ambitious and different than integrating vertically, moreover. Managers deciding whether to make or buy will start with end products and look upstream to the efficiencies of the supply chain and downstream toward distribution and customers. They do not take inventory of skills and look forward to applying them in non-traditional ways. (Of course, decisions about competencies *do* provide a logic for vertical integration. Canon is not particularly integrated in its copier business, except in those aspects of the vertical chain that support the competencies it regards as critical.)

Identifying core competencies – and losing them

At least three tests can be applied to identify core competencies in a company. First, a core competence provides potential access to a wide variety of markets. Competence in display systems, for example, enables a company to participate in such diverse businesses as calculators, miniature TV sets, monitors for laptop computers, and automotive dashboards – which is why Casio's entry into the handheld TV market was predictable. Second, a core competence should make a significant contribution to the perceived customer benefits of the end product. Clearly, Honda's engine expertise fills this bill.

Finally, a core competence should be difficult for competitors to imitate. And it will be difficult if it is a complex harmonization of individual technologies and production skills. A rival might acquire some of the technologies that comprise the core competence, but it will find it more difficult to duplicate the more-or-less comprehensive pattern of internal coordination and learning. JVC's decision in the early 1960s to pursue the development of a videotape competence passed the three tests outlined here. RCA's decision in the late 1970s to develop a stylus-based video turntable system did not.

Few companies are likely to build world leadership in more than five or six fundamental competencies. A company that compiles a list of 20 to 30 capabilities has probably not produced a list of core competencies. Still, it is probably a good discipline to generate a list of this sort and to see aggregate capabilities as building blocks. This tends to prompt the search for licensing deals and alliances through which the company may acquire, at low cost, the missing pieces.

Most western companies hardly think about competitiveness in these terms at all. It is time to take a tough-minded look at the risks they are running. Companies that judge competitiveness, their own and their competitors', primarily in terms of the price/ performance of end products are courting the erosion of core competencies – or making too little effort to enhance them. The embedded skills that give rise to the next generation of competitive products cannot be 'rented in' by outsourcing and original equipment manufacturer (OEM) supply relationships. In our view, too many companies have unwittingly surrendered core competencies when they cut internal investment in what they mistakenly thought were just 'cost centres' in favour of outside suppliers.

Of course, it is perfectly possible for a company to have a competitive product line up but be a laggard in developing core competencies – at least for a while. If a company wanted to enter the copier business today, it would find a dozen Japanese companies more than willing to supply copiers on the basis of an OEM private label. But when fundamental technologies changed or if its supplier decided to enter the market directly and become a competitor, that company's product line, along with all of its investments in marketing and distribution, could be vulnerable. Outsourcing can provide a shortcut to a more competitive product, but it typically contributes little to building the people-embodied skills that are needed to sustain product leadership.

Nor is it possible for a company to have an intelligent alliance or sourcing strategy if it has not made a choice about where it will build competence leadership. Clearly, Japanese companies have benefited from alliances. They've used them to learn from western partners who were not fully committed to preserving core competencies of their own. Learning within an alliance takes a positive commitment of resources travel, a pool of dedicated people, test-bed facilities, and time to internalize and test what has been learned. A company may not make this effort if it doesn't have clear goals for competence building.

Another way of losing is foregoing opportunities to establish competencies that are evolving in existing businesses. In the 1970s and 1980s, many American and European companies – like General Electric, Motorola, GTE, Thorn and General Electric Company (GEC) – chose to exit the colour television business, which they regarded as mature. If by 'mature' they meant that they had run out of new product ideas at precisely the moment global rivals had targeted the TV business for entry, then yes, the industry was mature. But it certainly wasn't mature in the sense that all opportunities to enhance and apply video-based competencies had been exhausted.

In ridding themselves of their television businesses, these companies failed to distinguish between divesting the business and destroying their video media-based competencies. They not only got out of the TV business but they also closed the door on a whole stream of future opportunities reliant on video-based competencies.

There are two clear lessons here. First, the costs of losing a core competence can be only partly calculated in advance. The baby may be thrown out with the bath water in divestment decisions. Second, since core competencies are built through a process of continuous improvement and enhancement that may span a decade or longer, a company that has failed to invest in core competence building will find it very difficult to enter an emerging market, unless, of course, it will be content simply to serve as a distribution channel.

American semiconductor companies like Motorola learned this painful lesson when they elected to forego direct participation in the 256k generation of DRAM chips. Having skipped this round, Motorola, like most of its American competitors, needed a large infusion of technical help from Japanese partners to rejoin the battle in the 1-megabyte generation. When it comes to core competencies, it is difficult to get off the train, walk to the next station, and then reboard.

From core competencies to core products

The tangible link between identified core competencies and end products is what we call the core products – the physical embodiments of one or more core competencies. Honda's engines, for example, are core products, linchpins between design and development skills that ultimately lead to a proliferation of end products. Core products are the components or sub-assemblies that actually contribute to the value of the end products. Thinking in terms of core products forces a company to distinguish between the brand share it achieves in end product markets (for example, 40 per cent of the US refrigerator market) and the manufacturing share it achieves in any particular core product (for example, 5 per cent of the world share of compressor output).

It is essential to make this distinction between core competencies, core products and end products because global competition is played out by different rules and for different stakes at each level. To build or defend leadership over the long term, a corporation will probably be a winner at each level. At the level of core competence, the goal is to build world leadership in the design and development of a particular class of product functionality – be it compact data storage and retrieval, as with Philips's optical-media competence, or compactness and ease of use, as with Sony's micromotors and microprocessor controls.

To sustain leadership in their chosen core competence areas, these companies *seek to maximize their world manufacturing share in core products.* The manufacture of core products for a wide variety of external (and internal) customers yields the revenue and market feedback that, at least partly, determines the pace at which core competencies can be enhanced and extended. This thinking was behind JVC's decision in the mid-1970s to establish VCR supply relationships with leading national consumer electronics companies in Europe and the United States. In supplying Thomson, Thorn and Telefunken (all independent companies at that time) as well as US partners, JVC was able to gain the cash and the diversity of market experience that ultimately enabled it to outpace Philips and Sony. (Philips developed videotape competencies in parallel with JVC, but it failed to build a worldwide network of OEM relationships that would have allowed it to accelerate the refinement of its videotape competence through the sale of core products.)

JVC's success has not been lost on Korean companies like Goldstar, Samsung, Kia and Daewoo, who are building core product leadership in areas as diverse as displays, semiconductors and automotive engines through their OEM-supply contracts with western companies. Their avowed goal is to capture investment initiative away from potential competitors, often US companies. In doing so, they accelerate their competence-building efforts while 'hollowing out' their competitors. By focusing on competence and embedding it in core products, Asian competitors have built up advantages in component markets first and have then leveraged off their superior products to move downstream to build brand share. And they are not likely to remain the low-cost suppliers forever. As their reputation for brand leadership is consolidated, they may well gain price leadership. Honda has proven this with its Acura line, and other Japanese car makers are following suit.

Control over core products is critical for other reasons. A dominant position in core products allows a company to shape the evolution of applications and end markets. Such compact audio disc-related core products as data drives and lasers have enabled Sony and Philips to influence the evolution of the computer-peripheral business in optical-media storage. As a company multiplies the number of application arenas for its core products, it can consistently reduce the cost, time and risk in new product development. In short, well-targeted core products can lead to economies of scale and scope.

The tyranny of the SBU

The new terms of competitive engagement cannot be understood using analytical tools devised to manage the diversified corporation of 20 years ago, when competition was primarily domestic (GE versus Westinghouse, General Motors versus Ford) and all the key players were speaking the language of the same business schools and consultancies. Old prescriptions have potentially toxic side effects. The need for new

principles is most obvious in companies organized exclusively according to the logic of SBUs. The implications of the two alternate concepts of the corporation are summarized in Table 5.2.1.

Obviously, diversified corporations have a portfolio of products and a portfolio of businesses. But we believe in a view of the company as a portfolio of competencies as well. United States companies do not lack the technical resources to build competencies, but their top management often lacks the vision to build them and the administrative means for assembling resources spread across multiple businesses. A shift in commitment will inevitably influence patterns of diversification, skill deployment, resource allocation priorities, and approaches to alliances and outsourcing.

We have described the three different planes on which battles for global leadership are waged: core competence, core products and end products. A corporation has to know whether it is winning or losing on each plane. By sheer weight of investment, a company might be able to beat its rivals to blue-sky technologies yet still lose the race to build core competence leadership. If a company is winning the race to build core competencies (as opposed to building leadership in a few technologies), it will almost certainly outpace rivals in new business development. If a company is winning the race to capture world manufacturing share in core products, it will probably outpace rivals in improving product features and the price/performance ratio.

Determining whether one is winning or losing end-product battles is more difficult because measures of product market share do not necessarily reflect various companies' underlying competitiveness. Indeed, companies that attempt to build market share by relying

TABLE 5.2.1   Two concepts of the corporation

	SBU	Core competence
Basis for competition	Competiveness of today's products	Interfirm competition to build competencies
Corporate structure	Portfolio of businesses related in product – market terms	Portfolio of competencies, core products, and businesses
Status of the business unit	Autonomy is sacrosanct; the SBU 'owns' all resources other than cash	SBU is a potential reservoir of core competencies
Resource allocation	Discrete businesses are the unit of analysis; capital is allocated business by business	Businesses and competencies are the unit of analysis: top management allocates capital and talent
Value added of top management	Optimizing corporate returns through capital allocation trade-offs among businesses	Enunciating strategic architecture and building competencies to secure the future

on the competitiveness of others, rather than investing in core competencies and world core-product leadership, may be treading on quicksand. In the race for global brand dominance, companies like 3M, Black & Decker, Canon, Honda, NEC and Citicorp have built global brand umbrellas by proliferating products out of their core competencies. This has allowed their individual businesses to build image, customer loyalty and access to distribution channels.

When you think about this reconceptualization of the corporation, the primacy of the SBU – an organizational dogma for a generation – is now clearly an anachronism. Where the SBU is an article of faith, resistance to the seductions of decentralization can seem heretical. In many companies, the SBU prism means that only one plane of the global competitive battle, the battle to put competitive products on the shelf *today,* is visible to top management. What are the costs of this distortion?

Underinvestment in developing core competencies and core products

When the organization is conceived of as a multiplicity of SBUs, no single business may feel responsible for maintaining a viable position in core products or be able to justify the investment required to build world leadership in some core competence. In the absence of a more comprehensive view imposed by corporate management, SBU managers will tend to underinvest. Recently, companies such as Kodak and Philips have recognized this as a potential problem and have begun searching for new organizational forms that will allow them to develop and manufacture core products for both internal and external customers.

SBU managers have traditionally conceived of competitors in the same way as they've seen themselves. On the whole, they've failed to note the emphasis Asian competitors were placing on building leadership in core products or to understand the critical linkage between world manufacturing leadership and the ability to sustain development pace in core competence. They've failed to pursue OEM-supply opportunities or to look across their various product divisions in an attempt to identify opportunities for coordinated initiatives.

Imprisoned resources

As an SBU evolves, it often develops unique competencies. Typically, the people who embody this competence are seen as the sole property of the business in which they grew up. The manager of another SBU who asks to borrow talented people is likely to get a cold rebuff. SBU managers are not only unwilling to lend their competence carriers but they may actually hide talent to prevent its redeployment in the pursuit of new opportunities. This may be compared to residents of an underdeveloped country hiding most of their cash under their mattresses. The benefits of competencies, like the benefits of the money supply, depend on the velocity of their circulation as well as on the size of the stock the company holds.

Western companies have traditionally had an advantage in the stock of skills they possess. But have they been able to reconfigure them quickly to respond to new opportunities? Canon, NEC and Honda have had a lesser stock of the people and technologies that compose core competencies but could move them much quicker from one business unit to another. Corporate R&D spending at Canon is not fully indicative of the size of Canon's core competence stock and tells the casual observer nothing about the velocity with which Canon is able to move core competencies to exploit opportunities.

When competencies become imprisoned, the people who carry the competencies do not get assigned to the most exciting opportunities, and their skills begin to atrophy. Only by fully leveraging core competencies can small companies like Canon afford to compete with industry giants like Xerox. How strange that SBU managers, who are perfectly willing to compete for cash in the capital budgeting process, are unwilling to compete for people – the company's most precious asset. We find it ironic that top management devotes so much attention to the capital budgeting process yet typically has no comparable mechanism for allocating the human skills that embody core competencies. Top managers are seldom able to look four or five levels down into the organization, identify the people who embody critical competencies, and move them across organizational boundaries.

Bounded innovation

If core competencies are not recognized, individual SBUs will pursue only those innovation opportunities that are close at hand – marginal product-line extensions or geographic expansions. Hybrid opportunities like fax machines, laptop computers, handheld televisions or portable music keyboards will emerge only when managers take off their SBU blinkers. Remember, Canon appeared to be in the camera business at the time it was preparing to become a world leader in copiers. Conceiving of the corporation in terms of core competencies widens the domain of innovation.

Developing strategic architecture

The fragmentation of core competencies becomes inevitable when a diversified company's information systems, patterns of communication, career paths, managerial rewards and processes of strategy development do not transcend SBU lines. We believe that senior management should spend a significant amount of its time developing a corporate-wide strategic architecture that establishes objectives for competence-building. A strategic architecture is a road map of the future that identifies which core competencies to build and their constituent technologies.

By providing an impetus for learning from alliances and a focus for internal development efforts, a strategic architecture like NEC's C&C (computers and communication) can dramatically reduce the investment needed to secure future market leadership. How can a company make partnerships intelligently without a clear understanding of the core competencies it is trying to build and those it is attempting to prevent from being unintentionally transferred?

Of course, all of this begs the question of what a strategic architecture should look like. The answer will be different for every company. But it is helpful to think again of that tree, of the corporation organized around core products and, ultimately, core competencies. To sink sufficiently strong roots, a company must answer some fundamental questions: How long could we preserve our competitiveness in this business if we did not control this particular core competence? How central is this core competence to perceived customer benefits? What future opportunities would be foreclosed if we were to lose this particular competence?

The architecture provides a logic for product and market diversification, moreover. An SBU manager would be asked: Does the new market opportunity add to the overall goal of becoming the best player in the world? Does it exploit or add to the core competence? At Vickers, for example, diversification options have been judged in the context of becoming the best power and motion control company in the world.

The strategic architecture should make resource allocation priorities transparent to the entire organization. It provides a template for allocation decisions by top management. It helps lower-level managers understand the logic of allocation priorities and disciplines senior management to maintain consistency. In short, it yields a definition of the company and the markets it serves. 3M, Vickers, NEC, Canon and Honda all qualify on this score. Honda knew it was exploiting what it had learned from motorcycles – how to make high-revving, smooth-running, lightweight engines – when it entered the car business. The task of creating a strategic architecture forces the organization to identify and commit to the technical and production linkages across SBUs that will provide a distinct competitive advantage.

It is consistency of resource allocation and the development of an administrative infrastructure appropriate to it that breathes life into a strategic architecture and creates a managerial culture, teamwork, a capacity to change, and a willingness to share resources, to protect proprietary skills and to think long term. That is also the reason the specific architecture cannot be copied easily or overnight by competitors. Strategic architecture is a tool for communicating with customers and other external constituents. It reveals the broad direction without giving away every step.

Redeploying to exploit competencies

If the company's core competencies are its critical resource and if top management must ensure that competence carriers are not held hostage by some particular business, then it follows that SBUs should bid for core competencies in the same way they bid for capital. We've made this point glancingly. It is important enough to consider more deeply.

Once top management (with the help of divisional and SBU managers) has identified overarching competencies, it must ask businesses to identify the projects and people closely connected with them. Corporate officers should direct an audit of the location, number and quality of the people who embody competence.

This sends an important signal to middle managers: core competencies are corporate resources and may be reallocated by *corporate* management. An individual business doesn't own anybody. SBUs are entitled to the services of individual employees so long as SBU management can demonstrate that the opportunity it is pursuing yields the highest possible payoff on the investment in their skills. This message is further underlined if each year in the strategic planning or budgeting process, unit managers must justify their hold on the people who carry the company's core competencies.

Also, reward systems that focus only on product-line results and career paths that seldom cross SBU boundaries engender patterns of behaviour among unit managers that are destructively competitive. At NEC, divisional managers come together to identify next-generation competencies. Together they decide how much investment needs to be made to build up each future competence and the contribution in capital and staff support that each division will need to make. There is also a sense of equitable exchange. One division may make a disproportionate contribution or may benefit less from the progress made, but such short-term inequalities will balance out over the long term.

Incidentally, the positive contribution of the SBU manager should be made visible across the company. An SBU manager is unlikely to surrender key people if only the other business (or the general manager of that business who may be a competitor for promotion) is going to benefit from the redeployment. Cooperative SBU managers should be celebrated as team players. Where priorities are clear, transfers are less likely to be seen as idiosyncratic and politically motivated.

Transfers for the sake of building core competence must be recorded and appreciated in the corporate memory. It is reasonable to expect a business that has surrendered core skills on behalf of corporate opportunities in other areas to lose, for a time, some of its competitiveness. If these losses in performance bring immediate censure, SBUs will be unlikely to assent to skills transfers next time.

Finally, there are ways to wean key employees off the idea that they belong in perpetuity to any particular business. Early in their careers, people may be exposed to a variety of businesses through a carefully planned rotation programme.

Competence carriers should be regularly brought together from across the corporation to trade notes and ideas. The goal is to build a strong feeling of community among these people. To a great extent, their loyalty should be to the integrity of the core competence area they represent and not just to particular businesses. In travelling regularly, talking frequently to customers and meeting with peers, competence carriers may be encouraged to discover new market opportunities.

Core competencies are the wellspring of new business development. They should constitute the focus for strategy at the corporate level. Managers have to win manufacturing leadership in core products and capture global share through brand-building programmes aimed at exploiting economies of scope. Only if the company is conceived of as a hierarchy of core competencies, core products and market-focused business units will it be fit to fight.

Nor can top management be just another layer of accounting consolidation, which it often is in a regime of radical decentralization. Top management must add value by enunciating the strategic architecture that guides the competence acquisition process. We believe an obsession with competence building will characterize the global winners of the 1990s. With the decade underway, the time for rethinking the concept of the corporation is already overdue.

READING

5.3

Seeking synergies

By Andrew Campbell and Michael Goold[1]

A review of synergy management can be triggered in a number of ways. A parent manager may suspect that co-ordination opportunities are being missed, but may not be sure what is being missed, how important it is, or what to do about it. A new chief executive may sense that his predecessor's emphasis on decentralization has led unit managers to overlook sharing opportunities. A visit to other companies that sing the praises of co-ordination may raise concerns about what is being missed. Critical press comments about the company's failure to achieve synergies across its portfolio may prompt questions about what more could be achieved. Given our concern about 'synergy bias', we counsel caution in following up vague disquiets. But an audit of how well synergy management is working can be a useful step in allaying fears or pinpointing areas that need to be addressed.

A review can also be triggered by grumbles at lower levels in the company that current co-ordination efforts are pointless, damaging or contradictory. Business

[1]Source: This article was adapted from Chapter 7 of *Synergy: Why Links Between Business Units Often Fail and How to Make Them Work.* Reproduced with permission from John Wiley & Sons Ltd.. Copyright © 1998 Andrew Campbell and Michael Goold.

managers may complain that short-term budget targets prevent them from exploring potentially valuable synergy opportunities or about the pointlessness of corporate-wide conferences at expensive resorts to promote 'family feeling'. Corridor gossip about the negative influence of the parent may percolate up to the chief executive. More direct complaints may be received from frustrated business managers. Bottom-up pressures to think again about a company's approach to synergies should be taken seriously, and, if there are widespread or deep-seated concerns, a systematic and objective stock-taking may be in order.

Some companies build a periodic review of their cross-company initiatives into their regular planning processes. We are less enthusiastic about this practice, since it can easily lead either to superficial, year-by-year reiteration of what everyone already knows about the areas of overlap between businesses or to vain attempts to come up with new ideas. Unless there is a particular reason to review linkage management, it will probably cause more frustration than enlightenment. On the whole, therefore, we believe that a review should only be undertaken when there are identifiable reasons for doing so.

Good reasons to take stock of the current approach include:

- a belief that a major category of synergies such as international rationalization, sharing technical know-how or joint development of new business opportunities, is being systematically missed;
- visible and costly failures of several recent synergy initiatives;
- evidence that business units are favoring links with third parties in preference to internal links.

While it would be useful to have a way of objectively deciding when a stock take is necessary, our experience suggests that it is best judged subjectively by thinking about how well the current organization is working.

The purpose of a review should be to decide whether changes are needed in the overall corporate approach to synergies; to identify any specific opportunities that merit closer investigations; and to propose possible new linkage mechanisms or interventions.

A framework for a review

Our review framework is shown in Figure 5.3.1. It involves taking stock of both synergy opportunities available and the current corporate approach to

cross-company linkages. The effectiveness of the approach can be assessed by testing how well it fits with the opportunities. The assessment can then be used to pinpoint new initiatives that may be worth considering. The framework will bring out aspects of the overall approach that are working well or badly, and lead to proposals for changes.

The value of the framework is that it obliges companies to address some fundamental questions:

- What is our current attitude to co-ordination between our business units, and how do we go about managing it?
- What do we believe are the main synergy opportunities in our portfolio, and how fully are we grasping them?
- How well suited is our current approach, including structures, processes and staff support, to the opportunities we believe are on offer?
- What current synergy initiatives should we drop, what new opportunities should we go for, and what changes in processes and mechanisms should we consider?

These questions can be asked of the whole company or of a multi-business division within a larger company. The framework is equally applicable when applied to any level above that of the individual business unit. However, when working at a division level, it is valuable to understand some of the broader corporate context in which the division is operating.

Although the framework provides a systematic means of tackling these questions, it should not be treated either as a straitjacket or a panacea. The emphasis of a review should depend on the concerns that prompted it. Is it primarily a matter of fine-tuning the current mechanisms and processes to work more smoothly, or are we more concerned with the underlying philosophy or structure of the company? Did we get into the review to beat the bushes to create a wide agenda of all possible new opportunities, or was it really a means of legitimizing a fresh look at one or two specific issues? With different motivations for the review, the weight given to different areas of analysis will vary, the order in which activities take place will be different, and the level of effort and speed of the review will change.

We also recognize that the structured framework we suggest may not appeal to all companies. Some may have a culture that stresses a more intuitive assessment of issues, and may find the analytical approach we propose too constraining. Others may have their own

FIGURE 5.3.1   Reviewing synergy parenting

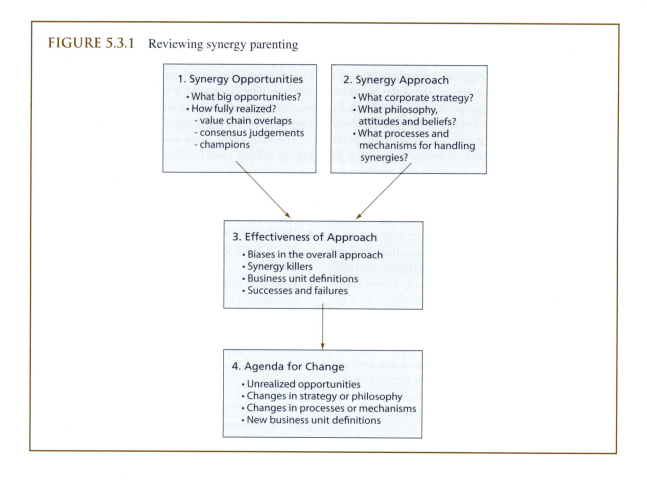

preferred analyses that we have not included in our framework. We recognize that our approach is not the only way to undertake a review of linkage parenting, and we advise each company to tailor its approach to its own needs, culture and preferences.

As we discuss the different steps in the framework, readers should accordingly view our proposals as building blocks from which to construct their own review process, rather than as an inflexible 'how to do it' manual. We have found the steps useful in our work with companies, but we are not dogmatic about the framework we put forward.

Synergy opportunities

The first step in the review involves developing a list of major synergy opportunities and judging how fully they are being realized. The purpose is to unearth any important opportunities that are not currently being successfully grasped. This may prompt ideas for changes in the overall approach or for specific new interventions.

To undertake detailed analysis for every linkage opportunity as part of a general review is clearly not feasible. It would take too long and cost too much. The challenge is to find efficient ways of homing in quickly on possible areas of high unexploited potential.

In our research, we have identified three useful prompts that can help to reveal neglected potential: rough modelling of value chain overlaps; interviews, focus groups or questionnaires designed to draw out consensus from business unit and parent managers; and identification of pet projects or initiatives that are being strongly championed by individual managers.

Value chain overlaps

Businesses with value chains that overlap, or could overlap, are obvious candidates for linkage opportunities. If two businesses purchase similar components, what benefits might be available by co-coordinating their purchases? If two businesses have overseas offices in the same country, what could be saved by sharing premises, sales forces, or management? We have found that rough modelling of the extent of overlaps and of the economies of scale or utilization available from sharing can rapidly yield a broad sizing of the benefits available in different areas. For example, a retail group was able to prioritize opportunities for joint purchasing by assessing the extent of overlaps in different product ranges between two of their chains, and estimating the level of extra purchase discounts that would be available from combined buying. Back-of-the-envelope calculations showed that there were only two product ranges with significant overlaps and, thus, real prospects for achieving better terms. More detailed analysis then focused on these prime candidates. Although there was nothing precise or sophisticated about the modelling that led to this conclusion, it was highly effective in narrowing down the opportunities to consider.

Even rough value chain modelling can, however, be hard to do or too time consuming at the review stage. The benefits may not yet be sufficiently well defined, or may be made up of several different component parts, or may be too numerous to analyse. An alternative is to rely on consensus judgments of informed managers.

Consensus judgment

When experienced managers agree that there is probably a worthwhile benefit to go for, their views deserve to be heard. If most of the marketing managers in different countries believe that they could benefit from sharing best practice in advertising, it is almost certainly worth trying to understand more about the opportunity. If, on the other hand, the corporate marketing director has suggested more sharing but the national marketing managers are lukewarm, it should probably be put on the backburner – at least unless the corporate director can argue convincingly that the national managers may be misjudging the opportunity. In the difficult field of synergies, the gut-feel and intuitive judgment of experienced managers should carry considerable weight.

In companies where information flows freely and managers are encouraged to express their views, it is comparatively easy for parent managers to discern an emerging consensus. In other companies, it can be much more difficult. Managers from different units may not meet together often enough to share views, or may not feel empowered to express their views to each other. They may also be constrained to follow prevailing corporate policies rather than challenge them. Whatever the reason, a structured approach to eliciting the consensus is frequently needed.

There are a variety of ways to draw out consensus judgments, ranging from questionnaires, through focus groups, to some form of systematic interviewing process. The method chosen needs to be tailored to the circumstances of the company – and we have adopted somewhat different methods in each of the companies we have worked with. In all cases, however, the objective is to discover whether informed managers generally feel that there are important unexplored opportunities going begging, and, if so, what priorities they should receive.

Championing

A third valuable prompt comes from championing. Strong and enthusiastic champions are important for the effective implementation of new interventions. We believe that they can also provide a short cut to identifying priority opportunity areas. If a manager feels so powerfully that an opportunity is worthwhile that he is willing to lobby for it, devote personal sweat equity to it, and risk the displeasure of his colleagues and bosses by repeatedly advocating it, it is usually worth taking notice.

There is little danger that strong champions will not be heard by the corporate parent. The danger is more that they will be too readily discounted. Persistent champions, particularly if their ideas challenge vested interests, can face strong opposition. Their views may be dismissed as unrealistic or irrelevant, or they may be labelled eccentrics or troublemakers. Prudent managers then pipe down, and learn to live with their frustrations. However, frustrated champions welcome any chance to promote their pet projects. A review of linkage parenting is a good opportunity to give them an objective hearing. Our advice is to listen carefully to what they have to say – even if the rest of the organization has long ago decided not to.

Creativity and realism

In drawing up the short-list of opportunities that merit detailed consideration, we need to balance creativity and open-mindedness with realism. We want managers with new ideas to come forward, we want to encourage brainstorming that will generate fresh thinking, and we want to give a hearing to highly motivated champions. Especially if the purpose of the review is to make sure we're not missing something, we should be positive about new suggestions and supportive of 'thinking the unthinkable'.

We should also be willing to accept that some promising ideas may be clouded by considerable uncertainty.

In Consco, for example, there was widespread support for more sharing of best practice in training and management development. But the benefits available were somewhat nebulous. Some managers had fairly specific ideas about how course designs or materials could be shared better. Others were simply reflecting a sense that this was an increasingly important area, in which they did not feel that their units were doing a very good job. Some had anecdotes or examples to support their views. But there was considerable uncertainty about where the real opportunities lay and how they should be pursued. And, in some situations, there is intrinsic uncertainty about the nature of the benefits. In businesses in the middle of rapid technological change, such as media and communications, the benefits of collaborating to develop new businesses to some extent depend on market and technology developments that are simply not predictable. The review should encourage managers to put forward speculative or uncertain opportunities: on closer examination they may turn out to contain real nuggets of gold. But any interventions to pursue them will probably have to be exploratory, designed to find out whether there are solid benefits to be obtained or not.

In creating a short-list of ideas to examine more closely, we should, however, guard against pursuing mirages, and question whether there really are likely to be parenting opportunities to address. When we assess the short-listed ideas, we shall need to be rigorous in applying the mental disciplines to them. In drawing up the short-list, we should therefore reject ideas if there is insufficient logic or evidence to support them. For example, if the champion of a shared salesforce appears to have given little serious consideration to important details, such as salesmen's calling patterns or the purchase criteria of customers, his proposal should receive less weight. Or if, on reflection, no-one can see any possible parenting opportunities associated with the targeted benefit, we should avoid wasting time with further investigation of it. We need to blend support for fresh thinking with the reality checks and tough-mindedness that the mental disciplines provide. It is the ideas that will stand up under closer analysis that we are interested in.

Synergy approach

The next step in the review is to lay out the main features of the company's approach to synergy management. It should cover the role that synergies play within the corporate strategy. It should bring out the company's underlying philosophy, attitudes and beliefs concerning the units' relationships to each other and to the centre. And it should make explicit the mechanisms and processes that the company typically uses to deal with these issues.

Corporate strategy

In our research on corporate strategy, we have found that different companies place very different emphases on the horizontal and vertical linkages that they foster. Some companies, such as Hanson (before the breakup), Emerson, RTZ and BTR (prior to 1995), place much more weight on the value that they add through stand-alone parenting than through linkage parenting. Others, such as Banc One, Unilever, 3M, ABB and Canon, have always seen the management of synergies as a key part of their corporate strategies. Business managers in organizations such as Hanson know that the main focus of the parent's attention will be on opportunities to improve the performance of each business as a stand-alone entity, and that they will receive few brownie points for collaborative efforts with other units. By contrast, business managers in Canon or Unilever know that their bosses expect and require them to seek out and participate in opportunities for working together with other units. Furthermore, they know what sorts of synergies the parent typically promotes most energetically. In Canon, for example, the strongest drive is for new product developments that require cooperation across business unit boundaries, while in Unilever the transfer of product and market information across geographic boundaries is critical.

Exhibit 5.3.1 summarizes the main sources of value creation identified in one international manufacturing and marketing company. This way of summarizing the corporate strategy into a list of parenting tasks helps position the importance of synergy initiatives versus other forms of parenting.

In summary, the review should document the priority given to linkage issues versus other forms of parenting and record the types of linkages that feature most prominently as key sources of added value. The review should also record the direction of movement in the corporate strategy. Is the company looking to build more synergies in the future or unwind some of the links and coordinated activities that currently exist? The current corporate strategy and the perceived direction of movement influence the sort of synergies that managers are likely to pursue and the priority they give them.

EXHIBIT 5.3.1 SOURCES OF PARENTING VALUE CREATION

- Transferring know-how about products, markets, marketing, manufacturing and other functions from/to business units around the world.

- Helping businesses (mainly in developed economies) avoid the pitfall of under investment in new product development and consumer understanding.

- Creating a value-based performance culture that has low tolerance of unnecessary costs or weak performance, yet is capable of investing where necessary.

- Orchestrating pools of mobile management talent so that businesses can draw on them in times of need.

- Developing and appointing outstanding managers to lead each business, with skills appropriate to the particular challenges of that business.

- Helping businesses (mainly in emerging markets) to avoid common pitfalls, such as insufficient investment in local management or poor timing of major commitments.

- Developing valuable relationships with potential partners and influential governments, and building the company brand into one of the world's leading corporate brands.

- Providing cost effective central services and corporate governance activities.

Philosophy, attitudes and beliefs

Companies also have different underlying attitudes and beliefs about how best to handle linkages. Often these differences concern the advantages of centralization or decentralization. To achieve benefits from pooled purchasing power, for example, a parent with a belief in the efficacy of central initiatives may set up a central purchasing department and insist that all purchases of certain items are handled by this department. Conversely, a parent that favours decentralized networking may simply circulate data on the purchasing terms and conditions being achieved by each unit, maintaining strong pressure on the businesses to reduce their individual unit costs. Such an intervention leaves the businesses much freer to determine whether and how they wish to work with other businesses to improve their purchasing power, but gives them no direct help or guidance about what to do. Between these extremes, there are a variety of other possibilities, such as establishing joint purchasing teams with members from different businesses, nominating selected businesses to act as lead units in purchasing for different items, centralizing certain aspects of negotiations on terms and conditions but allowing each business to make its own buying decisions, and hiring a central purchasing expert who is available to the businesses, but need only be used by them if they choose.

For any synergy benefit, a range of possible intervention options can be arrayed along a spectrum of more versus less centralist interventions (see Table 5.3.1). Some companies, such as Mars and Unilever, are philosophically committed to the decentralized,

networking end of the spectrum. They believe that it is vital to preserve business-unit autonomy and leave decisions to business-unit managements. Wary of central interference, they prefer to rely on the 'enlightened self-interest' of unit managers to guide linkages. Other companies, such as Canon or Rentokil, are more comfortable mandating policies or decisions from the centre on a range of issues. Although they accept the importance of unit motivation and initiative, they believe that there are many important benefits that will not be realized unless the parent makes the decisions.

Differences in attitudes concerning the appropriate degree of centralization affect the range of intervention options that a parent is likely to perceive. Those who favour decentralized solutions will tend to give little or no consideration to more mandatory central interventions. Those who typically mandate central policies and decisions will be less sensitive to how much can be accomplished through a variety of measures that encourage networking. Corporate linkage philosophies represent blinkers that constrain the options that receive attention.

Another important factor is the corporate parent's attitude to central staff resources. Should large, heavyweight staff groups be set up or not? Should the businesses be forced to work with the corporate staff, or should their use by the businesses be voluntary? As with centralization/decentralization choices, companies tend to have a dominant philosophy which governs the role of staff in managing linkages. Companies such as ABB are strenuously opposed to the use of corporate staff, wherever possible relying on decisions and resources in the business units. They

TABLE 5.3.1   Differences in linkage philosophy

	Belief in decentralization	Mixed	Belief in central direction
Know-how sharing	■ Network facilitation	■ Some central policies ■ Centres of excellence ■ Lead units ■ Franchise	■ Mandatory central policies and directives
Tangible resources sharing	■ Internal JVs/contracts ■ Voluntary use of shared resource units ■ Set up as profit centres	■ Limited central functions and resources ■ Service level agreements	■ Mandatory central functions and resources ■ Incomplete SBUs
Pooled negotiating power	■ Information sharing ■ Joint SBU teams and initiatives	■ Lead units	■ Central functions experts
Vertical integration	■ Third party trading relationships, but first refusal in-house	■ Negotiated transfer prices ■ In-house preference ■ Centre influences relationship	■ Centre sets transfer prices and manages relationships for corporate benefit
Co-ordinated strategies	■ Centre arbitrates ■ Minimal constraints on scope/strategy	■ Restrained central role ■ Matrix structure ■ Task forces ■ Franchise	■ Centre directs ■ Low SBU autonomy
New business creation	■ SBU driven	■ Task forces drawn from centre and SBUs	■ Centrally driven

fear that, lacking direct profit responsibility, staff can easily lose touch with the needs of the businesses and take on a life of their own, in which power and empire-building take precedence over the benefits delivered to the corporation. Other companies, 3M or Cooper for instance, believe that corporate staff, at least in selected areas, are the best way to ensure that specialist expertise is developed and shared among units. They are therefore a source of valuable linkages. These beliefs will be reflected in the synergy interventions that the parent makes.

Different philosophies therefore influence the sorts of synergies that will be pursued and the means which will be used to pursue them. Take, for example, a new product-development initiative involving joint work between two or more business units. At one extreme, a 'Hanson' approach, suspicious of shared responsibilities of this sort, would likely press for the initiative to be pursued within one of the businesses or else dropped. By contrast, a 'Unilever' approach would be to provide encouragement and, if necessary, expert assistance, while allowing the businesses to pursue the matter in their own way, within a framework of strong corporate cultural norms to guide decision-making. A 'Canon' approach would be different again, entailing willingness to give high corporate priority to the project, including assignment of numbers of both corporate and business staff to work full-time on the project to see it through to commercialization. Some assessment of the underlying corporate attitudes and beliefs about linkages should therefore form part of the review.

Mechanisms and processes

Companies also differ in the nature of the specific mechanisms and processes that they typically use to manage co-ordination. The review should identify the mechanisms and processes that are most frequently used, and should articulate the impact that they have on synergy management. What is the nature and importance of the budget and planning processes and how, if at all, do they affect cross-company initiatives? What sort of cross-business committees are in place and how do they work? What staff groups exist and what role do they play in linkages?

We argue that 'well-grooved' mechanisms are an important factor in gauging the ease with which a company's synergy intervention will be implemented. Equally, ineffective or ill-suited mechanisms and processes can account for failure to realize some opportunities.

'Five lenses analysis'

As a means of describing and analysing the parent's approach to synergy issues, we have found that a display that views the characteristics of the parent through five interlinked lenses is useful (see Goold, Campbell and Alexander, 1994 and Figure 5.3.2). The five lenses are:

- The beliefs, knowledge or mental maps that guide the behaviour and decisions of senior managers in the parent organization. These mental maps determine the corporate linkage strategy and philosophy, and guide the parent's thinking about the selection and implementation of linkage mechanisms and interventions.

- The structure of the company, including the way in which the business units are defined and the nature of parenting structures to which they report, and the systems and processes through which parent managers mainly exercise influence, pressure and control. The business-unit definitions determine what links between units need to be managed; the nature of the parenting structure, for example whether there are product divisions, geographical divisions, or a matrix structure, influences the parenting opportunities that will be pursued; and the systems and processes that are in place determine how they are most likely to be handled.

- The functional staff, central service groups and corporate resources that are important in synergy management. The size, composition and strengths of the corporate staff and the way in which they operate are key components of the overall approach to cross-company working.

- The people in the parent organization. The experience, skills and biases of key individuals in the parent have a major impact on synergy management.

- The extent to which authority is delegated to business managers, together with the criteria by which their performance is judged and the rewards or sanctions for good or poor performance; we refer to this as the 'decentralization contract' for each business. The manner in which decentralization contracts are defined influences the sorts of linkage intervention

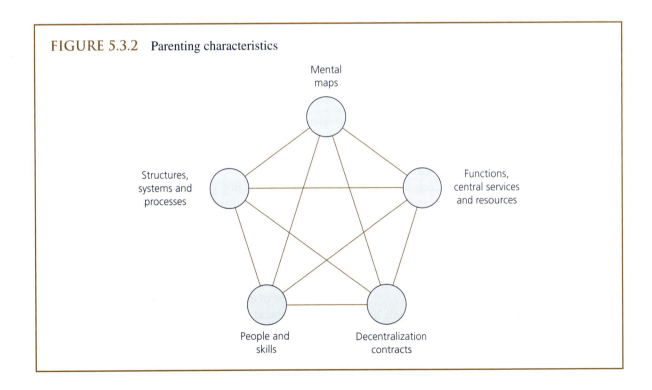

FIGURE 5.3.2   Parenting characteristics

that the parent is likely to make and that the businesses are likely to accept.

We have found that these five lenses provide a useful checklist for itemizing those features of the corporate parent's approach to the management of synergies that matter most. By running through each of these headings and taking stock of the key features under each, a picture of the overall approach can be built up and made explicit. The five lenses can also be used to bring out ways in which the approach is changing, giving a direction of movement as well as a static picture.

Effectiveness of approach

The third step is to assess the effectiveness of the current synergy approach. How well does the approach match up with the opportunities? Is it working reasonably well, apart from a few specific problems? Are there any fundamental shortcomings that need to be tackled? Once the approach and the opportunities have been laid out in the first two steps of the review, the answers to these questions may be readily apparent. There are, however, some more structured questions that it may be useful to ask. These include:

- Are there biases in the overall approach that condition which opportunities will be realized?

- Are there any aspects of the approach which are impeding linkages; are there any 'synergy killers'?

- Do any business unit definitions need to be changed?

- What have been the successes and failures of the approach, and what problems need addressing?

Biases in the overall approach

Earlier in this reading, we contrasted the corporate strategies and philosophies of different companies, including Hanson, Unilever, ABB and Canon. The differences in these companies' approaches to synergies mean that they will each steer away from certain sorts of interventions and towards others: their approaches bias both the types of linkages they are likely to emphasize and the means by which they will be pursued.

Nearly all companies have biases in their linkage parenting, and a value of the review is to lay out what they are. What does the corporate strategy emphasize? What are the dominant mental maps that are driving the linkage interventions that the parent chooses to make? What are the well-grooved processes that are

usually chosen as the preferred way to intervene? If we can make these biases explicit, we may be able to see why certain synergy opportunities are grasped, while others are systematically overlooked; why some initiatives run smoothly, while others are always contentious and difficult.

- In one manufacturer of automotive components, the corporate strategy stressed the importance of global co-ordination across different national companies. This strategy led to cost savings and superior customer service in many areas. However, it also led to pressure for rationalization of the product range that carried high opportunity costs in some countries. The basic presumption in favour of international coordination made it very difficult for the countries in question to get a fair hearing on these costs. Instead, they were accused of NIH thinking and told to fall into line with global policy. The bias in favour of international co-ordination in the corporate strategy prevented the parent from taking a balanced view of the advantages and disadvantages of product-range rationalization.

- In a building products company, there was a strong commitment to decentralized networking as the best way to capture synergies, based partly on history and partly on a belief in the need to respect differences in each business unit's markets. When the corporate parent wanted to encourage all the businesses to adopt a common MIS system, the networking bias resulted in an endless sequence of project-team meetings, in which it was impossible to reach agreement on a new standard system for all the businesses. It was only after literally years of delay that the parent insisted on a choice being made and pushed it through. The bias in favour of networking prevented a stronger corporate lead from being taken earlier.

The biases in a company's overall approach will make it especially effective at handling certain sorts of linkages, but ineffective at others. For example, there are some parenting opportunities that require mandated central decisions and are unlikely to be grasped through interventions that simply aim to promote networking between the businesses. Hence, a parent with a bias in favour of decentralized networking is unlikely to be successful at realizing these sorts of parenting opportunities. Similarly, a staff-averse company that always tends to use cross-business project teams to handle linkages will find it difficult to push through parenting opportunities for which central staff are needed. By making explicit any biases in the approach, we may be able to understand better why some opportunities are being successfully realized while others are proving problematic. We can then decide whether to maintain the approach and endorse its biases or to consider making changes.

Synergy killers

Most discussions of synergy concern ways in which the corporate parent can make linkages between business units work better. Unfortunately, the harsh reality is that the corporate parent often inadvertently makes these connections more difficult, not easier. We need to recognize this fact, and can use a review of linkage parenting as a means of rooting out things that are impeding linkages. We refer to policies or characteristics of the parent that are systematically inhibiting linkages as 'synergy killers'.

The effectiveness of the approach to linkages will be compromised if any of the following synergy killers are present:

- **Inhibiting corporate strategy.** The most common way in which the corporate-level strategy can work against synergy is through lack of clarity. Lack of clarity about corporate priorities leads managers to be excessively cautious about when they collaborate and with whom. If managers in the businesses are unsure whether the corporate parent expects them to be coordinating their technical efforts or looking for cost savings in marketing, the uncertainty can leave them paralysed. A more obvious, if rarer, problem stems from corporate strategies that actively discourage linkages of any sort. In a notorious memorandum written after GEC's acquisition of English Electric, Lord Weinstock informed the managers of the English Electric businesses that all cross-unit committees and projects were to be disbanded forthwith. In future, they would have only one responsibility: the performance of their own units. Though few companies today take such a radical stance against synergies between businesses, some corporate-level strategies still discourage cooperation. 'In my view', stated one chief executive, 'synergy is always an illusion. What is more, it fatally damages accountability.' Not surprisingly, this attitude had a dampening effect on unit managers' attempts to work together.

- **Infighting between the barons.** In some companies, there are battles raging between senior managers. The battles may be about differences in corporate strategy or management philosophy. They may be about competition between managers for the top job. They may be due to personality clashes. They may be due to previous collaborations where one party felt let down. Whatever the reason, these battles have a huge negative impact on cooperation. Managers lower down are often aware of lost opportunities, but the climate of hostility between their bosses means that cooperation to pursue them is stifled. It is simply not acceptable to be seen to be 'working with the enemy'.

- **Culture of secrecy.** In secretive companies, people play their cards close to their chests. Information about business unit performance, new product plans, operating issues and organization structures is given out reluctantly. In these circumstances, cooperation is hard, not only because it is difficult to find out what is going on in other units, but also because the free flow of information and communication that is needed to oil the wheels of synergies is inhibited. Why do these cultures occur? Sometimes it is fear of competitor espionage. Sometimes it is a result of resisting corporate information requests and interference. Sometimes it is associated with baronial infighting. Whatever the cause, a culture of secrecy reduces synergy.

- **Misaligned incentives.** In many companies, bonus systems and promotion criteria depend largely or exclusively on the results managers achieve in their own businesses, and give no credit for contributions to other businesses or the corporate whole. The personal incentive system then makes it more difficult for business managers to cooperate, unless they can structure a deal that rewards all the units involved. Where the synergy involves a sacrifice by one unit to help others, and there is no ready process by which to compensate the loser, the incentive system will block progress. Again and again, we encountered situations in which this prevented managers from helping colleagues in other businesses, even though there was a clear net benefit. Where win/lose trade-offs exist, reward systems should aim to make it easier for business managers to cooperate; all too often, they have precisely the reverse effect.

- **Excessive performance pressure.** When managers are hounded by close-to-impossible targets, they are apt to become defensive and inward-looking. In companies where business unit performance is paramount and where targets are set too high, managers often concentrate exclusively on things within their own immediate control and cease to be comfortable with situations where they must rely on their colleagues' cooperation. Oppressive targets damp down the spirit of mutuality and collaboration from which synergies flow.

- **Insulation from performance pressure.** At the opposite end of the spectrum from excessive performance pressure is insulation from performance pressure. If business units are insulated from performance pressures, the basic drive of enlightened self-interest, on which so many beneficial sharing initiatives depend, will be weakened. In companies where synergies thrive, such as Mars or Canon, senior managers keep up the pressure for constant improvement, knowing that this leads to more energy from working together. In companies where the parent insulates the businesses from such pressures, the businesses are less likely to seek out mutually rewarding synergies.

- **Domineering corporate staff.** If corporate staff groups have domineering or insensitive attitudes, business managers will automatically reject their ideas for improving linkages, however sound they may be. In a major chemical company with old established functional baronies, the heads of the corporate staff departments were inclined to issue policies and guidelines to the businesses with little consultation or recognition of inter-company differences. Over time, the business heads became adept at passive resistance and non-cooperation, spending much more time on the tactics of opposition than on assessing whether the proposed policies were, in fact, beneficial. As a result, genuine synergy opportunities were resisted as strenuously as misguided attempts at standardization.

- **Mistrust.** An atmosphere of mistrust undermines cooperation. If the businesses believe that their sister units are out to take advantage of them, or are always unwilling to put themselves out to help, relations are quickly soured to the point where even well-intentioned initiatives are blocked. Equally, if a climate of opinion has grown up where business managers believe that corporate management or staff are incompetent or untrustworthy, synergy interventions are likely to be resisted in principle. Expensive, high profile failures seriously undermine the credibility and prospects of any future proposal. Particular problems arise when the parent is suspected of having a hidden agenda, since all initiatives will be scrutinized for ulterior motives, and interpreted in the worst possible light.

All companies have some synergy killers. Our concern should be with pathological characteristics that may be causing widespread damage, not with minor irritants. Is there a strong sense that some of the parent's characteristics are really preventing collaboration? Can we see evidence from the unrealized opportunities that indicates that these synergy killers are having a real impact? How can the parent adjust the corporate context to make linkages work better?

While synergy killers inhibit linkages, their opposites create the sort of fertile ground in which cooperation flourishes. Clear corporate strategies that support high priority synergies; good personal relationships between senior managers in the businesses; an open culture that promotes sharing; incentive systems that reward attempts to create synergies; corporate pressure to raise performance through sharing best practices; competent staff units that are sensitive in their relationships with the businesses; and an atmosphere of mutual trust and support are all conducive to perceiving synergy opportunities and implementing them successfully. The parent should aim to nurture synergies through creating these fertile ground conditions. Hence, even if no real synergy killers exist, the review may still pinpoint ways in which the corporate context could be made more fertile for synergies.

Business unit definitions

The boundaries established around a group's business units are fundamental for the approach to synergies. By changing the definition of the business units, the parent automatically changes the nature of the potential links between business units. If a new European unit is set up out of previously separate national units, issues of manufacturing co-ordination that used to be handled as linkages between separate units are now managed within a single larger entity. 'Internalizing' the linkages in this way makes a big difference, because there is now a single general manager for the combined business who is in a position to decide on trade-offs between the subunits and who will be held responsible for the results of the integrated entity. This makes certain interventions much easier to push through, although it may involve some reduction in focus on the product-market niches within the larger entity.

The trade-offs between breadth and focus in business-unit definition are complex. There are, however, some business-unit definition issues that should be addressed in a review of synergy management. In particular, it is important to raise the following questions:

- Are there some important synergies that are never likely to be realized with the current business-unit definitions? If so, are there alternative definitions that should be considered?

- Are certain synergies harder to achieve because of the manner in which the boundaries around the business units are set up and managed?

There are some circumstances in which coordination between separate businesses is never likely to be achieved, however beneficial it may be for the group. If, for example, the collective net benefits involve costs to one or more units that are hard or impossible to compensate for, the initiative is likely to be blocked. Thus, it may be almost impossible to bring about coordinated production planning between separate units if it involves one or more units shutting their factories and transferring production to another. To avoid the consequent reduction in power and status, the general managers of the units in question will be likely to go to any lengths to block or undermine the initiative. Conclusion: the best way to achieve this synergy benefit will probably be to redefine the business to encompass all the previously separate units, giving responsibility for optimizing performance to a single management team.

Other situations in which managers should consider a redefinition of the businesses to achieve desirable synergies include the following:

- **Deeply embedded hostility and mistrust between senior managers in the different units.** If the rivalry between the general managers of the units is intense, they may simply be unwilling to work together, whatever the benefits. The solution may be to redefine the business units and give responsibility for both of them to one or other of the managers.

- **Hard-to-allocate costs and revenues.** If shared production facilities or the lack of an open third-party market for products traded between the units make it difficult to agree a split of costs and revenues, any form of cooperation is likely to suffer, since underlying disputes about transfer prices and allocated costs will dominate everything else. In such circumstances, it is often better to expand the business definition to include both units, with a single bottom line. Coordination issues then become a means to maximize aggregate profitability rather than the pretext for haggling over how to divide up the results.

- **Need for speedy and continuous resolution of trade-off judgments.** Concerns about contamination and lack of focus have led many companies to create more and more separate profit centres, each with its own management and strategy. This drive for business focus creates major difficulties if the separate businesses need to be in constant touch with each

other and have to resolve a series of difficult day-to-day trade-offs. For example, if two petrochemical businesses share a process plant and continuous decisions about output mix are needed to achieve the optimum overall profitability, taking account of the shifting relative prices of different inputs and of different end products, the two businesses will be locked in constant complex negotiations about how to run the plant. A structure in which a single management team is responsible for optimizing both businesses is likely to work more smoothly.

The underlying issue is whether, for whatever reason, co-ordination between the separate businesses' management teams will always be much less effective than co-ordination under a single management team. Managers should therefore examine the current business-unit boundaries to see if they are preventing any important synergies from taking place. If they are, consider altering the boundaries.

Judgments about whether a redefinition of the businesses is necessary should also reflect the nature of the boundaries. If decentralization contracts emphasize the autonomy of the business heads and provide few incentives or opportunities for them to work together, potential problems resulting from separate business definitions will be magnified. If, however, business heads do not expect to have full control over all the functions and resources they need in their businesses, and work in a context that encourages and requires frequent liaison with colleagues from other businesses and from central functions, the boundaries around the separate businesses will be more naturally permeable. In Canon, for example, business managers are very ready to work on cross-business project teams, to draw on corporate staff support, and to co-ordinate with other businesses: the corporate approach to coordination stresses the connections between the businesses, not the boundaries that separate them. With more permeable boundaries around the businesses, there is more flexibility to make different business definitions work well. With more separation between businesses, there is a greater premium on drawing the boundaries in ways that will internalize linkages that would otherwise become problematic.

Successes and failures

Last, but not least, the effectiveness of the overall approach can be tested in terms of evident successes and failures: well and poorly rated mechanisms and processes, fully and less fully realized synergy opportunities, patterns of success and failure that cast light on organizational strengths and weaknesses.

As part of the audit of the current approach, it is essential to canvas opinion about the effectiveness of the main systems and processes for managing synergies, and of the key staff groups that promote them. Surveys, in-depth discussions or focus groups can bring well-grooved and successful mechanisms into relief and pinpoint areas of friction or dissatisfaction. Poorly rated mechanisms should then be examined more carefully. What are the causes of dissatisfaction? Is it a mechanism for chasing mirages? Are the parenting opportunities on which it is targeted clear, or is it being driven by parenting bias? Is it wasting the time of managers at the centre or in the businesses? Should we consider other ways of intervening to realize the target benefits, or should we simply discontinue our efforts if they are not working?

Another way into the successes and failures analysis is via the synergy opportunities review. Do the unrealized opportunities indicate some underlying gap or shortcoming in our approach? Is there some mismatch between the processes or interventions we use for getting at the opportunities and the nature of the opportunities? If, for example, we are consistently failing to achieve the benefits of better capacity utilization that vertical integration should provide, is this because there is something wrong with our transfer-pricing processes or with our approach to combined investment planning? Or are our business-specific performance measures to blame? Our quest should be to unearth new or different mechanisms for intervening that are better suited for the parenting opportunities open to us, in order to reduce the number of important unrealized opportunities.

We have also found that a retrospective analysis of patterns of success and failure with previous synergy interventions can be useful. Which synergies have we managed well – and probably taken for granted? What notorious initiatives have caused the most trouble and yielded the least benefit? What can we learn from these successes and failures?

By examining the successes, we will be able to see more clearly what mechanisms work best for us. What opportunities have we derived most benefit from? By what means did we realize these opportunities? Answers to these questions will reveal what the organization's well-grooved mechanisms and processes are, and will help to shape thinking about how to tackle new opportunities. By examining the failures, we may discover underlying weaknesses in our skills or processes, or organizational blockages and

synergy killers that lie behind our inability to implement certain types of synergies successfully. A sense of these underlying patterns is useful in assessing the effectiveness of the approach.

Agenda for change

The output from the review should be a short-list of possible new initiatives for more detailed consideration. Since the review is a broadly based stock take, the purpose is to create an agenda of possible changes, not to arrive at firm conclusions about how to move forward. Each of the possible initiatives that emerge from the review will then need to be subjected to detailed scrutiny.

The short-list should embrace:

- high priority unrealized synergy opportunities, including ways to address them;

- changes in underlying strategy or philosophy that may increase the effectiveness of the overall approach;

- changes in specific coordination processes or mechanisms, including elements that should be discontinued because they may be having a damaging effect, as well as new initiatives that should be considered;

- possible changes in business unit definitions.

Prioritization of the ideas that emerge from the review is essential. The front-runners normally select themselves, either because of the size of the potential benefits (or disbenefits) or the strength of feeling among managers. But the cut-off on what to take forward is more a matter for judgment. We have four pieces of advice in forming the judgment.

First, be selective. A focused follow-through on three or four key initiatives is much more likely to yield tangible benefits than a long drawn-out survey of a couple of dozen possibly attractive options. And if the review is not seen to lead on fairly quickly to action, its credibility will suffer and managers will lose enthusiasm.

Second, look forward, not back. Give preference to ideas that anticipate breaking trends and build links that will become increasingly valuable in the future. Avoid focusing on initiatives that deal with yesterday's problems or with issues that are likely to become less significant. Concentrate, for example, on putting in place pricing coordination mechanisms to avoid arbitrage in what will become an increasingly integrated European marketplace. Don't struggle to promote common design and manufacturing of components that more and more of the business units are already tending to outsource.

Third, use your rivals and competitors to guide your sense of priorities. If your main competitors are deriving much more benefit from sharing know-how than you are, move it up your priority list, unless there are good reasons why it is always likely to be less important to you than to them. If others have tried and failed with a shared-purchasing initiative, be cautious about pushing ahead with it. The concern should be with the specific achievements of known competitors, not with current general management fads and fashions. Of course, this presumes a certain level of competitive intelligence, which is not always present. However,

we believe that efforts to find out about competitors' initiatives can play a valuable role in establishing a final short-list.

Fourth, recognize system effects. The five-lenses analysis brings out the connections between different aspects of the synergy approach. Successes and failures often stem from deeply rooted attitudes that underlie the use of certain mechanisms rather than others. Proposals to make changes in a given process or to address a specific opportunity may therefore entail consequential changes in other areas. Consider whether specific initiatives will work in the whole context in which they will be taken; assess the possibility that a systematic change programme to shift the overall culture may be required as a pre-condition for success in specific areas.

REFERENCES

Amit, R. and Livnat, J. (1988) 'Diversification and the Risk-Return Trade-off', *Academy of Management Journal*, 31(1, March), pp. 154–165.

Anslinger, P.L. and Copeland, T.E. (1996) 'Growth Through Acquisitions: A Fresh Look', *Harvard Business Review*, 74(1, January–February), pp. 126–135.

Bartlett, C.A. and Ghoshal, S. (2003) 'What is a Global Manager?', *Harvard Business Review*, 81(8), pp. 101–108.

Baum, J.A.C. and Greve, H.R. (eds) (2001) *Multiunit Organization and Multimarket Strategy*, Vol. 18, Stamford, CT: JAI Press.

Calori, R. and de Woot, P. (eds) (1994) *A European Management Model: Beyond Diversity*, Hemel Hempstead: Prentice Hall.

Campbell, A. and Goold, M. (1998) *Synergy: Why Links Between Business Units Often Fail and How to Make Them Work*, Oxford: Capstone Publishing.

Campbell, A., Goold, M. and Alexander, M. (1995) 'The Value of the Parent Company', *California Management Review*, 38(1, Fall), pp. 79–97.

Cavusgil, S.T., Knight, G., Riesenberger, J.R., Rammal, H.G. and Rose, E.L. (2014) *International Business: The New Realities* (2nd edn), Melbourne: Pearson Australia.

Chatterjee, S. (1986) 'Types of Synergy and Economic Value: The Impact of Acquisitions on Merging and Rival Firms', *Strategic Management Journal*, 7(2, March–April), pp. 119–139.

Eisenhardt, K.M. and Galunic, D.C. (2000) 'Coevolving: At Last, a Way to Make Synergies Work', *Harvard Business Review*, 78(1, January–February), pp. 91–101.

Fieldhouse, D.K. (1978) *Unilever Overseas: The Anatomy of a Multinational 1895–1965*, London: Croom Helm.

Ghoshal, S. and Mintzberg, H. (1994) 'Diversification and Diversifact', *California Management Review*, 37(1, Fall), pp. 8–27.

Goold, M. and Campbell, A. (1987) *Strategies and Styles: The Role of the Centre in Managing Diverse Corporations*, Oxford: Basil Blackwell.

Goold, M. and Lansdell, S. (1997) *Survey of Corporate Strategy Objectives, Concepts and Tools*, Ashridge Strategic Management Centre.

Goold, M., Campbell, A. and Alexander, M. (1994) *Corporate-Level Strategy: Creating Value in the Multibusiness Company*, New York: Wiley.

Hamel, G. and Prahalad, C.K. (1993) 'Strategy as Stretch and Leverage', *Harvard Business Review*, 71(2, March–April), pp. 75–84.

Hamel, G. and Prahalad, C.K. (1994) *Competing for the Future: Breakthrough Strategies for Seizing Control of Your Industry and Creating the Markets of Tomorrow*, Harvard Business School Press.

Harrigan, K.R. (1985) 'Vertical Integration and Corporate Strategy', *Academy of Management Journal*, 28(2, June), pp. 397–425.

Haspeslagh, P. (1982) 'Portfolio Planning: Uses and Limits', *Harvard Business Review*, 60(1, January–February), pp. 58–73.

Hedley, B. (1977) 'Strategy and the "Business Portfolio"', *Long Range Planning*, 10(1, February), pp. 9–15.

Helfat, C.E. and Eisenhardt, K.M. (2004) 'Inter-temporal Economies of Scope, Organizational Modularity, and the Dynamics of Diversification', *Strategic Management Journal*, 25(13), pp. 1217–1296.

Henderson, B.D. (1979) *On Corporate Strategy*, Cambridge, MA: Abt Books.

Hofer, C. and Schendel, D. (1978) *Strategy Formulation: Analytical Concepts*, St. Paul: West.

Hofstede, G. (1993) 'Cultural Constraints in Management Theories', *Academy of Management Executive*, 7(1), pp. 8–21.

Jayachandran, S., Gimeno, J. and Varadarajan, P.R. (1999) 'Theory of Multimarket Competition: A Synthesis and Implications for Marketing Strategy', *Journal of Marketing*, 63(3), pp. 49–66.

Kaplan, S. (1989) 'The Effects of Management Buyouts on Operating Performance and Value', *Journal of Financial Economics*, 24(2, October), pp. 217–254.

Kono, T. (1999) 'A Strong Head Office Makes a Strong Company', *Long Range Planning*, 32(2), pp. 225–236.

Lawrence, P.R. and Lorsch, J.W. (1967) *Organization and Environment,* Cambridge, MA: Harvard University Press.

Long, W.F. and Ravenscraft, D.J. (1993) 'Decade of Debt: Lessons from LBOs in the 1980s', in: M.M. Blair (ed.) *The Deal Decade: What Takeovers and Leveraged Buyouts Mean for Corporate Governance*, Washington: Brookings Institution.

Lubatkin, M. and Chatterjee, S. (1994) 'Extending Modern Portfolio Theory into the Domain of Corporate Diversification: Does It Apply?', *Academy of Management Journal*, 37(1), pp. 109–136.

Mahoney, J.T. (1992) 'The Choice of Organizational Form: Vertical Financial Ownership versus Other Methods of Vertical Integration', *Strategic Management Journal*, 13(8), pp. 559–584.

Miyashita, K. and Russell, D. (1994) *Keiretsu. Inside the Hidden Japanese Conglomerates*, Maidenhead: McGraw Hill.

Morikawa, H. (1992). *Zaibatsu: The Rise and Fall of Family Enterprise Groups in Japan*. Tokyo: University of Tokyo Press.

Perlmutter, H.V. (1969) 'The Tortuous Evolution of Multi-National Enterprises', *Columbia Journal of World Business*, 1, pp. 9–18.

Porter, M.E. (1987) 'From Competitive Advantage to Corporate Strategy', *Harvard Business Review*, 65(3, May–June), pp. 43–59.

Porter, M.E. (ed.) (1986) *Competition in Global Industries*, Harvard Business Press.

Prahalad, C.K. and Bettis, R.A. (1986) 'The Dominant Logic: A New Linkage Between Diversity and Performance', *Strategic Management Journal*, 7(6, November–December), pp. 485–601.

Prahalad, C.K. and Doz, Y. (1987) *The Multinational Mission: Balancing Local Demands and Global Vision*, New York: Free Press.

Prahalad, C.K. and Hamel, G. (1990) 'The Core Competence of the Corporation', *Harvard Business Review*, 68(3, May–June), pp. 79–91.

Ramachandran, J., Manikandan, K.S. and Pant, A. (2013) 'Why Conglomerates Thrive (Outside the U.S.)', *Harvard Business Review*, 91(12), 110–119.

Ramanujam, V. and Varadarajan, P. (1989) 'Research on Corporate Diversification: A Synthesis', *Strategic Management Journal*, 10(6, November–December), pp. 523–551.

Raynor, M.E. and Bower, J.L. (2001) 'Lead from the Center: How to Manage Diverse Businesses', *Harvard Business Review*, 80(5, May), pp. 93–100.

Rumelt, R.P. (1974) *Strategy, Structure, and Economic Performance,* Cambridge, MA: Harvard University Press.

Rumelt, R.P. (1982) 'Diversification Strategy and Profitability', *Strategic Management Journal*, 3(4, October–December), pp. 359–369.

Seth, A. (1990) 'Value Creation in Acquisitions: A Re-Examination of Performance Issues', *Strategic Management Journal*, 11(2, February), pp. 99–115.

Sirower, M.L. (1997) *The Synergy Trap: How Companies Lose the Acquisition Game*, New York: Free Press.

Stalk, G., Evans, P. and Schulman, L.E. (1992) 'Competing on Capabilities: The New Rules of Corporate Strategy', *Harvard Business Review*, 70(2, March–April), pp. 57–69.

Steers, R.M., Shin, Y.K. and Ungson, G.R. (1991) *The Chaebol: Korea's New Industrial Might*, New York: Harper Collins.

Suetorsak, R. (2007) 'Keiretsu and Risk: An Examination of the Risk Exposure of Keiretsu Banks in Japan', *Journal of Economics and Finance*, 31(2), 268–282.

Trautwein, F. (1990) 'Merger Motives and Merger Prescriptions', *Strategic Management Journal*, 11(4, May–June), pp. 283–295.

Verluyten, S.P. (2000) *Intercultural Communication in Business and Organisations*, Leuven: Acco.

Weston, J.F., Chung, K.S. and Hoag, S.E. (1990) *Mergers, Restructuring, and Corporate Control*, Englewood Cliffs, NJ: Prentice Hall.

Williamson, O.E. (1975) *Markets and Hierarchies: Analysis and Antitrust Implications*, New York: Free Press.

Yergin, D. (2011) *The Quest. Energy, Security and the Remaking of the Modern World*, New York: Penguin Books.

NETWORK LEVEL STRATEGY

When bad men combine, the good must associate; else they will fall, one by one, an unpitied sacrifice in a contemptible struggle.

Edmund Burke (1729–1797) British political writer

INTRODUCTION

A business unit can have a strategy, while a group of business units can also have a strategy together – this joint course of action at the divisional or corporate level was discussed in the previous chapter. What has not been examined yet, is whether a group of companies can also have a strategy together. Is it possible that companies do not develop their strategies in 'splendid isolation', but rather coordinate their strategies to operate as a team? And is it a good idea for firms to link up with others for a prolonged period of time to try to achieve shared objectives together?

Where two or more firms move beyond a mere transactional relationship and work jointly towards a common goal, they form an alliance, partnership or network. Their shared strategy is referred to as a network level strategy. In such a case, strategy is not only 'concerned with relating a firm to its environment', as was stated in Chapter 4, but also with relating a network to its broader environment.

The existence of networks does raise a range of questions, not the least of which is whether they make strategic sense or not. Is it beneficial to engage in long-term collaborative relationships with other firms or is it more advantageous for firms to 'keep their distance' and to interact with one another in a more market-like, transactional way? Is it viable to manage a web of partnership relations or is it preferable to keep it simple, by having the firm operate more or less independently? To address these questions is to raise the issue of inter-organizational relationships – what should be the nature of the relationship between a firm and other organizations in its surroundings? This issue will be the focus of further discussion in this chapter.

THE ISSUE OF INTER-ORGANIZATIONAL RELATIONSHIPS

No firm exists that is autarchic. All firms must necessarily interact with other organizations (and individuals) in their environment and therefore they have inter-organizational (or inter-firm) relationships. These relationships can evolve without any clear strategic intent or tactical calculation, but most managers agree that actively determining the nature of their external relations is a significant part of what strategizing is about. Even avoiding relations with some external parties can be an important strategic choice.

FIGURE 6.1   Aspects of inter-organizational relations

To gain a better understanding of the interaction between firms, four aspects are of particular importance and will be reviewed here – the who, why, what and how of inter-organizational relationships (see Figure 6.1). The first aspect is the question of who – who are the potential counterparts with whom a firm can actually have a relationship? This is referred to as the topic of 'relational actors'. The second aspect is the question of why – why do the parties want to enter into a relationship with one another? This is referred to as the topic of 'relational objectives'. The third aspect is the question of what – what type of influences determine the nature of the relationship? This is referred to as the topic of 'relational factors'. The fourth aspect is the question of how – how can relationships be structured into a particular organizational form to let them function in the manner intended? This is referred to as the topic of 'relational arrangements'.

Relational actors

In Figure 6.2 an overview is given of the eight major groups of external parties with whom the firm can, or must, interact. A distinction has been made between industry and contextual actors. The industry actors are those individuals and organizations that perform value-adding activities or consume the outputs of these activities. The contextual actors are those parties whose behaviour, intentionally or unintentionally, sets the conditions under which the industry actors must operate. The four main categories of relationships between the firm and other industry parties are the following (e.g. Porter, 1980; Reve, 1990):

■ Upstream vertical (supplier) relations. Every company has suppliers of some sort. In a narrow definition these include the providers of raw materials, parts, machinery and business services. In a broader definition the providers of all production factors (land, capital, labour, technology, information and entrepreneurship) can be seen as suppliers, if they are not part of the firm itself. All these suppliers can either be the actual producers of the input, or an intermediary (distributor or agent) trading in the product or service. Besides the suppliers with which the firm transacts directly (first-tier suppliers), the firm may also have relationships with suppliers further upstream in the industry. All these relationships are traditionally referred to as upstream vertical relations, because economists commonly draw the industry system as a column.

■ Downstream vertical (buyer) relations. On the output side, the firm has relationships with its customers. These clients can either be the actual users of the product or service, or intermediaries trading the output. Besides the buyers with which the firm transacts directly, it may also have relationships with parties further downstream in the industry column.

■ Direct horizontal (industry insider) relations. This category includes the relations between the firm and other industry incumbents. Because these competitors produce similar goods or services, they are said to be at the same horizontal level in the industry column.

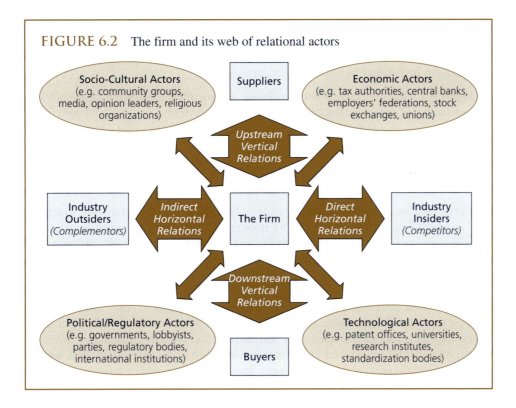

FIGURE 6.2   The firm and its web of relational actors

- **Indirect horizontal (industry outsider) relations.** Where a firm has a relationship with a company outside its industry, this is referred to as an indirect horizontal relation. Commonly, companies will have relationships with the producers of complementary goods and services (e.g. hardware manufacturers with software developers). Such a relationship can develop with the producer of a substitute good or service, either as an adversary or as an ally. A relationship can also exist between a firm and a potential industry entrant, whereby the incumbent firm can assist or attempt to block the entry of the industry outsider. Furthermore, a firm can establish a relationship with a firm in another industry, with the intention of diversifying into that, or a third, industry. In reality, where industry boundaries are not clear, the distinction between direct and indirect horizontal relations is equally blurry.

Besides relationships with these industry actors, there can be many contacts with condition-setting parties in the broader environment. Employing the classic SEPTember distinction, the following rough categories of contextual actors can be identified:

- **Socio-cultural actors.** Individuals or organizations that have a significant impact on societal values, norms, beliefs and behaviours may interact with the firm. These could include the media, community groups, charities, religious organizations and opinion leaders.

- **Economic actors.** There can also be organizations influencing the general economic state of affairs, with which the firm interacts. Among others, tax authorities, central banks, employers' federations, stock exchanges and unions may be of importance.

- **Political/legal actors.** The firm may also interact with organizations setting or influencing the regulations under which companies must operate. These could include governments, political parties, special interest groups, regulatory bodies and international institutions.

■ Technological actors. There are also many organizations that influence the pace and direction of technological development and the creation of new knowledge. Among others, universities, research institutes, patent offices, government agencies and standardization bodies may be important to deal with.

As Figure 6.2 visualizes, companies can choose, but are often also forced, to interact with a large number of organizations and individuals in the environment. This configuration of external actors with which the organization interacts is referred to as the company's group of 'external stakeholders'.

Relational objectives

How organizations deal with one another is strongly influenced by what they hope to achieve (e.g. Dyer and Singh, 1998; Preece, 1995). Both parties may have clear, open and mutually beneficial objectives, but it is also possible that one or both actors have poorly defined intentions, hidden agendas and/or mutually exclusive goals. Moreover, it is not uncommon that various people within an organization have different, even conflicting, objectives and expectations with regard to an external relationship (e.g. Allison, 1969; Doz and Hamel, 1998).

Where two or more firms seek to work together with one another, they generally do so because they expect some value added – they assume more benefit from the interaction than if they had proceeded on their own. This expectation of value creation as a driver for cooperation was also discussed in Chapter 5, where two or more business units worked together to reap synergies. In fact, the same logic is at play between business units and between companies. In both cases, managers are oriented towards finding sources of added value in a potential relationship with another – either across business unit boundaries or across company boundaries. Hence, the same sources of synergy identified in the discussion on corporate level strategy are just as relevant when examining the objectives for inter-organizational cooperation (see Figure 6.3).

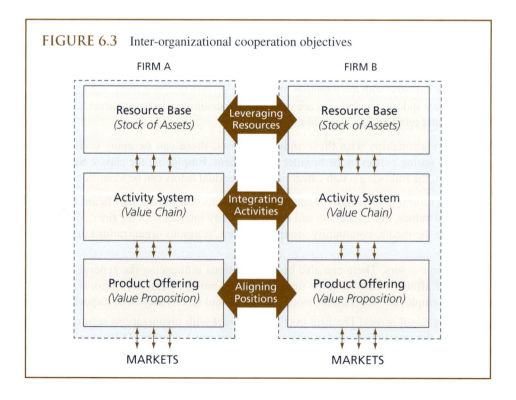

FIGURE 6.3   Inter-organizational cooperation objectives

Relations oriented towards leveraging resources. The first area where companies can cooperate is at the level of their resource bases. By sharing resources with one another, companies can improve either the quantity or quality of the resources they have at their disposal. There are two general ways for firms to leverage resources to reap mutual benefit:

- Learning. When the objective is to exchange knowledge and skills, or to engage in the joint pursuit of new know-how, the relationship is said to be learning-oriented. Firms can enter into new learning relationships with industry outsiders, but can also team up with industry incumbents, for instance to develop new technologies or standards (e.g. Hamel, Doz and Prahalad, 1989, Reading 6.1; Shapiro and Varian, 1998). However, firms can add a learning objective to an already existing relationship with a buyer or supplier as well.

- Lending. Where one firm owns specific resources that it cannot make full use of, or another firm can make better use of, it can be attractive for both to lend the resource to the other. Lending relationships happen frequently in the areas of technology, copyrights and trademarks, where licensing is commonplace. But physical resources can also be lent, usually in the form of lease contracts. In all cases the benefit to lenders can be financial or they receive other resources in return.

Relations oriented towards integrating activities. The second area where companies can cooperate is at the level of their activity systems. Few companies can span an entire industry column from top to bottom and excel at every type of activity. Usually, by integrating their value chains with other organizations, firms can be much more efficient and effective than if they were totally separated. There are two general ways for firms to integrate their activities with others:

- Linking. The most common type of relationship in business is the vertical link between a buyer and a seller. All relationships in which products or services are exchanged fall into this category. Most firms have many linking relationships, both upstream and downstream, because they want to focus on only a limited number of value-adding activities, but need a variety of inputs, as well as clients to purchase their finished goods.

- Lumping. Where firms bring together their similar activities to gain economies of scale, the relationship is said to be oriented towards lumping. Sharing operations (e.g. airline alliances), sales infrastructure (e.g. software cross-selling deals), logistics systems (e.g. postal partnerships) or payment facilities (e.g. inter-bank settlement agreements) are examples of where firms can lump their activities together. Because the activities need to be more or less the same to be able to reap scale economies, lumping relationships are usually found between two or more industry insiders.

Relations oriented towards aligning positions. The third area where companies can cooperate is at the level of their market positions. Even where companies want to keep their value-adding activities separate, they can coordinate their moves in the environment with the intention of strengthening each other's position. Usually, this type of coalition-building is directed at improving the joint bargaining power of the cooperating parties. These position-enhancing relationships can be further subdivided into two categories:

- Leaning. Where two or more firms get together to improve their bargaining position vis-à-vis other industry actors, it is said that they lean on each other to stand stronger. Leaning can be directed at building up a more powerful negotiation position towards suppliers, or to offer a more attractive package of products and services towards buyers. Getting together with other companies to form a consortium to launch a new industry standard can also bolster the position of all companies involved. At the same time, the cooperation can be directed at weakening the position of an alternative group of companies or even heightening the entry barriers for interested industry outsiders.

■ Lobbying. Firms can also cooperate with one another with the objective of gaining a stronger position vis-à-vis contextual actors. Such lobbying relationships are often directed at strengthening the firms' voice towards political and regulatory actors, such as governments and regulatory agencies. However, firms can get together to put pressure on various other contextual actors, such as standard setting bodies, universities, tax authorities and stock exchanges.

In practice, cooperative relationships between organizations can involve a number of these objectives simultaneously. Moreover, it is not uncommon for objectives to shift over time and for various participants in the relationship to have different objectives.

Relational factors

How inter-organizational relationships develop is strongly influenced by the objectives pursued by the parties involved. However, a number of other factors also have an impact on how relationships unfold. These relational factors can be grouped into four general categories (e.g. Gulati, 1998; Mitchell, Agle and Wood, 1997):

■ Legitimacy. Relationships are highly impacted by what is deemed to be legitimate. Written and unwritten codes of conduct give direction to what is viewed as acceptable behaviour. Which topics are allowed on the agenda, who has a valid claim, how interaction should take place and how conflicts should be resolved, are often decided by what both parties accept as 'the rules of engagement'. There is said to be 'trust', where it is expected that the other organization or individual will adhere to these rules. However, organizations do not always agree on 'appropriate behaviour', while what is viewed as legitimate can shift over time as well. It can also be (seen as) advantageous to act opportunistically by not behaving according to the unwritten rules (e.g. Gambetta, 1988; Williamson, 1991).

■ Urgency. Inter-organizational relations are also shaped by the factor 'timing'. Relationships develop differently when one or both parties are under time pressure to achieve results, as opposed to a situation where both organizations can interact without experiencing a sense of urgency (e.g. James, 1985; Pfeffer and Salancik, 1978).

■ Frequency. Inter-organizational relations also depend on the frequency of interaction and the expectation of future interactions. Where parties expect to engage in a one-off transaction they usually behave differently than when they anticipate a more structural relationship extending over multiple interactions. Moreover, a relationship with a low rate of interaction tends to develop differently than one with a high regularity of interaction (e.g. Axelrod, 1984; Dixit and Nalebuff, 1991).

■ Power. Last but not least, relations between organizations are strongly shaped by the power held by both parties. Power is the ability to influence others' behaviour and organizations can have many sources of power. Most importantly for inter-organizational relationships, a firm can derive power from having resources that the other organization requires. In relationships with a very high level of resource dependence, firms tend to behave differently towards each other than when they are interdependent or relatively independent of one another (e.g. Pfeffer and Salancik, 1978; Porter, 1980).

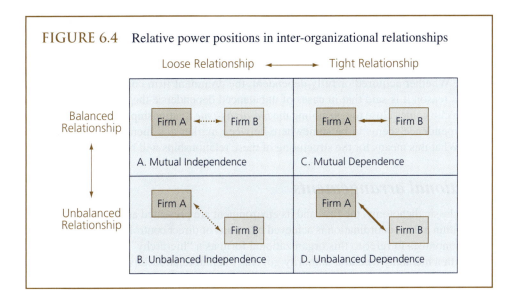

FIGURE 6.4   Relative power positions in inter-organizational relationships

Especially the impact of power differences on inter-organizational relationships is given extensive attention in the strategic management literature. Many authors (e.g. Chandler, 1990; Kay, 1993; Pfeffer and Salancik, 1978; Porter, 1980; Schelling, 1960) stress that for understanding the interaction between firms it is of the utmost importance to gain insight into their relative power positions. One way of measuring relative power in a relationship is portrayed in Figure 6.4, where a distinction is made between the closeness of the relationship (loose vs tight) and the distribution of power between the two parties involved (balanced vs unbalanced). This leads to a categorization of four specific types of inter-firm relationships from the perspective of relative power position. These four categories (adapted from Ruigrok and Van Tulder, 1995) are:

A Mutual independence. Organizations are independent in a relationship if they have full freedom to act according to their own objectives. Independence in an inter-organizational relationship means that organizations will only interact on their own terms and that they have the ability to break off the relationship without any penalty. In a situation of mutual independence, neither organization has significant influence over the other.

B Unbalanced independence. When two organizations work together in a loose relationship, one side (Firm A) can have more power than the other (Firm B). In such a case, it is said that Firm A is more independent than Firm B – Firm A's power gives it more freedom to act, while Firm B can be influenced by the powerful Firm A. This situation is called unbalanced independence, as both sides are independent, but one more so than the other.

C Mutual dependence. Two organizations can have a tight relationship, in which they are mutually dependent, while having an equal amount of sway over their counterpart. This type of situation, where there is a substantial, yet balanced, relationship between two or more parties, is also called interdependence.

D Unbalanced dependence. Where a tight relationship is characterized by asymmetrical dependence, one party will be able to dominate the other. In this situation of unbalanced dependence, the organization with the lower level of dependence will have more freedom to manoeuvre and impose its conditions than its counterpart.

The first category, mutual independence, is what is typically expected of a *market* relationship, although it is not strange to also witness market relationships that fit more in the second category, unbalanced independence. At the other extreme, unbalanced dependence is very close to the situation that would occur if the dominant firm acquired its counterpart. Whether acquired or fully dependent, the dominant firm controls its behaviour. For this reason it is said that in cases of unbalanced dependence the inter-organizational relationship comes close to resembling the *hierarchy-type* relationship found within a firm. Interdependence seems to be somewhere between market and hierarchy-type relationships. What this means for the structuring of these relationships will be examined below.

Relational arrangements

In the classic dichotomy, the firm and its environment are presented as rather distinct entities. Within a firm, coordination is achieved by means of direct control, leading transaction cost economists to refer to this organizational form as a "hierarchy" (Williamson, 1975, 1985). In a hierarchy a central authority governs internal relationships and has the formal power to coordinate strategy and solve inter-departmental disputes. In the environment, relationships between firms are non-hierarchical, as they interact with one another without any explicit coordination or dispute settlement mechanism. This organizational form is referred to as a 'market'.

In Chapter 5 it was argued that there are all types of activities that companies should not want to internalize and run themselves, but should leave up to the marketplace. In many situations, it is much more efficient to buy inputs in the market than to make them yourself – where activities are performed by autonomous parties and outputs are sold in the marketplace, costs will often be lowest. As summarized by Ouchi (1980, p. 130), "In a market relationship, the transaction takes place between the two parties and is mediated by a price mechanism in which the existence of a competitive market reassures both parties that the terms of exchange are equitable".

Integration of activities into the firm is only necessary where 'markets do not function properly' – where doing it yourself is cheaper or better. The firm must internalize activities, despite the disadvantages of hierarchy, where the 'invisible hand' of the market cannot be trusted to be equitable and effective. Control over activities by means of formal authority – the 'visible hand' – is needed under these conditions. This is particularly true of all of the synergy advantages mentioned in Chapter 5 that the corporation would not be able to reap if the various business activities were not brought together under one 'corporate roof'.

In reality, however, there are many organizational forms between markets and hierarchies (e.g. Hakansson and Johanson, 1993; Powell, 1990; Thorelli, 1986). These are the networks, partnerships or alliances introduced at the start of this chapter. In networks, strategies are coordinated and disputes resolved, not through formal top-down power, but by mutual adaptation. To extend the above metaphor, networks rely neither on the visible nor invisible hand to guide relationships, but rather employ the 'continuous handshake' (Gerlach, 1992).

The organizations involved in networks can employ different sorts of collaborative arrangements to structure their ties with one another. In Figure 6.5, an overview of a number of common types of collaborative arrangements is presented. Two major distinctions are made in this overview. First, between bilateral arrangements, which only involve two parties, and multilateral arrangements, which involve three or more. Commonly, only the multilateral arrangements are referred to as networks, although here the term is employed to cover all groupings of two or more cooperating firms. The second distinction is between non-contractual, contractual and equity-based arrangements. Noncontractual arrangements are cooperative agreements that are not binding by law, while contractual arrangements do have a clear legal enforceability. Neither, however, involve taking a financial stake in each other or in a new joint venture, while the equity-based arrangements do.

FIGURE 6.5 Examples of collaborative arrangements

	Non-Contractual Arrangements	Contractual Arrangements	Equity-based Arrangements
Multilateral Arrangements	• Lobbying coalition (e.g. European Roundtable of Industrialists) • Joint standard setting (e.g. Linux coalition) • Learning communities (e.g. Strategic Management Society)	• Research consortium (e.g. Symbian in PDAs) • International marketing alliance (e.g. Star Alliance in airlines) • Export partnership (e.g. Netherlands Export Combination)	• Shared payment system (e.g. Visa) • Construction consortium (e.g. Eurotunnel) • Joint reservation system (e.g. Galileo)
Bilateral Arrangements	• Cross-selling deal (e.g. between pharmaceutical firms) • R&D staff exchange (e.g. between IT firms) • Market information sharing agreement (e.g. between hardware and software makers)	• Licensing agreement (e.g. Disney and Coca-Cola) • Co-development contract (e.g. Disney and Pixar in movies) • Co-branding alliance (e.g. Coca-Cola and McDonald's)	• New product joint venture (e.g. Sony and Ericsson in cellphones) • Cross-border joint venture (e.g. Daimler-Benz and Beijing Automotive) • Local joint venture (e.g. CNN Turk in Turkey)

The intent of these collaborative arrangements is to profit from some of the advantages of vertical and horizontal integration, without incurring their costs. Networks are actually hybrid organizational forms that attempt to combine the benefits of hierarchy with the benefits of the market. The main benefits of hierarchy are those associated with the structural coordination of activities. In non-market relational arrangements, all parties collaborate on a more long-term basis with the intent of realizing a common goal. They will organize procedures, routines and control systems to ensure effective and efficient functioning of their joint activities and a smooth transition at their organizational interfaces. The benefits of the market that these collaborative arrangements retain are flexibility and motivation. By not being entirely locked into a fixed hierarchy, individual firms can flexibly have multiple relationships of varying length and intensity, and can change these relationships more easily where circumstances require adaptation. The market also provides the motivation to be efficient and to optimize the pursuit of the organization's self-interest. This entrepreneurial incentive can be a strong spur for risk-taking, innovation and change.

A significant advantage of collaborative arrangements is that such relationships facilitate the process of 'co-specialization'. Much of humanity's economic progress is based on the principle of specialization by means of a division of labour. As people and firms focus more closely on performing a limited set of value-adding activities, they become more effective and efficient in their work. This division of labour assumes, however, that the value-adding activities that are outsourced by one become the specialization of another, hence co-specialization. Yet, many activities cannot be outsourced to outsiders on the basis of normal market relations, either due to the risk of dependence or because of the need for the structural coordination of activities. Under these conditions, collaborative arrangements can act as a synthesis of hierarchy and market relations, thus catalysing the process of specialization (e.g. Axelsson and Easton, 1992; Best, 1990).

Such co-specialization can progress to such an extent that clusters of firms work together in more or less permanent networks. Such symbiotic groups of collaborating firms can actually function as 'virtual corporations' (e.g. Chesbrough and Teece, 1996; Quinn, 1992). In such networks, the relationships between the participating firms are often very tight and durable, based on a high level of trust and perceived mutual interest. While each organization retains its individual identity, the boundaries between them become fuzzy, blurring the clear distinction between 'the organization' and 'its environment'. When a high level of trust and reciprocity has been achieved, relations can move far beyond simple contractual obligations. The collaborative relations can become more open-ended, with objectives, responsibilities, authority and results not fully determined in advance in a written contract, but evolving over time, given all parties' sincere willingness to 'work on their relationship' (e.g. Jarillo, 1988; Kanter, 1994).

While the intention of collaborative arrangements may be to blend the advantages of hierarchy with the qualities of the market, it is also possible that the weaknesses of both are actually combined. The main weakness of hierarchy is bureaucracy – creating red tape, unnecessary coordination activities and dulling the incentive to perform. In reality, collaborative arrangements might be mechanisms for structuring static relationships and dampening entrepreneurial behaviour. A further danger is that the mutual dependence might become skewed, shifting the balance of power to one of the partners. Under such conditions, one or more organizations can become dependent on a dominant party, without much influence (voice) or the possibility to break off the relationship (exit). Such unbalanced dependency relationships (see Figure 6.4) might be a great benefit for the stronger party, but can easily lead to the predominance of its interests over the interests of the weaker partners (e.g. Oliver and Wilkinson, 1988; Ruigrok and Van Tulder, 1995).

Simultaneously, such partnerships are vulnerable to the main disadvantage of the market, namely opportunism. Companies run the risk of opportunism, which is (according to Williamson, 1985: 47):

> ... *self-interest seeking with guile. This includes but is scarcely limited to more blatant forms, such as lying, stealing and cheating ... More generally, opportunism refers to the incomplete or distorted disclosure of information, especially to calculated efforts to mislead, distort, disguise, obfuscate, or otherwise confuse.*

Such behaviour can be limited by clearly defining objectives, responsibilities, authority and expected results ahead of time, preferably in an explicit contract. Even then collaborative arrangements expose companies to the risk of deception, the abuse of trust and the exploitation of dependence, making their use by no means undisputed.

THE PARADOX OF COMPETITION AND COOPERATION

We have no eternal allies and we have no perpetual enemies. Our interests are eternal and perpetual, and those interests it is our duty to follow.
Lord Palmerston (Henry John Temple) (1784–1865); British prime minister

When former CEO of KLM Royal Dutch Airlines, Pieter Bouw, teamed up with Northwest Airlines in 1989, he was thrilled to have the first major transatlantic strategic alliance in the industry, involving joint flights, marketing and sales activities, catering, ground handling, maintenance and purchasing. Northwest was the fourth largest American carrier at that time, but was in 'Chapter 11', balanced on the verge of bankruptcy, and in dire need of cash. To help their new ally, KLM gave a US$400 million capital injection, in return for 20 per cent of the shares and the option to increase this to a majority stake within a few years. KLM and Northwest were on their way to becoming a virtual transatlantic company – a marriage 'made in the heavens'.

Commercially the deal was a success, but relationally the alliance was a Shakespearean drama. KLM gave up its hopes of an alliance with Swissair, SAS and Delta to remain loyal to Northwest, but as soon as Northwest emerged from Chapter 11, it blocked KLM's efforts to increase its shareholding. In the resulting two-year legal shooting match between 1995 and 1997, relations deteriorated sharply and the goose laid the golden eggs was threatened to be killed in the cross fire. Disappointed and dismayed, Bouw decided to give in, selling Northwest back its shares in return for a prolongation of the alliance, after which he immediately resigned. His successor, Leo van Wijk, has managed the alliance since then and it is still 'up in the air', in both senses of the expression. His most important conclusion has been that a collaborative alliance is not only about working together towards a common interest, but equally about being assertive with regard to one's own interests. Alliances are not only *cooperative*, but also have *competitive* aspects.

What this example of KLM and Northwest illustrates is that firms constantly struggle with the tension created by the need to work together with others, while simultaneously needing to pursue their own interests. Firms cannot isolate themselves from their environments, but must actively engage in relationships with suppliers and buyers, while selectively teaming up with other firms inside and outside their industry to attain mutual benefit. But while they are collaborating to create joint value, firms are also each other's rivals when it comes to dividing the benefits. These opposite demands placed on organizations are widely referred to as the pressures for competition and cooperation (e.g. Brandenburger and Nalebuff, 1996; Lado, Boyd and Hanlon, 1997). In the following sections both pressures will be examined in more detail.

The demand for inter-organizational competition

Competition can be defined as the act of working against others, where two or more organizations' goals are mutually exclusive. In other words, competition is the rivalry behaviour exhibited by organizations or individuals where one's win is the other's loss.

Organizations need to be competitive in their relationships with others. As the interests or objectives of different organizations are often mutually exclusive, each organization needs to be determined and assertive in pursuing its own agenda. Each organization needs to be willing to confront others to secure its own interests. Without the will to engage in competitive interaction, the organization will be at the mercy of more aggressive counterparts, e.g. suppliers will charge excessively for products, buyers will express stiff demands for low prices, governments will require special efforts without compensation, and rival firms will poach from among existing customers. Taking a competitive posture towards these external parties means that the organization is determined to assert its own interests and fight where necessary.

The resulting competitive relations can vary between open antagonism and conflict on the one hand, and more subtle forms of friction, tension and strain on the other. Blatant competitive behaviour is often exhibited towards organizations whose objectives are fully in conflict – most clearly other producers of the same goods, attempting to serve the same markets (aptly referred to as 'the competition'). Highly competitive behaviour can also be witnessed where a supplier and a buyer confront each other for dominance in the industry value chain (e.g. Porter, 1980; Van Tulder and Junne, 1988). A more restrained competitive stance can be observed where organizations' objectives are less at odds, but assertiveness is still important to protect the organization's interests. Negotiation and bargaining will commonly be employed under these circumstances.

To be competitive an organization must have the power to overcome its rivals and it must have the ability and will to use its power. Many factors shape the power of an organization, but its relative level of resource dependence is one of the most important determining elements. The more independent the organization, and the more others are dependent on it, the more power the organization will wield. In competitive relationships, manoeuvring the other party into a relatively dependent position is a common approach. In general, calculation, bargaining, manoeuvring, building coalitions and outright conflict are all characteristic of the competitive interaction between organizations.

The demand for inter-organizational cooperation

Cooperation can be defined as the act of working together with others, where two or more organizations' goals are mutually beneficial. In other words, cooperation is the collaborative behaviour exhibited by organizations or individuals where both sides need each other to succeed.

Organizations need to be cooperative in their relationships with others. The interests or objectives of different organizations are often complementary and working together can be mutually beneficial. Therefore, organizations must be willing to behave as partners, striving towards their common good. Without the will to engage in cooperative interaction, the organization will miss the opportunity to reap the advantages of joint efforts, e.g. developing new products together with suppliers, creating a better service offering together with buyers, improving the knowledge infrastructure together with government and setting new technical standards together with other firms in the industry. Taking a cooperative posture towards these external parties means that the organization is determined to leverage its abilities through teamwork.

The resulting cooperative relations can vary between occasional alliances on the one hand, to tight-knit, virtual integration on the other. Strongly cooperative behaviour can be witnessed where the long-term interests of all parties are highly intertwined. This type of symbiotic relationship can be found between the producers of complementary goods and services, where success by one organization will positively impact its partners – aptly referred to as the "network effect" (Arthur, 1994; Shapiro and Varian, 1998). Highly cooperative behaviour can also be observed where suppliers and buyers face a joint challenge (such as government regulation, an innovative technology or a new market entrant) that can only be tackled by significant mutual commitment to a shared objective.

More restrained cooperative behaviour is common where there is potential for a 'positive sum game', but some parties seek to optimize their own returns to the detriment of others. Under such circumstances, exhibiting cooperative behaviour does not mean being naive or weak, but creating conditions under which the long-term shared interests prevail over the short-term temptation by some to cheat their partners. An important ingredient for overcoming the lure of opportunism is to build long-term commitment to one another, not only in words and mentality, but also practically, through a high level of interdependence. Where organizations are closely linked to one another, the pay-off for cooperative behaviour is usually much more enticing than the possibility to profit from the dependence of one's partner. But to be willing to commit to such a high level of interdependence, people on both sides of a relationship need to trust each other's intentions and actions, while there must be coordination and conflict-resolution mechanisms in place to solve evolving issues (e.g. Dyer, Kale and Singh, 2001; Simonin, 1997).

EXHIBIT 6.1   SHORT CASE

ETIHAD: COOPERATING AGAINST ALLIANCES

If a passenger makes an intercontinental flight, chances are high she/he will end up transferring somewhere in the Gulf area. Instead of international airlines which rely mostly on travellers going to and from their home countries, the Gulf's 'super-connectors' attract passengers from all over the world to change planes at the carriers' hub airports. Thanks to geography and pro-aviation government policies, three giants in the commercial airline industry manage to pull this off. Two of these, Emirates and Qatar Airways, follow similar strategies. With home bases in big cities, Dubai and Doha respectively, the streamlined airlines pursue organic growth by slowly expanding their fleet and destinations. Etihad, the youngest of the Gulf trio, takes the road less travelled.

Set up in 2003 by royal decree, Etihad Airways is the second flag carrier of the United Arab Emirates and is the carrier of Abu Dhabi. But what is a flagship without a decent fleet? A US$8 billion order for five Boeing 777s and 24 Airbus aircraft in 2004 was followed by the largest aircraft order in the history of commercial aviation in 2008. A US$43 billion order included the effective purchase of 100 airplanes. Etihad does not call itself the fastest-growing airline in commercial aviation history for nothing. Today, Abu Dhabi's carrier serves 117 destinations with over 120 aeroplanes, resulting in revenues close to US$10 billion.

James Hogan, a bullish Australian who earned his spurs at British Midland International and Gulf Air, can be held responsible for Etihad's reach for the sky. He was personally plucked by Abu Dhabi's government in 2006 to oversee the expansion of Etihad as its CEO. Etihad started decades after its major competitors, so how can it catch up? When airlines from one region are arguably heavily funded by their oil-rich governments and manage to scoop up global traffic, this does not create friends; not among governments abroad nor among competing airlines. Europe does not have Open Skies treaties with the United Arab Emirates and there are no plans to sign any. When Etihad tried to join the major global alliances – Star Alliance, Sky Team

and OneWorld – it discovered there were no membership options for the airline. Nevertheless, Hogan decided to follow a partnership strategy – albeit an aggressive one.

Hogan pursues investments in minority stakes in struggling regional carriers operating in key strategic markets. Restrictions on foreign ownership of airlines prevent Etihad from gaining total control, but these partners do serve to create closer bonds and gain benefits. Etihad currently has shares in Virgin Australia, Air Berlin, India's Jet Airways, Air Serbia, Alitalia, Aer Lingus and a stake in a Swiss regional carrier it renamed Etihad Regional. With 'skin in the game', as Etihad calls it, these investments open doors to new network alignment and timetable coordination. They also help Etihad to get more passengers and cargo through its Abu Dhabi hub and to feed them into its long-haul routes. As regulations limit the number of destinations – and flights – per country the Gulf carrier is allowed to serve, these partners can fly from secondary cities and connect them to Abu Dhabi instead. The poorly connected cities served by these partners, such as Leipzig and Florence, can now bring passengers to Etihad's hub; creating a web of Etihad services as a result.

This strategy is not without risks however. Etihad is not actually able to grab the joystick and control its partners; it is limited to a hands-off approach. As an investor, cash injections are the only incentive to make Etihad's partners change their course. For example, in return for an investment from Etihad, Alitalia agreed to cut 20 per cent of its workforce in 2014. This strategy has an ill-fated precedent. The attempts of Swissair to carry out similar techniques – even though the airline had more control over its stable – resulted in its bankruptcy in 2002.

In addition to his unorthodox endeavours, Hogan also pursues a more conventional strategy concerning industry cooperation, visible in the way he deals with the heavy competition of the big airline alliances. Hogan's rhetoric is that if there is no good access to markets and if it is impossible to join overarching alliances, then you strike partnerships with its members. Etihad managed to establish code share partners with 49 airlines, covering over 400 destinations. This allows passengers seats on the planes of other airlines. Code sharing increases the number of occupied seats and it allows Etihad to offer connecting flights, even to places it does not officially fly to itself. Etihad's own code sharing collection is small fry compared to the global alliances, but Etihad argues it does provide the airline with a viable alternative to the big alliance trio.

What goes up, can come down and while Etihad is still flying high, there are a number of dangers that can take down the airline. Running an airline as efficient as Etihad is difficult, but factoring in the strategic interests of its partners is a different case altogether. This goes for its own collection of collaborating share coding partners, but it is even more pressuring for the partner airlines of which it holds shares. How should Etihad proceed? Throwing money around to change their course does not seem like a viable long-term option, especially if Etihad continues to receive government subsidies. The ensuing backlash of airline competitors and foreign governments might bring about irreversible consequences for Etihad's endeavours. If it does not receive subsidies, the airline can at least publish

full accounts like Emirates does. This might open doors to future cooperation with current competitors. Etihad also needs to realize how it can continue to thrive among fellow regional giants Qatar and Emirates and their respective hub cities. In addition, the rise of Turkish Airlines brings new competition to the skies and the Gulf hubs. With which parties Hogan competes and with which he cooperates, are tricky questions. Should Etihad continue going alone, gaining precious market access via stakes in regional airlines? Or should it avoid the territory of the American and European markets dominated and saturated by the global alliances and seek collaboration with others, such as the other Gulf airlines or regional airlines in upcoming economies? Whatever decision Hogan ultimately makes, it is clear that if he can find the right mix of cooperation and competition, he can continue to prove that for Etihad the sky is the limit.

Co-author: Wester Wagenaar

Sources: www.etihad.com; *Economist*, 3 June 2010, 28 June 2014 and 25 April 2015; *Forbes*, 24 August 2015 and 28 June 2016.

PERSPECTIVES ON NETWORK LEVEL STRATEGY

Concordia discors (discordant harmony).
Horace (65–8 BC); Roman poet

Firms need to be able to engage in competition and cooperation simultaneously, even though these demands are each other's opposites. Firms need to exhibit a strongly cooperative posture to reap the benefits of collaboration, and they need to take a strongly competitive stance to ensure that others do not hamper their interests. Some theorists conclude that what is required is 'co-opetition' (Brandenburger and Nalebuff, 1996). While a catchy word, managers are still left with the difficult question of how to deal with these conflicting demands. To meet the pressure for cooperation, firms must actually become part of a broader 'team', spinning a web of close collaborative relationships. But to meet the pressure for competition, firms must not become too entangled in restrictive relationships, but rather remain free to manoeuvre, bargain and attack, with the intention of securing their own interests. In other words, firms must be *embedded* and *independent* at the same time – embedded in a network of cooperative interactions, while independent enough to wield their power to their own advantage.

The question dividing strategizing managers is whether firms should be more embedded or more independent. Should firms immerse themselves in broader networks to create strong groups, or should they stand on their own? Should firms willingly engage in long-term interdependence relationships or should they strive to remain as independent as possible? Should firms develop network level strategies at all, or should the whole concept of multi-firm strategy-making be directed to the garbage heap?

While strategy writers generally agree about the need to manage the paradox of competition and cooperation, they come to widely differing prescriptions on how to do so. Views within the field of strategic management are strongly at odds with regard to the best approach to inter-organizational relations. As before, here the two diametrically opposed positions will be identified and discussed to show the scope of differing ideas. On one side of the spectrum, there are strategists who believe that it is best for companies to be primarily competitive in their relationships to all outside forces. They argue that firms should remain independent and interact with other companies under market conditions as much as possible. As these strategists emphasize the discrete boundaries separating the firm from its 'competitive environment', this point of view is called the 'discrete organization perspective'. At the other end of the spectrum, there are strategists who believe that companies should strive to build up more long-term cooperative relationships with key organizations in their environment. They argue that firms can reap significant benefits by surrendering a part of their independence and developing close collaborative arrangements with a group of other organizations. This point of view will be referred to as the 'embedded organization perspective'.

The discrete organization perspective

Managers taking the discrete organization perspective, view companies as independent entities competing with other organizations in a hostile market environment. In line with neoclassical economics, this perspective commonly emphasizes that individuals, and the organizations they form, are fundamentally motivated by aggressive self-interest and therefore that competition is the natural state of affairs. Suppliers will try to enhance their bargaining power vis-à-vis buyers with the aim of getting a better price, while conversely, buyers will attempt to improve their negotiation position to attain better quality at lower cost. Competing firms will endeavour to gain the upper hand against their rivals if the opportunity arises, while new market entrants and manufacturers of substitute products will consistently strive to displace incumbent firms (e.g. Porter, 1980, 1985).

In such a hostile environment it is a strategic necessity for companies to strengthen their competitive position in relation to the external forces. The best strategy for each organization is to obtain the market power required to get good price/quality deals, ward off competitive threats, limit government demands and even determine the development of the industry. Effective power requires independence and therefore heavy reliance on specific suppliers, buyers, financiers or public organizations should be avoided.

The label 'discrete organization' given to this perspective refers to the fact that each organization is seen as being detached from its environment, with sharp boundaries demarcating where the outside world begins. The competitive situation is believed to be *atomistic*, that is, each self-interested firm strives to satisfy its own objectives, leading to rivalry and conflict with other organizations. Vertical interactions between firms in the industry column tend to be transactional, with an emphasis on getting the best possible deal. It is generally assumed that under such market conditions the interaction will be of a zero-sum nature, that is, a fight for who gets how much of the pie. The firm with the strongest bargaining power will usually be able to appropriate a larger portion of the 'economic rent' than will the less potent party. Therefore, advocates of the discrete organization perspective emphasize that the key to competitive success is the ability to build a powerful position and to wield this power in a calculated and efficient manner. This might sound Machiavellian to the faint-hearted, but it is the reality of the marketplace that is denied at one's own peril.

Essential for organizational power is the avoidance of resource dependence. Where a firm is forced to lean on a handful of suppliers or buyers, this can place the organization in a precariously exposed position. To managers taking a discrete organization perspective, such dependence on a few external parties is extremely risky, as the other firm will be tempted to exploit their position of relative power to their own advantage. Wise firms will therefore not let themselves become overly dependent on any external organization, certainly not for any essential resources. This includes keeping the option open to exit from the relationship at will – with low barriers to exit, the negotiating position of the firm is significantly stronger. Therefore the firm must never become so entangled with outsiders that it cannot rid itself of them at the drop of a hat. The firm must be careful that in a web of relationships it is the spider, not the fly (e.g. Pfeffer and Salancik, 1978; Ruigrok and Van Tulder, 1995).

Keeping other organizations at arm's-length also facilitates clear and business-like interactions. Where goods and services are bought or sold, distinct organizational boundaries help to distinguish tasks, responsibilities, authority and accountability. But as other firms will always seek to do as little as possible for the highest possible price, having clear contracts and a believable threat to enforce them will serve as a method to ensure discipline. Arm's-length relations are equally useful in avoiding the danger of vital information leaking to the party with whom the firm must (re)negotiate.

In their relationships with other firms in the industry it becomes even clearer that companies' interests are mutually exclusive. More market share for one company must necessarily come at the expense of another. Coalitions are occasionally formed to create power blocks if individual companies are not strong enough to compete on their own. Such tactical alliances bring together weaker firms, not capable of doing things independently. But 'competitive collaboration' is usually short-lived – either the alliance is unsuccessful and collapses, or it is successful against the common enemy, after which the alliance partners become each other's most important rivals.

Proponents of the discrete organization perspective argue that collaborative arrangements are always second best to doing things independently. Under certain conditions, weakness might force a firm to choose an alliance, but it is always a tactical necessity, never a strategic preference. Collaborative arrangements are inherently risky, fraught with the hazard of opportunism. Due to the ultimately competitive nature of relationships, allies will be tempted to serve their own interests to the detriment of the others, by manoeuvring, manipulating or cheating. The collaboration might even be a useful ploy, to cloak the company's aggressive intentions and moves. Collaboration, it is therefore concluded, is merely 'competition in a different form' (Hamel, Doz and Prahalad, 1989, Reading 6.1). Hence, where collaboration between firms really offers long-term advantages, a merger or acquisition is preferable to the uncertainty of an alliance.

Where collaboration is not the tool of the weak, it is often a conspiracy of the strong to inhibit competition. If two or more formidable companies collaborate, chances are that the alliance is actually ganging up on a third party – for instance on buyers. In such cases the term 'collaboration' is just a euphemism for collusion and not in the interest of the economy at large.

Worse yet, collaboration is usually also bad for a company's long-term health. A highly competitive environment is beneficial for a firm, because it provides the necessary stimulus for companies to continually improve and innovate. Strong adversaries push companies towards competitive fitness. A more benevolent environment, cushioned by competition-inhibiting collaboration, might actually make a firm more content and less eager to implement tough changes. In the long run this will make firms vulnerable to more aggressive companies, battle-hardened by years of rivalry in more competitive environments.

In conclusion, the basic assumption of the discrete organization perspective is that companies should not develop network level strategies, but should strive for 'strategic self-sufficiency'. Collaborative arrangements are a tactical tool, to be selectively employed. The sentiment of this perspective has been clearly summarized by Porter (1990; 224): "Alliances are rarely a solution ... no firm can depend on another independent firm for skills and assets that are central to its competitive advantage ... Alliances tend to ensure mediocrity, not create world leadership".

EXHIBIT 6.2   THE DISCRETE ORGANIZATION PERSPECTIVE

DANGOTE: WAGING WARS ON THE AFRICAN CONTINENT

Aliko Dangote, born, raised and doing business in Nigeria, was named Africa's richest man for the last six years in a row. His empire was founded over three decades ago when Mr Dangote started trading in commodities, an enterprise he expanded in the early 2000s to a fully-fledged production business. His take on producing local, value-added products that meet the needs of the African population, is a rather warlike one. Although the subject matter, ranging from cement to pasta, might seem mundane, Mr Dangote's approach to growing his business certainly is not.

Dealing with competitors and governments can be a tiresome business. Whereas most businessmen and women try diplomacy to deal with such issues, Mr Dangote started a fully-fledged war campaign in order to gain market dominance. Doing so didn't leave the ability to make good deals to chance, good arguments or charisma. Instead, he forced the market to bend to his wishes, making sure that failure was no longer an option. His weapon of choice was to be siege his competitors by undercutting their prices on major commodities. This forced his adversaries to either give up or sell their goods with negative margins. With a net worth of US$75 billion, the Dangote group time and again turned out to have the longest breath, thus taking out many of its rivals and creating a near monopoly in most commodities in Nigeria.

Besides siege tactics, Mr Dangote has developed the ability to make the right allies, but doesn't let them get too close. Being in good favour with Olugegun Obasanjo by generously funding his presidential campaign would certainly have helped him to take part in the rapid privatization of failing state businesses. Buying these failing businesses cheaply and making them profitable was one of the major early sources of his financial wealth. Another example has to do with the recent collaboration with GE to improve Nigeria's infrastructure. Western companies are anxious to expand into Africa's untapped markets, a dream that Mr Dangote certainly can make reality by using his power, connections and experience in navigating the Nigerian landscape. While GE will make a pretty penny from this building contract, the long-term benefits for Mr Dangote's commodity business and the deal's success depending on his ability to navigate Nigeria's upper echelons, surely makes clear who calls the shots.

Mr Dangote's current-day empire maintains clear similarities with its early beginnings. As a commodity trader, he was dependent on no one and was able to act as he thought best. Although he certainly made friends as his business expanded, the Dangote group never became dependent on any of them but used them as a lever to reach increasingly greater heights. While his competitors that did make alliances had to take each other's interests into account, without strategic partners Mr Dangote is as free in making business decisions as he ever was. Many wars are waged to retain freedom, a practice the Dangote group managed to successfully convey into the business realm.

Co-author: Jasper de Vries

Sources: '5 Machiavellian Business Lessons From Billionaire Aliko Dangote', Forbes, July 13, 2011; 'Cementing a fortune: The king of concrete has ambitions beyond Nigeria', *The Economist,* June 23, 2012; 'GE partners Dangote on power, transportation, Oil & Gas', *The Sun,* February 4, 2013; 'Meet the richest man in Africa – the only black billionaire among the world's 50 richest people', *Business Insider,* February 1, 2016.

The embedded organization perspective

 Strategists taking an embedded organization perspective are fundamentally at odds with the assumption that competition is the predominant factor determining the interaction between organizations. Business isn't war, so to approach all interactions from an antagonistic angle is seen as overly pessimistic, even cynical. On the contrary, it is argued that business is about value creation, which is inherently a positive-sum activity. Creating value brings together organizations towards a common goal, as they can achieve more by working together than by behaving autonomously. In the modern economy, no organization can efficiently perform all activities in-house, as the division of labour has encouraged companies to specialize and outsource as many non-core activities as possible. Companies are necessarily cogs in the larger industrial machine and they can achieve little without working in unison with the other parts of the system. In the embedded organization perspective, atomistic competition is a neoclassical theoretical abstraction that seriously mischaracterizes the nature of relationships between organizations. In reality, cooperation is the predominant factor determining inter-organizational relations. Symbiosis, not aggression, is the fundamental nature of economic functioning (e.g. Jarillo, 1988; Moore, 1996, Reading 6.3).

A company can always find many organizations in its environment with which it shares an interest and whose objectives are largely parallel to its own (Child and Faulkner, 1998). A company might want to develop new products together with its buyers, optimize the logistical system together with its suppliers, expand the industry's potential together with other manufacturers, link technological standards with other industries and improve employment conditions together with the government. In general, most organizations have a stronger interest in increasing the size of the pie, than in deciding who gets what – keeping the focus on making a success of value creation eases the process of finding an equitable solution to the issue of value distribution.

The label 'embedded organization' given to this perspective refers to the fact that firms are becoming increasingly integrated into webs of mutually dependent organizations (e.g. Gnyawali and Madhavan, 2001; Granovetter, 1985). As companies strive to focus on a limited set of core competencies and core business processes, they have moved to outsource as many non-core activities as possible. But as firms have attempted to further specialize by outsourcing activities that are close to their core business, they have become more vulnerable to outside suppliers and the need for explicit coordination of activities has often remained high. The outsourcing of such essential and coordination-intensive activities can only take place where the other party can be trusted to closely collaborate with the joint interests in mind. Of course, a company will not quickly move to such dependence on an outside supplier. But as experience and trust build over time, a strategic partnership can develop, where both sides come to accept the value of the close cooperation (e.g. Axelsson and Easton, 1992; Lorenzoni and Baden-Fuller, 1995, Reading 6.2).

For a firm to willingly surrender a part of its independence, it must be certain that its partners are also willing to invest in the relationship and will not behave opportunistically. Ideally, therefore, durable partnerships are based on mutual dependence and reciprocity. Both sides of the relationship must need each other, which gives an important incentive for both to find solutions to the disputes that will inevitably pop up. A balance in the benefits to be gained and the efforts to be exerted will also contribute to the success of a long-term collaborative relationship.

While such close collaborative relationships place a firm in a position of resource dependence, the benefits are well worth it. By specializing in a certain area, the firm can gain scale and experience advantages much faster. Specialization helps the firm to focus on a more limited set of core competencies, which can be developed more efficiently and rapidly than if the firm were a 'conglomerate' of activities. At the same time the firm can tap into the complementary resources (Richardson, 1972) developed by its co-specialized partners. These complementary resources will usually be of higher quality and lower price than if the firm had built them up independently.

Specialized firms also use collaborative arrangements to quickly combine their resources with industry outsiders, to create new products and services. As product and business innovation are high paced and usually require the combination of various types of resources, developing everything in isolation is unworkable for most firms. By teaming up with other firms that have complementary resources, a company can make the most of its own resource base, without having to build up other resources from scratch. But again, trust is needed to engage in such a joint venture, as there are significant downside risks that the firm needs to take into account.

So, from the embedded organization perspective, collaboration is not competition in disguise, but a real alternative means of dealing with other organizations (e.g. Contractor and Lorange, 1988; Piore and Sabel, 1984). Successful firms embed themselves in webs of cooperative relationships, developing strategies together with their partners. These networks might compete against other networks (e.g. Gomes-Casseres, 1994; Hamilton and Woolsey Biggart, 1988; Weidenbaum and Hughes, 1996), but even here the relationships need not be fundamentally antagonistic. Proponents of the embedded organization perspective do not believe that firms should become obsessed with 'putting the competition out of business', as this again reduces business to a win–lose, zero-sum game. Firms should be focused on creating value and avoiding direct confrontation with other manufacturers, emphasizing the opportunity for a win–win, positive-sum game (e.g. Kim and Mauborgne, 2004; Moore, 1996, Reading 6.3). With this approach, firms in the same industry will recognize that they often have parallel interests as well. Setting industry standards, lobbying the government, finding solutions to joint environmental problems, improving the image of the industry, investing in fundamental research and negotiating with the unions are just a few of the issues where cooperation can be fruitful.

EXHIBIT 6.3   THE EMBEDDED ORGANIZATION PERSPECTIVE

NIKE: RUNNING NETWORK FOR GOLD

No sporting event in the world attracts more global viewers than the Olympics, with 3.6 billion people worldwide tuning into the 2016 Olympic Games in Rio de Janeiro, Brazil. Old records being broken dominate headlines, like runner Wayde van Niekerk smashing Michael Johnson's 17-year-old record on the 400-metre dash. With all these viewers, the Olympics provide a great opportunity to market products; but becoming an official sponsor requires footing a 100 to 200 million dollar fee. Any non-sponsoring brand that promotes products at the Olympics can expect a visit from the IOC's fierce pack of lawyers, suing anyone who breaks their tight marketing rules.

These strict rules originated 20 years ago at the 1996 Olympics in Atlanta, when Nike pulled off an excellent marketing trick. They offered the Olympic sprinter Michael Johnson, the same who saw his 1999 record broken in Rio, a pair of gold-coloured lightweight racing shoes (worth US$30 000) that he used while setting his gold medal winning time on the 400-metre dash. Millions of people saw the shoes the day of the race and even more people saw them on the cover of *Time* magazine a few days later. Michael Johnson turned out to be a very profitable partner for Nike. What Nike did in 1996, besides prompting the IOC to come up with more stringent marketing guidelines, demonstrates their excellence in marketing. It is their expertise in marketing, as well as in R&D, that makes Nike one of the world's leading footwear and apparel companies. By focusing on just a few core competencies, Nike can demonstrate greatness exactly there.

Of course there is more to Nike's value chain than R&D and marketing; in 2014 Nike moved roughly 900 million units through its manufacturing network. This network partially consists of over 700 factories, yet none of them are owned by Nike. The manufacturing process is outsourced to third parties who specialize in this process, while the raw materials are sourced by independent contractors. The company is considered to be one of the pioneers in manufacturing outsourcing strategy and is currently focusing on new, innovative ways of manufacturing to allow for more customized products. In November 2015, Nike announced a partnership with Flex, a global manufacturer with experience in design, engineering and manufacturing in industries other than footwear and apparel. At the same time, Nike partnered with Nova, a company with 3D digital design system experience, enabling Nike to enhance its digital design capabilities. While these two partnerships are intended to give Nike a competitive advantage, another element of Nike's strategy focuses on sustainability. In 2013 Nike opened a water-free dyeing facility at its Taiwan-based manufacturer 'Far Eastern New Century Corp'. It employs dyeing

▶

technology from a small Dutch company called DyeCoo, which uses carbon dioxide as a replacement for water to dye polyester.

Part of Nike's vision is to bring advanced innovation to its manufacturing supply chain. This is a prerequisite for meeting ever-changing customer needs, which currently demand customized solutions, quick delivery and products that communicate with each other. Nike has demonstrated that it is very capable of managing relationships with its network partners while specializing in its core competencies, but it may be up for a network challenge on a different level. Platform businesses are disrupting the traditional business landscape, so if Nike hopes to fend off this platform disruption it should re-evaluate its business model. Instead of focusing on vertical

integration with its suppliers or distributors, it should now focus on partnering up with its end user. By offering a platform that creates value for its end consumer, Nike can reinvent its partnership strategy and continue to hold its number one position. Yet speed is of the essence, so a pair of gold-coloured lightweight racing shoes would be more than welcome.

Co-author: Adriaan de Bruijn

Sources: 'How Nike Brilliantly Ruined Olympic Marketing Forever', *Adweek,* August 10, 2016; 'Nike's manufacturing revolution accelerated by new partnership with Flex', www.news.nike.com, October 14, 2015; 'An Overview Of Nike's Supply Chain and Manufacturing Strategies', *Marketrealist*, December 2, 2014; 'Nike & Adidas Strategic Partners for Dyecoo's Business model', www.between-us.com; 'Here's How Nike Became a Platform Business', *Fortune,* April 10, 2016.

MANAGING THE PARADOX OF COMPETITION AND COOPERATION

All for one, one for all.

The Three Musketeers, Alexandre Dumas Jr (1824–1895); French novelist

So, should managers form network level strategies or not? Should firms consciously embed themselves in a web of durable collaborative relationships, emphasizing the value of cooperative inter-organizational interactions for realizing their long-term aims? Or should firms try to remain as independent as possible, emphasizing the value of competitive power in achieving their strategic objectives? Is it 'all for one, one for all' or must the strong truly stand alone? (see Table 6.1).

TABLE 6.1   Discrete organization versus embedded organization perspective

	Discrete organization perspective	Embedded organization perspective
Emphasis on	Competition over cooperation	Cooperation over competition
Preferred position	Independence	Interdependence
Environment structure	Discrete organizations (atomistic)	Embedded organizations (networked)
Firm boundaries	Distinct and defended	Fuzzy and open
Inter-organizational relations	Arm's-length and transactional	Close and structural
Interaction outcomes	Mainly zero-sum (win/lose)	Mainly positive-sum (win/win)
Interaction based on	Bargaining power and calculation	Trust and reciprocity
Network level strategy	No	Yes
Use of collaboration	Temporary coalitions (tactical alliance)	Durable partnerships (strategic alliance)
Collaborative arrangements	Limited, well-defined, contract-based	Broad, open, relationship-based

The debate on this issue within the field of strategy is far from being concluded. Many perspectives exist on how to reconcile the conflicting demands of competition and cooperation, and many 'best practices' have been put forward. Therefore strategists need to determine their own point of view, with a number of suggestions from the literature in mind. From all the discussed strategy issues in this book, the number of available options to manage the paradox of cooperation and competition is highest. Three options have been brought forward: navigating, parallel processing and juxtaposing.

Navigating

By focusing on one contrary element at a time, the paradox is managed by a series of contrary initiatives. In network level strategy, Gary Hamel, Yves Doz and C.K. Prahalad have suggested the route for strategists to cooperate first and compete later in their *Harvard Business Review* (*HBR*) article: "Collaborate with your competitor and win" (1989; Reading 6.1). They describe how Japanese strategists collaborate with competitors from the West with the explicit intention to learn, and then beat them as competitors. In this case, vertical (cooperative supply chain) relations become horizontal (competitive). But also without this specific change of relationship, navigating vertical partnering is an option. For example, in the retail industry it is common practice that suppliers (A-Brand manufacturers) cooperate with clients (supermarkets) to jointly develop logistical processes and technologies to enhance efficiency. Both parties benefit, but once the new technology and process are in place, parties start negotiating prices and conditions again. This cycle of cooperating and competing is repeated many times.

Other suggestions have also been made. Under the guidance of the Japanese Ministry of International Trade and Industry (MITI), groups of (Japanese) companies have been brought together to jointly develop new technologies, stimulated with government money. The intention was to cooperate in the 'pre-competitive stage', and once the technology was developed to compete in the marketplace. This industrial policy has been adopted by the European Union with initiatives such as ESPRIT and EUREKA, to promote innovation and to introduce new standards in the telecommunications sector (Gastells, 2006; Van Tulder and Junne, 1988).

Cooperating first and competing later is not an exclusive industrial policy option. Companies have learned that on some occasions it makes strategic sense to join forces with competitors in the early phase of developing technologies and industry standards. Well-described in the literature is the case of developing an industry standard for video devices (e.g. Bartlett *et al.,* 2008). Three competitors had been competing for the world standard, Philips with V2000, Sony with Betamax, and Matsushita with VCR. The victor was VCR in this winner-takes-all game (Arthur, 1994); the contestants learned the hard way that competing for standards may be heroic and exciting, but often proves disappointing. For developing a world Wi-Fi standard, several stakeholders have participated in a standardization group; competition started after the new standard had created a level playing field.

Parallel processing

The term co-opetition, an astute portmanteau of cooperation and competition, has become popularized by game theorists (e.g. Brandenburger and Nalebuff, 1996). It is explained as companies interacting with partial congruence of interests. For example, the French car manufacturer PSA Peugeot Citroën and the Japanese firm Toyota share components of city cars, the Peugeot 107, Toyota Aygo and Citroën C1, while competing fiercely for market share. Cooperating to reduce costs while competing for market share is being executed in different organizational units, and hence are an example of parallel processing.

Companies can also separate competing and cooperating in different country units. For example, the French company Danone and the Japanese firm Yakult (see also the short case on Yakult in Exhibit 4.1), compete in Europe but cooperate in India. In this case, the arguments in the strategic decision making process to 'make, buy or cooperate' differ over country units, and therefore the decisions vary. Without an overarching corporate policy, the organizational units have the freedom to choose, and so parallel processing is possible.

Juxtaposing

Simultaneously managing competition and cooperation, even with the same network partners, is a next option for strategists. Lord Palmerston's quote earlier in this chapter articulates the position of a strategizing manager quite well: there are no eternal allies and perpetual enemies. Comparable to a cycling race, rival teams can become allies and then turn rivals again, depending on the situation during the race. Managers also keep their options open; rivals can become allies and rivals again, depending on the situation. For example, in the battle for mobile operating model standards some competing providers have a joint interest to defend the chosen platform and join forces, and after a cooperative meeting start competing again.

Juxtaposing is common in business ecosystems, as Moore (1996; Reading 6.3) points out. Moore argues that the pattern of business co-evolution consists of "a complex network of choices, which depend, at least in part, on what participants are aware of". In other words, managers can not afford to label firms as definite rivals or allies. Positions within the ecosystem can change so fast that allies can turn into rivals within days and vice versa. Ecosystems are often described in innovation contexts, with eroding industry boundaries and companies often unexpectedly finding themselves in fierce competition with the most unlikely of rivals.

NETWORK LEVEL STRATEGY IN INTERNATIONAL PERSPECTIVE

Co-authors: Gep Eisenloeffel and Wester Wagenaar

Do as adversaries in law, strive mightily, but eat and drink as friends.
William Shakespeare (1564–1616); English dramatist and poet

Of all the debates in the field of strategic management, the one on network level strategy has received the most attention from comparative management researchers. Almost all of them have concluded that firms from different countries display widely divergent propensities to compete and cooperate. Many authors suggest there are recognizable national inclinations, even national styles, when it comes to establishing inter-firm relationships (Contractor and Lorange, 1988; Kagono *et al.*, 1985).

Since there can be significant variance within a country, it is difficult to generalize at the national level. Nevertheless it is challenging to debate these observed international dissimilarities. Are there really national inter-organizational relationship styles and what factors might influence their existence? As a stimulus to the international dimension of this debate, a number of country characteristics are put forward as possible influences on how the paradox of competition and cooperation is dealt with in different national settings. In addition to analyses on the societal level, preferences on the industry merit discussion.

On the societal level

It is generally argued that most countries have developed an idiosyncratic economic system – that is, their own brand of capitalism – with a different emphasis on competition and cooperation. One prominent analysis is that of historian Chandler (1986, 1990), who has described the historical development of 'personal capitalism' in the United Kingdom, 'managerial capitalism' in the United States, 'group capitalism' in Japan and 'cooperative capitalism' in Germany from 1850 to 1950. We can also identify other types of institutional environments, such as what can be dubbed 'bureaucratic capitalism' in France and 'familial capitalism' in Italy. The legacy of these separately evolving forms of capitalism is that, to this day, there are significantly different institutional philosophies, roles and behaviour in each of these countries. It goes without saying that not only institutions define general preferences of countries, but that social networks and cultural values also have an influence.

In the English-speaking nations, governments have generally limited their role to the establishment and maintenance of competitive markets (Hampden-Turner and Trompenaars, 1993). A shared belief in the basic tenets of classical economies has led these governments to be suspicious of competition-undermining collusion masquerading under the term 'cooperation'. For instance, in the US the Sherman Antitrust Act was passed in 1890 and has been applied with vigour since then to guard the functioning of the market. Many companies that would like to cooperate have been discouraged or barred from doing so (Teece, 1992). On the cultural level, Hofstede's research found the US to be the highest scoring nation in the world on the individualism scale, closely followed by the other English-speaking countries. In the socially atomistic Anglo-Saxon nations, individuals are seen as the building blocks of society and each person is inclined to optimize his own interests (Hofstede, 1993; Lessem & Neubauer, 1994). One result is that in the US cooperation tends to only exist "under a system of formal rules and regulations, which have to be negotiated, agreed to, litigated and enforced, sometimes by coercive means" (Fukuyama, 1995). Not surprisingly, the US has the highest number of corporate lawyers in the world and transaction costs are high.

Japan is generally put at the opposite side of the spectrum, emphasizing group affiliation instead of individualism (Lessem and Neubauer, 1994). In more collectivist societies, a relationship is "not calculative, but moral: It is based not on self-interest, but on the individual's loyalty toward the clan, organization, or society – which is supposedly the best guarantee of that individual's ultimate interest" (Hofstede, 1993). Japan's 'group capitalism' is characterized by partnerships between business and social institutions to promote mutually beneficial developments. On the multi-company level Japan's collectivist bent manifests itself in the bank-led *keiretsu* system. Firms within a *keiretsu* are familiar with one another through long historical association and have had durable, open-ended relationships, partially cemented by multilateral shareholdings. Collectivism, resulting in different modes of group-orientation, correlates with importance adhered to trust-building and social capital, a characteristic also observable in many other countries in Asia (Fukuyama, 1995). In China, for instance, longstanding informal relationships form the basis for the functioning of business networks, or *guanxi* in Chinese. Without the proper *guanxi*, doing business is particularly difficult.

The German system and culture are often compared with those of Japan. Lessem and Neubauer argue that both cultures exhibit a holistic worldview, in which "management and banker, employer and employee, government and industry combine forces rather than engage in adversarial relations", to the benefit of the entire system (1994). In Germany's 'cooperative capitalism' the government has major shareholdings in hundreds of companies outside the public services. In particular, the large German banks have played an important role in guiding industrial development, promoting cooperation and defusing potentially dangerous conflicts between companies. Since the late 1990s this system has been unravelling, but trade associations and unions, like the German banks, also employ a long-term, cooperative perspective.

Similar to German and Japanese, Italian culture is also characterized by a strong group orientation, but in the 'familial capitalism' of Italy the affiliations valued by Italians tend to be mostly family-like. These are based on blood ties, friendships or ideological bonds between individuals. There is strong loyalty and trust within these communities, but distrust prevails towards the outside world, among which are institutions like the central government, tax authorities, bankers and trade unions. Therefore, the role of the government tends to be small and trading associations, purchasing cooperatives, educational institutions and cooperative marketing are often created to support a large number of small, specialized firms working together as a loose federation. Family-like cooperation tends to be high within these communities and it is thus unsurprising that Italy is often cited for its high number of networked companies (Piore and Sabel, 1984). Besides the well-known example of Benetton, examples can be found in the textile industry of Prato, the ceramics industry of Sassuolo, the farm machine industry of Reggio Emilia and the motorcycle industry of Bologna.

The 'bureaucratic capitalism' system observable in France focuses strongly on the state as industrial strategist, coordinating many major developments in the economy. It is the planners' job "to maintain a constant pressure on industry – as part industrial consultant, part banker, part plain bully – to keep it moving in some desired direction" (Lessem and Neubauer, 1994). This was for instance the case in France's state-supported *filière* policy, supporting the national communication industry in the mid-1980s (Groenewegen and Beije, 1989). The unions, on the other hand, tend to be more antagonistic, particularly in their relationship to the government. On the work floor, however, a more cooperative attitude prevails. There is a strong sense that cooperation in economic affairs is important. Generally, however, there is a preference to impose such cooperation in a top-down manner by integrating companies into efficiently working bureaucracies. Such structuring of the economy usually takes place under the influence, or by direct intervention, of the French government. The extent of this French philosophy is deep: even relationships with firms not absorbed into the hierarchy are of a bureaucratic nature – that is, formal, rational and depersonalized.

On the industry level

The nature of some industries makes inter-organizational competition more likely than cooperation and vice versa. Industries where available projects are limited can be expected to fall in the category with a preference for competition. For example, the construction industry is one of the most highly competitive industries worldwide and "is characterized by opportunistic behaviour and the lack of vertical cooperation" (Welling and Kamann, 2001). One reason is the competition contractors have to engage in to obtain contracts. Usually, contractors who submit the lowest bids get selected, but even when other methods to find a contractor are employed, the stakes to secure projects remain high. In addition, the specialized nature of some of the tasks in the industry makes diversification outside of construction fairly difficult. The limited options of players in the construction industry and the intense competition to secure contracts generally result in a zero sum game.

Oligopoly industries are also dominated by a focus on competition. If one company in such a setting changes its organization, strategy or price, this will have a significant impact on its rivals. The aircraft manufacturing industry is arguably the most well-known example of a highly competitive arena controlled by just a few players. Airbus and Boeing practically own the jet airliner market together, but as a result they engage in fierce competition over the limited number of orders. Other global oligopolies are the steel, oil, wholesale beer, photo camera and cellular phone market industries.

Inter-organizational cooperation, on the other hand, can generally be expected in high technology or knowledge-based industries. Here, collaborative projects are considered fairly commonplace. Examples are the space and biotechnology industries. For instance, since 1990, the EU-US Task Force on Biotechnology Research has shared, cooperated on and promoted biotechnology research. The knowledge gained can then be turned into products (Aguilar, Bochereau and Matthiessen-Guyader, 2008). Higher education can also be considered a cooperative industry: universities can be found collaborating in order to provide student exchange programmes, share research findings and engage in projects.

Cooperation is at the heart of industries that are – partly or wholly – organized as business ecosystems, such as international sourcing (Alibaba), the music industry (Spotify) and the taxi industry (Uber). Here companies create platforms, establishing partnerships with other companies and individuals. The quality of these platforms generally increases along with a higher number of platform partnerships.

To the strategist

There is a variety of ways to deal with the paradox of cooperation and competition, as showcased by differences in the perceptions of companies, industries and countries. A strategist can and should learn from the ways others around the world and across industries perceive these seemingly opposing concepts, but also has to be aware of international differences when her or his company wishes to reach across borders. Research by Bleeke and Ernst found that only half of the cross-border alliances succeed, fuelling the need for accurately predicting a company's ability to collaborate and having a good understanding of international differences (1991, 1993). Since companies, countries and industries vary widely, there is not one given answer.

INTRODUCTION TO THE READINGS

To help strategists gain more insight into the variety of perspectives on this issue, three readings have been selected that each take a different angle on the debate. As in previous chapters, the first two readings will be representative of the two poles in this debate, while the third will combine both perspectives.

To open on behalf of the discrete organization perspective, the classic, 'Collaborate with Your Competitors – and Win', has been selected as Reading 6.1. The authors, Gary Hamel, Yves Doz and C.K. Prahalad, basically take the same stance that inter-firm relations are largely competitive and governed by power and calculation. The authors see collaboration as a useful tool for improving the firm's competitive profile. They argue that alliances with competitors "can strengthen both companies against outsiders even if it weakens one partner vis-a-vis the other", and therefore that the net result can be positive. Yet they emphasize that companies should not be naive about the real nature of alliances – "collaboration is competition in a different form". An alliance is "a constantly evolving bargain", in which each firm will be fending for itself, trying to learn as much as possible from the other, while attempting to limit the partner's access to its knowledge and skills.

The authors advise firms to proceed cautiously with alliances, only when they have clear objectives of what they wish to learn from their allies, a well-developed capacity to learn, and defences against their allies' probing of their skills and technologies. While Hamel, Doz and Prahalad only focus on horizontal relationships in this reading, their message is similar to that of Porter – competition in the environment is paramount and cooperation is merely an opportunistic move in the overall competitive game.

As representative of the embedded organization perspective, an article by Gianni Lorenzoni and Charles Baden-Fuller has been selected for Reading 6.2, entitled 'Creating a Strategic Centre to Manage a Web of Partners'. Lorenzoni and Baden-Fuller are particularly interested in how companies structure their vertical relationships, balancing pressures for competition and cooperation. In their view, where a group of firms works together closely, they can form a 'virtual company'. This type of network can benefit from most of the advantages of being a large vertically integrated company, while avoiding most of the pitfalls of integration. But Lorenzoni and Baden-Fuller articulate that it is necessary for a network of firms to have a strategic centre that can act as builder and coordinator. As builder, the strategic centre can deliberately design and assemble the network components, and as coordinator it can regulate activities and resolve disputes. The authors carry on to specify the conditions under which a network of firms can be an advantageous organizational form and what is required to make them work. Overall, their main message is that durable partnerships between multiple firms are not easy, but if this interdependence is managed well, it can give the group a strong competitive edge against others.

Reading 6.3, 'Coevolution in Business Ecosystems', by James Moore, describes how both perspectives are combined in business ecosystems. This reading is from Moore's best-selling book *The Death of Competition,* in which he places the paradox of competition and cooperation in the broader context of 'business ecosystems'. He defines a business ecosystem as a part of the business environment where a variety of firms co-exist with one another and co-evolve on the basis of their ongoing interaction. He explains the functioning of a business ecosystem by drawing a parallel with biological ecosystems – plants and animals cannot be understood in isolation, as they co-evolve with one another in an endless cycle of change and selection. So too, the success or failure of companies cannot be understood without understanding how they have been able to nestle into the business ecosystem and how well the entire system is doing. Great companies, like great animal species, will still face extinction if their ecosystem goes into decline. Similarly, companies that want to create a new market must recognize that they actually need to create a new business ecosystem, with a lush variety of suppliers, distributors, service providers and customers. If a firm only 'plants' its new product without engendering a broader ecosystem, it will be just as successful as a new species of tropical tree in the desert. Moore's point is that you should try to "understand the economic systems evolving around you and find ways to contribute". He concludes that "competitive advantage stems principally from … cooperative, co-evolving relationships with a network of other contributors to the overall economic scene". In other words, cooperation and systems level thinking are essential to the strategist – not to substitute competitive behaviour, but rather to complement it.

READING

6.1

Collaborate with your competitors – and win

By Gary Hamel, Yves Doz and C.K. Prahalad[1]

Collaboration between competitors is in fashion. General Motors and Toyota assemble automobiles, Siemens and Philips develop semiconductors, Canon supplies photocopiers to Kodak, France's Thomson and Japan's JVC manufacture videocassette recorders. But the spread of what we call 'competitive collaboration' – joint ventures, outsourcing agreements, product licensing, cooperative research – has triggered unease about the long-term consequences. A strategic alliance can strengthen both companies against outsiders even as it

[1]Source: Reprinted by permission of *Harvard Business Review.* From 'Collaborate with your competitors – and win' by G. Hamel, Y.L. Doz and C.K. Prahalad, January–ebruary 1989, Vol. 67. © 1989 by the Harvard Business School Publishing Corporation, all rights reserved.

weakens one partner vis-a-vis the other. In particular, alliances between Asian companies and western rivals seem to work against the western partner. Cooperation becomes a low-cost route for new competitors to gain technology and market access.

Yet the case for collaboration is stronger than ever. It takes so much money to develop new products and to penetrate new markets that few companies can go it alone in every situation. ICL, the British computer company, could not have developed its current generation of mainframes without Fujitsu. Motorola needs Toshiba's distribution capacity to break into the Japanese semiconductor market. Time is another critical factor. Alliances can provide shortcuts for western companies racing to improve their production efficiency and quality control.

We have spent more than five years studying the inner workings of 15 strategic alliances and monitoring scores of others. Our research involves cooperative ventures between competitors from the United States and Japan, Europe and Japan, and the United States and Europe. We did not judge the success or failure of each partnership by its longevity – a common mistake when evaluating strategic alliances – but by the shifts in competitive strength on each side. We focused on how companies use competitive collaboration to enhance their internal skills and technologies while they guard against transferring competitive advantages to ambitious partners.

There is no immutable law that strategic alliances *must* be a windfall for Japanese or Korean partners. Many western companies do give away more than they gain – but that's because they enter partnerships without knowing what it takes to win. Companies that benefit most from competitive collaboration adhere to a set of simple but powerful principles:

- **Collaboration is competition in a different form.** Successful companies never forget that their new partners may be out to disarm them. They enter alliances with clear strategic objectives, and they also understand how their partners' objectives will affect their success.

- **Harmony is not the most important measure of success.** Indeed, occasional conflict may be the best evidence of mutually beneficial collaboration. Few alliances remain win–win undertakings forever. A partner may be content even as it unknowingly surrenders core skills.

- **Cooperation has limits.** Companies must defend against competitive compromise. A strategic alliance is a constantly evolving bargain whose real terms go beyond the legal agreement or the aims of top management. What information gets traded is determined day to day, often by engineers and operating managers. Successful companies inform employees at all levels about what skills and technologies are off-limits to the partner and monitor what the partner requests and receives.

- **Learning from partners is paramount.** Successful companies view each alliance as a window on their partners' broad capabilities. They use the alliance to build skills in areas outside the formal agreement and systematically diffuse new knowledge throughout their organizations.

Why collaborate?

Using an alliance with a competitor to acquire new technologies or skills is not devious. It reflects the commitment and capacity of each partner to absorb the skills of the other. We found that in every case in which a Japanese company emerged from an alliance stronger than its western partner, the Japanese company had made a greater effort to learn.

Strategic intent is an essential ingredient in the commitment to learning. The willingness of Asian companies to enter alliances represents a change in competitive tactics, not competitive goals. NEC, for example, has used a series of collaborative ventures to enhance its technology and product competences. NEC is the only company in the world with a leading position in telecommunications, computers and semiconductors – despite its investing less in research and development (R&D) (as a percentage of revenues) than competitors like Texas Instruments, Northern Telecom and L.M. Ericsson. Its string of partnerships, most notably with Honeywell, allowed NEC to leverage its in-house R&D over the last two decades.

Western companies, on the other hand, often enter alliances to avoid investments. They are more interested in reducing the costs and risks of entering new businesses or markets than in acquiring new skills. A senior US manager offered this analysis of his company's venture with a Japanese rival: 'We complement each other well – our distribution capability and their manufacturing skill. I see no reason to invest upstream if we can find a secure source of product. This is a comfortable relationship for us.'

An executive from this company's Japanese partner offered a different perspective: 'When it is necessary to collaborate, I go to my employees and say, "This is bad, I wish we had these skills ourselves. Collaboration is second best. But I will feel worse if after four years we do not know how to do what our partner knows how to do." We must digest their skills.'

The problem here is not that the US company wants to share investment risk (its Japanese partner does too) but that the US company has no ambition beyond avoidance. When the commitment to learning is so one-sided, collaboration invariably leads to competitive compromise.

Many so-called alliances between western companies and their Asian rivals are little more than sophisticated outsourcing arrangements. General Motors buys cars and components from Korea's Daewoo. Siemens buys computers from Fujitsu. Apple buys laser printer engines from Canon. The traffic is almost entirely one way. These original equipment manufacturer (OEM) deals offer Asian partners a way to capture investment initiative from western competitors and displace customer–competitors from value-creating activities. In many cases this goal meshes with that of the western partner: to regain competitiveness quickly and with minimum effort.

Consider the joint venture between Rover, the British automaker, and Honda. Some 25 years ago, Rover's forerunners were world leaders in small car design. Honda had not even entered the automobile business. But in the mid-1970s, after failing to penetrate foreign markets, Rover turned to Honda for technology and product development support. Rover has used the alliance to avoid investments to design and build new cars. Honda has cultivated skills in European styling and marketing as well as multinational manufacturing. There is little doubt which company will emerge stronger over the long term.

Troubled laggards like Rover often strike alliances with surging latecomers like Honda. Having fallen behind in a key skills area (in this case, manufacturing small cars), the laggard attempts to compensate for past failures. The latecomer uses the alliance to close a specific skills gap (in this case, learning to build cars for a regional market). But a laggard that forges a partnership for short-term gain may find itself in a dependency spiral: as it contributes fewer and fewer distinctive skills, it must reveal more and more of its internal operations to keep the partner interested. For the weaker company, the issue shifts from, 'Should we collaborate?' to 'With whom should we collaborate?' to 'How do we keep our partner interested as we lose the advantages that made us attractive to them in the first place?'

There's a certain paradox here. When both partners are equally intent on internalizing the other's skills, distrust and conflict may spoil the alliance and threaten its very survival. That's one reason joint ventures between Korean and Japanese companies have been few and tempestuous. Neither side wants to 'open the kimono'. Alliances seem to run most smoothly when one partner is intent on learning and the other is intent on avoidance – in essence, when one partner is willing to grow dependent on the other. But running smoothly is not the point; the point is for a company to emerge from an alliance more competitive than when it entered it.

One partner does not always have to give up more than it gains to ensure the survival of an alliance. There are certain conditions under which mutual gain is possible, at least for a time:

■ **The partners' strategic goals converge while their competitive goals diverge.** That is, each partner allows for the other's continued prosperity in the shared business. Philips and Du Pont collaborate to develop and manufacture compact discs, but neither side invades the other's market. There is a clear upstream/downstream division of effort.

■ **The size and market power of both partners is modest compared with industry leaders.** This forces each side to accept that mutual dependence may have to continue for many years. Long-term collaboration may be so critical to both partners that neither will risk antagonizing the other by an overtly competitive bid to appropriate skills or competences. Fujitsu's 1 to 5 size disadvantage with IBM means it will be a long time, if ever, before Fujitsu can break away from its foreign partners and go it alone.

■ **Each partner believes it can learn from the other and at the same time limit access to proprietary skills.** JVC and Thomson, both of whom make VCRs, know that they are trading skills. But the two companies are looking for very different things. Thomson needs product technology and manufacturing prowess; JVC needs to learn how to succeed in the fragmented European market. Both sides believe there is an equitable chance for gain.

How to build secure defences

For collaboration to succeed, each partner must contribute something distinctive: basic research, product development skills, manufacturing capacity, access to distribution. The challenge is to share enough skills to create advantage vis-a-vis companies outside the alliance while preventing a wholesale transfer of core skills to the partner. This is a very thin line to walk. Companies must carefully select what skills and technologies they pass to their partners. They must develop safeguards against unintended, informal transfers of information. The goal is to limit the transparency of their operations.

The type of skill a company contributes is an important factor in how easily its partner can internalize the skills. The potential for transfer is greatest when a partner's contribution is easily transported (in engineering drawings, on computer tapes, or in the heads of a few technical experts); easily interpreted (it can be reduced to commonly understood equations or symbols); and easily absorbed (the skill or competence is independent of any particular cultural context).

Western companies face an inherent disadvantage because their skills are generally more vulnerable to transfer. The magnet that attracts so many companies to alliances with Asian competitors is their manufacturing excellence – a competence that is less transferable than most. Just-in-time inventory systems and quality circles can be imitated, but this is like pulling a few threads out of an oriental carpet. Manufacturing excellence is a complex web of employee training, integration with suppliers, statistical process controls, employee involvement, value engineering and design for manufacture. It is difficult to extract such a subtle competence in any way but a piecemeal fashion.

So companies must take steps to limit transparency. One approach is to limit the scope of the formal agreement. It might cover a single technology rather than an entire range of technologies; part of a product line rather than the entire line; distribution in a limited number of markets or for a limited period of time. The objective is to circumscribe a partner's opportunities to learn.

Moreover, agreements should establish specific performance requirements. Motorola, for example, takes an incremental, incentive-based approach to technology transfer in its venture with Toshiba. The agreement calls for Motorola to release its microprocessor technology incrementally as Toshiba delivers on its promise to increase Motorola's penetration in the Japanese semiconductor market. The greater Motorola's market share, the greater Toshiba's access to Motorola's technology.

Many of the skills that migrate between companies are not covered in the formal terms of collaboration. Top management puts together strategic alliances and sets the legal parameters for exchange. But what actually gets traded is determined by day-to-day interactions of engineers, marketers and product developers: who says what to whom, who gets access to what facilities, who sits on what joint committees. The most important deals ('I'll share this with you if you share that with me') may be struck four or five organizational levels below where the deal was signed. Here lurks the greatest risk of unintended transfers of important skills.

Consider one technology-sharing alliance between European and Japanese competitors. The European company valued the partnership as a way to acquire a specific technology. The Japanese company considered it a window on its partner's entire range of competences and interacted with a broad spectrum of its partner's marketing and product development staff. The company mined each contact for as much information as possible.

For example, every time the European company requested a new feature on a product being sourced from its partner, the Japanese company asked for detailed customer and competitor analyses to justify the request. Over time, it developed a sophisticated picture of the European market that would assist its own entry strategy. The technology acquired by the European partner through the formal agreement had a useful life of three to five years. The competitive insights acquired informally by the Japanese company will probably endure longer.

Limiting unintended transfers at the operating level requires careful attention to the role of gatekeepers, the people who control what information flows to a partner. A gatekeeper can be effective only if there are a limited number of gateways through which a partner can access people and facilities. Fujitsu's many partners all go through a single office, the 'collaboration section,' to request information and assistance from different divisions. This way the company can monitor and control access to critical skills and technologies.

We studied one partnership between European and US competitors that involved several divisions of each company. While the US company could only access its partner through a single gateway, its partner had unfettered access to all participating divisions. The European company took advantage of its free rein. If one division refused to provide certain information, the European partner made the same request of another division. No single manager in the US company could tell how much information had been transferred or was in a position to piece together patterns in the requests.

Collegiality is a prerequisite for collaborative success. But *too much* collegiality should set off warning bells to senior managers. CEOs or division presidents should expect occasional complaints from their counterparts about the reluctance of lower level employees to share information. That's a sign that the gatekeepers are doing their jobs. And senior management should regularly debrief operating personnel to find out what information the partner is requesting and what requests are being granted.

Limiting unintended transfers ultimately depends on employee loyalty and self-discipline. This was a real issue for many of the western companies we studied. In their excitement and pride over technical achievements, engineering staff sometimes shared information that top management considered sensitive. Japanese engineers were less likely to share proprietary information.

There are a host of cultural and professional reasons for the relative openness of western technicians. Japanese engineers and scientists are more loyal to their company than to their profession. They are less steeped in the open give-and-take of university research since they receive much of their training from employers. They consider themselves team members more than individual scientific contributors. As one Japanese manager noted, 'We don't feel any need to reveal what we know. It is not an issue of pride for us. We're glad to sit and listen. If we're patient we usually learn what we want to know.'

Controlling unintended transfers may require restricting access to facilities as well as to people. Companies should declare sensitive laboratories and factories off-limits to their partners. Better yet, they might house the collaborative venture in an entirely new facility. IBM is building a special site in Japan where Fujitsu can review its forthcoming mainframe software before deciding whether to license it. IBM will be able to control exactly what Fujitsu sees and what information leaves the facility.

Finally, which country serves as 'home' to the alliance affects transparency. If the collaborative team is located near one partner's major facilities, the other partner will have more opportunities to learn – but less control over what information gets traded. When the partner houses, feeds and looks after engineers and operating managers, there is a danger they will 'go native'. Expatriate personnel need frequent visits from headquarters as well as regular furloughs home.

Enhance the capacity to learn

Whether collaboration leads to competitive surrender or revitalization depends foremost on what employees believe the purpose of the alliance to be. It is self-evident: to learn, one must want to learn. Western companies won't realize the full benefits of competitive collaboration until they overcome an arrogance borne of decades of leadership. In short, western companies must be more receptive.

We asked a senior executive in a Japanese electronics company about the perception that Japanese companies learn more from their foreign partners than vice versa. 'Our western partners approach us with the attitude of teachers', he told us. 'We are quite happy with this, because we have the attitude of students.'

Learning begins at the top. Senior management must be committed to enhancing their companies' skills as well as to avoiding financial risk. But most learning takes place at the lower levels of an alliance. Operating employees not only represent the front lines in an effective defence but also play a vital role in acquiring knowledge. They must be well briefed on the partner's strengths and weaknesses and understand how acquiring particular skills will bolster their company's competitive position.

This is already standard practice among Asian companies. We accompanied a Japanese development engineer on a tour through a partner's factory. This engineer dutifully took notes on plant layout, the number of production stages, the rate at which the line was running, and the number of employees. He recorded all this despite the fact that he had no manufacturing responsibility in his own company, and that the alliance didn't encompass joint manufacturing. Such dedication greatly enhances learning.

Collaboration doesn't always provide an opportunity to fully internalize a partner's skills. Yet just acquiring new and more precise benchmarks of a partner's performance can be of great value. A new benchmark can provoke a thorough review of internal performance levels and may spur a round of competitive innovation. Asking questions like, 'Why do their semiconductor logic designs have fewer errors than ours?' and 'Why are they investing in this technology and we're not?' may provide the incentive for a vigorous catch-up programme.

Competitive benchmarking is a tradition in most of the Japanese companies we studied. It requires many of the same skills associated with competitor analysis: systematically calibrating performance against external targets; learning to use rough estimates to determine where a competitor (or partner) is better, faster, or cheaper; translating those estimates into new internal targets; and recalibrating to establish the rate of improvement in a competitor's performance. The great advantage of competitive collaboration is that proximity makes benchmarking easier.

Indeed, some analysts argue that one of Toyota's motivations in collaborating with GM in the much-publicized NUMMI venture is to gauge the quality of GM's manufacturing technology. GM's top manufacturing people get a close look at Toyota, but the reverse is true as well. Toyota may be learning whether its giant US competitor is capable of closing the productivity gap with Japan.

Competitive collaboration also provides a way of getting close enough to rivals to predict how they will behave when the alliance unravels or runs its course. How does the partner respond to price changes? How does it measure and reward executives? How does it prepare to launch a new product? By revealing a competitor's management orthodoxies, collaboration can increase the chances of success in future head-to-head battles.

Knowledge acquired from a competitor – partner is only valuable after it is diffused through the organization. Several companies we studied had established internal clearinghouses to collect and disseminate information. The collaborations manager at one Japanese company regularly made the rounds of all employees involved in alliances. He identified what information had been collected by whom and then passed it on to appropriate departments. Another company held regular meetings where employees shared new knowledge and determined who was best positioned to acquire additional information.

Proceed with care – but proceed

After World War II, Japanese and Korean companies entered alliances with western rivals from weak positions. But they worked steadfastly toward independence. In the early 1960s, NEC's computer business was one-quarter the size of Honeywell's, its primary foreign partner. It took only two decades for NEC to grow larger than Honeywell, which eventually sold its computer operations to an alliance between NEC and Group Bull of France. The NEC experience demonstrates that dependence on a foreign partner doesn't automatically condemn a company to also-ran status. Collaboration may sometimes be unavoidable; surrender is not.

Managers are too often obsessed with the ownership structure of an alliance. Whether a company controls 51 per cent or 49 per cent of a joint venture may be much less important than the rate at which each partner learns from the other. Companies that are confident of their ability to learn may even prefer some ambiguity in the alliance's legal structure. Ambiguity creates more potential to acquire skills and technologies. The challenge for western companies is not to write tighter legal agreements but to become better learners.

Running away from collaboration is no answer. Even the largest western companies can no longer outspend their global rivals. With leadership in many industries shifting toward the east, companies in the United States and Europe must become good borrowers – much like Asian companies did in the 1960s and 1970s. Competitive renewal depends on building new process capabilities and winning new product and technology battles. Collaboration can be a low-cost strategy for doing both.

Creating a strategic centre to manage a web of partners

By Gianni Lorenzoni and Charles Baden-Fuller[1]

Strategic alliances and inter-firm networks have been gaining popularity with many firms for their lower overhead costs, increased responsiveness and flexibility, and greater efficiency of operations. Net-works that are *strategically guided* are often fast-growing and on the leading edge. In 10 years, Sun Microsystems (founded in 1982) grew to $3.2 billion in sales and $284 million in profits. This remarkable growth has been achieved by Sun's strategic direction of a web of alliances.

Few would expect such rapid growth and technological success in an older and mature industry such

[1]Source: This article © 1995, by the Regents of the University of California. Adapted from *California Management Review*, Vol. 37, No. 3. By permission of the Regents. All rights reserved. Permission conveyed through Copyright Clearance Center, Inc..

as textiles. Yet Benetton, the famous global textile empire, is in many ways like Sun. Founded in 1964, it had by 1991 achieved more than $2 billion in sales and $235 million in profits. Benetton is widely admired in Europe and the Far East for its rapid growth and ability to change the industry's rules of the game through its strategy of 'mass fashion to young people'.

What creates and guides the successful, innovative, leading-edge inter-firm network? Most research into inter-firm networks has emphasized how they can reconcile the flexibility of market relationships with the long-term commitment of hierarchically centralized management. Although all networks reflect the conscious decisions of some managers, it is becoming increasingly apparent that those networks that are not guided strategically by a 'centre' are unable to meet the demanding challenges of today's markets. In this reading, we are concerned with those strategic centres that have had a very significant impact on their sectors, especially as regards innovation. They are not confined to just a few isolated sectors, but have been observed in a wide variety of circumstances, some of which are listed in Table 6.2.1.

In this reading, we examine three dimensions of the strategic centre:

- as a creator of value for its partners;
- as leader, rule setter and capability builder;
- as simultaneously structuring and strategizing.

The role of the strategic centre

The strategic centre (or central firm) plays a critical role as a creator of value. The main features of this role are:

- Strategic outsourcing. Outsource and share with more partners than the normal broker and traditional firm. Require partners to be more than doers, expect them to be problem-solvers and initiators.
- Capability. Develop the core skills and competencies of partners to make them more effective and competitive. Force members of the network to share their expertise with others in the network and with the central firm.
- Technology. Borrow ideas from others which are developed and exploited as a means of creating and mastering new technologies.
- Competition. Explain to partners that the principle dimension of competition is between value chains and networks. The network is only as strong as its weakest link. Encourage rivalry between firms inside the network, in a positive manner.

From subcontracting to strategic outsourcing

All firms that act as brokers or operate networks play only a limited role in undertaking the production and delivery of the good or service to the markets in which the system is involved. What distinguishes central firms is both the extent to which they subcontract, and the way that they collect together partners who contribute to the whole system and whose roles are clearly defined in a positive and creative way.

Many organizations see their subcontractors and partners as passive doers or actors in their quest for competitive advantage. They typically specify exactly what they want the partners to do, and leave little to the creative skills of others. They reserve a special creative role for only a few 'critical' partners. In strategic networks, it is the norm rather than an exception for partners to be innovators.

Typically each of these partnerships extends beyond a simple subcontracting relationship. Strategic centres expect their partners to do more than follow the rules, they expect them to be creative. For example, Apple worked with Canon and Adobe to design and create a laser jet printer which then gave Apple an important position in its industry. In all the cases we studied, the strategic centre looked to the partners to be creative in solving problems and being proactive in the relationships. They demanded more – and obtained more – from their partners than did their less effective counterparts that used traditional subcontracting.

Developing the competencies of the partners

How should the central firm see its own competencies vis-a-vis its partners? Most writers argue that current competences should guide future decisions. Many have warned of the dangers in allowing the other partners in a joint venture or alliance to exploit the skills of the host organization. For example, Reich and Mankin (1986) noted that joint ventures between Japanese and US firms often result in one side (typically the Japanese) gaining at the expense of the other. Bleeke and Ernst (1991) found similar disappointment in that in only 51 per cent of the cases they studied did both firms gain from alliances. In a study of cross border alliances, Hamel (1991) found that the unwary partner typically found that its competencies were 'hollowed out' and that its collaborator became a more powerful competitor. Badaracco (1991) examined the experiences of GM and IBM, who have signed multiple agreements, and explored the difficulties they face.

TABLE 6.2.1   Some central firms and their activities

Name of company and its industry	Activities of strategic centre	Activities of the network
Apple (computers)	■ Hardware design ■ Software design ■ Distribution	■ Principal subcontractors manufacture ■ 3000 software developers
Benetton (apparel)	■ Designing collections ■ Selected production ■ Developing new technology systems	■ 6000 shops ■ 400 subcontractors in production ■ Principal joint ventures in Japan, Egypt, India and others
Corning (glass, medical products and optical fibres)	■ Technology innovation ■ Production	■ More than 30 joint ventures worldwide
Genentech (biotechnology/DNA)	■ Technology innovation	■ JVs with drug companies for production and distribution, licensing in from universities
McDonald's (fast food) in many foreign countries	■ Marketing ■ Prototyping technology and systems	■ 9000 outlets, joint ventures in many foreign countries
McKesson (drug distribution)	■ Systems ■ Marketing ■ Logistics ■ Consulting advice	■ Thousands of retail drug outlets, and ties with drug companies and government institutions
Nike (shoes and sportswear)	■ Design ■ Marketing	■ Principal subcontractors
Nintendo (video games)	■ Design ■ Prototyping ■ Marketing	■ 30 principal hardware subcontractors ■ 150 software developers
Sun (computers and computer systems)	■ Innovation of technology ■ Software ■ Assembly	■ Licensor/licensees for software and hardware
Toyota (automobiles)	■ Design ■ Assembly ■ Marketing	■ Principal subcontractors for complex components ■ Second tier for other components ■ Network of agents for distribution

Traditional brokers and large integrated firms do not 'hand out' core skills, but the central firms we studied have ignored this advice and won. While keeping a very few skills and assets to themselves, the central firms were remarkable in their desire to transfer skill and knowledge adding value to their partners. Typically, they set out to build up the partners' ability and competencies. At Benetton, site selection and sample selection were skills which Benetton would offer to the new retail partners, either directly or through the agents. Skill transfers were also evident in the machinery networks and at Apple.

Nike brings its partners to its research site at Beaverton to show them the latest developments in materials, product designs, technologies and markets. Sometimes the partners share some of the costs, but the prime benefit is to shorten cycle times and create a more vibrant system. Toyota's subcontractors may receive training from Toyota and are helped in their development of expertise in solving problems pertaining to their particular component. Not only does this encourage them to deliver better quality parts to the Toyota factories, but it also allows the Toyota system to generate an advantage over other car manufacturers.

In contrast to these companies, the less successful organizations we studied did not have groups of specialists to transfer knowledge to partners – nor, it seems, did they appreciate its importance. They did not enlist all their suppliers and customers to fight a common enemy. Moreover, their experiences did not encourage exploration of this approach. They spoke of past difficulties in alliances. Skill transfers between parties did not always result in mutual benefit. One defence contractor explained that their experience of skill transfers nearly always meant that the partner was strengthened and became a stronger rival.

Borrowing–developing–lending new ideas

While all firms bring in new ideas from outside, the central firms we studied have adopted an unusual and aggressive perspective in this sphere. They scan their horizons for all sorts of opportunities and utilize a formula we call *borrow–develop–lend*. 'Borrow' means that the strategic centre deliberately buys or licenses some existing technological ideas from a third party; 'develop' means that it takes these outside ideas and adds value by developing them further in its own organization. This commercialization can then be exploited or 'lent' with great rapidity through its stellar system, creating new adjuncts to leverage to the greatest advantage. Borrowing ideas, which are subsequently developed and exploited, stretches the organization and forces it to grow its capabilities and competencies. It demands a new way of thinking.

In the Italian packaging machinery sector, lead producers follow this strategy. They borrow designs of a new machine from specialist designers or customers. These designs are then prototyped. From these prototypes, small and medium-sized partners or specialists often improve the design in a unique way, such as improving the flows and linkages. The focal firm then re-purchases and exploits the modified design, licensing to producers for the final development and marketing phase. Thus we see a 'to-and-fro' pattern of development between the central firm and its many partners.

Sun also used the borrow–develop–lend approach in their project to build a new workstation delivering 'more power with less cost'. They borrowed existing technology from other parties, re-combined and developed them further inside Sun, and then licensed them to third parties for development and sale under the Sun brand.

The borrow–develop–lend principle helps the central firm reduce the cost of development, make progress more quickly, and, most importantly, undertake projects which would normally lie outside its scope. This approach contrasts with the procedures used by other large firms. Although these firms may buy ideas from other sources, large firms usually have a slower pace of development and rarely match the speed of exploitation achieved through networking and relending the idea to third parties. The strategic centre seems to avoid the *not-invented-here* syndrome, where innovations and ideas are rejected because they are not internally created and developed.

From the view of independent inventors, the strategic centre is an attractive organization with which to do business. The central firms have a track record of rapid commercialization (usually offering large incentives to those with ideas). They emphasize moving quickly from ideas to market by a simultaneous learning process with partners, thereby offering a competitive advantage over other developers. Finally, the willingness to involve others means rapid diffusion with fast payback, thus lessening the risks.

Perceptions of the competitive process

Firms in the same industry experience varying degrees of competitive rivalry. The joint venture, formal agreements, or the use of cross shareholdings are mechanisms used to create common ties, encourage a common view and unite firms against others in the industry. Strategic centres also create this sense of cooperation across competing enterprises.

Competitive success requires the integration of multiple capabilities (e.g. innovation, productivity, quality, responsiveness to customers) across internal and external organizational boundaries. Such integration is a big challenge to most organizations. Strategic centres rise to this challenge and create a sense of common purpose across multiple levels in the value chain and across different sectors. They achieve a combination of specialized capability and large-scale integration at the same time, despite the often destructive rivalry between buyers and customers. Strategic purchasing partnerships are commonly used to moderate this rivalry, but few firms are able to combine both horizontal and vertical linkages.

In building up their partner's capabilities and competencies, strategic centres convey an unusual perspective to their partners on the nature of the competitive process. This perspective permits the partners to take a holistic view of the network, seeing the collective as a unit that can achieve competitive advantage. In this respect, the whole network acts like a complex integrated firm spanning many markets.

TABLE 6.2.2   Different kinds of competition across sectors and stages of the value chain

	Single units within the sector	Multiple units within the sector or across related sectors
Multiple stages of the value chain	■ Vertical integration; or ■ Value-added partnerships	■ Strategic centres and their webs of partners; or ■ Large integrated multi-market organizations
Single stages of the value chain	■ Traditional adversarial firm	■ Chain stores; or ■ Simple networks

Table 6.2.2 illustrates how the actions of the strategic centre differ from other organizations. Chain stores are a good example of organizations that co-ordinate activities across many actors, yet at a single stage of the value chain. In contrast, the narrowly defined, vertically integrated firm coordinates across many stages but not across many markets or actors. Only the strategic centre and the large multi-market, vertically integrated organization are able to co-ordinate across many markets and many stages of the value chain.

Beyond the hollow organization

Although the strategic centre outsources more activities than most organizations, it is not hollow. Unlike the traditional broker that is merely a glorified arranger, the central firms we studied understand that they have to develop some critical core competencies. These competencies are, in general, quite different from those stressed by most managers in traditional firms. The agenda for the central firm consists of:

■ The idea. Creating a vision in which partners play a critical role.

■ The investment. A strong brand image and effective systems and support.

■ The climate. Creating an atmosphere of trust and reciprocity.

■ The partners. Developing mechanisms for attracting and selecting partners.

Sharing a business idea

Most of the central firms we studied are small, lean and focused operations. They employ comparatively few people and are very selective in what they do. Yet, they have an unusual ability to conceptualize a business idea that can be shared not only internally, but with other partners.

In the case of Benetton, this idea has a few key elements such as: mass fashion for young people, and the notion of a strategic network to orchestrate and fulfil this vision. In food-machinery, the key idea of the central firms is to solve the client's problems, rather than selling existing competencies, while new partners are developed in response to customer needs – a novel notion in this sector. These simple ideas are not easy to create or sustain.

These ideas have been able to capture the imagination of the employees and their partners. They also encapsulate strategy and so contain, in the language of Prahalad and Hamel (1990), the features of a clear strategic intent. Common to all the business ideas we studied, there is a notion of partnership which includes the creation of a learning culture and the promotion of systems experiments so as to outpace rival competing organizations. The strategic centres view their role as one of leading and orchestrating their systems. Their distinctive characteristics lie in their ability to perceive the full business idea and understand the role of all the different parties in many different locations across the whole value chain. The managers in the strategic centre have a dream and they orchestrate others to fulfil that dream.

This vision of the organization is not just an idea in the minds of a few managers, it is a feature that is shared throughout the organization. Many of the strategic centres we studied admit that their visions have emerged over time, they are not the work of a moment. Their vision is dynamic, for as their network grows and as the environment changes, the organizational vision also changes. This is not the case in the less successful alliances. They showed the typical characteristics of most organizations, multifaceted views of the world and a less-than-clear expression of their vision.

Clearly, vision is reinforced by success. The ability of central firms to deliver profits and growth for the partners helps cement a vision in their minds and makes their claims credible. It creates a cycle where success breeds clarity, which in turn helps breed more success.

Brand power and other support

To maintain the balance of power in the network, all central firms retain certain activities. The control of the brand names and the development of the systems that integrate the network are two activities that give the organization a pivotal role and allow it to exercise power over the system.

Some of the firms we observed were involved in consumer markets where branding is important. The brand name, owned by the central firm, was promoted by the activities of the partners, who saw the brand as a shared resource. They were encouraged to ensure its success, and quite often these efforts helped the brand become famous in a short period of time. While the brand and marketing are not so vital in producer goods markets, they are still important – and the strategic centre neglects these at its peril. Its importance is highlighted by the experiences of one of the less successful organizations we studied. This aerospace firm had problems as a result of the inability of its members to relinquish many of the aspects of marketing to a single central firm.

To retain its power, the central firm must ensure that the information between partners flows freely and is not filtered. Communication is a costly activity, and developing effective communication systems is always the responsibility of the strategic centre. These systems are not only electronically-based, but include all other methods of communication. Often there is a style for meeting among the partners, which is set and monitored by the central firm. The quality of information is a key requirement if the central firm is to mandate effectively the stream of activities scattered among different firms.

Trust and reciprocity

Leveraging the skills of partners is easy to conceive but hard to implement. The difficulties occur because it takes many partners operating effectively to make the system work, but the negative behaviour of only a few can bring the whole system to a halt. The strategic vision requires all its members to contribute all the time without fail. This is a considerable demand. The typical organizational response to such a need is to circumscribe the contracts with outsiders in a tight legalistic manner. But this is not always wise; contract making and policing can be difficult and expensive. Formal contracts are relatively inflexible and are suitable only where the behaviour is easy to describe and is relatively inflexible. But the relationships are creative and flexible and so very difficult to capture and enforce contractually.

The approach of the central firms we studied is to develop a sense of trust and reciprocity in the system. This trust and reciprocity is a dynamic concept and it can be very tight. The tightness is apparent in each party agreeing to perform its known obligations. This aspect has similarities to contracts in the sense that obligations are precisely understood. But Anglo-Saxon contracts are typically limited in the sense that partners are not expected to go beyond the contract. In contrast, in a network perspective, the behaviour is prescribed for the unknown, each promising to work in a particular manner to resolve future challenges and difficulties as they arise. This means that each partner will promise to deliver what is expected, and that future challenges will also be addressed positively. If there are uncertainties and difficulties in the relationships, these will be resolved after the work is done. If one party goes beyond (in the positive sense) the traditional contract, others will remember and reciprocate at a later date.

Trust and reciprocity are complements, not substitutes, to other obligations. If partners do not subscribe to the trust system, they can hold the whole system hostage whenever they are asked to do something out of the ordinary, or even in the normal course of events. Such behaviour will cause damage to all, and the system will break up. Only with trust can the system work in unison.

The Benetton franchising system is perhaps an extreme version of this trust system. On the continent of Europe, Benetton does not use legal contracts, rather it relies on the unwritten agreement. This, it claims, focuses everyone's attention on making the expectations clear. It also saves a great deal of time and expense. Many other strategic centres also rely on trust, but utilize contracts and formal controls as a complement. Central firms develop rules for settling disputes (for there will be disputes even in a trust system). The central firm also ensures that rewards are distributed in a manner which encourages partners to reinforce the positive circle. Benetton has encountered limits to its approach in the US, where the cultural emphasis on law and contracts has come into conflict with Benetton's strategy.

In sharp contrast are the other less successful systems we studied. There, trust was used on a very limited scale, since most organizations had difficulty in getting partners to deliver even that which was promised. Broken promises and failed expectations were common in the defence systems. Very low anticipated expectations of partner reciprocity were a common feature of the Scottish network and appliance sectors. Most organizations believed that anything crucial had to be undertaken in-house.

Trust is delicate, and it needs fostering and under-pinning. One of the ways in which positive behaviour is encouraged is to ensure that the profit-sharing relationships give substantial rewards to the partners. None of the central firms we studied seeks to be the most profitable firm in the system; they are happy for others to take the bulk of the profit. In Benetton, a retailer may find his or her capital investment paid back in three years. In Corning, some partners have seen exceptional returns. This seemingly altruistic behaviour, however, does not mean that the rewards to the central firm are small.

Partner selection

The central firms we studied recognize that creating success and a long-term perspective must begin with the partner selection process. In building a network, partners must be selected with great care. Initially, the central firms followed a pattern of trial and error, but following successful identification of the key points in the selection process, they became more deliberate. The many new styles of operation and new ways of doing things are not easy to grasp, and they are quite difficult to codify – especially at the early stages of the selection process. As time passes, a partner profile emerges together with a selection procedure aimed at creating the correct conditions for the relationships. These relationships require coordination among all the partners, a common long-term perspective, an acceptance of mutual adaptation and incremental innovation. When we looked at the details of the selection procedure, there was a difference between those central firms that had a few large partners and those that had many small-scale partners. In the case of the network composed of a few, large firm alliances, the selection criterion is typically based on careful strategic considerations. There is the question of matching capabilities and resources, as well as considerations of competition. However, most important are the organizational features based on a compatibility of management systems, decision processes and perspectives – in short, a cultural fit.

The selection process must also be tempered by availability. Typically, there are few potential partners to fit the ideal picture. Perhaps it is for this reason that some Japanese and European firms start the process early on by deliberately spinning off some of their internal units to create potential partners. Typically these units will contain some of their best talents. However, these units will have a cultural affinity and a mutual understanding, which makes the partnership easier.

In the case of the large network composed of many small partners, the centre acts as a developer of the community. Its managers must assume a different role. Apple called some of its managers 'evangelists' because they managed the relationships with 3000 third-party developers. So that they could keep constant contact with them, they used images of the 'Figurehead' and the 'Guiding Light'.

Simultaneous structuring and strategizing

Of all the battles firms face, the most difficult is not the battle for position, nor is it even the battle between strong firms and weak firms following the same strategic approaches. Rather, it is the battle between firms adopting different strategies and different approaches to the market. In these battles, the winners are usually those who use fewer and different resources in novel combinations. The central firms we studied fit this category, for they have typically dominated their sectors by stretching and leveraging modest resources to great effect. In trying to understand these battles of stretch and leverage, others have stressed the technical achievements of central firms such as lean production, technical innovation, or flexible manufacturing and service delivery. To be sure, these advances are important and provide partial explanations for the success of Sun, Nintendo, Benetton, Apple and others. Equally important, if not more important, are new ideas on the nature of strategizing and structuring. Strategizing is a shared process between the strategic centre and its partners; structuring of the relationships between the partners goes hand in hand and is seen as a key part of the strategy.

Strategy conception and implementation of ideas is shared between central firms and their webs of partners. Here they differ from most conventional organizations, which neither share their conceptions of strategy with other organizations nor insist that their partners share their ideas with them in a constructive dialogue. While all firms form partnerships with some of their suppliers and customers, these linkages rarely involve sharing ideas systematically. Subcontracting relationships are usually deeper and more complex, and many firms share their notions of strategy with their subcontractors, but the sharing is nearly always limited. Alliances demand even greater levels of commitment and interchange, and it is common for firms involved in alliances to exchange ideas about strategy and to look for strategic fit and even reshaping of strategic directions. Networks can be thought of as a higher stage of alliances, for in the strategic centre there is a conscious desire to influence and shape the strategies of the partners, and to obtain from partners ideas and influences in return.

This conscious desire to share strategy is reflected in the way in which central firms conceive of the boundaries of their operations. Most organizations view their joint ventures and sub-contractors as beyond the boundaries of their firm, and even those involved in alliances do not think of partners as an integral part of the organization. Even firms that are part of a franchise system (and thus have a more holistic perspective) do not view their relationships as a pattern of multilateral contracts. Going beyond the franchise view, central firms and their participants communicate multilaterally across the whole of the value chain. In the words of Johanson and Mattsson (1992), they have a 'network theory,' a perception of governing a whole system.

Strategizing and structuring in the central firms we studied reverses Chandler's famous dictum about structure following strategy. When partner's competencies are so crucial to the developments of the business idea of the strategic centre, the winners are building strategy and structure simultaneously whereas the losers are signing agreements without changing their organizational forms to match them. When each partner's resources and competencies are so essential to the success of the enterprise, new forms must be designed. To achieve this, structuring must come earlier, alongside strategizing, and both require an interaction among partners to create a platform of flexibility and capability. This behaviour challenges much of what is received managerial practice and avoids some of the traps that webs of alliances face.

Like the large integrated cohesive organization, networked firms are able to behave as a single competitive entity which can draw on considerable resources. However, the network form avoids many of the problems of large integrated firms, who typically find themselves paralysed in the struggle between freedom and control. By focusing attention on the matters where commonality is important (e.g. product design) and by allowing each unit to have freedom elsewhere, cooperation is fostered, time and energy spent in monitoring is reduced, and resources are optimized. In this way, the networked organization succeeds in bridging the gap between centralization and decentralization. But cooperation can dull the edge of progress, and the organizations in our study have avoided this trap by fostering a highly competitive spirit.

Marketing and information sharing

The way in which information is collected and shared in the system reveals how structure and strategy go hand in hand. The gathering of information is a central activity in any organization. A strategic feature of a network of alliances is that the firms in the system are closely linked for the sharing of information. Members of the network exchange not only hard data about best practice, but also ideas, feelings and thoughts about customers, other suppliers and general market trends.

The central firm structures the information system so that knowledge is funneled to the areas that need it the most. Members specializing in a particular function have access to others in the system performing similar tasks, and share their knowledge. This creates a level playing field within the network system. It also provides the opportunity for the members to focus and encourage the development of competitive advantage over rivals.

One of the basic premises in our network view is that new information leading to new ways of doing things emerges in a process of interaction with people and real-life situations. It follows that the 'information ability' of the firm depends critically on a scheme of interactions. The difficulty is that the generation of new information cannot be planned, but has to emerge. Thus, the task of the manager is one of designing a structure which provides an environment favourable for interactions to form, and for new information to be generated. Such a structure is a network.

Our study found, as have others, that the availability of large amounts of high quality information on many aspects of the business facilitated more rapid responses to market opportunities. Information condensed through the network is 'thicker' than that condensed through the brokerage market, but is 'freer' than in the hierarchy.

The need for a sophisticated system was clear when we contrasted the central firms we studied with other firms. In these other firms, we often found that critical information was guarded, not shared. As is so common among organizations, individual players are either afraid of being exploited or they have a desire to exploit the power they have through knowledge. Even in traditional franchise systems, information is typically passed to the centre for filtering before being shared. In the large integrated firm, centralization also causes unnecessary filtering. With centralization, the process of collecting and distributing information can be cumbersome and slow. Moreover, power to manipulate the information can be accidentally or intentionally misused by a small central group.

Some of the 'control group' of firms we studied did share their information, with adverse consequences. For example, defence contractors, unable to create an effective strategic network, found the partners sometimes used the shared information to their own advantage, and then did not reciprocate. The knowledge was exploited by partners to create superior bargaining positions. Opportunities to foster collective interest were missed, and in extreme cases, partners used the information to bolster a rival alliance to the detriment of the original information provider.

Learning races

Whereas identifying opportunities for growth is facilitated by information sharing, responding to the opportunity is more difficult. Here we see some of the clearest evidence that structure and strategy go hand in hand. First and foremost, the central firms we studied reject the idea of doing everything themselves. Instead, they seek help from others to respond to the opportunities they face. When the knowledge and capabilities exist within the network, the role of the centre is to orchestrate the response so that the whole system capitalizes on the opportunity.

It frequently happens that opportunities require an innovative response, and it is common for strategic centres to set up 'learning races'. Here, partners are given a common goal (say a new product or process development) with a prize for the first to achieve the target. The prize may be monetary, but more commonly it is the opportunity to lead off the exploitation of the new development. There is a catch, the development must be shared with others in the network. Learning races create a sense of competition and rivalry, but within an overall common purpose.

Nintendo uses carefully nurtured learning races with its partners to create high quality rapid innovation. Partners are typically restricted in the number of contributions they can make. In the case of software design, the limit may be three ideas a year. These restrictions force a striving for excellence, and the consequence is a formidable pace of progress.

Learning races can be destructive rather than constructive if the partners do not have the skills and resources. The strategic centres we studied get around these difficulties by sharing knowledge and in effect allowing the whole network to 'borrow' skills and competencies from each other.

It is important to understand the role of new members in the process of creating innovations. Many central firms follow the twin strategies of internal and external development. Internal development involves offering existing partners a possibility of sharing in the growth markets. External development involves the finding of new partners to fill the gaps and accelerate the possibilities. New partners typically fit the pattern set by existing partners. These newly found 'look alike' firms allow the strategic centre to truncate development of the necessary capabilities, leveraging off earlier experiences developed by the existing partners. By making growth a race between old and new partners, speed is assured and scale effects exploited. Our strategic centres fostered positive rivalry rather than hostility by ensuring that both old and new partners share in the final gains. When pursuing rapid growth, the twin tracks of internal and external development can lessen tensions. Because they are independent, existing members can respond to the new demands as they wish. But, if they do not respond positively, the central firm can sign up new partners to fill the gaps. The stresses and strains of growth can thus be reduced for each of the members of the network.

Conclusions

The strategically minded central firms in our study view the boundaries of the organization differently because their conception and implementation of strategy are shared with a web of partners. This attitude contrasts sharply with most organizations, which view their joint ventures and sub-contractors as existing beyond the boundaries of their firm. Even those involved in alliances typically do not think of partners as an integral part of their organization; they rarely share their conceptions of strategy and even fewer insist that their partners share their strategy with them in a constructive dialogue. In contrast, strategic centres communicate strategic ideas and intent multilaterally across the whole of the value chain. They have a network view of governing a whole system.

Strategic centres reach out to resolve classic organizational paradoxes. Many sub-contracting and alliance relationships seemed to be mired in the inability to reconcile the advantages of the market with those of the hierarchy. Strategic centres are able to create a system that has the flexibility and freedom of the market coupled with long-term holistic relationships, ensuring the requisite strategic capabilities across the whole system. Another paradox exists between creativity and discipline. Most organizations oscillate between having ample creativity and little discipline, or too much discipline and not enough creativity. Through their unusual attitude to structuring and strategizing, strategic centres attain leading-edge technological and market developments while retaining rapid decision making processes.

All organizations have much to learn from studying strategic centres and their unusual conception of the managerial task. Strategic centres have taken modest resources and won leadership positions in a wide variety of sectors. They have brought a new way of thinking about business and organizing. Much of what they do is at the cutting edge, and they are shining examples of how firms can change the rules of the game by creative and imaginative thinking.

Coevolution in business ecosystems

By James F. Moore[1]

During the past decade, a great deal of insight has been gleaned about complex biological communities – illuminated by biologists poking around in Central American jungles, collecting insects in Asia and observing birds in the Arctic. Much of this work has focused on the intricate and far-reaching relationships among species: predator and prey, pollinator and plant, protector and herd. What has become clear is that some ecosystems, notably those besieged by wave after wave of potential settlers, develop a special resiliency, flexibility and resistance to catastrophes. In contrast, those that develop in isolation like Hawaii can become highly vulnerable to ecological disasters, and may even face mass extinctions.

Recent work in community ecology has dwelled on topics like 'keystone' species, the most critical of the species in an ecosystem. When they disappear from an ecosystem, life within the system itself changes radically. One example is the sea otter. Sea otters on the California coast prey on sea urchins. The urchins feast on kelp beds and other seaweeds along the ocean floor. When the otters were hunted almost to extinction during the nineteenth century, urchin populations grew exponentially and consumed much of the kelp beds, diminishing the biodiversity of the ecosystem. The ocean floor became almost barren. Through aggressive efforts, conservationists re-introduced the sea otter to the area. The urchins have now been harvested and the rich complexity along the coast restored.

Biologists have also concentrated on highly aggressive 'exotic' species that can have a particularly disruptive effect when injected into an ecosystem. The hydrilla plant, for instance, was introduced into Florida from Asia in the 1950s. Today hydrilla infests over 40 per cent of the waterways in the state – choking lakes and rivers, killing native fish and other wildlife. The hydrilla is almost impossible to control and seems destined to have a permanently damaging effect on biological diversity and robustness in the region.

Unfortunately, the study of business communities lags well behind the biological. Yet close examination of the history of business innovation and the creation of wealth shows that there are important parallels between these two seemingly dissimilar worlds.

While biological analogies are often applied to the study of business, they are frequently applied much too narrowly. Almost invariably, the recurring focus is on the evolution of species. For example, some argue that in a market economy a Darwinian selection occurs in which the fittest products and companies survive. More recently, as businesses have been dissected into processes through the quality and re-engineering movements, some now maintain that the fittest processes and systems of processes drive out the weak. In either instance, the 'species' are seen to be subject to genetic mutation and selection that gradually transforms them.

I have become convinced that the world is more complicated than that, and that we must think in grander terms. Species-level improvement of business processes is unquestionably crucial for keeping companies successful, and creates unmistakable value for society. But there are complementary forms of evolution that play

[1]Source: This article © 1996 by James F. Moore. Adapted from Chapter One of James F. Moore, *The Death of Competition: Leadership and Strategy in the Age of Business Ecosystems,* by permission of HarperCollins Publishers Inc..

vital but grossly underrated roles in both biology and business. They encompass the ecological and evolutionary interactions that occur across an entire ecosystem, comprising all the organisms of a particular habitat as well as the physical environment itself. Leaders who learn to understand these dimensions of ecology and evolution will find themselves equipped with a new model for devising strategy, and critical new options for shaping the future of their companies.

In biological ecosystems, changes take place over different time scales: many ecological changes occur within the lifetime of the individual organism, whereas evolutionary changes transpire over numerous generations. In business ecosystems, these two time scales collapse into one, because, unlike biological species, a business can guide its own evolution and effect dramatic evolutionary changes during its lifetime. A leader in a business ecosystem has an important edge over the species in a biological ecosystem: the ability to see the big picture and understand the dynamics of the ecosystem as a whole. This enables a business to alter its traits to better fit its ecosystem. What is more, a business can anticipate future changes in its ecosystem and evolve now so that it is well prepared to face future challenges.

Coevolution: Working together to create the future

The late anthropologist Gregory Bateson, who had a lifelong obsession with the workings of complex systems, greatly influenced my thinking. His thought-provoking theories of coevolution, culture and addiction as they applied to natural and social systems are very intriguing, and I was struck by how he often studied systems in biological terms and then tried to understand how consciousness played its part in those systems.

In his thinking, Bateson focused on patterns. One of his observations was that behaviours within systems – companies, societies, species, and families – coevolve. What does 'coevolve' mean in this context? In his book *Mind and Nature*, Bateson (1979) describes coevolution as a process in which interdependent species evolve in an endless reciprocal cycle – 'changes in species A set the stage for the natural selection of changes in species B', and vice versa. Take the caribou and the wolf. The wolf culls the weaker caribou, which strengthens the herd. But with a stronger herd, it is imperative for wolves to evolve and become stronger themselves to succeed. And so the pattern is not simply competition or cooperation, but coevolution. Over time, as coevolution proceeds, the whole system becomes more hardy.

From Bateson's standpoint, coevolution is more important a concept than simply competition or cooperation. The same holds true in business. Too many executives focus their time primarily on day-to-day product and service-level struggles with direct competitors. Over the past few years, more managers have also emphasized cooperation: strengthening key customer and supplier relationships, and in some cases working with direct competitors on initiatives like technical standards and shared research to improve conditions for everyone.

A small number of the most effective firms in the world develop new business advantages by learning to lead economic coevolution. These companies – such as Intel, Hewlett-Packard, Shell, Wal-Mart, Creative Artists Agency and others – recognize that they live in a rich and dynamic environment of opportunities. The job of their top management is to seek out potential centres of innovation where, by orchestrating the contributions of a network of players, they can bring powerful benefits to bear for customers and producers alike. Their executives must not only lead their current competitors and industries – whether by competition or cooperation – but hasten the coming together of disparate business elements into new economic wholes from which new businesses, new rules of competition and cooperation, and new industries can emerge.

Obliterating industry boundaries

There are certain spots on the earth – Amazon rain forests, for instance – where biological evolution proceeds at madcap speed. In these hyperdomains, nature brazenly experiments with new evolutionary loops and wrinkles, as well as new strategies for genetic invention. As a consequence, new organisms are spawned that, in due course, crawl out and populate the rest of the world.

Similar and unprecedented upheaval is astir in the world of business. There are certain identifiable hot spots of rapidly accelerating evolutionary activity in the global economy, places where the speed of business is exceedingly fast and loose. New technologies, deregulation and changes in customer behaviour are the metaphorical equivalent of floods and fires, opening up new competitive landscapes. On such newly cleared and fertile grounds, embryonic or transformed businesses are sprouting.

These new renditions are businesses with an edge. In a sense, they are renegades. In their marauding ways, they do not respect traditional industry paradigms and partitions. Indeed, what they share is a tendency to upend business and industry models and to redraw increasingly porous boundaries.

What we are seeing, in fact, is the end of industry. That's not to say that we now need to mourn the dissolution of the airline industry or the cement industry. Rather, it means the end of industry as a useful concept in contemplating business. The notion of 'industry' is really an artefact of the slowly paced business evolution during the middle of this century. The presumption that there are distinct, immutable businesses within which players scramble for supremacy is a tired idea whose time is past. It has little to do with what is shaping the world. The designation itself is simplistic, describing certain players better than others. But, in truth, the label is not much more than a crude grid used to compare and contrast businesses, a fiction conjured up by policymakers and regulators, investment analysts, and even academic students of business strategy.

There has been a profound change in management thinking of senior executives over recent years. Earlier, many senior managers could rightfully be accused of living in denial about the structural transformations of the world economy and its impact on their businesses. Today, very few senior management teams can really be charged with living in such a state. There is no need to argue that the economic times have shifted – there is widespread agreement that this is true. The traditional industry boundaries that we've all taken for granted throughout our careers are blurring – and in many cases crumbling.

Enter a new logic to guide action

The important question for management today is not whether such changes are upon us but how to make strategy in this new world. Few management teams have been able to put together systematic approaches for dealing with the new business reality. Most find themselves struggling with varying degrees of effectiveness, but with no clear way to think about and communicate, let alone confront, the new strategic issues.

What is most needed is a new language, a logic for strategy, and new methods for implementation. Many of the old ideas simply don't work any more. For instance, diversification strategies that emphasize finding 'attractive' industries often assume the fixedness of industry structure, yet our experience tells us that industry structures evolve very rapidly. Our traditional notions of vertical and horizontal integration fail us in the new world of cooperating communities. Competitive advantage no longer accrues necessarily from economies of scale and scope. Many firms can attain the volume of production to be efficient. Flexible systems are widely available that enable firms to customize their offers, proliferate variety, and do so at little additional cost. In the new world, scale and scope matter, but only as they contribute to a continuing innovation trajectory so that a company continually lowers its costs while increasing its performance.

Companies agitating to be leaders in the volatile new world order must transform themselves profoundly and perpetually so as to defy categorization. Is Wal-Mart a retailer, a wholesaler, or an information services and logistics company? Is Intel governed by the economic realities of the semiconductor industry, or does it lead one of several coevolving, competing personal computer-centred ecosystems? Are its competitors Texas Instruments and NEC or Microsoft and Compaq?

In place of 'industry', I suggest an alternative, more appropriate term: *business ecosystem.* The term circumscribes the microeconomies of intense coevolution coalescing around innovative ideas. Business ecosystems span a variety of industries. The companies within them coevolve capabilities around the innovation and work cooperatively and competitively to support new products, satisfy customer needs, and incorporate the next round of innovation. Microsoft, for example, anchors an ecosystem that traverses at least four major industries: personal computers, consumer electronics, information and communications. Centred on innovation in microprocessing, the Microsoft ecosystem encompasses an extended web of suppliers including Intel and Hewlett-Packard and myriad customers across market segments.

A second new term is 'opportunity environment,' a space of business possibility characterized by unmet customer needs, unharnessed technologies, potential regulatory openings, prominent investors and many other untapped resources. Just as biological ecosystems thrive within a larger environment, so do business ecosystems. As traditional industry boundaries erode around us, companies often unexpectedly find themselves in fierce competition with the most unlikely of rivals. At the same time, the most creative and aggressive companies exploit these wider territories, transforming the landscape with new ecosystems.

Thus, shaping cohesive strategy in the new order starts by defining an opportunity environment. Within such an environment, strategy-making revolves around devising novel ways to seize opportunities and create viable networks with other business ecosystems.

Unfortunately, most prevailing ideas on strategy today begin with the wrong-headed assumption that competition is bounded by clearly defined industries. As a result, these ideas are nearly useless in the current business climate and are sure to be even less valid in the future. Can one understand the economic events of tomorrow relying on these ideas? I very much doubt it. It is more important to see a company within its food web than in competition with superficially similar firms bundled together in an industry.

We compete in a bifurcated world. Executives today really must view strategy from two perspectives: They must pay attention to the wider opportunity environment and strive to lead in establishing the business ecosystems that will best utilize it. The dominant new ecosystems will likely consist of networks of organizations stretching across several different industries, and they will joust with similar networks, spread across still other industries.

At the same time, executives must continue to see their companies in the traditional sense, as members of homogenous industries clawing away at rivals for market share and growth. In terms of strategy, it no longer matters if the industries are old and venerable like banking and automobiles, or frisky new ones like cable television and personal computers. So understanding one's industry will be only the first step to pursuing customers, innovation and the creation of wealth.

Learn from companies investing in the new approach

I believe that this change in conceptualizing is vitally important for three reasons. First, the conditions and challenges prevalent in the fastest-moving sectors of the global economy are spreading inexorably to all the others. The dynamics of these centres, and the challenges confronting their feistiest companies and leaders, are now relevant to us all.

Second, some of the hottest centres of economic competition – computers, communications, media, retailing, health care – are now devising fresh approaches to strategy and leadership. These approaches are not very well understood, even by many of their creators, and they surely are not appreciated by the wider public. Nevertheless, the scope of the strategic ambitions are truly breathtaking. If their creators succeed in their endeavours, their initiatives will have profound implications in our daily lives. What it already means is the end of competition as we know it.

Third, these ideas are already propagating across the general business landscape and thus are guaranteed to have a dramatic and irreversible impact on how we do business from now on. Because of these reasons, business people, no matter what business they conduct, must comprehend at least the broad outlines of what is afoot.

The special task of business leadership: Creating communities of shared imagination

In one significant respect, a strictly biological metaphor does not apply to business. Unlike biological communities of coevolving organisms, business communities are social systems. And social systems are composed of real people who make decisions. A powerful shared imagination, focused on envisioning the future, evolves in a business ecosystem that is unlike anything in biology. Conscious choice does play an important role in ecology. Animals often choose their habitats, their mates and their behaviour. In the economic world, however, strategists, policymakers and investors spend a great deal of time trying to understand the overall game and find fruitful ways to play it or change it. This consciousness is central to economic relationships.

Even more, shared imagination is what holds together economies, societies and companies. Therefore, a great deal of leadership and business strategy relies on creating shared meaning, which in turn shapes the future. For example, during 1995 millions of people from diverse backgrounds became convinced that the Internet would become a major locus for commerce, entertainment and personal communication. They rushed to become involved and, in the act of so doing, established a foundation for the very reality they believed was coming about. While many other factors encouraged the exponential growth of interest in the Internet, Sun Microsystems played a powerful role by introducing a software language called Java. Java made it possible to create appealing animated experiences across the Internet.

Sun makes a wide range of computers. Java was the result of a small research project, outside the company mainstream. Nonetheless, Sun executives saw Java's potential to enliven the community. Sun executives chose not to treat Java as just another product. Instead, they essentially gave away Java to the rest of the world in order to feed the Internet frenzy and reinforce Sun's image as a leader of the movement. What mattered was Java the campaign – not Java the product. A widespread perception formed that Sun was prescient and well positioned for the future. Sun's sales rose, its stock appreciated, and it became more able to get other stakeholders to follow its lead.

It is the mind that imparts the harmony and the sense and the syncopation to the business ecosystem. The larger patterns of business coevolution are maintained by a complex network of choices, which depend, at least in part, on what participants are aware of. As Gregory Bateson stressed, if you change the ideas in a social system, you change the system itself. We are seeing the birth of ideas. The very fact that new ideas are coming into existence is changing the conditions. If you don't follow these new ideas, you will be totally lost.

As companies get more sophisticated in creating new ecosystems, become more like the guiding hand of a forester or gardener in an ecological environment, the more this new level of consciousness will become the dominant reality of business strategy. The game of leadership will evolve to new levels. There is a wonderful book of business history by Alfred Chandler (1977) called *The Visible Hand*. It chronicles the rise of the multidivisional organization between 1900 and 1930 and the consciousness of people like Alfred Sloane who made the development of this then new organization possible. We are witnessing the next revolution beyond multidivisional organizations and beyond the visible hand. It is the ability in an environment of immense resources, immense plasticity, and powerful information systems to make and break microeconomic relationships with enormous subtlety and velocity. We are entering an age of imagination.

In an age of imagination, the ultimate struggle among companies is for the souls of customers and the hearts of vast communities of suppliers and other associated companies. Strange things can happen in the new world of virtual organizations. In the new world, strategy based on conventional competition and cooperation gives way to strategy based on coevolution – which in turn defines a new level of competition. At this

higher level, competition defines attractive futures and galvanizes concerted action. We can vividly see the tremendous power of a company like Microsoft, which leads and shapes the collective behaviour of thousands of associated suppliers, even though during most of the years of its most powerful influence, Microsoft never had more than $6 billion in sales.

But heightened consciousness of the benefits of ecosystem power and influence can also make prospective partners wary of committing to a leader. Competition to lead coevolution can bring its own peculiar paranoia – and fragment a community of companies. We already see this sort of effect within the PC business, where the heightened consciousness of Microsoft's role in overturning IBM's dominion has put all participants in the computer, communications and even the entertainment business on notice.

Now prospective allies and partners of Microsoft appreciate the costs as well as the benefits of allegiance to the company from Redmond. Many of them have become reluctant co-adventurers. Worries over Microsoft's motives and leadership outweighed the genuine benefits that appeared to be achieved by working together. Such worries also helped Sun Microsystems and Java. Java appealed to some stakeholders in part because it did not originate from Microsoft. The success of Sun and Java was welcomed as a limiter of Microsoft's influence on the future.

The new ecology of business

The heart of strategy is understanding these evolutionary patterns. What is consistent from business to business is the process of coevolution, the complex interplay between competitive and cooperative business strategies.

The immense changes that have taken place in business are minor compared to what is yet to come. When an ecological approach to management becomes more common, and when an increasing number of executives become conscious of coevolution, the pace of business change will accelerate at an exponential rate. Executives whose horizons are bounded by traditional industry perspectives will miss the real challenges and opportunities facing their companies. Shareholders and directors, who perceive the new reality, will eventually oust them. For companies caught up in dynamic business ecosystems, the stakes are considerable, but the rewards are commensurate and the challenges exhilarating as never before.

REFERENCES

Aguilar, A., Bochereau, L. and Matthiessen-Guyader, L. (2008) 'Biotechnology and sustainability: The role of transatlantic cooperation in research and innovation', *Trends in Biotechnology*, 26(4), 163–165.

Albert, M. (1991) *Capitalisme contre Capitalisme*, Paris: Seuil.

Allison, G.T. (1969) 'Conceptual Models and The Cuban Missile Crisis', *The American Political Science Review*, 3(September), pp. 689–718.

Arthur, W.B. (1994) *Increasing Returns and Path Dependence in the Economy*, Ann Arbor, MI: University of Michigan Press.

Axelrod, R. (1984) *The Evolution of Cooperation*, New York: Basic Books.

Axelsson, B. and Easton, G. (1992) *Industrial Networks: A New View of Reality*, New York: Wiley.

Badaracco, J.L. (1991) *The Knowledge Link: How Firms Compete Through Strategic Alliances*, Boston, MA: Harvard Business School Press.

Bartlett, C.A., Ghoshal, S. and Beamish, P. (2008) *Transnational Management: Text, Cases and Readings in Cross Border Management*, Burr Ridge, IL: McGraw-Hill/Irwin, 5th edition.

Bateson, G. (1979) *Mind and Nature: A Necessary Unity*, New York: Dutton.

Best, M.H. (1990) *The New Competition: Institutions of Industrial Restructuring*, Cambridge: Polity.

Bleeke, J. and Ernst, D. (1991) 'The Way to Win in Cross Border Alliances', *Harvard Business Review*, 69(6, November–December), pp. 127–135.

Bleeke, J. and Ernst, D. (1993) *Collaborating to Compete: Using Strategic Alliances and Acquisitions in the Global Marketplace*. New York: John Wiley & Sons.

Brandenburger, A.M. and Nalebuff, B.J. (1996) *Co-opetition*, New York: Currency Doubleday.

Chandler, A.D. (1986) 'The Evolution of Modern Global Competition', in: M.E. Porter (ed.) *Competition in Global Industries*, Boston, MA: Harvard Business School Press, pp. 405–448.

Chandler, A.D. (1990) *Scale and Scope*, Cambridge, MA: Belknap.

Chandler, A.D. Jr. (1977) *The Visible Hand: The Managerial Revolution in American Business*, Cambridge, MA: Harvard University Press.

Chesbrough, H.W. and Teece, D.J. (1996) 'Organizing for Innovation: When is Virtual Virtuous?', *Harvard Business Review*, 74(1, January–February), pp. 65–73.

Child, J. and Faulkner, D. (1998) *Strategies for Cooperation: Managing Alliances, Networks, and Joint Ventures*, Oxford: Oxford University Press.

Contractor, F.J. and Lorange, P. (1988) *Cooperative Strategies in International Business*, Lexington, MA: Lexington Books.

Dixit, A.K. and Nalebuff, B.J. (1991) *Thinking Strategically: The Competitive Edge in Business, Politics, and Everyday Life*, New York: WW Norton.

Doz, Y. and Hamel, G. (1998) *The Alliance Advantage: The Art of Creating Value Through Partnering*, Boston, MA: Harvard Business School Press.

Dunning, J.H. (1958) *American Investment in British Manufacturing Industry*, London: George Allen & Unwin.

Dyer, J.H. and Ouchi, W.G. (1993) 'Japanese-Style Partnerships: Giving Companies a Competitive Edge', *Sloan Management Review*, Fall, pp. 51–63.

Dyer, J.H. and Singh, H. (1998) 'The Relational View: Cooperative Strategy and Sources of Inter-organizational Competitive Advantage', *Academy of Management Review*, 23(4), pp. 660–679.

Dyer, J.H., Kale, P. and Singh, H. (2001) 'How to Make Strategic Alliances Work', *Sloan Management Review*, 42(4, Summer), pp. 37–43.

Fukuyama, F. (1995) *Trust: Social Virtues and the Creation of Prosperity*, New York: Free Press.

Gambetta, D. (ed.) (1988) *Trust: Making and Breaking Cooperative Relations*, New York: Blackwell.

Gastells, M. (2006) *The Rise of The Network Society*, Oxford: Blackwell.

Gerlach, M. (1992) *Alliance Capitalism: The Social Organization of Japanese Business*, Berkeley, CA: University of California Press.

Gnyawali, D.R. and Madhavan, R. (2001) 'Cooperative Networks and Competitive Dynamics: A Structural Embeddedness Perspective', *Academy of Management Review*, 26(3), pp. 431–445.

Gomes-Casseres, B. (1994) 'Group versus Group: How Alliance Networks Compete', *Harvard Business Review*, 72(4, July–August), pp. 62–74.

Granovetter, M.S. (1985) 'Economic Action and Social Structure: The Problem of Embeddedness', *American Journal of Sociology*, 91, pp. 481–501.

Greenhalgh, L. (2001) *Managing Strategic Relationships*, New York: Free Press.

Groenewegen, J. and Beije, P.R. (1989) 'The French Communication Industry Defined and Analyzed through the Social Fabric Matrix, the Filière Approach, and Network Analysis', *Journal of Economic Issues*, 23(4, December), pp. 1059–1074.

Gulati, R. (1998) 'Alliances and Networks', *Strategic Management Journal*, 19(4), pp. 293–317.

Hakansson, H. and Johanson, J. (1993) 'The Network as a Governance Structure: Interfirm Cooperation beyond Markets and Hierarchies', in: G. Grabner (ed.) *The Embedded Firm: On the Socioeconomics of Industrial Networks*, London: Routledge, pp. 35–51.

Hall, E.T. (1976) *Beyond Culture*, New York: Knopf Doubleday Publishing Group.

Hamel, G. (1991) 'Competition for Competence and Inter-Partner Learning Within International Strategic Alliances', *Strategic Management Journal*, 12(Special Issue, Summer), pp. 83–103.

Hamel, G., Doz, Y.L. and Prahalad, C.K. (1989) 'Collaborate with Your Competitors – and Win', *Harvard Business Review*, 67(1, January–February), pp. 133–139.

Hamilton, G.G. and Woolsey Biggart, N. (1988) 'Market, Culture and Authority: A Comparative Analysis of Management and Organization in the Far East', *American Journal of Sociology*, 94, p. 52.

Hampden-Turner, C. and Trompenaars, A. (1993) *The Seven Cultures of Capitalism: Value Systems for Creating Wealth in the United States, Japan, Germany, France, Britain, Sweden and the Netherlands*, New York: Doubleday.

Henry, J. (2003) *Understanding Japanese Society*, London: Routledge.

Hofstede, G. (1993) 'Cultural Constraints in Management Theories', *Academy of Management Executive*, 7(1), pp. 8–21.

James, B.G. (1985) *Business Wargames*, Harmondsworth: Penguin.

Jarillo, J.C. (1988) 'On Strategic Networks', *Strategic Management Journal*, 9(1, January–February), pp. 31–41.

Johanson, J. and Mattsson, L.G. (1992) 'Network Position and Strategic Action: An Analytical Framework', in: B. Axelsson and G. Easton (eds) *Industrial Networks: A New View of Reality*, London: Routledge.

Kagono, T., Nonaka, I., Sakakibara, K. and Okumara, A. (1985) *Strategic vs. Evolutionary Management*, Amsterdam: North-Holland.

Kanter, R.M. (1994) 'Collaborative Advantage: The Art of Alliances', *Harvard Business Review*, 72(4, July–August), pp. 96–108.

Kay, J.A. (1993) *Foundations of Corporate Success*, Oxford: Oxford University Press.

Kim, N.K., Sengupta, S. and Kim, D. (2009) 'How Can Non-Chaebol Companies Thrive in the Chaebol Economy?', *Journal of Global Academy of Marketing Science*, 19(3), 28–36.

Kim, W.C. and Mauborgne, R. (2004) 'Blue Ocean Strategy', *Harvard Business Review*, October, pp. 2–11.

Koen, C. (2005) *Comparative International Management*, Berkshire: McGraw Hill.

Lado, A.A., Boyd, N.G. and Hanlon, S.C. (1997) 'Competition, Cooperation and the Search for Economic Rents: A Syncretic Model', *Academy of Management Review*, 22(1, January), pp. 110–141.

Lessem, R. and Neubauer, F.F. (1994) *European Management Systems*, London: McGraw-Hill.

Lorenzoni, G. and Baden-Fuller, C. (1995) 'Creating a Strategic Center to Manage a Web of Partners', *California Management Review*, 37(3, Spring), pp. 146–163.

Meyer, E. (2014). *The Culture Map: Decoding how people think, lead, and get things done across cultures*, New York: Public Affairs.

Mitchell, R.K., Agle, B.R. and Wood, D.J. (1997) 'Toward a Theory of Stakeholder Identification and Salience: Defining the Principle of Who and What Really Counts', *Academy of Management Review*, 22(4, October), pp. 853–886.

Miwa, Y. and Ramseyer, J.M. (1996) *The Fable of the Keiretsu*, Chicago, IL: Chicago University Press.

Miyashita, K. and Russell, D. (1994) *Keiretsu: Inside the Hidden Japanese Conglomerates*, New York: McGraw-Hill, pp. 21–33.

Moore, J.F. (1996) *The Death of Competition: Leadership and Strategy in the Age of Business Ecosystems*, New York: HarperBusiness.

Oliver, N. and Wilkinson, B. (1988) *The Japanization of British Industry*, London: Basil Blackwell.

Ostrom, E. (1990) *Governing the Commons: The Evolution of Institutions for Collective Action*, Cambridge University Press.

Ouchi, W.G. (1980) 'Markets, Bureaucracies, and Clans', *Administrative Science Quarterly*, 25(1), pp. 129–142.

Pascale, R.T. and Athos, A.G. (1981) *The Art of Japanese Management*, New York: Simon & Schuster.

Pfeffer, J. and Salancik, G.R. (1978) *The External Control of Organizations: A Resource Dependency Perspective*, New York: Harper & Row.

Piore, M. and Sabel, C.F (1984) *The Second Industrial Divide*, New York: Basic Books.

Porter, M.E. (1980) *Competitive Strategy: Techniques for Analyzing Industries and Competitors*, New York: Free Press.

Porter, M.E. (1985) *Competitive Advantage*, New York: Free Press.

Porter, M.E. (1990) *The Competitive Advantage of Nations*, London: Macmillan.

Powell, W. (1990) 'Neither Market nor Hierarchy: Network Forms of Organization', *Research in Organizational Behavior*, 12, pp. 295–336.

Prahalad, C.K. and Hamel, G. (1990) 'The Core Competence of the Corporation', *Harvard Business Review*, 68(3, May–June), pp. 79–91.

Preece, S.B. (1995) 'Incorporating International Strategic Alliances into Overall Firm Strategy: A Typology of Six Managerial Objectives', *The International Executive*, 37(3, May–June), pp. 261–277.

Quinn, J.B. (1992) *The Intelligent Enterprise: A Knowledge and Service Based Paradigm for Industry*, New York: Free Press.

Reich, R. and Mankin, E. (1986) 'Joint Ventures with Japan Give Away Our Future', *Harvard Business Review*, 64(2, March–April), pp. 78–86.

Reve, T. (1990) 'The Firm as a Nexus of Internal and External Contracts', in: M. Aoki B. Gustafsson and O.E. Williamson (eds) *The Firm as a Nexus of Treaties*, London: Sage.

Richardson, G. (1972) 'The Organization of Industry', *Economic Journal*, 82, pp. 833–896.

Ruigrok, W. and Van Tulder, R. (1995) *The Logic of International Restructuring*, London: Routledge.

Schelling, T. (1960) *The Strategy of Conflict*, Cambridge, MA: Harvard University Press.

Schneider, S. and Barsoux, J. (1999) *Managing Across Cultures*, Pearson Education Limited.

Shapiro, C. and Varian, H. (1998) *Information Rules: A Strategic Guide to the Network Economy*, Cambridge, MA: Harvard Business School Press.

Simonin, B. (1997) 'The Importance of Collaborative Know-How', *Academy of Management Journal*, 40(5), pp. 1150–1174.

Teece, D.J. (1992) 'Competition, Cooperation, and Innovation: Organizational Arrangements for Regimes of Rapid Technological Progress', *Journal of Economic Behavior and Organization*, 18, pp. 1–25.

Teranishi, J. (1994) 'Loan syndication in war time Japan and the origins of the main bank system', in: N. Aoki and H. Patrick (eds) *The Japanese Main Bank System*, Oxford: Clarendom Press.

Thorelli, H.B. (1986) 'Networks: Between Markets and Hierarchies', *Strategic Management Journal*, 7(1, January–February), pp. 37–51.

Thurow, L. (1991) *Head to Head*, Cambridge, MA: MIT Press.

Trompenaars, F. (2003) *Did the Pedestrian Die: Insights from the World's Greatest Culture Guru*, Oxford: Capstone.

Van Tulder, R. and Junne, G. (1988) *European Multinationals and Core Technologies*, London: Wiley.

Verluyten, S.P. (2010) *Intercultural Skills for International Business and International Relations*, Leuven: Acco.

Weidenbaum, M. and Hughes, S. (1996) *The Bamboo Network: How Expatriate Chinese Entrepreneurs Are Creating a New Economic Superpower in Asia*, New York: Free Press.

Welling, D.T. and Kamann, D.-J.F. (2001) 'Vertical Cooperation in the Construction Industry: Size Does Matter', *Journal of Supply Chain Management*, 37(3), 28–33.

Williamson, O.E. (1975) *Markets and Hierarchies: Analysis and Antitrust Implications*, New York: Free Press.

Williamson, O.E. (1985) *The Economic Institutions of Capitalism*, New York: Free Press.

Williamson, O.E. (1991) 'Strategizing, Economizing, and Economic Organization', *Strategic Management Journal*, 12(Winter, Special Issue), pp. 75–94.

STRATEGY PROCESS

Follow the course opposite to custom and you will almost always do well.

Jean-Jacques Rousseau (1712–1778) French philosopher

Given the variety of perspectives on strategy, finding a precise definition with which all people agree is probably impossible. Therefore, in this book we will proceed with a very broad conception of strategy as 'a course of action for achieving an organization's purpose'. In this section, it is the intention to gain a better insight into how such a course of action comes about – how is, and should, strategy be made, analysed, dreamt-up, formulated, implemented, changed and controlled; who is involved; and when do the necessary activities take place?

The process by which strategy comes about can be dissected in many ways. Here, the strategy process has been unravelled into three partially overlapping issues, each of which requires managers to make choices, and each of which is (therefore) controversial (see Figure III.1):

- **Strategy formation.** This issue focuses on the question of how managers should organize their strategizing activities to achieve a successful strategy formation process.
- **Strategic change.** This issue focuses on the question of how managers should organize their strategizing activities to achieve a successful change process.
- **Strategic innovation.** This issue focuses on the question of how managers should organize their strategizing activities to achieve a successful strategic innovation process.

The most important term to remember throughout this section is *process*. In each chapter the discussion is not about one-off activities or outcomes – a formed strategy, a strategic change or a strategic innovation – but about the ongoing processes of forming, changing and innovating. These processes need to be organized, structured, stimulated, nurtured and/or facilitated over a prolonged period of time and the question concerns which approach will be successful in the long term, as well as in the short term.

FIGURE III.1   The strategy process chapters

STRATEGY FORMATION

Nothing in progression can rest on its original plan. We may as well think of rocking a grown man in the cradle of an infant.

Edmund Burke (1729–1797) Irish-born politician and man of letters

INTRODUCTION

There are many definitions of strategy and many ideas of how strategies should be made. In the introduction to Section III of this book on 'Strategy Process', our definition of strategy was kept basic to encompass the large majority of these different views – 'strategy is a course of action for achieving an organization's purpose'. Taking this definition as a starting point, a major distinction can be observed between people who see strategy as an *intended* course of action and those who regard strategy as a *realized* course of action. Mintzberg and Waters (1985) have remarked that these two views of strategy are not contradictory, but complementary. Intended strategy is what individuals or organizations formulate prior to action (a *pattern of decisions*), while realized strategy refers to the strategic behaviour exhibited in practice (a *pattern of actions*). Of course, not all behaviour is necessarily strategic – if the actions do not follow a pattern directed at achieving the organization's purpose, it does not qualify as strategy.

The process by which an intended strategy is created is called 'strategy formulation'. Normally strategy formulation is followed by strategy implementation. However, intentions sometimes end up not being put into practice – plans can be changed or cancelled along the way. The process by which a realized strategy is formed is called 'strategy formation'. What is realized might be based on an intended strategy, but it can also be the result of unplanned actions as time goes by. In other words, the process of strategy formation encompasses both formulation and action. Strategy formation is the entire process leading to strategic behaviour in practice.

For managers with the responsibility for getting results, it would be too limited to only look at the process of strategy formulation and to worry about implementation later. Managers must ask themselves how the entire process of strategy formation should be managed to get their organizations to act strategically. Who should be involved, what activities need to be undertaken and to what extent can strategy be formulated in advance? In short, for managers, finding a way to realize a strategic pattern of actions is the key issue.

THE ISSUE OF REALIZED STRATEGY

Getting an organization to exhibit strategic behaviour is what all strategists aim to achieve. Preparing detailed analyses, drawing up plans, making extensive slide presentations and holding long meetings might all be necessary means to achieve this end, but ultimately it is the organization's actions directed at the marketplace that count. The key issue facing managers is, therefore, how this strategic behaviour can be attained. How can a successful course of action be realized in practice?

To answer these questions, it is first necessary to gain a deeper understanding of the 'who' and 'what' of strategy formation – 'what type of strategy formation activities need to be carried out?' and 'what type of strategy formation roles need to be filled by whom?' Both questions will be examined in the following sections.

Strategy formation activities

In Chapter 2 it is argued that the process of strategic reasoning could be divided into four general categories of activities – identifying, diagnosing, conceiving and realizing. These strategic problem-solving activities, taking place in the mind of the strategist, are in essence the same as those encountered in organizations at large. Organizations also need to 'solve strategic problems' and achieve a successful pattern of actions. The difference is that the organizational context – involving many more people, with different experiences, perspectives, personalities, interests and values – leads to different requirements for structuring the process. Getting people within an organization to exhibit strategic behaviour necessitates the exchange of information and ideas, decision-making procedures, communication channels, the allocation of resources and the coordination of actions.

When translated to an organizational environment, the four general elements of the strategic reasoning process can be further divided into the eight basic building blocks of the strategy formation process, as illustrated in Figure 7.1.

Strategic issue identification activities. If a strategy is seen as an answer to a perceived 'problem' or 'issue', managers must have some idea of what the problem is. 'Identifying' refers to all activities contributing to a better understanding of what should

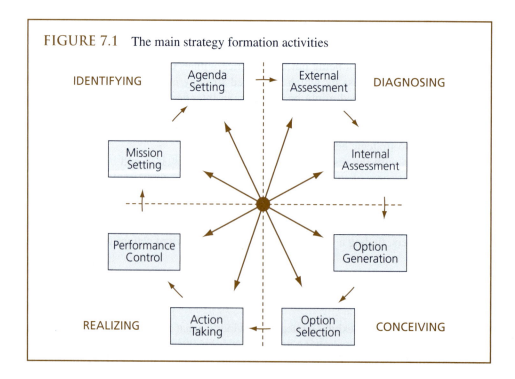

FIGURE 7.1   The main strategy formation activities

be viewed as problematic – what constitutes an important opportunity or threat that must be attended to if the organization's purpose is to be met. The key activities here are:

- **Mission setting.** What the organization sees as an issue will in part depend on its mission – the enduring set of fundamental principles outlining what purpose the organization wishes to serve, in what domain and under which conditions. A company's mission, encompassing its core values, beliefs, business definition and purpose, forms the basis of the organization's identity and sets the basic conditions under which the organization wishes to function. Where a company has a clearly developed mission, shared by all key players in the organization, this will strongly colour its filtering of strategic issues. The mission does not necessarily have to be formally captured in a mission statement, but can be informally internalized as part of the company culture. The topic of mission has been discussed at more length in Chapter 3.

- **Agenda setting.** Besides the organizational mission as a screening mechanism, many other factors can contribute to the focusing of organizational attention on specific strategic issues. For instance, the cognitive map of each strategist will influence which environmental and organizational developments are identified as issues. Furthermore, group culture will have an impact on which issues are discussible, which are off-limits to open debate, and under what conditions discussions should take place. Getting people to sit up and take notice will also depend on each actor's communication and political skills, as well as their sources of power, both formal and informal. Together these attention-focusing factors determine which issues are picked up on the 'organizational radar screen', discussed and looked into further. It is said that these issues make it on to the 'organizational agenda', while all other potential problems receive less or no attention. Many of these organizational factors are discussed more extensively in Chapters 8 and 11.

Strategic issue diagnosis activities.   To come to grips with a 'problem' or 'issue', managers must try to comprehend its structure and its underlying causes. Especially since most strategic issues are not simple and straightforward, but complex and messy, it is very important to gain a deeper understanding of 'what is going on' – which 'variables' are there and how are they interrelated? This part of the strategy formation processes can be divided into the following activities:

- **External assessment.** The activity of investigating the structure and dynamics of the environment surrounding the organization is commonly referred to as an external assessment or analysis. Typically, such a diagnosis of the outside world includes both a scan of the direct (market) environment and the broader (contextual) environment. In both cases the analyst wants to move beyond observed behaviour, to understand 'what makes the system tick'. What is the underlying structure of the industry and the market that is conditioning each party's behaviour? And what are the characteristics and strategies of each important actor, including customers, competitors, suppliers, distributors, unions, governments and financiers? Furthermore, only understanding the current state of affairs is generally insufficient; it is also necessary to analyse in which direction external circumstances are developing. Which trends can be discerned, which factors seem to be driving the industry and market dynamics, and can these be used to forecast or estimate future developments? In Chapters 4, 6 and 10, these questions surrounding external assessment are discussed in more detail.

- **Internal assessment.** The activity of investigating the capabilities and functioning of the organization is commonly referred to as an internal assessment or analysis. Typically such a diagnosis of the inner workings of the organization includes an assessment of the *business system* with which the firm creates value and the *organizational system* that has been developed to facilitate the business system. When dissecting the business system, attention is directed at understanding the resources and chain of value-adding activities that enable the firm to offer a set of products and services. To gain insight into the functioning of the organizational system, it is necessary to determine the structure of the organization, the processes used to control and coordinate the various people and units, and the organizational culture. In all these analyses a mere snapshot of the firm is generally insufficient – the direction in which the organization is developing must also be examined, including a consideration of the main change drivers and change inhibitors. Furthermore, for strategy-making it is important to compare how the organization scores on all aforementioned factors compared to rival firms. In Chapters 4 and 8 these topics are investigated in more depth.

Strategy conception activities.   To deal with a strategic 'problem' or 'issue', managers must come up with a potential solution. A course of action must be found that will allow the organization to relate itself to the environment in such a way that it will be able to achieve its purpose. 'Conceiving' refers to all activities that contribute to determining which course of action should be pursued. In this part of the strategy formation process, the following categories of activities can be discerned:

■ Option generation. Creating potential strategies is what option generation is about. Sometimes managers will immediately jump at one specific course of action, limiting their strategic option generation activities to only one prime candidate. However, many managers will be inclined to explore a number of different avenues for approaching a specific strategic issue, thereby generating multiple strategic options. Each option can range in detail from a general outline of actions to be taken, up to a full-blown strategic plan, specifying goals, actions, tasks, responsibilities, resource allocation, milestones and performance measures. Which questions each strategic option should address is the main focus of discussion in the strategy content section of this book.

■ Option selection. The potential 'solutions' formulated by managers must be evaluated to decide whether they should be acted upon. It must be weighed whether the strategic option generated will actually lead to the results required and then it must be concluded whether to act accordingly. Especially where two or more strategic options have come forward, managers need to judge which one of them is most attractive to act on. This screening of strategic options is done on the basis of evaluation criteria, for instance perceived risk, anticipated benefits, the organization's capacity to execute, expected competitor reactions and follow-up possibilities. Sometimes a number of the evaluation criteria used are formally articulated, but generally the evaluation will at least be partially based on the experience and judgement of the decision makers involved. Together, these activities of assessing strategic options and arriving at a selected course of action are also referred to as 'strategic decision making'.

Strategy realization activities.   A strategic 'problem' or 'issue' can only be resolved if concrete actions are undertaken that achieve results. Managers must make adjustments to their business or organizational system, or initiate actions in the market – they must not only think, talk and decide, but also do, to have a tangible impact. 'Realizing' refers to all these practical actions performed by the organization. If there is a clear pattern to these actions, it can be said that there is a realized strategy. In this part of the strategy formation process, the following activities can be distinguished:

■ Action taking. A potential problem solution must be carried out – intended actions must be implemented to become realized actions. This performing of tangible actions encompasses all aspects of a firm's functioning. All hands-on activities, more commonly referred to as 'work', fall into this category – everything from setting up and operating the business system to getting the organizational system to function on a day-to-day basis.

■ Performance control. Managers must also measure whether the actions being taken in the organization are in line with the option selected and whether the results are in line with what was anticipated. This reflection on the actions being undertaken can be informal, and even unconscious, but it can be formally structured into a performance monitoring and measuring system as well. Such performance measurement can be employed to assess how well certain people and organizational units are doing vis-à-vis set objectives. Incentives can be linked to achieving targets, and corrective steps can be taken to ensure conformance to an intended course of action. However, deviation from the intended strategy can also be a signal to re-evaluate the original solution or even to re-evaluate the problem definition itself. An important issue when engaging in performance control is to determine which performance indicators will be used – micro-measuring all aspects of the organization's functioning is generally much too unwieldy and time-consuming. Some managers prefer a few simple measures, sometimes quantitative (e.g. financial indicators), sometimes qualitative (e.g. are clients satisfied?), while others prefer more extensive and varied measures, such as a balanced scorecard (Kaplan and Norton, 2001; Simons, 1995).

Note that these strategy formation activities have not been labelled 'steps' or 'phases'. While these eight activities have been presented in an order that seems to suggest a logical sequence of steps, it remains to be seen in which order they should be carried out in practice. In Figure 7.1 the outer arrows represent the logical clockwise sequence, similar to the analytic reasoning process discussed in Chapter 2. The inner arrows represent the possibility to jump back and forth between the strategy formation activities, similar to the irregular pattern exhibited in the holistic reasoning process in Chapter 2.

Strategy formation roles

In all strategy formation processes the activities discussed above need to be carried out. However, there can be significant differences in who carries out which activities. Roles in the strategy formation process can vary as tasks and responsibilities are divided in alternative ways. The main variations are due to a different division of labour along the following dimensions:

■ Top vs middle vs bottom roles. Strategy formation activities are rarely the exclusive domain of the CEO. Only in the most extreme cases will a CEO run a 'one-man show', carrying out all activities except realization. Usually some activities will be divided among members of the top management team, while other activities will be pushed further down to divisional managers, business unit managers, and department managers (e.g. Bourgeois and Brodwin, 1983; Floyd and Wooldridge, 2000). Some activities might be delegated or carried out together with people even further down the hierarchy, including employees on the work floor. For activities such as external and internal assessment and option generation it is more common to see participation by people lower in the organization, while top management generally retains the responsibility for selecting, or at least deciding on, which strategic option to follow. The recurrent theme in this question of the vertical division of activities is how far down activities can and should be pushed – how much *empowerment* of middle and lower levels is beneficial for the organization?

■ Line vs staff roles. By definition, line managers are responsible for realization of strategic options pertaining to the primary process of the organization. Because they are responsible for achieving results, they are often also given the responsibility to participate in conceiving the strategies they will have to realize. Potentially, line managers can carry out all strategy formation activities without staff support. However, many organizations do have staff members involved in the strategy formation process. Important staff input can come from all existing departments, while some organizations institute special strategy departments to take care of strategy formation activities. The responsibilities of such strategy departments can vary from general process facilitation, to process ownership to full responsibility for strategy formulation.

- **Internal vs external roles.** Strategy formation activities are generally seen as an important part of every manager's portfolio of tasks. Yet, not all activities need to be carried out by members of the organization, but can be 'outsourced' to outsiders (e.g. Robinson, 1982). It is not uncommon for firms to hire external agencies to perform diagnosis activities or to facilitate the strategy formation process in general. Some organizations have external consultants engaged in all aspects of the process, even to the extent that the outside agency has the final responsibility for drawing up the strategic options.

In organizing the strategy formation process, a key question is how formalized the assignment of activities to the various potential process participants should be. The advantage of formalization is that it structures and disciplines the strategy formation process (e.g. Chakravarthy and Lorange, 1991, Reading 7.1 in this book; Hax and Maljuf, 1984). Especially in large organizations, where many people are involved, it can be valuable to keep the process tightly organized. Formalization can be achieved by establishing a strategic planning system. In such a system, strategy formation steps can be scheduled, tasks can be specified, responsibilities can be assigned, decision-making authority can be clarified, budgets can be allocated and evaluation mechanisms can be put in place. Generally, having unambiguous responsibilities, clearer accountability and stricter review of performance will lead to a better functioning organization. The added benefit of formalization is that it gives top management more control over the organization, as all major changes must be part of approved plans and the implementation of plans is checked.

Yet, there is a potential danger in using formal planning systems as a means to make strategy. Formalization strongly emphasizes those aspects that can be neatly organized such as meetings, writing reports, giving presentations, making decisions, allocating resources and reviewing progress, while having difficulty with essential strategy-making activities that are difficult to capture in procedures. Important aspects such as creating new insights, learning, innovation, building political support and entrepreneurship can be sidelined or crushed if rote bureaucratic mechanisms are used to produce strategy. Moreover, planning bureaucracies, once established, can come to live a life of their own, creating rules, regulations, procedures, checks, paperwork, schedules, deadlines and double-checks, making the system inflexible, unresponsive, ineffective and demotivating (e.g. Marx, 1991; Mintzberg, 1994a).

THE PARADOX OF DELIBERATENESS AND EMERGENCE

The ability to foretell what is going to happen tomorrow, next week, next month and next year. And to have the ability afterwards to explain why it didn't happen.
Winston Churchill (1874–1965) British prime minister and writer

Strategy has to do with the future. And the future is unknown. This makes strategy a fascinating, yet frustrating, topic. Fascinating because the future can still be shaped and strategy can be used to achieve this aim. Frustrating because the future is unpredictable, undermining the best of intentions, thus demanding flexibility and adaptability. To managers, the idea of creating the future is highly appealing, yet the prospect of sailing for *terra incognita* without a compass is unsettling at best.

This duality of wanting to intentionally design the future, while needing to gradually explore, learn and adapt to an unfolding reality, is the tension central to the topic of strategy formation. It is the conflicting need to figure things out in advance, versus the need to find things out along the way. On the one hand, managers would like to forecast the future and to orchestrate plans to prepare for it. Yet, on the other hand, managers understand that experimentation, learning and flexibility are needed to deal with the fundamental unpredictability of future events.

In their influential article, 'Of strategies: Deliberate and emergent', Mintzberg and Waters (1985) were one of the first to explicitly focus on this tension. They argued that a distinction should be made between deliberate and emergent strategy (see Figure 7.2). Where realized strategies were fully intended, one can speak of 'deliberate strategy'. However, realized strategies can also come about 'despite, or in the absence of, intentions', which Mintzberg and Waters labelled 'emergent strategy'. In their view, few strategies were purely deliberate or emergent, but usually a mix between the two.

Hence, in realizing strategic behaviour managers need to blend the conflicting demands for deliberate strategizing and strategy emergence. In the following paragraphs both sides of this paradox of deliberateness and emergence will be examined further.

The demand for deliberate strategizing

Deliberateness refers to the quality of acting intentionally. When people act deliberately, they 'think' before they 'do'. They make a plan and then implement the plan. A plan is an intended course of action, stipulating which measures a person or organization proposes to take. In common usage, plans are assumed to be articulated (made explicit) and documented (written down), although strictly speaking this is not necessary to qualify as a plan.

As an intended course of action, a plan is a means towards an end. A plan details which actions will be undertaken to reach a particular objective. In practice, however, plans can exist without explicit objectives. In such cases, the objectives are implicitly wrapped up in the plan – the plan incorporates both ends and means.

FIGURE 7.2   Deliberate and emergent strategy

Source: Mintzberg and Waters, 1985; reprinted with permission from *Strategic Management Journal*, © 1985 John Wiley and Sons Ltd.

All organizations need to plan. At the operational level, most firms will have some degree of production planning, resource planning, manpower planning and financial planning, to name just a few. When it comes to strategic behaviour, there are also a number of prominent advantages that strongly pressure organizations to engage in deliberate strategizing:

■ Direction. Plans give organizations a sense of direction. Without objectives and plans, organizations would be adrift. If organizations did not decide where they wanted to go, any direction and any activity would be fine. People in organizations would not know what they were working towards and therefore would not be able to judge what constitutes effective behaviour (e.g. Ansoff, 1965; Chakravarthy and Lorange, 1991, Reading 7.1).

■ Commitment. Plans enable early commitment to a course of action. By setting objectives and drawing up a plan to accomplish them organizations can invest resources, train people, build up production capacity and take a clear position within their environment. Plans allow organizations to mobilize themselves and to dare to take actions that are difficult to reverse and have a long payback period (e.g. Ghemawat, 1991; Marx, 1991).

■ Coordination. Plans have the benefit of coordinating all strategic initiatives within an organization into a single cohesive pattern. An organization-wide master plan can ensure that differences of opinion are ironed out and one consistent course of action is followed throughout the entire organization, avoiding overlapping, conflicting and contradictory behaviour (e.g. Ackoff, 1981; Andrews, 1987).

■ Optimization. Plans also facilitate optimal resource allocation. Drawing up a plan disciplines strategizing managers to explicitly consider all available information and consciously evaluate all available options. This allows managers to choose the optimal course of action before committing resources. Moreover, documented plans permit corporate level managers to compare the courses of action proposed by their various business units and to allocate scarce resources to the most promising initiatives (e.g. Ansoff and McDonnell, 1990; Bower, 1970).

■ Programming. Last, but not least, plans are a means for programming all organizational activities in advance. Having detailed plans allows organizations to be run with the clockwork precision, reliability and efficiency of a machine. Activities that might otherwise be plagued by poor organization, inconsistencies, redundant routines, random behaviour, helter-skelter fire fighting and chaos, can be programmed and controlled if plans are drawn up (e.g. Grinyer *et al.*, 1986; Steiner, 1979).

Given these major advantages, it can come as no surprise that organizations feel the pressure to engage in deliberate strategizing. Deliberateness is a quality that the strategy formation process cannot do without.

The demand for strategy emergence

Emergence is the process of becoming apparent. A strategy emerges when it comes into being along the way. Where there are no plans, or people divert from their plans but their behaviour is still strategic, it can be said that the strategy is emergent – gradually shaped during an iterative process of 'thinking' and 'doing'.

Emergent strategy differs from ad hoc behaviour in that a coherent pattern of action does evolve. While managers may have no prior intentions, they can explore, learn and piece together a consistent set of behaviours over time. Such an approach of letting strategy emerge has a number of major advantages that organizations also need to consider:

■ Opportunism. As the future is unknown and therefore unpredictable, organizations must retain enough mental freedom to grab unforeseen opportunities as they emerge. Organizations must keep an open mind to sense where positive and negative circumstances are unfolding, so that they can respond rapidly to these new conditions – proactively riding the wave of opportunity, using the momentum in the environment and/or the organization to their advantage. This ability to 'play the field' is an important factor in effective strategy formation (e.g. Quinn, 2002; Stacey, 2001).

- Flexibility. Not only must managers keep an open mind, they must keep their options open as well, by not unnecessarily committing themselves to irreversible actions and investments. Letting strategy emerge means not prematurely locking the organization into a preset course of action, but keeping alternatives open for as long as practically possible. And where commitments must be made, managers need to select 'robust' options, which permit a lot of leeway to shift along with unfolding events. This pressure to remain flexible is also an important demand on strategizing managers (e.g. Beinhocker, 1999; Evans, 1991).

- Learning. Often, the best way to find out what works is to give it a try – to act before you know. Letting strategy emerge is based on the same principle, that to learn what will be successful in the market must be discovered by experimentation, pilot projects, trial runs and gradual steps. Through the feedback obtained by hands-on 'doing', a rich insight can grow into what really works. As Thomas Alva Edison is well-known for remarking, invention is 5 per cent inspiration and 95 per cent perspiration, and this is probably equally true for 'inventing the corporate future'. Learning is hard work, but it is an essential part of strategy formation (e.g. Mintzberg, 1994b; Pascale, 1984).

- Entrepreneurship. Building on the previous point, often the best way to find out what works is to let various people give it a try – to tap into the entrepreneurial spirits within the organization. Different people in the organization will have different strategic ideas and many of them will feel passionately about proving that their idea 'can fly'. By providing individuals, teams and/or entire units with a measure of autonomy to pursue innovative initiatives, firms can use the energy of 'intrapreneurs' within the organization, instead of forcing them to conform or start on their own (e.g. Amabile, 1998; Pinchot, 1985). As true incubators, firms can facilitate various divergent projects simultaneously, increasing commitment or closing them down as their potential unfolds (e.g. Burgelman, 1983, 1991; Lyon, Lumpkin and Dess, 2000).

- Support. A major shift in strategy generally requires a major shift in the political and cultural landscape of an organization – careers will be affected, vested departmental interests will be impacted and cultural values and beliefs will be challenged. Rarely can such shifts be imposed top-down by decree. Getting things done in organizations includes building coalitions, blocking rivals, convincing wavering parties, confronting opposing ideas and letting things 'sink in', all with the intention of gradually building enough support to move forward. Yet, finding out where enough support can be mustered to move forward, and where side steps or even reversals are needed, is an ongoing process and cannot be predicted in advance. Hence, strategizing managers must understand the internal political and cultural dynamics of their organizations and pragmatically shape strategy depending on what is feasible, not on what is ideal (e.g. Allison, 1971; Quinn, 1980).

Each of these points seems to be the opposite counterpart of the advantages of deliberate strategizing – while deliberateness creates commitment, emergence allows for flexibility; while deliberateness gives direction, emergence allows for opportunism; while deliberateness facilitates fixed programming, emergence allows for ongoing learning. This places managers in a paradoxical position. While both deliberate strategizing and strategy emergence seem to have advantageous characteristics, they are each other's opposites and are to a certain extent contradictory – a firm cannot be fully committed to detailed and coordinated long-term plans, while simultaneously adapting itself flexibly and opportunistically to unfolding circumstances, ongoing learning and unpredictable political and cultural processes. With two conflicting demands placed on the strategy formation process at the same time, managers need to choose one at the expense of the other, trying to strike the best possible balance between deliberateness and emergence.

EXHIBIT 7.1   SHORT CASE

TOMTOM: NAVIGATING THROUGH UNCHARTED WATERS

Few companies can claim to have navigated clients to exactly the right spot. TomTom can. The Dutch company has sold millions of navigation devices and continues to do so. This travelled road was hardly evident when CEO Harold Goddijn founded the company in 1991 however. TomTom started out as a small software firm, developing mobile applications for personal digital assistants (PDAs). When more accurate GPS satellite readings became available, the company quickly recognized the potential of this technology, and developed its first in-car navigation for PDAs: the TomTom Navigator. Although innovative, the real breakthrough came when the decision was made to put the software in its own box. It was this all-in-one Portable Navigation Device (PND), the TomTom GO, that was almost solely responsible for the company's massive sudden growth. In two years, revenues increased from €39 million in 2003 to €720 million in 2005. The TomTom GO quickly managed to pave the road to further success.

Being well aware that neither products, nor software, have eternal life, CEO Goddijn decided to invest in areas that would broaden the company's revenue base. Goddijn knew that the mobile platform for navigation products is not a stable basis for a sustainable business model. A diversity of platforms and various hardware suppliers, in addition to the threat of piracy, make up a volatile environment indeed. Goddijn was in search of new growth areas to broaden the firm's base.

He did so with a couple of strategic acquisitions. In August 2005 the German telematics company Datafactory AG was acquired, laying the foundation for the business unit 'Telematics', currently Europe's fastest-growing telematics service provider for fleet management. The acquisition of Applied Generics, specializing in using data from mobile networks for advanced routing of vehicles, formed the basis of TomTom's traffic services. As it was expected that within a few years each car would have built-in navigation by default, an automotive engineering team from the Siemens research and development division was attracted in June 2007. They became the core of TomTom's Automotive business unit, geared towards developing these built-in navigation systems.

Since TomTom's core business remained its navigation devices, maps were of utmost importance to the company's activities. In July 2007 TomTom made a bid of €2.0 billion for digital map developer Tele Atlas. Nokia responded by making an even bigger bid for geographic information provider Navteq, currently known as Here, for $8.1 billion in October 2007. Garmin, TomTom's biggest competitor, felt threatened by this development and offered €2.3 billion for Tele Atlas. TomTom raised its bid to €2.9 billion after which Garmin pulled out. TomTom now consisted of four market-facing business units: Consumer (organized around the PND and GPS Sport products), Automotive (built-in navigation software, map content and services), Licensing (selling map content and services), and Telematics (offering fleet management solutions), in addition to two centralized Technology units.

The storm had not calmed down for TomTom yet though. The financial crisis commenced, and Google announced they would be offering Google Maps for free, based on their own content. The combination of crisis and free maps resulted in an immense decline in sales of PNDs, TomTom's main source of revenues. Google's announcement, the firm's largest licensing client, had another effect: the scarcity value of its maps deteriorated and TomTom's stock value made a dive. TomTom went through financial restructuring and had to reduce its workforce by 7 per cent.

Goddijn had to respond to stronger competition in the PND market and the 'free' business models that were shrinking the market. He answered by attracting a new Chief Technology Officer (CTO), Charles

Davies. After 20 years of being software director at PDA developer Psion, Davies had been CTO of Symbian, Nokia's mobile operating system. He was expected to not only understand the future need for mapping and navigation technology, but also bring in a more deliberate strategy mode. Although Tom-Tom fared fairly well in 2010, the same could not be said for the next year. In 2011, economic decline had weakened the consumer electronics markets, a trend that was expected to last. The European PND market was expected to continue to shrink and in four months' time, TomTom's shares lost half their value.

This new wake-up call gave Goddijn and his fellow board members another impetus to do something to act on this negative trend. TomTom's top management held various meetings. Tough decisions were needed on the group structure, the firm's activities, reporting lines and review processes, as well as on how to achieve the highly needed savings. The process was top-down driven; only a limited number of organizational members were involved. The main outcomes were a new organization structure and savings in support activities. The newly created structure would bring more transparency and accountability, speed up making innovation choices and reduce time to market.

In addition, the company decided to change its internal structure, emphasizing its diversification. Products would continue to be delivered to the market through the existing Consumer, Automotive, Licensing and Telematics business units. Furthermore, existing R&D activities would be regrouped into various smaller product units within the Technology Units Maps and Location Technology Products. Each product unit is mandated to invest in ongoing development of a well-defined product category to deliver the best products to TomTom's customers.

In the new structure – still in place today – product units are imposed to develop a business plan based on a standardized strategy template, including coherent actions, a product roadmap and a financial paragraph. Templates were provided by a corporate staff organization, headed by CTO Charles Davies. Every product unit is supposed to follow the ideas of Richard Rumelt's book *Good Strategy/Bad Strategy*, in which good planning is emphasized. Review sessions with the product units are planned three times a year. Furthermore, the business of each business unit and product unit is updated annually and presented to TomTom's management board and CTO.

Clearly, a much more formal strategy approach has been installed. This strategy has proven to navigate TomTom to a renewed state of growth and stability, but that does not mean it will last. After all, the firm's history has proven that the industry is in constant flux. This holds especially true for the next step TomTom is undertaking: delivering products to support autonomous driving. However, this raises some obvious questions. How soon will autonomous driving be taken on the road on a mass scale and what technologies will be used? Who will be the future competitors? Next to existing competitors like Here – nowadays owned by Audi, BMW and Daimler – companies like Nvidea and Mobileye might play a role as well. And what will be the role of Apple, Uber and Google in autonomous driving?

With its future uncertain, it is clear that a good strategy is imperative to navigate through these unchartered waters successfully. Should TomTom continue with its current structured strategy, or should the company prepare for stormy waters and build in an additional emergency response unit?

Co-authors: Claudia Janssen and Wester Wagenaar

Source: Company information.

PERSPECTIVES ON STRATEGY FORMATION

It is impossible for a man to learn what he thinks he already knows.
Epictetus (c. 60–120) Roman philosopher

In Hollywood, most directors do not start shooting a movie until the script and storyboard are entirely completed – the script details each actor's words, expression and gestures, while the storyboard graphically depicts how each scene will look in terms of camera angles, lighting, backgrounds and stage props. Together they form a master plan, representing the initial intentions of the director. However, it frequently happens that a director has a new insight, and changes are made to the script or storyboard 'on the fly'. Yet, on the whole, most 'realized movies' are fairly close to directors' initial intentions.

For some directors this is madness. They might have a movie idea, but in their mind's eye they cannot yet picture it in its final form. Some elements might have already crystallized in their thoughts, but other parts of the film can only be worked out once the cameras are rolling and the actors start playing their roles. In this way, directors can let movies emerge without having a detailed script or storyboard in advance to guide them. It can be said that such movies are shaped by gradually blending together a number of small intentional steps over a long period of time, instead of taking one big step of making a master plan and implementing it. This approach of taking many small steps is called 'incrementalism'.

The question is how this works for managers making strategy. Is it best to deliberately draw up a storyboard for the film and trust that the 'actors' are flexible enough to adapt to minor changes in the script as time goes by? Or is the idea of a master plan misplaced, and are the best results achieved by developing a strategy incrementally, emergently responding to opportunities and threats as they unfold along the way? In short, how should strategizing managers strike a balance between deliberateness and emergence?

Unfortunately, the strategic management literature does not offer a clear-cut answer to this question. In both the academic journals and the practitioner-oriented literature, a wide spectrum of views can be observed on how managers should engage in strategy formation. While some writers suggest that there might be different styles in balancing deliberateness and emergence (e.g. Chaffee, 1985; Hart, 1992), most seem intent on offering 'the best way' to approach the issue of strategy formation – which often differs significantly from 'the best way' advised by others.

To come to grips with this variety of views, here the two diametrically opposed pole positions will be identified and discussed. On the basis of these two 'points of departure' the debate on how to deal with the paradox of deliberateness and emergence can be further explored. At one pole we find those managers and theorists who strongly emphasize deliberateness over emergence. They argue that organizations should strive to make strategy in a highly deliberate manner, by first explicitly formulating comprehensive plans, and only then implementing them. In accordance with common usage, this point of view will be referred to as the 'strategic planning perspective'. At the other pole are those who strongly emphasize emergence over deliberateness, arguing that in reality most new strategies emerge over time and that organizations should facilitate this messy, fragmented, piece-meal strategy formation process. This point of view will be referred to as the 'strategic incrementalism perspective'.

The strategic planning perspective

Advocates of the strategic planning perspective argue that strategies should be deliberately planned and executed. In their view, anything that emerges unplanned is not really strategy. A successful pattern of action that was not intended cannot be called strategy, but should be seen for what it is – brilliant improvization or just plain luck (Andrews, 1987). However, managers cannot afford to count on their good fortune or skill at muddling through. They must put time and effort into consciously formulating an explicit plan, making use of all available information and weighing all of the strategic alternatives. Tough decisions need to be made and priorities need to be set, before action is taken. 'Think before you act' is the strategic planning perspective's motto. But once a strategic plan has been adopted, action should be swift, efficient and controlled. Implementation must be secured by detailing the activities to be undertaken, assigning responsibilities to managers and holding them accountable for achieving results (e.g. Ansoff and McDonnell, 1990; Chakravarthy and Lorange, 1991, Reading 7.1).

Hence, in the strategic planning perspective, strategies are intentionally designed, much as an engineer designs a bridge. Building a bridge requires a long formulation phase, including extensive analysis of the situation, the drawing up of a number of rough designs, evaluation of these alternatives, choice of a preferred design, and further detailing in the form of a blueprint. Only after the design phase has been completed do the construction companies take over and build according to plan. Characteristic of such a planning approach to producing bridges and strategies is that the entire process can be disassembled into a number of distinct steps that need to be carried out in a sequential and orderly way. Only by going through these steps in a conscious and structured manner will the best results be obtained (e.g. Armstrong, 1982; Powell, 1992).

For advocates of the strategic planning perspective, the whole purpose of strategizing is to give organizations direction, instead of letting them drift. Organizations cannot act rationally without intentions – if you do not know where you are going, any behaviour is fine, which soon degenerates into 'muddling through' (e.g. Ansoff, 1991; Steiner, 1979). By first setting a goal and then choosing a strategy to get there, organizations can get 'organized'. Managers can select actions that are efficient and effective within the context of the strategy. A structure can be chosen, tasks can be assigned, responsibilities can be divided, budgets can be allotted and targets can be set. Not unimportantly, a control system can be created to measure results in comparison to the plan, so that corrective action can be taken.

Another advantage of the planning approach to strategy formation is that it allows for the *formalization* and *differentiation* of strategy tasks. Because of its highly structured and sequential nature, strategic planning lends itself well to formalization. The steps of the strategic planning approach can be captured in planning systems (e.g. Kukalis, 1991; Lorange and Vancil, 1977), and procedures can be developed to further enhance and organize the strategy formation process. In such strategic planning systems, not all elements of strategy formation need to be carried out by one and the same person, but can be divided among a number of people. The most important division of labour is often between those formulating the plans and those implementing them. In many large companies the managers proposing the plans are also the ones implementing them, but deciding on the plans is passed up to a higher level. Often other tasks are spun off as well, or shared with others, such as diagnosis (strategy department or external consultants), implementation (staff departments) and evaluation (corporate planner and controller). Such task differentiation and specialization, it is argued, can lead to a better use of management talent, much as the division of labour has improved the field of production. At the same time, having a formalized system allows for sufficient coordination and mutual adjustment, to ensure that all specialized elements are integrated back into a consistent organizationwide strategy (e.g. Grinyer *et al.*, 1986; Jelinek, 1979).

Last, but not least, an advantage of strategic planning is that it encourages long-term thinking and commitment. 'Muddling through' is short-term oriented, dealing with issues of strategic importance as they come up or as a crisis develops. Strategic planning, on the other hand, directs attention to the future. Managers making strategic plans have to take a more long-term view and are stimulated to prepare for, or even create, the future (Ackoff, 1981). Instead of just focusing on small steps, planning challenges managers to define a desirable future and to work towards it. Instead of wavering and opportunism, strategic planning commits the organization to a course of action and allows for investments to be made at the present that may only pay off in the long run (e.g. Ansoff, 1991; Miller and Cardinal, 1994).

One of the difficulties of strategic planning, advocates of this perspective will readily admit, is that plans will always be based on assumptions about how future events will unfold. Plans require forecasts. And as the Danish physicist Niels Bohr once joked, "prediction is very difficult, especially about the future". Even enthusiastic planners acknowledge that forecasts will be inaccurate. As Makridakis, the most prolific writer on the topic of forecasting, writes (1990: 66), "the future can be predicted only by extrapolating from the past, yet it is fairly certain that the future will be different from the past". Consequently, it is clear that rigid long-range plans based on such unreliable forecasts would amount to nothing less than Russian roulette. Most proponents of the strategic planning perspective therefore caution for overly deterministic plans. Some argue in favour of 'contingency planning', whereby a number of alternative plans are held in reserve in case key variables in the environment suddenly change. These contingency plans are commonly based on different future 'scenarios' (Van der Heijden, 1996; Wilson, 2000; Bodwell and Chermack, 2010, Reading 7.3). Others argue that organizations should stage regular reviews, and realign strategic plans to match the altered circumstances. This is usually accomplished by going through the planning cycle every year and adapting strategic plans to fit with the new forecasts.

The strategic planning perspective shares many of the assumptions underlying the analytic reasoning perspective discussed in Chapter 2. Both perspectives value systematic, orderly, consistent, logical reasoning and assume that humans are capable of forming a fairly good understanding of reality. And both are based on a calculative and optimizing view of strategy-making. It is, therefore, not surprising that many managers who are rationally inclined also exhibit a distinct preference for the strategic planning perspective.

EXHIBIT 7.2   THE STRATEGIC PLANNING PERSPECTIVE

KOOYMAN: BUILDING ISLANDS

For three generations, Kooyman has been building much of the Caribbean islands. Doing business with big do-it-yourself stores for building materials, hardware and home improvement, the Kooyman family business is the largest player on the islands of Curaçao, Bonaire, Aruba and St Maarten. It has to cope with unique small island economies where logistics require complex knowledge of supply and demand, and where markets are generally small and very mature. With little growth potential and a thoroughly competitive market, Kooyman fends off the challenges that come with operating in island economies by efficiency and good planning.

The company's planning used to follow a straightforward yearly procedure. Kooyman's board of directors updated their analysis of the current and future situation and changed strategic directions accordingly. The company's middle management then had to carry out a sanity check. This yearly update was subsequently translated by board members and middle management into more practical action plans. There was one problem though:

with little public information on island economics available, assumptions on business environments and customers are often not accurate enough, and strategic planning turns out to be less than effective. In order to connect better to the wishes and expectations of Kooyman's customers, the company decided to bring its planning process to the next level.

Because middle management is closer to consumer's needs, Kooyman's CEO Herbert van der Woude has decided to involve them more closely when creating the company's yearly plans. Middle management first outlines their understanding of the current situation, emphasizing Kooyman's strengths and weaknesses, and then proposes their desired future for the company. The inputs are discussed by the board of directors and related to other available sources, and then consolidated in the strategic plan. In a joint meeting with middle management, the board explains how and why their inputs are being included or not, and what future objectives have been decided upon. Since the inputs from middle management form the basis for the company's assumptions, Kooyman's new planning procedure manages to create more robust strategic plans that are also more widely embraced among the firm's management. One result of this strategy process has been the key finding of middle management – based on customer meetings – that another strategic pillar needs to be developed: customers want Kooyman to engage in e-tailing.

However, the tricky part with e-tailing strategies is that these are extremely hard to plan. In Kooyman's case, this is even more so. Although e-tailing has similarities with the company's core competencies, such as logistics, it also requires several yet underdeveloped Internet-related skills. In addition, e-tailing on an island is even more difficult to establish. Since deep market knowledge, complex logistics channels and strategic alliances with suppliers are necessary to operate on Kooyman's islands, Amazon and Ali Baba do not actively operate there. This means that Kooyman possesses a competitive advantage, but also that the firm has few examples to get inspired by.

In order to deal with the difficulty of incorporating e-tailing into its planning, Kooyman decided to push a similar strategy as it did with its corporate strategy: focus on what customers want and expect. The firm therefore decided to create customer panels, divided into key customer segments, and asked them how they experience different aspects of the Kooyman experience. From here the company deduces what is required to improve and expand upon this experience through online means. Kooyman then makes use of its regular strategic planning process to define what has to be carried out exactly and how to do so efficiently.

Kooyman shows the merits of strategic planning in small island economies due to their static nature. In this context it is more difficult to imitate partnerships, logistics channels and the indispensable deep market knowledge. To properly channel this know-how into appropriate action, the company's middle management was given a leading role in the strategy formation process. This leads to planning more in accordance with customers' expectations, ensuring Kooyman can continue to assist islanders building and improving houses for years to come.

Co-authors: Jasper de Vries and Wester Wagenaar

Source: Company information.

The strategic incrementalism perspective

 To advocates of the strategic incrementalism perspective, the planners' faith in deliberateness is misplaced and counter-productive. In reality, incrementalists argue, new strategies largely emerge over time, as managers proactively piece together a viable course of action or reactively adapt to unfolding circumstances. The strategy formation process is not about rigidly *setting* the course of action in advance, but about flexibly *shaping* the course of action by gradually blending together initiatives into a coherent pattern of actions. Making strategy involves sense-making, reflecting, learning, envisioning, experimenting and changing the organization, which cannot be neatly organized and programmed. Strategy formation is messy, fragmented and piecemeal – much more like the unstructured and unpredictable processes of exploration and invention rather than the orderly processes of design and production (e.g. Mintzberg, 1990; Quinn, 1978, Reading 7.2).

Yet proponents of the strategic planning perspective prefer to press strategy formation into an orderly, mechanistic straightjacket. Strategies must be intentionally designed and executed. According to strategic incrementalists, this excessive emphasis on deliberateness is due to planners' obsession with rationality and control (e.g. Mintzberg, 1993;

Wildavsky, 1979). Planners are often compulsive in their desire for order, predictability and efficiency. It is the intention of strategic planning to predict, analyse, optimize and programme – to deliberately fine-tune and control the organization's future behaviour. For them, 'to manage' is 'to control' and therefore only deliberate patterns of action constitute good strategic management.

Incrementalists do not question the value of planning and control as a means for managing some organizational processes, but point out that strategy formation is not one of them. In general, planning and control are valuable for routine activities that need to be efficiently organized (e.g. production or finance). But planning is less suitable for non-routine activities – that is, for doing new things. Planning is not appropriate for innovation (e.g. Hamel, 1996; Kanter, 2002). Just as R&D departments cannot plan the invention of new products, managers cannot plan the development of new strategies. Innovation, whether in products or strategies, is not a process that can be neatly structured and controlled. Novel insights and creative ideas cannot be generated on demand, but surface at unexpected moments, often in unexpected places. Nor are new ideas born fully grown, ready to be evaluated and implemented. In reality, innovation requires brooding, tinkering, experimentation, testing and patience, as new ideas grow and take shape. Throughout the innovation process it remains unclear which ideas might evolve into blockbuster strategies and which will turn out to be miserable disappointments. No one can objectively determine ahead of time which strategic initiatives will 'fly' and which will 'crash'. Therefore, managers engaged in the formation of new strategies must move incrementally, letting novel ideas crystallize over time, and increasing commitment as ideas gradually prove their viability in practice. This demands that managers behave not as planners, but as 'inventors' – searching, experimenting, learning, doubting and avoiding premature closure and lock-in to one course of action (e.g. Stacey, 1993, Reading 11.2 in this book; Beinhocker, 1999).

Recognizing that strategy formation is essentially an innovation process has more consequences. Innovation is inherently subversive, rebelling against the status quo and challenging those who are emotionally, intellectually or politically wedded to the current state of affairs. Creating new strategies involves confronting people's cognitive maps, questioning the organizational culture, threatening individuals' current interests and disrupting the distribution of power within the organization (e.g. Hamel, 1996; Johnson, 1988). None of these processes can be conducted in an orderly fashion, let alone be incorporated into a planning system. Changing people's cognitive maps requires complex processes of unlearning and learning. Cultural and political changes are also difficult processes to programme. Even for the most powerful CEO, managing cognitive, cultural and political changes is not a matter of deliberate control, but of incremental shaping. Less powerful managers will have an even weaker grip on the unfolding cognitive, cultural and political reality in their organization and therefore will be even less able to plan. In short, managers who understand that strategy formation is essentially a disruptive process of organizational change will move incrementally, gradually moulding the organization into a satisfactory form. This demands that managers behave not as commanders, but as 'organizational developers' – questioning assumptions, challenging ideas, getting points on the strategic agenda, encouraging learning, championing new initiatives, supporting change and building political support.

Incrementalists point out that planning is particularly inappropriate when dealing with wicked problems (see Chapter 1). While solving tame problems can often be planned and controlled, strategizing managers rarely have the luxury of using generic solutions to fix clearly recognizable strategic problems. Strategic problems are inherently wicked – they are essentially unique, highly complex, linked to other problems, can be defined and interpreted in many ways, and have no correct answer, nor a delimited set of possible solutions. The planning approach of recognizing the problem, fully analysing the situation, formulating a comprehensive plan and then implementing the solution, is sure to choke on a wicked problem. A number of weaknesses of planning show up when confronted with a wicked problem:

■ Problems cannot be simply recognized and analysed, but can be interpreted and defined in many ways, depending on how the manager looks at them. Therefore, half the work of the strategizing manager is *making sense* out of complex problems. Or, as Rittel and Webber (1973) put it, the definition of a wicked problem is the problem! Managers must search for new ways for understanding old problems and must be aware of how others are reinterpreting what they see (e.g. Liedtka, 2000; Smircich and Stubbart, 1985). This inhibits strategic planning and encourages strategic incrementalism.

■ A full analysis of a wicked problem is impossible. Due to a wicked problem's complexity and links to other problems, a full analysis would take, literally, forever. And there would always be more ways of interpreting the problem, requiring more analysis. Strategic planning based on the complete understanding of a problem in advance therefore necessarily leads to paralysis by analysis (e.g. Langley, 1995; Lenz and Lyles, 1985). In reality, however, managers move proactively despite their incomplete understanding of a wicked problem, learning as they go along. By acting and thinking at the same time, strategizing managers can focus their analyses on what seems to be important and realistic in practice, gradually shaping their understanding along the way.

■ Developing a comprehensive plan to tackle a wicked problem is asking for trouble. Wicked problems are very complex, consisting of many subproblems. Formulating a master plan to solve all subproblems in one blow would require a very high level of planning sophistication and an organization with the ability to implement plans in a highly coordinated manner – much like circus performers who can keep ten plates twirling at the ends of poles at the same time. Such organizations are rare at best, and the risk of a grand strategy failing is huge – once one plate falls, the rest usually come crashing down. This is also known as Knagg's law: the more complex a plan, the larger the chance of failure. Incrementalists therefore argue that it is wiser to tackle subproblems individually, and gradually blend these solutions into a cohesive pattern of action.

■ Planners who believe that formulation and implementation can be separated underestimate the extent to which wicked problems are interactive. As soon as an organization starts to implement a plan, its actions will induce counteractions. Customers will react, competitors will change behaviour, suppliers will take a different stance, regulatory agencies might come into action, unions will respond, the stock markets will take notice and company employees will draw conclusions. Hence, action by the organization will change the nature of the problem. And since the many counterparties are intelligent players capable of acting strategically, their responses will not be entirely predictable. Planners will not be able to forecast and incorporate other parties' reactions into the plans. Therefore, plans will be outdated as soon as implementation starts. For this reason, incrementalists argue that action must always be swiftly followed by redefinition of the problem and reconsideration of the course of action being pursued. Over time, this iterative process of action–reaction–reconsideration will lead to the emergence of a pattern of action, which is the best possible result given the interactive nature of wicked problems.

■ This last point, on the unpredictability of external and internal reactions to a plan, leads to a weakness of strategic planning that is possibly its most obvious one – strategy has to do with the future and the future is inherently unknown. Developments cannot be clearly forecast, future opportunities and threats cannot be predicted, nor can future strengths and weaknesses be accurately foreseen. In such unknown terrain, it is foolhardy to commit oneself to a preset course of action unless absolutely necessary. It makes much more sense in new and unpredictable circumstances to remain flexible and adaptive, postponing fixed commitments for as long as possible. An unknown future requires not the mentality of a train conductor, but of an explorer – curious, probing, venturesome and entrepreneurial, yet moving cautiously, step-by-step, ready to shift course when needed.

To proponents of the strategic incrementalism perspective, it is a caricature to call such behaviour ad hoc or muddling through. Rather, it is behaviour that acknowledges the fact that strategy formation is a process of innovation and organizational development in the face of wicked problems in an unknown future. Under these circumstances, strategies must be allowed to emerge and 'strategic planning' must be seen for what it is – a contradiction in terms.

EXHIBIT 7.3   THE STRATEGIC INCREMENTALISM PERSPECTIVE

PIXAR: "GOING FROM SUCK TO NON-SUCK"

From its early beginnings with *Toy Story* all the way to its latest movie iteration *Finding Dory*, Pixar has consistently churned out blockbusters. All of its 17 movies to date have been remarkable successes at the box office and most have been highly praised by critics all over the world. One of the key factors contributing to the unblemished record of Pixar's movies is the company's emergent strategy. The assumption that the first ideas on new products are likely to be wrong or incomplete is embedded in the way Pixar approaches its movies. Pixar co-founder and President Ed Catmull refers to this as "going from suck to non-suck".

Hollywood generally approaches film productions with deliberate planning. The work begins with a script, after which resources are devoted to the project and studios produce the movie. This can work out fine, but there is also a real possibility it leads to mediocrity or flops. When problems arise while creating the film, usually more money is used to solve it. Pixar's answer? As Andrew Stanton, Director of *Finding Nemo* and *WALL-E*, puts it: "Be wrong as fast as we can, which basically means, we're gonna screw up, let's just admit that. Let's not be afraid of that".

Pixar thus does not initiate new movies with a script. Instead, ideas start with rough story ideas. Small 'incubation teams' work with directors to find holes in these ideas and to refine them. Then storyboards are made and extensively revised. These get developed and thousands of problems are met and dealt with on the way. As a result, Pixar used an astounding 43 536 storyboards for *Finding Nemo*,

69 562 for *Ratatouille* and 98 173 for *WALL-E*. The storyboards are then converted into story reels, improved storyboards with a voice track. Here feedback and iteration also play a key role. According to Catmull, "Every time we show a film for the first time, it sucks", but the comments people provide to the director make sure substantial changes are made throughout the moviemaking process. If a project manages to pass through all of Pixar's internal processes, it moves to the costly digital animation phase. This is how the studio can continue to breed original movies that "would all fail an elevator pitch", but still end up as multimillion blockbusters.

Sometimes this constant struggle for 'non-suck' can result in painful decisions, but even these can end on a happy note. The cancellation of the movie *Newt* is an example of this process. The idea of this film, which was supposed to come out in 2011, did not seem to work and the project was given to someone else to direct. Pete Docter, director of *Up*, took it on but completely turned it around. This ultimately resulted in a completely different film altogether: the critically acclaimed 2015 hit *Inside Out*, Pixar's take on human emotions.

Of course Pixar's way of operating is slow; creating one movie can easily take more than 5 years. Even then, as chief creative officer of Pixar John Lasseter states, "We don't actually finish our films, we release them". Pixar's successful emergent strategy follows the same idea.

Co-author: Wester Wagenaar

Sources: Catmull, Ed. 'Creativity, Inc.: Overcoming the Unseen Forces That Stand in the Way of True Inspiration', 2014; *Fast Company*, 19 March 2014; *Forbes*, 11 September 2014; *Innoblog*, 6 April 2011.

MANAGING THE PARADOX OF DELIBERATENESS AND EMERGENCE

Those who triumph compute at their headquarters a great number of factors prior to a challenge. Little computation brings defeat. How much more so with no computation at all!

Sun Tzu (5th century BC) Chinese military strategist

So, how should strategies be formed in practice? Should managers strive to formulate and implement strategic plans, supported by a formalized planning and control system? Or should managers move incrementally, behaving as inventors, organizational developers and explorers? (See Table 7.1).

No consensus has yet developed within the field of strategic management on how to manage deliberateness and emergence, which is understandable as it – among other things such as personal and culture differences (see also the next paragraph on the international perspective) – depends on the company's context. For example, strategy formation in hypercompetitive and stable environments will differ significantly. Yet, a number of suggestions have been made by scholars in the strategy and organizational behaviour fields. Taking the taxonomy of Chapter 1, the following options can be considered.

Balancing

In balancing opposite demands, elements of the opposing demands are traded off to find the most appropriate balance. The demand for deliberate strategizing and strategy emergence often differs over departments within the organization; depending on the organizational unit's primary process (see Chapter 4 on Business level strategy). Within business units production departments are generally more planning-oriented, product development units take a more incremental process, and research and development takes a bit of both.

In large organizations, the strategy process not only differs over departments but also between the business units. Strategists of business units that are active in stable industries

TABLE 7.1   Strategic planning versus strategic incrementalism perspective

	Strategic planning perspective	*Strategic incrementalism perspective*
Emphasis on	Deliberateness over emergence	Emergence over deliberateness
Nature of strategy	Intentionally designed	Gradually shaped
Nature of formation	Figuring out	Finding out
View of future	Forecast and anticipate	Partially unknown and unpredictable
Posture towards the future	Make commitments, prepare	Postpone commitments, remain flexible
Formation process	Formally structured and comprehensive	Unstructured and fragmented
Formation process steps	First think, then act	Thinking and acting intertwined
Decision-making	Hierarchical	Dispersed
Decision-making focus	Optimal resource allocation and coordination	Experimentation and parallel initiatives
Implementation focused on	Programming (organizational efficiency)	Learning (organizational development)
Strategic change	Implemented top-down	Requires broad cultural and cognitive shifts

prefer deliberateness over emergence, while in hypercompetitive industries the reverse occurs. The balance between demands in large firms also depends on the firm's perspective on corporate level strategy: in portfolio organizations more variety of strategy processes can be noticed than in integrated organizations (see Chapter 5 on corporate level strategy).

Balancing the paradox of deliberateness and emergence can also be institutionalized into a formal process. Popular in many organizations is the scenario process (see also Reading 7.3 by Grant, 2003). This method, popularized by Royal Dutch Shell, intentionally combines elements of deliberateness and emergence. It is a formal process, but by developing multiple scenarios and providing opportunity for intuitive and entrepreneurial inputs, it provides a balanced approach to strategy formation.

Juxtaposing

From the perspective of a business level manager the paradox of deliberateness and emergence is managed by balancing the two opposite demands; however, a corporate level manager needs to engage in different strategy formation processes. Apart from participating in the corporate strategy process, the strategizing manager is also involved in formation processes in other corporate units – divisions and business units – and company-wide initiatives, international activities and ad hoc projects. Being engaged in such a variety of processes the strategizing manager needs to be juxtaposing, managing opposites or different blends simultaneously. This requires specific dynamic capabilities (Teece, 2007, Reading 2.1; Teece, Pisano and Shuen, 1997, Reading 4.3).

In professional firms the situation for strategists complicates even further. Managing a professional firm is one thing, delivering services is yet another. With multiple clients, professionals need flexibility to juxtapose between clients and their own firm. For example, King (2008) reports that venture capitalists are 'bifurcated strategists', using planning for their portfolio companies, while using emergent strategies on their own behalf.

STRATEGY FORMATION IN INTERNATIONAL PERSPECTIVE

Co-authors: Gep Eisenloeffel and Wester Wagenaar

What we anticipate seldom occurs; what we least expect generally happens.
Benjamin Disraeli (1804–1881) British prime minister and novelist

Whether there are specific national preferences for strategic planning or the strategic incrementalism perspective seems like a legitimate question, yet it is not often asked. It has generally been assumed that international differences are a non-issue, but the few international comparative studies that have been carried out – albeit not conducted recently – suggest the opposite. There are also studies suggesting international similarities, most notably when it comes to the size of firms. Of course the position of a strategist is not only bound by the international or industrial playing field and there is variance among individuals as well. Nevertheless, it is important for a strategist to take heed of differences in order to best understand strategy across countries and industries.

On the national level

Among others, international comparative studies show significantly different levels of formal planning across various industrialized countries. Planning was found to be the most common and most formalized in the United States, with other English-speaking countries – Australia, Britain, Canada and New Zealand respectively – also exhibiting a high score (Steiner and Schollhammer, 1975). The popularity of formal planning systems in these societies seems odd, given their high level of individualism and strong preference for a market economy. One might expect that the English-speaking countries' fondness of unplanned markets would be a reflection of a general dislike of planning. Yet, so concludes Ohmae, strangely "most large US corporations are run like the Soviet economy" of yesteryear, emphasizing central planning and top-down control (1982, p. 224). One explanation for this behaviour is a strong labour division. Nowhere in the industrialized world, with the exception of France, has there been a stronger development of a distinct managerial class than in the English-speaking countries (Hampden-Turner and Trompenaars, 1993; Lessem and Neubauer, 1994). In the division of labour, managers are the officers who formulate the strategies and the workforce concentrates their efforts on implementing them. The general preference for planning, however, is typically limited to the predictable, not-too-distant future. As such, English-speaking countries belong to the category of short-term oriented cultures (Hofstede, 1993).

At the other extreme, according to the research by Steiner and Schollhammer (1975), are Italy and Japan. Here very little formal planning was witnessed and, in the case of Japan, the low propensity to engage in formalized strategic planning has been noted by a number of others as well (e.g. Kagono *et al.*, 1985). Hayashi (1978) remarks that Japanese firms "distrust corporate planning in general", while Ohmae (1982) characterizes Japanese companies as "less planned, less rigid, but more vision- and mission-driven" than their Western counterparts. Japanese giants Canon, Honda and Komatsu did not commit to long-term plans for global leadership positions, instead prioritizing "strategic intent" over strategic planning (Hamel & Prahalad, 2005).

Preferences for different *types* of internal control and related organizational models have been discussed above, yet countries can also differ with regard to the *level* of internal control their citizens favour. In some societies, people have a strong desire for order and structure, with clear tasks, responsibilities, power rules and procedures. Ambiguous situations and uncertain outcomes are shunned and therefore management strives to control organizational processes. Management can reduce uncertainty in a number of ways. Structure can be offered by strictly following traditions or by imposing top-down paternalistic rule. Uncertainty can also be reduced by planning (Kagono *et al.*, 1985; Schneider, 1989). By setting direction, coordinating initiatives, committing resources and programming activities, structure can be brought to the organization. In societies that are more tolerant towards ambiguity and uncertainty, one can expect a weaker preference for planning.

It is not only preferences for internal control that can have an impact on inclinations towards certain views on strategy formation; societies also differ with regard to the level of control they wish to have over their environment. At the one extreme are countries in which people strive to manage or even dominate their surroundings. The consequence is that organizations in these nations are drawn to proactive and deliberate strategy-making, under the motto "plan or be planned for" (Ackoff, 1981). This characteristic is particularly pronounced in Western countries (Trompenaars and Hampden-Turner, 2012). At the other extreme are fatalistic cultures in which most people passively accept their destiny. As people here approach opportunities and threats reactively on a day-to-day basis, this muddling rarely leads to successful emergent strategies but can be characterized more as disjointed, unpatterned action. In between are societies where people accept that events are unpredictable and that the environment cannot be tightly controlled, yet trust that individuals and organizations can proactively seek and pave their own path. This requires firms to "develop an attitude of receptivity and high adaptability to changing conditions" (Maruyama, 1984). This way of thinking is particularly pronounced in South-East Asia, and leads towards a stronger inclination towards the strategic incrementalism perspective (Kagono *et al.*, 1985; Schneider, 1989).

On the industry level

Theoretical studies on strategy emergence are plentiful, but empirical data remain scarce. As such, there has been little research confirming industry preferences for strategic incrementalism or strategic planning. Nevertheless, some studies have suggested that generalizations can be made on the impact of the size of firms; the strategy process in smaller companies is mainly emergent (e.g. Harris, Forbes and Fletcher, 2000). In small- and medium-sized enterprises (SMEs) emergent strategies are particularly important regarding product and market-related decisions (Leitner, 2014). Industries where the majority of incumbents are SMEs can be expected to have a higher tendency towards emergent strategy formation. In contrast, strategic development in large firms has traditionally been described as more planned at the higher echelons, with middle managers functioning more as the facilitators of emergent strategies (e.g. Wooldridge and Floyd, 1990).

To the strategist

As previously highlighted, there is international variance when it comes to the degree to which people aim to regulate the environment, but individual propensities also play a role. Strategy formation is the interplay between two forces: an unstable environment and an organizational operating system seeking to stabilize. The role of leadership is to mediate between the two and enforce a correct strategy (Mintzberg, 1978). Yet, because the understanding of the surroundings is subject to perceptions and interpretations, the disposition of a strategist has a significant impact on strategy formation (Schneider, 1989). The strategist should be aware of his own preferences and those of others around him. In the international playing field, such as at an international company with multiple subsidiaries, it is particularly important to be aware of differing international preferences and act accordingly.

INTRODUCTION TO THE READINGS

As an input to the process of assessing the variety of perspectives, three readings have been selected that each shed their own light on this issue. As in the previous chapters, the first two readings will be representative of the two poles in this debate, while the third reading will bring in a middle way to combine perspectives.

As opening reading in this debate, 'Managing the Strategy Process', by Balaji Chakravarthy and Peter Lorange, has been selected to represent the strategic planning perspective. Lorange is one of the most well-known writers on the topic of formal planning systems (Lorange, 1980; Lorange and Vancil, 1977) and this reading is taken from the 1991 textbook he co-authored with Chakravarthy, entitled *Managing the Strategy Process: A Framework for a Multibusiness Firm*. As with most proponents of the strategic planning perspective, Chakravarthy and Lorange do not actively defend their assumption that formal planning is beneficial. Rather, basing themselves on this supposition, they concentrate on outlining a framework for effectively structuring strategic planning activities. Their ideal is an extensive strategic planning system, comprised of a number of distinct steps, procedures, mechanisms and roles. However, they go further than only structuring strategic planning. In their view, a formal planning system will not lead to effective strategy formation if it is not linked to other organizational systems. In particular, the strategic planning system needs to interact with the monitoring, control and learning system, the incentives system and the staffing system. As such, Chakravarthy and Lorange champion a highly comprehensive and structured approach to strategic planning.

James Brian Quinn has been chosen as spokesman for the strategic incrementalism perspective. Together with Henry Mintzberg, Quinn has been one of the most influential pioneers on the topic of emergent strategy. Quinn's article, 'Logical Incrementalism', which is reprinted here as Reading 7.2, and his subsequent book *Strategies for Change* (1980), are widely accepted as having been instrumental in developing the strategic incrementalism perspective. In his reading, Quinn explains some of the key shortcomings of formal strategic planning and goes on to make a case for strategic incrementalism. Important in his argumentation is that strategic incrementalism is distinguished from muddling through. Incrementalism is a proactive approach to strategy formation – managers can intentionally choose to let unintended strategies emerge. Muddling through is also incremental in nature, but reactive and ad hoc – improvised decisions are made to deal with unplanned and poorly controllable circumstances. To make this distinction more explicit, Quinn refers to the proactive strain of incremental behaviour as 'logical incrementalism'. By 'logical' he means 'reasonable and well-considered'. However, logical incrementalism is not always logical by the definition used in Chapter 2 – incremental behaviour is not necessarily 'dictated by formal logic'. Therefore, for the sake of accuracy and clarity, the term strategic incrementalism will be used in this book instead of logical incrementalism.

Reading 7.3 is 'Strategic Planning in a Turbulent Environment: Evidence from the Oil Majors' by Robert M. Grant. The debate between the strategic planning perspective (which Grant refers to as the 'rational design school') and the strategic incrementalism perspective (dubbed by Grant as the 'emergent process school') has involved caricatures of firms' strategic planning processes, but little empirical evidence of whether and how companies actually organize strategy formation. Grant's paper aims at filling this empirical gap by describing the characteristics of the strategic planning systems of multinational, multi-business companies faced with volatile, unpredictable business environments. Case studies of the planning systems of eight of the world's largest oil companies identified fundamental changes in the nature and role of strategic planning since the end of the 1970s. The findings point to a possible reconciliation of 'design' and 'process' approaches to strategy formation. The study points to a process of *planned emergence* in which strategic planning systems provide a mechanism for coordinating decentralized strategy formulation within a structure of demanding performance targets and clear corporate guidelines. The study shows that these planning systems foster adaptation and responsiveness, but also limited innovation and analytical sophistication.

Managing the strategy process

By Balaji Chakravarthy and Peter Lorange[1]

There are five distinct steps in the strategy process (see Figure 7.1.1). The first three steps involve the strategic planning system; the final two steps cover the role of the monitoring, control and learning system, and the incentives and staffing systems, respectively.

The strategic planning system

The purpose of the first step in the planning system, *objectives setting*, is to determine a strategic direction for the firm and each of its divisions and business units.

Objectives setting calls for an open-ended reassessment of the firm's business environments and its strengths in dealing with these environments. At the conclusion of this step, there should be agreement at all levels of the organization on the goals that should be pursued and the strategies that will be needed to meet them. It is worth differentiating here between objectives and goals. Objectives refer to the strategic intent of the firm in the long run. Goals, on the other hand, are more specific statements of the achievements targeted for certain deadlines – goals can be accomplished, and when that

[1]Source: This article was adapted from Chapter 1 of Chakravarty and Lorange, *Managing the Strategy Process: A Framework for a Multi business Firm*, 1st Edition. © 1991, reprinted by permission of Pearson Education, Inc., Upper Saddle River, NJ.

FIGURE 7.1.1   The strategy process

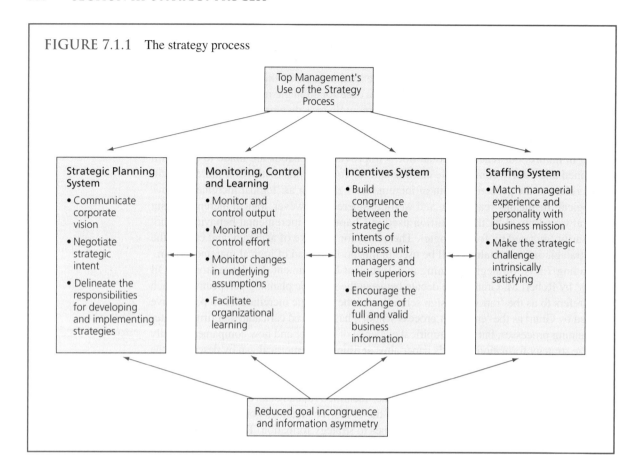

happens the firm moves closer to meeting its objectives. Objectives represent a more enduring challenge.

The second step, *strategic programming,* develops the strategies identified in the first step and defines the cross-functional programmes that will be needed to implement the chosen strategies. Cross-functional cooperation is essential to this step. At the end of the strategic programming step a long-term financial plan is drawn up for the firm as a whole and each of its divisions, business units and functions. On top of the financial projections from existing operations, the long-term financial plan overlays both the expenditures and revenues associated with the approved strategic programmes of an organizational unit. The time horizon for these financial plans is chosen to cover the typical lead times that are required to implement the firm's strategic programmes. A five-year financial plan is, however, very common. The purpose of the five-year financial plan is to ensure that the approved strategic programmes can be funded through either the firm's internally generated resources or externally financed resources.

The third step, *budgeting,* defines both the strategic and operating budgets of the firm. The strategic budget helps identify the contributions that the firm's functional departments, business units and divisions will be expected to make in a given fiscal year in support of the firm's approved strategic programmes. It incorporates new product-market initiatives. The operating budget, on the other hand, provides resources to functional departments, business units and divisions so that they can sustain their existing momentum. It is based on projected short-term activity levels, given past trends. Failure to meet the operating budget will hurt the firm's short-term performance, whereas failure to meet the strategic budget will compromise the firm's future.

The monitoring, control, and learning system

The fourth step in the strategy process is *monitoring, control and learning.* Here the emphasis is not on output but on meeting key milestones in the strategic budget and on adhering to planned spending schedules. Strategic programmes, like strategic budgets, are monitored for the milestones reached and for adherence to spending schedules. In addition, the key assumptions underlying these programmes are validated periodically. As a natural extension to this validation process, even the agreed-on goals at various levels are reassessed in the light of changes to the resources of the firm and its business environment.

The incentives and staffing systems

The fifth and final step in the strategy process *is incentives and staffing*. One part of this is the award of incentives as contracted to the firm's managers. If the incentives system is perceived to have failed in inducing the desired performance, redesigning the incentives system and reassessing the staffing of key managerial positions are considered at this step.

Linking organizational levels and steps in strategic planning

An effective strategy process must allow for interactions between the organizational levels and iterations between the process steps. Figure 7.1.2 describes

some of the interactions and iterations in the strategic planning steps. The formal interactions in the process are shown in the figure by the solid line that weaves up and down through the organizational levels and across the three steps. The informal interactions that complement the formal interactions are shown by dotted loops.

Objectives setting

The first formal step of the strategy process commences soon after top management reaffirms or modifies the firm's objectives at the beginning of each fiscal year. Embedded in these objectives should be the vision of the chief executive officer (CEO) and his or her top management team. Top management's vision helps specify what will make the firm great. An elaboration of this vision can be done through a formal statement of objectives. However, it is not the formality of a firm's objectives but rather the excitement and challenge that top management's vision can bring to a firm's managers that is important to the strategy process.

Along with its communication of corporate objectives, top management must provide a forecast on

FIGURE 7.1.2   Steps in the strategy process

key environmental factors. Assumptions on exchange rates, inflation and other economic factors – as well as projections on the political risks associated with each country – are best compiled centrally so as to ensure objectivity and consistency. These objectives and forecasts are then discussed with a firm's divisional and business unit managers.

Once the corporate objectives are decided, top management negotiates, for each division and business unit in the firm, goals that are consistent with these objectives. The nature of these negotiations can vary. In some firms, top management may wish to set goals in a top-down fashion; in others, it may invite subordinate managers to participate in the goal-setting process.

Managers are encouraged to examine new strategies and modify existing ones in order to accomplish their goals. The proposed strategies are approved at each higher level in the organizational hierarchy, then eventually by top management. Top management tries to make certain that the strategies as proposed are consistent with the firm's objectives and can be supported with the resources available to the firm. Modifications, where necessary, are made to the objectives, goals and strategies in order to bring them in alignment. Another important outcome of the objectives-setting step is to build a common understanding across the firm's managerial hierarchy of the goals and strategies that are intended for each organizational unit.

The objectives-setting step in Figure 7.1.2 does not include the functional departments. As we observed earlier, the primary role of these departments is a supporting one. They do not have a profit or growth responsibility, and their goals cannot be decided until the second step, when strategic programmes in support of approved business unit goals begin to be formed. It is not uncommon, however, for key functional managers to be invited to participate in the objectives-setting step either as experts in a corporate task force or, more informally, as participants in the deliberations that are held at the business unit level.

It is important that divisional proposals be evaluated on an overall basis as elements of a corporate portfolio and not reviewed in a sequential mode. In the latter case, the resulting overall balance in the corporate portfolio would be more or less incidental, representing the accumulated sum of individual approvals. It makes little sense to attempt to judge in isolation whether a particular business family or business strategy is attractive to the corporate portfolio. That will depend on a strategy's fit with the rest of the portfolio and on the competing investment opportunities available to the firm in its business portfolio.

Strategic programming

The second step in the process has two purposes:

1 To forge an agreement between divisional, business unit and functional managers on the strategic programmes that have to be implemented over the next few years.

2 To deepen the involvement of functional managers in developing the strategies that were tentatively selected in the first step.

The strategic programming step begins with a communication from top management about the goals and strategies that were finally approved for the firm's divisions and business units. The divisional manager then invites his or her business unit and functional managers to identify programme alternatives in support of the approved goals and strategies. Examples of strategic programmes include increasing market share for an existing product, introducing a new product, and launching a joint marketing campaign for a family of divisional products. As in these examples, a strategic programme typically requires the cooperation of multiple functional departments.

However, the functional specialties within a firm often represent different professional cultures that do not necessarily blend easily. Further, day-to-day operating tasks can be so demanding that the functional managers may simply find it difficult to participate in the time-consuming cross-functional teamwork. A key challenge for both divisional and business managers is to bring about this interaction.

The proposed strategic programmes travel up the hierarchy for approval at each level. At the division level, the programmes are evaluated not only for how well they support the approved strategies but also for how they promote synergies within the firm. Synergies can come from two sources: through economies of scale or economies of scope. The creation of synergies based on economies of scale calls for a sharing of common functional activities – such as research and development (R&D), raw materials procurement, production and distribution – so as to spread over a larger volume the overhead costs associated with these functions. The creation of economies of scope, on the other hand, requires a common approach to the market. Examples of such an approach include the development of a common trademark, the development of products/services that have a complementary appeal to a customer group, and the ability to offer a common regional service organization for the firm's diverse businesses.

At the corporate level, the proposed strategic programmes provide an estimate of the resources that will be required to support the divisional and business unit goals. These goals, as well as their supporting strategies, are once again reassessed; and where needed, modifications are sought in the proposed strategic programmes. As noted earlier, a long-term financial plan is drawn up at this stage for the firm as a whole and each of its organizational units. The approved strategic programmes are communicated to the divisions, business units and functional departments at the beginning of the budgeting cycle.

Budgeting

When top management decides on the strategic programmes that the firm should pursue, it has *de facto* allocated all of the firm's human, technological and financial resources that are available for internal development. This allocation influences the strategic budgets that may be requested at each level in the organizational hierarchy.

The strategic budgets, together with the operating budgets of the various organizational units, are consolidated and sent up for top management approval. When top management finally approves the budgets of the various organizational units, before the start of a new budget year, it brings to a close what can be a year-long journey through the three steps of the strategy-making subprocess. The strategy implementation subprocess is then set into motion. Even though the two subprocesses are described sequentially here, it is important to mention that even as the budget for a given year is being formed, the one for the prior year will be under implementation. Midcourse corrections to the prior year's budget can have an impact on the formulation of the current budget.

If the actual accomplishments fall short of the strategic budget, in particular, the negative variance may suggest that the firm's managers failed to implement its chosen strategy efficiently. But it can also suggest that the strategic programmes that drive this budget may have been ill-conceived or even that the goals underlying these programmes may have been specified incorrectly. The monitoring, control and learning system provides continuous information on both the appropriateness of a strategic budget and the efficiency with which the budget is implemented. This information, based on the implementation of the prior year's strategic budget, can trigger another set of iterations between the three strategy-making steps, calling into question the goals and strategies on which the current year's budget are based. These iterations are shown by the dotted rectangles in Figure 7.1.2.

Logical incrementalism

By James Quinn[1]

When I was younger I always conceived of a room where all these [strategic] concepts were worked out for the whole company. Later I didn't find any such room ... The strategy [of the company] may not even exist in the mind of one man. I certainly don't know where it is written down. It is simply transmitted in the series of decisions made.
Interview quotation

Introduction

When well-managed major organizations make significant changes in strategy, the approaches they use frequently bear little resemblance to the rational-analytical systems so often touted in the planning literature. The full strategy is rarely written down in any one place. The processes used to arrive at the total strategy are typically fragmented, evolutionary and largely intuitive. Although one can usually find embedded in these fragments some very refined pieces of formal strategic analysis, the real strategy tends to evolve as internal decisions and external events flow together to create a new, widely shared consensus for action among key members of the top management team. Far from being an abrogation of good management practice, the rationale behind this kind of strategy formulation is so powerful that it perhaps provides the normative model for strategic decision-making, rather than the step-by-step 'formal systems planning' approach so often espoused.

[1]Source: This article was originally published as 'Strategic change: logical incrementalism' in *Sloan Management Review,* Fall, 1978, pp. 7–21. Reproduced by permission. © 1978 from MIT Sloan Management Review/Massachusetts Institute of Technology. All rights reserved.

The formal systems planning approach

A strong normative literature states what factors should be included in a systematically planned strategy and how to analyse and relate these factors step-by-step. The main elements of this 'formal' planning approach include:

■ analysing one's own internal situation: strengths, weaknesses, competencies, problems;

■ projecting current product lines, profits, sales, investment needs into the future;

■ analysing selected external environments and opponents' actions for opportunities and threats;

■ establishing broad goals as targets for subordinate groups' plans;

■ identifying the gap between expected and desired results;

■ communicating planning assumptions to the divisions;

■ requesting proposed plans from subordinate groups with more specific target goals, resource needs and supporting action plans;

■ occasionally asking for special studies of alternatives, contingencies, or longer-term opportunities;

■ reviewing and approving divisional plans and summing these for corporate needs;

■ developing long-term budgets presumably related to plans;

■ implementing plans;

■ monitoring and evaluating performance (presumably against plans, but usually against budgets).

While this approach is excellent for some purposes, it tends to focus unduly on measurable quantitative factors and to underemphasize the vital qualitative, organizational and power-behavioural factors that so often determine strategic success in one situation versus another. In practice, such planning is just one building block in a continuous stream of events that really determine corporate strategy.

The power-behavioral approach

Other investigators have provided important insights on the crucial psychological, power and behavioural relationships in strategy formulation. Among other things, these have enhanced understanding about the multiple goal structures of organizations, the politics of strategic decisions, executive bargaining and negotiation processes, 'satisficing' (as opposed to maximizing)

in decision making, the role of coalitions in strategic management, and the practice of 'muddling' in the public sphere. Unfortunately, however, many power-behavioural studies have been conducted in settings far removed from the realities of strategy formulation. Others have concentrated solely on human dynamics, power relationships and organizational processes, and ignored the ways in which systematic data analysis shapes and often dominates crucial aspects of strategic decisions. Finally, a few have offered much normative guidance for the strategist.

The study

Recognizing the contributions and limitations of both approaches, I attempted to document the dynamics of actual strategic change processes in some ten major companies as perceived by those most knowledgeably and intimately involved in them. Several important findings have begun to emerge from these investigations:

■ Neither the power-behavioural nor the formal systems planning paradigm adequately characterizes the way successful strategic processes operate.

■ Effective strategies tend to emerge from a series of 'strategic subsystems', each of which attacks a specific class of strategic issue (e.g. acquisitions, divestitures, or major reorganizations) in a disciplined way, but which blends incrementally and opportunistically into a cohesive pattern that becomes the company's strategy.

■ The logic behind each subsystem is so powerful that to some extent it may serve as a normative approach for formulating these key elements of strategy in large companies.

■ Because of cognitive and process limits, almost all of these subsystems – and the formal planning activity itself – must be managed and linked together by an approach best described as logical incrementalism.

■ Such incrementalism is not muddling. It is a purposeful, effective, proactive management technique for improving and integrating both the analytical and behavioural aspects of strategy formulation.

This article will document these findings, suggest the logic behind several important subsystems for strategy formulation, and outline some of the management and thought processes executives in large organizations use to synthesize them into effective corporate strategies. Such strategies embrace those patterns of high-leverage decisions (on major goals, policies and action sequences) that affect the viability and direction of the entire enterprise or determine its competitive posture for an extended time period.

Critical strategic issues

Although certain 'hard data' decisions (e.g. on product- market position or resource allocations) tend to dominate the analytical literature, executives identified other 'soft' changes that have at least as much importance in shaping their concern's strategic posture. Most often cited were changes in the company's:

- overall organizational structure or its basic management style;
- relationships with the government or other external interest groups;
- acquisition, divestiture, or divisional control practices;
- international posture and relationships;
- innovative capabilities or personnel motivations as affected by growth;
- worker and professional relationships reflecting changed social expectations and values;
- past or anticipated technological environments.

When executives were asked to 'describe the processes through which their company arrived at its new posture' vis-a-vis each of these critical domains, several important points emerged. First, a few of these issues lent themselves to quantitative modelling techniques or perhaps even formal financial analyses. Second, successful companies used a different subsystem to formulate strategy for each major class of strategic issues, yet these subsystems were quite similar among companies even in very different industries. Finally, no single formal analytical process could handle all strategic variables simultaneously on a planned basis. Why?

Precipitating events

Often external or internal events over which managements had essentially no control would precipitate urgent, piecemeal, interim decisions that inexorably shaped the company's future strategic posture. One clearly observes this phenomenon in the decisions forced on General Motors by the 1973–74 oil crisis; the shift in posture pressed upon Exxon by sudden nationalizations; or the dramatic opportunities allowed for Haloid Corporation and Pilkington Brothers Ltd by the unexpected inventions of xerography and float glass.

In these cases, analyses from earlier formal planning cycles did contribute greatly, as long as the general nature of the contingency had been anticipated. They broadened the information base available (as in Exxon's case), extended the options considered (Haloid-Xerox), created shared values to guide decisions about precipitating events in consistent directions (Pilkington), or built up resource bases, management flexibilities, or active search routines for opportunities whose specific nature could not be defined in advance (General Mills, Pillsbury). But no organization – no matter how brilliant, rational, or imaginative – could possibly foresee the timing, severity, or even the nature of all such precipitating events. Further, when these events did occur there might be neither time, resources nor information enough to undertake a full formal strategic analysis of all possible options and their consequences. Yet early decisions made under stress conditions often meant new thrusts, precedents, or lost opportunities that were difficult to reverse later.

An incremental logic

Recognizing this, top executives usually consciously tried to deal with precipitating events in an incremental fashion. Early commitments were kept broadly formative, tentative and subject to later review. In some cases neither the company nor the external players could understand the full implications of alternative actions. All parties wanted to test assumptions and have an opportunity to learn from and adapt to the others' responses. For example: Neither the potential producer nor user of a completely new product or process (like xerography or float glass) could fully conceptualize its ramifications without interactive testing. All parties benefited from procedures that purposely delayed decisions and allowed mutual feedback. Some companies, like IBM or Xerox, have formalized this concept into 'phase programme planning' systems. They make concrete decisions only on individual phases (or stages) of new product developments, establish interactive testing procedures with customers, and postpone final configuration commitments until the latest possible moment. Similarly, even under pressure, most top executives were extremely sensitive to organizational and power relationships and consciously managed decision processes to improve these dynamics. They often purposely delayed initial decisions, or kept such decisions vague, in order to encourage lower-level participation, to gain more information from specialists, or to build commitment to solutions.

Even when a crisis atmosphere tended to shorten time horizons and make decisions more goal oriented than political, perceptive executives consciously tried to keep their options open until they understood how the crisis would affect the power bases and needs of their key constituents.

Incrementalism in strategic subsystems

One also finds that an incremental logic applies in attacking many of the critical subsystems of corporate strategy. Those subsystems for considering diversification moves, divestitures, major reorganizations, or government-external relations are typical and will be described here. In each case conscious incrementalism helps to:

1 cope with both the cognitive and process limits on each major decision;
2 build the logical-analytical framework these decisions require;
3 create the personal and organizational awareness, understanding, acceptance and commitment needed to implement the strategies effectively.

The diversification subsystem

Strategies for diversification, either through research and development (R&D) or acquisitions, provide excellent examples. The formal analytical steps needed for successful diversification are well documented. However, the precise directions in which R&D may project the company can only be understood step-by-step as scientists uncover new phenomena, make and amplify discoveries, build prototypes, reduce concepts to practice, and interact with users during product introductions. Similarly, only as each acquisition is sequentially identified, investigated, negotiated for and integrated into the organization can one predict its ultimate impact on the total enterprise.

A step-by-step approach is clearly necessary to guide and assess the strategic fit of each internal or external diversification candidate. Incremental processes are also required to manage the crucial psychological and power shifts that ultimately determine the programme's overall direction and consequences. These processes help unify both the analytical and behavioural aspects of diversification decisions. They create the broad conceptual consensus, the risk-taking attitudes, the organizational and resource flexibilities, and the adaptive dynamism that determine both the timing and direction of diversification strategies. Most important among these processes are:

■ Generating a genuine, top-level psychological commitment to diversification. General Mills, Pillsbury and Xerox all started their major diversification programmes with broad analytical studies and goal-setting exercises designed both to build top-level consensus around the need to diversify and to establish the general directions for diversification. Without such action, top-level bargaining for resources would have continued to support only more familiar (and hence apparently less risky) old lines, and this could delay or undermine the entire diversification endeavour.

■ Consciously preparing to move opportunistically. Organizational and fiscal resources must be built up in advance to exploit candidates as they randomly appear. And a 'credible activist' for ventures must be developed and backed by someone with commitment power. All successful acquirers created the potential for profit-centred divisions within their organizational structures, strengthened their financial-controllership capabilities, took action to create low-cost capital access, and maintained the shortest possible communication lines from the acquisitions activist to the resource-committing authority. All these actions integrally determined which diversifications actually could be made, the timing of their accession and the pace at which they could be absorbed.

■ Building a 'comfort factor' for risk taking. Perceived risk is largely a function of one's knowledge about a field. Hence well-conceived diversification programmes should anticipate a trial-and-error period during which top managers reject early proposed fields or opportunities until they have analysed enough trial candidates to 'become comfortable' with an initial selection. Early successes tend to be 'sure things' close to the companies' past (real or supposed) expertise. After a few successful diversifications, managements tend to become more confident and accept other candidates – farther from traditional lines – at a faster rate. Again, the way this process is handled affects both the direction and pace of the actual programme.

■ Developing a new ethos. If new divisions are more successful than the old – as they should be – they attract relatively more resources and their political power grows. Their most effective line managers move into corporate positions, and slowly the company's special competency and ethos change. Finally, the concepts and products that once dominated the company's culture may decline in importance or even disappear. Acknowledging these ultimate consequences to the organization at the beginning of a diversification programme would clearly be impolitic, even if the manager both desired and could predict the probable new ethos. These factors must be handled adaptively, as opportunities present themselves and as individual leaders and power centres develop.

Each of the above processes interacts with all others (and with the random appearance of diversification candidates) to affect action sequences, elapsed time and ultimate results in unexpected ways. Complexities are so great that few diversification programmes end up as initially envisioned. Consequently, wise managers recognize the limits to systematic analysis in diversification, and use formal planning to build the 'comfort levels' executives need for risk taking and to guide the programme's early directions and priorities. They then modify these flexibly, step-by-step, as new opportunities, power centres and developed competencies merge to create new potentials.

The divestiture subsystem

Similar practices govern the handling of divestitures. Divisions often drag along in a less-than-desired condition for years before they can be strategically divested. In some cases, ailing divisions might have just enough yield or potential to offer hoped-for viability. In others, they might represent the company's vital core from earlier years, the creations of a powerful person nearing retirement, or the psychological touchstones of the company's past traditions.

Again, in designing divestiture strategies, top executives had to reinforce vaguely felt concerns with detailed data, build up managers' comfort levels about issues, achieve participation in and commitment to decisions, and move opportunistically to make actual changes. In many cases, the precise nature of the decision was not clear at the outset. Executives often made seemingly unrelated personnel shifts or appointments that changed the value set of critical groups, or started a series of staff studies that generated awareness or acceptance of a potential problem. They might then instigate goal assessment, business review, or 'planning' programmes to provide broader forums for discussion and a wider consensus for action. Even then they might wait for a crisis, a crucial retirement, or an attractive sale opportunity to determine the timing and conditions of divestiture. In some cases, decisions could be direct and

analytical. But when divestitures involved the psychological centres of the organization, the process had to be much more oblique and carefully orchestrated.

The major reorganization subsystem

It is well recognized that major organizational changes are an integral part of strategy. Sometimes they constitute a strategy themselves, sometimes they precede and/or precipitate a new strategy, and sometimes they help to implement a strategy. However, like many other important strategic decisions, macro-organizational moves are typically handled incrementally and outside of formal planning processes. Their effects on personal or power relationships preclude discussion in open forums and reports of such processes.

In addition, major organizational changes have timing imperatives (or 'process limits') all their own. In making any significant shifts, executives must think through the new roles, capabilities and probable individual reactions of the many principals affected. They may have to wait for the promotion or retirement of a valued colleague before consummating any change. They then frequently have to bring in, train, or test new people for substantial periods before they can staff key posts with confidence. During this testing period they may substantially modify their original concept of the reorganization, as they evaluate individuals' potentials, their performance in specific roles, their personal drives, and their relationships with other team members.

Because this chain of decisions affects the career development, power, affluence and self-image of so many, executives tend to keep close counsel in their discussions, negotiate individually with key people and make final commitments as late as possible in order to obtain the best matches between people's capabilities, personalities and aspirations and their new roles. Typically, all these events do not come together at one convenient time, particularly the moment annual plans are due. Instead executives move opportunistically, step-by-step, selectively moving people toward a broadly conceived organizational goal, which is constantly modified and rarely articulated in detail until the last pieces fit together.

The government-external relations subsystem

Almost all companies cited government and other external activist groups as among the most important forces causing significant changes in their strategic postures during the periods examined. However, when asked 'How did your company arrive at its own strategy vis-a-vis these forces?' it became clear that few companies had cohesive strategies (integrated sets of goals, policies and programmes) for government-external relations, other than lobbying for or against specific legislative actions. To the extent that other strategies did exist, they were piecemeal, ad hoc and had been derived in a very evolutionary manner. Yet there seemed to be very good reasons for such incrementalism. The following are two of the best short explanations of the way these practices develop:

> We are a very large company, and we understand that any massive overt action on our part could easily create more public antagonism than support for our viewpoint. It is also hard to say in advance exactly what public response any particular action might create. So we tend to test a number of different approaches on a small scale with only limited or local company identification. If one approach works, we'll test it further and amplify its use. If another bombs, we try to keep it from being used again. Slowly we find a series of advertising, public relations, community relations actions that seem to help. Then along comes another issue and we start all over again. Gradually the successful approaches merge into a pattern of actions that becomes our strategy.

> I [the president] start conversations with a number of knowledgeable people ... I collect articles and talk to people about how things get done in Washington in this particular field. I collect data from any reasonable source. I begin wide-ranging discussions with people inside and outside the corporation. From these a pattern eventually emerges. It's like fitting together a jigsaw puzzle. At first the vague outline of an approach appears like the sail of a ship in a puzzle. Then suddenly the rest of the puzzle becomes quite clear. You wonder why you didn't see it all along. And once it's crystallized, it's not difficult to explain to others.

In this realm, uncontrollable forces dominate. Data are very soft, often can be only subjectively sensed and may be costly to quantify. The possible responses of individuals and groups to different stimuli are difficult to determine in advance. The number of potential opponents with power is very high, and the diversity in their viewpoints and possible modes of attack is so substantial that it is physically impossible to lay out probabilistic decision diagrams that would have much meaning. Results are unpredictable and error costs

extreme. Even the best intended and most rational-seeming strategies can be converted into disasters unless they are thoroughly and interactively tested.

Formal planning in corporate strategy

What role do classical formal planning techniques play in strategy formulation? All companies in the sample do have formal planning procedures embedded in their management direction and control systems. These serve certain essential functions. In a process sense, they:

- provide a discipline forcing managers to take a careful look ahead periodically;
- require rigorous communications about goals, strategic issues and resource allocations;
- stimulate longer-term analyses than would otherwise be made;
- generate a basis for evaluating and integrating short-term plans;
- lengthen time horizons and protect long-term investments such as R&D;
- create a psychological backdrop and an information framework about the future against which managers can calibrate short-term or interim decisions.

In a decision-making sense, they:

- fine-tune annual commitments;
- formalize cost-reduction programmes;
- help implement strategic changes once decided on (for example, coordinating all elements of Exxon's decision to change its corporate name).

Formal plans also 'increment'

Although individual staff planners were often effective in identifying potential problems and bringing them to top management's attention, the annual planning process itself was rarely (if ever) the initiating source of really new key issues or radical departures into new product-market realms. These almost always came from precipitating events, special studies, or conceptions implanted through the kinds of 'logical incremental' processes described above.

In fact, formal planning practices actually institutionalize incrementalism. There are two reasons for this. First, in order to utilize specialized expertise and to obtain executive involvement and commitment, most planning occurs from the bottom up in response to broadly defined assumptions or goals, many of which are longstanding or negotiated well in advance. Of necessity, lower-level groups have only a partial view of the corporation's total strategy, and command only a fragment of its resources. Their power bases, identity, expertise and rewards also usually depend on their existing products or processes. Hence, these products or processes, rather than entirely new departures, should and do receive their primary attention. Second, most managements purposely design their plans to be 'living' or 'evergreen'. They are intended only as frameworks to guide and provide consistency for future decisions made incrementally. To act otherwise would be to deny that further information could have a value. Thus, properly formulated formal plans are also a part of an incremental logic.

Special studies

Formal planning was most successful in stimulating significant change when it was set up as a special study on some important aspect of corporate strategy. For example, when it became apparent that Pilkington's new float glass process would work, the company formed a Directors' Float Glass Committee consisting of all internal directors associated with float glass 'to consider the broad issues of float glass [strategy] in both the present and the future'. The committee did not attempt detailed plans. Instead, it tried to deal in broad concepts, identify alternate routes, and think through the potential consequences of each route some 10 years ahead. Of some of the key strategic decisions it was later remarked, 'It would be difficult to identify an exact moment when the decision was made ... Nevertheless, over a period of time a consensus crystallized with great clarity.'

Such special strategic studies represent a subsystem of strategy formulation distinct from both annual planning activities and the other subsystems exemplified above. Each of these develops some important aspect of strategy, incrementally blending its conclusions with those of other subsystems, and it would be virtually impossible to force all these together to crystallize a completely articulated corporate strategy at any one instant.

Total posture planning

Occasionally, however, managements do attempt very broad assessments of their companies' total posture. Shortly after becoming CEO of General Mills, James McFarland decided that his job was 'to take a very good company and move it to greatness', but that it was up to his management group, not himself alone, to decide what a great company was and how to get there. Consequently he took some 35 of the company's topmost managers away for a three-day management retreat. On the first day, after agreeing to broad financial goals, the group broke up into units of six to eight people. Each unit was to answer the question, 'What is a great company?' from the viewpoints of stockholders, employees, suppliers, the public and society. Each unit reported back at the end of the day, and the whole group tried to reach a consensus through discussion.

On the second day the groups, in the same format, assessed the company's strengths and weaknesses relative to the defined posture of 'greatness.' The third day focused on how to overcome the company's weaknesses and move it toward a great company. This broad consensus led, over the next several years, to the surveys of fields for acquisition, the building of management's initial comfort levels with certain fields, and the acquisition-divestiture strategy that characterized the McFarland era at General Mills.

Yet even such a major endeavour is only a portion of a total strategic process. Values that had been built up over decades stimulated or constrained alternatives. Precipitating events, acquisitions, divestitures, external relations and organizational changes developed important segments of each strategy incrementally. Even the strategies articulated left key elements to be defined as new information became available, polities permitted, or particular opportunities appeared. Major product thrusts proved unsuccessful. Actual strategies therefore evolved as each company overextended, consolidated, made errors and rebalanced various thrusts over time. And it was both logical and expected that this would be the case.

Logical incrementalism

All of the above suggest that strategic decisions do not lend themselves to aggregation into a single massive decision matrix where all factors can be treated relatively simultaneously in order to arrive at a holistic optimum. Many have spoken of the cognitive limits that prevent this. Of equal importance are the process limits – that is, the timing and sequencing imperatives necessary to create awareness, build comfort levels, develop consensus, select and train people and so forth – that constrain the system yet ultimately determine the decision itself. Unlike the preparation of a fine banquet, it is virtually impossible for the manager to orchestrate all internal decisions, external environmental events, behavioural and power relationships, technical and informational needs, and actions of intelligent opponents so that they come together at any precise moment.

Can the process be managed?

Instead, executives usually deal with the logic of each subsystem of strategy formulation largely on its own merits and usually with a different subset of people. They try to develop or maintain in their own minds a consistent pattern among the decisions made in each subsystem. Knowing their own limitations and the unknowability of the events they face, they consciously try to tap the minds and psychic drives of others. They often purposely keep questions broad and decisions vague in early stages to avoid creating undue rigidities and to stimulate others' creativity. Logic, of course, dictates that they make final commitments as late as possible consistent with the information they have.

Consequently, many successful executives will initially set only broad goals and policies that can accommodate a variety of specific proposals from below, yet give a sense of guidance to the proposers. As they come forward the proposals automatically and beneficially attract the support and identity of their sponsors. Being only proposals, the executives can treat these at less politically charged levels, as specific projects rather than as larger goal or policy precedents. Therefore, they can encourage, discourage, or kill alternatives with considerably less political exposure. As events and opportunities emerge, they can incrementally guide the pattern of escalated or accepted proposals to suit their own purposes without getting prematurely committed to a rigid solution set that unpredictable events might prove wrong or that opponents find sufficiently threatening to coalesce against.

A strategy emerges

Successful executives link together and bring order to a series of strategic processes and decisions spanning years. At the beginning of the process it is literally impossible to predict all the events and forces that will shape the future of the company. The best executives can do is to forecast the forces most likely to impinge on the company's affairs and the ranges of their possible impact. They then attempt to build a resource base and a corporate posture so strong in selected areas that the enterprise can survive and prosper despite all but the most devastating events. They consciously select market/technological/product segments the concern can dominate given its resource limits, and place some side bets in order to decrease the risk of catastrophic failure or to increase the company's flexibility for future options.

They then proceed incrementally to handle urgent matters, start longer-term sequences whose specific future branches and consequences are perhaps murky, respond to unforeseen events as they occur, build on successes and brace up or cut losses on failures. They constantly reassess the future, find new congruencies as events unfurl and blend the organization's skills and resources into new balances of dominance and risk aversion as various forces intersect to suggest better – but never perfect – alignments. The process is dynamic, with neither a real beginning nor end.

Strategy deals with the unknowable, not the uncertain. It involves forces of such great number, strength and combinatory powers that one cannot predict events in a probabilistic sense. Hence logic dictates that one proceeds flexibly and experimentally from broad concepts toward specific commitments, making the latter concrete as late as possible in order to narrow the bands of uncertainty and to benefit from the best available information. This is the process of logical incrementalism.

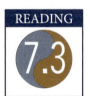

Strategic planning in a turbulent environment: Evidence from the oil majors

By Robert M. Grant[1]

Since the early 1980s, strategic planning – systematic, formalized approaches to strategy formulation – has come under heavy attack from management scholars. Criticisms have addressed the theoretical foundations of strategic planning, particularly the impossibility of forecasting (Mintzberg, 1994b: 110), while empirical evidence – both longitudinal case studies (e.g., Mintzberg and Waters, 1982; Pascale, 1984) and investigations of

[1]Source: Robert M. Grant (2003) 'Strategic planning in a turbulent environment: Evidence from the oil majors', *Strategic Management Journal*, 24: pp. 491–517. Copyright © 2003, reprinted with permission from John Wiley & Sons Ltd..

strategic decision making (e.g., Bower, 1970; Burgelman, 1983) – points to strategies emerging from the weakly coordinated decisions of multiple organizational members. Increased volatility of the business environment makes systematic strategic planning more difficult. Rapid change requires strategies that are flexible and creative – characteristics which, according to Hamel, are seldom associated with formalized planning: 'In the vast majority of companies, strategic planning is a calendar-driven ritual ... [which assumes] that the future will be more or less like the present' (Hamel, 1996: 70). Eisenhardt's research into 'high velocity environments' points to the advantages of 'semi-coherent' strategic decision-making processes that are unpredictable, uncontrolled, inefficient, proactive, continuous, and diverse (Brown and Eisenhardt, 1997; Eisenhardt, 1989). If complexity and uncertainty render decision making impossible, then self-organization may be more conducive to high performance than hierarchical direction (Pascale, 1999). The goal of this paper is to explore whether and how companies' strategic planning practices have adapted to a world of rapid, unpredictable change. The study identifies the key features of strategic planning systems in an industry that transitioned from stability to turbulence – the world petroleum industry. It explores the changing characteristics of the oil majors' strategic planning processes and the changing role of strategic planning within the companies. The study fills a gap in the literature: despite the intense debate over the merits of strategic planning and continued interest in strategic decision processes within firms, we know little about the formal systems through which companies formulate their strategic plans. The paper contributes to strategic management knowledge in three areas. First, it provides descriptive data on the strategic planning practices of some the world's largest and most complex companies during the late 1990s and how these practices changed in response to increasing environment turbulence. Second, it informs the long-running debate between the 'design' and 'process' schools of strategic management and suggests a possible reconciliation of the two. Third, it sheds light upon the coordination and control in large, complex enterprises operating in fast-changing business environments.

Planning and environmental turbulence: Theory and evidence

The literature

Interest in strategy as an area of management study followed the diffusion of strategic planning ('long-range planning') among large companies during the 1950s and 1960s. Articles on long range planning began appearing in the *Harvard Business Review* during 1956–61 (Ewing, 1956; Payne, 1957; Platt and Maines, 1959; Quinn, 1961; Wrap, 1957) and by 1965 the first systematic, analytically based frameworks for strategy formulation appeared (Ansoff, 1965; Learned *et al.*, 1965). Empirical studies of corporate planning practices included, in the United States, Cleland (1962), Henry (1967), the US House of Representatives Committee on Science and Technology (1976), Ang and Chua (1979), and Capon, Farley, and Hulbert (1987); and in the United Kingdom, Denning and Lehr (1971, 1972) and Grinyer and Norburn (1975). As strategic management developed as an area of academic study, interest in companies' strategic planning practices waned. By the 1980s empirical research in strategic planning systems focused upon just two areas: the impact of strategic planning on firm performance and the role of strategic planning in strategic decision making. The first area spawned many studies but no robust findings. Ramanujam, Ramanujam, and Camillus (1986: 347) observed: 'The results of this body of research are fragmented and contradictory,' while Boyd's (1991) survey concluded: 'The overall effect of planning on performance is very weak'. The second area of research explored the organizational processes of strategy formulation. Longitudinal studies of strategy formation (Mintzberg, Brunet, and Waters, 1986; Mintzberg and McHugh, 1985; Mintzberg and Waters, 1982) and Pascale (1984) identified a process of emergence that bore little resemblance to formal, rational, strategic planning processes. Corporate-level strategic decisions emerged from complex interactions between individuals with different interests and different perceptions (Bower, 1970; Burgelman, 1983). The resulting debate pitted the advocates of systematic, rational analysis (Ansoff, 1991; Chakravarthy and Lorange, 1991, Reading 7.1; Goold, 1992) against those who favored the empirical validity and normative merits of emergent processes (Mintzberg, 1991, 1994a; Quinn, 1978, Reading 7.2). The contribution of both areas of research has been limited by lack of empirical investigation of the phenomenon itself. Planning-performance studies relied upon largely superficial characterizations of strategic planning practices based mainly upon questionnaire data. The 'design vs. process' debate has centered on a few well-known case examples – notably Honda's entry into the US motorcycle market (Mintzberg *et al.*, 1996; Pascale, 1984); yet the validity of the Honda case remains dubious – its author described it as a 'small foundation of anecdote' arising from a 'quest for amusement rather than scholarly ambition' (Mintzberg *et al.*, 1996: 112).

The impact of environmental turbulence

Changes in the business environment reinforced the case against formal strategic planning. In the last quarter of the twentieth century, macroeconomic disequilibrium, exchange rate volatility, the microelectronics revolution, and the emergence of newly industrializing countries marked the end of postwar economic stability. Since economic and market forecasts provided the foundation for strategic planning, inability to predict demand, prices, exchange rates and interest rates represented a fundamental challenge to companies' ability to plan. The challenge of making strategy when the future is unknowable encouraged reconsideration of both the processes of strategy formulation and the nature of organizational strategy. Attempts to reconcile systematic strategic planning with turbulent, unpredictable business environments included the following.

Scenario planning

Multiple scenario planning seeks not to predict the future but to envisage alternative views of the future in the form of distinct configurations of key environmental variables (Schoemaker, 1993, 1995). Abandoning single-point forecasts in favor of alternative futures implies forsaking single-point plans in favor of strategy alternatives, emphasizing strategic flexibility that creates option values. However, as recognized by Shell – the foremost exponent of scenario planning within the corporate sector – the primary contribution of scenario planning is not so much the creation of strategic plans as establishing a process for strategic thinking and organizational learning. Shell's former head of planning observed: 'the real purpose of effective planning is not to make plans but to change the mental models that decision makers carry in their heads' (De Geus, 1988: 73). With scenario analysis, strategic planning is a process where decision makers share and synthesize their different knowledge sets and surface their implicit assumptions and the mental models.

Strategic intent and the role of vision

If uncertainty precludes planning in any detailed sense, then strategy is primarily concerned with establishing broad parameters for the development of the enterprise with regard to 'domain selection' and 'domain navigation' (Bourgeois, 1980). Uncertainty requires that strategy is concerned less with specific actions and the more with establishing clarity of direction within which short-term flexibility can be reconciled with overall coordination of strategic decisions. This requires that long term strategic goals are established, articulated through statements of 'vision' and 'mission' (Van Der Heijden, 1993), and committed to through 'strategic intent' (Hamel and Prahalad, 1989).

Strategic innovation

If established companies are to prosper and survive, new external environments require new strategies (Baden-Fuller and Stopford, 1994; Markides, 1998). Strategic planning may be a source of institutional inertia rather than innovation: 'Search all those strategic planning diagrams, all those interconnected boxes that supposedly give you strategies, and nowhere will you find a single one that explains the creative act of synthesizing experiences into a novel strategy' (Mintzberg, 1994b: 109); 'The essential problem in organizations today is a failure to distinguish planning from strategizing' (Hamel, 1996: 71). Yet, systematic approaches to strategy can encourage managers to explore alternatives beyond the scope of their prior experiences: 'Good scenarios challenge tunnel vision by instilling a deeper appreciation for the myriad factors that shape the future' (Schoemaker, 1995: 31). Strategic inertia may be more to do with the planners than of planning per se. If top management teams are characterized by lack of genetic diversity and heavy investments of emotional equity in the past, breaking the conservative bias of strategic planning may require involving younger organizational members who are further from the corporate HQ (Hamel, 200: 148). Strategic innovation can also be enhanced through sensitivity to emerging discontinuities in a company's evolution – these strategy/environment misalignments ('strategic inflection points') offer the potential for radical strategic change (Burgelman and Grove, 1996).

Complexity and self-organization

Mintzberg and Pascale's arguments in favor of strategy making as an organic, unsystematic, informal process have received conceptual reinforcement from complexity theory. Models of complex adaptive systems developed mainly for analyzing biological evolution have also been applied to the evolution of organizations (Anderson, 1999). These models offer interesting implications for organizational strategy. For example, faced with a constantly changing fitness landscape, maximizing survival (reaching high fitness peaks) implies constant exploration, parallel exploration efforts by different organizational members, and the combination of incremental steps ('adaptive walks') with occasional major leaps (Beinhocker, 1999). What kinds of strategy can achieve this adaptation? Brown and Eisenhardt's (1997) study of six computer firms points to the role of 'limited probes into the future' that involve experimentation, strategic alliances, and 'time-based transition processes' that link the present with the future. A key feature of strategic processes is the presence of 'semi-structures' that create plans, standards, and responsibilities for certain activities, while allowing freedom elsewhere (Brown and Eisenhardt, 1997: 28–29). One application of the semi-structure concept to strategy formulation concerns the use of simple rules that permit adaptation while establishing bounds that can prevent companies from falling off the edge of chaos (Eisenhardt and Sull, 2001).

Empirical evidence

Empirical evidence points to the coexistence of formal and informal strategic planning processes. Most large companies maintain some form of formal strategic planning. Bain & Company's annual survey of business techniques consistently identifies strategic planning as the most popular and widely utilized of any management tool (Rigby, 1999), while studies by the American Productivity and Quality Center (1996a, 1996b) report features of strategic planning systems among leading-edge US corporations. Yet most strategic decisions appear to be made outside of formal strategic planning systems. Analyzing 1087 decisions by 127 Fortune 500 companies, Sinha concluded: 'the overall contributions of formal strategic planning systems ... are modest' (Sinha, 1990: 489). In unstructured and fast-moving contexts, strategies tend to emerge: Mintzberg and McHugh (1985) identified a 'grass roots' process of strategy formulation, while Burgelman's study of Intel's exit from DRAM chips (Burgelman, 1994, 1996) pointed to the smooth and timely adaptation to external change that resulted from unplanned decision processes forming an 'internal selection mechanism.' Evidence of the impact of environmental turbulence upon strategic planning is limited. Cross-sectional studies have produced inconsistent findings. Longitudinal evidence is fragmented, but more consistent: in response to increasing environmental turbulence, strategic planning systems have changed substantially from the highly formalized processes of the 1960s and 1970s. *BusinessWeek*'s (1996: 46) proclamation that 'strategic planning is back with a vengeance' acknowledged that 'it's also back with a difference.' Details of how strategic planning systems have been adapted to increasingly unstable, unpredictable business environments are sparse. Descriptions of strategic planning practices are available for some companies, e.g., General Electric (Aguilar, Hamermesh and Brainard, 1993; Slater, 1999), Royal Dutch Shell (De Geus, 1997), MCI (Simons and Weston, 1990), and PowerGen (Jennings, 2000), while Wilson (1994) provides more general evidence on changes in strategic planning practices. Overall, the evidence points less to a 'decline of strategic planning' (Mintzberg, 1994a), than to fundamental changes in the ways in which companies undertake their strategic planning.

Investigating these changes in companies' strategic planning practices is likely to require richer data than that used in most prior studies. Boyd and Reuning-Elliot (1998) observed that researchers have represented strategic planning – a complex, multidimensional construct – by a few indicators. However, despite their finding that 'strategic planning is a construct that can be reliably measured through seven indicators: mission statement, trend analysis, competitor analysis, long-term goals, annual goals, short-term action plans, and on-going evaluation' (Boyd and Reuning-Elliot, 1998: 189), even multiple indicators may fail to recognize the characteristics of overall strategic planning configurations and their links with other processes of decision making and control.

Evidence from the oil majors

I selected the international oil majors for my research site for four reasons. First, the oil majors were among the world's largest industrial corporations. By 1996, even after a decade of downsizing and depressed oil prices, 10 of the world's 40 largest industrial corporations (ranked by revenues) were oil companies. Second, the companies were unusual in their complexity. They were vertically integrated, diversified, and multinational, and the close linkages between their activities gave rise to complex coordination problems. Third, the companies had traditionally been at the leading edge of strategic planning practices: they had pioneered the creation of corporate planning departments and application of economic forecasting, risk analysis, portfolio planning, and scenario analysis. Finally, they had experienced a radical transformation of their industry environment from one of stability

TABLE 7.3.1   The world's 10 biggest oil and gas corporations, 1996

Company	Country	Sales revenue 1996 ($m)	Employees 1996
Royal Dutch/Shell[a]	Neth./UK	128 174	101 000
Exxon[a]	US	119 434	79 000
Mobil[a]	US	72 267	43 000
British Petroleum[a]	UK	69 852	53 150
Elf Aquitaine[a]	France	46 818	85 400
Texaco[a]	US	44 561	28 957
ENI[a]	Italy	38 844	83 424
Chevron[a]	US	38 691	40 820
Total	France	34 513	57 555
Amoco[a]	US	32 726	41 723

[a]Included in study sample.

Source: *Fortune Global 500*, 1997.

and continuity to one of uncertainty and turbulence. After several decades of stability and growth when they had been masters of their destiny, their competitive environment was thrown into turmoil by the oil shocks of 1973–74 and 1979–80, the nationalization of the reserves, and the growth of competition (Grant and Cibin, 1996). The 10 leading oil and gas oil majors (as listed in the 1997 Fortune Global 500) which formed my study sample, included the six surviving 'Seven Sisters' – Exxon, Shell, BP, Mobil, Texaco, and Chevron – together with four comparative newcomers to the ranks of the international majors – Elf Aquitaine, ENI, Total, and Amoco. They are shown in Table 7.3.1.

The main features of strategic planning among the oil majors

The strategic planning cycle

All the companies in the sample engaged in a formal, strategic planning process built around an annual planning cycle. Each company's planning cycle (with the exception of BP, which declined to make available its planning framework) is shown in Figure 7.3.1. Despite differences between companies in the depiction of their planning processes and the terminology they used to describe it, the similarities were sufficient to identify a 'generic' strategic planning cycle (see Figure 7.3.2.). The principal stages of the planning process common to all the companies were the following:

1   Planning guidelines. The starting point for the annual planning cycle was an announcement by the corporate headquarters of guidelines and assumptions to be used by the businesses in preparing their business-level strategic plans. These guidelines and assumptions comprised two major elements. First, a view of the external environment. This typically included guidance as to some features of energy markets over the planning period – demand, supply, prices, and margins – which were not so much forecasts as a set of assumptions relating to prices and supply and demand conditions that provided a common basis for strategic planning across the company. Some companies put greater emphasis on scenarios – alternative views of possible developments in the energy sector. Second, corporate management provided overall direction to the planning process through a statement of priorities, guidelines, and expectations. A key aspect of this direction was setting companywide performance targets (e.g., 'raise return on capital employed to 12 per cent,' 'reduce costs per barrel by 10 per cent,' 'a 110 per cent reserve replacement rate,' 'reduce the ratio of debt to equity ratio to 25 per cent by 2000'). Guidance often related to resource allocation, e.g., 'to shift investment from downstream to upstream,' 'to refocus on core businesses,' 'to take advantage of opportunities in China and East Asia,' 'to increase the proportion of gas in our hydrocarbon reserves.'

2   Draft business plans. Strategic plans were formulated bottom-up: the individual businesses took the initiative in formulating their strategic plans.

3   Discussion with corporate. The draft business plans were submitted to the corporate headquarters. After

FIGURE 7.3.1   The companies' strategic planning cycles

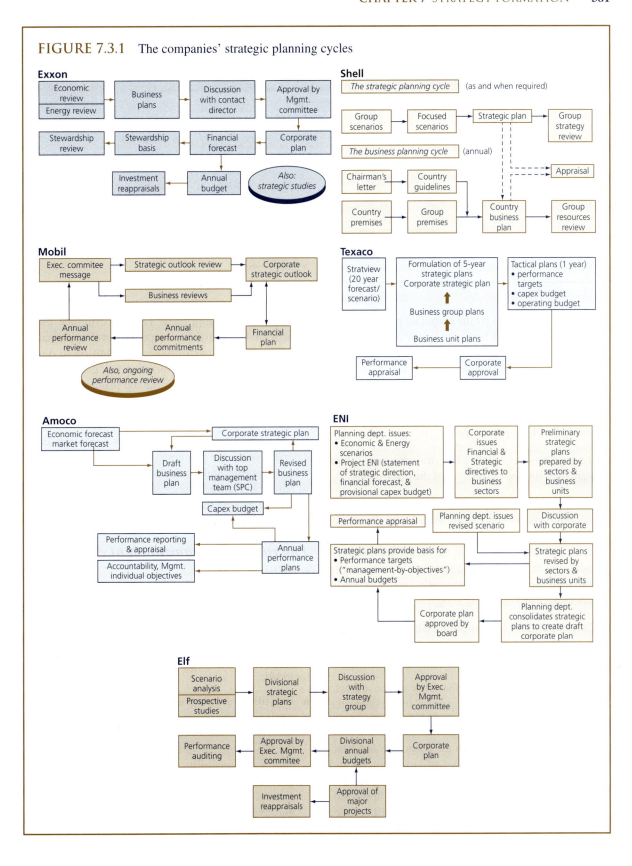

FIGURE 7.3.2   The generic strategic planning cycle among the oil majors

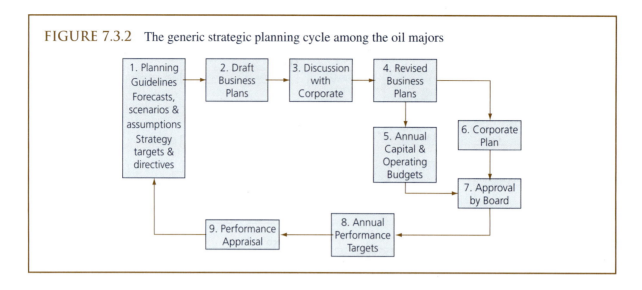

some initial analysis by the corporate planning staff, a meeting was held between senior corporate and senior divisional management. These face-to-face meetings lasted between 2 hours and a full day and discussed the rationale for the strategies being pursued, the performance implications of these strategies, and the compatibility of the business strategy with corporate goals.

4 Revised business plans. The draft business plans were then revised in the light of the discussions.

5 Annual capital and operating budgets. The strategic planning process was closely linked with the annual budgeting process. Although budgeting is coordinated and administered by the controller's department, the first year of the strategic plan typically provided the basis for next year's capital expenditure budget and operating budget.

6 Corporate plan. The corporate plan resulted from the aggregation of the business plans, which was undertaken by the corporate planning department.

7 Board approval. The final formality of the strategic planning formulation was approval of the corporate and business plans by the board of directors.

8 Performance targets. From the corporate and business plans a limited number of key financial and strategic targets were extracted to provide the basis for performance monitoring and appraisal. Targets related to the life of the plan with a more detailed emphasis on performance targets for the coming year.

9 Performance appraisal. The performance plans provided the basis for corporate-level appraisal of business-level performance. In addition to ongoing performance monitoring, a key event was the annual meeting between the top management team and divisional senior managers to discuss each business's performance during the prior year.

For companies whose financial years corresponded to calendar years, the planning cycle began in the spring, with corporate and business plans finally approved in November or December, and performance reviews occurring around the beginning of the following year (see Figure 7.3.3.).

The role and organization of corporate planning staffs

All of the companies possessed a corporate staff unit responsible for strategic planning headed by a vice president or a director of corporate planning or strategy (or, in the case of Exxon, a general manager). The functions of these corporate planning departments included:

■ Providing technical and administrative support to strategic management activities. In all the companies, responsibility for corporate strategy lay with the top management team. The corporate planning staff's responsibility was to support the corporate executive team in its strategic management role (for example, in providing information and analysis, and exploring the impacts of alternative assumptions and courses of action) and to administer the planning process.

FIGURE 7.3.3   Timing of the planning cycle

- Preparing economic, political, and market forecasts, risk analysis, competitor analysis, and other investigations of the business environment to assist strategic planning through the company.

- Fostering communication between corporate and business management. In some of the companies – notably Shell, Mobil, ENI, and Amoco – corporate planners liaised with divisional managers and divisional planners, and fostered dialog through a common format and terminology for strategic plans. In other companies – notably Exxon and BP – high levels of involvement by corporate planning staff was viewed as a barrier to strategy dialog between business-level chief executives and corporate top management.

- Internal consulting. To the extent that corporate planning departments became repositories of expertise about strategy analysis and strategic planning techniques, they tended to develop internal consulting roles in relation to the businesses and other functions.

Who are the corporate planners?

Unlike certain other corporate functions (finance, law, and information systems), none of the companies recognized strategic planning as a career track. Corporate planners were drawn from line management positions within the businesses and, in some cases, from other staff functions (e.g., finance and IT). Planners typically spent between 3 and 5 years in corporate planning posts before returning to a line management position. The only

examples of career track planners were, first, the few professional economists that resided in corporate planning departments and, second, some corporate planning managers in two companies with significant public ownership, ENI and Elf, who spent 15 years or more within the planning function. Several companies explained that their staffing of corporate planning departments reflected their intention to combine the analytic skills of younger staff with the deep experiential knowledge of longer-serving managers. At all the companies corporate planning assignments were viewed as important career development stages offering corporate-level exposure and a 'big-picture' perspective for 'fast track' executives.

Differences between the companies

Within this common framework, there were some notable differences between the companies. In particular:

1 Formality and regularity. Several companies, notably Elf Aquitaine and ENI, had planning systems that were more formal (e.g., greater reliance upon written reports and formal presentations), more regular (in terms of a fixed annual cycle), and less flexible than those of the other companies. These differences were related primarily to differences in overall management styles – Elf and ENI had retained more traditional hierarchical structures and formal administrative styles, in contrast to the other companies (most notably BP and Texaco) that had encouraged a more entrepreneurial management style. The degree of formalization of the

planning process was also linked to the emphasis given to performance targets in the strategic planning process. The companies that placed the biggest emphasis on establishing rigorous financial targets for their businesses – BP, Texaco, and Exxon, in particular – also had planning processes that were comparatively informal. Conversely, companies that emphasized strategic control – ENI, Elf, and Shell – placed greater emphasis on written strategic plans and formal approval processes. In terms of regularity, all the companies pursued an annual planning cycle; however, some companies – notably Amoco, Shell, and Mobil – had moved away from standardized, calendar-driven annual cycles; they updated environmental analysis and performance targets annually (or more frequently), but called for revision of business strategies only when circumstances required.

2   The time horizon of strategic plans. Strategic plans were typically for 4–5 years, although in upstream planning horizons tended to be longer – up to 15 years in the case of Exxon. Several companies – notably Shell, Texaco and Elf – operated a dual system of planning: long-term planning that extended for 10 years or more and was typically qualitative and scenario based, and medium-term planning that was more detailed and quantitative and involved a greater level of commitment. Shell had the longest horizon for its strategic plans – up to 20 years – however, these long-term strategic plans took the forms of long-term views of the business and the environment where the primary object was to encourage long term thinking about the business in the light of underlying technological, political, and business trends. Texaco maintained 15- to 20-year strategic views, though, like Shell, Texaco's long-term plans involved no formal resource commitment.

3   Differences in the role and activities of planning departments. The emphasis placed upon different strategic planning activities varied across the companies. Among companies that had undergone major internal reorganizations, such as Amoco and ENI, the strategic planning function played a prominent role as a coordinating and integrating mechanism. Thus, following Amoco's 1995 reorganization around 17 business separate groups, the strategic planning department was actively involved in developing cooperation across the different business, e.g., in creating cross-business 'umbrella strategies' for individual countries. A more interventionist role of corporate planning departments

was also apparent within those companies whose corporate planners fulfilled an internal consulting role. Although Shell's internal consulting unit was disbanded in 1992, Shell's planning group maintained an active role in promoting and diffusing strategic management ideas and techniques. Similarly, ENI's planning department maintained a strong advisory role and was active in disseminating corporate-level goals and priorities. Companies with the broadest roles for their corporate planners also had the biggest corporate planning departments.

Table 7.3.3 summarizes key features of the individual companies' strategic planning systems.

Changes in strategic planning systems

All eight companies acknowledged major changes in their strategic planning practices over the previous decade and a half. While the basic framework of strategic planning – in terms of the strategic planning cycle and its key phases – remained little changed, the content of strategic plans, the strategic planning process, and the role of planning within the companies' management systems changed considerably.

The planning heritage of 'Big Oil'

Corporate planning had been adopted by most of the companies during the early 1960s, in response to the increasing difficulties of coordination and control that the companies faced as they expanded their vertical, geographical, and product scope during the postwar period. Strategic planning began within their supply departments, where planning of international flows of oil and refined products had developed expertise in forecasting prices and market trends. By the late 1960s, most of the oil majors had established corporate planning departments.

The primary task of these corporate planning departments was forecasting trends in energy markets and the general economy. Macroeconomic forecasts provided the basis for predictions of the demand, supply, and prices of oil and refined products upon which outputs, revenues, profits, and capital investment requirements were projected. Hence, all the planning departments included an economics unit typically headed by a professional economist. Diversification during the 1970s expanded the role of the corporate planning departments. By 1980 the corporate planning departments were involved in: forecasting demand, supply, prices, and profit margins; creating scenarios; undertaking country risk analysis;

building corporate financial models to link economic and market forecasts to company financial performance; administering the annual strategic planning cycle; developing planning methodologies and techniques; advising corporate and divisional management on strategic issues; and providing strategic analysis of major capital investment projects. In administering the strategic planning process, the corporate planning departments became important intermediaries between corporate and divisional management communicating corporate goals and priorities to divisional managers, assessing business-level plans presented to top management, and aggregating business-level plans into corporate plans. This pivotal role resulted in them exerting significant influence not just over the process of strategy formulation, but in many instances over its content as well.

Forces for change

The transformation of energy majors' market environment from stability and continuity to uncertainty and turbulence also created a far more hostile environment. The catastrophic fall in the price of oil in 1986 and increased competition at all stages of the companies' value chains put profits under considerable pressure. Simultaneously, a surge in acquisitions and leveraged buyouts created a more active market for corporate control that pressured top management to improve returns to shareholders. This transformation had far-reaching implications for the companies' strategies, structures, and management processes (Cibin and Grant, 1996) – including their strategic planning systems.

The changing foundations of strategic planning

The dangers of using medium-term forecasts as a foundation for business and corporate plans became painfully apparent during the 1980s, when the accuracy of macroeconomic and market forecasts – especially of crude oil prices – declined precipitously. As late as 1992, BP was brought to the brink of catastrophe as the result of a strategy that had assumed an oil price of $20 a barrel. CEO John Browne subsequently remarked:

> We gave up trying to forecast what would happen some time ago – we'd just learned from experience that even the most sophisticated models can't predict the reality of oil prices or any of the other key variables. All you can do is to look at the current reality, and the recent pattern of the economic cycle and from that set

> yourself some guidelines against which you can judge your own performance.

During the 1980s and 1990s, all the companies reduced their forecasting efforts and downsized or eliminated their economist staff. Exxon's economic forecasting and analysis unit was reduced to a single staff economist. In place of forecasts, the companies' external analysis shifted in two directions. The first was scenario planning. While Shell was the only company to base its entire strategic planning process upon multiple scenario analysis, other companies adopted scenario planning to a more limited extent, for example, to explore particular issues (such as the future of OPEC or strategies for the former Soviet Union). Replacing single-point forecasts with alternative scenarios of the future had important implications for the nature of strategic planning. Instead of a single basis for competitive positioning and resource deployment, scenario analysis was a tool for contingency planning that fostered alertness and responsiveness among decision-makers to changing market circumstances. The reluctance of some companies to use scenarios more widely as a basis for strategy formulation was partly the result of the perceived costs of developing and disseminating scenarios in terms of management time. The second response was to replace forecasts of key variables with assumptions about these variables. Thus, in relation to the prices of crude oil, natural gas, and refined products and key currency exchange rates, all the companies introduced 'reference prices' which provided a basis for financial projections and performance targets. Again, this shifting basis for planning had far-reaching implications for the nature of strategic planning. The purpose of reference prices and other fixed assumptions about the environment was not to provide a basis for strategic decisions, but to provide a consistent foundation against which financial performance could be targeted and monitored. This shift of planning from 'strategy-as-resource-deployment' to 'strategy-as-aspirations-and-performance-goals' is a key transition that I return to below.

Growing informality of the planning process

The planning systems of the 1970s and 1980s were highly formalized in terms of documentation, formal presentations, emphasis on techniques and quantitative analysis, and the central role of specialist planners. By 1996–97, planning systems were far more informal: there was less emphasis on written documentation, strategic plans were shorter, and there was less emphasis on set-piece presentations and more on open discussion. To encourage discussion and the exchange of ideas, new rules-of-play were adopted: BP discouraged the use of multiple graphs at strategy meetings; Amoco limited the number of slides at strategy presentations. Meetings between business-level and corporate executives became shorter and the balance shifted from presentation to discussion. All the companies reported that the annual meetings between corporate and business executives to discuss business-level strategic plans were increasingly focused around discussion of a few underlying issues. Similarly, at strategy and performance review meetings, discussion became focused around just a smaller set of performance variables. As a result, meetings become shorter:

- At Mobil performance reviews were downsized from 2-day meetings with each division with formal presentations by business managers to shorter, more informal interactions where business group management reported to the Executive Committee on 'How we did. What we did. What we didn't do.'

- At Exxon, the annual 'stewardship reviews' between the divisional president and the Management Committee were cut from 3 or 4 days down to a half-day. These meetings focused upon reports of key performance indicators and 'Things we feel good about, and things we feel bad about.'

Less formality was also evident in a move from a regular, standardized planning cycle to more flexible and ad hoc process. As noted above, Amoco allowed its business groups to develop new strategic plans as and when needed, while the long-term, scenario-based projections by Shell and Texaco became less regular.

Shifting strategic planning responsibilities

Increasing volatility and uncertainty of the external environment was accompanied by two changes in strategic planning responsibilities: first, a shift of decision-making responsibility from corporate to business-level managers; second, a shift of planning responsibilities from planning staff to line managers.

From corporate management to business management

By the late 1990s, strategic planning was primarily a bottom-up process. The content of the strategic plans

was determined mainly at the business unit and divisional levels under the principle that business-level chief executives were responsible for their businesses – including their business strategies. This concept of business-level management 'owning' the business and being responsible to shareholders and corporate executives for its management was a particularly strong philosophy at Exxon and BP. The corporate influence was primarily in establishing the context for business strategy formulation and intervening to question, criticize, and cajole business managers. Decentralization of strategic management authority was indicated by the increasing levels of discretion exercised by business unit and divisional managers over capital expenditures. As Table 7.3.2 shows, during the 1990s all the companies raised authorization levels of individual executives. This transfer of strategic planning responsibilities from corporate to divisional level was part of a broader shift in the relationship between corporate and divisional management. The key priorities of the 1990s were speedier decision making to respond to fast-changing external circumstances and the increasing returns of shareholders. Strategic planning systems became less about planning the majors' long-run growth and stability, and more about squeezing increased profitability from mature, slow growth businesses. If business-level managers were to take responsibility for strategic decisions, while corporate management was to be responsible for shareholder returns, decentralization of strategic decision making needed to be matched by divisional executives being unambiguously accountable for divisional performance. By 1996, the primary focus of the strategic planning processes of the majors was medium-term performance targets. If the primary responsibility of divisional management was to achieve the levels of performance expected by corporate management, the inevitable corollary was that divisional management must be free to select strategies capable of delivering the required performance. The role of the corporate headquarters in strategic planning focused less on endorsing and approving business-level strategies and more on negotiation with the divisions over expected performance levels and questioning and challenging the thinking behind the proposed strategies in order to improve the quality of divisional strategic decision making.

From staff to line managers

Decentralization of strategic planning from corporate to business levels coincided with a declining role of planning staff as corporate and divisional line managers became increasingly responsible for strategic planning.

TABLE 7.3.2   A summary of the key features of the individual comapnies' strategic planning systems

Company	Position (at the time of interview)
Royal Dutch/Shell	Head of Group Planning Senior Strategist Manager, Group Planning Group Treasurer Head, Management Development
Exxon	General Manager, Corporate Planning Department Former General Manager, Corporate Planning Department Manager, Corporate Strategy Division, Corporate Planning Department Assistant Treasurer
Mobil	Vice President, Strategic Planning Global Industry Analyst, Strategic Planning Vice President, Planning, Downstream Division
British Petroleum	Strategic Coordinator Manager, Upstream Strategy Former head of Chairman's office
ELF Aquitaine	Director, Direction Prospective Economie Strategic Manager, Direction Prospective Economie Strategic
Texaco	Vice President, Corporate Strategy and Planning Director of Planning Manager, Corporate Strategy and Planning Director of Organization and Executive Development
ENI	Director, Planning and Control Department Deputy Director, Planning and Control Department Deputy Director, Personnel and Organization
Amoco	Director, Market Analysis, Strategic Planning Practice Leader, Competency Modeling Organization Effectiveness Consultant Practice Leader, Competency Modeling Organization Effectiveness Consultant

This diminishing role of strategic planning staff reflected the increasing personal responsibility on executives at all levels. As chief executives became more accountable to shareholders for corporate performance and divisional heads became increasingly responsible to their chief executives for divisional performance, so these executives became individually responsibility for strategy. The shift of responsibility from staff planners to executives is indicated by the shrinking size of corporate planning departments (see Table 7.3.3). This downsizing of corporate planning staffs was reinforced by the reduction in economic forecasting activities and the outsourcing of intelligence activities and analysis to consulting companies. In addition, planning staff became increasingly located within the operating divisions. For example, at Mobil in 1996, corporate planning staff numbered only 12; however, each of Mobil's 13 business groups had its own planning units, and throughout the (approximately) 100 'natural businesses' there were some 470 planning staff. Similarly, at ENI, at the beginning of 1993, the 72 corporate planning staff were outnumbered by the 416 strategic planning staff located in the operating companies.

TABLE 7.3.3 Numbers employed in corporate planning departments

	1990	1993	1996
Amoco	90	60	30
BP	48[a]	12	3
Elf	n.a.	15	14
ENI	n.a.	72	65
Exxon	42[a]	20	17
Mobil	38	n.a.	12
Shell	48[b]	23	17
Texaco	40	n.a.	27

[a]Estimated. In 1986 Exxon's corporate planning staff numbered 60.

[b]Estimated. In 1985 Shell's corporate planning staff numbered 54.

The content of strategic plans

A detailed analysis of the content of strategic plans was not possible owing to the reluctance of the companies to make available their plans. Only two of the companies made available recent planning documents. Nonetheless, it was clear from the interviews that some significant changes had occurred in the content of strategic plans over the previous decade. Three trends were common to all the companies:

1 Shortening time horizons. Table 7.3.2 shows the periods for which the companies prepared their strategic plans. All the companies reported a shortening of their planning horizons over the previous decade. Among my sample, five out of the eight companies had planning periods of 5 years or less. However, the major contraction of companies' strategy horizons resulted, not from formal changes to their planning periods, but from shifting their emphasis from the long term to the short and medium term. For example, the companies that engaged in both medium-term strategic planning and longer-term scenario planning (Shell, Texaco, and Elf) increased their emphasis on medium-term planning at the expense of longer-term projections. Foreshortened planning horizons were most apparent among companies whose strategic priorities were dominated by restructuring, cost cutting, and the need to boost shareholder return (e.g., ENI's strategic plans period was only 4 years). A second trend was to link planning periods more closely to the lives of investment. Thus, Exxon and Elf each required their upstream sector to plan for 10–15 years as compared to 5 years for their downstream and chemical sectors.

2 A shift from detailed planning to strategic direction. Increased environmental instability resulted not only in less formality and rigidity of the planning process, but also in less precision and greater flexibility in the content of strategic plans. Strategic plans became less concerned with detailed programs of action, commitments to particular projects, and resource deployments, and placed greater emphasis upon more broadly defined goals. For example, Amoco's strategic plan of 1995–99 was specified almost entirely in terms of 'strategic themes' and 'specific strategies and goals'. These strategies and goals related to themes that included financial targets ('net income to exceed $3 billion by 1998') and cost reduction ('achieve cost savings of $1–2 billion from restructuring') and international expansion (e.g., 'to develop a global gas business'). This shift to broad strategic direction is also indicated by the adoption by all the companies (with the exception of Exxon and Elf Aquitaine) of statements of 'mission' and/or 'vision' to communicate and guide their strategies. Although these mission and vision statements were partly exercises in image management, the interviewees pointed to their significant role in the strategy-making process in terms of creating a sense of corporate, identity-setting boundaries for corporate scope and establishing long-term strategic intent.

3 Increased emphasis on performance planning. In discussing the shifting relationship between corporate and divisional levels in the planning processes, I noted the increasing emphasis placed on performance targets. During the 1990s, the strategic plans of all the companies shifted their focus away from forecasts and specific strategic decisions that specified timetables and resource deployments, and towards targets relating to financial and operational performance targets. Thus, of Amoco's six strategic themes of 1995–99, four were couched entirely in terms of performance outcomes rather than commitments to take specific actions. The growing preoccupation with performance goals was also evident in the increasing emphasis placed upon short and medium performance planning within the strategic planning process. Despite different terminology – 'performance plans' (Amoco), 'management by objectives' (ENI), 'stewardship basis' (Exxon), and 'performance commitments' (Mobil) – the elements were similar.

■ Financial targets. These focused upon total profit (typically net profit and/or operating profit, and in some cases economic profit, e.g. EVA) and profitability ratios (return on capital employed was the most widely used). Several companies set targets for shareholder return (typically defining targets in relation to the sector as a whole, e.g., 'to achieve a return to shareholders in the top quartile of the industry').

- Operating targets. For upstream these might include production, wells drilled, lease agreements signed, reserves added. For downstream these might include throughput, capacity utilization, inventories.
- Safety and environmental objectives.
- Strategic mileposts – intermediate objectives which were indicators that a strategy was on track. For a division, strategic mileposts might relate to entry into specific countries, specific cost reduction targets, new product introductions, and divestments of specified assets.
- Capital expenditure limits.

Among these different objectives, the overwhelming priority for all the companies was financial targets. This emphasis was evident in the tools and techniques used by the companies' planning departments. Despite all the strategy concepts, tools, and techniques developed during the 1990s – from competitive analysis to the analyses of resources and capabilities – most of the new tools and techniques deployed by the oil majors during the 1990s were financial in nature. These included new measures of profitability (e.g., EVA), techniques of shareholder value analysis, and real options analysis.

The companies were acutely aware of the problems of reconciling short-term (annual) performance targets with longer-term performance goals – while effective performance monitoring required quarterly and annual appraisal, maximization of shareholder value required long-term profit maximization. Hence all the companies sought to combine short-term profit targets with strategic and operational targets that were consistent with building longer-term competitive advantage (e.g., the operating targets and strategic mileposts referred to above). Mobil, Texaco, and Amoco used 'balanced scorecards' for achieving consistency between short-term performance targets and longer-term strategic goals. At Mobil, balanced scorecards played a key role in 'cascading down' corporate and divisional strategies to business units and individual departments.

The essential complements to performance plans were performance reviews. At all the companies, reviews of business performance against performance targets and strategic plan were central elements of the strategic planning process. Most companies had quarterly performance reviews based on the businesses submitting written performance reports with informal discussion between divisional and corporate management. The major business-corporate interactions were at the annual performance reviews that took place in the early part of the calendar year and involved face-to-face meetings between divisional and corporate top management.

The role of strategic planning

Changes in the oil majors' strategic planning practices pointed to a different role for strategic planning within the companies. The strategic planning systems of the 1960s and 1970s were mechanisms for formulating strategy – they planned growth and allocated resources. By the late 1990s, strategy formulation was occurring, for the most part, outside of the companies' strategic planning systems. When interviewees were asked to identify the sources of critical strategic decisions that their companies had made in recent years – acquisitions, divestments, restructuring measures, and cost-cutting initiatives – it was apparent that few had their origins in the plans that emerged from the companies' strategic planning systems. The typical sequence was the other way round: strategic decisions were made in response to the opportunities and threats that appeared, and were subsequently incorporated into strategic plans. If the purpose of the strategic planning system was not primarily to take strategic decisions, what role did it play within the companies' management? The interview data pointed to three key roles.

Strategic planning as a context for strategic decision making

Even if strategic planning systems were no longer the primary decision paths for making strategy, they created contexts that influenced the content and quality of strategic decisions. Even here, the mechanisms through which the corporate center conventionally influenced business-level strategies – providing forecasts and detailed scrutiny – had progressively eroded. This left two key processes through which the corporate planning processes contributed to the quality of business-level strategic management:

1 Influencing the methodologies and techniques of strategic planning. Although corporate planning departments continued to act as centers of excellence for strategy methods and strategy techniques, downsizing of planning departments downsized and

increased reliance upon outside consultants for analytical expertise constrained this role. Some tools of strategy analysis were widely used, including Porter-type industry analysis, shareholder value analysis, game theory, appraisals of competencies and capabilities, PIMS analysis, and the identification of critical success factors. However, several companies, Exxon in particular, were skeptical of most formal strategy techniques and the jargon associated with them, believing that they created a barrier to deploying experience-based knowledge and hampered the shift of strategic planning responsibility from planning staff to line managers.

2 Providing channels and forums for communication and knowledge sharing. All the companies placed greater emphasis on the communication and knowledge sharing role of planning processes. Indeed, the desire to promote dialog between businesses and the corporate executives on fundamental strategy issues was the main motive for reducing the formality of the planning process. This involved shifting emphasis of strategy meetings from formal presentations to face-to-face discussion where assumptions and beliefs were challenged and critical issues identified. Shell and Exxon provide contrasting examples of this trend:

■ Shell has placed particular weight upon strategic planning as a vehicle for organizational learning. Shell's scenario planning process was primarily a process for sharing and integrating multiple knowledge bases from both within and outside the Shell group. Shell's 'scenario-to-strategy' framework involved discussion workshops in which scenarios would provide the foundation for an interactive strategy formulation. To maximize the organizational learning occurring through the strategic planning process, Shell has attempted to make explicit the perceptions and judgments of the various decision makers within the strategy process through techniques such as 'mental mapping.'

■ Exxon's emphasis was upon a strategic planning process that was tightly integrated within a management structure that stressed the close bonds of communication and accountability between each divisional president and the corresponding 'contact director' on the corporate management committee. Thus, while Exxon had a well-defined strategic planning system, the formalities relating to the submission, discussion, and approval of divisional strategic plans were inseparable from the regular communication and interaction between the division

presidents and the management committee that allowed strategic plans to be informed and guided by the continual integration of divisional and corporate level knowledge.

Strategic planning as a mechanism for coordination

Increased emphasis on planning as a process of communication and knowledge sharing was intended not only to influence and improve strategic decisions, but also to provide a basis for coordinating decentralized decision making. The interview data suggested that increased environmental turbulence had enhanced the role of the strategic planning system as a coordinating device. As decision making had become increasingly decentralized, there was a growing need for a structured process of dialog, adjustment, and agreement to coordinate these dispersed decisions. This increased emphasis on coordination was evident from a number of the changes already described, notably the transition by the corporate center from detailed control towards more general direction and guidance, and the increased emphasis placed upon business-corporate dialog and consensus building. The priority accorded to this coordinating role of strategic planning varied between the companies. In general, the more decentralized was strategic decision making, the greater the emphasis on strategic planning as a coordinating device. Thus, Shell with its 200 separate operating companies had long regarded its strategic planning process as primarily a vehicle for coordination and consensus within its far-flung business empire. Similarly, once Amoco reorganized as 17 separate business groups, the corporate planning department became increasingly concerned with providing vertical coordination between corporate and business levels, and developing horizontal coordination, e.g., through involving different business groups in country 'umbrella strategies.' Exxon's emphasis upon strategic planning as a coordinating device was a central rationale for embedding its strategic planning process within ongoing dialog between the divisional presidents and 'contact directors.' Exxon's head of corporate planning described Exxon's strategic planning as having evolved from a 'product-based' to a 'process-based' system.

Strategic planning as a mechanism for control

Hierarchical control in organizations can be exerted through behavioral control which manages the inputs into decisions through supervision and approval, and output control which manages the performance outcomes of decisions (Eisenhardt, 1985; Ouchi, 1979). Establishing control over increasing large and unwieldy corporate empires was a major motive for the adoption of strategic planning. Corporate planning provided a medium- and long-term control mechanism that complemented the short-term controls provided by budgeting systems. Under the 'old model' corporate management's ability to approve (or reject) business-level strategic and the resource allocations to support these plans represented a form of input control. By the late 1990s, strategic planning's function as a control system had shifted from one based upon strategy content to one based upon strategy outcomes defined in terms of the performance that the strategy would deliver. This shift was apparent from three types of evidence. First, the corporate guidelines that shaped business-level strategic planning (stage 1 of the generic strategic planning cycle) places increased emphasis on company-wide financial performance goals. This shift was also evident in the ways in which the companies revised their statements of mission, vision, and business principles. By the late 1990s, pride of place was given to shareholder return and superior profitability. Second, most companies reported that the meetings to discuss business-level strategic plans (stage 3 of the generic planning cycle) had become increasingly focused around performance targets (especially for operating profit and return on capital employed). Third, as attention shifted to the setting and monitoring of performance targets, so the performance planning process (stage 8 of the generic strategic planning cycle) became increasingly prominent.

Preoccupation with shareholder return was translated into rising aspirations for ROCE. Belief in the efficacy of 'stretch goals' also influenced thinking about the role of strategy. Hamel and Prahalad's (1989, 1994) analysis of 'strategic intent' and 'strategy as leverage and stretch' suggests that strategy's biggest contribution to company's performance is not so much through superior strategic decisions as in raising levels of aspiration and commitment through setting challenging goals.

Increasing emphasis on performance and quantification of performance targets was accompanied by less detailed strategic plans. This was most evident among the companies that placed the biggest emphasis on performance planning – BP, Exxon, and Texaco. These companies argued that commitments by divisional presidents to ambitious performance targets required their taking responsibility for divisional strategy. The more corporate was involved in influencing divisional strategies, the greater the erosion of divisional responsibility and accountability. Increasingly the corporate message was: 'Here's the performance we require. You figure out how to deliver it.' This shift from strategic control to performance planning (supported by stronger performance incentives) was typically described by the companies in terms of 'empowerment' – divisional and business unit managers were accorded greater decision-making discretion, while becoming more individually accountable for results.

Discussion

Implications for design vs process debate

The evidence on the strategic planning practices of the major oil companies suggests that the long running debate over the roles of rational design and organizational emergence in strategy formulation has been perpetuated by misconceptions of the reality of strategic planning. The vivid caricatures presented by each side of the other's conceptualization of strategy making bear little resemblance to the realities of strategic planning as pursued by large companies during the late 1990s. Although hierarchical in structure with decision-making power ultimately vested in the top management team and critical inputs provided by corporate planning staff, the major oil companies' strategic planning systems of the late 1990s had little in common with the highly bureaucratized, top-down processes caricatured by Henry Mintzberg. In particular, strategic planning was primarily a bottom-up process in which corporate management provided direction, but primary inputs came from the business units and operating divisions. However, consistent with the process view of strategy formation, it was clear that the strategies of the oil majors were not created by their strategic planning systems. Strategic planning systems were mechanisms for improving the quality of strategic decisions, for coordinating strategic decision making, and for driving performance improvement. However, the critical strategic decisions that fundamentally affected the business portfolios and direction of development of the companies were, for the most part, taken outside formal systems of strategic planning. By disbanding aspects of strategic planning conventionally associated with rational, top-down strategy design and embracing adaptive, emergent aspects of strategy making, none of the oil majors appeared to be deluded by Mintzberg's (1994b: 110–112) 'fallacies of strategic planning.' In terms of the 'fallacy of prediction,' none of the strategic planning systems relied upon precise predictions of key external variables. In terms of the 'fallacy of detachment,' all the companies located primary strategy responsibilities with line managers. In terms of 'fallacy of formalization,' all the companies had substantially reduced the formality of their planning procedures. In short, the strategic planning systems of the international majors could be described as processes of 'planned emergence.' The primary direction of planning was bottom-up – from the business units to the corporate headquarters – and with business managers exhibiting substantial autonomy and flexibility in strategy making. At the same time, the structure of the planning systems allowed corporate management established constraints and guidelines in the form of vision and mission statements, corporate initiatives, and performance expectations. In bringing together these bottom-up and top-down initiatives through dialog, debate, and compromise, the systems displayed aspects of the 'generative planning model' that Liedtka (2000) suggests is conducive to strategic change. To what extent do these systems of 'both incremental learning and deliberate planning' (Goold, 1992: 169) assist the companies in adapting effectively to the challenges and opportunities of the 1990s? Distinguishing the contribution of strategic planning as distinct from other aspects of the companies' management processes is difficult. What is apparent, however, is that the major oil companies were exceptionally successful in adapting to the challenges of the decade. Key strategic adjustments by the oil majors included: rationalization of downstream and chemical businesses

in the face of chronic excess capacity (especially through joint ventures and asset swaps), refocusing upon core energy businesses, upstream expansion into new geographical areas (especially China, the Former Soviet Union and Latin America), the adoption of new technologies (e.g., deep-water exploration, directional drilling, 3D seismic analysis, and environmentally friendlier fuels), adaptation to social and political pressures, and responsiveness to the demands of owners (especially Elf and ENI's transformation from state to shareholder ownership). Perhaps the strongest evidence of the effectiveness of strategic adjustment lies in bottom-line performance: despite the low oil prices that prevailed for most of the 1990s, profitability for most of the companies was higher than during earlier periods when oil prices were significantly higher (see Table 7.3.4). However, as mechanisms for aligning the companies more closely and effectively with their changing environment and guiding their long-term development, the effectiveness of the companies' strategic planning may also have deteriorated in three respects:

1 The foreshortening of planning horizons may reflect a shift in top management priority from long-term development to short- and medium-term performance goals. When investment projects have lives that extended to 40 years, strategic planning horizons of 4 and 5 years limited the potential for companies to relate their current resource allocations with their longer-term vision.

TABLE 7.3.4 The oil majors' return on equity, 1970s, 1980s and 1990s

	1970–79	1980–89	1990–98
Return on equity			
Shell Group	10.76	13.87	13.82
Exxon	13.63	15.30	16.14
Mobil	11.15	11.57	12.87
BP	9.07	12.08	11.09
ENI	4.83	0.13	10.20
Elf Aquitaine	6.24	11.91	9.37
Texaco	10.30	8.93	12.30
Amoco	11.57	14.56	12.54
Average price of crude oil (US wellhead purchase price at constant 1996 $ per barrel)	17.1	28.6	17.4

Source: *Fortune Global 500*; WTRG Economics.

2 The transfer of strategic planning responsibilities from staff planners to line managers, while resolving problems of formalization and detachment, also entailed a loss of analytical capability. One of the ancillary observations of our study was the limited use by the companies of recently developed strategy concepts and techniques. Despite the rapid diffusion of the tools and techniques of strategic management during the 1980s and 1990s, few of these found application in the strategic planning processes of the oil majors. Although performance management tools – shareholder value analysis, EVA, balanced scorecards, and the like – had achieved significant uptake, the same was not apparent for concepts and techniques of strategy analysis. For example, while interviewees frequently referred to 'building competitive advantage,' 'exploiting key strengths,' and 'leveraging core competences,' only one of the companies (Amoco) had introduced any systematic process for assessing and developing organizational capabilities. It is possible that the priority accorded to financial performance targets in strategic planning squeezed out analysis. For example, the reluctance of several of the majors to introduce option valuation into their capital budgeting procedures stemmed from the fear that adding greater complexity might result in losing the discipline associated with unambiguous hurdle rates of return.

3 While breaking down the rigidities of the old formalized planning systems and embracing emergent strategy-making processes, the companies had done little in terms of positive measures to encourage innovation in strategy making. If competitive advantage in changing markets depends critically upon strategic innovation (Baden-Fuller and Stopford, 1994; Hamel, 2000; Markides, 1998), then the sources of strategic innovation need to be considered. While bottom-up, informal strategic planning systems offer the potential for innovative strategies to emerge, the absence of impediments to such innovation is not the same as positive measures to foster such innovation.

Implications for the management of complexity

In discussing the literature on the implications of environmental turbulence for strategic planning, I noted the potential contribution of complexity theory in providing a bridge between the opposing views of the strategy-as-design and strategy-as-process camps. Several of the features of the oil majors' strategic planning systems are consistent with the observations of other management scholars regarding the implications of complexity theory for business management. If scaling fitness peaks requires combining incremental steps with occasional major leaps (Anderson, 1999; Beinhocker, 1999), performance-focused strategic planning may facilitate this goal. Bottom-up strategic planning is conducive to incremental adaptation. Yet, as Shell, BP, ENI, and Texaco demonstrated, when realized performance falls far short of targeted level, the natural bias towards incrementalism is supplanted by pressures for more radical strategic changes. My characterization of the companies' strategic planning processes as ones of 'planned emergence' corresponds closely to Brown and Eisenhardt's (1997) concept of 'semi-structures': the planning systems created an organizational structure, a fixed time schedule, and defined goals and responsibilities, while offering considerable freedom for experimentation, entrepreneurship, and initiative at the business level. Two aspects of this 'semi-structure' character of strategic planning systems were particularly apparent. First, the strategy planning processes embodied the concept of simple rules which models of complex adaptive systems suggest can be remarkably effective in predicting and guiding the adaptation of nonhierarchical systems to changing environmental conditions (Eisenhardt and Sull, 2001; Gell-Mann, 1994). The strategy initiatives and guidelines established by corporate management in the form of mission and vision statements and targets for cost reduction, reserve replacement, and debt/equity ratios represented a framework of constraints and objectives that bounded and directed strategic choices. Second, existence of rigid annual planning cycles and the emphasis on breaking down longer-term strategic goals into short-term objectives in the form of strategic milestones, programmed targets, and scorecards corresponded to Brown and Eisenhardt's (1997) concept of time-paced transition from the present to the future.

Conclusion

The findings from this study, together with other recent evidence, show that strategic planning continues to play a central role in the management systems of large companies. At the same time, strategic planning practices have changed substantially over the past two decades in response to the challenges of strategy formulation in turbulent and unpredictable environments.

Strategic planning processes have become more decentralized, less staff driven, and more informal, while strategic plans themselves have become shorter term, more goal focused, and less specific with regard to actions and resource allocations. The role of strategic planning systems within companies' overall management has also changed. Strategic planning had become less about strategic decision making and more a mechanism for coordination and performance managing. The growing prominence of performance targets within strategic plans has changed the role of strategic planning as a corporate control system, permitting increased decentralization of strategic decision making and greater adaptability and responsiveness to external change.

Despite the apparently successful adaptation of strategic planning systems to unstable, uncertain environments, the study pointed to the limited impact of strategic planning processes upon the quality of strategic decisions. Decentralization and informality of strategic planning processes permitted access to a broader range of expertise, but there was limited use of new tools and concepts of strategic analysis and little evidence that the systems of strategic planning were conducive to strategic innovation.

The study has implications for the study of strategic management. The features of strategic planning revealed by the study suggest that much of the debate between the 'strategy-as-rational-design' and 'strategy-as-emergent-process' schools has been based upon a misconception of how strategic planning works in the real world. The process of 'planned emergence' evident in the companies' strategic planning systems is consistent with management principles derived from complexity theory and observations of complex adaptive systems.

REFERENCES

Ackoff, R.L. (1981) *Creating the Corporate Future*, Chichester: Wiley.

Aguilar, F.J., Hamermesh, R.G. and Brainard, C.E. (1993) *General Electric Co.: 1984, Case 385315*, Boston, MA: Harvard Business School.

Allaire, Y. and Firsirotu, M. (1990) 'Strategic Plans as Contracts', *Long Range Planning*, 23(1), pp. 102–115.

Allison, G.T. (1971) *The Essence of Decision: Explaining the Cuban Missile Crisis*, Boston, MA: Little Brown.

Amabile, T.M. (1998) 'How to Kill Creativity', *Harvard Business Review*, 76(5, September–October), pp. 76–87.

American Productivity and Quality Center (1996) *Reinventing Strategic Planning for a Dynamic Environment*, Houston, TX: APQC's International Benchmarking Clearinghouse.

Anderson, P. (1999) 'Complexity theory and organizational science', *Organization Science*, 10, pp. 216–232.

Andrews, K.R. (1987) *The Concept of Corporate Strategy* (3rd edn), Homewood, IL: Irwin.

Ang, J.S. and Chua, J.H. (1979) 'Long-range planning in large United States corporations: a survey', *Long Range Planning*, 12(April), pp. 99–102.

Ansoff, H.I. (1965) *Corporate Strategy: An Analytic Approach to Business Policy for Growth and Expansion*, New York: McGraw-Hill.

Ansoff, H.I. (1991) 'Critique of Henry Mintzberg's The "Design School": Reconsidering the Basic Premises of Strategic Management', *Strategic Management Journal*, (September), pp. 449–461.

Ansoff, H.I. and McDonnell, E. (1990) *Implanting Strategic Management* (2nd edn), New York: Prentice Hall.

Armstrong, J.S. (1982) 'The Value of Formal Planning for Strategic Decisions: Review of Empirical Research', *Strategic Management Journal*, 3, pp. 197–211.

Baden-Fuller, C. and Stopford, J.M. (1994) *Rejuvenating the Mature Business: The Competitive Challenge*, Boston, MA: Harvard Business School Press.

Barber, H., Freeland, G. and Brownell, D. (2002) 'A survivor's guide to organization redesign', in: M.S. Deimler (ed.) *The Boston Consulting Group on Strategy* (2nd edn), Classic Concepts and New Perspectives, pp. 302–309.

Beinhocker, E.D. (1999) 'Robust Adaptive Strategies', *Sloan Management Review*, 40(3, Spring), pp. 95–106.

Bodwell, W. and Chermack, T.J. (2010) 'Organizational ambidexterity: Integrating deliberate and emergent strategy with scenario planning', *Technological Forecasting & Social Change*, 77, pp.193–202.

Bourgeois, L.J. (1980) 'Strategy and the environment: a conceptual integration', *Academy of Management Review*, 5, pp. 25–39.

Bourgeois, L.J. and Brodwin, D.R. (1983) 'Putting Your Strategy into Action', *Strategic Management Planning*, March–May.

Bower, J.L. (1970) *Managing the Resource Allocation Process*, Boston, MA: Harvard Business School Press.

Boyd, B.K. (1991) 'Strategic planning and financial performance: a meta-analysis', *Journal of Management Studies*, 28, pp. 353–374.

Boyd, B.K. and Reuning-Elliot, E. (1998) 'A measurement model of strategic planning', *Strategic Management Journal*, 19(2), pp. 181–192.

Brews, P.J. and Hunt, M. (1999) 'Learning to plan and planning to learn: resolving the planning school/learning school debate', *Strategic Management Journal*, 20(10), pp. 889–914.

Brown, S. and Eisenhardt, K.M. (1997) 'The art of continuous change: linking complexity theory and time-paced evolution in relentlessly shifting organizations', *Adm. Science Quarterly*, 42(1), pp. 1–34.

Bungay, S. and Goold, M. (1991) 'Creating a Strategic Control System', *Long Range Planning*, 24(6), pp. 32–39.

Burgelman, R.A. (1983) 'Corporate Entrepreneurship and Strategic Management: Insights from a Process Study', *Management Science*, 29(12), pp. 1349–1364.

Burgelman, R.A. (1991) 'Intraorganizational Ecology of Strategy Making and Organizational Adaptation: Theory and Field Research', *Organization Science*, 2(3), pp. 239–262.

Burgelman, R.A. (1994) 'Fading memories: a process theory of strategic business exit in dynamic environments', *Administrative Science Quarterly*, 39, pp. 24–36.

Burgelman, R.A. (1996) 'A process model of strategic business exit: implications of an evolutionary perspective on strategy', *Strategic Management Journal*, 17, (Summer, Special Issue), pp. 193–214.

Burgelman. R.A. and Grove, A. (1996) 'Strategic dissonance', *California Management Review*, 38(2), pp. 8–28.

Burt, G. and Van der Heijden, K. (2003) 'First steps: towards purposeful activities in scenario thinking and future studies', *Futures*, 35(10), pp. 1011–1026.

Business Week (1996) *Strategic planning*, 26 August, pp. 45–52.

Calori, R., Valla, J-P. and De Woot, P. (1994) 'Common Characteristics: The Ingredients of European Management', in: R. Calori and P. De Woot (eds) *A European Management Model: Beyond Diversity*, Hemel Hempstead: Prentice Hall.

Capon, N., Farley, J.U. and Hulbert, J.M. (1987) *Corporate Strategic Planning*, New York: Columbia University Press.

Chaffee, E.E. (1985) 'Three Models of Strategy', *Academy of Management Review*, 10(1, January), pp. 89–98.

Chakravarthy, B.S. and Lorange, P. (1991) *Managing the Strategy Process: A Framework for a Multibusiness Firm*, Englewood Cliffs, NJ: Prentice Hall.

Chermack, T.J. (2007) 'Assessing the quality of scenarios in scenario planning', *Futures Res. Q.*, 22(4), pp. 23–35.

Cibin, R. and Grant, R.M. (1996) 'Restructuring among the world's leading oil companies', *British Journal of Management*, 7, pp. 283–307.

Cleland, D.I. (1976) *The Origin and Development of a Philosophy of Long-Range Planning in American Business*, New York: Arno Press. (Original PhD thesis submitted Ohio State University, 1962.)

De Geus, A. (1988) 'Planning as learning', *Harvard Business Review*, 66(2), pp. 70–74.

De Geus, A. (1997) *The Living Company*, Boston, MA: Harvard Business School Press.

Denning, B.W. and Lehr, M.E. (1971) 'The extent and nature of long-range planning in the United Kingdom', *I. Journal of Management Studies*, 8, pp. 145–161.

Eisenhardt, K.M. (1985) 'Control: organizational and economic approaches', *Management Science*, 31, pp. 134–149.

Eisenhardt, K.M. (1989) 'Making fast strategic decisions in high-velocity environments', *Academy of Management Journal*, 32, pp. 543–559.

Eisenhardt, K.M. and Brown, S.L. (1998) 'Time pacing: competing in markets that won't stand still', *Harvard Business Review*, 76(2), p. 59.

Eisenhardt, K.M. and Sull, D.N. (2001) 'Strategy as simple rules', *Harvard Business Review*, 79(1), pp. 107–116.

Evans, J.S. (1991) 'Strategic Flexibility for High Technology Manoeuvres: A Conceptual Framework', *Journal of Management Studies*, 28(January), pp. 69–89.

Ewing, D.W. (1956) 'Looking around: long-range business planning', *Harvard Business Review,* 56(4), pp. 135–146.

Floyd, S.W. and Wooldridge, B. (2000) *Building Strategy from the Middle Reconceptualizing Strategy Process*, Thousand Oaks, CA: Sage.

Gell-Mann, M. (1994) *The Quark and the Jaguar*, New York: Freeman.

Ghemawat, P. (1991) *Commitment: The Dynamic of Strategies*, New York: Free Press.

Ghemawat, P. (2002) 'Competition and business strategy in historical perspective', *Bus. Hist. Rev.*, 76(1), pp. 37–74.

Gilbert, X. and Lorange, P. (1995) 'National Approaches to Strategic Management: A Resource-based Perspective', *International Business Review*, 3(4), pp. 411–423.

Goold, M. (1992) 'Design, learning and planning: a further observation on the design school debate', *Strategic Management Journal*, 13(2), pp. 169–170.

Goold, M. and Quinn, J.J. (1990) 'The paradox of strategic controls', *Strategic Management Journal*, 11, pp. 43–57.

Grant, R.M. and Cibin, R. (1996) 'Strategy, structure and market turbulence: the international oil majors, 1970–91', *Scandinavian Journal of Management*, 12, pp. 165–188.

Grayson, L.E. (1987) *Who and How in Planning for Large Companies: Generalizations from the Experiences of Oil Companies*, New York: St Martin's Press.

Grinyer, P.H. and Norburn, D. (1975) 'Strategic planning in 21 UK companies', *Long Range Planning*, 7(August), pp. 80–88.

Grinyer, P.H., Al-Bazzaz, S. and Yasai-Ardekani, M. (1986) 'Towards a Contingency Theory of Corporate Planning: Findings in 48 U.K. Companies', *Strategic Management Journal*, 7, pp. 3–28.

Hamel, G. (1996) 'Strategy as Revolution', *Harvard Business Review*, 74(4, July–August), pp. 69–82.

Hamel, G. (2000) *Leading the Revolution*, Boston, MA: Harvard Business School Press.

Hamel, G. and Prahalad, C.K. (1989, 2005) 'Strategic Intent', *Harvard Business Review*, 83(7), pp. 148–161.

Hamel, G. and Prahalad, C.K. (1994) *Competing for the Future*, Boston, MA: Harvard Business School Press.

Hampden-Turner, C. and Trompenaars, A. (1993) *The Seven Cultures of Capitalism: Value Systems for Creating Wealth in the United States, Japan, Germany, France, Britain, Sweden and the Netherlands*, New York: Doubleday.

Hannan, M.T. and Freeman, J. (1989) *Organizational Ecology*, Cambridge, MA: Harvard University Press.

Harris, S., Forbes, T., & Fletcher, M. (2000). Taught and enacted strategic approaches in young enterprises. *International Journal of Entrepreneurial Behavior & Research*, 6(3), 125–145.

Hart, S.L. (1992) 'An Integrative Framework for Strategy-Making Processes', *Academy of Management Review*, 17(2), pp. 327–351.

Hax, A.C. and Majluf, N.S. (1984) *Strategic Management: An Integrative Approach*, Englewood Cliffs, NJ: Prentice Hall.

Hayashi, K. (1978) 'Corporate Planning Practices in Japanese Multinationals', *Academy of Management Journal*, 21(2), pp. 211–226.

Henry, H.W. (1967) *Long-Range Planning Practices in 45 Industrial Companies*, Englewood Cliffs, NJ: Prentice Hall.

Hofstede, G. (1993) 'Cultural Constraints in Management Theories', *Academy of Management Executive*, 7(1), pp. 81–94.

Holland, J.H. (1998) *Emergence. From Chaos to Order*, Reading, MA: Perseus Books.

Javidan, M. (1984) 'The impact of environmental uncertainty on long-range planning practices of the U.S. savings and loan industry', *Strategic Management Journal*, 5(4), pp. 381–392.

Jelinek, M. (1979) *Institutionalizing Innovation*, New York: Praeger.

Jennings, D. (2000) 'PowerGen: the development of corporate planning in a privatized utility', *Long Range Planning*, 33(2), pp. 201–218.

Jett, Q.R. and George, J.M. (2005) 'Emergent strategies and their consequences: a process study of competition and complex decision making', *Adv. Strategic Management*, 22, pp. 387–411.

Johnson, G. (1988) 'Rethinking Incrementalism', *Strategic Management Journal*, 9(1, January–February), pp. 75–91.

Kagono, T, Nonaka, I., Sakakibara, K. and Okumara, A. (1985) *Strategic vs. Evolutionary Management*, Amsterdam: North-Holland.

Kahn, H. and Wiener, A.J. (1967) 'The next thirty-three years: a framework for speculation', *Daedalus*, 96(3), pp. 705–732.

Kanter, R.M. (2002) 'Strategy as Improvisational Theater', *Sloan Management Review*, 43(2), pp. 76–81.

Kaplan, R.S. and Norton, D.P. (2001) *The Strategy-Focused Organization: How Balanced Scorecard Thrive in the New Business Environment*, Boston, MA: Harvard Business School Press.

King, B.L. (2008) 'Strategizing at leading venture capital firms: of planning, opportunism and deliberate emergence', *Long Range Planning*, 41, pp. 345–366.

Korte, R.F. (2008) 'Applying scenario planning across multiple levels of analysis', *Adv. Dev. Human Resources*, 10(2), pp.179–197.

Kukalis, S. (1991) 'Determinants of Strategic Planning Systems in Large Organizations: A Contingency Approach', *Journal of Management Studies*, 28, pp. 143–160.

Langley, A. (1995) 'Between "Paralysis and Analysis" and "Extinction by Instinct"', *Sloan Management Review*, 36(3, Spring), pp. 63–76.

Learned, E., Christensen, C.R., Andrews, K.R. and Guth, W.D. (1965) *Business Policy: Text and Cases*, Homewood, IL: Irwin.

Leitner, K.-H. (2014) 'Strategy formation in the innovation and market domain: emergent or deliberate?', *Journal of Strategy and Management*, 7(4), 354–375.

Lenz, R.T. and Lyles, M. (1985) 'Paralysis by Analysis: Is Your Planning System Becoming Too Rational?', *Long Range Planning*, 18(4), pp. 64–72.

Lessem, R. and Neubauer, F.F. (1994) *European Management Systems*, London: McGraw-Hill.

Liedtka, J. (2000) 'In Defense of Strategy as Design', *California Management Review*, 42(3), pp. 8–30.

Lindblom, C.E. (1959) 'The Science of Muddling Through', *Public Administration Review*, Spring, pp. 79–88.

Lindsay, W.M. and Rue, L.W. (1980) 'Impact of organization environment on the long-range planning process: a contingency view', *Academy of Management Journal*, 23, pp. 385–404.

Lorange, P. (1980) *Corporate Planning: An Executive Viewpoint*, Englewood Cliffs, NJ: Prentice Hall.

Lorange, P. and Vancil, R.F. (1977) *Strategic Planning Systems*, Englewood Cliffs, NJ: Prentice Hall.

Lyon, D.W., Lumpkin, G.T. and Dess, G.G. (2000) 'Enhancing Entrepreneurial Orientation Research: Operationalizing and Measuring a Key Strategic Decision Making Process', *Journal of Management*, 26, pp. 1055–1085.

Makridakis, S. (1990) *Forecasting, Planning and Strategy for the 21st Century*, New York: Free Press.

Marginson, D. and McAulay, L. (2008) 'Exploring the debate on short-termism: a theoretical and empirical analysis', *Strategic Management Journal*, 29, pp. 273–292.

Markides, C. (1998) 'Strategic innovation in established companies', *Sloan Management Review*, 39(Spring), pp. 27–36.

Maruyama, M. (1984) 'Alternative Concepts of Management: Insights from Asia and Africa', *Asia Pacific Journal of Management*, 1(January), pp. 100–111.

Marx, T.G. (1991) 'Removing the Obstacles to Effective Strategic Planning', *Long Range Planning*, 24(4, August), pp. 21–28.

McCarthy, B. (2003a) 'Strategy is personality-driven, strategy is crisis-driven: insights from entrepreneurial firms', *Management Decision*, 41(4), 327–339.

McCarthy, B. (2003b) 'The Impact of the Entrepreneur's Personality on the Strategy-Formation and Planning Process in SMEs', *Irish Journal of Management*, 24(1), 154–172.

Miller, C.C. and Cardinal, L.B. (1994) 'Strategic Planning and Firm Performance: A Synthesis of more than Two Decades of Research', *Academy of Management Journal*, 37(6), pp. 1649–1665.

Mintzberg, H. (1978) 'Patterns in Strategy Formation', *Management Science*, 24(9), 934–948.

Mintzberg, H. (1979) *The Structuring of Organizations: A Synthesis of the Research*, Englewood Cliffs, NJ: Prentice Hall.

Mintzberg, H. (1990) 'The Design School: Reconsidering the Basic Premises of Strategic Management', *Strategic Management Journal*, 11, pp. 171–195.

Mintzberg, H. (1991) 'Learning 1, planning 0: reply to Igor Ansoff', *Strategic Management Journal*, 12(6), pp. 463–466.

Mintzberg, H. (1993) 'The Pitfalls of Strategic Planning', *California Management Review*, 36(1, Fall), pp. 32–45.

Mintzberg, H. (1994a) 'The Fall and Rise of Strategic Planning', *Harvard Business Review*, 73(1, January–February).

Mintzberg, H. (1994b) *The Rise and Fall of Strategic Planning*, Englewood Cliffs, NJ: Prentice Hall.

Mintzberg, H. (2005) *Managers not MBAs: A Hard Look at the Soft Practice of Managing and Management Practice*, San Francisco, CA: Berrett-Koehler.

Mintzberg, H. and Waters, J.A. (1985) 'Of Strategy: Deliberate and Emergent', *Strategic Management Journal*, 6(3, July–September), pp. 257–272.

Mintzberg, H. and Waters, J.A. (1982) 'Tracking strategy in an entrepreneurial firm', *Academy of Management Journal*, 15, pp. 465–499.

Mintzberg, H., Ahlstrand, B. and Lampel, J. (1998) *Strategy Safari: A Guided Tour Through the Wilds of Strategic Management*, New York: Free Press.

Mintzberg, H. Brunet, P. and Waters, J. (1986) 'Does planning impede strategic thinking? Tracking the strategies of Air Canada from 1937 to 1976', in: R.B. Lamb and P. Shivastava (eds) *Advances in Strategic Management, Vol. 4*, Greenwich, CT: JAI Press, pp. 3–41.

Mintzberg, H. and McHugh, A. (1985) 'Strategy formulation in an adhocracy', *Administrative Science Quarterly,* 30, pp. 160–197.

Moncrieff, J. (1999) 'Is strategy making a difference?' *Long Range Planning*, 32(2), pp. 273–276.

Nag, R., Hambrick, D.C. and Chen, M.J. (2007) 'What is strategic management, really? Inductive derivation of a consensus definition of the field', *Strategic Management Journal*, 28, pp. 935–955.

Nonaka, I. and Johansson, J.K. (1985) 'Japanese Management: What about "Hard" Skills?' *Academy of Management Review*, 10(2), pp. 181–191.

Ohmae, K. (1982) *The Mind of the Strategist*, New York: McGraw-Hill.

Olson, E.E. and Eoyang, G.H. (2001) *Facilitating Organization Change. Lessons from Complexity Science*, San Francisco, CA: Jossey-Bass.

Ouchi, W. (1979) 'A conceptual framework for design of organizational control mechanisms', *Management Science*, 25, pp. 833–848.

Pascale, R.T. (1984) 'Perspectives on Strategy: The Real Story Behind Honda's Success', *California Management Review*, 26(3), pp. 47–72.

Pascale, R.T. (1999) 'Surfing the edge of chaos', *Sloan Management Review*, Spring, pp. 83–94.

Payne, B. (1957) 'Steps in long-range planning', *Harvard Business Review*, 35(2), pp. 95–101.

Pinchot, G., III (1985) *Intrapreneuring: Why You Don't Have to Leave the Company to Become an Entrepreneur*, New York: Harper & Row.

Platt, W.J. and Maines, N.R. (1959) 'Pretest your long-range plans', *Harvard Business Review*, 37(1), pp.119–127.

Powell, T.C. (1992) 'Strategic Planning as Competitive Advantage', *Strategic Management Journal*, 13, pp. 551–558.

Quinn, J.B. (1961) 'Long-range planning of industrial research', *Harvard Business Review*, 39(4), pp. 88–102.

Quinn, J.B. (1978) 'Strategic Change: "Logical Incrementalism"', *Sloan Management Review*, Fall, pp. 7–21.

Quinn, J.B. (1980) *Strategies for Change,* Homewood, IL: Irwin.

Quinn, J.B. (2002) 'Strategy, Science and Management', *Sloan Management Review*, 43(4).

Ramanujam, V., Ramanujam, N. and Camillus, J.C. (1986) 'Multi-objective assessment of effectiveness of strategic planning: a discriminant analysis approach', *Academy of Management Journal,* 29(2), pp. 347–472.

Rigby, D. (1999) *Management Tools and Techniques*, Boston, MA: Bain.

Rittel, H.W. and Webber, M.M. (1973) 'Dilemmas in a General Theory of Planning', *Policy Sciences*, 4, pp. 155–169.

Robinson, R.B. (1982) 'The Importance of Outsider in Small Firm Strategic Planning', *Academic Management Journal*, 25(2), 80–93.

Schneider, S.C. (1989) 'Strategy Formulation: The Impact of National Culture', *Organization Studies*, 10(2), pp. 149–168.

Schoemaker, P.J. (1993) 'Multiple scenario development: its conceptual and behavioral basis', *Strategic Management Journal*, 14(3), pp. 193–213.

Schoemaker, P.J. (1995) 'Scenario planning: a tool for strategic thinking', *Sloan Management Review,* 23(2), pp. 25–34.

Simons, R. (1995) *Levers of Control: How Managers Use Innovative Control Systems to Drive Strategic Renewal*, Boston, MA: HBS Press.

Simons, R.L. and Weston, H.A. (1990) *MCI Communications Corp.: planning for the 1990s, Case number 1–90136*, Boston, MA: Harvard Business School.

Sinha, D.K. (1990) 'The contribution of formal planning to decisions', *Strategic Management Journal*, 11(6), pp. 479–492.

Slater, R. (1999) *Jack Welch and the GE Way*, New York: McGraw Hill.

Smircich, L. and Stubbart, C. (1985) 'Strategic Management in an Enacted World', *Academy of Management Review*, 10(4), pp. 724–736.

Stacey, R.D. (1993) 'Strategy as Order Emerging from Chaos', *Long Range Planning*, 26(1), pp. 10–17.

Stacey, R.D. (2001) *Complex Responsive Processes in Organizations: Learning and Knowledge Creation*, London: Routledge.

Steiner, G.A. (1979) *Strategic Planning: What Every Manager Must Know*, New York: Free Press.

Steiner, G.A. and Schollhammer, H. (1975) 'Pitfalls in Multi-National Long-Range Planning', *Long Range Planning*, 8(2, April), pp. 2–12.

Teece, D.J. (2007) 'Explicating dynamic capabilities: The nature and microfoundations of (sustainable) enterprise performance', *Strategic Management Journal*, 28, pp. 1319–1350.

Teece, D.J., Pisano, G. and Shuen, A. (1997) 'Dynamic Capabilities and Strategic Management', *Strategic Management Journal*, 18(7), pp. 509–533.

Trompenaars, A. (1993) *Riding the Waves of Culture: Understanding Cultural Diversity in Business*, London: The Economist Books.

Trompenaars, A. and Hampden-Turner, C. (2012) *Riding the Waves of Culture: Understanding Diversity in Global Business*, London: Hodder & Stoughton General Division.

Tuna, C. (2009) 'Pendulum is swinging back on "scenario planning"', July 6, *Wall Street Journal*.

US House of Representatives, Committee on Science and Technology (1976) *Long Range Planning*, Washington, DC: US Government Printing Office.

Van Der Heijden, K. (1993) 'Strategic vision at work: discussing strategic vision in management teams', in: J. Hendry, G. Johnson and J. Newton (eds) *Strategic Thinking: Leadership and the Management of Change*, New York: Wiley, pp. 137–150.

Van der Heijden, K. (1996) *Scenarios: The Art of Strategic Conversation*, New York: Wiley.

Van der Heijden, K. (1997) *Scenarios: Strategies and the Strategy Process*, Nyenrode University Press, The Netherlands.

Van der Heijden, K. (2004) 'Can internally generated futures accelerate organizational learning?', *Futures*, 36, pp.145–159.

Veliyath, R. (1992) 'Strategic planning: balancing short-run performance and longer term prospects', *Long Range Planning*, 25(3), pp. 86–97.

Wack, P. (1985a) 'Scenarios: Unchartered Waters Ahead', *Harvard Business Review*, 64(5, September–October), pp. 73–89.

Wack, P. (1985b) 'Scenarios: Shooting the Rapids', *Harvard Business Review*, 64(6, November–December), pp. 139–150.

Weidenbaum, M. and Hughes, S. (1996) *The Bamboo Network: How Expatriate Chinese Entrepreneurs Are Creating a New Economic Superpower in Asia*, New York: Free Press.

Wildavsky, A. (1979) *Speaking Truth to Power: The Art and Craft of Policy Analysis,* Toronto: Little, Brown & Co.

Wilson, I. (1994) 'Strategic planning isn't dead—it changed', *Long Range Planning*, 27(4), pp. 12–24.

Wilson, I. (2000) 'From Scenario Thinking to Strategic Action', *Technological Forecasting and Social Change*, 65(1, September), pp. 23–29.

Wilson, I. and Ralston, W. (2006) *Scenario Planning Handbook: Developing Strategies in Uncertain Times,* Belmont, CA: South-Western Educational Publishers.

Wooldridge, B. and Floyd, S.W. (1990) The strategy process, middle management involvement, and organizational performance, *Strategic Management Journal*, 11(3), pp. 231–241.

Wrap H.E. (1957) 'Organization for long-range planning', *Harvard Business Review*, 35(1), pp. 37–47.

STRATEGIC CHANGE

Alteration, movement without rest,
Flowing through the six empty places,
Rising and sinking without fixed law,
It is only change that is at work here.

I Ching, Book of Changes, appr. 2000 BCE

INTRODUCTION

In a world of new technologies, transforming economies, shifting demographics, re-forming governments, fluctuating consumer preferences and dynamic competition, it is not a question of whether firms *should* change, but of where, how and in what direction they *must* change. For 'living' organizations, change is a given. Firms must constantly be aligned with their environments, either by reacting to external events, or by proactively shaping the businesses in which they operate.

While change is pervasive, not all change in firms is strategic in nature. Much of the change witnessed is actually the ongoing operational kind. To remain efficient and effective, firms constantly make 'fine-tuning' alterations, whereby existing procedures are upgraded, activities are improved and people are reassigned. Such operational changes are directed at increasing the performance of the firm within the confines of the existing system – within the current basic set-up used to align the firm with the environment. Strategic changes, on the contrary, are directed at creating a new type of alignment – a new fit between the basic set-up of the firm and the characteristics of the environment. Strategic changes have an impact on the way the firm does business (its 'business model') and on the way the organization has been configured (its 'organizational system').

For managers the challenge is to implement strategic changes on time, to keep the firm in step with the shifting opportunities and threats in the environment. Some parts of the firm's business model and organizational system can be preserved, while others need to be transformed for the firm to stay up-to-date and competitive. This process of constantly enacting strategic changes to remain in harmony with external conditions is called 'strategic alignment'. This chapter examines the issue of the series of strategic change steps required in order to bring about a process of ongoing strategic alignment.

THE ISSUE OF STRATEGIC ALIGNMENT

There are many actions that constitute a strategic change – a reorganization, a diversification move, a shift in core technology, a business process redesign and a product portfolio reshuffle, to name a few. Each one of these changes is fascinating in itself. Yet, here

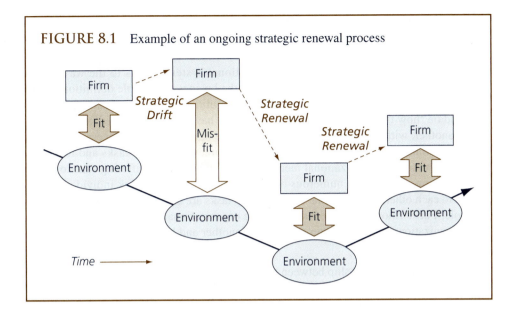

FIGURE 8.1   Example of an ongoing strategic renewal process

the discussion will be broader than just a single strategic change, looking instead at the process of how a series of strategic changes can be used to keep the firm in sync with its surroundings (see Figure 8.1). How can 'a path of strategic changes' be followed to constantly align the firm and avoid a situation whereby the firm 'drifts' too far away from the demands of the environment (Johnson, 1988)?

To come to a deeper understanding of the issue of strategic alignment, the first step that must be taken is to examine what is actually being aligned during a process of strategic change. The areas of strategic alignment have been explored in the previous section. After this initial analysis of 'what' is being changed, a distinction will be made between the magnitude and the pace of change. The magnitude of change refers to the size of the steps being undertaken, whereby the question is whether managers should move in bold and dramatic strides, or in moderate and undramatic ones. The pace of change refers to the relative speed at which the steps are being taken, whereby the question is whether managers should move quickly in a short period of time, or more gradually over a longer time span.

Areas of strategic alignment

Firms are complex systems, consisting of many different elements, each of which can be changed. Therefore, to gain more insight into the various areas of potential change, firms need to be analytically disassembled into a number of component parts. The most fundamental distinction that can be made within a firm is between the business model and the organizational system:

- Business model. The term 'business model' refers to the way a firm conducts its business (for an extensive explanation see Chapter 4). A simple definition would be 'how a firm makes money'. A more formal definition of a business model is 'the specific configuration of resources, value-adding activities and product/service offerings directed at creating value for customers'. Each firm has its own specific system for taking certain resources as inputs (e.g. materials and know-how), adding value to them in some type of manner (e.g. production and branding) and then selling a particular package of products and/or services as output. As such, a firm's business model (or 'value creation system') is particular to the type of business that the firm is in – an airplane manufacturer conducts its business differently from an airline.

■ Organizational system. The term 'organizational system' refers to the way a firm gets its people to work together to carry out the business. A simple definition would be 'how a firm is organized'. A more formal definition of the organizational system would be 'how the individuals populating a firm have been configured, and relate to one another, with the intention of facilitating the business model'. Every firm needs to determine some type of organizational structure, dividing the tasks and responsibilities among the organizational members, thereby instituting differing functions and units. Firms also require numerous organizational processes to link individual members to each other, to ensure that their separate tasks are coordinated into an integrated whole. Furthermore, firms necessarily have organizational cultures and subcultures, as organizational members interact with one another and build up joint beliefs, values and norms.

In Figure 8.2 the relationship between the business model and the major components of the organizational system is depicted. As this figure illustrates, the business model is 'supported' by the organizational system, with the organizational members 'at its base'. While each firm's business model and organizational system are essentially unique, their general configuration can be fairly similar to that of other firms. Where firms have a comparable business 'formula', it is said that they share the same business model. Likewise, where firms have a similar organizational 'form', they are said to subscribe to the same organizational system.

Both the business model and the organizational system can be further disaggregated into component parts and examined in more detail. With this aim in mind, the business model has been at the centre of attention in Chapter 4. In this chapter the organizational system will be further dissected. Actually, the term 'dissection' conjures up images of the organizational system as 'corporate body', which is a useful metaphor for distinguishing the various components of an organizational system (Morgan, 1986).

Following Bartlett and Ghoshal (1995), the organizational system can be divided into its anatomy (structure), physiology (processes) and psychology (culture). Each of these components, summarized in Figure 8.3, will be examined in the following subsection.

FIGURE 8.2 General view of the business model and the organizational system

Business Model

Organizational Structure

Organizational Processes

Organizational Culture

Organizational Members

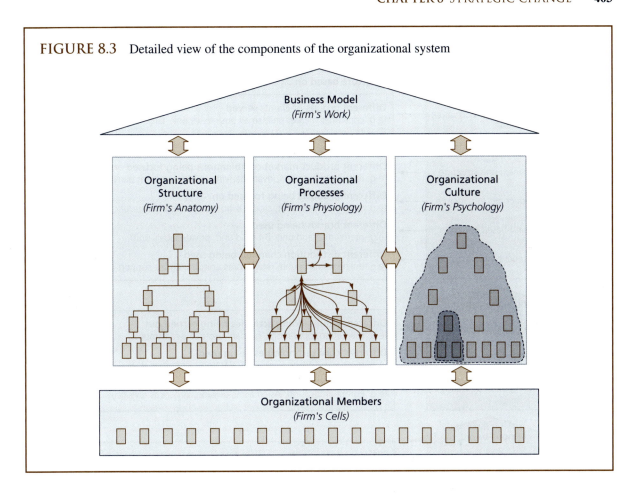

FIGURE 8.3   Detailed view of the components of the organizational system

Organizational structure.   Organizational structure refers to the clustering of tasks and people into smaller groups. All organizations need at least some division of labour in order to function efficiently and effectively, requiring them to structure the organization into smaller parts. The main question when determining the organizational structure is which criteria will be used to differentiate tasks and to cluster people into particular units. While there are numerous structuring (or decomposition) criteria, the most common ones are summarized in Figure 8.4. In a simple organization tasks might be divided according to just one criterion, but in most organizations multiple criteria are used (either sequentially or simultaneously).

To balance this horizontal differentiation of tasks and responsibilities, all organizations also have integration mechanisms intended to get the parts to function well within the organizational whole (Lawrence and Lorsch, 1967). While some of these integration mechanisms are found in the categories of organizational processes and culture, the most fundamental mechanism is usually built into the organizational structure – formal authority. In organizations, managers are appointed with the specific task of supervising the activities of various people or units and to report to managers higher up in the hierarchy.

Depending on the span of control of each manager (the number of people or units reporting to him/her), an organizational structure will consist of one or more layers of management. At the apex of this vertical structure is the board of directors, with the ultimate authority to make decisions or ratify decisions made at lower levels in the hierarchy. The most important questions in this context are the number of management layers needed

FIGURE 8.4   Organizational structuring criteria

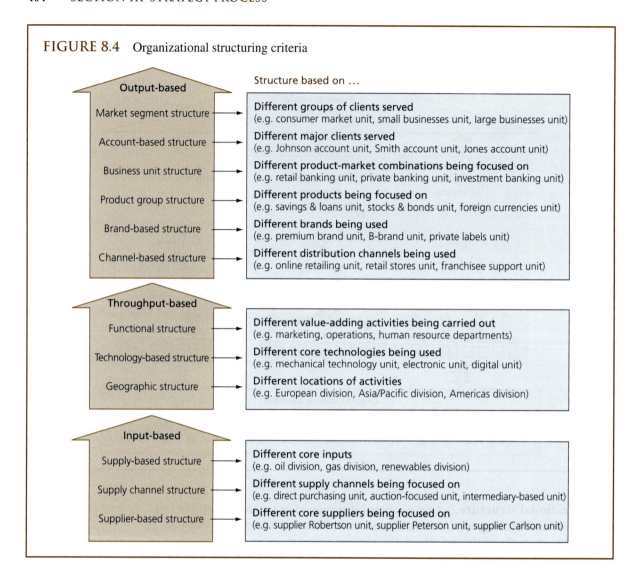

and the amount of authority delegated to lower levels of management. It should be noted that the organizational charts used to represent the formal structure of an organization (see Figure 8.3) need not be an accurate reflection of the informal organizational structure as it operates in reality.

Organizational processes.   Organizational processes refer to the arrangements, procedures and routines used to control and coordinate the various people and units within the organization. Some formalized processes span the entire organization, such as business planning and control procedures, and financial budgeting and reporting processes. Other control and coordination processes have a more limited scope, such as new product development meetings, yearly sales conferences, weekly quality circles, web-based expert panels and quarterly meetings with the board of directors. But not all organizational processes are institutionalized as ongoing integration mechanisms. Often, integration across units and departments is needed for a short period, making it useful to employ task forces, committees, working groups, project teams and even joint lunches as means for ensuring coordination.

While all of these processes are formalized to a certain degree, many more informal organizational processes exist, such as communicating via hallway gossip, building support through personal networking, influencing decision making through informal negotiations and solving conflicts by means of impromptu meetings.

Organizational culture.   Organizational culture refers to the worldview and behavioural patterns shared by the members of the same organization (e.g. Schein, 1985; Trice and Beyer, 1993). As people within a group interact and share experiences with one another over an extended period of time, they construct a joint understanding of the world around them. This shared belief system will be emotionally charged, as it encompasses the values and norms of the organizational members and offers them an interpretive filter with which to make sense of the constant stream of uncertain and ambiguous events around them. As this common ideology grows stronger and becomes more engrained, it will channel members' actions into more narrowly defined patterns of behaviour. As such, the organizational culture can strongly influence everything, from how to behave during meetings to what is viewed as ethical behaviour.

As part of the organizational system, culture can act as a strong integration mechanism, controlling and coordinating people's behaviour, by getting them to abide by 'the way we do things around here'. Having a common 'language', frame of reference and set of values also makes it easier to communicate and work together. However, an organizational culture is not always homogeneous – in fact, strongly divergent subcultures might arise in certain units, creating 'psychological' barriers within the organization.

The magnitude of change

Strategic change is by definition far-reaching. We speak of strategic change when fundamental alterations are made to the business model or the organizational system. Adding a lemon-flavoured Coke to the product portfolio was interesting, maybe important, but not a strategic change, while branching out into bottled water was – it was a major departure from Coca-Cola's traditional business model. Hiring a new CEO is also important, but is in itself not a strategic change, while his consequent reorientation towards a new vision is.

Strategic alignment is often even more far-reaching, as a number of strategic changes are executed in a variety of areas to keep the firm aligned with market demands. But while the result of all these strategic changes is far-reaching, this says nothing about the size of the steps along the way. The strategic alignment process might consist of a few large change steps or numerous small ones. This distinction is illustrated in Figure 8.5. The total amount of strategic changes envisaged is measured along the Y-axis. Change Path A shows the change path taken by a firm that has implemented all changes in two big steps, while Change Path B shows the change path followed by a firm taking numerous smaller steps. Both organizations have completed the same alignment, but via distinctly different routes.

The size of the change steps is referred to as the magnitude of change. This issue of change magnitude can be divided into two component parts:

- Scope of change. The scope of change in a firm can vary from broad to narrow. Change is broad when many aspects and parts of the firm are aligned at the same time. In the most extreme case the changes might be comprehensive, whereby the business model is entirely revised, and the organizational structure, processes, culture and people are changed in unison. However, change can also be much more narrowly focused on a specific organizational aspect (e.g. new product development processes) or department (e.g. marketing). If many changes are narrowly targeted, the total result will be a more piecemeal change process.

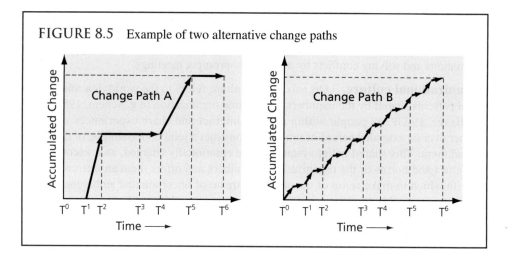

FIGURE 8.5   Example of two alternative change paths

■ Amplitude of organizational changes. The amplitude of change in firms can vary from high to low. The amplitude of change is high when the new business model, organizational culture, structure, processes or people are a radical departure from the previous situation. The amplitude of change is low when the step proposed is a moderate adjustment to the previous circumstances.

Where a change is comprehensive and radical, the magnitude of the change step is large. In Figure 8.5 this is represented as a large jump along the Y-axis. Where a change is narrow and moderate, the magnitude of the step is small. However, the above distinction also clarifies that there are two rather different types of medium-sized change steps – a focused radical change (narrow scope, high amplitude) and a comprehensive moderate change (broad scope, low amplitude). Both changes are 'mid-sized', yet significantly different to manage in practice.

The pace of change

Strategic alignment takes time. Yet, there are a variety of ways by which the strategic alignment process can take place over time. Strategic change measures can be evenly spread out over an extended period, allowing the organization to follow a relatively steady pace of strategic alignment. However, it is also possible to cluster all changes into a few short irregular bursts, giving the alignment process an unsteady, stop-and-go pace.

This distinction is seen in Figure 8.5 as well. The total time period needed for achieving a strategic change is measured along the X-axis. Change Path A shows the change path taken by a firm that has had an unsteady pace of change, while Change Path B tracks the path taken by a firm on a more steady change trajectory. Both organizations have completed the same strategic alignment process by T^3 and by T^6, but have distributed their change activities differently during the period.

In Figure 8.5 it also becomes apparent that the pace of organizational changes can be decomposed into two related parts:

■ Timing of change. First, the pace of change depends on the moment at which changes are initiated. The timing of change can vary from intermittent to constant. Where change is intermittent, it is important for a firm to determine the right moment for launching a new initiative (for example, T^1 and T^4 in Change Path A). The need to 'wait for the right timing' is often a reason for spreading change activities unevenly over time. On the other hand, change can be constant, so that the exact moment for kicking off any new set of measures is less important, as long as there is no peak at any one moment in time (see Change Path B).

■ Speed of change. The pace of change also depends on the time span within which changes take place. The speed of change can vary from high to low. Where a major change needs to be implemented within a short period of time, the speed of change must be high. A short burst of fast action can bring about the intended changes. In Figure 8.5, the speed can be seen by the slope of the arrow (in Change Path A, the speed between T^1 and T^2 is higher than between T^4 and T^5). On the other hand, where the change measures are less formidable and the time span for implementation is longer, the speed of change can be lower.

The variables of timing and speed of change, together with the variables of scope and amplitude of change, create a wide range of possible strategic alignment paths. Firms have many different ways of bringing about strategic change. Unavoidably, this raises the question of which route is best. Why should a firm choose one trajectory over another?

THE PARADOX OF REVOLUTION AND EVOLUTION

It is not the strongest of the species that survive, nor the most intelligent, but the one most responsive to change.

Charles Darwin (1809–1882); English naturalist

In selecting an approach to strategic change, most managers struggle with the question of how bold they should be. On the one hand, they usually realize that to fundamentally transform the organization, a break with the past is needed. To achieve strategic alignment, it is essential to turn away from the firm's heritage and to start with a clean slate. On the other hand, they also recognize the value of continuity, building on past experiences, investments and loyalties. To achieve lasting strategic alignment, people in the organization will need time to learn, adapt and grow into a new organizational reality.

This distinction between disruptive change and gradual change has long been recognized in the strategic management and organizational behaviour literature (e.g. Greiner, 1972; Tushman and O'Reilly, 1996, Reading 8.3 in this book). Disruptive change is variably referred to as 'frame-breaking' (e.g. Baden-Fuller and Stopford, 1992; Grinyer, Mayes and McKiernan, 1987), 'radical' (e.g. Greenwood and Hinings, 1996; Stinchcombe, 1965) and 'revolutionary' (e.g. Gersick, 1991; Tushman, Newman and Romanelli, 1986). Gradual change is variably referred to as 'incremental' (e.g. Johnson, 1987; Quinn, 1980) and 'evolutionary' (e.g. Nelson and Winter, 1982; Tushman and O'Reilly, 1996, Reading 8.3 in this book). Here the labels revolutionary and evolutionary change will be used, in keeping with the terminology used by Greiner (1972) in his classic work.

It is widely accepted among researchers that firms need to balance revolutionary and evolutionary change processes. However, most authors see this as a balancing of strategic (revolutionary) change and operational (evolutionary) change. As strategic change is far-reaching, it is often automatically equated with radical means, while gradual means are reserved for smaller-scale operational changes. Yet, in the previous section it was made clear that a radical result (a strategic change) can be pursued by both revolutionary and evolutionary means (e.g. Hayes, 1985; Krüger, 1996; Nonaka, 1988; Strebel, 1994).

While these two change processes are each other's opposites, and they seem to be at least partially contradictory, both approaches are needed within firms. In practice both change processes have valuable, yet conflicting, qualities. The tension that this creates between revolution and evolution will be explored in the following sections.

The demand for revolutionary change processes

Revolution is a process whereby an abrupt and radical change takes place within a short period of time. Revolutionary change processes are those that do not build on the status quo, but overthrow it. 'Revolutionaries' revolt against the existing business model and organizational system, and attempt to push through changes that will reinvent the firm. Thus, revolution leads to a clear break with the past – a discontinuity in the firm's development path.

Such a 'big bang' approach to strategic change is generally needed when organizational rigidity is so deeply rooted that smaller pushes do not bring the firm into movement. If the firm threatens to become paralysed by these inherited rigidities in the business model and organizational system, the only way to get moving can be to radically break with the past. Typical sources of organizational rigidity include:

■ Psychological resistance to change. Many people resist change because of the uncertainty and ambiguity that unavoidably accompanies any shift in the old way of doing business (e.g. Argyris, 1990; Pondy, Boland and Thomas, 1988). As people become accustomed to fixed organizational routines and established habits, their ability to learn and gradually adapt invariably recedes. New business methods or job descriptions are not seen as a challenging opportunity to learn, but as an unwelcome interference in the existing system. It can be necessary to break through this psychological resistance to change by imposing a new business model and/or organizational system on people (e.g. Hammer, 1990, Reading 8.1 in this book; Powell, 1991).

■ Cultural resistance to change. As discussed in Chapter 2, people can easily become immune to signals that their cognitive maps are outdated, especially if they are surrounded by others with the same flawed belief system. Once an organizational culture develops that perpetuates a number of obsolete assumptions about the market or the organization, it is very difficult for organizational members to challenge and gradually reshape the organizational belief system. It can be necessary to break through this cultural resistance to change by exposing the organization to a shocking crisis or by imposing a new organizational system (e.g. Senge, 1990a, Reading 8.2; Tushman, Newman and Romanelli, 1986).

■ Political resistance to change. Change is hardly ever to everyone's advantage. Each organizational change leads to a different constellation of winners and losers. Generally, the potential losers reject a strategic change, although they are likely to think of some seemingly objective reasons for their opposition. Even a situation in which a person or department thinks that it might run the risk of losing power to others can be enough to block a change. Since strategic changes invariably have a significant impact on all people within an organization, there will always be a number of open and hidden opponents. It can be necessary to break through this political resistance by imposing a new business model and reshuffling management positions (e.g. Allison, 1969; Krüger, 1996).

■ Investment lock-in. Once a firm has committed a large amount of money and time to a certain product portfolio, activity system or technology, it will find that this fixed investment locks the organization in. Any gradual movement away from the past investment will increase the risk of not earning back the sunk cost. Therefore, it can be necessary to break through the lock-in by radically restructuring or disposing of the investment (e.g. Bower and Christensen, 1995; Ghemawat, 1991).

■ Competence lock-in. The better a firm becomes at something, the more a firm becomes focused on becoming even better still – which is also known as the virtuous circle of competence-building. Once a competitive advantage has been built on a particular type of competence, the natural tendency of firms is to favour external opportunities based on these competencies. New people are hired that fit the corporate competence profile and R&D spending further hones the firm's skill. But if the firm's competence base threatens to become outdated due to market or technological changes, its former advantage could become its downfall – the firm could become caught in a vicious 'competence trap', unable to gradually shift the organization to an alternative set of competencies, because the entire business model and organizational system have been aligned to the old set (e.g. Leonard-Barton, 1995; Teece, Pisano and Shuen, 1997). Changing the core competence of the corporation in a comprehensive and radical manner can be the only way to 'migrate' from one competence profile to another.

- Systems lock-in. Firms can also become locked into an open standard (e.g. sizes in inches, GAAP accounting rules) or a proprietary system (e.g. Windows operating system, SAP enterprise resource planning software). Once the firm has implemented a standard or system, switching to another platform cannot be done gradually or at low cost. Therefore, the lock-in can usually only be overcome by a big bang transition to another platform (e.g. Arthur, 1996; Shapiro and Varian, 1998).

- Stakeholder lock-in. Highly restrictive commitments can also be made towards the firm's stakeholders. Long-term contracts with buyers and suppliers, warranties, commitments to governments and local communities and promises to shareholders can all lock firms into a certain strategic direction. To break through the stakeholders' resistance to change, it can be necessary to court a crisis and aim for a radical restructuring of the firm's external relationships (e.g. Freeman, 1984; Oliver, 1991).

Besides the use of revolutionary change to overcome organizational rigidity, such a radical approach to strategic alignment is often also necessary given the short time span available for a large change. The 'window of opportunity' for achieving a strategic change can be small for a number of reasons. Some of the most common triggers for revolutionary strategic change are:

- Competitive pressure. When a firm is under intense competitive pressure and its market position starts to erode quickly, a rapid and dramatic response might be the only approach possible. Especially when the organization threatens to slip into a downward spiral towards insolvency, a bold turnaround can be the only option left to the firm.

- Regulatory pressure. Firms can also be put under pressure by the government or regulatory agencies to push through major changes within a short period of time. Such externally imposed revolutions can be witnessed among public sector organizations (e.g. hospitals and schools) and highly regulated industries (e.g. banks and utilities), but in other sectors of the economy as well (e.g. antitrust break-ups, public health regulations).

- First mover advantage. A more proactive reason for instigating revolutionary change is to be the first firm to introduce a new product, service or technology and to build up barriers to entry for late movers. Especially for know-how that is dissipation-sensitive, or for which the patent period is limited, it can be important to cash in quickly before others arrive on the market (e.g. Kessler and Chakrabarthi, 1996; Lieberman and Montgomery, 1988, 1998).

To some extent all managers recognize that their organizations are prone to inertia, and most will acknowledge that it is often vital to move quickly, either in response to external pressures or to cash in on a potential first mover advantage. It should therefore come as no surprise that most managers would like their organizations to have the ability to successfully pull off revolutionary strategic changes.

The demand for evolutionary change processes

Evolution is a process whereby a constant stream of moderate changes gradually accumulates over a longer period of time. Each change is in itself small, but the cumulative result can be large. Evolutionary change processes take the current firm as a starting point, constantly modifying aspects through extension and adaptation. Some 'mutations' to the firm prove valuable and are retained, while other changes are discarded as dysfunctional. Thus, a new business model and/or organizational system can steadily evolve out of the old, as if the organization were shedding its old skin to grow a new one (e.g. Aldrich, 1999; Kagono *et al.*, 1985).

This 'metamorphosis' approach to strategic change is particularly important where the strategic alignment hinges on widespread organizational learning. Learning is not a process that is easily compressed into a few short bursts of activity (as anyone who has studied knows). Learning is a relatively slow process, whereby know-how is accumulated over an extended period of time. It can take years to learn things, especially if the necessary knowledge is not readily available but must be acquired 'on the job' (e.g. Argyris, 1990; Senge, 1990a, Reading 8.2). This is true for both individuals and firms. When groups of people in a firm need to develop new routines, new competencies, new processes, as well as new ways of understanding the world, time is needed to experiment, reflect, discuss, test and internalize. Even in the circumstances where individuals or departments are merely asked to adjust their behaviours to new norms, the learning process is often protracted and difficult (e.g. Nelson and Winter, 1982; Pfeffer and Sutton, 1999).

While the evolutionary nature of learning is a positive factor stimulating gradual change, the organizational reality is often also that power is too dispersed for revolutionary changes to be imposed upon the firm. Where no one has enough sway in the organization to push through radical changes, a more evolutionary approach can be the only viable route forward.

To some extent all managers recognize that their firms need to continuously learn and adapt, while most will acknowledge that they do not have the absolute power to impose revolutionary changes at will. For these reasons, managers generally would like their organizations to have the ability to pursue evolutionary changes.

Yet, engaging in evolutionary change is the opposite of revolutionary change. On the one hand, being opposites might make revolution and evolution complementary. Some authors suggest that organizations should be 'ambidextrous', using both revolution and evolution, contingent upon internal and external conditions (e.g. Duncan, 1976; Krüger; 1996, Tushman and O'Reilly, 1996, Reading 8.3). On the other hand, the above discussion makes clear that the two are, to a certain extent, mutually incompatible. Once the one form of change has been chosen, this will seriously limit the ability of the strategist to simultaneously, or even subsequently, use the other. Hence, managers are once again faced with a paradox, between revolution and evolution.

EXHIBIT 8.1   SHORT CASE

CHINA COSCO: CHANGING SHIPS?

Thanks to the rise of the Internet, distance has rapidly decreased and communication has become easier and faster. There are, however, things the Internet is not capable of: sending physical goods. Even now,

the primary means of transporting products is still shipping. A lot of goods need to be transported from China in particular, the country being the world's main production site. Large amounts of products, 'Made in China', are shipped around the globe. Even though many industries are in flux, there is no alternative for shipping bulk products. This would suggest that shipping is an oasis of stability in a world of change; yet, even giants in seemingly calm waters have no guarantee of stable income. The state-owned China Ocean Shipping Company (COSCO), China's largest corporate group in global shipping, modern logistics and ship building, has encountered restless waters, which its subsidiary China COSCO in particular has to circumnavigate. For China COSCO, this is the final call to choose the right speed and the correct direction.

Founded in 1961, COSCO was China's first international shipping company. What started out as a passenger transportation company, quickly diversified to container shipping. COSCO gathered steam with purchasing and operating ships, financed by long-term bank loans. By the end of 1975, the company proudly announced that the capacity of its fleet had surpassed five million deadweight tons (DWT), the sum of the weights a ship can safely carry. Yet, COSCO's international activities remained limited and it was only during the 1980s that COSCO really gained momentum.

After the death of Mao Zedong in 1976, his successor, Deng Xiaoping, embarked on a wave of economic reforms and steered China towards trade liberalization and a free market-oriented economy. Also attracted by the country's cheap labour, Western companies began manufacturing products in China, and the demand for shipping started booming. Through government-established Special Economic Zones – coastal areas given more flexible regulation and other preferential treatment – inflow of foreign capital and exports started to grow, along with COSCO's profits. China's economy was only partially opened to the global market and ministries overlooking COSCO cleverly mobilized resources to enhance the company's position. Ample use was made of domestic trade linkages, while the influx of foreign currency and technological know-how through regional and global linkages were utilized for various high-value adding activities, such as the production of technologically advanced ships.

Possessing a large share of the Chinese shipping market, COSCO expanded its overseas activities by establishing partnerships and setting up transnational business operations. The company created its first overseas joint venture in 1980 in Rotterdam, the Netherlands, and set up a wholly owned subsidiary in London in 1988 by purchasing the remaining shares held by its business partner. Although growth

continued in the 1990s, COSCO was also forced to respond to an important change in its environment.

In anticipation of China's WTO ascension in 1997, successive waves of state legislation were enacted. State-owned enterprises lost virtually all types of government subsidies, could now go bankrupt, and COSCO's ties with the Chinese government disintegrated further. COSCO lost its monopoly over China's overseas transport. These upcoming shifts prompted COSCO's management to re-adjust their strategy. It decided to pursue a dynamic strategy of investing in core businesses through vertical linkages, while enhancing horizontal linkages to support the former. COSCO severed its ties with partners that relied heavily on global alliances and networks and instead decided to create a network of its own. It turned into the China Ocean Shipping (Group) Company, or COSCO Group for short. The Group's first overseas-listed subsidiary was COSCO Corporation (Singapore), followed by COSCO Hong Kong, COSCO Korea and COSCO Container Lines (Japan), among others. The businesses of COSCO were further expanded by adding modern logistics, the building of vessels and ship maintenance to its activities. Yet, the pursuit of expansion does not necessarily result in better performances, as is highlighted by China COSCO.

This subsidiary, established in 2005, forms the flagship of the COSCO Group, providing core services like dry bulk shipping, terminal operations and the manufacturing, leasing and shipping of containers. As such, the subsidiary basically covers the whole shipping value chain. All seemed to go well for China COSCO, especially profiting from the dry bulk unit that it purchased in 2007 from its parent. With 45 per cent of its 2007 revenues coming from dry bulk shipping, the company's management believed the future was bright. China COSCO's CEO stated in the annual report of 2007 that "it is expected that the overall dry bulk shipping market supply and demand conditions will remain favourable". Unfortunately, this was not to be.

In 2008, economies suffered from the global financial crisis and the international shipping industry, a barometer of the global economy, was adversely affected. Still, the COSCO Group was able to keep its head above water, making minor profits during a challenging time for global shipping. However, the same could not be said for China COSCO. In 2009 revenues decreased by 48 per cent, with immense operating losses of 144 per cent. Nevertheless, a turnaround seemed to dawn during the next year. Due to a modest recovery from the global financial crisis, while also minimizing costs, cancelling new ships and selling a 49 per cent stake in COSCO Logistics to its parent, China COSCO was able to announce an annual profit of US$361 million in 2010.

Whereas China COSCO's logistics unit and terminal operations continued to make profits, its dry bulk shipping rebounded to losses. Its chairman ascribed this to rising fuel prices and overcapacity in the sector, but also pointed to "oversupply in the market, low freight rate, high cost and [an] imbalanced fleet composition". Although China COSCO's debts racked up – in 2012 alone it had to endure a loss of US$1.54 billion – this was the least of the company's worries. China COSCO last recorded annual profit stemmed from 2010, and according to the Shanghai stock exchange rules a company could well be de-listed after three consecutive annual losses. The stock exchange regulations could make China COSCO sink, fuelling the necessity for strategic change.

In order to regain profitability in 2013, solutions were sought by following an evolutionary path to carefully reforming the company. For instance, China COSCO had to focus on strengthening coordination among internal departments and centralizing procurement. These measures were backed up by downsizing the company's assets in a prudent fashion: one by one. The lucrative COSCO Logistics was sold to its parent company for US$1.1 billion, providing a one-off pre-tax gain of approximately US$316 million for 2013. China COSCO also sold its stakes in a container manufacturer and office properties, so that dry bulk shipping – China COSCO's core business – could remain intact. When the 2013 fiscal year ended, it managed to scrape together a minor profit of US$37.9 million, sparing the company a disaster.

This bought China COSCO three more years but does not ensure its future; it could very well be a reprieve. The chairman of the group indicated in 2014 that he was not sure how China COSCO could return to profits, since "there aren't that many ways left to tackle losses through asset disposal". The chosen answer was to consolidate. A merger of China COSCO and China Shipping Container Lines (CSCL) resulted in China COSCO Shipping, the biggest shipping fleet in the world with over 800 vessels. This is almost three times the number owned by competitor Maersk Line.

The worst downturn of the shipping industry since the financial crisis was met with a merger of two companies in the midst of heavy weather. Yet, is efficiency the right direction to deal with the oversupply and weak demand in the bulk shipping sector or does the group have to sell more of its assets and take other cautious measures? Perhaps bolder actions are necessary. Should the troublesome core business perhaps be discarded, thus giving up the position as the world's largest bulk cargo fleet operator? Time is running out again, and given the difficult situation of the shipping industry the bulk assets are difficult to value, and therefore hard to sell at a reasonable price. Continuing on the evolutionary path or pursuing a revolutionary direction: change is eminent at any rate. China COSCO has to be steered in a direction that will prevent the company from rebounding to losses and keep the boat afloat.

Co-author: Wester Wagenaar

Sources: www.en.cosco.co; www.chinacosco.com; China COSCO Annual Reports 2007–2015; *Bloomberg,* 13 March 2013 and 28 March 2013; *Financial Times,* 30 August 2012; Joseph, William A., *Politics in China: An Introduction,* Second Edition, 2014; Moore, 2002; Naughton, Barry J., *The Chinese Economy: Transitions and Growth,* 2006; Pinder, David, and Brian Slack, *Shipping and Ports in the Twenty-first Century,* 2004; *Reuters,* 29 March 2012, 27 March 2014 and 18 February 2016; *The Wall Street Journal,* 23 March 2011, 20 May 2013 and 2 July 2013.

PERSPECTIVES ON STRATEGIC CHANGE

Although the demand for both revolutionary and evolutionary change is clear, this does place managers in the difficult position of having to determine how both must be combined and balanced in a process of ongoing strategic alignment. Revolutionary change is necessary to create *discontinuity* in the alignment process – radical and swift breaks with the past. Evolutionary change is necessary to ensure *continuity* in the alignment process – moderate and gradual metamorphosis from one state into another. In finding a balance between these two demands, the question is which of the two must play a leading role and what type of change path this leads to. Does successful strategic alignment hinge on a few infrequent big bangs, with some minor evolutionary changes in the intervening time span, or is successful strategic alignment essentially a gradual process of mutation and selection, where revolutionary changes are used only in case of emergency?

Yet, as in previous chapters, we see that the strategic management literature comes up with a wide variety of answers to this question. Both among business practitioners and strategy researchers, views differ sharply about the best way of dealing with the paradox of revolution and evolution. To gain insight into the major points of disagreement between people on the issue of strategic alignment, we will again outline the two diametrically opposed perspectives here.

At one end of the virtual continuum of views, are the strategists who argue that real strategic alignment can only be achieved by radical means. Revolutionary change, although difficult to achieve, is at the heart of alignment, while evolutionary changes can only figure in a supporting role. This point of view will be referred to as the 'discontinuous alignment perspective'. At the other end of the spectrum are the strategists who argue that real strategic alignment is not brought about by an 'axe', but must grow out of the existing firm, in a constant stream of small adjustments. Evolutionary change, although difficult to sustain, is at the heart of alignment, while revolutionary changes are a fall-back alternative, if all else fails. This point of view will be referred to as the 'continuous alignment perspective'.

The discontinuous alignment perspective

 According to advocates of the discontinuous alignment perspective, it is a common misconception that firms develop gradually. It is often assumed that organizations move fluidly from one state to the next, encountering minimal friction. In reality, however, strategic change is arduous and encounters significant resistance. Pressure must be exerted, and tension must mount, before a major shift can be accomplished. Movement, therefore, is not steady and constant, as a current in the sea, but abrupt and dramatic, as in an earthquake, where resistance gives way and tension is released in a short shock. In general, the more significant a change is, the more intense the shock will be.

Proponents of this perspective argue that people and organizations exhibit a natural reluctance to change. Humans have a strong preference for stability. Once general policy has been determined, most firms are inclined to settle into a fixed way of working. The organizational structure will solidify, formal processes will be installed, standard operating procedures will be defined, key competence areas will be identified, a distribution of power will emerge and a corporate culture will become established. The stability of an organization will be especially high if all of these elements form a consistent and cohesive configuration (e.g. Mintzberg, 1991; Waterman, Peters and Philips, 1980). Moreover, if a firm experiences a period of success, this usually strongly reinforces the existing way of working (e.g. Markides, 1998; Miller, 1990).

It must be emphasized that stability is not inherently harmful, as it allows people to 'get to work'. A level of stability is required to function efficiently (e.g. March and Simon, 1958; Thompson, 1967). Constant change would only create an organizational mess. There would be prolonged confusion about tasks and authority, poorly structured internal communication and coordination, and a lack of clear standards and routines. The instability brought on by such continuously changing processes and structures would lead to widespread insecurity, political manoeuvring and inter-departmental conflicts.

Advocates of the discontinuous alignment perspective, therefore, argue that long periods of relative stability are necessary for the proper functioning of firms. However, the downside of stability is rigidity – the unwillingness and/or inability to change, even when it is urgently required. To overcome rigidity and get the firm in motion, a series of small nudges will by no means be sufficient. Instead, a big shove will be needed. For strategic changes to really happen, measures must be radical and comprehensive. A coordinated assault is usually required to decisively break through organizational defences and 'shock therapy' is needed to fundamentally change people's cognitive maps. Solving lock-in problems generally also demands a quick, firm-wide switchover to a new system. For instance, business process reengineering must involve all aspects of the value chain at once (e.g. Hammer, 1990, Reading 8.1; Hammer and Champy, 1993). However, proponents of the discontinuous alignment perspective emphasize that the period of turmoil must not take too long. People cannot be indefinitely confronted with high levels of uncertainty and ambiguity, and a new equilibrium is vital for a new period of efficient operations.

Some proponents of the discontinuous change perspective argue that episodes of revolutionary change are generally not chosen freely, but are triggered by crises. A major environmental jolt can be the reason for a sudden crisis (e.g. Meyer, 1982; Meyer, Brooks and Goes, 1990) – for example, the introduction of a new technology, a major economic recession, new government regulations, a novel market entrant or a dramatic event in international political affairs. However, misalignment between the firm and its environment often grows over a longer period of time, causing a mounting sense of impending crisis (e.g. Johnson, 1988; Strebel, 1992). As tension increases, people in the firm become more receptive to submitting to the painful changes that are necessary. This increased willingness to change under crisis circumstances coincides with the physical law that 'under pressure things become fluid'. As long as the pressure persists, revolutionary change is possible, but as soon as the pressure lets up the firm will resolidify in a new form, inhibiting any further major changes (e.g. Lewin, 1947; Miller and Friesen, 1984). For this reason, managers often feel impelled to heighten and prolong the sense of crisis, to keep organization members receptive to the changes being pushed through. Where a crisis is lacking, some managers will induce one, to create the sense of urgency and determination needed to get people into the change mindset.

It can be concluded that strategic changes, whether proactive or reactive, require an abrupt break with the status quo. Change management demands strong leadership to rapidly push through stressful, discomforting and risky shifts in the business and organizational system. Battling the sources of rigidity and turning crisis into opportunity are the key qualities needed by managers implementing strategic change. Ultimately, strategizing managers should know when to change and when it is wiser to seek stability – they should know when to trigger an 'earthquake' and when to avoid one.

EXHIBIT 8.2   THE DISCONTINUOUS ALIGNMENT PERSPECTIVE

CHANGE BANKING FOR GOOD

In 2012, with the £133 billion financial crisis still echoing, UK citizens again received surprising news: banks had manipulated their Libor rates (London Inter-Bank Offered Rate) to appear more creditworthy or to profit from trades. The Houses of Parliament responded by installing a 'Parliamentary Commission on Banking Standards'. The commission was founded to conduct an inquiry into professional standards and culture in the UK banking sector, and to formulate recommendations for future legislation. Those expecting minor measures were in shock. If the commission could find support from the UK treasury, top bankers who had enriched themselves during the financial crisis would face colossal penalties or even time in jail: the price the industry had to pay to restore trust in banking.

The commission concluded that too many bankers were not personally accountable, taking shelter in collective decision making, with sanctions being disproportionate to the severity of the consequences of failure. In addition, many bank staff had been paid too much for doing the wrong things: bonuses provoked short-term personal gain and long-term societal pain. This has led the commission to develop a new framework for individuals working in the industry, the main element being a Senior Persons Regime which will ensure that the key responsibilities within banks are assigned to specific individuals. The bankers will be made fully and unambiguously aware of their responsibilities and held accountable for carrying them out. Regulators will apply the civil powers of fines, restrictions on responsibilities and a ban from the industry.

The new rigorous regime will restore trust in banking – crucial for the UK's dominant position within the global financial services industry. A reformed banking industry with higher standards has the potential, once again, to be a great asset to the United Kingdom. For good.

Co-author: Adriaan de Bruijn

Sources: *House of Lords, House of Commons Parliamentary Commission on Banking Standards. June 2013. Volume 1: Summary, and Conclusions and recommendations.* www.parliament.uk/business/committees/committees-a-z/joint-select/professional-standards-in-the-banking-industry/news/changingbanking-for-good-report/. *The Economist,* 22 June 2013.

The continuous alignment perspective

According to proponents of the continuous alignment perspective, if firms shift by 'earthquake' it is usually their own 'fault'. The problem with revolution is that it commonly leads to the need for further revolution at a later time – discontinuous change creates its own boom-and-bust cycle. Revolutionary change is generally followed by a strong organizational yearning for stability. The massive, firm-wide efforts to implement agonizing changes can often be sustained for only a short period of time, after which change momentum collapses. Any positive inclination towards change among employees will have totally disappeared by the time the reorganizations are over. Consequently, the firm lapses back into a stable state in which only minor changes occur. This stable situation is maintained until the next round of shock therapy becomes necessary, to jolt the organization out of its ossified state.

To supporters of the continuous alignment perspective, the boom-and-bust approach to strategic change is like running a marathon by sprinting and then standing still to catch one's breath. Yet, marathons are not won by good sprinters, but by runners with endurance and persistence, who can keep a steady pace – runners who are more inspired by the tortoise than by the hare. The same is true for companies in the marathon of competition. Some companies behave like the hare in Aesop's fable, showing off their ability to take great leaps, but burdened by a short span of attention. Other companies behave more like the tortoise, moving gradually and undramatically, but unrelentingly and without interruption, focusing on the long-term goal. In the short run, the hares might dash ahead, suggesting that making big leaps forward is the best way to compete. But in the long run, the most formidable contenders will be the diligent tortoises, whose ability to maintain a constant speed will help them to win the race.

Therefore, the 'big ideas' and 'quantum leaps' that so mesmerize proponents of the discontinuous alignment perspective are viewed with suspicion by supporters of continuous alignment. Revolution not only causes unnecessary disruption and dysfunctional crises, but also is usually the substitute for diligence. If organizations do not have the stamina to continuously improve themselves, quick fix radical change can be used as a short-term remedy. Where firms do not exhibit the drive to permanently upgrade their capabilities, revolutionary alignment can be used as the short cut to improved competitiveness. In other words, the lure of revolutionary change is that of short-term results. By abruptly and dramatically making major changes, managers hope to rapidly book tangible progress – and instantly win recognition and promotion.

To advocates of the continuous alignment perspective, a preference for revolution usually reflects an unhealthy obsession with the short term. Continuous alignment, on the other hand, is more long-term in orientation. Development is gradual, piecemeal and undramatic, but as it is constantly maintained over a longer period of time, the aggregate level of change can still be significant.

Everyone in the firm must be motivated to continuously learn. People within the organization must constantly update their knowledge base, which not only means acquiring new information, but challenging accepted company wisdom as well. Learning goes hand in hand with unlearning – changing the cognitive maps shared within the organization. In this respect, it is argued that an atmosphere of crisis actually inhibits continuous alignment. In a situation of crisis, it is not a matter of 'under pressure things become fluid', but 'in the cold everything freezes'. Crisis circumstances might lower people's resistance to imposed change, but it also blunts their motivation for experimenting and learning, as they brace themselves for the imminent shock. Crisis encourages people to seek security and to focus on the short term, instead of opening up and working towards long-term development (e.g. Bate, 1994; Senge, 1990a, Reading 8.2).

Everyone in the firm must not only continuously learn, but also be motivated to continuously adapt. Constant adjustment to external change and fluid internal realignment should be pursued. To this end, the organization must actively avoid inertia, by combatting the forces of ossification. Managers should strive to create flexible structures and processes (e.g. Bartlett and Ghoshal, 1995; Eisenhardt and Brown, 1997), to encourage an open and tolerant corporate culture, and to provide sufficient job and career security for employees to accept other forms of ambiguity and uncertainty (e.g. Kagono *et al.*, 1985; Nonaka, 1988).

In an evolutionary firm basically everyone in the organization is involved. Revolutionary change can be initiated by top management, possibly assisted and urged on by a few external consultants, and carried by a handful of change agents or champions (e.g. Day, 1994; Maidique, 1980). Evolutionary change, on the other hand, requires a firm-wide effort. Leaders cannot learn on behalf of their organizations, nor can they orchestrate all of the small adaptations needed for continuous alignment. Managers must realize that evolution can be led from the top, but not be imposed from the top. For strategizing managers to realize change, hands-on guidance of organizational developments is more important than commanding organizational actions.

EXHIBIT 8.3   CONTINUOUS ALIGNMENT PERSPECTIVE

STORA ENSO: CENTURIES OF CHANGE

Like no other, Stora Enso knows how to adapt. The company has not only coped with social and political changes throughout the ages, but also has the foresight to change its business when necessary. Swedish mining company Stora Kopparberg – Swedish for Big Copper Mountain – started operating in the 13th century, its first share dating from 1288. This effectively makes the firm the oldest limited liability company, and the oldest still existing corporation, in the world.

Stora rose to prominence during the 17th century. For some periods in this age, the company's mine in Falun produced around two-thirds of the world's production of copper. When copper mining gradually lost its importance in the next century, the company decided to purchase an iron ore mine. Its foresight proved successful as it did not take long before iron ore proved more profitable for the company than copper. Another century passed, but towards the end of the 19th century Stora decided to switch its business once again. The company kept operating in the primary sector of the economy, but divested its mining and steel mill businesses and entered paper and pulp production instead. In home country Sweden, where forests are plentiful and the country is thinly populated, Stora quickly accumulated a big chunk of territory of its own and a turnover to match. In 1997 the company owned 1.6 million hectares of forest in Sweden and 0.7 million hectares in Portugal, Canada and Brazil. The next year the company merged with Finnish forest giant Enso Oyj to form Stora Enso. But it did not take long before the company needed to shed its skin again.

In an era in which consumers increasingly move from paper to digital media, the demand for paper continues to decline. Stora Enso thus had to scale down its global workforce by about 10 per cent in 2013, most notably in the Nordic region, and restructured by putting the paper and wood products business into one division. As a response to the decline in Western markets, Stora Enso now invests heavily in pulp and packaging production outside of Europe. The company is part of a pulp mill joint venture in Uruguay and owns a cardboard plant in China's Guangxi province.

Stora Enso is well aware this is no viable long-term solution; it honours its history by divesting and exploring once again. Increasing awareness among consumers for the environment and renewable solutions creates growth opportunities, and Stora Enso aims to ride that wave. It reinvigorated its packaging by making it increasingly renewable and is developing alternatives for cardboard and pulp. One of its projects involves Nutella spread producer, Ferrero. This company produces 180 million kilograms of Nutella every year, resulting in an enormous amount of hazelnut shell waste. Stora Enso and Ferrero are now developing EcoPaper, in which hazelnut fibres are used to create an alternative to carton board.

To keep Stora Enso even more relevant, the company is also shifting into biochemistry, biomaterials and green construction products. All of these measures are to prevent Stora Enso from getting beaten to a pulp by a changing environment, and to ensure that the centuries-old company will continue to be the world's oldest firm in the future.

Co-author: Wester Wagenaar

Sources: www.storaenso.com; Stora Enso Financial Report 2015; *The Economist*, 16 December 2004; *Financial Times*, 10 November 2015; *The Guardian*, 21 April 2015; *The Wall Street Journal*, 18 June 2013.

MANAGING THE PARADOX OF REVOLUTION AND EVOLUTION

Slow and steady wins the race.

The Hare and the Tortoise, Aesop (c. 620–560 BC); Greek writer

So, how should managers align their organizations? Should managers strive to align abruptly, by emphasizing radical, comprehensive and dramatic changes? Or should they try to align in a more continuous fashion by learning and adaptation? How can strategists best manage the paradox of revolution and evolution (see Table 8.1)?

No consensus has yet been developed within the field of strategic management on how to balance revolution and evolution. In the end, strategic managers have to make up their mind, taking into consideration their specific situation. Fortunately, some researchers have brought forward their views on how to manage the paradox of revolution and evolution. The starting point is the set of arguments put forward in the taxonomy in the first chapter.

Navigating

Strategizing managers have to deal with technological developments, political changes, economic crises and competitive moves, to mention just a few, that differ in their pace and magnitude. Over the long term, the pattern of environmental change is episodic. Periods of relative stability are interrupted by short and dramatic periods of instability, a pattern of development that has been recognized in a variety of other sciences as well

TABLE 8.1   Discontinuous alignment versus continuous alignment perspective

	Discontinuous alignment perspective	Continuous alignment perspective
Emphasis on	Revolution over evolution	Evolution over revolution
Strategic alignment as	Disruptive turnaround	Uninterrupted improvement
Magnitude of change	Radical, comprehensive and dramatic	Moderate, piecemeal and undramatic
Pace of change	Abrupt, unsteady and intermittent	Gradual, steady and constant
Lasting alignment requires	Sudden break with status quo	Permanent learning and flexibility
Reaction to external jolts	Shock therapy	Continuous adjustment
View of organizational crises	Under pressure things become fluid	In the cold everything freezes
Long-term alignment dynamics	Stable and unstable states alternate	Persistent transient state
Long-term alignment pattern	Punctuated equilibrium	Gradual development

(Gersick, 1991). Following the natural historians Eldredge and Gould, this pattern is often called 'punctuated equilibrium' – stability punctuated by episodes in which many changes take place simultaneously (Tushman and O'Reilly, 1996, Reading 8.3).

When the environment is in flux, organizations must align. Therefore strategizing managers must possess a variety of options in dealing with environmental change. In periods of relative stability, gradual change is the appropriate alignment pattern, while during discontinuous change more drastic measures are needed (Greiner, 1972). Although the strategic alignment process does not precisely mirror environmental developments, it somehow relates to the pace and magnitude of change. Often with a delay and sometimes overly reacting, strategists aim at catching up with the long-term development of the environment.

Management scholars have been looking into this long-term alignment process (Anderson and Tushman, 1990; Tushman, Newman and Romanelli, 1986; Tushman and O'Reilly, 1996). They argue that to be successful during periods of relative stability, the emphasis should be on evolutionary adaptation to the always changing demands in the market. But during discontinuous changes, firms also need to be able to be revolutionary, adapting to whatever external change comes their way. In other words, comparable with a captain of a ship strategists need to navigate the company during sunny weather and occasionally through stormy waters, with one hand on the wheel and one on the throttle.

STRATEGIC CHANGE IN INTERNATIONAL PERSPECTIVE

Co-author: Gep Eisenloeffel

Wisdom lies neither in fixity nor in change, but in the dialectic between the two.
Octavio Paz (1914–1998); Mexican poet and essayist

Authors from different countries, as well as from similar ones, exhibit divergent perspectives on how to deal with the paradox of revolution and evolution. Why do firms in different countries prefer such significantly different approaches to strategic change? Which factors determine the existence of national strategic change styles? Answers to these questions might assist in defining the most appropriate context for revolutionary change, as opposed to circumstances in which evolutionary change would be more fitting. Understanding international dissimilarities and their roots would clarify whether firms in different countries can borrow practices from one another or are limited by their national context.

As a stimulus to the international dimension in this debate, an overview will be given of the country characteristics mentioned in the literature as the major influencers on how the paradox of revolution and evolution is dealt with in different national settings. It should be noted, however, that cross-cultural research on this topic has not been extensive. Therefore, the propositions brought forward here should be viewed as tentative explanations, intended to encourage further discussion and research.

Prevalence of mechanistic organizations

In Chapter 7, the international differences in organizing work were briefly discussed. It was argued that in some countries the machine bureaucracy is a particularly dominant form of organization, while in other countries organizations can be characterized as more organic. The machine bureaucracy that is more predominant in English-speaking countries and France, is characterized by clear hierarchical authority relationships, strict differentiation of tasks, and highly formalized communication, reporting, budgeting, planning and decision-making processes. In such organizations, there is a relatively clear line separating the officers (management) from the troops, and internal relationships are depersonalized and calculative. In more organic forms of organization, management and production activities are not strictly separated, leading to less emphasis on top-down decision making, and more on bottom-up initiatives. Job descriptions are less strictly defined and control systems are less sophisticated. Integration within the organization is not achieved by these formal systems, but by extensive informal communication and consultation, both horizontally and vertically, and by a strong common set of beliefs and a shared corporate vision. Internal relationships are based on trust, cooperation and a sense of community, leading Ouchi (1981) to call such organizations 'clans'. This type of organization is more prevalent in Japan, and to a lesser extent in, for example, Germany, the Netherlands and the Nordic countries.

Various researchers have suggested that machine bureaucracies exhibit a high level of inertia (e.g. Kanter, 1989; Mintzberg, 1994). Once formal systems have been created, they become difficult to change. As soon as particular tasks are specified and assigned to a person or group, it becomes their turf, while all else is 'not their business'. Once created, hierarchical positions, giving status and power, are not easily abolished. The consequence, it is argued, is that machine bureaucracies are inherently more resistant to change than clan-like organizations (Kagono *et al.*, 1985). Therefore, revolution is usually the potent mode of change needed to make any significant alterations. It can be expected that in countries where organizations are more strongly mechanistic, the preference for the discontinuous alignment perspective will be more pronounced.

Clan-like organizations, on the other hand, are characterized by a strong capacity for self-organization – the ability to exhibit organized behaviour without a boss being in control (Nonaka, 1988; Stacey, 1993, Reading 11.2). They are better at fluidly and spontaneously reorganizing around new issues because of a lack of rigid structure, the close links between management and production tasks, the high level of group-oriented information-sharing and consensual decision making, and the strong commitment of individuals to the organization, and vice versa. In countries where organizations are more organic in this way, a stronger preference for continuous alignment can be expected. This issue will be discussed at greater length in Chapter 11.

Position of employees

This second factor is linked to the first. A mechanistic organization, it could be said, is a system into which groups of people have been brought, while an organic organization is a group of people into which some system has been brought. In a machine bureaucracy, people are human resources *for* the organization, while in a clan, people *are* the organization. These two conceptions of organization represent radically different views on the position and roles of employees within organizations.

In mechanistic organizations, employees are seen as valuable, yet expendable resources utilized by the organization. Salaries are determined by prices on the labour market and the value added by the individual employee. In the contractual relationship between employer and employee, it is a shrewd bargaining tactic for employers to minimize their dependence on employees. Organizational learning should, therefore, be captured in formalized systems and procedures, to avoid the irreplaceability of their people. Employees, on the other hand, will strive to make themselves indispensable for the organization, for instance by not sharing their learning. Furthermore, calculating employees will not tie themselves too strongly to the organization, but will keep their options open to job-hop to a better-paying employer. None of these factors contribute to the long-term commitment and receptiveness for ambiguity and uncertainty needed for continuous alignment.

In clan-like organizations the tolerance for ambiguity and uncertainty is higher, because employees' positions within the organization are more secure. Information is more readily shared, as it does not need to be used as a bargaining chip and acceptance within the group demands being a team player. Employers can invest in people instead of systems, since employees are committed and loyal to the organization. These better-trained people can consequently be given more decision-making power and more responsibility to organize their own work to fit with changing circumstances. Therefore, clan-like organizations, with their emphasis on employees as permanent co-producers, instead of temporary contractors, are more conducive to evolutionary change.

A number of factors have been brought forward to explain these international differences in the structuring of work and the position of employees. Some authors emphasize cultural aspects, particularly the level of individualism. It is argued that the mechanistic-organic distinction largely coincides with the individualism-collectivism division (e.g. Ouchi, 1981; Pascale and Athos, 1981). In this view, machine bureaucracies are the logical response to calculative individuals, while clans are more predominant in group-oriented cultures. Other authors point to international differences in labour markets (e.g. Calori, Valla and De Woot, 1994; Kagono *et al.*, 1985). High mobility of personnel is thought to coincide with the existence of mechanistic organizations, while low mobility (e.g. life time employment) fits with organic forms. Yet others suggest that the abundance of skilled workers is important. Machine bureaucracies are suited to deal with narrowly trained individuals, requiring extensive supervision. Clan-like organizations, however, need skilled, self-managing workers, who can handle a wide variety of tasks with relative autonomy. Kogut (1993, p. 11) reports that the level of workers within a country with these qualifications "has been found to rest significantly upon the quality of education, the existence of programmes of apprenticeship and worker qualifications, and the elimination of occupational distinctions".

Role of top management

Various researchers have observed important international differences in leadership styles and the role of top management. In some countries, top management is considered the 'central processing unit' of the company, making the key decisions and commanding the behaviour of the rest of the organizational machine. Visible top-down leadership is the norm, and therefore, strategic change is viewed as a top management responsibility (e.g. Hambrick and Mason, 1984; Hitt *et al.*, 1997). Strategic changes are formulated by top managers and then implemented at lower levels. Top managers are given significant power and discretion to develop bold new initiatives and to overcome organizational resistance to change. If organizational advances are judged to be insufficient or if an organization ends up in a crisis situation, a change of top management is often considered to be a necessary measure to transform or turn around the company (e.g. Boeker, 1992; Fredrickson, Hambrick and Baumrin, 1988). In nations where people exhibit a strong preference for this commander type of leadership, an inclination towards the discontinuous alignment perspective can be expected.

In other countries, top managers are viewed as the captains of the team and leadership is less direct and less visible (e.g. Hofstede, 1993, Reading 1.3; Kagono *et al.,* 1985). The role of top managers is to facilitate change among the members of the group. Change comes from within the body of the organization, instead of being imposed upon it by top management. Therefore, change under this type of leadership will usually be more evolutionary than revolutionary. In nations where people exhibit a strong preference for this servant type of leadership, an inclination towards the continuous alignment perspective is more likely.

Time orientation

Earlier in the text, a distinction was made between cultures that are more oriented towards the past, the present and the future. Obviously, it can be expected that cultural inclination to either past or present will perceive change to be much less favourable than future-oriented cultures. Among these future-minded cultures, a further division can be made between those with a long-term and a short-term orientation.

Various researchers have argued that short-term oriented cultures exhibit a much stronger preference for fast, radical change than cultures with a longer time horizon. In short-term oriented cultures, such as most English-speaking countries, there are significant pressures for rapid results, which predispose managers towards revolutionary change. Especially sensitivity to stock prices is often cited as a major factor encouraging firms to focus on short spurts of massive change and pay much less attention to efforts and investments with undramatic long-term benefits. Other contributing factors include short-term oriented bonus systems, stock option plans and frequent job-hopping (e.g. Calori, Valla and De Woot, 1994; Kagono *et al.*, 1985).

In long-term oriented cultures, such as Japan, China and South Korea, there is far less pressure to achieve short-term results. There is broad awareness that firms are running a competitive marathon and that a high, yet steady, pace of motion is needed. Generally, more emphasis is placed on facilitating long-term change processes, instead of intermittently shifting between one short-term change and another. Frequently mentioned factors contributing to this long-term orientation include long-term employment relationships, the lack of short-term bonus systems and, most importantly, the accent on growth as opposed to profit, as the firms' prime objective (e.g. Abegglen and Stalk, 1985; Hitt *et al.*, 1997). This topic is discussed at length in Chapter 3.

INTRODUCTION TO THE READINGS

No great thing is created suddenly, any more than a bunch of grapes or a fig. If you tell me that you desire a fig, I answer that there must be time. Let it first blossom, then bear fruit, then ripen.
Epictetus (c. 60–120); Roman philosopher

As an input to the process of assessing the variety of perspectives on this issue, three readings have been selected that can each help readers to make up their own minds. Again, the first two readings will be representative of the two poles in this debate, while the third reading will highlight arguments to find a balance between the opposing demands.

As the opening reading, Michael Hammer's 'Reengineering Work: Don't Automate, Obliterate' has been selected to represent the discontinuous alignment perspective. This paper was published in *Harvard Business Review* in 1990 and was followed in 1993 by the highly influential book *Reengineering the Corporation: A Manifesto for Business Revolution,* that Hammer co-authored with James Champy. In this article, Hammer explains the concept of reengineering in much the same way as in his best-selling book. "At the heart of reengineering," he writes, "is the notion of discontinuous thinking – of recognizing and breaking away from the outdated rules and fundamental assumptions that underlie operations." In his view, radically redesigning business processes "cannot be planned meticulously and accomplished in small and cautious steps. It's an all-or-nothing proposition with an uncertain result." He exhorts managers to "think big", by setting high goals, taking bold steps and daring to accept a high risk. In short, he preaches business revolution, and the tone of his article is truly that of a manifesto – impassioned, fervent, with here and there "a touch of fanaticism".

The second reading, 'Building Learning Organizations' by Peter Senge has been selected to represent the continuous alignment perspective. This reading summarizes many of the major points of Senge's (1990b) acclaimed book *The Fifth Discipline: The Art and Practice of the Learning Organization.* In his view, leaders must facilitate organizational learning – leaders "are responsible for building organizations where people are continually expanding their capabilities to shape their future". Creating organizations that want to adapt, learn and evolve means avoiding the traditional sources of inertia. Senge believes that one of the keys to continuous learning is motivation. He suggests that the drive to learn can best be stimulated by establishing a creative tension between the current reality and a compelling vision of the future. But, Senge points out, creating a shared vision and designing the organization in a way that enables learning, instead of impeding it, are clearly leadership tasks. In his opinion, leaders are needed to perform these important formative tasks, as well as to act as organizational teachers. A teacher is not someone with all the right answers, but a leader who can ask challenging questions and can shake up existing cognitive maps. Together, these 'new tasks' of leaders give them plenty of scope to influence the future direction of the firm, while at the same time leaving enough room for organizational members to also contribute to the organization's continuous alignment process.

The articles by Hammer and Senge on the fundamentals of revolution and evolution are followed by the third reading, describing how to manage the paradox of revolution and evolution: 'Ambidextrous Organizations: Managing Evolutionary and Revolutionary Change' by Michael Tushman and Charles O'Reilly (1996). While Hammer presents revolution as the radical measure needed to break the shackles of antiquated business models, it is unclear what the corporation must do after it is re-engineered. Tushman and O'Reilly look beyond a single episode of revolution, to the longer-term pattern of development. In their view, short periods of revolutionary change are usually followed by longer periods of gradual change, similar to the pattern found in nature, which scientists have dubbed 'punctuated equilibrium'. They argue that during periods of relative stability, firms need to commit themselves to a certain strategy, structure and culture, to create a strong fit with the environment, with an emphasis on evolutionary adaptation to the ever changing demands in the market. But as soon as discontinuous changes happen in the environment, firms need to be able to be revolutionary as well. Hence they conclude that the paradox of revolution and evolution needs to be managed by being ambidextrous, i.e. being able to do both, sometimes sequentially, sometimes even at the same time. This can be achieved by stimulating internal diversity, allowing different strategies, structures and cultures to blossom side-by-side, making a firm more robust in adapting to whatever external change comes its way.

Reengineering work: Don't automate, obliterate

By Michael Hammer[1]

Despite a decade or more of restructuring and downsizing, many US companies are still unprepared to operate in the 1990s. In a time of rapidly changing technologies and ever-shorter product life cycles, product development often proceeds at a glacial pace. In an age of the customer, order fulfilment has high error rates and customer enquiries go unanswered for weeks. In a period when asset utilization is critical, inventory levels exceed many months of demand.

The usual methods for boosting performance – process rationalization and automation – haven't yielded the dramatic improvements companies need. In particular, heavy investments in information technology have delivered disappointing results – largely because companies tend to use technology to mechanize old ways of doing business. They leave the existing processes intact and use computers simply to speed them up.

But speeding up those processes cannot address their fundamental performance deficiencies. Many of our job designs, workflows, control mechanisms and organizational structures came of age in a different competitive environment and before the advent of the computer. They are geared toward efficiency and control. Yet the watchwords of the new decade are innovation and speed, service and quality.

It is time to stop paving the cow paths. Instead of embedding outdated processes in silicon and software, we should obliterate them and start over. We should 'reengineer' our businesses: use the power of modern information technology to radically redesign our business processes in order to achieve dramatic improvements in their performance.

Every company operates according to a great many unarticulated rules. 'Credit decisions are made by the credit department.' 'Local inventory is needed for good customer service.' 'Forms must be filled in completely and in order.' Reengineering strives to break away from the old rules about how we organize and conduct business. It involves recognizing and rejecting some of them and then finding imaginative new ways to accomplish work. From our redesigned processes, new rules will emerge that fit the times. Only then can we hope to achieve quantum leaps in performance.

Reengineering cannot be planned meticulously and accomplished in small and cautious steps. It's an all-or-nothing proposition with an uncertain result. Still, most companies have no choice but to muster the courage to do it. For many, reengineering is the only hope for breaking away from the antiquated processes that threaten to drag them down. Fortunately, managers are not without help. Enough businesses have successfully reengineered their processes to provide some rules of thumb for others.

What Ford and MBL did

Japanese competitors and young entrepreneurial ventures prove every day that drastically better levels of process performance are possible. They develop products twice as fast, utilize assets eight times more productively and respond to customers ten times faster. Some large, established companies also show what can be done. Businesses like Ford Motor Company and Mutual Benefit Life Insurance (MBL) have reengineered their processes and achieved competitive leadership as a result. Ford has reengineered its accounts payable processes, and Mutual Benefit Life its processing of applications for insurance.

In the early 1980s, when the American automotive industry was in a depression, Ford's top management put accounts payable – along with many other departments – under the microscope in search of ways to cut costs. Accounts payable in North America alone employed more than 500 people. Management thought that by rationalizing processes and installing new computer systems, it could reduce the head count by some 20 per cent.

Ford was enthusiastic about its plan to tighten accounts payable – until it looked at Mazda. While Ford was aspiring to a 400-person department, Mazda's accounts payable organization consisted of a total of five people. The difference in absolute numbers

[1]Source: This article was adapted by permission of *Harvard Business Review*. From 'Reengineering work: Don't automate, obliterate' by M. Hammer, July/August 1990, Vol. 68. © 1990 by the Harvard Business School Publishing Corporation, all rights reserved.

was astounding, and even after adjusting for Mazda's smaller size, Ford figured that its accounts payable organization was five times the size it should be. The Ford team knew better than to attribute the discrepancy to calisthenics, company songs, or low interest rates.

Ford managers ratcheted up their goal: accounts payable would perform with not just a hundred but many hundreds fewer clerks. It then set out to achieve it. First, managers analysed the existing system. When Ford's purchasing department wrote a purchase order, it sent a copy to accounts payable. Later, when material control received the goods, it sent a copy of the receiving document to accounts payable. Meanwhile, the vendor sent an invoice to accounts payable. It was up to accounts payable, then, to match the purchase order against the receiving document and the invoice. If they matched, the department issued payment.

The department spent most of its time on mismatches, instances where the purchase order, receiving document and invoice disagreed. In these cases, an accounts payable clerk would investigate the discrepancy, hold up payment, generate documents, and all-in-all gum up the works.

One way to improve things might have been to help the accounts payable clerk investigate more efficiently, but a better choice was to prevent the mismatches in the first place. To this end, Ford instituted 'invoiceless processing'. Now when the purchasing department initiates an order, it enters the information into an online database. It doesn't send a copy of the purchase order to anyone. When the goods arrive at the receiving dock, the receiving clerk checks the database to see if they correspond to an outstanding purchase order. If so, he or she accepts them and enters the transaction into the computer system. (If receiving can't find a database entry for the received goods, it simply returns the order.)

Under the old procedures, the accounting department had to match 14 data items between the receipt record, the purchase order and the invoice before it could issue payment to the vendor. The new approach requires matching only three items – part number, unit of measure and supplier code – between the purchase order and the receipt record. The matching is done automatically, and the computer prepares the check, which accounts payable sends to the vendor. There are no invoices to worry about since Ford has asked its vendors not to send them.

Ford didn't settle for the modest increases it first envisioned. It opted for radical change – and achieved dramatic improvement. Where it has instituted this new process, Ford has achieved a 75 per cent reduction in

head count, not the 20 per cent it would have gotten with a conventional programme. And since there are no discrepancies between the financial record and the physical record, material control is simpler and financial information is more accurate.

Mutual Benefit Life, the country's eighteenth largest life carrier, has reengineered its processing of insurance applications. Prior to this, MBL handled customers' applications much as its competitors did. The long, multistep process involved credit checking, quoting, rating, underwriting and so on. An application would have to go through as many as 30 discrete steps, spanning five departments and involving 19 people. At the very best, MBL could process an application in 24 hours, but more typical turnarounds ranged from five to 25 days – most of the time spent passing information from one department to the next. (Another insurer estimated that while an application spent 22 days in process, it was actually worked on for just 17 minutes.)

MBL's rigid, sequential process led to many complications. For instance, when a customer wanted to cash in an existing policy and purchase a new one, the old business department first had to authorize the treasury department to issue a check made payable to MBL. The check would then accompany the paperwork to the new business department.

The president of MBL, intent on improving customer service, decided that this nonsense had to stop and demanded a 60 per cent improvement in productivity. It was clear that such an ambitious goal would require more than tinkering with the existing process. Strong measures were in order, and the management team assigned to the task looked to technology as a means of achieving them. The team realized that shared databases and computer networks could make many different kinds of information available to a single person, while expert systems could help people with limited experience make sound decisions. Applying these insights led to a new approach to the application handling process, one with wide organizational implications and little resemblance to the old way of doing business.

MBL swept away existing job definitions and departmental boundaries and created a new position called a case manager. Case managers have total responsibility for an application from the time it is received to the time a policy is issued. Unlike clerks, who performed a fixed task repeatedly under the watchful gaze of a supervisor, case managers work autonomously. No more hand-offs of files and responsibility, no more shuffling of customer enquiries.

Case managers are able to perform all the tasks associated with an insurance application because they are supported by powerful PC-based workstations that run an expert system and connect to a range of automated systems on a mainframe. In particularly tough cases, the case manager calls for assistance from a senior underwriter or physician, but these specialists work only as consultants and advisers to the case manager, who never relinquishes control.

Empowering individuals to process entire applications has had a tremendous impact on operations. MBL can now complete an application in as little as four hours, and average turnaround takes only two to five days. The company has eliminated 100 field office positions, and case managers can handle more than twice the volume of new applications the company previously could process.

The essence of reengineering

At the heart of reengineering is the notion of discontinuous thinking – of recognizing and breaking away from the outdated rules and fundamental assumptions that underlie operations. Unless we change these rules, we are merely rearranging the deckchairs on the *Titanic*. We cannot achieve breakthroughs in performance by cutting fat or automating existing processes. Rather, we must challenge old assumptions and shed the old rules that made the business underperform in the first place.

Every business is replete with implicit rules left over from earlier decades. 'Customers don't repair their own equipment.' 'Local warehouses are necessary for good service.' 'Merchandising decisions are made at headquarters.' These rules of work design are based on assumptions about technology, people and organizational goals that no longer hold. The contemporary repertoire of available information technologies is vast and quickly expanding. Quality, innovation and service are now more important than cost, growth and control. A large portion of the population is educated and capable of assuming responsibility, and workers cherish their autonomy and expect to have a say in how the business is run.

It should come as no surprise that our business processes and structures are outmoded and obsolete: our work structures and processes have not kept pace with the changes in technology, demographics and business objectives. For the most part, we have organized work as a sequence of separate tasks and employed complex mechanisms to track its progress.

This arrangement can be traced to the Industrial Revolution, when specialization of labour and economies of scale promised to overcome the inefficiencies of cottage industries. Businesses disaggregated work into narrowly defined tasks, reaggregated the people performing those tasks into departments, and installed managers to administer them.

Our elaborate systems for imposing control and discipline on those who actually do the work stem from the post-war period. In that halcyon period of expansion, the main concern was growing fast without going broke, so businesses focused on cost, growth and control. And since literate, entry-level people were abundant but well-educated professionals hard to come by, the control systems funneled information up the hierarchy to the few who presumably knew what to do with it.

These patterns of organizing work have become so ingrained that, despite their serious drawbacks, it's hard to conceive of work being accomplished any other way. Conventional process structures are fragmented and piecemeal, and they lack the integration necessary to maintain quality and service. They are breeding grounds for tunnel vision, as people tend to substitute the narrow goals of their particular department for the larger goals of the process as a whole. When work is handed off from person to person and unit to unit, delays and errors are inevitable. Accountability blurs, and critical issues fall between the cracks. Moreover, no one sees enough of the big picture to be able to respond quickly to new situations. Managers desperately try, like all the king's horses and all the king's men, to piece together the fragmented pieces of business processes.

Managers have tried to adapt their processes to new circumstances, but usually in ways that just create more problems. If, say, customer service is poor, they create a mechanism to deliver service but overlay it on the existing organization. Bureaucracy thickens, costs rise and enterprising competitors gain market share.

In reengineering, managers break loose from outmoded business processes and the design principles underlying them and create new ones. Ford had operated under the old rule that 'we pay when we receive the invoice.' While no one had ever articulated or recorded it, that rule determined how the accounts payable process was organized. Ford's reengineering effort challenged and ultimately replaced the rule with a new one: 'We pay when we receive the goods.'

Reengineering requires looking at the fundamental processes of the business from a cross-functional perspective. Ford discovered that reengineering only the accounts payable department was futile. The appropriate focus of the effort was what might be called the goods acquisition process, which included purchasing and receiving as well as accounts payable.

One way to ensure that reengineering has a cross-functional perspective is to assemble a team that represents the functional units involved in the process being reengineered and all the units that depend on it. The team must analyse and scrutinize the existing process until it really understands what the process is trying to accomplish. The point is not to learn what happens to form 73B in its peregrinations through the company but to understand the purpose of having form 73B in the first place. Rather than looking for opportunities to improve the current process, the team should determine which of its steps really add value and search for new ways to achieve the result.

The reengineering team must keep asking Why? and What if? Why do we need to get a manager's signature on a requisition? Is it a control mechanism or a decision point? What if the manager reviews only requisitions above $500? What if he or she doesn't see them at all? Raising and resolving heretical questions can separate what is fundamental to the process from what is superficial. The regional offices of an East Coast insurance company had long produced a series of reports that they regularly sent to the home office. No one in the field realized that these reports were simply filed and never used. The process outlasted the circumstances that had created the need for it. The re-engineering study team should push to discover situations like this.

In short, a reengineering effort strives for dramatic levels of improvement. It must break away from conventional wisdom and the constraints of organizational boundaries and should be broad and cross-functional in scope. It should use information technology not to automate an existing process but to enable a new one.

Principles of reengineering

Creating new rules tailored to the modern environment ultimately requires a new conceptualization of the business process – which comes down to someone having a great idea. But reengineering need not be haphazard. In fact, some of the principles that companies have already discovered while reengineering their business processes can help jump start the effort for others.

Organize around outcomes, not tasks

This principle says to have one person perform all the steps in a process. Design that person's job around an objective or outcome instead of a single task. The redesign at Mutual Benefit Life, where individual case managers perform the entire application approval process, is the quintessential example of this.

The redesign of an electronics company is another example. It had separate organizations performing each of the five steps between selling and installing the equipment. One group determined customer requirements, another translated those requirements into internal product codes, a third conveyed that information to various plants and warehouses, a fourth received and assembled the components and a fifth delivered and installed the equipment. The process was based on the centuries-old notion of specialized labour and on the limitations inherent in paper files. The departments each possessed a specific set of skills, and only one department at a time could do its work.

The customer order moved systematically from step to step. But this sequential processing caused problems. The people getting the information from the customer in step one had to get all the data anyone would need throughout the process, even if it wasn't needed until step five. In addition, the many hand-offs were responsible for numerous errors and misunderstandings. Finally, any questions about customer requirements that arose late in the process had to be referred back to the people doing step one, resulting in delay and rework.

When the company reengineered, it eliminated the assembly-line approach. It compressed responsibility for the various steps and assigned it to one person, the 'customer service representative'. That person now oversees the whole process – taking the order, translating it into product codes, getting the components assembled, and seeing the product delivered and installed. The customer service rep expedites and coordinates the process, much like a general contractor. And the customer has just one contact, who always knows the status of the order.

Have those who use the output of the process perform the process

In an effort to capitalize on the benefits of specialization and scale, many organizations established specialized departments to handle specialized processes. Each department does only one type of work and is a 'customer' of other groups' processes. Accounting does only accounting. If it needs new pencils, it goes to the purchasing department, the group specially equipped with the information and expertise to perform that role. Purchasing finds vendors, negotiates price, places the order, inspects the goods and pays the invoice – and eventually the accountants get their pencils. The process works (after a fashion), but it's slow and bureaucratic.

Now that computer-based data and expertise are more readily available, departments, units and individuals can do more for themselves. Opportunities exist to reengineer processes so that the individuals who need the result of a process can do it themselves. For example, by using expert systems and databases, departments can make their own purchases without sacrificing the benefits of specialized purchasers. One manufacturer has re-engineered its purchasing process along just these lines. The company's old system, whereby the operating departments submitted requisitions and let purchasing do the rest, worked well for controlling expensive and important items like raw materials and capital equipment. But for inexpensive and non-strategic purchases, which constituted some 35 per cent of total orders, the system was slow and cumbersome; it was not uncommon for the cost of the purchasing process to exceed the cost of the goods being purchased.

The new process compresses the purchase of sundry items and pushes it on to the customers of the process. Using a database of approved vendors, an operating unit can directly place an order with a vendor and charge it on a bank credit card. At the end of the month, the bank gives the manufacturer a tape of all credit card transactions, which the company runs against its internal accounting system.

When an electronics equipment manufacturer re-engineered its field service process, it pushed some of the steps of the process on to its customers. The manufacturer's field service had been plagued by the usual problems: technicians were often unable to do a particular repair because the right part wasn't on the van, response to customer calls was slow, and spare parts inventory was excessive.

Now customers make simple repairs themselves. Spare parts are stored at each customer's site and managed through a computerized inventory management system. When a problem arises, the customer calls the manufacturer's field-service hot line and describes the symptoms to a diagnostician, who accesses a diagnosis support system. If the problem appears to be something the customer can fix, the diagnostician tells the customer what part to replace and how to install it. The old part is picked up and a new part left in its place at a later time. Only for complex problems is a service technician dispatched to the site, this time without having to make a stop at the warehouse to pick up parts.

When the people closest to the process perform it, there is little need for the overhead associated with managing it. Interfaces and liaisons can be eliminated, as can the mechanisms used to coordinate those who perform the process with those who use it. Moreover, the problem of capacity planning for the process performers is greatly reduced.

Subsume information-processing work into the real work that produces the information

The previous two principles compress linear processes. This principle suggests moving work from one person or department to another. Why doesn't an organization that produces information also process it? In the past, people didn't have the time or weren't trusted to do both. Most companies established units to do nothing but collect and process information that other departments created. This arrangement reflects the old rule about specialized labour and the belief that people at lower organizational levels are incapable of acting on information they generate. An accounts payable department collects information from purchasing and receiving and reconciles it with data that the vendor provides. Quality assurance gathers and analyses information it gets from production.

Ford's redesigned accounts payable process embodies the new rule. With the new system, receiving, which produces the information about the goods received, processes this information instead of sending it to accounts payable. The new computer system can easily compare the delivery with the order and trigger the appropriate action.

Treat geographically dispersed resources as though they were centralized

The conflict between centralization and decentralization is a classic one. Decentralizing a resource (whether people, equipment, or inventory) gives better service to those who use it, but at the cost of redundancy, bureaucracy and missed economies of scale. Companies no longer have to make such trade-offs. They can use databases, telecommunications networks and standardized processing systems to get the benefits of scale and coordination while maintaining the benefits of flexibility and service.

At Hewlett-Packard, for instance, each of the more than 50 manufacturing units had its own separate purchasing department. While this arrangement provided excellent responsiveness and service to the plants, it prevented HP from realizing the benefits of its scale, particularly with regard to quantity discounts. HP's solution was to maintain the divisional purchasing organizations and to introduce a corporate unit to coordinate them. Each purchasing unit has access to a shared database on vendors and their performance and issues its own purchase orders. Corporate purchasing maintains this database and uses it to negotiate contracts for the corporation and to monitor the units. The payoffs have come in a 150 per cent improvement in on-time deliveries, 50 per cent reduction in lead times, 75 per cent reduction in failure rates, and a significantly lower cost of goods purchased.

Link parallel activities instead of integrating their results

HP's decentralized purchasing operations represent one kind of parallel processing in which separate units perform the same function. Another common kind of parallel processing is when separate units perform different activities that must eventually come together. Product development typically operates this way. In the development of a photocopier, for example, independent units develop the various subsystems of the copier. One group works on the optics, another on the mechanical paper-handling device, another on the power supply, and so on. Having people do development work simultaneously saves time, but at the dreaded integration and testing phase, the pieces often fail to work together. Then the costly redesign begins.

Or consider a bank that sells different kinds of credit – loans, letters of credit, asset-based financing – through separate units. These groups may have no way of knowing whether another group has already extended credit to a particular customer. Each unit could extend the full $10 million credit limit.

The new principle says to forge links between parallel functions and to coordinate them while their activities are in process rather than after they are completed. Communications networks, shared databases and teleconferencing can bring the independent groups together so that coordination is ongoing. One large electronics company has cut its product development cycle by more than 50 per cent by implementing this principle.

Put the decision point where the work is performed and build control into the process

In most organizations, those who do the work are distinguished from those who monitor the work and make decisions about it. The tacit assumption is that the people actually doing the work have neither the time nor the inclination to monitor and control it and that they lack the knowledge and scope to make decisions about it. The entire hierarchical management structure is built on this assumption. Accountants, auditors and supervisors check, record and monitor work. Managers handle any exceptions.

The new principle suggests that the people who do the work should make the decisions and that the process itself can have built-in controls. Pyramidal management layers can therefore be compressed and the organization flattened.

Information technology can capture and process data, and expert systems can to some extent supply knowledge, enabling people to make their own decisions. As the doers become self-managing and self-controlling, hierarchy – and the slowness and bureaucracy associated with it – disappears.

When Mutual Benefit Life reengineered the insurance application process, it not only compressed the linear sequence but also eliminated the need for layers of managers. These two kinds of compression – vertical and horizontal – often go together; the very fact that a worker sees only one piece of the process calls for a manager with a broader vision. The case managers at MBL provide end-to-end management of the process, reducing the need for traditional managers. The managerial role is changing from one of controller and supervisor to one of supporter and facilitator.

Capture information once and at the source

This last rule is simple. When information was difficult to transmit, it made sense to collect information repeatedly. Each person, department or unit had its own requirements and forms. Companies simply had to live with the associated delays, entry errors and costly overhead. But why do we have to live with those problems now? Today when we collect a piece of information, we can store it in an online database for all who need it. Bar coding, relational databases and electronic data interchange (EDI) make it easy to collect, store and transmit information. One insurance company found that its application review process required that certain items be entered into 'stovepipe' computer systems supporting different functions as many as five times. By integrating and connecting these systems, the company was able to eliminate this redundant data entry along with the attendant checking functions and inevitable errors.

Think big

Reengineering triggers changes of many kinds, not just of the business process itself. Job designs, organizational structures, management systems – anything associated with the process must be refashioned in an integrated way. In other words, reengineering is a tremendous effort that mandates change in many areas of the organization.

When Ford reengineered its payables, receiving clerks on the dock had to learn to use computer terminals to check shipments, and they had to make decisions about whether to accept the goods. Purchasing agents also had to assume new responsibilities – like making sure the purchase orders they entered into the database had the correct information about where to send the check. Attitudes toward vendors also had to change: vendors could no longer be seen as adversaries; they had to become partners in a shared business process. Vendors too had to adjust. In many cases, invoices formed the basis of their accounting systems. At least one Ford supplier adapted by continuing to print invoices, but instead of sending them to Ford threw them away, reconciling cash received against invoices never sent.

The changes at Mutual Benefit Life were also widespread. The company's job-rating scheme could not accommodate the case manager position, which had a lot of responsibility but no direct reports. MBL had to devise new job-rating schemes and compensation policies. It also had to develop a culture in which people doing work are perceived as more important than those supervising work. Career paths, recruitment and training programmes, promotion policies – these and many other management systems are being revised to support the new process design.

The extent of these changes suggests one factor that is necessary for reengineering to succeed: executive leadership with real vision. No one in an organization wants reengineering. It is confusing and disruptive and affects everything people have grown accustomed to. Only if top-level managers back the effort and outlast the company cynics will people take reengineering seriously. As one wag at an electronics equipment manufacturer has commented, 'Every few months, our senior managers find a new religion. One time it was quality, another it was customer service, another it was flattening the organization. We just hold our breath until they get over it and things get back to normal.' Commitment, consistency – maybe even a touch of fanaticism – are needed to enlist those who would prefer the status quo.

Considering the inertia of old processes and structures, the strain of implementing a reengineering plan can hardly be overestimated. But by the same token, it is hard to overestimate the opportunities, especially for established companies. Big, traditional organizations aren't necessarily dinosaurs doomed to extinction, but they are burdened with layers of unproductive overhead and armies of unproductive workers. Shedding them a layer at a time will not be good enough to stand up against sleek start-ups or streamlined Japanese companies. US companies need fast change and dramatic improvements.

We have the tools to do what we need to do. Information technology offers many options for reorganizing work. But our imaginations must guide our decisions about technology – not the other way around. We must have the boldness to imagine taking 78 days out of an 80-day turnaround time, cutting 75 per cent of overhead, and eliminating 80 per cent of errors. These are not unrealistic goals. If managers have the vision, reengineering will provide a way.

Building learning organizations

By Peter Senge[1]

Over the past two years, business academics and senior managers have begun talking about the notion of the learning organization. Ray Stata of Analog Devices put the idea succinctly in these pages last spring: 'The rate at which organizations learn may become the only substantial source of competitive advantage.' And in late May of this year, at an MIT-sponsored conference entitled 'Transforming Organizations', two questions arose again and again: How can we build organizations in which continuous learning occurs, and what kind of person can best lead the learning organization? This article, based on Senge's (1990b) book, *The Fifth Discipline: The Art and Practice of the Learning Organization,* begins to chart this new territory, describing new roles, skills and tools for leaders who wish to develop learning organizations.

[1]Source: This article reprinted with permission from Peter Senge (1990) 'The Leader's New Work: Building Learning Organizations', *Sloan Management Review*, Fall, 1990 pp.7–23. © 1990 from MIT *Sloan Management Review*/Massachusetts Institute of Technology. All rights reserved. Distributed by Tribune Media Services.

Human beings are designed for learning. No one has to teach an infant to walk, talk, or master the spatial relationships needed to stack eight building blocks that don't topple. Children come fully equipped with an insatiable drive to explore and experiment. Unfortunately, the primary institutions of our society are oriented predominantly toward controlling rather than learning, rewarding individuals for performing for others rather than for cultivating their natural curiosity and impulse to learn. The young child entering school discovers quickly that the name of the game is getting the right answer and avoiding mistakes – a mandate no less compelling to the aspiring manager.

'Our prevailing system of management has destroyed our people', writes W. Edwards Deming, leader in the quality movement. 'People are born with intrinsic motivation, self-esteem, dignity, curiosity to learn, joy in learning. The forces of destruction begin with toddlers – a prize for the best Halloween costume, grades in school, gold stars, and on up through university. On the job, people, teams, divisions are ranked – reward for the one at the top, punishment at the bottom. Management by Objectives (MBO), quotas, incentive pay, business plans, put together separately, division by division, cause further loss, unknown and unknowable.'

Ironically, by focusing on performing for someone else's approval, corporations create the very conditions that predestine them to mediocre performance. Over the long run, superior performance depends on superior learning.

If anything, the need for understanding how organizations learn and accelerating that learning is greater today than ever before. The old days when a Henry Ford, Alfred Sloan, or Tom Watson learned for the organization are gone. In an increasingly dynamic, interdependent and unpredictable world, it is simply no longer possible for anyone to 'figure it all out at the top'. The old model, 'the top thinks and the local acts', must now give way to integrating thinking and acting at all levels. While the challenge is great, so is the potential payoff.

Adaptive learning and generative learning

The prevailing view of learning organizations emphasizes increased adaptability. Given the accelerating pace of change, or so the standard view goes, 'the most successful corporation of the 1990s', according to *Fortune* magazine, 'will be something called a learning organization, a consummately adaptive enterprise'.

But increasing adaptiveness is only the first stage in moving toward learning organizations. The impulse to learn in children goes deeper than desires to respond and adapt more effectively to environmental change. The impulse to learn, at its heart, is an impulse to be generative, to expand our capability. This is why leading corporations are focusing on *generative* learning, which is about creating, as well as *adaptive* learning, which is about coping.

The total quality movement in Japan illustrates the evolution from adaptive to generative learning. With its emphasis on continuous experimentation and feedback, the total quality movement has been the first wave in building learning organizations. But Japanese firms' view of serving the customer has evolved. In the early years of total quality, the focus was on 'fitness to standard', making a product reliably so that it would do what its designers intended it to do and what the firm told its customers it would do. Then came a focus on 'fitness to need', understanding better what the customer wanted and then providing products that reliably met those needs. Today, leading-edge firms seek to understand and meet the 'latent need' of the customer – what customers might truly value but have never experienced or would never think to ask for.

Generative learning, unlike adaptive learning, requires new ways of looking at the world, whether in understanding customers or in understanding how to better manage a business. For years, US manufacturers sought competitive advantage in aggressive controls on inventories, incentives against overproduction, and rigid adherence to production forecasts. Despite these incentives, their performance was eventually eclipsed by Japanese firms who saw the challenges of manufacturing differently. They realized that eliminating delays in the production process was the key to reducing instability and improving cost, productivity and service. They worked to build networks of relationships with trusted suppliers and to redesign physical production processes to reduce delays in materials procurement, production setup and in-process inventory – a much higher-leverage approach to improving both cost and customer loyalty.

As Boston Consulting Group's George Stalk has observed (Stalk, Evans and Shulman, 1992), the Japanese saw the significance of delays because they saw the process of order entry, production scheduling, materials procurement, production and distribution as an integrated system. 'What distorts the system so badly is time', observes Stalk – the multiple delays between events and responses. 'These distortions reverberate throughout the system, producing disruptions, waste and inefficiency.' Generative learning requires seeing the systems that control events. When we fail to grasp the systemic source of problems, we are left to 'push on' symptoms rather than eliminate underlying causes. The best we can ever do is adaptive learning.

The leader's new work

Our traditional view of leaders – as special people who set the direction, make the key decisions and energize the troops – is deeply rooted in an individualistic and non-systemic worldview. Especially in the West, leaders are heroes – great men (and occasionally women) who rise to the fore in times of crisis. So long as such myths prevail, they reinforce a focus on short-term events and charismatic heroes rather than on systemic forces and collective learning.

Leadership in learning organizations centres on subtler and ultimately more important work. In a learning organization, leaders' roles differ dramatically from that of the charismatic decision maker. Leaders are designers, teachers and stewards. These roles require new skills: the ability to build shared vision, to bring to the surface and challenge prevailing mental models, and to foster more systemic patterns of thinking. In short, leaders in learning organizations are responsible for building organizations where people are continually expanding their capabilities to shape their future – that is, leaders are responsible for learning.

Creative tension: The integrating principle

Leadership in a learning organization starts with the principle of creative tension. Creative tension comes from seeing clearly where we want to be, our 'vision', and telling the truth about where we are, our 'current reality'. The gap between the two generates a natural tension.

Creative tension can be resolved in two basic ways: by raising current reality toward the vision, or by lowering the vision toward current reality. Individuals, groups and organizations who learn how to work with creative tension learn how to use the energy it generates to move reality more reliably toward their visions.

Without vision there is no creative tension. Creative tension cannot be generated from current reality alone. All the analysis in the world will never generate a vision. Many who are otherwise qualified to lead fail to do so because they try to substitute analysis for vision. They believe that, if only people understood current

reality, they would surely feel the motivation to change. They are then disappointed to discover that people resist the personal and organizational changes that must be made to alter reality. What they never grasp is that the natural energy for changing reality comes from holding a picture of what might be that is more important to people than what is.

But creative tension cannot be generated from vision alone; it demands an accurate picture of current reality as well. Vision without an understanding of current reality will more likely foster cynicism than creativity. The principle of creative tension teaches that *an accurate picture of current reality is just as important as a compelling picture of a desired future.*

Leading through creative tension is different from solving problems. In problem solving, the energy for change comes from attempting to get away from an aspect of current reality that is undesirable. With creative tension, the energy for change comes from the vision, from what we want to create, juxtaposed with current reality. While the distinction may seem small, the consequences are not. Many people and organizations find themselves motivated to change only when their problems are bad enough to cause them to change. This works for a while, but the change process runs out of steam as soon as the problems driving the change become less pressing. With problem solving, the motivation for change is extrinsic. With creative tension, the motivation is intrinsic. The distinction mirrors the distinction between adaptive and generative learning.

New roles

The traditional authoritarian image of the leader as 'the boss calling the shots' has been recognized as oversimplified and inadequate for some time. According to Edgar Schein (1985), 'Leadership is intertwined with culture formation.' Building an organization's culture and shaping its evolution is the 'unique and essential function' of leadership. In a learning organization, the critical roles of leadership – designer, teacher and steward – have antecedents in the ways leaders have contributed to building organizations in the past. But each role takes on new meaning in the learning organization and, as will be seen in the following sections, demands new skills and tools.

Leader as designer

The functions of design, or what some have called social architecture, are rarely visible; they take place behind the scenes. The consequences that appear today are the result of work done long in the past, and work today will show its benefits far in the future. Those who aspire to lead out of a desire to control, gain fame, or simply to be at the centre of the action will find little to attract them to the quiet design work of leadership.

But what, specifically, is involved in organizational design? 'Organization design is widely misconstrued as moving around boxes and lines', says Hanover's O'Brien. 'The first task of organization design concerns designing the governing ideas of purpose, vision and core values by which people will live.' Few acts of leadership have a more enduring impact on an organization than building a foundation of purpose and core values.

If governing ideas constitute the first design task of leadership, the second design task involves the policies, strategies and structures that translate guiding ideas into business decisions. Leadership theorist Philip Selznick (1957) calls policy and structure the 'institutional embodiment of purpose.' 'Policy making (the rules that guide decisions) ought to be separated from decision making', says Jay Forrester. 'Otherwise, short-term pressures will usurp time from policy creation.'

Traditionally, writers like Selznick and Forrester have tended to see policy-making and implementation as the work of a small number of senior managers. But that view is changing. Both the dynamic business environment and the mandate of the learning organization to engage people at all levels now make it clear that this second design task is more subtle. Henry Mintzberg has argued that strategy is less a rational plan arrived at in the abstract and implemented throughout the organization than an 'emergent phenomenon'. Successful organizations 'craft strategy' according to Mintzberg, as they continually learn about shifting business conditions and balance what is desired and what is possible. The key is not getting the right strategy but fostering strategic thinking.

Behind appropriate policies, strategies and structures are effective learning processes; their creation is the third key design responsibility in learning organizations. This does not absolve senior managers of their strategic responsibilities. Actually, it deepens and extends those responsibilities. Now they are not only responsible for ensuring that an organization has well developed strategies and policies but also for ensuring that processes exist whereby these are continually improved.

In the early 1970s, Shell was the weakest of the big seven oil companies. Today, Shell and Exxon are arguably the strongest, both in size and financial health. Shell's ascendance began with frustration. Around 1971, members of Shell's Group Planning in London began to foresee dramatic change and unpredictability in world oil markets. However, it proved impossible to persuade managers that the stable world of steady growth in oil demand and supply they had known for 20 years was about to change. Despite brilliant analysis and artful presentation, Shell's planners realized, in the words of Pierre Wack (1985), that they 'had failed to change behaviour in much of the Shell organization'. Progress would probably have ended there, had the frustration not given way to a radically new view of corporate planning.

As they pondered this failure, the planners' view of their basic task shifted: 'We no longer saw our task as producing a documented view of the future business environment five or ten years ahead. Our real target was the microcosm (the "mental model") of our decision makers.' Only when the planners reconceptualized their basic task as fostering learning rather than devising plans did their insights begin to have an impact. The initial tool used was 'scenario analysis', through which planners encouraged operating managers to think through how they would manage in the future under different possible scenarios. It mattered not that the managers believed the planners' scenarios absolutely, only that they became engaged in ferreting out the implications. In this way, Shell's planners conditioned managers to be mentally prepared for a shift from low prices to high prices and from stability to instability. The results were significant. When the Organisation of Petroleum Exporting Countries (OPEC) became a reality, Shell quickly responded by increasing local operating company control (to enhance manoeuverability in the new political environment), building buffer stocks, and accelerating development of non-OPEC sources – actions that its competitors took much more slowly or not at all.

Somewhat inadvertently, Shell planners had discovered the leverage of designing institutional learning processes whereby, in the words of former planning director De Geus, 'Management teams change their shared mental models of their company, their markets, and their competitors.' Since then, 'planning as learning' has become a byword at Shell, and Group Planning has continually sought out new learning tools that can be integrated into the planning process. Some of these are described below.

Leader as teacher

Leader as teacher does *not* mean leader as authoritarian expert whose job it is to teach people the 'correct' view of reality. Rather, it is about helping everyone in the organization, oneself included, to gain more insightful views of current reality. This is in line with a popular emerging view of leaders as coaches, guides, or facilitators. In learning organizations, this teaching role is developed further by virtue of explicit attention to people's mental models and by the influence of the systems perspective.

The role of leader as teacher starts with bringing to the surface people's mental models of important issues. No one carries an organization, a market, or a state of technology in his or her head. What we carry in our heads are assumptions. These mental pictures of how the world works have a significant influence on how we perceive problems and opportunities, identify courses of action, and make choices.

One reason that mental models are so deeply entrenched is that they are largely tacit. Ian Mitroff, in his study of General Motors, argues that an assumption that prevailed for years was that, in the United States, 'Cars are status symbols. Styling is therefore more important than quality.' The Detroit automakers didn't say, 'We have a mental model that all people care about is styling.' Few actual managers would even say publicly that all people care about is styling. So long as the view remained unexpressed, there was little possibility of challenging its validity or forming more accurate assumptions.

But working with mental models goes beyond revealing hidden assumptions. Reality, as perceived by most people in most organizations, means pressures that must be borne, crises that must be reacted to, and limitations that must be accepted. Leaders as teachers help people *restructure their views of reality* to see beyond the superficial conditions and events into the underlying causes of problems, and therefore to see new possibilities for shaping the future.

Specifically, leaders can influence people to view reality at three distinct levels: events, patterns of behaviour, and systemic structure.

Systemic Structure (Generative)

↓

Patterns of Behaviour (Responsive)

↓

Events (Reactive)

The key question becomes 'Where do leaders predominantly focus their own and their organization's attention?'

Contemporary society focuses predominantly on events. The media reinforces this perspective, with almost exclusive attention to short-term, dramatic events. This focus leads naturally to explaining what happens in terms of those events: 'The Dow Jones average went up 16 points because high fourth-quarter profits were announced yesterday.'

Pattern-of-behaviour explanations are rarer in contemporary culture than event explanations, but they do occur. Trend analysis is an example of seeing patterns of behaviour. A good editorial that interprets a set of current events in the context of long-term historical changes is another example. Systemic, structural explanations go even further by addressing the question 'What causes the patterns of behaviour?'

In some sense, all three levels of explanation are equally true. But their usefulness is quite different. Event explanations – who did what to whom – doom their holders to a reactive stance toward change. Pattern-of-behaviour explanations focus on identifying long-term trends and assessing their implications. They at least suggest how, over time, we can respond to shifting conditions. Structural explanations are the most powerful. Only they address the underlying causes of behaviour at a level such that patterns of behaviour can be changed.

By and large, leaders of our current institutions focus their attention on events and patterns of behaviour, and under their influence, their organizations do likewise. That is why contemporary organizations are predominantly reactive, or at best responsive – rarely generative. On the other hand, leaders in learning organizations pay attention to all three levels, but focus especially on systemic structure; largely by example, they teach people throughout the organization to do likewise.

Leader as steward

This is the subtlest role of leadership. Unlike the roles of designer and teacher, it is almost solely a matter of attitude. It is an attitude critical to learning organizations.

While stewardship has long been recognized as an aspect of leadership, its source is still not widely understood. I believe Robert Greenleaf (1977) came closest to explaining real stewardship, in his seminal book *Servant Leadership*. There, Greenleaf argues that 'the servant leader *is* servant first … It begins with the natural feeling that one wants to serve, to serve *first*. This conscious choice brings one to aspire to lead. That person is sharply different from one who is leader first, perhaps because of the need to assuage an unusual power drive or to acquire material possessions.'

Leaders' sense of stewardship operates on two levels: stewardship for the people they lead and stewardship for the larger purpose or mission that underlies the enterprise. The first type arises from a keen appreciation of the impact one's leadership can have on others. People can suffer economically, emotionally and spiritually under inept leadership. If anything, people in a learning organization are more vulnerable because of their commitment and sense of shared ownership. Appreciating this naturally instills a sense of responsibility in leaders. The second type of stewardship arises from a leader's sense of personal purpose and commitment to the organization's larger mission. People's natural impulse to learn is unleashed when they are engaged in an endeavour they consider worthy of their fullest commitment. Or, as Lawrence Miller puts it, 'Achieving return on equity does not, as a goal, mobilize the most noble forces of our soul.'

New skills

New leadership roles require new leadership skills. These skills can only be developed, in my judgment, through a lifelong commitment. It is not enough for one or two individuals to develop these skills. They must be distributed widely throughout the organization. This is one reason that understanding the disciplines of a learning organization is so important. These disciplines embody the principles and practices that can widely foster leadership development.

Three critical areas of skills (disciplines) are building shared vision, surfacing and challenging mental models, and engaging in systems thinking.

Building shared vision

The skills involved in building shared vision include the following:

- Encouraging personal vision. Shared visions emerge from personal visions. It is not that people only care about their own self-interest – in fact, people's values usually include dimensions that concern family, organization, community and even the world. Rather, it is that people's capacity for caring is personal.

- Communicating and asking for support. Leaders must be willing to continually share their own vision, rather than being the official representative of the corporate vision. They also must be prepared to ask, 'Is this vision worthy of your commitment?' This can be difficult for a person used to setting goals and presuming compliance.

- Visioning as an ongoing process. Building shared vision is a never-ending process. At any one point there will be a particular image of the future that is predominant, but that image will evolve. Today, too many managers want to dispense with the 'vision business' by going off and writing the Official Vision Statement. Such statements almost always lack the vitality, freshness and excitement of a genuine vision that comes from people asking, 'What do we really want to achieve?'

- Blending extrinsic and intrinsic visions. Many energizing visions are extrinsic – that is, they focus on achieving something relative to an outsider, such as a competitor. But a goal that is limited to defeating an opponent can, once the vision is achieved, easily become a defensive posture. In contrast, intrinsic goals like creating a new type of product, taking an established product to a new level, or setting a new standard for customer satisfaction can call forth a new level of creativity and innovation. Intrinsic and extrinsic visions need to coexist; a vision solely predicated on defeating an adversary will eventually weaken an organization.

- Distinguishing positive from negative visions. Many organizations only truly pull together when their survival is threatened. Similarly, most social movements aim at eliminating what people don't want: for example, anti-drug, anti-smoking, or anti-nuclear arms movements. Negative visions carry a subtle message of powerlessness: people will only pull together when there is sufficient threat. Negative visions also tend to be short term. Two fundamental sources of energy can motivate organizations: fear and aspiration. Fear, the energy source behind negative visions, can produce extraordinary changes in short periods, but aspiration endures as a continuing source of learning and growth.

Surfacing and testing mental models

Many of the best ideas in organizations never get put into practice. One reason is that new insights and initiatives often conflict with established mental models. The leadership task of challenging assumptions without invoking defensiveness requires reflection and inquiry skills possessed by few leaders in traditional controlling organizations.

- Seeing leaps of abstraction. Our minds literally move at lightning speed. Ironically, this often slows our learning, because we leap to generalizations so quickly that we never think to test them. We then confuse our generalizations with the observable data upon which they are based, treating the generalizations as if they were data.

■ **Balancing enquiry and advocacy.** Most managers are skilled at articulating their views and presenting them persuasively. While important, advocacy skills can become counterproductive as managers rise in responsibility and confront increasingly complex issues that require collaborative learning among different, equally knowledgeable people. Leaders in learning organizations need to have both enquiry and advocacy skills.

■ **Distinguishing espoused theory from theory in use.** We all like to think that we hold certain views, but often our actions reveal deeper views. For example, I may proclaim that people are trustworthy, but never lend friends money and jealously guard my possessions. Obviously, my deeper mental model (my theory in use), differs from my espoused theory. Recognizing gaps between espoused views and theories in use (which often requires the help of others) can be pivotal to deeper learning.

■ **Recognizing and defusing defensive routines.** As one CEO (chief executive officer) in our research programme puts it, 'Nobody ever talks about an issue at the eight o'clock business meeting exactly the same way they talk about it at home that evening or over drinks at the end of the day.' The reason is what Chris Argyris calls defensive routines; entrenched habits used to protect ourselves from the embarrassment and threat that come with exposing our thinking. For most of us, such defences began to build early in life in response to pressures to have the right answers in school or at home. Organizations add new levels of performance anxiety and thereby amplify and exacerbate this defensiveness. Ironically, this makes it even more difficult to expose hidden mental models, and thereby lessens learning. The first challenge is to recognize defensive routines, then to enquire into their operation. Those who are best at revealing and defusing defensive routines operate with a high degree of self-disclosure regarding their own defensiveness.

Systems thinking

We all know that leaders should help people see the big picture. But the actual skills whereby leaders are supposed to achieve this are not well understood. In my experience, successful leaders often are 'systems thinkers' to a considerable extent. They focus less on day-to-day events and more on underlying trends and forces of change. But they do this almost completely intuitively. The consequence is that they are often unable to explain their intuitions to others and feel frustrated that others cannot see the world the way they do. One of the most significant developments in management science today is the gradual coalescence of managerial systems thinking as a field of study and practice. This field suggests some key skills for future leaders:

■ **Seeing interrelationships, not things, and processes, not snapshots.** Most of us have been conditioned throughout our lives to focus on things and to see the world in static images. This leads us to linear explanations of systemic phenomenon.

■ **Moving beyond blame.** We tend to blame each other or outside circumstances for our problems. But it is poorly designed systems, not incompetent or unmotivated individuals that cause most organizational problems. Systems thinking shows us that there is no outside – that you and the cause of your problems are part of a single system.

■ **Distinguishing detail complexity from dynamic complexity.** Some types of complexity are more important strategically than others. Detail complexity arises when there are many variables. Dynamic complexity arises when cause and effect are distant in time and space, and when the consequences over time of interventions are subtle and not obvious to many participants in the system. The leverage in most management situations lies in understanding dynamic complexity, not detail complexity.

■ **Focusing on areas of high leverage.** Some have called systems thinking the 'new dismal science' because it teaches that most obvious solutions don't work – at best, they improve matters in the short run, only to make things worse in the long run. But there is another side to the story. Systems thinking also shows that small, well-focused actions can produce significant, enduring improvements, if they are in the right place. Systems thinkers refer to this idea as the principle of leverage. Tackling a difficult problem is often a matter of seeing where the high leverage lies, where a change – with a minimum of effort – would lead to lasting, significant improvement.

■ **Avoiding symptomatic solutions.** The pressures to intervene in management systems that are going awry can be overwhelming. Unfortunately, given the linear thinking that predominates in most organizations, interventions usually focus on symptomatic fixes, not underlying causes. This results in only temporary relief, and it tends to create still more pressures later on for further, low-leverage intervention. If leaders acquiesce to these pressures, they can be sucked into an endless spiral of increasing intervention. Sometimes the most difficult leadership acts are to refrain from intervening through popular quick fixes and to keep the pressure on everyone to identify more enduring solutions.

The consequences of leaders who lack systems-thinking skills can be devastating. Many charismatic leaders manage almost exclusively at the level of events. They deal in visions and in crises, and little in between. Under their leadership, an organization hurtles from crisis to crisis. Eventually, the world-view of people in the organization becomes dominated by events and reactiveness. Many, especially those who are deeply committed, become burned out. Eventually, cynicism comes to pervade the organization. People have no control over their time, let alone their destiny.

Similar problems arise with the 'visionary strategist', the leader with vision who sees both patterns of change and events. This leader is better prepared to manage change. He or she can explain strategies in terms of emerging trends, and thereby foster a climate that is less reactive. But such leaders still impart a responsive orientation rather than a generative one.

Many talented leaders have rich, highly systemic intuitions but cannot explain those intuitions to others. Ironically, they often end up being authoritarian leaders, even if they don't want to, because only they see the decisions that need to be made. They are unable to

conceptualize their strategic insights so that these can become public knowledge, open to challenge and further improvement.

Developing leaders and learning organizations

In a recently published retrospective on organization development in the 1980s, Marshall Sashkin and N. Warner Burke (1990) observe the return of an emphasis on developing leaders who can develop organizations. They also note Schein's critique that most top executives are not qualified for the task of developing culture. Learning organizations represent a potentially significant evolution of organizational culture. So it should come as no surprise that such organizations will remain a distant vision until the leadership capabilities they demand are developed. 'The 1990s may be the period', suggest Sashkin and Burke, 'during which organization development and (a new sort of) management development are reconnected.'

I believe that this new sort of management development will focus on the roles, skills and tools for leadership in learning organizations. Undoubtedly, the ideas offered above are only a rough approximation of this new territory. The sooner we begin seriously exploring the territory, the sooner the initial map can be improved – and the sooner we will realize an age-old vision of leadership:

> *The wicked leader is he who the people despise. The good leader is he who the people revere. The great leader is he who the people say, 'We did it ourselves.'*

> Lao Tsu

Ambidextrous organizations: Managing evolutionary and revolutionary change

By Michael L. Tushman and Charles A. O'Reilly III[1]

All managers face problems in overcoming inertia and implementing innovation and change. But why is this problem such an enduring one? Organizations are filled with sensible people and usually led by smart managers. Why is anything but incremental change often so difficult for the most

successful organizations? And why are the patterns of success and failure so prevalent across industries and over time? To remain successful over long periods, managers and organizations must be ambidextrous – able to implement both incremental and revolutionary change.

Patterns in organization evolution

Across industries there is a pattern in which success often precedes failure. But industry-level studies aren't very helpful for illustrating what actually went wrong. Why are managers sometimes ineffective in making the transition from strength to strength? To understand this we need to look inside firms and understand the forces impinging on management as they wrestle with managing innovation and change. To do this, let's examine the history of two firms, RCA semiconductors and Seiko watches, as they dealt with the syndrome of success followed by failure.

The stark reality of the challenge of discontinuous change can be seen in Figure 8.3.1. This is a listing of the leading semiconductor firms over a 40-year period. In the mid-1950s, vacuum tubes represented roughly a $700 million market. At this time, the leading firms in the then state-of-the-art technology of vacuum tubes included great technology companies such as RCA, Sylvania, Raytheon and Westinghouse. Yet between 1955 and 1995, there was almost a complete turnover in industry leadership. With the advent of the transistor, a major technological discontinuity, we see the beginnings of a remarkable shake-out. By 1965, new firms such as Motorola and Texas Instruments had become important players while Sylvania and RCA had begun to fade. Over the next 20 years still other upstart companies like Intel, Toshiba and Hitachi became the new leaders while Sylvania and RCA exited the product class.

Why should this pattern emerge? Is it that managers and technologists in 1955 in firms like Westinghouse, RCA and Sylvania didn't understand the technology? This seems implausible. In fact, many vacuum tube producers did enter the transistor market, suggesting that they not only understood the technology, but saw it as important. RCA was initially successful at making the transition. While from the outside it appeared that they had committed themselves to transistors, the inside picture was very different.

Within RCA, there were bitter disputes about whether the company should enter the transistor business and cannibalize their profitable tube business. On one side, there were reasonable arguments that the transistor business was new and the profits uncertain. Others, without knowing whether transistors would be successful, felt that it was too risky not to pursue the new technology. But even if RCA were to enter the solid-state business, there were thorny issues about how to organize it within the company. How could they manage both technologies? Should the solid-state division report to the head of the electronics group, a person steeped in vacuum tube expertise?

With its great wealth of marketing, financial and technological resources, RCA decided to enter the business. Historically, it is common for successful firms to experiment with new technologies. Xerox, for

FIGURE 8.3.1   Semiconductor industry 1955–1995

	1955 (Vacuum Tubes)	1955 (Transistors)	1965 (Semiconductors)	1975 (Integrated Circuits)	1982 (VLSI)	1995 (Submicron)
1.	RCA	Hughes	TI	TI	Motorola	Intel
2.	Sylvania	Transitron	Fairchild	Fairchild	TI	NEC
3.	General Electric	Philco	Motorola	National	NEC	Toshiba
4.	Raytheon	Sylvania	GI	Intel	Hitachi	Hitachi
5.	Westinghouse	TI	GE	Motorola	National	Motorola
6.	Amperex	GE	RCA	Rockwell	Toshiba	Samsung
7.	National Video	RCA	Sprague	GI	Intel	TI
8.	Rawland	Westinghouse	Philco	RCA	Philips	Fujitsu
9.	Eimac	Motorola	Transitron	Philips	Fujitsu	Mitsubishi
10.	Lansdale	Clevite	Raytheon	AMD	Fairchild	Philips

Source: Adapted from R. Foster, *Innovation: The Attacker's Advantage* (New York, NY 1986).

example, developed user-interface and software technologies, yet left it to Apple and Microsoft to implement them. Western Union developed the technology for telephony and allowed American Bell (AT&T) to capture the benefits. Almost all relatively wealthy firms can afford to explore new technologies. Like many firms before them, RCA management recognized the problems of trying to play two different technological games but were ultimately unable to resolve them. In the absence of a clear strategy and the cultural differences required to compete in both markets, RCA failed.

In his study of this industry, Richard Foster (then a Director at McKinsey & Company) notes, 'Of the 10 leaders in vacuum tubes in 1955 only two were left in 1975. There were three variants of error in these case histories. First is the decision not to invest in the new technology. The second is to invest but picking the wrong technology. The third variant is cultural. Companies failed because of their inability to play two games at once: To be both effective defenders of what quickly became old technologies and effective attackers with new technologies.' Senior managers in these firms fell victim to their previous success and their inability to play two games simultaneously. New firms, like Intel and Motorola, were not saddled with this internal conflict and inertia. As they grew, they were able to re-create themselves, while other firms remained trapped.

In contrast to RCA, consider Hattori-Seiko's watch business. While Seiko was the dominant Japanese watch producer in the 1960s, they were a small player in global markets. Bolstered by an aspiration to be a global leader in the watch business, and informed by internal experimentation between alternative oscillation technologies (quartz, mechanical and tuning fork), Seiko's senior management team made a bold bet. In the mid-1960s, Seiko transformed itself from being merely a mechanical watch firm into being both a quartz and mechanical watch company. This move into low-cost, high-quality watches triggered wholesale change within Seiko and, in turn, within the worldwide watch industry. As transistors replaced vacuum tubes (to RCA's chagrin), quartz movement watches replaced mechanical watches. Even though the Swiss had invented both the quartz and tuning fork movements, at this juncture in history they moved to reinvest in mechanical movements. As Seiko and other Japanese firms prospered, the Swiss watch industry drastically suffered. By 1980, SSIH, the largest Swiss watch firm, was less than half the size of Seiko. Eventually, SSIH and Asuag, the two largest Swiss firms, went bankrupt. It would not be until after these firms were taken over by the Swiss

banks and transformed by Nicholas Hayek that the Swiss would move to recapture the watch market.

The real test of leadership, then, is to be able to compete successfully by both increasing the alignment or fit among strategy, structure, culture and processes, while simultaneously preparing for the inevitable revolutions required by discontinuous environmental change. This requires organizational and management skills to compete in a mature market (where cost, efficiency and incremental innovation are key) *and* to develop new products and services (where radical innovation, speed and flexibility are critical). A focus on either one of these skill sets is conceptually easy. Unfortunately, focusing on only one guarantees short-term success but long-term failure. Managers need to be able to do both at the same time, that is, they need to be ambidextrous. Juggling provides a metaphor. A juggler who is very good at manipulating a single ball is not interesting. It is only when the juggler can handle multiple balls at one time that his or her skill is respected.

These short examples are only two illustrations of the pattern by which organizations evolve: periods of incremental change punctuated by discontinuous or revolutionary change. Long-term success is marked by increasing alignment among strategy, structure, people and culture through incremental or evolutionary change punctuated by discontinuous or revolutionary change that requires the simultaneous shift in strategy, structure, people and culture. These discontinuous changes are almost always driven either by organizational performance problems or by major shifts in the organization's environment, such as technological or competitive shifts. Where those less successful firms (e.g., SSIH, RCA) react to environmental jolts, those more successful firms proactively initiate innovations that reshape their market (e.g., Seiko).

What's happening? Understanding patterns of organizational evolution

These patterns in organization evolution are not unique. Almost all successful organizations evolve through relatively long periods of incremental change punctuated by environmental shifts and revolutionary change. These discontinuities may be driven by technology, competitors, regulatory events, or significant changes in economic and political conditions. For example, deregulation in the financial services and airline industries led to waves of mergers and failures as firms scrambled to reorient themselves to the new competitive environment. Major political changes in Eastern Europe and South Africa have had a similar impact. The combination of the European Union and the emergence of global competition in the automobile and electronics industries has shifted the basis of competition in these markets. Technological change in microprocessors has altered the face of the computer industry.

The sobering fact is that the cliché about the increasing pace of change seems to be true. Sooner or later, discontinuities upset the congruence that has been a part of the organization's success. Unless their competitive environment remains stable – an increasingly unlikely condition in today's world – firms must confront revolutionary change. The underlying cause of this pattern can be found in an unlikely place: evolutionary biology.

Innovation patterns over time

For many years, biological evolutionary theory proposed that the process of adaptation occurred gradually over long time periods. The process was assumed to be one of variation, selection and retention. Variations occurred naturally within species across generations. Those variations that were most adapted to the environment would, over time, enable a species to survive and reproduce. This form would be selected in that it endured while less adaptable forms reproduced less productively and would diminish over time. For instance, if the world became colder and snowier, animals who were whiter and had heavier coats would be advantaged and more likely to survive. As climatic changes affected vegetation, those species with longer necks or stronger beaks might do better. In this way, variation led to adaptation and fitness, which was subsequently retained across generations. In this early view, the environment changed gradually and species adapted slowly to these changes. There is ample evidence that this view has validity.

But this perspective missed a crucial question: What happened if the environment was characterized, not by gradual change, but periodic discontinuities? What about rapid changes in temperature, or dramatic shifts in the availability of food? Under these conditions, a reliance on gradual change was a one-way ticket to extinction. Instead of slow change, discontinuities required a different version of Darwinian theory – that of punctuated equilibria in which long periods of gradual change were interrupted periodically by massive discontinuities. What then? Under these conditions, survival or selection goes to those species with the characteristics needed to exploit the new environment.

Evolution progresses through long periods of incremental change punctuated by brief periods of revolutionary or discontinuous change.

So it seems to be with organizations. An entire subfield of research on organizations has demonstrated many similarities between populations of insects and animals and populations of organizations. This field, known as 'organizational ecology', has successfully applied models of population ecology to the study of sets of organizations in areas as diverse as wineries, newspapers, automobiles, biotech companies and restaurants. The results confirm that populations of organizations are subject to ecological pressures in which they evolve through periods of incremental adaptation punctuated by discontinuities. Variations in organizational strategy and form are more or less suitable for different environmental conditions. Those organizations and managers who are most able to adapt to a given market or competitive environment will prosper. Over time, the fittest survive – until there is a major discontinuity. At that point, managers of firms are faced with the challenge of reconstituting their organizations to adjust to the new environment. Managers who try to adapt to discontinuities through incremental adjustment are unlikely to succeed. The processes of variation, selection and retention that winnow the fittest of animal populations seem to apply to organizations as well.

To understand how this dynamic affects organizations, we need to consider two fundamental ideas; how organizations grow and evolve, and how discontinuities affect this process. Armed with this understanding, we can then show how managers can cope with evolutionary and revolutionary change.

Organizational growth and evolution. There is a pattern that describes organizational growth. All organizations evolve following the familiar S-curve. For instance, consider the history of Apple Computers and how it grew. In its inception, Apple was not so much an organization as a small group of people trying to design, produce and sell a new product, the personal computer. With success, came the beginnings of a formal organization, assigned roles and responsibilities, some rudimentary systems for accounting and payroll, and a culture based on the shared expectations among employees about innovation, commitment and speed. Success at this stage was seen in terms of congruence among the strategy, structure, people and culture. Those who fitted the Apple values and subscribed to the cultural norms stayed. Those who found the Jobs and Wozniak vision too cultish left. This early structure was aligned with the strategy and the critical tasks needed to implement it. Success flowed not only from having a new product with desirable features, but also from the ability of the organization to design, manufacture, market and distribute the new PC. The systems in place tracked those outcomes and processes that were important for the implementation of a single product strategy. Congruence among the elements of the organization is a key to high performance across industries.

As the firm continued its successful growth, several inexorable changes occurred. First, it got larger. As this occurred, more structure and systems were added. Although this trend toward professionalization was resisted by Jobs (who referred to professional managers as 'bozos'), the new structures and procedures were required for efficiency and control. Without them, chaos would have reigned. As Apple got older, new norms were developed about what was important and acceptable and what would not be tolerated. The culture changed to reflect the new challenges. Success at Apple and at other firms is based on learning what works and what doesn't.

Inevitably, even Apple's strategy had to change. What used to be a single-product firm (selling the Apple PC and then its successor, the Apple II) now sold a broader range of products in increasingly competitive markets. Instead of a focused strategy, the emphasis shifted to a market-wide emphasis. Not only was Apple selling to personal computer users, but also to the educational and industrial markets. This strategic shift required further adjustment to the structure, people, culture and critical tasks. What worked in a smaller, more focused firm was no longer adequate for the larger, more differentiated Apple. Success at this phase of evolution required management's ability to realign the organization to insure congruence with the strategy. The well-publicized ousting of Steve Jobs by Apple's board of directors reflected the board's judgement that John Sculley had the skills necessary to lead a larger, more diversified company. Jobs's approach was fine for a smaller, more focused firm but inappropriate for the challenges Apple faced in the mid-1980s.

Over an even longer period of success, there are inevitably more changes – sometimes driven by technology, sometimes by competition, customers, or regulation, sometimes by new strategies and ways of competing. As the product class matures, the basis of competition shifts. While in the early stages of a product class, competition is based on product variation, in the later stages competition shifts to features, efficiency, and cost. In the evolution of Apple, this can be seen as the IBM PC and the clones emerged. The Windows operating system loosened the grip Apple had

maintained on the easy-to-use graphical interface and triggered a battle between three incompatible operating systems – the Mac, IBM's OS/2, and Microsoft Windows. Once Windows became the industry standard in operating systems, the basis of competition shifted to cost, quality and efficiency. Faced with these realities, Apple managers once again had to re-balance the congruence among strategy, structure, people and culture. Success comes from being able to outdo the competition in this new environment. So the board of directors replaced Sculley as CEO in 1994 with Michael Spindler, who was seen as having the operational skills needed to run the company in a mature market. Spindler's task was to emphasize the efficiencies and lower margins required in today's markets and reshape Apple to compete in this new market. With Apple's performance stagnant, its board chose a turnaround expert, Gil Amelio, to finish what Spindler could not do.

Notice how Apple evolved over a 20-year period. Incremental or evolutionary change was punctuated by discontinuous or revolutionary change as the firm moved through the three stages of growth in the product class; innovation, differentiation and maturity. Each of these stages required different competencies, strategies, structures, cultures and leadership skills. These changes are what drive performance. But while absolutely necessary for short-term success, incremental change is not sufficient for long-term success. It is not by chance that Steve Jobs was successful at Apple until the market became more differentiated and demanded the skills of John Sculley. Nor is it surprising that, as the industry consolidated and competition emphasized costs, operations-oriented managers such as Michael Spindler and, in turn, Gil Amelio were selected to reorient Apple.

To succeed over the long haul, firms have to periodically reorient themselves by adopting new strategies and structures that are necessary to accommodate changing environmental conditions. These shifts often occur through discontinuous changes – simultaneous shifts in strategy, structures, skills and culture. If an environment is stable and changes only gradually, as is the case in industries such as cement, it is possible for an organization to evolve slowly through continuous incremental change. But, many managers have learned (to their stockholders' chagrin) that slow evolutionary change in a fast-changing world is, as it was for the dinosaurs, a path to the boneyard.

Technology cycles.   Although organizational growth by itself can lead to a periodic need for discontinuous change, there is another more fundamental process occurring that results in punctuated change. This is a pervasive phenomenon that occurs across industries and is not widely appreciated by managers. Yet it is critical to understanding when and why revolutionary change is necessary: this is the dynamic of product, service and process innovation, dominant designs, and substitution events which together make up technology cycles. Figure 8.3.2 shows the general outline of this process.

In any product or service class (e.g., microprocessors, automobiles, baby diapers, cash management accounts) there is a common pattern of competition that describes the development of the class over time. As shown in Figure 8.3.2, technology cycles begin with a proliferation of innovation in products or services as the new product or service gains acceptance. Think, for example, of the introduction of VCRs. Initially, only a few customers bought them. Over time, as demand increased, there was increasing competition between Beta and VHS. At some point, a design emerged that became the standard preferred by customers (i.e., VHS). Once this occurred, the basis of competition shifted to price and features, not basic product or service design. The emergence of this *dominant design* transforms competition in the product class. Once it is clear that a dominant design has emerged, the basis of competition shifts to process innovation, driving down costs and adding features. Instead of competing through product or service innovation, successful strategies now emphasize compatibility with the standard and productivity improvement. This competition continues until there is a major new product, service or process

substitution event and the technology cycle kicks off again as the basis of competition shifts back again to product or service variation (e.g., CDs replacing audio tapes). As technology cycles evolve, bases of competition shift within the market. As organizations change their strategies, they must also realign their organizations to accomplish the new strategic objectives. This usually requires a revolutionary change.

A short illustration from the development of the automobile will help show how dramatic these changes can be for organizations. At the turn of the century, bicycles and horse-driven carriages were threatened by the 'horseless carriage', soon to be called the automobile. Early in this new product class there was substantial competition among alternative technologies. For instance, there were several competing alternative energy sources – steam, battery and internal combustion engines. There were also different steering mechanisms and arrangements for passenger compartments. In a fairly short period of time, however, there emerged a consensus that certain features were to be standard – that is, a dominant design emerged. This consisted of an internal combustion engine, steering wheel on the left (in the US), brake pedal on the right, and clutch on the left (this dominant design was epitomized in the Ford Model T). Once this standard emerged, the basis of competition shifted from variations in what an automobile looked like and how it was powered, to features and cost. The new competitive arena emphasized lower prices and differentiated market segments, not product

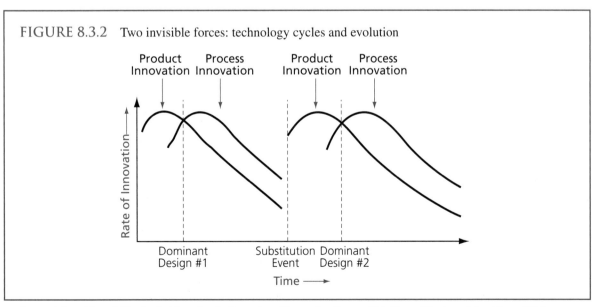

FIGURE 8.3.2   Two invisible forces: technology cycles and evolution

Source: Adapted from J. Utterback, *Mastering the Dynamics of Innovation* (Boston, MA; Harvard Business School Press, 1994).

variation. The imperative for managers was to change their strategies and organizations to compete in this market. Those that were unable to manage this transition failed. Similar patterns can be seen in almost all product classes (e.g., computers, telephones, fast foods, retail stores).

With a little imagination, it is easy to feel what the managerial challenges are in this environment. Holding aside the pressures of growth and success, managers must continually readjust their strategies and realign their organizations to reflect the underlying dynamics of technological change in their markets. These changes are not driven by fad or fashion but reflect the imperatives of fundamental change in the technology. This dynamic is a powerful cause of punctuated equilibria and can demand revolutionary rather than incremental change. This pattern occurs across industries as diverse as computers and cement, the only issue is the frequency with which these cycles repeat themselves. Faced with a discontinuity, the option of incremental change is not likely to be viable. The danger is that, facing a discontinuous change, firms that have been successful may suffer from life-threatening inertia – inertia that results from the very congruence that made the firm successful in the first place.

The success syndrome: Congruence as a managerial trap

Successful companies learn what works well and incorporate this into their operations. This is what organizational learning is about; using feedback from the market to continually refine the organization to get better and better at accomplishing its mission. A lack of congruence (or internal inconsistency in strategy, structure, culture and people) is usually associated with a firm's current performance problems. Further, since the fit between strategy, structure, people and processes is never perfect, achieving congruence is an ongoing process requiring continuous improvement and incremental change. With evolutionary change, managers are able to incrementally alter their organizations. Given that these changes are comparatively small, the incongruence injected by the change is controllable. The process of making incremental changes is well known and the uncertainty created for people affected by such changes is within tolerable limits. The overall system adapts, but it is not transformed.

When done effectively, evolutionary change of this sort is a crucial part of short-term success. But there is a dark side to this success. As we described with Apple,

success resulted in the company becoming larger and older. Older, larger firms develop structural and cultural inertia – the organizational equivalent of high cholesterol. As companies grow, they develop structures and systems to handle the increased complexity of the work. These structures and systems are interlinked so that proposed changes become more difficult, more costly and require more time to implement, especially if they are more than small, incremental modifications. This results in *structural inertia* – a resistance to change rooted in the size, complexity and interdependence in the organization's structures, systems, procedures and processes.

Quite different and significantly more pervasive than structural inertia is the *cultural inertia* that comes from age and success. As organizations get older, part of their learning is embedded in the shared expectations about how things are to be done. These are sometimes seen in the informal norms, values, social networks and in myths, stories and heroes that have evolved over time. The more successful an organization has been, the more institutionalized or ingrained these norms, values and lessons become. The more institutionalized these norms, values and stories are, the greater the cultural inertia – the greater the organizational complacency and arrogance. In relatively stable environments, the firm's culture is a critical component of its success. Culture is an effective way of controlling and coordinating people without elaborate and rigid formal control systems. Yet, when confronted with discontinuous change, the very culture that fostered success can quickly become a significant barrier to change. When Lou Gerstner took over as CEO at IBM, he recognized that simply crafting a new strategy was not the solution to IBM's predicament. In his view, 'Fixing the culture is the most critical – and the most difficult – part of a corporate transformation.' Cultural inertia, because it is so ephemeral and difficult to attack directly, is a key reason managers often fail to successfully introduce revolutionary change – even when they know that it is needed.

Ambidextrous organizations: Mastering evolutionary and revolutionary change

The dilemma confronting managers and organizations is clear. In the short run they must constantly increase the fit or alignment of strategy, structure and culture. This is the world of evolutionary change. But this is not enough for sustained success. In the long run, managers may be required to destroy the very alignment that has made their organizations successful. For managers, this means operating part of the time in a world characterized by periods of relative stability and incremental innovation, and part of the time in a world characterized by revolutionary change. These contrasting managerial demands require that managers periodically destroy what has been created in order to reconstruct a new organization better suited for the next wave of competition or technology.

Ambidextrous organizations are needed if the success paradox is to be overcome. The ability to simultaneously pursue both incremental and discontinuous innovation and change results from hosting multiple contradictory structures, processes and cultures within the same firm. There are good examples of companies and managers who have succeeded in balancing these tensions. To illustrate more concretely how firms can do this, consider three successful ambidextrous organizations, Hewlett-Packard, Johnson & Johnson and ABB (Asea Brown Boveri). Each of these has been able to compete in mature market segments through incremental innovation and in emerging markets and technologies through discontinuous innovation. Each has been successful at winning by engaging in both evolutionary and revolutionary change.

At one level they are very different companies. HP competes in markets like instruments, computers and networks. J&J is in consumer products, pharmaceuticals and professional medical products ranging from sutures to endoscopic surgical equipment. ABB sells power plants, electrical transmission equipment, transportation systems and environmental controls. Yet each of them has been able to periodically renew itself and to produce streams of innovation. HP has gone from an instrument company to a minicomputer firm to a personal computer and network company. J&J has moved from consumer products to pharmaceuticals. ABB transformed itself from a slow heavy engineering company based primarily in Sweden and Switzerland to an aggressive global competitor with major investments in Eastern Europe and the Far East. In spite of their differences, each has been ambidextrous in similar ways.

Organizational architectures

Although the combined size of these three companies represents over 350,000 employees, each has found a common way to remain small by emphasizing autonomous groups. For instance, J&J has over 165 separate operating companies that scramble relentlessly for new products and markets. ABB relies on over 5,000 profit centres with an average of 50 people in each.

These centres operate like small businesses. HP has over 50 separate divisions and a policy of splitting divisions whenever a unit gets larger than a thousand or so people. The logic in these organizations is to keep units small and autonomous so that employees feel a sense of ownership and are responsible for their own results. This encourages a culture of autonomy and risk taking that could not exist in a large, centralized organization. In the words of Ralph Larsen, CEO of J&J, this approach 'provides a sense of ownership and responsibility for a business you simply cannot get any other way'.

But the reliance on small, autonomous units is not gained at the expense of firm size or speed in execution. These companies also retain the benefits of size, especially in marketing and manufacturing. ABB continually re-evaluates where it locates its worldwide manufacturing sites. J&J uses its brand name and marketing might to leverage new products and technologies. HP uses its relationships with retailers developed from its printer business to market and distribute its new personal computer line. But these firms accomplish this without the top-heavy staffs found at other firms. Barnevik reduced ABB's hierarchy to four levels and a headquarters staff of 150, and purposely keeps the structure fluid. At J&J headquarters, there are roughly a thousand people, but no strategic planning is done by corporate. The role of the centre is to set the vision and review the performance of the 165 operating companies. At HP, the former CEO, John Young, recognized in the early 1990s that the more centralized structure that HP had adopted in the 1980s to coordinate their minicomputer business had resulted in a suffocating bureaucracy that was no longer appropriate. He wiped it out, flattening the hierarchy and dramatically reducing the role of the centre.

In these companies, size is used to leverage economies of scale and scope, not to become a checker and controller that slows the organization down. The focus is on keeping decisions as close to the customer or the technology as possible. The role of headquarters is to facilitate operations and make them go faster and better. Staff have only the expertise that the field wants and needs. Reward systems are designed to be appropriate to the nature of the business unit and emphasize results and risk taking. Barnevik characterizes this as his 7-3 formula; better to make decisions quickly and be right seven out of ten times than waste time trying to find a perfect solution. At J&J this is expressed as a tolerance for certain types of failure; a tolerance that extends to congratulating managers who take informed risks, even if they fail. There is a delicate balance among size, autonomy, teamwork and speed which these ambidextrous organizations are able to engineer. An important part of the solution is massive decentralization of decision making, but with consistency attained through individual accountability, information sharing and strong financial control. But why doesn't this result in fragmentation and a loss of synergy? The answer is found in the use of social control.

Multiple cultures

A second commonality across these firms is their reliance on strong social controls. They are simultaneously tight and loose. They are tight in that the corporate culture in each is broadly shared and emphasizes norms critical for innovation such as openness, autonomy, initiative and risk taking. The culture is loose in that the manner in which these common values are expressed varies according to the type of innovation required. At HP, managers value the openness and consensus needed to develop new technologies. Yet, when implementation is critical, managers recognize that this consensus can be fatal. One senior manager in charge of bringing out a new workstation prominently posted a sign saying, 'This is not a democracy.' At J&J, the emphasis on autonomy allows managers to routinely go against the wishes of senior management, sometimes with big successes and sometimes with failures. Yet, in the changing hospital supply sector of their business, managers recognized that the cherished J&J autonomy was stopping these companies from coordinating the service demanded by their hospital customers. So, in this part of J&J, a decision was made to take away some of the autonomy and centralize services. CEO Larsen refers to this as J&J companies having common standards but unique personalities.

A common overall culture is the glue that holds these companies together. The key in these firms is a reliance on a strong, widely shared corporate culture to promote integration across the company and to encourage identification and sharing of information and resources – something that would never occur without shared values. The culture also provides consistency and promotes trust and predictability. Whether it is the Credo at J&J, the HP Way, or ABB's Policy Bible, these norms and values provide the glue that keeps these organizations together. Yet, at the same time, individual units entertain widely varying subcultures appropriate to their particular businesses. For example, although the HP Way is visible in all HP units worldwide, there are distinct differences between the new video server unit and an old line instrument division.

What constitutes risk taking at a mature division is different than the risk taking emphasized at a unit struggling with a brand new technology. At J&J, the Credo's emphasis on customers and employees can be seen as easily in the Philippines as in corporate headquarters in New Brunswick, New Jersey. But the operating culture in the Tylenol division is distinctly more conservative than the culture in a new medical products company.

This tight–loose aspect of the culture is crucial for ambidextrous organizations. It is supported by a common vision and by supportive leaders who both encourage the culture and know enough to allow appropriate variations to occur across business units. These companies promote both local autonomy and risk taking and ensure local responsibility and accountability through strong, consistent financial control systems. Managers aren't second-guessed by headquarters. Strategy flows from the bottom up. Thus, at HP the $7 billion printer business emerged not because of strategic foresight and planning at HP's headquarters, but rather due to the entrepreneurial flair of a small group of managers who had the freedom to pursue what was believed to be a small market. The same approach allows J&J and ABB to enter small niche markets or develop unproven technologies without the burdens of a centralized bureaucratic control system. On the other hand, in return for the autonomy they are granted, there are strong expectations of performance. Managers who don't deliver are replaced.

Ambidextrous managers

Managing units that pursue widely different strategies and that have varied structures and cultures is a juggling act not all managers are comfortable with. At ABB, this role is described as 'preaching and persuading'. At HP, managers are low-key, modest, team players who have learned how to manage this tension over their long tenures with the company. At HP, they also lead by persuasion. 'As CEO my job is to encourage people to work together, to experiment, to try things, but I can't order them to do it', says Lew Platt. Larsen at J&J echoes this theme, emphasizing the need for lower level managers to come up with solutions and encouraging reasonable failures. Larsen claims that the role is one of a symphony conductor rather than a general.

One of the explanations for this special ability is the relatively long tenure managers have in these organizations and the continual reinforcement of the social control system. Often, these leaders are low-keyed but embody the culture and act as visible symbols of it. As a group the senior team continually reinforces the core values of autonomy, teamwork, initiative, accountability and innovation. They ensure that the organization avoids becoming arrogant and remains willing to learn from its competitors. Observers of all three of these companies have commented on their modesty or humility in constantly striving to renew themselves. Rather than becoming complacent, these organizations are guided by leaders who venerate the past but are willing to change continuously to meet the future.

The bottom line is that ambidextrous organizations learn by the same mechanism that sometimes kills successful firms: variation, selection and retention. They promote variation through strong efforts to decentralize, to eliminate bureaucracy, to encourage individual autonomy and accountability, and to experiment and take risks. This promotes wide variations in products, technologies and markets. It is what allows the managers of an old HP instrument division to push their technology and establish a new division dedicated to video servers. These firms also select 'winners' in markets and technologies by staying close to their customers, by being quick to respond to market signals, and by having clear mechanisms to 'kill' products and projects. This selection process allowed the development of computer printers at HP to move from a venture that was begun without formal approval to the point where it now accounts for almost 40 per cent of HP's profits. Finally, technologies, products, markets, and even senior managers are retained by the market, not by a remote, inwardly focused central staff many hierarchical levels removed from real customers. The corporate vision provides the compass by which senior managers can make decisions about which of the many alternative businesses and technologies to invest in, but the market is the ultimate arbiter of the winners and losers. Just as success or failure in the marketplace is Darwinian, so too is the method by which ambidextrous organizations learn. They have figured out how to harness this power within their companies and organize and manage accordingly.

Summary

Managers must be prepared to cannibalize their own business at times of industry transitions. While this is easy in concept, these organizational transitions are quite difficult in practice. Success brings with it inertia and dynamic conservatism. Four hundred years ago, Niccolo Machiavelli noted, 'There is no more delicate matter to take in hand, nor more dangerous to conduct, nor more doubtful in its success, than to be a leader in the introduction of changes. For he who innovates will have for enemies all those who are well off under the old order of things, and only lukewarm supporters in those who might be better off under the new.'

While there are clear benefits to proactive change, only a small minority of far-sighted firms initiate discontinuous change before a performance decline. Part of this stems from the risks of proactive change. One reason for RCA's failure to compete in the solid-state market or for SSIH's inability to compete in quartz movements came from the divisive internal disputes over the risks of sacrificing a certain revenue stream from vacuum tubes and mechanical watches for the uncertain profits from transistors and quartz watches. However, great managers are willing to take this step. Andy Grove of Intel puts it succinctly, 'There is at least one point in the history of any company when you have to change dramatically to rise to the next performance level. Miss the moment and you start to decline.'

REFERENCES

Abegglen, J.C. and Stalk, G. (1985) *Kaisha, The Japanese Corporation*, New York: Basic Books.

Aldrich, H. (1999) *Organizations Evolving*, London: Sage.

Allison, G.T. (1969) 'Conceptual Models and The Cuban Missile Crisis', *The American Political Science Review*, 3(September), pp. 689–718.

Anderson, P. and Tushman, M. (1990) 'Technological discontinuities and dominant designs: A cyclical model of technological change', *Administrative Science Quarterly*, 35, pp. 604–633.

Argyris, C. (1990) *Overcoming Organizational Defenses: Facilitating Organizational Learning*, Boston, MA: Prentice Hall.

Arthur, W.B. (1996) 'Increasing Returns and the New World of Business', *Harvard Business Review*, 74(4, July–August), pp. 100–109.

Baden-Fuller, C. and Stopford, J.M. (1992) *Rejuvenating the Mature Business*, London: Routledge.

Bartlett, C.A. and Ghoshal, S. (1995) *Transnational Management: Text, Cases, and Readings in Cross-Border Management* (2nd edn), Homewood, IL: R.D. Irwin Inc.

Bate, P. (1994) *Strategies for Cultural Change*, Oxford: Butterworth-Heinemann.

Boeker, W. (1992) 'Power and Managerial Dismissal: Scapegoating at the Top', *Administrative Science Quarterly*, 37(4), pp. 538–547.

Bower, J.L. and Christensen, C.M. (1995) 'Disruptive Technologies: Catching the Wave', *Harvard Business Review*, 73(1, January–February), pp. 43–53.

Calori, R., Valla, J-P. and de Woot, P. (1994) 'Common Characteristics: The Ingredients of European Management', in: R. Calori and P. de Woot (eds) *A European Management Model: Beyond Diversity*, Hemel Hempstead: Prentice Hall.

Day, D.L. (1994) 'Raising Radicals: Different Processes for Championing Innovative Corporate Ventures', *Organization Science*, 5(2, May), pp. 148–172.

Duncan, R.B. (1976) 'The Ambidextrous Organization: Designing Dual Structures for Innovation', in: R.H. Kilmann, L.R. Pondy and D.P. Slevin (eds) *The Management of Organizational Design*, New York: Elsevier North Holland, pp. 167–188.

Eisenhardt, K.M. and Brown, S.L. (1997) 'The Art of Continuous Change: Linking Complexity Theory and Time-Paced Evolution in Relentlessly Shifting Organizations', *Administrative Science Quarterly*, 42(1, March), pp. 1–34.

Forrester, J.W. (2003) 'Dynamic models of economic systems and industrial organizations', *System Dynamics Review*, 19(4), pp. 329–345.

Foster, R. (1986) *Innovation: The Attacker's Advantage*, New York: Summit Books.

Fredrickson, J.W., Hambrick, D.C. and Baumrin, S. (1988) 'A Model of CEO Dismissal', *Academy of Management Review*, 13(2, April), pp. 255–270.

Freeman, R.E. (1984) *Strategic Management: A Stakeholder Approach*, Boston: Pitman/Ballinger.

Gersick, C.J.G. (1991) 'Revolutionary Change Theories: A Multilevel Exploration of the Punctuated Equilibrium Paradigm', *Academy of Management Review*, 17(1, January), pp. 10–36.

Ghemawat, P. (1991) *Commitment: The Dynamic of Strategy*, New York: Free Press.

Greenleaf, R.K. (1977) *Servant Leadership: A Journey into the Nature of Legitimate Power and Greatness*, New York: Paulist Press.

Greenwood, R. and Hinings, C.R. (1996) 'Understanding Radical Organizational Change: Bringing Together the Old and the New Institutionalism', *Academy of Management Review*, 21(4, October), pp. 1022–1054.

Greiner, L.E. (1972) 'Evolution and Revolution as Organizations Grow', *Harvard Business Review*, 50(4, July–August), pp. 37–46.

Grinyer, P.H., Mayes, D. and McKiernan, P. (1987) *Sharpbenders: The Secrets of Unleashing Corporate Potential*, Oxford: Blackwell.

Hambrick, D.C. and Mason, P. (1984) 'Upper Echelons: The Organization as a Reflection of Its Top Managers', *Academy of Management Review*, 9(2, April), pp. 193–206.

Hamel, G. (1996) 'Strategy as Revolution', *Harvard Business Review*, 74(4, July–August), pp. 69–82.

Hammer, M. (1990) 'Reengineering Work: Don't Automate, Obliterate', *Harvard Business Review*, 68(4, July–August), pp. 104–111.

Hammer, M. and Champy, J. (1993) *Reengineering the Corporation: A Manifesto for Business Revolution*, New York: HarperCollins.

Hannan, M.T. and Freeman, J. (1984) 'Structural Inertia and Organizational Change', *American Sociological Review*, 49(2, April), pp. 149–164.

Hayes, R.H. (1985) 'Strategic Planning: Forward in Reverse?', *Harvard Business Review*, 63(6, November–December), pp. 111–119.

Hitt, M.A., Dacin, M.T., Tyler, B.B. and Park, D. (1997) 'Understanding the Differences in Korean and US Executives' Strategic Orientations', *Strategic Management Journal*, 18, pp. 159–167.

Hofstede, G. (1993) 'Cultural Constraints in Management Theories', *Academy of Management Executive*, 7(1), pp. 8–21.

Johnson, G. (1987) *Strategic Change and the Management Process*, Oxford: Basil Blackwell.

Johnson, G. (1988) 'Rethinking Incrementalism', *Strategic Management Journal*, 9(1, January–February), pp. 75–91.

Kagono, T., Nonaka, I., Sakakibara, K. and Okumura, A. (1985) *Strategic vs. Evolutionary Management: A US-Japan Comparison of Strategy and Organization*, Amsterdam: North Holland.

Kanter, R.M. (1989) *When Giants Learn to Dance*, New York: Simon & Schuster.

Kessler, E.H. and Chakrabarthi, A.K. (1996) 'Innovation Speed: A Conceptual Model of Context, Antecedents, and Outcomes', *Academy of Management Review*, 21(4, October), pp. 1143–1191.

Kogut, B. (ed.) (1993) *Country Competitiveness: Technology and the Organizing of Work*, Oxford: Oxford University Press.

Krüger, W. (1996) 'Implementation: The Core Task of Change Management', *CEMS Business Review*, 1, pp. 77–96.

Lawrence, P.R. and Lorsch, J.W. (1967) *Organization and the Environment*, Boston, MA: Harvard Business School.

Leonard-Barton, D. (1995) *Wellsprings of Knowledge*, Boston, MA: Harvard Business School Press.

Lewin, K. (1947) 'Frontiers in Group Dynamics: Social Equilbria and Social Change', *Human Relations*, 1, pp. 5–41.

Lieberman, M.B. and Montgomery, D.B. (1988) 'First Mover Advantages', *Strategic Management Journal*, 9(1, January–February), pp. 41–58.

Lieberman, M.B. and Montgomery, D.B. (1998) 'First-Mover (Dis)Advantages: Retrospective and Link with the Resource-Based View', *Strategic Management Journal*, 19(12, December), pp. 1111–1126.

Maidique, M.A. (1980) 'Entrepreneurs, Champions, and Technological Innovation', *Sloan Management Review*, 21, pp. 18–31.

March, J.G. and Simon, H.A. (1958) *Organizations*, New York: Wiley.

Markides, C. (1998) 'Strategic Innovation in Established Companies', *Sloan Management Review*, 39(3), pp. 31–42.

Meyer, A., Brooks, G. and Goes, J. (1990) 'Environmental Jolts and Industry Revolutions: Organizational Responses to Discontinuous Change', *Strategic Management Journal*, 11(2, February), pp. 93–110.

Meyer, A.D. (1982) 'Adapting to Environmental Jolts', *Administrative Science Quarterly*, 27(4, December), pp. 515–537.

Miller, D. (1990) *The Icarus Paradox: How Excellent Companies Bring About Their Own Downfall*, New York: Harper Business.

Miller, D. and Friesen, P. (1984) *Organizations: A Quantum View*, Englewood Cliffs, NJ: Prentice Hall.

Mintzberg, H. (1991) 'The Effective Organization: Forces and Forms', *Sloan Management Review*, 32(2, Winter), pp. 54–67.

Mintzberg, H. (1994) *The Rise and Fall of Strategic Planning*, Englewood Cliffs, NJ: Prentice Hall.

Mintzberg, H. and Norman, R.A. (2001) *Reframing Business: When the Map Changes the Landscape*, New York: Wiley.

Morgan, G. (1986) *Images of Organization*, London: Sage.

Nelson, R.R. and Winter, S.G. (1982) *An Evolutionary Theory of Economic Change*, Cambridge, MA: Harvard University Press.

Nonaka, I. (1988) 'Creating Organizational Order Out of Chaos: Self-Renewal in Japanese Firms', *California Management Review*, 30(3, Spring), pp. 9–18.

Oliver, C. (1991) 'Strategic Responses to Institutional Processes', *Academy of Management Review*, 16(1, January), pp. 145–179.

Ouchi, W. (1981) *Theory Z: How American Business Can Meet the Japanese Challenge*, Reading, MA: Addison-Wesley.

Pascale, R.T. and Athos, A.G. (1981) *The Art of Japanese Management*, New York: Simon & Schuster.

Pettigrew, A.M. (1988) *The Management of Strategic Change*, Oxford: Basil Blackwell.

Pfeffer, J. and Sutton, R.I. (1999) 'Knowing "What" to Do is Not Enough: Turning Knowledge Into Action', *California Management Review*, 42(1, Fall), pp. 83–108.

Pondy, L.R., Boland, J.R. and Thomas, H. (eds) (1988) *Managing Ambiguity and Change*, New York: Wiley.

Powell, W.W. (1991) 'Expanding the scope of Institutional Analysis', in: W.W. Powell and P.J. DiMaggio (eds) *The New Institutionalism in Organizational Analysis*, Chicago, IL: University of Chicago Press, pp. 183–123.

Quinn, J.B. (1980) *Strategies for Change*, Homewood, IL: Irwin.

Sashkin, M. and Burke, W.W. (1990) 'Organization development in the 1980s', *Journal of Management*, 13(2), pp. 393–417.

Schein, E.H. (1985) *Organizational Culture and Leadership*, San Francisco, CA: Jossey-Bass.

Schumpeter, J.A. (1950) *Capitalism, Socialism and Democracy* (3rd edn), New York: Harper and Brothers.

Selznick, P. (1957) *Leadership in Administration*, New York: Harper & Row.

Senge, P.M. (1990a) 'The Leader's New Work: Building Learning Organizations', *Sloan Management Review*, 32(1, Fall), pp. 7–23.

Senge, P. (1990b) *The Fifth Discipline: The Art and Practice of the Learning Organization*, New York: Doubleday/Currency.

Shapiro, C. and Varian, H. (1998) *Information Rules: A Strategic Guide to the Network Economy*, Cambridge, MA: Harvard Business School Press.

Stacey, R.D. (1993) 'Strategy as Order Emerging from Chaos', *Long Range Planning*, 26(1), pp. 10–17.

Stalk, G., Evans, P. and Shulman, L.E. (1992) 'Competing on Capabilities: The New Rules of Corporate Strategy', *Harvard Business Review*, 70(2, March–April), pp. 57–69.

Stinchcombe, A.L. (1965) 'Social Structure and Organizations', in: J.G. March (ed.) *Handbook of Organizations*, Chicago, IL: Rand McNally, pp. 142–193.

Strebel, P. (1992) *Breakpoints: How Managers Exploit Radical Business Change*, Boston, MA: Harvard Business School Press.

Strebel, P. (1994) 'Choosing the Right Change Path', *California Management Review*, 36(2, Winter), pp. 29–51.

Teece, D.J., Pisano, G. and Shuen, A. (1997) 'Dynamic Capabilities and Strategic Management', *Strategic Management Journal*, 18(7, August), pp. 509–533.

Thompson, J.D. (1967) *Organizations in Action*, New York: McGraw-Hill.

Tidd, J., Bessant, J. and Pavitt, K. (1997) *Managing Innovation: Integrating Technological, Market and Organizational Change*, Chichester: Wiley.

Trice, H.M. and Beyer, J.M. (1993) *The Cultures of Work Organizations*, Englewood Cliffs, NJ: Prentice Hall.

Tushman, M.L. and O'Reilly III, C.A. (1996) 'Ambidextrous Organizations: Managing Evolutionary and Revolutionary Change', *California Management Review*, 38(4, Summer), pp. 8–30.

Tushman, M.L. and O'Reilly III, C.A. (1997) *Winning Through Innovation: A Practical Guide to Leading Organizational Change and Renewal*, Boston, MA: Harvard Business School.

Tushman, M.L., Newman, W.H. and Romanelli, E. (1986) 'Convergence and Upheaval: Managing the Unsteady Pace of Organizational Evolution', *California Management Review*, 29(1, Fall), pp. 29–44.

Utterback, J. (1994) *Mastering the Dynamics of Innovation*, Boston, MA: Harvard Business School Press.

Wack, P. (1985) 'Scenarios: Uncharted Waters Ahead', *Harvard Business Review,* September–October.

Waterman, R.H., Peters, T.J. and Phillips, J.R. (1980) 'Structure is Not Organization', *Business Horizons*, 23(June), pp. 14–26.

STRATEGIC INNOVATION

There is nothing more difficult to take in hand, more perilous to conduct, or more uncertain in its success, than to take the lead in the introduction of a new order of things. Because the innovator has for enemies all those who have done well under the old conditions, and lukewarm defenders in those who may do well under the new.

Niccolo Machiavelli (1469–1527); Florentine statesman and political philosopher

INTRODUCTION

In Chapter 8, the magnitude and pace of strategic change in aligning the business model and organizational system to the external environment have been addressed. The distinction has been made between operational change that aims at maintaining the current business model and organizational system, and strategic changes that are directed at aligning them with the firm's environment. Strategizing managers are particularly concerned with business model changes, as this affects the way the company creates value and competes in the business environment (see also Chapter 4).

Changing a firm's business model to defend and create a sustainable advantage over the competition is referred to as strategic innovation. It relates to all technologies, resources, activities and processes by which new ideas are generated and converted into products and services that increase satisfaction of current customers and attract new customers. Strategists innovate to strengthen the firm's competitive position, a process that is both necessary and unending due to the dynamics of the competitive game. Hence this chapter deals with the enduring, and arguably the most challenging, topic for strategizing managers of strategic innovation.

Although a large and increasing number of studies address the topic of strategic innovation, definitions either differ widely or remain implicit. In this chapter, strategic innovation is defined as renewing the firm's business model to create or sustain a competitive advantage (Amit and Zott, 2001, 2012). Ultimately, strategic innovation aims to achieve a successful long-term corporate life.

THE ISSUE OF STRATEGIC RENEWAL

The idea of eternal life has always appealed to people in many parts of the world, including Europe, China and India. For centuries, people have been searching for the golden formula of an elixir of life that would provide eternal life and eternal youth. Indeed, it is a fascinating thought that by just consuming a drink, even if it would only work at a defined moment, in a specific place and from a certain cup, we would live forever. Because the idea is so appealing, there have been blooming markets of supply – the alchemists – and demand – usually rich and powerful people. It is unlikely that an elixir of life has even been found efficacious, however we are quite sure that people have died after consuming an acclaimed elixir. The British historian Joseph Needham (Needham *et al.,* 1976) compiled a list of Chinese emperors whose death was likely caused due to elixir poisoning. Chinese interest in alchemy and the elixir of life vanished with the rise of Buddhism, which claimed to have alternative avenues to eternity.

Although the health industry is working hard on lengthening human life through research and technological innovations, eternal life is most likely not achievable. For organizations the situation is different, but not in the sense that they can exist forever. Yet, organizations have the ability to stay young and vital for hundreds of years. In a study, initiated by Royal Dutch Shell, on large companies older than 100 years and important in their industry, De Geus (1997) found 40 large and dominant companies over 100 years old. The oldest company that De Geus and his team found is the Swedish paper, pulp and chemical manufacturer Stora (that in 1998 merged with the Finnish company Enzo to form the new entity Stora Enzo), which started as a copper mine in central Sweden over 700 years ago. As second-oldest company, De Geus nominated the Japanese Sumitomo with origins in a copper casting shop founded by Riemon Soga in the year 1590. Furthermore, De Geus estimated the average life expectancy of multinational Fortune 500 corporations between 40 and 50 years, and speculated that the natural average lifespan of a corporation could be as long as two or three centuries. So firms can potentially become much older than humans, yet the average age of companies turns out to be much lower. The question is thus, why is it so difficult to renew the company?

Characteristics of strategic innovation

Strategic renewal processes are arguably *the* most complex processes to bring to a successful ending, the main reason being that strategic innovation consists of four different processes that are already challenging on their own, and therefore extremely demanding in combination. The following paragraph discusses the constituting elements of strategic innovation: strategizing, entrepreneuring, changing and investing processes (see Figure 9.1).

Strategic innovation as a strategizing process.   In strategic renewal processes, strategizing managers must be aware of the unfolding opportunities and threats in the environment, and the evolving strengths and weaknesses of the organization. They must be able to constantly re-evaluate their views and generate a new understanding of the competitive situation, often against the company's dominant logic. For strategists a fundamental question in renewal processes is how to avoid getting stuck with an outdated cognitive map (see also Chapter 2). How can they avoid the danger of building up a flawed picture of their industry, their markets and themselves?

While creative thinking is imperative for generating a new understanding of the current situation, it is at the essence of developing a new business model. Creativity is in every human being, albeit at different levels as not everyone is equally talented and lives a life that pushes their creative talent to the limit. Everyone can learn to paint, but few will find their paintings displayed in a museum. Likewise the level of creativity that business model innovation requires is quite scarce. Moreover, creativity appears in a variety of modes. While artists have the freedom to choose any kind of material, form and subject with no imposed time constraints, architects are bound by available space, functionality, budget and time. Being engaged in strategic renewal, strategists are like architects, working in a context of 'bounded creativity'. Constrained by, for example, lead time and resource availability, the context of strategic renewal processes is usually framed by more or less articulated input and output criteria.

FIGURE 9.1   Strategic innovation

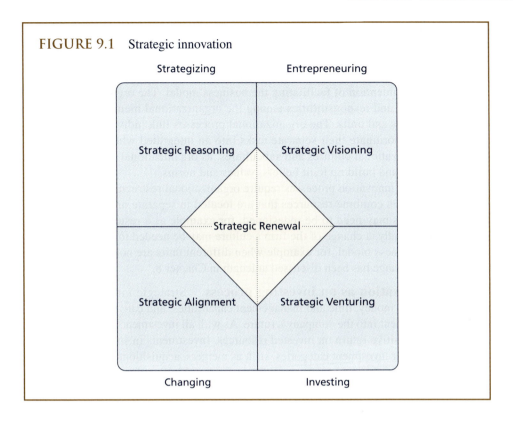

Strategic innovation as an entrepreneurial process.   Each year, thousands of individuals start a new business, expecting to have identified an opportunity that can be exploited. The backgrounds and basic ideas of these entrepreneurs differ widely. For example, some entrepreneurs may have just graduated, others hold many years of experience in an industry they know well; some build their newly established company on the basis of a new technology, others start serving a group of customers that has been overlooked. With all the differences, entrepreneurs share the aim to change the environment and take a personal risk in starting their own business as the vehicle for their dreams. Many, but not all, entrepreneurs succeed and some of their businesses grow large as a family company or public firm. The importance of entrepreneurial activity is widely recognized as the driving force of creating new industries and renewing existing ones.

Not everyone with an entrepreneurial capability likes to take the risks, nor the personal consequences that come with starting a business however. Many prefer a less risky life and start working with an established firm. These people are entrepreneurial but not entrepreneurs, and their entrepreneurial capabilities become a company resource for entrepreneurial initiatives. Entrepreneurial people do not own the company, but they do take ownership over the firm's future. This phenomenon has become known as corporate entrepreneurship.

Established companies make use of entrepreneurial managers for various strategic activities, such as finding new markets for existing products and services, applying new technologies in current markets and setting up new businesses. Entrepreneurial managers realize in established companies what entrepreneurs achieve on their own account: finding growth opportunities. Unique for corporate entrepreneurs, however, is that they often also have to change the company's internal conditions, along with finding avenues for strategic innovation.

Strategic innovation as a change process. Along with changing the company's business model, one or more elements of the company's organizational system (Figure 9.2, see also Chapter 8) also need to be adjusted. The term 'organizational system' refers to how the individuals in the firm have been configured and relate to one another, with the intention of facilitating the business model. The organizational structure divides tasks and responsibilities among the organizational members, by forming different functions and units. The organizational processes link individual members to each other and coordinate their separate tasks into an integrated whole. Furthermore, firms have organizational cultures and subcultures, as organizational members interact with one another and build up joint beliefs, values and norms.

Some strategic innovation processes require organizational restructuring, for example when new products combine resources that are located in separate units. Also, organizational processes may need to be redesigned, for example as a result of new product offerings. And finally, a change of the firm's culture may be needed to enable strategists renewing the business model, for example when different units are not inclined to share ideas. Strategic change has been discussed at length in Chapter 8.

Strategic innovation as an investing process. Strategic innovation requires resources, such as money, time and management capabilities, and can, therefore, be considered an investment into the company's future. As with all investments, strategic innovation requires a positive return on invested resources. Investments in strategic innovation compete with other investment categories, such as mergers, acquisitions and entering new countries. Consequently, companies engage in decision making routines to decide whether or not to allocate scarce resources for proposed strategic innovation projects.

Generally, investments that promise to generate returns in the long term are riskier than short term options and therefore harder to take. The same applies to innovation options. In addition, investing in an enhanced long-term competitive position involves more uncertainty about the expected effects as the company environment changes along the way. So, investing in strategic innovation becomes both riskier and more uncertain as the results are to be expected over a longer term.

Managers with the responsibility for innovation processes cannot afford to develop ideas only. They must think of the entire process, from generating ideas and managing the renewal process up to successfully implementing innovations. Managers must ask

FIGURE 9.2   General view of the business model and the organizational system

themselves upfront how the entire process of strategic innovation should be managed to renew their organizations. Who should be involved, what activities need to be undertaken and to what extent can the results be described in advance? For strategizing managers, strategic innovation encompasses the entire process to arrive at the best possible position to achieve a positive return on the innovation investment.

In sum, strategic innovation is complex for strategizing managers as it combines four processes that separately are, in themselves challenging, to bring to a successful ending: strategizing, entrepreneuring, changing and investing processes. Strategic innovation is equally challenging for management scholars, as the topic crosses and combines several academic disciplines such as Organizational Behaviour, Technology Management, Marketing, Finance and of course Strategy. The multi-disciplinary character of the topic thwarts researchers in understanding strategic innovation in full, with diverse academic contributions as an understandable result. The diverse research findings point to a number of factors that further complicate strategic innovation.

Inhibitors of strategic innovation

As described above, strategic innovation is a difficult process to manage. Although companies may potentially exist for over a century, there are good reasons why only a few companies succeed in surviving for such an extensive period. Some obvious reasons include bad management and unfortunate consequences of wars and natural disasters. But even in the absence of such occasions, strategic renewal is hard to accomplish as strategists face several inhibitors of strategic renewal. The following paragraphs discuss such inhibitors of strategic renewal: the effects of innovation results, inertia and bias, and feedback.

Effects of innovation results.   The advantage of start-up innovators is a blank cognitive map, as there have not been past innovation successes and failures that influence perceptions on the viability of innovation options. Over time, however, the innovator collects experiences of past projects, both positive and negative. Successes stimulate going forward on this path, while disappointing results lead to reconsidering the choices that have been made. The results influence future innovating behaviour and strategic choices. Innovators continue on routes that lead to success, while changing direction when results prove disappointing. Radical innovations that have paid off in terms of strengthened competitive position, stimulate strategists to replicate bold innovative moves, while disappointing results urge strategists to rethink the choices that have been made. The same applies to incremental improvement successes leading to continued gradual innovation, while disappointing effects on the company's competitive position prompt for evaluating innovation policies.

Established companies do not have the advantage of blank cognitive maps. When considering innovation options, past experiences influence how alternatives are valued and evaluated. Strategists become reluctant to explore alternatives that had been tried before with disappointing pay-offs. They have learned what works and what doesn't; as a result, they develop perceptions and opinions on the viability of certain options. Past experiences lead to following the proven innovation routines in which they become increasingly more effective – a phenomena that has been commonly termed path dependency (Nelson and Winter, 1982). In other words, positive results of certain innovation routines lead to replicating these routines and building up relevant innovation process competencies. Such competencies lead to increased chances of success, and ultimately come to define the way the company innovates.

As the organization develops innovation routines and institutionalizes successful practices, the chances of inertia magnify. The organization increasingly comes to rely on patterns of actions it has had sustainable success with in the past (Hannan and Freeman, 1984; Tripsas and Gavetti, 2000), thus becoming less likely to change course (Kelly and

Amburgey, 1991). As the organization becomes older, it tends to select innovation routines that have proved to be fruitful (Rahmandad, 2008). Successes lead to bias in evaluating innovation options and outcomes, inertia builds up over time, and the organization loses the ability to value different innovation patterns.

The effects of inertia and bias.   Building up inertia and bias over time prohibits organizations from appreciating the potential of innovation options outside the dominant organizational logic and managers' cognitive maps. As a consequence, successful innovations of competitors are hardly noticed, the importance of these innovations is not understood in full and the organization might miss a crucial industry development. For example, the US retailer Sears Roebuck has missed the advent of discount retailers and home centres (Christensen, 1997, 2011, Reading 9.2).

The effects of inertia and bias apply to all innovation routines. Organizations that continuously improve the current business model have a high chance of missing a breakthrough technology, such as Kodak missing the digital imaging revolution, or a revolutionary new business model, as the Sears Roebuck reading illustrates. In contrast, companies focusing on the 'next big thing', concentrating key resources on the new breakthrough innovation, build up a blind spot for continuous improvements of competitors. As a result, they may well end up with products that are too expensive or which, when compared with alternatives, lack differentiation value. For example, by continuously improving products, the Japanese electronics firms have come to dominate the market of television sets in the United States, the TV country par excellence.

The effects of feedback.   When innovation results are satisfying according to higher level managers, strategists are not challenged to explore innovations that could be even more promising. Innovations are evaluated according to the current dominant logic and based on existing mental models (see also Chapter 2). As long as the results meet the criteria, there is no compelling reason to change course. The company's absorption of innovations that are 'good enough' is reinforced when the full potential of different innovation options is not fully understood or valued.

Continuous feedback of the innovation portfolio complicates business model renewal processes, especially for innovations with a longer development time. During the innovation period, innovations with an extensive lead time are evaluated in multiple intermediate states. Since in each state disappointing progress might be noted, innovations with a long lead time are vulnerable to being discontinued. For example, promising process improvement initiatives can prematurely be abandoned (Repenning and Sterman, 2002), and product development capability can be compromised by reduced investments in concept design activities (Repenning, 2001). The effect of intermediate evaluations is that innovation projects with a relatively short duration, delivering immediate payoffs, become dominant (Rahmandad, 2008). Process improvements in manufacturing pay off relatively fast, while it takes some time before the results of business development become visible.

Of course, strategizing managers do not merely focus on the immediate payback of innovations. The expected future value continues to be a significant factor while evaluating innovations with long lead times. The problem is, however, that in allocating resources priorities may change. For example, some resources may be needed in urgent innovation projects with immediate payoffs and temporal budget cuts may eliminate long term investments. If intermediate moments of evaluation become more frequent, innovations are, thus, more likely to be abandoned.

The key to bringing long-term investment projects to a successful end is to define milestones with clearly described mid-term targets. However, the end state of long-term innovations can usually not be clearly envisioned, making intermediate states difficult to define. In sum, investment projects with long lead times have the highest chance of being abandoned along the way, especially when intermediate feedback occurs more frequently.

The combination of four challenging processes – strategizing, entrepreneuring, changing and investing – in conjunction with the three main inhibitors may well explain why most companies are unable to approach a century-enduring corporate life, which De Geus' study has proven to be possible. The question is, thus, how can strategizing managers extend corporate life? Is there a magic formula for sustained youth, a corporate elixir from magicians in academia or consulting? While this can not be fully excluded, a much more likely answer is that companies should master the ability to renew themselves. This would indicate that strategic renewal is the key strategic issue for a company's long-term success.

Business model renewal

Strategizing managers striving for long-term success are well aware that many factors may change the competitive arena. Although strategists can not predict the future, they know that it will differ from today. Customer needs, competitor's actions and technological advancements are among the many elements that may create a future misfit between the current business model and the company's environment. In order to prepare for a competitive future that is yet unknown, strategizing managers need to renew several elements of the business model. Not only current products and services are to be improved; to create future demands new products and services must also be developed. Strategists are not only *reacting* to changes, they can also *initiate* changes by innovating activities, effectively creating an environmental misfit for competitors.

As strategic innovation is defined as renewing the business model that creates a competitive advantage, the term business model renewal needs to be introduced. Strategists can renew each element of the company's business model. A business model is the configuration of resources (inputs), activities (throughput) and product/service offerings (output) intended to create value for customers – it is the way a firm conducts its business (see Chapter 4). The first element in a successful business model (*product offering*) is a superior 'value proposition'. A firm must be able to supply a product or service that has a superior mix of attributes (e.g. price, availability, reliability, technical specifications, image, colour, taste, ease of use, etc.). The second element (*value chain*) is the ability to actually develop and supply the superior product offering. It needs to have the capability to perform the necessary value-adding activities in an effective and efficient manner. These value-adding activities, such as R&D, production, logistics, marketing and sales, are jointly referred to as a firm's value chain. The third element of a business model (*resource base*) consists of the resources required to perform the value-adding activities. Resources such as know-how, patents, facilities, money, brands and relationships make up the stock of assets that can be employed to create the product offering. If these firm-specific assets are distinctive and useful, they can form the basis of a superior value proposition. Strategizing managers can choose between outside-in renewal, inside-out renewal and value chain renewal (see Figure 9.3.).

Outside-in renewal.   Strategizing managers can renew their value proposition to customers by increasing the perceived product and service value, and by lowering prices. Reliability, for example, is highly valued by customers in most industries. By continuously improving the reliability of its products, the Korean car maker Hyundai has become known as a company offering high quality yet affordable products (see also the short case in Chapter 5). Another case of outside-in renewal, usually coined marketing innovation or product offering renewal, has to do with the creation of new markets or market segments with existing products. For example, Unilever created new market demand by offering instant soup to the corporate market and by repositioning ice cream to increase adult consumption.

FIGURE 9.3   Three business model renewal alternatives

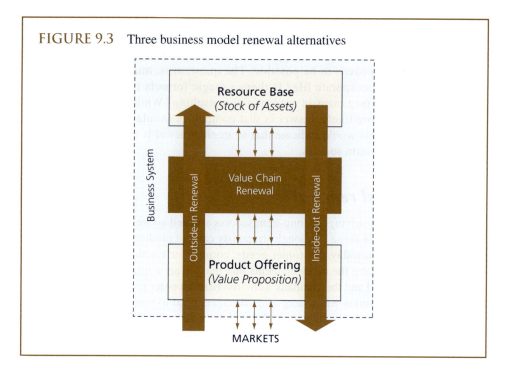

Inside-out renewal.   By renewing the company's resource base, new products and services can be created and existing ones can be improved. New technologies are often the prime starting point for inside-out renewal. For example, companies like Philips (medical technology, lighting and household appliances), Merck (pharmaceuticals), and Toyota (motorized vehicles) invest heavily in technological research and development. The know-how and patents add to the firm's resource base, and from there new technologies will create and improve new products and services. Other resources can also be renewed. For example, brands can be renewed by an intensive marketing campaign, and the firm's human resources by training.

Value chain renewal.   Along with renewing the firm's value proposition or resource base, strategists can renew some, or even all, elements of the value chain. For example, IKEA has become the world's largest furniture retailer by redesigning the end-to-end value chain, from standardizing production processes to developing flat pack designs and lowering transportation costs. The value chain innovation of Amazon has prompted competitors and firms in other industries to rethink and renew their chain of value-adding activities.

THE PARADOX OF EXPLOITATION AND EXPLORATION

If you realize that all things change, there is nothing you will try to hold on to.
If you are not afraid of dying there is nothing you cannot achieve.
Lao Tsu (6th century BC); Chinese philosopher and author

Many management theorists have addressed the tension between exploitation and exploration (Gupta *et al.,* 2006; March, 1991, Reading 9.3; Raisch *et al.,* 2009; Tushman and O'Reilly, 1996; Zott and Amit, 2013). The question being addressed is whether the company should renew itself by improving the current organization (exploitation) or by radically rejuvenating the organization through disrupting technologies and processes (exploration). On the one hand, they realize that ongoing improvement of products and services will increase customer satisfaction and therefore strengthens the company's competitive position. When ongoing improvement becomes an organizational routine, the company becomes better and faster, which would, in the long run, wear out competitors. On the other hand, they recognize the effects of changing the competitive rules with radically new products, technologies and novel ways of organizing the company. Rule changers leave competitors in the awkward position of catching up with their rules; a feat at which they often fail.

Researchers agree that companies need both exploitative and explorative processes (March, 1991). The problem is, however, that these renewal processes are each other's opposites and are at least partially contradictory. Improving the current business model starts with defining how the company can become more efficient and effective. Customers are asked how the current products and services may become even better than they are today, and what changes would meet their demands even more; employees are invited to come up with ideas on how to streamline production and distribution processes, and how to adapt the sales organization to increase effectiveness. On the basis of these data, the business model is incrementally improved and becomes more efficient and effective. The point of departure for radically rejuvenating firms, on the other hand, is not a list of today's possible improvements, but an imagined future of a different industry. It does not start with asking customers what they need, because customers generally do not know if they need something that does not exist yet. The starting point is either a new technology or a radically new idea of how future customers may be served. From this vision, new products, services and business models are being developed, and new customer needs are shaped. Customers need to adapt to the firm's great new offerings, not the other way around. The company *shapes* the future; it doesn't *build* on the present situation.

Both renewal processes have value, however the problem is that processes to improve current products, services and technologies are very different and often even opposite to processes to explore breakthrough innovations. It requires a different mindset, different people, different processes and a different time horizon. Even the criteria of measuring success differ. Renewal processes aimed at improving current products and services can be measured in terms of realized client value (lower price and higher quality). The success of radical renewal with disrupting technologies and new processes is measured by the extent to which a new industry is created or new customer value is realized. The resulting tension between exploitation and exploration will be explored in the following sections.

The demand for sustained renewal

Sustained renewal refers to the process of permanently improving products and services to strengthen the company's competitive position. It is the never-ending quest for raising quality standards and increasing efficiency, achieving ever better and cheaper value propositions – including after-sales, marketing and sales. Each time a higher standard has been reached, the bar is raised to the next level. Quality standards include not only technologies, materials and other physical inputs into the renewal process, but also people – the human resources. People are also developed at ever higher levels.

Sustained renewal is based on factual information, such as customer feedback and market research as well as on ideas from anyone within and outside of the firm. Anything that may bring the current products and services to a higher level is included in the renewal process. The higher level then becomes the new standard both for the company and for competitors and customers. A company needs to improve, even to maintain its current position, because without engaging in this permanent process of improvement, the firm would lag behind competitors and eventually deteriorate. People do not want to read yesterday's newspaper or buy outdated products, and therefore without sustained renewal there is no long-term future for a company.

Ideas for improvement arrive from different internal and external stakeholders. The areas of improvement can widely vary, yet these are usually based on the current understanding of the business the company is in and what kinds of products and services the company relates to the dominant logic (see also Chapter 2). Thinking within the boundaries of a shared paradigm is generally accepted and people tend to proceed accordingly – that is, they renew to sustain the current business model. The downside of a dominant logic is that it usually locks people into shared paradigms that have been tried and tested, and thus becomes immune to external signals that may not fit. This is where the need for disruptive renewal comes in.

The demand for disrupting renewal

Disrupting renewal refers to a process in which current competitive positions are challenged by introducing new technologies and business models. As described above, when improving products and services, a strategist defines each renewing activity on the basis of facts while following the dominant logic. However, when searching for an innovation that will disrupt the industry, a strategist needs to take leaps of imagination. Disruptive innovations do not follow from the facts, but need to be invented. They are not analysed into existence, but need to be generated if they are to be distinctive and rule-changing.

When generating disrupting solutions, creative thinking is not just important, it is the essence. In disrupting creative thinking, the strategist abandons the rules governing sound argumentation and draws a conclusion that is not justified based on prior arguments. In this way, the strategist generates a new understanding, but without objective proof that the new idea 'makes sense'. Creative thinking takes liberty in following thinking rules. One idea might lead to another idea, without formal logic interfering. One variable might be linked to another, without a sound explanation of why a correlation is assumed. Creativity in effect creates a new understanding, with little attention paid to supporting evidence. Often logic is used afterwards to justify an idea that was actually generated by creative means.

Disruptive renewal does not follow from the dominant logic, but is the unexpected outcome that emerges when the dominant logic is challenged. Changing a shared paradigm requires strategists to imagine new ways of understanding the world that do not follow from current beliefs. Strategic thinkers need to be willing and able to break with orthodoxy and make leaps of imagination, to generate novel ways of looking at old problems.

The conclusion must be that sustained renewal and disruptive renewal are not only opposites, but they are partially incompatible as well. They are based on methods that are at odds with one another. Strategizing managers would probably love to exploit and explore at the same time, yet both require such a different mindset and range of cognitive skills that in practice it is very difficult to achieve both simultaneously (March, 1991, Reading 9.3). The demand for sustained renewal and disruptive renewal is not only contradictory for each individual, but also within teams, departments and the overall firm. While strategizing groups would like to be fully capable of both exploiting and exploring, finding ways of incorporating both into a workable renewal process is extremely challenging. Conflicting styles often lead to mutual misunderstanding and conflicts among people. Therefore, a blend between the two is not that simple. It is for this reason that we speak of the 'paradox of exploitation and exploration' – the two demands on innovating managers seem to be contradictory, yet both are required at the same time. Inspired by Christensen (1997, 2011, Reading 9.2 in this chapter), this can be called *the innovator's paradox.*

EXHIBIT 9.1 SHORT CASE

3M: IN SEARCH OF RENEWAL

If one organization can be said to represent 20th century innovations and technological break-throughs it would probably be 3M. The Minnesota Mining and Manufacturing Company has managed to conquer the world with products such as cello tape and Post-it notes, and has become famous for its innovative culture. Yet, while in 2004 still the world's most innovative company, 3M was no longer listed on the BCG Top 50 of most innovative companies when Inge Thulin took the helm as the new CEO in 2012. Shareholders were happy though: with a steady growth and expanding sales in emerging markets such as China and Brazil, 3M had gradually climbed the ranks of best perform-ing companies from place 110 to 95. But could this be sustained? 3M was facing tough competition, increased environmental regulations and a versa-tile global market, while the firm's strong financial performance was largely the result of past innova-tions – and 3M seemed to have lost its innovation capability. Inge Thulin was wondering how he could keep shareholders satisfied, while also rebuilding the innovation capability that had made 3M famous and had created strong growth.

The Minnesota Mining and Manufacturing Com-pany was founded in 1902 by five entrepreneurs with the initial objective to mine and market a rela-tively rare mineral known as *corundum* to be sold as an abrasive. When the mine called *Crystal Bay* proved to contain insufficient amounts of minerals, the founders' focus changed. They had noted cus-tomers' great need for better processing materials, and so they developed high-quality sandpaper that caused less dust than the hitherto conventional abra-sives. From there 3M worked itself to one of the most successful companies it is today, in roughly four phases.

3M's first phase consisted of building an inno-vation-centred company. The focal point in the first decades of success was CEO William McKnight, an engineer who stood at the base of the first 3M prod-ucts. He defined 3M's mission as: *solving unsolved problems in innovative ways.* In 1948 he laid the management foundation for 3M's innovative culture:

As our business grows, it becomes increas-ingly necessary to delegate responsibility and to encourage men and women to exercise their initiative. This requires considerable tol-erance. Those men and women, to whom we delegate authority and responsibility, if they are good people, are going to want to do their jobs in their own way.

Mistakes will be made. But if a person is essentially right, the mistakes he or she makes are not as serious in the long run as the mis-takes management will make if it undertakes to tell those in authority exactly how they must do their jobs.

Management that is destructively critical when mistakes are made kills initiative. And it's essential that we have many people with initiative if we are to continue to grow.

3M employees gained independence and space to experiment and investigate. Staff were allowed to spend 15 per cent of their working time on self-initiated projects; exploring became part of each employee's job. An endless array of new products and variants thereof were developed. Examples of breakthrough innovations were the cellotape, magnetic tape, and not to be forgotten: the Post-it note. By combining competencies, 3M had entered different industries such as the pharmaceutical sector with new generation patches, and electronics where 3M materials allowed for higher resolution flat-screens.

The eight divisions had the autonomy to develop new products within their sector and bring them to the market. From 1914 to 1966 – when McKnight acted as CEO – the company's sales exploded from $264 000 to an astonishing $1.15 billion. His internal successors continued this policy: renewal remained paramount and the bottom-up organiza-tion was sustained. In the early 1990s however, 3M seemed to have lost its grip on financial and intel-lectual resources. Costly investments in people and products failed to generate the desired results, while no new breakthrough product had been launched since the Post-it note in 1980. Time to market for new products had been too lengthy, managers were insufficiently challenged, and the company that relied heavily on innovative initiatives had been characterized as reactive. At the end of the 1990s 3M missed focus and was sensitive to all kinds of fads and fashions. Shareholders were murmuring. It was time for a change.

▶

As such, the second phase welcomed an increased focus and an accelerated time to market of 3M's products. In early 2000, on the initiative of shareholders, outsider James McNerney was appointed CEO. Unlike his engineering predecessors McNerney had a marketing background, and had previously worked under the leadership of General Electric's CEO Jack Welch where he had gained credits in creating and transforming lean organizations. McNerney's arrival at 3M was the start of a transformation process in search of hidden costs. In a short time period he managed to bring focus to both the manufacturing and R&D departments. Focusing on the mindset of 3M employees he imported the GE Six Sigma program, a series of management techniques aimed at reducing production errors and increasing efficiency. And not without results: performance at 3M improved significantly.

In parallel, McNerney took some – for 3M – unprecedented steps. He increased competition within the company, while existing plants and research laboratories were downsized and some activities were transferred to low-wage countries. In a short time, the US workforce was reduced by 8000 employees – over 10 per cent of the total employment. Never before in the existence of the organization had worker job security at the Minnesota plants been threatened. These events had a negative impact on the open and innovative culture of 3M that had been built on the strong bond between company and employees. In addition, innovation focused on only those R&D projects that promised the highest and safest return. The time from idea to product was shortened, which resulted in an expanded product portfolio in a relatively short time period. Sales increased by 10 per cent annually, delighting the shareholders. In 2005, McNerney decided to leave the company and moved to Boeing.

The third phase of 3M consisted of accelerating growth by acquisitions and the strengthening of new markets. George Buckley, a former engineer from Brunswick Company was appointed CEO at the end of 2005. After a detailed study of the firm he concluded that 3M was a highly scientific engineering and manufacturing company with conservative values, successfully participating in many niche markets. Success, he concluded, was related to collaboration within the company, and therefore sharing and transferring technologies across products

and markets became a key ingredient of the company's strategy. Buckley decided to restore the original 3M innovative culture by rehabilitating the 15 per cent rule without restrictions for R&D operations. A technology-market architecture was set up, in which nine technology platforms (such as adhesives and non-woven materials) were distinguished as the fundament for 3M's core assets and interconnected with the various markets (such as aerospace and health care) in which 3M was active. This way the gap between research and customers had been narrowed.

Expansion of the product portfolio had mainly been realized by Buckley's choice for an acquisition strategy, focused on booming sectors and emerging markets such as China and Brazil. In 2006, only 16 acquisitions were made – representing 24 per cent of the company's annual turnover – and more acquisitions followed suit. When Buckley retired in 2012, he had increased revenues by 40 per cent to $29.6 billion in his CEO term, yet only 3 per cent of the increase had resulted from internal organic growth.

3M's final phase is thus a possible restoration of organic growth. Buckley's successor Inge Thulin joined 3M in 1979, and climbed the ranks through the company's health care business. Thulin was the first company insider after a period of 12 years in which outsiders held sway at 3M. He had run international operations, for which he had expanded sales to almost $20 billion, two-thirds of 3M's $29.6 billion total revenues. When taking the helm in 2012, Thulin had challenging shareholder expectations and inherited his predecessor's ambition of 7 to 8 per cent annual sales growth. Four years later, in 2016, shareholders were happy: 3M had gradually climbed on the Fortune 500 list of best performing companies from position 102 in 2012 to number 93 in 2016.

Not all went well, though. While in 2014 the company had gained position 22 on the BCG top-50 of the world's most innovative companies after many years of re-instating 3M's innovative power, a year later in 2015 it had plummeted again: to position 40. The company that was once the 20th century champion of innovation, then dropped to position 22 in 2008 and out of BCG's list of the world's most innovative companies in 2010. In his CEO letter, Thulin described his motto as "finding the balance between a microscope view focusing on the day-to-day challenges and a telescope view focusing on strengthening 3M for the future". With 5.8 per cent of its sales spent on R&D in 2015, slightly above the industrial average, Thulin seemed not to have found the desired balance between short and long term yet. Future value comes from invention and innovation – even one single idea may create the company's future – while short-term value relates to operational excellence. How should Thulin glue the present to the future? He has one advantage over competitors: there is no shortage of cello tape and Post-it notes.

Co-author: Jeroen van der Velden

Sources: www.3m.com; 3M Annual report 2012; 3M Annual report 2015; *Business Week* 2007 'At 3M, a struggle between efficiency and creativity'; *Business Week* 2012 '3M's Thulin to keep Buckley focus on research, emerging markets'; www.bcgperspectives.com (innovative companies 2005–2015) www.fortune500.com; IBS (3M Cultivating Core Competency)

PERSPECTIVES ON STRATEGIC INNOVATION

Innovation opportunities do not come with the tempest but with the rustling of the breeze.

Peter Drucker (1909–2005); Austrian-American writer, management thinker and consultant

The demand for both sustained and disruptive renewal puts strategizing managers in the difficult position of having to determine how these two must be combined and balanced in a process of ongoing renewal. Sustained renewal is necessary to ensure ongoing improvement of the current business model – elevating current products and services to ever higher levels of customer satisfaction. Disruptive renewal is necessary to create new business models – forcing competitors to follow the new rules of the competitive game. The question is how strategizing managers go about the demands of renewing the company.

The strategic management literature comes up with a variety of answers to this question. Both among business practitioners and strategy researchers, views differ sharply about the best way of dealing with the paradox of exploitation and exploration. To gain insight into the major points of disagreement on the issue of strategic renewal, the two diametrically opposed perspectives will be outlined here.

At one end of the virtual continuum of views are the strategists who argue that strategic innovation must be achieved by ongoing renewal of the existing firm. Continuous improvement, although difficult to sustain, is at the heart of strategic innovation. This point of view will be referred to as the '*strategic improvement perspective*'. At the other end of the spectrum are the strategists who argue that real strategic innovations are radical departures from the current business model, disrupting the industry in which the firm is active. Minor improvements are not at the heart of strategic innovation, but are instead striving for a significant rejuvenation towards a next state. Disrupting renewal, although difficult to achieve, is at the heart of strategic innovation. This point of view will be referred to as the '*radical rejuvenation perspective*'.

The strategic improvement perspective

Proponents of the strategic improvement perspective advocate that companies should focus on improving their business model. The point of departure is the permanent battle between rivalling companies that fight for the same customer group. With customers having a choice between comparable products

and services that may satisfy their needs, competitive success requires offering the best, cheapest and most novel value propositions. Improved products and services attract more customers, increase market share and generate more returns, and therefore are the key success factors in the competitive game.

The attitude that things can always be advanced is important for the strategic improvement perspective. Everyone within the firm should be driven by constructive dissatisfaction with the status quo. Furthermore, all employees within the firm should be committed to improving all elements of the business model. Company leaders are facilitative in the sustained renewal process; their main role is to coordinate several renewal initiatives. They must also be aware of the danger of the 'success trap': "sustained renewal often leads to early success, which in turn reinforces further renewal along the same trajectory" (Gupta *et al.*, 2006).

Proponents of the strategic improvement perspective agree that game-changing innovations provide a significant competitive advantage for the innovator. They point out, however, that although the benefits of success can be considerable, it is a risky route with a moderate chance of success at best. In order to increase the chance of a successful breakthrough innovation, the company must allocate the best resources, leaving ample capacity for engaging in continuous improvements that generate immediate competitive success. As the chance of breakthrough success is low, all innovation efforts may well be without results, while the company's rivals have progressed to higher standards. The conclusion must be that radical innovation initiatives absorb the most precious resources for corporate renewal while, due to the high chance of failure, the most likely outcome is that the company loses competitive position, or worse gets kicked out of business by rivals (Imai, 1986, Reading 9.1).

EXHIBIT 9.2   THE STRATEGIC IMPROVEMENT PERSPECTIVE

WEBER-STEPHEN PRODUCTS: HOT FOR GRILLS

In the 1940s, brick-made grills were the norm. Surrounded by low walls with a grill rack in the middle, these open-air grills were a staple of American life. Although hugely popular at the time, these types of grills are far from perfect. They cannot be moved, the grill rusts from constant exposure to the elements, bad weather extinguishes the fire and wind can cause ash to blow up and attach itself to food and the occasional piece of clothing.

This annoyed George Stephen Sr, who was working at Weber Brothers Metal Works in Chicago at the time. So much so that he tried to fix it. George went to his workplace, grabbed a metal half-sphere used to make marine buoys and turned it into a tight-fitting lid for his grill. In order to fuel the fire, a neighbour suggested poking holes in the kettle. The result was a dome-shaped grill that protects food from the elements, keeps the fire burning and all the while sealing in that distinct barbeque flavour. Thus

the Weber grill was born, a charcoal kettle grill that would bring about a backyard revolution.

The invention caught fire among George Stephen's friends. They raved on about his grill and the taste of the dishes his invention helped make. The kettle design also allows heat to circulate around the food evenly and this has a profound effect on the food. The enthusiastic responses made Stephen sell the first ever kettle grills in 1952 and soon did this under his own brand: Weber-Stephen Products. It did not take long before the spherical grill became the most popular grill in the United States and the majority of Americans gave their meat the kettle treat. The company is now the world's largest grill manufacturer and holds about 35 per cent of the US grill market.

Weber-Stephen Products is continuously looking for ways to improve its grill offering. In the 1970s it started producing electric grills and kettles fitted with propane tanks. These did not sell like hotcakes however, for the kettle shape was associated too much with charcoal grilling. Setting his sights on creating a better gas grill, Weber-Stephen launched the Genesis line. These rectangular gas-based grills are fitted with triangular 'Flavorizer' cooking bars, designed to distribute heat more evenly, reduce flare-ups and mimic the sizzling of food on hot coals. The company kept improving its grill assortment, by introducing the Handle Light to illuminate the grilling surface and came up with built-in charcoal buckets for its coal-based grills. More compact grills were also designed for dense urban areas in order to better serve the South-East Asian market.

Resembling General Motors' Chevy-to-Caddy product range, Weber-Stephen offers different priced grills. As consumers climb the income ladder, they can start off with the miniature Smokey Joe kettle for $30 and keep purchasing better, more expensive grills, such as the $2000 Genesis gas models. With a wide product range and continued improvement, Weber-Stephen aims to keep firing up audiences worldwide and let the grilling continue.

Co-author: Wester Wagenaar

Sources: weber.com; weberstephen.nl; *Bloomberg*, 27 June 2013; *The Wall Street Journal*, 21 May 2015.

The radical rejuvenation perspective

According to proponents of the radical rejuvenation perspective, companies should focus on breakthrough innovations that change the rules of the competitive game rather than becoming better at playing by the current rules. Game-changing innovations provide innovators with a significant competitive advantage, forcing rivals to follow and play by their rules. The more radical the departure from the industry rules, the more difficult it will be for competitors to follow and the higher the benefits for the innovator are likely to be.

If a firm decides to use a breakthrough technology or a new business model to strengthen its competitive position vis-à-vis rivals, this requires some major changes in a short period of time, as such innovations to the business model are inherently disrupting. Creating novel products and developing a unique business formula require a sharp break with the past. Old ways must be discarded before new methods can be adopted. This is the essence of what Schumpeter (1950) referred to as the process of 'creative destruction', inherent in the capitalist system. This process is not orderly and protracted, but disruptive and intense. Therefore, it is argued, successful firms must learn to master the skill of radical innovation (e.g. D'Aveni, 1994; Hamel, 1996). Rapid implementation of system-wide change is an essential organizational capability.

In the radical rejuvenation perspective, strong company leadership is essential (Leifer, 2000). Break-through renewal is not only disrupting for rivals, but also for the organization itself. The business model needs to be renewed, usually in conjunction with the organizational system. Such dramatic alterations can only be successful when a strong company leader is in the position to get things done. This is even more prominent as a disruptive renewal project usually takes extensive time to be developed from an idea into an actual product, which makes the continuity of the project vulnerable for feedback sessions along the way. It is crucial that the disruptive renewal project will be a success, because in the absence, there is the danger of the 'failure trap': "failure promotes the search for even newer ideas and thus more exploration" (Gupta *et al.*, 2006).

Proponents of the radical rejuvenation perspective agree that improvements are useful to help companies defend and strengthen their competitive positions; however, they argue that it comes at a high price. Sustained improvement and allocating key company resources on projects that enhance existing products, services and technologies, comes at the expense of strategically more effective game-changing innovations. Focusing on serving current customers with better propositions at lower costs, leads to maximizing short-term return on innovation budgets, and diminishes the capacity to engage in breakthrough innovations to serve customers in the future. Indeed, many well-managed companies that continuously improve on the basis of customer needs fail *exactly because* they are well managed, a phenomena dubbed by Christensen (1997, 2011, Reading 9.2) as the Innovator's Dilemma.

EXHIBIT 9.3   THE RADICAL REJUVENATION PERSPECTIVE

CHOBANI: KEEPING THE YOGHURT MARKET FRESH

Born in Turkey to a Kurdish dairy farmer, Hamdi Ulukaya used his childhood knowledge to build a Greek yoghurt empire that made him a billionaire in just six years. While his original intent of coming to America was to study business and English, he soon got side-tracked by an ad in the paper offering an old dairy plant for sale. He dropped out of his studies, a parallel that might have contributed to his officious title, the 'Steve Jobs of Yoghurt', to buy the 80-year-old plant that he restored himself. He sold his first container of yoghurt just 18 months later and went on to expand at an impressive pace, today employing over 2000 people.

Until a decade ago, a very sweet type of yoghurt dominated the American supermarket shelves. The alternative to this popular breakfast item, Greek yoghurt, containing more protein and less fat, had never been available outside specialty shops. Recession-weary and health-conscious shoppers took very warmly to Mr Ulukaya's efforts to extend their breakfast choices with his traditional Greek product, consequently growing Greek yoghurt sales from 1 to 60 per cent of the total yoghurt business.

One might wonder why yoghurt giants Stark or Danone did not act upon these trends, as retailers certainly welcomed Mr Ulukaya's products with open arms, right from the start. In fact, the Greek yoghurt invasion was not the first time that food and beverage incumbents were caught by surprise. Plum Organics revolutionized baby food packaging, resulting in 20 per cent of American babies now being fed by squirting food out of a container instead of being spoon-fed, while Koppert Cress commoditized decorative foodstuffs to liven up

plates in restaurants all over the world; a very profitable niche in which it still maintains a monopoly.

The common practice in the food and beverage industry is that successful start-ups are being acquired by incumbents. Mr Ulukaya, however, has never accepted any of the lucrative offers he has received for his Greek yoghurt empire, keeping all shares under his own control. This resulted in him not just disrupting the market once and then being integrated in a large bureaucracy, but allowed him to keep going. After his first success of introducing Greek yoghurt to the American public, he opened a store in Soho, one of New York's most fashionable neighbourhoods, selling the most exquisite combinations of Greek yoghurt with peach, dates and much more. With his unique and healthy snacks – nearly as exclusive and expensive as the neighbouring VIP bars' cocktails – Mr Ulukaya tried to vamp up the image of breakfast items. Other savvy moves, in a similar vein, are a new line of healthy products for children and healthy alternatives to Red Bull or coffee.

Mr Ulukaya is an innovator *par excellence*. He has been able to keep surprising the establishment with new and exciting ways to position his products. Whether he can keep momentum once his company has reached a similar size as the yoghurt giants he is competing with remains to be seen, but based on his passion and continuous streak of awards, we can look forward to many more delicious market disruptions.

Co-author: Jasper de Vries

Sources: 'At Chobani, the Turkish King of Greek Yogurt', Bloomberg, January 31, 2013; 'Cultural revolution: The Greek-yogurt phenomenon in America left big food firms feeling sour. They are trying to get better at innovation', *The Economist*, August 31, 2013; 'At Chobani, Now It's Not Just the Yoghurt That's Rich', *The New York Times*, April 26, 2016.

MANAGING THE PARADOX OF EXPLOITATION AND EXPLORATION

He that will not apply new remedies must expect new evils, for time is the greatest innovator.

Francis Bacon (1561–1626); English philosopher, statesman, scientist, jurist, orator and author

So, how should managers go about renewing their organizations? Should strategizing managers focus on sustained renewal by ongoing improvement of their current business model? Or should they strive for disruptive renewal by focusing on radical, breakthrough innovations? There is no consensus within the field of strategic management on how to balance exploitation and exploration; however a number of scholars have discussed different ways of dealing with the arguments put forward in the debate (see Table 9.1). Depending on the situation, strategizing managers can assess the arguments and develop their own way of dealing with the paradox.

While the general notion of strategy paradoxes and competing demands is often not – or not fully – embraced among scholars, it is one of the key research areas in innovation research. Initiated by March's (1991) pioneering article, the paradox of exploitation and exploration has become highly influential in the fields of organizational learning and organizational behaviour, and currently also enjoys attention from many strategy researchers. As strategic innovation concerns the future of the company, it is at the core of what strategizing managers are actually doing. The question is thus, how can they best manage the paradox of exploitation and exploration? Taking the taxonomy in Chapter 1 (Figure 1.9) the following options have been discussed in the literature.

Parallel processing

Parallel processing involves separating exploitation and exploration processes in different organizational units (differentiation), while integration takes place at a different – usually higher – organizational level. This option has been coined 'spatial separation' – an

TABLE 9.1   Strategic improvement versus strategic rejuvenation perspective

	Strategic improvement perspective	Radical rejuvenation perspective
Emphasis on	Exploitation over exploration	Exploration over exploitation
Strategic innovation as	Sustained improvements	Disruptive rejuvenation
Innovation effects	Undramatic and long-lasting	Dramatic and short-term
Innovation ideas come from	All internal and external company stakeholders	Entrepreneurial company leaders
Innovation investments are	Low-risk, small returns	High-risk, high returns
Main reinforcement mechanism	Success trap	Failure trap
Strategic renewal process	Organic adaptation	Creative destruction
View on the future	Building the future	Shaping the future
Lasting renewal requires	Continuous learning	Radical breakthrough series
Long-term renewal dynamics	Persistent transient state	Stable and unstable states alternate

academic term still used by organization behaviour scholars. Organizations that employ both exploitation – for example, by improving production processes – and exploration – such as technological research and development – as the means of dealing with the paradox of exploitation and exploration are called ambidextrous organizations (Benner and Tushman, 2003). Ambidextrous organizations separate exploitative and explorative processes in different organizational units. The literature has suggested two distinct parallel processing practices:

Parallel processing internally. A well-known practice is to build a separate research and development (R&D) unit that develops new technologies. The outcomes are then transferred to other organizational units, such as business units or market groups. Some researchers have indicated, however, that differentiating may be easy but integrating often fails. The problems are many, for example when researchers have developed technologies and patents, while managers have difficulties matching the technologies to client demands.

Parallel processing with external partners. Exploitation and exploration can also be separated by outsourcing one of the processes to an external strategic partner. When exploitation is outsourced, partners take responsibility to adopt the firm's exploitative processes, such as manufacturing products, including the ongoing improvement of current processes and products. In this case, the company is able to focus the key organizational resources on exploration processes, creating the new generation of products and services. Conversely, the firm can also outsource exploration to specialized companies, and stay focused on efficient and effective exploitation. Strategizing managers then integrate the partner's deliverables within the company processes. A main advantage of parallel processing with external partners is that it effectively combines the contradicting core capabilities of two firms; a main pitfall is, however, that the partner's strategic objectives may change and become conflicting.

Navigating

Entrepreneurs often separate exploration and exploitation over time in the early start-up phase. When starting a new business on the basis of a new idea for a new technology (such as a new app) or a novel market proposition, the entrepreneur first explores and then exploits – hence navigates over time, also called temporal separation.

In this case, the start-up entrepreneur is not renewing as there is not yet an organization to be renewed; however when this initiative is being taken by a corporate entrepreneur or a business development manager, the entrepreneurial activity may well intend to renew the current company. The new activity is then meant to replace or improve established businesses. This process had become known by the famous CEO from General Electric, Jack Welch, who introduced the 'Destroy your business dot com' programme in the year 2000. The general practice is that the renewing unit stays at a distance from the established company in order to prevent managers from the current business killing the initiative in its infancy. This practice has been advocated by Peters and Waterman (1982), who dubbed these promising corporate start-ups 'skunk works' as the initiative may threaten the current organization and thus 'stinks'.

Balancing

One of the differences between exploitation and exploration is time orientation: sustaining renewal processes (exploitation) has a short-term focus, while disrupting processes (exploration) is long-term oriented. Notwithstanding the differences, it is suggested in the literature that the processes may be combined in the same unit. The strategic agenda then consists of both short-term and long-term innovation projects. The balance between the two is not only company-specific, but also dynamic as priorities can change. Although balancing exploitation and exploration is more complex than parallel processing, some scholars prefer balancing because, although differentiating is relatively easy and fast, the integrating part is usually a problem (Smith *et al.*, 2016).

When balancing takes place at the individual level, some strategists are expected to fulfil roles in both sustaining and disrupting renewal processes. For example, knowledge workers both build their professional practice at higher levels and also explore radically different ways to serve future clients. Being able to do so requires personal characteristics that not all individuals possess. Smith and Tushman (2005, Reading 1.2) argue that "the ability to engage in paradoxical thinking may be vital for effectively managing exploitation and exploration".

The human factor in balancing the paradox, in particular the composition of the company's leadership team, has been explored by Peter Robertson. In a book, provocatively entitled *Always Change a Winning Team* (2005), Robertson combines insights from ethology – a field strongly related to neuroanatomy, ecology and evolution theory – with the dynamics of the well-known S-curve. Robertson argues that the composition of a successful leadership team should differ over the S-curve. In the early phase, the leadership team should mainly be composed of leaders employing visionary feedforward-thinking with a passion to explore the unknown, while in the mature phase, the leadership team should mainly consist of analytic feedback-thinking leaders (see Figure 9.4). Over the S-curve, the composition of the leadership team should be changed in anticipation of the next phase. According to Robertson, the key role in permanently changing the leadership team is a 'chairperson', the CEO, who connects the feedforward and feedback thinkers and who is in charge of continuously rebalancing the 'winning team'. This individual needs to have what Robertson calls high 'complexity maturity', a term that relates to what Smith and Tushman (2005) describe as "the ability to engage in paradoxical thinking".

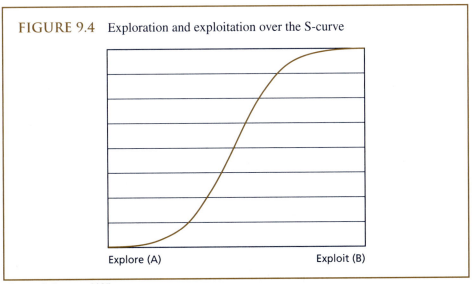

FIGURE 9.4   Exploration and exploitation over the S-curve

Explore (A)   Exploit (B)

Source: Robertson, 2005.

STRATEGIC INNOVATION IN INTERNATIONAL PERSPECTIVE

Co-authors: Gep Eisenloeffel and Wester Wagenaar

Imagination is more important than knowledge.

Albert Einstein (1879–1955); German–American physicist

Pronounced international variance on inclinations towards exploitation or exploration are apparent across countries. For what reason do firms in different societies prefer different views on strategic innovation? Are there any country-specific factors that lead to divergent perspectives? Understanding international differences and their causes helps get a better grip on the extent to which companies are able to learn from international practices or are limited by their national context. In addition to national differences, some industries focus more on radical breakthroughs than do others. A strategist can learn from both the national level as well as international industry similarities.

On the national level

Strategic innovation is responsible for turning small firms into industry leaders and for falling giants that fail to successfully renew (Bilton and Cummings, 2010; Utterback, 1994). This is true for the national level as well as for the global scale. Although most agree that innovation is important, preferences on how to innovate differ across societies. Imai (1986) explicitly introduces specific national preferences in his approach to strategic innovation. He argues that "Japanese companies generally favour the gradualist approach and Western companies the great-leap approach – an approach epitomized by the term innovation". This general, yet fundamental, distinction is supported by other research, although these studies are relatively old (e.g. Kagono *et al.*, 1985; Ouchi, 1981; Pascale and Athos, 1981). Nevertheless, the common suggestion is that the US and Japan represent two extremes, with most other industrialized countries somewhere in between (e.g. Calori, Valla and De Woot, 1994; Krüger, 1996).

Elucidating the differences in preferences for innovation styles generally boils down to cultural explanations. For example, studies claim a correlation between individualism and innovation (e.g. Goncalo and Staw, 2006; Hampden-Turner and Trompenaars, 2000). Individualistic-minded teams foster internal competition, which improves innovation (Tellis, Prabhu and Chandy, 2009, p. 8). The two countries considered most individualistic, the US and Great Britain, also show tremendous capacity to realize radical frame-breaking innovations. Furthermore, the US leads the world ranking of Nobel Prizes won, in the practical application of scientific principles.

Another cultural explanation can be found in national preferences towards uncertainty avoidance. Because radical innovation inherently yields unexpected and unintended outcomes (Starbuck, 2014), a natural tendency towards feeling threatened by the unknown may limit possibilities. Especially adopting radical changes can be expected to be met with a degree of reluctance in countries scoring high on Hofstede's uncertainty avoidance index (1980).

Culture cannot explain everything, however. Government support and prevailing rules and regulations may also play a decisive role in the transition from one technological platform to another. For instance, since the Second World War, the European Union has been crucial in the transition from coal to an oil- and gas-based energy supply. In China, the government promotes solar power batteries to reduce emissions from two- to four-wheeled motor vehicles.

Traditionally, most recent radical innovations have originated from the West, but a shift seems to be imminent. A good indicator of shifting technological innovations from the traditional industrialized countries in the North West to the upcoming economies in the South East is the number of patents granted per country. This concentration of patents is highly uneven. Between 2000 and 2006, applicants from Japan, the US, the Republic of Korea and Germany received 73 per cent of total patents worldwide. In that same period, the number of patents granted to applicants from China and South Korea grew with an average annual growth rate of 26.5 per cent and 23.2 per cent respectively (WIPO, 2008). China is now the country with the most filed patents per year, although it is the Republic of Korea where the highest number of patents per unit of GDP are filed. High-income countries in total still account for about 60 per cent of the applications filed. This reflects their high R&D spending (WIPO, 2015). The rapid growth of Chinese patents matches the emergence of this country as the second largest producer of scientific knowledge as revealed by a Thomson Reuters analysis of 10 500 scientific journals worldwide for the period 1981–2008 (Cookson, 2010).

On the industry level

Are there industries with a preference for radical rejuvenation and industries where a focus on strategic improvement can be observed? Every industry follows an S-curve of exploration and exploitation. It depends on the industry how long it takes before a radical innovation changes the game and traditional processes or technologies become outdated. Furthermore, there is not a strict distinction between disruptive and evolutionary industries, because innovation is by nature inter-disciplinary (Story *et al.*, 2014, p. 1272). Nevertheless, some industries do display a stronger focus on exploring possibilities for disruptive innovations, such as the high-tech sector. Capital often proves essential for innovative technological breakthroughs and this is especially true for these high-tech industries. Collaboration or coopetition is thus a common way to advance promising technological initiatives. Nevertheless, it is important to note that collaboration among those with complementary technology and processes contributes to developing radical innovations, while partners with similar technologies innovate incrementally (Quintana-García and Benavides-Velasco, 2011).

Because of the power of capital to find and develop drastic breakthroughs, it is not surprising that proactive government support is often responsible for radical innovation. One straightforward example is the military industry. The development of aviation, for example, was made possible because of war. Dutch engineer Anthony Fokker, working for the Germans during the First World War, was one of the first great pioneers in the field exploiting opportunities presented as a result of conflict. Many other entrepreneurs, like American Lockheed and French Dassault followed suit. The Cold War is both responsible for the improvement of helicopters and the development of stealth technology. Helicopters were used for the first time in the Korean War and stealth technology was developed in the late 1950s after earlier attempts by the Soviet Union to prevent radar tracking of US spy planes had been unsuccessful. DARPA research teams (The Defense Advanced Research Projects Agency) made computer networking possible, paving the way for the development of the Internet, and present-day drones were primarily invented for war and not for commercial purposes.

Although many of the inventions by the military are adopted by other industries, non-military sectors can also profit directly from government support. For example, Japan's Ministry of International Trade and Industry (MITI) is highly influential in developing industries and the European Commission promotes technological development programs in the field of information technologies.

To the strategist

Increasingly, the innovator is not merely seen as an individual. He plays a role in a team, organization and network in fostering innovation (Fichter and Beucker, 2012). Nevertheless, the individual strategist still has a powerful role to play in the innovation process. He/she should not see their context, national and international, as eternally stable, but as in flux and malleable. In order to make the right strategic decisions, he needs to be able to continuously adapt to a changing industry environment. Not only does this mean having the ability to abandon processes, products and services when these prove outdated, the strategist also needs to shift between leadership styles when the need arises. Making radical changes may make some previous commitments and policies obsolete, so a versatile strategist is necessary when dealing with innovation – both during the exploration and in the exploitation phase (Starbuck, 2014).

INTRODUCTION TO THE READINGS

Every act of creation is first of all an act of destruction.
Pablo Picasso (1881–1973); Spanish artist

So, how should managers go about renewing their organizations? The debate will be kicked off in the first reading (9.1), 'Kaizen', by Masaaki Imai, which has been selected to represent the strategic improvement perspective. This article has been taken from Imai's famous book *Kaizen: The Key to Japan's Competitive Success*. Kaizen (pronounced Ky'zen) is a Japanese term that is best translated as continuous improvement. Imai argues that it is this continuous improvement philosophy that best explains the competitive strength of so many Japanese companies. In his view, Western companies have an unhealthy obsession with one-shot innovations. They are fixated on the great leap forward, while disregarding the power of accumulated small changes. Imai believes that disruptive innovations are also important for competitive success, but that they should be embedded in an organization that is driven to continuously improve.

The radical rejuvenation perspective is represented by Clayton Christensen. In Reading 9.2, adapted from his popular book, *The Innovator's Dilemma, When New Technologies Cause Great Firms to Fail,* Christensen explains why outstanding companies lost their market leadership when confronted with disruptive changes in technology and market structure. This phenomenon applies particularly to excellent firms with an excessive customer focus, Christensen argues, *exactly because* their excessive customer focus prevents them from creating new markets and finding new customers for the products of the future. His argument follows Burgelman, who wrote in 1991: "Paradoxically, adaptation to existing environmental demands may reduce the organization's capacity to adapt to future changes in the environment or to seek our new environments" (1991: 251). Christensen has termed this strategic innovation paradox 'the innovator's dilemma'.

While the third reading in other chapters predominantly represents recent insights in how to deal with strategy paradoxes, in this chapter the article that actually started the debate on the paradox of exploitation and exploration has been chosen. March's 1991 pioneering and seminal article 'Exploitation and Exploration in Organizational Learning' (Reading 9.3) started a new research stream and stimulated many scholars in several academic fields to understand how companies do and should manage the paradox of exploitation and exploration to achieving long-term success. The first movers were scholars in the field of Organizational Learning and Organizational Behaviour, such as the currently prominent Harvard professor Michael Tushman (e.g. Benner and Tushman (2002; 2003).

March argues that "companies require both exploitation and exploration to achieve persistent success", and have to manage both by finding a balance, because "the two are fundamentally incompatible". These propositions have been – and still are for that matter – subject to scientific debate. However, while alternative avenues have been described and suggested (see for a thorough discussion Gupta *et al.* (2006)), March's proposition still holds. Stronger even: the popular term 'ambidextrous organization' takes March's proposition as a more general characteristic of organizations. From here, the fundamental idea that companies have to manage multiple tensions hallmarks a significant portion of present day research in the organization and strategy sciences.

Kaizen

By Masaaki Imai[1]

Back in the 1950s, I was working with the Japan Productivity Center in Washington, DC. My job mainly consisted of escorting groups of Japanese businessmen who were visiting American companies to study 'the secret of American industrial productivity'. Toshiro Yamada, now Professor Emeritus of the Faculty of Engineering at Kyoto University, was a member of one such study team visiting the United States to study the industrial vehicle industry. Recently, the members of his team gathered to celebrate the silver anniversary of their trip.

At the banquet table, Yamada said he had recently been back to the United States in a 'sentimental journey' to some of the plants he had visited, among them the River Rouge steelworks in Dearborn, Michigan. Shaking his head in disbelief, he said, 'You know, the plant was exactly the same as it had been 25 years ago.'

These conversations set me to thinking about the great differences in the ways Japanese and Western managers approach their work. It is inconceivable that a Japanese plant would remain virtually unchanged for over a quarter of a century.

I had long been looking for a key concept to explain these two very different management approaches, one that might also help explain why many Japanese companies have come to gain their increasingly conspicuous competitive edge. For instance, how do we explain the fact that while most new ideas come from the West and some of the most advanced plants, institutions and technologies are found there, there are also many plants there that have changed little since the 1950s?

Change is something which everybody takes for granted. Recently, an American executive at a large multinational firm told me his company chairman had said at the start of an executive committee meeting: 'Gentlemen, our job is to manage change. If we fail, we must change management.' The executive smiled and said, 'We all got the message!'

In Japan, change is a way of life, too. But are we talking about the same change when we talk about managing change or else changing management? It dawned on me that there might be different kinds of change: gradual and abrupt. While we can easily observe both gradual and abrupt changes in Japan, gradual change is not so obvious a part of the Western way of life. How are we to explain this difference?

This question led me to consider the question of values. Could it be that differences between the value systems in Japan and the West account for their different attitudes toward gradual change and abrupt change? Abrupt changes are easily grasped by everyone concerned, and people are usually elated to see them. This is generally true in both Japan and the West. Yet what about the gradual changes? My earlier statement that it is inconceivable that a Japanese plant would remain unchanged for years refers to gradual change as well as abrupt change.

Thinking all this over, I came to the conclusion that the key difference between how change is understood in Japan and how it is viewed in the West lies in the Kaizen concept – a concept that is so natural and obvious to many Japanese managers that they often

[1]Source: This article was adapted with permission from Chapters 1 and 2 of *Kaizen: The Key to Japan's Competitive Success,* McGraw-Hill, New York, 1986. Copyright © 1986 by The McGraw-Hill Companies, Inc.. Reproduced by permission of The McGraw-Hill Companies, Inc..

do not even realize that they possess it! The Kaizen concept explains why companies cannot remain the same for long in Japan. Moreover, after many years of studying Western business practices, I have reached the conclusion that this Kaizen concept is non-existent, or at least very weak, in most Western companies today. Worse yet, they reject it without knowing what it really entails. It's the old 'not invented here' syndrome. And this lack of Kaizen helps explain why an American or European factory can remain exactly the same for a quarter of a century.

The essence of Kaizen is simple and straightforward: Kaizen means improvement. Moreover, Kaizen means ongoing improvement involving everyone, including both managers and workers. The Kaizen philosophy assumes that our way of life – be it our working life, our social life, or our home life – deserves to be constantly improved.

In trying to understand Japan's post-war 'economic miracle,' scholars, journalists and businesspeople alike have dutifully studied such factors as the productivity movement, total quality control, small-group activities, the suggestion system, automation, industrial robots and labour relations. They have given much attention to some of Japan's unique management practices, among them the lifetime employment system, seniority-based wages and enterprise unions. Yet I feel they have failed to grasp the very simple truth that lies behind the many myths concerning Japanese management.

The essence of most 'uniquely Japanese' management practices – be they productivity improvement, TQC (total quality control) activities, QC (quality control) circles or labour relations – can be reduced to one word: Kaizen. Using the term Kaizen in place of such words as productivity, TQC, ZD (zero defects), *kanban* and the suggestion system paints a far clearer picture of what has been going on in Japanese industry. Kaizen is an umbrella concept covering most of those 'uniquely Japanese' practices that have recently achieved such worldwide fame.

The implications of TQC or CWQC (companywide quality control) in Japan have been that these concepts have helped Japanese companies generate a process oriented way of thinking and develop strategies that assure continuous improvement involving people at all levels of the organizational hierarchy. The message of the Kaizen strategy is that not a day should go by without some kind of improvement being made somewhere in the company.

The belief that there should be unending improvement is deeply ingrained in the Japanese mentality. As the old Japanese saying goes, 'If a man has not been seen for three days, his friends should take a good look at him to see what changes have befallen him.' The implication is that he must have changed in three days, so his friends should be attentive enough to notice the changes.

After World War II, most Japanese companies had to start literally from the ground up. Every day brought new challenges to managers and workers alike, and every day meant progress. Simply staying in business required unending progress, and Kaizen has become a way of life. It was also fortunate that the various tools that helped elevate this Kaizen concept to new heights were introduced to Japan in the late 1950s and early 1960s by such experts as W.E. Deming and J.M. Juran.

However, most new concepts, systems and tools that are widely used in Japan today have subsequently been developed in Japan and represent qualitative improvements upon the statistical quality control and total quality control of the 1960s.

Kaizen and management

Figure 9.1.1 shows how job functions are perceived in Japan. As indicated, management has two major components: maintenance and improvement. Maintenance refers to activities directed toward maintaining current technological, managerial and operating standards; improvement refers to those directed toward improving current standards.

Under its maintenance functions, management performs its assigned tasks so that everybody in the company can follow the established SOP (Standard

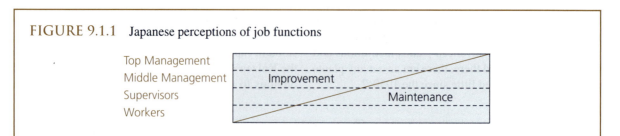

FIGURE 9.1.1   Japanese perceptions of job functions

Top Management
Middle Management
Supervisors
Workers

Improvement

Maintenance

Operating Procedure). This means that management must first establish policies, rules, directives and procedures for all major operations and then see to it that everybody follows SOP. If people are able to follow the standard but do not, management must introduce discipline. If people are unable to follow the standard, management must either provide training, or review and revise the standard so that people can follow it.

In any business, an employee's work is based on existing standards, either explicit or implicit, imposed by management. Maintenance refers to maintaining such standards through training and discipline. By contrast, improvement refers to improving the standards. The Japanese perception of management boils down to one precept: maintain and improve standards.

The higher up the manager is, the more he is concerned with improvement. At the bottom level, an unskilled worker working at a machine may spend all his time following instructions. However, as he becomes more proficient at his work, he begins to think about improvement. He begins to contribute to improvements in the way his work is done, either through individual suggestions or through group suggestions.

Ask any manager at a successful Japanese company what top management is pressing for, and the answer will be, 'Kaizen' (improvement). Improving standards means establishing higher standards. Once this is done, it becomes management's maintenance job to see that the new standards are observed. Lasting improvement is achieved only when people work to higher standards. Maintenance and improvement have thus become inseparable for most Japanese managers.

What is improvement? Improvement can be broken down between Kaizen and innovation. Kaizen signifies small improvements made in the status quo as a result of

ongoing efforts. Innovation involves a drastic improvement in the status quo as a result of a large investment in new technology or equipment. Figure 9.1.2 shows the breakdown among maintenance, Kaizen and innovation as perceived by Japanese management.

On the other hand, most Western managers' perceptions of job functions are as shown in Figure 9.1.2. There is little room in Western management for the Kaizen concept.

Sometimes, another type of management is found in the high-technology industries. These are the companies that are born running, grow rapidly, and then disappear just as rapidly when their initial success wanes or markets change.

The worst companies are those which do nothing but maintenance, meaning there is no internal drive for Kaizen or innovation, change is forced on management by market conditions and competition and management does not know where it wants to go.

Implications of QC for Kaizen

While management is usually concerned with such issues as productivity and quality, the thrust of this article is to look at the other side of the picture – at Kaizen.

The starting point for improvement is to recognize the need. This comes from recognition of a problem. If no problem is recognized, there is no recognition of the need for improvement. Complacency is the arch enemy of Kaizen. Therefore, Kaizen emphasizes problem awareness and provides clues for identifying problems.

Once identified, problems must be solved. Thus Kaizen is also a problem-solving process. In fact, Kaizen requires the use of various problem-solving tools. Improvement reaches new heights with every

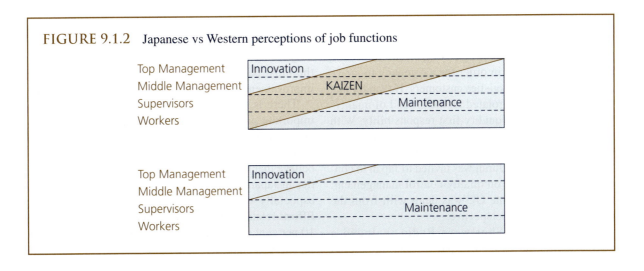

FIGURE 9.1.2 Japanese vs Western perceptions of job functions

problem that is solved. In order to consolidate the new level, however, the improvement must be standardized. Thus Kaizen also requires standardization.

Such terms as QC (quality control), SQC (statistical quality control), QC circles, and TQC (or CWQC) often appear in connection with Kaizen. To avoid unnecessary confusion, it may be helpful to clarify these terms here. The word *quality* has been interpreted in many different ways, and there is no agreement on what actually constitutes quality. In its broadest sense, quality is anything that can be improved. In this context, quality is associated not only with products and services but also with the way people work, the way machines are operated and the way systems and procedures are dealt with. It includes all aspects of human behaviour. This is why it is more useful to talk about Kaizen than about quality or productivity.

The English term *improvement* as used in the Western context more often than not means improvement in equipment, thus excluding the human elements. By contrast, Kaizen is generic and can be applied to every aspect of everybody's activities. This said, however, it must be admitted that such terms as quality and quality control have played a vital role in the development of Kaizen in Japan.

In March 1950, the Union of Japanese Scientists and Engineers (JUSE) started publishing its magazine *Statistical Quality Control*. In July of the same year, W.E. Deming was invited to Japan to teach statistical quality control at an eight-day seminar organized by JUSE. Deming visited Japan several times in the 1950s, and it was during one of those visits that he made his famous prediction that Japan would soon be flooding the world market with quality products.

Deming also introduced the 'Deming cycle', one of the crucial QC tools for assuring continuous improvement, to Japan. The Deming cycle is also called the Deming wheel or the PDCA (Plan-Do-Check-Action) cycle (see Figure 9.1.3.) Deming stressed the importance of constant interaction among research, design, production and sales in order for a company to arrive at better quality that satisfies customers. He taught that this wheel should be rotated on the ground of quality-first perceptions and quality-first responsibility. With this process, he argued, the company could win consumer confidence and acceptance and prosper.

In July 1954, J.M. Juran was invited to Japan to conduct a JUSE seminar on quality-control management. This was the first time QC was dealt with from the overall management perspective.

In 1956, Japan Shortwave Radio included a course on quality control as part of its educational

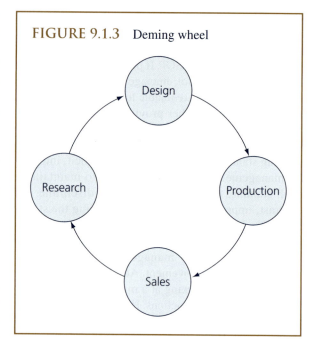

FIGURE 9.1.3   Deming wheel

programming. In November 1960, the first national quality month was inaugurated. It was also in 1960 that Q-marks and Q-flags were formally adopted. Then in April 1962 the magazine *Quality Control for the Foreman* was launched by JUSE, and the first QC circle was started that same year.

A QC circle is defined as a small group that *voluntarily* performs quality-control activities within the shop. The small group carries out its work continuously as part of a company-wide programme of quality control, self-development, mutual education, and flow-control and improvement within the workshop. The QC circle is only *part* of a company-wide programme; it is never the whole of TQC or CWQC.

Those who have followed QC circles in Japan know that they often focus on such areas as cost, safety and productivity, and that their activities sometimes relate only indirectly to product-quality improvement. For the most part, these activities are aimed at making improvements in the workshop.

There is no doubt that QC circles have played an important part in improving product quality and productivity in Japan. However, their role has often been blown out of proportion by overseas observers who believe that QC circles are the mainstay of TQC activities in Japan. Nothing could be further from the truth, especially when it comes to Japanese management. Efforts related to QC circles generally account for only 10 per cent to 30 per cent of the overall TQC effort in Japanese companies.

What is less visible behind these developments is the transformation of the term quality control, or QC, in Japan. As is the case in many Western companies, quality control initially meant quality control applied to the manufacturing process, particularly the inspections for rejecting defective incoming material or defective outgoing products at the end of the production line. But very soon the realization set in that inspection alone does nothing to improve the quality of the product, and that product quality should be built at the production stage. 'Build quality into the process' was (and still is) a popular phrase in Japanese quality control. It is at this stage that control charts and the other tools for statistical quality control were introduced after Deming's lectures.

Juran's lectures in 1954 opened up another aspect of quality control: the managerial approach to quality control. This was the first time the term QC was positioned as a vital management tool in Japan. From then on, the term QC has been used to mean both quality control and the tools for overall improvement in managerial performance.

At a later stage, other industries started to introduce QC for such products as consumer durables and home appliances. In these industries, the interest was in building quality in at the design stage to meet changing and increasingly stringent customer requirements. Today, management has gone beyond the design stage and has begun to stress the importance of quality product development, which means taking customer related information and market research into account from the very start.

All this while, QC has grown into a fully-fledged management tool for Kaizen involving everyone in the company. Such company-wide activities are often referred to as TQC (total quality control) or CWQC (company-wide quality control). No matter which name is used, TQC and CWQC mean company-wide Kaizen activities involving everyone in the company, managers and workers alike. Over the years, QC has been elevated to SQC and then to TQC or CWQC, improving managerial performance at every level. Thus it is that such words as QC and TQC have come to be almost synonymous with Kaizen. This is also why I constantly refer to QC, TQC and CWQC in explaining Kaizen.

On the other hand, the function of quality control in its original sense remains valid. Quality assurance remains a vital part of management, and most companies have a QA (quality assurance) department for this.

To confuse matters, TQC or CWQC activities are sometimes administered by the QA department and sometimes by a separate TQC office. Thus it is

important that these QC-related words be understood in the context in which they appear.

Kaizen and TQC

Considering the TQC movement in Japan as part of the Kaizen movement gives us a clearer perspective on the Japanese approach. First of all, it should be pointed out that TQC activities in Japan are not concerned solely with quality control. People have been fooled by the term 'quality control' and have often construed it within the narrow discipline of product-quality control. In the West, the term QC is mostly associated with inspection of finished products, and when QC is brought up in discussion, top managers, who generally assume they have very little to do with quality control, lose interest immediately.

It is unfortunate that in the West TQC has been dealt with mainly in technical journals when it is more properly the focus of management journals. Japan has developed an elaborate system of Kaizen strategies as management tools within the TQC movement. These rank among this century's most outstanding management achievements. Yet because of the limited way in which QC is understood in the West, most Western students of Japanese QC activities have failed to grasp their real significance and challenge. At the same time, new TQC methods and tools are constantly being studied and tested.

TQC in Japan is a movement centered on the improvement of managerial performance at all levels. As such, it has typically dealt with:

1 quality assurance;
2 cost reduction;
3 meeting production quotas;
4 meeting delivery schedules;
5 safety;
6 new-product development;
7 productivity improvement;
8 supplier management.

More recently, TQC has come to include marketing, sales and service as well. Furthermore, TQC has dealt with such crucial management concerns as organizational development, cross-functional management, policy deployment and quality deployment. In other words, management has been using TQC as a tool for improving overall performance.

Those who have closely followed QC circles in Japan know that their activities are often focused on such areas as cost, safety and productivity, and that their activities may only indirectly relate to product-quality improvement. For the most part, these activities are aimed at making improvements in the workplace.

Management efforts for TQC have been directed mostly at such areas as education, systems development, policy deployment, cross-functional management and, more recently, quality deployment.

Kaizen and the suggestion system

Japanese management makes a concerted effort to involve employees in Kaizen through suggestions. Thus, the suggestion system is an integral part of the established management system, and the number of workers' suggestions is regarded as an important criterion in reviewing the performance of these workers' supervisor. The manager of the supervisors is in turn expected to assist them so that they can help workers generate more suggestions.

Most Japanese companies active in Kaizen programmes have a quality-control system and a suggestion system working in concert. The role of QC circles may be better understood if we regard them collectively as a group-oriented suggestion system for making improvements.

One of the outstanding features of Japanese management is that it generates a great number of suggestions from workers and that management works hard to consider these suggestions, often incorporating them into the overall Kaizen strategy. It is not uncommon for top management of a leading Japanese company to spend a whole day listening to presentations of activities by QC circles, and giving awards based on predetermined criteria. Management is willing to give recognition to employees' efforts for improvements and makes its concern visible wherever possible. Often, the number of suggestions is posted individually on the wall of the workplace in order to encourage competition among workers and among groups.

Another important aspect of the suggestion system is that each suggestion, once implemented, leads to a revised standard. For instance, when a special foolproof device has been installed on a machine at a worker's suggestion, this may require the worker to work differently and, at times, more attentively.

However, inasmuch as the new standard has been set up by the worker's own volition, he takes pride in the new standard and is willing to follow it. If, on the contrary, he is told to follow a standard imposed by management, he may not be as willing to follow it.

Thus, through suggestions, employees can participate in Kaizen in the workplace and play a vital role in upgrading standards. In a recent interview, Toyota Motor Chairman Eiji Toyoda said, 'One of the features of the Japanese workers is that they use their brains as well as their hands. Our workers provide 1.5 million suggestions a year, and 95 per cent of them are put to practical use. There is an almost tangible concern for improvement in the air at Toyota.'

Kaizen vs innovation

There are two contrasting approaches to progress: the gradualist approach and the great-leap-forward approach. Japanese companies generally favour the gradualist approach and Western companies the great-leap approach – an approach epitomized by the term 'innovation'.

Western management worships at the altar of innovation. This innovation is seen as major change in the wake of technological breakthroughs, or the introduction of the latest management concepts or production techniques. Innovation is dramatic, a real attention-getter. Kaizen, on the other hand, is often undramatic and subtle, and its results are seldom immediately visible. While Kaizen is a continuous process, innovation is generally a one-shot phenomenon.

In the West, for example, a middle manager can usually obtain top management support for such projects as CAD (computer-aided design), CAM (computer-aided manufacture), and MRP (materials requirements planning), since these are innovative projects that have a way of revolutionizing existing systems. As such, they offer ROI (return on investment) benefits that managers can hardly resist.

However, when a factory manager wishes, for example, to make small changes in the way his workers use the machinery, such as working out multiple job assignments or realigning production processes (both of which may require lengthy discussions with the union as well as re-education and retraining of workers), obtaining management support can be difficult indeed.

Table 9.1.1 compares the main features of Kaizen and of innovation. One of the beautiful things about Kaizen is that it does not necessarily require sophisticated technique or state-of-the-art technology. To implement Kaizen, you need only simple, conventional techniques. Often, common sense is all that is needed. On the other hand, innovation usually requires highly sophisticated technology, as well as a huge investment.

TABLE 9.1.1   Features of Kaizen and innovation

	Kaizen	Innovation
1. *Effect*	Long-term and long-lasting but undramatic	Short-term but dramatic
2. *Pace*	Small steps	Big steps
3. *Timeframe*	Continuous and incremental	Intermittent and non-incremental
4. *Change*	Gradual and constant	Abrupt and volatile
5. *Involvement*	Everybody	Select few 'champions'
6. *Approach*	Collectivism, group efforts, systems approach	Rugged individualism, individual ideas and efforts
7. *Mode*	Maintenance and improvement	Scrap and rebuild
8. *Spark*	Conventional know-how and state of the art	Technological breakthroughs, new inventions, new theories
9. *Practical requirements*	Requires little investment but great effort to maintain it	Requires large investment but little effort to maintain it
10. *Effort orientation*	People	Technology
11. *Evaluation criteria*	Process and efforts for better results	Results and profits
12. *Advantage*	Works well in slow-growth economy	Better suited to fast-growth economy

Kaizen is like a hotbed that nurtures small and ongoing changes, while innovation is like magma that appears in abrupt eruptions from time to time. One big difference between Kaizen and innovation is that while Kaizen does not necessarily call for a large investment to implement it, it does call for a great deal of continuous effort and commitment. The difference between the two opposing concepts may thus be likened to that of a staircase and a slope. The innovation strategy is supposed to bring about progress in a staircase progression. On the other hand, the Kaizen strategy brings about gradual progress. I say the innovation strategy 'is supposed to' bring about progress in a staircase progression, because it usually does not. Instead of following the staircase pattern, the actual progress achieved through innovation will generally follow the

pattern shown in Figure 9.1.4, if it lacks the Kaizen strategy to go along with it. This happens because a system, once it has been installed as a result of new innovation, is subject to steady deterioration unless continuing efforts are made first to maintain it and then to improve on it.

In reality, there can be no such thing as a static constant. All systems are destined to deteriorate once they have been established. One of the famous Parkinson's Laws is that an organization, once it has built its edifice, begins its decline. In other words, there must be a continuing effort for improvement to even maintain the status quo.

When such effort is lacking, decline is inevitable (see Figure 9.1.4). Therefore, even when an innovation makes a revolutionary standard of performance

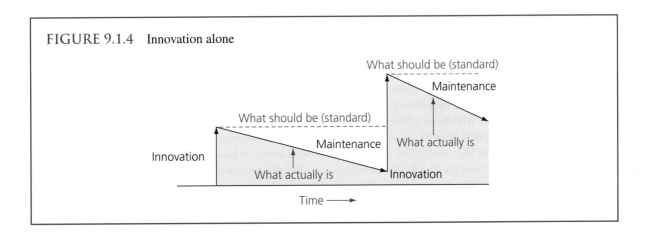

FIGURE 9.1.4   Innovation alone

FIGURE 9.1.5   Innovation plus Kaizen

attainable, the new performance level will decline unless the standard is constantly challenged and upgraded. Thus, whenever an innovation is achieved, it must be followed by a series of Kaizen efforts to maintain and improve it (see Figure 9.1.5).

Whereas innovation is a one-shot deal whose effects are gradually eroded by intense competition and deteriorating standards, Kaizen is an ongoing effort with cumulative effects marking a steady rise as the years go by. If standards exist only in order to maintain the status quo, they will not be challenged so long as the level of performance is acceptable. Kaizen, on the other hand, means a constant effort not only to maintain but also to upgrade standards. Kaizen strategists believe that standards are by nature tentative, akin to stepping stones, with one standard leading to another as continuing improvement efforts are made. This is the reason why QC circles no sooner solve one problem than they move on to tackle a new problem. This is also the reason why the so-called PDCA (plan-do-check-action) cycle receives so much emphasis in Japan's TQC movement.

Another feature of Kaizen is that it requires virtually everyone's personal efforts. In order for the Kaizen spirit to survive, management must make a conscious and continuous effort to support it. Such support is quite different from the fanfare recognition that management accords to people who have achieved a striking success or breakthrough. Kaizen is concerned more with the process than with the result. The strength of Japanese management lies in its successful development and implementation of a system that acknowledges the ends while emphasizing the means.

Thus Kaizen calls for a substantial management commitment of time and effort. Infusions of capital are no substitute for this investment in time and effort.

Investing in Kaizen means investing in people. In short, Kaizen is people-oriented, whereas innovation is technology- and money-oriented.

Finally, the Kaizen philosophy is better suited to a slow-growth economy, while innovation is better suited to a fast-growth economy. While Kaizen advances inch-by-inch on the strength of many small efforts, innovation leaps upward in hopes of landing at a much higher plateau in spite of gravitational inertia and the weight of investment costs. In a slow-growth economy characterized by high costs of energy and materials, overcapacity and stagnant markets, Kaizen often has a better payoff than innovation does. As one Japanese executive recently remarked, 'It is extremely difficult to increase sales by 10 per cent. But it is not so difficult to cut manufacturing costs by 10 per cent to even better effect.'

I argued that the concept of Kaizen is non-existent or at best weak in most Western companies today. However, there was a time, not so long ago, when Western management also placed a high priority on Kaizen-like improvement-consciousness. Older executives may recall that before the phenomenal economic growth of the late 1950s and early 1960s, management attended assiduously to improving all aspects of the business, particularly the factory. In those days, every small improvement was counted and was seen as effective in terms of building success.

People who worked with small, privately owned companies may recall with a touch of nostalgia that there was a genuine concern for improvement 'in the air' before the company was bought out or went public. As soon as that happened, the quarterly P/L (profit/loss) figures suddenly became the most important criterion, and management became obsessed with the bottom line, often at the expense of pressing for constant and unspectacular improvements.

For many other companies, the greatly increased market opportunities and technological innovations that appeared during the first two decades after World War II meant that developing new products based on the new technology was much more attractive or 'sexier' than slow, patient efforts for improvement. In trying to catch up with the ever-increasing market demand, managers boldly introduced one innovation after another, and they were content to ignore the seemingly minor benefits of improvement.

Most Western managers who joined the ranks during or after those heady days do not have the slightest concern for improvement. Instead, they take an offensive posture, armed with professional expertise geared toward making big changes in the name of innovation, bringing about immediate gains, and winning instant recognition and promotion. Before they knew it, Western managers had lost sight of improvement and put all their eggs in the innovation basket.

Another factor that has abetted the innovation approach has been the increasing emphasis on financial controls and accounting. By now, the more sophisticated companies have succeeded in establishing elaborate accounting and reporting systems that force managers to account for every action they take and to spell out the precise payout or ROI of every managerial decision. Such a system does not lend itself to building a favourable climate for improvement.

Improvement is by definition slow, gradual and often invisible, with effects that are felt over the long run. In my opinion, the most glaring and significant shortcoming of Western management today is the lack of improvement philosophy. There is no internal system in Western management to reward efforts for improvement; instead, everyone's job performance is reviewed strictly on the basis of results. Thus it is not uncommon for Western managers to chide people with, 'I don't care what you do or how you do it. I want the results – and now!' This emphasis on results has led to the innovation-dominated approach of the West. This is not to say that Japanese management does not care about innovation. But Japanese managers have enthusiastically pursued Kaizen even when they were involved in innovation.

The innovator's dilemma

By Clayton M. Christensen[1]

This reading is about the failure of companies to stay atop their industries when they confront certain types of market and technological change. It's not about the failure of simply any company, but of *good* companies – the kinds that many managers have admired and tried to emulate, the companies known for their abilities to innovate and execute. Companies stumble for many reasons, of course, among them bureaucracy, arrogance, tired executive blood, poor planning, short-term investment horizons, inadequate skills and resources, and just plain bad luck. But this reading is not about companies with such weaknesses: It is about well-managed companies that have their competitive antennae up, listen astutely to their customers, invest aggressively in new technologies, and yet still lose market dominance.

Such seemingly unaccountable failures happen in industries that move fast and in those that move slow; in those built on electronics technology and those built on chemical and mechanical technology; in manufacturing and in service industries. Sears Roebuck, for example, was regarded for decades as one of the most astutely managed retailers in the world. At its zenith Sears accounted for more than 2 per cent of all retail sales in the United States. It pioneered several innovations critical to the success of today's most admired retailers: for example, supply chain management, store brands, catalogue retailing and credit card sales. The esteem in which Sears' management was held shows in this 1964 excerpt from *Fortune:* "How did Sears do it? In a way, the most arresting aspect of its story is that there was

[1]Source: Reprinted by permission of Harvard Business School Press. From *The Innovator's Dilemma* by Clayton M. Christensen. Boston, MA 1997, pp. ix–xxvi. Copyright © 1997 by the Harvard Business School Publishing Corporation; all rights reserved.

no gimmick. Sears opened no big bag of tricks, shot off no skyrockets. Instead, it looked as though everybody in its organization simply did the right thing, easily and naturally. And their cumulative effect was to create an extraordinary powerhouse of a company."

Yet no one speaks about Sears that way today. Somehow, it completely missed the advent of discount retailing and home centres. In the midst of today's catalogue retailing boom, Sears has been driven from that business. Indeed, the very viability of its retailing operations has been questioned. One commentator has noted that "Sears' Merchandise Group lost $1.3 billion (in 1992) even before a $1.7 billion restructuring charge. Sears let arrogance blind it to basic changes taking place in the American marketplace." Another writer has complained:

> Sears has been a disappointment for investors who have watched its stock sink dismally in the face of unkept promises of a turnaround. Sears' old merchandising approach – a vast, middle-of-the-road array of mid-priced goods and services – is no longer competitive. No question, the constant disappointments, the repeated predictions of a turnaround that never seems to come, have reduced the credibility of Sears' management in both the financial and merchandising communities.

It is striking to note that Sears received its accolades at exactly the time – in the mid-1960s – when it was ignoring the rise of discount retailing and home centres, the lower-cost formats for marketing name-brand hard goods that ultimately stripped Sears of its core franchise. Sears was praised as one of the best-managed companies in the world at the very time it let Visa and MasterCard usurp the enormous lead it had established in the use of credit cards in retailing.

In some industries this pattern of leadership failure has been repeated more than once. Consider the computer industry. IBM dominated the mainframe market but missed by years the emergence of minicomputers, which were technologically much simpler than mainframes. In fact, no other major manufacturer of mainframe computers became a significant player in the minicomputer business. Digital Equipment Corporation created the minicomputer market and was joined by a set of other aggressively managed companies: Data General, Prime, Wang, Hewlett-Packard and Nixdorf. But each of these companies in turn missed the desktop personal computer market. It was left to Apple Computer, together with Commodore, Tandy and IBM's stand-alone PC division, to create the personal-computing market. Apple, in particular, was

uniquely innovative in establishing the standard for user-friendly computing. But Apple and IBM lagged five years behind the leaders in bringing portable computers to market. Similarly, the firms that built the engineering workstation market – Apollo, Sun and Silicon Graphics – were all newcomers to the industry.

As in retailing, many of these leading computer manufacturers were at one time regarded as among the best-managed companies in the world and were held up by journalists and scholars of management as examples for all to follow. Consider this assessment of Digital Equipment, made in 1986: "Taking on Digital Equipment Corp. these days is like standing in front of a moving train. The $7.6 billion computer maker has been gathering speed while most rivals are stalled in a slump in the computer industry." The author proceeded to warn IBM to watch out, because it was standing on the tracks. Indeed, Digital was one of the most prominently featured companies in the McKinsey study that led to the book *In Search of Excellence* (Peters and Waterman, 1982).

Yet a few years later, writers characterized DEC quite differently:

> Digital Equipment Corporation is a company in need of triage. Sales are drying up in its key minicomputer line. A two-year-old restructuring plan has failed miserably. Forecasting and production planning systems have failed miserably. Cost-cutting hasn't come close to restoring profitability.... But the real misfortune may be DEC's lost opportunities. It has squandered two years trying halfway measures to respond to the low-margin personal computers and workstations that have transformed the computer industry.

In Digital's case, as in Sears, the very decisions that led to its decline were made at the time it was so widely regarded as being an astutely managed firm. It was praised as a paragon of managerial excellence at the very time it was ignoring the arrival of the desktop computers that besieged it a few years later.

Sears and Digital are in noteworthy company. Xerox long dominated the market for plain paper photocopiers used in large, high-volume copying centres. Yet it missed huge growth and profit opportunities in the market for small tabletop photocopiers, where it became only a minor player. Although steel mini mills have now captured 40 per cent of the North American steel market, including nearly all of the region's markets for bars, rods and structural steel, not a single integrated steel company – American, Asian, or European – had by 1995 built a plant using mini mill technology. Of the thirty manufacturers of cable-actuated power shovels, only four survived the industry's twenty-five-year transition to hydraulic excavation technology.

The list of leading companies that failed when confronted with disruptive changes in technology and market structure is a long one. At first glance, there seems to be no pattern in the changes that overtook them. In some cases the new technologies swept through quickly; in others, the transition took decades. In some, the new technologies were complex and expensive to develop. In others, the deadly technologies were simple extensions of what the leading companies already did better than anyone else. One theme common to all of these failures, however, is that the decisions that led to failure were made when the leaders in question were widely regarded as among the best companies in the world.

There are two ways to resolve this paradox. One might be to conclude that firms such as Digital, IBM, Apple, Sears, Xerox and Bucyrus Erie must never have been well managed. Maybe they were successful because of good luck and fortuitous timing, rather than good management. Maybe they finally fell on hard times because their good fortune ran out. Maybe. An alternative explanation, however, is that these failed firms were as well-run as one could expect a firm managed by mortals to be – but that there is something about the way decisions get made in successful organizations that sows the seeds of eventual failure.

Our research supports this latter view: It shows that in the cases of well-managed firms such as those cited above, good management was the most powerful reason they failed to stay atop their industries. Precisely because these firms listened to their customers, invested aggressively in new technologies that would provide their customers more and better products of the sort they wanted, and because they carefully studied market trends and systematically allocated investment capital to innovations that promised the best returns, they lost their positions of leadership.

What this implies at a deeper level is that many of what are now widely accepted principles of good management are, in fact, only situationally appropriate. There are times at which it is right not to listen to customers, right to invest in developing lower-performance products that promise lower margins, and right to aggressively pursue small, rather than substantial, markets. This book derives a set of rules, from carefully designed research and analysis of innovative successes and failures in the disk drive and other industries that managers can use to judge when the widely accepted principles of good management should be followed and when alternative principles are appropriate.

These rules, which I call *principles of disruptive innovation,* show that when good companies fail, it often has been because their managers either ignored these principles or chose to fight them. Managers can be extraordinarily effective in managing even the most difficult innovations if they work to understand and harness the principles of disruptive innovation. As in many of life's most challenging endeavours, there is great value in coming to grips with "the way the world works," and in managing innovative efforts in ways that accommodate such forces. *The Innovator's Dilemma* applies to manufacturing and service businesses – high tech or low – in slowly evolving or rapidly changing environments.

Technology means the processes by which an organization transforms labour, capital, materials and information into products and services of greater value. All firms have technologies. A retailer like Sears employs a particular technology to procure, present, sell and deliver products to its customers, while a discount warehouse retailer like PriceCostco employs a different technology. This concept of technology therefore extends beyond engineering and manufacturing to encompass a range of marketing, investment and managerial processes. *Innovation* refers to a change in one of these technologies.

The failure framework: Why good management can lead to failure

The failure framework is built upon three findings from our study. The first is that there is a strategically important distinction between what I call *sustaining* technologies and those that are *disruptive*. These concepts are very different from the incremental – versus – radical distinction (as described in Chapter 8 of this book) that has characterized many studies of this problem. Second, the pace of technological progress can, and often does, outstrip what markets need. This means that the relevance and competitiveness of different technological approaches can change with respect to different markets over time. And third, customers and financial structures of successful companies colour heavily the sorts of investments that appear to be attractive to them, relative to certain types of entering firms.

Sustaining versus disruptive technologies

Most new technologies foster improved product performance. I call these *sustaining technologies.* Some sustaining technologies can be discontinuous or radical in character, while others are of an incremental nature.

What all sustaining technologies have in common is that they improve the performance of established products, along the dimensions of performance that mainstream customers in major markets have historically valued. Most technological advances in a given industry are sustaining in character. An important finding revealed in this book is that rarely have even the most radically difficult sustaining technologies precipitated the failure of leading firms.

Occasionally, however, *disruptive technologies* emerge: innovations that result in worse product performance, at least in the near-term. Ironically, in each of the instances studied in this book, it was disruptive technology that precipitated the leading firms' failure.

Disruptive technologies bring to a market a very different value proposition than had been available previously. Generally, disruptive technologies underperform established products in mainstream markets. But they have other features that a few fringe (and generally new) customers value. Products based on disruptive technologies are typically cheaper, simpler, smaller and, frequently, more convenient to use. There are many examples in addition to the personal desktop computer and discount retailing examples cited above. Small off-road motorcycles introduced in North America and Europe by Honda, Kawasaki and Yamaha were disruptive technologies relative to the powerful, over-the-road cycles made by Harley-Davidson and BMW. Transistors were disruptive technologies relative to vacuum tubes.

Health maintenance organizations were disruptive technologies to conventional health insurers.

Trajectories of market need versus technology improvement

The second element of the failure framework, the observation that technologies can progress faster than market demand, illustrated in Figure 9.2.1, means that in their efforts to provide better products than their competitors and earn higher prices and margins, suppliers often "overshoot" their market: They give customers more than they need or ultimately are willing to pay for. And more importantly, it means that disruptive technologies that may underperform today, relative to what users in the market demand, may be fully performance-competitive in that same market tomorrow.

Many who once needed mainframe computers for their data processing requirements, for example, no longer need or buy mainframes. Mainframe performance has surpassed the requirements of many original customers, who today find that much of what they need to do can be done on desktop machines linked to file servers. In other words, the needs of many computer users have increased more slowly than the rate of improvement provided by computer designers. Similarly, many shoppers who in 1965 felt they had to shop at department stores to be assured of quality and selection now satisfy those needs quite well at Target and Wal-Mart.

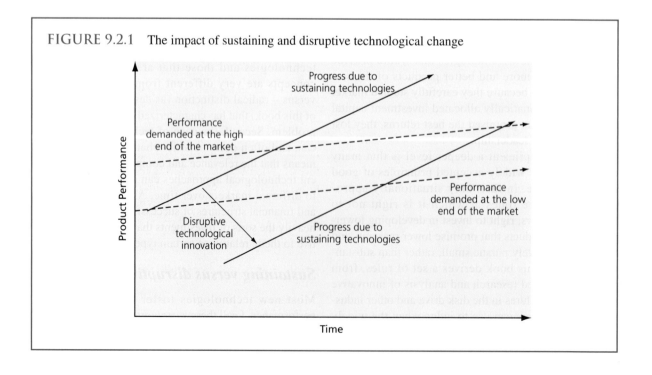

FIGURE 9.2.1   The impact of sustaining and disruptive technological change

Disruptive technologies versus rational investments

The last element of the failure framework, the conclusion by established companies that investing aggressively in disruptive technologies is not a rational financial decision for them to make, has three bases. First, disruptive products are simpler and cheaper; they generally promise lower margins, not greater profits. Second, disruptive technologies typically are first commercialized in emerging or insignificant markets. And third, leading firms' most profitable customers generally don't want, and indeed initially can't use, products based on disruptive technologies. By and large, a disruptive technology is initially embraced by the least profitable customers in a market. Hence, most companies with a practiced discipline of listening to their best customers and identifying new products that promise greater profitability and growth are rarely able to build a case for investing in disruptive technologies until it is too late.

Harnessing the principle of disruptive innovation

Colleagues who have read my academic papers were struck by their near-fatalism. If good management practice drives the failure of successful firms faced with disruptive technological change, then the usual answers to companies' problems – planning better, working harder, becoming more customer-driven and taking a longer-term perspective – all *exacerbate* the problem. Sound execution, speed-to-market, total quality management and process reengineering are similarly ineffective. Needless to say, this is disquieting news to people who teach future managers!

I suggest, however, that although the solution to disruptive technologies cannot be found in the standard tool kit of good management, there are, in fact, sensible ways to deal effectively with this challenge. Every company in every industry works under certain forces – laws of organizational nature – that act powerfully to define what that company can and cannot do. Managers faced with disruptive technologies fail their companies when these forces overpower them.

By analogy, the ancients who attempted to fly by strapping feathered wings to their arms and flapping with all their might as they leapt from high places invariably failed. Despite their dreams and hard work, they were fighting against some very powerful forces of nature. No one could be strong enough to win this fight. Flight became possible only after people came to understand the relevant natural laws and principles that defined how the world worked: the law of gravity, Bernoulli's principle, and the concepts of lift, drag and resistance. When people then designed flying systems that recognized or harnessed the power of these laws and principles, rather than fighting them, they were finally able to fly to heights and distances that were previously unimaginable.

I propose the existence of five laws or principles of disruptive technology. As in the analogy with manned flight, these laws are so strong that managers who ignore or fight them are nearly powerless to pilot their companies through a disruptive technology storm. If managers can understand and harness these forces, rather than fight them, they can in fact succeed spectacularly when confronted with disruptive technological change. I am very confident that great managers will be very capable on their own of finding the answers that best fit their circumstances. But they must first understand what has caused those circumstances and what forces will affect the feasibility of their solutions. The following paragraphs summarize these principles and what managers can do to harness or accommodate them.

Principle #1: Companies depend on customers and investors for resources

The history of the disc drive industry shows that the established firms stayed atop wave after wave of sustaining technologies (technologies that their customers needed), while consistently stumbling over simpler disruptive ones. This evidence supports the *theory of resource dependence* (Pfeffer and Salancik 1978) which states that while managers may think they control the flow of resources in their firms, in the end it is really customers and investors who dictate how money will be spent because companies with investment patterns that don't satisfy their customers and investors don't survive. The highest-performing companies, in fact, are those that are the best at this; that is, they have well-developed systems for killing ideas that their customers don't want. As a result, these companies find it very difficult to invest adequate resources in disruptive technologies – lower margin opportunities that their customers don't want – until their customers want them. And by then it is too late.

I suggest a way for managers to align or harness this law with their efforts to confront disruptive technology. With few exceptions, the only instances in which mainstream firms have successfully established a timely position in a disruptive technology were those in which the firms' managers set up an autonomous organization charged with building a new and independent business around the disruptive technology. Such organizations, free of the power of the customers of the mainstream company, ensconce themselves among a different set of customers – those who want the products of the disruptive technology. In other words, companies can succeed in disruptive technologies when their managers align their organizations *with* the forces of resource dependence, rather than ignoring or fighting them.

The implication of this principle for managers is that, when faced with a threatening disruptive technology, people and processes in a mainstream organization cannot be expected to allocate freely the critical financial and human resources needed to carve out a strong position in the small, emerging market. It is very difficult for a company whose cost structure is tailored to compete in high-end markets to be profitable in low-end markets as well. Creating an independent organization, with a cost structure honed to achieve profitability at the low margins characteristic of most disruptive technologies, is the only viable way for established firms to harness this principle.

Principle #2: Small markets don't solve the growth needs of large companies

Disruptive technologies typically enable new markets to emerge. There is strong evidence showing that companies entering these emerging markets early have significant first-mover advantages over later entrants. And yet, as these companies succeed and grow larger, it becomes progressively more difficult for them to enter the even newer small markets destined to become the large ones of the future.

To maintain their share prices and create internal opportunities for employees to extend the scope of their responsibilities, successful companies need to continue to grow. But while a $40 million company needs to find just $8 million in revenues to grow at 20 per cent in the subsequent year, a $4 billion company needs to find $800 million in new sales. No new markets are that large. As a consequence, the larger and more successful an organization becomes, the weaker the argument that emerging markets can remain useful engines for growth.

Many large companies adopt a strategy of waiting until new markets are "large enough to be interesting". But the evidence shows why this is not often a successful strategy. Those large established firms that have successfully seized strong positions in the new markets enabled by disruptive technologies have done so

by giving responsibility to commercialize the disruptive technology to an organization whose size matched the size of the targeted market. Small organizations can most easily respond to the opportunities for growth in a small market. The evidence is strong that formal and informal resource allocation processes make it very difficult for large organizations to focus adequate energy and talent on small markets, even when logic says they might be big someday.

Principle #3: Markets that don't exist can't be analyzed

Sound market research and good planning followed by execution according to plan are hallmarks of good management. When applied to sustaining technological innovation, these practices are invaluable; they are the primary reason, in fact, why established firms led in every single instance of sustaining innovation in the history of the disc drive industry. Such reasoned approaches are feasible in dealing with sustaining technology because the size and growth rates of the markets are generally known, trajectories of technological progress have been established, and the needs of leading customers have usually been well articulated. Because the vast majority of innovations are sustaining in character, most executives have learned to manage innovation in a sustaining context, where analysis and planning were feasible.

In dealing with disruptive technologies leading to new markets, however, market researchers and business planners have consistently dismal records. In fact, based upon the evidence from the disc drive, motorcycle and microprocessor industries, the only thing we may know for sure when we read experts' forecasts about how large emerging markets will become is that they are wrong.

In many instances, leadership in sustaining innovations – about which information is known and for which plans can be made – is not competitively important. In such cases, technology followers do about as well as technology leaders. It is in disruptive innovations, where we know least about the market, that there are such strong first-mover advantages. This is the innovator's dilemma.

Companies whose investment processes demand quantification of market sizes and financial returns before they can enter a market get paralysed or make serious mistakes when faced with disruptive technologies. They demand market data when none exists and make judgments based upon financial projections when neither revenues nor costs can, in fact, be known. Using planning and marketing techniques that were developed to manage sustaining technologies in the very different context of disruptive ones is an exercise in flapping wings.

A different approach to strategy and planning recognizes the law that the right markets, and the right strategy for exploiting them, cannot be known in advance. Called discovery-based planning, it suggests that managers assume that forecasts are wrong, rather than right, and that the strategy they have chosen to pursue may likewise be wrong. Investing and managing under such assumptions drives managers to develop plans for learning what needs to be known, a much more effective way to confront disruptive technologies successfully.

Principle #4: An organization's capabilities define its disabilities

When managers tackle an innovation problem, they instinctively work to assign capable people to the job. But once they've found the right people, too many managers then assume that the organization in which they'll work will also be capable of succeeding at the task. And that is dangerous – because organizations have capabilities that exist independently of the people who work within them. An organization's capabilities reside in two places. The first is in its processes – the methods by which people have learned to transform inputs of labour, energy, materials, information, cash and technology into outputs of higher value. The second is in the organization's values, which are the criteria that managers and employees in the organization use when making prioritization decisions. People are quite flexible, in that they can be trained to succeed at quite different things. An employee of IBM, for example, can quite readily change the way he or she works, in order to work successfully in a small start-up company. But processes and values are not flexible. A process that is effective at managing the design of a minicomputer, for example, would be ineffective at managing the design of a desktop personal computer. Similarly, values that cause employees to prioritize projects to develop high-margin products, cannot simultaneously accord priority to low-margin products. The very processes and values that constitute an organization's capabilities in one context, define its disabilities in another context.

Principle #5: Technology supply may not equal market demand

Disruptive technologies, though they initially can only be used in small markets remote from the mainstream, are disruptive because they subsequently can become fully performance-competitive within the mainstream market against established products. As depicted in Figure 9.2.1, this happens because the pace of technological progress in products frequently exceeds the rate of performance improvement that mainstream customers demand or can absorb. As a consequence, products whose features and functionality closely match market needs today often follow a trajectory of improvement by which they overshoot mainstream market needs tomorrow. And products that seriously underperform today, relative to customer expectations in mainstream markets, may become directly performance-competitive tomorrow.

When this happens, in markets as diverse as disc drives, accounting software and diabetes care, the basis of competition – the criteria by which customers choose one product over another – changes. When the performance of two or more competing products has improved beyond what the market demands, customers can no longer base their choice upon which is the higher performing product. The basis of product choice often evolves from functionality to reliability, then to convenience, and, ultimately, to price.

Many students of business have described phases of the product life cycle in various ways. But the phenomenon in which product performance overshoots market demands is the primary mechanism driving shifts in the phases of the product life cycle.

In their efforts to stay ahead by developing competitively superior products, many companies don't realize the speed at which they are moving up-market, over-satisfying the needs of their original customers as they race the competition toward higher-performance, higher-margin markets. In doing so, they create a vacuum at lower price points into which competitors employing disruptive technologies can enter. Only those companies that carefully measure trends in how their mainstream customers use their products can catch the points at which the basis of competition will change in the markets they serve.

Lessons from spotting disruptive threats and opportunities

Some managers and researchers familiar with these ideas have arrived at this point in the story in an anxious state because the evidence is very strong that even the best managers have stumbled badly when their markets were invaded by disruptive technologies. Most urgently, they want to know whether their own businesses are targets for an attacking disruptive technologist and how they can defend their business against such an attack before it is too late. Others, interested in finding entrepreneurial opportunities, wonder how they can identify potentially disruptive technologies around which new companies and markets can be built.

"Good" companies often begin their descent into failure by aggressively investing in the products and services that their most profitable customers want. No automotive company is currently threatened by electric cars, and none contemplates a wholesale leap into that arena. The automobile industry is healthy. Gasoline engines have never been more reliable. Never before has such high performance and quality been available at such low prices. Indeed, aside from governmental mandates, there is no reason why we should expect the established car makers to pursue electric vehicles.

But the electric car *is* a disruptive technology and potential future threat. The innovator's task is to ensure that this innovation – the disruptive technology that doesn't make sense – is taken seriously within the company without putting at risk the needs of present customers who provide profit and growth. The problem can be resolved only when new markets are considered and carefully developed around new definitions of value – and when responsibility for building the business is placed within a focused organization whose size and interest are carefully aligned with the unique needs of the market's customers.

TABLE 9.2.1

Established technology	Disruptive technology
Silver halide photographic film	Digital photography
Wireline telephony	Mobile telephony
Circuit-switched telecommunications networks	Packet-switched communications network
Notebook computers	Hand-held digital appliances
Desktop personal computers	Sony Playstation II, Internet appliances
Full-service stock brokerage	Online stock brokerage
New York and NASDAQ stock exchanges	Electronic Communications Network (ECNs)
Full-free underwriting of new equity and debt issues	Dutch auctions of new equity and debt issues, conducted on the Internet
Credit decisions based upon the personal judgement of bank lending officers	Automated lending decisions based upon credit scoring systems
Bricks and mortar retailing	Online retailing
Industrial materials distributors	Internet-based sites such as Chemdex and E-steel
Printed greeting cards	Free greeting cards, downloadable over the Internet
Electric utility companies	Distributed power generation (gas turbines, micro-turbines, fuel cells)
Graduate school of management	Corporate universities and in-house management training programmes
Classroom and campus-based instruction	Distance education, typically enabled by the Internet
Standard textbooks	Custom-assembled, modular digital textbooks
Offset printing	Digital printing
Manned fighter and bomber aircraft	Unmanned aircraft
Microsoft Windows operating systems and applications software written in C++	Internet Protocols (IP), and Java software protocols
Medical doctors	Nurse practitioners
General hospitals	Outpatient clinics and in-home patient care
Open surgery	Arthroscopic and endoscopic surgery
Cardiac bypass surgery	Angioplasty
Magnetic resonance imaging (MRI) and Computer tomography (CT) Scanning	Ultrasound – initially floor-standing machines, ultimately portable machines

Where disruptions are happening today

One of the most gratifying aspects of my life since the first edition of *The Innovator's Dilemma* was published has been the number of people who have called, representing industries that I had never thought about, who have suggested that forces similar to those historical examples I described in these pages are disrupting their industries as well. Some of these are described in Table 9.2.1. Not surprisingly, the Internet looms as an infrastructural technology that is enabling the disruption of many industries.

Each of the innovations in the right column – in the form of a new technology or a new business model – is now in the process of disrupting the established order described in the left column. Will the companies that currently lead their industries using the technologies in the left column survive these attacks? My hope is that the future might be different than the past. I believe that the future can be different, if managers will recognize these disruptions for what they are, and address them in a way that accounts for or harnesses the fundamental principles.

Exploration and exploitation in organizational learning

By James G. March[1]

A central concern of studies of adaptive processes is the relation between the exploration of new possibilities and the exploitation of old certainties (Holland, 1975; Kuran, 1988; Schumpeter, 1934). Exploration includes things captured by terms such as search, variation, risk taking, experimentation, play, flexibility, discovery, innovation. Exploitation includes such things as refinement, choice, production, efficiency, selection, implementation, execution. Adaptive systems that engage in exploration to the exclusion of exploitation are likely to find that they suffer the costs of experimentation without gaining many of its benefits. 'They exhibit too many undeveloped new ideas and too little distinctive competence. Conversely, systems that engage in exploitation to the exclusion of exploration are likely to find themselves trapped in suboptimal stable equilibria. As a result, maintaining an appropriate balance between exploration and exploitation is a primary factor in system survival and prosperity.

This paper considers some aspects of such problems in the context of organizations. Both exploration and exploitation are essential for organizations, but they compete for scarce resources. As a result, organizations make explicit and implicit choices between the two. The explicit choices are found in calculated decisions about alternative investments and competitive strategies.

The implicit choices are buried in many features of organizational forms and customs, for example, in organizational procedures for accumulating and reducing slack, in search rules and practices, in the ways in which targets are set and changed, and in incentive systems. Understanding the choices and improving the balance between exploration and exploitation are complicated by the fact that returns from the two options vary not only with respect to their expected values, but also with respect to their variability, their timing, and their distribution within and beyond the organization. Processes for allocating resources between them, therefore, embody intertemporal, interinstitutional, and interpersonal comparisons, as well as risk preferences. The difficulties involved in making such comparisons lead to complications in specifying appropriate trade-offs, and in achieving them.

1. The exploration/exploitation trade-off

Exploration and exploitation in theories of organizational action

In rational models of choice, the balance between exploration and exploitation is discussed classically

[1]Source: This article was adapted with permission of INFORMS. From: 'Exploration and exploitation in organizational learning' by James G. March, *Organization Science,* Vol. 2, No. 1, February 1991.

SECTION III STRATEGY PROCESS

in terms of a theory of rational search (Hey, 1982; Radner and Rothschild, 1975). It is assumed that there are several alternative investment opportunities, each characterized by a probability distribution over returns that is initially unknown. Information about the distribution is accumulated over time, but choices must be made between gaining new information about alternatives and thus improving future returns (which suggests allocating part of the investment to searching among uncertain alternatives), and using the information currently available to improve present returns (which suggests concentrating the investment on the apparently best alternative). The problem is complicated by the possibilities that new investment alternatives may appear, that probability distributions may not be stable, or that they may depend on the choices made by others.

In theories of limited rationality, discussions of the choice between exploration and exploitation emphasize the role of targets or aspiration levels in regulating allocations to search (Cyert and March, 1963). The usual assumption is that search is inhibited if the most preferred alternative is above (but in the neighbourhood of) the target. On the other hand, search is stimulated if the most preferred known alternative is below the target. Such ideas are found both in theories of satisficing (Simon, 1955) and in prospect theory (Kahneman and Tversky, 1979). They have led to attempts to specify conditions under which target-oriented search rules are optimal (Day, 1967). Because of the role of targets, discussions of search in the limited rationality tradition emphasize the significance of the adaptive character of aspirations themselves (March, 1988).

In studies of organizational learning, the problem of balancing exploration and exploitation is exhibited in distinctions made between refinement of an existing technology and invention of a new one (Levinthal and March, 1981; Winter, 1971). It is clear that exploration of new alternatives reduces the speed with which skills at existing ones are improved. It is also clear that improvements in competence at existing procedures make experimentation with others less attractive (Levitt and March, 1988). Finding an appropriate balance is made particularly difficult by the fact that the same issues occur at levels of a nested system – at the individual level, the organizational level and the social system level.

In evolutionary models of organizational forms and technologies, discussions of the choice between exploration and exploitation are framed in terms of balancing the twin processes of variation and selection (Ashby, 1960; Hannan and Freeman, 1987). Effective selection among forms, routines or practices is essential to survival, but so also is the generation of new alternative practices, particularly in a changing environment. Because of the links among environmental turbulence, organizational diversity and competitive advantage, the evolutionary dominance of an organizational practice is sensitive to the relation between the rate of exploratory variation reflected by the practice and the rate of change in the environment. In this spirit, for example, it has been argued that the persistence of garbage-can decision processes in organizations is related to the diversity advantage they provide in a world of relatively unstable environments, when paired with the selective efficiency of conventional rationality (Cohen, 1986).

Vulnerability of exploration

Compared to returns from exploitation, returns from exploration are systematically less certain, more remote in time, and organizationally more distant from the locus of action and adaption. What is good in the long run is not always good in the short run. What is good at a particular historical moment is not always good at another time. What is good for one part of an organization is not always good for another part. What is good for an organization is not always good for a larger social system of which it is a part. As organizations learn from experience how to divide resources between exploitation and exploration, this distribution of consequences across time and space affects the lessons learned. The certainty, speed, proximity and clarity of feedback ties exploitation to its consequences more quickly and more precisely than is the case with exploration. The story is told in many forms. Basic research has less certain outcomes, longer time horizons and more diffuse effects than does product development. The search for new ideas, markets or relations has less certain outcomes, longer time horizons and more diffuse effects than does further development of existing ones.

Because of these differences, adaptive processes characteristically improve exploitation more rapidly than exploration. These advantages for exploitation cumulate. Each increase in competence at an activity increases the likelihood of rewards for engaging in that activity, thereby further increasing the competence and the likelihood (Argyris and Schön, 1978; David, 1985). The effects extend, through network externalities, to others with whom the learning organization interacts (David and Bunn, 1988; Katz and Shapiro, 1986). Reason inhibits foolishness; learning and imitation inhibit experimentation. This is not an accident but is a consequence of the temporal and spatial proximity of the effects of exploitation, as well as their precision and interconnectedness.

Since performance is a joint function of potential return from an activity and present competence of an organization at it, organizations exhibit increasing returns to experience (Arthur, 1996). Positive local feedback produces strong path dependence (David, 1990) and can lead to suboptimal equilibria. It is quite possible for competence in an inferior activity to become great enough to exclude superior activities with which an organization has little experience (Herriott, Levinthal and March, 1985). Since long-run intelligence depends on sustaining a reasonable level of exploration, these tendencies to increase exploitation and reduce exploration make adaptive processes potentially self-destructive.

The social context of organizational learning

The trade-off between exploration and exploitation exhibits some special features in the social context of organizations. The next two sections of the present paper describe two simple models of adaptation, use them to elaborate the relation between exploitation and exploration, and explore some implications of the relation for the accumulation and utilization of knowledge in organizations. The models identify some reasons why organizations may want to control learning and suggest some procedures by which they do so.

Two distinctive features of the social context are considered. The first is the mutual learning of an organization and the individuals in it. Organizations store knowledge in their procedures, norms, rules and forms. They accumulate such knowledge over time, learning from their members. At the same time, individuals in an organization are socialized to organizational beliefs. Such mutual learning has implications for understanding and managing the trade-off between exploration and exploitation in organizations. The second feature of organizational learning considered here is the context of competition for primacy. Organizations often compete with each other under conditions in which relative position matters. The mixed contribution of knowledge to competitive advantage in cases involving competition for primacy creates difficulties for defining and arranging an appropriate balance between exploration and exploitation in an organizational setting.

2. Mutual learning in the development of knowledge

Organizational knowledge and faiths are diffused to individuals through various forms of instruction, indoctrination and exemplification. An organization socializes recruits to the languages, beliefs and practices that comprise the organizational code (Van Maanen, 1973; Whyte, 1957). Simultaneously, the organizational code is adapting to individual beliefs. This form of mutual learning has consequences both for the individuals involved and for an organization as a whole. In particular, the trade-off between exploration and exploitation in mutual learning involves conflicts between short-run and long-run concerns and between gains to individual knowledge and gains to collective knowledge.

A model of mutual learning

Consider a simple model of the development and diffusion of organizational knowledge. There are four key features to the model:

1 There is an external reality that is independent of beliefs about it. Reality is described as having m dimensions, each of which has a value of 1 or –1. The (independent) probability that any one dimension will have a value of 1 is 0.5.

2 At each time period, beliefs about reality are held by each of n individuals in an organization and by an organizational code of received truth. For each of the m dimensions of reality, each belief has a value of 1, 0, or –1. This value may change over time.

3 Individuals modify their beliefs continuously as a consequence of socialization into the organization and education into its code of beliefs. Specifically, if the code is 0 on a particular dimension, individual belief is not affected. In each period in which the code differs on any particular dimension from the belief of an individual, individual belief changes to that of the code with probability, $p1$. Thus, $p1$ is a parameter reflecting the effectiveness of socialization, i.e., learning *from* the code. Changes on the several dimensions are assumed to be independent of each other.

4 At the same time, the organizational code adapts to the beliefs of those individuals whose beliefs correspond with reality on more dimensions than does the code. The probability that the beliefs of the code will be adjusted to conform to the dominant belief within the superior group on any particular dimension

depends on the level of agreement among individuals in the superior group and on $p2$. Thus, $p2$ is a parameter reflecting the effectiveness of learning *by* the code. Changes on the several dimensions are assumed to be independent of each other.

Within this system, initial conditions include: a reality m-tuple (m dimensions, each of which has a value of 1 or –1, with independent equal probability); an organizational code m-tuple (m dimensions, each of which is initially 0); and n individual m-tuples (m dimensions, with values equal 1, 0, or –1, with equal probabilities).

Thus, the process begins with an organizational code characterized by neutral beliefs on all dimensions and a set of individuals with varying beliefs that exhibit, on average, no knowledge. Over time, the organizational code affects the beliefs of individuals, even while it is being affected by those beliefs. The beliefs of individuals do not affect the beliefs of other individuals directly but only through affecting the code. The effects of reality are also indirect. Neither the individuals nor the organizations experience reality. Improvement in knowledge comes by the code mimicking the beliefs (including the false beliefs) of superior individuals and by individuals mimicking the code (including its false beliefs).

Basic properties of the model in a closed system

Consider such a model of mutual learning first within a closed system having fixed organizational membership and a stable reality. Since realizations of the process are subject to stochastic variability, repeated simulations using the same initial conditions and parameters are used to estimate the distribution of outcomes. In all of the results reported here, the number of dimensions of reality (m) is set at 30, the number of individuals (n) is set at 50, and the number of repeated simulations is 80. The quantitative levels of the results and the magnitude of the stochastic fluctuations reported depend on these specifications, but the qualitative results are insensitive to values of m and n.

Since reality is specified, the state of knowledge at any particular time period can be assessed in two ways. First, the proportion of reality that is correctly represented in the organizational code can be calculated for any period. This is the knowledge level of the code for that period. Second, the proportion of reality that is correctly represented in individual beliefs (on average) can be calculated for any period. This is the average knowledge level of the individuals for that period.

Within this closed system, the model yields time paths of organizational and individual beliefs, thus knowledge levels that depend stochastically on the initial conditions and the parameters affecting learning. The basic features of these histories can be summarized simply: Each of the adjustments in beliefs serves to eliminate differences between the individuals and the code. Consequently, the beliefs of individuals and the code converge over time. As individuals in the organization become more knowledgeable, they also become more homogeneous with respect to knowledge. Equilibrium is reached at which all individuals and the code share the same (not necessarily accurate) belief with respect to each dimension. The equilibrium is stable.

Effects of learning rates.   Higher rates of learning lead, on average, to achieving equilibrium earlier. The equilibrium level of knowledge attained by an organization also depends interactively on the two learning parameters. Figure 9.3.1 shows the results when we assume that $p1$ is the same for all individuals. Slower socialization (lower $p1$) leads to greater knowledge at equilibrium than does faster socialization, particularly when the code learns rapidly (high $p2$). When socialization is slow, more rapid learning by the code leads to greater knowledge at equilibrium but when socialization is rapid, greater equilibrium knowledge is achieved through slower learning by the code. By far the highest equilibrium knowledge occurs when the code learns rapidly from individuals whose socialization to the code is slow.

The results pictured in Figure 9.3.1 confirm the observation that rapid learning is not always desirable (Herriott, Levinthal and March, 1985; Lounamaa and March, 1987).

In previous work, it was shown that slower learning allows for greater exploration of possible alternatives and greater balance in the development of specialized competencies. In the present model, a different version of the same general phenomenon is observed. The gains to individuals from adapting rapidly to the code (which is consistently closer to reality than the average individual) are offset by second-order losses stemming from the fact that the code can learn only from individuals who deviate from it. Slow learning on the part of individuals maintains diversity longer, thereby providing the exploration that allows the knowledge found in the organizational code to improve.

Effects of learning rate heterogeneity.   The fact that fast individual learning from the code tends to have a favourable first-order effect on individual knowledge but an adverse effect on improvement in organizational knowledge and thereby on long-term individual

FIGURE 9.3.1   Effect of learning rates on equilibrium knowledge

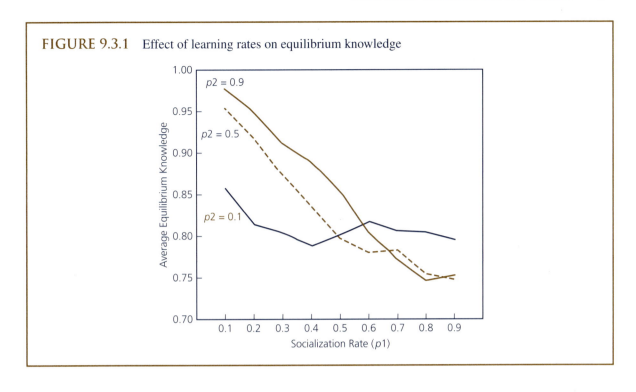

improvement suggests that there might be some advantage to having a mix of fast and slow learners in an organization. Suppose the population of individuals in an organization is divided into two groups, one consisting of individuals who learn rapidly from the code ($p1 = 0.9$) and the other consisting of individuals who learn slowly ($p1 = 0.1$).

If an organization is partitioned into two groups in this way, the mutual learning process achieves an equilibrium in which all individuals and the code share the same beliefs. As would be expected from the results above with respect to homogeneous socialization rates, larger fractions of fast learners result in the process reaching equilibrium faster and in lower levels of knowledge at equilibrium than do smaller fractions of fast learners. However, as Figure 9.3.2 shows, for "any average rate of learning from the code, it is better from the point of view of equilibrium knowledge to have that average reflect a mix of fast and slow learners rather than a homogeneous population." For equivalent average values of the socialization learning parameter ($p1$), the heterogeneous population consistently produces higher equilibrium knowledge.

On the way to equilibrium, the knowledge gains from variability are disproportionate due to contributions by slow learners, but they are disproportionately realized (in their own knowledge) by fast learners. Figure 9.3.3 shows the effects on period-20 knowledge

of varying the fraction of the population of individuals who are fast learners ($p1 = 0.9$) rather than slow learners ($p1 = 0.1$). Prior to reaching equilibrium, individuals with a high value for $p1$ gain from being in an organization in which there are individuals having a low value for $p1$, but the converse is not true.

These results indicate that the fraction of slow learners in an organization is a significant factor in organizational learning. In the model, that fraction is treated as a parameter. Disparities in the returns to the two groups and their interdependence make optimizing with respect to the fraction of slow learners problematic if the rates of individual learning are subject to individual control. Since there are no obvious individual incentives for learning slowly in a population in which others are learning rapidly, it may be difficult to arrive at a fraction of slow learners that is optimal from the point of view of the code if learning rates are voluntarily chosen by individuals.

Basic properties of the model in a more open system

These results can be extended by examining some alternative routes to selective slow learning in a somewhat more open system. Specifically, the role of turnover in the organization and turbulence in the environment are considered. In the case of turnover, organizational

FIGURE 9.3.2   Effect of heterogeneous socialization rates on equilibrium knowledge

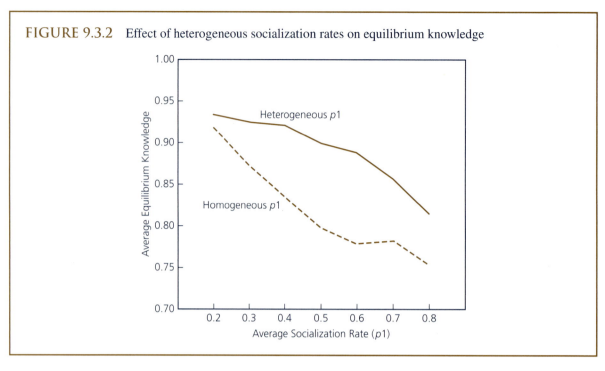

FIGURE 9.3.3   Effect of heterogeneous socialization rates on period-20 knowledge

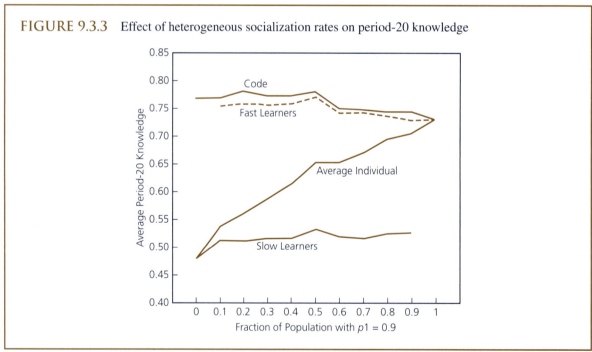

membership is treated as changing. In the case of turbulence, environmental reality is treated as changing.

Effects of personnel turnover.   In the previous section, it was shown that variability is sustained by low values of $p1$. Slow learners stay deviant long enough for the code to learn from them. An alternative way of producing variability in an organization is to introduce personnel turnover. Suppose that each time period each individual has a probability, $p3$, of leaving the organization and being replaced by a new individual with a set of naive beliefs described by an *m*-tuple, having values equal to 1, 0, or −1, with equal probabilities. As might be expected, there is a consistent negative first-order effect of turnover on average individual knowledge. Since there is a positive relation between lengths of service in the organization and individual knowledge, the greater the turnover, the shorter the average length of service and the lower the average individual knowledge at any point. This effect is strong.

The effect of turnover on the organizational code is more complicated and reflects a trade-off between learning rate and turnover rate. Figure 9.3.4 shows the period-20 results for two different values of the socialization rate ($p1$). If $p1$ is relatively low, period-20 code knowledge declines with increasing turnover. The combination of slow learning and rapid turnover leads to inadequate exploitation. However, if $p1$ is relatively high, moderate amounts of turnover improve the organizational code. Rapid socialization of individuals into the procedures and beliefs of an organization tends to reduce exploration. A modest level of turnover, by introducing less socialized people, increases exploration, and thereby improves aggregate knowledge. The level of knowledge reflected by the organizational code is increased, as is the average individual knowledge of those individuals who have been in the organization for some time. Note that this effect does not come from the superior knowledge of the average new recruit. Recruits are, on average, less knowledgeable than the individuals they replace. The gains come from their diversity.

Turnover, like heterogeneity in learning rates, produces a distribution problem. Contributions to improving the code (and subsequently individual knowledge) come from the occasional newcomers who deviate from the code in a favourable way. Old-timers, on average, know more, but what they know is redundant with knowledge already reflected in the code. They are less likely to contribute new knowledge on the margin. Novices know less on average, but what they know is less redundant with the code and occasionally better, thus more likely to contribute to improving the code.

Effects of environmental turbulence. Since learning processes involve lags in adjustment to changes, the contribution of learning to knowledge depends on the amount of turbulence in the environment. Suppose that the value of any given dimension of reality shifts (from 1 to −1 or −1 to 1) in a given time period with probability $p4$. This captures in an elementary way the idea that understanding the world may be complicated by turbulence in the world. Exogenous environmental change makes adaptation essential, but it also makes learning from experience difficult (Weick, 1979). In the model, the level of knowledge achieved in a particular (relatively early) time period decreases with increasing turbulence.

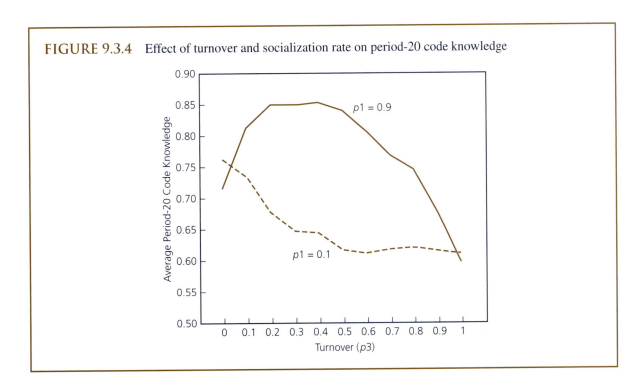

FIGURE 9.3.4   Effect of turnover and socialization rate on period-20 code knowledge

In addition, mutual learning has a dramatic long-run degenerative property under conditions of exogenous turbulence. As the beliefs of individuals and the code converge, the possibilities for improvement in either decline. Once a knowledge equilibrium is achieved, it is sustained indefinitely. The beliefs reflected in the code and those held by all individuals remain identical and unchanging, regardless of changes in reality. Even before equilibrium is achieved, the capabilities for change fall below the rate of change in the environment. As a result, after an initial period of increasing accuracy, the knowledge of the code and individuals is systematically degraded through changes in reality. Ultimately, the accuracy of belief reaches chance (i.e., where a random change in reality is as likely to increase accuracy of beliefs as it is to decrease it). The process becomes a random walk.

The degeneracy is avoided if there is turnover. Figure 9.3.5 plots the average level of code knowledge over time under conditions of turbulence ($p4 = 0.02$). Two cases of learning are plotted, one without turnover ($p3 = 0$), the other with moderate turnover ($p3 = 0.1$). Where there is turbulence without turnover, code knowledge first rises to a moderate level, and then declines to 0, from which it subsequently wanders randomly. With turnover, the degeneracy is avoided and a moderate level of code knowledge is sustained in the face of environmental change. The positive effects of

moderate turnover depend, of course, on the rules for selecting new recruits. In the present case, recruitment is not affected by the code. Replacing departing individuals with recruits closer to the current organizational code would significantly reduce the efficiency of turnover as a source of exploration.

Turnover is useful in the face of turbulence, but it produces a disparity between code knowledge and the average knowledge of individuals in the organization. As a result, the match between turnover rate and level of turbulence that is desirable from the point of view of the organization's knowledge is not necessarily desirable from the point of view of the knowledge of every individual in it, or individuals on average. In particular, where there is turbulence, there is considerable individual advantage to having tenure in an organization that has turnover. This seems likely to produce pressures by individuals to secure tenure for themselves while restricting it for others.

3. Knowledge and ecologies of competition

The model in the previous section examines one aspect of the social context of adaptation in organizations, the ways in which individual beliefs and an organizational code draw from each other over time. A second major feature of the social context of organizational learning

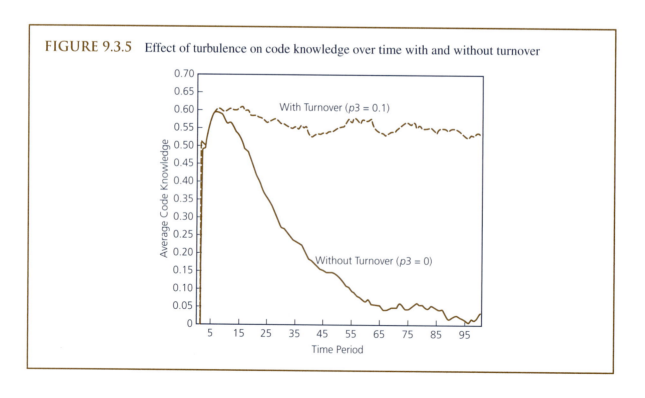

FIGURE 9.3.5   Effect of turbulence on code knowledge over time with and without turnover

is the competitive ecology within which learning occurs and knowledge is used. External competitive processes pit organizations against each other in pursuit of scarce environmental resources and opportunities. Examples are competition among business firms for customers and governmental subsidies. Internal competitive processes pit individuals in the organization against each other in competition for scarce organizational resources and opportunities. Examples are competition among managers for internal resources and hierarchical promotion. In these ecologies of competition, the competitive consequences of learning by one organization depend on learning by other organizations. In this section, these links among learning, performance and position in an ecology of competition are discussed by considering some ways in which competitive advantage is affected by the accumulation of knowledge.

Competition and the importance of relative performance

Suppose that an organization's realized performance on a particular occasion is a draw from a probability distribution that can be characterized in terms of some measure of average value and some measure of variability. Knowledge, and the learning process that produces it, can be described in terms of their effects on these two measures. A change in an organization's performance distribution that increases average performance will often be beneficial to an organization, but such a result is not assured when relative position within a group of competing organizations is important. Where returns to one competitor are not strictly determined by that competitor's own performance but depend on the relative standings of the competitors, returns to changes in knowledge depend not only on the magnitude of the changes in the expected value but also on changes in variability and on the number of competitors.

In bilateral competition involving normal performance distributions, learning that increases the mean always pays off, and changes in the variance – whether positive or negative – have no effect. The situation changes as N increases. If N is greater than 1 (but finite), increases in either the mean or the variance have a positive effect on competitive advantage, and sufficiently large increases in either can offset decreases in the other. The trade-off between increases in the mean and increases in the variance is strongly affected by N. As the number of competitors increases, the contribution of the variance to competitive advantage increases until at the limit, as N goes to infinity, the mean becomes irrelevant.

Learning, knowledge, and competitive advantage

The effects of learning are realized in changes in the performance distribution. The analysis indicates that if learning increases both the mean and the variance of a normal performance distribution, it will improve competitive advantage in a competition for primacy. The model also suggests that increases in the variance may compensate for decreases in the mean; decreases in the variance may nullify gains from increases in the mean. These variance effects are particularly significant when the number of competitors is large.

The underlying argument does not depend on competition being only for primacy. Such competition is a special case of competition for relative position. The general principle that relative position is affected by variability, and increasingly so as the number of competitors increases, is true for any position. In competition to achieve relatively high positions, variability has a positive effect. In competition to avoid relatively low positions, variability has a negative effect.

Nor does the underlying argument depend on the assumption of normality or other symmetry in the performance distributions. Normal performance distributions are special cases in which the tails of the distribution are specified when the mean and variance are specified. For general distributions, as the number of competitors increases, the likelihood of finishing first depends increasingly on the right-hand tail of the performance distribution, and the likelihood of finishing last depends increasingly on the left-hand tail (David, 1981). If learning has different effects on the two tails of the distribution, the right-hand tail effect will be such more important in competition for primacy among many competitors. The left-hand tail will be much more important in competition to avoid finishing last.

Some learning processes increase both average performance and variability. A standard example would be the short-run consequences from adoption of a new technology. If a new technology is so clearly superior as to overcome the disadvantages of unfamiliarity with it, it will offer a higher expected value than the old technology. At the same time, the limited experience with the new technology (relative to experience with the old) will lead to an increased variance. A similar result might be expected with the introduction of a new body of knowledge or new elements of cultural diversity to an organization, for example, through the introduction of individuals with untypical skills, attitudes, ethnicity, or gender.

Learning processes do not necessarily lead to increases in both average performance and variation, however. Increased knowledge seems often to reduce the variability of performance rather than to increase it. Knowledge makes performance more reliable. As work is standardized, as techniques are learned, variability, both in the time required to accomplish tasks and in the quality of task performance, is reduced. Insofar as that increase in reliability comes from a reduction in the left-hand tail, the likelihood of finishing last in a competition among many is reduced without changing the likelihood of finishing first. However, if knowledge has the effect of reducing the right-hand tail of the distribution, it may easily decrease the chance of being best among several competitors even though it also increases average performance. The question is whether you can do exceptionally well, as opposed to better than average, without leaving the confines of conventional action. The answer is complicated, for it depends on a more careful specification of the kind of knowledge involved and its precise effects on the right-hand tail of the distribution. But knowledge that simultaneously increases average performance and its reliability is not a guarantee of competitive advantage.

Consider, for example, the case of modern information and decision technology based on computers. In cases where time is particularly important, information technology has a major effect on the mean, less on the variance. Some problems in environmental scanning for surprises, changes or opportunities probably fall into such a category. Under such conditions, appropriate use of information technology seems likely to improve competitive position. On the other hand, in many situations the main effect of information technology is to make outcomes more reliable. For example, additional data, or more detailed analyses, seem likely to increase reliability in decisions more rapidly than they will increase their average returns. In such cases, the effects on the tails are likely to dominate the effects on the mean. The net effect of the improved technology on the chance of avoiding being the worst competitor will be positive, but the effect on the chance of finishing at the head of the pack may well be negative.

Similarly, multiple independent projects may have an advantage over a single, coordinated effort. The average result from independent projects is likely to be lower than that realized from a coordinated one, but their right-hand side variability can compensate for the reduced mean in a competition for primacy. The argument can be extended more generally to the effects of close collaboration or cooperative information exchange. Organizations that develop effective instruments of coordination and communication probably can be expected to do better (on average) than those that are more loosely coupled, and they also probably can be expected to become more reliable, less likely to deviate significantly from the mean of their performance distributions. The price of reliability, however, is a smaller chance of primacy among competitors.

Competition for relative position and strategic action

The arguments above assume that the several individual performances of competitors are independent draws from a distribution of possible performances, and that the distribution cannot be arbitrarily chosen by the competitors. Such a perspective is incomplete. It is possible to see both the mean and the reliability of a performance distribution (at least partially) as choices made strategically. In the long run, they represent the result of organizational choices between investments in learning and in consumption of the fruits of current capabilities, thus the central focus of this paper. In the short run, the choice of mean can be seen as a choice of effort or attention. By varying effort, an organization selects a performance mean between an entitlement (zero-effort) and a capability (maximum-effort) level. Similarly, in the short run, variations in the reliability of performance can be seen as choices of knowledge or risk that can be set wilfully within the range of available alternatives.

These choices, insofar as they are made rationally, will not, in general, be independent of competition. If relative position matters, as the number of competitors increases, strategies for increasing the mean through increased effort or greater knowledge become less attractive relative to strategies for increasing variability. In the more general situation, suppose organizations face competition from numerous competitors who vary in their average capabilities but who can choose their variances. If payoffs and preferences are such that finishing near the top matters a great deal, those organizations with performance distributions characterized by comparatively low means will (if they can) be willing to sacrifice average performance in order to augment the right-hand tails of their performance distributions. In this way, they improve their chances of winning, thus force their more talented competitors to do likewise, and thereby convert the competition into a right-hand tail "race" in which average performance (due to ability and effort) becomes irrelevant. These dynamics comprise powerful countervailing forces to the tendency for experience to eliminate exploration and are a reminder that the learning dominance of exploitation is, under some circumstances, constrained not only by slow learning and turnover but also by reason.

4. Little models and old wisdom

Learning, analysis, imitation, regeneration and technological change are major components of any effort to improve organizational performance and strengthen competitive advantage. Each involves adaptation and a delicate trade-off between exploration and exploitation. The present argument has been that these trade-offs are affected by their contexts of distributed costs and benefits and ecological interaction. The essence of exploitation is the refinement and extension of existing competencies, technologies and paradigms. Its returns are positive, proximate and predictable. The essence of exploration is experimentation with new alternatives. Its returns are uncertain, distant and often negative. Thus, the distance in time and space between the locus of learning and the locus for the realization of returns is generally greater in the case of exploration than in the case of exploitation, as is the uncertainty.

Such features of the context of adaptation lead to a tendency to substitute exploitation of known alternatives for the exploration of unknown ones, to increase the reliability of performance rather more than its mean. This property of adaptive processes is potentially self-destructive. As we have seen, it degrades organizational learning in a mutual learning situation. Mutual learning leads to convergence between organizational and individual beliefs. The convergence is generally useful both for individuals and for an organization. However, a major threat to the effectiveness of such learning is the possibility that individuals will adjust to an organizational code before the code can learn from them. Relatively slow socialization of new organizational members and moderate turnover sustains variability in individual beliefs, thereby improving organizational and average individual knowledge in the long run.

An emphasis on exploitation also compromises competitive position where finishing near the top is important. Knowledge-based increases in average performance can be insufficient to overcome the adverse effects produced by reductions in variability. The ambiguous usefulness of learning in a competitive race is not simply an artefact of representing knowledge in terms of the mean and variance of a normal distribution. The key factor is the effect of knowledge on the right-hand tail of the performance distribution. Thus, in the end, the effects stem from the relation between knowledge and discovery. Michael Polanyi, commenting on one of his contributions to physics, observed (Polanyi 1963, p. 1013) that "I would never have conceived my theory, let alone have made a great effort to verify it, if I had been more familiar with major developments in physics that were taking place. Moreover, my initial ignorance of the powerful, false objections that were raised against my ideas protected those ideas from being nipped in the bud."

These observations do not overturn the renaissance. Knowledge, learning and education remain as profoundly important instruments of human well-being. At best, the models presented here suggest some of the considerations involved in thinking about choices between exploration and exploitation and in sustaining exploration in the face of adaptive processes that tend to inhibit it. The complexity of the distribution of costs and returns across time and groups makes an explicit determination of optimality a non-trivial exercise. But it may be instructive to reconfirm some elements of folk wisdom asserting that the returns to fast learning are not all positive, that rapid socialization may hurt the socializers even as it helps the socialized, that the development of knowledge may depend on maintaining an influx of the naive and ignorant, and that competitive victory does not reliably go to the properly educated.

REFERENCES

Amit, R. and Zott, C. (2001) 'Value creation in e-business', *Strategic Management Journal*, 22(6–7), pp. 493–520.

Amit, R. and Zott, C. (2012) 'Creating Value Through Business Model Innovation', *Sloan Management Review*, Spring, 53, pp. 41–49.

Argyris, C. (1990) *Overcoming Organizational Defenses: Facilitating Organizational Learning*, Boston, MA: Prentice Hall.

Argyris, C. and Schon, D. (1978) *Organizational Learning: A Theory of Action Approach*, Reading, MA: Addison Wesley.

Arthur, W.B. (1996) 'Increasing Returns and the New World of Business', *Harvard Business Review*, 74(4, July–August), pp. 100–109.

Ashby, W.R. (1960) *Design for a Brain* (2nd edn), New York: Wiley.

Benner, M.J. and Tushman, M.L (2002) 'Process management and technological innovation: A longitudinal study of the photography and paint industries', *Administrative Science Quarterly*, 47, pp. 676–706.

Benner, M.J. and Tushman, M.L. (2003) 'Exploitation, exploration, and process management: The productivity dilemma revisited', *Academy of Management Review*, 2, pp. 238–256.

Bilton, C. and Cummings, S. (2010) *Creative Strategy: Reconnecting Business and Innovation,* Chichester: John Wiley & Sons.

Braudel, F. (1949) *The Mediterranean and the Mediterranean World in the Age of Philip II*, Scranton, PA: HarperCollins.

Burgelman, R. (1991) 'Intraorganizational Ecology of Strategy Making and Organizational Adaptation: Theory and Field Research', *Organization Science*, 2(3, August), pp. 239–262.

Calori, R. and de Woot, P. (eds) (1994) *A European Management Model: Beyond Diversity*, Hemel Hempstead: Prentice Hall.

Calori, R., Valla, J.-P. and de Woot, P. (1994) 'Common Characteristics: The Ingredients of European Management', in: R. Calori and P. de Woot (eds) *A European Management Model: Beyond Diversity*, Hemel Hempstead: Prentice Hall.

Cantwell, J. (1989) *Technological Innovations in Multinational Corporations*, Oxford: Blackwell.

Chen, C.C. and Lee Y.T. (eds) (2008) *Leadership and Management in China*, Cambridge: Cambridge University Press.

Christensen, C.M. (1997, 2011) *The Innovator's Dilemma, When New Technologies Cause Great Firms to Fail*, New York: Harper Business.

Cohen, E.G. (1986) 'Artificial Intelligence and the Dynamic Performance of Organizational Designs', in: J.G. March and R. Weissinger-Baylon (eds) *Ambiguity and Command: Organizational Perspectives on Military Decision Making*, Boston, MA: Ballinger.

Cookson, C. (2010) 'China set for global lead in scientific research', *Financial Times*, January 26.

Cyert, R.M. and March, J. (1963) *A Behavioral Theory of the Firm*, Englewood Cliffs, NJ: Prentice Hall.

D'Aveni, R. (1994) *Hypercompetition: Managing the Dynamics of Strategic Maneuvering*, New York: Free Press.

David, H.A. (1981) *Order Statistics* (2nd edn), New York: John Wiley.

David, P.A. (1985) 'Clio and the Economics of QWERTY', *The American Economic Review*, 75(2), pp. 332–337.

David, P.A. (1990) 'The Hero and the Herd in Technological History: Reflections on Thomas Edison and The Battle of the Systems', in: P. Higgonet and H. Rosovski (eds) *Economic Development Past and Present: Opportunities and Constraints*, Cambridge, MA: Harvard University Press.

David, P.A. and Bunn, J.A. (1988) 'The Economics of Gateway Technologies and Network Evolution: Lessons from Electricity Supply History', *Information Economics and Policy*, 3(2), pp. 165–202.

Day, R.H. (1967) 'Profits, Learning and the Convergence of Satisficing to Marginalism', *The Quarterly Journal of Economics*, 81, pp. 302–311.

De Geus, A. (1997) 'The Living Company', *Harvard Business Review*, March, pp. 51–59.

Diamond, J.M. (1997) *Guns, Germs and Steel: The Fates of Human Societies*, New York: Norton.

Dosi, G. (1984) *Technical Change and Industrial Transformation*, London, Macmillan.

Dunning, J.H. (1958) *American Investment in British Manufacturing Industry*, London: George Allen & Unwin.

Fichter, K. and Beucker, S. (2012) *Innovation Communities: Teamworking of Key Persons - A Success Factor in Radical Innovation*, Berlin and New York: Springer Science & Business Media.

Freeman, C. and Perez, C. (1988) 'Structural Crises of Adjustment, Business Cycles and Investment Behavior', in: G. Dosi, C. Freeman, R. Nelson, G. Silverberg and L. Soete (eds) *Technical Change And Economic Theory*, London and New York: Pinter Publishers.

Goncalo, J.A. and Staw, B.M. (2006) 'Individualism–collectivism and group creativity', *Organizational Behavior and Human Decision Processes*, 100(1), 96–109.

Gupta, A.K., Smith, K.G. and Shalley, C.E. (2006) 'The interplay between exploration and exploitation', *Academy of Management Journal*, 49(4), pp. 693–706.

Hamel, G. (1996) 'Strategy as Revolution', *Harvard Business Review*, 74(4, July–August), pp. 69–82.

Hamel, G. and Prahalad, C.K. (1994) *Competing for the Future*, Boston, MA: Harvard Business School Press.

Hampden-Turner, C. and Trompenaars, F. (2000) *Building Cross-Cultural Competence: How to Create Wealth from Conflicting Values*, New Haven, CT: Yale University Press.

Hannan, M.T. and Freeman, J. (1984) 'Structural Inertia and Organizational Change', *American Sociological Review*, 49(2, April), pp. 149–164.

Hannan, M.T. and Freeman, J. (1987) 'The Ecology of Organizational Foundings: American Labor Unions, 1836–1985', *American Journal of Sociology*, 92, pp. 910–943.

Herriott, S.R., Levinthal, D.A. and March, J.G. (1985) 'Learning from Experience in Organizations', *The American Economic Review*, 75(2), pp. 298–302.

Hey, J.D. (1982) 'Search for Rules for Search', *Journal of Economic Behavior and Organization*, 3(1), pp. 65–81.

Hofstede, G. (1980) *Culture's Consequences: International Differences in Work-Related Values*, Newbury Park, CA: Sage.

Holden, N. (2002) *Cross Cultural Management a Knowledge Based Perspective*, London: Pearson Education.

Holland, J.H. (1995) *Adaptation in Natural and Artificial Systems*, Ann Arbor, MI: University of Michigan Press.

Imai, M. (1986) *Kaizen: The Key to Japan's Competitive Success*, New York: McGraw-Hill.

Kagono, T., Nonaka, I., Sakakibara, K. and Okumura, A. (1985) *Strategic vs. Evolutionary Management: A US-Japan Comparison of Strategy and Organization*, Amsterdam: North Holland.

Kahneman, D. and Tversky, A. (1979) 'Prospect Theory: An Analysis of Decision under Risk', *Econometrica*, pp. 263–291.

Katz, M.L. and Shapiro, C. (1986) 'Technology Adoption in the Presence of Network Externalities', *Journal of Political Economy*, 9, pp. 822–841.

Kelly, D. and Amburgey, T. (1991) 'Organizational inertia and momentum: a dynamic model of strategic change', *Academy of Management Journal*, 34(3), pp. 591–612.

Krüger, W. (1996) 'Implementation: The Core Task of Change Management', *CEMS Business Review*, 1, pp. 77–96.

Kuran, T. (1998) 'The Tenacious Past: Theories of Personal and Collective Conservatism', *Journal of Economic Behavior and Organization*, 10, pp. 143–171.

Lee, C.C.K. (2010) *Thought and Governance of East Asia: Confucian Humanism, Human Rights and Business Ethics*, Seoul: PerDream.

Leifer, M. (2000) *The Political and Security Outlook for Southeast Asia*, Institute of Southeast Asian Studies.

Levinthal, D. and March, J.G. (1981) 'A Model of Adaptive Organizational Search', *Journal of Economic Behavior & Organization*, 2(4), pp. 307–333.

Levitt, B. and March, J.G. (1988) 'Organizational Learning', *Annual Review of Sociology*, 14, pp. 319–340.

Levitt, T. (1983) 'The Globalization of Markets', *Harvard Business Review*, 61(3, May–June), pp. 92–102.

Lounamaa, P.H. and March, J.G. (1987) 'Adaptive Coordination of a Learning Team', *Management Science*, 33(1), pp. 107–123.

March, J.G. (1988) 'Variable Risk Preferences and Adaptive Aspirations', *Journal of Economic Behavior and Organization*, 9, pp. 5–24.

March, J.G. (1991) 'Exploitation and Exploration in Organizational Learning', *Organization Science*, 2(1), pp. 71–87.

McLuhan, M. (1964) *Understanding Media: The Extensions of Man*, New York: McGraw-Hill.

Morris, I. (2010) *Why the West Rules – For Now: The Patterns of History, and What They Reveal About the Future*, Farrar, Straus and Giroux.

Needham, J., Ho, P.Y. and Lu, G.D. (1976) *Science and Civilisation in China*, Volume V, Part III, London: Cambridge University Press.

Nelson, R.R. and Winter, S.G. (1982) *An Evolutionary Theory of Economic Change*, Cambridge, MA: Harvard University Press.

Ouchi, W. (1981) *Theory Z: How American Business Can Meet the Japanese Challenge*, Reading, MA: Addison-Wesley.

Pascale, R.T. and Athos, A.G. (1981) *The Art of Japanese Management*, New York: Simon & Schuster.

Peters, T.J. and Waterman, R.H. (1982) *In Search of Excellence*, New York: Warner Books.

Pfeffer, J. and Salancik, G.R. (1978) *The External Control of Organizations: A Resource Dependence Perspective*, New York: Harper and Row.

Polanyi, M. (1963) 'The Potential Theory of Adsorption: Authority in Science Has Its Uses and Its Dangers', *Science*, 141, pp. 1010–1013.

Poole, M.S. and Van de Ven, A.H. (1989) 'Using Paradox to Build Management and Organization Theories', *Academy of Management Review*, 14(4), pp. 562–578.

Porter, M.E. (1990) *The Competitive Advantage of Nations*, London: Macmillan.

Quintana-García, C., and Benavides-Velasco, C. A. (2011). Knowledge organisation in R&D alliances: its impact on product innovation. *Technology Analysis & Strategic Management*, 23(10), pp. 1047–1061.

Radner, R. and Rothschild, M. (1975) 'On the Allocation of Effort', *Journal of Economic Theory*, 10(3), pp. 358–376.

Rahmandad, H. (2008) 'Effects of Delays on Complexity of Organizational Learning', *Management Science*, 54(7, July), pp. 1297–1312.

Raisch, S., Birkinshaw, J., Probst, G. and Tushman, M.L. (2009) 'Organizational Ambidexterity: Balancing Exploitation and Exploration for Sustained Performance', *Organization Science*, 20(4), pp. 685–695.

Repenning, N.P. (2001) 'Understanding fire fighting in new product development', *Journal of Product Innovation Management*, 18, pp. 285–300.

Repenning, N.P. and Sterman, J.D. (2002) 'Capability traps and self-confirming attribution errors in the dynamics of process improvement', *ASQ*, 47, pp. 265–295.

Robertson, P. (2005) *Always Change a Winning Team, Why Reinvention and Change Are Prerequisite for Business Success,* Singapore: Marshall Cavendish Business.

Schneider, S. and Barsoux, J. (2003) *Managing Across Cultures* (2nd edn), Pearson Education Limited.

Schumpeter, J.A. (1934) *The Theory of Economic Development*, Cambridge, MA: Harvard University Press.

Schumpeter, J.A. (1950) *Capitalism, Socialism and Democracy* (3rd edn), New York: Harper and Brothers.

Simon, H.A. (1955) 'A Behavioral Model of Rational Choice', *Quarterly Journal of Economics*, 69(1), pp. 99–118.

Smith, W.K. and Tushman, M.L. (2005) 'Managing Strategic Contradictions: A Top Management Model for Managing Innovation Streams', *Organization Science*, 16(5), pp. 522–536.

Smith, W.K., Lewis, M.W., and Tushman, M.L. (2016) 'Both/And' Leadership', Harvard Business Review, May, pp. 62–70.

Starbuck, W. H. (2014). Five stories that illustrate three generalizations about radical innovations. *Industrial Marketing Management*, 43(8), pp. 1278–1283.

Story, V. M., Daniels, K., Zolkiewski, J., and Dainty, A. R. J. (2014). The barriers and consequences of radical innovations: Introduction to the issue. *Industrial Marketing Management*, 43, pp. 1271–1277.

Tellis, G.J. (2013) *Unrelenting Innovation: How to Build a Culture for Market Dominance*, San Francisco, CA: Jossey-Bass.

Tellis, G. J., Prabhu, J. C., and Chandy, R. K. (2009). Radical Innovation Across Nations: The Preeminence of Corporate Culture. *Journal of Marketing*, 73(1), pp. 3–23.

Tripsas, M. and Gavetti, G. (2000) 'Capabilities, Cognition, and Inertia: Evidence from Digital Imaging', *Strategic Management Journal*, 21(10/11, October–November), Special Issue: The Evolution of Firm Capabilities, pp. 1147–1161.

Trompenaars, F. and Hampden-Turner, C. (2000) *Building Cross-Cultural Competence*, New Haven, CT: Yale University Press.

Tushman, M.L. and O'Reilly III, C.A. (1996) 'Ambidextrous Organizations: Managing Evolutionary and Revolutionary Change', *California Management Review*, 38(4, Summer), pp. 8–30.

Utterback, J. (1994). *Mastering the Dynamics of Innovation*. Boston, MA.: Harvard Business School Press.

Van Maanen, J. (1973) 'Observation of the Making of Policemen', *Human Relations*, 32, pp. 407–418.

Van Tulder, R. and Junne, G. (1988) *European Multinationals in Core Technologies*, London: Wiley & Sons.

Vernon, R. (1966) 'International Investment and International Trade in the Product Life Cycle', *Quarterly Journal of Economics*, 80(2, May), pp. 190–207.

Waterman, R.H., Peters, T.J. and Phillips, J.R. (1980) 'Structure is Not Organization', *Business Horizons*, 23(June), pp. 14–26.

Weick, K. (1979) *The Social Psychology of Organizing* (2nd edn), Reading, MA: Addison-Wesley.

Whyte, W.H. Jr. (1957) *The Organization Man*, Garden City, New York: Doubleday.

WIPO (2008) *World Patent Report: A Statistical Review*, World Intellectual Property Organization.

WIPO (2015) *World Intellectual Property Indicators 2015*, World Intellectual Property Organization.

Zott, C. and Amit, R. (2013) 'The Business Model: A Theoretically Anchored Robust Construct for Strategic Analysis', *Strategic Organization*, 11, pp. 403–411.

STRATEGY CONTEXT

Circumstances? I make circumstances!

Napoleon Bonaparte (1769–1821); French emperor

The strategy context is the set of circumstances surrounding strategy-making – the conditions under which both the strategy process and the strategy content are formed. It could be said that strategy context is concerned with the *where* of strategy – where (i.e. in which firm and which environment) the strategy process and strategy content are embedded.

Most strategizing managers have an ambivalent relationship with their strategy context. On the one hand, strategizing is about creating something new, and for this, a healthy level of disregard, or even disrespect, for the present circumstances is required. Much like Napoleon, managers do not want to hear about current conditions limiting their capability to shape the future – they want to create their own circumstances. On the other hand, managers recognize that many contextual limitations are real and that wise strategists must take these circumstances into account. In this section, this fundamental tension between *shaping* the context and *adapting* to it is at the centre of attention.

As visualized in Figure IV.1, the strategy context can be dissected along two different dimensions: industry versus organization, and national versus international. This gives the three key contexts that are explored in Chapters 10, 11 and 12:

- The industry context. The key issue here is how industry development takes place. Can the individual firm influence its industry and to what extent does the industry context dictate particular types of firm behaviour?

- The organizational context. The key issue here is how organizational development takes place. Can strategizing managers influence their own organizational conditions and to what extent does the organizational context determine particular types of firm behaviour?

- The international context. The key issue here is how the international context is developing. Must firms adapt to ongoing global convergence or will international diversity remain a characteristic with which firms will need to cope?

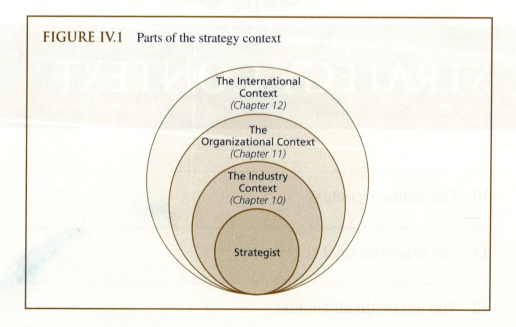

FIGURE IV.1   Parts of the strategy context

THE INDUSTRY CONTEXT

Know the other and know yourself: Triumph without peril.
Know nature and know the situation: Triumph completely.

Sun Tzu (5th century BC); Chinese military strategist

INTRODUCTION

If strategic management is concerned with relating a firm to its environment, then it is essential to know this environment well. In the previous chapters the factors and actors that shape the external context of the firm have been thoroughly reviewed. While the entire outside world was taken into consideration, emphasis was placed on the direct environment in which a firm needs to compete – its industry context. It has been concluded that an understanding of competitors, buyers, suppliers, substitutes and potential new entrants, as well as the structural factors that influence their behaviour, is invaluable for determining a successful strategy.

A constant theme in the strategy content and strategy process sections was industry change. Knowing the current industry context, it became clear, is not enough to secure an ongoing alignment between a firm and its environment. Strategizing managers need to recognize in which direction the industry is developing to be able to maintain a healthy fit. However, what was not addressed in these discussions is how industry development actually takes place. Important questions such as 'what are the drivers propelling industry development?' and 'what patterns of development do industries exhibit?' have not yet been examined. Nor has it been established whether industries develop in the same way and at the same speed, and whether change is always accompanied by the same opportunities and threats. In this chapter, these questions surrounding the issue of industry development are the centre of attention.

For strategizing managers, however, the most important question linked to the issue of industry development is how a firm can move beyond *adapting* to *shaping*. How can a firm, or a group of collaborating firms, modify the structure and competitive dynamics in their industry to gain an advantageous position? How can the industry's evolutionary path be proactively diverted into a particular direction? If a firm is capable of shaping its industry environment instead of following it, this will give it the potential for creating a strong competitive advantage – it can 'set the rules of the competitive game' instead of having to 'play by the rules' set by others. This topic of industry leadership – shaping events as opposed to following them – will be the key focus throughout this chapter.

THE ISSUE OF INDUSTRY DEVELOPMENT

When strategists look at an industry, they are interested in understanding 'the rules of the game' (e.g. Hamel, 1996; Prahalad and Doz, 1987). The industry rules are the demands dictated to the firm by the industry context, limiting the scope of potential strategic behaviours. In other words, industry rules stipulate what must be done to survive and thrive in any chosen line of business – they determine under what conditions the competitive game will be played. For example, an industry rule could be 'must have significant scale economies', 'must have certain technology' or 'must have strong brand'. Failure to adhere to the rules leads to being selected out.

The industry rules arise from the structure of the industry (e.g. McGahan, 2000; Porter, 1980; Tirole, 1988). All of Porter's five forces can impose constraints on a firm's freedom of action. Where the rules are strict, the degrees of freedom available to the strategist are limited. Strict rules imply that only very specific behaviour is allowed – firms must closely follow the rules of the game or face severe consequences. Where the rules are looser, firms have more room to manoeuvre and exhibit distinctive behaviour – the level of managerial discretion is higher (e.g. Carpenter and Golden, 1997; Hambrick and Abrahamson, 1995).

As industries develop, the rules of competition change – vertical integration becomes necessary, certain competencies become vital or having a global presence becomes a basic requirement. To be able to play the competitive game well, strategizing managers need to identify which characteristics in the industry structure and which aspects of competitive interaction are changing. This is the topic of 'dimensions of industry development', which is reviewed in more detail below. To determine their response, it is also essential to understand the nature of the change. Are the industry rules gradually shifting or is there a major break with the past? Is the industry development more evolutionary or more revolutionary? A process of slow and moderate industry change demands a different strategic reaction than a process of sudden and dramatic disruption of the industry rules. This topic of 'paths of industry development' is also examined more closely.

As strategists generally like to have the option to shape instead of always being shaped, they need to recognize the determinants of industry development as well. What are the factors that cause the industry rules to change? This subject can be divided into two parts. First, the question of what the drivers of industry development are, pushing the industry in a certain direction. Second, the question of what the inhibitors of industry development are, placing a brake on changes. Together, these forces of change and forces for stability will determine the actual path of development that the industry will follow. How these four topics are interrelated is outlined in Figure 10.1.

Dimensions of industry development

Industry development means that the structure of the industry changes. In Chapter 4, the key aspects of the industry structure have already been discussed. Following Porter (1980), five important groups of industry actors were identified (i.e. competitors, buyers, suppliers, new entrants and substitutes) and the underlying factors determining their behaviour were reviewed. Industry development (which Porter calls "industry evolution"; see also McGahan, 2000, Reading 10.1) is the result of a change in one or more of these underlying factors.

As Porter already indicates, the industry structure can be decomposed into dozens of elements, each of which can change, causing a shift in industry rules. Here it is not the intention to go through all of these elements, but to pick out a number of important

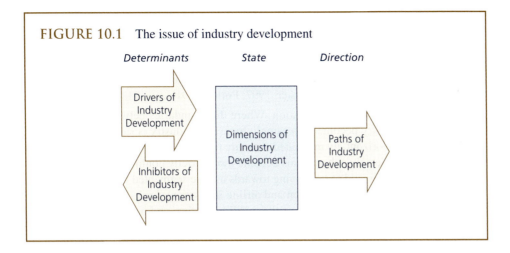

FIGURE 10.1   The issue of industry development

structural characteristics that require special attention. Each of these structural characteristics represents a dimension along which significant industry developments can take place:

- Convergence–divergence. Where the business models that firms employ increasingly start to resemble each other, the industry is said to be moving towards convergence (e.g. insurance and airline industries). In contrast, where many firms introduce new business models, the industry is said to be developing towards more diversity (e.g. car retailing and restaurant industries). Higher diversity can result from the 'mutation' of existing firms, as they strive to compete on a different basis, or the result of new entrants with their own distinct business model. Convergence is the consequence of adaptation by less successful firms to a 'dominant design' in the industry and the selecting out of unfit firms incapable of adequate and timely adaptation (e.g. Hannan and Freeman, 1977; Porter, 1980). Generally, patterns of divergence and convergence can be witnessed in all industries, although the amount of mutation and the pressure for convergence can greatly differ, as can the overall cycle time of an "evolutionary phase" of mutation and selection (e.g. Aldrich, 1999; Baum and Singh, 1994).

- Concentration–fragmentation. Where an increasing share of the market is in the hands of only a few companies, the industry is said to be developing towards a more concentrated structure (e.g. aircraft and food retailing industries). Conversely, where the average market share of the largest companies starts to decrease, the industry is said to be moving towards a more fragmented structure (e.g. airline and telecom services industries). Concentration can be due to mergers and acquisitions, or result from companies exiting the business. Fragmentation can happen when new companies are formed and grab a part of the market, or through the entry of existing companies into the industry. In a concentrated industry it is much more likely that only one or two firms are dominant than in a fragmented industry, but it is also possible that the industry structure is more balanced.

- Vertical integration–fragmentation. Where firms in the industry are becoming involved in more value-adding activities in the industry column, the industry is said to be developing towards a more vertically integrated structure (e.g. media and IT service providers). Conversely, where firms in the industry are withdrawing from various value-adding activities and 'go back to the core', the industry is said to be moving towards a more disintegrated, layered or vertically fragmented structure (e.g. telecom and automotive industries). It is even possible that the entire vertical structure changes if a new business model has major upstream and/or downstream consequences. In recent years, technological changes surrounding IT and the Internet have triggered a number of such instances of industry reconfiguration (e.g. travel and encyclopedia industries). However, even though we are now equipped with more fashionable terms (e.g. 'deconstruction'), such industry-wide transformations of the value-creation process are in themselves not new (e.g. PCs and the computer industry in the 1980s; airplanes and the travel industry in the 1950s) (e.g. Evans and Wurster, 1997; Porter, 2001).

- Horizontal integration–fragmentation. Where the boundaries between different businesses in an industry become increasingly fuzzy, the industry is said to be developing towards a more horizontally integrated structure (e.g. consumer electronics and defence industries). Conversely, where firms become more strictly confined to their own business, the industry is said to be moving towards a more segmented or horizontally fragmented structure (e.g. construction and airline industries). Links between businesses can intensify or wane, depending on the mobility barriers and potential cross-business synergies. However, horizontal integration and fragmentation are not limited to the intra-industry domain. Inter-industry integration between two or more industries can also increase, creating a more or less open competitive space (Hamel and Prahalad, 1994) with few mobility barriers (e.g. the digital industries). Inter-industry integration can also occur where the producers of different products and services are complementary or converge on a common standard or platform (e.g. Android and Linux), making them 'complementers' (e.g. Cusumano and Gawer, 2002; Moore, 1996). Yet, the opposite trend is possible as well, whereby an industry becomes more isolated from neighbouring sectors (e.g. accountancy).

- International integration–fragmentation. Where the international boundaries separating various geographic segments of an industry become increasingly less important, the industry is said to be developing towards a more internationally integrated structure (e.g. food retailing and business education industries). Conversely, where the competitive interactions in an industry are increasingly confined to a region (e.g. Europe) or country, the industry is said to be moving towards a more internationally fragmented structure (e.g. satellite television and internet retailing). These developments are more thoroughly examined in Chapter 12, which deals with the international context.

- Expansion–contraction. Industries can also differ with regard to the structural nature of the demand for their products and/or services. Where an industry is experiencing an ongoing increase in demand, the industry is said to be in growth or expansion. Where demand is constantly receding, the industry is said to be in decline or contraction. If periods of expansion are followed by periods of contraction, and vice versa, the industry is said to be cyclical. A prolonged period of expansion is usually linked to the growth phase of the industry life cycle (e.g. McGahan, 2000, Reading 10.1; Moore, 2000; Porter, 1980), while contraction is linked to the decline phase. Often, however, it is rather difficult to apply the 'life cycle' concept to an entire industry (as opposed to a product or technology). As industry growth (expansion) can easily follow a period of industry decline (contraction), the life cycle model has little descriptive value – what does it mean to be mature? – and even less predictive value.

Paths of industry development

The development of an industry can be mapped along any one of the dimensions listed above. The most popular is to track the pattern of expansion and contraction, to gain some indication of the life cycle phase in which the industry might have arrived. Another frequently analysed characteristic is the level of concentration, commonly using a concentration index to measure the market share of the four or eight largest companies. But it is

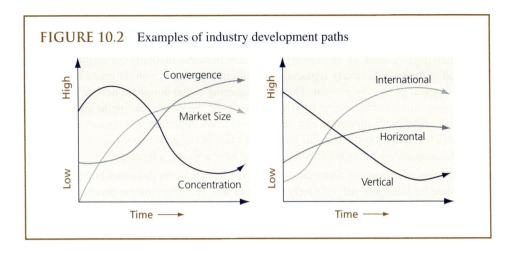

FIGURE 10.2   Examples of industry development paths

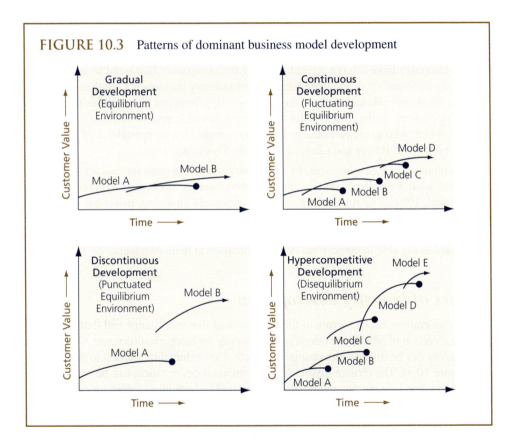

FIGURE 10.3   Patterns of dominant business model development

equally viable to trace the trajectory of vertical, horizontal or international integration. In Figure 10.2 examples of these paths of industry development are given.

In Figure 10.3 one particular element of the convergence–divergence dimension has been selected for further magnification. As discussed above, in the development of an industry a particular business model can become the dominant design around which the rest of the industry converges. A strategically relevant development occurs when the dominant business model is replaced by a new business model that offers customers higher value. In Figure 10.3, four generic patterns of industry development are outlined, each describing a different type of transition from the old dominant model to the new (Burgelman and Grove, 1996; D'Aveni, 1999):

- **Gradual development.** In an industry where one business model is dominant for a long period of time and is slowly replaced by an alternative that is a slight improvement, the development process is gradual. The firms adhering to the dominant design will generally have little trouble adapting to the new rules of the game, leading to a situation of relative stability. Competition can be weak or fierce, depending on the circumstances, but will take place on the basis of the shared rules of the game. In this type of environment, companies with an established position have a strong advantage.

- **Continuous development.** In an industry where changes to the dominant business model are more frequent, but still relatively modest in size, the development process is continuous. While firms need not have difficulties adjusting to each individual change to the rules of the game, they can fall behind if they do not keep up with the pace of improvement. In this type of environment, rapid adaptation to developments will strengthen the competitive position of firms vis-à-vis slow movers.

- **Discontinuous development.** In an industry where one business model is dominant for a long period of time and is then suddenly displaced by a radically better one, the development process is discontinuous. The firms riding the wave of the new business model will generally have a large advantage over the companies that need to adjust to an entirely different set of industry rules. Where industry incumbents are themselves the "rule breakers" (Hamel, 1996), they can strongly improve their position vis-à-vis the "rule takers" in the industry. But the business model innovator can also be an industry outsider, who gains entrance by avoiding competition with established players on their terms (e.g. Bower and Christensen, 1995; Slywotsky, 1996).

- **Hypercompetitive development.** In an industry where business models are frequently pushed aside by radically better ones, the development process is hypercompetitive (D'Aveni, 1994). The rules of the game are constantly changing, making it impossible for firms to build up a sustainably dominant position. The only defence in this type of environment is offence – being able to outrun existing competitors, being innovative first and being able to outperform new rule breakers at their own game.

Drivers of industry development

There is an endless list of factors in the environment that can change and that can influence the direction of industry development. Following the categorization made in Chapter 6, these factors can be divided into change drivers that are external or internal to the industry (see Figure 10.4). The change drivers in the contextual environment can be roughly split into socio-cultural, economic, political/regulatory and technological forces for change. The change drivers in the industry environment can be divided into groups surrounding suppliers, buyers, incumbent rivals, new entrants, and substitutes and complementors.

As the arrows indicate (Figure 10.4), change in a complex system like an industry does not always start in one discernible part and then reverberate throughout the whole. Rather, change can also be the result of the interplay of various elements in the system, without any clear start or ending point. Yet, for the discussion on shaping industry development it is important to recognize the distinction between industry changes that are largely triggered by an individual firm, as opposed to broader, system-wide changes for which no one actor can claim responsibility. Where one firm is the major driver of industry development, it can claim industry leadership. However, if there is no industry leader and the evolution of the industry is due to the complex interaction of many different change drivers, it is said that the industry dynamics determine the path of industry development.

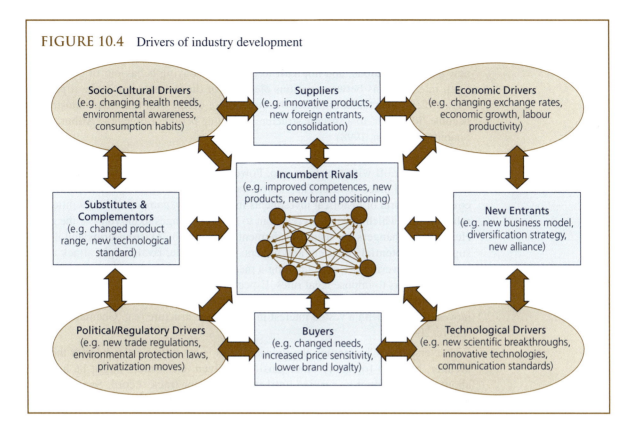

FIGURE 10.4   Drivers of industry development

Inhibitors of industry development

Forces of change do not always go unopposed. In the discussion on strategic change in Chapter 8, the sources of organizational rigidity have been reviewed, each of which acts as an inhibitor to organizational change. In the same way, there are many sources of industry rigidity, making the industry rules much more difficult to bend or break. Industry rigidity can be defined as the lack of susceptibility to change. If an industry is rigid, the rules of the game cannot be altered and competitive positions are relatively fixed. The opposite term is industry plasticity – an industry's susceptibility to change.

A large number of factors can contribute to rigidity, thereby inhibiting industry development. Some of the most important ones are the following:

■ **Underlying conditions.** Basically, some rules might be immutable because the underlying industry conditions cannot be changed. In some industries economies of scale are essential (e.g. airplane manufacturing, merchant shipping), while in others economies of scale are not of importance (e.g. wedding services, dentistry services). In some industries buyers are fragmented (e.g. newspapers, moving services), while in others they are highly concentrated (e.g. defence systems, harbour construction). In some industries buyers value product differentiation (e.g. clothing, restaurants), while in others bulk producers must compete on price (e.g. chemicals, general construction). Many of these structural factors are inherent to the industry and defy any attempts to change them (e.g. Bain, 1959; Porter, 1980).

■ **Industry integration.** Besides the limited plasticity of individual aspects of the industry context, it is also important to recognize that some industries are particularly rigid because of the complex linkages between various aspects of the industry. For example, to be a rule-breaking music company not only requires developing new delivery methods via the Internet, but also getting electronics manufacturers to adopt the new standards, finding ways to safeguard copyrights, working together with governments to find new policing methods, and not least to change the buying behaviour of consumers. Such interrelations between various elements of the industry can make it particularly difficult to actually influence the direction of events over time. The industry can become 'locked in' to a specific structure for a long period of time (e.g. Arthur, 1994; Shapiro and Varian, 1998).

■ Power structures. The industry rules can also be kept in place by those who feel they are better off with the status quo. Powerful industry incumbents often have little to gain and much to lose. They have established positions and considerable sunk costs, in the form of historical investments in technology, competencies, facilities and relationships, which make them reluctant to support changes to the rules of the game. Hence, rule changers are usually vehemently resisted by existing firms and denied support by potential suppliers and buyers. For example, rivals might attack a rule breaker by lowering prices, launching a media campaign, or even lobbying government regulators to impose legal rules. Especially where a rule breaker needs allies to secure supplies, distribution or a new standard, it will be vulnerable to the countermoves of parties with a vested interest in the current structure (e.g. Ghemawat, 1991; Moore, 2000).

■ Risk averseness. Challenging the industry rules is not only a risky step for the rule breaker, but also for many other parties involved. Customers might be hesitant about a new product or service until it has a firmer track record. Suppliers and distributors might worry whether the initial investments will pay off and what the countermoves of the established companies will be. The more risk averse the parties in the industry, the more rigid will be the industry rules (e.g. Christensen, 1997; Parolini, 1999).

■ Industry recipes. An industry recipe is a widely held perception among industry incumbents regarding the actual rules of the game in the industry. In other words, an industry recipe is the cognitive map shared by industry incumbents about the structure and demands of an industry. Such a common understanding of the rules of the game can develop over time through shared experiences and interaction – the longer people are in the industry and converse with each other, the greater the chance that a consensus will grow about 'what makes the industry tick'. Thus, the industry recipe can limit people's openness to rule changers who challenge the industry orthodoxy (e.g. Baden-Fuller and Stopford, 1992; Spender, 1989).

■ Institutional pressures. While the industry recipe is a shared understanding of how the industry actually functions, industry incumbents usually also share norms of what constitutes socially acceptable economic behaviour. Companies experience strong pressures from governments, professional associations, customers, consultants, trade unions, pressure groups and other industry incumbents prescribing permissible strategies and actions, and generally internalize these behavioural standards. Such conformity to institutional pressures gives companies legitimacy, but makes them less willing to question industry conventions, let alone work together with a maverick rule breaker (e.g. Aldrich and Fiol, 1994; Oliver, 1997).

Taken together, these historically determined factors inhibit developments in the industry. It is said that industry evolution is path dependent – the path that the industry has travelled in the past will strongly limit how and in which direction it can develop in the future. In other words, 'history matters', setting bounds on the freedom to shape the future.

THE PARADOX OF COMPLIANCE AND CHOICE

When people are free to do as they please, they usually imitate each other.

Eric Hoffer (1902–1983); American philosopher

Yet, the question is whether firms should attempt to shape their industries at all, given the required effort and apparent risk of failure. There might be attractive rewards if a firm can lead industry developments, but trying to break industry rules that turn out to be immutable can be a quick way to achieve bankruptcy. Being an industry leader might sound very proactive, and even heroic, but it is potentially suicidal if the industry context defies being shaped.

This duality of wanting to change the industry rules that are malleable, while needing to adapt to the industry rules that are fixed, is the tension central to dealing with the industry context. On the one hand, managers must be willing to irreverently transgress widely acknowledged industry rules, going against what they see as the industry recipe. On the other hand, managers must respectfully accept many characteristics of the industry structure and play according to existing rules of the competitive game. Yet, these conflicting demands of being irreverent and respectful towards the industry rules are difficult for strategists to meet at the same time.

Where firms cannot influence the structure of their industry, *compliance* with the rules of the game is the strategic imperative. Under these circumstances, the strategic demand is for managers to adapt the firm to the industry context. Where firms do have the ability to manipulate the industry structure, they should exercise their freedom of *choice* to break the industry rules. In such a case, the strategic demand is for managers to try to change the terms of competition in their own favour.

This tension between compliance and choice has been widely acknowledged in the strategic management literature (e.g. Hrebiniak and Joyce, 1985; McGahan, 2000, Reading 10.1; Porter, 1980). The pressure for compliance has usually been presented as a form of environmental determinism, as the industry developments force firms to adapt or be selected out (e.g. Astley and Van der Ven, 1983; Wilson, 1992). The freedom of choice has often been labelled as organizational voluntarism, to convey the notion that industry developments can be the result of the wilful actions of individual organizations (e.g. Bettis and Donaldson, 1990; Child, 1972). In the following sections both compliance and choice are further examined.

The demand for firm compliance

It goes almost without saying that organizations must, to a large extent, adapt themselves to their environments. No organization has the ability to shape the entire world to fit its needs. Therefore, to be successful, all organizations need to understand the context in which they operate and need to play by most of the rules of the game.

After all, the alternative of ignoring the rules is fraught with danger. Probably the most common cause of 'corporate death' is misalignment between the organization and its environment (discussed in Chapter 8). And misalignment can happen very quickly, as most industries are constantly in flux. Companies can misinterpret the direction of the changes, can fail to take appropriate corrective action, or can be plainly self-centred, paying insufficient attention to external developments. Most companies have enough difficulty just staying attuned to the current rules of the competitive game, let alone anticipating how the industry context will change in the future.

To achieve compliance with the industry rules, firms must develop structures, processes and a culture in which listening and adapting to the environment become engrained. Firms must learn to become customer and market-oriented, reacting to the 'pull' of the market instead of 'pushing' their standard approach and pet projects at an unwilling audience. Firm compliance means avoiding the pitfall of organizational arrogance – knowing better than the market and imposing an approach that no one desires (e.g. Miller, 1990; Whitley, 1999).

The demand for strategic choice

While compliance with the industry rules can be very beneficial, contradicting them can also be strategically valuable. If firms only play by the current rules, it is generally very difficult to gain a significant competitive advantage over their rivals. After all, adapting to the current industry structure means doing business in more or less the same way as competitors, with few possibilities to distinguish the organization. In other words, 'compliance' might be another way of saying 'follow a me-too strategy'.

To be unique and develop a competitive advantage, firms need to do something different, something that does not fit within the current rules of the game. The more innovative the rule breaker, the larger will be the competitive advantage over rivals stuck with outdated business models. The more radical the departure from the old industry recipe, the more difficult it will be for competitors to imitate and catch up. Where companies are capable of constantly leading industry developments, they will have the benefit of capturing attractive industry positions before less proactive competitors eventually follow. In other words, there is a strong pressure for firms to attempt to shape the industry rules.

To achieve organizational choice, firms must find ways of escaping the pitfall of organizational conformity – the strict adherence to current industry rules. Firms must develop structures, processes and a culture in which the current industry recipe is constantly questioned, challenged and changed. Managers must come to see that in the long run the easy path of following the industry rules will be less productive than the rocky road of innovation and change (e.g. Hamel and Prahalad, 1994; Kim and Mauborgne, 2005, Reading 10.2).

EXHIBIT 10.1   SHORT CASE

NINTENDO: PRESS START TO CONTINUE

Founded in 1889, Nintendo's journey is one that charts a humble playing card manufacturer becoming the most well-known video game company of all time. Producing both hardware and software – video game systems and their games – with a portfolio of multimillion franchises ranging from Mario and Donkey Kong to Pokémon and The Legend of Zelda, the company has repeatedly inspired, innovated and revolutionized the video game industry. The Japanese firm has not done so without its fair share of challenges.

When Nintendo entered the video game market with its first dedicated video game console in 1983 (1985 in the West), it did so with a bang. The Family Computer, known as Nintendo Entertainment System (NES) abroad, was to be the first console

with a revolutionary business model. Instead of only producing games for the hardware itself, Nintendo licensed and encouraged external game developers to produce and distribute products for Nintendo's hardware. This authorization process provided Nintendo with its share, increased the platform's software library and provided the company with quality control. It became a standard in the video game industry and it would take years before Nintendo's monopoly position was challenged. The NES managed to achieve lifetime sales of 61.9 million units worldwide.

As hardware improved and competitors started adopting Nintendo's business model, competition grew fiercer. Having proven itself with the NES and a winning streak of high quality self-published titles such as *Super Mario Bros.*, *The Legend of Zelda* and *Metroid*, the Japanese video game company did more of the same in terms of its hardware.

Owing mostly to the high quality of its software, Nintendo systems managed to remain relevant. When Sony entered the game with its PlayStation, this new system introduced players to 3D graphics and emphasized more mature games. This proved a lethal combination: it went on to sell more than 102 million units over more than a decade. Its successor, the PlayStation 2 (2000), would become the most successful video game platform in history with a sales record of 155 million sold units. In an effort to challenge Sony's new hegemonic position, Nintendo released the GameCube (2001); technically a better machine than the second PlayStation, but a system that did nothing new. It performed poorly, ending its run with a measly 21.7 million units sold. Even the new kid, Microsoft's Xbox (2001), which catered towards older consumers and introduced its own well-run Internet service to consoles, exceeded that figure by a couple of million. Competitors played Nintendo's game and started winning.

Thanks to acclaimed software on Nintendo's platforms, the company maintained a share of dedicated fans, but it was not enough to sell sufficient hardware units. Nintendo's only consistent success story proved to be its portable video game devices. The Game Boy (1989) and its improved Color version (1998), sold a combined 118.7 million units. At a time when Nintendo had difficulty appealing to consumers, the follow-up to its blockbuster handheld, the Game Boy Advance (2001), achieved lifetime sales of 81.5 million sold units. Nintendo had the means to continue, but playing by the rules of the industry proved not to do Nintendo any favours. It was up to Satoru Iwata, newly crowned CEO of the company, to turn things around.

Iwata needed to change Nintendo's game and he did so with an unprecedented strategy. He would approach radically new demographics. In 2004 Nintendo released the DS, the newest addition to its portable game system portfolio. This piece of hardware features two screens, the lower one functioning as a touch screen, introducing a whole new way to play. To compare: the iPhone, which introduced touch screens on a big scale to the smartphone market, only came out in 2007. The launch of the Nintendo DS was Iwata's first big product release, but he was not present in Tokyo to promote the system. Instead, he was visiting neuroscientist Ryuta Kawashima. Iwata thought his 'train

the brain' exercise books could form the foundations of a game that had the potential to appeal to gamers and non-gamers alike. He guessed right. The resulting *Brain Age: Train Your Brain in Minutes a Day!* – known as *Dr Kawashima's Brain Training* outside of the US – became an industry phenomenon and helped introduce many adults to gaming. Nintendo also captured the previously underestimated girl demographic, releasing successful titles such as *Nintendogs*, *Animal Crossing: Wild World* and *Super Princess Peach*. Iwata soon proved that he could also change the playing field in which Nintendo had struggled the most: the home console market.

The codename for Nintendo's follow-up to the poor performing GameCube was 'Revolution', an apt premonition of what was to come. Instead of just making games look better and better, Nintendo once again wanted to change the way people played. Released as the Nintendo Wii in late 2006, the system did not focus on traditional button-based gameplay, but introduced motion controls. No need to remember tricky button combinations: you swing the remote-shaped controller like a tennis racket and so does the character on-screen. The games were social, intuitive and fun. As a result, the barrier between gamers and non-gamers dissolved and the Wii became an instant must-have for families.

Nintendo had truly altered the rules of the game. While most hardware is initially expensive and only gets adopted by the mainstream relatively late in their lifecycle, the Wii was sold at a budget price and appealed to everyone from its inception. Gamers wanted to try something new, while consumers new to gaming met an accessible and fun device. The Wii left its technically superior competitors in the dust – by mid-2007, Nintendo's system had sold more units than Sony and Microsoft's newest consoles put together. The me-too products Microsoft and PlayStation launched as a response to Nintendo's new-found success, never managed to get off the ground.

Nevertheless, smartphones and tablets slowly entered the fray, eating into the handheld console market, Nintendo's safe card. Why buy an expensive gaming handheld with expensive software, when smartphones allow you to play at significantly lower cost? With the successor to the DS, Nintendo tried to offer something not possible on mobiles: stereoscopic 3D. With its Nintendo 3DS it offered an improved DS, with the addition of 'glasses-free 3D'. This seemingly magic feat did not prevent the system from selling poorly at launch. Iwata took personal responsibility. Nintendo's CEO apologised, cut his own salary by 50 per cent and gave early adopters of the handheld 10 Nintendo games for free. Owing to a significant price drop and a steady stream of quality games later in its life cycle, the 3DS luckily turned out to be a slow-burner – as of 2016 the system has been sold almost 59 million times.

The same could not be said for the successor of the Wii. Nintendo was ahead of the curve with the Wii, but its follow-up ended up stuck in the middle. It did not appeal to its existing fans, nor to the more casual gamers. The confusingly named Wii U followed the tablet trend, a phenomenon introduced to the mass market by Apple and Google. It came with a tablet-like controller with buttons, but Nintendo had a hard time explaining to consumers what actually made the Wii U different. As the reveal to the console was unclear and Wii controllers are compatible with the Wii U, many were under the impression that the new system was a mere upgrade. Nintendo also struggled to make good use of its new hardware as many of the systems' more successful games, such as *Mario Kart 8* and *Super Smash Bros. for Wii U*, did not use the features of the tablet. As a response to the poor results of the Wii U – Nintendo only managed to sell about 13 million units of the system in total compared to more than 100 million Wiis – investors pressed Iwata to lay off employees. He refused to do so, under the philosophy that employees who fear they may get fired are in no state to develop impressive software.

He did however listen to a different demand, one that investors had been repeatedly making: Nintendo decided to also start releasing games on smartphones. Iwata had been cautious about separating Nintendo hardware and software, claiming the company would then "cease to be Nintendo" – its business strategy had thus far consisted of making compelling exclusive software to prompt people to buy hardware. However, Iwata soon declared that the "era has ended when people play all kinds of games only on dedicated gaming systems". Nintendo would form partnerships to publish applications and games on smartphones.

Iwata did not live to see the first app released; Nintendo's CEO died in 2015 from a tumour in his bile duct.. This was the same year that Nintendo finally entered the black again with an operating income of US$206 million, after three years of consecutive losses. One of the last ideas Iwata can be held responsible for helped establish this feat. He envisioned a line of toy figures based on Nintendo characters that can be connected to Nintendo games for in-game bonuses and extra options. In itself the idea was not new; companies such as Activision and Disney had done the same with *Skylanders* and *Disney Infinity* respectively. Nintendo's so-called Amiibo figures proved appealing enough to sell over 6 million units in their first month. By March 2016, the sales of Amiibo exceeded 64 million units. Sometimes a catch up strategy could be beneficial for Nintendo as well.

This was also true for the first two smartphone apps Nintendo released. While its first application, the social app *Miitomo*, turned profitable rather quickly, it failed to remain relevant over the long run. The second one, however, became a truly global phenomenon. *Pokémon Go*, developed by independent American company Niantic, lets people all over the world catch little monsters in the real environment using augmented reality. The game became so popular that Nintendo's market value doubled in a matter of days – from about US$20 billion to more than US$40 billion – marking the biggest daily turnover in stock ever on the Tokyo Stock Exchange. Nintendo however only had about a 13 per cent interest in *Pokémon Go* and the app would thus ultimately not have a big impact on the company's profits. After Nintendo made a financial statement about this, its shares plunged.

Nevertheless, it did prove a point: So long as it can make good use of its intellectual properties, playing follow-up also has potential for Nintendo. Its first smartphone endeavours can easily be called successful, and jumping on the so-called 'toys-to-life' market with Amiibo also turned out to be lucrative. The danger of being neither an industry leader nor a good follower, was proven by the Nintendo Wii U however. Nintendo's newest system, codenamed NX, is set to release in 2017 and much is riding on the success of the console. It is thus necessary for Nintendo to decide: what now? Can Nintendo find ways to shape the video game industry once again or can it find a way to play by the rules of others? Will the NX manage to put Nintendo alongside Sony and Microsoft again? And how long can the 3DS and similar future products remain relevant in a smartphone dominated environment? If Nintendo can make the right decisions, it will not reach 'game over' any time soon.

Co-author: Wester Wagenaar

Sources: nintendo.co.jp; nintendo.com; Nintendo Annual Report 2015; *Bloomberg*, 19 July 2016 and 25 July 2016; *Fortune*, 5 December 2014; *Gamesindustry.biz*, 15 July 2016; *Gamespot*, 25 July 2016; *Games Radar*, 29 April 2016; *The Guardian*, 13 July 2015; *The Japan Times*, 16 July 2016; Sheff, David, 'Game Over: How Nintendo Conquered the World', 1994.

PERSPECTIVES ON THE INDUSTRY CONTEXT

A wise man will make more opportunity than he finds.

Francis Bacon (1561–1624); Lord Chancellor of England

Once again the strategizing manager seems 'stuck between a rock and a hard place'. The pressures for both compliance and choice are clear, but as opposites they are at least partially incompatible. Developing an organizational culture, structure and processes attuned to compliance will to some extent be at odds with the culture, structure and processes needed to shape an industry. An organization well-rehearsed in the art of adaptation and skilful imitation is usually quite different from one geared towards business innovation and contrarian behaviour. How should managers actually deal with the issue of industry development – should they lead or follow?

In the strategic management literature many answers to this question are given – unfortunately, many contradictory ones. The views among management theorists differ sharply, as they emphasize a different balance between the need to comply and the need to choose. To gain a better overview of the range of conflicting opinions, the two diametrically opposed positions will be identified and discussed. On the one hand, there are strategists who argue that industry development is an autonomous process, which individual firms can hardly hope to shape. They believe that compliance to shifting industry characteristics is mandatory – adjust or risk being selected out. This point of view is referred to as the 'industry dynamics perspective'. On the other hand, many strategists believe that the industry context can be shaped in an infinite variety of ways by innovative firms. Therefore, industry development can be driven by firms willing and able to take a leading role. This point of view is referred to as the 'industry leadership perspective'.

The industry dynamics perspective

 To those taking an industry dynamics perspective, the popular notion that individual firms have the power to shape their industry is an understandable, but quite misplaced, belief. Of course, the illusion of control is tempting – most people, especially strategists, would like to control their own destiny. Most individuals assume they have a free will and can decide their own future. Many governments suppose that they can shape society and many cultures assume that they control nature. In the same way, it is seductive to believe that the individual firm can matter by influencing the development of its industry.

Unfortunately, this belief is largely a fallacy, brought on by a poor understanding of the underlying industry dynamics. In reality, according to advocates of the industry dynamics perspective, industries are complex systems, with a large number of forces interacting simultaneously, none of which can significantly direct the long-term development of the whole. Firms are relatively small players in a very large game – their behaviours may have some impact on industry development, but none can fundamentally shape the direction of changes. On the contrary, as industries evolve, all firms that do not meet the changing demands of the environment are weeded out. Firms not suited to the new circumstances die, while firms complying with the changing rules prosper. Hence, through selection the industry context determines the group of industry survivors, and through the pressures for adaptation, the behaviour of the remaining firms is determined. In short, the industry shapes the firm, not the other way around.

The industry dynamics perspective is often also referred to as the industry evolution perspective, due to the strong parallel with biological evolution. Both evolutionary processes, it is argued, share a number of basic characteristics. In nature, as in business, the survival and growth of entities depends on their fit with the environment. Within each environment variations on a successful theme might come about. These new individuals will thrive, as long as they suit the existing circumstances, but as the environment changes, only those that meet the new demands will perish. Hence, Darwin's well-known principle of 'survival of the fittest' is based on a cycle of variation and environmental selection. Many proponents of the industry dynamics perspective believe that this biological view of evolution is a good model for what happens in industries – new organizations arise as mutations and only the fittest mutations survive. However, it is usually pointed out that in a business environment, organizations do not vary 'at random', but purposefully, and they possess the ability to adapt to selection pressures during the evolution process (e.g. Baum and Singh, 1994; Nelson and Winter, 1982). Therefore, organizations have much more flexibility to evolve along with the unfolding industry dynamics than lifeforms generally do. This process of mutual adaptation and development between entities in the system is called 'co-evolution' (e.g. Aldrich, 1999; Moore, 1996, Reading 6.3). To proponents of the industry dynamics perspective, the objective of a firm should be to co-evolve with its environment, instead of trying to conquer it.

Supporters of the industry dynamics perspective do not deny that every once in a while a rule breaker comes along, turning an industry upside down and spawning dozens of case studies by admiring business professors and hours of television interviews. But these successes must be put into perspective, just as a lottery winner should not encourage everyone to invest their life savings into buying lottery tickets. Yes, some business innovators are successful, but we have no idea how many challengers were weeded out along the way – only the most spectacular failures make it into the media, most go unreported. This is called the 'survivor's bias', and the emphasis on case-based reasoning in the field of strategy makes theorists and practitioners equally susceptible to fall into this trap. But even where a firm has been able to pull off a major industry change once, this does not make them the industry leader of the future. They might have been the right company in the right place at the right time, able to push the industry in a certain direction once, but to assume that they will win the lottery twice is not particularly realistic.

The conclusion drawn by advocates of the industry dynamics perspective is that 'winning big' by changing the rules of the game sounds easy, fast and spectacular – but isn't. If one thing has been learnt from the Internet bubble, it is that changing the rules of the game is extremely difficult, slow and hazardous, and should be left up to those 'high rollers' willing to play for 'high stakes' with only a low chance of success (i.e. venture capitalists and entrepreneurs). For regular companies, such an approach cannot be the mainstay of their strategy. Their basic approach must be to stick closely to the shifting currents in their industry, which is challenging enough in most cases. Competitive advantage can be sought, but requires hard work within the rules of the game.

The bad news is that this leaves limited freedom to manoeuvre and that the general level of profitability that a firm can achieve is largely predetermined. Once in a poor industry, a firm's growth and profit potential are significantly limited (Porter, 1980). The good news is that this still leaves plenty of room for a firm to score above the industry average, by positioning better than competitors, but also by adapting better to the ongoing industry changes, or even anticipating changes more skilfully and reacting appropriately.

EXHIBIT 10.2   THE INDUSTRY DYNAMICS PERSPECTIVE

AB-INBEV: DOWNSTREAM GLOBAL BEER

One of the biggest beer conglomerates of the 21st century once had to sell ice cream to keep its brewing business afloat. Anheuser-Busch – renowned for its Budweiser label – was no ordinary company to begin with: it had co-evolved better with shifts in the beer industry than virtually any of its adversaries. Established in the mid-1800s in St Louis, founders Adolphus Busch and Eberhard Anheuser employed a lager style of beer, brought to the US through the influx of fellow German immigrants. This type of beer has a smoother aftertaste than traditional beers in US society and became a local hit across multiple cities. Meanwhile, the Industrial Age brought marvels of its own. The advent of motor-, railroad-, and pasteurization technology allowed for beer to be transported over vast distances without getting spoilt. These factors combined contributed to the proliferation of bottled beer – rather than barrel-aged beer – both at home and abroad. Not just Anheuser-Busch, but many other big names such as Miller, Pabst, Schlitz and Coors hopped on these trends in order to expand their local businesses across the nation. Ample use was made of economies of scale stemming from technological progress, increasing the firm size of manufacturers as they increased their scale of production and scope of distribution. A total of 750 000 barrels were produced in 1850 by breweries in the US, while in 1910 this amounted to 59.6 million barrels. This rise in production was not solely reflected in a growing population, but it was also mirrored by a rise in beer consumption per capita, as it soared from approximately 3.5 gallons in 1850 to 21 gallons in 1910. These shifts would foreshadow the dawning of the US domestic beer industry and at the turn of the 20th century many had bright prospects for its unfolding future.

Beer history took a turn though. In 1920 a 'war on alcohol' commenced under the banner of Prohibition – a constitutional ban on the manufacturing, sales and distribution of alcoholic beverages across the nation. Armed with mandates of Prohibition, one state after the other ratified the convention, obliterating breweries by the thousands. Yet, there were some who endured. A select few cheated corporate death by producing 'near beer' products – low percentage alcoholic content often used for culinary purposes. Other breweries such as Anheuser-Busch reinvented themselves as soft drink or ice cream manufacturers. Once Prohibition's reign ended after repeal in 1933 these newly gained experiences paved the way for mass consumption. Brewers had acquired expertise to produce canned beer, craft new beer recipes, and to diversify their businesses. Although only 45 survivors were left standing in the aftermath of Prohibition, in ensuing years new breweries spawned on an unprecedented scale, able to thrive throughout the decades as the industry had found peace in the wake of war. Nevertheless, this live and let live principle which dominated until the 1950s was not meant to last; it soon converted into a live and let die policy adopted by the bigger firms, as they charted a course of mergers and acquisitions. Anheuser-Busch, Miller, Pabst, Schlitz, Coors, and other beer giants who lasted through Prohibition, grew ever bigger as they swallowed smaller companies, while they utilized the economies of scale at their disposal for aggressive marketing strategies. In 1950 the top ten producers controlled 38 per cent of beer sales in the US, while in 1980 this number had risen to 93 per cent. These ten giants had in common that they were founded in the 1800s and had lived through Prohibition. Yet, several decades later none of these companies exist anymore as a separate entity.

Similar to the evolving patterns of the US market, its West European counterpart also became increasingly consolidated and matured, as regional champions such as Heineken (Holland), Interbrew (Belgium), and Carlsberg (Denmark) had engaged in a series of mergers, acquisitions and joint ventures. Prompted by the descent of the Iron Curtain and the rise of China, local and regional practices increasingly turned global, as giant beer conglomerates were eager to capitalize on opportunities provided by new markets in emerging economies. Heineken and Carlsberg reinvigorated their acquisition strategies by deploying divide and conquer tactics where both parties partially swallow other big conglomerates, in order to sway antitrust legislators across regions. The Belgian champion Interbrew and the regional champion of Latin America AmBev added momentum to their international endeavours, by establishing InBev after a mega merger in 2004. Brewing legends Miller and Coors combined their efforts in order to repel foreign takeovers, yet were swallowed by South African Breweries (SAB) nonetheless. In 2004, after 15 years of accelerated mergers and acquisitions, it was none other than Anheuser-Busch which was in global leadership position, as it commanded an 8.5 per cent global market share by volume. The beer giant was not new to all-out warfare, as its road to dominance was paved by the acquisition of past companies. Yet even for giants this cut-throat competition was hard to swallow, as Anheuser-Busch fell prey to InBev through a hostile takeover of US$52 billion in 2008 – forming AB InBev. Even though Anheuser-Busch had survived throughout Prohibition and both World Wars, it could not last in the hypercompetitive environment triggered by globalization. Within their regions, giants could be relatively safe of a dominant position in consolidated markets, yet their stability was rendered obsolete through the advent of globalization, as the global market still remained highly splintered.

Consolidating the global market continued with a wave of mergers, acquisitions and joint ventures, similar to what had occurred earlier in the US and Western Europe on a more regional scale. In 2005, ten companies controlled 48.4 per cent of the global market by volume, with InBev (10.8 per cent), Anheuser-Busch (9.4 per cent), SABMiller (7.3 per cent), Heineken (5.7 per cent), and

Carlsberg (2.9 per cent) claiming the top five positions. In 2012, after Anheuser-Busch and InBev had mega merged into AB-InBev, four global beer goliaths remained, accounting for approximately 50 per cent of beer sales in volume, reeling in 70 per cent of the revenues. In 2016 AB-InBev swallowed SAB-Miller, then the world's second largest, consolidating its global leadership position with a portfolio of blockbuster brands such as Stella Artois, Budweiser, Brahma, Skol, Harbin, Hoegaarden, and many more.

No time to chill though. Japanese breweries Asahi and Kirin are climbing the ladder, and so are Chinese breweries China Resources Enterprise and Tsingtao. Especially the latter are growing at an unprecedented pace after Snow and Tsingtao replaced AB-InBev's Budweiser brands as top selling beers in the world. Additionally, SABMiller had to sell 49 per cent of its stake in Snow to China Resources Enterprise, paving the way for enormous revenues for the colossal Chinese brewer. As opposed to the US- and European markets, China's domestic market remains largely untapped, providing novel ways to generate profits in China's flourishing economy.

Co-author: Sander Wisman

Sources: www.ab-inbev.com; www.sabmiller.com; www.heineken.com; AB-InBev Annual Reports 2009–2015; AB-InBev Second Quarter and Half Year 2016 Results; *Bloomberg,* 29 July 2016; Brock, James, 'The Structure of American Industry', twelth edn, 2013; Carlsberg Annual Report 2008; *The Economist,* 19 September 2015 and 17 October 2015; *Financial Times,* 10 February 2016; Guo, Yuantao., 'Global Big Business and the Chinese Brewing Industry', 2006; Martin, Scott, 'The SAGE Encyclopedia of Alcohol: Social, Cultural, and Historical Perspectives', 2014. Patterson, Mark W. and Nancy Hoalst, 'The Geography of Beer: Regions, Environment and Societies', 2014; SABMiller plc Annual Report 2012; *Reuters,* 2 March 2016, 6 July 2016 and 21 July 2016.

The industry leadership perspective

 Strategists taking an industry leadership perspective fundamentally disagree with the determinism inherent in the industry dynamics perspective. Even in biology, breeders and genetic engineers consistently attempt to shape the natural world. Of course, in industries, as in biology, some rules are immutable. Certain economic, technological, social and political factors have to be accepted as hardly changeable. But the remaining environmental factors can be manipulated leave strategists with an enormous scope for moulding the industry of the future. This belief is reflected in the remark by the Dutch poet Jules Deelder that "even within the limits of the possible, the possibilities are limitless". It is up to the strategist to identify which rules of the game must be respected and which can be ignored in the search for new strategic options. The strategist must recognize both the limits of the possible and the limitless possibilities.

Advocates of the industry leadership perspective do not deny that in many industries the developments are largely an evolutionary result of industry dynamics. For an understanding of the development paths of these 'leaderless' industries, the industry dynamics perspective offers a powerful explanatory 'lens' – many industries do evolve without a clear industry leader. However, these industries have only followed this path because no firm was creative and powerful enough to actively shape the direction of change. A lack of leadership is not the 'natural state of affairs', but simply weakness on behalf of the industry incumbents. Industry developments can be shaped, yet do require innovative companies willing to take on the leadership role (e.g. Baden-Fuller and Stopford, 1992; Hamel and Prahalad, 1994).

A leadership role, supporters of this perspective argue, starts with envisioning what the industry of tomorrow might look like. The firm's strategists must be capable of challenging the existing industry recipe and building a new conception of how the industry could function in the future. They must test their own assumptions about which industry rules can be changed and must, in fact, think of ways of "destroying their current business". Hamel and Prahalad (1994) refer to this as intellectual leadership, noting that smart strategists also develop "industry foresight", anticipating which trends are likely to emerge, so that they can be used to the firm's advantage.

Not only must a firm have the intellectual ability to envision the industry's future, but it must also be able to communicate this vision in a manner that other firms and individuals are willing to buy into. If a vision of the industry of tomorrow is compelling enough, people inside and outside the company will start to anticipate, and will become committed to, that future, making it a self-fulfilling prophecy. This "inevitability" of an industry vision can be important in overcoming risk averseness and resistance from industry incumbents (e.g. Levenhagen, Porac and Thomas, 1993; Moore, 2000, Reading 10.3).

To actually change the rules of the competitive game in an industry, a firm must move beyond a compelling vision and work out a new competitive business model. If this new business model is put into operation and seems to offer a competitive advantage, this can attract sufficient customers and support to gain 'critical mass' and break through as a viable alternative to the older business models. To shape the industry, the firm will also need to develop new competencies and standards required to make the new business model function properly. The better the firm is at building new competencies and setting new standards, alone or in cooperation with others, the more power it will have to determine the direction of industry development (e.g. D'Aveni, 1999; Hamel, 1996).

All of the above points together add up to quite a considerable task. But then, industry leadership is not easy and changing the industry rules rarely happens overnight. Rather, it can take years, figuring out which rules can be broken and which cannot. It can be a marathon, trying to get the business model right, while building competencies and support. Therefore, organizations require perseverance and commitment if they are to be successful industry shapers (Hamel and Prahalad, 1994).

EXHIBIT 10.3   THE INDUSTRY LEADERSHIP PERSPECTIVE

SPOTIFY: WHO PAYS THE PIPER CALLS THE TUNE

Revenues have been declining in the music industry for many years, a trend that started when the illegal download site Napster entered the scene in 1999. At first glance, iTunes was hailed as the solution, but this changed people's buying behaviour from purchasing entire albums to simply buying single songs. Revenues continued to drop, and it became clear that a revolution was needed to save the music industry. Daniel Ek came up with the solution: give it away for free.

In 1999 the music industry was shocked when Napster reached 80 million users in only two years, all of whom had access to free (illegal) music. This fascinated Daniel Ek, who found his two favourite bands on the website: the Beatles and Led Zeppelin. Daniel wanted to find a way to let music inspire people, just as it inspired him. The new status quo was characterized by illegal downloads, but could there be a legal approach to serving freely available music while making people willing to pay for it again?

In 2008 Daniel Ek came up with an innovative *freemium* business model for the music industry in Sweden. With fellow entrepreneur Martin Lorentzon he launched the music service Spotify, containing a large catalogue of songs, which had grown to over 30 million in 2015. The service and the music itself is offered for free, but ads are inserted between songs to fund the 'free music'. Paying subscribers experience higher quality music without ads and paying a monthly fee also allows them to download songs of choice to be played back offline.

Daniel Ek started with Spotify in Sweden and quickly started to conquer the world. Spotify is a game changer; a new industry leader with new ideas and new innovations. This is supported by the fact that others – such as Apple Music, Google Play and Amazon's Prime Music in addition to private companies like Deezer – quickly tried to follow in Spotify's tracks. Although there are some minor differences these initiatives are all trying to find their way into this new era of experiencing music.

Spotify remains the undisputed industry leader however. The company is valued at US$8.4 billion and it entertains a paid user base surpassing 30 million subscribers. An additional 70 million make use of the ad-based free version of the service. Meanwhile its biggest competitor, Apple Music, is only half as big as the Swedish streaming giant, having accumulated 15 million paid subscriptions.

Spotify is set to keep expanding as long as musicians continue to co-operate with the service. That is also where it sometimes goes wrong. Some artists, such as Taylor Swift and Radiohead's Thom Yorke, have removed their songs from the service, as they consider the business model unfairly compensates artists, producers and writers. One problem is that Spotify pays artists based on their 'market share', or the number of streams for an artist's songs relative to the service's total number of streams. This comes down to Spotify paying as little as US$0.006 to US$0.008 per stream on average. Another issue is that revenues go to the publishers – about 70 per cent of its turnover – who then distribute to their musicians on their own terms.

Nevertheless, Spotify could well have established a more sustainable business model for the previously dying music industry. The firm fits perfectly in this age's spirit; offering free streaming music to the masses. Since it can never outspend Apple or Google, it has to stay on its toes however. If Spotify manages to keep ahead of its competitors, it might well set the tone of the music industry for years to come.

Co-authors: Jeroen Brinkhuis and Wester Wagenaar

Sources: Spotify.com; *The Economist*, 5 May 2016 and 27 May 2016; *Forbes*, 16 January 2012 and 21 July 2013; *The Guardian*, 16 January 2013; *Pocket-lint*, 16 May 2013; *TechRadar*, 20 November 2015.

MANAGING THE PARADOX OF COMPLIANCE AND CHOICE

The reasonable man adapts himself to the world; the unreasonable one persists in trying to adapt the world to himself. Therefore, all progress depends on the unreasonable man.

George Bernard Shaw (1856–1950); Irish playwright and critic

So, how should managers deal with the industry context? Should they concentrate on adapting to the dynamics in the industry, honing their ability to respond to changing demands and to adjust their business model to meet new requirements? Or should they take a more proactive role in shaping the future of the industry, changing the rules of the competitive game to suit their own needs? Within the field of strategic management, the

TABLE 10.1   Industry dynamics versus industry leadership perspective

	Industry dynamics perspective	Industry leadership perspective
Emphasis on	Compliance over choice	Choice over compliance
Industry development	Uncontrollable evolutionary process	Controllable creation process
Change dynamics	Environment selects fit firms	Firm creates fitting environment
Firm success due to	Fitness to industry demands	Manipulation of industry demands
Ability to shape industry	Low, slow	High, fast
Normative implication	Play by the rules (adapt)	Change the rules (innovate)
Development path	Convergence towards dominant design	Divergence, create new design
Firm profitability	Largely industry-dependent	Largely firm-dependent

views are far apart and no consensus seems to be emerging on how to manage the paradox of compliance and choice (see Table 10.1 for the main arguments).

With so many competing opinions on the nature of the industry context, readers may now want to 'select the fittest one'. Or maybe readers conclude that one view has rewritten the rules of competition in the strategy industry. In the international context especially, a much more strategizing stance would be to challenge one's own cognitive map, as perspectives on the industry context are closely related to the well-described and culturally skewed voluntarism versus determinism debate.

Balancing

Even rule-breaking companies cannot make or break all industry rules. Some industry rules – such as the importance of brands in consumer markets and economies of scale in capital-intensive industries – are not to be moulded. Strategists then need to follow some rules while trying to change others. The balancing act is common, while the balance itself is industry-specific. In other words, larger firms that are active in multiple businesses are also multi-balancing.

Parallel processing

While business unit managers have to play by the industry rules as they have little influence on the company's context, corporate strategists of large firms are often engaged in initiatives that may well change the industry context. For example, as members of national and supra-national (e.g. European) industrial policy boards, corporate strategists are involved in government initiatives to formulate policy priorities which would lead to innovation funds and subsidies for particular technologies. By influencing governments, corporate strategists change the industry rules, while business managers have to play by the rules.

Juxtaposing

As described in this chapter, industry characteristics determine which industry rules are malleable by strategists' actions. Attempts to break particular industry rules – such as scale advantages in the steel industry – are outright dangerous, while others may well be successful. Even when the large majority of industry rules cannot be broken, the important attribute of corporate strategists is to know which ones can. So from the perspective of the strategizing manager, the industry dynamics perspective is applicable in some occasions while the industry leadership perspective is preferred in others. The proportion of compliance and choice differs between both perspectives, yet independent from perspectives strategists need to juxtapose between firm compliance and strategic choice.

In the international context, managing the paradox of compliance and choice becomes even more challenging. Not only does the strategist need to find the right combination of rules that need to be followed and can be moulded, the combination often also differs over countries. As will be further explained in the next paragraph 'The industry context in international perspective', in many businesses the industry context is country-specific. For example, industrial policies may influence industry forces, and local or national networks determine the strategic window of opportunities. Hence, the conclusion must be that strategists not only need to juxtapose; in international firms they need to 'country specifically' juxtapose between demands for firm compliance and strategic choice.

It goes without saying that it takes special capabilities of strategizing managers to juxtapose the paradox. In Chapter 4 on business level strategy it was discussed that strategists need *dynamic capabilities* (Teece, 2007; Teece, Pisano and Shuen, 1997) to juxtapose between demands for firm compliance and strategic choice, which would 'higher-level' dynamic capabilities. In the international human resources field the scarcity of such strategists is well-known. In most cases firms choose to manage the paradox by appointing local managers, or expatriates that know the local culture very well.

THE INDUSTRY CONTEXT IN INTERNATIONAL PERSPECTIVE

Co-authors: Gep Eisenloeffel and Wester Wagenaar

When I hear any man talk of an unalterable law, the only effect it produces on me is to convince me that he is an unalterable fool.
Sydney Smith (1771–1845); English writer and Anglican cleric

In the field of strategy, views differ sharply on whether the industry context can be shaped or not. These differences of opinion usually remain implicit – few practising managers or strategy theorists make a point of expounding their assumptions about the nature of the environment. For this reason, it is difficult to identify whether there are national preferences when it comes to industry context perspectives. Yet, it seems not unlikely that strategists in different countries have different inclinations regarding this issue. Strategists in some nations gravitate more towards an industry leadership perspective than they do in others. Interestingly, there are distinct differences in preferences within industries as well.

On the national level

Culture researchers have tried to understand differences in how people perceive the power of individuals to shape their environment. In some cultures the view prevails that the individual is at the mercy of external forces, while in other cultures there is a strong belief in the freedom of individuals to act independently of the environment and even to create their own circumstances (Hampden-Turner and Trompenaars, 2000). Psychologists refer to this as the perceived 'locus of control' (e.g. Miller, Kets de Vries and Toulouse, 1982). People with an internal locus of control believe they mostly are in control of their own fate. Their efforts will shape their circumstances – success is earned and failure is one's own fault. People with an external locus of control, on the other hand, believe their fate is largely the result of circumstances beyond their control. Any effort to improve one's position, if at all possible, should be directed towards complying with external demands – fortune favours those who go with the flow. In countries with a culture that is more inclined towards an internal locus of control, such as the United States, the industry leadership perspective is more widespread. In cultures in which people exhibit a strong emphasis for an external locus of control, as in most Asian countries, the industry dynamics perspective is likely to be more predominant.

The role that governments can play in encouraging the shaping of industries also differs internationally. In some countries the predominant view is that governments should facilitate industry development by creating supportive business circumstances and then staying out of the way of company initiatives. Governments are needed to set basic rules of business conduct, but firms should not be impeded by other governmental intervention in the functioning of industries and markets. Individual companies are seen as the primary drivers of industry development and if companies are given enough leeway, game-changing firms can shake the industry context. Such economic liberalism is particularly strong in the English-speaking nations, where governments facilitate the industry-shaping efforts of companies.

In other nations the predominant view is that Adam Smith's free market ideal often proves to be dysfunctional. A fully liberal market, it is believed, can lead to short-termism, negative social consequences, mutually destructive competition and an inability to implement industry-wide changes. Governments must therefore adopt a more proactive role. They must protect weaker parties, such as workers and the environment, against the negative side of the market system, and actively create a shared infrastructure for all companies. Furthermore, the government can develop an industrial policy to encourage the development of new industries, force companies to work together where this is more effective and push through industry-wide changes, otherwise a stalemate would occur. This 'managed competition' view has been prevalent in Japan and France, and to a lesser extent in Germany (e.g. Hampden-Turner and Trompenaars, 1993; Lessem and Neubauer, 1994). In these countries the industry leadership perspective is not as strongly held as in the English-speaking nations – industries can be shaped, but few companies have the power to do so without a good industrial policy and government backing.

In countries where the discrete organization perspective (Chapter 6) is predominant, companies often strive to retain their independence and power position vis-à-vis other companies. As these firms are not embedded in complex networks but operate free from constraining relationships, they are more at liberty to challenge the existing rules of the game. In other words, where firms are not entangled in a web of long-term relationships, they are better positioned for rule-breaking behaviour – every firm can make a difference. In these countries an industry leadership perspective is more prevalent. However, in nations where firms are more inclined to operate in networks, each individual firm surrenders a part of its freedom in exchange for long-term relationships. Even though a group of firms, once in agreement, is often more powerful than each individual firm, it is difficult to get network partners to agree. As all changes must be negotiated with partners, the ability to shape an industry declines.

On the industry level

In some countries an inclination towards the industry leadership or the industry dynamics perspective is apparent, but are there industries for which the same can be said? Many industries develop along evolutionary paths and here there are no leaders who have managed to bend the rules of the game – or at least not yet. Incumbents in a 'leaderless' industry adapt to the changing environment, but do not attempt to drastically alter the context of the industry themselves. There are a variety of reasons why an industry can have more or less strategists aiming to change the rules and win big.

Industries are complex systems, but some are more complex than others. The heterogeneity and concentration within an industry provides challenges in the information process to come to the right strategy. When many stakeholders are involved in an industry, this further constrains strategic decisions (Chen *et al.*, 2015). The more complex the industry, the more rigid its players. The industry context can also be more rigid because of regulations. Some industries, such as the pharmaceutical industry, are constrained and the rules of the game are strongly enforced.

Business-model innovation hardly originates from established big companies; their common response is to imitate (Markides, 2013). As such, the more difficult it is to enter an industry – for example because of high sums of venture capital required to play along – the industry dynamics are most prevalent. Entrepreneurs and venture capitalists, who are willing to play a high stakes game in the hope of winning big, have a hard time participating in an industry which they can only enter with the utmost difficulty.

To the strategist

The individual strategist can also have different opinions on the strategic paradox of the industry context. The individual disposition of a leader and supposed preferable character traits that go along with it have received much attention (e.g. Bass and Steidlmeier, 1999; Bennis, 1989; Cromie, 2000; Olson-Buchanan, Bryan and Thompson, 2013). Not every strategist is able to develop proper 'industry foresight' (Hamel and Prahalad, 1994) and not every individual is necessarily out there to change the rules of the game.

Regardless of the individual disposition of a strategist, it is also simply difficult to mitigate the industry context paradox internationally. An international firm has to analyse the demands for firm compliance and choice on a country-by-country basis and found his strategy on that. Becoming an industry leader on a global scale through juxtaposing nation-specific requirements is a tough cookie to bake.

INTRODUCTION TO THE READINGS

As an input to the process of assessing the variety of perspectives on this issue, three readings have been selected that each shed their own light on the debate. As in previous chapters, the first two readings will be representative of the two poles in this debate (see Table 10.1), while the third has been chosen to bridge the arguments of both perspectives.

The first reading representing the industry dynamics perspective (Reading 10.1) is 'How Industries Evolve', by Anita McGahan. Building on Michael Porter's seminal works on industry evolution (1980), McGahan argues that firms can improve their performance by riding industry trends rather than trying to fight them. She argues that better corporate performance hinges on understanding how industries evolve and that the main frameworks currently in use (the five forces and the S-curve/product life cycle models) are incomplete for this purpose. The author identifies four basic models of industry evolution which she calls 'receptive', 'blockbuster', 'radical organic' and 'intermediating'. Each kind of evolution involves specific kinds of risks, and each carries different implications for the relevance of established capabilities and investment priorities.

The second article representing the industry leadership perspective (Reading 10.2) is 'Blue Ocean Strategy', by W. Chan Kim and Renée Mauborgne. This *Harvard Business Review* article is a summary of the arguments they put forward in their similarly entitled book. Their core idea is that companies should not focus on competing in existing overcrowded markets, which they call red oceans, bloodied by battle, but should create new uncontested market spaces – blue oceans. Staying in a red ocean means accepting the existing industry conditions and finding a way to survive in this harsh environment, while breaking out into blue oceans means leaving competition behind and having a sea all to yourself. As such, Kim and Mauborgne are fully in line with the industry leadership perspective; rule breaking is superior to rule taking. Looking at a wide range of industries, stretching from automobiles and computers to movie theatres and circuses, Kim and Mauborgne conclude that much of the business innovation comes from fundamentally new and superior ways of creating value for buyers, which they call 'value innovation'. The authors, thus, make an infrequently heard point, namely that industry incumbents can also be rule breakers. The headline grabbing innovators are often new entrants that disrupt the existing industry pecking order, but many of the value innovators reviewed by Kim and Mauborgne are actually industry incumbents who have been able to revolutionize their industries from the inside.

The third reading, 'Living on the Fault Line', has been taken from a book with the same name (note that there are more Moores; Geoffrey's namesake in the previous chapter was James Moore). This reading has been added to introduce an issue of vital importance to industry development – the introduction of new technology. Of all the drivers of industry development, the adoption of disruptive technologies is probably the most prominent. Disruptive technologies are those that do not complement established technologies, but displace them. As such, Moore points out, disruptive technologies can cause dramatic shifts in an industry as "competitive advantage positions that once seemed secure are abruptly overthrown and management teams … must scramble to recover". Moore's central thesis is that for the innovators, championing a new technology, creating a mainstream market requires going through a number of phases, each with its own inherent strategic logic. He describes these phases of market development, making use of the widely known technology adoption life cycle. The first phase, or 'early market', is where technology enthusiasts and visionaries adopt the innovation. This phase is generally followed by a 'chasm', which is a period of no adoption, which needs to be bridged to get to the second phase, called the 'bowling alley', where early pragmatists 'knock' others into also adopting the new technology. Once adoption starts picking up speed, the third phase is entered, the 'tornado', where high growth is experienced. Finally, the technology achieves the fourth phase of broad acceptance, called 'Main Street'. Key to success in each phase, Moore concludes, is realizing that the strategy of the previous phase is no longer appropriate and that a new strategy must be developed. In his argumentation Moore focuses his attention on customer acceptance, paying less attention to the reactions of competitors and other industry actors. As such, his contribution is more to understanding market development and less to highlighting overall industry development. However, this reading still provides invaluable insight into the difficult process of changing the rules of the game based on technological innovation, and how the strategist needs to juxtapose over time.

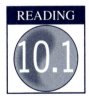

How industries evolve

By Anita M. McGahan[1]

Over the last two decades, the profitability of US firms dropped by nearly a third while stock market values soared to create a huge financial market premium on corporate assets. The absolute level of the financial market premium today puts unprecedented pressure on managers to generate real returns on invested capital. Either fundamental operating performance must improve, or shareholder value will not rise at historic rates.

There is no shortage of theories on how to relieve the pressure. Many of them involve technology. Some

[1]Source: Anita M. McGahan (2000) 'How industries evolve', *Business Strategy Review*, Vol.11 (3) pp. 1–16. Copyright © 2000 London Business School. Reproduced with permission of John Wiley & Sons Ltd..

optimists believe that the blanket introduction of new technology across the whole economy will somehow result in new value, almost by osmosis. Others look for more specific links between strategy, investment and increased profitability. Building on the five-forces framework (Porter 1980) and on the S-curve framework (Abernathy and Utterback 1978; Foster 1986), the fundamental premise of this article is that you cannot increase profitability without a thorough understanding of the structural changes shaping the industry concerned.

The five-forces framework is essentially static: it provides an approach for determining the financial performance of an industry, and thus its attractiveness for investors, *at a specific point in time.* Although the S-curve framework (Figure 10.1.1) is dynamic – it focuses on how industries evolve over time – it does not deal with how companies move across product generations, i.e. across S-curves. Using a large body of fieldwork and statistical research, this article introduces a new framework that identifies four models of industry evolution. The approach is complementary to the five-forces and S-curve frameworks. How an individual should tackle the problem of increasing profitability in his or her own firm depends largely on which of the four models best characterizes the nature of innovation in the industry.

A major distinction in this new framework is between 'architectural' and non-architectural change. Architectural change (Henderson and Clark 1990) is here defined as any innovation that disrupts the industry's established relationships with *both* suppliers *and* customers. Often this is based on new technology but it can also involve the redeployment of existing technology (Markides, 1999). For instance, the department store and the supermarket represented architectural

changes in retailing, but neither was based on radical technology. Non-architectural change involves innovation through established customer or supplier relationships. Examples include new supermarket layouts or the introduction of a new pharmaceutical product.

Two of the four models of industry evolution identified in this article are non-architectural, with firms innovating within the structure of established relationships. The other two are architectural, with firms innovating outside the structure of the industry's established customer and supplier relationships. Before describing them in detail I first show why we need to go beyond the S-curve.

Beyond the S-curve

The S-curve and the closely-related product life cycle (PLC) frameworks are based on the idea that industries move through periods of emergence, shake-out, maturity and decline. Although the models are appealing, they are hard to use on their own for corporate planning, and may even be misleading in some situations (Foster 1986). Industry leaders may become trapped in a kind of self-fulfilling logic of maturity if they take action based on an oversimplified S-curve; if they believe that an industry has reached the 'mature' phase of the S-curve, they may wrongly assume it is past innovation.

This perspective threatened toy retailers in the early 1990s (Coxe *et al.*, 1996). At the time, many studies of toy retailing reported that the industry was mature. Toys-R-Us, Wal-Mart, K-Mart and Kaybee dominated the US mass market. Given the stability in the industry structure, the leading firms invested incrementally to build out their store networks and to improve their information systems. Neighbourhood Mom-and-Pop

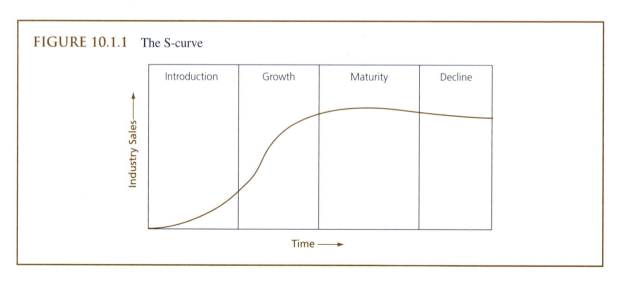

FIGURE 10.1.1 The S-curve

| Introduction | Growth | Maturity | Decline |

Industry Sales →

Time →

toy stores exited steadily as the mass marketers grew. A few upstart educational stores – like the Discovery Zone, the Learning Place, and LearningSmith – gained a toehold, but these innovative retail outlets were perceived as too small to threaten the market leaders.

The maturity mindset offered little insight into the impending industry change. By the late 1990s, toy retailing was transformed by new technology, new products and new kinds of customer relationships. Companies like eToys and Amazon.com satisfied customer needs for quick, reliable, convenient and inexpensive access to exciting new products. Old pricing and merchandising formulas no longer reflected competitive conditions. The new systems also affected toy *manufacturing* by making available extensive personalized information about customer preferences. The mass marketers had to preserve their surviving advantages while retrenching to compete effectively against the new retailers. By mid-2000, Toys-R-Us had announced a partnership with Amazon.com to unify convenient access with established distribution capability and manufacturer relationships.

Why the S-curve and product life cycle models are difficult to use

What was wrong with the idea that the industry was in maturity? Conventional wisdom held that maturity was driven by the ageing of the baby boomers and the stability of toy design. The reality of tough price competition at the retail level underscored this perception. Many industry leaders had a sense that new technology might some day support innovation but the possibilities appeared remote and futuristic. Why didn't people foresee that the industry was about to be transformed?

Life cycle phases are difficult to see

First, it was hard to get the timing right on technology and demographic trends. While radical innovation was a theoretical possibility, it was hard to imagine in practice. Upstart entrants that challenged the incumbents typically failed because of high costs and inadequate consumer response. The reality of the industry underscored the hard-edged economics of faddish toys and retail price competition.

Industry boundaries are hard to identify

Second, the S-curve analysis did not capture subtle changes in industry boundaries. Indeed, it reinforced the incumbents' view that toy retailing required

storefronts backed by complex distribution networks and tight manufacturer relationships. As toy e-tailing emerged, many incumbents saw it as a separate industry, like catalogue distribution. Catalogues had been limited in their effectiveness mainly because mailing costs were so high and response rates were so low. Unlike traditional retailing, catalogues offered no opportunity for prepurchase play. Traditional retailers soon learned that the touch-and-feel requirement was not nearly as important to online retailers as they had thought, however.

The S-curve and PLC models offer little help for adapting an organization across generations

Third, the models did not offer toy-retailing executives a point of view on how to survive into the next industry generation when it did finally arrive. Many of the mass merchants kept their core revenue streams even when new entrants like eToys and Amazon began to attract customers. Questions arose about whether the upstarts could fulfil orders. Lingering concerns about the customer's need for touch-and-feel suggested that the traditional bricks-and-mortar retailers should not overreact to the threat. Organizational conflict made it confusing and difficult to go for clicks-and-bricks.

The difficulties are widespread

Across many industries, executives in leading firms have perceived their industries as mature and have later been blindsided by innovative rivals. The problems in applying the S-curve and PLC frameworks in toy retailing are also common in other settings. Challenges of misplaced investment can also arise when executives perceive their industries as emerging or as declining. Field research on industry transitions shows that the most persistent challenges are organizational. Without a better view on how the environment is changing, firms cannot fully commit to organizational adaptation.

Four models of industry evolution

Figure 10.1.2 illustrates the four models of industry evolution: 'receptive', 'blockbuster', 'radical organic' and 'intermediating'. Among the two non-architectural models, the distinction is between those where the customer and supplier markets provide continuous feedback (Model 1, 'Receptive') and those where profitability is mainly determined by the outcome of major projects for which feedback is delayed and unpredictable (Model 2,

FIGURE 10.1.2   The four models of industry evolution

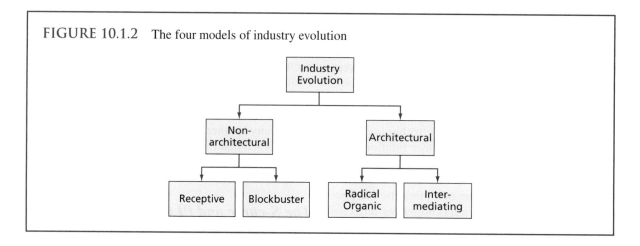

'Blockbuster'). When industry evolution involves blockbuster change, firms sustain superior performance if they use long-term relationships to create more value from successful projects than can outsiders. In contrast, firms in receptive industries create value by systematically translating incremental improvements into formulas for success that can be replicated across their businesses. Discount consumer-goods retailing is an industry undergoing 'receptive' change while ethical pharmaceutical manufacture is on a 'blockbuster' path. Within a sector's supply chain, the downstream industries (i.e. pharmacies, movie theatres and gas stations) often evolve receptively even if the upstream industries (i.e. pharmaceuticals, movie production, and oil/gas exploration) undergo blockbuster evolution.

Architectural industry change is less common but may lead to major shifts in the overall character of an industry. It occurs in two ways. The third model, 'radical organic' evolution, encompasses approaches that provide a quantum improvement in customer or supplier value (performance, ease of use, mode of use) big enough to disrupt existing customer and supplier relationships. A classic example is the personal computer, which appealed to a whole new set of customers and engaged a new cadre of components suppliers and employees. The personal computer quickly transformed both the horizontal industry structure (yielding winners and losers among computer manufacturers) and the vertical value chain (including software suppliers, sales and distribution channels, purchasing processes, etc).

The fourth model of industry evolution, 'intermediating' change, describes architectural innovation that originates within established relationships. Intermediating change occurred during the late nineteenth century in consumer-goods retailing, when Sears and Montgomery Ward pioneered mail-order catalogues to create new ways of buying and selling for households. Today, online auctions create intermediating change in the markets for used cars.

Each of the four models has distinctive characteristics in terms of industry structure, historic innovation paths, investment opportunities and performance drivers (Figure 10.1.2). Every industry evolves by one of these models, although industries may move between evolutionary models over time (and especially over long periods of time). An industry may rapidly move from non-architectural change into radical organic change, as in the launch of electronic watches. In most cases, this kind of rapid change is preceded by a long period in which pressure for major change builds in the old industry structure. Similarly, an industry may move from a period of architectural change into a relatively stable period of non-architectural evolution.

Model 1: Receptive evolution

Receptive innovation paths are more stable than other trajectories for industry evolution. Examples of receptive evolution commonly arise in the distribution, transportation and manufacturing sectors. Firms with superior performance in these industries typically grow by expanding their activity systems outward steadily. The characteristic quality of receptive industries is that firms achieve returns on their investments incrementally as the investments are made. Information quickly arrives on whether the firm's approach is viable in the market. In general, investment is less risky than under other evolutionary models. It is as if the industry's leaders have conceived of winning formulas, and their success depends on the steady radiation of the formula into new contexts. In these industries, sustained outstanding performers are rare; but so also are sustained low performers. Incumbent firms typically become steady moderate performers that yield excellent long-run returns on investments, especially after accounting for the lower risks.

Industry structure.   Receptive evolution typically involves a different kind of industry structure from blockbuster evolution. Under receptive evolution, firm characteristics and firm performance tend to cluster around the industry average. However, the underlying structures of Model 1 industries do vary. Florists, local restaurants and dry cleaning are fragmented while discount retailing, express delivery and long-haul trucking are consolidated. In many situations, the attractiveness of the industry depends on whether established firms are being overtaken by the more efficient systems of their rivals. During most of the 1980s, the discount retailing industry in the US was unattractive largely because Wal-Mart was expanding its operations and creating excess capacity in the systems of many of its major rivals. Today, many Mom-and-Pop restauranteurs are exiting for similar reasons. Modern restaurant chains expand into their local markets and offer customers similar experiences at lower prices. As these examples suggest, the profitability of Model 1 industries usually involves shorter and shallower periods of loss than among industries on other evolutionary paths. Under receptive industry evolution, disadvantaged firms normally have trouble surviving unless they can quickly adapt to more efficient approaches.

Historic innovation path.   Industries undergoing receptive evolution may have very different histories. Often, however, a long initial period of fragmentation occurs and in some cases industries remain fragmented. (Even fragmentation is not normally associated with substantial losses, however.) Receptive industries tend to consolidate when particularly efficient competitors come to dominate the industry.

Dominating firms often have grown slowly over long periods. Steady radiation from a geographic base is common. Starbucks, Wal-Mart and Federal Express all evolved this way. These successful firms grow by continuously investing in a number of core assets simultaneously. For example, Wal-Mart has added stores, distribution capacity, transportation systems, information-technology features, employee-recognition programmes and merchandise all at the same time. The company innovates by extending its system rather than by looking for a big-hit return on investment in a single capability. Wal-Mart's entire distribution system differs from that of Sears, K-Mart and other competitors.

In both fast food and discount retailing, differences in the formulas pursued by the major competitors extend across a broad range of activities. Companies become archrivals because of fundamental differences in their philosophies for approaching both customers and suppliers. The pattern of growth is distinctive from the blockbuster model because the company gets immediate feedback (and immediate return on its investment) as it builds out its network.

Investment opportunities.   Competition tends to occur at the boundaries between systems in product or geographic space. Over the past three decades, McDonald's and Burger King became famous for basic differences in the way they make burgers, with McDonald's adopting a batch process and Burger King cooking to order. (Recent announcements indicate that McDonald's may be moving to a cook-to-order system, which may reflect convergence in strategies as the industry consolidates.)

When industries on a receptive evolutionary path consolidate, they tend to encompass economies of scale and scope based on relationships across specific activities, with continuous feedback from markets. They do not engage in major bets on new technologies in isolation from market forces. Receptive industries are substantially more favourable to mid-course corrections than blockbuster industries, with more market testing of new ideas and less background research and development.

Performance drivers.   The highest-performing firms in Model 1 industries continually develop new efficiencies. They are rigorous, disciplined and clear in their willingness to turn away opportunities that may compromise the existing approach. Leading firms also find ways to extend themselves incrementally without directly confronting competitors with equally efficient approaches. High performers avoid price wars as they come into contact with competitors through incremental growth.

Industries on receptive paths are vulnerable to price wars because customers and suppliers tend to be less loyal than in blockbuster industries. Starbucks, Wal-Mart and Federal Express offer more-or-less standardized products and services. The companies generally avoid customizing their approaches to remain efficient and to offer low prices. (Although these firms may be differentiated, the absolute standards for efficiency in their industries are high.) As a result, customers and suppliers (including employees) have low switching costs. When two leaders come into contact, they often face powerful incentives to win customers by cutting price because they cannot rely on customer loyalty. These conditions have plagued the airline industry for years.

Model 2: Blockbuster evolution

Examples of industries on a blockbuster trajectory include pharmaceuticals, applications software, cellular-telephone service, oil-and-gas extraction and movie production. The characteristic quality of a blockbuster industry is that nearly all the costs of developing new products and technologies are incurred before the sponsor learns whether markets will respond favourably. Critical resources are created through risky investment over long periods before they generate profits. Once the new project is developed, it is commercialized in concert with complementary assets that are already in place.

A film studio cannot truly resolve its uncertainty about a film's market value until the project is finished. However, big box-office hits rarely come from independent film-makers. Established studios use their relationships with key actors and their distribution systems to secure important advantages in bringing their films to market. In this context, the innovation occurs within the framework of these complementary assets. Great new value may be created by innovative film projects like *Titanic*, but the industry is not changed architecturally.

The structural platform for innovation is similar in the pharmaceutical industry, where companies must invest for years in R&D before obtaining reliable estimates of a product's viability. Once a drug passes through the approval process, however, the company may make hundreds of millions. Typically, the innovating company brings the approved drug to market through an established salesforce and distribution system. These complementary assets are critical to the stability of the industry.

Industry structure.   What are the structural characteristics of blockbuster industries? It depends on whether incumbents are currently engaged in significant development expenditures or whether dominant designs have emerged. For decades, the cellular-telephone industry was unattractive as firms built out their networks. The payoff is occurring now, as firms begin to achieve above-average returns on their invested capital.

After a dominant design emerges, blockbuster industries typically generate above-average returns. A five-forces analysis normally reveals a low threat of entry, low buyer or supplier power, low rivalry and moderate threats of substitution. What makes buyers

and suppliers tolerate high profits on average among industry incumbents? What keeps the industry's rivals from gravitating to similar competitive positions?

First, firms in the industry bear significant operating risk. Film profits are notoriously volatile. Occasionally film companies go out of business by overfunding ill-fated projects. Similarly, the high profits of pharmaceutical leaders may be significantly threatened when drugs go off patent. Buyers and suppliers tolerate the industry's profit as a reward to innovation.

Second, blockbuster industries typically create enormous value for both buyers and suppliers. Firms often adhere to high standards in customer service and in supplier partnering. Successful blockbuster firms create so much value in partnership with buyers and suppliers that all are satisfied with returns on their investments.

Third, the industry's incumbents tend to pursue projects that are distinctive by repeatedly reinvesting in basic technologies. Leading companies generally try to avoid imitating one another because the stakes in blockbuster investment are so high. This taste for distinctiveness in project definition tends to support ongoing differentiation once commercialization occurs.

Blockbuster industries remain stable when the industry's incumbents, its customers and its suppliers earn more from exchange than through the best alternatives that emerge over time. What can jar these industries into architectural change? The underlying technology no longer delivers enough value to keep customers and suppliers interested, or the incremental innovation no longer makes buyers willing to compensate the industry for the risks undertaken in development. For a blockbuster industry to remain stable, customers and suppliers have to perceive more value by continuing to deal with the industry than by pursuing the best alternatives.

Historic innovation path.   There are no simple rules for the historical innovation path in blockbuster industries, but many of these industries share common experiences. They tend to have had an early period of extensive development, fragmentation and losses as inventors experiment with new technology. With successful development, firms acquire the complementary assets necessary to realize the commercial potential of their innovations. A shakeout often occurs, and the surviving leaders become positioned for significant returns on their investments.

In the film-production industry during the early decades of the twentieth century, firms experimented

FIGURE 10.1.3 The four models: Summary

Evolutionary model	Architectural change	Defining characteristics	Industry structure	Historic innovation path	Investment opportunities	Performance drivers	Examples
1. Receptive	No	Incremental returns as investments are made	Firm performance may cluster around the industry average; firms develop integrated systems of activities	Long initial periods of fragmentation sometimes followed by consolidation around efficient leaders	Incremental at geographic boundaries or at product-attribute boundaries	Constant search for new efficiencies	Retailing before the Web, fast food
2. Blockbuster	No	Risky projects with delayed feedback	Firm performance may vary widely; firms seek to dominate riches	Early periods of loss followed by consolidation around leaders that hold complementary assets	Risky and rare over a single specialized asset	Constant risk management on big projects	Film production, pharmaceuticals, oil exploration
3. Radical Organic	Yes	Radical innovation in the capabilities that support both customer and supplier relationships	Often depressed average profitability with attractive pockets	Built-up resistance among incumbents to new technologies; lagging reinvestment by critical customers and suppliers	Risky and rare over many specialized assets	First-mover advantage through commercialization of new product and process technologies	News services, high-end leisure travel
4. Intermediating	Yes	Radical shift in the information available when transactions occur	Often depressed average profitability with attractive layers	Built-up compromises among incumbents in transactions; tough negotiations by critical customers and suppliers	Incremental over both customer and supplier transactions	First-mover advantage through reshaping ways of interacting with customers and suppliers	Autodealing, retail banking, agricultural supplies

with approaches to delivering feature films. Should movies be personalized for individual viewing? How long should they be? Would new documentaries dominate fiction? What production values would be acceptable? After a few big feature-film successes, producers began to develop structural rules that continue to influence the industry today: films are usually between one-and-a-quarter and three hours long; exhibitors pay producers according to a standard formula related to box-office receipts and typically cannot preview a film before committing to show it; all viewers are charged about the same price for admission; previews of forthcoming films are shown before the featured presentation; and theatre lobbies contain candy stands. Once this basic structure was established, the industry launched a major programme to develop complementary assets in distribution and actor relationships.

Investment opportunities. To find out whether architectural change is imminent, look at the current investments. Are firms continuing to invest in blockbuster technology? Are customers and suppliers renewing the platforms for their interaction with the industry?

The big studios are still developing feature films by decades-old rules. Actors, directors and other talent suppliers continue to hone their skills over long periods and to follow the industry's norms for delivering value to the producers. Despite diminishing financial performance, the exhibitors continue to build multiplex theatres in new locations. Why? By some accounts, the exhibition industry is engaged in a war of attrition. Through consolidation, exhibitors hope to exert countervailing power against the producers in negotiations over film rights. Exhibitors may not be satisfied with their financial returns, but their next-best alternatives still do not swamp their incentives to reinvest. These conditions suggest that film production is likely to remain relatively stable over a five- to ten-year time horizon.

Performance drivers. For blockbuster firms, the most common route to superior returns is by innovating within a specialized niche while also owning the complementary assets necessary for successful commercialization. High-performance film producers develop specialized skills in particular categories (animated features, documentaries, or action films). Leading pharmaceutical firms dominate therapeutic categories. High-performance cellular operators dominate specific geographic regions. Within each of these categories, the leading firms also own and deploy the complementary assets critical for quick commercialization of new technology.

While domination of a niche is prevalent, a second blockbuster approach involves the sale of supporting activities to industry incumbents. In some cases, the support may even cover core resources. For example, independent film makers may sell innovative scripts or even finished films to mainstream film producers.

Yet another approach involves partnering with leading firms to maintain and extend complementary assets. Consultants and agents often assist film producers in identifying promising new actors. Lobbyists work with cellular-telephone providers to assure their representation in regulatory hearings that affect their geographic coverage.

What does this mean for a potential entrant that seeks industry leadership? Most established industries resist entry by outsiders. Despite this fact, the potential for massive returns often attracts new entrants anyway. Often, upstart firms begin by trying to innovate within an established niche. Traditional biotechnology firms are a classic example. If an organization beats the odds and is successful at development, it then faces extraordinary challenges of commercialization because it does not hold the complementary assets necessary to bring products to market. At this stage, firms often sell or link up with industry leaders to gain access to critical resources. In cellular-telephone service, for example, entrants with key licences were often bought by larger firms with established customer relationships. Companies tend to perform poorly when they underestimate the power of the established firms' complementary assets.

Model 3: Radical organic evolution

Under radical organic industry evolution, change is driven by radical innovation in the capabilities that support both customer and supplier relationships. The entire system of old capabilities may be dismantled and a new system rebuilt. Although some old capabilities may retain their relevance, major architectural change occurs in the ways that firms interact with both customers and suppliers. What firms do is changing radically, and, as a result, how they interact changes too. Intermediation may be part of the change, but, in Model 3 evolution, intermediation itself is driven by the availability of innovative new technologies for creating value. One consequence is that the new industry's boundaries may be quite different from the old industry's. Indeed, old industry boundaries may be barely distinguishable after the change fully takes hold. As a result, former leaders may lose position and new leaders often emerge.

In high-end leisure travel, for example, old systems for booking traditional vacations are giving way to new options that may make old assets obsolete. New forms and styles of travel that merge leisure with business blur the old boundaries of the industry. Fully integrated provider-agents offer customized packages tailored to the interests of the vacationer. Just enough of the old services may retain their relevance to induce a transition from established incumbents. Even if they make the transition, though, industry boundaries are likely to be very different over the long run.

At present, the news-services industry is undergoing organic industry evolution. In news services, unprecedented technologies – and especially the Internet – create opportunities to provide more accurate, relevant and timely information to customers. Information is transmitted so quickly to so many people that demand is growing for services to help us cope. Cultural and community organizations are emerging to service this demand. New information-processing vehicles are developing to generate sifted information for news organizations. Some of the news services' old reporting, editing and broadcasting capabilities are relevant in the new environment, but there is no doubt that they must change in character to retain their relevance. Why are news services classified as 'organic' rather than as 'intermediating' (Model 4)? Because this industry's *product* is information. In this case, the core assets, all oriented around information flows, are what is being changed.

Model 3 industries offer significant opportunities for penetration by new entrants. Although CNN was established as a news service in the mid-1970s, it gained attention during the Gulf War as viewers came to value its distributed news-gathering capabilities. Analysis suggests that no dominant design has developed for many of the industry's important capabilities. Continuing component and architectural change will likely reshape the news-services industry for decades.

Industry structure. Industries undergoing architectural change are often less attractive than stable industries. Excess capacity, blurring industry boundaries and races for first-mover advantage all depress profitability. Unlike intermediating industry evolution, however, organic evolution hosts the potential for new approaches that bring together new customers and new suppliers. As a result, pockets of very high profitability may arise, especially among new entrants.

Historic innovation path. Organically-evolving industries are often populated by firms that have resisted the adoption of new technologies for long periods,

typically because of strong incentives to preserve established resources. In many cases, the marginal cost of operating from established platforms is lower than the fixed cost of implementing a new approach, giving new entrants a strong advantage over incumbents. These advantages may be partly offset, however, if some of the incumbent's resources can be translated into the new environment. This possibility may create difficult questions about the optimal timing of migration.

Investment opportunities. Firms often announce major new investment programmes that have big implications for the industry. For example, the invention of fiber-optic cable in the 1970s made obsolete copper cable and other technologies for carrying long-distance telephone calls. Current examples include e-mail and express mail, which promise to change the face of the mail-delivery business.

Performance drivers. High performers develop first-mover advantages by bearing the considerable risk of introducing new technologies before they know if customers are going to buy the product which results. Incumbent firms take on massive new investment programmes that may involve interacting with new kinds of customers as well as new suppliers.

Model 4: Intermediating evolution

Under Model 4 evolution, architectural change alters the way transactions occur. Intermediating change describes industries in which there are discontinuities in the value chain itself. This sort of change is topical because information technology is lowering transaction costs in some industries and creating potential for disintermediation/ reintermediation.

The characteristic quality of intermediating change is a radical shift in the overall information available in the industry's transactions. These transactions may take place either within established firms or between the industry and its customers or suppliers. Better information tends to reduce transaction costs and diminish the benefits of vertical integration as new layers of intermediate customers and suppliers emerge. In some situations, established firms find new efficiencies through subcontracting. Lower transaction costs can also create incentives to develop new capabilities.

The emergence of eMarketplaces and business-to-business (B2B) commerce on the Web often represents intermediating change. A new B2B exchange in PC devices has emerged to support local resellers and assemblers. No longer do resellers stockpile hard drives, CD-ROM drives and other peripherals: through the B2B exchange, a reseller can obtain a precisely specified peripheral within 24 hours, often at lower prices than direct from the manufacturer. The new exchange represents architectural change because it shifts the level at which the transaction occurs. The exchange's owner has a chance to build new capabilities for handling transaction volume and for assuring fair access across buyers and sellers; resellers can build new capabilities that will allow seamless ordering and inventory control; peripheral manufacturers can create value by becoming more efficient. Of course, the PC-peripherals B2B exchange also creates challenges for established customers and firms because it makes many of their old capabilities obsolete. Other industries going through intermediating change at present include retail banking and agricultural supplies.

Industry structure. Again, the characteristics of industry structure may vary widely. In many cases, however, changes in the distribution of information make old capabilities obsolete. As the industry structure shifts, excess capacity arises and firms scramble to dominate new layers of transaction. If transaction efficiency is compromised, then customers and suppliers may turn to new entrants. Eventually, several new industries may emerge to displace an old industry. As these changes take place, industries often are unattractive.

Auto dealing is currently undergoing major changes in the transaction costs that had linked activities. Formerly, auto dealerships performed a broad range of activities that included stocking new cars, preparing cars for sale, advertising, reselling used cars, informing prospective customers, market research, negotiating price and financing. Intermediating change began in auto dealing even before the World Wide Web.

Specialized services emerged for financing, market research and even price negotiations. With the Web, more and more activities that were traditionally performed by dealers are now organized in separate entities. What makes intermediation possible in this context? The exchange of credible information on the Web allows activities to be coordinated in arm's-length relationships where once they would have been integrated. As the system evolves, a number of separate new industries are likely to emerge for auto financing, inventory management, credible quality verification and perhaps even price negotiation. During the transition, the traditional auto-dealing industry is likely to continue to be unattractive.

Historic innovation path. Industries on an intermediating evolutionary path typically have accumulated compromises in transactions between the industry's incumbents, their customers and their suppliers. In many cases, these compromises reflect efforts to balance incentives for investment with bargaining strength on either side of the exchange.

Companies may have tried to induce their customers to accept low prices by partially integrating forward, for example.

Over time, the accumulation of compromises creates pressure. Customers, suppliers and some dissatisfied incumbents may seek alternative mechanisms for governing how they interact. Old assets that support both customer transactions and supplier relationships become obsolete. In the case of auto dealers, the reputational capital built up between the auto dealers and the auto manufacturers has become obsolete, at least in part. Some manufacturers have sought to break many of their dealer franchise agreements. At the same time, relationships between auto dealers and customers have suffered. Just a few years ago, customers were typically more loyal to dealerships than to car brands. This loyalty is quickly eroding as intermediating change occurs.

Investment opportunities. Under Model 4 change, innovation often starts with experimentation in different mechanisms for organizing transactions. Upstart firms may enter at low scale to test market acceptance for new ways of interacting. Leading firms also may shed activities in an effort to become more efficient, although these efforts may be plagued with difficulty. General Motors' efforts at intermediation led to a major strike in the summer of 1998.

Performance drivers. High performers rely on new technologies to reshape ways of interacting with customers, suppliers and newly-emerging intermediate suppliers. Companies must design mechanisms for decoupling traditional relationships, and especially complex internal transfer-pricing mechanisms that insulate activities from market pressure. The highest performers in this environment find ways to integrate established resources with new transaction mechanisms.

How to analyse industry evolution

Which type of industry are you in? It is worth approaching this question rigorously. Analysis of industry evolution involves taking three different perspectives, and then putting them together. The perspectives are:

- assessment of the current environment,
- evaluation of historical trends, and
- evaluation of prospective returns.

The entire process focuses on the industry's durable, specialized and economically-important investments, because they shape the incentives of the relevant players (Ghemawat 1991). A comprehensive analysis also assesses investments by the industry's customers and its suppliers. The next step is to take a view on whether the industry is undergoing architectural change. The final step is an assessment of the implications for the firm.

Who should do the analysis? The process within the firm can be as important as the results. Analysing industry evolution can generate compelling insights about emerging opportunities, which may reveal critical weaknesses in the firm's old approaches. This means that the most successful attempts to analyse industry evolution are those which involve full attention over several weeks (or even months) of senior managers from different functions across the company. So the first rule is to assign a senior, cross-functional team which brings together wide-ranging information on customer preferences, supplier technologies and competitive behaviour. The process also requires intellectual flexibility and a capacity to imagine alternative paths of industry evolution, and of the role that the firm might play. Choosing the right team members is a critical preliminary step.

1. Map the existing industry structure and competitive environment

The first analytical step involves taking a snapshot of the current environment. This becomes the foundation for the rest of the study. By looking back from this vantage point, the team later assesses whether accumulated compromises create an incentive for large-scale, punctuated change. By looking forward, the team later evaluates the potential of new kinds of investments.

Begin with an examination of the financial performance of the industry's incumbents. What accounts for current returns on invested capital in the business? Is the industry structurally attractive (Porter, 1980)? What approaches have been used to balance buyer power and supplier power? How do partnerships and strategic alliances influence relationships? Are there significant switching costs for customers, incumbents, or suppliers? Has rivalry generated excess capacity in key activities?

After analysing industry structure, evaluate the competitive position of the firm relative to its direct rivals. Does the firm hold a competitive advantage or disadvantage? Which activities account for differences between the financial performance of the firm and its rivals? Are some competitors saddled with excess capacity? Is the firm locked into specific activities?

In the end, the purpose of this step is to generate a list of strategically-important resources across the industry and within the firm. Each of the resources relies on an underlying technology, and each was acquired to allow a firm to be more efficient at delivering value to customers or suppliers.

2. Look back at how critical resources have developed

Once the team identifies the durable resources created by customers, incumbents and suppliers, the next step is to look historically at how they developed. The relevance of the industry's resources is often revealed through close inspection of customer and supplier behaviour. If customers are making specialized investments that are tailored to specific competitors, then there is evidence that their approaches are still relevant. When customers minimize their exposure to long-term relationships, then they are signaling a desire to lower switching costs. Even if customers (and suppliers) are locked in, the team should assess whether their preferences have shifted since the industry's resources were initially designed and established. Are customers and suppliers seeking fresh approaches?

The team should also assess whether the resources that support scale economies are outdated. When was the technology established? When did scale economies first arise? Have customer tastes and supplier preferences shifted so that the efficiencies are no longer realized in the same way? Has the industry been able to adapt its approach to efficiencies so that established resources are preserved as they are updated? Have some firms in the industry sought trading partnerships that have siphoned volume from firms that pursue efficiency approaches? Mature efficiency approaches may be especially vulnerable to firms that lead with partnership opportunities for customers and suppliers.

In sum, this part of the analysis allows the observer to understand how specific resources developed historically within the industry. Which are most important? Which are mature and vulnerable to radical innovation? Which resources are still in development? Ultimately, the objective is to identify whether customers, incumbents and suppliers have an incentive to transform the underlying business models that shape their interaction.

3. Identify major investment initiatives

After looking historically, the team should look forward to understand the prospective economic impact of newly-formed investments both by incumbents and outsiders. The objective is to look at new investment activity with a clean slate. What major investments in both tangible and intangible assets have been created to meet needs that are currently served within the industry? It is important to consider investments that may originate outside conventional industry boundaries.

The team should also assess the nature of the investment risk associated with innovation. Risks occur whenever the return on investment is deferred. It is risk that creates the prospect of future profitability, however. Without risk, the cost of investment would reflect the entire net-present-value of the return. How much risk are entrepreneurs taking as they pursue major investments? How much investment has to occur before the entrepreneur learns whether the innovation will create value in the marketplace? What early signals are available for assessing market acceptance? Does the investing entrepreneur have contingency plans for redeploying investment if market acceptance is low?

4. Decide whether innovation is architectural

Industries tend to be slow to change. Compromises accumulate because the parties are locked in by their prior commitments. The fourth step involves integrating the historical and prospective points of view to evaluate the accumulated compromises in value-creation strategies. These compromises stimulate innovation because they create incentives for change in the economic relationships between the industry, its customers and its suppliers. When an industry is profitable, and when its customers and its suppliers are also earning high returns on their invested capital, then the incentive for architectural change can be quite low. Occasionally, however, architectural innovation occurs. In this step of the analysis, the team must assess whether the investment activities identified through the analysis amount to architectural change over a five- to ten-year horizon.

It is easy to overestimate the prospective impact of technological change over a moderate time horizon. Technological change is almost certain to create architectural change in an industry over the very long run, but architectural innovation can occur only if the results of the historical analysis point to incentives for change for the industry's customers and its suppliers.

5. Evaluate the implications

The final step is to evaluate the implications for the firm. There are several ways in which the organization may be challenged. The firm may be investing in projects that are either behind or ahead of their time. Invariably, incentives arise to preserve the value of established capital. Executives may be struggling with whether to abandon profitable old approaches in order to develop unprofitable new ones. An organization may find it optimal to invest minimally to preserve old capital at the same time as it invests for the future. Managing the path of innovation requires deep knowledge of economic incentives as well as technology requirements. By looking historically as well as prospectively, the team can assess how quickly customers and suppliers will respond to new opportunity.

The challenges of industry evolution are even more complex if the firm is engaged in close rivalry over the opportunity. A war of attrition may arise over the old approach. These wars are pernicious because they often lead the firm into an unprofitable battle to serve outdated customers. They are also dangerous when they drain capital and keep attention fixed on the old paradigm. A similar kind of war can emerge if the firm competes too closely with a rival for dominance in a new industry structure. Too much competition can rush investment in technologies that may not be optimally suited to long-run opportunities. Worse yet, the rivals may become committed to similar strategies, and may consequently invest inefficiently once the new technologies become established.

Organizational resistance to change can arise regardless of whether innovation is architectural. Companies have devised a broad variety of mechanisms for dealing with this kind of resistance: aligning incentives, making arm's-length financial investments and adjusting formal hierarchical structure. By examining how resources and relationships are changing, the team can identify a range of potential approaches for reorganizing, and then recommend which carries appropriate levels of risk and reward.

Implications

What does all this mean? Understanding industry evolution is important because firms are much more likely to survive and to earn high rates of return if their investment strategies are aligned with industry evolution than if they resist it. Extensive analysis on broad patterns of performance suggests that industries evolve on one of the four major models: receptive, blockbuster, radical organic, or intermediating. Companies typically fail when they attempt to jar the path of industry evolution from one model to another.

Evolution is driven by powerful incentives that affect an industry's customers and suppliers as well as its incumbents. When an industry is architecturally stable, change follows either a 'receptive' or 'blockbuster' path. Architecturally unstable industries undergo redefinition, and may offer greater opportunities to displace industry leaders. The risks of pursuing first-mover advantage are also great. Organic and intermediating industries host many more casualties than successes.

Rigorous, disciplined analysis of industry evolution is necessary to anticipate when different kinds of opportunities are likely to emerge over time. Begin with a comprehensive map of existing industry conditions, and then look retrospectively and prospectively to understand how technology may take hold. Assess the accumulated pressure on industry structure that may have emerged as customers, incumbents and suppliers have compromised to preserve the value of established capabilities. Careful analysis frames the viable opportunities for successfully commercializing new technologies. Understanding industry evolution sets the stage for evaluating competitive threats and organizational challenges. Thus, understanding industry evolution is just the first step toward building a comprehensive plan for an organization's development.

Blue ocean strategy

By W. Chan Kim and Renee Mauborgne[1]

A one time accordion player, stilt walker and fire-eater, Guy Laliberté is now CEO of one of Canada's largest cultural exports, Cirque du Soleil. Founded in 1984 by a group of street performers, Cirque has staged dozens of productions seen by some 40 million people in 90 cities around the world. In 20 years, Cirque has achieved revenues that Ringling Bros. and Barnum & Bailey – the world's leading circus – took more than a century to attain.

Cirque's rapid growth occurred in an unlikely setting. The circus business was (and still is) in long-term decline. Alternative forms of entertainment – sporting events, TV and video games – were casting a growing shadow. Children, the mainstay of the circus audience, preferred PlayStations to circus acts. There was also rising sentiment, fuelled by animal rights groups, against the use of animals, traditionally an integral part of the circus. On the supply side, the star performers that Ringling and the other circuses relied on to draw in the crowds could often name their own terms. As a result, the industry was hit by steadily decreasing audiences and increasing costs. What's more, any new entrant to this business would be competing against a formidable incumbent that for most of the last century had set the industry standard.

How did Cirque profitably increase revenues by a factor of 22 over the last ten years in such an unattractive environment? The tagline for one of the first Cirque productions is revealing: 'We reinvent the circus.' Cirque did not make its money by competing within the confines of the existing industry or by stealing customers from Ringling and the others. Instead it created uncontested market space that made the competition irrelevant. It pulled in a whole new group of customers who were traditionally non-customers of the industry – adults and corporate clients who had turned to theatre, opera or ballet and were, therefore, prepared to pay several times more than the price of a conventional circus ticket for an unprecedented entertainment experience.

To understand the nature of Cirque's achievement, you have to realize that the business universe consists of two distinct kinds of space, which we think of as red and blue oceans. Red oceans represent all the industries in existence today – the known market space. In red oceans, industry boundaries are defined and accepted, and the competitive rules of the game are well understood. Here, companies try to outperform their rivals in order to grab a greater share of existing demand. As the space gets more and more crowded, prospects for profits and growth are reduced. Products turn into commodities, and increasing competition turns the water bloody.

Blue oceans denote all the industries *not* in existence today – the unknown market space, untainted by competition. In blue oceans, demand is created rather than fought over. There is ample opportunity for growth that is both profitable and rapid. There are two ways to create blue oceans. In a few cases, companies can give rise to completely new industries, as eBay did with the online auction industry. But in most cases, a blue ocean is created from within a red ocean when a company alters the boundaries of an existing industry. As will become evident later, this is what Cirque did. In breaking through the boundary traditionally separating circus and theatre, it made a new and profitable blue ocean from within the red ocean of the circus industry.

Cirque is just one of more than 150 blue ocean creations that we have studied in over 30 industries, using data stretching back more than 100 years. We analysed companies that created those blue oceans and their less successful competitors, which were caught in red oceans. In studying these data, we have observed a consistent pattern of strategic thinking behind the creation of new markets and industries, what we call blue ocean strategy. The logic behind blue ocean strategy parts with traditional models focused on competing in existing market space. Indeed, it can be argued that managers' failure to realize the differences between red and blue ocean strategy lies behind the difficulties many companies encounter as they try to break from the competition.

In this article, we present the concept of blue ocean strategy and describe its defining characteristics. We assess the profit and growth consequences of blue oceans and discuss why their creation is a rising imperative for companies in the future. We believe that an understanding of blue ocean strategy will help today's companies as they struggle to thrive in an accelerating and expanding business universe.

Blue and red oceans

Although the term may be new, blue oceans have always been with us. Look back 100 years and ask yourself which industries known today were then unknown. The answer: Industries as basic as automobiles, music recording, aviation, petrochemicals, pharmaceuticals and management consulting were unheard-of or had just begun to emerge. Now turn the clock back only 30 years and ask yourself the same question. Again, a plethora of multibillion-dollar industries jump out: mutual funds, cellular telephones, biotechnology, discount retailing, express package delivery, snowboards, coffee bars and home videos, to name a few. Just three decades ago, none of these industries existed in a meaningful way.

This time, put the clock forward 20 years. Ask yourself: How many industries that are unknown today will

exist then? If history is any predictor of the future, the answer is many. Companies have a huge capacity to create new industries and re-create existing ones, a fact that is reflected in the deep changes that have been necessary in the way industries are classified. The half-century-old Standard Industrial Classification (SIC) system was replaced in 1997 by the North American Industry Classification System (NAICS). The new system expanded the ten SIC industry sectors into 20 to reflect the emerging realities of new industry territories – blue oceans. The services sector under the old system, for example, is now seven sectors ranging from information to health care and social assistance. Given that these classification systems are designed for standardization and continuity, such a replacement shows how significant a source of economic growth the creation of blue oceans has been.

Looking forward, it seems clear to us that blue oceans will remain the engine of growth. Prospects in most established market spaces – red oceans – are shrinking steadily. Technological advances have substantially improved industrial productivity, permitting suppliers to produce an unprecedented array of products and services. And as trade barriers between nations and regions fall and information on products and prices becomes instantly and globally available, niche markets and monopoly havens are continuing to disappear. At the same time, there is little evidence of any increase in demand, at least in the developed markets, where recent United Nations statistics even point to declining populations. The result is that in more and more industries, supply is overtaking demand.

This situation has inevitably hastened the commoditization of products and services, stoked price wars and shrunk profit margins. According to recent studies, major American brands in a variety of product and service categories have become more and more alike. And as brands become more similar, people increasingly base purchase choices on price. People no longer insist, as in the past, that their laundry detergent be Tide. Nor do they necessarily stick to Colgate when there is a special promotion for Crest, and vice versa. In overcrowded industries, differentiating brands becomes harder both in economic upturns and in downturns.

The paradox of strategy

Unfortunately, most companies seem becalmed in their red oceans. In a study of business launches in 108 companies, we found that 86 per cent of those new ventures were line extensions – incremental improvements to existing industry offerings – and a mere 14 per cent were aimed at creating new markets or industries. While line extensions did account for 62 per cent of the total revenues, they delivered only 39 per cent of the total profits. By contrast, the 14 per cent invested in creating new markets and industries delivered 38 per cent of total revenues and a startling 61 per cent of total profits.

So why the dramatic imbalance in favour of red oceans? Part of the explanation is that corporate strategy is heavily influenced by its roots in military strategy. The very language of strategy is deeply imbued with military references – chief executive 'officers' in 'headquarters', 'troops' on the 'front lines'. Described this way, strategy is all about red ocean competition. It is about confronting an opponent and driving him off a battlefield of limited territory. Blue ocean strategy, by contrast, is about doing business where there is no competitor. It is about creating new land, not dividing up existing land. Focusing on the red ocean therefore means accepting the key constraining factors of war – limited terrain and the need to beat an enemy to succeed. And it means denying the distinctive strength of the business world – the capacity to create new market space that is uncontested.

The tendency of corporate strategy to focus on winning against rivals was exacerbated by the meteoric rise of Japanese companies in the 1970s and 1980s. For the first time in corporate history, customers were deserting Western companies in droves. As competition mounted in the global marketplace, a slew of red ocean strategies emerged, all arguing that competition was at the core of corporate success and failure. Today, one hardly talks about strategy without using the language of competition. The term that best symbolizes this is 'competitive advantage'. In the competitive-advantage worldview, companies are often driven to outperform rivals and capture greater shares of existing market space.

Of course competition matters. But by focusing on competition, scholars, companies and consultants have ignored two very important – and, we would argue, far more lucrative – aspects of strategy: One is to find and develop markets where there is little or no competition – blue oceans – and the other is to exploit and protect blue oceans. These challenges are very different from those to which strategists have devoted most of their attention.

Toward blue ocean strategy

What kind of strategic logic is needed to guide the creation of blue oceans? To answer that question, we looked back over 100 years of data on blue ocean creation to see what patterns could be discerned. Some of our data are presented in Exhibit 10.2.1 'A Snapshot of Blue Ocean Creation'. It shows an overview of key blue ocean creations in three industries that closely touch people's lives: autos – how people get to work; computers – what people use at work; and movie theatres – where people go after work for enjoyment. We found that:

- Blue oceans are not about technology innovation. Leading-edge technology is sometimes involved in the creation of blue oceans, but it is not a defining feature of them. This is often true even in industries that are technology intensive. As the exhibit reveals, across all three representative industries, blue oceans were seldom the result of technological innovation per se; the underlying technology was often already in existence. Even Ford's revolutionary assembly line can be traced to the meat-packing industry in America. Like those within the auto industry, the blue oceans within the computer industry did not come about through technology innovations alone but by linking technology to what buyers valued. As with the IBM 650 and the Compaq PC server, this often involved simplifying the technology.

- Incumbents often create blue oceans – and usually within their core businesses. GM, the Japanese auto-makers, and Chrysler were established players when they created blue oceans in the auto industry. So were CTR and its later incarnation, IBM, and Compaq in the computer industry. And in the cinema industry, the same can be said of Palace Theatres and AMC. Of the companies listed here, only Ford, Apple, Dell and Nickelodeon were new entrants in their industries; the first three were start ups, and the fourth was an established player entering an industry that was new to it. This suggests that incumbents are not at a disadvantage in creating new market spaces. Moreover, the blue oceans made by incumbents were usually within their core businesses. In fact, as the exhibit shows, most blue oceans are created from within, not beyond, red oceans of existing industries. This challenges the view that new markets are in distant waters. Blue oceans are right next to you in every industry.

- Company and industry are the wrong units of analysis. The traditional units of strategic analysis – company and industry – have little explanatory power when it comes to analysing how and why blue oceans are created. There is no consistently excellent company; the same company can be brilliant at one time and wrongheaded at another. Every company

EXHIBIT 10.2.1   A SNAPSHOT OF BLUE OCEAN CREATION

	Key blue ocean creations	Was the blue ocean created by a new entrant or an incumbent?	Was it driven by technology pioneering or value pioneering?*	At the time of the blue ocean creation, was the industry attractive or unattractive?
Automobiles	**Ford Model T** Unveiled in 1908, the Model T was the first mass-produced car, priced so that many Americans could afford it.	New entrant	Value pioneering (mostly existing technologies)	Unattractive
	GM's 'car for every purse and purpose' GM created a blue ocean in 1924 by injecting fun and fashion into the car.	Incumbent	Value pioneering (some new technologies)	Attractive
	Japanese fuel-efficient autos Japanese automakers created a blue ocean in the mid-1970s with small, reliable lines of cars.	Incumbent	Value pioneering (some new technologies)	Unattractive
	Chrysler minivan With its 1984 minivan, Chrysler created a new class of automobile that was as easy to use as a car but had the passenger space of a van.	Incumbent	Value pioneering (mostly existing technologies)	Unattractive
Computers	**CTR's tabulating machine** In 1914, CTR created the business machine industry by simplifying, modularizing and leasing tabulating machines. CTR later changed its name to IBM.	Incumbent	Value pioneering (some new technologies)	Unattractive
	IBM 650 electronic computer and System/360 In 1952, IBM created the business computer industry by simplifying and reducing the power and price of existing technology. And it exploded the blue ocean created by the 650 when in 1964 it unveiled the System/360, the first modularized computer system.	Incumbent	Value pioneering (650: mostly existing technologies) Value and technology pioneering (System/360: new and existing technologies)	Non-existent
	Apple personal computer Although it was not the first home computer, the all-in-one, simple-to-use Apple II was a blue ocean creation when it appeared in 1978.	New entrant	Value pioneering (mostly existing technologies)	Unattractive
	Compaq PC servers Compaq created a blue ocean in 1992 with its ProSignia server, which gave buyers twice the file and print capability of the minicomputer at one-third the price.	Incumbent	Value pioneering (mostly existing technologies)	Non-existent
	Dell built to order computers In the mid-1990s, Dell created a blue ocean in a highly competitive industry by creating a new purchase and delivery experience for buyers.	New entrant	Value pioneering (mostly existing technologies)	Unattractive

Key blue ocean creations	Was the blue ocean created by a new entrant or an incumbent?	Was it driven by technology pioneering or value pioneering?*	At the time of the blue ocean creation, was the industry attractive or unattractive?
Nickelodeon The first Nickelodeon opened its doors in 1905, showing short films around the clock to working class audiences for five cents.	New entrant	Value pioneering (mostly existing technologies)	Non-existent
Palace theatres Created by Roxy Rothapfel in 1914, these theatres provided an opera-like environment for cinema viewing at an affordable price.	Incumbent	Value pioneering (mostly existing technologies)	Attractive
AMC multiplex In the 1960s, the number of multiplexes in America's suburban shopping malls mushroomed. The multiplex gave viewers greater choice while reducing owners' costs.	Incumbent	Value pioneering (mostly existing technologies)	Unattractive
AMC megaplex Megaplexes, introduced in 1995, offered every current blockbuster and provided spectacular viewing experiences in theatre complexes as big as stadiums, at a lower cost to theatre owners.	Incumbent	Value pioneering (mostly existing technologies)	Unattractive

(Movie Theatres)

*Driven by value. Pioneering does not mean that technologies were not involved. Rather, it means that the defining technologies used had largely been in existence, whether in that industry or elsewhere.

rises and falls over time. Likewise, there is no perpetually excellent industry; relative attractiveness is driven largely by the creation of blue oceans from within them. The most appropriate unit of analysis for explaining the creation of blue oceans is the strategic move – the set of managerial actions and decisions involved in making a major market-creating business offering. Compaq, for example, is considered by many people to be 'unsuccessful' because it was acquired by Hewlett-Packard in 2001 and ceased to be a company. But the firm's ultimate fate does not invalidate the smart strategic move Compaq made that led to the creation of the multibillion-dollar market in PC servers, a move that was a key cause of the company's powerful comeback in the 1990s.

■ Creating blue oceans builds brands. So powerful is blue ocean strategy that a blue ocean strategic move can create brand equity that lasts for decades. Almost all of the companies listed in the exhibit are remembered in no small part for the blue oceans

they created long ago. Very few people alive today were around when the first Model T rolled off Henry Ford's assembly line in 1908, but the company's brand still benefits from that blue ocean move. IBM, too, is often regarded as an 'American institution' largely for the blue oceans it created in computing; the 360 series was its equivalent of the Model T.

Our findings are encouraging for executives at the large, established corporations that are traditionally seen as the victims of new market space creation. For what they reveal is that large R&D budgets are not the key to creating new market space. The key is making the right strategic moves. What's more, companies that understand what drives a good strategic move will be well placed to create multiple blue oceans over time, thereby continuing to deliver high growth and profits over a sustained period. The creation of blue oceans, in other words, is a product of strategy and as such is very much a product of managerial action.

The defining characteristics

Our research shows several common characteristics across strategic moves that create blue oceans. We found that the creators of blue oceans, in sharp contrast to companies playing by traditional rules, never use the competition as a benchmark. Instead they make it irrelevant by creating a leap in value for both buyers and the company itself. (Exhibit 10.2.2 compares the chief characteristics of these two strategy models.)

Perhaps the most important feature of blue ocean strategy is that it rejects the fundamental tenet of conventional strategy: that a trade-off exists between value and cost. According to this thesis, companies can either create greater value for customers at a higher cost or create reasonable value at a lower cost. In other words, strategy is essentially a choice between differentiation and low cost. But when it comes to creating blue oceans, the evidence shows that successful companies pursue differentiation and low cost simultaneously.

To see how this is done, let us go back to Cirque du Soleil. At the time of Cirque's debut, circuses focused on benchmarking one another and maximizing their shares of shrinking demand by tweaking traditional circus acts. This included trying to secure more and better-known clowns and lion tamers, efforts that raised circuses' cost structure without substantially altering the circus experience. The result was rising costs without rising revenues and a downward spiral in overall circus demand. Enter Cirque. Instead of following the conventional logic of outpacing the competition by offering a better solution to the given problem – creating a circus with even greater fun and thrills – it redefined the problem itself by offering people the fun and thrill of the circus *and* the intellectual sophistication and artistic richness of the theatre.

In designing performances that landed both these punches, Cirque had to re-evaluate the components of the traditional circus offering. What the company found was that many of the elements considered essential to the fun and thrill of the circus were unnecessary and in many cases costly. For instance, most circuses offer animal acts. These are a heavy economic burden, because circuses have to shell out not only for the animals but also for their training, medical care, housing, insurance and transportation. Yet Cirque found that the appetite for animal shows was rapidly diminishing because of rising public concern about the treatment of circus animals and the ethics of exhibiting them.

Similarly, although traditional circuses promoted their performers as stars, Cirque realized that the public no longer thought of circus artists as stars, at least not in the movie star sense. Cirque did away with traditional three-ring shows, too. Not only did these create confusion among spectators forced to switch their attention from one ring to another, they also increased the number of performers needed, with obvious cost implications. And while aisle concession sales appeared to be a good way to generate revenue, the high prices discouraged parents from making purchases and made them feel they were being taken for a ride.

Cirque found that the lasting allure of the traditional circus came down to just three factors: the clowns, the tent and the classic acrobatic acts. So Cirque kept the clowns, while shifting their humour away from slapstick to a more enchanting, sophisticated style. It glamourized the tent, which many circuses had abandoned in favour of rented venues. Realizing that the tent, more than anything else, captured the magic of the circus, Cirque designed this classic symbol with a glorious external finish and a high level of audience comfort. Gone were the sawdust and hard benches. Acrobats and other thrilling performers were retained, but Cirque reduced their roles and made their acts more elegant by adding artistic flair.

EXHIBIT 10.2.2   RED OCEAN VERSUS BLUE OCEAN STRATEGY

Red ocean strategy	Blue ocean strategy
■ Compete in existing market space.	■ Create uncontested market space.
■ Beat the competition.	■ Make the competition irrelevant.
■ Exploit existing demand.	■ Create and capture new demand.
■ Make the value/cost trade-off.	■ Break the value/cost trade-off.
■ Align the whole system of a company's activities with its strategic choice of differentiation or low cost.	■ Align the whole system of a company's activities in pursuit of differentiation and low cost.

Even as Cirque stripped away some of the traditional circus offerings, it injected new elements drawn from the world of theatre. For instance, unlike traditional circuses featuring a series of unrelated acts, each Cirque creation resembles a theatre performance in that it has a theme and story line. Although the themes are intentionally vague, they bring harmony and an intellectual element to the acts. Cirque also borrows ideas from Broadway. For example, rather than putting on the traditional 'once and for all' show, Cirque mounts multiple productions based on different themes and story lines. As with Broadway productions, too, each Cirque show has an original musical score, which drives the performance, lighting and timing of the acts, rather than the other way around. The productions feature abstract and spiritual dance, an idea derived from theatre and ballet. By introducing these factors, Cirque has created highly sophisticated entertainments. And by staging multiple productions, Cirque gives people reason to come to the circus more often, thereby increasing revenues.

Cirque offers the best of both circus and theatre. And by eliminating many of the most expensive elements of the circus, it has been able to dramatically reduce its cost structure, achieving both differentiation and low cost.

By driving down costs while simultaneously driving up value for buyers, a company can achieve a leap in value for both itself and its customers. Since buyer value comes from the utility and price a company offers, and a company generates value for itself through cost structure and price, blue ocean strategy is achieved only when the whole system of a company's utility, price and cost activities is properly aligned. It is this whole-system approach that makes the creation of blue oceans a sustainable strategy. Blue ocean strategy integrates the range of a firm's functional and operational activities.

A rejection of the trade-off between low cost and differentiation implies a fundamental change in strategic mindset – we cannot emphasize enough how fundamental a shift it is. The red ocean assumption that industry structural conditions are a given and firms are forced to compete within them is based on an intellectual worldview that academics call the *structuralist* view, or *environmental determinism*. According to this view, companies and managers are largely at the mercy of economic forces greater than themselves. Blue ocean strategies, by contrast, are based on a worldview in which market boundaries and industries can be reconstructed by the actions and beliefs of industry players. We call this the *reconstructionist* view.

The founders of Cirque du Soleil clearly did not feel constrained to act within the confines of their industry. Indeed, is Cirque really a circus with all that it has eliminated, reduced, raised and created? Or is it theatre? If it is theatre, then what genre – Broadway show, opera, ballet? The magic of Cirque was created through a reconstruction of elements drawn from all of these alternatives. In the end, Cirque is none of them and a little of all of them. From within the red oceans of theatre and circus, Cirque has created a blue ocean of uncontested market space that has, as yet, no name.

Barriers to imitation

Companies that create blue oceans usually reap the benefits without credible challenges for 10 to 15 years, as was the case with Cirque du Soleil, Home Depot, Federal Express, Southwest Airlines and CNN, to name just a few. The reason is that blue ocean strategy creates considerable economic and cognitive barriers to imitation.

For a start, adopting a blue ocean creator's business model is easier to imagine than to do. Because blue ocean creators immediately attract customers in large volumes, they are able to generate scale economies very rapidly, putting would-be imitators at an immediate and continuing cost disadvantage. The huge economies of scale in purchasing that Wal-Mart enjoys, for example, have significantly discouraged other companies from imitating its business model. The immediate attraction of large numbers of customers can also create network externalities. The more customers eBay has online, the more attractive the auction site becomes for both sellers and buyers of wares, giving users few incentives to go elsewhere.

When imitation requires companies to make changes to their whole system of activities, organizational politics may impede a would-be competitor's ability to switch to the divergent business model of a blue ocean strategy. For instance, airlines trying to follow Southwest's example of offering the speed of air travel with the flexibility and cost of driving would have faced major revisions in routing, training, marketing and pricing, not to mention culture. Few established airlines had the flexibility to make such extensive organizational and operating changes overnight. Imitating a whole-system approach is not an easy feat.

The cognitive barriers can be just as effective. When a company offers a leap in value, it rapidly earns brand buzz and a loyal following in the marketplace.

Experience shows that even the most expensive marketing campaigns struggle to unseat a blue ocean creator. Microsoft, for example, has been trying for more than ten years to occupy the centre of the blue ocean that Intuit created with its financial software product Quicken. Despite all of its efforts and all of its investment, Microsoft has not been able to unseat Intuit as the industry leader.

In other situations, attempts to imitate a blue ocean creator conflict with the imitator's existing brand image. The Body Shop, for example, shuns top models and makes no promises of eternal youth and beauty. For the established cosmetic brands like Estée Lauder and L'Oréal, imitation was very difficult, because it would have signaled a complete invalidation of their current images, which are based on promises of eternal youth and beauty.

A consistent pattern

While our conceptual articulation of the pattern may be new, blue ocean strategy has always existed, whether or not companies have been conscious of the fact. Just consider the striking parallels between the Cirque du Soleil theatre-circus experience and Ford's creation of the Model T.

At the end of the nineteenth century, the automobile industry was small and unattractive. More than 500 automakers in America competed in turning out handmade luxury cars that cost around $1,500 and were enormously *un*popular with all but the very rich. Anticar activists tore up roads, ringed parked cars with barbed wire and organized boycotts of car-driving businessmen and politicians. Woodrow Wilson caught the spirit of the times when he said in 1906 that 'nothing has spread socialistic feeling more than the automobile'. He called it 'a picture of the arrogance of wealth'.

Instead of trying to beat the competition and steal a share of existing demand from other automakers, Ford reconstructed the industry boundaries of cars and horse-drawn carriages to create a blue ocean. At the time, horse-drawn carriages were the primary means of local transportation across America. The carriage had two distinct advantages over cars. Horses could easily negotiate the bumps and mud that stymied cars – especially in rain and snow – on the nation's ubiquitous dirt roads. And horses and carriages were much easier to maintain than the luxurious autos of the time, which frequently broke down, requiring expert repairmen who were expensive and in short supply. It was Henry Ford's understanding of these advantages that showed him how he could break away from the competition and unlock enormous untapped demand.

Ford called the Model T the car 'for the great multitude, constructed of the best materials'. Like Cirque, the Ford Motor Company made the competition irrelevant. Instead of creating fashionable, customized cars for weekends in the countryside, a luxury few could justify, Ford built a car that, like the horse-drawn carriage, was for everyday use. The Model T came in just one colour, black, and there were few optional extras. It was reliable and durable, designed to travel effortlessly over dirt roads in rain, snow, or sunshine. It was easy to use and fix. People could learn to drive it in a day. And like Cirque, Ford went outside the industry for a price point, looking at horse-drawn carriages ($400), not other autos. In 1908, the first Model T cost $850; in 1909, the price dropped to $609, and by 1924 it was down to $290. In this way, Ford converted buyers of horse-drawn carriages into car buyers – just as Cirque turned theatregoers into circusgoers. Sales of the Model T boomed. Ford's market share surged from 9 per cent in 1908 to 61 per cent in 1921, and by 1923, a majority of American households had a car.

Even as Ford offered the mass of buyers a leap in value, the company also achieved the lowest cost structure in the industry, much as Cirque did later. By keeping the cars highly standardized with limited options and interchangeable parts, Ford was able to scrap the prevailing manufacturing system in which cars were constructed by skilled craftsmen who swarmed around one workstation and built a car piece by piece from start to finish. Ford's revolutionary assembly line replaced craftsmen with unskilled labourers, each of whom worked quickly and efficiently on one small task. This allowed Ford to make a car in just four days – 21 days was the industry norm – creating huge cost savings.

Blue and red oceans have always co-existed and always will. Practical reality, therefore, demands that companies understand the strategic logic of both types of oceans. At present, competing in red oceans dominates the field of strategy in theory and in practice, even as businesses' need to create blue oceans intensifies. It is time to even the scales in the field of strategy with a better balance of efforts across both oceans. For although blue ocean strategists have always existed, for the most part their strategies have been largely unconscious. But once corporations realize that the strategies for creating and capturing blue oceans have a different underlying logic from red ocean strategies, they will be able to create many more blue oceans in the future.

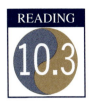

READING
10.3

Living on the fault line

By Geoffrey Moore[1]

The technology adoption life cycle models the response of any given population to the offer of a discontinuous innovation, one that forces the abandonment of traditional infrastructure and systems for the promise of a heretofore unavailable set of benefits.

It represents this response as a bell curve, separating out five subpopulations, as illustrated in Figure 10.3.1.

The bell curve represents the total population of people exposed to a new technology offer. The various segments of the curve represent the percentage of people predicted to adopt one or another of the five different strategies for determining when and why to switch allegiance from the old to the new. The five strategies unfold sequentially as follows:

1 The *technology enthusiast strategy* is to adopt the new technology upon its first appearance, in large part just to explore its properties to determine if it is 'cool'. The actual benefits provided may not even be of interest to this constituency, but the mechanism by which they are provided is of great interest. If they are entertained by the mechanism, they often adopt the product just to be able to show it off.

2 The *visionary strategy* is to adopt the new technology as a means for capturing a dramatic advantage over competitors who do not adopt it. The goal here is to be first to deploy an advantaged system and use that head start to leapfrog over the competition, establishing a position so far out in front that the sector realigns around its new leader. Visionaries are mavericks who want to break away from the herd and differentiate themselves dramatically.

3 The *pragmatist strategy* is directly opposed to the visionary. It wants to stay with the herd, adopting the new technology if and only if everyone else does as well. The goal here is to use the wisdom of the marketplace to sort out what's valuable and then to be a fast follower once the new direction has clearly emerged. Pragmatists consult each other frequently about who's adopting what in an effort to stay current but do not commit to any major change without seeing successful implementations elsewhere first.

4 The *conservative strategy* is to stick with the old technology for as long as possible (a) because it works, (b) because it is familiar, and (c) because it is paid for. By putting off the transition to the new platform, conservatives conserve cash and avoid hitting the learning curve, making themselves more productive in the short run. Long term, when they do switch, the system is more completely debugged, and that works to their advantage as well. The downside of the strategy is that they grow increasingly out of touch for the period they don't adopt and can, if they wait too long, get isolated in old technology that simply will not map to the new world.

5 Finally, the *sceptic strategy* is to debunk the entire technology as a false start and refuse to adopt it at all. This is a winning tactic for those technologies that never do gain mainstream market acceptance. For those that do, however, it creates extreme versions of the isolation problems conservatives face.

Each of these strategies has validity in its own right, and a single individual is perfectly capable of choosing different strategies for different offers. But for any given technology, the market will develop in a characteristic pattern due to the aggregate effects of a population distributing its choices in the proportions outlined by the bell curve. The resulting market development model is shown in Figure 10.3.2.

The model segments the evolution of a technology-based market as follows:

■ The first phase, or *early market,* is a time when early adopters (technology enthusiasts and visionaries) take up the innovation while the pragmatic majority holds back. The market development goal at this stage is to gain a few prestigious flagship customers who help publicize the technology and celebrate its potential benefits.

■ The early market is followed by a *chasm,* a period of no adoption, when the early adopters have already made their choices, but the pragmatist majority is still holding back. The barrier to further progress

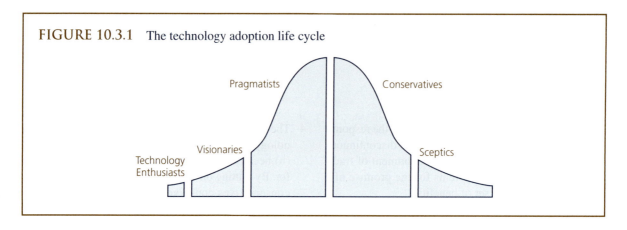

FIGURE 10.3.1   The technology adoption life cycle

FIGURE 10.3.2   Technology-enabled market development

is that pragmatists are looking to other pragmatists to be references, but no one wants to go first. The market development goal at this stage is to target an initial beachhead segment of pragmatists who can lead the second wave of adoption.

■ In the development of most technology-enabled markets, specific niches of pragmatic customers adopt the new technology before the general pragmatist population. We call this period the *bowling alley* because the market development goal is to use the first group of adopters as references to help win over the next group, and the next, and so on. Typically the 'head bowling pin' is a niche of pragmatists who have a major business problem that cannot be solved with current technology but that does respond to a solution built around the new innovation. These are the *department managers in charge of a broken, mission-critical process.*

Once this first group starts to move it takes much less of a motive to overcome the inertia of the next group.

■ As pragmatist adoption builds in niches, one of two futures emerges. In one, adoption continues to remain localized to niche markets, creating a pattern we call 'bowling alley forever'. In this pattern, each niche's solution is relatively complex and differentiated from every other niche's. As a result, no mass market emerges, and the market development goal is simply to expand existing niches and create new ones as the opportunity arises. In the other pattern, a 'killer app' emerges – a single application of the innovative technology that provides a compelling benefit that can be standardized across multiple niches. The killer app transforms niche adoption into mass adoption, creating an enormous uptick in demand for the new technology across a wide range of sectors. We call this period the *tornado* because the onrush of mass demand is so swift it creates a vortex that sucks the supply out of the market and puts the category into hypergrowth for a number of years. The market development goal here is to win as much market share as possible during a period when the entire market is choosing its supplier for the new class of technology-enabled offering.

■ Once the supply side of the market finally catches up with the backlog of demand, the tornado phase subsides and the market reaches a state we call *Main Street*. The new technology has been broadly deployed and, with the support of conservatives, now settles down to a (hopefully) long engagement as the incumbent technology. The market development goal here is to continuously improve the value of the offering, decreasing its base costs and recouping margins by increasing the number of value-adding extensions that can supplement it. The ultimate extension in many cases is to convert the offering from a product sale to a services subscription, allowing the customer to gain the benefit of the product without having to take on the responsibility for maintaining it.

It is important to note that the end of the technology adoption life cycle does not represent the end of technology's productive market life. The category of offering can be sustained indefinitely on Main Street, coming to an end only when the next discontinuous innovation renders the prior technology obsolete. Indeed, despite all the emphasis on shortening life cycles, Main Street markets normally last for decades

after complete absorption of the enabling technology – witness the car, the telephone, the television, the personal computer and the cell phone. Importantly, however, the marketplace pecking order set by market share that emerges during the bowling alley and tornado phases tends to persist for the life of Main Street. That is, while Main Street represents the final and lasting distribution of competitive advantage, its boundaries get set prior to arrival. Thus success in every prior stage in the life cycle is key to building sustainable Main Street market success.

Stage-one adoption: The early market

The early market begins with the ambitions of two constituencies who live at opposite ends of the value chain (see Figure 10.3.3). On the left is the *technology provider*, the supplier of the discontinuous innovation, with ambitions of constructing an entirely new marketplace based on a new platform. On the right are one or more visionary executives, in the role of *economic buyer*, who also have ambitions of their own. They want to re-architect the marketplaces they participate in to install their company as the new market leader – and they want to do it fast. They see in the new technology an opportunity to disrupt the established order and insert themselves into the lead.

Between these two poles, however, there is at present no existing value chain that can link their ambitions. Indeed, the existing value chain is appalled by them. There is, however, one institution in the market

FIGURE 10.3.3 Early-market value chain

that can bridge the gulf between the two, can transform the technology provider's magic into the economic buyer's dream, and that is the *consulting firm*. Rather than try to incubate a value chain in the marketplace, this consultancy will instead create a temporary value chain to serve a single project's specific needs. That is, they will pull together the products, the applications, the sales and support, the customer service, and in extreme cases even substitute their own people for the customer's technical buyer (and even for the customer's end users), all to make the value chain work *in a single instance for a single customer.*

Needless to say, this is an expensive proposition. But if it pays off, if the sponsoring company really does leapfrog over its competition in a new market order, then the visionary becomes a hero, and whatever money was spent was pocket change by comparison to the appreciation in the customer company's stock price.

Competitive advantage in the early market

The primary competitive advantage strategy for the early market consists of being first to catch the new technology wave. This is often called *first-mover advantage*. Amazon.com, by catching the Web retail wave first, has created a powerful brand that its competitors cannot hope to replicate, regardless of how much they spend. By being first to introduce auctions onto the Web, eBay gained first-mover advantage also, so that even when assaulted by an alliance of extremely powerful companies – Microsoft, Dell, Lycos, Excite – it has been able to sustain market share. Four years into Web advertising, the top ten sites, with Yahoo! leading the list, garner as much as 85 per cent of the total spending – largely because of first-mover advantage. The Sabre system for airline and other travel-related reservations has had a similar track record, even as Apollo and Galileo and others have entered the market. Same with United Airlines' and American Airlines' frequent-flyer systems.

In every case, first-mover advantage equates to getting the market started around your unique approach and making the others play catch-up. It is a great strategy – when it works. The risk, of course, is that the market never goes forward to adopt the paradigm. At the time when the visionaries make their moves, this is a high probability. Visionaries are always bucking the odds in that most markets, like most mutations, die out before they can reproduce themselves sufficiently to gain persistence. Indeed, market creation is very much

like the origin of species in nature, with the early market equating to the emergence of at least a few vital representatives of the new order.

The key metric of competitive advantage at this stage is simply the existence of proof of having one or more such representatives. For the technology provider, the test is one or more major corporate commitments from prestigious customers who champion the new paradigm as a platform for change in their industries. For the customer, the test is whether on top of this new platform an industry-changing offer can be promulgated. Neither measure is financial. Neither measure uses market share. The goal in both cases is just to validate the category. That puts the new wave on the map, enters it in the race.

The benefit to the company sponsoring this new initiative is that it gets a lot of attention. This attracts prospective customers to it at no additional cost of marketing. It also positions it as something of a thought leader in its industry. At the same time, however, it starts a timer ticking, with the expectation that within some definable period dramatic results will appear. If they do not, then the customers lose face and the technology providers lose their company.

Value disciplines for the early market

In order to execute on a winning agenda, management teams must understand that the early market rewards discontinuous innovation and product leadership and penalizes customer intimacy and operational excellence. Thus optimal results are gained by elevating the former and suppressing the latter, as follows:

- Elevate discontinuous innovation and product leadership. The early market is driven by the demands of visionaries for offerings that create dramatic competitive advantages of the sort that would allow them to leapfrog over the other players in their industry. Only discontinuous innovation offers such advantage. In order to field that innovation, however, it must be transformed into a product offering that can be put to work in the real world. Hence the need for product leadership.

- Suppress customer intimacy and operational excellence. When technologies are this new, there are no target markets as yet and thus customer intimacy is not practical. Moreover, discontinuous innovations demand enormous customer tolerance and sacrifice as they get debugged, again not a time for celebrating putting the customer first. At the same time, because everything is so new and so much is yet to be discovered, it is equally impractical to target operational excellence. There is just too much new product, process and procedure to invent and then shake out before pursuing this value discipline would be reasonable. Instead, one has to make peace with the strategy 'Go ugly early.'

Looking at the above, it is not surprising that engineering-led organizations, who resonate with the value disciplines in favour, are much more successful at early-market initiatives than marketing-led or operations-led organizations, who lean toward the value disciplines that should be suppressed. Going forward, as we look at each subsequent phase of the life cycle, we will see that the rewarded and penalized disciplines change and so will the types of organizations that can be most successful.

Stage-two adoption: Crossing the chasm into the bowling alley

For technologies to gain persistent marketplace acceptance, they must cross the chasm and take up a position on the other side. Now we are in the realm of the pragmatists. To get pragmatists to move at all, companies must rethink their marketing objective from the early market. There the goal was to win a customer, and then another and another. To cross the chasm, however, you have to *win a herd*. Here's why:

- Pragmatists only feel comfortable moving in herds. That's why they ask for references and use word of mouth as their primary source of advice on technology purchase decisions. Selling individual pragmatists on acting ahead of the herd is possible but very painful, and the cost of sales more than eats up the margin in the sale itself.

- Pragmatists evaluate the entire value chain, not just the specific product offer, when buying into a new technology. Value chains form around herds, not individual customers. There has to be enough repeatable business in the pipeline to reward an investment in specializing in the new technology. Sporadic deals, regardless of how big they are, do not create persistent value chains.

The visible metric for crossing the chasm, therefore, is to *make a market* and *create a value chain* where there was no market and no value chain before. This is a difficult undertaking. To increase its chances for success, and to decrease the time it takes to achieve, it is best to focus the effort on creating a niche market first before trying to create a mass market. It is simply prudent to minimize the number of variables at risk.

Think of a niche market as a self-contained system of commerce with its own local set of specialized needs and wants. Isolated from the mainstream market, which does not serve these special needs, it offers a *value-chain incubator* for emerging technology-enabled markets. That is, its isolation protects the fragile new chain from direct competitive attacks from the incumbent value chain. The customer community, in effect, nurtures the fledgling enterprise because it hopes to gain great benefit from it.

Value-chain strategy

To visualize the changes in moving from the early market to the bowling alley, let us return to our value-chain diagram, this time focusing on a new set of market makers (see Figure 10.3.4).

At the right-hand end of the chain, the *managers* in the customer domain represent the pre-assembled herd, an aggregation of relatively homogeneous demand. These are the department managers in charge of a broken, mission-critical process, all huddled in a mass. At the other end, the *application provider* in the product domain offers a relatively homogeneous solution to this herd's problem. It will bring its solution to market through a sales and support organization where it is the *support function* that really counts. That is because at the outset of a market the remaining value-chain partners are just getting recruited and cannot be relied upon to assemble the whole product correctly on their own. Later on these same partners will compete to take over the support function – and the enlightened application provider will let them, as it will greatly expand its market and its reach – but for now it is all just too new. So the application provider's support team must take the lead in working through all the glitches until a working whole product is in place, even when the problem is with someone else's part of the offering and not their own.

Note that the money-recycling arrow has now been restored to the diagram. This is the whole point of the niche-market strategy. We are now creating for the first time a self-funding persistent market where the economic gains of the customer lead to increasing and ongoing investment in the products and services that bring them about. Even if no other market ever adopts this technology, it will still be economically viable to maintain this niche. To be sure, the returns will not be all that the investors hoped for, but it

FIGURE 10.3.4 Bowling alley value chain

will not be a total bust either. That is because niche markets have persistent competitive advantages that allow them to sustain themselves even when the marketplace in general is unsupportive of their efforts. Moreover, if the value chain extends its reach into additional niches, then it can add market growth to its already attractive price margins to produce highly attractive returns indeed.

The major beneficiaries of this strategy are the application providers. It is they who harness the new wave of technology to the specific needs of the target segment, and they who rally the rest of the value chain to support this effort. Because the application provider is the company that really does 'make the market', it gains a dominant market-specific competitive advantage during this market formation period. This advantage will persist indefinitely, even after the technology adoption life cycle goes forward, since once any market falls into a particular pecking order, it is loath to change.

Everyone else in the value chain – the core technology providers, the hardware and software product companies, the business consultants and the systems integrators, the customer service staff and even the client's own technical staff – all happily take a backseat. That's because they will all be operating primarily as cost-effective generalists, making relatively minor modifications to their way of doing business, whereas the application vendor, interacting intimately with the problem-owning department managers, must operate as a value-creating specialist and invest significantly to be able to do so effectively.

Competitive advantage in the bowling alley

The ability to harness the technology wave to solve the critical problem of one or more specific niche markets is what creates power at this stage, and that power goes primarily to the application provider. As more and more of the pragmatist department managers in the niches see their colleagues getting out of the soup, they, too, will come forward and insist on buying this vendor's application. Thus every other company in the value chain becomes dependent on that one vendor's good graces to get into the good deals. In effect, this creates a form of value-chain domination, but it is restricted solely to the niches served, and so it has very different properties – and a very different valuation – from the kind of broad horizontal-market domination we will see develop inside the tornado.

Because they reap the bulk of the rewards, it is relatively easy for application providers to understand and adopt niche marketing, especially if the alternative is to spend another year in the chasm. It is much more problematic, however, for a platform product or a transaction services company to embrace it. Their business plans are normally predicated on either broad horizontal adoption across a multitude of business segments or a broad cross-section of consumers. They are not well positioned to go after niche markets. Vertical industry domain expertise holds little value for them, and voluntarily subordinating themselves to an application vendor just to gain entry into one little niche seems like a huge price to pay. Moreover, even if the tactic proves successful, the resulting order stream will be relatively modest, and worse, may inappropriately cause the rest of the market to misperceive the company as a niche player. For all these very good reasons, platform-products and transaction services vendors tend to shy away from taking the niche approach to crossing the chasm. And yet it is still a mistake. Here's why.

As we shall see shortly, platform products are optimized for tornado markets, and transaction-services offers are optimized for Main Street markets. Those are the phases of the life cycle in which they will shine. So their strategy should be to accelerate technology adoption to get to 'their' phase as quickly as possible. Time spent in the chasm for either strategy represents a huge opportunity cost, giving their competitors a chance to catch up to first-mover advantage while making no progress for themselves at all. This makes exiting the chasm as quickly as possible their top strategic imperative – hence their need to perform the admittedly unnatural act of niche marketing. To be sure, it is a little bit like asking a caterpillar who has a stated goal to be a butterfly to first spin itself into a cocoon and melt – the intermediate step is so disconnected from the end result that it is hard to warrant taking it. But there is now sufficient history to show that not taking the step is fatal – as demonstrated by the market development failures of ISDN networking, object-oriented databases, IBM's OS/2 operating system, pen-based PCs, infrared connectivity protocols and artificial intelligence.

To be sure, once an initial niche market is established, the winning strategy for platform products and transaction services does indeed split off from the application providers. For the latter, the most powerful path forward is to stay in the bowling alley – this is their sweet spot – expanding niche to niche, following a bowling pin strategy. In this manner, such companies can chew their way through multiple markets with a very high probability of securing dominant positions in the majority of their niches. It is a 'bowling alley forever' strategy focused on *preserving complexity* in order to create a source of profit margins for themselves and their service partners. It ends up trading off massive scale in favour of locally dominant roles and eventually makes the transition to Main Street as a leader in a set of mature vertical markets.

By contrast, for platform-product and transaction-services companies, the goal should be to get beyond niches altogether as soon as possible. Their quest instead should be for a single, general-purpose 'killer app' – a word-processing program, a spreadsheet, e-mail, voice-mail, a Web site, an e-commerce

server – something that can be adopted by whole sectors of the economy all at once, thereby leveraging their horizontal business models' strength in being able to scale rapidly. But students of the life cycle should note that in the era prior to pervasive word processing, there were segment-specific solutions for lawyers, doctors, consultants and governmental functions. These were a critical stepping stone toward getting to a mass market.

Value disciplines for the bowling alley

To execute on a niche strategy in an emerging technology-enabled market, companies must realign their value discipline orientation to meet a new set of market priorities, as follows:

- Elevate product leadership and customer intimacy. The bowling alley is driven by the demands of pragmatists for a whole product that will fix a broken mission-critical business process. The fact that the process will not respond to conventional treatment calls out the need for product leadership. The fact that the required whole product will have to integrate elements specific to a particular vertical segment calls out the need for customer intimacy.

- Suppress discontinuous innovation and operational excellence. Pragmatist department managers under pressure to fix a broken process have neither the time nor the resources to support debugging a discontinuous innovation. At the same time, their need for special attention is incompatible with the kind of standardization needed for operational excellence.

Marketing-led organizations are best at crossing the chasm, specifically those that combine strong domain expertise in the targeted market segment with a solutions orientation. Operations-led organizations struggle with the amount of customization required that cannot be amortized across other segments, all of which offends their sense of efficiency. Engineering-led organizations struggle with the lack of product symmetry resulting from heavily privileging one niche's set of issues over a whole raft of other needed enhancements.

To win with this strategy, the critical success factor is focus – specifically, focus on doing whatever it takes to get that first herd of pragmatist customers to adopt en masse the new technology. Hedging one's bet by sponsoring forays targeted at additional herds at the same time is bad strategy. Both engineering- and operations-oriented organizations, however, are drawn to this approach because they fear that the company is putting all its eggs into one basket. Of course, that is precisely what it *is* doing. The reason it is good strategy to do so is that only by creating critical mass can one move a market and bring into existence a new value chain. Unless they can leverage tornado winds blowing in other markets, alternative initiatives subtract from the needed mass and, ironically, increase rather than decrease market risk.

Stage-three adoption: inside the tornado

A tornado occurs whenever pragmatists across a variety of market sectors all decide simultaneously that it is time to adopt a new paradigm – in other words, when the pragmatist herd stampedes. This creates a dramatic spike in demand, vastly exceeding the currently available supply, calling entire categories of vendors to reconfigure their offerings to meet the needs of a new value chain.

Value-chain strategy

The overriding market force that is shaping the tornado value chain is the desire for everyone in the market, beginning with the customer but quickly passing through to all vendors, to drive the transition to a new paradigm as quickly as possible. That calls to the fore the three constituencies highlighted in Figure 10.3.5. Each of these constituencies is well positioned to benefit from standardization for rapid deployment.

- In the product sphere, it is *products,* not technology and not applications, that get the privileged position. The problem with technology is that it is too

malleable to be mass-produced and thus does not lend itself to rapid proliferation of common, standard infrastructure. The problem with applications is that they must be customized to sector-specific processes, and so again they do not deploy as rapidly as desired. By contrast, products, and specifically those that serve as platforms for a broad range of applications, are the ideal engine for paradigm proliferation.

- Now, to be sure, there must be at least one application that warrants the purchase of the platform in the first place, but in a tornado that application must be essentially the same for every sector. Such an application is called 'the killer app', and it becomes the focus for horizontal expansion across multiple sectors of the economy. *Accounting* was the killer app for mainframes, *manufacturing automation* for minicomputers, *word processing* for PCs, *computer-aided design* for workstations and *electronic mail* for local area networks. But in every case, it was the platform product providers, not the killer app vendors, who were ultimately the big tornado winners because as other applications came online, they created still more demand for their platforms.

- In the services sphere, it is the sales and support function, with the emphasis on *sales*, that carries the day. The drawback with consulting is that its projects are too complex, take too long and require resources that are too scarce to ever permit a tornado to go forward. The drawback with customer service is that it is too focused on serving existing

FIGURE 10.3.5   Tornado value chain

customers at a time when the overwhelming emphasis has to be on acquiring new customers.

- Generating sales in the tornado is not a problem of winning over the customer so much as it is of beating the competition. It is critical, therefore, to field the most competitive sales force you can at this time. Because so much wealth is changing hands, and because the long-term consequences of market share are so great, tornado sales tactics are brutal and sales aggressiveness is the core discipline. This is the time when nice guys do finish last.

- On the support side, the key issue is to get new customers up and running on a minimal system as quickly as possible and then move on to the next new customer. The more cookie-cutter the process, the faster it replicates and the more new customers you can absorb. The push is for operational excellence, not customer intimacy. This is not a normal support profile, so once again focusing the team on the right value discipline is a critical executive responsibility.

- On the customer side of the value chain, it is the *technical buyer,* not the end-user departments and not the economic buyer, who becomes the key focus. The problem with end users is that they inevitably seek customization to meet their department-specific needs. Not only is such complexity contrary to the vendor's wishes, it also works against the host institution's imperative to roll out the new infrastructure to everyone in the company as quickly as possible. Such rapid deployment requires a one-size-fits-all approach for the initial roll-out, something that the technical buyer understands far better than the end user. It is also not the time to court senior executives in their role as economic buyers. Once the tornado is under way, they sense the need to get over to the new infrastructure and delegate the task, including the selection process, to their technical staff.

- When technical buyers become the target customer, their compelling reason to buy drives sales outcomes. High on their list is conformance to common standards, followed by market leadership status, which initially is signaled by partnerships with other market leaders, and later on confirmed by market share. The technical buyers' biggest challenge is systems integration, and this is where the support function can contribute to faster roll-outs by building standard interfaces to the most prevalent legacy systems.

The tornado, in essence, is one big land grab – a fierce struggle to capture as many new customers as possible during the pragmatist stampede to the new paradigm. Increasing shareholder value revolves entirely around maximizing market share, and to that end there are three sources of competitive-advantage leverage to exploit.

Competitive advantage in the tornado

The primary source of competitive advantage is simply to be riding the new technology wave as it enters into its tornado phase. Mass-market adoption is an awesome market creation force that wreaks havoc on installed bases rooted in old technology. As the incumbents retreat under the impact of this force to protect their increasingly conservative installed bases, your company advances with the new wave of adoption to occupy their lost ground. This is *category advantage* at work, and it alone will enhance your stock price – hence the scramble of every vendor in the sector to position themselves on the bandwagon of whatever this hot new category is.

The second element of competitive advantage derives from the potential institutionalization of key market-making companies as value-chain leaders or dominators. That is, for each element in the value chain, tornado markets seek out a single market leading provider to set the de facto standards for that component. That role normally goes to the company that garners the most new customers early in the race. In addition, when a single company can gain power over the rest of the value chain, typically by leveraging the power to withhold its proprietary technology and thereby stymie the entire offer, the market accords even more privilege to it.

The power of market-share leadership is rooted in the pragmatist preference to make the safe buy by going with the market leader. That is, rather than rely on their own judgement, pragmatists prefer to rely on the group's. Once that judgement has been made clear, once one vendor has emerged as the favourite, then pragmatists naturally gravitate to that choice, which of course further increases that company's market share, intensifying its gravitational attraction.

This cycle of positive feedback not only spontaneously generates market leaders, but once they are generated, works to keep them in place. That is, the value chain advantage a market leader gains over its direct competitors is that it has become the default choice for any other company in the chain to round out its offers.

Thus the company gains sales that it never initiated and gets invited into deals its competitors never see. Such sales not only add to revenues but to margins, since the absence of competition removes much of the pressure to discount price. In short, winning the market-share prize is a very sweet deal, which, if it is not working for you, is working against you. Hence the need to focus all guns on market share.

Thus the essence of tornado strategy is simply to capture the maximum number of customers in the minimum amount of time and to minimize all other efforts. At each moment the winning strategy is to strike and move on, strike and move on. Anything you can do to slow down a competitor along the way is gravy. What you must not do is voluntarily slow yourself down, not even for a customer. That is, during the tornado *customer acquisition* takes temporary priority over *customer satisfaction*. The entire pragmatist herd is switching from the old to the new – not a frequent event. As customers, in other words, they are temporarily 'up for grabs'. Once they choose their new vendor, they will be highly reluctant to consider changing yet again. So either you win these customers now, or you risk losing them *for the life of the paradigm.*

And then there is the super grand prize bonanza of tornado market development to which we have already alluded, namely, gaining *value-chain power over the other vendors in the value chain.* As noted, this occurs when a single vendor has monopoly control of a crucial element in the value chain, the way Microsoft and Intel each do for the personal computer, the way Cisco does for the Internet, the way Qualcomm appears to do for the future of wireless telephony. In such cases, as the market tornado unfolds, the standard whole product that forms around the killer app incorporates a piece of your proprietary technology. Going forward, for the value-chain offering as a whole to evolve, it must take your technology along with it – and there is no substitute for it. This makes everyone in the chain dependent upon you, which in turn allows you to orchestrate the behaviour of the rest of the chain. This can include pressuring value-chain partners to adopt or support some of your less successful products so that you gain power across a much broader portion of your product line than its actual features and benefits would normally merit.

Value disciplines for the tornado

Elevate product leadership and operational excellence. Whatever position one achieves during the tornado market depends largely on your company's ability to execute a market-share land-grab strategy. To this end, the market rewards a third alignment of value disciplines, as follows:

- Elevate product leadership and operational excellence. The tornado is driven by the demands of infrastructure buyers for standard, reliable offerings suitable for rapid mass deployment. Here product leadership gets translated into shipping the next release with the new set of features ahead of the competition and thereby grabbing additional market share from them. Operational excellence is critical to this effort because if there is any hiccup in the process, the market can still shift to an alternative vendor, with major market-share consequences that will last for the duration of the paradigm.

- Suppress discontinuous innovation and customer intimacy. Any form of discontinuous innovation during a tornado creates opportunity for error, putting rapid mass deployment at risk, and is thus anathema. Customer intimacy is also suppressed for the duration of the roll-out for the same reason, sacrificed to the end of achieving reliable, consistent deployment. Once the infrastructure is set in place, then there will be time to come back and meet customer-specific requests.

Operations-led organizations tend to have the edge in a tornado, where meeting deadlines, shipping in quantity and minimizing returns all take priority over innovation and customer delight. Marketing-led organizations, by contrast, typically flounder because they cannot bear to relinquish their commitment to customer intimacy and customer satisfaction. They need to realize that, in a tornado, just getting the new systems installed and working properly is grounds for customer satisfaction.

Stage-four adoption:
On Main Street

Main Street begins as the market-share frenzy that drives tornado winds subsides. The overwhelming bulk of the pragmatists in the market have chosen their vendor, made their initial purchases, and rolled out the first phase of a multiphase deployment. Only a fraction of the total forecastable sales in the segment has actually been made at this point, but from here on out the market-share boundaries are relatively fixed. This has significant implications for the value chain.

FIGURE 10.3.6   Main Street value chain

Value-chain strategy

Here is the fourth and final mutation in the value chain. This one will endure for the life of the paradigm. In effect, it is the value chain we have been setting up all along (see Figure 10.3.6).

There is a key change underlying this entire value chain, which is that the technology adoption life cycle as a whole has evolved from the pragmatist to the conservative agenda, and every constituency in the value chain is affected by this change. Let's start with the customer.

When companies adopt new paradigms, conservative customers at first hang back, preferring to eke out some last bit of value from the old system. But once it is clear that the new system must supplant the old one, then they seek to put their stamp on the new vendor relationship. They remind all these new arrivals that most of the promises that were made on behalf of their products and services are as yet far from true, and they work to keep everyone focused on making incremental improvements going forward. In effect, they transform what heretofore was a discontinuous innovation into what will from now on be a system of continuous innovation.

In mature – or maturing – markets, both the economic buyer and the technical buyer recede in importance. The economic buyer is no longer looking for competitive advantage or to support a manager in fixing a broken business process; now the issue is simply staying within budget, and that can be delegated.

And the technical buyer is no longer concerned about how to either manage or postpone the introduction of a disruptive technology; now the concern is simply to stay compliant with established standards, and that, too, can be delegated. Even within the user community, the managers are now taking the new systems for granted, assuming that it must be doing pretty much what it was bought to do (a naive, but all too frequent point of view). Thus it is only *end users,* the people who actually interact with the system on a frequent basis, that (a) know anything about how it really works, and (b) have a stake in sponsoring improvements to it.

If these end users do not voice their desires, then the offering becomes a complete commodity, with the purchasing department driving a *supplier relationship* going forward. If they do voice their desires, however, and gain their managers' approval, then end users can drive a *vendor relationship,* a condition that allows a company to earn margins above commodity levels. We are long past the time for customers to embrace you in a *strategic partner relationship,* something that is confined to earlier phases in the life cycle.

To earn preferred margins from end-user sponsorship, focus shifts to those aspects of the value chain that end users can directly experience. On the product side, this suppresses the importance of technology, platform products and even the core of the application. All these are still important, but they are more directly experienced by the technical buyer than the end user.

By contrast, any product element that is consumable, is highly user visible. It is here that minor enhancements for a modest increase in price can generate dramatic changes in gross profit margin, the way, for example, the cup holder has done in the automotive industry.

Lucrative as the accessories and consumables business is on Main Street, however, an even bigger opportunity lies in the product-service shift. What customers used to value and buy as products becomes reconceived as service offerings – shifting the burden of system maintenance from the customer back to the vendor. Thus the move from answering machine to voice-mail, from videotapes to pay-per-view, from bar bells to health clubs.

The primary organization tasked with masterminding this shift is *customer service*. Historically this has been a challenge because that organization was not constructed, nor were its personnel recruited with the thought that it would eventually become a lead contributor to the P&L and market valuation of the company. In the age of the Internet, however, investors are now actively pursuing companies that have been founded from day one with just such an agenda in mind.

Competitive advantage on Main Street

The technology wave has crested and broken and no longer provides market development leverage. The value chain is already formed, and whatever place you have in it is not going to change without massive and usually unwarranted investment. There is always the possibility of you finding an underserved market segment here or there, but the speed of market penetration now will be much slower, the impact on any local value chain much less, and thus the rewards more modest than they would have been during the bowling alley phase. And so it is that we get to the domain of company execution, to which we shall turn in a moment, and differentiated offerings.

There are classically two types of differentiation strategies that succeed on Main Street. The first is being the low-cost provider, a strategy that works best in commodity markets where it is not the end user but the purchasing manager acting as economic buyer who is the real decision maker. The other type is a customer-delight strategy, which works best in consumer markets or in business markets where the end user is permitted to behave as a consumer. The more a market matures, the more opportunity your company has to deliver on both of these propositions to be competitive. To do so it must gravitate toward a product or service deployment strategy called *mass customization*.

Mass customization separates any offering into a *surface* and a *substructure*. The surface is what the end user experiences. It is here that changes are made to enhance that experience. This is the *customization* portion of the offer. By contrast, the substructure is the necessary delivery vehicle for the entire performance, but it is not directly experienced by the end user. The goal here is to provide maximum reliability at the lowest possible cost, and the preferred tactic is to reduce variability and increase standardization to achieve high volume. This is the *mass* portion of the offer.

To combine the two without sacrificing the benefits of either, the customizing portion must often be done downstream in the value chain in a separate step from the mass portion. This typically leads to a need to redesign the value chain, creating new opportunities for service providers to create customization value at the point of customer contact. Think of how cell phones are provided, and you get the idea. Everything upstream from the retail outlet is totally standardized; everything downstream is customizable – the phone itself, its accessories, service options, program pricing, and the like. Prior to retail, everything is sold as a commodity; after retail, it is a value-added offering.

The implications of this restructuring of the market are far-reaching, and not just for service providers. Consumables have the same potential to deliver customized value. Consider, for example, the razor-to-razor-blade transition in Gillette's history, or Kodak's move from cameras to film, or HP's transition from inkjet printers to inkjet cartridges. In every case once Main Street is reached, it is the consumable at the surface, and not the underlying engine at the core, that becomes the basis of differentiation and the locus of high profit margins.

Alternatively, service transactions can also replace the serviced commodity as the locus of value creation. This has been the case in the automobile industry, where the bulk of the profits are made not from selling new cars but from financing the purchase, insuring the vehicle, supplying the consumables and providing the maintenance services. In every case margins are affected by the end user's experience during these transactions. That is why companies like Lexus have been so successful with their customer-care offers. It is also why traditional car dealerships are failing with their customer-unfriendly approach to purchase and financing, driving their customers to brokers and to the Web instead.

In large part the promise of the Internet is based on it being a universal platform for value-adding customization in Main Street value chains. The systems are not yet completely in place to fulfill this proposition today, but forward-thinking executives and enlightened investors can see how with incremental improvements they will be able to generate scalable, low-cost, high-touch offerings of the sort that create attractive profit margins on Main Street.

Value disciplines

To execute on this strategy of mass customization, companies as elsewhere in the life cycle must learn to elevate one pair of value disciplines and suppress the other:

- Elevate operational excellence and customer intimacy. Main Street markets are supported by conservative customers seeking incremental gains in value. These can be achieved either through decreasing the costs of the current set of offers – the domain of operational excellence – or by introducing a new set of offers improved through readily absorbed continuous innovations – the domain of customer intimacy.

- Suppress discontinuous innovation and product leadership. Discontinuous innovation runs directly contrary to the interests of Main Street customers and is simply not welcome. Even offers based on product leadership are problematic. If they require re-tooling the existing infrastructure, they usually just aren't worth it. What development teams must realize is that now product improvements should be focused either on keeping the core product viable, with operational excellence as a guide, or on making cosmetic changes at the surface, with customer intimacy providing the direction.

Of all the pairings, this particular set should be the most familiar to established companies in mature markets. They should see themselves as the champions of the first pair, and those wretched dotcoms assaulting their marketplace as the purveyors of the second. Note that in this pairing the established company's existing customers are very much on its side, not on the dotcoms'. That's because they, like the company itself, are ruled by conservative interests. It is instead the flock of new customers who are entering the tornado for the next big thing that are undermining this company's stock price going forward.

Implications of living on the fault line

The four market states are set out in a side-by-side comparison in Table 10.3.1. The table maps the working out of the competitive advantage hierarchy over the course of a technology-enabled market's development. The columns lay out the life-cycle phases these markets evolve through. The rows lay out the changes in focus that organizations must make to adapt to this evolution. The first row sets forth the layer in the competitive-advantage hierarchy that has the most impact during each phase. The next three rows highlight the value-chain elements that create the most impact during the phase because they are best suited to leveraging the type of competitive advantage available.

Even a cursory glance shows that the changes companies have to make in order to adapt to these forces are dramatic indeed. Moreover, the time allotted to make them is painfully short. As a result, it should surprise no one that few real-world organizations are very good at actually making them. Indeed, the larger and more successful a company becomes, the less likely it is to attempt making them at all.

TABLE 10.3.1   Comparison of market states

	Early market	*Bowling alley*	*Tornado*	*Main Street*
Primary competitive advantage	Catching technology wave	Market-segment domination	Market-share leadership	Differentiated offerings
Product focus	Technology	Applications	Platform products	Consumables
Service focus	Consulting	Support	Sales	Customer service
Customer focus	Economic buyer	Department manager	Technical buyer	End user

REFERENCES

Abernathy, W.J. and Utterback, J.M. (1978) 'Patterns of Industrial Innovation', *Technological Review*, 80(7 June–July), pp. 40–47.

Aldrich, H.E. (1999) *Organizations Evolving*, London: Sage.

Aldrich, H.E. and Fiol, C.M. (1994) 'Fools Rush In? The Institutional Context of Industry Creation', *Academy of Management Review*, 19(4), pp. 645–670.

Arthur, W.B. (1994) *Increasing Returns and Path Dependence in the Economy*, Ann Arbor, MI: University of Michigan Press.

Astley, W.G. and van der Ven, A.H. (1983) 'Central Perspectives and Debates in Organization Theory', *Administrative Science Quarterly*, 28(2, June), pp. 245–273.

Baden-Fuller, C.W.F. and Stopford, J.M. (1992) *Rejuvenating the Mature Business*, London: Routledge.

Bain, J.S. (1959) *Industrial Organizations*, New York: Wiley.

Bass, B.M. and Steidlmeier, P. (1999) 'Ethics, character, and authentic transformational leadership behavior', *The Leadership Quarterly*, 10(2), 181–217.

Baum, A.C. and Singh, J.V. (eds) (1994) *Evolutionary Dynamics of Organizations*, New York: Oxford University Press.

Bennis, W. (1989). *On Becoming a Leader*, New York: Addison-Wesley.

Bettis, R.A. and Donaldson, L. (1990) 'Market Discipline and the Discipline of Management', *Academy of Management Review*, 15(3, July), pp. 367–368.

Bower, J.L. and Christensen, C.M. (1995) 'Disruptive Technologies: Catching the Wave', *Harvard Business Review*, 73(1, January–February), pp. 43–53.

Bradley, F. (2005) *International Marketing Strategy*, Pearson Education.

Burgelman, R.A. and Grove, A.S. (1996) 'Strategic Dissonance', *California Management Review*, 38(2), pp. 106–131.

Carpenter, M.A. and Golden, B.R. (1997) 'Perceived Managerial Discretion: A Study of Cause and Effect', *Strategic Management Journal*, 18(3, March), pp. 187–206.

Chen, H., Zeng, S., Lin, H. and Ma, H. (2015) 'Munificence, Dynamism, and Complexity: How Industry Context Drives Corporate Sustainability', *Business Strategy and the Environment*, doi:10.1002/bse.1902

Child, J. (1972) 'Organizational Structure, Environment, and Performance: The Role of Strategic Choice', *Sociology*, January, pp. 2–22.

Christensen, C.M. (1997) *The Innovator's Dilemma*, New York: Harper Business.

Cox, D. and Harris, R. (1985) 'Trade liberalization and industrial organization: Some estimates for Canada', *Journal of Political Economy*, 93, pp. 115–145.

Coxe D.O., Ganot, I., Keller G. and McGahan, A.M. (1996) 'Passion for Learning', HBS 9-796-057.

Cromie, S. (2000) 'Assessing entrepreneurial inclinations: Some approaches and empirical evidence', *European Journal of Work and Organizational Psychology*, 9(1), 7–30.

Cusumano, M.A. and Gawer, A. (2002) 'The Elements of Platform Leadership', *Sloan Management Review*, 43(3, Spring), pp. 51–58.

D'Aveni, R.A. (1994) *Hypercompetition: Managing the Dynamics of Strategic Maneuvering*, New York: Free Press.

D'Aveni, R.A. (1999) 'Strategic Supremacy through Disruption and Dominance', *Sloan Management Review*, 40(3), pp. 127–135.

Dicken, P. (2011) *Global Shift, Mapping the Changing Contours of the World Economy*, New York: The Guilford Press.

Evans, P.B. and Wurster, T.S. (1997) 'Strategy and the New Economics of Information', *Harvard Business Review*, 76(5, September–October), pp. 71–82.

Foster, R. (1986) *Innovation: The Attacker's Advantage*, New York: Summit Books.

Frank, A.G. (1966) *The Development of Underdevelopment*. Monthly Review Press.

Friedman, T.L. (2005) *The World is Flat*, New York: Straus & Giroux.

Ghemawat, P. (1991) *Commitment: The Dynamic of Strategy*, New York: Free Press.

Greider, W. (1997) *One World, Ready or Not: The Manic Logic of Global Capitalism*, San Francisco: Jossey-Bass.

Hambrick, D.C. and Abrahamson, E. (1995) 'Assessing the Amount of Managerial Discretion in Different Industries: A Multi-Method Approach', *Academy of Management Journal*, 38(5, October), pp. 1427–1441.

Hamel, G. (1996) 'Strategy as Revolution', *Harvard Business Review*, 74(4, July–August), pp. 69–82.

Hamel, G. and Prahalad, C.K. (1994) *Competing for the Future*, Boston, MA: Harvard Business School Press.

Hampden-Turner, C. and Trompenaars, A. (1993) *The Seven Cultures of Capitalism: Value Systems for Creating Wealth in the United States, Japan, Germany, France, Britain, Sweden and the Netherlands*, New York: Doubleday.

Hampden-Turner, C. and Trompenaars, F. (2000) *Building Cross-Cultural Competence: How to Create Wealth from Conflicting Values*, New Haven, CT: Yale University Press.

Hannan, M.T. and Freeman, J. (1977) 'The Population Ecology of Organizations', *American Journal of Sociology*, 82(5, March), pp. 929–964.

Henderson, R.M. and Clark, K.B. (1990) 'Architectural Innovation: The Reconfiguration of Existing Product Technologies and the Failure of Established Firms', *Administrative Science Quarterly*, 35(March), pp. 9–30.

Hrebiniak, L.G. and Joyce, W.F. (1985) 'Organizational Adaptation: Strategic Choice and Environmental Determinism', *Administrative Science Quarterly*, 30(3, September), pp. 336–349.

Kim, W.C. and Mauborgne, R. (2004) 'Blue Ocean Strategy', *Harvard Business Review*. October.

Kim, W.C. and Mauborgne, R. (2005) 'Blue Ocean Strategy: From Theory to Practice', *California Management Review*, 47(3), pp. 105–121.

Kindleberger, A. (1962) *Foreign Trade and the National Economy*, New Haven, CT: Yale University Press.

Kotler, P. (1967) *Marketing Management: Analysis, Planning and Control*, Englewood Cliffs, NJ: Prentice-Hall.

Krugman, P. (1980) 'Scale Economies, Product Differentiation, and the Pattern of Trade', *The American Economic Review*, 70(5, December), pp. 950–959.

Krugman, P. (1985) 'International debt strategies in an uncertain World', in: G. Smith and J. Cuddington (eds) *International Debt and the Developing Countries*, Washington, DC: World Bank.

Lessem, R. and Neubauer, F.F. (1994) *European Management Systems*, London: McGraw-Hill.

Levenhagen, M., Porac, J.F. and Thomas, H. (1993) 'Emergent Industry Leadership and the Selling of Technological Visions: A Social Constructionist View', in: J. Hendry, G. Johnson and J. Newton (eds) *Strategic Thinking: Leadership and the Management of Change*, Chichester: Wiley.

Markides, C. (1999) *All the Right Moves: A Guide to Crafting Breakthrough Strategy*, Harvard Business School Press.

Markides, C.C. (2013) *Game-Changing Strategies: How to Create New Market Space in Established Industries by Breaking the Rules*, John Wiley & Sons.

McGahan, A. (2000) How Industries Evolve, *Business Strategy Review*, 11(3), pp. 1–16.

McGahan, A. and Porter, M.E. (1997) 'How Much Does Industry Matter, Really?', *Strategic Management Journal*, 18(S1), pp. 15–30.

Miller, D. (1990) *The Icarus Paradox: How Excellent Companies Bring About Their Own Downfall*, New York: Harper Business.

Miller, D., Kets de Vries, M. and Toulouse, J.M. (1982) 'Top Executive Locus of Control and its Relationship to Strategy-making, Structure and Environment', *Academy of Management Journal*, 25, pp. 237–253.

Moore, G.A. (2000) *Living on the Fault Line: Managing for Shareholder Value in the Age of the Internet*, New York: HarperBusiness.

Moore, J.F. (1996) *The Death of Competition: Leadership & Strategy in the Age of Business Ecosystems*, New York: Harper Business.

Morris, I. (2010) *Why The West Rules For Now, The Patterns of History and What They Reveal About the Future*, London: Profile Books.

Nelson, R.R. and Winter, S.G. (1982) *An Evolutionary Theory of Economic Change*, Reading, MA: Harvard University Press.

Oliver, C. (1997) 'Sustainable Competitive Advantage: Combining Institutional and Resource-based Views', *Strategic Management Journal*, 18(9, October), pp. 697–713.

Olson-Buchanan, J.B., Bryan, L.L.K. and Thompson, L.F. (2013) *Using Industrial-Organizational Psychology for the Greater Good: Helping Those Who Help Others*. Routledge.

Parolini, C. (1999) *The Value Net*, Chichester: Wiley.

Porter, M.E. (1980) *Competitive Strategy: Techniques for Analyzing Industries and Competitors*, New York: Free Press.

Porter, M.E. (1985) *Competitive Advantage: Creating and Sustaining Superior Performance*, New York: Free Press.

Porter, M.E. (1990) *The Competitive Advantage of Nations*, New York: Free Press.

Porter, M.E. (2001) 'Strategy and the Internet', *Harvard Business Review*, 80(3, March), pp. 62–78.

Prahalad, C.K. and Doz, Y.L. (1987) *The Multinational Mission: Balancing Local Demands and Global Vision*, New York: Free Press.

Prebisch, R. (1950) *The Economic Development of Latin America and Its Principal Problems*, New York: United Nations.

Ricardo, D. (1817) *On the Principles of Political Economy and Taxation*, London: John Murray.

Rugman, A.M. and Verbeke (1993) 'The Double Diamond Model of International Competitiveness: The Canadian Experience', *Management International Review*, 33(Special Issue), pp. 17–39.

Rumelt, R. (1991) 'How Much Does Industry Matter?', *Strategic Management Journal*, 12(3, March), pp. 167–186.

Shapiro, C.E. and Varian, H.R. (1998) *Information Rules*, Boston, MA: Harvard Business School Press.

Slywotsky, A.J. (1996) *Value Migration*, Boston, MA: Harvard Business School Press.

Smith, A. (1776) *An Inquiry into the Nature and Causes of the Wealth of Nations*, London: printed for W. Strahan and T. Cadell, in the Strand.

Smith, A. and Venables, J. (1988) 'Completing the Internal Market in the European Community: Some Industry Simulations', *European Economic Review*, 32(7, September), pp. 1501–1525.

Spender, J.C. (1989) *Industry Recipe: An Enquiry into the Nature and Sources of Managerial Judgement*, New York: Basil Blackwell.

Teece, D.J. (2007) 'Explicating Dynamic Capabilities: The Nature and Microfoundations of (Sustainable) Enterprise Performance', *Strategic Management Journal*, 28(13), pp. 1319–1350.

Teece, D.J., Pisano, G. and Shuen, A. (1997) 'Dynamic Capabilities and Strategic Management', *Strategic Management Journal*, 18(7), pp. 509–533.

Tirole, J. (1988) *The Theory of Industrial Organization*, Cambridge, MA: MIT Press.

Trompenaars, F. and Hampden-Turner, C. (2000) *Building Cross-Cultural Competence*, New Haven, CT: Yale University Press.

Vernon, R. (1966) 'International Investment and International Trade in the Product Cycle', *The Quarterly Journal of Economics*, 80(2), pp. 190–207.

Wallerstein, I. (1974) *The Modern World-System, Vol. I: Capitalist Agriculture and the Origins of the European World-Economy in the Sixteenth Century*, New York/London: Academic Press.

Whitley, R.D. (1999) *Divergent Capitalisms: The Social Structuring and Change of Business Systems*, Oxford: Oxford University Press.

Wilson, D.C. (1992) *A Strategy of Change*, London: Routledge.

THE ORGANIZATIONAL CONTEXT

We shape our environments, then our environments shape us.

Winston Churchill (1874–1965); British statesman and writer

INTRODUCTION

In organizations, just as in families, each new generation does not start from scratch but inherits properties of their predecessors. In families, a part of this inheritance is in the form of genetic properties, but other attributes are also passed down such as family traditions, myths, habits, connections, feuds, titles and possessions. People might think of themselves as unique individuals, but to some degree they are an extension of the family line, and their behaviour is influenced by this inheritance. In firms the same phenomenon is observable. New top managers may arrive on the scene, but they inherit a great deal from the previous generation. They inherit traditions and myths in the form of an organizational culture. Habits are passed along in the form of established organizational processes, while internal and external relationships and rivalries shape the political constellation in which new managers must function. They are also handed the family jewels – brands, competencies and other key resources.

In Chapter 8, it is pointed out that such inheritance is often the source of organizational rigidity and inertia (e.g. Hannan and Freeman, 1977; Rumelt, 1995). Inheritance limits 'organizational plasticity' – the capacity of the organization to change shape. As such, organizational inheritance can partially predetermine a firm's future path of development – which is referred to as path dependency, or sometimes simply summed up as 'history matters' (e.g. Aldrich, 1999; Nelson and Winter, 1982). Therefore, it was concluded that for strategic alignment to take place, some inherited characteristics could be preserved, but others needed to be changed, by either evolutionary or revolutionary means.

What is not discussed in Chapter 8 is *who* should trigger the required strategic changes. Who should initiate adaptations to the firm's business model and who should take steps to reshape the organizational system? Typically, managers have some role to play in all developments in the organizational context, but the question is what role? It is unlikely that any manager will have complete influence over all organizational developments, or would even want to exert absolute control. Inheritance and other organizational factors limit 'organizational malleability' – the capacity of the organization to be shaped by someone. As such, managers need to determine what power they have and where this power should be applied to achieve the best results. At the same time, managers will generally also look for opportunities to tap into the capabilities of other people in the firm to contribute to ongoing organizational adaptation.

So, the question can be summarized as: 'What is the role of managers in achieving a new alignment with the environment and what input can be garnered from other organizational members?' This question is also referred to as the issue of organizational development and is the central topic of further discussion in this chapter.

THE ISSUE OF ORGANIZATIONAL DEVELOPMENT

When it comes to realizing organizational development, managers generally acknowledge that they have some type of leadership role to play. Leadership refers to the act of influencing the views and behaviours of organizational members with the intention of accomplishing a particular organizational aim (e.g. Bass, 1990; Selznick, 1957). Stated differently, leadership is the act of getting organizational members to follow. From this definition it can be concluded that not all managers are necessarily leaders, and not all leaders are necessarily managers. Managers are individuals with a formal position in the organizational hierarchy, with associated authority and responsibilities. Leaders are individuals who have the ability to sway other people in the organization to get something done.

To be able to lead organizational developments, managers need power: the capability to influence. They also need to know how to get power, and how and where to exert it. In the following sections, these three topics are examined in more detail. First, the sources of leadership influence are described, followed by the levers of leadership influence. Finally, the arenas of leadership influence are explored.

Sources of leadership influence

To lead means to use power to influence others. Leaders can derive their potential influence from two general sources – their position and their person (Etzioni, 1961). 'Position power' comes from a leader's formal function in the organization. 'Personal power' is rooted in the specific character, knowledge, skills and relationships of the leader. Managers always have some level of position power, but they do not necessarily have the personal power needed to get organizational members to follow them. These two main types of power can be further subdivided into the following categories (French and Raven, 1959):

- Legitimate power. Legitimate power exists when a person has the formal authority to determine certain organizational behaviours and other employees agree to comply with this situation. Examples of legitimate power are the authority to assign work, spend money and demand information.

- Coercive power. People have coercive power when they have the capability to punish or withhold rewards to achieve compliance. Examples of coercive power include giving a poor performance review, withholding a bonus and dismissing employees.

- Reward power. Reward power is derived from the ability to offer something of value to a person in return for compliance. Examples of reward power include giving praise, awarding wage raises and promoting employees.

- Expert power. Expert power exists when organizational members are willing to comply because of a person's superior knowledge or skills in an important area. Such expert power can be based on specific knowledge of functional areas (e.g. marketing, finance), technologies (e.g. pharmaceuticals, information technology), geographic areas (e.g. South-East Asia, Florida) or businesses (e.g. mining, automotive).

- Referent power. When organizational members let themselves be influenced by a person's charismatic appeal, this is called referent power. This personal attraction can be based on many attributes, such as likeableness, forcefulness, persuasiveness, visionary qualities and image of success.

The first three types of power are largely determined by the organizational position of leaders and their willingness to exert them – coercive and reward capabilities without the credibility of use are not a viable source of power. The last two sources of power, expert and referent power, are largely personal in nature and therefore more subjective. Whether someone is seen as an expert, and therefore accorded a certain level of respect and influence, depends strongly on the perceptions of the people being led. Expert power can be made more tangible by wearing a white lab coat, putting three pens in your breast pocket or writing a book, but still perceived expertise will be in the eyes of the beholder. The same is true for referent power, as people do not find the same characteristics equally charismatic. What is forceful to one follower might seem pushy to someone else; what is visionary to one person might sound like the murmurings of a madman to others (e.g. Klein and House, 1998; Waldman and Yammarino, 1999).

In practice, leaders will employ a mix of all five types of power to achieve the influence they desire. However, leadership styles can differ greatly depending on the relative weight placed on the various sources of power within the mix.

Levers of leadership influence

The sources of power available to the leader need to be used to have influence. There are three generic ways for leaders to seek influence, each focused on a different point in the activities of the people being influenced. These levers of leadership influence are:

- Throughput control. Leaders can focus their attention directly at the actions being taken by others in the organization. Throughput control implies getting involved hands-on in the activities of others, either by suggesting ways of working, engaging in a discussion on how things should be done, leading by example or simply by telling others what to do. This form of direct influence does require sufficiently detailed knowledge about the activities of others to be able to point out what should be done.

- Output control. Instead of directly supervising how things should be done, leaders can set objectives that should be met. Output control implies reaching agreement on certain performance targets and then monitoring how well they are being lived up to. The targets can be quantitative or qualitative, financial or strategic, simple or complex, realistic or stretch-oriented. And they can be arrived at by mutual consent or imposed by the leader. The very act of setting objectives can have an important influence on people in the organization, but the ability to check ongoing performance and to link results with punishment and rewards can further improve a person's impact.

- Input control. Leaders can also choose to influence the general conditions under which activities are carried out. Input control implies shaping the circumstances preceding and surrounding the actual work. Before activities start a leader can influence who is assigned to a task, which teams are formed, who is hired, where they will work and in what type of environment. During the execution of activities the leader can supply physical and financial resources, mobilize relationships and provide support. Not unimportantly, the leader can also be a source of enthusiasm, inspiration, ambition, vision and mission.

Of these three, throughput control is the most direct in its impact and input control the least. However, throughput control offers the lowest leverage and input control the highest, allowing a leader to influence many people over a longer period of time, while leaving more room for organizational members to take on their own responsibilities as well. In practice, leaders can combine elements of all three of the above, although leadership styles differ greatly with regard to the specific mix.

Arenas of leadership influence

As leaders attempt to guide organizational development, there are three main organizational arenas where they need to direct their influence to achieve strategic changes. These three overlapping arenas are the parts in the organization most resistant to change – they are the subsystems of the firm where organizational inheritance creates its own momentum, resisting a shift into another direction (e.g. Miller and Friesen, 1980; Tushman, Newman and Romanelli, 1986):

■ The political arena. While most top managers have considerable position power with which they can try to influence the strategic decision-making process within their organization, very few top managers can impose their strategic agenda on the organization without building widespread political support. Even the most autocratic CEO will need to gain the commitment and compliance of key figures within the organization to be able to successfully push through significant changes. In practice, however, there are not many organizations where the 'officers and the troops' unquestioningly follow the general into battle. Usually, power is more dispersed throughout organizations, with different people and units having different ideas and interests, as well as the assertiveness to pursue their own agenda. Ironically, the more leaders that are developed throughout the organization, the more complex it becomes for any one leader to get the entire organization to follow – broad leadership can easily become fragmented leadership, with a host of strong people all pointing in different directions. For top management to gain control of the organization, they must build coalitions of supporters, not only to get favourable strategic decisions made, but also to ensure acceptance and compliance during the period of implementation. Otherwise strategic plans will be half-heartedly executed, opposed or silently sabotaged. However, gaining the necessary political support in the organization can be very difficult if the strategic views and interests of powerful individuals and departments differ significantly. Cultural and personality clashes can add to the complexity. Yet, top managers cannot recoil from the political arena, for it is here that new strategic directions are set (e.g. Allison, 1969; Pfeffer, 1992).

■ The cultural arena. Intertwined with the process of gaining political influence in the organization, there is the process of gaining cultural influence. After all, to be able to change the organization, a leader must be able to change people's beliefs and associated behavioural patterns. Yet, affecting cultural change is far from simple. A leader must be capable of questioning the shared values, ideas and habits prevalent in the organization, even though the leader has usually been immersed in the very same culture for years. Leaders must also offer an alternative worldview and set of behaviours to supersede the old. All of this requires exceptional skills as visionary – to develop a new image of a desired future state for the firm – and as missionary – to develop a new set of beliefs and values to guide the firm. Furthermore, the leader needs to be an excellent teacher to engage the organizational members in a learning process to adapt their beliefs, values and norms to the new circumstances. In practice, this means that leaders often have to 'sell' their view of the new culture, using a mix of rational persuasion, inspirational appeal, symbolic actions, motivational incentives and subtle pressure (e.g. Ireland and Hitt, 1999; Senge, 1990, Reading 8.2).

■ The psychological arena. While leaders need to influence the political process and the cultural identity of the organization, attention also needs to be paid to the psychological needs of individuals. To affect organizational change, leaders must win both the hearts and minds of the members of the organization. People must be willing to, literally, 'follow the leader' – preferably not passively, but actively, with commitment, courage and even passion (e.g. Bennis and Nanus, 1985; Kelley, 1988). To achieve such 'followership', leaders must gain the respect and trust of their colleagues. Another important factor in winning people over is the ability to meet their emotional need for certainty, clarity and continuity, to offset the uncertainties, ambiguities and discontinuities surrounding them (e.g. Argyris, 1990; Pfeffer and Sutton, 1999).

Even where political, cultural and psychological processes make the organization difficult to lead, managers might still be able to gain a certain level of control over their organizations. Yet, there will always remain aspects of the organizational system that managers cannot control, and should not even want to control, which are discussed in the following section.

THE PARADOX OF CONTROL AND CHAOS

Of all men's miseries the bitterest is this, to know so much and to have control over nothing.

Herodotus (5th century BC); Greek historian

In general, managers like to be in control. Managers like to be able to shape their own future, and by extension, to shape the future of their firm. Managers do not shy away from power – they build their power base to be able to influence events and steer the development of their organization. In short, to be a manager is to have the desire to be in charge.

Yet, at the same time, most managers understand that their firms do not resemble machines, where one person can sit at the control panel and steer the entire system. Organizations are complex social systems, populated by numerous self-thinking human beings, each with their own feelings, ideas and interests. These people need to decide and act for themselves on a daily basis, without the direct intervention of the manager. They must be empowered to weigh situations, take initiatives, solve problems and grab opportunities. They must be given a certain measure of autonomy to experiment, do things differently and even constructively disagree with the manager. In other words, managers must also be willing to 'let go' of some control for the organization to function at its best.

Moreover, managers must accept that in a complex system, like an organization, trying to control everything would be a futile endeavour. With so many people and so many interactions going on in a firm, any attempt to run the entire system top-down would be an impossible task. Therefore, letting go of some control is a pure necessity for normal organizational functioning.

This duality of wanting to control the development of the organization, while understanding that letting go of control is often beneficial, is the key strategic tension when dealing with the organizational context. On the one hand, managers must be willing to act as benevolent 'philosopher kings', autocratically imposing on the company what they consider to be best. On the other hand, managers must be willing to act as constitutional monarchs, democratically empowering organizational citizens to take their own responsibilities and behave more like entrepreneurs. The strategic paradox arises from the fact that the need for top-down *imposition* and bottom-up *initiative* are conflicting demands that are difficult for managers to meet at the same time.

On one side of this strategy paradox is 'control', which can be defined as the power to direct and impose order. On the other side of the paradox is the need for 'chaos', which can be defined as disorder or the lack of fixed organization. The paradox of control and chaos is a recurrent theme in the literature on strategy, organization, leadership and governance.

In most writings the need for control is presented as a pressure for a directive leadership style or an autocratic governance system (e.g. Tannenbaum and Schmidt, 1958; Vroom and Jago, 1988). The need for chaos is presented as a pressure for a participative leadership style and/or a democratic governance system (e.g. Ackoff, 1980; Stacey, 1992). In the following subsections both control and chaos are further examined.

The demand for top management control

As Herodotus remarked, it would be bitter indeed to have control over nothing. Not only would it be a misery for the frustrated managers, who would be little more than mere administrators or caretakers, it would also be a misery for their organizations, which would need to constantly adjust course without a helmsman to guide the ship. Managers cannot afford to let their organizations drift on the existing momentum. It is a manager's task and responsibility to ensure that the organization changes in accordance with the environment, so that the organizational purpose can still be achieved.

Top management cannot realize this objective without some level of control. They need to be able to direct developments in the organization. They need to have the power to make the necessary changes in the organizational structure, processes and culture, to realign the organization with the demands of the environment. This power, whether positional or personal, needs to be applied towards gaining sufficient support in the political arena, challenging existing beliefs and behaviours in the cultural arena, and winning the hearts and minds of the organizational members in the psychological arena.

The control that top management needs is different from the day-to-day control built in to the organizational structure and processes – they need *strategic control* as opposed to *operational control*. While operational control gives managers influence over activities within the current organizational system, strategic control gives managers influence over changes to the organizational system itself (e.g. Goold and Quinn, 1990; Simons, 1994). It is this power that managers require to be able to steer the development of their organization.

The demand for organizational chaos

To managers the term 'chaos' sounds quite menacing – it carries connotations of rampant anarchy, total pandemonium and a hopeless mess. Yet, chaos only means disorder, coming from the Greek term for the unformed original state of the universe. In the organizational context, chaos refers to situations of disorder, where phenomena have not yet been organized, or where parts of an organizational system have become 'unfrozen'. In other words, something is chaotic if it is unformed or has become 'disorganized'.

While this still does not sound particularly appealing to most managers, it should, because a period of disorganization is often a prerequisite for strategic renewal. Unfreezing existing structures, processes, routines and beliefs, and opening people up to different possibilities might be inefficient in the short run, as well as making people feel uncomfortable, but it is usually necessary to provoke creativity and to invent new ways of seeing and doing things. By allowing experimentation, skunk works, pilot projects and out-of-the-ordinary initiatives, managers accept a certain amount of disorder in the organization, which they hope will pay off in terms of organizational innovations.

But the most appealing effect of chaos is that it encourages 'self-organization'. To illustrate this phenomenon, one should first think back to the old Soviet 'command economy', which was based on the principle of control. It was believed that a rational, centrally planned economic system, with strong top-down leadership, would be the most efficient and effective way to organize industrial development. In the West, on the other hand, the 'market economy' was chaotic – no one was in control or could impose order. Everyone could go ahead and start a company. They could set their own production levels and even set their own prices! As entrepreneurs made use of the freedom offered to them, the economy 'self-organized' bottom-up. Instead of the 'visible hand' of the central planner controlling and regulating the economy, it was the 'invisible hand' of the market that created relative order out of chaos.

As the market economy example illustrates, chaos does not necessarily lead to pandemonium, but can result in a self-regulating interplay of forces. A lack of top-down control frees the way for a rich diversity of bottom-up ventures. Managers who also want to release the energy, creativity and entrepreneurial potential pent up in their organizations must therefore be willing to let go and allow some chaos to exist. In this context, the role of top management is comparable to that of governments in market economies – creating suitable conditions, encouraging activities and enforcing basic rules.

EXHIBIT 11.1   SHORT CASE

GAZPROM: BUILT TO DREAM

Although the slogan *mechty sbyvayutsya* or 'dreams come true' will probably not be familiar to most, the owner of the motto most likely is. The open joint-stock company Gazprom is Russia's national champion and one of the world's largest energy companies. It has over 270 000 employees, its latest shareholder count exceeds 461 600 and with a length of 171 200 kilometres of pipelines in Russia alone it could wrap the globe more than four times. Its core business consists of geological exploration, production, transportation and storage processing of hydrocarbons, as well as generating heat and electric power. Gazprom equals big business, with the company accounting for about 8 per cent of Russia's GDP and generating about one-fifth of the Russian government's revenues. In others words: if Gazprom suffers, Russia does as well.

Gazprom was an offshoot of the Soviet Gas Ministry, created by Viktor Chernomyrdin, the last Soviet Minister of Gas Industry, in 1989. This young professional made an enterprise association that was granted special privileges, such as favourable taxes and a full monopoly over the foreign trade in piped gas. For years the state corporate enterprise enjoyed sky-high gas prices with a net profit of US$25 billion in 2007. No matter what difficulties came across the company's path, it could always, as Natalia Volchkova of the New Economic School in Moscow phrased it, "drown it with money". In May 2008, Gazprom's market capitalization peaked at US$350 billion, making it the third most valuable company in the world. Investment banks and energy consultants foresaw a dazzling future and its officials predicted that the giant would become the biggest in the world, worth US$1 trillion.

Unfortunately for Gazprom, all good things eventually come to an end. The global financial crisis hit oil prices in 2009, which resulted in Gazprom's production plummeting by about 16 per cent. The company not only suffered a decline in revenues, structural management problems also showed their face. With financial crises proven to bring structural weaknesses to light, Russia's national champion seemed no exception to the rule.

Because of recent events, Gazprom faces several challenges, with its reliability as a supplier being one of them. Whereas Gazprom considers itself a trustworthy gas supplier to Russia and foreign countries, its purchasers tend to see this differently. Few need to be reminded of the trick it pulled with Ukraine by cutting off gas in 2006, leaving 16 other European countries in the cold. The conflict in eastern Ukraine from 2014 effectively reduced Gazprom's exports to Ukraine from 36 billion cubic metres in 2010 to zero on 1 July 2015. The energy blockade against Kiev ultimately failed, but it pushed European customers into further diversifying their energy imports. The unreliable gas supply makes Gazprom's consumers eager for alternative routes to meet their demands.

And these exist. Normally a warned man counts for two, but CEO Alexei Miller clearly underestimated the development of shale gas in North America by calling it a 'myth' and 'shale fever' in 2010. Shale gas production in Europe is off to a slow start; nevertheless, it offers an affordable alternative to Russian gas. Furthermore, Norway manages to further exploit its oil reserves. In fact, in the winter of 2014 Norway overtook Russia as Western Europe's top gas supplier. In addition, Gazprom not only has to deal with more pressure in the European market, it is challenged by fierce competition in the domestic market as well. Unlike Gazprom, independent producers are now capable of selling gas volumes with high profits.

Gazprom is not only losing ground, but faces more problems with less money at the same time. If it wants to remain a global player, drowning obstacles with money will not be an option any more. An answer seems to lie in one particular area: Gazprom's management. During the last couple of years, its corporate governance has been criticized for being incompetent, bureaucratic, inert and mismanaged. When bearing Russia's history in mind, this summary does not come as a total surprise. During the Soviet regime, Joseph Stalin introduced the concept of the 'command economy', with planned and centralized production replacing a free market. The corporate governance of the current Gazprom illustrates that shaking off the past is more easily said than done.

When looking at the enterprise's structure, one might say it resembles an authoritarian system. Gazprom's holding group is comprised of the parent company OAO Gazprom and its seven subsidiaries engaged in gas processing, oil, transmission, power industry, ancillary activities, marketing and gas exploration, exploitation and distribution. The Chairman of Gazprom Group forms the broad policy for the CEO and his directors to execute. The CEO is next in line of command, followed by the board of directors that execute the chairman's policy by passing this through to the company's various departments. The responsibility of managers is to ensure the observance of the decisions taken by the board of directors, who can thus be called foot soldiers, rather than leaders.

For Alexei Miller, Gazprom's current head, there was no need to choose between the two top positions; he became Gazprom's chairman as well as its CEO. Although decision making within Gazprom is controlled and centralized by top-down focused management, he is not in total control of the company. The Russian government possesses over 50 per cent of Gazprom's shares, making it the most powerful shareholder and thus allowing it to exert pressure while also ensuring a certain degree of command.

Whether Miller is actually in control, is becoming an increasingly poignant question, however. Gazprom seems to increasingly be one of Putin's most favoured geopolitical instruments. In 2015, the Kremlin decided to block energy to Ukraine during the conflict in the eastern part of that country, effectively reducing Gazprom's exports to Ukraine from 36 billion cubic metres in 2010 to zero on 1 July 2015. While the energy blockade against Kiev ultimately failed, it did cost Gazprom about US$6 billion in lost revenues. In addition, the Putin administration pushed the company into purchasing major media outlets, sponsoring the expensive Sochi Olympic Games and embarking on big projects.

One of these is the grand Power of Siberia project, a 4000 km pipeline through East Siberia to the Russian Pacific Coast. Although a project accompanied by a US$46 billion bill can be called rather pricey, even for companies Gazprom's size, government support makes it feasible. Power of Siberia is able to create a valuable opportunity for the company as it could lessen the dependence of Gazprom on European markets, especially with talks on connecting the project with the extensive Chinese market in the pipeline. In this case, Gazprom might actually profit from its bureaucratic, state-centred position, since no commercial company would ever attempt or accomplish something like this.

Nevertheless, the idea that a rational and centralized system would be the most efficient and effective way to organize Gazprom has not fully proven itself. The Gazprom management did not truly understand the severity of recent economic changes, with it calling the decline in gas demand a 'temporary inconvenience'. Therefore, the top-down leadership within Gazprom seems unfit at adapting to changes on the global stage. Perhaps when managers, as opposed to external shareholders, are given more control, they can allow for more internal organizational freedom to stimulate self-regulating departments.

On the other hand: is it advisable for Gazprom to adapt to the industry and is it realistic to expect Gazprom's customers' stance to change in the upcoming years even if Miller changes his management? Though his top-down focused organization has proven to inherit flaws, one can argue that Gazprom is actually in need of strict control in order to successfully compete in the oil and gas industry, especially in Russia. In order to best preserve its monopoly, playing it hard seems like a logical option, something that can best be accomplished with a more autocratic company.

With a changing oil and gas industry, decreasing revenues and increasing competition, something needs to change. Disorganizing the extremely organized company and disconnecting it more from the Russian state might help accomplish strategic renewal and herewith better adapt itself to the industry. Yet, keeping management control exclusive to the top provides Gazprom with merits as well, with a large company demanding a certain level of control. And that is without even considering the difficulty tinkering with Gazprom's management would bring. While both options embody disadvantages as well, making the right decision is definitely challenging. It is up to Miller to decide, but what choice can ultimately make Gazprom's dreams come true?

Co-authors: Larissa Kalle and Wester Wagenaar

Sources: www.gazprom.com; Åslund (2010); *Economist*, 23 March 2013; *EurasiaNet*, 3 August 2015; *Financial Times*, 5 June 2013 and 17 June 2013; *Forbes*, 2 June 2005.

PERSPECTIVES ON THE ORGANIZATIONAL CONTEXT

I claim not to have controlled events, but confess plainly that events have controlled me.

Abraham Lincoln (1809–1865); American president

While the pressures for both control and chaos are clear, this does leave managers with the challenging question of how they must reconcile two opposite, and at least partially incompatible, demands. Gaining a considerable level of top management control over the development of the organization will to some extent be at odds with a policy of accepting, or even encouraging, organizational chaos. To control or not to control, that is the question.

And yet again managers should not hope to find widespread consensus in the strategic management literature on what the optimal answer is for dealing with these two conflicting pressures. For among strategy academics and business practitioners alike, opinions differ strongly with regard to the best balance between control and chaos. Although many writers do indicate that there may be different styles in dealing with the paradox and that these different styles might be more effective under different circumstances (e.g. Strebel, 1994; Vroom and Jago, 1988), most authors still exhibit a strong preference for a particular approach – which is duly called the 'modern' or 'new' style, or better yet, '21st Century practices' (Ireland and Hitt, 1999).

Following the dialectical enquiry method used in previous chapters, here the two diametrically opposed positions are identified and discussed. On the one hand, there are those who argue that top managers should lead from the front. Top managers should dare to take on the responsibility of imposing a new strategic agenda on the organization and should be at the forefront in breaking away from organizational inheritance where necessary. This point of view, with its strong emphasis on control and leading top-down, is referred to as the 'organizational leadership perspective'. This view is also known as the strategic leadership perspective (e.g. Cannella and Monroe, 1997; Rowe, 2001), but to avoid confusion with the industry leadership perspective discussed in Chapter 10, here the prefix 'organizational' is preferred. On the other hand, there are people who believe that managers rarely have the ability to shape their organizations at will, but rather that organizations develop according to their own dynamics. These strategists argue that in most organizations no one is really in control and that managers should not focus their energy on attempting to impose developments top-down, but rather focus on facilitating processes of self-organization. This point of view, with its strong emphasis on chaos and facilitating bottom-up processes, is referred to as the 'organizational dynamics perspective'.

The organizational leadership perspective

 To proponents of the organizational leadership perspective, top management can – and should – take charge of the organization. In their view, organizational inertia and a growing misfit between the organization and its environment are not an inevitable state of affairs, but result from a failure of leadership. Bureaucracy, organizational fiefdoms, hostile relationships, inflexible corporate cultures, rigid competencies and resistance to change – all of these organizational diseases exist, but they are not unavoidable facts of organizational life. 'Healthy' organizations guard against falling prey to such degenerative illnesses, and when symptoms do arise it is a task of the leader to address them. If organizations do go 'out of control', it is because weak leadership has failed to deal with a creeping ailment. The fact that there are many sick, poorly controlled companies does not mean that sickness should be accepted as the natural condition.

At the basis of the organizational leadership perspective lies the belief that if people in organizations are left to 'sort things out' by themselves, this will inevitably degenerate into a situation of strategic drift (see Chapter 8). Without somebody to quell political infighting, set a clear strategic direction, force through tough decisions and supervise disciplined implementation, the organization will get bogged down in protracted internal bickering. Without somebody to champion a new vision, rally the troops and lead from the front, the organization will never get its heavy mass in motion. Without somebody who radiates confidence and cajoles people into action, the organization will not be able to overcome its risk averseness and conservatism. In short, leaders are needed to counteract the inherent inertia characteristic of human organization.

As organizational order and direction do not happen spontaneously, the 'visible hand' of management is indispensable for the proper functioning of the organization (e.g. Child, 1972; Cyert, 1990, Reading 11.1). And this hand must be firm. Managers cannot afford to take a laissez-faire attitude towards their task as leader – to lead means to get the organizational members to follow, and this is usually plain hard work (e.g. Bennis and Nanus, 1985; Kelley, 1988). To convince people in the organization to let themselves be led, managers cannot simply fall back on their position power. To be able to steer organizational developments managers need considerable personal power. To be successful, managers must be trusted, admired and respected. The forcefulness of their personality and the persuasiveness of their vision must be capable of capturing people's attention and commitment. And as leaders, managers must also be politically agile, able to build coalitions where necessary to get their way.

Of course, not all managers have the qualities needed to be effective leaders – either by nature or nurture. Some theorists emphasize the importance of 'nature', arguing that managers require specific personality traits to be successful leaders (e.g. House and Aditya, 1997; Tucker, 1968). Yet, other theorists place more emphasis on 'nurture', arguing that most effective leadership behaviour can be learned if enough effort is exerted (e.g. Kotter, 1990; Nanus, 1992). Either way, the importance of having good leadership makes finding and developing new leaders one of the highest priorities of the existing top management team.

To proponents of the organizational leadership perspective, being a leader does not mean engaging in simple top-down, command-and-control management. There are circumstances where the CEO or the top management team design strategies in isolation and then impose them on the rest of the organization. This type of direct control is sometimes necessary to push through reorganizations or to make major acquisitions. In other circumstances, however, the top managers can control organizational behaviour more indirectly. Proposals can be allowed to emerge bottom-up, as long as top management retains its power to approve or terminate projects as soon as they become serious plans (e.g. Bourgeois and Brodwin, 1983; Quinn, 1980, Reading 7.2). Some authors suggest that top management might even delegate some decision-making powers to lower level managers, but still control outcomes by setting clear goals, developing a conducive incentive system and fostering a particular culture (e.g. Senge, 1990; Tichy and Cohen, 1997).

What leaders should not do, however, is relinquish control over the direction of the organization. The strategies do not have to be their own ideas, nor do they have to carry out everything themselves. But they should take upon themselves the responsibility for leading the organization in a certain direction and achieving results. If leaders let go of the helm, organizations will be set adrift, and will be carried by the prevailing winds and currents in directions unknown. Someone has to be in control of the organization, otherwise its behaviour will be erratic. Leadership is needed to ensure that the best strategy is followed.

In conclusion, the organizational leadership perspective holds that the upper echelons of management can, and should, control the strategy process and by extension the strategy content. The CEO, or the top management team (e.g. Finkelstein and Hambrick, 1996; Hambrick and Mason, 1984), should have a grip on the organization's process of strategy formation and should be able to impose their will on the organization. Leaders should strive to overcome organizational inertia and adapt the organization to the strategic direction they intend. This type of controlled strategic behaviour is what Chandler (1962) had in mind when he coined the aphorism "structure follows strategy" – the organizational structure should be adapted to the strategy intended by the decision maker. In the organizational leadership perspective it would be more fitting to expand Chandler's maxim to "organization follows strategy" – all aspects of the company should be matched to the strategist's intentions.

EXHIBIT 11.2 THE ORGANIZATIONAL LEADERSHIP PERSPECTIVE

LEADING BY ITALIAN EXAMPLE AT CHRYSLER

One of the most talked about change-makers in the automobile industry is Sergio Marchionne, who miraculously saved the left-for-dead Fiat – with Alfa Romeo, Maserati and Ferrari a distinctive Italian car maker – in just a couple of years after taking control in 2004. Then, Mr Marchionne aimed at applying his tried and tested method at Chrysler in which Fiat gained a 20 per cent stake at close to no cost. With Chrysler he chose not the easiest of challenges as the German firm Daimler – the parent company of Mercedes Benz – had failed in the same job only a couple of years earlier.

Central to the approach employed by Fiat's saviour is a monumental turnaround in leadership. Management should control the strategy process, focusing on dealing quickly with the volatile yet hardly growing industry. To do so, overheads must be cut quickly and old managers that hold on to top-down management need to be replaced by younger executives. This creates an accountable, open, quickly communicating and less politics-ridden eco-system at the top, capable of steering a firm through the industry's testing challenges.

Mr Marchionne's 60-day 'killing spree', which he initiated after taking over at Chrysler, is a good illustration of the new leadership style. Just as he did with Fiat, he redefined the structure and replaced people himself to become more responsive. This left many of the upper echelons of management being startled with new opportunities or, alternatively, anxiously looking for different jobs. Having forward thinking and flexible leaders at the helm of an organization in an industry as pressured as the car industry is no excessive luxury. The market is expected to become increasingly volatile and the benefits of scale, although necessary for mutual survival, bring about a new class of challenges. For this reason, a sudden jolt given by renewing the upper echelons of management is not enough. Instead, to be able to continuously benefit from its newfound boons, Mr Marchionne is visibly leading his senior staff, who in turn need to be visible to the rest of the organization. Only by continuously displaying the right behaviour can a sustainable competitive advantage be maintained.

Leading by example and being visible is something Mr Marchionne does not shy away from. In June 2013, he visited Fiat and Chrysler's headquarters in Turin and Auburn Hills in addition to visiting half a dozen other places around the world. While there he was far from enjoying the tourist locations, but instead visibly busying himself with quenching labour union issues, boosting productivity in Italy as well as his stake in Chrysler and setting up cooperative ventures in China.

According to Mr Marchionne, faulty leadership is underlying a firm's immediate problems, which one should not hesitate to replace. Saving hundreds of thousands of jobs worldwide surely weighs up to getting rid of a handful of senior executives that are partly responsible for creating the problems in the first place. His second stroke of genius, to make abundantly visible the upper ranks of managers including himself while showing the desired behaviour, might have been even more impressive. Not fearing structure changes and replacing people while being consistent and visible is what sets him apart. Will Mr Marchionne succeed where even the renowned car maker Daimler couldn't? Consecutive years of profits and growing car sales suggest that this Italian pilot has successfully tuned up Chrysler's economic engine.

Co-author: Jasper de Vries

Sources: 'The Italian solution: Fiat chief executive, Sergio Marchionne, has gone merger mad', *The Economist*, May 7, 2009; 'Sergio Marchionne's high-wire act at Fiat–Chrysler', *CNN Money*, July 12, 2013; 'Lessons from Chrysler: how to rev up a purpose-driven corporate culture', *The Guardian*, July 31, 2014; FCA Annual Report, 2013–2015.

The organizational dynamics perspective

To proponents of the organizational dynamics perspective, such a heroic depiction of leadership is understandable, but usually more myth than reality. There might be a few great, wise, charismatic managers that rise to the apex of organizations, but unfortunately, all other organizations have to settle for regular mortals. Strong leaders are an exception, not the norm, and even their ability to mould the organization at will is highly exaggerated – good stories for best-selling autobiographies, but legend nevertheless (e.g. Chen and Meindl, 1991; Kets de Vries, 1994). Yet, the belief in the power of leadership is quite popular among managers and the managed alike (e.g. Meindl, Ehrlich and Dukerich, 1985; Pfeffer, 1977). Managers like the idea that as leaders of an organization or organizational unit, they can make a difference. To most, 'being in control' is what management is all about. They have a penchant for attributing organizational results to their own efforts (e.g. Hayward, Rindova and Pollock, 2004; Sims and Lorenzi, 1992). As for 'the managed', they too often ascribe organizational success or failure to the figurehead leader, whatever that person's real influence has been – after all, they too like the idea that somebody is in control. In fact, both parties are subscribing to a seductively simple 'great person model' of how organizations work. The implicit assumption is that an individual leader, by the strength of personality, can steer large groups of people, like a present-day Alexander the Great.

However seductive, this view of organizational functioning is rarely satisfactory. A top manager does not resemble a commander leading the troops into battle, but rather a diplomat trying to negotiate peace. The top manager is not like a jockey riding a thoroughbred horse, but more like a cowboy herding mules. Organizations are complex social systems, made up of many 'stubborn individuals' with their own ideas, interests and agendas (e.g. Greenwood and Hinings, 1996; Stacey, 1993). Strategy formation is therefore an inherently political process that leaders can only influence depending on their power base.

The more dispersed the political power, the more difficult it is for a leader to control the organization's behaviour. Even if leaders are granted, or acquire, significant political power to push through their favoured measures, there may still be considerable resistance and guerrilla activities. Political processes within organizations do not signify the derailment of strategic decision making – politics is the normal state of affairs and few leaders have real control over these political dynamics.

Besides such political limitations, a top manager's ability to control the direction of a company is also severely constrained by the organization's culture. Social norms will have evolved, relationships will have been formed, aspirations will have taken root and cognitive maps will have been shaped. A leader cannot ignore the cultural legacy of the organization's history, as this will be deeply etched into the minds of the organization's members. Any top manager attempting to radically alter the direction of a company will find out that changing the underlying values, perceptions, beliefs and expectations is extremely difficult, if not next to impossible. As Weick (1979) puts it, an organization does not have a culture, it is a culture – shared values and norms are what make an organization. And just as it is difficult to change someone's identity, it is difficult to change an organization's culture (e.g. Schein, 1993; Smircich and Stubbart, 1985). Moreover, as most top managers rise through the ranks to the upper echelons, they themselves are a product of the existing organizational culture. Changing your own culture is like pulling yourself up by your own bootstraps – a great trick, too bad that nobody can do it.

In Chapters 4 and 5, a related argument was put forward, as part of the resource-based view of the firm. One of the basic assumptions of the resource-based view is that building up competencies is an arduous task, requiring a relatively long period of time. Learning is a slow process under the best of circumstances, but even more difficult if learning one thing means unlearning something else. The stronger the existing cognitive maps (knowledge), routines (capabilities) and disposition (attitude), the more challenging it is to 'teach an old dog new tricks'. The leader's power to direct and speed up such processes, it was argued, is quite limited (e.g. Barney, 1991, Reading 4.2; Leonard-Barton, 1995).

Taken together, the political, cultural and learning dynamics leave top managers with relatively little direct power over the system they want to steer. Generally, they can react to this limited ability to control in one of two basic ways – they can squeeze tighter or let go. Many managers follow the first route, desperately trying to acquire more power, to gain a tighter grip on the organization, in the vain attempt to become the heroic leader of popular legend. Such a move to accumulate more power commonly results in actions to assert control, including stricter reporting structures, more disciplined accountability, harsher punishment for non-conformists and a shakeout among managers. In this manner, control comes to mean restriction, subordination or even subjugation. Yet, such a step towards authoritarian management will still not bring managers very much further towards having a lasting impact on organizational development.

The alternative route is for managers to accept that they cannot, but also should not try to, tightly control the organization. As they cannot really control organizational dynamics, all heavy-handed control approaches will have little more result than making the organization an unpleasant and oppressive place to work. If managers emphasize control, all they will do is run the risk of killing the organization's ability to innovate and learn. Innovation and learning are very difficult to control, especially the business innovation and learning happening outside of R&D labs. Much of this innovation and learning is sparked by organizational members, out in the markets or on the work floor, questioning the status quo. New ideas often start 'in the margins' of the organization and grow due to the room granted to offbeat opinions. Fragile new initiatives often need to be championed by their owners lower down in the hierarchy and only survive if there is a tolerance for unintended 'misfits' in the organization's portfolio of activities. Only if employees have a certain measure of freedom and are willing to act as intrapreneurs, will learning and innovation be an integral part of the organization's functioning (e.g. Amabile, 1998; Quinn, 1985).

In other words, if managers move beyond their instinctive desire for control and recognize the creative and entrepreneurial potential of self-organization, they will not bemoan their lack of control. They will see that a certain level of organizational chaos can create the conditions for development (e.g. Levy, 1994; Stacey, 1993, Reading 11.2). According to the organizational dynamics perspective, the task for managers is to use their limited powers to facilitate self-organization (e.g. Beinhocker, 1999; Wheatley and Kellner-Rogers, 1996). Managers can encourage empowerment, stimulate learning and innovation, bring people together, take away bureaucratic hurdles – all very much like the approach by most governments in market economies, who try to establish conditions conducive to entrepreneurial behaviour instead of trying to control economic activity. Managers' most important task is to ensure that the 'invisible hand of self-organization' functions properly and does not lead to 'out-of-hand disorganization'.

So, does the manager matter? Yes, but in a different sense than is usually assumed. The manager cannot shape the organization – it shapes itself. Organizational developments are the result of complex internal dynamics, which can be summarized as strategy follows organization, instead of the other way around. Managers can facilitate processes of self-organization and thus indirectly influence the direction of development, but at the same time managers are also shaped by the organization they are in.

EXHIBIT 11.3   ORGANIZATIONAL DYNAMICS PERSPECTIVE

MIGROS: BY AND FOR THE PEOPLE

It is 1925, Zürich, Switzerland. Money is scarce, and healthy yet affordable groceries are hard to find in what has currently become the economic centre of a wealthy country. It was at that time when Gottlieb Duttweiler, a man with a vision and a kind heart, founded Migros, a firm that would later leave a mark on the Swiss retailing industry, as well as on Swiss society. His objective was to meet the demand for low-priced basic food by cutting out the middleman. He would sell a few basic products to households that didn't have easy access to markets, but as demand for his services grew, so did the company. This led to a dilemma for Mr Duttweiler: should he keep control of the growing company and ownership of its potential profits, or become a company 'by and for the people'? In 1941 Mr Duttweiler decided to put the customers in charge and transfer the branches into regional cooperatives.

The Migros community organizes itself bounded by a very society-oriented way of doing business. There is still a board as well as a Federation of Migros Cooperatives heading the different enterprises, but this governance structure takes more of a facilitating or coordinating form. The two million strong customer base, amounting to over a quarter of the Swiss population, effectively run the firm, meaning that it is owned by the same people that it serves. Every 2 years, 100 members of the cooperative are elected to take a seat in the Assembly of Delegates. The powers of the Assembly of Delegates includes defining and amending the statutes, electing or dismissing board members and defining and amending business policy.

One of the collectively taken decisions is to refrain from selling alcoholic beverages in the Migros flagship supermarkets. Offering products at the lowest price possible has always been a major objective, but when applying this policy to potentially harmful products, the well-being of individuals could be compromised. While a profitability-focused firm may perceive this as an acceptable consequence, for the consumer-operated Migros it is not.

In 1996 Migros initiated the M-Budget brand, aimed at individuals with a lower income, which follows tradition. In 2015, the M-Budget brand was voted Switzerland's second favourite brand, just behind the Migros brand itself which came in first. As it turns out, the idealistic philosophy behind this M-Budget initiative resulted in these items not only appealing to those living on a budget, but also to trendy shoppers sharing this philosophy. Migros followed up on this development by initiating M-budget parties where people were challenged to cook high-end, gastronomic meals using only

M-budget products. Naturally, the beverages served at those parties were non-alcoholic.

Co-author: Adriaan de Bruijn

Sources: Migros Annual Report 2012, report.migros.ch/2015/en/; Peter Gloor and Scott Cooper, 'The New Principles of a Swarm Business', *Sloan Management Review*, April 2007.

MANAGING THE PARADOX OF CONTROL AND CHAOS

Chaos often breeds life, when order breeds habit.

Henry Brooks Adams (1838–1919); American writer and historian

So, how should organizational development be encouraged? Can the top management of a firm shape the organization to fit with their intended strategy or does the organizational context determine the strategy that is actually followed? And should top management strive to have a tight grip on the organization, or should they leave plenty of room for self-organization? (See Table 11.1.)

As before, views differ strongly, both in business practice and in academia; not only in the field of strategy, but also in neighbouring fields such as organizational behaviour, human resource management and innovation management, and more broadly in the humanities, including sociology, economics, political science and psychology. The economic sociologist Duesenberry once remarked that "economics is all about how people make choices; sociology is all about how they don't have any choices to make." Although half in jest, his comment does ring true. Much of the literature within the field of economics assumes that people in organizations can freely make choices and have the power to

TABLE 11.1   Organizational leadership versus organizational dynamics perspective

	Organizational leadership perspective	Organizational dynamics perspective
Emphasis on	Control over chaos	Chaos over control
Organizational development	Controllable creation process	Uncontrollable evolutionary process
Development metaphor	The visible hand	The invisible hand
Development direction	Top-down, imposed organization	Bottom-up, self-organization
Decision making	Authoritarian (rule of the few)	Democratic (rule of the many)
Change process	Leader shapes new behaviour	New behaviour emerges from interactions
Change determinants	Leader's vision and skill	Political, cultural and learning dynamics
Organizational malleability	High, fast	Low, slow
Development driver	Organization follows strategy	Strategy follows organization
Normative implication	Strategize, then organize	Organize, then strategize

shape their strategy, while possible restraints on their freedom usually come from the environment. Sociological literature, but also psychological and political science work, often features the limitations on individual's freedom. These different disciplinary inclinations are not absolute, but can be clearly recognized in the debate.

With so many conflicting views and incompatible prescriptions on the issue of organizational development, the question is how to manage the paradox of control and chaos. Following the taxonomy in Chapter 1, strategizing managers have the following options at their disposal.

Balancing

Depending on the organization, strategists blend elements of opposite demands for top management control and organizational chaos into a balance. As has been discussed in Chapter 7 on strategy formation, the primary process of the firm or organizational unit is a key factor. For example, the demand for top management control is higher in production units than in a professional services firm, while the demand for organizational chaos prevails in business development units.

Organizational culture is another factor influencing the blend of opposite demands. For example, the founder's leadership style and the firm's native country are among the factors that create an organization-specific culture (further discussed in the next section on the international perspective on the organizational context).

Juxtaposing

Within the organization, strategists are leading many groups, projects and corporate initiatives. The larger the organization, the more variety of organizational processes strategizing leaders participate in. For example, a manager may be heading a product innovation project, a cost-cutting operation and an acquisition process at the same time. These activities require different organizational leadership styles, and thus the strategizing manager needs to juxtapose between different opposites or blends simultaneously. This requires high flexibility of leadership styles and specific dynamic capabilities (Teece, Pisano and Shuen, 1997, Reading 4.3).

Embracing

The tension between the demand for top management control and organizational chaos can also be exploited at the leadership team level, by intentionally bringing together opposite individuals. Diverse leadership teams, bringing together different disciplines and cultures for example, are not the easiest of organizational configurations. Yet, tensions can be exploited as sources of creativity and opportunity.

One specific manifestation of an intentionally designed tension is the phenomenon of 'dynamic duos' who have built large firms such as Hewlett and Packard, and Walt and Roy Disney. Actually some authors argue that a large number of new ventures are successful *exactly because* of the combination of two contrary individuals forming the leadership team. They argue that while the attention of academics and journalists is directed to the more outgoing member of the leadership team, the correct level of analysis should be the duo, the yin and yang of success.

One such author was the late David Thomson (2006; Reading 11.3) who analysed the 387 high growth companies that have IPO'd since 1980 and concluded that success often depends on dynamic duos, one of them being the external part and the other the internal half of the effort. Together they are able to combine change and stability.

THE ORGANIZATIONAL CONTEXT IN INTERNATIONAL PERSPECTIVE

Co-authors: Gep Eisenloeffel and Wester Wagenaar

So long as men worship the Caesars and Napoleons, Caesars and Napoleons will duly arise and make them miserable.

Aldous Huxley (1894–1963); English novelist

Views on the nature of the organizational context are diverse and research indicates divergent national preferences. A variety of factors can be held responsible for inclinations on how the paradox of control and chaos is viewed in different countries. When discussing the international perspective of the organizational context, dealing with national preferences is self-evident. Yet, not every perceptional difference should be attributed to international differences; preferences in industries taken on a global scale and individual dispositions should not be ignored.

On the national level

In large scale fieldwork carried out by researchers at Cranfield Business School in the United Kingdom (Myers *et al.*, 1995), significantly different leadership styles were recognized among European executives. The research notes that the predominant approach in Sweden and Finland can be typified as the 'consensus' style – with low power distance and low masculinity. This finding can be generalized for all of the Nordic countries, where cooperation and consensus are often valued over individualistic decision making (Goldsmith and Larsen, 2004). Executives in Germany and Austria have a style labelled 'working towards a common goal', where specialists work together within a rule-bound structure. In France, the most popular style is 'managing from a distance' where planning is emphasized in a hierarchic setting. Executives from the United Kingdom, Ireland and Spain prefer 'leading from the front'. According to the researchers, the latter leadership style relies on the belief that it is the skills and charisma of particular individuals at the top that are responsible for the success or failure of an organization. This suggests that the organizational leadership perspective is more popular in these three countries as well as in other Anglo-Saxon and Latin cultures, than in the rest of Europe. Other cross-cultural theorists support this supposition (e.g. Hampden-Turner and Trompenaars, 1993; Lessem and Neubauer, 1994).

The perceived locus of control can also explain international preferential differences. People with an internal locus of control believe that they can shape events and have an impact on their environment, while those with an external locus of control believe they are caught up in events they can hardly influence. In countries where the culture is more inclined towards an internal locus of control, it is reasonable to expect that the organizational leadership perspective will be more widespread. Managers in such societies will be more strongly predisposed to believe that they can shape organizational circumstances. In cultures that are characterized by a predominantly external locus of control, more support for the organizational dynamics perspective can be expected.

A cultural characteristic related to perceived loci of control is the preference for order and structure that prevails in some countries. Hofstede (1993) refers to this issue as uncertainty avoidance. In some cultures, there is a low tolerance for unstructured situations, poorly defined tasks and responsibilities, ambiguous relationships and unclear rules.

People in these nations exhibit a distinct preference for predictability – they need to feel they are in control. In other cultures however, people are less nervous about uncertain settings. The tolerance for situations that are unorganized or self-organizing is much higher – even in relatively chaotic circumstances, the call for 'law and order' will not be particularly strong. It can be expected that there will be a more pronounced preference for the organizational leadership perspective in countries that score high on uncertainty avoidance, than in nations with a low score on this cultural dimension.

Another distinction that can be made is between two types of organizations. In the mechanistic view, organizations exist as systems that are staffed with people, while in the organic view organizations exist as groups of people into which some system has been brought. Taking the former perspective, leaders will be regarded as mechanics – the organizational system can be redesigned, re-engineered and restructured to pursue another course of action where necessary. In countries where the mechanistic view of organizations is more predominant, an inclination towards the organizational leadership can be expected. The organic view, however, sees the leader as the head of the clan – bound by tradition and loyalty, but able to count on the emotional commitment of the members. Important in reorienting and rejuvenating the organization is the leader's ability to challenge orthodox ideas, motivate people and manage the political processes. Countries where this view is more predominant will likely lean towards the organizational dynamics perspective.

Closely related to the distinction between mechanistic and organic organizations, is the level of formalization of a firm. If companies aim to govern the activities and behaviours of employees through imposing extensive rules and procedures, an organizational leadership perspective is taken. When little formalization is in place and employees are encouraged to self-organize, this indicates the organizational dynamics perspective. Some countries show distinct differences in the level of formalization. For example, Japanese firms are quite formalized, while companies in the Nordic countries are often less so (Dobbin and Boychuk, 1999; Horváth et al., 1976).

On the industry level

Although the average level of formalization of companies correlates with country-specific preferences, it is a common rule that the bigger the firm, the more formalized it becomes. This is true regardless of the country of origin of the company. Only big companies can develop and produce trains, airplanes, spacecraft, national defence systems and oil platforms for instance. Industries requiring a large scale to properly operate can thus be expected to have an inclination towards the organizational leadership perspective.

Reluctant to call it chaos, most researchers do agree organizations need a decent degree of disorder to foster the flow of innovative ideas. As such, many companies in the creative sector try to refrain from imposing authoritarian control and instead see the value of self-organization.

To the strategist

It is not just culture that plays a role in the organizational context, research has suggested behaviours of leaders to be gender stereotypic. The heroic, individualized depiction of leadership is an association particularly strong among men. Leadership styles have traditionally been grouped as a dichotomy between task orientation as opposed to relations orientation; men are commonly associated with task-oriented leadership and women with the interpersonally-oriented style (e.g. Eagly and Johannesen-Schmidt, 2001; Eagly and Johnson, 1990; Gevedon, 1992; Gibson, 1995; Oshagbemi and Gill, 2003; Rigg and Sparrow, 1994; Taleb, 2010). The country of origin of a leader does not appear to influence this gendered perception much, as these gender preferences have been confirmed across a variety of countries – even in more 'feminine', less patriarchal, societies (e.g. Bellou, 2011; Gibson, 1995; Oshagbemi and Gill, 2003; Taleb, 2010).

Another individual characteristic that can influence a preference for either the organizational dynamics or the organizational leadership perspective is the leader's age. Studies in the UK, US and India suggest that the higher the age of a manager, the more participative he is, preferring collective decision making over the authoritarian kind. This in contrast to younger managers who take decisions that may not necessarily be popular among the majority of the workers (e.g. Kotur and Anbazhagan, 2014; Mitchell, 2000; Oshagbemi, 2004, 2008).

A strategist has to be aware of his own disposition and what the environmental demands are. Does a strategist need to adapt to internal or external needs and is a bit of chaos then beneficial to the development of the firm? Or is it the vision and skill of the leader that needs to guide the organization? Operating on the international level brings along more difficulties, for employees from different countries are likely to have divergent opinions on what behaviour the organizational context is supposed to encourage and facilitate.

INTRODUCTION TO THE READINGS

To help strategists to come to grips with the variety of perspectives on this issue, three readings have been selected that each shed their own light on the topic. As in previous chapters, the first two readings are representative of the two poles in this debate, while the third reading relates the two contrary perspectives.

To open the debate on behalf of the organizational leadership perspective, Reading 11.1 has been selected entitled 'Defining Leadership and Explicating the Process', which is written by one of the 'godfathers' of organizational theory, Richard Cyert. In this article, Cyert starts by summarizing the functions of a leader: determining the organizational structure, selecting managers, setting strategic objectives, controlling internal and external information flows, maintaining morale and making important decisions. But while some authors take an organizational leadership perspective and tend to conjure up an image of the leader as an octopus, with many long arms performing all of these tasks at the same time, Cyert has a more human, two-armed individual in mind. His view of the leader is not the control freak who wants to run the organization single-handedly, but a person who can "heavily influence the process of determining the goals of the organization", and then can "have the participants in the organization behave in the ways that the leader believes are desirable". This definition of leadership has two important ingredients. First, Cyert argues that leaders need to take the initiative in determining a vision and organizational goals, although they do this in interaction with other organizational members. Second, Cyert argues that leaders need to focus on modifying the people's behaviours. To get people to move in the desired direction, he states that it is not so important what a leader decides or tells people to do. Rather, an effective leader "controls the allocation of the attention focus of the participants in the organization … so that their attention is allocated to the areas that the leader considers important". In this way, Cyert believes, organizational members will voluntarily align their behaviours with where the leader wants to go. He admits that "this conception of leadership might strike some as making the leader a manipulative person", but feels that if leaders have a genuine belief in what they are doing and have an honest dedication to the people in the organization, exerting this type of leadership is justified. Although Cyert is well aware that organizations are complex systems of interacting human beings, his unquestioned supposition throughout the reading is that leadership is *possible* and *necessary*. As many writers take an organizational leadership perspective, the demand for top management control is an implicit assumption – the main issue discussed is how to get power and how to exert control. Cyert's preference is for more indirect control, implicitly leaving some room for bottom-up self-organization.

As the opening reading to represent the organizational dynamics perspective (Reading 11.2), an article by Ralph Stacey has been selected, entitled 'Strategy as Order Emerging from Chaos'. Stacey argues that top managers cannot, and should not even try, to control the organization and its strategy. In his view, the organizational dynamics involved in strategy formation, learning and change are too complex to simply be controlled by managers. He states that "sometimes the best thing a manager can do is to let go and allow things to happen". The resulting chaos, he argues, does not mean that the organization will be a mess – a lack of control, he assures, does not mean that the organization will be adrift. His reasoning is that non-linear feedback systems, such as organizations, have a self-organizing ability, which "can produce controlled behaviour, even though no one is in control". In his view, real strategic change requires the chaos of contention and conflict to destroy old recipes and to encourage the quest for new solutions. The "self-organizing processes of political interaction and complex learning" ensure that chaos does not result in disintegration. Hence, in Stacey's opinion, it is management's task to help create a situation of bounded instability in which strategy can emerge. Managers do have a role in organizations, but it can hardly be called leadership – 'leaders' must direct their efforts at influencing the organizational context in such a way that the right conditions prevail for self-organization to take place. 'Leaders' are largely facilitators, making it possible for new and unexpected strategies to develop spontaneously.

The third reading (11.3), combining the two perspectives, is adapted from the book *Blueprint to a Billion: 7 essentials to achieve exponential growth* by David Thomson. The late writer researched America's 387 highest growth companies, the 5 per cent that have IPO'd since 1980 and grown to $1 billion in revenue. One surprising finding was that dynamic duos – often visible in the company's naming as in Sears and Roebuck, and Hewlett and Packard – as an essential success factor of high growth companies, is more than corporate myth. Thomson found that dynamic duos, "two individuals who worked tightly together to build the firm from dreams to a billion dollars in revenue" drove many of the star-performing companies, including Yahoo!, Microsoft, Tractor Supply, eBay, Siebel Systems, Starbucks and Broadcom. For the duo to be dynamic, one of them had to excel in the *external* part while the other had the *internal* focus. Together, Thomson observes, they "are the yin and yang, the weave and warp, the bacon and eggs – and without this dynamic of compatibility their companies could not have made it to the top. As a pair, they were the highest of performance teams". The duos were able to manage tensions such as the creative tension between the flat and somewhat chaotic innovative organization and the more top-down and structured execution of ideas. The importance of this reading is that if dynamic duos are the key to success in an extremely demanding context it may, more generally, also be essential in strategic leadership.

Defining leadership and explicating the process
By Richard M. Cyert[1]

It is true that organizations, whether for-profit or not-for-profit, are in need of leadership. Most people in leadership positions in organizations tend to be managers rather than leaders. They administer, allocate resources, resolve conflicts and go home at night convinced that they have done a good day's

[1]Source: This article was adapted from Richard M. Cyert, (2006) 'Defining leadership and explicating the process' *Nonprofit Management and Leadership* vol. 1(1) pp. 29–38. Copyright © John Wiley & Sons, Inc. 1990. Reproduced with permission of John Wiley & Sons, Inc..

work. They may have, but they have not provided the organization with the critical ingredient that every organization needs – leadership (Zalesnik, 1977; Bavelas, 1964).

It is possible to generalize three broad functions that a leader performs. I specify these functions as organizational, interpersonal and decisional. The organizational function involves the development of the organizational structure and the selection of people to manage the various segments of an organization. It involves the determination of the goal structure and the control of the internal and external information flows. This function requires the leader to make certain that the participants in the organization and the relevant groups external to the organization are knowledgeable about the organization.

The interpersonal function involves the maintenance of morale in the organization. It reflects the degree of concern about the humanness of the organization. It requires the leader to pay attention to individual concerns.

The decision function involves the making of decisions that must be made in order for the organization to progress toward the achievement of its goals. This is the function that has traditionally been associated with leadership.

Nature of leadership

Although there is little agreement on the definition of leadership, most students of leadership would agree that the three functions just described are clearly a part of the definition. In a broad sense, the leader is attempting to have the participants in the organization behave in the ways that the leader believes are desirable. A major step in performing the organizational function is to define desirable behaviour.

Desirability is determined by the goals of the organization. The leader should heavily influence the process of determining the goals of the organization. The determination of a goal structure for an organization is the result of a series of interactions among the participants and between the participants and the leader. The goal structure represents the vision of the leader and of the organization's other members. Projecting a vision for the organization is another characteristic that is commonly associated with leadership.

The vision embedded in the goal structure is essentially a map that is used as a guide for the direction of the organization. Clearly, the map is more detailed as one's view shifts to subunits within the organization. At the top leadership position, a number of broad principles are specified to guide the overall construction of the vision.

These principles relate to the process by which the organization's vision can be constantly modified and reshaped. The specification of strategic principles and of the process by which the vision is modified is another characteristic of leadership. The leader is the helmsman, and the goal structure, together with the strategic principle, is the means by which the leader steers the organization. But, an organization is an interactive system of human beings, and its performance depends on the behaviour of individuals. Regardless of the policies that are promulgated, the participants in the organization will determine the destiny of the organization by their productivity.

The goal structure is important in the leading of an organization. However, organizations can have conflicting goals (Cyert and March, 1963), primarily because they tend to goals sequentially. Also, each unit in an organization can focus on different goals. These goals may conflict, but they can all be embraced by the organization (Birnbaum, 1988).

A definition of leadership

The concept of attention focus is one of the most important variables in organization theory (March and Simon, 1958; Cyert and March, 1963). Participants in an organization allocate their attention to a variety of matters. The amount of attention allocated to each matter has been a subject of study. It can affect the organization in crucial ways. For example, if attention is not given to problems concerned with the future, the organization may flounder from myopia – too much attention to immediate problems. Clearly, the problems, concerns, ideas, concepts and so on to which the participants pay attention will determine the long-run viability of the organization. The control of this allocation of attention is vital to the organization.

In discussing the formation of the organizational coalition, Cyert and March (1963, p. 39) argue that one of the five basic mechanisms for a theory of coalition formation is 'an attention-focus mechanism'; however, 'we know rather little about the actual mechanisms that control this attention factor.' In this paper, I argue that the leadership function is one of the mechanisms that control the attention factor.

In fact, my definition of leadership is that the leader controls the allocation of the attention focus of the participants in the organization. The leader of any organization, no matter how small or large it is, affects the allocation of attention by participants. In a decentralized, structured organization, standard operating procedures determine the allocation of attention if the leader does not intervene. In general, in any organization where managers dominate, structured rules tend to influence the allocation of attention, but the leader will try to capture the attention focus of the participants so that their attention is allocated to the areas that the leader considers important.

The issues or problems on which the leader attempts to focus attention reflect, at least in part, the vision of the organization that exists in the leader's mind. This vision will generally have been developed from discussions with relevant participants, from the leader's experience and knowledge, and from his or her assessment of the organization's future in the light of existing information. This vision will change over time as the leader gets feedback from the organization's performance. As the vision changes, so does the priority of individual issues and problems to which the leader wishes to allocate the attention of participants. Organizations are dynamic, and attention allocation is an ongoing and always necessary process. Leadership, in the sense in which I have defined it here, must also be continuous.

Leadership, as I define it here, must also have substance. A leader cannot succeed in allocating attention without a strong intellectual position for a particular attention focus. This position can only come from a knowledge of the organization and of the area in which it functions. This need for specific knowledge is one of the reasons why it is difficult for executives to move from an organization in one industry to an organization in a different industry. The executive may be able to function as a manager, but he or she will have more difficulty functioning as a leader.

A second definition of leadership

Subgroups develop in every organization. Participants involved in the same department or in similar endeavours form a natural alliance (March and Simon, 1958). Important individuals in an organization can constitute subgroups in and of themselves. The point is that subgroups can develop a goal structure of their own, and this goal structure may conflict with that of the central organization.

The leader must bring about conformity between subgroup goals and the goals of the central organization. In other words, the leader must convince the members of the subgroup to give up or modify their goals and adopt the central organization's goals. In some cases, of course, the leader may decide that the central goals should be changed in the direction of the subgroup's goals. The point is that the leader cannot tolerate conflicting goals in the organization (Vroom and Jago, 1988). There must be a single goal structure, and everyone in the organization must accept it if the organization's goals are to be achieved. The concept of teamwork – of everyone working together – is a necessity for any organization.

Definitions of leadership and the three leadership functions

Having defined leadership, it is now logical for us to discuss the methods that one uses in the act of leadership. However, before we move to that topic, it will be useful to relate our two definitions of leadership – which really are essentially one – to the three functions of leadership discussed earlier.

In order to understand the leader's role, we need to go back to the distinction between managers and leaders. Every leader must perform some managerial functions, even though every manager cannot take a leadership role.

For example, in an effort to change organizational performance, many managers attempt to change the structure of their organizations. Currently, in an effort to reduce costs, many managers are attempting to reduce the number of hierarchical levels. Sometimes, the structure is changed by modifying the reporting relationship among units. The level at which decisions are made can also be changed. The organization can become more centralized or more decentralized with respect to decision making. Yet, changes in organizational structure alone are not likely to have any lasting impact on the organization's performance unless the structure affects the basic desire of participants to improve their performance.

The leader recognizes that it is necessary to focus the attention of participants on factors that will change performance. Thus, the leader makes changes in structure for their effect on attention focus, not because he or she believes that organizational structure alone can change the performance of participants. If the leader wishes to focus attention on costs, he or she looks at changes in the organization's structure that will encourage participants to allocate their attention to costs. Increased decentralization will often accomplish such a shift. The point is that leaders look at organizational tasks with a view to the impact that their actions will have on the attention focus of participants. Attention focus is central to the performance of the organizational function of leadership.

A similar statement can be made about the interpersonal function. The leader's role is to relate to the participants in ways that will affect their attention focus. The interpersonal function of leadership is sometimes viewed as one that holds the leader responsible for making everyone in the organization feel good. Friendliness and openness can be good for an organization if they help participants to focus their attention on the elements that the leader deems to be important. The interpersonal function is extremely important, but the leader must relate his or her actions in this area to the desired impact on attention focus. There is ample evidence that there is a low correlation between high morale and high productivity (Misumi, 1985).

The relation between the decisional function and attention focus is perhaps the most interesting of the three. Bavelas (1964, p. 206) defined leadership in terms of decision making: 'leadership consists of the continuous choice-making process that permits the organization as a whole to proceed toward its objectives despite all sorts of internal and external perturbations.' More explicitly, he regards leadership as consisting of the reduction of uncertainty; this reduction is achieved by making choices.

This definition, which is close to the commonly accepted view of leadership, is quite different from those propounded here. My definitions focus on the leader's responsibility for modifying the behaviour of participants in the organization. They assume that behaviour is affected by the items to which individuals allocate their attention. The leader is able to capture the attention focus of participants. The leader gets participants to allocate attention to the items that he or she deems to be important. There is no question that the decisions that a leader makes are ways of making the priorities for attention clear. That is the aspect of decision making that in my view is part of leadership, not the fact that decision making reduces uncertainty. Nevertheless, it could be argued that influencing the allocation of attention tends to reduce uncertainty.

Studies of decision making tend to show that decisions are rarely made by a single individual without regard to the views of the members of the organization. Leadership in an organization has to be less individualistic than it is in a combat situation where the leader may single-handedly eliminate a machine gun nest. Decision making in an organization must take into account the fact that members of the organization are interested in the direction that the organization takes. If the leader has captured the attention focus of the members, then it is possible to demonstrate 'the highest expressions of personal leadership' (Bavelas, 1964) and carry the organization along with those expressions.

Methods of leadership

If leadership is adequately encompassed by my definitions, we may ask how leadership is actually implemented in an organization. How does a person act in an organization when he or she plays a leadership role and wants to exert leadership?

There are at least three general approaches that are taken. They can be classified as communication, role modelling, and reward systems. I will discuss each of these approaches.

Communication

The first action that influences attention focus is oral interaction. These talks are ways of capturing the attention focus of participants. The ultimate aim is to change the behaviour of people in the organization by influencing their focus. The underlying theory is that individuals' behaviour is controlled by their attention focus. Put another way, the leader brings about the behaviour that he or she desires by convincing participants to focus their attention on the ideas and actions that the leader considers important.

The interesting and difficult problem is that the methods of communication in organizations are not well defined (March and Simon, 1958). In general, it is best to use a variety of communication channels. These channels can vary from one-on-one discussions to departmental meetings and meetings of the whole faculty and staff.

The leader also uses written communication. Again, different approaches must be found. Written communications can vary from personal letters to letters to the whole organization and formal reports. Even articles written for newspapers or other publications can be used to explicate the leader's desired priorities for the allocation of attention among participants.

Communication is perhaps the most important mechanism of leadership. The leader must have a clear understanding of the message that he or she is communicating, and he or she must be aware that the goal of communication is to influence the allocation of attention of the organization's members.

Role model

As a way of continuing to communicate with members of the organization, the leader must take into account the impact of his or her behaviour on the attention focus of participants. The actions of the leader clearly represent the ideas that he or she considers to be important. If a university president is trying to emphasize research as an activity of importance, he or she should engage in research activity as well as emphasize research in the direct communications that he or she makes. Role modelling is a case in which actions speak as loudly as words.

The leader's activities are widely known among the members of any organization. Thus, the leader has ample opportunity to affect the attention focus of participants by demonstrating the factors that are important in his or her own behaviour. In other words, role modelling is a form of communication. The leader's behaviour exerts leadership whether the leader intends it or not.

Reward system

The reward system that the leader establishes is another way of reinforcing the attention focus of members. The relationship between particular rewards and performance is not well established. An organization cannot offer a specific monetary award and achieve a particular performance. However, a leader can use rewards to reinforce the priority system for attention allocation that he or she has established. The reward system can lead to both honour and money for recipients. The reward system is also a means of communicating the leader's priorities to participants. Obviously, a reward system cannot guarantee that performance in teaching will improve, but it can supplement the leader's effort to capture the attention focus of participants and allocate attention to areas that the leader considers important.

Conclusion

The theory of leadership just outlined is essentially a simple one. It assumes that participants in an organization behave in accordance with their focus attention.

Behaviour follows from the items on which they focus. From this perspective, leadership is the effort to capture the attention focus of the members of an organization. Three mechanisms help to perform the leadership function: communication between leader and participants, role modelling and reward systems. The three mechanisms are alike in that all are ways of communicating the matters on which the leader wants members to focus their attention. There are other, related mechanisms. My list is not exhaustive. In all cases, the effort is to capture the attention focus of participants.

This conception of leadership might strike some as making the leader a manipulative person (Glassman, 1986). The key is that the leader must believe in what he or she is expressing. Mintzberg (1989) has put it exactly right: 'To my mind, key to the development of an organization ideology, in a new or existing organization, is a leadership with a genuine belief in mission and an honest dedication to the people who must carry it out.'

It is obvious, although I have not emphasized it, that a leader must have the ability and the knowledge needed to select the right items for the attention focus of participants (Mintzberg, 1982). That is, the items singled out for attention must enable the organization to attain its goals. The process of capturing the attention focus is also a dynamic one. The items on which the leader wishes participants to focus will change, and the leader must be perceptive enough to select the new items properly.

Although I have simplified the nature of leadership and the methods by which leadership can be exerted, I do not mean to imply that leadership is anything but complex. In any organization of significant size, the leader uses a system composed of many variables. To attend to the appropriate constituencies and focus their attention on the appropriate items requires thought, planning, energy, conviction and an ability to persuade.

Strategy as order emerging from chaos

By Ralph Stacey[1]

There are four important points to make on the recent discoveries about the complex behaviour of dynamic systems, all of which have direct application to human organizations.

[1]Source: This article was reprinted from *Long Range Planning*, Vol. 26, No. 1, R. Stacey, 'Strategy as order emerging from chaos', pp. 3–9, © 1993. With permission from Elsevier.

Chaos is a form of instability where the specific long-term future is unknowable

Chaos in its scientific sense is an irregular pattern of behaviour generated by well defined non-linear feedback rules commonly found in nature and human society. When systems driven by such rules operate away from equilibrium, they are highly sensitive to selected tiny changes in their environments, amplifying them into self-reinforcing virtuous and vicious circles that completely alter the behaviour of the system. In other words, the system's future unfolds in a manner dependent upon the precise detail of what it does, what the systems constituting its environments do, and upon chance. As a result of this fundamental property of the system itself, specific links between cause and effect are lost in the history of its development, and the specific path of its long-term future development is completely unpredictable. Over the short term, however, it is possible to predict behaviour because it takes time for the consequences of small changes to build up.

Is there evidence of chaos in business systems? We would conclude that there was if we could point to small changes escalating into large consequences; if we could point to self-reinforcing vicious and virtuous circles; if we could point to feedback that alternates between the amplifying and the damping. It is not difficult to find such evidence.

Creative managers seize on small differences in customer requirements and perceptions to build significant differentiators for their products. Customers may respond to this by switching from other product offerings, leading to a virtuous circle; or they may switch away, causing the kind of vicious circle that Coca-Cola found itself caught up in when it made that famous soft drink slightly sweeter.

Managers create, or at the very least shape, the requirements of their customers through the product offerings they make. Sony created a requirement for personal hi-fi systems through its Walkman offering, and manufacturers and operators have created requirements for portable telephones. Sony and Matsushita created the requirement for video recorders, and when companies supply information systems to their clients, they rarely do so according to a complete specification – instead, the supplier shapes the requirement. When managers intentionally shape customer demands through the offerings they make, this feeds back into customer responses, and managers may increase the impact by intentionally using the copying and spreading effects through which responses to product offerings feed back into other customers' responses. When managers do this, they are deliberately using positive feedback – along with negative feedback controls to meet cost and quality targets, for example – to create business success.

A successful business is also affected by many amplifying feedback processes that are outside the control of its managers and produce effects that they did not intend. Successful businesses are quite clearly characterized by feedback processes that flip between the negative and the positive, the damping and the amplifying; that is, they are characterized by feedback patterns that produce chaos. The long-term future of a creative organization is absolutely unknowable, and no one can intend its future direction over the long term or be in control of it. In such a system long-term plans and visions of future states can be only illusions.

But in chaos there are boundaries around the instability

While chaos means disorder and randomness in the behaviour of a system at the specific level, it also means that there is a qualitative pattern at a general, overall level. The future unfolds unpredictably, but it always does so according to recognizable family-like resemblances. This is what we mean when we say that history repeats itself, but never in the same way. We see this combination of unpredictable specific behaviour within an overall pattern in snowflakes. As two nearby snowflakes fall to the earth, they experience tiny differences in temperature and air impurities. Each snowflake amplifies those differences as they form, and by the time they reach the earth they have different shapes – but they are still clearly snowflakes. We cannot predict the shape of each snowflake, but we can predict that they will be snowflakes. In business, we recognize patterns of boom and recession, but each time they are different in specific terms, defying all attempts to predict them.

Chaos is unpredictable variety within recognizable categories defined by irregular features, that is, an inseparable intertwining of order and disorder. It is this property of being bounded by recognizable qualitative patterns that makes it possible for humans to cope with chaos. Numerous tests have shown that our memories do not normally store information in units representing the precise characteristics of the individual shapes or events we perceive. Instead, we store information about the strength of connection between individual units perceived. We combine information together into categories or concepts using family resemblance-type features. Memory emphasizes general structure, irregular category features, rather than specific content. We remember the irregular patterns rather than the specific features and we design our next actions on the basis of these memorized patterns. And since we design our actions in this manner, chaotic behaviour presents us with no real problem. Furthermore, we are adept at using analogical reasoning and intuition to reflect upon experience and adapt it to new situations, all of which is ideally suited to handling chaos.

Unpredictable new order can emerge from chaos through a process of spontaneous self-organization

When non-linear feedback systems in nature are pushed far from equilibrium into chaos, they are capable of creating a complex new order. For example, at some low temperatures the atoms of a particular gas are arranged in a particular pattern and the gas emits no light. Then, as heat is applied, it agitates the atoms causing them to move, and as this movement is amplified through the gas it emits a dull glow. Small changes in heat are thus amplified, causing instability, or chaos, that breaks the symmetry of the atoms' original behaviour. Then at a critical point, the atoms in the gas suddenly all point in the same direction to produce a laser beam. Thus, the system uses chaos to shatter old patterns of behaviour, creating the opportunity for the new. And as the system proceeds through chaos, it is confronted with critical points where it, so to speak, makes a choice between different options for further development. Some options represent yet further chaos and others lead to more complex forms of orderly behaviour, but which will occur is inherently unpredictable. The choice itself is made by spontaneous self-organization amongst the components of the system in which they, in effect, communicate with each other, reach a consensus, and commit to a new form of behaviour. If a more complex form of orderly behaviour is reached, it has what scientists call a dissipative structure, because continual attention and energy must be applied if it is to be sustained – for example, heat has to be continually pumped into the gas if the laser beam is to continue. If the system is to develop further, then the dissipative structure must be short-lived; to reach an even more complex state, the system will have to pass through chaos once more.

It is striking how similar the process of dealing with strategic issues in an organization is to the self-organizing phenomenon just outlined. The key to the effectiveness with which organizations change and develop new strategic directions lies in the manner in which managers handle what might be called their strategic issue agenda. That agenda is a dynamic, unwritten list of issues, aspirations and challenges that key groups of managers are attending to. Consider the steps managers can be observed to follow as they handle their strategic issue agenda:

- **Detecting and selecting small disturbances.** In open-ended strategic situations, change is typically the result of many small events and actions that are unclear, ambiguous and confusing, with consequences that are unknowable. The key difficulty is to identify what the real issues, problems or opportunities are, and the challenge is to find an appropriate and creative aspiration or objective. In these circumstances the organization has no alternative but to rely on the initiative of individuals to notice and pursue some issue, aspiration or challenge. In order to do this, those individuals have to rely on their experience-based intuition and ability to detect analogies between one set of ambiguous circumstances and another.

- **Amplifying the issues and building political support.** Once some individual detects some potential issue, that individual begins to push for organizational attention to it. A complex political process of building special interest groups to support an issue is required before it gains organizational attention and can thus be said to be on the strategic issue agenda.

- **Breaking symmetries.** As they build and progress strategic issue agendas, managers are in effect altering old mental models, existing company and industry recipes, to come up with new ways of doing things. They are destroying existing perceptions and structures.

- **Critical points and unpredictable outcomes.** Some issues on the agenda may be dealt with quickly, while others may attract attention, continuous or periodic, for a very long time. How quickly an issue is dealt with depends upon the time required to reach enough consensus and commitment to proceed to action. At some critical point, an external or internal pressure in effect forces a choice. The outcome on whether and how to proceed to action over the issue is unpredictable because it depends upon the context of power, personality and group dynamic within which it is being handled. The result may or may not be action, and action will usually be experimental at first.

587 THE ORGANIZATIONAL CONTEXT

■ Changing the frame of reference. Managers in a business come to share memories of what worked and what did not work in the past – the organizational memory. In this way they build up a business philosophy or culture, establishing a company recipe and in common with their rivals an industry recipe too. These recipes have a powerful effect on what issues will subsequently be detected and attended to; that is, they constitute a frame of reference within which managers interpret what to do next. The frame of reference has to be continually challenged and changed because it can easily become inappropriate to new circumstances. The dissipative structure of consensus and commitment is therefore necessarily short-lived if an organization is to be innovative.

These phases constitute a political and learning process through which managers deal with strategic issues, and the key point about these processes is that they are spontaneous and self-organizing: no central authority can direct anyone to detect and select an open-ended issue for attention, simply because no one knows what it is until someone has detected it; no one can centrally organize the factions that form around specific issues; nor can anyone intend the destruction of old recipes and the substitution of new ones since it is impossible to know what the appropriate new ones are until they are discovered. The development of new strategic direction requires the chaos of contention and conflict, and the self-organizing processes of political interaction and complex learning.

Chaos is a fundamental property of non-linear feedback systems, a category that includes human organizations

Feedback simply means that one action or event feeds into another; that is, one action or event determines the next according to some relationship. For example, one firm repackages its product and its rival responds in some way, leading to a further action on the part of the first, provoking in turn yet another response from the second, and so on. The feedback relationship may be linear or proportional, and when this is the case, the first firm will repackage its product and the second will respond by doing much the same. The feedback relationship could be non-linear, or non-proportional, however, so that when the first firm repackages its product, the second introduces a new product at a lower price; this could lead the first to cut prices even further, so touching off a price war. In other words, non-linear

systems are those that use amplifying (positive) feedback in some way. To see the significance of positive feedback, compare it with negative feedback.

All effective businesses use negative or damping feedback systems to control and regulate their day-to-day activities. Managers fix short-term targets for profits and then prepare annual plans or budgets, setting out the time path to reach the target. As the business moves through time, outcomes are measured and compared with annual plan projections to yield variances. Frequent monitoring of those variances prompts corrective action to bring performance indicators back onto their planned paths; that is, variances feed back into corrective action and the feedback takes a negative form, so that when profit is below target, for example, offsetting action is taken to restore it. Scheduling, budgetary and planning systems utilize negative feedback to keep an organization close to a predictable, stable equilibrium path in which it is adapted to its environment. While negative feedback controls a system according to prior intention, positive feedback produces explosively unstable equilibrium where changes are amplified, eventually putting intolerable pressure on the system until it runs out of control.

The key discovery about the operation of non-linear feedback systems, however, is that there is a third choice. When a non-linear feedback system is driven away from stable equilibrium toward explosive unstable equilibrium, it passes through a phase of bounded instability – there is a border between stability and instability where feedback flips autonomously between the amplifying and the damping to produce chaotic behaviour; a paradoxical state that combines both stability and instability.

All human interactions take the form of feedback loops simply because the consequences of one action always feed back to affect a subsequent one. Furthermore, all human interactions constitute non-linear feedback loops because people under- and overreact. Since organizations are simply a vast web of feedback loops between people, they must be capable of chaotic, as well as stable and explosively unstable, behaviour. The key question is which of these kinds of behaviours leads an organization to success. We can see the answer to this question if we reflect upon the fundamental forces operating on an organization.

All organizations are powerfully pulled in two fundamentally different directions:

■ Disintegration. Organizations can become more efficient and effective if they divide tasks, segment markets, appeal to individual motivators, empower people, promote informal communication and separate production processes in geographic and other terms. These steps lead to fragmenting cultures and dispersed power that pull an organization toward disintegration, a phenomenon that can be seen in practice as companies split into more and more business units and find it harder and harder to maintain control.

■ Ossification. To avoid this pull to disintegration, and to reap the advantages of synergy and coordination, all organizations are also pulled to a state in which tasks are integrated, overlaps in market segments and production processes managed, group goals stressed above individual ones, power concentrated, communication and procedures formalized, and strongly shared cultures established. As an organization moves in this direction it develops more and more rigid structures, rules, procedures and systems until it eventually ossifies, consequences that are easy to observe as organizations centralize.

Thus, one powerful set of forces pulls every organization toward a stable equilibrium (ossification) and another powerful set of forces pulls it toward an explosively unstable equilibrium (disintegration). Success lies at the border between these states, where managers continually alter systems and structures to avoid attraction either to disintegration or to ossification. For example, organizations typically swing to centralization in one period, to decentralization in another, and back again later on. Success clearly lies in a non-equilibrium state between stable and unstable equilibria; and for a non-linear feedback system, that is chaos.

Eight steps to create order out of chaos

When managers believe that they must pull together harmoniously in pursuit of a shared organizational intention established before they act, they are inevitably confined to the predictable – existing strategic directions will simply be continued or innovations made by others will simply be imitated. When, instead of this, managers create the chaos that flows from challenging existing perceptions and promote the conditions in which spontaneous self-organization can occur, they make it possible for innovation and new strategic direction to emerge. Managers create such conditions when they undertake actions of the following kind.

Develop new perspectives on the meaning of control

The activity of learning in a group is a form of control that managers do not normally recognize as such. It is a self-organizing, self-policing form of control in which the group itself discovers intention and exercises control. Furthermore, we are all perfectly accustomed to the idea that the strategic direction of local communities, nation-states and international communities is developed and controlled through the operation of political systems, but we rarely apply this notion to organizations. When we do, we see that a sequence of choices and actions will continue in a particular direction only while those espousing that direction continue to enjoy sufficient support. This constitutes a form of control that is as applicable to an organization when it faces the conflicts around open-ended change, as it is to a nation. The lesson is that self-organizing processes can produce controlled behaviour even though no one is in control – sometimes the best thing a manager can do is to let go and allow things to happen.

Design the use of power

The distribution of power and the way in which it is used provide very important boundaries around the group learning process from which new strategic directions emerge. The application of power in particular forms has fairly predictable consequences for group dynamics. Where power is applied as force and consented to out of fear, the group dynamic will be one of submission, or where such power is not consented to, the group dynamic will be one of rebellion, either covert or overt. Power may be applied as authority, and the predictable group dynamic here is one in which members of the group suspend their critical faculties and accept instructions from those above them. Groups in states of submission, rebellion or conformity are incapable of complex learning, that is, the development of new perspectives and new mental models.

The kind of group dynamics that are conducive to complex learning occur when highly competitive win/lose polarization is removed and open questioning and public testing of assertions encouraged. When this happens, people use argument and conflict to move toward periodic consensus and commitment to a particular issue. That consensus and commitment cannot, however, be the norm when people are searching for new perspectives – rather, they must alternate between conflict and consensus, between confusion and clarity. This kind of dynamic is likely to occur when they most powerfully alternate the form in which they use their power: sometimes withdrawing and allowing conflict; sometimes intervening with suggestions; sometimes exerting authority.

Encourage self-organizing groups

A group will be self-organizing only if it discovers its own challenges, goals and objectives. Mostly, such groups need to form spontaneously – the role of top managers is simply to create the atmosphere in which this can happen. When top managers do set up a group to deal with strategic issues, however, they must avoid the temptation to write terms of reference, set objectives or prod the group to reach some predetermined view. Instead top managers must present ambiguous challenges and take the chance that the group may produce proposals they do not approve of. For a group of managers to be self-organizing, it has to be free to operate as its members jointly choose, within the boundaries provided by their work together. This means that when they work together in this way, the normal hierarchy must be suspended for most of the time. Members are there because of the contributions they are able to make and the influence they can exert through those contributions and their own personalities. This suspension of the normal hierarchy can take place only if those on higher levels behave in a manner that indicates that they attach little importance to their position for the duration of the work of the group.

Provoke multiple cultures

One way of developing the conflicting countercultures required to provoke new perspectives is to rotate people between functions and business units. The motive here is to create cultural diversity as opposed to the current practice of using rotation to build a cadre of managers with the same management philosophy. Another effective way of promoting countercultures is that practised by Canon and Honda, where significant numbers of managers are hired at the same time, midway through their careers in other organizations, to create sizeable pockets of different cultures that conflict with the predominant one.

Present ambiguous challenges instead of clear long-term objectives or visions

Agendas of strategic issues evolve out of the clash between different cultures in self-organizing groups. Top managers can provoke this activity by setting ambiguous challenges and presenting half-formed issues for others to develop, instead of trying to set clear long-term objectives. Problems without objectives should be intentionally posed to provoke the emotion and conflict that lead to active search for new ways of doing things. This activity of presenting challenges should also be a two-way activity, where top executives hold themselves open to challenge from subordinates.

Expose the business to challenging situations

Managers who avoid taking chances face the certainty of stagnation and therefore the high probability of collapse in the long term, simply because innovation depends significantly on chance. Running for cover because the future is unknowable is in the long run the riskiest response of all. Instead, managers must intentionally expose themselves to the most challenging of situations. In his study of international companies, Michael Porter concludes that those who position themselves to serve the world's most sophisticated and demanding customers, who seek the challenge of competing with the most imaginative and competent competitors, are the ones who build sustainable competitive advantage on a global scale.

Devote explicit attention to improving group learning skills

New strategic directions emerge when groups of managers learn together in the sense of questioning deeply held beliefs and altering existing mental models rather than simply absorbing existing bodies of knowledge and sets of techniques. Such a learning process may well be personally threatening and so arouse anxiety that leads to bizarre group dynamics – this is perhaps the major obstacle to effective organizational learning. To overcome it, managers must spend time explicitly exploring how they interact and learn together – the route to superior learning is self-reflection in groups.

Create resource slack

New strategic directions emerge when the attitudes and behaviour of managers create an atmosphere favourable to individual initiative and intuition, to political interaction, and to learning in groups. Learning and political interaction are hard work, and they cannot occur without investment in spare management resources. A vital precondition for emergent strategy is thus investment in management resources to allow it to happen.

Conclusion

Practising managers and academics have been debating the merits of organizational learning as opposed to the planning conceptualization of strategic management. That debate has not, however, focused clearly on the critical unquestioned assumptions upon which the planning approach is based, namely, the nature of causality. Recent discoveries about the nature of dynamic feedback systems make it clear that cause and effect links disappear in innovative human organizations, making it impossible to envisage or plan their long-term futures. Because of this lack of causal connection between specific actions and specific outcomes, new strategic directions can only emerge through a spontaneous, self-organizing political and learning process. The planning approach can be seen as a specific approach applicable to the short-term management of an organization's existing activities, a task as vital as the development of a new strategic direction.

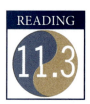

READING 11.3

Dual leadership

By David G. Thomson[1]

In 1994 Jerry Yang and David Filo, two doctoral candidates in Stanford University's electrical engineering programme, spent as much time surfing the newly created World Wide Web as they were pursuing their doctoral studies. They even created their own website, "Jerry's Guide to the World Wide Web," which linked Internet users to their favourite places in cyberspace.

"Jerry's Guide," however, did not make the Yang and Filo site sound very interesting, so one night they changed the name. Teeing off the phrase Yet Another Compiler Compiler (YACC) – a favourite among Unix computer code programmers – they came up with Yet Another Hierarchical Officious Oracle – or YAHOO! for short because Yang and Filo considered themselves a couple of major yahoos after all, and thus a famous brand name was born.

Then in 1995 Marc Andreessen, cofounder of Netscape Communications, invited Yang and Filo to move Yahoo! from the Stanford University computer system, which Yahoo! had outgrown, to Netscape's big facility. Commercialization soon followed. Advertising revenues began to rise – and Yang and Filo soon realized that they could not manage the business by themselves anymore.

That is when they recruited an experienced technology professional and former Stanford PhD, Tim Koogle, to serve as CEO. Koogle, in turn, recruited Jeff Mallett as COO, who had already cut his teeth at Reference Software and WordPerfect and was Vice President and General Manager of Novell Inc.'s consumer division. Together, Koogle and Mallett began transforming Yahoo!, turning it into one of the most popular stops along the information highway.

While Yang and Filo would arrive at work wearing T-shirts and sneakers, Koogle and Mallett preferred suits. Many viewed the foursome's working relationship as one of children with ideas and their parents who could turn their children's ideas into action. As analyst Andrea Williams of Volpe Brown Whelan & Co. noted, "Americans are captivated by the idea of two college kids like Yang and Filo starting an incredible service. But Mallet and Koogle have turned it into a business that advertisers and investors understand and respect."

Indeed, the relationship between Mallett and Koogle helped turn Yahoo! into a winning High Growth Company for the first five years of its development. Mallett was a strong internal leader and responsible for running operations. Koogle was an ideal outside-facing CEO. In the first 12 months on the job, Koogle took a startup and signed 50 alliances, hired a sales team and several crucial top management team members, and took the company public.

Koogle essentially guided the company through tremendous growth as he contributed to building its management team, creating its adventurous organizational culture and signing up alliance partners. Together the two men made Yahoo! into one of the few profitable, high-growth Internet companies of the late 1990s. After the dot.com meltdown, however, and Yahoo!'s well-chronicled falters, another team turned around

[1]Source: This article was adapted from David G. Thomson (2006) Chapter 7 'Dual leadership' *Blueprint To A Billion: 7 essentials to achieve exponential growth*, John Wiley & Sons. Copyright © David G Thomson 2006. Reproduced with permission of John Wiley & Sons, Inc..

the company and got it onto its present track. Current Chairman and CEO Terry Semel and COO Dan Rosensweig have also made a compelling team – with all the requisite external and internal skills needed to get Yahoo! onto the fast lane of the enormous Internet search-and advertising industry.

To pin all the early success of Yahoo! on Koogle and Mallett – and where it is today on Semel and Rosensweig – would oversimplify a complex corporate history. But teams of such effective pairs do, in fact, perform much of the work that catapults their companies to record-breaking success. The following sections explain why.

The importance of dynamic duos

Among High Growth Companies, we found that "dynamic duos" drove many of the star-performing companies. These are two individuals who worked tightly together to build the firm from dreams to a billion dollars in revenue.

More surprises surfaced as we drilled deeper into this finding. We learned that for the duo to be dynamic, one of them had to excel in the *external* part of the effort – in marketing and sales. The other had to be the *internal* – keeping the operations purring or, perhaps, inventing new products. Together, they had to explore and innovate continuously – whether it was in product innovation or marketing innovation. They had to make swift decisions – and often quick and nimble correction of their mistakes. Most important they had to have complete trust in and respect for one another.

The Koogle-Mallett combo at Yahoo! is typical of what we found in the High Growth Companies: an Internal–External leadership pair (working in partner- ship with the founding team) who managed to execute all the essentials simultaneously. This particular pair, like others we have seen repeatedly in High Growth Companies, had a unique chemistry that electrified the evolution of their service. Cisco, eBay, Nike, Starbucks and many others have applied the same pattern, as shown by the list of dynamic duos in Table 11.3.1.

Dynamic duos are the stuff of corporate legend: Sears and Roebuck, Roy and Walt Disney, Hewlett and Packard, and the like. What we found is that in High Growth Companies it is more than corporate myth – High Growth Companies *do* spring from such pairings.

There is one other thing that struck us. These dynamic duos who lead High Growth Companies are not just colleagues or even just friends. They have a remarkable chemistry between them, built on a very high level of respect and trust. They benefit from having complementary skills and talents. They are the yin and yang, the weave and warp, the bacon and eggs, and without this dynamic of compatibility their companies could not have made it to the top. Their relationship is dynamic in the way that they use their complementary strengths. Any individual weaknesses or flip-flops went unseen by outside observers because they used each other's strengths in ways that compensated for what the other lacked or could not do. As a pair, they were the highest of performance teams.

The essentials of high growth leadership

To get from an early High Growth to an actual billion dollars in revenue, you need a breakthrough value proposition, Launching Customers, and a powerhouse business model. What about leadership? What kind of management does it take to propel a company from a High Growth to a billion dollars in a few years? What are the roles of the CEO in a High Growth Company, the COO, the engineering team – even the founders themselves?

To answer these questions, we – in collaboration with Peter Robertson of the London-based consulting firm Human Insight – took a closer look at the best High Growth Companies. With Robertson's help we assessed a sample of the top High Growth Companies. There we found patterns in – and answers about – High Growth Companies leadership.

TABLE 11.3.1   Internal–External leadership pairs

Company	Leadership pair examples
Yahoo!	Jeff Mallett and Tim Koogle
Microsoft	Jon Shirley and Bill Gates
Tractor Supply	Jim Wright and Joe Scarlett
eBay	Maynard Webb and Meg Whitman
Siebel Systems	Patricia House and Tom Siebel
Starbucks	Orin Smith and Howard Schultz
Broadcom	Harry Samueli and Henry Nicholas III

Source: Company reports

In addition to these assessments, we studied published interviews and articles that featured the leaders of top High Growth Companies. Their statements gave us clues to the best management practices. We conducted our own interviews with numerous founders, CEOs, COOs and investors. These individuals helped identify the elements of management that they believed drove their success. After a year of this kind of exploration, we had a much clearer understanding about this unique set of leadership dimensions.

Three leadership dimensions of the internal-outside leadership duo

High Growth leadership, it turns out, has three dimensions:

1 *Focus on relationships and products.* One member of the dynamic duo is focused on company-shaping relationships – that is, building relationships with Launching Customers, Big Brother alliances, strategic investors, board members and outsiders such as other High Growth CEOs, suppliers and community leaders. The other half of the duo focuses on logical ideas concerned with product development, processes and systems that fuel the company's product or service pipeline.

2 *Drive to innovate and explore.* While one member of the duo manages for internal structure, that is, problem solving for disciplined and predictable responses, the other is forward looking by exploring and shaping opportunities. This is a delicate balance between preserving the past and exploring in order to innovate. That said, there is a useful back-and-forth and, sometimes, even a brief exchange of roles that keeps this chemistry dynamic and replenishing.

3 *The ability to manage simultaneously.* Most important, we learned the importance of management's ability to balance the execution of the essentials. In such a high-powered environment, there are always many balls to juggle and it takes a particularly talented, collegial team to keep those balls in the air. Dropping one can cause a High Growth Company to risk falling off trajectory. Successful High Growth management teams learn how to do it all – how to deal with the simultaneous execution of the essentials and still keep the corporate trajectory heading rapidly toward a billion dollars and more.

The first two leadership dimensions, focus and drive, form the basis for clearly defining the roles of the Internal–External leadership pair (see Figure 11.3.1).

When we started our research for this book, we sensed that High Growth Companies had a unique management style. What we learned was that *High Growth* management is unique. With limited resources these teams execute "1 + 1 = 3" miracles. What can we learn from these impressive leaders?

Breakaway marketing leaders

First, High Growth leaders are superb communicators. They possess the personal chemistry, even charisma, which lets them bridge the gaps between alliance members, Launching Customers, community leaders and important investors. They are accomplished at finding, qualifying and shaping the deals and relationships that ultimately shape the company.

One member of the leadership pair, typically the CEO, fills this role. The CEO could be an external hire, typically brought in early – or a founding member. Meg Whitman was brought in early; Bill Gates, Howard Schultz and Phil Knight are founding members.

The role of the leader depends on the value proposition of the company. Nike's Phil Knight was a showcase of breakaway marketing leadership. Knight constantly pushed the boundaries and changed the ground rules. Instead of marketing shoes, he marketed the athletes who wore the shoes and what they achieved in their Nikes.

As new market segments emerged, Knight tried to be the first to spot them. In 1984, when the National Basketball Association (NBA) games began televising in prime time, Knight was instrumental in getting an endorsement from Michael Jordan, then just a promising player. The Air Jordan shoes helped make Nike's

---

External-facing CEOs are highly exploratory – particularly with relationships and creating opportunities. This forward-thinking style is critical to proactively developing Launching Customers and Big Brother alliances, securing the right board members and evangelizing the company's vision to employees and the community. This leader affects the forward-thinking approaches of the person whose role is focused more primarily on the Internal, who is usually responsible for innovation leadership.

FIGURE 11.3.1   The Internal–External leadership pairs

Yahoo: perceived founding dynamics

Focus & Drive: form the basis for defining the roles of the Internal–External leadership pair

Drive is related to the contribution of roles to the standard Growth-curve. This is shown in the right picture, where the explore (A) – Preserve (B) characteristics of the Growth-curve correlate reversely with the role positions in the left and middle picture. The vertical axis (left picture) relates to the capacity to manage simultaneously. The higher a role scores, the more this role is capable of aligning the contribution of other roles to the Growth-curve. This makes these roles more generalistic, as contrast to roles that score lower, which relates to being more specialist (managing less, but more in depth).

basketball shoes into a $500 million business by 1990. No wonder that a recent *Fortune* magazine cover read: "Nike After Knight: The maverick built a company like no other. Can anyone fill his shoes?"

Tom Siebel aggressively shaped Launching Customer relationships with Charles Schwab and General Electric, shaped a Big Brother alliance with Microsoft and Andersen Consulting, and shaped his board by adding Charles Schwab and the head of Andersen as a result of an investment in Siebel.

Breakaway innovation leaders

While the dynamic duo is evangelizing customers, conceiving a brilliant marketing strategy and managing the business, a third critical leader is what we call *Breakaway Innovation Leadership*. These leaders, typically the founders of the company, focus more on the product rather than on External relationships. They are often highly creative, with a broad range of interests, perhaps skipping from mathematics to biology to music in a single thought. They have a need for innovation because they have a passion for extremely creative inventions. They work with others, but mostly because of a mutual interest in the subject. Rather than personal charm or charisma, they often use brilliant new ideas and the lure of exploration to keep their teams working together.

Company founders often assume this leadership role. They are pivotal in shaping the innovation-based value proposition, creating and leading the core engineering team, and contributing to the fundamental principles by which the business model is based. They serve to provide a consistent trajectory of innovation aligned to the company's core value proposition.

These leaders are an important link to customers, partners and markets in terms of getting product feedback from them. They are highly regarded by their specialist colleagues, who exist as customers and partners in the same technical community, and who breathe the same air. As corporations grow with new employees, these product-centred innovators act as a critical adhesive element by spurring the team on to higher levels of innovation.

More key roles in high growth management

If you relied on the covers of the business magazines, you would think that it takes only an individual or two to run a High Growth Company. No single CEO can possibly keep all of the essentials in motion without help. In fact, the more our team debated the unique qualities of High Growth Companies, the more we realized that the successful corporation was much more like an *eco-system* than a cult of personality or personalities.

High Growth Companies need steady-handed managers who bring stability to the enterprise. These individuals exhibit control, discipline and predictability. With this keel beneath them, High Growth marketing and product innovators can feel secure enough to keep their minds out on the cutting edge.

Process Managers, for instance, typically are the captains of supply chain leadership. They are controlling and process focused. They can either operate within existing boundaries or shape new boundaries within

THREE SURPRISING INSIGHTS

As we looked into the histories of the High Growth Companies, three counterintuitive insights dawned on us:

1 Most people assume that most High Growth leaders had previous experience working in smaller companies. That, we found, is not true. Of the top companies that we studied, the Internal–External leaders came from varied backgrounds.

2 There seems to be a belief that the founders rarely stayed with the company all the way to the $1 billion revenue mark. That is not true with these companies. A significant number of the original leaders were still at the helm when the High Growth start-up crossed the billion dollar line: Bill Gates, Larry Ellison, Tom Sternberg and Pierre Omidyar to name a few.

3 The third misconception is that High Growth founders are of the same breed, that stereotype of the young, tousle-haired, pizza-gobbling, brilliant college dropout – or some variation of the theme. However, High Growth leaders did not have a common background. They came from all walks of professional life – from college dropouts to college grads, from small company leaders to large company leaders. They came as business professionals or customer advocates with little marketing and sales expertise or with a lot of it.

which to operate. They tend to be the key team to support the COO and CEO. Of course, not every High Growth Company needs to invest in its own supply chain to get to the top. Many of them, on the faster four- and six-year trajectory, tended to outsource manufacturing. That allowed them to grow quickly, to minimize capital costs and to achieve lower product costs. Cisco, for instance, outsourced its manufacturing early. Broadcom also outsourced its semiconductor manufacturing. Nike moved its manufacturing to several Asian footwear producers.

Organization Managers are another role. These leaders are at home in the caring role. They foster a more congenial atmosphere in the organization and will do their best to maintain it. Especially important in high-growth and services companies, these leaders believe that caring for employees is fundamental for the company to provide a highly differentiated service to customers. This leadership style is typically humble. They are leaders by example, great listeners who pick up on feedback and quickly resolve issues. Typically, they support the CEO and COO.

A third role is *Operational Leadership,* the Chief Operating Officer. This role forms the complementary half of the Dynamic Duo – and is the internal counterpart to the outside-facing CEO. COOs are known as Mr. /Ms. Internal and are at the right hand of the outside-facing CEO. Operational leaders are centred and well balanced. Often, they are so far behind the scenes that you hardly hear about them in the business press or notice them when you walk in the door of a company. As shown in Figure 11.3.1, they are highly versatile across all of the leadership styles. They have a trust-based relationship with a very high propensity to effective and efficient problem solving. They are real partners. If you can envision a high performance team of two, this would be it.

The number-one Internal–External pair of the 1990s

Today, people often think of the prototypical Internal– External pair as Bill Gates and Steve Ballmer. But another great example of the Internal–External dynamic pair can be found in the evolution of Microsoft. Back in 1983, when Microsoft was at the inflection point, the company outgrew its small-time style faster than Bill Gates could handle it. Gates had tried to take charge of five product lines. As a result, he paid little attention to tailoring programmes to meet customers' needs. Key planning decisions were often delayed or not made.

Gates recognized his own shortcomings. He tried to hire a president, but that individual did not work out. He tried again in August 1983, and this time he hit gold – Jon Shirley, a 25-year career veteran at Tandy Corp. who had known Gates as a customer.

Shirley recalled, "The company lacked a lot of systems that it needed to grow to become big. It was nothing like an ideal organizational setup and it had no MIS system. They were using a Tandy Model 2 for the general ledger." Shirley also discovered that Microsoft lacked key statistical data about its products, its markets and its sales. "We were totally out of manufacturing space, and we had no one who knew how to run the manufacturing side," he said looking back, adding that he threw himself into developing "a whole lot of structures and systems that would give us the tools we needed."

Shirley had performed many of the same operations for the much larger Tandy and felt comfortable operating within Microsoft's "get-it-done" corporate culture. Shirley viewed his role as one of building up the support side of the business, hiring the chief financial officer (Francis Gaudette, who would later play a critical role in shepherding Microsoft's initial public offering through Wall Street in 1986), and honing the management team, whose members had almost all been hired from within the company.

In August 1984 the management team took serious action. It reorganized around two divisions: (1) systems software, the programmes that control a computer's internal operations; and (2) business applications, programmes that tell a machine to do specific tasks, such as word processing. Four years later, in 1988, Microsoft restructured the Applications Division into five business units. The business units would have profit and loss responsibility for their product lines and would be responsible for marketing and documentation of their products, said Shirley. "It gave them a great deal of control to run as a small business," he noted.

Analysts give Shirley credit for quarterbacking many of the key strategic alliances that helped catapult Microsoft to industry prominence (though Shirley said they naturally evolved from simple customer relationships). In contrast, Gates played the market and standards leadership role, shaping the technologies for various product areas. "Gates and Shirley absolutely occupied different ends of the business," said Arthur Block, Manufacturers Hanover Trust VP in charge of end-user support. "Bill focused on the IBM alliance while Shirley focused on Hewlett-Packard (HP). Gates talked to user groups while Shirley talked to the financial community. Gates linked product/market opportunities to technology, while Jon applied structure and process to the business so that it could scale."

On the day-to-day level, Shirley mirrored a management style that was supportive and didactic, well-suited to Microsoft's campus ambience. "I believe in delegation and teaching," Shirley said. "You've got to give people sufficient authority to make mistakes."

Shirley retired in 1989 – after Microsoft passed $800 million revenue (on the way to $1 billion next year). He had essentially guided the company from the inflection point to $1 billion as Bill Gates' "Mr. Internal."

A leading Internal–External pair today

Tractor Supply is a wonderful case study of a similar management pair in today's management world. Tractor Supply is the number one US farm and ranch store, with sales of $1.7 billion and over 7,000 team members. The company is known for its great customer service, which it provides to full- and part-time farmers and ranchers as well as the general public. Tractor Supply carries a complete line of livestock and pet products; maintenance products for agricultural and rural use; hardware and tools; lawn-and-garden power equipment; truck, trailer and towing gear; and work clothing. Despite the wide variety of products that Tractor Supply offers, the most popular item it sells harkens back to the roots of the business: the simple lynchpin, that basic item that connects the farm tractor to what it pulls.

While Joe Scarlett's official title is Chairman, he is more often described by those he works with as coach, cheerleader, company's conscience and chief missionary of the gospel at Tractor Supply. Scarlett provided us with a unique perspective on the dynamic duo leadership paradigm. During his tenure, he worked with an internal counterpart – and without one:

Before I became Chairman and my right hand, Jim Wright, became President and CEO in 2004, we served as the CEO and COO team. Then and today, we are on the same page at all times. We share the same values. We finish each other's sentences. Just the other day someone remarked that we are "like an old married couple." The chemistry started during the interviewing process.

When I hired Jim, we spent hours interviewing. We went to Florida and walked the stores for hours at a time. We attended a manager's meeting in Florida together. We spent two days walking through Wal-Mart, Lowe's, Home Depot and a score of other stores learning from them. In each of these settings, we asked questions of one another, we talked strategy, we discussed values, we discussed the competition, we problem solved. We would ask each other "How would you handle this situation?" in merchandising, operations, logistics, competition, people and training. We got into each others heads so well that when we are in meetings today and look at each other across the room we often know what the other is thinking.

Today, when Jim and I get the same email and I send a follow up I often find that Jim independently sent a similar follow up to the same people. What makes us successful is that we have similar but different backgrounds. We each managed a lot of different parts of the business over the years. We both have merchandising and operations experience, which we believe are critical factors for leadership success in high growth retailing. We both have run businesses before. Jim was previously the CEO of a smaller company. We are honest with one another. We are quick problem solvers. No problem lingers.

Scarlett explained that Wright is process driven and more inside facing. He can take a problem and determine the right priority, the right person, and the right process to get it solved. In contrast, Scarlett said he is more focused on big picture strategies and people issues. He spends much time preaching the message and interacting with employees – even though he is ostensibly more externally facing. "Of course," said Scarlett, "both of us are committed to our people first. Leadership in each store is our top priority." Scarlett spends 50 per cent of his time coaching, mentoring, career planning and training. Together they just brought in their 22 top high-potential store managers, with whom Scarlett spent two days discussing the business and customers. In fact, Scarlett personally visits about 150 stores a year.

Scarlett continued to elaborate on the differences of style in Tractor Supply's leadership pair:

In contrast there was a time before Jim [was at Tractor Supply] when it was a struggle. I am

not process oriented. We found ourselves talking a lot and didn't execute. I would unrealistically expect people to do things based on how I thought it should get done. We would "take three steps forward and two back." He could get things done realistically. He could break down problems into tasks with a process. With Jim on board we take three steps forward and stay there. I found that when I wore both hats, I simply did not have enough time for it all!

There was another aspect of this High Growth winner that impressed me. "We are very close to our suppliers," Scarlett said and continued in some detail:

I am on a first-name basis with our 50 top supplier CEOs. We bring the Presidents and CEOs in each year to share leadership, business strategy, direction, plans, philosophy and values. We share confidential information with them so that they can partner with us to innovate and be first to market. We count on our suppliers to help us offer products that are both key to our target customer and not part of the offering from the big-box retailers such as Wal-Mart and Home Depot. We work with our suppliers to serve as a guide for them so that we are first to market. We become their "Test kitchen." Today we are very proud of the fact that 35 per cent of our business is from new products that weren't in the product line three years earlier. We listen to our customers carefully to offer them higher quality and better lifestyle products.

Finally Scarlett explained that his company espouses some down-home, old-fashioned values and they have paid off. Scarlett said the company mission statement is *"Work hard, have fun, and make money by providing legendary service and great products at everyday low prices"* – and there is not a meeting where he or Jim do not discuss the values of the company in terms of everyday decision making. *"When I visit stores, I am consistently preaching our values,"* he explained. *"For example, we will discuss ethics with the store teams, what are breaches, how not to get in these situations. I preach and repeat our values consistently."*

"Why preach and repeat?" I asked.

"We continually have a lot of new people," he replied with a country man's grin, *"and people naturally only retain a small portion of what they hear!"*

Calm in the midst of the storm

In contrast to the intense stress environment that typically comes with high-energy innovation for both products and marketing, High Growth Companies share another trait: The ability to remain calm in the midst of the storm, to stay consistent and fairly unflappable even under the onslaught of chaos and ever increasing change. The "secret weapon" is having consistent values with the ability to self-correct.

One of the most important tasks of management is ensuring a climate in which people feel safe to explore. Exploration can only be achieved if leadership values are consistent. Leadership values are not one action, but a demonstrated set of actions over time in all kinds of situations that demonstrate consistency of values. There are two equally weighted drivers of consistency.

Consistent behaviours, communications and messaging

Marshall Goldsmith, world-renowned executive coach whose skills are in demand by many major CEOs, shared his perspective on this important leadership aspect. "What matters in leadership," Goldsmith said, "is not the words hanging on the wall; it is the behaviour demonstrated in the hall." This is the case in High Growth Companies, given the consistent nature of the communications that we found in which CEOs are always "on message."

For Joe Scarlett, Tractor Supply's Mission and Values are integrated into all of his communications and messages. This leads him to be consistent and aligned with communicating corporate values. As already mentioned, Scarlett spends much of his time with employees discussing the application of values to behaviours and customer service.

Consistent values at defining moments

Consistency means that personal values and organizational aims will largely dictate what a manager does. These are best illustrated during defining moments

> Leaders who lay out a consistent communications plan and vision – and act with upright values even in crisis – are critical to mobilizing an organization into consistent behaviours.

– times when an organization is facing a crisis. All eyes are on the leader. Consistency is tested when there is a worrisome opportunity for the leader to act in *opposition* to stated values – and a broader sense of ethics. If he or she demonstrates consistent values, they are not only proven a good leader, they have reinforced the culture of the company and, hence, the conditions for continued growth.

We found often that, early in the company's trajectory, many leaders of High Growth Companies are pretty unimpressed by the wealth and fame that might follow. They are focused on the business – or even how it might help the community. eBay's IPO, for example, established a charitable fund. Instead of focusing on themselves, High Growth leaders focus on the company. Mark Leslie, who built Veritas software to over $1 billion in revenue, came to this understanding: "I wasn't a great CEO until I realized it was about everybody *but* me."

High Growth leaders are goal- and results-oriented. They manage for long-term results. They know how to leverage customers and alliance partners to shape products and services, thereby creating exponential revenue growth. In certain sectors, software for example, it was paramount that these companies dominate their markets. These leaders, therefore, placed a high value on beating the competition.

We found that High Growth leaders communicate consistent messages about the company's value proposition. Their passion is aligned to the value proposition and the priorities that they must execute, as in the case of Meg Whitman.

In 1999, when eBay's website crashed for 22 hours, Meg Whitman stepped up. She called this event eBay's "near-death experience" – the young company risked losing its entire trove of customer and transaction data. The outage exposed a glaring weakness for an Internet company – and eBay did not have the in-house talent to fix the site. What saved her, and eBay too, was a new technology chief. "I was like a crazed woman on a mission," she recalled about her meeting with Maynard Webb, then Gateway Computer's tech boss, a few days after the outage. Whitman successfully pleaded with him to come over to eBay and the infrastructure that he built now handles, in a typical day, more transactions than NASDAQ – with no major outages in almost six years.

The defining moment does not stop there. Everyone at eBay was given a list of 100 customers to call and apologize to. It turned into a defining moment of another nature. The customers were genuinely touched

PASSION OVER PAIN

Although the management world has been taught that pain, crisis and the need to overcome deficiencies motivate change, High Growth Companies reveal a different picture. Top High Growth Companies innovate because they have an inner drive to explore. This exploration is not limited to products. It includes new markets, new alliances, new customers and new business models. Although pain can drive change, it often comes too late to be of much use.

and the company reconnected to the community. If you ask any eBay employee, this defining moment is one that is often described as part of the company's lore. In 2005, six years later, when the pricing changes were not understood by the community, the employees again picked up the phone to call the community and Meg Whitman joined the town hall meeting that week to explain the changes to customers.

Having your values in place also means that you can move fast to acquire an opportunity. For Tractor Supply, this happened in the summer of 2001. A competitor had gone bankrupt, and Tractor Supply had the chance to buy its stores. The problem was that the investment banker for the creditor said that Tractor Supply would have to buy all of them, not the 40 that Tractor Supply wanted. Tractor Supply could have lost the opportunity, but instead it came up with what CEO Joe Scarlett described as Project 110, in which the company had to open up all 110 stores by the end of 2002, with 87 of them opened in 110 days.

"Project 110 galvanized the whole organization," recalled Scarlett. "We brought the top 20 leaders in Tractor Supply together. Jim Wright ran the project. The teams met every week to read out the status: on target, nearly on target, or screwed up. No one wanted to report screwed up. This lifted the confidence of the management team. We opened 87 stores in 110 days – when the maximum we had ever opened was 30 in a year. Jim and I spent hours in each of the 87 stores talking with the entire team, sitting around in a circle on those five-gallon buckets and talking about the values of our company, relationship with our customers, our value over Wal-Mart, and the things we can do to continue making our culture very special. Since then, we have never looked back."

A change in leadership can also become a defining moment. It may be the need to change senior management or the search for a successor when "the shoes are hard to fill." The spotlight is on the board, founders or CEO at this defining moment. Yahoo!'s founding team was wise to recognize early on that they could not shape the business themselves. Their defining moment – bringing in Koogle as an Outside leader – brought increased talent and structure to the business. Koogle then brought his Internal counterpart, Mallett, into the company. And what would eBay be without Meg Whitman brought in as CEO in 1998? Not nearly as big a success.

The ability to quickly self-correct

When growing to $1 billion, whether you are a four-, six-, or twelve-year trajectory company, at the inflection point you should expect revenues to double every 4, 9, or 24 months, respectively. The speed at which four- and six-year companies double revenues particularly requires that these companies exhibit the ability to not only self-correct, but to do so with speed. Failure to correct quickly increases the likelihood that a company can fall off trajectory.

Joe Scarlett passed this lesson on to other leaders at Tractor Supply. "Drill down if you don't know a lot about a problem or opportunity. Ask a lot of questions," he said, describing his style of self-correction.

"Once I failed to do that when we bought a computer system. We bought too large a system when we could only manage a fraction of it. It wouldn't have happened if I had asked more questions." Scarlett says you have to challenge the status quo, and not "fall in love with your own thinking." Scarlett offers another homily: "Get close to everyone in the organization – customers and suppliers, too. Any CEO spending over 50 per cent of his or her time in the office is doing a disservice. Go where the action is."

The third leadership dimension: managing simultaneously

We have already noted that High Growth leaders must demonstrate breakaway marketing and breakaway product innovation leadership. Their third challenge is the toughest of them all: Managing simultaneously. Yet the leaders of our top High Growth Companies have proven themselves to be shapers – leaders who can effectively shape their company's destiny in the face of intense uncertainty.

These leaders are problem solvers. But even more, they have a comfort level for problems with a lot of moving parts. Beyond that they have a superior capacity to recognize patterns – the pattern of Launching Customer behaviour, the pattern of Big Brother alliances, patterns of linkages between the essentials, to name a few. As in crewing a racing shell, all oars dip and swing simultaneously. The rowing team is comfortable managing scale, scope and complexity – balanced in a single stroke and aligned.

Second, they are also *collaborators*. They keep the team, employees, customers, partners and investors passionate about the company's direction and execution. They develop a balanced board (as an extension of themselves for execution).

These CEOs shape the company and its opportunity through their exploratory passion, which leads them to new markets, new strategic customer and alliance deals, and new standards. Just as Bill Gates shaped the IBM alliance, Tom Siebel shaped Launching Customers early on with the Andersen alliance and Phil Knight shaped new markets for running shoes, the most notable being the game of basketball with Nike's groundbreaking Air Jordan.

Passion for the company

In truth, passion is present in both High Growth Companies *and* failed start-ups. In all of these cases, founders loved their companies. They were willing to sacrifice for their success. They poured their heart and souls (and real money) into the enterprise. So what's different?

We found three big differences.

First, High Growth Company leaders articulate their passion as one that is also relevant to customers, often in terms that will deliver higher-order benefits. By this we mean that their passion is tightly aligned with the value proposition; a pursuit for higher-order benefits. For Bill Gates it was "conceiving ideas to make personal computers easier to use and to programme." Gates envisioned a computer on every desk and in every home." He was known for having a one-track mind – microcomputers.

> The Internal–External team is critical. They determine the cross-functional initiatives. More important, they balance the mix of preservation of the past and exploration for the future as the company experiences exponential growth.

For John Morgridge, Cisco's original CEO, it was "realizing Cisco had a solution in anticipation of customer demand." Morgridge passionately drove to be early and dominant in capturing the big advantage. For Howard Schultz, it was about becoming the "third place" for the Starbucks community after home and work. In other words, the passion of the leader could also be viewed as a valued passion of the customer.

Second, such leaders had a consistent strength of will to execute. As Cisco's former VP Sales, Terry Eger said, "In the face of limited resources, you have to have superior strength of will to execute. You have to have superior energy to execute ahead of the growth curve."

Third, these leaders are intensely committed to the company, not to the position they fill. They are hands-on managers. They get involved in shaping deals with partners and customers. They serve as an important link between the engineering team and the customer. They work incredibly hard at the details.

Superior problem solvers

High Growth leaders are superior problem solvers. They can navigate and execute in the context of a growth strategy. They can break problems down in the height of uncertain outcomes. They can best define and lead strategic initiatives enabling teams to link execution to strategy. These might sound like traits of all leaders, but they are not.

High Growth leaders can qualify, shape and execute deals with partners that shape the company. When Starbucks' Howard Schultz entered into a relationship with Pepsi to co-develop their first product together, it failed. So Schultz suggested they try working on another idea together: Frappuccino. It became a $500 million-plus business opportunity. Tenacity, stubborn optimism and the ability to shape markets with their own hands mark High Growth winners. When we interviewed companies that had failed or were on the slippery slope downward, we didn't pick up the same vibes. They just weren't closing in on the big opportunities.

Ever see a "hands-off" leader who focuses only on process with little understanding of the details of the business? Ever find leaders who are focused only on cost reduction at the expense of growth? Ever find leaders who are simply maxed-out with no time to manage all the moving parts? Not the leader of a High Growth Company.

REFERENCES

Åslund (2010); *Economist,* 23 March 2013; *EurasiaNet*, 3 August 2015; *Financial Times*, 5 June 2013 and 17 June 2013; *Forbes*, 2 June 2005.

Ackoff, R.L. (1980) *Creating the Corporate Future*, Chichester: Wiley.

Aldrich, H. (1999) *Organizations Evolving*, London: Sage.

Ali, A.J. (1995) 'Cultural Discontinuity and Arab Management Thought', *International Studies of Management & Organization*, 25(3), pp. 7–30.

Allison, G. (1969) 'Conceptual Models and The Cuban Missile Crisis', *The American Political Science Review,* 63(3, September), pp. 689–718.

Amabile, T.M. (1998) 'How to Kill Creativity', *Harvard Business Review*, 76(5, September–October), pp. 76–87.

Argyris, C. (1990) *Overcoming Organizational Defenses: Facilitating Organizational Learning*, Needham, MA: Allyn & Bacon.

Barney, J.B. (1991) 'Firm Resources and Sustained Competitive Advantage', *Journal of Management*, 17(1), pp. 99–120.

Bass, B.M. (1990) *Bass and Stogdill's Handbook of Leadership* (3rd edn), New York: Free Press.

Bavelas, A. (1964) 'Leadership: Man and Function', in: H.H. Leavitt and L.R. Pondy (eds) *Readings in Managerial Psychology*, Chicago, IL: University of Chicago Press.

Beinhocker, E.D. (1999) 'Strategy at the Edge of Chaos', *The McKinsey Quarterly*, 1, pp. 24–39.

Bellou, V (2011) 'Do women followers prefer a different leadership style than men?', *The International Journal of Human Resource Management*, 22(13), pp. 2818–2833.

Bennis, W. and Nanus, B. (1985) *Leaders: The Strategies for Taking Charge*, New York: Harper & Row.

Birnbaum, R. (1988) *How Colleges Work: The Cybernetics of Academic Organization and Leadership*, San Francisco, CA: Jossey-Bass.

Bourgeois, L.J. and Brodwin, D.R. (1983) 'Putting Your Strategy into Action', *Strategic Management Planning,* March–May.

Cannella, A.A. and Monroe, M.J. (1997) 'Contrasting Perspectives on Strategic Leaders: Toward a More Realistic View of Top Managers', *Journal of Management*, 23(3), pp. 213–237.

Century: The Role of Strategic Leadership', *Academy of Management Executive*, 13(1, February), pp. 43–57.

Chandler, A.D. (1962) *Strategy and Structure: Chapters in the History of the American Industrial Enterprise,* Cambridge, MA: MIT Press.

Chen, C.C. and Meindl, J.R. (1991) 'The Construction of Leadership Images in the Popular Press: The Case of Donald Burr and People Express', *Administrative Science Quarterly,* 36(4, December), pp. 521–551.

Child, J. (1972) 'Organizational Structure, Environment, and Performance: The Role of Strategic Choice', *Sociology,* January, pp. 2–22.

Cyert, R.M. (1990) 'Defining Leadership and Explicating the Process', *Non-Profit Management and Leadership,* 1(1, Fall), pp. 29–38.

Cyert, R.M. and March, J.G. (1963) *A Behavioral Theory of the Firm*, Englewood Cliffs, NJ: Prentice Hall.

Dobbin, F. and Boychuk, T. (1999) 'National Employment Systems and Job Autonomy: Why Job Autonomy is High in the Nordic Countries and Low in the United States, Canada, and Australia', *Organization Studies*, 20(2), pp. 257–291.

Eagly, A.H. and Johannesen-Schmidt, M.C. (2001) 'The leadership styles of women and men', *Journal of Social Issues*, 57(4), pp. 781–797.

Eagly, A.H. and Johnson, B.T. (1990) 'Gender and leadership style: A meta-analysis', *Psychological Bulletin*, 108(2), p. 233.

Etzioni, A. (1961) *A Comparative Analysis of Complex Organizations*, New York: Free Press.

Finkelstein, S. and Hambrick, D.C. (1996) *Strategic Leadership: Top Executives and Their Effects on Organizations*, St. Paul, MN: West.

French, J. and Raven, B.H. (1959) 'The Bases of Social Power', in: D. Cartwright (ed.) *Studies of Social Power*, Ann Arbor, MI: Institute for Social Research.

Gevedon, S.L. (1992) 'Leadership Behaviors of Deans of Top-Ranked Schools of Nursing', *Journal of Nursing Education*, 31(5), pp. 221–224.

Gibson, C.B. (1995) 'An investigation of gender differences in leadership across four countries', *Journal of International Business Studies*, 26(2), pp. 255–279.

Glassman, R.M. (1986) 'Manufactured Charisma and Legitimacy', in: R.M. Glassman and W.H. Swatos, Jr. (eds) *Charisma, History, and Social Structure*, New York: Glenwood Press.

Goldsmith, M. and Larsen, H. (2004) 'Local Political Leadership: Nordic Style', *International Journal of Urban and Regional Research*, 28(1), pp. 121–133.

Goold, M. and Quinn, J.J. (1990) *Strategic Control: Milestones for Long-Term Performance*, London: Hutchinson.

Greenwood, R. and Hinings, C.R. (1996) 'Understanding Radical Organizational Change: Bringing Together the Old and the New Institutionalism', *Academy of Management Review*, 21(4, October), pp. 1022–1054.

Greiner, L.E. (1972) 'Evolution and Revolution as Organizations Grow', *Harvard Business Review,* July–August, pp. 37–46.

Hambrick, D.C. and Mason, P.A. (1984) 'Upper Echelons: The Organization as a Reflection of Its Top Managers', *Academy of Management Review*, 9(2, April), pp. 193–206.

Hampden-Turner, C. and Trompenaars, A. (1993) *The Seven Cultures of Capitalism: Value Systems for Creating Wealth in the United States, Japan, Germany, France, Britain, Sweden, and the Netherlands*, New York: Doubleday.

Hannan, M.T. and Freeman, J. (1977) 'The Population Ecology of Organizations', *American Journal of Sociology*, 82(5, March), pp. 929–964.

Hayward, M.L.A., Rindova, V.P. and Pollock, T.G. (2004) 'Believing One's Own Press: The Causes and Consequences of CEO Celebrity', *Strategic Management Journal*, 25(7), pp. 637–653.

Hofstede, G. (1993) 'Cultural Constraints in Management Theories', *Academy of Management Executive*, 7(1), pp. 8–21.

Horváth, D., McMillan, C.J., Azumi, K. and Hickson, D.J. (1976) 'The Cultural Context of Organizational Control: An International Comparison', *International Studies of Management & Organization*, 6(3), pp. 60–86.

House, R.J. and Aditya, R.N. (1997) 'The Social Science Study of Leadership: Quo Vadis?', *Journal of Management*, 23(3, May–June), pp. 409–474.

Ireland, R.D. and Hitt, M.A. (1999) 'Achieving and Maintaining Strategic Competitiveness in the 21ˢᵗ Kakabadse, A., Myers, A., McMahon, T. and Spony, G. (1995) 'Top Management Styles in Europe: Implications for Business and Cross-National Teams', *European Business Journal*, 7(1), pp. 17–27.

Kelley, R.E. (1988) 'In Praise of Followers', *Harvard Business Review*, 66(6, November–December), p. 142.

Kets de Vries, M.F.R. (1994) 'The Leadership Mystique', *Academy of Management Executive*, 8(3, August), pp. 73–92.

Klein, K.J. and House, R.J. (1998) 'Further Thoughts on Fire: Charismatic Leadership and Levels of Analysis', in: F. Dansereauand and F.J. Yammarino (eds) *Leadership: The Multi-Level Approaches*, Volume 2, Stamford, CT: JAI Press, pp. 45–52.

Kotter, J.P. (1990) 'What Leaders Really Do', *Harvard Business Review*, 68(3, May–June), p. 103.

Kotur, B.R. and Anbazhagan, S. (2014) 'The Influence of Age and Gender on the Leadership Styles', *Journal of Business and Management*, 16(1), pp. 30–36.

Leonard-Barton, D. (1995) *Well-Springs of Knowledge: Building and Sustaining the Sources of Innovation,* Boston, MA: Harvard Business School Press.

Lessem, R. and Neubauer, F.F. (1994) *European Management Systems*, London: McGraw-Hill.

Levy, D. (1994) 'Chaos Theory and Strategy: Theory, Application, and Managerial Implications', *Strategic Management Journal*, 15, pp. 167–178.

March, J.G. and Simon, H.A. (1958) *Organizations*, New York: Wiley.

Meindl, J.R., Ehrlich, S.B. and Dukerich, J.M. (1985) 'The Romance of Leadership', *Administrative Science Quarterly*, 30(1, March), pp. 78–102.

Miles, R.E. and Snow, C.C. (1978) *Organizational Strategy: Structure and Process*, New York: McGraw-Hill.

Miller, D. and Friesen, P.H. (1980) 'Momentum and Revolution in Organizational Adaptation', *Academy of Management Journal*, 23(4, December), pp. 591–614.

Mintzberg, H. (1982) 'If You're Not Serving Bill and Barbara, Then You're Not Serving Leadership', in: J.G. Hunt, U. Sekaran, and C.A. Schreisheim (eds) *Leadership: Beyond Establishment Views*, Carbondale, IL: Southern Illinois University.

Mintzberg, H. (1989) *Mintzberg on Management*, New York: Free Press.

Misumi, J. (1985) *The Behavioral Science of Leadership*, Ann Arbor, MI: University of Michigan Press.

Mitchell, S. (2000) *American Generations: Who They Are, How They Live, What They Think* (3rd edn), Ithaca, NY: New Strategists.

Myers, A., Kakabadse, A., McMahon, T. and Spony, G. (1995) 'Top Management Styles in Europe: Implications for Business and Cross-National Teams', *European Business Journal*, 7(1), pp. 17–27.

Nanus, B. (1992) *Visionary Leadership: Creating a Compelling Sense of Direction for Your Organization*, San Francisco, CA: Jossey-Bass.

Nelson, R.R. and Winter, S.G. (1982) *An Evolutionary Theory of Economic Change*, Reading, MA: Harvard University Press.

Oshagbemi, T. (2004) 'Age influences on the leadership styles and behaviour of managers', *Employee Relations*, 26(1), pp. 14–29.

Oshagbemi, T. (2008) 'The impact of personal and organisational variables on the leadership styles of managers', *The International Journal of Human Resource Management*, 19(10), pp. 1896–1910.

Oshagbemi, T. and Gill, R. (2003) 'Gender differences and similarities in the leadership styles and behaviour of UK managers', *Women in Management Review*, 18(6), pp. 288–298.

Pfeffer, J. (1977) 'The Ambiguity of Leadership', *Academy of Management Review*, 2(1, January), pp. 104–112.

Pfeffer, J. (1982) *Organizations and Organization Theory,* Boston, MA: Pitman.

Pfeffer, J. (1992) *Managing With Power: Politics and Influence in Organizations,* Boston, MA: Harvard Business School Press.

Pfeffer, J. and Salancik, G. (1978) *The External Control of Organizations: A Resource Dependency Perspective*, New York: Harper & Row.

Pfeffer, J. and Sutton, R.I. (1999) *The Knowing–Doing Gap: How Smart Companies Turn Knowledge Into Action,* Boston, MA: Harvard Business School Press.

Porter, M.E. (1990) *The Competitive Advantage of Nations*, London: Macmillan.

Quinn, J.B. (1980) 'Managing Strategic Change', *Sloan Management Review*, Summer, pp. 3–20.

Quinn, J.B. (1985) 'Managing Innovation: Controlled Chaos', *Harvard Business Review*, 63 (3, May–June), pp. 73–84.

Rigg, C. and Sparrow, J. (1994) 'Gender, diversity and working styles', *Women in Management Review*, 9(1), pp. 9–16.

Rowe, W.G. (2001) 'Creating Wealth in Organizations: The Role of Strategic Leadership', *Academy of Management Executive*, 15(1, February), pp. 81–94.

Rumelt, R.P. (1995) 'Inertia and Transformation', in: C.A. Montgomery (ed.) *Resource-based and Evolutionary Theories of the Firm: Towards a Synthesis,* Boston, MA: Kluwer Academic Publishers, pp. 101–132.

Sabri, H. (2008) 'Jordanian managers' leadership styles in comparison with the International Air Transport Association (IATA) and prospects for knowledge management in Jordan', *International Journal of Commerce and Management*, 17(1/2), pp. 56–72.

Schein, E.H. (1985) *Organizational Culture and Leadership*, San Francisco, CA: Jossey-Bass.

Schein, E.H. (1993) 'On Dialogue, Culture, and Organizational Learning', *Organizational Dynamics*, 22(2), pp. 40–51.

Selznick, P. (1957) *Leadership in Administration: A Sociological Interpretation*, New York: Harper & Row.

Senge, P.M. (1990) 'The Leader's New Work: Building Learning Organizations', *Sloan Management Review*, 32(1, Fall), pp. 7–23.

Simons, R. (1994) 'How New Top Managers Use Control Systems as Levers of Strategic Renewal', *Strategic Management Journal,* 15(3, March), pp. 169–189.

Sims, H.P. and Lorenzi, P. (1992) *The New Leadership Paradigm: Social Learning and Cognition in Organizations*, London: Sage.

Smircich, L. and Stubbart, C. (1985) 'Strategic Management in an Enacted World', *Academy of Management Review*, 10(4), pp. 724–736.

Stacey, R.D. (1992) *Managing Chaos: Dynamic Business Strategies in an Unpredictable World*, London: Kogan Page.

Stacey, R.D. (1993) 'Strategy as Order Emerging from Chaos', *Long Range Planning*, 26(1), pp. 10–17.

Strebel, P. (1994) 'Choosing the Right Change Path', *California Management Review*, 36(2, Winter), pp. 29–51.

Taleb, H.M. (2010) 'Gender and leadership styles in single-sex academic institutions', *International Journal of Educational Management*, 24(4), pp. 287–302.

Tannenbaum, R. and Schmidt, W.H. (1958) 'How to Choose a Leadership Pattern', *Harvard Business Review*, 36(2, March–April), pp. 95–101.

Teece, D.J., Pisano, G. and Shuen, A. (1997) 'Dynamic Capabilities and Strategic Management', *Strategic Management Journal*, 18(7), pp 509–533.

Thomson, D.G. (2006) *Blueprint To A Billion: 7 Essentials to Achieve Exponential Growth*, New Jersey: John Wiley & Sons.

Tichy, N. and Cohen, E. (1997) *The Leadership Engine: How Winning Companies Build Leaders at Every Level*, New York: Harper Collins.

Tucker, R.C. (1968) 'The Theory of Charismatic Leadership', *Daedalus*, 97(3), pp. 731–756.

Tushman, M.L., Newman, W.H. and Romanelli, E. (1986) 'Convergence and Upheaval: Managing the Unsteady Pace of Organizational Evolution', *California Management Review*, 29(1, Fall), pp. 29–44.

Vroom, V.H. and Jago, A.G. (1988) *The New Leadership: Managing Participation in Organizations*, Englewood Cliffs, NJ: Prentice Hall.

Waldman, D.A. and Yammarino, F.H. (1999) 'CEO Charismatic Leadership: Levels-of-Management and Levels-of-Analysis Effects', *Academy of Management Review*, 24(2), pp. 266–285.

Weick, K.E. (1979) *The Social Psychology of Organizing*, New York: Random House.

Wheatley, M.J. and Kellner-Rogers, M. (1996) 'Self-Organization: The Irresistible Future of Organizing', *Strategy, and Leadership*, 24(4), pp. 18–25.

Zalesnik, A. (1977) 'Managers and Leaders: Are They Different?' *Harvard Business Review*, 55(3, May–June), pp. 67–78.

THE INTERNATIONAL CONTEXT

There never were, since the creation of the world, two cases exactly parallel.

Philip Dormer Stanhope (1694–1773); English Secretary of State

INTRODUCTION

As firms move out of their domestic market on to the international stage, they are faced with differing business arenas. The nations they expand to can vary with regard to consumer behaviour, language, legal system, technological infrastructure, business culture, educational system, labour relations, political ideology, distribution structures and fiscal regime, to name just a few. At face value, the plurality of the international context can seem daunting. Yet, the question is how important the international differences are for firms operating across borders. Do firms need to adapt to the international diversity encountered, or can they find ways of overcoming the constraints imposed by distinct national systems, structures and behaviours? This matter of understanding and dealing with international variety is one of the key topics for managers operating across borders.

A second question with regard to the international context is that of international linkages. To what extent do events in one country have an impact on what happens in other countries? When a number of nations are tightly linked to one another in a particular area, this is referred to as a case of international integration. If, on the other hand, there are very weak links between developments in one country and developments elsewhere, this is referred to as a situation of international fragmentation. The question for managers is how tightly linked nations around the world actually are. Countries might be quite different, yet developments in one nation might significantly influence developments elsewhere. For instance, if interest rates rise in the United States, central bankers in most other countries cannot ignore this. If the price of oil goes down on the spot market in Rotterdam, this will have a 'spill over effect' towards most other nations. And if a breakthrough chip technology is developed in Taiwan, this will send a shockwave through the computer industry around the world. If nations are highly integrated, the manager must view all countries as part of the same system – as squares on a chessboard, not to be judged in isolation.

When looking at the subjects of international variety and linkages, it is also important to know in which direction they have been moving, and will develop further, over time. Where a development towards lower international variety and tighter international linkages on a worldwide scale can be witnessed, a process of globalization is at play. Where a movement towards more international variety and a loosening of international linkages is apparent, a process of localization is taking place.

For managers operating in more than one nation, it is vital to understand the nature of the international context. Have their businesses been globalizing or localizing, and what can be expected in the future? Answers to these questions should guide strategizing managers in choosing which countries to be active in and how to manage their activities across borders. Taken together, these international context questions constitute the issue of international configuration, and are the focus of further discussion in this chapter.

THE ISSUE OF INTERNATIONAL CONFIGURATION

How a firm configures its activities across borders is largely dependent on how it deals with the fundamental tension between the opposite demands of globalization and localization. To understand these forces, pulling the organization in contrary directions, it is first necessary to further define them. Globalization and localization are terms used by many, but explained by few. This lack of uniform definition often leads to an unfocused debate, as different people employ the same terms, but actually refer to different phenomena. Therefore, this discussion starts with a clarification of the concepts of globalization and localization. Subsequently, attention will turn to the two central questions facing the international manager: which countries should the firm be active in and how should this array of international activities be managed? This first question, deciding the geographic areas where the organization should be involved, is the issue of international composition. The second question, deciding the organizational structure and systems needed to run the multi-country activities, is the issue of international management.

Dimensions of globalization

Clearly, globalization refers to the process of becoming more global. But what is global? Although there is no agreement on a single definition, most writers use the term to refer to one or more of the following elements (see Figure 12.1):

- Worldwide scope. 'Global' can simply be used as a geographic term. A firm with operations around the world can be labelled a global company, to distinguish it from firms that are local (not international) or regional in scope. In such a case, the term 'global' is primarily intended to describe the spatial dimension – the broadest possible international scope is to be global. When this definition of global is employed, globalization is the process of international expansion on a worldwide scale (e.g. Patel and Pavitt, 1991).

- Worldwide similarity. 'Global' can also refer to homogeneity around the world. For instance, if a company decides to sell the same product in all of its international markets, it is often referred to as a global product, as opposed to a locally tailored product. In such a case, the term 'global' is primarily intended to describe the variance dimension – the ultimate level of worldwide similarity is to be global. When this definition of global is employed, globalization is the process of declining international variety (e.g. Levitt, 1983, Reading 12.1 in this book).

- Worldwide integration. 'Global' can also refer to the world as one tightly linked system. For instance, a global market can be said to exist if events in one country are significantly impacted by events in other geographic markets. This contrasts with local markets, where price levels, competition, demand and fashions are hardly influenced by developments in other nations. In such a case, the term 'global' is primarily intended to describe the linkages dimension – the ultimate level of worldwide integration is to be global. When this definition of global is employed, globalization is the process of increasing international interconnectedness (e.g. Porter, 1986).

So, for example, is McDonald's a global company? That depends along which of the above three dimensions the company is measured. When judging the international scope of McDonald's, it can be seen that the company is globalizing, but far from global. The

FIGURE 12.1   Internationalization and globalization of the firm

Internationalization as
increasing international scope

Globalization as
increasing worldwide scope

Globalization as
increasing worldwide similarity

Globalization as
increasing worldwide integration

company operates in approximately half the countries in the world, but in many of these only in one or a few large cities. Of McDonald's worldwide revenues, more than half is still earned in the United States. This predominance of the home country is even stronger if the composition of the company's top management is looked at (Ruigrok and Van Tulder, 1995). However, when judging McDonald's along the dimension of international similarity, it is simple to observe that the company is relatively global, as it takes a highly standardized approach to most markets around the world. Although it should be noted that on some aspects, such as menu and interior design, there is leeway for local adaptation. Finally, when judging McDonald's along the dimension of international integration, the company is only slightly global, as it is not very tightly linked around the world. Some activities are centralized or coordinated, but in general there is relatively little need for concerted action.

As for localization – the opposite of the process of globalization – it is characterized by decreasing international scope, similarity and integration. From the angle of international strategy, the most extreme form of localness is when firms operate in one country and there is no similarity or integration between countries (e.g. the hairdressing and driving school businesses). However, this equates local with national, while firms and businesses can be even more local, all the way down to the state/province/department/district and municipal playing fields.

Levels of globalization

The second factor complicating a clear understanding of the concept of globalization is that it is applied to a variety of subjects, while the differences are often not made explicit. Some people discuss globalization as a development in the economy at large, while others debate globalization as something happening to industries, markets, products, technologies, fashions, production, competition and organizations. In general, debates on globalization tend to concentrate on one of three levels of analysis:

- **Globalization of companies.** Some authors focus on the micro level, debating whether individual companies are becoming more global. Issues are the extent with which firms have a global strategy, structure, culture, workforce, management team and resource base. The globalization of specific products and value-adding activities is often discussed in more detail. Here it is of particular importance to acknowledge that the globalization of one product or activity (e.g. marketing) does not necessarily entail the globalization of all others (e.g. Bartlett and Ghoshal, 1987; Prahalad and Doz, 1987).

- **Globalization of businesses.** Other authors are more concerned with the meso level, debating whether particular businesses are becoming more global. Here it is important to distinguish those who emphasize the globalization of markets, as opposed to those accentuating the globalization of industries (see Chapter 4 for this distinction). The issue of globalizing markets has to do with the growing similarity of worldwide customer demand and the growing ease of worldwide product flows (e.g. Douglas and Wind, 1987, Reading 12.2; Levitt, 1983, Reading 12.1). For example, the crude oil and foreign currency markets are truly global – the same commodities are traded at the same rates around the world. The markets for accountancy and garbage collection services, on the other hand, are very local – demand differs significantly, there is little cross-border trade and consequently prices vary sharply. The globalization of industries is quite a different issue, as it has to do with the emergence of a set of producers that compete with one another on a worldwide scale (e.g. Porter, 1990a, 1990b; Prahalad and Doz, 1987). So, for instance, the automobile and consumer electronics industries are quite global – the major players in most countries belong to the same set of companies that compete against each other all around the world. The accountancy industry is relatively global, even though the markets for accountancy services are very local. On the other hand, the hairdressing and retail banking industries are very local – the competitive scene in each country is relatively uninfluenced by competitive developments elsewhere.

- **Globalization of economies.** Yet other authors take a macro level of analysis, arguing whether or not the world's economies in general are experiencing a convergence trend. Many authors are interested in the macroeconomic dynamics of international integration and its consequences in terms of growth, employment, inflation, productivity, trade and foreign direct investment (e.g. Kay, 1989; Krugman, 1990). Others focus more on the political realities constraining and encouraging globalization (e.g. Klein, 2000; McGrew and Lewis, 1992). Yet others are interested in the underlying dynamics of technological, institutional and organizational convergence (e.g. Dunning, 1986; Kogut, 1993).

Ultimately, the question in this chapter is not only whether economies, businesses and companies are actually globalizing, but also whether these developments are a matter of choice. In other words, is global convergence or continued international diversity an uncontrollable evolutionary development to which firms (and governments) must comply, or can managers actively influence the globalization or localization of their environment?

International composition

An international firm operates in two or more countries. When a firm starts up value-adding activities in yet another country, this process is called internationalization. In Figure 12.2 an overview is presented of the most common forms of

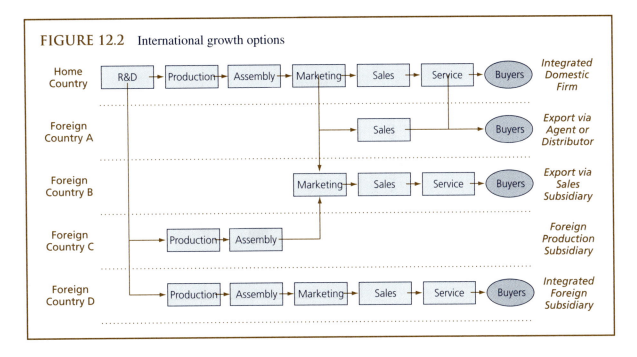

FIGURE 12.2   International growth options

internationalization. One of the earliest international growth moves undertaken by firms is to sell their products to foreign buyers, either directly (Internet or telephone sales), through a travelling salesperson, or via a local agent or distributor. Such types of export activities are generally less taxing for the organization than the establishment of a foreign sales subsidiary (or sales unit). Serving a foreign market by means of a sales subsidiary often requires a higher level of investment in terms of marketing expenditures, sales force development and after-sales service provision. A firm can also set up a foreign production subsidiary (or 'off-shore' production unit), where activities are focused on manufacturing goods to be exported back to the firm's other markets. Alternatively, a firm can begin an integrated foreign subsidiary that is responsible for a full range of value-adding activities, including production and sales. In practice, there are many variations to these basic forms of internationalization, depending on the specific value-adding activities carried out in different countries. For example, some subsidiaries have R&D, assembly and marketing as part of their portfolio of activities, while others do not (Birkinshaw and Hood, 1998).

When establishing a foreign subsidiary, the firm must decide whether to purchase an existing local company (entry by acquisition) or to start from scratch (greenfield entry). In both cases the firm can work independently or by means of a joint venture with a local player or foreign partner. It is also possible to dispense with the establishment of a subsidiary at all, by networking with local manufacturers, assemblers, sales agents and distributors (as discussed in Chapter 6).

The issue of international composition deals with the question of where the firm wants to have a certain level of involvement. The firm's strategists must decide where to allocate resources, build up activities and try to achieve results. The issue of international composition can be further subdivided into two parts:

■ International scope. The international composition of the firm depends first of all on the countries selected to do business in. The geographic spectrum covered by the firm is referred to as its international scope. The firm's strategists must decide how many countries they want to be active in, and which countries these should be.

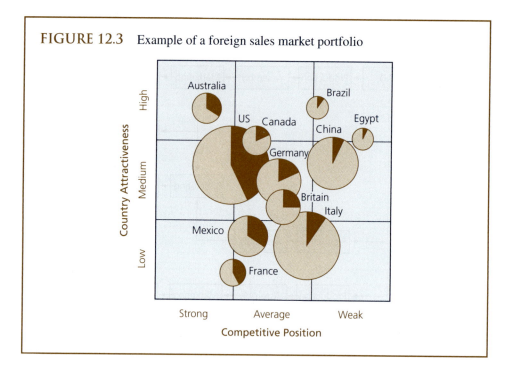

FIGURE 12.3 Example of a foreign sales market portfolio

- International distribution. The international composition of the firm also depends on how it has distributed its value-adding activities across the countries selected. In some firms all national subsidiaries carry out similar activities and are of comparable size. However, in many firms activities are distributed less symmetrically, with, for example, production, R&D and marketing concentrated in only a few countries (Porter, 1986). Commonly, some countries will also contribute much more revenue and profits than others, but these might not be the countries where new investments can best be made. It is the task of the firm's strategists to determine how activities can best be distributed and how resources can best be allocated across the various countries.

Just as a corporation's portfolio of businesses can be visualized by means of a portfolio grid, so too can a business's portfolio of foreign sales markets be displayed using such a matrix. In Figure 12.3 a fictitious example is given of a firm's international sales portfolio using the GE business screen as analysis tool. Instead of industry attractiveness along the vertical axis, country attractiveness is used, calculating items such as market growth, competitive intensity, buyer power, customer loyalty, government regulation and operating costs. Following a similar logic, firms can also evaluate their international portfolios of, for instance, production locations and R&D facilities.

Deciding which portfolio of countries to be active in, both in terms of international scope and distribution, will largely depend on the strategic motives that have stimulated the firm to enter the international arena in the first place. After all, there must be some good reasons why a firm is willing to disregard the growth opportunities in its home market and to enter into uncertain foreign adventures. There must be some advantages to being international that offset the disadvantages of foreignness and distance. These advantages of having activities in two or more countries – cross-border synergies – are discussed in more detail later, after an account of the second international configuration question: the issue of international management.

International management

A firm operating in two or more countries needs to find some way of organizing itself to deal with its border-spanning nature. As managing across borders is difficult and costly, the simplest solution would be to organize all operations on a country-by-country basis, and to leave all country units as autonomous as possible. Yet, internationalization is only economically rational if 'the international whole is more than the sum of the country parts' (see Chapter 5). In other words, internationalization only makes sense if enough cross-border synergies can be reaped to offset the extra cost of foreignness and distance.

Therefore, the firm needs to have international integration mechanisms to facilitate the realization of cross-border synergies. The three most important integration mechanisms used in international management are:

- Standardization. An easy way to reap cross-border synergies is to do the same thing in each country, without any costly adaptation. Such standardization can be applied to all aspects of the business model (see Chapter 4) – the product offerings, value-adding activities and resources employed. Standardization is particularly important for achieving economies of scale (e.g. Hout, Porter and Rudden, 1982; Levitt, 1983), but can be equally valuable for serving border-crossing clients who want to encounter a predictable offering (e.g. Hamel and Prahalad, 1985; Yip, 1993).

- Coordination. Instead of standardizing products or activities, international firms can align their varied activities in different countries by means of cross-border coordination. Getting the activities in the various countries aligned is often inspired by the need to serve border-crossing clients in a coordinated manner (e.g. global service level agreements), or to counter these clients' policy of playing off the firm's subsidiaries against one another (e.g. cross-border price shopping). International coordination can be valuable when responding to, or attacking, competitors as well. A coordinated assault on a few markets, financed by the profits from many markets (i.e. cross-subsidization), can sometimes lead to competitive success (Prahalad and Doz, 1987).

- Centralization. Of course, activities within the firm can also be integrated at one central location, either in the firm's home country or elsewhere. Such centralization is often motivated by the drive for economies of scale (e.g. Buckley and Casson, 1985; Dunning, 1981), but might be due to the competitive advantage of a particular country as well. For example, production costs might be much lower, or quality much higher, in a certain part of the world, making it a logical location for centralized production. Centralization of knowledge-intensive activities is sometimes also needed, to guard quality or to ensure faster learning than could be attained with decentralized activities (e.g. Dunning, 1993; Porter, 1990b).

It is up to the firm's strategists to determine the most appropriate level of standardization, coordination and centralization needed to function efficiently and effectively in an international context. The level chosen for each of these three characteristics will largely determine the organizational model adopted by the international firm.

In their seminal research, Bartlett and Ghoshal (1989) distinguish four generic organizational models for international firms, each with its own mix of standardization, coordination and centralization (see Figure 12.4):

- Decentralized federation. In a decentralized federation, the firm is organized along geographic lines, with each full-scale country subsidiary largely self-sufficient and autonomous from international headquarters in the home country. Few activities are centralized and little is coordinated across borders. The level of standardization is also low, as the country unit is free to adapt itself to the specific circumstances in its national

FIGURE 12.4 Generic organizational models for international firms (adapted from Bartlett and Ghoshal, 1995)

Decentralized Federation

Coordinated Federation

Mainly knowledge
flows (technology,
processes, systems)

Mainly
financial
flows

Loose, simple controls
(strategic decisions decentralized)

Formal system controls
(some centralization and standardization)

Centralized Hub

Integrated Network

Large flows of info,
components, products,
resources and people

Mainly flows
of goods

Tight, simple controls
(strategic decisions centralized)

Complex coordination
(strategic decision-making shared)

environment. Bartlett and Ghoshal refer to this organizational model as 'multinational'. Another common label is 'multi-domestic' (e.g. Prahalad and Doz, 1987; Stopford and Wells, 1972).

■ **Coordinated federation.** In a coordinated federation, the firm is also organized along geographic lines, but the country subsidiaries have a closer relationship with the international headquarters in the home country. Most of the core competencies, technologies, processes and products are developed centrally, while other activities are carried out locally. As a consequence, there is some standardization and coordination, requiring some formalized control systems (i.e. planning, budgeting, administration). Another name employed by Bartlett and Ghoshal to refer to this organizational model is 'international'.

■ **Centralized hub.** In a centralized hub, national units are relatively unimportant, as all main activities are carried out in the home country. Generally a highly standardized approach is used towards all foreign markets. As centralization and standardization are high, foreign subsidiaries are limited to implementing headquarters' policies in the local markets. Coordination of activities across countries is made easy by the dominance of headquarters. Bartlett and Ghoshal use the term 'global' to describe this organizational model.

■ **Integrated network.** In an integrated network, the country subsidiaries have a close relationship with international headquarters, just as in the coordinated federation, but also have a close relationship with each other. Very little is centralized at the international headquarters in the home country, but each national unit can become the worldwide centre for a particular competence, technology, process or product. Thus subsidiaries need to coordinate the flow of components, products, knowledge and people between one other. Such a networked organization requires a certain level of standardization to function effectively. Another name used by Bartlett and Ghoshal for this organizational model is 'transnational'.

Which international organizational model is adopted depends strongly on what the corporate strategist wishes to achieve. The preferred international management structure will be largely determined by the type of cross-border synergies that the strategists envisage. This topic of multi-country synergies is examined more closely in the following section.

THE PARADOX OF GLOBALIZATION AND LOCALIZATION

The axis of the earth sticks out visibly through the center of each and every town or city.

Oliver Wendell Holmes (1809–1894); American physician, poet and essayist

It requires almost no argumentation that internationally operating companies are faced with a tension between treating the world as one market and acknowledging national differences. During the last few decades, achieving a balance between international uniformity and meeting local demands has been the dominant theme in the literature on international management. All researchers have recognized the tension between international standardization and local adaptation. The key question has been whether international firms have the *liberty* to standardize or face the *pressure* to adapt.

However, since the mid-1980s, this standardization-adaptation discussion has progressed significantly as strategy researchers have moved beyond the organizational design question, seeking the underlying strategic motives for standardization and adaptation (e.g. Bartlett and Ghoshal, 1987; Porter, 1986; Prahalad and Doz, 1987). It has been acknowledged that international standardization is not a matter of organizational convenience that companies naturally revert to when the market does not demand local adaptation. Rather, international standardization is a means for achieving cross-border synergies. A firm can achieve cross-border synergies by leveraging resources, integrating activities and aligning product offerings across two or more countries. Creating additional value in this way is the very *raison d'etre* of the international firm. If internationalizing companies fully adapted to local conditions, without leveraging a homegrown quality, they would have no advantage over local firms, while they would be burdened by the extra costs of international business (e.g. overcoming distance and foreignness). Therefore, international companies need to realize at least enough cross-border synergies to compensate for the additional expenses of operating in multiple countries.

Much of the theoretical discourse has focused on the question of which cross-border synergies can be achieved on the ultimate, global scale. Most researchers identify various potential opportunities for worldwide synergy, yet recognize the simultaneous demands to meet the specific conditions in each local market (e.g. Dicken, 1992; Yip, 1993). These possibilities for reaping global synergy will be examined first, followed by the countervailing pressures for local responsiveness.

The demand for global synergy

Striving for cross-border synergies on as large a scale as possible can be an opportunity for an international firm to enhance its competitive advantage. However, realizing global synergies is often less an opportunity than a competitive demand. If rival firms have already

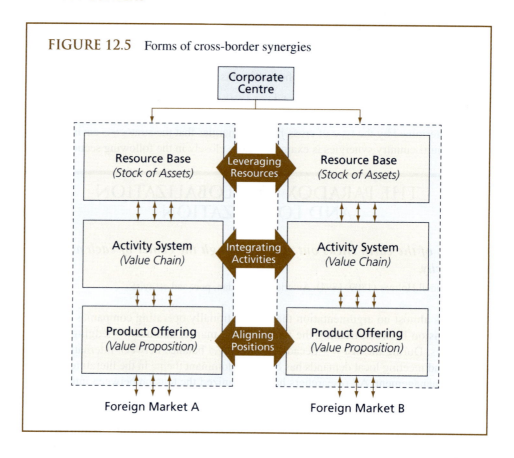

FIGURE 12.5   Forms of cross-border synergies

successfully implemented a global strategy, there can be a severe pressure to also reap the benefits of globalization through standardization, coordination or centralization.

There are many different types of cross-border synergies. In accordance with the business model framework described in Chapter 4, these synergies can be organized into three categories: aligning product offerings, integrating activities and leveraging resources (see Figure 12.5).

Synergy by aligning positions.   The first way to create cross-border synergies is to align market positions in the various countries in which the firm operates. Taking a coordinated approach to different national markets can be necessary under two circumstances – namely to provide a concerted cross-border product offering to customers and to stage a concerted cross-border attack on competitors:

- Dealing with cross-border customers. An international firm is ideally placed to offer border-crossing customers an internationally coordinated product or service offering. Whether it is for a tourist who wants to have the same hotel arrangements around the world, or for an advertiser who wants to stage a globally coordinated new product introduction, it can be important to have a standardized and coordinated offering across various nations. It might be equally necessary to counter the tactics of customers shopping around various national subsidiaries for the best deals, or to meet the customer's demand to aggregate all global buying via one central account.

- Dealing with cross-border competition. An international firm is also in an ideal position to successfully attack locally oriented rivals if it does not spread its resources too thinly around the world, but rather focuses on only a few countries at a time. By coordinating its competitive efforts and bringing its global power to bear on a few national markets, an international firm can push back or even defeat local rivals country-by-country. Of course, an international company must also have the capability of defending itself against such a globally coordinated attack by a rival international firm.

Synergy by integrating activities.   Cross-border synergies can also be achieved by linking the activity systems of the firm in its various national markets. Integrating the value-creation processes across borders can be useful to realize economies of scale and to make use of the specific competitive advantages of each nation:

- Reaping scale advantages. Instead of organizing the international firm's activity system on a country-by-country basis, certain activities can be pooled to reap economies of scale. Commonly this means that activities must be centralized at one or a few locations, and that a certain level of product and/or process standardization must be accepted. Economies of scale can be realized for many activities, most notably production, logistics, procurement and R&D. However, scale advantages might be possible for all activities of the firm. Although scale advantages are often pursued by means of centralization, it is often possible to achieve economies by standardizing and coordinating activities across borders (e.g. joint procurement, joint marketing campaigns).

- Reaping location advantages. For some activities certain locations are much more suited than others, making it attractive to centralize these activities in the countries that possess a particular competitive advantage. A national competitive advantage can consist of inexpensive or specialist local inputs, such as raw materials, energy, physical infrastructure or human resources, but can also be due to the presence of attractive buyers and related industries (Porter, 1990a).

Synergy by leveraging resources.   A third manner in which cross-border synergies can be realized is by sharing resources across national markets. Such resource leveraging can be achieved by physically reallocating resources to other countries where they can be used more productively, or by replicating them so they can be used in many national markets simultaneously:

- Achieving resource reallocation. Instead of leaving resources in countries where they happen to be, international firms have the opportunity to transfer resources to other locations, where they can be used to more benefit. For example, money, machinery and people can be reallocated out of countries where the return on these resources is low, into countries where they can reap a higher return. Managers specializing in market development might be sent to new subsidiaries, while older machinery might be transferred to less advanced markets (Buckley and Casson, 1976; Vernon, 1966).

- Achieving resource replication. While leveraging tangible resources requires physical reallocation or sharing (see reaping scale advantages), intangible resources can be leveraged by means of replication. Intangibles such as knowledge and capabilities can be copied across borders and reused in another country. This allows international companies to leverage their know-how with regard to such aspects as technology, production, marketing, logistics and sales (Kogut and Zander, 1993; Liebeskind, 1996).

For all of these cross-border synergies it holds that the wider the geographic scope, the greater the potential benefit. Where possible, realizing these synergies on a global scale would result in the highest level of value creation.

These opportunities for global synergy represent a strong demand on all companies, both international and domestic. If a company can reap these synergies more quickly and successfully than its competitors, this could result in a strong offensive advantage. If other companies have a head start in capturing these global synergies, the firm must move quickly to catch up. Either way, there is a pressure on companies to seek out opportunities for global synergy and to turn them to their advantage.

The demand for local responsiveness

Yet the pressure to pursue global synergies is only half the equation. Simultaneously, companies must remain attuned to the specific demands of each national market and retain the ability to respond to these particular characteristics in a timely and adequate manner. In other words, firms must have the capability to be responsive to local conditions. If they lose touch with the distinct competitive dynamics in each of their national markets, they might find themselves at a competitive disadvantage compared to more responsive rivals.

While business responsiveness is always important, it becomes all the more pressing when the differences between various national markets are large. The more dissimilar the national markets, the more pressure on the international firm to be attuned to these distinct characteristics. The most important differences between countries include:

- Differences in market structure. Countries can differ significantly with regard to their competitive landscape. For example, in some national markets there are strong local competitors, requiring the international firm to respond differently than in countries where it encounters its 'regular' international rivals. Another difference is that in some countries there are only a few market parties, while in other countries the market is highly fragmented among numerous competitors. There can also be large differences from country to country in the background of competitors – in some countries conglomerates dominate the business scene, while in other countries single business competitors are more frequent.

- Differences in customer needs. Customers in each national market can have needs that are significantly different from the needs exhibited in other countries. The nature of these customer differences can vary from divergent cultural expectations and use circumstances, to incompatible technical systems and languages employed.

- Differences in buying behaviour. Not only can the customers' needs differ across countries, but so can their buying behaviour. For example, customers can be different with regard to the way they structure buying decisions, the types of information they consider and the relationship they wish to have with their suppliers.

- Differences in substitutes. National markets can also differ with regard to the types of indirect competition that needs to be faced. In some countries, for instance, beer brewers have to deal with wine as an important rival product, while in other markets tea or soft drinks might be the most threatening substitutes.

- Differences in distribution channels. Countries can exhibit remarkable differences in the way their distribution channels work. For example, countries can vary with regard to the kinds of distribution channels available, the number of layers in the distribution structure, their level of sophistication, their degree of concentration and the negotiating power of each player.

- Differences in media structure. National markets can have very different media channels available for marketing communication purposes. In the area of television, for instance, countries vary widely with regard to the number of stations on the air (or on the cable), the types of regulation imposed, the amount of commercial time available, and its cost and effectiveness. In the same way, all other media channels may differ.

- Differences in infrastructure. Many products and services are heavily dependent on the type of infrastructure available in a country. For example, some products rely on a digital telephone system, high-speed motorways, 24-hour convenience stores, or a national health care system. Some services require an efficient postal service, public transport, electronic banking or cable television.

- Differences in supply structure. If a company has local operations, the differences between countries with regard to their supply structures can also force the company to be more locally responsive. Not only the availability, quality and price of raw materials and components can vary widely between countries, but the same is true for other inputs such as labour, management, capital, facilities, machinery, research, information and services.

- **Differences in government regulations.** As most government regulations are made on a country-by-country basis, they can differ significantly. Government regulations can affect almost every aspect of a company's operations, as they range from antitrust and product liability legislation, to labour laws and taxation rules.

Responsiveness to these local differences is not only a matter of adaptation. Simple adaptation can be reactive and slow. Being responsive means that the firm has to have the ability to be proactive and fast. As each market develops in a different way and at a different pace, the international firm needs to be able to respond quickly and adequately to remain in tune.

It is clear that international managers cannot afford to neglect being responsive to local conditions. Yet, at the same time, they need to realize cross-border synergies to create additional value. Unfortunately for managers, these two key demands placed on the international firm are, at least to some extent, in conflict with one another. Striving for cross-border synergies on a global scale will interfere with being locally responsive and vice versa. Therefore, the question is how these two conflicting demands can be reconciled – how can the international manager deal with the paradox of globalization and localization?

EXHIBIT 12.1   SHORT CASE

NESPRESSO IN CHINA: WHERE ELSE?

Ever since the Swiss company Nestlé created a new market segment by developing an innovative system for premium portioned coffee under the Nespresso brand, it has seen remarkable growth in the global coffee market. Nespresso launched its products on the international market in 1991 and is currently operating in 64 countries worldwide. In pursuit of new growth markets, the company's focus has recently shifted towards the huge upcoming Chinese market. This seems an obvious choice, but how to become successful is not an easy question. While coffee is gaining popularity as a hot beverage in China, consumption is still very low and the age-old tradition of tea consumption in China is deeply embedded in the national culture. The company's question, expressed in several commercials by actor George Clooney: "Nespresso: what else?" is easily answered in China.

Nespresso's journey started in 1976 when one of Nestlé's employees, Eric Favre, developed and patented the Nespresso System. During the following years, the system went through several improvements and the company started selling different varieties of coffee flavours and machine models to the business sector in Switzerland, Japan and Italy. Due to low sales in the early years, the company was forced to reposition Nespresso as a premium quality brand targeted at households, with an emphasis on individuals with high incomes. A new and successful business model was born, based on three important elements: individually portioned aluminium coffee capsules, specially designed coffee machines that are exclusively compatible with the Nespresso capsules, and unique customer service through the Nespresso Club and Nespresso Boutiques. Nespresso products still cannot be purchased in ordinary stores or supermarkets; the company uses its own distribution channels (web-shop, e-mail, telephone) and transport service to sell and deliver its products with an emphasis on personal attention for the customer. Since 2000, the company has opened over 450 Nespresso Boutiques around the world, situated at carefully selected locations to give consumers the opportunity to 'experience the brand with all their senses'. After purchasing Nespresso products, consumers automatically become members of the Nespresso Club. Club members receive information and advice on all grand cru coffees, technical problems, special offers and new machine models. With the Nespresso Club, the company hopes to build stronger brand loyalty, thereby encouraging repeat purchasing among its consumers. The company's decision to reposition Nespresso has resulted in a period of rapid expansion and can be marked as the start of developing a strong global brand. Nowadays, Nespresso is the market leader in the single serve portioned coffee market and has seen an average double digit annual profit growth between 2000 and 2010 with revenues exceeding US$2.5 billion. Challenges also arise: in recent years Nespresso's growth has slowed down as dozens of rivals offer coffee pods that fit into its machines.

Aware of the growth potential in China, Nespresso decided to enter the Chinese market in 2007. Six Nespresso Boutiques have been established since then, in Shanghai, Beijing and Chengdu. Country manager of Nespresso China, Alfonso Troisi, is convinced of the huge possibilities for Nespresso in China, as coffee consumption is expected to rise by 18 per cent between 2014 and 2019. However, the choice is not as obvious as it seems, considering the strong preference for tea as both a hot and cold beverage in China's domestic market. Tea symbolizes an important cultural element in Chinese society and has been enjoyed by the Chinese for thousands of years. Originally tea was mainly appreciated for its medical effects, in particular because it helps to digest food. Nowadays, the Chinese drink tea at almost any time of the day, especially during and after every meal. Moreover, the majority of the Chinese are not used to the bitter taste of pure coffee. Of 1.28 billion kilograms of hot drinks consumed in 2014, hot tea holds a share of approximately 82 per cent. Coffee only accounts for 5.7 per cent, but it is estimated that coffee will gain a market share of 8.4 per cent in 2019.

American coffee house Starbucks was one of the first coffee companies to enter the Chinese market in 1998, successfully introducing high-end premium coffee to Chinese consumers, and making them more familiar with drinking and appreciating coffee. The consumption of regular and quality coffee is gaining popularity in China, in accordance with the rising living standards of the growing urban middle class who are becoming increasingly accustomed to Western standards and ways of living. This growing middle class is looking for quality brands and a variety of flavours. But still, Chinese consumers only drink an average of five cups of coffee per person per year, compared to, for example, the Americans or Swiss who drink respectively 400 and 1117 cups of coffee annually. In Shanghai and Beijing, only 20 to 30 per cent of the consumers drink coffee and as there is a general lack of knowledge on how to prepare coffee, drinking instant coffee at home and ready-to-drink coffee at coffee houses is much more common in China. Instant coffee accounts for 84 per cent of the Chinese coffee market, with 3–1 instant coffee (coffee-powder, milk, sugar) as the most popular beverage of choice, while preparing ground coffee at home is a rare habit.

Nespresso's country manager, Alfonso Troisi, is facing a difficult challenge in China. Should Nespresso maintain its way of doing business as the company does in other countries? Nespresso has developed itself as one of the most famous brands for premium coffee, with an important focus on its global status, brand image and exclusive customer service. The company's business model and marketing strategy are homogeneous worldwide, which is manifested in, for example, the Nespresso Club and Boutiques. This uniform strategy proved to be a successful formula in Europe and the United States. In addition, the Chinese upcoming urban middle-class consumers increasingly attach importance to popular Western brands to boost their image and enhance their social position. The exclusivity and premium quality of the Nespresso brand could contribute to this image. Should Nespresso maintain its winning global formula?

On the other hand, it could also be a sagacious move for Nespresso to adapt its comprehensive business model to the Chinese market, since the market is not that familiar with Nespresso's core product: high quality ground coffee for individual households. Chinese consumers have specific preferences compared to other consumers in the global marketplace. Former Nespresso Market Director for South East Asia, Greater China and Korea, Mark Leenders, already acknowledged the difficulty of selling pricey coffee machines and coffee capsules in a country with an entrenched tea culture. Should Nespresso adjust its products to meet, for example, the dislike of the bitter taste of pure coffee by Chinese consumers? Or should it change its marketing strategy and focus its attention on providing more information about brewing coffee for its Chinese customers?

In attempting to create a higher brand loyalty among its Chinese customers and generate a greater demand for its coffee products, Nespresso has a number of coffee beans to crack. Should the company put effort in to making Chinese consumers more accustomed to drinking high quality, pure ground coffee and keep its homogeneous business model? Or should the company offer new varieties of coffee flavours and machine designs, especially developed for Chinese consumer preferences? For example, in 2012 Nespresso collaborated with the Hong Kong-based company *Shanghai Tang* to develop a red coffee machine with a dragon integrated in the design to adapt to the Chinese taste. Red is a very important colour in the Chinese culture and is associated with prosperity, while the dragon was the zodiac sign of the year 2012 and symbolizes good fortune. It could also be an interesting option for Nespresso to target another market, namely the business sector. For example, in 2016, Nespresso launched a new coffee machine model in China, which is specially designed for restaurants, hotels and bars, in order to offer their customers high-end quality coffee with the least amount of effort. Will it be useful for Nespresso to target the business-to-business sector as well, or should the company stick to the market of individual households?

Alfonso Troisi needs to decide which road the company has to follow and how to position it in the Chinese market. The Chinese market has a huge potential in several ways and it is definitely worth the try. Whether he decides to stick to Nespresso's homogeneous business model and brand image, adapt to local differences, or even decide to deviate from its core product and focus on tea instead, each decision will have important implications for the company's future position in the Chinese market.

Co-authors: Laura Kamsma and Maria Hu

Sources: www.nestle-nespresso.com; Lu Chang, 'Pod People', *China Daily,* Oct. 1, 2012; *Marketing Channels,* Cengage, 2012; Analysis of the China Coffee Market, *SPR coffee,* 2009; Mintel Global Market Navigator, *Coffee in China,* Mintel 2012; Xu Junqian, 'Chinese Have Got Drinking Coffee Down To a Tee', *The Telegraph,* Jan. 27, 2016; Lucy Craymer, 'Chinese Changing Taste Offer Upside for Coffee', *Wall Street Journal,* Sept. 16, 2015; 'Tea Is Still Most Consumed Hot Drink in China; but Coffee Making Inroads', *Canadean,* Aug. 17, 2015; Corinne Gretler, 'Nestle's Coffee Business Is Competing With Itself', *Bloomberg,* Jun. 28, 2016.

PERSPECTIVES ON THE INTERNATIONAL CONTEXT

You may say I'm a dreamer, but I'm not the only one; I hope some day you'll join us, and the world will live as one.

John Lennon (1940–1980); British musician and songwriter

When doing business in an international context, it is generally accepted that the challenge for firms is to strive for cross-border synergies, while simultaneously being responsive to the local conditions. It is acknowledged that international managers need to weigh the specific characteristics of their business when reconciling the paradox of globalization and localization – some businesses are currently more suited for a global approach than others. Where opinions start to diverge is on the question of which businesses will become more global, or can be made more global, in the near future. To some managers it is evident that countries are rapidly becoming increasingly similar and more closely interrelated. To them globalization is already far advanced and will continue into the future, wiping out the importance of nations as it progresses. Therefore, they argue that it is wise to anticipate, and even encourage, a 'nationless' world, by focusing on global synergies over local responsiveness. Other managers, however, are more sceptical about the speed and impact of globalization. In their view, much so-called globalization is quite superficial, while at a deeper level important international differences are not changing quickly and cross-border integration is moving very slowly. They also note that there are significant counter-currents creating more international variety, with the potential of loosening international linkages. Therefore, wise managers should remain highly responsive to the complex variety and fragmentation that characterizes our world, while only carefully seeking out selected cross-border synergy opportunities.

These differing opinions among international strategists are reflected in differing views in the strategic management literature. While there is a wide spectrum of positions on the question of how the international context will develop, here the two opposite poles in the debate will be identified and discussed. On one side of the spectrum there are the managers who believe that globalization is bringing Lennon's dream of the 'world living as one' closer and closer. This point of view is called the 'global convergence perspective'. At the other end of the spectrum are the managers who believe that deep-rooted local differences will continue to force firms to 'do in Rome as the Romans do'. This point of view is referred to as the 'international diversity perspective'.

The global convergence perspective

According to proponents of the global convergence perspective, the growing similarity and integration of the world can be argued by pointing to extensive economic statistics showing significant rises in foreign direct investment and international trade. Yet, it is simpler to observe things directly around you. For instance, are you wearing clothing unique to your country, or could you mingle in an international crowd without standing out? Is the television you watch, the vehicle you drive, the telephone you use and the timepiece you wear specific to your nation, or based on the same technology and even produced by the same companies as those in other countries? Is the music you listen to made by local bands, unknown outside your country, or is this music equally popular abroad? Is the food you eat unique to your region, or is even this served in other countries? Now compare your answers with what your parents would have answered 30 years ago – the difference is due to global convergence.

Global convergence, it is argued, is largely driven by the ease, low cost and frequency of international communication, transport and travel. This has diminished the importance of distance. In the past world of large distances, interactions between countries were few and international differences could develop in relative isolation. But the victory of technology over distance has created a 'global village', in which goods, services and ideas are easily exchanged, new developments spread quickly and the 'best practices' of one nation are rapidly copied in others. Once individuals and organizations interact with one another as if no geographic distances exist, an unstoppable process towards cultural, political, technological and economic convergence is set in motion – countries will become more closely linked to one another and local differences will be superseded by new global norms.

Of course, in the short run there will still be international differences and nations will not be fully integrated into a 'world without borders'. Managers taking a global convergence perspective acknowledge that such fundamental and wide-ranging changes take time. There are numerous sources of inertia, e.g. vested interests, commitment to existing systems, emotional attachment to current habits and fear of change. The same type of change inhibitors could be witnessed during the Industrial Revolution, as well. Yet, these change inhibitors can only slow the pace of global convergence, not reverse its direction – the momentum caused by the shrinking of distance can only be slowed down, but not stopped. Therefore, firms thinking further than the short term should not let themselves be guided too much by current international diversity, but rather by the emerging global reality (Ohmae, 1990).

For individual firms, global convergence is changing the rules of the competitive game. While in the past most countries had their own distinct characteristics, pressuring firms to be locally responsive, now growing similarity offers enormous opportunities for leveraging resources and sharing activities across borders, e.g. production can be standardized to save costs, new product development can be carried out on an international scale to reduce the total investments required, and marketing knowledge can easily be exchanged to avoid reinventing the wheel in each country. Simultaneously, international integration has made it much easier to centralize production in large-scale facilities at the most attractive locations and to supply world markets from there, unrestrained by international borders. In the same manner, all types of activities, such as R&D, marketing, sales and procurement, can be centralized to profit from worldwide economies of scale.

An equally important aspect of international integration is that suppliers, buyers and competitors can also increasingly operate as if there were no borders. The ability of buyers to shop around internationally makes the world one global market, in which global bargaining power is very important. The ability of suppliers and competitors to reap global economies of scale and sell everywhere around the world creates global industries in which competition takes place on a worldwide stage, instead of in each nation separately. To deal with such global industries and global markets, the firm must be able to align its market activities across nations.

These demands of standardization, centralization and coordination require a global firm, with a strong centre responsible for the global strategy, instead of a federation of autonomous national subsidiaries focused on being responsive to their local circumstances. According to proponents of the global convergence perspective, such global organizations, or 'centralized hubs' (Bartlett and Ghoshal, 1995), will become increasingly predominant over time. And as more companies switch to a global strategy and a global organizational form, this will in turn speed up the general process of globalization. By operating in a global fashion, these firms will actually contribute to a further decrease of international variety and fragmentation. In other words, globalizing companies are both the consequence and a major driver of further global convergence.

EXHIBIT 12.2   GLOBAL CONVERGENCE PERSPECTIVE

UNILEVER: ONE FOR ALL AND ALL FOR ONE

Unilever is currently the world's third-largest consumer-products company, generating over US€50 billion in annual revenue. Seven out of every ten households across the world contain at least one Unilever product, while 2 billion people use Unilever's products on a daily basis. Its global brands include 13 'billion dollar brands' such as Dove, Knorr, Lipton, Magnum, Omo, Axe and Sunsilk. From the bustling city of São Paulo to the rural plains of northern Vietnam, people can spill Knorr soup on their shirts, wash them with Omo detergent, use Axe or Dove products to freshen themselves up, and celebrate tidiness with Magnum ice cream.

Unilever was formed on 2 September 1929 with one of the largest mergers of that time between Margarine Unie from The Netherlands and Lever Brothers from the UK. Margarine Unie was established by the two Dutch family businesses of butter merchants Van den Bergh and Jurgens who picked up the new product 'margarine' made from beef fat and milk that promised to replace butter – their core business. Lever Brothers, on the other hand, was a British manufacturing company that produced a new kind of soap by replacing animal fats with copra and pine kernel oil. The merger was formed to stop producing the same kind of products and combine forces in international expansion.

Growing the diverse portfolio internationally paid off for the newly formed multinational, as joint production saved costs and the joint internationalization leveraged investments. When the world economy expanded, Unilever followed suit. It developed new products, entered new markets and countries, and ran an ambitious acquisition programme. The corporate basis was also strengthened. Higher R&D spending enhanced product quality and enabled continuous product innovations, while the new and improved products were introduced faster and more effectively by professionalizing the sales and marketing functions. Unilever's bargaining power vis-à-vis its customers – shops and supermarkets – increased with the company's growing scale and product portfolio, and as a result its products were better positioned in the supermarkets.

Unilever's scale was also beneficial in other areas. As it became one of the world's largest buyers of raw materials, increased buying power reduced the costs of these inbound resources. Palm oil in particular was used in almost all of Unilever's products in food, detergents and beauty products. The higher margins were invested in sales and marketing campaigns, which increased the value of Unilever's brands and – again – the products' positioning in outlets. Unilever spends around US$9 billion annually on marketing campaigns, making it the second-biggest spender on adverts in the world. Global presence in products and product categories not only reduced relative marketing costs but also increased marketing quality. The strong competitive position of Unilever products increased further, particularly vis-à-vis local brands.

Not all of Unilever's products were global brands though. While most customer needs are comparable throughout the globe, local preferences in smell and taste restricted the company's potential of global synergy advantages in many products. Hard economic conditions and high inflation in the 1970s drove the company into a rationalization programme in which the performance of Unilever's product portfolio was analysed. While thriving on 'global jewels', the majority of the products appeared to be 'local brands', and thus it was decided to sell or withdraw most of the non-core brands. The newly adopted 'compass strategy' imbued principles of 'winning with brands and innovation' and 'winning with the people'. These notions were reinforced by

Unilever's R&D development throughout nations in every continent of the world. To date, Unilever operates in over 190 countries with a the guise of 400 different brands.

Selling consumer products globally does makes a company vulnerable to global developments. Especially the unfolding importance of sustainability could well be threatening Unilever's position, being one the world's largest users of palm oil. This crop plays a significant role in deforestation, as tropical forests are often cleared illegally to make way for palm-oil plantations. Unilever's 'Polman Plan', a 'Sustainable Living Plan' named after its CEO, aims to "help a billion people to take steps to improve their health and well-being, halve the environmental impact of its products; and source all its agricultural raw materials sustainably, meaning that they should meet requirements covering everything from forest protection to pest control" by 2020. These are not mere words, as contracts with IOI, a Malaysian palm oil company which supplies palm oil to more than 300 companies, have been cancelled. IOI has been accused of nearly all elements of the Polman Plan, including the destruction of orangutan habitat, the wrecking of peatland forest and serious labour issues on its Malaysian plantations. While being a global citizen capturing global synergies, Unilever is taking care of us all. Profits must be protected by saving People and Planet.

Co-author: Sander Wisman

Sources: www.unilever.com; Unilever sustainable palm oil sourcing policy, 2016; Full Year Results 2013–2015; K. Taufik, 'Unilever palm oil supplier must suspend all plantation expansion to save reputation', *The Guardian*, 9 April 2016; 'In search of the good business', *The Economist*, 9 August, 2014; L. O'Reilly, 'Almost a quarter of Unilever's $8 billion ad budget is now spent on digital', *Business Insider UK*, 28 January 2016.

The international diversity perspective

 To managers taking an international diversity perspective, the 'brave new world' outlined in the previous subsection is largely science fiction. People around the world might be sporting a Swatch or a Rolex, munching Big Macs and drinking Coke, while sitting in their Toyota or Nissan, but to conclude that these are symptoms of global convergence is a leap of faith. Of course, there are some brand names and products more or less standardized around the world, and their numbers might actually be increasing. The question is whether these manufacturers are globalizing to meet increasing worldwide similarity, or whether they are actually finally utilizing the similarities between countries that have always existed. The actual level of international variety may really be quite consistent.

It is particularly important to recognize in which respects countries remain different. For instance, the world might be drinking the same soft drinks, but they are probably doing it in different places, at different times, under different circumstances and for different reasons in each country. The product might be standardized worldwide, but the cultural norms and values that influence its purchase and use remain diverse across countries. According to proponents of the international diversity perspective, it is precisely these fundamental aspects of culture that turn out to be extremely stable over time – habits change slowly, but cultural norms and values remain rigid. Producers might be lucky to find one product that fits in with such cultural diversity, but it would be foolish to interpret this as worldwide cultural convergence.

Other national differences are equally resilient against the tides of globalization. No countries have recently given up their national language in favour of Esperanto or English. On the contrary, there has been renewed emphasis on the local language in many countries (e.g. Ireland and the Baltic countries) and regions (e.g. Catalonia and Quebec). In the same way, political systems have remained internationally diverse, with plenty of examples of localization, even within nations. For instance, in Russia and the United States the shift of power to regional governments has increased policy diversity within the country. Similar arguments can be put forward for legal systems, fiscal regimes, educational systems and technological infrastructure – each is extremely difficult to change due to the lock-in effects, vested interests, psychological commitment and complex decision-making processes.

For each example of increasing similarity, a counter-example of local initiatives and growing diversity could be given. Some proponents of the international diversity perspective argue that it is exactly this interplay of divergence and convergence forces that creates a dynamic balance preserving diversity. While technologies, organizing principles, political trends and social habits disperse across borders, resulting in global convergence, new developments and novel systems in each nation arise causing international divergence (Dosi and Kogut, 1993). Convergence trends are usually easier to spot than divergence – international dispersion can be more simply witnessed than new localized developments. To the casual observer, this might suggest that convergence trends have the upper hand, but after more thorough analysis, this conclusion must be cast aside.

Now add to this enduring international diversity the reality of international economic relations. Since World War II, attempts have been made to facilitate the integration of national economies. There have been some regional successes (e.g. the North American Free Trade Association and the European Union) and some advances have been made on a worldwide scale (e.g. the World Trade Organization). However, progress has been slow and important political barriers remain.

The continued existence of international diversity and political obstacles, it is argued, will limit the extent to which nations can become fully integrated into one borderless world. International differences and barriers to trade and investment will frustrate firms' attempts to standardize and centralize, and will place a premium on firms' abilities to adapt and decentralize. Of course, there will be some activities for which global economies of scale can be achieved and for which international coordination is needed, but this will not become true for all activities. Empowering national managers to be responsive to specific local conditions will remain an important ingredient for international success. Balancing globalization and localization of the firm's activities will continue to be a requirement in the future international context.

Ideally, the internationally operating company should neither deny nor regret the existence of international diversity, but regard it as an opportunity that can be exploited. Each country's unique circumstances will pose different challenges, requiring the development of different competencies. Different national 'climates' will create opportunities for different innovations. If a company can tap into each country's opportunities and leverage the acquired competencies and innovations to other countries, this could offer the company an important source of competitive advantage. Naturally, these locally leveraged competencies and innovations would subsequently need to be adapted to the specific circumstances in other countries. This balancing act would require an organization that combined strong local responsiveness with the ability to exchange and coordinate internationally, even on a worldwide scale. International organizations blending these two elements are called 'transnational' (Bartlett and Ghoshal, 1995), or 'heterarchical' (Hedlund, 1986). However, in some businesses the international differences will remain so large that an even more locally responsive organizational form might be necessary, operating on a federative basis.

EXHIBIT 12.3   THE INTERNATIONAL DIVERSITY PERSPECTIVE

WALKING DOWN SESAME STREET IN AFGHANISTAN

Ever since its creation, *Sesame Street* has educated children with colourful puppets. The TV show is broadcast in over 140 countries, yet it is not the same everywhere. Because Sesame Workshop specifically adapts its formula to the countries it operates in, its expansion has been especially successful. In 2011, the non-profit organization started with a new group production, this time aimed towards Afghanistan. With around 45 per cent of the population under 15 and less than two-thirds of Afghan children enrolled in primary school, teaching children numbers, letters and messages of love, tolerance and equal treatment, seems like a logical step.

The series, known locally as *Baghch-e-Simsim*, is a co-production between Sesame Workshop and Moby Media, an Afghan company operating some of the leading television channels in Afghanistan as well as possessing some of the biggest brands in the country. This partner is responsible for making *Sesame Street* palatable to the local audience by picking shots from the vast amount of already puppeteered videos from other international *Sesame Street* productions, which are then dubbed over. The rest consists of locally recorded mini-documentaries, aimed at delivering educational messages.

Due to the probability of cultural misunderstandings, some important changes are made to the *Sesame Street* formula. For example, the Afghan script writers feared parents might frown upon encouraging their young viewers to dance in front of the television, since such activity is often perceived as something sexual in Afghanistan. Instead, children are invited to 'exercise'.

The producers of *Baghch-e-Simsim* have a certain degree of freedom when deciding what is acceptable, most noticeably with picking the puppet videos with the likes of Bert, Ernie, Elmo and Grover. For example, after testing an episode in which Ernie is barking like a dog and getting Bert to copy this, the producers found out that this could encourage indecent behaviour, since a dog is considered to be an unclean animal by many Afghans. Moby Media is also able to leave out characters which are deemed inappropriate altogether. In this regard, The Count has been omitted, since Afghans were thought to not understand why the vampire figure bears fangs, according to Tania Farzana, the Afghan-American executive producer of the show.

It is not just the local producers of Moby Media deciding what is okay and what is not though, since the Sesame Workshop aims to maintain a tight watch on how its international partners handle the show. When trying to film a scene on a building site, the producers struggled with finding one where workers wore clothes in accordance with the health and safety norms Sesame Workshop was accustomed to. Another shot that had to be dropped involved a car ride, because no one in it was actually wearing a seatbelt.

However, some locals might argue that the series still consists of inappropriate scenes. As is quite common for *Sesame Street*, the Afghan edition also occasionally borders on the line of controversy with the messages it tries to convey. When showing the experience of a first day at school, the producers picked a little girl as the main character – a role model – instead of a boy. In a country in which females attending school is still relatively rare, this can be considered quite daring. Furthermore, in 2016 *Bagch-e-Simsim* welcomed Zari, the series' first Afghan Muppet. This 6-year-old female puppet focuses on girls' health and empowerment. Still, as Lilith Dollard, content specialist for the US *Sesame Street*, explains: "We don't want to overload the programme with messages – we want it to be fun".

Since November 2011, the series has been broadcast on TOLO and LEMAR television stations. In order to best fit with the country's cultural diversity, the series is shown in both the Dari and Pashto languages.

Co-author: Wester Wagenaar

Sources: www.mobygroup.com; www.sesameworkshop.org; *AFP*, 29 March 2013; *The Guardian*, 30 November 2011; *The Huffington Post*, 8 December 2011; *The New York Times*, 11 April 2016; *Reuters*, 30 November 2011.

MANAGING THE PARADOX OF GLOBALIZATION AND LOCALIZATION

When I am in Milan, I do as they do in Milan; but when I go to Rome, I do as Rome does.

St. Augustine (354–430); Roman theologian and philosopher

So, what does the paradox of global synergy and local responsiveness mean for the international configuration of firms? Should managers anticipate and encourage global convergence by emphasizing global standardization, centralization and coordination? They would choose to place more emphasis on realizing value creation by means of global synergies, accepting some value destruction due to a loss of local responsiveness. Or should managers acknowledge international diversity by emphasizing local adaptation, decentralization and autonomy? They would then focus on being locally responsive, accepting that this will frustrate the realization of cross-border synergies. See Table 12.1 for the main differences.

Again, the strategic management literature does not provide a uniform answer to the question of which international strategy firms can best pursue, however four suggestions have been brought forward to manage the paradox of globalization and localization: balancing, navigating, resolving and embracing.

TABLE 12.1   Global convergence versus international diversity perspective

	Global convergence perspective	International diversity perspective
Emphasis on	Globalization over localization	Localization over globalization
International variety	Growing similarity	Remaining diverse
International linkages	Growing integration	Remaining fragmented
Major drivers	Technology and communication	Cultural and institutional identity
Diversity and fragmentation	Costly, convergence can be encouraged	Reality, can be exploited
Strategic focus	Global-scale synergies	Local responsiveness
Organizational preference	Standardize/centralize	Adapt/decentralize
Innovation process	Centre-for-global	Locally leveraged
Organizational structure	Global (centralized hub)	Transnational (integrated network)

Balancing

The Coca-Cola example illustrates well the paradox of globalization and localization: it had to give up advantages of global scale and worldwide standardization to become more locally adapted. There are, of course, many different possibilities to be attuned to local conditions, but they are all achieved at the expense of global advantages. In other words, companies have to trade off their demands for global synergy and local responsiveness to find a balance. However, the tension remains when companies have found a balance, and so strategizing managers will continue to search for a more favourable balance.

It should be kept in mind that while companies are trading off global synergy and local responsiveness, international firms do capture the advantages of global operations in local markets. Market presence in many countries leads to economies of scale in production and higher R&D and branding budgets, as the Unilever example illustrates (Exhibit 12.2). So while firms have to trade off global synergy and local responsiveness, they reap the benefits of global presence, which is being used as a source of competitive advantage in local markets.

Navigating

In Chapter 5 on corporate level strategy it has been discussed that companies manage the paradox of multi-business synergy and business responsiveness by means of a series of corporate initiatives that sequentially focus on capturing synergy, responsiveness and then synergy again. In the same vein, international strategists navigate multinational companies with international initiatives. Actually, successfully managing the tension of global synergy and local responsiveness is more difficult, as local differences – such as cultural and institutional varieties – come on top of the complexity of managing the corporate level paradox.

Resolving

If one would be satisfied with a fast resolution for the paradox of globalization and localization, the term *glocalization*, widely used by academics, consultants and journalists, would do well. It suggests that the paradox can be resolved with a synthesis. After taking a closer look at how the term is usually explained, however, a more likely conclusion would be that the solution is not only fast but also rather superficial: going global while adapting to local conditions. With examples such as Coca-Cola that had to adapt to local circumstances as its globally standardized strategy had run its course, and McDonald's introducing local products such as Veggie McNuggets in India and McLobster in Canada, the term glocalization is used for companies going global while to some extent adapting locally. Yet, it is hard if not impossible to find a global company that does not need any local adaptations, and so the new term is close to empty.

Glocalization, the semantic compilation of the words globalization and localization, originates from the Japanese word *dochakuka* which means global localization, and originally referred to adapting farming techniques to local conditions. In the strategy field, the term has been picked up from one of many Japanese presenters in the 1980s on Japanese management techniques and globalization. These were two hot topics, particularly in the United States, for two reasons. First, Japanese companies had become extremely successful overseas from the 1970s with, for example, cars and electronic products, and American companies and scholars wanted to understand Japanese success. And since demand creates supply, Japanese writers were invited to share some valuable insights. Second, globalization was a popular subject as new technological innovations changed the firm's understanding of international expansion dramatically (further explained in the next section 'The international context in international perspective').

The Japanese McKinsey consultant Kenichi Ohmae contributed to this topic with his book *Triad of Economic Power* (1985). Humans need language to exchange and discuss ideas; however, the words' connotations are not always understood, including the Japanese word *dochakuka*, which had to be understood as Yin Yang Balancing, and not as a quick solution.

Still, companies can capture the advantages of both global synergies and local responsiveness. In Chapter 5 on corporate level strategy, one prominent synthesis between business responsiveness and multi-business synergy has been discussed: the franchise. Franchises can also be – and actually often are – internationally organized, such as Pizza Hut, McDonald's and Kentucky Fried Chicken. Franchises are even more advantageous in the international context, as many complicating issues can be handled in an elegant way, such as specific local characteristics in the local food culture – for example with the above mentioned Veggie McNuggets in India – and import restrictions.

Embracing

Tensions between global synergy and local responsiveness are felt by the employees of the international firms. Not only frictions between head office and business units (see also Chapter 5), but also between people from different countries within the country unit often lead to misunderstandings, while some culture-related values are hardly compatible. For example, while drinking coffee is irrelevant for some, it is crucial for others (never install the company's standard English coffee machine at an Italian branch!). Most international firms provide culture training to prepare managers for emerging culture issues to manage the cultural tensions.

Yet, international operations create not only tensions, they can also be exploited. In the next section, 'The international context in international perspective', the so-called *New International Division of Labour* (Fröbel, Heinrichs and Kreye, 1980) is discussed. This paradigm claims that labour intensive production will be concentrated in countries with an abundance of cheap labour, while R&D will be concentrated in countries with superior levels of education, income and infrastructure. For example, the Japanese Uniqlo produces labour-intensive cashmere clothes in China while developing high-tech garments in Japan. This new division of labour includes much more than just production and research. International firms settle in Silicon Valley to become part of the next technological revolution, have designer teams in Italy, software engineers in India, media innovators in South Korea, lawyers in London and production facilities in Germany.

The importance of the global division of labour is that companies are not searching for one global standard, but instead combine countries' relative advantages. By blending country-specific differences, the tensions that arise from the paradox of global synergy and local responsiveness are seen as an opportunity (Beech *et al.*, 2004).

THE INTERNATIONAL CONTEXT IN INTERNATIONAL PERSPECTIVE

Co-authors: Gep Eisenloeffel and Wester Wagenaar

A truth on this side of the Pyrenees, a falsehood on the other.
Michel Eyquem de Montaigne (1533–1592); French philosopher, statesman and essayist

'The international context in international perspective.' What a curious title one might think. Is not this a case of the snake biting itself in its own tail? The answer is no. An international angle can be used to view the debate between proponents of the global convergence perspective and those of the international diversity perspective. In other words, are there countries where a focus on attaining global synergies is more prevalent, while in others answering the demand for local responsiveness is more widespread?

For a long time it was mostly companies from industrialized countries that operated on a global scale, utilizing cheap labour from other countries. Knowledge and capital are the crucial inputs in the early stages of product manufacturing; labour intensity dominates in the latter ones. This has a large effect on the location of industries as the comparative advantage in production shifts across countries. After the Second World War, foreign direct investment (FDI) accelerated at an unprecedented rate, eventually outpacing the growth of international trade (Dicken, 2015). Now a global shift is occurring.

Most notably after the turn of the century a profound change in the balance of economic power came about. Labour-intensive production found its way from the first generation of newly industrializing countries – Singapore, Hong Kong, Taiwan and South Korea – to second and third tier locations like Indonesia, Thailand, Malaysia and Bangladesh. In addition, new economic powerhouses, such as China, India, Russia, Turkey and Brazil made their presence felt. These awakening giants attracted FDI because of cheap labour, but as the middle class in countries like China increased, they also became interesting markets for Western consumer products. Rising income levels and technological developments in these countries changed locational conditions while markets matured. Now regions within China, like greater Beijing or Shanghai, attract not just cheap labour but also high end production geared for both export and their own home market. Companies from the developing countries have not only risen, they have done so fast. For example, between 2006 and 2015 the number of enterprises from the four major developing countries – Brazil, Russia, India and China, or the BRIC countries – has increased from 20 to 61 on the Financial Times Global 500 list (*Financial Times*, 2006, 2015). As it stands, more and more internationalizing firms from developing countries are starting to operate on a global scale. Economic interdependencies have only increased in the last 30 years.

It is important to note that much of the global trade is still limited to the United States, Europe and East Asia. This triad of economic power as the main markets for the influx of FDI makes clear that the much-used term globalization should be put into perspective. Many companies do not make a distinct trade-off between the international and the local level; FDI still mainly takes place in a relatively small number of countries and only a minority of MNEs have an equal share of their production and sales in all countries of the triad (Ghemawat, 2005; Rugman, 2005). Many multinational enterprises do not truly operate globally, but often stick to a region. Moreover, the more strategic the assets, the less global the activities: R&D, headquarter location and stock ownership are mainly concentrated in the MNEs' home countries (Rugman, 2005; Ruigrok and Van Tulder, 1995).

On the national level

History matters in terms of which countries historically had the resources to operate globally, but preferences as to how to deal with international strategy have not been discussed. Which nation-specific factors determine international differences when it comes to preferences for the global convergence or the international diversity perspective? If the proponents of the global convergence perspective are right, history and other factors will play a less and less important role as countries grow more similar. However, if international diversity remains a characteristic of our world, the way strategy paradoxes are dealt with differently in each country will continue to be an important issue to discuss.

One nation-specific factor that plays a role in strategies in the international context is the level of nationalism. In some countries the belief is widespread that the country's ability to decide its own fate is being compromised. Foreign values, norms, habits and behaviours are being imposed, undermining the national culture. This leads many to argue that global convergence should be, and will be, curtailed. In other countries such nationalism is far less pronounced, and the advantages of globalization are more widely accepted. In general, it can be expected that strategists from countries with a strong streak of nationalism will gravitate more towards the international diversity perspective, while strategists from less nationalist countries will be more inclined towards the global convergence perspective.

The size of a country can also have an impact on national inclinations towards either one of the perspectives on the international context paradox. In general, smaller countries are more exposed to the international context than larger countries. Smaller countries commonly export more of their gross domestic product than larger countries, and import more as well. Hence, their companies are more used to dealing with, and adapting to, a high number of foreign suppliers, customers and competitors. Moreover, companies from smaller countries, confronted with a limited home market, are forced to seek growth in foreign markets earlier than their counterparts in larger countries. During this early internationalization, these companies do not have the benefit of scale economies in the home market and therefore are usually more inclined to adapt themselves to the demands of foreign markets. Companies in larger markets normally grow to a significant size at home, thereby achieving certain economies of scale through national standardization, while also establishing a domestically oriented management style. When they do move abroad, as a more mature company, their international activities will tend to be modest compared to domestic operations and therefore they will be less inclined to be locally adaptive. It stands to reason that this difference in exposure to the international context has an influence on how strategists from different countries perceive developments in the international context. Generally, strategists from smaller countries, to whom adaptation to international variety has become second nature, will favour the view that international diversity will remain. Strategists from larger countries will be more inclined to emphasize the growing similarities and to seek opportunities for international standardization.

Technology and a well-functioning IT infrastructure also play an important role. Some propose that internationalization is an incremental process that unfolds over time as a company shifts from an established domestic market to the international (Johanson and Vahlne, 1977). This so-called Uppsala model is now challenged by a new phenomenon. Entrepreneurial ventures, labelled as Born Globals (BGs), start out more or less globally from their inception, seizing opportunities offered by an increasingly interconnected and integrated global economy (Dicken, 2015; Mathews and Zander, 2007). Born Globals are typically companies that take advantage of the global IT infrastructure, such as Airbnb and Alibaba. They tend to be endowed with distinguishing intangible capabilities and superior technological and relational resources (Hennart, 2014; Knight and Liesch, 2016). Most of the software or Internet-focused companies are capturing global synergies in the tech industry, such as social media platforms and firms offering mobile entertainment. Yet the phenomenon is not exclusive to those industries. Logitech, HTC and Zara are all examples of successful companies that went global almost right away. Born Globals are emerging all over the world and as time progresses many more across a variety of industries can be expected.

On the industry level

Some industries naturally operate more globally than others. This was already hinted at when discussing Born Globals, where for instance Internet-focused firms can easily provide a similar product internationally. Some companies have a hard time going global, even if they want to. Jean-François Hennart argues that the reason why Born Globals are able to go internationally fast is that their business model allows them to do so. They often "sell niche products at low information, transportation, and adaptation costs to expert customers dispersed throughout the world". When Logitech transitioned from a niche to a mass market, a significant amount of time was needed to increase foreign sales, as the Uppsala model predicts (2014).

Whether an industry has a preference for the global convergence perspective over the international diversity perspective, largely has to do with culture. Whether a company needs to adapt or not, mostly has to do with national cultures and tastes. European consumers prefer cars with good engines, while Americans tend to pick large and comfortable ones. In Japan, smaller cars are the norm. Local adaptation is a prerequisite and as such, some products are more suitable for unaltered global distribution than others.

A similar case can be made for the pharmaceutical industry, although barriers prevent companies from employing a truly global strategy. Here regulation plays a key role. Local and regional rules can have a big impact on a firm's possibilities. The pharmaceutical industry, for instance, is heavily regulated by regional and national governments. Differences in the drug approval process, liability for damage and price controls complicates international sales of pharmaceuticals (Rugman, 2005). Nevertheless, the pharmaceutical industry does aim for global, or at least regional, synergies. Since pharmaceutical products hardly have to be adapted for each geographic market and since the large pharmaceutical companies own the rights to brand-name drugs, the firms can sell their products basically anywhere – as long as regulations do not stop them.

To the strategist

Whether a strategist opts to standardize or adapt on the international level is not always a personal choice. It is also influenced by external factors such as local pressure to adapt to local demand and regulations. The pressure to locally adapt is something strategists who operate internationally should take heed of. Nevertheless, even if a firm decides to remain operating locally it will still have to compete with others who might gain competitive advantages through international synergies. A strategist can then choose to offer more localized products and services and pursue a more responsive strategy.

INTRODUCTION TO THE READINGS

To help strategizing managers to come to grips with the variety of perspectives on this issue, three readings have been selected that each shed their own light on the debate. As in previous chapters, the first two readings are representative of the two poles in this debate (see Table 12.1), while the third reading bridges the perspectives.

Reading 12.1, representing the global convergence perspective, is 'The Globalization of Markets' by Theodore Levitt. This article, published in the early 1980s, has probably been the most influential at starting the debate about globalization in the business literature. Levitt's thesis is that the world is quickly moving towards a converging commonality.

He believes that "the world's needs and desires have been irrevocably homogenized". The force driving this process is technology, which has facilitated communication, transport and travel, while allowing for the development of superior products at low prices. His conclusion is that "the commonality of preference leads inescapably to the standardization of products, manufacturing and the institutions of trade and commerce". The old-fashioned multinational corporation, that adapted itself to local circumstances is "obsolete and the global corporation absolute". While a clear proponent of the global convergence perspective, it should be noted that Levitt's bold prediction of global convergence is focused on the globalization of markets. In particular, he is intent on pointing out that converging consumer demand in international markets facilitates – even necessitates – the reaping of economies of scale through the standardization of products, marketing and production. With this emphasis on the demand side, Levitt pays far less attention to the supply side – the globalization of industries and the competition within industries – that other global convergence proponents tend to accentuate. And although he strongly advises companies to become "global corporations", he does not further detail what a global company should look like. Overall, Levitt views globalization more as growing international similarity, while paying less attention than some other authors to the possibility of growing international integration.

As a direct response to "the sweeping and somewhat polemic character" of Levitt's argumentation, Susan Douglas and Yoram Wind's article, 'The Myth of Globalization', has been selected for Reading 12.2 representing the international diversity perspective. Douglas and Wind believe that many of the assumptions underlying Levitt's global standardization philosophy are contradicted by the facts. They argue that the convergence of customer needs is not a one-way street; divergence trends are noticeable as well. Furthermore, they believe that Levitt is mistaken in arguing that economies of scale in production and marketing are an irreversible force driving globalization. According to Douglas and Wind, many new technologies have actually lowered the minimum efficient scale of operation, while there are also plenty of industries where economies of scale are not an important issue. The authors conclude by outlining the specific circumstances under which a strategy of global standardization might be effective. Under all other circumstances, Douglas and Wind reiterate, the international strategist will have to deal with the existence of international diversity and search for the right balance between global standardization and local adaptation.

In the third reading, 'Clusters and the New Economics of Competition', Michael E. Porter argues that today's economic map of the world is dominated by what he calls clusters: "critical masses – in one place – of unusual competitive success in particular fields". Well-known clusters such as Silicon Valley and Hollywood are not exceptions but rather the rule in economically advanced nations. Porter describes the paradox of global synergy and local responsiveness as the enduring competitive advantages in a global economy that increasingly lies in local things – knowledge, relationships, motivation – that distant rivals cannot match. Obviously, what happens inside companies is important, yet the immediate business environment outside companies plays a vital role as well. This role of locations has been long overlooked.

READING
12.1

The globalization of markets

By Theodore Levitt[1]

A powerful force drives the world toward a converging commonality, and that force is technology. It has proletarianized communication, transport and travel. It has made isolated places and impoverished peoples eager for modernity's allurements. Almost everyone everywhere wants all the things they have heard about, seen, or experienced via the new technologies.

The result is a new commercial reality – the emergence of global markets for standardized consumer products on a previously unimagined scale of magnitude. Corporations geared to this new reality benefit from enormous economies of scale in production, distribution, marketing and management. By translating these benefits into reduced world prices, they can decimate competitors that still live in the disabling grip of old assumptions about how the world works.

Gone are accustomed differences in national or regional preference. Gone are the days when a company could sell last year's models – or lesser versions of advanced products – in the less developed world. And gone are the days when prices, margins and profits abroad were generally higher than at home.

The globalization of markets is at hand. With that, the multinational commercial world nears its end, and so does the multinational corporation.

The multinational and the global corporation are not the same thing. The multinational corporation operates in a number of countries, and adjusts its products and practices in each – at high relative costs. The global corporation operates with resolute constancy – at low relative cost – as if the entire world (or major regions of it) were a single entity; it sells the same things in the same way everywhere.

Which strategy is better is not a matter of opinion but of necessity. Worldwide communications carry everywhere the constant drumbeat of modern possibilities to lighten and enhance work, raise living standards, divert and entertain. The same countries that ask the world to recognize and respect the individuality of their cultures insist on the wholesale transfer to them of modern goods, services and technologies. Modernity is not just a wish but also a widespread practice among those who cling, with unyielding passion or religious fervour, to ancient attitudes and heritages.

Who can forget the televised scenes during the 1979 Iranian uprisings of young men in fashionable French-cut trousers and silky body shirts thirsting with raised modern weapons for blood in the name of Islamic fundamentalism?

In Brazil, thousands swarm daily from preindustrial Bahian darkness into exploding coastal cities, there quickly to install television sets in crowded corrugated huts and, next to battered Volkswagens, make sacrificial offerings of fruit and fresh-killed chickens to Macumban spirits by candlelight.

A thousand suggestive ways attest to the ubiquity of the desire for the most advanced things that the world makes and sells – goods of the best quality and reliability at the lowest price. The world's needs and desires have been irrevocably homogenized. This makes the multinational corporation obsolete and the global corporation absolute.

Living in the Republic of Technology

Daniel J. Boorstin, author of the monumental trilogy *The Americans* (1973), characterized our age as driven by 'the Republic of Technology (whose) supreme law is convergence, the tendency for everything to become more like everything else'.

In business, this trend has pushed markets toward global commonality. Corporations sell standardized products in the same way everywhere – autos, steel, chemicals, petroleum, cement, agricultural commodities and equipment, industrial and commercial construction, banking and insurance services, computers, semiconductors, transport, electronic instruments, pharmaceuticals and telecommunications, to mention some of the obvious.

Nor is the sweeping gale of globalization confined to these raw material or high-tech products, where the universal language of customers and users facilitates standardization. The transforming winds whipped up by the proletarianization of communication and travel enter every crevice of life.

Commercially, nothing confirms this as much as the success of McDonald's from the Champs Elysees to the Ginza, of Coca-Cola in Bahrain and Pepsi-Cola in Moscow, and of rock music, Greek salad, Hollywood movies, Revlon cosmetics, Sony televisions and Levi jeans everywhere. 'High-touch' products are as ubiquitous as high-tech.

Starting from opposing sides, the high-tech and the high-touch ends of the commercial spectrum gradually consume the undistributed middle in their cosmopolitan orbit. No one is exempt and nothing can stop the process. Everywhere everything gets more and more like everything else as the world's preference structure is relentlessly homogenized.

Consider the cases of Coca-Cola and Pepsi-Cola, which are globally standardized products sold everywhere and welcomed by everyone. Both successfully cross multitudes of national, regional and ethnic taste buds trained to a variety of deeply ingrained local preferences of taste, flavour, consistency, effervescence and aftertaste. Everywhere both sell well. Cigarettes, too, especially American-made, make year-to-year global inroads in territories previously held in the firm grip of other, mostly local, blends.

These are not exceptional examples. (Indeed their global reach would be even greater were it not for artificial trade barriers.) They exemplify a general drift toward the homogenization of the world and how companies distribute, finance and price products. Nothing is exempt. The products and methods of the industrialized world play a single tune for all the world, and all the world eagerly dances to it.

Ancient differences in national tastes or modes of doing business disappear. The commonality of preference leads inescapably to the standardization of products, manufacturing, and the institutions of trade and commerce. Small nation-based markets transmogrify and expand. Success in world competition turns on efficiency in production, distribution, marketing and management, and inevitably becomes focused on price.

The most effective world competitors incorporate superior quality and reliability into their cost structures. They sell in all national markets the same kind of products sold at home or in their largest export market. They compete on the basis of appropriate value – the best combinations of price, quality, reliability and delivery for products that are globally identical with respect to design, function and even fashion.

That, and little else, explains the surging success of Japanese companies dealing worldwide in a vast variety of products – both tangible products like steel, cars, motorcycles, hi-fi equipment, farm machinery, robots, microprocessors, carbon fibres and now even textiles, and intangibles like banking, shipping, general contracting, and soon computer software. Nor are high-quality and low-cost operations incompatible, as a host of consulting organizations and data engineers argue with vigorous vacuity. The reported data are incomplete, wrongly analysed and contradictory. The truth is that low-cost operations are the hallmark of corporate cultures that require and produce quality in all that they do. High quality and low costs are not opposing postures. They are compatible, twin identities of superior practice.

To say that Japan's companies are not global because they export cars with left-side drives to the United States and the European continent, while those in Japan have right-side drives, or because they sell office machines through distributors in the United States but directly at home, or speak Portuguese in Brazil, is to mistake a difference for a distinction. The same is true of Safeway and Southland retail chains operating effectively in the Middle East, and to not

only native but also imported populations from Korea, the Philippines, Pakistan, India, Thailand, Britain and the United States. National rules of the road differ, and so do distribution channels and languages. Japan's distinction is its unrelenting push for economy and value enhancement. That translates into a drive for standardization at high quality levels.

Vindication of the Model T

If a company forces costs and prices down and pushes quality and reliability up – while maintaining reasonable concern for suitability – customers will prefer its world-standardized products. The theory holds at this stage in the evolution of globalization, no matter what conventional market research and even common sense may suggest about different national and regional tastes, preferences, needs and institutions. The Japanese have repeatedly vindicated this theory, as did Henry Ford with the Model T. Most important, so have their imitators, including companies from South Korea (television sets and heavy construction), Malaysia (personal calculators and microcomputers), Brazil (auto parts and tools), Colombia (apparel), Singapore (optical equipment) and yes, even from the United States (office copiers, computers, bicycles, castings), Western Europe (automatic washing machines), Romania (housewares), Hungary (apparel), the former Yugoslavia (furniture) and Israel (pagination equipment).

Of course, large companies operating in a single nation or even a single city don't standardize everything they make, sell, or do. They have product lines instead of a single product version, and multiple distribution channels. There are neighbourhood, local, regional, ethnic and institutional differences, even within metropolitan areas. But although companies customize products for particular market segments, they know that success in a world with homogenized demand requires a search for sales opportunities in similar segments across the globe in order to achieve the economies of scale necessary to compete.

Such a search works because a market segment in one country is seldom unique; it has close cousins everywhere precisely because technology has homogenized the globe. Even small local segments have their global equivalents everywhere and become subject to global competition, especially on price.

The global competitor will seek constantly to standardize his offering everywhere. He will digress from this standardization only after exhausting all possibilities to retain it, and he will push for reinstatement of standardization whenever digression and divergence have occurred. He will never assume that the customer is a king who knows his own wishes.

Trouble increasingly stalks companies that lack clarified global focus and remain inattentive to the economics of simplicity and standardization. The most endangered companies in the rapidly evolving world tend to be those that dominate rather small domestic markets with high-value-added products for which there are smaller markets elsewhere. With transportation costs proportionately low, distant competitors will enter the now sheltered markets of those companies with goods produced more cheaply under scale-efficient conditions. Global competition spells the end of domestic territoriality, no matter how diminutive the territory may be.

When the global producer offers his lower costs internationally, his patronage expands exponentially. He not only reaches into distant markets, but also attracts customers who previously held to local preferences and now capitulate to the attractions of lesser prices. The strategy of standardization not only responds to worldwide homogenized markets but also expands those markets with aggressive low pricing.

The new technological juggernaut taps an ancient motivation – to make one's money go as far as possible. This is universal – not simply a motivation but actually a need.

The hedgehog knows

The difference between the hedgehog and the fox, wrote Sir Isaiah Berlin in distinguishing between Dostoevsky and Tolstoy, is that the fox knows a lot about a great many things, but the hedgehog knows everything about one great thing. The multinational corporation knows a lot about a great many countries and congenially adapts to supposed differences. It willingly accepts vestigial national differences, not questioning the possibility of their transformation, not recognizing how the world is ready and eager for the benefit of modernity, especially when the price is right. The multinational corporation's accommodating mode to visible national differences is medieval.

By contrast, the global corporation knows everything about one great thing. It knows about the absolute need to be competitive on a worldwide basis as well as nationally and seeks constantly to drive down prices by standardizing what it sells and how it operates. It treats the world as composed of few standardized markets rather than many customized markets. It actively seeks

and vigorously works toward global convergence. Its mission is modernity and its mode, price competition, even when it sells top-of-the-line, high-end products. It knows about the one great thing all nations and people have in common: scarcity.

Nobody takes scarcity lying down; everyone wants more. This in part explains division of labour and specialization of production. They enable people and nations to optimize their conditions through trade. The median is usually money.

Experience teaches that money has three special qualities: scarcity, difficulty of acquisition and transience. People understandably treat it with respect. Everyone in the increasingly homogenized world market wants products and features that everybody else wants. If the price is low enough, they will take highly standardized world products, even if these aren't exactly what mother said was suitable, what immemorial custom decreed was right, or what market-research fabulists asserted was preferred.

The implacable truth of all modern production – whether of tangible or intangible goods – is that large-scale production of standardized items is generally cheaper within a wide range of volume than small-scale production. Some argue that CAD/CAM (computer aided design/computer aided manufacturing) will allow companies to manufacture customized products on a small scale – but cheaply. But the argument misses the point. If a company treats the world as one or two distinctive product markets, it can serve the world more economically than if it treats it as three, four, or five product markets.

Different cultural preferences, national tastes and standards, and business institutions are vestiges of the past. Some inheritances die gradually; others prosper and expand into mainstream global preferences. So-called ethnic markets are a good example. Chinese food, pitta bread, country and western music, pizza and jazz are everywhere. They are market segments that exist in worldwide proportions. They don't deny or contradict global homogenization but confirm it.

Many of today's differences among nations as to products and their features actually reflect the respectful accommodation of multinational corporations to what they believe are fixed local preferences. They believe preferences are fixed, not because they are but because of rigid habits of thinking about what actually is. Most executives in multinational corporations are thoughtlessly accommodating. They falsely presume that marketing means giving the customer what he says he wants rather than trying to understand exactly what he'd like. So they persist with high-cost, customized multi-national products and practices instead of pressing hard and pressing properly for global standardization.

I do not advocate the systematic disregard of local or national differences. But a company's sensitivity to such differences does not require that it ignore the possibilities of doing things differently or better.

With persistence and appropriate means, barriers against superior technologies and economics have always fallen. There is no recorded exception where reasonable effort has been made to overcome them. It is very much a matter of time and effort.

A failure in global imagination

Many companies have tried to standardize world practice by exporting domestic products and processes without accommodation or change – and have failed miserably. Their deficiencies have been seized on as evidence of bovine stupidity in the face of abject impossibility. Advocates of global standardization see them as examples of failures in execution.

In fact, poor execution is often an important cause. More important, however, is failure of nerve – failure of imagination.

Consider the case for the introduction of fully automatic home laundry equipment in Western Europe at a time when few homes had even semi-automatic machines.

The growing success of small, low-powered, low-speed, low-capacity, low-priced Italian machines, even against the preferred but highly priced and highly promoted brand in West Germany, was significant. It contained a powerful message that was lost on managers confidently wedded to a distorted version of the marketing concept according to which you give the customer what he says he wants. In fact the customers said they wanted certain features, but their behaviour demonstrated they'd take other features provided the price and the promotion were right.

In this case it was obvious that under prevailing conditions, people preferred a low-priced automatic over any kind of manual or semi-automatic machine and certainly over higher priced automatics, even though the low-priced automatics failed to fulfil all their expressed preferences. The supposedly meticulous and demanding German consumers violated all expectations by buying the simple, low-priced Italian machines.

This case illustrates how the perverse practice of the marketing concept and the absence of any kind of marketing imagination let multinational attitudes survive when customers actually want the benefits of global standardization. People were asked what features they wanted in a washing machine rather than what they wanted out of life. Selling a line of products individually tailored to each nation is thoughtless. Managers who took pride in practising the marketing concept to the fullest did not, in fact, practise it at all. Data do not yield information except with the intervention of the mind. Information does not yield meaning except with the intervention of imagination.

Cracking the code of Western markets

Since the theory of the marketing concept emerged a quarter of a century ago, the more managerially advanced corporations have been eager to offer what customers clearly want rather than what is merely convenient. They have created marketing departments supported by professional market researchers of awesome and often costly proportions. And they have proliferated extraordinary numbers of operations and product lines – highly tailored products and delivery systems for many different markets, market segments and nations.

Significantly, Japanese companies operate almost entirely without marketing departments or market research of the kind so prevalent in the West. Yet, in the colourful words of General Electric's chairman, John F. Welch Jr., the Japanese, coming from a small cluster of resource-poor islands, with an entirely alien culture and an almost impenetrably complex language, have cracked the code of Western markets. They have done it not by looking with mechanistic thoroughness at the way markets are different but rather by searching for meaning with a deeper wisdom. They have discovered the one great thing all markets have in common – an overwhelming desire for dependable, world-standard modernity in all things, at aggressively low prices. In response, they deliver irresistible value everywhere, attracting people with products that market-research technocrats described with superficial certainty as being unsuitable and uncompetitive.

The wider a company's global reach, the greater the number of regional and national preferences it will encounter for certain product features, distribution systems, or promotional media. There will always need to be some accommodation to differences.

In its highly successful introduction of Contac 600 (the timed-release decongestant) into Japan, Smith-Kline Corporation used 35 wholesalers instead of the 1000-plus that established practice required. Daily contacts with the wholesalers and key retailers, also in violation of established practice, supplemented the plan, and it worked.

Denied access to established distribution institutions in the United States, Komatsu, the Japanese manufacturer of lightweight farm machinery, entered the market through over-the-road construction equipment dealers in rural areas of the Sunbelt, where farms are smaller, the soil sandier and easier to work. Here inexperienced distributors were able to attract customers on the basis of Komatsu's product and price appropriateness.

In cases of successful challenge to prevailing institutions and practices, a combination of product reliability and quality, strong and sustained support systems, aggressively low prices, and sales-compensation packages, as well as audacity and implacability, circumvented, shattered and transformed very different distribution systems. Instead of resentment, there was admiration.

The differences that persist throughout the world despite its globalization affirm an ancient dictum of economics – that things are driven by what happens at the margin, not at the core. Thus, in ordinary competitive analysis, what's important is not the average price but the marginal price, what happens not in the usual case but at the interface of newly erupting conditions. What counts in commercial affairs is what happens at the cutting edge. What is most striking today is the underlying similarities of what is happening now to national preferences at the margin. These similarities at the cutting edge cumulatively form an overwhelming, predominant commonality everywhere.

To refer to the persistence of economic nationalism (protective and subsidized trade practices, special tax aids, or restrictions for home market producers) as a barrier to the globalization of markets is to make a valid point. Economic nationalism does have a powerful persistence. But, as with the present almost totally smooth internationalization of investment capital, the past alone does not shape or predict the future.

Reality is not a fixed paradigm, dominated by immemorial customs and derived attitudes, heedless of powerful and abundant new forces. The world is becoming increasingly informed about the liberating and enhancing possibilities of modernity. The persistence of the inherited varieties of national preferences rests uneasily on increasing evidence of, and restlessness regarding, their inefficiency, costliness and confinement. The historic past, and the national differences respecting commerce and industry it spawned and fostered everywhere, is now subject to relatively easy transformation.

Cosmopolitanism is no longer the monopoly of the intellectual and leisure classes; it is becoming the established property and defining characteristic of all sectors everywhere in the world. Gradually and irresistibly it breaks down the walls of economic insularity, nationalism and chauvinism. What we see today as escalating commercial nationalism is simply the last violent death rattle of an obsolete institution.

The successful global corporation does not abjure customization or differentiation for the requirements of markets that differ in product preferences, spending patterns, shopping preferences and institutional or legal arrangements. But the global corporation accepts and adjusts to these differences only reluctantly, only after relentlessly testing their immutability, after trying in various ways to circumvent and reshape them.

The myth of globalization

By Susan Douglas and Yoram Wind[1]

In recent years, globalization has become a key theme in every discussion of international strategy. Proponents of the philosophy of 'global' products and brands, such as Professor Theodore Levitt of Harvard, and the highly successful advertising agency, Saatchi & Saatchi, argue that in a world of growing internationalization, the key to success is the development of global products and brands, in other words, a focus on

[1]Source: This article was published in *Columbia Journal of World Business*, Winter 1987, Susan Douglas and Yoram Wind, 'The myth of globalization', pp. 19–29. Copyright © Elsevier 1987.

standardized products and brands worldwide. Others, however, point to the numerous barriers to standardization, and suggest that greater returns are to be obtained from adapting products and marketing strategies to the specific characteristics of individual markets.

The growing integration of international markets as well as the growth of competition on a worldwide scale implies that adoption of a global perspective has become increasingly imperative in planning strategy. However, to conclude that this mandates the adoption of a strategy of universal standardization appears naive and over simplistic. In particular, it ignores the inherent complexity of operations in international markets, and the formulation of an effective strategy to penetrate these markets. While global products and brands may be appropriate for certain markets and in targeting certain segments, adopting such an approach as a universal strategy in relation to all markets may not be desirable, and may lead to major strategic blunders. Furthermore, it implies a product orientation, and a product-driven strategy, rather than a strategy grounded in a systematic analysis of customer behaviour and response patterns and market characteristics.

The purpose of this article is thus to examine critically the notion that success in international markets necessitates adoption of a strategy of global products and brands. Given the restrictive characteristic of this philosophy, a somewhat broader perspective in developing global strategy is proposed which views standardization as merely one option in the range of possible strategies which may be effective in global markets.

The traditional perspective on international strategy

Traditionally, discussion of international business strategy has been polarized around the debate concerning the pursuit of a uniform strategy worldwide versus adaptation to specific local market conditions. On the one hand, it has been argued that adoption of a uniform strategy worldwide enables a company to take advantage of the potential synergies arising from multicountry operations, and constitutes the multinational company's key competitive advantage in international markets. Others however, have argued that adaptation of strategy to idiosyncratic national market characteristics is crucial to success in these markets.

Fayerweather (1969), in his seminal work in international business strategy, described the central issue as one of conflict between forces toward unification and those resulting in fragmentation. He pointed out

that within a multinational firm, internal forces created pressures toward the integration of strategy across national boundaries. On the other hand, differences in the sociocultural, political and economic characteristics of countries as well as the need for effective relations with the host society, constitute fragmenting influences that favour adaptation to the local environment.

Recent discussion of global competitive strategy echoes the same theme of the dichotomy between the forces that have triggered the globalization of markets and those that constitute barriers to global competition. Factors such as economies of scale in production, purchasing, faster accumulation of learning from operating worldwide, decrease in transportation and distribution costs, reduced costs of product adaptation, and the emergence of global market segments have encouraged competition on a global scale. However, barriers such as governmental and institutional constraints, tariff barriers and duties, preferential treatment of local firms, transportation costs, differences in customer demand and so on, call for nationalistic or 'protected niche' strategies.

Compromise solutions such as 'pattern standardization' have also been proposed. In this case, a global promotional theme or positioning is developed, but execution is adapted to the local market. Similarly, it has been pointed out that even where a standardized product is marketed in a number of countries, its positioning may be adapted in each market. Conversely, the positioning may be uniform across countries, but the product itself adapted or modified.

Although this debate first emerged in the 1960s, it has recently taken on a new vigour with the widely publicized pronouncements of proponents of 'global standardization' such as Professor Levitt and Saatchi & Saatchi.

The sweeping and somewhat polemic character of their argument has sparked a number of counterarguments as well as discussion of conditions under which such a strategy may be most appropriate. It has, for example, been pointed out that the potential for standardization may be greater for certain types of products such as industrial goods or luxury personal items targeted to upscale consumers, or products with similar penetration rates. Opportunities for standardization are also likely to occur more frequently among industrialized nations, and especially the Triad countries where customer interests as well as market conditions are likely to be more similar than among developing countries.

The role of corporate philosophy and organizational structure in influencing the practicality of implementing a strategy of global standardization has also been recognized. Here, it has been noted that few companies pursue the extreme position of complete standardization with regard to all elements of the marketing mix, and business functions such as R&D, manufacturing and procurement in all countries throughout the world. Rather, some degree of adaptation is likely to occur relative to certain aspects of the firm's operations or in certain geographic areas. In addition, the feasibility of implementing a standardized strategy will depend on the autonomy accorded to local management. If local management has been accustomed to substantial autonomy, considerable opposition may be encountered in attempting to introduce globally standardized strategies.

An examination of such counterarguments suggests that there are a number of dangers in espousing a philosophy of global standardization for all products and services, and in relation to all markets worldwide. Furthermore, there are numerous difficulties and constraints to implementing such a strategy in many markets, stemming from external market conditions (such as government and trade regulation, competition, the marketing infrastructure and so on), as well as from the current structure and organization of the firm's operations.

The global standardization philosophy: The underlying assumptions

An examination of the arguments in favour of a strategy of global products and brands reveals three key underlying assumptions:

- Customer needs and interests are becoming increasingly homogeneous worldwide.
- People around the world are willing to sacrifice preferences in product features, functions, design and the like, for lower prices at high quality.
- Substantial economies of scale in production and marketing can be achieved through supplying global markets.

There are, however, a number of pitfalls associated with each of these assumptions. These are discussed here in more detail.

Homogenization of the world's wants

A key premise of the philosophy of global products is that customers' needs and interests are becoming increasingly homogeneous worldwide. But while global segments with similar interests and response patterns may be identified in some product markets, it is by no means clear that this is a universal trend. Furthermore, there is substantial evidence to suggest an increasing diversity of behaviour within countries, and the emergence of idiosyncratic country-specific segments.

Lack of evidence of homogenization. In a number of product markets ranging from watches, perfume and handbags to soft drinks and fast foods, companies have successfully identified global customer segments, and developed global products and brands targeted to these segments. These include such stars as Rolex, Omega and Le Baume & Mercier watches, Dior, Patou or Yves St Laurent perfume. But while these brands are highly visible and widely publicized, they are often, with a few notable exceptions such as Classic Coke or McDonald's, targeted to a relatively restricted upscale international customer segment.

Numerous other companies, however, adapt lines to idiosyncratic country preferences, and develop local brands or product variants targeted to local market segments. The Findus frozen food division of Nestle, for example, markets fish cakes and fish fingers in the United Kingdom, but beef bourguignon and coq au vin in France, and vitello con funghi and braviola in Italy. Similarly, Coca-Cola in Japan markets Georgia, cold coffee in a can, and Aquarius, a tonic drink, as well as Classic Coke and Hi-C.

Growth of intracountry segmentation price sensitivity. Furthermore, there is a growing body of evidence that suggests substantial heterogeneity within countries. In the United States, for example, the VALS (Value of American Lifestyles) study has identified nine value segments, while other studies have identified major differences in behaviour between regions and subcultural segments. Many other countries are also characterized by substantial regional differences as well as different lifestyle and value segments.

Similarly, in industrial markets, while some global segments, often consisting of firms with international operations, can be identified, there also is considerable diversity within and between countries. Often local businesses constitute an important market segment and, especially in developing countries, may differ significantly in technological sophistication, business philosophy and strategy, emphasis on product quality, and service and price, from large multinationals.

The evidence thus suggests that the similarities in customer behaviour are restricted to a relatively limited number of target segments or product markets, while for the most part, there are substantial differences between countries. Proponents of standardization counter that the international strategist should focus on similarities among countries rather than differences. This may, however, imply ignoring a major part of a local market, and the potential profits that may be obtained from tapping other market segments.

Universal preference for low price at acceptable quality

Another critical component of the argument for global standardization is that people around the world are willing to sacrifice preferences in product features, functions, design and the like for lower prices, assuming equivalent quality. Aggressive low pricing for quality products that meet the common needs of customers in markets around the world is believed to further expand the global markets facing the firm. Although an appealing argument, this has three major problems.

Lack of evidence of increased price sensitivity. Evidence to suggest that customers are universally willing to trade off specific product features for a lower price is largely lacking. While in many product markets there is invariably a price-sensitive segment, there is no indication that this is on the increase. On the contrary, in many product and service markets, ranging from watches, personal computers and household appliances to banking and insurance, an interest in multiple product features, product quality and service appears to be growing.

Low price positioning is a highly vulnerable strategy. Also, from a strategic point of view, emphasis on price positioning may be undesirable, especially in international markets, since it offers no long-term competitive advantage. A price-positioning strategy is always vulnerable to new technological developments that may lower costs, as well as to attack from competitors with lower overhead, and lower operating or labour costs. Government subsidies to local competitors may also undermine the effectiveness of a price-positioning strategy. In addition, price-sensitive customers typically are not brand or source loyal.

Standardized low price can be overpriced in some countries and underpriced in others. Finally, a strategy based on a combination of a standardized product at a low price, when implemented in countries that vary in their competitive structure as well as the level of economic development, is likely to result in products that are overdesigned and overpriced for some markets and underdesigned and underpriced for others. Cost advantages may also be negated by transportation and distribution costs as well as tariff barriers or price regulation.

Economies of scale of production and marketing

The third assumption underlying the philosophy of global standardization is that a key force driving strategy is product technology, and that substantial economies of scale can be achieved by supplying global markets. This does, however, neglect three critical and interrelated points:

1 Technological developments in flexible factory automation enable economies of scale to be achieved at lower levels of output and do not require production of a single standardized product.

2 Cost of production is only one and often not the critical component in determining the total cost of the product.

3 Strategy should not be solely product-driven but should take into account the other components of a marketing strategy, such as positioning, packaging, brand name, advertising, PR, consumer and trade promotion and distribution.

Developments in flexible factory automation. Recent developments in flexible factory automation methods have lowered the minimum efficient scale of operation and have thus enabled companies to supply smaller local markets efficiently, without requiring operations on a global scale. However, diseconomies may result from such operations due to increased transportation and distribution costs, as well as higher administrative overhead, and additional communication and coordination costs.

Furthermore, decentralization of production and establishment of local manufacturing operations enables diversification of risk arising from political events, fluctuations in foreign exchange rates, or economic instability. Recent swings in foreign exchange rates, coupled with the growth of offshore sourcing have underscored the vulnerability of centralizing production in a single location. Government regulations relating to local component or offset requirements create additional pressures for local manufacturing. Flexible automation not only implies that decentralization of manufacturing and production may be cost efficient but also makes minor modifications in products or models in the latter stages of production feasible, so that a variety of model versions can be produced without major retooling. Adaptations to product design can thus be made to meet differences in preferences from one country to another without loss of economies of scale.

Production costs are often a minor component of total cost. In many consumer and service industries, such as cosmetics, detergents, pharmaceuticals or financial institutions, production costs are a small fraction of total cost. The key to success in these markets is an understanding of the tastes and purchase behaviour of target customers' distribution channels, and tailoring products and strategies to these rather than production efficiency. In the detergent industry, for example, mastery of mass-merchandising techniques and an effective brand management system are typically considered the key elements in the success of the giants in this field, such as Procter & Gamble (P&G) or Colgate-Palmolive.

The standardization philosophy is primarily product driven. The focus on product- and brand-related aspects of strategy in discussions of global standardization is misleading since it ignores the other key strategy variables. Strategy in international markets should also take into consideration other aspects of the marketing mix, and the extent to which these are standardized across country markets rather than adapted to local idiosyncratic characteristics.

Requisite conditions for global standardization

The numerous pitfalls in the rationale underlying the global standardization philosophy suggests that such a strategy is far from universally appropriate for all products, brands or companies. Only under certain conditions is it likely to prove a 'winning' strategy in international markets. These include:

- the existence of a global market segment;
- potential synergies from standardization;
- the availability of a communication and distribution infrastructure to deliver the firm's offering to target customers worldwide.

Existence of global market segments

As noted previously, global segments may be identified in a number of industrial and consumer markets. In consumer markets these segments are typically luxury- or premium-type products. Global segments are, however, not limited to such product markets, but also exist in other types of markets, such as motorcycle, record, stereo equipment and computer, where a segment with similar needs and wants can be identified in many countries.

In industrial markets, companies with multinational operations are particularly likely to have similar needs and requirements worldwide. Where the operations are integrated or coordinated across national boundaries, as in the case of banks or other financial institutions, compatibility of operational systems and equipment may be essential. Consequently, they may seek vendors who can supply and service their operations worldwide, in some cases developing global contrasts for such purchases. Similarly, manufacturing companies with worldwide operations may source globally in order to ensure uniformity in quality, service and price of components and other raw materials throughout their operations.

Marketing of global products and brands to such target segments and global customers enables development of a uniform global image throughout the world. In some markets such as perfume or fashions, association with a specific country of origin or a foreign image in general may carry a prestige connotation. In other cases, for example, Sony electronic equipment, McDonald's hamburgers, Hertz or Avis car rental, IBM computers, or Xerox office equipment, it may help to develop a worldwide reputation for quality and service. Just as multinational corporations may seek uniformity in supply worldwide, some consumers who travel extensively may be interested in finding the same brand of cigarettes and soft drinks or hotels, in foreign countries. This may be particularly relevant in product markets used extensively by international travellers.

While the existence of a potential global segment is a key motivating factor for developing a global product and brand strategy, it is important to note that the desirability of such a strategy depends on the size and economic viability of the segment in question, the strength of the segment's preference for the global brand, as well as the ability to reach the segment effectively and profitably.

Synergies associated with global standardization

Global standardization may also have a number of synergistic effects. In addition to those associated with a global image noted above, opportunities may exist for the transfer of good ideas for products or promotional strategies from one country to another.

The standardization of strategy and operations across a number of countries may also enable the acquisition or exploitation of specific types of expertise that would not be feasible otherwise. Expertise in assessing country risk or foreign exchange risk, or in identifying and interpreting information relating to multiple country markets, for example, may be developed.

Such synergies are not, however, unique to a strategy of global standardization, but may also occur wherever operations and strategy are coordinated or integrated across country markets. In fact, only certain scale economies associated with product and advertising copy standardization, and the development of a global image as discussed earlier, are unique to global standardization.

Availability of an international communication and distribution infrastructure

The effectiveness of global standardization also depends to a large extent on the availability of an international infrastructure of communications and distribution. As many corporations have expanded overseas, service organizations have followed their customers abroad to supply their needs worldwide.

Advertising agencies such as Saatchi & Saatchi, McCann Erickson and Young & Rubicam now have an international network of operations throughout the world, while many research agencies can also supply services in major markets worldwide. With the growing integration of financial markets, banks, investment firms, insurance and other financial institutions are also becoming increasingly international in orientation and are expanding the scope of their operations in world markets. The physical distribution network of shippers, freight forwarding, export and import agents, customs clearing, invoicing and insurance agents is also becoming increasingly integrated to meet demand for international shipment of goods and services.

Improvements in telecommunications and in logistical systems have considerably increased capacity to manage operations on a global scale and hence facilitate adoption of global standardization strategies. The spread of telex and fax systems, as well as satellite linkages and international computer linkages, all contribute to the shrinking of distances and facilitate globalization of operations. Similarly, improvements in transportation systems and physical logistics such as containerization and computerized inventory and handling systems have enabled significant cost savings as well as reducing time required to move goods across major distances.

Operational constraints to effective implementation of a standardization strategy

While adoption of a standardized strategy may be desirable under certain conditions, there are a number of constraints that severely restrict the firm's ability to develop and implement a standardized strategy.

External constraints to effective standardization

The numerous external constraints that impede global standardization are well recognized. Here, four major categories are highlighted, namely:

1 government and trade restrictions;
2 differences in the marketing infrastructure, such as the availability and effectiveness of promotional media;
3 the character of resource markets, and differences in the availability and costs of resources;
4 differences in competition from one country to another.

Government and trade restrictions. Government and trade restrictions, such as tariff and other trade barriers, product, pricing or promotional regulation, frequently hamper standardization of the product line, pricing or promotional strategy. Tariffs or quotas on the import of key materials, components or other resources may, for example, affect production costs and thus hamper uniform pricing or alternatively result in the substitution of other components and modifications in product design. Local content requirements or compensatory export requirements, which specify that products contain a certain proportion of components manufactured locally or that a certain volume of production is exported to offset imports of components or other services, may have a similar impact.

The existence of cartels such as the European steel cartel, or the Swiss chocolate cartel, may also impede or exclude standardized strategies in countries covered by these agreements. In particular, they may affect adoption of a uniform pricing strategy as the cartel sets prices for the industry. Cartel members may also control established distribution channels, thus preventing use of a standardized distribution strategy. Extensive grey markets in countries such as India, Hong Kong and South America may also affect administered pricing systems, and require adjustment of pricing strategies.

The nature of the marketing infrastructure. Differences in the marketing infrastructure from one country to another may hamper use of a standardized strategy. These may, for example, include differences in the availability and reach of various promotional media, the availability of certain distribution channels or retail institutions, or in the existence and efficiency of the communication and transportation network. Such factors may, therefore, require considerable adaptation of strategy of local market conditions.

Interdependencies with resource markets. Yet another constraint to the development of standardized strategies is the nature of resource markets, and their operation in different countries throughout the world as well as the interdependency of these markets with marketing decisions. Availability and cost of raw materials, as well as labour and other resources in different locations, will affect not only decisions regarding sourcing of and hence the location of manufacturing activities but also marketing strategy decisions such as product design. For example, in the paper industry, availability of cheap local materials such as jute and sugar cane may result in their substitution for wood fibre.

Cost differentials relative to raw materials, labour, management and other inputs may also influence the trade-off relative to alternative strategies. For example, high packaging costs relative to physical distribution may result in use of cheaper packaging with a shorter shelf life and more frequent shipments. Similarly, low labour costs relative to media may encourage a shift from mass media advertising to labour-intensive promotion such as personal selling and product demonstration.

Availability of capital, technology and manufacturing capabilities in different locations will also affect decisions about licensing, contract manufacturing, joint ventures and other 'make-buy' types of decisions for different markets, as well as decisions about countertrade, reciprocity and other long-term relations.

The nature of the competitive structure. Differences in the nature of the competitive situation from one country to another may also suggest the desirability of adaptation strategy. Even in markets characterized by global competition, such as agricultural equipment and motorcycles, the existence of low-cost competition in certain countries may suggest the desirability of marketing stripped-down models or lowering prices to meet such competition. Even where competitors are predominantly other multinationals, preemption of established distribution networks may encourage adoption of innovative distribution methods or direct distribution to

short-circuit an entrenched position. Thus, the existence of global competition does not necessarily imply a need for global standardization.

All such aspects thus impose major constraints on the feasibility and effectiveness of a standardized strategy, and suggest the desirability or need to adapt to specific market conditions.

Internal constraints to effective standardization

In addition to such external constraints on the feasibility of a global standardization strategy, there are also a number of internal constraints that may need to be considered. These include compatibility with the existing network of operations overseas, as well as opposition or lack of enthusiasm among local management toward a standardized strategy.

Existing international operations. Proponents of global standardization typically take the position of a novice company with no operations in international markets, and hence fail to take into consideration the fit of the proposed strategy with current international activities. In practice, however, many companies have a number of existing operations in various countries. In some cases, these are joint ventures or licensing operations, or involve some collaboration in purchasing, manufacturing or distribution with other companies. Even where foreign manufacturing and distribution operations are wholly owned, the establishment of a distribution network will typically entail relationships with other organizations, for example, exclusive distributor agreements.

Such commitments may be difficult if not impossible to change in the short run, and may constitute a major impediment to adoption of a standardized strategy. If, for example, a joint venture with a local company has been established to manufacture and market a product line in a specific country or region, resistance from the local partner (or government authorities) may be encountered if the parent company wishes to shift production or import components from another location. Similarly, a licensing contract will impede a firm from supplying the products covered by the agreement from an alternative location for the duration of the contract, even if it becomes more cost efficient to do so.

Conversely, the establishment of an effective dealer or distribution network in a country or region may constitute an important resource to a company. The addition of new products to the product line currently sold or distributed by this network may therefore provide a more efficient utilization of company resources than expanding to new countries or geographic regions with the existing line, as this would require substantial investment in the establishment of a new distribution network.

In addition, overseas subsidiaries may currently be marketing not only core products and brands from the company's domestic business, but may also have added or acquired local or regional products and brands in response to local market demand. In some cases, therefore, introduction of a global product or brand may be likely to cannibalize sales of local or regional brands.

Advocates of standardization thus need to take into consideration the evolutionary character of international involvement, which may render a universal strategy of global products and brands suboptimal. Somewhat ironically, the longer the history of a multinational corporation's involvement in foreign or international markets, and the more diversified and far-flung its operations, the more likely it is that standardization will not lead to optimal results.

Local management motivation and attitudes. Another internal constraint concerns the motivation and attitudes of local management with regard to standardization. Standardized strategies tend to facilitate or result in centralization in the planning and organization of international activities. Especially if input from local management is limited, this may result in a feeling that strategy is 'imposed' by corporate headquarters, and/or not adequately adapted or appropriate in view of specific local market characteristics and conditions. Local management is likely to take the view 'it won't work here – things are different', which will reduce their motivation to implement a standardized strategy effectively.

A framework for classifying global strategy options

The adoption of a global perspective should not be viewed as synonymous with a strategy of global products and brands. Rather, for most companies such a perspective implies consideration of a broad range of strategic options of which standardization is merely one.

In essence, a global perspective implies planning strategy relative to markets worldwide rather than on a country-by-country basis. This may result in the identification of opportunities for global products and brands or integrating and coordinating strategy across national boundaries to exploit potential synergies of operating on an international scale. Such opportunities should, however, be weighed against the benefits of adaptation to idiosyncratic customer characteristics.

The development of an effective global strategy thus requires a careful examination of all international options in terms of standardization versus adaptation open to the firm.

A firm's international operations are likely to be characterized by a mix of strategies, including not only global products and brands, but also some regional products and brands and some national products and brands. Similarly, some target segments may be global, others regional and others national. Hybrid strategies of this nature thus enable a company to take advantage of the benefits of standardization and potential synergies from operating on an international scale, while at the same time not losing those afforded by adaptation to specific country characteristics and customer preferences.

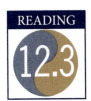

READING
12.3

Clusters and the new economics of competition

Michael E. Porter[1]

Now that companies can source capital, goods, information and technology from around the world, often with the click of a mouse, much of the conventional wisdom about how companies and nations compete needs to be overhauled. In theory, more open global markets and faster transportation and communication should diminish the role of location in competition. After all, anything that can be efficiently sourced from a

distance through global markets and corporate networks is available to any company and therefore is essentially nullified as a source of competitive advantage.

But if location matters less, why, then, is it true that the odds of finding a world-class mutual-fund company in Boston are much higher than in most any other place? Why could the same be said of textile-related companies in North Carolina and South Carolina, of high-performance auto companies in southern Germany, or of fashion shoe companies in northern Italy?

Today's economic map of the world is dominated by what I call clusters: critical masses – in one place – of unusual competitive success in particular fields. Clusters are a striking feature of virtually every national, regional, state, and even metropolitan economy, especially in more economically advanced nations. Silicon Valley and Hollywood may be the world's best-known clusters. Clusters are not unique, however; they are highly typical – and therein lies a paradox: the enduring competitive advantages in a global economy lie increasingly in local things – knowledge, relationships, motivation – that distant rivals cannot match.

Although location remains fundamental to competition, its role today differs vastly from a generation ago. In an era when competition was driven heavily by input costs, locations with some important endowment – a natural harbor, for example, or a supply of cheap labor – often enjoyed a comparative advantage that was both competitively decisive and persistent over time.

Competition in today's economy is far more dynamic. Companies can mitigate many input-cost disadvantages through global sourcing, rendering the old notion of comparative advantage less relevant. Instead, competitive advantage rests on making more productive use of inputs, which requires continual innovation.

Untangling the paradox of location in a global economy reveals a number of key insights about how companies continually create competitive advantage. What happens inside companies is important, but clusters reveal that the immediate business environment outside companies plays a vital role as well. This role of locations has been long overlooked, despite striking evidence that innovation and competitive success in so many fields are geographically concentrated – whether it's entertainment in Clusters affect competitiveness within countries as well as across national borders. Therefore, they lead to new agendas for all business executives – not just those who compete globally. More broadly, clusters represent a new way of thinking about location, challenging much of the conventional wisdom about how companies should be configured, how institutions such as universities can contribute to competitive success, and how governments can promote economic development and prosperity.

What is a cluster?

Clusters are geographic concentrations of interconnected companies and institutions in a particular field. Clusters encompass an array of linked industries and other entities important to competition. They include, for example, suppliers of specialized inputs such as components, machinery, and services, and providers of specialized infrastructure. Clusters also often extend downstream to channels and customers and laterally to manufacturers of complementary products and to companies in industries related by skills, technologies, or common inputs. Finally, many clusters include governmental and other institutions – such as universities, standards-setting agencies, think tanks, vocational training providers, and trade associations – that provide specialized training, education, information, research, and technical support.

The California wine cluster is a good example. It includes 680 commercial wineries as well as several thousand independent wine grape growers. An extensive complement of industries supporting both wine making and grape growing exists, including suppliers of grape stock, irrigation and harvesting equipment, barrels, and labels; specialized public relations and advertising firms; and numerous wine publications aimed at consumer and trade audiences. A host of local institutions is involved with wine, such as the world-renowned viticulture and enology program at the University of California at Davis, the Wine Institute, and special committees of the California senate and assembly. The cluster also enjoys weaker linkages to other California clusters in agriculture, food and restaurants, and wine-country tourism.

Consider also the Italian leather fashion cluster, which contains well-known shoe companies such as Ferragamo and Gucci as well as a host of specialized suppliers of footwear components, machinery, molds, design services, and tanned leather. It also consists of several chains of related industries, including those producing different types of leather goods (linked by common inputs and technologies) and different types of footwear (linked by overlapping channels and technologies). These industries employ common marketing media and compete with similar images in similar customer segments. A related Italian cluster in textile fashion, including clothing, scarves, and accessories, produces complementary products that often employ common channels. The extraordinary strength of the Italian leather fashion cluster can be attributed, at least in part, to the multiple linkages and synergies that participating Italian businesses enjoy.

A cluster's boundaries are defined by the linkages and complementarities across industries and institutions that are most important to competition. Although clusters often fit within political boundaries, they may cross state or even national borders. In the United

States, for example, a pharmaceuticals cluster straddles New Jersey and Pennsylvania near Philadelphia. Similarly, a chemicals cluster in Germany crosses over into German-speaking Switzerland.

Clusters rarely conform to standard industrial classification systems, which fail to capture many important actors and relationships in competition. Thus significant clusters may be obscured or even go unrecognized. In Massachusetts, for example, more than 400 companies, representing at least 39,000 high-paying jobs, are involved in medical devices in some way. The cluster long remained all but invisible, however, buried within larger and overlapping industry categories such as electronic equipment and plastic products. Executives in the medical devices cluster have only recently come together to work on issues that will benefit them all.

Clusters promote both competition and cooperation. Rivals compete intensely to win and retain customers. Without vigorous competition, a cluster will fail. Yet there is also cooperation, much of it vertical, involving companies in related industries and local institutions. Competition can coexist with cooperation because they occur on different dimensions and among different players.

Clusters represent a kind of new spatial organizational form in between arm's-length markets on the one hand and hierarchies, or vertical integration, on the other. A cluster, then, is an alternative way of organizing the value chain. Compared with market transactions among dispersed and random buyers and sellers, the proximity of companies and institutions in one location – and the repeated exchanges among them – fosters better coordination and trust. Thus clusters mitigate the problems inherent in arm's-length relationships without imposing the inflexibilities of vertical integration or the management challenges of creating and maintaining formal linkages such as networks, alliances, and partnerships. A cluster of independent and informally linked companies and institutions represents a robust organizational form that offers advantages in efficiency, effectiveness, and flexibility.

Why clusters are critical to competition

Modern competition depends on productivity, not on access to inputs or the scale of individual enterprises. Productivity rests on how companies compete, not on the particular fields they compete in. Companies can be highly productive in any industry – shoes, agriculture, or semiconductors – if they employ sophisticated methods, use advanced technology, and offer unique products and services. All industries can employ advanced technology; all industries can be knowledge intensive.

The sophistication with which companies compete in a particular location, however, is strongly influenced by the quality of the local business environment. Companies cannot employ advanced logistical techniques, for example, without a high-quality transportation infrastructure. Nor can companies effectively compete on sophisticated service without well-educated employees. Businesses cannot operate efficiently under onerous regulatory red tape or under a court system that fails to resolve disputes quickly and fairly. Some aspects of the business environment, such as the legal system, for example, or corporate tax rates, affect all industries. In advanced economies, however, the more decisive aspects of the business environment are often cluster specific; these constitute some of the most important microeconomic foundations for competition.

Clusters affect competition in three broad ways: first, by increasing the productivity of companies based in the area; second, by driving the direction and pace of innovation, which underpins future productivity growth; and third, by stimulating the formation of new businesses, which expands and strengthens the cluster itself. A cluster allows each member to benefit as if it had greater scale or as if it had joined with others formally – without requiring it to sacrifice its flexibility.

Clusters and productivity

Being part of a cluster allows companies to operate more productively in sourcing inputs; accessing information, technology, and needed institutions; coordinating with related companies; and measuring and motivating improvement.

Better access to employees and suppliers

Companies in vibrant clusters can tap into an existing pool of specialized and experienced employees, thereby lowering their search and transaction costs in recruiting. Because a cluster signals opportunity and reduces the risk of relocation for employees, it can also be easier to attract talented people from other locations, a decisive advantage in some industries.

A well-developed cluster also provides an efficient means of obtaining other important inputs. Such a cluster offers a deep and specialized supplier base. Sourcing locally instead of from distant suppliers lowers transaction costs. It minimizes the need for inventory, eliminates importing costs and delays, and – because local reputation is important – lowers the risk that suppliers will overprice or renege on commitments. Proximity improves communications and makes it easier for suppliers to provide ancillary or support services such as installation and debugging. Other things being equal, then, local outsourcing is a better solution than distant outsourcing, especially for advanced and specialized inputs involving embedded technology, information, and service content.

Formal alliances with distant suppliers can mitigate some of the disadvantages of distant outsourcing. But all formal alliances involve their own complex bargaining and governance problems and can inhibit a company's flexibility. The close, informal relationships possible among companies in a cluster are often a superior arrangement.

In many cases, clusters are also a better alternative to vertical integration. Compared with in-house units, outside specialists are often more cost effective and responsive, not only in component production but also in services such as training. Although extensive vertical integration may have once been the norm, a fast-changing environment can render vertical integration inefficient, ineffective, and inflexible.

Even when some inputs are best sourced from a distance, clusters offer advantages. Suppliers trying to penetrate a large, concentrated market will price more aggressively, knowing that as they do so they can realize efficiencies in marketing and in service.

Working against a cluster's advantages in assembling resources is the possibility that competition will render them more expensive and scarce. But companies do have the alternative of outsourcing many inputs from other locations, which tends to limit potential cost penalties. More important, clusters increase not only the demand for specialized inputs but also their supply.

Access to specialized information

Extensive market, technical, and competitive information accumulates within a cluster, and members have preferred access to it. In addition, personal relationships and community ties foster trust and facilitate the flow of information. These conditions make information more transferable.

Complementarities

A host of linkages among cluster members results in a whole greater than the sum of its parts. In a typical tourism cluster, for example, the quality of a visitor's experience depends not only on the appeal of the primary attraction but also on the quality and efficiency of complementary businesses such as hotels, restaurants, shopping outlets, and transportation facilities. Because members of the cluster are mutually dependent, good performance by one can boost the success of the others.

Complementarities come in many forms. The most obvious is when products complement one another in meeting customers' needs, as the tourism example illustrates. Another form is the coordination of activities across companies to optimize their collective productivity. In wood products, for instance, the efficiency of sawmills depends on a reliable supply of high-quality timber and the ability to put all the timber to use – in furniture (highest quality), pallets and boxes (lower quality), or wood chips (lowest quality). In the early 1990s, Portuguese sawmills suffered from poor timber quality because local landowners did not invest in timber management. Hence most timber was processed for use in pallets and boxes, a lower-value use that limited the price paid to landowners. Substantial improvement in productivity was possible, but only if several parts of the cluster changed simultaneously. Logging operations, for example, had to modify cutting and sorting procedures, while sawmills had to develop the capacity to process wood in more sophisticated ways. Coordination to develop standard wood classifications and measures was an important enabling step. Geographically dispersed companies are less likely to recognize and capture such linkages.

Other complementarities arise in marketing. A cluster frequently enhances the reputation of a location in a particular field, making it more likely that buyers will turn to a vendor based there. Italy's strong reputation for fashion and design, for example, benefits companies involved in leather goods, footwear, apparel, and accessories. Beyond reputation, cluster members often profit from a variety of joint marketing mechanisms, such as company referrals, trade fairs, trade magazines, and marketing delegations.

Finally, complementarities can make buying from a cluster more attractive for customers. Visiting buyers can see many vendors in a single trip. They also may perceive their buying risk to be lower because one location provides alternative suppliers. That allows them to multisource or to switch vendors if the need arises. Hong Kong thrives as a source of fashion apparel in part for this reason.

Access to institutions and public goods

Investments made by government or other public institutions such as public spending for specialized infrastructure or educational programs can enhance a company's productivity. The ability to recruit employees trained at local programs, for example, lowers the cost of internal training. Other quasi-public goods, such as the cluster's information and technology pools and its reputation, arise as natural by-products of competition.

It is not just governments that create public goods that enhance productivity in the private sector. Investments by companies – in training programs, infrastructure, quality centers, testing laboratories, and so on – also contribute to increased productivity. Such private investments are often made collectively because cluster participants recognize the potential for collective benefits.

Better motivation and measurement

Local rivalry is highly motivating. Peer pressure amplifies competitive pressure within a cluster, even among noncompeting or indirectly competing companies. Pride and the desire to look good in the local community spur executives to attempt to outdo one another.

Clusters also often make it easier to measure and compare performances because local rivals share general circumstances – for example, labor costs and local market access – and they perform similar activities. Companies within clusters typically have intimate knowledge of their suppliers' costs. Managers are able to compare costs and employees' performance with other local companies. Additionally, financial institutions can accumulate knowledge about the cluster that can be used to monitor performance.

Clusters and innovation

In addition to enhancing productivity, clusters play a vital role in a company's ongoing ability to innovate. Some of the same characteristics that enhance current productivity have an even more dramatic effect on innovation and productivity growth.

Because sophisticated buyers are often part of a cluster, companies inside clusters usually have a better window on the market than isolated competitors do. Computer companies based in Silicon Valley and Austin, Texas, for example, plug into customer needs and trends with a speed difficult to match by companies located elsewhere. The ongoing relationships with other entities within the cluster also help companies to learn early about evolving technology, component and machinery availability, service and marketing concepts, and so on. Such learning is facilitated by the ease of making site visits and frequent face-to-face contact.

Clusters do more than make opportunities for innovation more visible. They also provide the capacity and the flexibility to act rapidly. A company within a cluster often can source what it needs to implement innovations more quickly. Local suppliers and partners can and do get closely involved in the innovation process, thus ensuring a better match with customers' requirements.

Companies within a cluster can experiment at lower cost and can delay large commitments until they are more assured that a given innovation will pan out. In contrast, a company relying on distant suppliers faces greater challenges in every activity it coordinates with other organizations – in contracting, for example, or securing delivery or obtaining associated technical and service support. Innovation can be even harder in vertically integrated companies, especially in those that face difficult trade-offs if the innovation erodes the value of in-house assets or if current products or processes must be maintained while new ones are developed.

Reinforcing the other advantages for innovation is the sheer pressure – competitive pressure, peer pressure, constant comparison – that occurs in a cluster. Executives vie with one another to set their companies apart. For all these reasons, clusters can remain centers of innovation for decades.

Clusters and new business formation

It is not surprising, then, that many new companies grow up within an existing cluster rather than at isolated locations. New suppliers, for example, proliferate within a cluster because a concentrated customer base lowers their risks and makes it easier for them to spot market opportunities. Moreover, because developed clusters comprise related industries that normally draw on common or very similar inputs, suppliers enjoy expanded opportunities.

Clusters are conducive to new business formation for a variety of reasons. Individuals working within a cluster can more easily perceive gaps in products or services around which they can build businesses. Beyond that, barriers to entry are lower than elsewhere. Needed assets, skills, inputs, and staff are often readily available at the cluster location, waiting to be assembled into a new enterprise. Local financial institutions and investors, already familiar with the cluster, may require a lower risk premium on capital. In addition, the cluster often presents a significant local market, and an entrepreneur may benefit from established relationships. All of these factors reduce the perceived risks of entry – and of exit, should the enterprise fail.

The formation of new businesses within a cluster is part of a positive feedback loop. An expanded cluster amplifies all the benefits I have described – it increases the collective pool of competitive resources, which benefits all the cluster's members. The net result is that companies in the cluster advance relative to rivals at other locations.

Birth, evolution, and decline

A cluster's roots can often be traced to historical circumstances. In Massachusetts, for example, several clusters had their beginnings in research done at MIT or Harvard. The Dutch transportation cluster owes much to Holland's central location within Europe, an extensive network of waterways, the efficiency of the port of Rotterdam, and the skills accumulated by the Dutch through Holland's long maritime history.

Clusters may also arise from unusual, sophisticated, or stringent local demand. Israel's cluster in irrigation equipment and other advanced agricultural technologies reflects that nation's strong desire for self-sufficiency in food together with a scarcity of water and hot, arid growing conditions. The environmental cluster in Finland emerged as a result of pollution problems created by local process industries such as metals, forestry, chemicals, and energy.

Prior existence of supplier industries, related industries, or even entire related clusters provides yet another seed for new clusters. The golf equipment cluster near San Diego, for example, has its roots in southern California's aerospace cluster. That cluster created a pool of suppliers for castings and advanced materials as well as engineers with the requisite experience in those technologies.

New clusters may also arise from one or two innovative companies that stimulate the growth of many others. Medtronic played this role in helping to create the Minneapolis medical-device cluster. Similarly, MCI and America Online have been hubs for growing new businesses in the telecommunications cluster in the Washington, DC, metropolitan area.

Sometimes a chance event creates some advantageous factor that, in turn, fosters cluster development although chance rarely provides the sole explanation for a cluster's success in a location. The telemarketing cluster in Omaha, Nebraska, for example, owes much to the decision by the United States Air Force to locate the Strategic Air Command (SAC) there. Charged with a key role in the country's nuclear deterrence strategy,

SAC was the site of the first installation of fiber-optic telecommunications cables in the United States. The local Bell operating company (now US West) developed unusual capabilities through its dealings with such a demanding customer. The extraordinary telecommunications capability and infrastructure that consequently developed in Omaha, coupled with less unique attributes such as its central-time-zone location and easily understandable local accent, provided the underpinnings of the area's telemarketing cluster.

Once a cluster begins to form, a self-reinforcing cycle promotes its growth, especially when local institutions are supportive and local competition is vigorous. As the cluster expands, so does its influence with government and with public and private institutions.

A growing cluster signals opportunity, and its success stories help attract the best talent. Entrepreneurs take notice, and individuals with ideas or relevant skills migrate in from other locations. Specialized suppliers emerge; information accumulates; local institutions develop specialized training, research, and infrastructure; and the cluster's strength and visibility grow. Eventually, the cluster broadens to encompass related industries. Numerous case studies suggest that clusters require a decade or more to develop depth and real competitive advantage.

Cluster development is often particularly vibrant at the intersection of clusters, where insights, skills, and technologies from various fields merge, sparking innovation and new businesses. An example from Germany illustrates this point. The country has distinct clusters in both home appliances and household furniture, each based on different technologies and inputs. At the intersection of the two, though, is a cluster of built-in kitchens and appliances, an area in which Germany commands a higher share of world exports than in either appliances or furniture.

Clusters continually evolve as new companies and industries emerge or decline and as local institutions develop and change. They can maintain vibrancy as competitive locations for centuries; most successful clusters prosper for decades at least. However, they can and do lose their competitive edge due to both external and internal forces. Technological discontinuities are perhaps the most significant of the external threats because they can neutralize many advantages simultaneously. A cluster's assets – market information, employees' skills, scientific and technical expertise, and supplier bases – may all become irrelevant. New England's loss of market share in golf equipment is a good example. The New England cluster was based on steel shafts, steel irons, and wooden-headed woods.

When companies in California began making golf clubs with advanced materials, East Coast producers had difficulty competing. A number of them were acquired or went out of business.

A shift in buyers' needs, creating a divergence between local needs and needs elsewhere, constitutes another external threat. US companies in a variety of clusters, for example, suffered when energy efficiency grew in importance in most parts of the world while the United States maintained low energy prices. Lacking both pressure to improve and insight into customer needs, US companies were slow to innovate, and they lost ground to European and Japanese competitors.

Clusters are at least as vulnerable to internal rigidities as they are to external threats. Overconsolidation, mutual understandings, cartels, and other restraints to competition undermine local rivalry. Regulatory inflexibility or the introduction of restrictive union rules slows productivity improvement. The quality of institutions such as schools and universities can stagnate.

Groupthink among cluster participants – Detroit's attachment to gas-guzzling autos in the 1970s is one example – can be another powerful form of rigidity. If companies in a cluster are too inward looking, the whole cluster suffers from a collective inertia, making it harder for individual companies to embrace new ideas, much less perceive the need for radical innovation.

Such rigidities tend to arise when government suspends or intervenes in competition or when companies persist in old behaviors and relationships that no longer contribute to competitive advantage. Increases in the cost of doing business begin to outrun the ability to upgrade. Rigidities of this nature currently work against a variety of clusters in Switzerland and Germany.

As long as rivalry remains sufficiently vigorous, companies can partially compensate for some decline in the cluster's competitiveness by outsourcing to distant suppliers or moving part or all of production elsewhere to offset local wages that rise ahead of productivity. German companies in the 1990s, for example, have been doing just that. Technology can be licensed or sourced from other locations, and product development can be moved. Over time, however, a location will decline if it fails to build capabilities in major new technologies or needed supporting firms and institutions.

Implications for companies

In the new economics of competition, what matters most is not inputs and scale, but productivity – and that is true in all industries. The term high tech, normally used to refer to fields such as information technology and biotechnology, has distorted thinking about competition, creating the misconception that only a handful of businesses compete in sophisticated ways.

In fact, there is no such thing as a low-tech industry. There are only low-tech companies – that is, companies that fail to use world-class technology and practices to enhance productivity and innovation. A vibrant cluster can help any company in any industry compete in the most sophisticated ways, using the most advanced, relevant skills and technologies.

Thus executives must extend their thinking beyond what goes on inside their own organizations and within their own industries. Strategy must also address what goes on outside. Extensive vertical integration may once have been appropriate, but companies today must forge close linkages with buyers, suppliers, and other institutions.

Specifically, understanding clusters adds the following four issues to the strategic agenda.

1. Choosing locations. Globalization and the ease of transportation and communication have led many companies to move some or all of their operations to locations with low wages, taxes, and utility costs. What we know about clusters suggests, first, that some of those cost advantages may well turn out to be illusory. Locations with those advantages often lack efficient infrastructure, sophisticated suppliers, and other cluster benefits that can more than offset any savings from lower input costs. Savings in wages, utilities, and taxes may be highly visible and easy to measure up front, but productivity penalties remain hidden and unanticipated.

More important to ongoing competitiveness is the role of location in innovation. Yes, companies have to spread activities globally to source inputs and gain access to markets. Failure to do so will lead to a competitive disadvantage. And for stable, labor-intensive activities such as assembly and software translation, low factor costs are often decisive in driving locational choices.

For a company's "home base" for each product line, however, clusters are critical. Home base activities – strategy development, core product and process R&D, a critical mass of the most sophisticated production or service provision – create and renew the company's product, processes, and services. Therefore locational decisions must be based on both total systems costs and innovation potential, not on input costs alone. Cluster thinking suggests that every product line needs a home base, and the most vibrant cluster will offer the best location. Within the United States, for example,

Hewlett-Packard has chosen cluster locations for the home bases of its major product lines: California, where almost all of the world's leading personal computer and workstation businesses are located, is home to personal computers and workstations; Massachusetts, which has an extraordinary concentration of world-renowned research hospitals and leading medical instrument companies, is home to medical instruments.

As global competition nullifies traditional comparative advantages and exposes companies to the best rivals from around the world, a growing number of multinationals are shifting their home bases to more vibrant clusters – often using acquisitions as a means of establishing themselves as insiders in a new location. Nestlé, for example, after acquiring Rowntree Mackintosh, relocated its confectionary business to York, England, where Rowntree was originally based, because a vibrant food cluster thrives there. England, with its sweet-toothed consumers, sophisticated retailers, advanced advertising agencies, and highly competitive media companies, constitutes a more dynamic environment for competing in mass-market candy than Switzerland did. Similarly, Nestlé has moved its headquarters for bottled water to France, the most competitive location in that industry. Northern Telecom has relocated its home base for central office switching from Canada to the United States – drawn by the vibrancy of the US telecommunications-equipment cluster.

Cluster thinking also suggests that it is better to move groups of linked activities to the same place than to spread them across numerous locations. Colocating R&D, component fabrication, assembly, marketing, customer support, and even related businesses can facilitate internal efficiencies in sourcing and in sharing technology and information. Grouping activities into campuses also allows companies to extend deeper roots into local clusters, improving their ability to capture potential benefits.

2. Engaging locally.

The social glue that binds clusters together also facilitates access to important resources and information. Tapping into the competitively valuable assets within a cluster requires personal relationships, face-to-face contact, a sense of common interest, and "insider" status. The mere colocation of companies, suppliers, and institutions creates the potential for economic value; it does not necessarily ensure its realization.

To maximize the benefits of cluster involvement, companies must participate actively and establish a significant local presence. They must have a substantial local investment even if the parent company is headquartered elsewhere. And they must foster ongoing relationships with government bodies and local institutions such as utilities, schools, and research groups.

Companies have much to gain by engaging beyond their narrow confines as single entities. Yet managers tend to be wary, at least initially. They fear that a growing cluster will attract competition, drive up costs, or cause them to lose valued employees to rivals or spin-offs. As their understanding of the cluster concept grows, however, managers realize that many participants in the cluster do not compete directly and that the offsetting benefits, such as a greater supply of better trained people, for example, can outweigh any increase in competition.

3. Upgrading the cluster.

Because the health of the local business environment is important to the health of the company, upgrading the cluster should be part of management's agenda. Companies upgrade their clusters in a variety of ways.

Consider Genzyme. Massachusetts is home to a vibrant biotechnology cluster, which draws on the region's strong universities, medical centers, and venture capital firms. Once Genzyme reached the stage in its development when it needed a manufacturing facility, CEO Henri Termeer initially considered the pharmaceuticals cluster in the New Jersey and Philadelphia area because it had what Massachusetts lacked: established expertise in drug manufacturing. Upon further reflection, however, Termeer decided to influence the process of creating a manufacturing capability in Genzyme's home base, reasoning that if his plans were successful, the company could become more competitive.

Thus Genzyme deliberately chose to work with contractors committed to the Boston area, bypassing the many specialized engineering firms located near Philadelphia. In addition, it undertook a number of initiatives, with the help of city and state government, to improve the labor force, such as offering scholarships and internships to local youth. More broadly, Genzyme has worked to build critical mass for its cluster. Termeer believes that Genzyme's success is linked to the cluster's – and that all members will benefit from a strong base of supporting functions and institutions.

4. Working collectively.

The way clusters operate suggests a new agenda of collective action in the private sector. Investing in public goods is normally seen as a function of government, yet cluster thinking clearly demonstrates how companies benefit from local assets and institutions.

In the past, collective action in the private sector has focused on seeking government subsidies and special favors that often distort competition. But executives' long-term interests would be better served by working to promote a higher plane of competition. They can begin by rethinking the role of trade associations, which often do little more than lobby government, compile some statistics, and host social functions. The associations are missing an important opportunity.

Trade associations can provide a forum for the exchange of ideas and a focal point for collective action in overcoming obstacles to productivity and growth. Associations can take the lead in such activities as establishing university-based testing facilities and training or research programs; collecting cluster-related information; offering forums on common managerial problems; investigating solutions to environmental issues; organizing trade fairs and delegations; and managing purchasing consortia.

For clusters consisting of many small and mid-size companies – such as tourism, apparel, and agriculture – the need is particularly great for collective bodies to assume scale-sensitive functions. In the Netherlands, for instance, grower cooperatives built the specialized auction and handling facilities that constitute one of the Dutch flower cluster's greatest competitive advantages. The Dutch Flower Council and the Association of Dutch Flower Growers Research Groups, in which most growers participate, have taken on other functions as well, such as applied research and marketing.

Most existing trade associations are too narrow; they represent industries, not clusters. In addition, because their role is defined as lobbying the federal government, their scope is national rather than local. National associations, however, are rarely sufficient to address the local issues that are most important to cluster productivity.

By revealing how business and government together create the conditions that promote growth, clusters offer a constructive way to change the nature of the dialogue between the public and private sectors. With a better understanding of what fosters true competitiveness, executives can start asking government for the right

things. The example of MassMEDIC, an association formed in 1996 by the Massachusetts medical-devices cluster, illustrates this point. It recently worked successfully with the US Food and Drug Administration to streamline the approval process for medical devices. Such a step clearly benefits cluster members and enhances competition at the same time.

New public–private responsibilities

Economic geography in an era of global competition, then, poses a paradox. In a global economy – which boasts rapid transportation, high-speed communication, and accessible markets – one would expect location to diminish in importance. But the opposite is true. The enduring competitive advantages in a global economy are often heavily local, arising from concentrations of highly specialized skills and knowledge, institutions, rivals, related businesses, and sophisticated customers. Geographic, cultural, and institutional proximity leads to special access, closer relationships, better information, powerful incentives, and other advantages in productivity and innovation that are difficult to tap from a distance. The more the world economy becomes complex, knowledge based, and dynamic, the more this is true.

Leaders of businesses, government, and institutions all have a stake and a role to play in the new economics of competition. Clusters reveal the mutual dependence and collective responsibility of all these entities for creating the conditions for productive competition. This task will require fresh thinking on the part of leaders and the willingness to abandon the traditional categories that drive our thinking about who does what in the economy. The lines between public and private investment blur. Companies, no less than governments and universities, have a stake in education. Universities have a stake in the competitiveness of local businesses. By revealing the process by which wealth is actually created in an economy, clusters open new public–private avenues for constructive action.

REFERENCES

Bain, J.S. (1956) *Barriers to New Competition: Their Character and Consequences in Manufacturing*, Harvard University Press.

Bartlett, C.A. and Ghoshal, S. (1988) 'Organizing for worldwide effectiveness: the transnational solution', *California Management Review*, 31, pp. 54–74.

Bartlett, C.A. and Ghoshal, S. (1987) 'Managing across borders: new organizational responses', *Sloan Management Review*, 29(1, Fall), pp. 43–53.

Bartlett, C.A. and Ghoshal, S. (1989) *Managing Across Borders: The Transnational Solution*, New York: Harvard Business School Press.

Bartlett, C.A. and Ghoshal, S. (1995) *Transnational Management: Text, Cases and Readings in Cross-Border Management* (2nd edn), New York: R.D. Irwin Inc.

Beech, N., Burns, H., de Caestecker, L., Mackintosh, R. and MacLean, D. (2004) 'Paradox as invitation to act in problematic change situations', *Human Relations*, 57, pp. 1313–1332.

Birkinshaw, J. and Hood, N. (1998) *Multinational Corporate Evolution and Subsidiary Development*, London: Macmillan.

Boorstin, D.J. (1973) *The Americans: The Democratic Experience*, New Jersey: Random House.

Buckley, P.J. and Casson, M.C. (1976) *The Future of the Multinational Enterprise*, London: Macmillan.

Buckley, P.J. and Casson, M.C. (1985) *The Economic Theory of the Multinational Enterprise*, London: Macmillan.

Castells, M. (1996) *The Rise of the Network Society*, Oxford: Blackwell Publishers.

Caves, R.E. (1971) 'International corporations: the industrial economics of foreign investment', *Economica*, 38(149), pp. 1–27.

Chesnais, F. (1984) 'Marx's Crisis Theory Today', in: C. Freeman (ed.) *Design, Innovation and Long Cycles in Economic Development*, London: Frances Pinter.

Dicken, P. (1986) *Global Shift: Industrial Change in a Turbulent World*, London: Harper & Row.

Dicken, P. (1992) *Global Shift: The Internationalisation of Economic Activity*, London: Chapman.

Dicken, P. (2003) *Global Shift: Reshaping the Global Economic Map in the 21st Century*, London: Sage.

Dicken, P. (2011) *Mapping the Changing Contours of the World Economy* (2nd edn), New York: Guilford Press.

Dicken, P. (2015) *Global Shift: Mapping the Changing Contours of the World Economy* (7th edn), New York: Guilford Press.

Dosi, G. and Kogut, B. (1993) 'National Specificities and the Context of Change: The Co-evolution of Organization and Technology', in: B. Kogut (ed.) *Country Competitiveness: Technology and the Organizing of Work*, Oxford: Oxford University Press.

Douglas, S.P. and Wind, Y. (1987) 'The Myth of Globalization', *Columbia Journal of World Business*, 22(Winter), pp. 19–29.

Doz, Y. and Prahalad, C.K. (1984) 'Patterns of strategic control within multinational corporations', *Journal of International Business Studies*, 15(2), pp. 55–72.

Dunning, J. (1986) *Japanese Participation in British Industry: Trojan Horse or Catalyst for Growth?* Dover, NH: Croom Helm.

Dunning, J. (1993) *The Globalization of Business*, London: Routledge.

Dunning, J.H. (1980) 'Toward an eclectic theory of international production: some empirical tests', *Journal of International Business Studies*, 11(1), pp. 9–31.

Dunning, J.H. (1981), *International Production and the Multinational Enterprise*, London: Allen and Unwin.

Dunning, J.H. (1988) *Explaining international production*, London: Unwin Hyman.

Dunning, J.H. (1998) 'Location and the multinational enterprise: a neglected factor?', *Journal of International Business Studies*, 29(1), pp. 45–66.

Dunning, J.H. (2000) 'The eclectic paradigm as an envelope for economic and business theories of MNE activity', *International Business Review*, 9(2), pp.163–190.

Dunning, J.H. (2001) 'The Key Literature on IB activities: 1960–2000', in: A.M. Rugman and Th. L. Brewer, *The Oxford Handbook of International Business*, Oxford: Oxford University Press, pp. 36–68.

Fayerweather, J. (1969) 'International Business Management', *The International Executive*, 11(1), pp. 10–11.

Financial Times Global 500 (2006), *Financial Times* (June 9).

Financial Times Global 500 (2015), *Financial Times* (June 19).

Friedman, T.L. (2005) *The World is Flat: A Brief History of the Twenty-first Century*, New York: Farrar, Straus and Giroux.

Fröbel, F., Heinrichs, J. and Kreye, O. (1980) *The Tendency Towards a New International Division of Labor: The Utilization of a World-Wide Labor Force for Manufacturing Oriented to the World Market*, Cambridge: Cambridge University Press.

Fukuyama, F. (1992) *The End of History and the Last Man*, New York: Free Press.

Ghemawat, P. (2005) 'Regional Strategies for Global Leadership', *Harvard Business Review*, 83(12), p. 98.

Ghemawat, P. (2007) *Redefining Global Strategy*, Boston, MA: Harvard Business School Press.

Gramsci, A. (1934) 'Americanism and Fordism', in: A. Gramsci *The Prison Notebooks*, Columbia University Press.

Guillén, M. (2001) *The Limits of Convergence: Globalization and Organizational Change in Argentina, South Korea and Spain*, Princeton, NJ: Princeton University Press.

Hamel, G. and Prahalad, C.K. (1985) 'Do You Really Have a Global Strategy?', *Harvard Business Review*, 63(4, July–August), pp. 139–148.

Hedlund, G. (1986) 'The Hypermodern MNC – A Heterarchy?' *Human Resource Management*, 25, pp. 9–35.

Hennart, J-F. (1977) *A Theory of Foreign Direct Investment*, PhD dissertation, University of Maryland.

Hennart, J.-F. (2014) 'The Accidental Internationalists: A Theory of Born Globals', *Entrepreneurship Theory and Practice*, 38(1), pp. 117–135.

Hofstede, G. (1980) *Culture's Consequences: International Differences in Work-Related Values*, Newbury Park, CA: Sage.

Hout, T.M., Porter, M.E. and Rudden, E. (1982) 'How Global Companies Win Out', *Harvard Business Review*, 60(5, September–October), pp. 98–108.

Hymer, S (1960) *The International Operations of National Firms: A Study of Direct Investment*, PhD dissertation, Cambridge, MA: MIT Press.

Johanson, J. and Vahlne, J.-E. (1977) 'The internationalization process of the firm: A model of knowledge development and increasing foreign market commitments', *Journal of International Business Studies*, 8, pp. 23–32.

Kay, J. (1989) 'Myths and Realities', in: Davis, E. (ed.) *1992: Myths and Realities*, London: Centre for Business Strategy.

Kindleberger, C.P. (1973) *The World in Depression: 1929–1939*, London: Allen Lane.

Klein, N. (2000) *No Logo, Taking Aim at the Brand Bullies*, London: Flamingo.

Knight, G.A. and Liesch, P.W. (2016) 'Internationalization: From incremental to born global', *Journal of World Business*, 51(1), pp. 93–102.

Kogut, B. (ed.) (1993) *Country Competitiveness: Technology and the Organizing of Work*, Oxford: Oxford University Press.

Kogut, B. and Zander, U. (1993) 'Knowledge of the firm and the Evolutionary Theory of the Mul', *Journal of International Business Studies*, 24(4), pp. 625–645.

Krugman, P. (1990) *Rethinking International Trade*, Cambridge, MA: MIT Press.

Krugman, P. (1980) 'Scale Economies, Product Differentiation, and the Pattern of Trade', *The American Economic Review*, 70(5), pp. 950–959.

Levitt, T. (1983) 'The Globalization of Markets', *Harvard Business Review*, 61(3, May–June), pp. 92–102.

Liebeskind, J. (1996) 'Knowledge, Strategy and the Theory of the Firm', *Strategic Management Journal*, 17(Winter, Special Issue), pp. 93–107.

Markowitz, H.M. (1959) *Portfolio Selection: Efficient Diversification of Investments*, New York: John Wiley & Sons.

Mathews, J.A. and Zander, I. (2007) 'The International Entrepreneurial Dynamics of Accelerated Internationalisation', *Journal of International Business Studies*, 38, pp. 1–17.

McGrew, A.G. and Lewis, P.G. (eds) (1992) *Global Politics: Globalisation and the Nation-State*, Cambridge: Polity Press.

Meyer, K.E., Mudambi, R. and Narula, R. (2011) 'Multinational enterprises and local contexts: the opportunities and challenges of multiple embeddedness', *Journal of Management Studies*, 48(2), pp. 235–252.

Mudambi, R. and Navarra, P. (2004) 'Is knowledge power? Knowledge flows, subsidiary power and rentseeking within MNCs', *Journal of International Business Studies*, 35(5), pp. 385–406.

Ohmae, K. (1989) 'Managing in a Borderless World', *Harvard Business Review*, 67(3, May–June), pp. 152–161.

Ohmae, K. (1990) *The Borderless World: Power and Strategy in the Interlinked Economy*, London: Fontana.

Ohmae, K. (1985) *The Triad of Economic Power*, New York, Free Press.

Patel, P. and Pavitt, K. (1991) 'Large Firms in the Production of the World's Technology: An Important case of "Non-Globalisation"', *Journal of International Business Studies*, 22(1), pp. 1–21.

Penrose, E. (1959) *The Theory of the Growth of the Firm*, New York: John Wiley and Sons.

Porter, M.E. (1986) *Competition in Global Industries*, New York: Free Press.

Porter, M.E. (1990a) *The Competitive Advantage of Nations*, London: Macmillan.

Porter, M.E. (1990b) 'New Global Strategies for Competitive Advantage', *Planning Review*, 18(3, May–June), pp. 4–14.

Porter, M.E. (1998) 'Clusters and the New Economics of Competition', *Harvard Business Review*, November–December.

Prahalad, C.K. and Doz, Y. (1987) *The Multinational Mission: Balancing Local Demands and Global Vision*, New York: Free Press.

Prahalad, C.K. (2004) *The Fortune at the Bottom of the Pyramid*, Philadelphia, PA: Wharton School Publishing.

Rugman, A.M. and Verbeke, A. (2001) 'Location, Competitiveness and the Multinational Enterprise', in: A.M. Rugman and Th. L. Brewer, *The Oxford Handbook of International Business*, Oxford: Oxford University Press, pp. 150–177.

Rugman, A.M. (2005) *The Regional Multinational: MNEs and 'Global' Strategic Management*, Cambridge: Cambridge University Press.

Ruigrok, W. and Van Tulder, R. (1995) *The Logic of International Restructuring*, London: Routledge.

Servan-Schreiber, J.J. (1967) *Le Defi Americain*, Paris: Denoel.

Stopford, J.M. and Wells, L.T. (1972) *Strategy and Structure of Multinational Enterprise*, New York: Basic Books.

Taylor, F.W. (1911) *Principles of Scientific Management*, New York, London: Harper & Brothers.

UNCTAD (2010) *World Investment Report*.

Van Tulder, R. and Junne, G. (1988) *European Multinationals in Core Technologies*, London: Wiley & Sons.

Vernon, R. (1966) 'International Investment and International Trade in the Product Life Cycle', *Quarterly Journal of Economics*, 80(2, May), pp. 190–207.

Vernon, R. (1977) *Storm Over The Multinationals: The Real Issues*, Cambridge, MA: Harvard University Press.

Wilkins, M. (2003) 'The History of the International Enterprise', in: A.L. Rugman, and Th. L. Brewer, *The Oxford Handbook of International Business*, Oxford: Oxford University Press.

Williamson, O.E. (1975) *Markets and Hierarchies*, New York: Free Press.

Womack, J.P., Jones, D.T. and Roos, D. (1990) *The Machine That Changed The World*, New York: Harper Perennial.

Yip, G.S. (1993) *Total Global Strategy: Managing for Worldwide Competitive Advantage*, London: Prentice Hall.

CASES

Zara: The world's largest fashion retailer

By Kasra Ferdows, Jose A.D. Machuca and Michael A. Lewis

In 2014 Zara, and its parent company Inditex, were still the subject of intense curiosity. By all measures it was a phenomenal success story. Inditex' sales, with Zara still accounting for almost two-thirds, had grown from €3.25 billion in 2001 to €18.1 billion in 2014, making it the largest apparel company (by sales) in the world. Its profits had grown at an even faster rate: from €340 million in 2001 to €2.5 billion in 2014. The number of stores during this period increased from 1284 in 39 countries to 6683 in 88 countries. This translated into an average rate of more than one new Inditex store opening every working day during these 14 years, many of them in upscale locations such as Fifth Avenue in Manhattan, Champs-Elysees in Paris, Ginza in Tokyo, and West Nanjing Road in Shanghai or Pitt Street in Sidney.

How did a company with humble beginnings in La Coruña, a small city in the far north-west of Spain, become the world's largest apparel company, employing 128,000 people? How could its founder, Mr. Amancio Ortega, who had started his first business in the early 1960s with 15000 pesetas (€90), have become the richest man in Europe and third richest man in 2014 in the world according to the *Forbes* magazine? How could it continue its remarkable growth unabated, even during the post 2008 economic crisis?

Had Inditex discovered something that its powerful and indisputably competent peers, celebrated firms like Gap, H&M and Benetton, had missed? "There are really no secrets," explained Mr. Pablo Isla, CEO of Inditex. "Our strategy is clear: Find out what our customers want and design, produce and distribute it quickly." Mr. Jesús Echevarría,

Chief Communications & Corporate Affairs Officer, added, "The core of our business is not really *fast* fashion – it is *accurate* fashion." But what was not so clear was how this company managed to execute this strategy so well – remarkably better than its peers. What was the management system that supported this strategy?

According to Mr. Isla, even the management system was simple: "We empower our people at all levels to make thousands of decisions every day. They usually make good decisions, but even if they make a mistake, it is often not a serious problem and they can correct them quickly themselves. We are far from perfect. Whatever we analyze, we see lots of room for improvement. Continuous improvement is in the heart of the company." Mr. Miguel Díaz, Zara Finance Director, added, "We know that this business is an art, we try on a daily basis to add science to that art, but it is still an art." Mr. Echevarría also observed: "Many things here are decided *naturally*. There are not many formal processes for how to do things. The culture is not hierarchical – it is essentially entrepreneurial." Mr. Díaz stressed: "We give lots of responsibility to young people. You don't have to be a star to work here but you must be competent and have an entrepreneurial spirit."

However, many questions still remained. How could such a large company continue to react to fast moving global markets so accurately and rapidly? How could it design, produce, distribute, and sell its new products so quickly – in as little as two weeks if needed – when many firms in the industry still required several months? Could it continue to grow at such phenomenal pace?

Professors Kasra Ferdows (McDonough School of Business, Georgetown University), Jose A.D. Machuca (Department of Finance and Operations Management, University of Seville) and Michael A. Lewis (University of Bath School of Management) wrote this case for class discussion. It is partly based on the case "Zara" ECCH 603-002-01 they wrote in 2002. Continued cooperation of Inditex is gratefully acknowledged (particularly Mr. Pablo Isla (CEO), Jesús Echevarría (Chief Communications & Corporate Affairs Officer, Inditex), José M. Álvarez Gallego (Director of Corporate Development, Inditex), Miguel Díaz (Director of Finance, Zara), and Lorena Alba (General Director of Logistics, Inditex) for this case). Shahryar Kabir (Research Assistant at Georgetown University) and Dr. Pedro Garrido (Universidad de Sevilla) also helped in this research. Certain facts and figures have been disguised.

Note: This case is an updated and extended version of the prize-winning ZARA case (# 603-002-1, The Case Centre, 2003) by the same authors. It was ranked 15th in the top 40 best selling Case Centre cases (1973–2013).

Inditex

Amancio Ortega Gaona began working as a delivery boy for a shirt-maker when he was only 13 years old. He later managed a tailor shop where he made night-shirts and pajamas. In 1963, when still in his 20s, he started Confecciones GOA in La Coruña, to manufacture women's pajamas (and later lingerie products), initially for sale directly to garment wholesalers. In 1975, when a German customer cancelled a sizable order, the firm opened its first Zara retail shop in La Coruña. The original intent was simply to have an outlet for cancelled orders, but this experience taught Amancio Ortega the importance of the 'marriage' between manufacturing and retailing – a lesson that guided the evolution of the company from then on. As it was reiterated in 2001 by Mr. Miguel Díaz, a senior marketing executive at that time, "it is critical for us to have five fingers touching the factory and the other five touching the customer."

Starting with six stores in 1979, the company established retail operations in all the major Spanish cities during the 1980s. In 1988 Zara opened its first store abroad, in Porto, Portugal, followed shortly by New York City in 1989 and Paris in 1990. But the real 'step-up' in foreign expansion took place during the 1990s when Inditex entered 29 countries in Europe, the Americas and Asia (particularly during 1998

to 2001 when it entered 21 of these 29 countries). The pace of foreign expansion accelerated during the 2000s and early 2010s, particularly in Asia. (See Exhibit 1 for number of stores by brand and Exhibit 2 for geographic sales breakdown).

In parallel with its overseas expansion, Inditex had diversified its retail offering by adding and acquiring new brands in order to target different customer segments. The company introduced Pull & Bear in 1991 to offer low price men's casual wear with a "sporty" image. The same year saw the addition of the group's most upmarket concept, Massimo Dutti, offering more expensive (although still good value) stylish men's clothing. Inditex initially acquired 65 per cent of Massimo Dutti (which started trading in 1985) eventually taking full ownership by mid 1990s. In 1995, it added woman's wear to both brands. In 1998, the company opened Bershka, targeting very low price but 'cutting-edge' fashion at 14–24 year old young women. In 1999, Inditex acquired Stradivarius, strengthening its market presence in the young woman sector, and two years later, in the summer of 2001, it launched a new brand, Oysho, specializing in underwear, sportswear, accessories and cosmetics. In 2008 it introduced Zara Home, specializing in home decorations, and the latest addition, Uterque, selling fashion accessories, costume jewelry and a selection of fabric and leather garments, was launched in 2011.

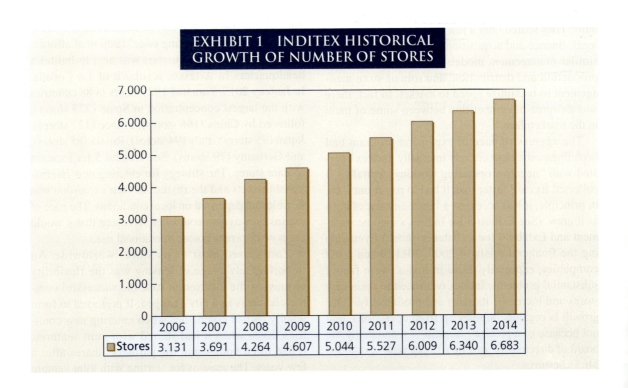

EXHIBIT 1 INDITEX HISTORICAL GROWTH OF NUMBER OF STORES

	2006	2007	2008	2009	2010	2011	2012	2013	2014
Stores	3.131	3.691	4.264	4.607	5.044	5.527	6.009	6.340	6.683

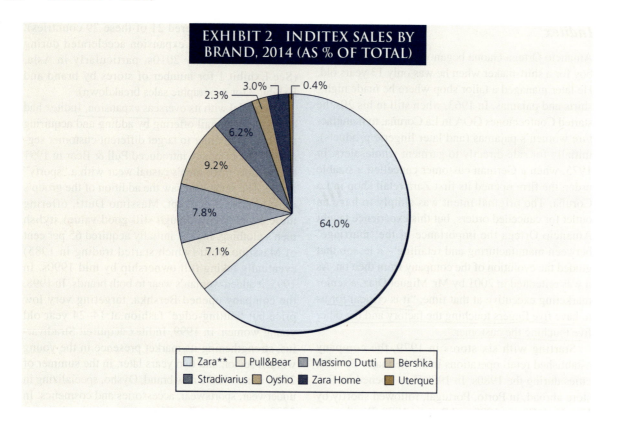

EXHIBIT 2 INDITEX SALES BY BRAND, 2014 (AS % OF TOTAL)

3.0% — 2.3% — 0.4%

6.2%

9.2%

7.8%

7.1%

64.0%

☐ Zara** ☐ Pull&Bear ☐ Massimo Dutti ☐ Bershka
☐ Stradivarius ☐ Oysho ☐ Zara Home ☐ Uterque

Each brand operated independently, with its own stores, ordering system, designers, factories, subcontractors, suppliers, warehousing and distribution systems. They shared only a few corporate services, like legal, finance and acquisitions, but they all followed similar management models for control of supply, production and distribution, and role of store management to maximize speed to market. In fact, there was a degree of competition between some of them in the marketplace.

The aggressive pace of expansion program had been financed almost entirely internally. Inditex operated with "negative operating working capital" – it collected its cash faster than it had to pay it out – so, in principle, it had access to a larger amount of cash as it grew. (See Exhibit 3 for Inditex's income statement and Exhibit 4 for its balance sheet.) Even during the financial crisis of 2009–2011, when most companies, especially those in Spain, were facing substantial problems, Inditex continued to open new stores and increased its sales and profitability. "Our growth is organic, bubbles up from operations, and not because of a precise blueprint or mandate by the board of directors to grow by x % per year," explained Mr. Echevarría.

Zara

Accounting for about two-thirds of total retail sales, Zara was the largest division of Inditex and was well-known for offering 'cutting edge' fashion at affordable prices. Zara's headquarters was next to Inditex's headquarters in Arteixo, a suburb of La Coruña. In January 2015, Zara had 1923 stores in 88 countries with the largest concentration in Spain (323 stores), followed by China (165 stores), France (127 stores), Japan (95 stores), Italy (94 stores), Russia (85 stores), and Germany (79 stores). See Exhibit 5 for location of Zara stores. The strategy for entering new international markets and the rhythm of their expansion was flexible and depended on local conditions. The pace of expansion was also controlled to ensure that it would not pose disproportionate operational risks.

Zara leased most of its stores worldwide. An important advantage of leasing was the flexibility of moving the location in case the successful commercial areas in a city changed. It preferred to form wholly owned companies when entering new countries. Even when it had started with joint ventures, it had often bought out the partners' shares after a few years. The reasons for starting with joint venture

EXHIBIT 3 INCOME STATEMENTS FY 2010–2014

Million Euros	FY2014	F2013	FY2012	FY 2011	FY 2010
Net sales	18,117	16,725	15,946	13,793	12,527
Cost of Merchandise	−7,548	−6,802	−6,417	−5,612	−5,105
Gross profit	**10,569**	**9,923**	**9,529**	**8,181**	**7,422**
Gross Margin	*58.34%*	*59.33%*	*59.76%*	*59.31%*	*59.25%*
Operating Expenses	−6,458	−5,998	−5,605	−4,919	−4,452
Other Net Operating income (losses)	8	1	−12	−3	0
Operating cash flow (EBITDA)	**4,103**	**3,926**	**3,912**	**3,259**	**2,970**
EBITDA margin	*22.65%*	*23.47%*	*24.53%*	*23.63%*	*23.71%*
Amortization and Depreciation	905	−855	−796	−736	−676
Net Operating Income (EBIT)	**3,198**	**3,071**	**3,116**	**2,523**	**2,294**
EBIT margin	*17.65%*	*18.36%*	*19.54%*	*18.29%*	*18.31%*
Financial results	14	−18	14	37	31
Income before taxes	**3,212**	**3,053**	**3,130**	**2,560**	**2,325**
EBT margin	*17.91%*	*18.25%*	*19.63%*	*18.56%*	*18.56%*
Taxes	−735	−671	−764	−613	−580
Net Profit	**2,510**	**2,382**	**2,366**	**1,947**	**1,745**
Net Income margin	*13.85%*	*14.24%*	*14.84%*	*14.12%*	*13.93%*

EXHIBIT 4 INDITEX BALANCE SHEETS FY 2010–2014

Thousand Euros	FY 2014	FY 2013	FY 2012	FY 2011	FY 2010
ASSETS					
Currents Assets	**7,105,953**	**6,764,961**	**6,692,150**	**5,437,289**	**5,202,512**
Cash & cash equivalents	3,797,930	3,846,726	3,842,918	3,466,752	3,433,452
Short Term Investments	222,259	212,890	260,632	0	0
Trade and other receivables	861,811	815,227	847,608	531,048	481,844
Inventories	1,859,516	1,676,879	1,581,297	1,277,009	1,214,623
Other Financial assets	168,947	13,022	7,831	50,684	0
Income Tax receivables	68,284	95,637	58,936	17,235	16,958
Other current assets	127,206	104,580	92,928	94,561	55,635
Non-current Assets	**8,271,047**	**6,991,300**	**6,198,166**	**5,521,889**	**4,623,568**
Property, Plant and equipment	6,040,573	5,137,581	4,662,407	4,063,066	3,397,083
Investment property	81,490	82,809	82,567	19,807	17,354
Rights over leased assets	531,115	508,919	487,474	499,960	526,306
Other tangible assets	152,995	133,364	125,326	114,148	29,444
Goodwill	197,901	203,458	207,089	218,094	131,685

Thousand Euros	FY 2014	FY 2013	FY 2012	FY 2011	FY 2010
Financial investments	151,253	20,634	3,992	9,501	8,921
Deferred Tax assets	643,574	529,664	382,554	356,372	299,350
Other non-current assets	472,146	374,871	246,757	240,941	213,424
TOTAL ASSETS	**15,377,000**	**13,756,261**	**12,890,316**	**10,959,178**	**9,826,079**
LIABILITIES AND EQUITY					
Current Liabilities	**3,748,828**	**3,462,292**	**3,485,064**	**2,702,774**	**2,674,907**
Trade and other payables	3,507,878	3,332,451	3,243,281	2,475,140	2,458,857
Financial debt	7,823	2,521	2,437	686	2,682
Other financial liabilities	83,222	38,339	73,918	22,880	0
Income tax payable	149,905	88,981	165,428	204,068	213,368
Non-current Liabilities	**1,159,471**	**1,015,605**	**923,391**	**800,827**	**728,005**
Financial debt	2,265	2,133	4,306	1,544	4,172
Deferred tax liabilities	240,825	217,291	191,654	182,531	172,648
Provisions	200,611	147,768	144,331	147,318	156,610
Other non-current liabilities	715,770	648,414	583,100	469,434	394,575
EQUITY	**10,468,701**	**9,278,363**	**8,481,861**	**7,455,577**	**6,423,167**
Equity attributable to the parent	10,430,655	9,246,244	8,445,936	7,414,806	6,386,183
Equity attributable to non-controlling interests	38,046	32,119	35,925	40,771	36,984
TOTAL EQUITY AND LIABILITIES	15,377,000	13,756,261	12,890,316	10,959,178	9,826,079

varied. In Japan and Italy, for example, the main reason was to gain access to prime real-estate; in Germany, having seen that other global retailers had often failed, it was access to local expertise and being cautious; in India, which in 2014 was essentially the only notable remaining joint venture, it was to comply with the legal requirement (as well as to access local expertise). "We don't mind investing in joint ventures to learn, but prefer to go alone," explained Mr. Jose M. Álvarez Gallego, Director of Corporate Development at Inditex.

Less than 10 per cent of the stores worldwide were franchises. These included the stores in most of the Middle East (Arab countries and Israel), Indonesia, Central America and Venezuela. Again the reasons were a mix of legal requirements, access to local knowledge (both about retailing and dealing with local government, customs and regulations), access to prime real-estate, and reducing investment risks. Zara sometimes bought the franchisee's operations after gaining local experience. For example, it did that in Russia. In Venezuela, interestingly, it did the reverse: started with its own stores but changed them to franchisees.

Franchised and JV stores operated essentially like other stores. "Real-estate and stocks belong to the 'local partner,' but we are deeply involved in managing the stores' 'commerce' [orders, inventories, and sales information]. The feeling is the same," according to Miguel Díaz. Mr. Echevarría summarized the philosophy behind these policies as "Our model depends on having information about the customer in *our* hands."

The decision to open a new store anywhere in the world was made in La Coruña by an expansion team headed by the CEO, Pablo Isla. Locations were selected after extensive market research, and usually in the most prominent commercial areas, high traffic, and prestigious locations available. "Store is the heart of our company," emphasized Mr. Isla. Zara preferred to invest in its stores than in advertising. Unlike its peers, Zara did not advertise in the mass media. According to Mr. Miguel Díaz, "Our stores and word-of-mouth, do the advertising for us. We

EXHIBIT 5   ZARA STORES AROUND THE WORLD – 2014

Africa		Asia		Europe			
South Africa	6	China	165	Spain	323	Slovakia	3
Egypt	5	Japan	95	France	127	Armenia	2
Morocco	4	South Korea	43	Italy	94	Azerbaijan	2
Tunisia	2	India	15	Russia	85	Bosnia and Herzegovina	2
Algeria	1	Indonesia	13	Germany	79	Denmark	2
Total:	*18*	Malaysia	9	United Kingdom	66	Estonia	2
		Thailand	9	Portugal	63	Georgia	2
Americas		Philippines	8	Poland	47	Iceland	2
Mexico	64	Singapore	8	Greece	40	Albania	1
Brazil	53	Taiwan	7	Turkey	37	Andorra	1
United States	53	Kazakhstan	4	Belgium	27	Macedonia	1
Canada	26	*Total:*	*376*	Netherlands	25	Malta	1
Colombia	11			Romania	21	Monaco	1
Argentina	10	**Middle East**		Switzerland	17	Montenegro	1
Venezuela	10	Saudi Arabia	28	Austria	13	*Total:*	*1,178*
Chile	9	Israel	23	Sweden	10		
Costa Rica	2	UAE	11	Croatia	9	*Total:*	*1,923*
Dominican Republic	2	Lebanon	7	Ireland	9	*In 88 Countries*	
Ecuador	2	Kuwait	6	Ukraine	9		
El Salvador	2	Bahrain	2	Hungary	8		
Guatemala	2	Jordan	2	Czech Republic	7		
Honduras	2	Qatar	2	Bulgaria	6		
Panama	2	Oman	1	Cyprus	6		
Peru	2	*Total:*	*82*	Slovenia	5		
Puerto Rico	2			Finland	4		
Uruguay	2	**Australia**		Latvia	4		
Total:	*256*	Australia	13	Lithuania	4		
		Total	*13*	Serbia	4		
				Luxembourg	3		
				Norway	3		

want our products to pull the customers to our stores; we don't want to push them there by ads."

Zara stores also reflected the evolving, and strategically planned, image of the company. As Mr. Álvarez Gallego explained, "We are constantly optimizing and differentiating our retail proposition. A notable recent development is the enlargement of our global flagship stores." A clear example was the store in Manhattan opened on March 15, 2012. Located on the Fifth Avenue and 52nd Street, one of the most exclusive

shopping areas in New York City, the store occupied the entire four storeys of an impressive and highly visible building which offered 3000 square meters of floor space, double the size of the average Zara store. Another example was the store opened in Hong Kong on June 24, 2014. This one was a six-storey building in the heart of Hong Kong on Queens Road with 5200 square meters of floor space.

Inside the stores, Zara paid careful attention to create a pleasant, spacious and uncluttered shopping environment that invited customers to walk around and browse. The layout of the stores, the furniture, and even the window displays were all designed centrally to give the same image worldwide and a "flying team" from headquarters was usually dispatched to a new site to set up the store. Even after startup, stores still relied heavily on central staff, located in either La Coruña or their region, to assist with major refurbishment and other construction-related issues.

A typical Zara store had women's, men's and children's sections, with a manager in charge of each. Women's wear usually accounted for more than half of the store's sales, with the rest of the turnover equally divided between men's wear and children's wear. The store manager was usually also the head of the women's section. Zara placed a great deal of emphasis on the training of its sales force and correspondingly emphasized internal promotion. The primary responsibility of store managers was to increase sales. All the investment decisions, merchandizing decisions (both for new and existing products), retail prices, discounts, sale and promotion campaigns were essentially made by La Coruña. La Coruña also tracked the inventory at every store and generally determined which items should be replenished, especially if the item was temporarily in short supply and had to be allocated among stores. The store manager could of course influence the process by providing better forecasts and qualitative information about the demand at their stores and the trends they had captured in the preferences of their customers.

Zara's strategy required generation of a great deal of product variety throughout the year. "We are in the *fashion* business – not clothing. Our customers buy our products because they like it – not because it is Zara," explained Mr. Díaz. To many of its customers, Zara stores were places to go to see latest affordable fashion trend, a place for shopping pleasure rather than searching for specific items. The garments were not displayed in the usual way (i.e. skirts together, pants together, shirts etc.) but often mixed together for better presentation and encouraging customers to buy combined outfits. Typically only a few pieces of each item were displayed, which reinforced the image of newness, and since the displayed items were often the entire stock held at the store, it also promoted an image of exclusivity. However, holding such low levels of inventory meant that the stores depended on regular and rapid replenishment of their inventory.

Operations

Creating a supply chain that allowed Zara stores to offer cutting edge fashion at affordable prices required the firm to exert a strong influence over all stages of design, production, distribution, and retailing of clothes.

Retailing

All stores worldwide placed orders and received shipments twice per week. Orders had to be placed at pre-designated times: stores in Spain, southern Europe and few other zones on Wednesdays before 3 p.m. and Saturdays before 6 p.m. and in rest of the world on Tuesdays by 3 p.m. and Fridays by 6 p.m. If a store, say in Belgium, missed the Wednesday deadline, then it would have to wait until Saturday. "We are very strict about these deadlines. Orders must be on time," emphasized Mr. Díaz.

The composition of these orders was usually the result of discussion between store managers and country managers in La Coruña. They had very frequent and direct communications (by Skype, phone, email, and other methods) and generally developed personal relationships. Zara referred to each store by name – not a number – to reinforce this personal relationship. The team in La Coruña had access to store's inventory level and made the pricing decisions. (See the next section, "Design," for more detail about the team in La Coruña.)

Most items did not stay in the stores more than two weeks. Zara sought to minimize the risk of oversupply by keeping production volumes low at the beginning of the season and reacting quickly to orders and new trends during the season. It operated with much smaller average "pre-season inventory commitment" than its peers. Pre-season inventory commitment is the level of production and procurement that has to be committed in the supply chain before the start of the "season" (for example, in late July for the fall/winter season). The average for the industry was 80 per cent to 100 per cent of the anticipated sales during the season; for Zara it was only 15 per cent to 20 per cent for the difficult-to-forecast "fashion products" and about 40 per cent for "basic products". Zara's policy was to wait until the season had started before making more commitments. The "in-season commitments" for Zara were 40 per cent to 45 per cent whereas the industry average ranged from almost nothing to a maximum of 20 per cent. Zara had to react faster but worked with more reliable market information, coming from the stores and from the evolution of tendencies.

Zara refreshed the presentation at the store regularly. Items that remained on the shelves for more than two or three weeks were normally taken out of the store and shipped to another store in the same country region (occasionally very small amounts were sent back to Spain which were then usually shipped to other regions in the world.) Rapid movement of products through the store and the knowledge that some of the products may not be replenished created an additional incentive for customers to buy on the spot. However, Mr. Díaz emphasized: "You can change the collection in the store frequently, but that is not an end in itself. You must react to what the customers are or are not buying as accurately as possible." For example, warm weather in October 2013 in parts of Europe had increased the sales of lighter garments (and reduced the sales of heavier ones), which had required quick adjustments in orders and shipments to these stores. "Perhaps our production and distribution system can react faster to changes because we started as a manufacturer," suggested Mr. Díaz.

All this meant that Zara managed to carry less overall inventory per unit of sales than its peers and had less unsold items that had to be discounted at end of season. In an industry where the average product fetched usually only 60 per cent to 70 per cent of its full price, Zara sold 80 per cent to 85 per cent of its products at full price and even for the rest offered less discounts at end of the season. "Our *model is built to minimize the operational risk,* sending to the stores exactly what the customer wants in the correct amount. We build and update the required capacities in the rest of the Chain as needed. This allows us to maximize the sales at full price and to maintain a very stable margin, perhaps the most stable in the industry. But that is not the goal; it is a consequence of our business model," said Mr. Álvarez.

Design and order administration

Zara designed all its products itself. In 2013, Zara had 350 people in the "commercial team" at its La Coruña headquarters, including designers, country managers (also known as "market specialists"), and buyers. About 100 of them were considered to be designers (although it was difficult to pinpoint the exact number because many members of the "commercial team" participated in different tasks). Designers were generally young – in their late 20s – and Zara encouraged a collegial atmosphere amongst them (there were no design "prima donnas"). Design inspirations came from many sources from around the world – trade fairs, clubs, catwalks, magazines – and close follow up of recent trends in popularity of new fabrics and colors. Extensive feedback from the store network was an integral part of the design process. "Unlike many other companies, the designers at Zara can get quick feedback from customers at the store, and refine and improve their creations rapidly," explained Mr. Echevarría.

Zara introduced approximately 18000 new products annually, which reflected combined works of designers (who were the creative type), the buyers (who dealt with sourcing and production), and the country managers (who dealt with merchandizing at stores). Zara management considered that the continuous interaction between these three groups was critical to make quick and balanced decisions about what and how much to produce following the information from the stores. The designers for women, men and children wear sat in different halls in a modern building attached to the Inditex headquarters. In each of these big open spaces, the designers, organized by products (e.g., dresses, T-shirts and denim, accessories) occupied the perimeter areas of the room and country managers and buyers sat around a long table in the middle area. The layout of the hall was designed to encourage impromptu meetings with an air of informality and openness. For example, Eduardo Sabater, head of a product group in the women's section explained the process in his section:

We have many meetings all the time. We are working simultaneously on new collections and supplementing existing ones. For new collections, we meet to decide which trends we are going to follow, then how to put the collection together, then select which items to make a prototype, which items to produce and in what quantity. Many different people are involved formally and informally in these meetings. For example, in the section that designs our "basic collection," the design team may come up with 500 design ideas, and after a few meetings with others in the room (reviewing selection of fabrics, colors, textures), and checking that the new designs could be produced and sold at a profit, we may arrive at 40 designs to move forward, and we may actually choose to go ahead with only a few of them. We don't discard the remaining designs, of course, since we are constantly adding to the collection.

EXHIBIT 6   COMPARISON WITH PEERS

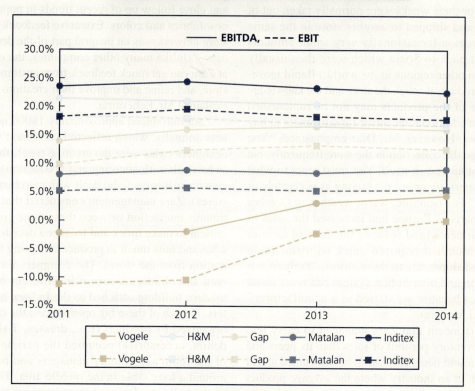

EBITDA, ---- EBIT

Legend: Vogele, H&M, Gap, Matalan, Inditex (EBITDA solid); Vogele, H&M, Gap, Matalan, Inditex (EBIT dashed)

Earnings (EBITDA and EBIT)

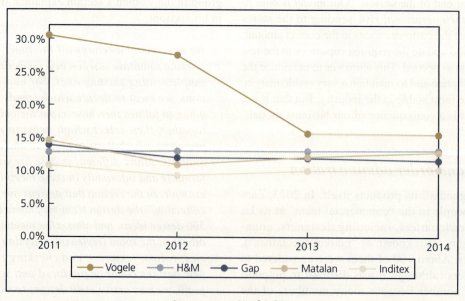

Legend: Vogele, H&M, Gap, Matalan, Inditex

Inventory as % of Sales

The designers usually drew their sketches using a CAD system where further changes and adjustments (for better matching of weaves, textures, and colors etc.) were made. Samples were made by skilled workers located in the small prototype shops – consisting of simple equipment for patterns, cutting and sewing – in a corner of each hall. If there were any questions or problems, these workers could just walk over to the designers and discuss and resolve them on the spot.

Each of the country managers had a responsibility for dealing with a number of specific stores in a country or region. As experienced employees, who had often been store managers themselves, they recognized that it was crucial to establish personal relationships with the managers of stores assigned to them. They were in constant contact, especially by phone or Skype, with these managers, discussing sales, orders, new lines and other matters. They represented many nationalities – Chinese, Moroccan, Greek, Indian, Polish and may others – working with stores in countries that matched their language and cultural knowledge. Store managers relied heavily on discussions with country managers before they finalized their orders. Given the time differences, those dealing with Asia would come to work earlier in the morning and those dealing with the Americas would stay late in the room. Store managers also used digital devices for communicating with La Coruña; they had used custom-designed hand-held devices but had recently replaced them with tablets.

The third group in the hall, the buyers, managed sourcing, procurement and production planning. They planned procurement and production requirements, monitored the inventories, allocated production to various factories and third-party suppliers and kept track of shortages and oversupplies.

Production

Zara produced its time sensitive fashion products "in proximity". This term was not referring to distance but to fast response. Most of them were produced in Spain, Portugal and Morocco, and the rest in a number of European countries. Eleven of these factories belonged to Zara, of which ten were located in and around its complex in Arteixo. The share of in-house production had traditionally been substantial, larger than most of its competitors, but was becoming a smaller proportion because of its rapid rate of growth and development of close relationships with competent suppliers worldwide. These factories generally worked a single shift, and occasionally on two shifts, and were managed as profit centers. Zara sourced the rest of its products from around 1600 suppliers around the world. A third of this volume came from Eastern Europe, including Turkey, Bulgaria and Romania. From Asia, Zara procured "basic" products and those for which the region had a clear advantage. With its relatively large and stable orders, Zara was a preferred customer for almost all its suppliers. "Our relationship with most of our suppliers is based on trust. There is an understanding between us: we have placed orders with them for many years and they can rely on us to continue to do that; and we expect them to meet our required quality and speed as well as availability of sufficient capacity," explained Mr. Álvarez.

The make or buy decisions were made, as mentioned earlier, by the buyers (in the commercial team). The key criteria in making these decisions were having the capability and available capacity to meet the required speed, quality, and cost. However, such decisions were made carefully, paying great attention to minimizing the risks associated with the particular fashion and the sensitivity of speed to market.

Zara purchased its raw materials from suppliers worldwide. Some of the fabrics were purchased undyed and dyed in the desired color later in the production process. The first step in the production process was cutting. A typical factory had several cutting machines with long tables, where typically 30 to 50 layers of fabric were laid out under a top paper layer. The cutting pattern was generated by special software that helped the skilled operators arrange the pieces in a pattern that minimized fabric waste. "Although the CAD software can generate the cutting pattern automatically, we prefer to do the final step manually because skilled operators can still do a better job in minimizing fabric waste. They can do it because they have a feel for the fabric and understand the design," said Mr. Mendoza, a supervisor in one of Zara's factories for men's apparel.

Once the pattern was generated, it was sent to the cutting machine and drawn by the machine onto the top layer (so that cut pieces can be identified later). After a final visual check by the operator, the machine cut the multiple layers into hundreds of different small pieces. Operators then marked each piece and packed them into clear plastic bags (with the identifying paper layer on top). This was a time consuming and laborious task that had to be done carefully because it was very easy to mix up the pieces. The bags were then sent to sewing contractors.

Zara used contractors for all sewing operations. There were some 200 sewing contractors, some around La Coruña, others in rest of the Galicia region and a few even as far as Portugal. Contractors, often using their own trucks, usually collected the bagged cut pieces at the factory, along with appropriate components (like buttons and zippers). Most were small and medium size companies and Zara was their main customer. However, as one of the senior managers at Zara said, "We prefer not to be the only customer; a very important customer, yes, but not the only one." Zara monitored contractors' operations closely to ensure quality, compliance with labor laws, and especially adherence to the production schedule. Zara believed that outsourcing a highly labor intensive operation, like sewing, helped its own factories to remain focused and increased their flexibility to change production volumes quickly.

Contractors brought back the sewn items to the same factory, where factory employees inspected every piece during ironing (by machine and by hand). Finished products were labelled and placed in plastic bags before sending them to the distribution center (DC). The labels included price in local currency and even store security pins, making the product ready to be placed on shelves in the store. A system of aerial monorails through underground tunnels directly connected the factories on Zara's "campus" in Arteixo to the distribution center. Finished products procured from outside suppliers were also sent directly to one of the distribution centers in Spain.

Inditex paid increasing attention to the ethical and sustainability issues in its extended supply chain. A corporate philosophy, labeled "Right to Wear," captured its strategic intent to "guarantee the quality and sustainability of all our products and business activities." This philosophy went beyond compliance with health, safety and ethical standards. The goal was to be proactive in developing environmentally friendly products and investing in a range of social initiatives. This required transparency and frequent and systematic audits across the supply chain. Inditex had already progressed significantly and was being recognized as one of the leaders in these areas. For example, it was consistently rated the highest level of performance by the United Nation's Global Compact.

Distribution

Until 2003, Zara had only one distribution center next to its headquarters in Arteixo. It occupied a five storey building with 500,000 square meters of storage space and used the latest technology. Almost all products passed through this large and sophisticated distribution center. However continued expansion of the company had necessitated addition of new distribution capacity. In mid-2001, when Arteixo distribution center was working at essentially 50 per cent capacity, Zara announced that it would build an additional distribution center in Zaragoza (Spain). Costing €120 million, the 190,000-square meter Zaragoza distribution center was completed in October 2003. It was allocated to distribution of most women garments globally. In 2007, Zara opened a third major distribution center, with 180,000 square meters storage space, in Meco, near Madrid. Costing €150 million, Meco specialized in children garments and few other items.

The scale of operations in these distribution centers was impressive. The three DCs handled over a million pieces in a typical day in early 2014, and had the capacity to do much more. Fast changing fashion garments represented the major share of these items, resulting in a very large number of stock keeping units (SKUs), which created additional complexity in inventory management, order picking and fulfillment.

Zara had worked with some of the world's best suppliers of hardware and software to develop the systems for these warehouses and had modified them by its own teams to fit its operations. For example, at Arteixo, optical readers tracked the network of the overhead rails that connected the factories via underground tunnels to the distribution center and directed individual items and batches to specific areas. Orders for each store were packed automatically in boxes from moving conveyors, and matched, also automatically, with items on hangers for the same store in the shipping areas usually in 8 hours, with a higher activity overnight. Around a thousand persons worked in the Arteixo distribution center, supplemented by up to 200 additional temporary workers during peak periods. Zara had continued to deploy the latest and most technologically advanced systems in its newer distribution centers in Zaragoza and Meco, giving them comparable capacities to Arteixo even though they had smaller floor and fewer operators.

Zara used only trucks and air for transporting orders from its distribution centers to stores. Since orders for each store normally required items from all three distribution centers, they were consolidated in Zaragoza. The shipments did not stay more than a few hours in Zaragoza. Stores in most of Europe were supplied by trucks, carrying Zara's name but owned and operated by contractors. These trucks – from Arteixo and Meco to Zaragoza and from Zaragoza to stores – ran on published schedules (like bus timetables). Shipments by air were also on published timetables using scheduled flights. In some countries, the contractors had established "docking stations" where the shipments from Spain were transferred to smaller trucks for local distribution.

Typically, stores in Europe received their orders in 24 hours, in the United States in 48 hours and in Japan in 48 to 72 hours. Speed was clearly an overriding concern; as Lorena Alba (General Director of Logistics) put it: "For us, distance is not measured in kilometers, but in *time*." For example, orders from stores in Tokyo would be usually on the flight next morning and in Japan the following day, picked up by a third party contractor and delivered to the Zara stores the next day. The goods could be displayed as soon as they were taken out of the truck because they had already been labeled and priced.

Zara online

Zara's first foray into the online world was simply a catalogue; allowing customers to see a selection of products but still needing them to visit the store to make a purchase. By 2008 however, Zara decided that it was time to launch its own online offering. Zara's online store officially opened in September 2010 for customers in France, Germany, Spain, Italy, Portugal and the UK. Online sales grew quickly and there was no evidence of cannibalization of sales from stores. In fact, since many online customers picked up their orders at stores, it seemed that they were actually helping the store sales.

Talking to analysts in March 2013, Mr. Isla said "Inditex's online operations have seen a very rapid rollout in recent years. Our business model allows a swift expansion of our online sales platform globally." Zara quickly built an online presence in 18 European markets; presence in the US, Japan and China were added in 2012, and in Canada and Russia in 2013. When, in 2014, Greece, Romania, Mexico and South Korea were added, the online sales reached 27 markets. The ambition, for both Zara and the rest of the Inditex brands, was made clear by Mr. Isla, "We will continue to roll out online sales progressively in all the markets in which we are present with stores". Analysts at Citigroup concluded in 2013 that the results indicated that Inditex was "one of the few beneficiaries of the ongoing, rapid channel shift to online from store-based apparel sales." According to Mr. Isla, Zara' operating model fitted well with online sale: "It is as if, 30 years ago, we had decided to design a business model to support online retailing."

Online orders were supplied by "online stores." The decision to open an online store followed the same decision making process as for any other store. There was usually one online store per country or, if practical, a region, and it operated like any other store that placed orders and received shipments twice per week. The difference was that the orders were managed by a dedicated team in La Coruña, which saw all online orders and arranged the shipments to the appropriate "online store" using the standard system for distribution. Shipments for online sales in each country were sent to a "macro store" in that country – just like any other store. The macro stores were in reality rented warehouses, which were bigger than storage areas in a typical store but had no face-to-face contact with customers. They were operated by third party logistics providers who shipped the individual orders. Online customers could pick up their orders in a physical store for free (delivery in 3–5 days) or at home by standard delivery (2–3 days) or express delivery (48 hours) at additional costs.

Looking into the future

During the last decade, Zara had defied, repeatedly, the predictions of those who had suggested that it had reached the limit of its business model. In 2014, it seemed to be continuing its phenomenal growth into the future. Nevertheless, many observers still wondered whether it needed to modify its business model and operating systems to account for its increasing size and global footprint. For example, was its current system of design, production, and order fulfillment helping or hindering serving the growing markets in Asia? Would it facilitate growth of online sales? Did it require a major overhaul of its well-organized operating processes?

Snapchat: Fad or future?

By Sapna Malhotra

Abstract

S napchat, the brainchild of two University students, Evan Spiegel and Bobby Murphy created waves in the instant messaging sector since its inception in 2011. Snapchat was a picture-based messaging application where messages would automatically disappear after a few seconds of being sent. It enticed demography critical to advertisers, i.e. the teens and millennials. Snapchat became such a rage that Mark Zuckerberg, the CEO of Facebook offered a whopping $3 billion for a buyout. Snapchat declined his offer and received $20 million in funding from venture capital firm Kleiner Perkins Caufield & Byers that catapulted its valuation to $10 billion in 2014. Although the app started to experiment with methods to monetize, it was yet to make any substantial revenue. However, it raised $163 million in five funding rounds from a number of investors. Its user base grew close to 200 million and the brand was ranked third in the global list of top venture backed firms, becoming one of the most valued start-ups. By 2015, Snapchat was valued at $19 billion with further investments from Alibaba, among other heavyweights. However, industry analysts warned that Snapchat was reeling in a billion-dollar bubble, hinging only on initial investor confidence. They suggested that the billions with which 'apps' were being funded in Silicon Valley replicated the dotcom bubble of the 90s. Snapchat's biggest challenge would be the justification of its multibillion-dollar tag. Could the loss-making enterprise become a profitable messaging juggernaut? Was it a passing fad or the future of social media communication?

Case study

"I know it's an ephemeral platform, but my 14-year-old spends half her life there."[1]
     – Jeremy Zimmer[2]

"Snapchat is not valuable in the long-term because it is used by teens or because it is a threat to Facebook. It is valuable because it has fundamentally changed the nature of digital communication in <2 years and will continue to do so for the life of the Company."[3]
     – Evan Spiegel[4]

"At some point, we are going to see the momentum of investing dollars move against these high valuation private companies."[5]
     – Drew Nordlicht[6]

Snapchat was founded in 2011 by Evan Spiegel (Spiegel) and Bobby Murphy (Murphy). Unlike any other picture messaging application, Snapchat's differentiation lay in the fact that images would get deleted after being viewed for a few seconds. Teenagers thronged the platform with frenzy. Snapchat's user base grew by the millions, and the app earned billions in valuation along the way. While renowned brands took a liking for the application as a platform to reach out to customers, Snapchat was yet to devise fool-proof strategies to justify its latest valuation of $19 billion in 2015. Further, industry analysts feared the onset of a bubble, much like the dotcom era in the 90s. Was Snapchat ephemeral or could it stand strong among a plethora of other applications and also be immune to a bubble burst?

[1]J. De La Merced Michael and Isaac Mike, "Snapchat, Pinterest, Lyft: Investors create a billion-dollar-startup boom", http://economictimes. indiatimes.com/news/international/business/snapchat-pinterest-lyft-investors-create-a-billion-dollar-startup-boom/articleshow/46311042.cms, February 20th 2015.

[2]Head of the United Talent Agency.

[3]Lubin Gus, "Leaked 2013 Email Shows Snapchat CEO's Warning About A Tech Crash And A Brutal Fall For Facebook", http://uk.businessinsider. com/snapchat-ceo-on-tech-bubble-and-facebook-overvaluation-2014-12, December 18th 2014.

[4]Snapchat CEO.

[5]Quittner Jeremy, "Why Bill Gurley and Mark Cuban Don't Hate to Burst Your Bubble", http://www.inc.com/jeremy-quittner/tech-bubble-or-not-high-valuations-will-end.html, March 17th 2015.

[6]Partner and Managing Director of Hightower Advisors, San Diego.

Snapchat's exponential growth story

Instant messaging

Instant Messaging (IM) technology could be dated back to 1996. Four individuals from Israel created 'Mirabilis' that helped users to communicate through the internet so that the online community could be more interconnected.[7] The software behind IM essentially helped people to send text messages to one another that were received instantaneously at the other end. Over the years, IM caught the fancy of more and more people and in no time, it also made inroads into the workplace. Surveys in 2004 stated that IM was slated to surpass e-mail as the primary medium of electronic communication.[8]

Mobile phones remained at the forefront until the advent of the smartphone. Hence, text messages always took precedence. However, texts as opposed to 'social messages', cost money. Thus, the latter possessed a more universal appeal. In fact, social messaging apps catered to social networking and social media development. iPhones and iPads had 'iMessages', Microsoft had 'Skype', Google had 'Hangouts' and BlackBerry had 'BBM'. And as the global smartphone market grew, so did social messaging.[9]

"We've seen significant change across our stores as customers are more interested in enquiring about a tariff's data limits – and whether a phone comes with a free messaging app or function pre-installed – as opposed to the number of text messages and minutes available," said a Carphone Warehouse spokesperson[10] (Exhibit I). The Public IM market started to co-exist across desktops, web portals as well as mobiles. At the same time, it also became integrated with social networking sites.[11]

Interestingly, IM was winning in 'volume' while text messaging remained ahead in revenue generation mainly due to 'ubiquity, infrequency and price'. A number of IM services had largely been focused only on getting the maximum number of users on board. Deloitte stated they must have to start raising income through in-app purchases and/or advertising.[12]

In fact, in 2015, Mobile IM went beyond just text communication into more audio-visual forms.[13] With free messaging services becoming increasingly popular, it was estimated that global texting revenues would fall once they reach their peak in 2016.[14] According to a report by Juniper, instant messaging was expected to garner about 75 per cent of the entire mobile messaging market by 2018[15] and IM user base was expected to stand at 3.8 billion by 2019[16] (Exhibit II). The mobile app market was flooded with several IM services, among which Snapchat was touted as the 'next generation messaging service.' Even though the mobile application boasted of no particular business model, yet millions of messages were being sent through it. The messages would vanish in less than 10 seconds, making Snapchat an extremely instant service.

The Snapchat story

Evan Spiegel (Spiegel), the CEO of Snapchat, grew up in Los Angeles and studied product design at Stanford University. Spiegel and Bobby Murphy (Spiegel's senior by 2 years),[17] launched 'Snapchat' in the year 2011. It allowed users to communicate with one another through images that would get automatically deleted after being viewed for a few seconds.[18]

[7]"An Instant War, Just Add Chat: The Growth of Instant Messaging Technology", https://www.sans.org/reading-room/whitepapers/basics/instant-war-add-chat-growth-instant-messaging-technology-470.

[8]Walker Leslie, "Instant Messaging Is Growing Up, Going to Work", http://www.washingtonpost.com/wp-dyn/articles/A54261-2004Sep1.html, September 2nd 2004.

[9]"Instant messaging apps going mainstream in 2014", http://www.ctvnews.ca/sci-tech/instant-messaging-apps-going-mainstream-in-2014-1.1570030, December 2nd 2013.

[10]Curtis Sophie, "Instant messaging overtakes texting in the UK", http://www.telegraph.co.uk/technology/news/10568395/Instant-messaging-overtakes-texting-in-the-UK.html, January 13th 2014.

[11]Radicati Sara and Taitague Alex, "Instant Messaging Market, 2013–2017", http://www.radicati.com/wp/wp-content/uploads/2013/09/Instant-Messaging-Market-2013-2017-Executive-Summary.pdf.

[12]"Instant Messaging Market, 2013–2017", op. cit..

[13]"Instant Messaging Market, 2015–2019", http://www.radicati.com/wp/wp-content/uploads/2015/02/Instant-Messaging-Market-2014-2018-Executive-Summary.pdf.

[14]"WhatsApp Shows How Phone Carriers Lost Out On $33 Billion", op. cit..

[15]Calladine Dan, "Why brands must get to know instant messaging apps", http://www.marketingmagazine.co.uk/article/1312372/why-brands-know-instant-messaging-apps, September 17th 2014.

[16]"Instant Messaging Market, 2015–2019", op. cit..

[17]"The World's Billionaires", http://www.forbes.com/profile/evan-spiegel/.

[18]"Snapchat valued at $10bn by Californian investment firm", http://www.bbc.com/news/technology-28952245, August 27th 2014.

EXHIBIT I TEXT MESSAGING VS. IM COUNTRY

United Kingdom	Text messaging & IM (2012–2013–2014).
	Text Messages: 152 billion in 2012, 145 billion in 2013.
	IM: 57 million in 2012, 160 billion in 2013.
India	IM usage grew 113% in 2013. WhatsApp (52% Users), Facebook Messenger (42%), Skype (37%), WeChat (26%), Viber (18%).
China	Mobile instant messaging accounts approached 1.5 billion in 2013.
USA	Text-messaging income: $21 billion in 2013.
	Expected to drop 3–4% in 2014.
Global	Social messaging apps sent 27.5 trillion messages in 2013.
	Applications like iMessage, BBM, WeChat, Snapchat, Facebook Messenger, etc. would cater to 50 billion daily messages.
	MIM depleted SMS revenues by about $32 billion in 2013.
	IM accounts were 3.4 billion in 2013.
	Revenues generated for MIM service providers from games and other virtual goods like stickers were worth over $1 billion in 2014.

EXHIBIT II INSTANT MESSAGING: EXPECTED GROWTH (2015–2019)

Worldwide IM Accounts (M), 2015–2019

Source: "Instant Messaging Market, 2015–2019", http://www.radicati.com/wp/wp-content/uploads/2015/02/Instant-Messaging-Market-2014-2018-Executive-Summary.pdf.

The first version of Snapchat was a website, but the idea was soon taken onto the mobile platform. Headquartered at Spiegel's father's house, Snapchat progressed towards becoming a rage. Users inched towards the 1000 mark and numbers doubled and quadrupled, all at the cost of increasing server bills. Spiegel borrowed some money from his grandfather,

while Murphy gave up half of his salary. However, monthly bills touched $5,000 and the founders needed desperate aid.[19]

Luck struck in April 2012 when Lightspeed[20] invested $485,000 and Snapchat's valuation instantaneously ascended to $4.25 million. "That was the greatest feeling of all time. There is nothing that will

[19]Colao J.J., "The Inside Story Of Snapchat: The World's Hottest App Or A $3 Billion Disappearing Act?" http://www.forbes.com/sites/jjcolao/2014/01/06/the-inside-story-of-snapchat-the-worlds-hottest-app-or-a-3-billion-disappearing-act/, January 6th 2014.

[20]Lightspeed Venture Partners is a venture capital firm focusing on early and expansion stage investments.

replace that," proclaimed Spiegel. He quit Stanford the day the money was received.[21] By February 2013, Snapchat was sending about 60 million messages per day.[22] In fact, Pew Research Centre stated that 9 per cent of American smartphone users were engaged with Snapchat with nearly 26 per cent of them aged between 18 and 29.[23]

Notably, Snapchat was increasing its user base, especially teenagers who were leaving Facebook. Facebook was bleeding so Mark Zuckerberg (CEO, Facebook) offered $3 billion to Spiegel in 2013.[24] *"Come to Menlo Park and let's get to know each other,"* e-mailed Zuckerberg to loss-making Snapchat CEO Spiegel, to which Spiegel replied, *"I'm happy to meet you... if you come to me."*[25]

Interestingly, the idea behind Snapchat was once derided by Spiegel's classmates. However, Spiegel remained confident and rejected the buyout offer which was Facebook's highest bid ever until then, anticipating better offers as he expected Snapchat's user base to increase further.[26] He told Forbes, in late 2013, "There are very few people in the world who get to build a business like this. I think trading that for some short-term gain isn't very interesting."[27]

Going further from vanishing photos, Snapchat enabled a number of marketing based features such as 'Stories' – an amalgamation of images and videos weaved to make stories. Several brands jumped onto the Stories bandwagon, making 30–60 second long snippets. Unlike photos, Stories could be viewed multiple times within a 24-hour time frame. Renowned brands such as Audi, Taco Bell, McDonald's among others started to make use of Snapchat's services.[28]

By November 2013, about 400 million snaps were being shared each day. And by May 2014, the numbers rose to 700 million photos and videos every day. In fact, Snapchat's 'Stories' were being viewed about 500 million times daily. With explosive growth, analysts claimed Snapchat had aced the photo sharing mobile platform.[29] In fact, by 2014, Snapchat became an able competitor to the likes of WhatsApp and Instagram (both owned by Facebook) and also China-based WeChat and Line.[30]

Snapchat's popularity consistently increased among teens and millennials, especially girls aged 13–25 years (Exhibit III). The app also earned a coveted spot in the top three rankings of Apple's app store in several mature markets such as the U.S, Sweden, Australia, Canada and UK, among others. (Exhibit IV). It witnessed exponential growth, where sharing of 'Stories' grew 100 per cent in two months up to July 2014 and got a billion views daily. In fact, 760 million images and videos were being shared per day[31] (Exhibit V).

While Snapchat chose to be independent of tech giants that tried to buy it, the founders became billionaires in the process. Venture capital firm Kleiner Perkins Caufield & Byers invested $20 million into the app. The funding earned Snapchat a valuation of $10 billion. User count continued to swell and reached 100 million per month, while the app tried its hand in 'advertising, money transfer and content discovery'. By August 2014, Snapchat had successfully raised funding of $163 million in five rounds from several investors that also comprised $50 million[32] from Coatue Management[33] alone. This latest

[21]"The Inside Story Of Snapchat: The World's Hottest App Or A $3 Billion Disappearing Act?", op. cit..

[22]Shontell Alyson, "5 Months After Turning Down Billions, Snapchat's Growth Is Still Exploding With 700 Million Photos Shared Per Day", http://www.businessinsider.in/5-Months-After-Turning-Down-Billions-Snapchats-Growth-Is-Still-Exploding-With-700-Million-Photos-Shared-Per-Day/articleshow/34541258.cms, May 2nd 2014.

[23]Walker Tim, "The 23-year-old Snapchat co-founder and CEO who said no to a $3bn offer from Facebook", http://www.independent.co.uk/life-style/gadgets-and-tech/news/the-23yearold-snapchat-cofounder-and-ceo-who-said-no-to-a-3bn-offer-from-facebook-8940433.html, November 14th 2013.

[24]Bercovici Jeff, "Facebook Tried To Buy Snapchat For $3B In Cash. Here's Why", http://www.forbes.com/sites/jeffbercovici/2013/11/13/facebook-wouldve-bought-snapchat-for-3-billion-in-cash-heres-why/, November 13th 2013.

[25]"The Inside Story Of Snapchat: The World's Hottest App Or A $3 Billion Disappearing Act?", op. cit..

[26]"The 23-year-old Snapchat co-founder and CEO who said no to a $3bn offer from Facebook", op. cit..

[27]"The World's Billionaires", op. cit..

[28]Ballve Marcelo, "Snapchat's Explosive Growth Among Teens and Millennials Means It's Emerging As A Powerful Brand Platform", http://www.businessinsider.in/Snapchats-Explosive-Growth-Among-Teens-And-Millennials-Means-Its-Emerging-As-A-Powerful-Brand-Platform/articleshow/38149131.cms, July 10th 2014.

[29]"5 Months After Turning Down Billions, Snapchat's Growth Is Still Exploding With 700 Million Photos Shared Per Day", op. cit..

[30]"Snapchat valued at $10bn by Californian investment firm", op. cit..

[31]"Snapchat's Explosive Growth Among Teens and Millennials Means It's Emerging As A Powerful Brand Platform", op. cit..

[32]Olson Parmy, "Snapchat Founders Likely Billionaires With New, Reported Investment", http://www.forbes.com/sites/parmyolson/2014/08/26/report-snapchat-valued-at-10-billion-with-new-kleiner-investment/, August 27th 2014.

[33]Coatue Management is a global investment manager focused on public and private companies.

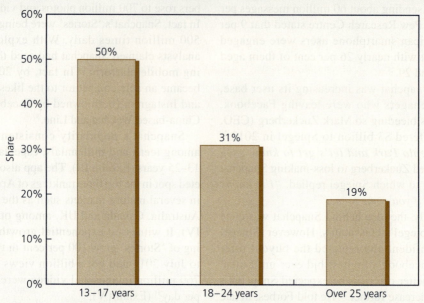

Source: Nolan Jonathan, "Is Snapchat Scrambling to Implement a Monetisation Plan to Avoid Collapse?", http://www.venturecapnews.com/technology/is-snapchat-scrambling-to-implement-a-monetization-plan-to-avoid-collapse/, March 4th 2015.

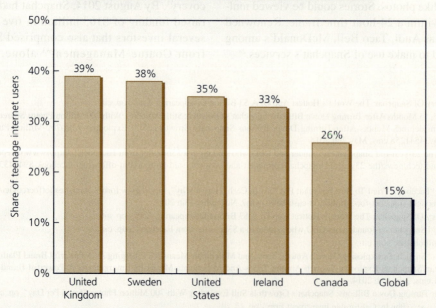

Source: Nolan Jonathan, "Is Snapchat Scrambling to Implement a Monetisation Plan to Avoid Collapse?", http://www.venturecapnews.com/technology/is-snapchat-scrambling-to-implement-a-monetization-plan-to-avoid-collapse/, March 4th 2015.

EXHIBIT V   SNAPCHAT: DEC 2012–JUNE 2014

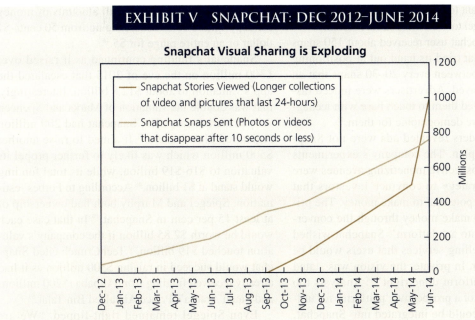

Snapchat Visual Sharing is Exploding

— Snapchat Stories Viewed (Longer collections of video and pictures that last 24-hours)

— Snapchat Snaps Sent (Photos or videos that disappear after 10 seconds or less)

Source: Ballve Marcelo, "Snapchat's Explosive Growth Among Teens And Millennials Means It's Emerging As A Powerful Brand Platform", http://www.businessinsider.in/Snapchats-Explosive-Growth-Among-Teens-And-Millennials-Means-Its-Emerging-As-A-Powerful-Brand-Platform/articleshow/38149131.cms, July 10th 2014.

valuation meant Snapchat's shareholder value had grown by $11 million each day in its initial years.[34]

In 2014, Snapchat partnered with Square[35] to start 'Snapcash'. It essentially allowed users to send money to the bank account of any contact. While mobile based payments had been gaining steam with Apple's introduction of Apple Pay, analysts wondered if Snapchat could reap revenue from Snapcash.[36] However, Snapchat had in place a monetisation plan that would showcase advertisements, TV/film clips, and also news.[37] It introduced channels for news bytes and entertainment from companies that included the likes of Vice and even National Geographic.[38] Further, it began to offer videos from well-known news

networks like Yahoo News and Sky. Analysts said it could also charge news networks for 'visibility'.[39]

At a Vanity Fair event in October 2014, while Spiegel revealed ads would debut within Snapchat, he also said they would be untargeted. While untargeted advertising (Spam) was considered the most irrelevant form, the fact that users had the right to choose whether to see the ad or not was expected to hold Snapchat in good stead.[40] For this, Snapchat created a product called Discover, wherein ads would be displayed within "curated" channels.[41] "We're cutting through a lot of the new technology stuff around ads to sort of the core of it, which I think has always been telling a story that leaves people with a new feeling. They're not fancy. You just

[34]Koetsier John, "There are now at least 25 billion-dollar mobile internet companies", http://venturebeat.com/2014/09/03/there-are-now-at-least-25-billion-dollar-mobile-internet-companies/, September 3rd 2014.

[35]*Square*, Inc. is a financial services, merchant services aggregator and mobile payments company based in San Francisco, California.

[36]Nolan Jonathan, "Is Snapchat Scrambling to Implement a Monetisation Plan to Avoid Collapse?", http://www.venturecapnews.com/vcn/is-snapchat-scrambling-to-implement-a-monetization-plan-to-avoid-collapse/, March 4th 2015.

[37]"Why brands must get to know instant messaging apps", op. cit..

[38]Frier Sarah and Picker Leslie, "Two Charts That Show How Fast Snapchat Is Growing", https://www.bloomberg.com/news/articles/2015-02-18/two-charts-that-show-how-fast-snapchat-is-growing, February 18th 2015.

[39]Arthur Charles, "Pinterest, Snapchat, BuzzFeed – here come tech's multibillion-dollar babies", http://uk.businessinsider.com/pinterest-snapchat-buzzfeed--here-come-techs-multibillion-dollar-babies-2015-3, March 22nd 2015.

[40]Edwards Jim, "Evan Spiegel Reveals His Business Plan For Snapchat, And It's Spam", http://www.businessinsider.in/Evan-Spiegel-Reveals-His-Business-Plan-For-Snapchat-And-Its-Spam/articleshow/44753059.cms, October 9th 2014.

[41]Frier Sarah, "Snapchat COO Emily White Leaving as It Builds Business Model", http://www.bloomberg.com/news/articles/2015-03-13/snapchat-coo-emily-white-leaving-amid-funding-revenue-plans, March 13th 2015.

look at it if you want to look at it, and you don't if you don't," Even Spiegel told the Wall Street Journal.[42]

An active Snapchat user received about 150 snaps each day. Snapchat tried its hand out at positioning video/photo ads between every 20–30 snaps that an average user received. Advertisers were indeed fascinated as it allowed them to touch base with teenagers, a very lucrative demographic for them.[43]

However, insiders revealed ads were not Snapchat's long term plan. The company's experiments with a slew of prospective monetizing avenues were all a part of a strategy to convince investors that Snapchat had the potential to make money. The primary plan was to make money through the conversion of the app into a 'platform'. Snapchat wished to monetize by selling services that users would be willing to pay for. In private, the vision was stated as 'Facebook platform done right'.[44] Analysts too endorsed the idea of a prospective 'platform' for utility services that could be integrated into Snapchat, somewhat like an 'app store'.[45]

Notably, the newest generation of internet users (teenagers) did not fancy the usage of the web, e-mail or Facebook. They preferred to connect through mobile apps such as WhatsApp, Instragram and Snapchat – precisely why a 'platform' seemed like a good bet. Hence, Snapchat planned to release an API (application programming interface) on the lines of the offerings of Facebook and Twitter. It would enable features of third party applications on Snapchat. Analysts suggested another prospective income source for Snapchat could be the sale of 'virtual goods'. Messaging companies made money by charging users small amounts of money for copyrighted emoticons, ranging from 50 cents-$1 dollar or an entire range for $5.[46]

Snapchat's funding continued as it raised over £300 million on the eve of 2015 that escalated the app's valuation to about $12.8 billion. Interestingly, that was double the valuation of Marks and Spencer. As per market statistics, Snapchat had 200 million registered global users.[47] It aimed to raise another $500 million which was likely to further propel its valuation to $16-$19 billion, while its total funding would stand at $1 billion.[48] According to Forbes' estimation, Spiegel and Murphy both had ownership of at least 15 per cent in Snapchat.[49] In that case each would be worth $2.85 billion if the company's valuation touched $19 billion.[50] TechCrunch cited Snapchat would succeed in raising $500 million as it had already received funding from Alibaba ($200 million) and Saudi Arabia's Prince Alwaleed Bin Talal.[51]

Evan Spiegel remained tight-lipped. "We are famous for not talking about the future", he said.[52] However, a Goldman Sachs executive stated that Snapchat's growth was 'abnormal'.[53]

Snapchat's fundraising spree: a billion-dollar bubble?

It may be noted that the in the era of modern technology, the worst crisis ever faced was that during the dotcom phase. The swift expansion of the internet brought along with it the mushrooming of one company after another, all of which wished to capitalise

---

[42]Goldstein Phil, "Facebook won't monetize WhatsApp now, but Snapchat is planning to debut ads", http://www.fiercewireless.com/wireless/facebook-won-t-monetize-whatsapp-now-but-snapchat-planning-to-debut-ads, October 9th 2014.

[43]Blodget Henry, "How Snapchat Plans To Make Money", http://www.businessinsider.com/how-snapchat-will-make-money-2013-11?IR=T, November 20th 2013.

[44]Dotan Tom, "Snapchat's Real Business Plan is Platform, Not Ads", https://www.theinformation.com/Snapchats-Real-Business-Plan-is-Platform-Not-Ads, October 14th 2014.

[45]"Pinterest, Snapchat, BuzzFeed – here come tech's multibillion-dollar babies", op. cit..

[46]"How Snapchat Plans To Make Money", op. cit..

[47]Campbell Peter, "Loss-making photo messaging company Snapchat fuels technology bubble fears – after being valued at almost £13bn", http://www.thisismoney.co.uk/money/markets/article-2893710/Loss-making-photo-messaging-company-Snapchat-fuels-technology-bubble-fears-valued-13bn.html, January 1st 2015.

[48]Kosoff Maya, "How to use Snapchat (the surprisingly complicated photo app) if you're old", http://www.businessinsider.in/How-to-use-Snapchat-the-surprisingly-complicated-photo-app-if-youre-old/articleshow/46294233.cms, February 19th 2015.

[49]"The World's Billionaires", op. cit..

[50]Neate Rupert, "Snapchat values itself at $19bn", http://www.theguardian.com/technology/2015/feb/17/snapchat-values-self-19bn, February 17th 2015.

[51]Strong Rebecca, "If This Really Is A Tech Bubble, Snapchat May Be The Best Proof", http://bostinno.streetwise.co/2015/03/12/snapchat-valuation-snapchat-worth-15b-with-new-funding/, March 12th 2015.

[52]"Snapchat 'worth $15bn' after Alibaba investment", http://www.theguardian.com/technology/2015/mar/12/snapchat-worth-15bn-after-alibaba-invesment, March 12th 2015.

[53]Shontell Alyson, "Snapchat Is A Lot Bigger Than People Realise And It Could Be Nearing 200 Million Active Users", http://www.businessinsider.com.au/snapchats-monthly-active-users-may-be-nearing-200-million-2014-12, January 3rd 2015.

EXHIBIT VI   THE BILLION-DOLLAR CLUB

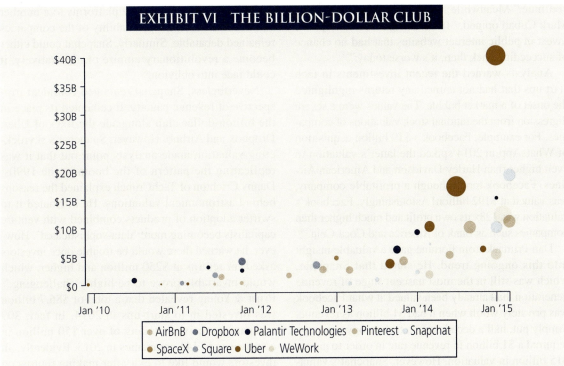

Source: Tiku Nitasha, "Look at how quickly the values of multi-billion-dollar startups have multiplied", http://www.theverge.com/2015/2/20/8075053/look-at-how-quickly-the-value-of-multi-billion-dollar-startups-have, February 20th 2015.

on the boom within the industry. The bubble burst and many a company sank without a trace. Certain analysts claimed that the technology market had yet again encompassed in a bubble. They warned that sustainability would be difficult especially in the mobile application market.[54] "A million dollars isn't cool. You know what's cool? A *billion* dollars." The now infamous line from the film "The Social Network" was being embraced by a multitude of ambitious apps[55] (Exhibit VI).

It would be interesting to know how valuations worked in Silicon Valley in this new era. Notably, the valuations were usually made-up. Investors concurred to high valuations for certain capable startups. The funding aided the company in employment and in marking a foothold in the market. The funding would come through only with the guarantee that

the investor shall get returns as soon as the company was sold or once it became public. However, Randy Komisar of Kleiner Perkins said, "These big numbers almost don't matter. Those numbers are just a middling shot at a valuation, and then it's adjusted later." In Snapchat's case, relying on public company metrics was not plausible due to the fact that it was yet to generate real revenue.[56]

Interestingly, in order to depict the rarity of billion-dollar companies, the term "unicorns" was coined. However, the new buzzword was "decacorn", attributed to companies over $10 billion. Ironically it was a word after a creature that was non-existent.[57] Todd Dagres from Spark Capital said, "We are definitely in a bubble. This one is not as bad as 2000. If you wake up in a room full of unicorns, you are dreaming and you can't expect the dream to

[54]"Are we teetering on the edge of an app bubble?", http://www.dailydot.com/via/tech-industry-app-bubble/, November 1st 2014.

[55]"Pinterest, Snapchat, BuzzFeed – here come tech's multibillion-dollar babies", op. cit..

[56]Frier Sarah and Newcomer Eric, "The Fuzzy, Insane Math That's Creating So Many Billion-Dollar Tech Companies", https://www.bloomberg.com/news/articles/2015-03-17/the-fuzzy-insane-math-that-s-creating-so-many-billion-dollar-tech-companies, March 17th 2015.

[57]ibid..

continue." Meanwhile, owner of Dallas Mavericks, Mark Cuban opined, "If we thought it was stupid to invest in public internet websites that had no chance of succeeding back then, it's worse today."[58]

Analysts warned the recent investments in tech start ups that had not earned any returns highlighted the onset of a market bubble. The values were a severe digression from the rational stock valuations of companies. For example, Facebook's $19 billion acquisition of WhatsApp in 2014 spiked the latter's valuation to even higher than Harley Davidson and American Airlines. Facebook too, although a profitable company, was valued at $192 billion! Astonishingly, Facebook's valuation was 128x its own profit and much higher than companies such as Bank of America and Coca-Cola.[59]

Dan Primack from Fortune gave a valuable insight into this ongoing trend. He stated that Snapchat, which was still in the most nascent stage of revenue generation, had already been valued at what Facebook was privately worth when it had $1 billion as revenue. Simply put, half a decade ago, a technology company required a $1 billion in revenue rate in order to garner $15 billion in valuation. However, Snapchat's valuation ascended to $15 billion two years earlier (within four years) in comparison to Facebook (within six years). Thus, it seemed evident that in current market conditions, a company did not require even $50 million in revenue to touch such valuations. Only a large user base was needed. However, the sudden surge in the number of entrants into the 'billion-dollar startup club' (78 in 2015 as against 49 in 2014) raised serious concerns regarding over-valuation.[60]

However, Snapchat maintained it was not concerned about valuation. The company stated, "The valuation of our business and our capital requirements are the least exciting aspects of supporting the Snapchat community." While Snapchat seemed to have the capability to make money due to high growth and user engagement, there remained questions on its value, primarily due to the quick pace at which technology trends had been changing. Silicon Valley had surely given able platforms to a number of firms. However, the profitability of the companies remained debatable. Similarly, Snapchat could either become a revolutionary empire or alternatively, it could fade into oblivion.[61]

Nevertheless, Snapchat remained confident irrespective of revenue paucity. It cemented its place in the billion-dollar club alongside the likes of Uber, Dropbox and Airbnb. However, Snapchat's skyrocketing valuation made analysts point out that it was replicating the pattern of the boom in the 1990s. Danny Crichton of TechCrunch explained the reasons behind astronomical valuations. He attributed it to swifter adoption of products combined with venture capitalists becoming more 'data-sophisticated'. However, he warned there would be trouble once investors asked for returns at $250 million and higher, which would invariably prove to be highly challenging.[62] Ernst & Young revealed that a total of $86.7 billion was invested in to start-ups in 2014. In fact, 309 companies received funding of over $50 million in comparison to 141 companies in 2013. Evidently, all investors would like to exit after making returns on the money invested into the companies.[63]

While Snapchat had no profits or revenue, at the same time, it was also exhausting £20 million per year. It had to fund research as well as make staff payments. Further, Snapchat was spending £2 million every month towards legal fees to cater to the several lawsuits it was embroiled in. Emerging technology companies raising large amounts of funding was no surprise. Snapchat had in fact raised money even from Yahoo and Alibaba, while it turned down takeover offers from Facebook and Google. However, the latest advances in funding sprees made technology analyst Rob Enderle comment about the Facebook-WhatsApp deal, "The deal reminds me so much of some of the strategies of the dotcom era, it's actually giving me chills."[64]

Analysts claimed the challenge would come at the point where Snapchat would have to make a transition from a revenue-less enterprise to a profitable

[58]"This VC says we have entered a tech bubble", http://www.crainsnewyork.com/article/20150305/TECHNOLOGY/150309919/this-vc-says-we-have-entered-a-tech-bubble, March 5th 2015.

[59]Chamorro-Premuzic Tomas, "Snapchat's $10bn valuation: inside the billion-dollar bubble", http://www.theguardian.com/media-network/media-network-blog/2014/sep/04/snapchat-message-valuation-technology-bubble, September 4th 2014.

[60]"If This Really Is A Tech Bubble, Snapchat May Be The Best Proof", op. cit..

[61]Aziz John, "Is Snapchat really worth $10 billion?", http://theweek.com/speedreads/447341/snapchat-really-worth-10-billion, August 27th 2014.

[62]Watts William, "Snapchat worth $10 billion? Start-up valuations stoke bubble fears", http://blogs.marketwatch.com/thetell/2014/08/27/snapchat-worth-10-billion-start-up-valuations-stoke-bubble-fears/, August 27th 2014.

[63]McGee Suzanne, "Snapchat and the 'T-Rex' venture: It all sounds like dotcom bubble 2.0", http://www.businessinsider.com/snapchat-and-the-t-rex-venture-it-all-sounds-like-dotcom-bubble-20-2015-2?IR=T, February 22nd 2015.

[64]"Loss-making photo messaging company Snapchat fuels technology bubble fears – after being valued at almost £13bn", op. cit..

one. There was a constant decline in advertising rates which were likely to come in the way of monetising. And even though Snapchat had been scouting ways to become profitable,[65] analysts were yet to fathom its $10 billion valuation. They questioned whether a company as young as Snapchat could truly be valued higher than established brands such as the Hyatt Hotels and even Burger King.[66] Jim Edwards of Business Insider felt the technology sector was indeed overvalued. He felt funding was increasing due to competitive interest rates. Due to this, all kinds of companies received funding, broken business models and zero revenue notwithstanding. This, he said, would prove to be problematic once the large investments failed in translating into requisite profits.[67]

In fact, Brian Blau, research director at Gartner said, "You have to think about where the revenue could come from to support that value, and it's hard to see that today because the company hasn't shown any user interfaces that are revenue-generating." Further, even if Snapchat won in competition against services such as Taptalk and Bolt, it still required to spruce up in data collection. As Bob Pearson of W20 Group pointed out, "I don't have a lot of clients asking about Snapchat, because how do you gather data? How do you get market research? How do you integrate it with search and e-commerce?" Evidently, Snapchat was yet to prove it was worthy of all the hype.[68]

Nevertheless, companies such as Facebook and Twitter had several engagement metrics such as 'Retweets', 'Followers' and 'Likes', in addition to elaborate reports that were handy to advertisers.

However, the only thing Snapchat users had were notifications about their snaps being viewed.[69] Notably, Snapchat would delete its most valuable data. And, even though advertisers could target potential clients on the basis of words in messages, it would require Snapchat to retain those messages. That would devalue the inherent quality that made the app a rage – the disappearance of messages.[70]

"The grand experiment that we are running right now is: Can you cram hundreds of millions of dollars into 80 or 90 different private companies and have it end up well? For some, I think it will end badly," said Bill Gurley, Partner at venture capital firm Benchmark.[71] Further, he also held the opinion that investors were distributing such large amounts of money that they could be compared to IPO's. However, he warned, "This replaces the IPO – but not all these companies are IPO-level candidates. Would you hand a teenager $200,000?" A great worry seemed to be that tech companies were predominantly concentrated in particular regions, which meant, if the bubble were to burst, Silicon Valley would be hit hard. Olivier Giovannoni, researcher at the Levy Economics Institute said, "If investors see a wave of earning reports that are below expectation and a movement of panic about the future of these technology firms sets in, the bubble may burst."[72]

In fact, Marc Andreessen, an investor in Airbnb and Foursquare opined, "When the market turns, and it will turn, we will find out who has been swimming without trunks on: many high burn rate companies will vaporise."[73]

---

[65]Sherman Erik, "Moneywatch: Is Snapchat really worth $10 billion?", http://www.cbsnews.com/news/is-snapchat-really-worth-10-billion/, August 27th 2014.

[66]O'Toole James, "Could Snapchat really be worth $10 billion?", http://money.cnn.com/2014/08/01/technology/social/snapchat-10-billion/, August 1st 2014.

[67]Arthur Charles, "Do high valuations for Uber, Snapchat and BuzzFeed herald a new tech bubble?", http://www.theguardian.com/technology/2014/aug/17/technology-bubble-uber-snapchat-buzzfeed, August 17th 2014.

[68]"Could Snapchat really be worth $10 billion?", op. cit..

[69]Fiegerman Seth, "Brands Are Coming To Snapchat. Will Users Disappear?", http://mashable.com/2014/01/09/snapchat-brands-future/, January 10th 2014

[70]"Even Spiegel Reveals His Business Plan For Snapchat, And It's Spam", op. cit..

[71]"Snapchat, Pinterest, Lyft: Investors create a billion-dollar-startup boom", op. cit..

[72]Rozenberg Norman, "Are we in a tech bubble worse than the '90's boom?", http://www.techpageone.co.uk/downtime-uk-en/tech-bubble-worse-90s-boom/.

[73]Thomas Daniel, "Silicon Valley's billion dollar start-up failures", http://www.bbc.com/news/business-29653830, October 24th 2014.

'Compassion vs competitiveness' dilemma at Novo Nordisk

By Debapratim Purkayastha

"*How to strike the right balance between business and global health? Again, we were challenged by stakeholders...,*"[1] quipped Lise Kingo (Kingo), Executive vice president and chief of staffs, Novo Nordisk. The Danish pharmaceutical company, Novo Nordisk, had gained global recognition as a champion of sustainability for a number of sustainability related initiatives that it had taken over the years.

Over the years, Novo Nordisk's business grew substantially and it emerged as a leader in the global insulin[a] market. In the new millennium, Novo Nordisk's new sustainability strategy placed global health at the center of its sustainability initiatives. According to Novo Nordisk's vision statement, the company strove to find the right balance between compassion and competitiveness. From then on, Novo Nordisk started selling its products at a subsidized price in some of the poorest countries around the world. Despite all the efforts that it took to protect the interests of all its stakeholders, in 2010, Novo Nordisk was severely criticized by patients and NGOs when it stopped selling its drugs in Greece when the crisis ridden government there ordered a 25 per cent cut in the prices of all medicines sold in the country. Novo Nordisk was accused of putting profits above corporate social responsibility. Though the issue was settled later with the resumption of the sale of all its products in Greece, the episode badly dented the image of Novo Nordisk as a company with a focus on sustainability.

Faced with increased regulatory scrutiny and stakeholder activism, the challenge before the senior management of Novo Nordisk was how to tackle the issue and embed sustainability further in the company. According to them, as a global healthcare company focused on diabetes treatment, they had to often face the compassion vs competitiveness dilemma and the conflicting demands of multiple stakeholders. This also led some analysts to question the readiness of the company to face the new challenging environment. The question before Novo Nordisk's CEO Lars Rebien Sorensen (Sorensen), Kingo and other members of the senior management team was, as a global healthcare company, how could Novo Nordisk strike the right balance between compassion and competitiveness?

About Novo Nordisk

Novo Nordisk, a global leader in insulin, was formed in 1989 through the merger of two Danish companies, Novo Industri A/S and Nordisk Gentofte A/S. Novo Nordisk's roots can be traced to Nordisk Insulinlaboratorium, which was founded in 1923 to produce insulin. Novo Nordisk pioneered many breakthroughs in diabetes treatment.

After the merger, Novo Nordisk A/S rolled out many innovations like prefilled insulin syringes, oral treatment syringes, rapid acting insulin, etc.. By the late 1990s, it started focusing more on international markets. In 2000, Novo Nordisk A/S was demerged into three separate companies – Novo Nordisk A/S (Novo Nordisk), Novozymes A/S, and Novo A/S. After the demerger of Novo Nordisk A/S, Novo A/S was made the holding company of the Novo Group and was wholly-owned by the Novo Nordisk Foundation. Majority shares in both Novo Nordisk and Novozymes A/S were transferred to Novo A/S. While Novo Nordisk continued to focus on pharmaceutical products and services, the enzymes business of Novo Nordisk A/S was transferred to Novozymes A/S. In the decade that followed the demerger, Novo Nordisk expanded its business across the globe and emerged as a leading pharmaceutical company in the area of diabetes care. By 2011, Novo Nordisk employed 32,000 people in 75 countries and marketed its products in 190 countries. For the financial year 2011,

[a] Insulin is used for the treatment of some forms of diabetes. Patients with Type 1 diabetes depend on external insulin (most commonly injected subcutaneously) for their survival because the hormone is no longer produced by their body. Certain patients with Type 2 diabetes may also require insulin if other medications fail to control blood glucose levels adequately.

EXHIBIT I   INCOME STATEMENT OF NOVO NORDISK (2007–2011)

(in DKK Million)	2011	2010	2009	2008	2007
Sales	66,346	60,776	51,078	45,553	41,831
Cost of goods sold	12,589	11,680	10,438	10,109	9,793
Gross profit	53,757	49,096	40,640	35,444	32,038
Sales and distribution costs	19,004	18,195	15,420	12,866	12,371
Research and development costs	9,628	9,602	7,864	7,856	8,538
Including costs related to discontinuation of all pulmonary diabetes projects	–	–	–	325	1,325
Administrative expenses	3,245	3,065	2,764	2,635	2,508
Licence fees and other operating income, net	494	657	341	286	321
Operating profit	22,374	18,891	14,933	12,373	8,942
Share of profit/(loss) of associated companies, net of tax	(4)	1,070	(55)	(124)	1,233
Financial income	514	382	375	1,127	1,303
Financial expenses	959	2,057	1,265	681	507
Profit before income taxes	21,925	18,286	13,988	12,695	10,971
Income taxes	4,828	3,883	3,220	3,050	2,449
Net profit for the year	17,097	14,403	10,768	9,645	8,522

Source: Novo Nordisk Annual Report, 2011; Novo Nordisk Annual Report, 2009.

Novo Nordisk's revenue was Danish Kroner[b] (DKK) 66.35 billion (See Exhibit I for the income statement of Novo Nordisk from 2007 to 2011; Exhibit II for Key Yearly statistics and Exhibit III for key quarterly statistics).[2] It was placed 18th on the list of top pharmaceutical companies of the world by revenue.

Novo Nordisk's primary market was insulin which was estimated to be US$15.4 billion in 2010, according to IMS Health. The market for insulin had quadrupled over the last decade and Novo Nordisk was the leader with US$7.1 billion in sales of insulin in 2010. The company faced tough competition in this market from the US-based Eli Lilly and France-based Sanofi-Aventis. The trio made up a *"hard-to-penetrate oligopoly"* in the insulin market.[3] Novo Nordisk also faced local competitors in some countries such as China and India.

Novo Nordisk and sustainability

Responding to stakeholder tension

In the late 1960s, Novo Nordisk faced severe stakeholder criticism for the first time in its history. During the 1960s, Novo Nordisk's predecessor, Novo, had started producing enzymes through new production processes of fermentation of microorganisms. These new processes used genetically engineered microorganisms and led to the evolution of a successful new product line of enzymes. These enzymes became important ingredients in many products like detergents. Environmental organizations and activists alleged that the use of enzymes developed by Novo could cause skin allergies in people who came into contact with them. They also alleged that the dust generated during the production process of the enzymes could have serious effects on the health of Novo Nordisk's workers. An activist called Ralph Nader started a movement against the laundry industry in the US which created a stir both in the US and around the world. The sales of Novo fell dramatically between 1970 and 1971 due to the concerns raised by activists. Nearly 700 employees of Novo lost their jobs due to the crisis. Novo responded swiftly and developed dust-free enzymes which did not pose any risk to its consumers or employees. The sales of Novo's enzyme products rose soon and enzyme production became an important part of Novo's business

[b] The Danish Kroner is the official currency of Denmark, Greenland, and the Faroe Islands. As of September 2012, one Danish Kroner was approximately equal to 0.1696 US$.

EXHIBIT II KEY STATISTICS FOR NOVO NORDISK (2007–2011)

(in € million)	2007	2008	2009	2010	2011
Sales	5,614	6,109	6,860	8,161	8,905
Sales by business segment:					
Modern insulins (insulin analogues)	1,880	2,323	2,883	3,572	3,861
Human insulins	1,687	1,583	1,520	1,588	1,448
VictozaR	–	–	12	311	804
Protein-related products	235	247	265	297	310
Oral antidiabetic products (OAD)	288	321	356	369	346
Diabetes care total	4,090	4,474	5,036	6,137	6,769
NovoSeven	788	858	950	1,078	1,120
Norditropin	471	518	591	645	677
Other products	41	43	49	47	63
Hormone replacement therapy	224	216	234	254	276
Biopharmaceuticals total	1,524	1,635	1,824	2,024	2,136
Sales by geographical segment:					
North America	1,845	2,032	2,454	3,170	3,569
Europe	2,194	2,309	2,356	2,506	2,573
International Operations	708	777	917	1,119	1,257
Japan & Korea	596	638	657	760	835
Region China	271	353	476	606	671

Adapted from Novo Nordisk's Annual Reports.

in many countries like Denmark, the US, and Japan. This episode made Novo realize the importance of keeping the interests of all stakeholders in mind. Since then, Novo, and subsequently, Novo Nordisk, focused on producing products which did not affect the health of consumers and which were environmental friendly.

Novo Nordisk took its first significant step toward sustainable development in 1989 when it conducted its first environmental management review. It took this significant step as an element of its proactive stakeholder strategy in the days when environmental reporting was not compulsory for companies like Novo Nordisk. From 1991, it started organizing visits of its laboratories and production facilities for representatives of NGOs as part of its stakeholder engagement strategy.[4] In 1992, some people from Novo Nordisk attended the United Nations Conference on Environment and Development (UNCED) Earth Summit organized in Rio de Janeiro. The summit made Novo

Nordisk realize the importance of environmental protection and led to its reinforcing its commitment to sustainable development. Commenting on the impact that the 1992 Earth Summit had on Novo Nordisk's commitment to sustainable development, Kingo said, *"We came back from Rio with a better understanding of how huge an agenda environmental protection was, how many stakeholders were involved, and that many other companies were taking an interest. It was a real eye-opener."*[5] In 1994, Novo Nordisk published its first environmental report. It became the first company in Denmark and one of the first in the world to publish an environmental report.[6] The report contained details regarding resource consumption, emissions in its production processes, and the use of animals in its experiments. The environmental report was followed by Novo Nordisk's first social report in 1998. And since 1999, Novo Nordisk started publishing annual reports on sustainability which integrated its environmental, social, and economic concerns.

EXHIBIT III KEY QUARTERLY STATISTICS FOR NOVO NORDISK (2009–2011)

(in DKK million)	2009				2010				2011			
	Q1	Q2	Q3	Q4	Q1	Q2	Q3	Q4	Q1	Q2	Q3	Q4
Sales	12,498	13,001	12,517	13,062	13,674	15,394	15,584	16,124	15,693	16,001	16,532	18,120
Sales by business segment:												
Modern insulins (insulin analogues)	4,990	5,414	5,353	5,714	5,862	6,792	6,820	7,127	6,705	6,972	7,232	7,856
Human insulins	3,004	2,879	2,747	2,685	2,773	3,099	2,963	2,992	2,655	2,642	2,698	2,790
VictozaR	–	–	28	59	370	296	700	951	1,098	1,250	1,547	2,096
Protein-related products	484	492	491	510	503	583	567	561	639	527	574	569
Oral antidiabetic products (OAD)	691	675	650	636	645	704	736	666	711	653	562	649
Diabetes care total	9,169	9,460	9,269	9,604	10,153	11,474	11,786	12,297	11,808	12,044	12,613	13,960
NovoSeven	1,805	1,874	1,651	1,742	1,914	2,155	1,965	1,996	2,032	2,140	2,044	2,131
Norditropin	1,034	1,122	1,074	1,171	1,083	1,245	1,233	1,242	1,252	1,180	1,275	1,340
Other products	81	110	83	85	81	70	83	107	109	124	99	141
Hormone replacement therapy	409	435	440	460	443	450	517	482	492	513	501	548
Biopharmaceuticals total	3,329	3,541	3,248	3,458	3,521	3,920	3,798	3,827	3,885	3,957	3,919	4,160
Sales by geographical segment:												
North America	4,532	4,710	4,527	4,510	5,221	5,988	6,114	6,286	6,035	6,165	6,804	7,582
Europe	4,195	4,375	4,376	4,594	4,432	4,671	4,675	4,886	4,595	4,847	4,728	4,998
International Operations	1,684	1,807	1,571	1,773	1,835	2,213	2,127	2,160	2,203	2,415	2,286	2,463
Japan & Korea	1,164	1,255	1,167	1,302	1,156	1,439	1,454	1,611	1,484	1,423	1,539	1,777
Region China	923	854	876	883	1,030	1,083	1,214	1,181	1,376	1,151	1,175	1,300

Adapted from Novo Nordisk's Annual Reports.

Novo Nordisk way of management

In 1996, Novo Nordisk introduced the 'Novo Nordisk Way of Management' (NNWM) to serve as an overall guidance system to reach its strategic goals. NNWM served as the value-based governance framework for the company. It described how people at Novo Nordisk put values into action and defined the principles to be followed by the company while doing business.[7] NNWM offered a broad framework of guidelines to the employees and covered Novo Nordisk's activities beyond the products and manufacturing operations. The central part of the goal was to integrate and implement the various sustainable business practices of Novo Nordisk. NNWM consisted of three parts, viz. the vision, the charter, and global company policies (See Exhibit IV for Novo Nordisk Way of Management).

The vision of NNWM set the direction for Novo Nordisk. It expressed what goals Novo Nordisk was striving to achieve, how the company wanted to achieve its goals, and how the company was guided by its values to strike the right balance between its commercial interests and acting as a responsible business. The Charter explained the company's

values, commitments, fundamentals, and follow-up methods. The values highlighted the company's commitment to the Triple Bottom Line and sustainable development. Fundamentals were a set of 11 management principles to ensure it stayed focused on its business objectives, customers, compliance, collaboration, and sharing of better practices, and quality mindset.[8] Follow-up methods provided a systematic documentation of the performance of all material areas of Novo Nordisk. The global company policies set global standards for its managers and gave operational guidelines on 13 specific areas related to its business.

In addition to coming out with an innovative way of managing its activities through NNWM, Novo Nordisk took steps to ensure that the entire organization understood and followed it. It had developed a methodology consisting of three elements: facilitators, sustainability reporting, and balanced scorecard. The facilitators were a group of 16 senior professionals at Novo Nordisk's holding company Novo A/S. These facilitators traveled in pairs and visited all the business units and levels of the whole organization once every three years. They performed a well-planned and structured

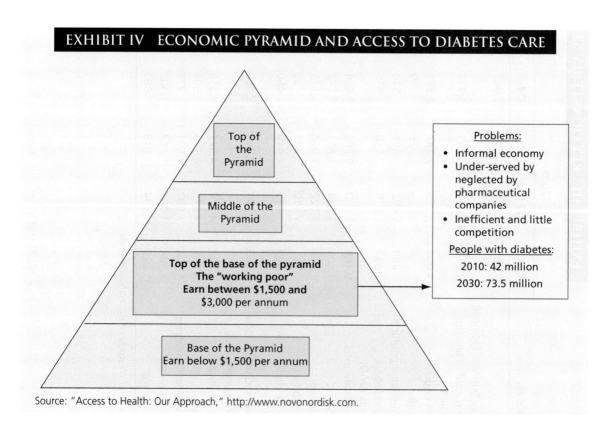

EXHIBIT IV   ECONOMIC PYRAMID AND ACCESS TO DIABETES CARE

Source: "Access to Health: Our Approach," http://www.novonordisk.com.

assessment of the implementation of NNWM within a project or unit. The main objective of the facilitation process was to develop agreed upon actions for improvement. The facilitation process consisted of three stages. The first was the pre-facilitation stage in which the scope of the facilitation process was identified. The second stage was the facilitation itself. In this stage, the facilitators met the unit and project members and arrived at an agreement regarding improvements to be made wherever non-compliance had been identified. In the third stage, the post-facilitation process was conducted in which the facilitator followed up on the progress and reports to the management team about the achievements and shortfalls, if any, from the facilitation process.

Sustainability reporting was used to ensure that sustainability became a part of Novo Nordisk's corporate culture. Novo Nordisk had come a long way in sustainability reporting since it first published its environmental report in 1994. From 1999, it started publishing annual reports on sustainability which integrated its environmental, social, and economic concerns. The reports documented Novo Nordisk's ambitions, initiatives, goals, and results related to environmental and social responsibility. From the year 2004, information on sustainability was integrated with its financial results and published as part of its annual report.

In 1996, Novo Nordisk started using the balanced scorecard. It was initially used as a finance initiative. Later, it began to be used to integrate the company's sustainability approach with all its business processes. One balanced scorecard was prepared for the organization as a whole and separate balanced scorecards were prepared at the executive VP, senior VP, and in some cases even at the sub-unit levels (e.g. a single factory). Novo Nordisk's balanced scorecard had a total of 24 objectives under four headings: customers and society, finance, business processes, and people and organization.

Triple bottom line

In 1997, just one year after it introduced NNWM, Novo Nordisk started another important initiative to help it evolve as an organization practicing sustainable business practices. It introduced the Triple Bottom Line (TBL) philosophy to maximize value to all its stakeholders. The TBL philosophy focused on

operating in a way that was financially, environmentally, and socially responsible. The main objective behind the introduction of the TBL philosophy was to balance its short-term profitability with the long-term interests of the society. In this way, Novo Nordisk aimed at optimizing its business performance in all the societies in which it had its operations. It made the TBL philosophy its top strategic priority as it believed from the beginning that being socially responsible, environmentally sound, and economically viable made good business sense. Simply put, the TBL philosophy was the way Novo Nordisk chose to interpret its commitment toward sustainable development. Commenting on the importance of the TBL philosophy, Sorensen, said, *"The main foundation for Novo Nordisk is the triple bottom line because that is what's protecting our license to operate. That begs and obliges everybody in the company not only to see that we become a good business – that's the financial bottom line – but that we do so in a way that is socially and environmentally responsible."*[9] Over time, Novo Nordisk embedded the TBL philosophy into the corporate governance structures, management tools, performance appraisal and reward schemes of its employees.[10]

Novo Nordisk formulated its first environmental policy in the early 1980s and made a lot of progress in its environmental performance from then on.[11] On the environmental front, Novo Nordisk committed itself to continuously improving its environmental performance. It aimed to achieve this by setting itself stiff targets and by merging environmental and bioethical considerations into its regular business activities. Novo Nordisk started to have an open dialogue with all its stakeholders regarding its commitment toward the conservation of the environment. It also initiated annual reporting of its progress in environmental performance. It supported the United Nations Convention on Biological Diversity[c] to emphasize its focus on sustainability. On the social front too, Novo Nordisk started to set high objectives and to integrate social, human rights, and health and safety considerations into its daily business activities. Like environment reporting, Novo Nordisk annually reported on its social performance. It offered a patient assistance program for those who did not have private health insurance and who did not get any medical assistance from their governments.[12] Under the program, patients were required to apply to Novo Nordisk for medical

---

[c] United Nations Convention on Biological Diversity is an international legal treaty with the three main goals of conserving biological diversity, sustainable use of its components, and equal sharing of benefits arising from genetic resources. The treaty was opened for signature at the Earth Summit in Rio de Janeiro in June 1992 and came into force in December 1993.

assistance and medicines were supplied free of cost to applicants who qualified. Under the TBL philosophy, Novo Nordisk also committed itself to focusing on continuously improving its financial performance by reaching new milestones in growth and to creating value for its shareholders. It complied with international reporting standards of its financial statements.

In 2004, Novo Nordisk updated its Articles of Association and bylaws and included in the objectives the words 'the company seeks to conduct its business in a way that is financially, environmentally, and socially responsible'.[13]

Patent rights vs patient's right

After the demerger of Novo Nordisk A/S, a new sustainability strategy focusing on the healthcare business of Novo Nordisk was developed. This new strategy marked the shift to Novo Nordisk's next stage of sustainability endeavors. According to the new strategy, Novo Nordisk would have global health at the heart of its sustainability initiatives.[14] Despite its focus on sustainability for such a long period of time, Novo Nordisk faced new criticism from activists and NGOs regarding its business practices after the demerger.

In 2001, a consortium of 38 pharmaceutical companies along with Novo Nordisk filed a lawsuit against the South African government for violating their intellectual property rights, mostly in relation to the medicines used in the treatment of AIDS. The South African government sought to deliver generic versions of some AIDS medicines in South Africa by using a 1997 law called the Medicines and Related Substances Control Amendment Act (MRSCA) which the consortium opposed.[15]

Generic medicines (or generics) are either copies or the basic form of a proprietary medicine (or "brand-named") medicines produced by research-based pharmaceutical companies. For example, Lipitor is the brand name owned and patented by Pfizer, Inc. It contains the molecule Atorvastatin. Any other drugs with the same composition made by other companies are called generics. Generic versions are priced much lower than the proprietary drug, and generally, when a drug loses patent protection, generic competition forces a drop in price of up to 80 per cent within one year. Research-based pharmaceutical companies such as Novo Nordisk develop proprietary medicines that are novel and obtain patent protection ranging from 15–20 years. These companies try to zealously safeguard their

intellectual property rights and extend it as long as possible. Usually the price of a drug put it out of reach of people with low income, particularly those living in developing countries. Activist charged that research-based pharmaceutical companies over-price their medicines and keep it away from the reach of people who needed it the most. Pharmaceutical companies, on the other hand, contended that if generic versions are allowed companies would have little incentive for innovation. They claimed that to bring a new drug into the market it took more than US$800 million and they had little time to recoup their expenses and earn profits. Moreover, they argued that the drug development process takes time (more than 15 years) and is fraught with many risks. Many of the drugs being investigated do not make it to the market as they fail at different stages of drug development process. Activists scoff at the US$800 million figure and argue that many of the drugs were discovered and developed with a significant investment of government and other public funds. They also harped on the ethics of keeping a medicine away from a patient who would die without treatment.

MRSCA allowed the South African government to procure the cheapest possible medicines for all purposes from both international and local suppliers. The law also gave the South African health ministry the right to override pharmaceutical patents whenever the government thought that public health was at stake. While the Agreement on Trade Related Aspects of Intellectual Property Rights[d] (TRIPS) allowed countries to produce generic versions of patented medicines in cases of national emergencies like the AIDS epidemic, the consortium members felt that MRSCA gave the South African government the right to infringe the patent rights of any pharmaceutical product even if there were no national emergencies.

Novo Nordisk and members of the consortium faced heavy criticism from activists and NGOs regarding the case. The consortium members were accused of giving more importance to profits than to the health of poor people living in the developing countries. The case also caused public concern in Denmark regarding the business practices of Novo Nordisk.

Sustainable pricing

Novo Nordisk was quick to react to the criticism and it started a dialogue with the NGOs. It came out with a new policy to increase its presence in developing

---

[d] The Agreement on Trade Related Aspects of Intellectual Property Rights (TRIPS) is an international agreement related to intellectual property administered by the World Trade Organization (WTO).

countries and to develop new medicines for combating diseases there. It adopted a new pricing policy under which it started supplying insulin to the 50 poorest countries designated by the United Nations at 20 per cent of the average price in North America, Europe, and Japan. Through this new pricing policy called sustainable pricing, Novo Nordisk ensured that it did not earn any profits on its sales in poor countries. It also ensured that the research and development costs for Novo Nordisk's drugs sold in poor countries were borne by its consumers in the developed world. In effect, Novo Nordisk started cross subsidizing its products sold in developing countries. The company had often stated in its communications to investors that the company had been able to steadily increase prices of its insulin products particularly in North America which resulted in higher profit margins of these products.

Commenting on the new pricing policy, Sorensen said, *"We advocate sustainable pricing. That means we will not levy a profit on these products sold to the developing world, but rather the costs of our research and development will be borne by the developed world. Of course, this hinges on a psychological contract – namely that developed countries are willing to subsidize developing countries."*[16] The case with the South African government was settled out of court with the consortium withdrawing the case and the South African government agreeing to honor its obligations under TRIPS. In 2001, Novo Nordisk established the World Diabetes Foundation with the objective of improving diabetes care in poor countries through education, capacity building, distribution, procurement of essential drugs, and monitoring of the care given.

The case filed against the South African government and the subsequent developments made Novo Nordisk think more about its role in increasing access to healthcare and essential medicines. It also highlighted the need to engage in continuous dialogue with its stakeholders and monitor their concerns. In 2001, Novo Nordisk started the Triple Bottom Line reporting (TBL). TBL reporting focused on the progress made by the company in its commitments toward the economy, society, and environment according to its TBL philosophy (See Exhibit VII for the Novo Nordisk learning curve). Novo Nordisk became a signatory to the United Nations Global Compact[e], a global platform for promoting good corporate principles and learning, in the year 2001.

Growing sustainably with a focus on global health

By the year 2005, Novo Nordisk had significantly grown its business around the world. In 2005, it emerged as the leader in the US insulin market for the first time since it had entered the market. By 2011, it got 40.1 per cent of its sales from North America and 28.9 per cent of its sales from Europe. Novo Nordisk also emerged as the leading producer of insulin in the world with a market share of 50 per cent.[17]

Over the years, Novo Nordisk changed the focus of its sustainability policy from the environment to health, safety, bioethics, and integrating issues related to social responsibility. In 2005, Novo Nordisk launched its 'Changing Diabetes' brand platform. Diabetes is a major cause of death with more than 80 per cent of diabetes deaths occurring in low- and middle-income countries. An estimated 347 million people worldwide suffered from diabetes and according to World Health Organization's estimates diabetes would be the seventh leading cause of death in 2030.[18] The Changing Diabetes initiative aimed at bringing about a change in the lives of people suffering from diabetes through several other ways apart from treatment like science, humanitarian outreach, education, and public policy.[19] The ultimate goal of the Changing Diabetes program initiative was to defeat the diabetes pandemic.[20] Novo Nordisk took up ambitious challenges to tackle diabetes globally which was not an easy task considering that a huge percentage of the people afflicted were from developing countries and were less able to afford the treatment (See Exhibit IV for economic pyramid and access to diabetes care, and Exhibit V for Novo Nordisk's ambitions in improving access to diabetes care up to 2015).

Manufacturing insulin was an energy intensive process. Therefore, another important area which Novo Nordisk focused on as part of its sustainable development initiatives was climate change. Novo Nordisk set long-term environmental targets in three areas, viz. CO_2 emissions from energy consumption, energy consumption, and water consumption. Over the years the company was able to make significant progress in these areas. To inculcate a sense of responsibility among its employees toward all the stakeholders, it started training its employees in Business Ethics. By 2011, nearly 99 per cent of the

---

[e] The United Nations Global Compact is a United Nations initiative to encourage businesses around the world to adopt policies which are sustainable and socially responsible and report on their implementation.

EXHIBIT V   NOVO NORDISK'S AMBITIONS IN IMPROVING ACCESS TO DIABETES CARE UP TO 2015

Ambition	Focus area	Approach
Availability of treatment: Develop quality-assured diabetes treatment for all	Make insulin available to people with diabetes globally	■ Ensure continued supply of human insulin to low- and middle-income countries for at least another 10 years ■ Support research to document consequences and implications of diabetes ■ Share discoveries and knowledge that could have application in infectious-disease areas
	Address distribution challenges at the base of pyramid (BOP)	Explore business models for people living with diabetes in the BOP segment
	Facilitate technology transfer	Work with public and private institutions in low- and middle-income countries to enhance healthcare provision to the benefit of all patients
Accessibility of healthcare: Work with partners to make diabetes care more accessible for those in need	Support strengthening of health-care systems	Contribute to the training of healthcare professionals
	Improve accessibility to insulin in remote areas	Reach out to people with diabetes in remote areas
	Improve access to diabetes care for women and children	■ Establish partnerships for the improved delivery of care to children with diabetes in low- and middle-income countries ■ Establish partnership-based interventions as part of a long-term commitment to the improvement of health of women and the next generation
Affordability of treatment: Work to improve affordability of treatment for patients, particularly in resource-poor settings	Improve funding for diabetes healthcare	Continue our annual endowment to the World Diabetes Foundation
	Improve affordability of insulin	■ Continue our differential pricing policy and provide insulin to the governments in least developed countries at maximum 20 US cents per patient per day ■ Work in partnership with governments and other organizations to increase the number of patients we reach in low- and middle-income countries

Ambition	Focus area	Approach
Quality for patients: Quality assurance in diabetes treatment for patients	Conduct responsible and ethical clinical trials	▪ Support and ensure full transparency of clinical-trial activities and results ▪ Ensure that all persons enrolled in Novo Nordisk-sponsored research are protected by the same rights, high ethical standards and regulations, regardless of geography
	Work for safe medicines	▪ Maintain one global quality standard ▪ Work against counterfeiting ▪ Work with ministries of health and distributors to establish effective supply chains for delivery of insulin
	Empower people with diabetes to achieve better health and quality of life	▪ Continue research into the understanding of patient needs, including the psycho-social barriers against adhering to treatment regimens ▪ Continue engaging with stakeholders, with a view to identifying areas for improvement in the management of diabetes ▪ Support healthcare professionals to deliver better quality healthcare, building on principles of patient involvement and ongoing support

Source: "Access to Health: Our Approach," http://www.novonordisk.com.

relevant employees had been trained in business ethics. Novo Nordisk also started to have diverse senior management teams to understand the needs of various sections of the society properly. By 2011, 62 per cent of its senior management teams had members from diverse backgrounds. It set a target of having 100 per cent of senior management teams from diverse backgrounds by the year 2014. *"We set out to show that it is possible to be a profitable and a responsible business. We strengthened our approach to sustainability, now revolving around the right to health and the need for improved diabetes care,* *actions to combat climate change, ethical business behavior, human rights, and how we can connect the dots, "*[21] said Kingo.

Novo Nordisk got several recognitions for its progress in sustainable development. It was named as the 'most sustainable company in the world' by the business magazine Corporate Knights[f] for the year 2012. Another Novo group company, Novozymes A/S was also ranked fourth in the list of global 100 most sustainable corporations in the world. Commenting on the recognition, Kingo said, *"This is a wonderful recognition of our Triple Bottom Line*

[f] Corporate Knights is a magazine focused on capitalism. The magazine focuses on how markets and companies can promote social and ecological sustainability.

EXHIBIT VI NOVO NORDISK'S COMMUNICATION TO PATIENTS AND DOCTORS REGARDING ITS DECISION

Important information about possible shortages of products (translated).

Novo Nordisk (Hellas Ltd) regretfully informs you of the temporary suspension of distribution of medicinal products in Greece. This will soon lead to shortages of certain products manufactured by Novo Nordisk.

Novo Nordisk came to this decision as a result of the adoption of new prices which required an average reduction of around 25 per cent. This is an unprecedented depreciation of its products and as prices in Greece are already among the lowest in Europe, Novo Nordisk cannot viably operate on a loss.

Novo Nordisk is confident that both the price schedule and the way it is implemented is unlawful to Greek and European legislation and will soon be withdrawn. For this purpose we are proceeding to take legal action.

Novo Nordisk is committed to providing treatment options for patients in Greece and is already moving to find a solution to this difficult situation, as the Greek branch (Greek Novo Nordisk Office) to become sustainable and to normalize the supply (of insulin on the) market. Unfortunately, we can not prevent this development from leading to a shortage of the following products in the Greek market:

1 ACTRAPID PENFILL INJ.SOL.FL 5x3ml x 100iu/ml

2 GLUCAGEN HYPOKIT

3 LEVEMIR INJ.SOL. 100u/ml FLEXPEN x 5PF. PEN x 3ml 100u/ml FLEXPEN x 5PF.PEN x 3ml

4 MIXTARD 30 PENFILL INJ.SOL FL 5x3ML

5 MIXTARD 40 PENFILL INJ.SOL FL 5x3ML

6 MIXTARD 50 PENFILL INJ.SOL FL 5x3ML

7 NORDITROPIN SIMPLEXX 5mg

8 NOVOMIX 30 FLEXPEN 5 PF PENx3mlx100u/ml

9 NOVONORM 0,5 mg 120TABS

10 NOVONORM 1,0 mg 120TABS

11 NOVONORM 2,0 mg 120TABS

12 NOVORAPID 1 VIAL 10ml x100u/ml

13 NOVORAPID INJ.SOL FLEXPEN 5 PENx3mlx100u/ml

14 PROTAPHANE PENFILL INJ.SOL.FL 5x3ml

15 TRISEQUENS FC tabl BT X 28

16 VAGIFEM 25pg 16. VAGIFEM 25 mg

17 VICTOZA IN.SO.PFP 6 mg/ml 2 PF PENS x 3ml

We (Novo Nordisk) advise patients using the above products to communicate with their physician to discuss alternative therapeutic options.

Health professionals whose patients are prescribed the above products are encouraged to inform their patients about this situation and discuss possible alternative treatment options.

Until further notice, and because of concerns for people with diabetes who use our products in Greece, Novo Nordisk will have unobstructed human insulin in vials of 10 ml at reduced prices set by the new price schedule.

- ACTRAPID
- PROTAPHANE
- MIXTARD 30

We understand the anxiety and truly regret the inconvenience caused to people with diabetes who use these products.

approach and a clear indication that Novo Nordisk is poised for long-term business success. But most importantly, it is an encouragement to continue to find new ways of growing our business in a way that is profitable, responsible, and valuable for patients, employees, and society. "[22] Novo Nordisk was listed in the 2010/2011 Dow Jones Sustainability Indices[g] (DJSI).[23] It was also awarded a gold class rating[h] by Sustainability Asset Management[i] (SAM) in its Sustainability Yearbook 2011 in recognition of its integrated reporting, stakeholder engagement, and its consistent high sustainability performance.[24]

[g] Dow Jones Sustainability indexers are a group of indexes which evaluate the world's leading companies in their sustainability practices.
[h] To qualify for the Gold Class distinction, a company's Dow Jones Sustainability Indexes score needs to be within the 5 per cent of the respective sector leader's score.
[i] Sustainable Asset Management, headquartered in Zurich, Switzerland is an international investment company with exclusive focus on sustainability investments.

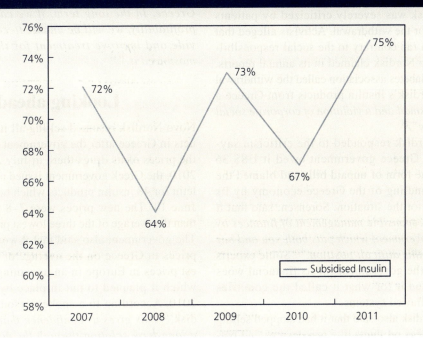

EXHIBIT VII   PERCENTAGE OF POOREST COUNTRIES WHERE NOVO NORDISK SOLD SUBSIDIZED INSULIN

Pricing issue in greece

Novo Nordisk had its presence in Greece through its wholly-owned subsidiary Novo Nordisk Hellas Ltd. The subsidiary was engaged in sales and marketing of the company's products in Greece where the company maintained prices that were among the lowest in Europe. The market generated annual sales of €48 million (US$58 million) in 2009.[25] In the end of May 2010, Novo Nordisk stopped selling some of its insulin products in Greece. These products included the 'modern insulins' (insulin analogues that were sold under the brands Novolog and Levemir) and other costly pen devices.

The decision to do so came after the government there decreed a 25 per cent cut in the prices of all the medicines sold effective May 3, 2010, due to the debt crisis[j] that the country was facing. Novo Nordisk said that the price cut would result in a loss to its

business. Commenting on the decision to stop selling its products in Greece, Mike Rulisthe, spokesperson of Novo Nordisk, said, *"A 25 per cent price cut does not allow us to run a sustainable business in Greece, and this is what we have told the government."*[26] Novo Nordisk further said that a price cut in Greece would lead to similar moves in other countries where the prices in Greece were taken as reference prices which would result in serious financial consequences for the company. At the time of their withdrawal from the market, more than 50,000 people suffering from Type 1 diabetes in Greece used Novo Nordisk's insulin products for their survival.

During the same time other European governments were also having a hard look at high drug prices in a bid to tackle runaway budget deficits. Countries including Germany, Italy and Spain had proposed or enacted price reductions or adopted other cost-control measures for various drugs.[27]

---

[j] The Greek government-debt crisis was a financial crisis that the Greek government was facing since 2009 due to many factors like high government debt and rising fiscal deficit. The Greek government had implemented several austerity measures to deal with the crisis.

Putting profits above corporate social responsibility?

Novo Nordisk was severely criticized by patients and NGOs for the withdrawal. Activists alleged that this decision ran contrary to the social responsibility that Novo Nordisk claimed in its annual reports. The Greek diabetes association called the withdrawal of Novo Nordisk's insulin products from Greece a *"brutal blackmail and a violation of corporate social responsibility".*[28]

Novo Nordisk responded to the criticism saying that the Greece government owed it US$ 36 million in the form of unpaid bills and blamed the improper handling of the Greece economy by its government for the situation. Sorensen, said that it was *"the irresponsible management of finances by the Greek government which puts both you and our company in this difficult position."*[29] Some experts too blamed the government for its financial woes and lambasted it for what it called the countries corrupt and flawed systems.

Novo Nordisk also said that it had stopped selling only its modern products like pen devices and patented insulin products in Greece. It said it continued to sell its other insulin product, Novolinbiosynthetic human insulin.[30] It also continued to provide another of its cheaper insulin products, Glucagen insulin, free of charge in Greece.[31] Novo Nordisk claimed that these products were sufficient for the survival of any person suffering from diabetes.

Activists alleged that Novo Nordisk was trying to shift the responsibility on to the Greece government while focusing only on profits. The company had been steadily raising the price of its insulin products for six consecutive quarters across the world which resulted in a higher profit margin for its insulin products, they said. Pavlos Panayotacos a Greek economist whose 10-year-old daughter suffered from diabetes, said in a letter to Novo Nordisk, *"As an economist I realize the importance of making a profit, but healthcare is more than just the bottom line. As you well may know, Greece is presently in dire economic and social straits, and you could not have acted in a more insensitive manner at a more inopportune time."*[32]

Explaining the challenging dilemma the company faced, CEO Sorensen said, *"This year, as several governments in Europe mandated price cuts to address their economic problems, we faced dilemmas between operating profitably and continuing to serve people who rely on our products... In a situation like this, there is a major dilemma for a company like ours. The proposed price reductions for patented products would not have allowed us to continue running a profitable business in Greece. In the long term, if we cannot maintain profitability, we will be unable to continue to provide and improve treatment for the people who most need it."*[33]

Looking ahead

Novo Nordisk resumed selling all its insulin products in Greece after the government agreed to raise the prices of its drugs there in July 2010.[34] In June 2010, the Greek government issued a new price bulletin for 48 insulin products which became effective June 14. The new prices were 7–8 per cent lower than the average of the three lowest prices in Europe. The government also said that it would base future prices in Greece on the average of the three lowest prices in Europe in an upcoming price decree, which it planned to put in place by September 1, 2010. According to a spokesperson of Novo Nordisk, *"This gives us confidence that we will reach a long-term solution through the dialogue we will be having with the government about the decree... To ensure that people with diabetes in Greece can continue to have access to our most modern insulin products, we have therefore accepted the new temporary prices."*[35] But, the new prices were still 10 per cent less than what they had been before the controversy erupted.

By the year 2011, Novo Nordisk was selling its insulin products at a subsidized price in 75 per cent of the least developed countries. And, it had a long-term target of making its cheaper insulin products available in 100 per cent of the least developed countries. However, despite the resumption of the sales of its products in Greece, the controversy regarding the Greek price cut was seen by many analysts as a big public relations disaster for Novo Nordisk. They said that the episode had dented its image as a champion of sustainable development. Some analysts raised questions on the readiness of the company to face the new challenging environment marked by increased regulatory scrutiny and stakeholder activism that companies around the world were facing in their operations. Even the senior management team at Novo Nordisk considered it a key challenge that they were facing particularly while operating in developing countries. In their words: *"Even though our core business philosophy requires us to make a difference where we can, there are significant dilemmas involved for us as a company. What role should we assume in developing countries? How can we develop new sustainable business models? How will our investors respond to such business models? How do we avoid creating unhealthy dependencies between us and our project partners?*[36]

End notes

[1]"20 Years in the Business of Sustainability," www.novonordisk.com, 2012.

[2]Novo Nordisk Annual Report, 2011.

[3]Robert Langreth, "Novo Nordisk's Medical Miracle," http://www.forbes.com/forbes/2011/0228/features-lars-sorensen-novo-nordisk-medical-miracle.html, February 9, 2011.

[4]"20 Years in the Business of Sustainability," www.novonordisk.com, 2012.

[5]Ibid.

[6]"Milestones in Novo Nordisk's History," www.novonordisk.com.

[7]"Novo Nordisk Way of Management," www.novonordisk.com.

[8]Ibid.

[9]Marc Gunther, "Novo Nordisk," www.corporateknights.com.

[10]"Triple Bottom Line," http://annualreport2008.novonordisk.com.

[11]"Case Study Collection: Novo Nordisk's Approach," www.partners-inprojectgreen.com.

[12]"Our Triple Bottom Line," www.novonordisk-us.com.

[13]Susanne Stormer, "Story: How Novo Nordisk's Corporate DNA – "to act responsibly" – Drives Innovation," www.managementexchange.com, April 30, 2012.

[14]"20 Years in the Business of Sustainability," https://www.novonordisk.com/content/dam/Denmark/HQ/Sustainability/documents/20-years-anniversary.pdf, 2012.

[15]"Novo Nordisk TBL Report 2001," http://tbl2001.novonordisk.com.

[16]"Annual Review 2001," www.novonordisk.com.

[17]"Novo-Nordisk: Diabetes and Dollars," http://money.msn.com, April 5, 2012.

[18] www.who.int/mediacentre/factsheets/fs312/en/

[19]"Changing Diabetes," www.novonordisk.co.in.

[20]"About Changing Diabetes," www.novonordisk.com.

[21]"20 Years in the Business of Sustainability," www.novonordisk.com, 2012.

[22]"Novo Nordisk Tops Global List of 100 Most Sustainable Companies," www.novonordisk.com/sustainability/news.

[23]"Novo Nordisk in the Lead of the Dow Jones Sustainability Index," www.novonordisk.com.

[24]Jessi Copeland, "ReportAlert.Info-Novo Nordisk (CPH: NOVO.B) Publishes 2010 Annual Report," www.businessfightspoverty.org, February 21, 2012.

[25]"Novo Nordisk to Resume Modern Insulin Sales to Greece on Better Terms," www.thepharmaletter.com, June 15, 2010.

[26]"Novo Nordisk Rejects Greek Drug Price Cut," http://www.reuters.com, May 31, 2010.

[27]Gustav Sandstrom, "Novo Nordisk, Greece Reach Drug Deal," http://online.wsj.com, June 14, 2010.

[28]Malcolm Brabant, "Insulin Giant Pulls Medicine from Greece over Price Cut," www.bbc.co.uk/news/10189367, May 29, 2010.

[29]Ibid.

[30]"The Business of Diabetes: Is Novo Nordisk's Pullback from Greece Really a Greek Tragedy?" http://blog.sstrumello.com, June 2, 2010.

[31]Ed Silverman, "Novo Nordisk Pulls Insulin from Greece over Money," www.pharmalot.com, May 29, 2010.

[32]Ibid.

[33]Novo Nordisk Annual Report 2010.

[34]Ed Silverman, "Novo Nordisk to Supply Greece with Diabetes Drug," www.pharmalot.com, June 15, 2010.

[35]"Novo Nordisk to Resume Modern Insulin Sales to Greece on Better Terms," www.thepharmaletter.com, June 15, 2010.

[36]Novo Nordisk, "Access to Health: Our Approach," www.novonordisk.com, September 2011.

Amazon.com's business model and its evolution

By Syeda Maseeha Qumer and Debapratim Purkayastha

Cash flow.

In 2015, Seattle-based e-commerce giant Amazon.com, Inc.(Amazon) surprised investors by posting an unanticipated second quarterly profit in a row after struggling with profitability the previous year. In the third quarter ended September 30, 2015, Amazon's revenues increased by 20 per cent to US$23.2 billion, while net income was US$79 million, compared with a net loss of US$437 million in the corresponding quarter of the previous year. The revenue growth was attributed to the company's rapidly growing cloud-computing business, higher sales in North America, and initiatives to attract more customers. On the back of these unexpected quarterly results, Amazon shares surged, making it the most valuable retailer in the world surpassing Wal-Mart Stores Inc[1] as of July 2015[i] (See Exhibit I and II). *"They are showing investors that if they want to deliver profits, they can. Amazon is a dominant online retailer, well on its way to becoming one of the world's largest retailers,"*[ii] said Michael Pachter, analyst at Wedbush Securities Inc[2].

Launched as an online bookstore in 1995, Amazon quickly expanded beyond books to include all types of consumer goods. The company constantly innovated with its business model and moved from consumer electronics to cloud computing services and later into the technology business. Amazon's business model was built around low prices, a vast selection, fast and reliable delivery, and a convenient online customer experience. Besides offering customers a vast selection of products at low prices, Amazon also provided marketing and promotional services for third-party retailers and web services for developers. It was Amazon's relentless focus on value and selection along with innovations around shipping and handling cost reductions that had made it a leader in e-commerce, opined analysts.

Amazon reinvested much of its free cash flow in its growth. The company's strategy was to put long-term investment, market gains, and value creation ahead of short-term profits. Amazon constantly plowed cash back into the business and continued building new businesses in the hope of getting greater returns in the future. *Market development* Though the strategy helped the company in capturing a larger share of the e-commerce sector, it was consistently reporting losses. In the third quarter of 2014, Amazon spent about 12 per cent of its revenues on technology and content including new-product development and licensing for music and video streaming. That led to the biggest quarterly loss the company had suffered in 14 years. Despite the lack of profits, Amazon's shareholders backed the strategy of the CEO, Jeff Bezos, of being indifferent to short-term earnings in anticipation of future profits.

According to some critics, if the huge investments made by Amazon did not work out, investors' patience would finally run out and the company would be in trouble. They felt that Amazon had boundless ambition, but going forward, the company would have to be selective about where it invested in order to turn profitable. Moreover, some analysts felt that between price-match guarantees, free shipping, and plans to go multi-channel, other competitors were finally catching up with Amazon in the online retail game. Amazon would need to work harder and meet the expectations of its customers to maintain its dominance in the highly competitive online retail sector, they added. Some analysts raised questions like: How can Amazon keep its prices low as it grows? Is it time for the company to adjust its "growth now profits later" formula? Should it stop entering new categories and markets and instead focus on making profits? Will Amazon shareholders continue to be patient?

This case was written by Syeda Maseeha Qumer and Debapratim Purkayastha, IBS Hyderabad. It was compiled from published sources, and is intended to be used as a basis for class discussion rather than to illustrate either effective or ineffective handling of a management situation.

© 2016, IBS Center for Management Research

[1]Wal-Mart was the largest retailer in the world with annual net sales of US$482 billion in the fiscal year ended January 31, 2015. It operates a chain of retail stores in various formats worldwide.

[2]Wedbush Securities Inc is a US-based financial services and investment firm.

EXHIBIT I   MOST VALUABLE S&P 500 COMPANIES (AS OF JULY 2015)

Company	Industry	Market Value (US$ Billions)
Apple	Technology	713.7
Google	Technology	462.5
Microsoft	Technology	370.1
Berkshire Hathaway	Financials	350.2
Exxon Mobil	Oil & Gas	339.3
Wells Fargo	Financials	299.5
Johnson & Johnson	Healthcare	277.9
Facebook	Technology	268
General Electric	Industrials	264.6
Amazon.com	**Retail**	**262.7**
JPMorgan Chase	Financials	258.4
Walmart	**Retail**	**233.5**

Source: http://www.usatoday.com/story/money/markets/2015/07/23/amazon-worth-more-walmart/30588783/.

EXHIBIT II   MARKET VALUE OF AMAZON.COM

Source: http://qz.com/462605/amazon-is-now-bigger-than-walmart/.

Background note

Amazon was founded in June 1994 by Bezos. At that time, the internet was gaining popularity and was being considered as a potential business medium. To cash in on this trend, Bezos came up with the idea of selling books to a mass audience through the internet. In June 1995, Bezos launched his online bookstore, Amazon.com, named after the river Amazon. Amazon officially opened for business on July 6, 1995. At the beginning, Amazon's business model was based on the "sell all, carry few"

strategy wherein Amazon offered more than a million books online, though it actually stocked only about 2000. The remaining titles were sourced predominantly through drop shipping wherein Amazon forwarded customer orders to book publishers, who then shipped the products directly to the consumers. By the end of 1996, Amazon was offering about 2.5 million book titles. In 1996, the company's net sales were about US$15.7 million and it reported a net loss of US$5.7 million.

To attract customers, Amazon launched the Amazon Associates Program in July 1996. This was an affiliate marketing program which allowed smaller websites to sell books through a link to Amazon posted on their sites. These sites in turn received a commission of 15 per cent for any referred purchase and 5 per cent for any other purchase made by that consumer. The program was successful as was evident from the fact that about 800,000 associates had signed up with Amazon by September 2002. As the scale of Amazon's operations grew, its partners found it difficult to fulfill the company's quick shipment promise. As a result, Amazon began to build its own warehouses. In 1997, sales grew to US$147.8 million, an 838 per cent increase compared to the previous year. Customer accounts too increased from 180,000 to 1,510,000, a 738 per cent increase over the preceding year.

Over a period of time, Bezos realised that his earlier business model would not sustain the kind of growth he was looking for and decided to diversify. In 1998, Amazon expanded beyond books to include all sorts of shippable consumer goods such as electronics, videos, and toys and games. This led to a reversal of its business model from a "sell all, carry few" strategy to a "sell all, carry more" model. The focus shifted to a business model built around excellent delivery and efficient logistics. Orders began to land quickly at the doorsteps of customers. To attract third party sellers, Amazon launched a feature called 'Zshops' in September 1999, which enabled merchants and customers to set up online stores on Amazon for a monthly fee of US$10 and a transaction cost of 1–5 per cent of the value of the sale. Retailers and third party sellers registered on Zshop could sell their products on Amazon's site. Through Zshops, the company devised a new value proposition and by the end of 1999, Amazon's sales surpassed the billion dollar mark to reach US$1.6 billion.

In early 2000, Amazon started offering technology services through its e-commerce platform called Amazon Enterprise Solutions. It entered into partnerships with traditional brick-and-mortar retailers such as Borders, Inc.[3] (Borders) and Target Corporation[4] (Target) and offered them its e-commerce and customer service infrastructure to sell their products. In 2000, Amazon's stock price dropped by more than two-thirds and analysts began to criticize the retailer for entering into too many product categories and spreading itself too thin. That year, the company posted a net loss of US$1.4 billion and was on the verge of bankruptcy. To save his company from insolvency, Bezos decided

to cut costs and restructure its business model. Amazon stopped selling products which were not profitable. As a cost-cutting measure, in January 2001, the company laid off 1300 workers, closed down two warehouses, and shut down the customer-service center at Seattle.

Bezos devised a strategy wherein Amazon decided not to expand its own warehouse inventory but to sell products through the warehouses of other companies. It allowed companies to sell their products online through Amazon and charged them a part of the sales. The strategy proved to be a success and Amazon posted a net profit of US$5.1 million in the fourth quarter of 2002. By the end of 2002, Amazon had about 22.3 million registered users on its site.

In 2002, Amazon identified a new area of growth by launching Amazon Web Services (AWS), a platform of computing services offered online for other websites or client-side applications by Amazon. These web services provided developers access to Amazon's technology infrastructure that they could use to run virtually any type of business. Serving the needs of these developer customers required different processes, resources, and a new business model. Though at that point it was risky for Amazon to invest in new business models, Bezos went ahead and launched AWS. The move was largely successful as within five years of its launch, AWS had grown into one of the largest computing services platforms in the world.

In 2003, Amazon expanded its overseas business by launching international websites in Asia-Pacific and European countries. To deliver goods to end consumers at a reasonable price, Amazon employed a business model called the 'Online Retailers of Physical Goods' wherein it obtained products directly from the distributors rather than stocking all the goods in its warehouse. In 2005, Amazon launched a free shipping program for its customers called Amazon Prime[5], wherein customers received free two-day shipping on their purchases for a fee of US$79 per year. According to industry observers, the program disrupted the retail industry by enveloping more customers into its fold and enhancing customer loyalty.

In 2006, Amazon developed a new business model aimed at serving an entirely different customer – third-party sellers. The company offered fulfillment services to sellers through the Fulfillment by Amazon (FBA) program where merchants sent cartons of

---

[3]Borders, Inc is an international bookseller based in Ann Arbor, Michigan, US.

[4]Target Corporation is one of the leading discount retailers in the US.

[5]In 2005, Bezos launched Amazon Prime, a membership program which offered customers a free two-day shipping on their purchases for a fee of US$79 per year. In 2014, Amazon raised the annual fee for the Amazon Prime membership by US$20 to US$99, attributing the hike to an increase in fuel and shipping costs.

their products to Amazon's warehouses while Amazon took the orders online, shipped the products, answered queries, and processed returns. Amazon gained a competitive advantage by publicly sharing its business model with small enterprises through the FBA program, said industry observers. By opening up its business to other retailers who were basically competitors, Amazon transformed its business from direct sales to a sales and service model, bringing many sellers under one roof and receiving commissions from their sales.

In late 2007, Amazon set up its research division Lab126 and launched the Kindle e-book reader. The e-book reader was a business model not only alien to Amazon but also potentially disruptive to the publishing industry. To launch Kindle, Amazon had to become an original equipment manufacturer (OEM) and partner with independent publishers to generate content for the Kindle. The Kindle was successful in

the market and in the first year of its launch, Amazon sold an estimated 500,000 Kindles.

In July 2009, Amazon acquired US-based online shoe retailer Zappos for US$847 million in stock and cash. In 2012, it forayed into the world of designer fashion, selling high end clothing, shoes, handbags, and accessories through its website Amazon Fashion. In April 2014, the company entered into the highly competitive video and games streaming market by releasing Fire TV[6]. Three months later, in an ambitious strategic move, Amazon debuted in the crowded smartphone market with the launch of Fire Phone. In order to bring the company closer to customers, Amazon opened its first physical store on the campus of Purdue University in West Lafayette, Indiana, in February 2015.

In 2014, Amazon's net sales increased 20 per cent to US$88.99 billion, compared to US$74.45 billion in 2013. Net loss was US$241 million, compared with net income of US$274 million in 2013[iii] (See Exhibit III).

EXHIBIT III   AMAZON.COM CONSOLIDATED INCOME STATEMENT (US$ IN MILLIONS)

12 months ended	Dec 31, 2014	Dec 31, 2013	Dec 31, 2012	Dec 31, 2011	Dec 31, 2010
Net product sales	70,080	60,903	51,733	42,000	30,792
Net services sales	18,908	13,549	9,360	6,077	3,412
Net sales	**88,988**	**74,452**	**61,093**	**48,077**	**34,204**
Cost of sales	−62,752	−54,181	−45,971	−37,288	−26,561
Gross profit	**26,236**	**20,271**	**15,122**	**10,789**	**7,643**
Fulfillment	−10,766	−8,585	−6,419	−4,576	−2,898
Marketing	−4,332	−3,133	−2,408	−1,630	−1,029
Technology and content	−9,275	−6,565	−4,564	−2,909	−1,734
General and administrative	−1,552	−1,129	−896	−658	−470
Other operating income (expense), net	−133	−114	−159	−154	−106
Income from operations	**178**	**745**	**676**	**862**	**1,406**
Interest income	39	38	40	61	51
Interest expense	−210	−141	−92	−65	−39
Other income (expense), net	−118	−136	−80	76	79
Non-operating income (expense)	**−289**	**−239**	**−132**	**72**	**91**
Income (loss) before income taxes	**−111**	**506**	**544**	**934**	**1,497**
Provision for income taxes	−167	−161	−428	−291	−352
Equity-method investment activity, net of tax	37	−71	−155	−12	7
Net income (loss)	**−241**	**274**	**−39**	**631**	**1,152**

Source: Amazon.com Inc., Annual Reports.

[6]Fire TV is a set-top box that plugs into HDTV for easy and instant access to Netflix, Prime Instant Video, Hulu Plus, and low-cost video rentals.

Building and evolving the business model

Over the years, Amazon had disrupted the online retail industry and transformed itself from an e-commerce player to a powerful digital media platform focused on growth and innovation. It constantly reinvented its business model and found new ways to create value for its customers. According to analysts, Amazon's business model was innovative because it combined the company's online retail expertise with its ability to understand the needs of its customers. Amazon moved beyond books to foray into completely new product categories such as e-readers and enterprise cloud computing services (See Exhibit IV). When he founded the company, Bezos was aware that there would be a constant need to modify Amazon's business model to survive in the highly competitive online retail market. Since then, Amazon had been consistently evaluating and experimenting with its business model by developing expertise in e-commerce innovation and investing in multiple businesses to differentiate itself from brick-and-mortar retailers. According to industry experts,

Amazon was successful largely because of its exceptional growth in new markets and adjoining markets. *"Amazon at its roots is built to transform. When it finds opportunities to serve new customers, or existing customers in new ways, it conceives and builds new business models to exploit them. Amazon has the unique ability to launch and run entirely new types of businesses while simultaneously extracting value from existing businesses,"*[iv] said Mark W. Johnson co-founder of Innosight LLC.[v]

Amazon's business model was based on capturing growth through innovative disruption as the company believed that innovation was the key to sustainability. The four pillars of Amazon's business model were – low prices, wide selection, convenience, and customer service. The attributes offered by Amazon, like low prices, vast selection, fast and reliable delivery, and a convenient online shopping experience, complemented each other. According to William C. Taylor, one of the founding editors of Fast Company, *"These value propositions are interrelated, and they all relate to the Web. We have the widest selection because we operate in the virtual world. We discount because we have a lower cost structure than physical stores do*

EXHIBIT IV AMAZON'S BUSINESS MODEL EVOLUTION

Amazon - Product and Business Model Evolution

Source: http://www.more-with-mobile.com/2014/02/google-nest-case-of-deja-vu.html.

…. We also want to "redecorate the store" for every customer. We can let people describe their preferences, analyze their past buying patterns, and create a home page specifically for them. These interactive features are going to be incredibly powerful. And you can't reproduce them in the physical world. Physical stores have to be designed for the lowest common denominator."[vi]

Low prices

Amazon's value proposition of low prices ensured that customers got the best deal. Over the years, Amazon had proactively cut prices and offered free shipping in order to attract customers. Reportedly, the prices of goods sold by Amazon were up to 13 per cent lower than those prevailing in other online and brick-and-mortar stores.[vii] According to industry observers, Amazon was able to offer the lowest prices possible to customers by improving its operating efficiencies, leveraging fixed costs, and allowing third party sellers to sell their products on the Amazon website and it passed on the savings to its customers in the form of lower prices. Moreover, Amazon had lower overhead costs as it did not have to maintain physical stores. The sales tax advantage it derived in some places where it did not have a physical presence also helped the company in keeping its prices low and gave it a cost advantage over brick-and-mortar stores. Also, 'Frugality', one of the core values of Amazon, created significant savings for the company and allowed it to lower its prices (See Exhibit V).

But some analysts felt that Amazon might not be as price competitive as it was perceived to be. According to them, Amazon gauged the most popular items in the online retail market and adjusted the prices of those items that shoppers were most likely to price compare. It offered huge discounts

---

EXHIBIT V AMAZON CORE VALUES

1 Customer Obsession: We start with the customer and work backward.

Invest in Customers First

"If you do build a great experience, customers tell each other about that. Word of mouth is very powerful." – **Jeff Bezoz**

Customer Focus	Frugality	Innovation
"We start with the customer and work backward."	*"Amazon is spending money on things that matter to customers."*	*"I think frugality drives innovation, just like other constraints do."*
Following a bottom-up approach, every decision at Amazon is driven by the customer's needs.	Frugality is part of the company's DNA. Amazon is continually looking for ways to do things cost-effectively.	Amazon is always looking for simple solutions in order to provide lower prices to its customer.

Amazon created a trusted, informative and loyal relationship with its customers.

Source: http://www.smartinsights.com.

2 Innovation: If you don't listen to your customers you will fail. But if you only listen to your customers you will also fail.

3 Bias for Action: We live in a time of unheralded revolution and insurmountable opportunity – provided we make every minute count.

4 Ownership: Ownership matters when you're building a great company. Owners think long-term, plead passionately for their projects and ideas, and are empowered to respectfully challenge decisions.

5 High Hiring Bar: When making a hiring decision we ask ourselves: "Will I admire this person? Will I learn from this person? Is this person a superstar?"

6 Frugality: We spend money on things that really matter and believe that frugality breeds resourcefulness, self-sufficiency, and invention!

Source: www.amazon.com/Values-Careers-Homepage.

on its most popular products, while making profits on less popular ones. For instance, Amazon priced a best-selling router 20 per cent below its competitor's price; at the same time, it priced a less popular model 29 per cent more than its competitor. Offering consistently low prices on the best-selling items led to a perception among consumers that Amazon had the best prices overall, pointed out experts.

Wide selection

Amazon offered customers the biggest selection of products. As of 2015, the Amazon website had about 20 product categories including Books; Movies; Music; Video Games; Electronics & Computers; Home & Garden; Tools; Toys; Kids & Baby; Grocery; Health & Beauty; Clothing; Shoes & Jewelry; Health & Beauty; Sports & Outdoors; and Automotive & Industrial. By purchasing large volumes of products directly from manufacturers, distributors, and publishers, Amazon received discounts from them. Amazon also expanded into new categories like film streaming and cloud computing. In order to expand the selection of new products available on its websites, Amazon launched programs such as the Merchants@ programs and the Syndicated Stores program wherein it enabled small businesses to offer their products for sale on its websites.

Amazon adopted a three-pronged strategy in order to widen its selection of products. It set up special teams' category-wise at its stores which focused on buying products, working with vendors, and expanding customers' selection. In its seller business where third parties were involved, Amazon appointed category managers who decided on the categories where they wanted sellers and subsequently invited them to do business. In certain categories like home décor where Amazon wanted to further augment the selection, it offered Product Ads, an advertising program that allowed sellers to promote their products on Amazon's website by uploading their catalogue. These Product Ads offered Amazon customers an unprecedented selection in a wide range of categories.

Convenience

The third pillar of the Amazon business model was convenience. Amazon offered customers hassle free anytime, anywhere ordering by using modern technology and ensuring that any product could be delivered cheaply and reliably through a simple order process accessible from customers' homes or offices. Amazon's website was browser friendly with easy-to-use

functionality, fast and reliable delivery, timely customer service, feature rich content, and a trusted transaction environment. The website offered a selection of search tools to find books, music, videos, and other products based on keyword, title, subject, author, artist, publication date, etc.. Amazon's website was designed to keep the download time to a minimum.

Customers could easily find products on the Amazon website through an easy to search format and also benefited from features such as user-generated reviews, product recommendations, browsing options, gift certificates, book excerpts, etc.. According to analysts, the product ratings and reviews on the Amazon site made consumers informed, perceptive, and price sensitive. At Amazon, product availability was a priority and shipping was completed as close to the time of order as possible. The company ensured that a first time user became a habitual customer. For instance, if a book was unavailable, it would try to find a used copy. If the wrong product was shipped, the company made sure it accepted returns and provided the correct items as quickly as possible.

To conveniently ship items to customers, Amazon relied on an entirely automated order management system, closely linked to its suppliers and payment networks. The website offered customers up-to-date inventory availability information, estimated delivery date, and delivery shipment notifications. Customers could send products to multiple locations through different modes of payments such as credit card, wire transfer, or checks. They could check the shipping costs of each item before deciding on the mode of delivery. As soon as a customer placed an order, he/she received an e-mail confirming all the details. The customer's credit card was charged only when the order was actually shipped. Customers could track their orders in process and view the complete order history at any time using the "Your Account" feature on the company's website. Additionally, customers could cancel unshipped items, change delivery instructions and payment options, combine orders, edit gift options, and return items using the same feature. In case customers wanted to contact customer service representatives, they could do so by e-mail or phone.

Amazon operated customer service centers globally and fulfilled customer orders through the US and international fulfillment centers and warehouses. About 95 per cent of the products were shipped on the day they were ordered. Products were packed in strong boxes with extra padding to ensure they reached customers in good condition. According to observers, the entire Amazon delivery system was so quick and convenient that it generated plenty of word-of-mouth recommendations. *"Consumers love Amazon because they can find whatever they want, order it with a click of a button, and get in within 24 hours, sometimes less. That presents an immense logistical challenge, which Amazon has solved with a vast, super-efficient, and super-expensive distribution system. These investments are driving Amazon forward and preventing rivals from catching up. More than that, they make up the essence of what the firm is,"*[viii] said Adam Gale (Gale), Section editor at *Management Today.*

Customer service

Customer service, loyalty, and customer retention were the three important aspects of Amazon's service culture. Offering compelling value to its customers had been the core strategy of Amazon since its inception. The company seduced customers through low prices, prompt delivery, a growing array of services and products, and exemplary customer attention. Amazon primarily focused on three primary customer groups – consumer customers, seller customers, and developer customers.

The company believed that a good customer experience would lead to repeat buyers. It worked relentlessly to develop and innovate ways by which customers could be served and satisfied. It provided easy-to-use functionality, fast and reliable fulfillment, and timely customer service. Amazon built a personal bond with customers by helping them make decisions through recommendations of items based on past purchases, user reviews and ratings, and suggestions on complementary purchases. Some of the customer-friendly features available on Amazon were a personalized shopping experience for each customer, book discovery through the "Search inside the Book" option, convenient checkout using "1-Click Shopping,"[7] and several community features such as Listmania[8], Gold Box,[9] and Windowshop View[10].

Amazon offered customers a variety of products and services, some of which it did not make any money on, but were more valuable to the customer. The company invested heavily in building advanced technological infrastructure and spent huge sums of money on customer service and loyalty programs, even though it affected the operating margins of the company (See Exhibit VI). Some of the popular customer service initiatives launched by Amazon were Amazon Prime, Mayday[11], One Day Delivery service[12], Amazon Dash[13], Amazon Lockers[14], and Automatic refunds[15]. In December 2013, Amazon began working on a drone-based delivery system in the US called Amazon Prime Air to deliver packages at customers' doorsteps within 30 minutes in urban areas.

According to analysts, Amazon had built a deeply loyal customer base over the years. By the end of 2014, Amazon had a customer base of 270 million.[ix] Experts attributed the increase in customer base mainly to the company's user-friendly website and excellent customer service. *"Amazon's customer service has always been recognized and applauded as world-class. This is remarkable, especially since it is a purely online retailer. Amazon has hardly any 'human' interactions – often considered crucial perception points for increasing customer satisfaction and loyalty – in the value delivery chain. Many companies try to emulate Amazon and cost-effectively provide higher levels of service through leveraging technology. But Amazon does not only 'deliver customer service' – they build powerful partnerships with their customers,"*[x] said Ron Kaufman, a leading customer service consultant.

---

[7]This feature allows registered users to place an order by clicking just one button. It is not necessary for the customer to repeatedly fill in shipping and credit card information while buying products.

[8]The Listmania feature allows customers to share compiled lists of products with other consumers. These lists may be created using any product sold or offered on Amazon.

[9]Gold Box highlights special deals offered by Amazon by the day, hour, or availability.

[10]Windowshop View allows users on the website to browse products and view them in a 3D-simulated environment to get the feel of walking through an aisle.

[11]A new customer support feature called Mayday was launched on the company's new Kindle Fire HDX tablet in September 2013. The Mayday button enables customers to connect to a live customer support professional for help with any type of product query within 15 seconds, 24/7, free of charge.

[12]In November 2013, Amazon in collaboration with US Postal Service rolled out its One Day Delivery service to deliver packages to Amazon Prime members on Sunday. The service was initially started in Los Angeles and New York and later extended to Dallas, Houston, New Orleans, and Phoenix.

[13]In April 2014, Amazon launched a new device called named Amazon Dash that allowed customers to add groceries and household goods to their shopping lists using the AmazonFresh service. The Dash is a wand-like wireless device that includes a microphone and a barcode scanner, enabling customers to add items to an AmazonFresh shopping list by scanning a product's bar code or speaking its name.

[14]Amazon Locker is a self-service delivery location where customers can pick up and return their Amazon orders at their convenience with no additional costs. These lockers are available in a variety of locations throughout the US.

[15]In 2013, Amazon launched a new customer service tool called Automatic refunds where it proactively refunded customers if it felt that its customer experience was not up to the mark.

EXHIBIT VI   FEATURES OFFERED TO CONSUMER CUSTOMERS*

Customer Reviews	Reviews by registered users helped customers make informed purchase decisions.
Online reviews	Amazon let customers submit feedback on books and other products sold on the site. It was a popular online feature as consumers could share their thoughts with other readers.
Personalized recommendations	Amazon.com suggested books that registered users might like, based on their past purchases, customer ratings, and authors preferred.
Instant Order Update	It informed customers when they were about to purchase a product that they had already purchased.
Amazon Prime	This was a free two-day shipping for US$79/year with no minimum purchase required. It could be upgraded to one-day/overnight shipping for US$3.99.
FREE Super Saver Shipping	This feature provided all customers with free shipping on orders over US$25 though some conditions applied.
1-Click Ordering	This allowed registered users to place an order by clicking just one button. It was not necessary for the customer to repeatedly fill in shipping and credit card information while buying products.
Where's My Stuff	This allowed customers to track the status of their shipment.
Wish List	Customers could make lists of products they would like to purchase or get as gifts. The list could be saved for online viewing by others.
Amazon.com Anywhere	This allowed customers to shop on Amazon using their wireless devices.
Purchase Circles	This showed lists of the most popular items purchased by customers in a given zip code.
Look Inside the Book	The shopper could browse through pages of books using this feature.
Search Inside the Book	Customers could search the text inside books for specific keywords.
Amazon Dash	A new device, this allowed customers to add groceries and household goods to their shopping lists using the AmazonFresh service.
May Day	The Mayday button enabled customers to connect to a live customer support professional for help with any type of product query within 15 seconds, 24/7, free of charge.

*the list is not exhaustive.

Compiled from various sources.

Amazon's growth wheel

In 2001, Bezos and his employees outlined a virtuous cycle called the "Amazon Flywheel", which they believed powered their business. Bezos once invited well-known author and business consultant Jim Collins (Collins) to participate in Amazon's executive retreat in 2001 to discuss the company's future. As part of the discussions, Collins told Bezos and his executives that they had to decide what they were best at. Drawing on Collins's concept of a flywheel, Bezos and his executives drew their own virtuous circle placing customer experience at the core of Amazon's flywheel. Internally, it was referred to as Bezos' napkin diagram as he drew it on a napkin.

Customer experience was at the core of Amazon's flywheel. According to the concept, growth would be faster when more customers visited the site. By offering low prices, a wide selection, and a great

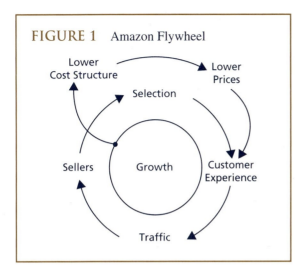

FIGURE 1   Amazon Flywheel

Kindle with a 35 per cent or 70 per cent royalty option. In addition, Amazon generated revenue from its cloud business by providing web technology infrastructure to developers and enterprises. It followed a high fixed costs and low marginal costs business model. According to Eugene Wei, a former Amazon employee, *"Amazon is a classic fixed cost business model, it uses the internet to get maximum leverage out of its fixed assets, and once it achieves enough volume of sales, the sum total of profits from all those sales exceed its fixed cost base, and it turns a profit."*[xii]

Amazon's strategy was to put long-term investment and value creation ahead of short-term profits. The company constantly reinvested profits in its business and made investment decisions based on long-term market leadership considerations rather than short-term profitability. Amazon spent significantly on future expansion, and according to Bezos, the company was still in 'Day One' of its growth. In a letter to shareholders in 1997, Bezos wrote, *"Long-term growth is what Amazon is about. Its focus is on years and decades, not quarters. It believes that if it has increased market leadership, it can get better deals on the goods it sells, and then increase its margins. That results in profits. This value will be a direct result of our ability to extend and solidify our current market leadership position. Market leadership can translate directly to higher revenue, higher profitability, greater capital velocity, and correspondingly stronger returns on invested capital."*[xiii]

Amazon adopted a profitless business model as it invested its free cash flow back into its business by expanding its operations and investing in new technology and customer service initiatives. Experts said that though Amazon generated profits on almost all transactions, it posted losses in some fiscal quarters due to significant investments in building new products, establishing warehouses, implementing and managing logistic systems, and offering free shipping. Amazon had spent about US$14 billion on building 50 new warehouses since 2010. In 2012, Amazon acquired Kiva Systems Inc. (Kiva) a maker of robots that moved items around warehouses, for US$775 million. In August 2014, it acquired Twitch Interactive, Inc. (Twitch), a videogame streaming company, for about US$970 million. On the product front, in

customer experience, Amazon was able to drive traffic (customers) and increase sales, which in turn attracted third party sellers and accelerated the wheel. By partnering with the best third party sellers, Amazon was able to offer a wide selection of products that added to economies of scale and allowed the company to benefit from a lower cost structure. This led to improvement in operating efficiencies and the savings were passed on to its customers in the form of lower prices and free shipping, which in turn attracted more customers (See Figure 1). When any part of this wheel was fed, it accelerated the loop and the cycle continued.

According to experts, Amazon focused on innovation, selection, price, and customer service that continuously improved the customer experience and resulted in market share gains. Commenting on the company's growth, Patrick O'Brien, a lead analyst at Verdict Retail,[16] said, *"They've managed to get top of mind on every category without doing anything creative – Amazon's 20 years isn't a marketing story, it's all about availability and scale."*[xi]

Growth now, profits later

Amazon generated revenues by selling millions of products to customers through its retail website and by charging third party sellers who sold products on Amazon's website. It also served as a platform for independent publishers to publish books on

---

[16]Verdict Retail is a UK-based retail consultancy.

2014, Amazon released its first smartphone, the Amazon Fire, and a video streaming box, Fire TV. It also spent US$1.3 billion on its online streaming service Prime Instant Video. Critics alleged that Amazon sacrificed profit margins to undercut competition and gain customer loyalty. For instance, to gain a competitive advantage in the tablet market, Amazon sold the Kindle e-reader at cost, and lost about US$11 per customer on its free shipping program, Amazon Prime, they said.

Despite growing sales, Amazon reported a loss in 2014. Apparently, a surge in spending on new product development and music and video licensing had resulted in a net loss of US$437 million in the third quarter of 2014, the company's largest quarterly loss in 14 years.[xiv] In 2014, Amazon reported three losing quarters out of four and posted a yearly loss of US$240 million against a net gain of US$274 million in 2013[xv] (See Exhibit VII and VIII). When Matthew Yglesias, a blogger from Slate[xvi] described the company as "a charitable organization being run by elements of the investment community for the benefit of consumers,"[xvii] Bezos took issue with this in a letter to shareholders and said that Amazon was a business whose strategy was to make its customers as happy as possible.

Resources and processes that support the strategy

Technology

Amazon was one of the most innovative companies in the US. From the beginning, it had been at the forefront of innovation, adding and refining technology and changing the way customers shopped. On invention being a second nature at Amazon, Bezos said, *"Invention comes in many forms and at many scales. The most radical and transformative of inventions are often those that empower others to unleash their creativity – to pursue their dreams. That's a big part of what's going on with Amazon Web Services, Fulfillment by Amazon, and Kindle Direct Publishing. With AWS, FBA, and KDP, we are creating powerful self-service platforms that allow thousands of people to boldly experiment and accomplish things that would otherwise be impossible or impractical. These innovative, large-scale platforms are not zero-sum – they create win-win situations and create significant value for developers, entrepreneurs, customers, authors, and readers."[xviii]*

Some of the company's technological advances pioneered by Amazon included 1-Click, Recommendations, Reviews, Wish List, Autorip[17], Kindle, Amazon Web Services, Amazon Cloud Drive[18],

EXHIBIT VII   AMAZON QUARTERLY RESULTS

Amazon's boom quarter

Amazon.com defied expectations in the second quarter, showing a strong sales gain and a surprise profit.

Source: www.seattletimes.com/business/amazon/amazon-crushes-quarterly-expectations-shares-soar-2/.

---

[17]Amazon AutoRip gives customers free MP3 versions of CDs and vinyl music they purchase from Amazon. More than 350,000 albums are available for AutoRip.

[18]Amazon Cloud Drive lets customers securely store their digital files on the Amazon cloud and access them anywhere using the Cloud Drive desktop client or any web browser.

EXHIBIT VIII

Amazon – Net Sales

(in US$ million)

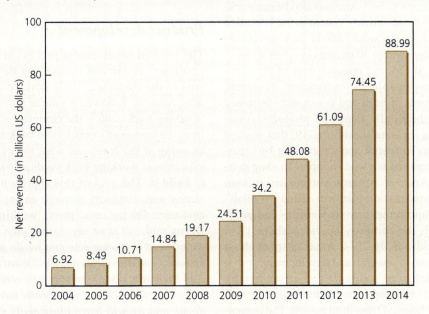

Amazon – Net Income

(in US$ billion)

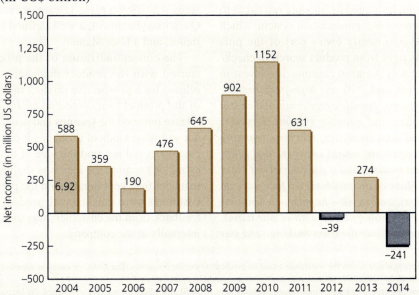

Source: www.statista.com.

Random Stow[19], The SLAM (Scan, Label, Apply, Manifest)[20], Amazon Storyteller[21], Amazon Studios[22], KDP[23], Fire TV, Fire Phone, and 3D printing[24]. Amazon had also come up with innovations that improved the customer experience such as May Day, Amazon Dash, and Amazon Echo[25]. Amazon also began working on a drone-based delivery system in the US called Amazon Prime Air that would deliver packages at customers' doorsteps within 30 minutes in urban areas.

Amazon Lab126, the research arm of the company, was responsible for innovation, research, and development of high-end consumer electronic devices like the Kindle family of products. Amazon also has a separate subsidiary, A9, that worked on innovations in search and advertising by creating mobile apps that allowed shoppers to shop conveniently on Amazon. Amazon also created its own internal experimentation platform called "Weblab" to evaluate improvements to its websites and products. In 2013, the company operated about 1976 Weblabs worldwide. In 2014, Amazon spent about US$8.72 billion on research and development.

Amazon achieved a competitive advantage by developing its own proprietary technologies, as well as technology licensed from third parties. The company's transaction-processing systems handled millions of items, multiple shipping addresses, and shipment methods. Amazon leveraged its big data resources to upgrade its customer recommendation system, which was integrated into nearly every part of the purchasing process right from product search to checkout. Explaining why Amazon continued to invest in technology, Bezos said, *"We use high-performance transactions systems, complex rendering and object caching, workflow and queuing systems, business intelligence and data analytics, machine learning and pattern recognition, neural networks and probabilistic decision making, and a wide variety of other techniques .... Many of the problems we face have no textbook solutions, and so we – happily – invent new approaches. ... Technology infuses all of our teams, all of our processes, our decision-making, and our approach to innovation in each of our businesses. It is deeply integrated into everything we do. Invention is in our DNA and technology is the fundamental tool we wield to evolve and improve every aspect of the experience we provide our customers."*[xix]

Product development ✓

The product development process at Amazon was customer-centric and focused on the value delivered to the customer. While developing new products, Amazon followed a unique philosophy called 'working backward' – the company always thought from the customer's perspective back to the product, knowing at the front-end what the customer could expect, and working backwards allowing the team to build it. The goal of this approach was to drive clarity and simplicity through an explicit focus on customer. On the concept of "working backward" Bezos said, *"It is to say, rather than ask what are we good at and what else can we do with that skill, you ask, who are our customers? What do they need? And then you say we're going to give that to them regardless of whether we currently have the skills to do so, and we will learn those skills no matter how long it takes."*[xx]

The 'working backward' concept involved four steps – writing a press release, a Frequently Asked Questions document, a well-defined customer experience, and a User Manual.

The conceptualization of the product generally started with the product manager writing a press release for a prospective product outlining the value of the product to its potential customers. The press release outlined the features and benefits of the product and what kinds of problems it could solve. If the customers did not find the idea of the product interesting or exciting, the idea was shelved. The product manager then kept iterating on the press release until customers were satisfied with product's benefits. The feedback from the customers was then passed around internally at the company.

---

[19]Random stow assigns products across the warehouse based on prediction of order frequency. The items are stored in a random order at fulfilment centers so that items on the same order are nearer to each other and could be picked up easily.

[20]At the end of the packing process, packages move along conveyor belts to the SLAM where the package is weighed, the barcode on the package is scanned, and an address label is printed and added to the package. The whole process takes less than 1 second per package.

[21]Amazon Storyteller is a new application from Amazon Studios that turns a movie script into a storyboard. Users can choose the backgrounds, characters, and props to visually tell a story.

[22]Amazon Studios is the movie and series production arm of Amazon.

[23]Kindle Direct Publishing provides authors the opportunity to publish their books and earn revenue.

[24]In July 2014, Amazon launched a new store for 3D printed products, which has over 200 listings that can be customized by material, color, style, text, or size.

[25]Echo is a hands-free device designed around voice wherein a user asks for information and gets answers instantly.

The next step involved preparing a Frequently Asked Questions document which included questions raised by the customers based on the press release. These questions were answered by the product team. The third step involved designing a well-defined customer experience to show the way a customer would use the product. For instance, for products with a user interface, the product development team built mock-ups of each screen that the customer used. The aim was to convey how a customer would fulfil his/her need using the product. The final step involved writing a user manual which offered details of the product and gave information to the customer on everything they needed to know to use the product.

Once the process was completed, it became clearer to the product development team what kind of product they would build. The concept of the new product was then explained to other teams within Amazon so that all the teams had a shared vision of the product. The "working backward" approach reduced the cycle time from concept-to-delivery with the customer at the forefront of every decision the company made. According to Ian McAllister, Director at Amazon, *"Once the project moves into development, the press release can be used as a touchstone; a guiding light. The product team can ask themselves, 'Are we building what is in the press release?' If they find they're spending time building things that aren't in the press release (overbuilding), they need to ask themselves why. This keeps product development focused on achieving the customer benefits and not building extraneous stuff that takes longer to build, takes resources to maintain, and doesn't provide real customer benefit."*[xxi]

Digitally driven supply chain

Amazon had one of the most well developed supply chains in the world which included warehouse and transportation management, inbound and outbound shipping, demand forecasts, and inventory planning. Amazon's supply chain was fast paced and tightly integrated and minimized the need for human intervention by adopting advanced technology. For instance, whenever a customer ordered books online, the order-management system immediately communicated with the inventory and warehouse-management systems to find the optimal distribution center to fulfill the order and in less than a minute, the customer

was informed about the delivery date of the items. The supply chain team at Amazon focused on customer experience and vendor management. This involved daily planning, analysis, metrics and communication, and managing operational relationships with vendors, fulfillment centers, and retail teams. In order to deliver products to customers quickly, Amazon installed robots in its warehouses. The robots cut out much of the hard picking work and brought items directly to workers, who then processed the orders. Though using robots was a costly investment, it resulted in cost advantages over time by streamlining operations and increasing the number of items being processed and shipped through Amazon warehouses. Amazon depended on shipping carriers such as UPS, FedEx, and USPS for delivering products to customers. The company also used drop shipping[26] wherein manufacturers shipped goods directly to consumers on its behalf.

Amazon boasted of one of the most advanced fulfillment networks in the world with large storage capacities. As of July 2015, Amazon managed about 149 active distribution centers the world over. In addition to warehouses, Amazon built sortation centers which took already packed orders from nearby Amazon fulfillment centers and sorted them according to the zip codes before sending them to shipping carriers for delivery to Amazon customers. Amazon had 19 sortation centers in the US as of November 2015.[xxii]

People

As of June 2015, Amazon had about 183,100 employees worldwide. These employees were empowered to make decisions quickly. Amazon was a decentralized company where independent ideas dominated over group thinking. Bezos instituted, as a company-wide rule, the concept of the "two-pizza team"- that is, any team should be small enough to be fed with two pizzas. Bezos used pizza as a metric for choosing the size of his teams. According to him, if a team could not be fed on two pizzas, then that team was too large. The concept limited the team to five to seven members. According to Bezos, the concept of the "two-pizza team" was not so much about the team size, as about autonomy and accountability and the team's fitness function[27]. Bezos felt that small teams tended to work better, communicate more effectively, move fast, and

---

[26]Drop shipping is a supply chain management technique in which the retailer does not keep goods in stock, but instead transfers customer orders and shipment details to either the manufacturer or a wholesaler who then directly ships the goods to the customer.

[27]A fitness function is a single key business metric to provide the team with focus and accountability that the senior executive team agrees on with the team lead.

innovate and test their ideas independently. The teams were free to execute ideas, pursue creative strategies, and set their own internal priorities. According to analysts, the model helped Amazon to be innovative and attract and retain entrepreneurial talent. The "two pizza" teams conceived some of the popular features on Amazon's website such as the GoldBox deals, Bottom of the Page deals, and daily bargains on staples.

While hiring, the company looked for innovative and smart people who would increase the average level of productivity on whichever team they joined. Amazon had in place a "bar raiser" program, wherein a select group of Amazon employees volunteered to be part of interview committees. These full-time employees, called "bar raisers", in addition to their responsibilities, spent about 20 to 30 hours each week interviewing prospective hires. Bar raisers who evaluated a particular candidate got together to decide whether the candidate would be a good fit for company. If any of them had any objection to hiring the candidate, he/she was not be selected. According to Amazon, the basic premise behind this approach was to raise the bar for the next hire, so that the overall talent pool was always improving.

Marketing

To attract customers, Amazon focused on online marketing channels. Customers were directed to the company's websites primarily through a number of targeted online marketing channels such as the Associates program, sponsored search, portal advertising, email marketing campaigns, and other initiatives like outdoor and TV advertising. Online advertising included paid search marketing, interactive ads on portals, e-mail campaigns, and search engine optimization.

The company also used free shipping offers such as Amazon Prime as effective marketing tools. The search feature on the Amazon site along with its product recommendation features allowed Amazon to connect its products with prospective customers.

Partnerships

Amazon partnered with or acquired a number of companies across different sectors such as Drugstore.com (pharmacy), Living.com (furniture), Pets.com (pet supplies), Wineshopper.com (wines), HomeGrocer.com (groceries), Sothebys.com (auctions), and Kozmo.com (urban home delivery). In most cases, Amazon purchased an equity stake in these partners and also charged them a fee for placement of their products on the Amazon site to promote and drive traffic to their sites. Amazon also facilitated formation of partnerships with smaller companies through its Associates programme. Amazon also offered its e-commerce platform to other retailers and to individual sellers including technology services, merchandising, customer service, and order fulfillment. Programs such as 'Merchants@' and 'Syndicated Stores' enabled third party merchants to sell their products through Amazon. This arrangement provided customers a wider choice of products from numerous suppliers while helping Amazon to extend its reach into the customer base of other suppliers. In 2014, Amazon introduced the Amazon Seller App to help on-the-go sellers manage their businesses on Amazon directly from their mobile devices. Amazon's third-party sellers shipped 2 billion units in 2014, double the 2013 figure.[xxiii] As of 2014, more than 40 per cent of units were sold by more than two million third-party sellers worldwide.[xxiv]

Challenges

According to industry observers, Amazon over the years had disrupted other online retailers and brick-and-mortar stores and leveraged its e-commerce operations to become a retail Goliath. However, some critics felt that Amazon was too ambitious as it had been growing alarmingly and investing heavily. They felt that the strategy could backfire and that Amazon needed to be selective about the opportunities it pursued as it could not take customers and the competition for granted.

While Amazon was trying to dominate the online retail sector with its aggressive strategies, its competitors were not far behind. Between price-match guarantees, free shipping, and efforts to go multi-channel, other retailers were finally catching up with Amazon in the online retail game. Its biggest rival, Wal-Mart, was making online sales a high priority, moving forward. Other large online retailers too, like Google Shopping[28] and Alibaba.com[29], were quickly gaining ground. Some experts felt that as the future favored multi-channel retail, Amazon would find it difficult to survive as a pure play retailer, going forward. In

[28]Google Shopping is a shopping search engine from Google that allows users to find products for sale from online merchants and compare prices between different vendors.
[29]Alibaba.com is one of the leading Chinese e-commerce companies.

the technology business, Amazon was facing tough competition from tech giants such as Apple Inc.[30] and Google Inc.[31] In order to stay competitive, Amazon would have to develop some path breaking products, analysts said.

One of the biggest challenges for Amazon was to keep prices low as it grew. Reportedly, some consumers found that prices at Amazon were less compelling than they had once been. Analysts opined that Amazon needed to stay competitively priced as other retailers were finally price matching it. They said in the future, Amazon might have to raise prices to generate a profit for its shareholders, and this would threaten its reputation as a low cost leader. According to some observers, Amazon's key free shipping service Amazon Prime too had lost some appeal as rivals like Walmart and Target were challenging the Amazon shipping advantage by providing free shipping and offering instant pick up. Though Amazon admitted that it faced limitations in its quest to provide lower prices, the increase in Prime subscription fee by US$20 in 2014 implied that it was facing problems from its low margin model. *"This is clearly a chink in the armor. Free shipping going from $25 to $35, a higher Prime membership rate, add-ons, slower Prime delivery, etc. seem to indicate that the business model is not as infallible as many believe. For me it all harks back to the dot-com bubble days, when huge losses for customer acquisition were acceptable, until, well – you know,"*[xxv] said Ken Lonyai, a digital innovative strategist.

Amazon's shipping carriers like the US Postal Service, UPS, and FedEx were considering increasing their shipping rates, a move that could affect the e-tailer's bottom line. In 2014, Amazon spent about US$6.6 billion on delivery and received US$3.1 billion in shipping fees,[xxvi] which according to some analysts, was unsustainable. *"The company has been investing heavily in delivery, which gives it an edge over other retailers. The company is betting that by investing in shipping and perfecting the fulfillment process, it will create a huge barrier to competition. That has worked so far, but is it possible that Amazon could have bet wrong? Is it possible the company's greatest strength could also be the biggest threat to its business?"*[xxvii] wondered Daniel B. Kline, editor of The Boston Globe.

For quite a considerable period of time, Amazon avoided paying local sales tax in states where it did not have a physical presence such as a warehouse. However, in October 2015, the US Senate passed the Bipartisan Marketplace Fairness Act, giving states the authority to collect sales taxes on online purchases even when the internet retailers were not based within their borders. If Amazon was forced to pay state sales taxes, which many analysts believed was inevitable, it would reduce its cost advantage and make it more vulnerable to competition.

Some observers criticized the fact that Amazon had a finger in every pie. According to them, the business was losing its shine as profits were dragged down by investments in fulfillment centers, updating products like the Kindle Fire tablet, and large acquisitions such as the takeover of Kiva and Twitch. Moreover, with the debacle of its Fire smartphone, Amazon took a US$170 million charge related to the write-down of costs associated with unsold Fire phones.

For years, shareholders had backed Bezos's view that big investments were required to gain market share as Amazon's business opportunity was huge and would pay off in the long run. While the shareholders had been tolerant with the company's investment strategy, some analysts felt that they were increasingly showing signs of their patience wearing out as Amazon disappointed them with poor profits in 2014. Someday, investors would demand profits and that may cause Amazon to increase prices for almost everything, leading to a reduced pace of growth. *"Bezos seems driven by legacy, so it's unlikely he'll be content until Amazon is the last giant standing. Unfortunately for that dream, there is a little thing called competition and anti-trust legislation, which puts an inevitable cap on how big Amazon can be without being split apart. Nothing lasts forever, let alone grows forever. Eventually, Amazon's growth will stop, and then Bezos won't be able to hold off his investors any more. They will want their pay off, which means the firm will no longer be able to hold onto the lead over its rivals on price and innovation,"*[xxviii] said Gale.

---

[30]Apple Inc. is a leading US-based technology company that designs, manufactures, and markets mobile communication and media devices, personal computers, and portable digital music players and sells a variety of related software, services, and third-party digital content and applications.

[31]Google Inc.is one of the biggest technology companies in the world involved in Internet-related services and products, computer software, and telecommunications equipment.

However, Bezos remained undaunted. He said Amazon's business model would continue to be to invest in its future. According to him, *"If you're going to take bold bets, they're going to be experiments. And if they're experiments you don't know ahead of time if they're going to work. Experiments are by their very nature prone to failure. But a few big successes compensate for dozens and dozens of things that didn't work. I've made billions of dollars of failures at Amazon.com. None of those things are fun, but they don't matter. What really matters is that companies that don't continue to experiment – companies that don't embrace failure – they eventually get in a* *desperate position, where the only thing they can do is make a 'Hail Mary' bet at the very end."*[xxix]

The road ahead

Going forward, the company planned to launch new digital products and service categories, build more fulfillment centers, power AWS, and expand the Kindle Fire Ecosystem. The company also planned to hire 100,000 people in North America for the holiday season.

In July 2015, Amazon surpassed Wal-Mart as the world's largest retailer by market value after a surprise second quarter profit that led to a surge in the company's stock value (See Exhibit IX). Amazon

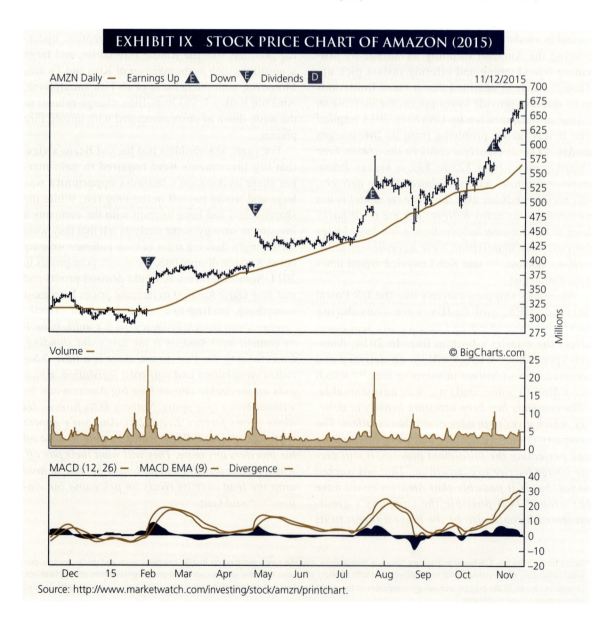

EXHIBIT IX   STOCK PRICE CHART OF AMAZON (2015)

Source: http://www.marketwatch.com/investing/stock/amzn/printchart.

shares rose 17 per cent, giving the company a market value of US$262.7 billion, compared to Wal-Mart's market capitalization of US$233.5 billion. After it posted two consecutive quarterly profits in 2015, analysts noted that Amazon was a company capable of both investing in itself and sustaining long-term profits. Though, according to them, going forward, Amazon had a number of competitive weapons in its arsenal to drive customer loyalty and sustain market position, the battle would be tough as competitors were set to give the company a hard fight. The challenges that the company faced could severely threaten its business model, they added. About the challenges facing Amazon, Semil Shah, a columnist, had once questioned, *"Will their research arm at A9 Labs continue to provide the company with better science and experimentation? Will AWS continue to mint money for the company as enterprise shifts to hybrid cloud management models? Will the company be able to maintain its ability to execute across so many different types of business lines, let alone maintain focus? What types of acquisitions will it make? Will they stumble with respect to logistics as they bring their brand offline and local? Will they be able to carve out a sustainable piece of the mobile device ecosystem where Apple and Google have a headstart, and where Facebook most likely has to enter?"*[xxx]

End notes

[i]Shannon Pettypiece, "Amazon Passes Wal-Mart as Biggest Retailer by Market Value," www.bloomberg.com, July 24, 2015.

[ii]Spencer Soper, "Amazon Posts Surprise Profit; Shares Soar," www.bloomberg.com, July 24, 2015.

[iii]"Amazon.com Announces Fourth Quarter Sales up 15 per cent to $29.33 Billion," http://phx.corporate-ir.net, January 29, 2015.

[iv]Mark W. Johnson, "Amazon's Smart Innovation Strategy," www.businessweek.com, April 12, 2010.

[v]Innosight LLC is a US-based strategic innovation consulting and investing company.

[vi]William C. Taylor, "Who's Writing the Book on Web Business?" www.fastcompany.com, October 31, 1996.

[vii]JP Mangalindan, "Amazon's Core? Frugality," http://fortune.com, March 26, 2012.

[viii]Adam Gale, "Will Amazon Ever be Profitable?" www.managementtoday.co.uk, July 15, 2015.

[ix]www.statista.com/statistics/237810/number-of-active-amazon-customer-accounts-worldwide/

[x]Ron Kaufman, "Amazon Does Not 'Deliver Customer Service', They Build Powerful Partnerships," http://ronkaufman.com, June 9, 2015.

[xi]Thomas Hobbs, "Amazon at 20: The Brand, the Challenges and the Future," www.marketingweek.com, July 15, 2015.

[xii]"Amazon and the "Profitless Business Model" Fallacy," www.eugenewei.com, October 26, 2013.

[xiii]Jacob Donnelly, "Amazon: Its Business Model Explained," http://seekingalpha.com, October 27, 2014.

[xiv]Greg Bensinger, "Amazon's Spending Leads to Biggest Quarterly Loss in 14 Years," www.wsj.com, October 23, 2014.

[xv]Megan Geuss, "Amazon Reports Modest Q4 Earnings and 2014 Loss, But Stock Soars," http://arstechnica.com, January 30, 2015.

[xvi]Slate is a daily online magazine.

[xvii]Matthew Yglesias "Amazon Profits Fall 45 Percent, Still the Most Amazing Company in the World," www.slate.com, January 29, 2013.

[xviii]h t t p : / / w w w . s e c . g o v / A r c h i v e s / e d g a r / d a t a /1018724/000119312512161812/d329990dex991.htm

[xix]"Why I, Jeff Bezos, Keep Spending Billions on Amazon R&D," www.businessinsider.com, April 27, 2011.

[xx]Daniel Lyons, "We Start with the Customer and We Work Backward," www.slate.com, December 24, 2009.

[xxi] _____ Amazon's Approach to Product _____ w.quora.com,

_____ " www.mwpvl. com, 2015.

[xxiii]Phil Wahba, "Amazon Gets Needed Boost in 2014 from Outside Sellers," http://fortune.com, January 5, 2015.

[xxiv]Ryan Mac, "Jeff Bezos' Letter to Shareholders: 'Don't Just Swipe Right, Get Married (A Lot)'," www.forbes.com, April 24, 2015.

[xxv]George Anderson, "Is Amazon Prime Suffering from Its Own Success?" www.forbes.com August 1, 2014.

[xxvi]Steve Denning, "The Future Of Amazon, Apple, Facebook And Google," www.forbes.com, April 9, 2015.

[xxvii]"Is This the Biggest Threat to Amazon's Business Model?" www.fool.com, June 8, 2015.

[xxviii]Adam Gale, "Will Amazon Ever be Profitable?" www.managementtoday.co.uk, July 15, 2015.

[xxix]Jillian D'onfro "Jeff Bezos: Here's Why It Wouldn't Matter if the Fire Phone Were a Flop," www.businessinsider.in, December 2, 2014.

[xxx]Semil Shah, "The Future of Amazon: Ambitious, Diverse, and Expansive," http://techcrunch.com, September 9, 2012.

Corporate restructuring at Google

By Aparna Venkatraman

Abstract

The search engine giant Google's core businesses were search, ads and apps. But over the years, Google diversified away from its main businesses and ventured into several blue sky projects like bio-tech, self-driving cars, smart homes and wearable technology. As Google moved to new markets and businesses, its investors were concerned about how the money from the cash cow businesses of Google were being wasted on such yet-to-be profitable projects. With the intent to spell clarity on the amount of investments in each of its business, the company announced that it would be restructuring with the creation of a new holding company called 'Alphabet'. Post the restructuring, Google would become one of the subsidiaries of the new parent Alphabet. Google would retain its search and advertising, YouTube, Chrome and Android businesses. Other business entities, such as Calico, Nest, Google Ventures, Google Capital and Google X would be managed under the holding company Alphabet, separately from Google business. Larry Page would be Alphabet's new CEO, while Sergey Brin would serve as the company's president and Sundar Pichai would be the new CEO of Google. But analysts cautioned that, with the restructuring, Alphabet's blue sky projects would be under close scrutiny from investors. If these projects failed to drive revenues, investors could call for pulling the plug on the funds invested on these projects, thereby thwarting the spirit of innovation at Alphabet. As Google 'swapped its tiles in the game of a corporate scrabble', what were the challenges ahead of the new company Alphabet?

Case study

"For Sergey and me this is a very exciting new chapter in the life of Google – the birth of Alphabet. We liked the name Alphabet because it means a collection of letters that represent language, one of humanity's most important innovations, and is the core of how we index with Google search! We also like that it means alpha-bet (Alpha is investment return above benchmark), which we strive for"![1]

– *Larry Page, Co-founder, Google Inc.*

"A rose by any other name is still a rose and Google by any other name is still the internet giant."[2]

– *John Simpson, Privacy Project Director, Consumer Watchdog*

Like a person turning over a new leaf and making a fresh start, corporations try to gain a second wind by restructuring. Whether the restructuring takes the form of splitting up a company, merging it with another company, reorganizing, or even taking on a new name, the goal is to end up with a more refined, more profitable entity. Both successful and failing companies may turn to restructuring to breathe fresh life and fresh profits into the business," opined Cynthia Myers[3], while explaining the rationale behind corporate restructuring.[4]

On August 10th 2015, Google announced a major reorganisation of the company, with the creation of

[1]"Google Announces Plans for New Operating Structure", https://abc.xyz/investor/news/releases/2015/0810.html, August 10th 2015.

[2]Rushe Dominic and Thielman Sam, "Inside Alphabet: why Google rebranded itself and what happens next", https://www.theguardian.com/technology/2015/aug/11/alphabet-google-rebranding-what-happens-next, August 11th 2015.

[3]Cynthia Myers is the author of numerous novels. She has a degree in economics from Sam Houston State University.

[4]Myers Cynthia, "What Are the Motives Behind Corporate Restructuring?", http://smallbusiness.chron.com/motives-behind-corporate-restructuring-34081.html, 2015.

Alphabet Inc., its new parent company. Google's different businesses such as Calico, Nest, Fiber, Google Ventures and Google Capital and Google X would be hived off from Google and will be treated as separate entities under the parent Alphabet. Google would continue with the company's core businesses such as search, ads, maps, apps, YouTube and Android. For the company, the reshuffling meant more dabble in its innovative and futuristic ventures, whereas for investors it was to provide improved corporate transparency and clarity.

Corporate restructuring at Google: an overview

Google's Q4 2014 earnings provided a picture of its strong financial performance for the quarter. Its gross revenue was $18.1 billion vis-à-vis $16.86 billion in 2013 and its net income was $4.76 billion compared to $3.38 billion in Q4 2013. It was observed, that as usual, Google AdWords made up the lion's share of the company's revenue with a staggering 89 per cent. Highlighting Google's Q4 financials, CFO Patrick Pichette stated that earnings from the 'other revenues' category[5] grew to $2 billion for the quarter with Google's Play Store driving the growth in this segment. The company also revealed that YouTube was the tech giant's star product and its revenue had increased significantly, over 100 per cent year over year, and the watch time on YouTube had increased by 50 per cent year-over-year.[6]

The philosophy of 'thinking10x' was the driving force behind all the innovations at Google (Annexure I). Its culture of innovation was driven by the thought that 'true innovation happens when you try to improve something by 10 times rather than by 10 per cent.'[7] The moon-shot projects at Google aimed to achieve the 10x improvements instead of 10 per cent

improvement.[8] (Annexure II). Besides X lab, Sidewalk Labs and Calico, Google's other businesses that were not tied to its main advertising business included 'Fiber', the Fiber optic network, which provided high-speed broadband internet and TV service and the smart-home business venture, Nest. Apart from this, Google had two investment divisions Google Capital and Google ventures. While Google Capital invested in 'late-stage growth companies', Google Ventures invested and funded 'early-stage companies.'[9]

Justin Post, analyst at Bank of America, noted that apart from Google's 'bread-and-butter' businesses[10] only a few of its other businesses were generating revenue. These included Fiber, Nest and Dropcam, which were collectively estimated to bring in about $400 million revenue in 2015. Analysts identified Calico, (its R&D biotech division that was yet make technological breakthrough in health care) and Google X, as among the company's non-revenue-generating non-core ventures. They estimated for a loss of between $2.7 billion and $4 billion from such moonshot projects in 2015. Analysts opined that Glass was the only product of Google X that could secure a place in the enterprise market, having sales estimated at $10 million.[11] For the FY 2014, Google's R&D expenses were $9.8 billion (Exhibit I), 14.9 per cent of its revenue $66 billion.[12] (Exhibit II).

Explaining the reasons why Google was investing significant capital in research and development, Jan Dawson (Dawson), Chief Analyst at Jackdaw Research, elaborated, "Google has to be looking for the next big thing and to be investing heavily in that." But he observed that there was very little correlation between the research outlay and innovation in its core products. Dawson said, "... In most companies, that investment would be in areas that seem like natural extensions of Google's existing business and that can leverage its existing skill sets and assets, whereas

[5]Revenues from Google Play Store and its hardware were included in its 'other revenue' category.

[6]Ingraham Nathan, "Google pulls in $4.76 billion in net income in the last quarter of 2014", http://www.theverge.com/2015/1/29/7947699/google-q4-2014-earnings, January 29th 2015.

[7]"Creating a Culture of Innovation", https://apps.google.com/learn-more/creating_a_culture_of_innovation.html.

[8]Yuwono Jeffrey, "The case for the high risk 10x moonshot strategy", http://cornerplay.com/2014/06/02/google-10x-moonshot/, June 2nd 2014.

[9]Reader Ruth, "Everything you need to know about Alphabet, Google's new holding company", http://venturebeat.com/2015/08/12/everything-you-need-to-know-about-alphabet-googles-new-holding-company/, August 12th 2015.

[10]Google's search, advertising business and YouTube.

[11]Drew Kate, "The big costs behind Google's moonshot start-ups", http://www.cnbc.com/2015/10/22/the-big-costs-behind-googles-moonshot-start-ups.html, October 22nd 2015.

[12]"FORM 10-K United States Securities And Exchange Commission", https://www.sec.gov/answers/form10k.htm, December 31st 2014.

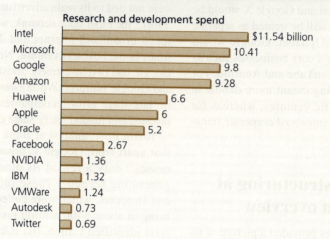

EXHIBIT I   GOOGLE'S R&D SPEND 2014

Research and development spend

Company	Spend (billion US$)
Intel	$11.54 billion
Microsoft	10.41
Google	9.8
Amazon	9.28
Huawei	6.6
Apple	6
Oracle	5.2
Facebook	2.67
NVIDIA	1.36
IBM	1.32
VMWare	1.24
Autodesk	0.73
Twitter	0.69

Source: Truong, Alice, "Huawei's R&D spend is massive even by the standards of American tech giants", http://qz.com/374039/huaweis-rd-spend-is-massive-even-by-the-standards-of-american-tech-giants/, March 31st 2015.

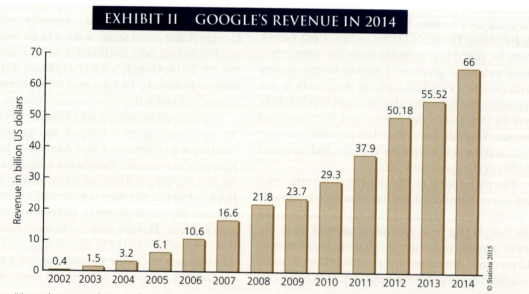

EXHIBIT II   GOOGLE'S REVENUE IN 2014

Revenue in billion US dollars

Year	Revenue
2002	0.4
2003	1.5
2004	3.2
2005	6.1
2006	10.6
2007	16.6
2008	21.8
2009	23.7
2010	29.3
2011	37.9
2012	50.18
2013	55.52
2014	66

© Statista 2015

Source: "Annual revenue of Google from 2002 to 2014 (in billion US dollars)", http://www.statista.com/statistics/266206/googles-annual-global-revenue/, 2014.

Google seems to be investing in such a wide range of projects with so little connection to its traditional business, that it's very hard to see a coherent strategy behind its investments."[13]

Naturally Google's investors were not happy with Google's 'free spending ways' as they felt these investments were out of Google's core businesses.[14] Dawson said, "Right now investors really have no idea how

[13]"FORM 10-K United States Securities And Exchange Commission", op. cit..

[14]Arce Nicole, "Google CFO Patrick Pichette Retiring In Six Months: Here's Why", http://www.techtimes.com/articles/38916/20150311/google-cfo-patrick-pichette-retiring-in-six-months-heres-why.htm, March 11th 2015.

the senior management at Alphabet/Google is making decisions about new areas to invest in, how long a leash these new businesses are given, how quickly they need to start producing revenue or profits, or ultimately what will determine whether Google continues to invest in these new projects if they're not meeting the company's goals." Furthermore Dawson noted Google's investments on its exotic moonshot projects were a source of anxiety to its investors. In his words, "It feels a bit too much as if Larry Page and Sergey Brin are being allowed to invest in pet projects without any broad strategic rationale behind them, and that would have me very concerned as a Google investor."[15]

While Google shareholders criticised the company's moonshots, analysts were quick to point out that Google's founders did not want Google to meet the same fate of the erstwhile business technology vendor titan, Microsoft, which now stared into the abyss of irrelevance. Microsoft was one of the companies which had not ploughed back its profits into fresher and relevant investments. The software behemoth was struggling in the mobile platform; it had lost its edge.[16] Page too emphasised on remaining technologically relevant to the public in the future and defended the company's investments in the moonshots. In a blog post on Google's blog, Page wrote, "We've long believed that over time companies tend to get comfortable doing the same thing, just making incremental changes. But in the technology industry, where revolutionary ideas drive the next big growth areas, you need to be a bit uncomfortable to stay relevant."

While staying technologically relevant to the public in the future was one concern at Google, the other was of retaining talented employees. Market analysts had observed, programmers at Silicon Valley were leaving big tech companies to join 'smaller, newer, faster-growing firms', while some prospective employees were declining job offers from large corporations.[17] Business analysts observed organisations needed to create a culture which made employees feel, purposeful and relevant to be a part of the organisation; Google's blue sky projects were doing that. A column in Reuters, stated, "Keeping a company on the cutting edge is about more than making workers happy. They have to feel relevant, heard and purposeful. One of the best ways to imbue work with a sense of purpose is to make people feel as though they are changing the world. Google's wackier projects have the potential to be earth-shaking: driverless cars could reinvent the way we get around; even the much-mocked Google Glass might turn out to be amazing in the next iteration. The Calico life-extention (*Sic.,* extension) project – which focuses on aging and age-related diseases – represents a push toward the holy grail of all technological research."[18]

With an intent to 'separate its core business from its ambitious research divisions'[19] the tech behemoth on August 10th 2015[20] in a filing with the Security and Exchange Commission,[21] announced its new corporate structure and management shake-up and rebranded itself as Alphabet Inc.[22] While Alphabet would be the holding company, Google would become its largest owned subsidiary. Google's different businesses such as Calico, Nest, and Fiber, Google Ventures and Google Capital, and Google X would spinoff from Google and will be treated as separate entities under the parent Alphabet. Google would include the company's core businesses such as 'search, ads, maps, apps, YouTube and Android and the related technical infrastructure.'[23] Following the restructuring, Page became the CEO of Alphabet, Brin president; Eric Schmidt became the executive chairman.[24] Sundar Pichai, who

[15]"The big costs behind Google's moonshot start-ups", op. cit..

[16]Waters, Richard and Platt, Eric, "Google transforms into new Alphabet tech conglomerate", http://www.ft.com/intl/cms/s/0/9a291bf8-3fa2-11e5-b98b-87c7270955cf.html#axzz3s7RDdKJ1, August 10th 2015.

[17]Vara Vauhini, "Google's New Alphabetical Order", http://www.newyorker.com/business/currency/googles-new-alphabetical-order, August 11th 2015.

[18]Schoenberger and R. Chana, "COLUMN-Why Google – and Larry Page – created their own Alphabet", http://uk.reuters.com/article/schoenberger-google-idUKL1N10O2MP20150813, August 13th 2015.

[19]Curtis, Sophie, "Sundar Pichai: Meet Google's new CEO", http://www.telegraph.co.uk/technology/google/11795673/Sundar-Pichai-Meet-Googles-new-CEO.html, August 11th 2015.

[20]Rushe, Dominic and Thielman, Sam, "Google to restructure into new holding company called Alphabet", https://www.theguardian.com/technology/2015/aug/10/google-alphabet-parent-company, August 11th 2015.

[21]Sharf, Samantha, "Goodbye Google? Search Giant Rebrands As Alphabet", http://www.forbes.com/sites/samanthasharf/2015/08/10/goodbye-google-search-giant-changing-its-name/, August 10th 2015.

[22]"Google to restructure into new holding company called Alphabet", op. cit..

[23]Rosoff, Matt, "What is Alphabet, Google's new company?", http://uk.businessinsider.com/what-is-alphabet-googles-new-company-2015-8, August 11th 2015.

[24]"Sundar Pichai: Meet Google's new CEO", op. cit..

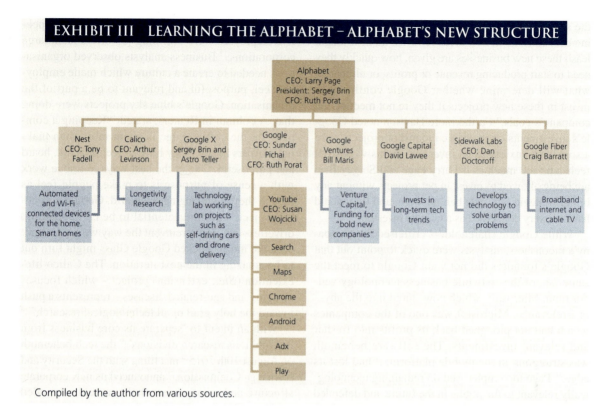

EXHIBIT III   LEARNING THE ALPHABET – ALPHABET'S NEW STRUCTURE

Compiled by the author from various sources.

had been senior vice president in charge of products[25], would be chief executive of Google and Ruth Porat would be chief financial officer for Alphabet and Google[26] (Exhibit III). While interpreting Page's blog post announcing Google's reshuffle, Richard Waters and Eric Platt of *Financial Times*, said, "the new name for the holding company was also a pun on 'alphabet' – a reference to the huge investment Google was willing to stake on ideas that had the chance to outperform other stock market investments, known in market terminology as 'alpha'."[27]

Business analysts noted that the restructuring was a response to the growing investor pressure over the use of Google's profits to finance high risk, long term projects. Analysts stated the

restructuring would help improve Google's corporate transparency and investors would get a deeper insight about how money was being spent.[28] Brian Wieser, an analyst with Pivotal Research spelled out Google's move; "The whole point is presumably to say to investors that we hear your calls for more transparency and we'll provide it."[29] Page in his blog post wrote that restructuring was to make Google a 'cleaner and more accountable' company. Beginning with the fourth quarter of 2015, Google said it would report separate financial results for the core Google business.[30] Alphabet subsidiaries, including Google, would be using 'segment reporting'[31] to report their financial results separately.[32] Colin Gillis, Technology Analyst at BGC

[25]Fung, Brian and Tsukayama, Hayley, "Seven quick facts about Sundar Pichai, Google's new CEO", https://www.washingtonpost.com/news/the-switch/wp/2015/08/11/seven-quick-facts-about-sundar-pichai-googles-new-ceo/, August 11th 2015.

[26]Huet, Ellen, "Google's Sundar Pichai To Replace Larry Page As CEO, Company Restructures As Alphabet", http://www.forbes.com/sites/ellenhuet/2015/08/10/googles-sundar-pichai-to-replace-larry-page-as-ceo/, August 10th 2015.

[27]"Google transforms into new Alphabet tech conglomerate", op. cit..

[28]"Google to restructure into new holding company called Alphabet", op. cit..

[29]Barr, Alistair And Winkler, Rolfe, "Google Creates Parent Company Called Alphabet in Restructuring", http://www.wsj.com/articles/google-creates-new-company-alphabet-1439240645, August 10th 2015.

[30]"Google transforms into new Alphabet tech conglomerate", op. cit..

[31]Segment reporting is the reporting of the operating segments of a company in the disclosures accompanying its financial statements. Segment reporting is required for publicly-held entities, and is not required for privately held ones.

[32]Cunningham, Andrew, "Google is now part of 'Alphabet,' Sundar Pichai steps up as CEO. [Updated]", http://arstechnica.com/gadgets/2015/08/google-is-now-part-of-alphabet-sundar-pichai-steps-up-as-ceo/, August 11th 2015.

Partners, said "the move would allow investors to assess Google's core business more clearly while allowing Google to highlight its other assets." He elaborated, "It'll give people a truer picture of the nature and specifics of Google's core operation."[33] A former Google executive observed that it was increasingly becoming difficult to withhold the costs of some of the company's far flung projects, whereas it was easier to take the core business and run it like a Fortune 500 company and spinning off its speculative ventures.[34]

With the restructuring, the Google's shareholders became Alphabet shareholders. The shares of Google will be traded under the same GOOG and GOOGL[35] ticker symbol. The only change would be company's name on shares (Alphabet Class A Common Stock and Alphabet Class C Common Stock).There was no change in the shareholders rights.[36] Google shares soared 5 per cent in after hours trading, after Google announced a new parent company, indicating that Google's business reshuffle resonated well with investor confidence.[37] (Exhibit IV).

Another impetus behind the reorganization was retaining top talent especially, Pichai. Pichai was seen as Page's right-hand man[38] and second in command at Google.[39] Pichai joined Google in 2004. It was Pichai who proposed the idea that Google should have its own browser 'Chrome'. Google Chrome browser eventually became a leader in world-wide browser usage. In 2014, he was promoted as the head of Google's products. Analysts observed that Pichai was sought after by other companies. An article in

EXHIBIT IV   INVESTORS REACTION POST THE ANNOUNCEMENT

Source: Roberts, John Jeff, "Google shares jump 5 per cent on bombshell CEO and restructuring news", http://fortune.com/2015/08/10/google-alphabet-share-price/, August 10th2015.

---

[33]"Google to restructure into new holding company called Alphabet", op. cit..

[34]"Google Creates Parent Company Called Alphabet in Restructuring", op. cit..

[35]There are two ticker symbols for Google Inc. (GOOG) on the NASDAQ Stock Market: GOOG and GOOGL. The two tickers represent two different share classes: A (GOOGL) and C (GOOG). The B shares are owned by insiders and don't trade on the public markets. Sergey Brin, Larry Page, Eric Schmidt and a couple other directors, hold the B class of shares.

[36]Alba, Davey, "After Today, Google Officially Becomes Alphabet", http://www.wired.com/2015/10/today-google-officially-becomes-alphabet/, October 2nd 2015.

[37]Roberts, John Jeff, "Google shares jump 5 per cent on bombshell CEO and restructuring news", http://fortune.com/2015/08/10/google-alphabet-share-price/, August 10th 2015.

[38]"PM Narendra Modi, Satya Nadella, Larry Page congratulate Sundar Pichai on new role", http://www.businesstoday.in/management/executives/satya-nadella-larry-page-eric-schmidt-congratulate-googles-pichai/story/222639.html, August 11th 2015.

[39]"Sundar Pichai: Meet Google's new CEO", op. cit..

Forbes observed, 'Pichai's success at Google reportedly attracted the attention of other technology powerhouses, including Twitter'. According to a 2011 article in AllThingsD that cited unnamed sources, Twitter tried to poach Pichai offering him the role of vice president of products at the micro-blogging site. In July 2015, Techcrunch listed him as one of the contenders for the CEO position at Twitter. Apart from this, he was also top choice for the position of CEO at Microsoft, after Steve Ballmer[40] retired. FBR Capital analyst William Bird observed that his promotion to CEO may have been a tactic by Page and Brin to keep Pichai on board. In his words, "The new structure offers an important way to promote and retain Sundar Pichai."[41] A Business Insider report also noted that to prevent Pichai from jumping ship and joining Twitter, "Google decided to pull the trigger on an organizational change it's been considering for some time, giving Pichai the CEO title while keeping the same set of duties." The report further theorised that Alphabet might likewise offer CEO titles to Tony Fadell, founder of Nest, and Arthur Levinson, who helms Calico.[42]

Analysts observed that the 'financial engineering from the new structure could give shareholders a boost too'. Google had almost no debt and could borrow funds to finance buy back of shares from investors. The new entity of Google could 'possibly find it cheaper to borrow once it is separated from expensive research projects'.[43]

Neil Irwin, Senior Economics Correspondent for *The New York Times* observed, "Google's decision to restructure is the strongest signal yet that it intends to be a 21st-century innovator, a bold creator of new products, not simply a harvester of profits from its lucrative search engine business."[44] This restructuring, analysts observed took a page from Warren Buffett's Berkshire Hathaway Inc. who transformed it from a struggling textile manufacturer to a sprawling conglomerate. Though the holding company Berkshire Hathaway's primary business was insurance[45], it managed diverse businesses that ranged from railroads, retail, jewelry, bricks, ice cream and even underwear.[46] Steve Wallman, a Wisconsin-based money manager noted, "They look at Warren as a hero and Berkshire as a template." Even fellow executives in the technology industry paralleled Google's strategy to Berkshire. Jeff Weiner, CEO of LinkedIn Corp, tweeted, "Google's Alphabet sounds like a 21st – century Berkshire Hathaway, but with a lot of very large venture bets."[47] Following Google's announcement many Wall Street analysts dubbed Google's reshuffle as "Berkshire Hathaway of the Internet."[48]

Google's 'a-bet': a risky move?

A section of analysts contrasted the business model of Berkshire Hathaway and Alphabet. They observed that though the portfolio of companies at Alphabet was operationally independent, they were financially dependent on the core Google business (advertisement). Though in his letter, Page committed to 'rigorously handle capital allocation and work to make sure each business is executing well' which emulated Buffett working style, but the fact was that the portfolio of businesses under Alphabet were unlike Berkshire Hathaway's cash generators and were 'speculative money losers with no clear future'.[49]

[40]Steve Ballmer was the chief executive officer of Microsoft from January 2000 to February 2014.

[41]Adams, Susan, "Who Is Google's New Chief, Sundar Pichai?", http://www.forbes.com/sites/susanadams/2015/08/12/who-is-googles-new-chief-sundar-pichai/, August 12th 2015.

[42]"What's Behind Google's Alphabet Restructuring?", http://knowledge.wharton.upenn.edu/artide/googles-alphabet-reorg-can-the-whole-live-up-to-one-of-its-parts/, August 14th 2015.

[43]Titcomb, James, "Google and Alphabet: What does this all mean?", http://www.telegraph.co.uk/technology/google/11796103/Google-and-Alphabet-What-does-this-aM-mean.html, August 12th 2015.

[44]Irwin, Neil, "Is the New Google More Like Berkshire Hathaway, General Electric or AT&T?", http://www.nytimes.com/2015/08/12/upshot/is-the-new-google-more-like-berkshire-hathaway-general-electric-or-att.html?_r=1, August 11th 2015.

[45]ibid.

[46]Barr, Alistair, "Will Google Become the Berkshire Hathaway of Tech?", http://blogs.wsj.com/digits/2014/10/31/will-google-become-the-berkshire-hathaway-of-tech/,October 31st 2014.

[47]Satariano, Adam and Buhayar, Noah,"B Is for Buffett' in Page's Plan to Mold Google After Berkshire", http://www.bloomberg.com/news/articles/2015-08-11/-b-is-for-buffett-in-page-s-plan-to-mold-google-after-berkshire, August 11th 2015.

[48]Udland, Myles, "Wall Street thinks Google just created the 'Berkshire Hathaway of the Internet", http://www.businessinsider.in/Wall-Street-thinks-Google-just-created-the-Berkshire-Hathaway-of-the-Internet/articleshow/48439544.cms, August 11th 2015.

[49]Nisen, Max, "No, Google's new 'Alphabet' structure is really nothing like Berkshire Hathaway", http://qz.com/477284/no-googles-new-alphabet-structure-is-really-nothing-like-berkshire-hathaway/, August 13th 2015.

Likewise, Todd Zenger, Professor of Strategy and Strategic Leadership at University of Utah's Eccles School of Business, stated "The important distinction is that Berkshire Hathaway's businesses are generally cash producers and Berkshire's task is to improve on the cash they already generate. Alphabet will be more like a cash cow coupled to a venture capital firm, investing in early stage and in some cases highly capital-intensive new ventures."[50] R. Jagannathan, the Editor-in-Chief of First post, succinctly stated his view, 'Berkshire is a capitalist; Alphabet will be a venture capitalist.'[51]

Business analysts stated businesses under Berkshire Hathaway focused on value creation; its investors were confident in the company's 'theory of value creation' (Exhibit V). The key challenge of Alphabet was to prove to its investors the added value of its multiple businesses under a single entity. It was unlikely of investors to be convinced to be investing in businesses of search engine, longevity research, thermostats, and drones simultaneously, where the theory of value creation made no or little sense.[52]

Wharton management professor David Hsu said that it would be challenging to have the two parts of the organization (Alphabet and Google) work together. He observed 'the new Google and the rest of Alphabet may need different staff, human resource incentives, culture, etc'. He predicted that these issues could become 'significant management challenges.'[53]

While the conglomerate model worked for companies like Berkshire Hathaway whose businesses

of financial services, energy, and manufacturing firms did not require R&D, such a model would not work well for technology companies like Google that flourished on cutting-edge discoveries. With Google financial results being reported separately from Alphabet, each of its divisions would face the glare of intense scrutiny from its shareholders 'by virtue of being separate and (at least collectively) more transparent'. This meant the company's cash burning, unprofitable entities would become more obvious, leading to such divisions to be sold or shut.[54] According to Wharton emeritus management professor Lawrence Hrebiniak, the start-ups under the Alphabet will have to yield results, although he was doubtful of seeing these results in the near future. In his words, "The negative thing would be if investors perceive no value on that side and just perceive them as doing nothing but draining cash from the cash cow, Google."[55]

According to Kumar, a tech and business commentator, Google's strategy of spinning of its ventures would 'encourage the company to pursue rational strategic alternatives for individual divisions and be good for optimization of the stock price, it could also put a serious damper on the spirit of innovation. Excessive analyst and shareholder focus on original R&D at Alphabet, especially when the payoff may be years away or indirect, could be detrimental to pure creativity.' He further noted, 'Google's move could also spur fundamental research by attracting (and allowing) outside investments for its

EXHIBIT V   THEORY OF VALUE CREATION

$$A = (a+b+c)*y$$

where y = the value add of the ownership structure

Source: Minter, Dial, "Google Alphabet: Spelling Success with Alphabet – Lovable Or Hatable?" http://myndset.com/2015/08/google-alphabet/, August 26th 2015.

[50]Zenger, Todd, "Why Google Became Alphabet", https://hbr.org/2015/08/why-google-became-alphabet, August 11th 2015.

[51]Jagannathan, R, "Google's Alphabet: Creating the tech version of Warren Buffett's Berkshire", http://www.firstpost.com/business/googles-alphabet-creating-tech-version-warren-buffetts-berkshire-2389012.html, August 12th 2015.

[52]"Why Google Became Alphabet", op. cit..

[53]"What's Behind Google's Alphabet Restructuring?", op. cit..

[54]Kumar, S, "Google's Alphabet could stifle innovation", http://fortune.com/2015/08/12/google-alphabet-sundar-pichai/, August 12th 2015.

[55]"What's Behind Google's Alphabet Restructuring?", op. cit..

explorative projects through private placements or tracking stocks, which are tied to discrete business lines within a larger company, and it's unclear just how granular the company's financial reporting will eventually be. It's entirely possible that the new structure will turn out to be mostly cosmetic and have little impact on how Google co-founders Larry Page and Sergey Brin spend Google's money'.[56]

Apart from the above, a section of business analysts raised significant questions with regards to Google's Alphabet transition. – "Can Alphabet create a soup of synergies and cross-pollination of sufficient efficiency to offset/warrant the cost and complexity of a holding company structure with its inherent risks? For example, what posture will the conglomerate have with regard to back-office and personnel sharing? Will data be sharable across the businesses? To what extent will Alphabet businesses favor one another? If one business unit has a catastrophe, will it/can it taint the rest of the organization?"[57]

Annexure I
Timeline of Events at Google

1995

The founders meet
Google founders Larry Page and Sergey Brin meet at Stanford University.

1996

The search engine project
The pair begin to work together on a search engine called BackRub as part of a research project.

1997

Google.com hits the web
Google.com is registered as a domain, the name having been chosen as a play on the word "googol", the number one followed by 100 zeroes, to represent the near-infinite amount of content on the web.

1998

The company is incorporated
Google as a company is launched, filing for incorporation in California. The first office is in a garage.

1999

New offices
The company outgrows the garage and moves to new premises in Palo Alto with eight employees, then later the same year another relocation takes the company to Mountain View, where Google employs its first chef. The company raises $25m in equity funding.

2000

The world's largest search engine
Google is launched in ten new languages. Today search is available in more than 150 languages. In June Google becomes the world's largest search engine, with an index of one billion pages.

2001

Eric Schmidt appointed CEO
Eric Schmidt, a former director of Apple, becomes chairman of the board of directors, then in August he is appointed CEO. Meanwhile Mr Page is president of products and Mr Brin president of technology. The same year, Google image search launches.

---

[56]"Google's Alphabet could stifle innovation", op. cit..

[57]Minter, Dial, "Google Alphabet: Spelling Success with Alphabet – Lovable Or Hatable?", http://myndset.com/2015/08/26/google-alphabet/.

2002

AdWords introduced
Google AdWords, first launched in 2000, is given an overhaul with cost-per-click pricing. Google News launches, as does Google Labs which allows users to try out beta technologies from the research and development team.

2003

Blogger creators acquired
The company acquires Pyra Labs, creators of Blogger. Google AdSense is launched.

2004

Google floats
Google launches its IPO with a share price of $85. The company is valued at $27bn. Email service Gmail is launched. Google acquires Keyhole, a digital mapping company which later helps create Google Earth. The European headquarters in Dublin open.

2005

Google maps the world
February sees the launch of Google Maps and in June Google Earth is introduced.

2006

Google buys YouTube
In October, the company announces the acquisition of video site YouTube. A number of new features launch this year including Google Calendar, Google Translate and Google Docs and Spreadsheets.

2007

Android launched
In November, Google announces Android, the first open platform for mobile devices. Also this year, Google is named the best company to work for by Fortune. Street View is started in five US cities. But Google Earth receives some bad press as intelligence sources warn terrorists are using aerial footage from the feature to target British bases in Basra.

2008

The introduction of Chrome
Web browser Google Chrome is launched. Google Suggest, now known as Autocomplete, is introduced on Google.com, predicting search queries.

2009

Google supports innovation
Google Ventures is announced, a fund aimed to support innovation and new technology companies.

2010

Nexus devices and driverless technology
The Nexus series of smartphone and tablet devices using the Android operating system is launched. Google announces the development of technology for self-driving cars.

2011

Larry Page reinstated as CEO
Larry Page becomes CEO, ten years after he passed the title to Eric Schmidt, who is now named executive chairman. Google+ is launched.

2012

Google campaigns against censorship
Google is part of the campaign against the SOPA and PIPA bills in the US, saying they would censor the internet and impede innovation. In April, Google Glass is unveiled, as is Google Drive, a file creation and sharing platform.

2013

Shares pass the $1,000 mark
Less than a decade after Google's flotation, shares hit $1,000. A milestone for Android as it passes one billion device activations.

2014

Stock split
A stock split creates a new level of non-voting shares and cements Mr Page and Mr Brin's control over the company.

2015

Alphabet becomes holding company in big corporate overhaul
A massive corporate overhaul separates Google's core business from its research divisions with a new holding company, Alphabet, of which Mr Page will be chief executive.

Source: Curtis, Sophie, "Sundar Pichai: Meet Google's new CEO", http://www.telegraph.co.uk/technology/google/11795673/Sundar-Pichai-Meet-Googles-new-CEO.html, August 11th2015.

Annexure II
Google's Moonshots

Google Glass

The first project and probably the most anticipated is called Google Glass; although this product was already announced and even being sold to developers for testing, numerous reasons made the company move back in development and change several key aspects of Glass. Many tech enthusiasts have become increasingly anxious to know what Google changed with the wearable computer for the next version.

Self-Driving Cars

Driverless cars is another service that is being thoroughly tested and currently developed by the Google X labs (an area at Google dedicated to these kind of "moonshot" projects). The future of driving, as numerous reports have called the project, is still far away from becoming a consumer product, but if you live in Mountain View, California, Google's self-driving cars are already a normal sight.

Project Loon

Since the year 2013, Google has been testing a project called Loon in New Zealand with the hopes to eventually launch the project worldwide. Google's Project Loon aims to provide users located in rural areas all around the world with an internet connection. The ambitious project will give users the ability to be connected with the rest of the world no matter where they live.

Smart Contact Lenses

Google is also developing smart contact lenses that will help users with diabetes to accurately monitor and control their sugar levels. This is achieved by measuring the level of glucose in their tears, which can actually describe the amount of sugar in the rest of their organism.

Drone Delivery

Drones have a wide variety of uses, one of which Google is taking advantage of. The internet giant is willing to directly compete with Amazon by using drones to deliver packages, although Google's approach aims to have more reach in order to deliver packages to the most remote places.

Tremor-Cancelling Spoon

Google has a history of buying out smaller companies that have innovative and useful products with a lot of promise to improve the lives of their customers. As it is the case with Lift Labs, a relatively small company acquired by Google in late 2014. Working with Google, Lift Labs developed a tremor-cancelling spoon to help patients with Parkinson's disease.

Clean Energy Kites

Google has always had a great concern for the environment, this becomes apparent with some of the company's innovations and ideas. Currently, Google is developing an unprecedented project which consists of a number of kites with built-in wind turbines to generate clean power.

Calico

Calico is a Google-owned company with one of the most ambitious goals in human history. With Calico, Google is researching how to essentially "cure death" by fighting the normal aging speed, ultimately extending the human lifespan.

Project Tango

Project Tango is a tablet with several sensors that are able to sense and track motion in a three-dimensional space, with many useful applications. This Google project was unveiled a while ago, but it is still undergoing development to improve its performance.

Project Ara

Project Ara is one of the most anticipated inventions that Google has announced. It basically allows the user to build their own smartphone by choosing from different components. The modular smartphone will let users have the latest hardware features without having to buy a brand new device.

Project Fi

Project Fi has been the under the spotlight for a while now and is currently going through a private testing phase. Project Fi is a hybrid network created in partnership with T-Mobile and Sprint, users will be able to pay only for the data they use instead of paying for a standard monthly fee.

Project Jacquard

There are several ways to control your smartphone, such as voice, touch. Project Jacquard aims to give users a new way to control their smartphones by touching their own clothes. This new kind of smart fabric has the goal to create smarter clothes that are able to interact with the wearer.

Project Vault

Project Vault is the next step in security. Vault consists of a completely secure computer that runs on our already existing computer's SD card.

Spotlight Stories

Google is also developing a new way to watch movies called Spotlight Stories. The already-available invention lets the user become more engaged with movies by watching them in a full 360-degree angle.

Compiled by the author from various sources.

CASE

6

Renault-Nissan alliance: Will further integration create more synergies?[1]

By Wiboon Kittilaksanawong and Caroline Palecki

Renault-Nissan Alliance (RNA) was the oldest of its kind in the automotive industry, celebrating its 15th anniversary in March 2014. As of April 2015, it sold more than one in 10 cars worldwide.[2] The alliance was formed on the principles of mutual respect while preserving each other's brands and corporate identities. On April 1, 2014, to accelerate synergies, RNA launched convergence projects in four key functions: research and development, manufacturing and logistics, purchasing, and human resources, expecting to realize at least €4.3 billion[3] in annualized synergies and cost reductions by 2016, an increase of 54 per cent since 2013.[4] However, the projects presented a number of important questions: Would this strategic move to enhance economies of scale through greater levels of product and process standardization limit quality and innovation? Would its benefits outweigh the costs of organizing common processes between the two culturally distant, independent entities? Would the move allow RNA to successfully compete in both developed and emerging target markets? Would further integration jeopardize the alliance's original spirit of respecting each other's distinctive identities, and thus undermine its competitiveness and sustainability in the long run? Should the alliance consider inviting new partners to strengthen its standing?

The global automotive industry

The automotive industry had become increasingly consolidated to meet the challenges of a wider product line, global presence and economies of scale. While in traditional developed markets like the United States and Western Europe, the industry had slowed down, emerging markets – particularly those in Brazil, Russia, India and China (BRIC) – had been growing, representing over 50 per cent of global light-vehicle sales.[5] The developed markets had seen expansion in substitute means such as public transportation, car sharing and used cars. Consumers were more cost conscious and less loyal to brands while lengthening the use of their cars. Automakers had to deal with new and more stringent regulations concerning safety and carbon dioxide emissions. Accordingly, manufacturers had to find a way to invest in new technologies while ensuring competitive prices. In emerging markets, the main challenge was to adapt existing models and technologies to the local markets, and localize production and distribution capacities to achieve lower prices. However, the common key success factors in both markets for the manufacturers were time to market, cost, quality and styling.[6]

[1]This case has been written on the basis of published sources only. Consequently, the interpretation and perspectives presented in this case are not necessarily those of Renault-Nissan Alliance or any of its employees.
[2]"The Renault-Nissan Alliance Reports Record Sales of 7,276,398 Units in 2010," January 28, 2011, www.nissan-global.com/EN/NEWS/2011/_STORY/110128-02-e.html (accessed August 20, 2015).
[3]€ = EUR.
[4]"Renault Nissan Alliance Facts and Figures 2014," http://www.nissan-global.com/EN/NEWS/2011/_STORY/110128-02-e.html (accessed August 20, 2015).
[5]"McKinsey Report – The Automotive Industry: 2020 and Beyond."
[6]J. H. Dyer, *Collaborative Advantage: Winning Through Extended Enterprise Supplier Networks*, Oxford University Press, Oxford, 2000.

The industry had a few large parts and components suppliers serving major automakers. There were also a number of small, highly specialized suppliers – mostly original equipment manufacturers (OEM) – who relied on relationships with a few automakers. These suppliers had increasingly been challenged by automakers to provide more added values but generally for the same price.[7] For example, suppliers were required to invest in highly specific assets or technologies dedicated to particular needs of their clients, and to ensure high production capacities at a global scale without reciprocal commitments.

The role of purchasing function

Automakers outsourced over half of the required parts and components.[8] Purchasing represented up to 70 per cent of the total cost of final vehicles.[9] The success of Toyota as the world's first automobile manufacturer to produce more than 10 million vehicles per year was often explained by relationship-specific investments with its suppliers.[10] Since the 1980s, automobile manufacturers had adopted "just-in-time" (JIT) production techniques, reducing the number of suppliers and investing in long-lasting collaborative relationships with only a few of them to ensure quality and product development time.

Japanese automakers were mostly familiar with developing long-term and strong informal relationships with suppliers under the "keiretsu." The keiretsu was a type of informal business group comprising companies with interlocking business relationships and shareholdings.[11] While large automakers in the West had shifted to arm's-length relationships with parts suppliers, Toyota invested significantly in its suppliers' capability development. These suppliers were, in turn, able to provide sophisticated system components tailored to Toyota's specific requirements at highly competitive prices.[12] The relationship between RNA and its suppliers was

in between such arm's-length and highly relationship-specific transactions. In particular, the alliance developed strong partnerships with suppliers of key components, while it employed arm's-length transactions with those supplying standardized, peripheral components.

The Renault-Nissan alliance

RNA was a strategic partnership between two automobile manufacturers: Renault, based in Paris, France, and Nissan, based in Yokohama, Japan. The alliance was officially established on March 27, 1999, with Renault acquiring 36.8 per cent of Nissan's outstanding stocks.[13] Carlos Ghosn had been appointed the chief executive officer of both companies. A key principle of the alliance's formation was that the parties respect each other's independent corporate identity. During the late 1990s and early 2000s, the automotive industry had undergone a period of consolidation, with numerous merger and acquisition deals.[14] RNA's top priority was to revive Nissan from the verge of bankruptcy. The revival plan drastically cut operating costs while implementing a clear strategic direction. In 2001, after the turnaround, Nissan bought a 15 per cent stake in Renault, while Renault increased its stake in Nissan to 43.4 per cent[15] (see Exhibit 1).

The main objective of RNA was to create synergies in each stage of the value chain, by fostering cost reduction and quality/innovation improvement (see Exhibit 2). The alliance allowed the parties to share technologies and best practices, and to enter new markets. Renault could benefit from Nissan's strong position in North America and Asia, while Nissan could learn from Renault's successful experience in Europe, Latin America and Russia (see Exhibit 3). The alliance aimed to be one of the top three automakers in terms of quality, technology and

[7]"Global Automotive Supplier Study," September 9, 2013, www.rolandberger.com/press_releases/Global_automotive_supplier_study.html (accessed August 20, 2015).

[8]F. Lettice, C. Wyatt and S. Evans, "Buyer-supplier Partnerships During Product Design and Development in the Global Automotive Sector: Who Invests, in What and When?" *International Journal of Production Economics*, 127(2), 2010, pp. 309–319.

[9]Dyer, op. cit..

[10]R. Vaghefi, "Creating Sustainable Competitive Advantage: The Toyota Philosophy and Its Effects," *FT.com*, 2001.

[11]K. Aoki and T.T. Lennerfors, "The New, Improved Keiretsu," *Harvard Business Review*, 91(9), 2013, pp. 109–113.

[12]Ibid.

[13]Renault-Nissan Alliance, Facts and Figures, 2014.

[14]J. MacDuffie and C. Benko, "Auto Industry Consolidation: Is There a New Model on the Horizon?" January 25, 2006, http://knowledge.wharton.upenn.edu/article/auto-industry-consolidation-is-there-a-new-model-on-the-horizon/ (accessed August 20, 2015).

[15]"Nissan and Renault Cement Ties," October 30, 2001, http://news.bbc.co.uk/2/hi/business/1627671.stm (accessed August 20, 2015).

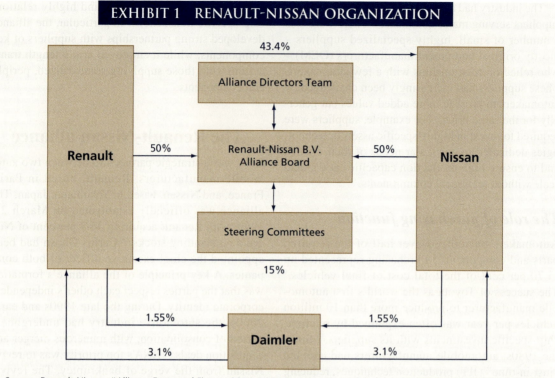

EXHIBIT 1 RENAULT-NISSAN ORGANIZATION

Source: Renault Nissan, "Alliance Facts and Figures 2014," 2014, www.nissan-global.com/EN/DOCUMENT/PDF/ALLIANCE/HANDBOOK/2014/BookletAlliance2014_GB.pdf (accessed August 20, 2015).

profitability, while upholding the imperative principle of respecting each other's brand image, culture and organizational processes. Both sides realized that the cooperation had to be based on trust and that strategic decisions had to be mutually beneficial.

Further integration strategies

Since its formation, RNA had developed through more integration between the two partners. RNA first established the Renault-Nissan Purchasing Organization (RNPO) in 2001 to maximize economies of scale. To better align strategies and realize more synergies, in 2002, the alliance created the Renault-Nissan BV (RNBV), a strategic management company with the stocks being held equally between the partners (see Exhibit 1). RNBV was an impartial platform for Renault and Nissan to exchange ideas, build strategy and leverage each other's competences and resources in a way that maximized their synergies.[16]

By 2009, RNBV had set up a dedicated team of alliance directors to accelerate the integration and sharing of best practices to create even more synergies. Such development allowed RNA's partners to open their first joint manufacturing plant and technical centre in Chennai, India in 2010.[17] The plant would begin the production of vehicles within the common module family – affordable (CMF-A), to be launched into the Indian market in 2015. CMF-A would cover the most affordable category of cars through the modular system of vehicle architecture. For maximum efficiency and brand differentiation, compatible parts and components within the modular system would be assembled into hundreds of possible configurations.

A significant step towards the integration was made on April 1, 2014, when the alliance began the four convergence projects.[18] Both companies jointly managed key project functions by appointing an alliance executive to lead each

---

[16]"The Alliance," op. cit..

[17]"Renault-Nissan Confirms New Vehicles Specifically Tailored for Growth Markets," July 16, 2013, http://blog.alliance-renault-nissan.com/content/renault-nissan-confirms-new-vehicles-specifically-tailored-growth-markets (accessed August 20, 2015).

[18]"The Alliance," op. cit..

EXHIBIT 2   EVOLUTION OF ALLIANCE SYNERGIES

Year	Synergies evolution	
1999	– Alliance Agreement	
2000	–	
2001	–	Nissan Revival
2002	–	1999–2003
2003	–	Exchange Best Practices and Exploit
2004	–	Synergies
2005	–	2003–2008
2006	–	Hard Synergies
2007	–	2008–2012
2008	–	Support Midterm Plans and Growth
2009	– €1.5 billion with RNBV Dedicated Team	2013–
2010	– €1.5 billion	
2011	– €1.7 billion Synergies with Announcement of New MTPs	
2012	– €2.7 billion Synergies	
2013	– €2.8 billion Synergies (estimated)	
2014	–	
2015	–	
2016	–	
2017	–	

Source: Renault Nissan, "Alliance Facts and Figures 2014," 2014, www.nissan-global.com/EN/DOCUMENT/PDF/ALLIANCE/ HANDBOOK/2014/BookletAlliance2014_GB.pdf (accessed August 20, 2015).

function, and a management committee to oversee the implementation.

The alliance clearly benefited both partners in terms of market shares, global presence, technology development and cost reduction. By 2013, RNA had sold nearly 8.3 million units, becoming the fourth-largest global automaker in the world[19] (see Exhibit 4). The alliance had met its global expansion target of achieving 10 per cent market share in the top five countries: Russia, France, Mexico, Turkey and Japan. However, RNA needed to strengthen its presence in China, Germany, the United States, the United Kingdom and Brazil. Through the alliance, both companies were able to share expertise and costs in developing new technologies that met future needs and trends of automobile markets. In particular, RNA was the world's leading plug-in electric vehicle manufacturer. It had a leading 58 per cent market share for zero-emissions cars with global sales of over 200,000 units in 2014.[20]

Inviting new partners

In parallel with these developments, RNA invited new partners to access new markets and technologies. In 2008, Renault and Nissan acquired 25 per cent and 17 per cent shares, respectively, in AvtoVAZ, the largest car manufacturer in Russia and an owner of the country's most sold brand, Lada.[21] The acquisition enabled RNA to enter the Russian automotive market. RNA also launched the AvtoVAZ-Renault-Nissan Purchasing Organization (ARNPO) in January 2015 to localize the procurement of parts while encouraging global suppliers to expand their operations in

[19]"Renault-Nissan: Can Anyone Succeed Carlos Ghosn?" December 29, 2014, http://fortune.com/2014/12/29/renault-nissan-carlos-ghosn (accessed August 20, 2015).

[20]"Renault-Nissan Sells Its 200,000th Electric Vehicle," November 26, 2014, www.nissan-global.com/EN/NEWS/2014/_ STORY/141126-02-e. html (accessed August 20, 2015).

[21]"Renault-Nissan and Russian Technologies Create Joint Venture to Finalize Strategic Partnership with AvtoVAZ," December 12, 2012, http:// www.media.blog.alliance-renault-nissan.com/news/renault-nissan-and-russian-technologies-create-joint-venture-to-finalize-strategic-partnership-with-avtovaz/ (accessed August 20, 2015).

EXHIBIT 3   FINANCIAL AND SALES FIGURES

Nissan financials, 1999–2014

Year	1999	2005	2013	2014	1999–2014
Net income (million ¥)	−684,363	518,000	389,000	457,600	+167%
Operating profit margin	1.4%	9.2%	4.8%	5.2%	+3.8 points

Renault financials, 1999–2014

Year	1999	2013	2014	1999–2014
Net income (million €)	534	695	1,998	+274%
Operating profit margin	5%	1.3%	2.2%	−2.8 pts

Nissan global sales, 1999–2014 (units)

Year	1999	2005	2013	2014	1999–2014
Japan	758,603	842,062	678,824	623,000	−18%
USA	874,160	1,075,097	1,248,421	1,400,000	+60%
Europe	500,836	540,945	651,476	755,000	+51%
Others	281,834	1,111,191	993,628	1,318,000	+368%
China	N/A	N/A	1,266,167	1,222,000	N/A
Mexico	N/A	N/A	264,463	N/A	N/A
TOTAL	2,415,433	3,569,295	5,102,979	5,318,000	+117%

Renault global sales, 2013–2014 (units)

Year	2013	2014
Europe	1,301,864	887,010
France	547,693	577,601
Russia	210,099	194,531
Brazil	236,360	237,187
India	64,368	44,849
Others	267,824	771,254
TOTAL	2,628,208	2,712,432

Source: Nissan, "Nissan Motor Corporation Annual Report 2015," 2015, http://www.nissan-global.com/EN/DOCUMENT/PDF/AR/2015/AR15_E_All.pdf, August 20, 2015; Renault, "Renault Annual Report 2014," 2014, https://group.renault.com/wp-content/uploads/2015/05/renault_ra_2014_en.pdf (accessed August 20, 2015).

Russia.[22] The expected benefits for both RNA and AvtoVAZ were technology upgrading, as well as quality improvement and cost reduction.

In 2010, RNA decided to partner with Daimler, a German luxury car manufacturer, by buying 3.1 per cent shares of the company to develop technologies that increased their mutual efficiency worldwide[23] (see Exhibit 1). In 2013, RNA and Daimler together partnered with a major industry player, Ford, to jointly develop a fuel-cell electric vehicle

[22]"Renault-Nissan Alliance and AVTOVAZ to Create New, Merged Purchasing Organization in Russia," December 15, 2014, http://blog.alliance-renault-nissan.com/content/renault-nissan-alliance-avtovaz-create-new-merged-purchasing-organization-russia (accessed August 20, 2015).

[23]"Renault-Nissan Alliance and Daimler AG Announce Wide-ranging Strategic Cooperation," April 7, 2010, https://www.daimler.com/documents/investors/nachrichten/kapitalmarktmeldungen/daimler-ir-release-en-20100407.pdf (accessed August 20, 2015).

EXHIBIT 4   RENAULT-NISSAN-AVTOVAZ SALES IN 2013

	2013 sales results (in million units)
Toyota	9.8
GM-Wuling	9.7
VAG-Porsche	9.5
Renault-Nissan	8.3
Hyundai-KIA	7.4
Ford	6.3
Fiat-Chrysler	4.4
Honda	4.3
PSA	2.8
Suzuki	2.7
BMW	2.0
Daimler	1.8
Mazda	1.3
Mitsubishi	1.0

Source: Renault, "Renault Nissan Alliance Facts and Figures 2014," 2014, www.nissan-global.com/EN/DOCUMENT/PDF/ALLIANCE/HANDBOOK/2014/BookletAlliance2014_GB.pdf (accessed August 20, 2015).

technology.[24] In the same year, Renault accelerated its global expansion through a 50–50 joint venture with a Chinese state-owned enterprise, Dongfeng to build a plant in Wuhan, which was expected to launch the first locally manufactured vehicle in 2016.[25] Because Dongfeng and Nissan had collaborated in China before for over 10 years, the Renault-Dongfeng joint venture would leverage their synergies in terms of plant construction and operations. In 2014, Nissan and Mitsubishi set up an equal-stake joint venture to pursue development of a mini car-based electric vehicle at the lowest price among major automakers, expecting to release a new model in 2016.[26] This joint venture also allowed Nissan and Mitsubishi to share technology and development costs.

Some of the challenges of partnering strategy included finding appropriate partners that would agree on the alliance's principles and implementing the effective collaboration. RNA experienced such difficulties in 2009, when it decided to create a low-cost mini car in India in partnership with local player Bajaj, which had expertise of developing low-cost products and knowledge of the Indian market. However, the parties could not reach agreements, particularly on the quality and safety of the mini car.[27] RNA then discontinued platform-sharing plans in India.

Broadening RNA's scope of purchasing and sharing best practices

Common purchasing activities

RNPO was the largest common organization between Renault and Nissan that significantly contributed to the creation of new synergies, covering all purchasing activities of Renault and Nissan worldwide. Since 2009, RNPO had managed 100 per cent of the partners' purchasing activities (compared to only 30 per cent when it was created in 2001).[28] As a result, the alliance had largely increased its bargaining power toward suppliers and thus effectively decreased direct and indirect costs of manufacturing inputs. Since the creation of RNPO, the most significant change for Nissan was that Ghosn had disbanded its traditional keiretsu, which was seen as costly, slow and inefficient.[29]

Before RNA's formation, Nissan and its suppliers under the keiretsu were linked through obligational and financial relationships. The suppliers were considered as a part of the Nissan group, while Nissan held some equity stakes in its suppliers. However, such relationships, based on trust and goodwill, did not prove to be efficient. The price of parts and components offered by these suppliers was usually higher

[24]"Daimler," January 28, 2013, https://www.daimler.com/documents/investors/nachrichten/kapitalmarktmeldungen/daimler-ir-release-en-20130128.pdf (accessed August 20, 2015).

[25]"Renault-Dongfeng One Year Later," December 16, 2014, http://blog.alliance-renault-nissan.com/blog/renault-dongfeng-one-year-later-0 (accessed August 20, 2015).

[26]"Nissan, Mitsubishi to Join Hands on Low-cost Electric Car," August 4, 2014, http://asia.nikkei.com/Business/Deals/Nissan-Mitsubishi-to-join-hands-on-low-cost-electric-car (accessed August 20, 2015).

[27]"Renault Not to Partner Bajaj; Holds Plans of Low-cost Cars," March 28, 2014, www.moneycontrol.com/news/ business/renault-not-to-partner-bajaj-holds-planslow-cost-cars_1060049.html (accessed August 20, 2015).

[28]"Renault-Nissan Alliance Recognizes Its 10-year Anniversary and Takes a New Step Forward," www.nissan-global.com/EN/DOCUMENT/PDF/AR/2009/AR09E_P14_Renault-Nissan_Alliance.pdf (accessed August 20, 2015).

[29]"The Renault-Nissan Alliance in 2008: Exploiting the Potential of a Novel Organizational Form," HBR.

than the global competitive price. As the automotive industry entered a period of consolidation, the keiretsu significantly weakened Nissan's competitive position in the industry. Renault, on the contrary, was among the most competitive automakers at the time in employing worldwide component outsourcing, particularly with the increasing number of electronic parts.[30] Through sharing of best practices, Nissan was highly encouraged to adopt Renault's supplier selection processes, in which the successful suppliers were likely to be those offering the best quality and delivery at the most competitive price.

Nissan was also encouraged to outsource many parts and components that were once manufactured in house or jointly produced with its suppliers. At the time, Renault helped Nissan to select the best suppliers, including those from Renault's portfolio. The combination of the partners' supplier pools strengthened the alliance's bargaining power with suppliers, which in turn enhanced efficiency and cost reduction. Since its creation, RNPO had become a major driver of synergy creation within the alliance. In 2013, through integrated purchasing processes, RNPO created €1.036 billion of synergies, accounting for about 37 per cent of total synergies generated by the alliance.[31] This success was based on the alliance's ability to achieve equal and equitable allocation of benefits between partners. While Renault shared its best practices in supplier selection processes and helped Nissan decrease its purchasing costs, Nissan contributed to improvements in the quality of Renault's manufacturing processes.

Following such successful experience, in India, the alliance built its largest common plant where the partners jointly sourced components to foster efficiency and cost reductions while decreasing the complexity of the purchasing processes.[32] In Russia, Renault, Nissan and AvtoVAZ merged their purchasing activities in January 2015.[33] The new AvtoVAZ-Renault-Nissan Purchasing Organization (ARNPO) managed the purchasing activities of all three partners in Russia under the standards of the original RNPO. With the combined purchasing volume of three partners, ARNPO was set to become the largest buyer in Russia, facilitating AvtoVAZ's further integration into the global automotive industry.

Standardization via shared platforms and the common module family

In 2013, the alliance launched the common module family (CMF), a modular architecture consisting of five common interchangeable modules, including engine bay, cockpit, front underbody and rear underbody, as well as electrical and electronic parts.[34] The CMF allowed engineers to mix and match a variety of common components in order to further facilitate the joint purchasing of parts. The objective was to produce 70 per cent of cars under the CMF by 2018. The CMF enabled the alliance to maximize the economies of scale in terms of number of vehicles and geographical regions coverage. This project was anticipated to generate at least 30 to 40 per cent of overall cost reduction per model. The innovative CMF allowed the alliance to significantly reduce purchasing costs, while ensuring each partner's distinct brand image and a diversity of products to better serve different markets.

Increased cooperation between Renault-Nissan alliance and other partners

Inspired by Nissan, RNA enhanced the practice of "monozukuri" in the development process of new cars. Monozukuri (meaning "making things" in Japanese) was embedded in Nissan's tightly integrated value chain, from design and manufacturing to delivery, so as to provide high quality products at a lower cost.[35] The critical functions to be integrated were purchasing, manufacturing, logistics and delivery. Thanks to the creation of cross-functional teams, the purchasing teams not only followed the decisions made by the engineers, but also took an active role in

[30]G. Douin, "Behind the Scenes of the Renault-Nissan Alliance," translated by Rachel Marlin, École de Paris du Management, Paris, 2002.

[31]"Renault-Nissan Alliance Posts Record €2.9b Synergies in 2013 ahead of Launch of First Common Module Family Vehicles," July 2, 2014, www.media.blog.alliance-renault-nissan.com/news/renault-nissan-alliance-posts-record-e2-9b-synergies-in-2013-ahead-of-launch-of-first-common-module-family-vehicles/ (accessed August 20, 2015).

[32]"The Renault-Nissan Alliance Inaugurates Plant in Chennai, India," March 17, 2010, www.nissan-global.com/EN/NEWS/2010/_STORY/100317-01-e.html (accessed August 20, 2015).

[33]"Renault-Nissan Alliance and AVTOVAZ to Create New, Merged Purchasing Organization in Russia," op. cit..

[34]"Common Module Family (CMF): A New Approach to Engineering for the Renault-Nissan Alliance," June 19, 2013, www.nissan-global.com/EN/NEWS/2013/_STORY/130619-01-e.html (accessed August 20, 2015).

[35]P. Pringle, "Monozukuri – Another Look at a Key Japanese Principle," July 23, 2010, www.japanintercultural.com/en/news/default.aspx?newsid=88 (accessed August 20, 2015).

making such decisions. Through the meetings in the early stages of product development, the purchasing teams were able to effectively influence the use of the cheapest and most common parts that would generate the highest cost savings to the alliance. The application of the monozukuri philosophy was expected to reduce direct costs by 4 per cent each year.[36]

Apart from improving existing technologies, Renault and Nissan also shared the costs of developing new technologies (e.g., electric cars and batteries). Both companies shared their research findings with their respective battery suppliers (LG Chem for Renault[37] and NEC for Nissan).[38] As a result, the alliance could produce quality electric cars at attractive prices. The Nissan Leaf, released in December 2010, was the world's first mass-produced zero-emissions vehicle. It became the best-selling electric car, with over 100,000 units sold in 2014, accounting for over 45 per cent of worldwide market share.[39]

The alliance also enhanced its adaptation experience through cooperation with local partners in new locations. In particular, Renault and Nissan learned to create "frugal innovations"[40] through cooperation on CMF-A in India, with the objective of launching ultra-low-cost cars in emerging markets.[41] By collaborating with Indian engineers, RNA was able to adapt its offers to the local market with fewer parts and materials, and less product development time. The use of a local supply base was critical in the alliance's strategy to reduce manufacturing costs in India. With the help of a local supplier, RNA even developed a scrap-recycling system to produce new parts from used materials.

Co-creation between the alliance and its suppliers

When Ghosn launched the revival plan in October 1999, one of the very first measures was to dismantle the keiretsu in Nissan's purchasing system. The alliance' parts and components procurement had since moved toward arm's-length relationships. However, in 2004, RNA had reintegrated some elements of the relationship-specific transactions in dealing with suppliers in its new purchasing policy.[42] The purchasing practices had since underlined the potential benefits of investing in the relationship with suppliers.

First, RNA established the continuous review of supplier performance, and shared review results with its suppliers. Each year, the best suppliers were publicly rewarded. This policy encouraged suppliers to continuously deliver quality and price-competitive parts. The suppliers were also given more confidence that they would benefit from investing in such relationship. Furthermore, the alliance judged the suppliers' performance according to their ability to make proposals and implement continuous improvement in terms of quality, cost and delivery.[43]

In exchange, RNA invested in its suppliers by collaborating with them to improve and optimize their products and manufacturing processes. The alliance created multi-functional teams to work with its suppliers to develop new parts and components or to improve existing ones. Such assistance included direct involvement in technical improvements or developments at the suppliers' production sites. To encourage supplier innovation, RNA built long-term relationships with its suppliers by developing common working teams with the alliance's specialists from the earliest phases of development.[44]

RNA used several incentives to successfully convince its suppliers to invest in such specific relationships. Suppliers could improve their own competitiveness by accessing RNA's valuable knowledge and expertise, increasing supply volumes to

[36]"Renault 2016 – Drive the Change," February 10, 2011, www.media.renault.com/global/en-gb/renaultgroup/media/pressrelease.aspx?mediaid=27137 (accessed August 20, 2015).

[37]"Renault Inks MOU with LG Chem to Jointly Develop Future EV Batteries," May 24, 2014, http://myrenaultzoe.com/index.php/2014/05/renault-inks-mou-with-lg-chem-to-jointly-develop-future-ev-batteries/ (accessed August 20, 2015).

[38]"Nissan Joins with NEC to Produce Lithium Ion Batteries," May 19, 2008, http://wot.motortrend.com/nissan-joins-with-nec-to-produce-lithium-ion-batteries-1002.html#__federated=1 (accessed August 20, 2015).

[39]"Nissan LEAF Global Sales Reach 100,000 Units," January 20, 2014, www.nissan-global.com/EN/NEWS/2014/_STORY/140120-03-e.html?rss (accessed August 20, 2015).

[40]"Frugal Innovation: Lessons from Carlos Ghosn," HBR.

[41]"Renault-Nissan Confirms New Vehicles Specifically Tailored for Growth Markets," op. cit..

[42]Aoki and Lennerfors, op. cit..

[43]"The Renault-Nissan Purchasing Way," www.nissan-global.com/EN/DOCUMENT/PDF/SR/Renault_Nissan_Purchasing_Way_English.pdf (accessed August 20, 2015).

[44]"The Renault-Nissan Purchasing Way," op. cit..

RNA's partners, and by following RNA in its international expansion. Importantly, suppliers also gained higher market recognition and spillover reputation.[45]

The co-creation benefited RNA as well, by delivering price-competitive components with better quality, shorter development time and tailor-made unique technologies. Through the strong partnership with its suppliers, RNA could focus more on its core competencies and invest in strategic projects with high growth potential, such as electric cars and mini cars for emerging markets. These partnerships were also crucial in some emerging markets, where skilled and flexible suppliers were lacking; e.g., by investing in the relationship with AvtoVAZ, RNA was able to secure enough quality parts in Russia.[46]

Challenges with integration

Cost reduction versus quality and innovation

While industry experts and the media initially doubted RNA's chances of success, the alliance had proven to be very successful. In 1999, Nissan reported a net income loss of ¥684 billion;[47] however, by 2014, it enjoyed a net income gain of ¥458 billion. Nissan's 2014 operating profit margin (5.2 per cent – two points above the industry average) was one of the best in the industry.[48] Similarly, Renault expanded into new countries, and realized cost reductions, technology developments and quality improvements. Its net income grew by 274 per cent between 1999 and 2014. The stock prices of both companies had risen: Nissan's by 50 per cent, while Renault's had more than doubled.[49]

However, both partners had to accept some trade-offs in exchange for benefits. Some of Nissan's engineers deplored what they saw as an excessive focus on cost reduction against quality

and innovation, and were reluctant to use Renault's suppliers.[50] While price was a major concern when consumers bought a new car, it was not the only criteria. Developed country consumers considered quality, safety, reputation and performance to be the four most important criteria when buying a car.[51] Increasing the number of common parts within RNA's different car models would also increase the probability of a defective component affecting more vehicles. This risk had been demonstrated in 2013, when Nissan had to recall one million cars in North America for airbag problems. The recall affected seven models, including some of the best sellers in the region. Also in 2013, about 841,000 vehicles worldwide were recalled due to a steering wheel glitch.[52] Higher standardization of parts in large production volumes increased risks not only in terms of financial performance, but also with respect to reputation and brand image.

A higher level of product standardization (e.g., predefined platforms and modules) could also compromise RNA's focus on innovation. The reluctance of Nissan's engineers to use Renault's suppliers implied that emphasizing costs might deteriorate creativity and innovation within RNA.[53] Engineers might be restricted to develop incremental innovations from traditional designs or existing models. Such drawbacks might hinder expansion in emerging markets where local adaptation was critical. For example, Renault decided to enter India with the Logan, an existing low-cost model within its portfolio. Due to this decision, Renault lacked localization of its suppliers. The company procured only 50 per cent of the necessary parts in India, which was a much lower rate than that of its competitors. The car's engine, one of the most expensive parts, was also imported from France.[54] The price of the Logan was thus not low enough to attract Indian consumers and to compete in the Indian automotive market.

[45]Faurecia, Activity Report 2012, http://www.faurecia.com/files/media/site_com_corporate/document/ANGLAIS%20internet/AMF%20REGULATED%20INFORMATION/Annual%20financial%20reports/ddr_2012_va_pour_mel.pdf (accessed August 20, 2015).

[46]"Renault-Nissan and AvtoVAZ Create Common Purchasing Organization in Russia," September 18, 2013, www.media.blog.alliance-renault-nissan.com/news/renault-nissan-avtovaz-create-common-purchasing-organization-in-russia/ (accessed August 20, 2015).

[47]¥= Japanese yen, ¥1=€.007 as of August 31, 2014.

[48]S&P 500 Sectors and Industries Profit Margins, December 31, 2014, www.yardeni.com/pub/sp500margin.pdf (accessed August 20, 2015).

[49]"Renault-Nissan: Can Anyone Succeed Carlos Ghosn?" op. cit..

[50]"Ghosn: Resistance to Renault Suppliers is Healthy," May 19, 2003, www.autonews.com/article/20030519/SUB/ 305190818/ghosn:-resistance-to-renault-suppliers-is-healthy (accessed August 20, 2015).

[51]"Consumer Reports: Car-buying Guide," www.cfah.org/file/Getting_Tools_Used/consumer.pdf (accessed August 20, 2015).

[52]"Nissan to Recall 841,000 Vehicles Worldwide due to Steering Wheel Glitch," May 24, 2013, www.reuters.com/article/2013/05/23/us-nissan-recall-idUSBRE94M06A20130523 (accessed August 20, 2015).

[53]"Ghosn: Resistance to Renault Suppliers is Healthy," op. cit..

[54]"What Went Wrong with Logan," November 10, 2009, www.business-standard.com/article/companies/what-went-wrong-with-logan-109111000042_1.html (accessed August 20, 2015).

As a long-term sustainable strategy, RNA was supposed to invest in several potential innovative projects. Instead, it focused only on plug-in electric cars. Management underestimated the opportunity of hybrid cars, which were growing in developed markets.[55] As a result, Toyota had successfully claimed its global leader position with the Prius model.[56] Arguably, RNA was overly optimistic about the potential of plug-in electric cars. In 2013, Ghosn acknowledged that sales of its electric cars were at least four years behind the target, which he blamed on slow infrastructure development.[57] In fact, RNA's management did not sufficiently study the suppliers of electricity and supporting infrastructure before investing in this project.

The revival of the Nissan Datsun in India to compete with the Tata Nano was another failure. The Global New Car Assessment Programme, an international car safety organization, awarded the car zero stars and recommended its withdrawal while Nissan argued that it met all local safety regulations.[58] Renault was also too late in entering the growing Chinese market. It entered China in 2013, when all other major competitors were already present. As a late mover in China, Renault hardly established strategic collaboration with local partners and suppliers to compete with the incumbent competitors.

Integration versus flexibility

Renault and Nissan had very different corporate cultures. Both required considerable time to reach common strategic decisions and implement them. Such compromise in the alliance's flexibility was further lessened when more partners were involved and integration among partners was emphasized. It would be increasingly difficult for partners in the alliance to maintain their status quo. For example, RNA would need much more time to reach common agreements not only within the alliance (e.g., cross-functional teams from Renault, Nissan, Daimler, AvtoVAZ, Dongfeng and Mitsubishi), but also with outside partners (e.g., suppliers and other auto manufacturers).

Time to market, a key success factor in the automotive industry, would undoubtedly worsen. The alliance's prerogative to ensure that all of its decisions were based on a win-win principle might be hard to achieve.

As the two companies increased their integration and convergence of organizational processes in order to realize more economies of scale, to what extent should they abandon their own corporate cultures and identities to strengthen the integration? In 2008, Nissan refused to use the Logan platform for the development of its low-cost car segment and decided to create its new platform, breaking the alliance strategy to increase the use of common modules.[59] Was the future strategy of RNA – i.e., relying on standardization and increasing common organizational processes – threatening the basic principle of its creation: mutual respect of each partner's identity?

The leadership of CEO and succession plan

RNA's success was largely based on Ghosn's leadership. He had given both companies the autonomy to act within certain boundaries and retain their own individuality, while joining to build mutual benefits. As RNA pushed to achieve even more integration and thus efficiencies, Ghosn used some coercion to persuade the management of both companies to share designs as well as parts and components. The downside of pushing integration was that it was hard to keep the companies separate and on equal footing.

The 61-year-old Ghosn was hoping that electric cars, autonomous vehicles and costs reductions would drive the alliance to a place among the world's top three automakers. Given his track record, even if he succeeded in this endeavour, could anyone successfully take his place? Most of the industry's top-line executives were over 50 years old. Neither Nissan nor Renault had a clear candidate lined up to run such a complex alliance. RNA ran at least three auto companies (e.g., Renault, Nissan, AvtoVAZ

---

[55]"Ghosn Says Not Time for Hybrids Yet," April 20, 2006, http://paultan.org/2006/04/20/ghosn-says-not-time-for-hybrids-yet/ (accessed August 20, 2015).

[56]"Worldwide Prius Sales Top 3-million Mark; Prius Family Sales at 3.4 million," July 3, 2013, www.greencarcongress.com/2013/07/prius-20130703.html (accessed August 20, 2015).

[57]"Cost of Electric Vehicles Outweighs Their 'Green' Credentials," November 20, 2014, www.ft.com/intl/cms/s/0/73ed8758-650f-11e4-ab2d-00144feabdc0.html#axzz3OOzCtR8K (accessed August 20, 2015).

[58]"Renault-Nissan: Can Anyone Succeed Carlos Ghosn?" op. cit..

[59]"The Renault-Nissan Alliance in 2008: Exploiting the Potential of a Novel Organizational Form," op. cit..

and a few others), with three different official languages. Its leader was responsible for 10 per cent of all worldwide cars sales, amounting to €115 billion in 2014.[60] RNA also owned 3.1 per cent of Daimler, which in turn owned 3.1 per cent each of both Nissan and Renault. Could anyone succeed Ghosn in managing such a vast and complex enterprise?

Next strategic moves of the alliance

Ghosn was considering integrating a third global car manufacturer into RNA to further increase synergies and raise the investment needed to adapt to new regulations, trends and needs in both developed and emerging markets.[61] RNA had engaged in talks with General Motors but its attempt to partner with this US manufacturer failed in 2006.[62] Given the long-term successful collaboration between Renault and Nissan, would its alliance knowledge and experience help it to identify the right partner(s) and to manage the new alliance portfolio effectively? Would inviting new partners dilute RNA's core values and

identities, and increase the complexity (and costs) of the organization?

As new synergies would require further integration, should the two partners merge? Both companies had denied the merge option since the alliance's formation. However, in light of increasing dependence and integration, merging seemed to be a possible option. Alternatively, the two companies could split up into two smaller entities, struggling to survive in the highly consolidated automotive industry.

At Renault's annual meeting in April 2014, Ghosn set a goal for RNA to become one of the top three global automakers. To achieve this goal, the company had less than three years to increase its market share and profits by 33 per cent in order to achieve 8 per cent global market share and 8 per cent operating margins by the end of fiscal year 2017/18. A large part of this ambition was to conquer the BRIC markets. However, Brazil and China's economies were starting to slow down, and the Russian economy tended to head for recession. Furthermore, the Nissan Leaf had not come close to paying off the €5 billion that had been invested in it. Ghosn had to admit that RNA still had a long way to go.

---

[60]"Renault-Nissan: Can Anyone Succeed Carlos Ghosn?" op. cit..

[61]"The Renault-Nissan Alliance in 2008: Exploiting the Potential of a Novel Organizational Form," op. cit..

[62]"GM Talks with Renault and Nissan End in Disagreement," Financial Times, October 5, 2006, www.ft.com/intl/cms/s/0/604ed924-540e-11db-8a2a-0000779e2340.html#axzz37OT4Gw9G (accessed August 20, 2015).

Time for a change at The Change Foundation

By Alexander Smith

It was January 2007, and Cathy Fooks had just accepted her new position as chief executive officer (CEO) of The Change Foundation, an independent charitable foundation founded in 1996 by the Ontario Hospital Association (OHA) with a mandate to promote, support and improve health and the delivery of health care in Ontario. After 10 years, the board had undertaken a renewal process to evaluate the strategic directions of the foundation and measure the value-add of progress to date. After reviewing the new board-approved strategic plan, Fooks had some concerns about how The Change Foundation should refocus its activities and transform itself going forward. Before she could start to rebuild the foundation, she had to decide what its future direction should be.

Origins of the change foundation: the Ontario Hospital Association

The OHA was a member association representing over 150 Ontario public hospitals. It had the broad vision of "achiev[ing] a high-performing health system."[1] The OHA achieved this by providing its member hospitals with high-quality products and services, leading innovation and performance improvement and influencing Ontario health system policy.

In 1996, the OHA received a one-time payout of approximately $50 million through the divestiture of Blue Cross Insurance. This opportunity provided a number of investment options; however, the OHA chose to set up an endowment fund and establish The Change Foundation to lead transformation in the Ontario health system. Sheila Jarvis, chair of the OHA board in 2005 and of The Change Foundation board from 2011 to 2013, explained that this money was designed to "enable the health care system in Ontario, through the lens of hospitals, to explore new and innovative ways of doing business."[2] The funds enabled the OHA to develop an opportunity to achieve a sustainable approach to health system innovation from which all organizations in the health system could benefit. The vision was to promote a high-achieving Ontario health care system for the future.

In 2006, the OHA itself developed a new strategic plan to better achieve a high-performing health system in the future. It consisted of five key strategic directions:

- Create strong and lasting partnerships that advance health system integration;
- Improve knowledge transfer of leading practices to strengthen health system performance;
- Strengthen governance throughout the health care sector;
- Improve executive and management leadership capacity within the health sector through a new leadership institute; and
- Provide thought leadership on health system issues based on facts, evidence and/or hospital expertise.[3]

Alexander Smith wrote this case under the supervision of Professor Anne Snowdon solely to provide material for class discussion. The authors do not intend to illustrate either effective or ineffective handling of a managerial situation. The authors may have disguised certain names and other identifying information to protect confidentiality.

[1]OHA, "About Us," 2013, www.oha.com/AboutUs/Pages/Default.aspx (accessed February 26, 2014).

[2]Sheila Jarvis interview with case authors January 17, 2014.

[3]OHA, "OHA Strategic Directions 2007–2010: A Look Back," 2013, http://www.oha.com/knowledgecentre/library/annualreportarchive/annualreport2010/Pages/Default.aspx (accessed February 26, 2014).

History of the change foundation

The Change Foundation began primarily as a granting agency offering small amounts of funding to a wide range of projects; its mandate was "promoting, supporting and improving health and the delivery of health care" (see Exhibits 1 and 2). Gail Donner, chair of The Change Foundation board from 2007 to 2009, explained:

> The organization would tell people, "get a good idea underway" with the idea that over time they would then be eligible for significant funding. That's why we have the name, "Change Foundation" – it was a jumpstart for projects with less experience or with a good idea but not enough resources to work it through.

The Change Foundation was a separate entity from the OHA. It had a separate board and CEO, who reported to the OHA on their progress every year to make sure that they were achieving the mandate

that the OHA had given them. However, despite the separation, the OHA remained in a position of control over The Change Foundation and had the ability to remove the board and change its bylaws if it was unhappy with the progress that was being achieved. The Change Foundation worked to achieve its mandate through two key core functions: knowledge creation and knowledge transfer.

Knowledge creation

Knowledge creation was achieved at The Change Foundation through two key programs: the Change Initiatives Grants Program and the Research Program.

The Change Initiatives Grants Program was a joint program between The Change Foundation and the Ontario Ministry of Health and Long-Term Care (MOHLTC). It was designed to broadly support innovations that improved health care in Ontario. Each year, The Change Foundation established priorities for health system innovation that were then released to the research community, and grant applications were

EXHIBIT 1   THE CHANGE FOUNDATION BALANCE SHEET

	March 31,	
	2006	2005
Assets		
Cash	12,379	872,638
Investments	57,981,932	54,881,106
Accounts Receivable	27,456	30,522
	58,021,767	55,784,266
Capital Assets	5,883	4,951
	58,027,650	**55,789,217**
Liabilities		
Accounts Payable	665,139	353,363
Deferred Revenue	1,398,342	1,533,847
Employee Future Benefits	110,300	110,300
	2,173,781	1,997,510
Fund Balances		
Invested in Capital Assets	5,883	4,951
Externally Restricted	44,625,008	44,020,082
Unrestricted	11,522,978	9,766,674
	55,853,869	53,791,707
	58,027,650	**55,789,217**

Source: The Change Foundation, "Annual Report 2005/2006," www.changefoundation.ca/about-us/annual-reports/ (accessed on February 26, 2014).

EXHIBIT 2 THE CHANGE FOUNDATION STATEMENT OF OPERATIONS

	Year ended March 31, 2006
Revenues	
Investment Income	2,515,918
Amortization of Deferred Revenue	735,005
Other	212,281
Realized Gain on Investments	2,015,267
Total Revenues	**5,478,471**
Expenditures	
Investment Expenses	
Investment Management Fees	34,465
Operating Expenses	
Grants	1,482,150
Research and Analysis	623,567
Education	220,196
Development Projects	844,458
Administrative	516,399
Total Expenses	**3,721,235**
Net Operating Income	**1,757,236**

Source: The Change Foundation, "Annual Report 2005/2006," www.changefoundation.ca/about-us/annual-reports/ (accessed February 26).

reviewed for strengths in achieving these priority targets. In 2005, for example, this goal was to "support Ontario Health System Transformation by enhancing organizational integration through LHINs [Local Health Integration Networks] and supporting disease management."[4] Ten research projects received funding totaling $822,000 in 2005 (see Exhibit 3). This funding was supported through additional matched funding from the MOHLTC. Between 1997 and 2005, 75 projects were funded at a total of $5.9 million.

The Research Program consisted of a series of research project publications by The Change Foundation. These projects varied greatly, from establishing the Provincial Disease Management Network to collecting best practices in hospital and community integration in mental health. Through partnering with external individuals and organizations, The Change Foundation completed research projects and produced policy papers consistent with its mandate. Since 2004, the Research Program had focused on "promoting system transformation through integration."[5]

Knowledge transfer

In addition to producing research both in-house and through grants, The Change Foundation promoted the transfer of health research into clinical practice. Specifically, it focused on the roles of social marketing, electronic media and complexity theory on research knowledge transfer. The Knowledge Transfer Program partnered with the OHA through participation in and co-sponsorship of OHA events and conferences. The majority of projects within this stream focused on education and leadership development. The Change Foundation offered international study tours for health executives to provide senior health leaders the opportunity to learn new health policy and practices from the United Kingdom, Australia, Sweden and Norway.[6]

In 2003, the mandate of the Knowledge Transfer Program was expanded to focus on developing leadership capacity among health executives and emerging health leaders. The Change Foundation partnered

[4]The Change Foundation, "Annual Report 2005/2006," www.changefoundation.ca/about-us/annual-reports/ (accessed February 26, 2014).

[5]Company records.

[6]The Change Foundation, Annual Report 2005/2006, op. cit..

EXHIBIT 3   SAMPLE GRANTS AWARDED IN 2005

- *Integrated Delivery of Community Health Information to the Hospitals through the CHIN [Community Health Information Network],* 2005: Community Care Access Centre (CCAC) of Waterloo Region with Grand River Hospital and the University of Waterloo, $43,000 grant.

- *Enhancing Self-Management of Diabetes and Depression in Primary Care through Peer Support,* 2005: Hamilton HSO Mental Health & Nutrition Program, a service of St. Joseph's Healthcare Hamilton with Hamilton Branch, Canadian Diabetes Association; Diabetes Hamilton; and Mental Health Rights Coalition (2005), $40,000 grant.

- *Virtual Tours of Placement Destinations,* 2005: Hotel-Dieu Grace Hospital with Windsor

Regional Hospital, Windsor Essex CCAC, Windsor-Essex County Real Estate Board and the Hospitality Network, $100,000 grant.

- *Time to Treat Initiative for Lung Cancer Patients and PERLA (Patients with Early Resected and Locally Advanced),* 2005: Lung Cancer Clinic Lung Cancer Canada with Toronto Sunnybrook Regional Cancer Centre (Sunnybrook & Women's Health Sciences Centre) and Toronto East General Hospital, $100,000 grant.

Note: Ten grants were funded in 2005. This list represents a sample only.

Source: The Change Foundation, "Annual Report 2005/2006," www.changefoundation.ca/about-us/annual-reports/ (accessed February 26).

with the University of Toronto's Rotman School of Management and the King's Fund to develop a four-week training program for future health leaders focused on change management and integrative thinking.

In 2005, the mandate of the Knowledge Transfer Program was further expanded with the OHAfrica Project. Initiated by the OHA, OHAfrica challenged Ontario hospitals and other health organizations to help manage the AIDS pandemic in Africa. This involved sending teams of health care practitioners to Lesotho to introduce antiretroviral drugs. The Change Foundation committed to contributions totaling $1.5 million over three years to start this work and ultimately establish the program's independence. By 2006, OHAfrica had placed over 1,200 people on life-saving antiretroviral drugs in Lesotho.[7]

Oha review of The Change Foundation

In 2004, nearing the tenth anniversary of The Change Foundation and with a new strategy for the OHA in development, a new strategic plan needed to reflect on achievements to date to determine the foundation's future role. The OHA had begun to question the foundation's effectiveness: was it making

the impact on health system transformation that had been anticipated? The association felt that the research projects that were being completed were too small in scale to achieve health system change. It began to question whether or not funding small grants was the right approach to achieve transformation and change, as the recipients did not always have the scientific research competencies to produce high-quality research. One of the core values of the OHA was to be evidence-based, so the quality of the evidence produced was of the utmost importance.

Ultimately, the OHA was also concerned with impact. The OHA and The Change Foundation had already had two joint board and executive committee meetings to discuss these issues. Several board members had been replaced in an attempt to lead organizational change, but without starting anew and removing the existing legacy structures and processes, change was limited.

The OHA decided that more significant change had to occur at The Change Foundation, and as part of this new strategy, it replaced members of the foundation's board with OHA members in an interim capacity. Jarvis explained:

This was a very typical governance strategy and the board of the OHA, we appointed some of our own board members to be the new board of The Change Foundation, recognizing it was

[7]Ibid.

really an interim measure, while we thought about a strategic plan for The Change Foundation and then went out to recruit a new CEO with a new and fresh mandate.[8]

The Change Foundation draft strategic plan 2006

With pressure coming from the OHA, The Change Foundation's interim CEO and board underwent a strategic planning process consisting of two main phases: a SWOT (strengths, weaknesses, opportunities, tensions) analysis and environmental scan to understand the climate at the time and a Strategic Directions Think Tank to select the key strategic priorities.

Draft Strategic Plan: Phase 1 – SWOT analysis

The strategic planning process consisted of over 30 interviews with key stakeholders and several focus groups to identify the organization's strengths, weaknesses, opportunities and tensions.

One of the key components of the strategic renewal process was to examine the state of health care research organization in Ontario in order to better understand The Change Foundation's contributions. A benchmarking review of foundations in Ontario revealed that health care research was funded by four main types of organizations: full-service foundations, granting and knowledge transfer organizations, research institutes and think tank/policy forums (see Exhibit 4). The provincial health research landscape was growing, with a broad range of organizations focused on health research that ranged in size from small players to large organizations with endowment funds in excess of $200 million. No single model of foundation existed, as each organization used different core processes and mechanisms to achieve its mandate.

Robin Osborn, vice-president and director of the International Program in Health Policy and Innovation at the Commonwealth Fund, outlined seven key components of a "value-added foundation":

- A clear mission;
- Determination to focus;
- Well-defined strategies;

	EXHIBIT 4 HEALTH CARE RESEARCH ORGANIZATION TYPES			
Type of organization	1. Full service "value added" foundations	2. Granting & knowledge transfer organizations	3. Research institutes	4. Think tanks/ policy forums
Core Activities	■ Grant making ■ Conduct in-house research, work with grantees ■ Knowledge translation and exchange ■ Policy analysis and forums ■ Leadership development and fellowships	■ Grant making ■ Support knowledge creation, capacity building ■ Knowledge transfer and exchange	■ Non granting ■ Conduct research using salaried, in-house researcher; compete for peer reviewed funding ■ Knowledge transfer and exchange	■ Non granting ■ Research synthesis & policy analysis ■ May commission research ■ Create forums for debate, discussion and informed decision making
Examples	■ The Commonwealth Fund ■ The King's Fund	■ CHSRF ■ CIHR Institute of Health Services & Policy Research	■ Institute for Clinical Evaluative Sciences (ICES) ■ Institute of Work & Health	■ Institute of Research & Public Policy (IRPP) ■ Nuffield Trust

Source: Company records.

[8]Sheila Jarvis interview, op. cit..

- Rigorous grant making;
- Solid intellectual grounding in chosen fields;
- Communication to influential audiences; and
- Concern for accountability and performance.[9]

The findings of the SWOT analysis can be found in Exhibit 5.

Draft Strategic Plan: Phase 2 – strategic directions think tank

In May 2006, after the initial SWOT analysis was complete, The Change Foundation held a Strategic Directions Think Tank, which included 40 senior health leaders, policy and decision makers, grant makers, educators and health services researchers, to define the strategic priorities of the organization going forward.

The outcomes of the strategic planning process solidified The Change Foundation as a hybrid between a granting and knowledge transfer organization and a think tank/policy forum organization. Guided by a new mission, vision and value statement (see Exhibit 6), The Change Foundation sought to achieve a more focused approach to granting, a renewed focus on developing a role as a think tank organization and a new focus on capacity building through five key strategic priorities.

Priority 1: Support the successful implementation of integrated health systems in Ontario. In 2006, Ontario established a new regionalized health care system with the implementation of LHINs. The 14 regional health authorities managed all planning, integration and funding for all Ontario hospitals, long-term care homes, community care access centres, mental health agencies and community support agencies. This was to be a major change in the Ontario health care system, and there was opportunity for research organizations to study its structural governance and support the transition.

EXHIBIT 5   THE CHANGE FOUNDATION SWOT ANALYSIS 2006

Strengths	*Weaknesses*
■ Secure financial base ($50 million+ endowment) ■ Capacity to connect with upper echelon of thought leaders in Ontario's health care system ■ Relationship with the OHA ■ Several strong partnerships established including MOHLTC, The King's Fund, Canadian College of Health Service Executives ■ Potential to recruit to renewed mandate and focus ■ Flexibility in by-laws	■ Lack of focus and priority setting, engaged in too many disparate activities for the size of the organization ■ Granting program has been criticized for lacking sufficient rigour, appropriate peer review and transparency in decision making ■ Limited internal capacity to deliver on high-profile, high-quality research projects

Opportunities	*Tensions/Challenges*
■ Changing environment, MOHLTC Transformation Agenda, advent of LHINs ■ Need for a provincial forum for analysis, debate of known and emerging health issues; need to engage decision makers in long-term sustainability of the health system ■ Appetite for greater understanding and innovations in health system delivery and design, need for synthesis/creation of knowledge on health system integration and change ■ Potential to engage thought leaders and health service researchers nationally and internationally ■ Interested intellectual and funding partners to tackle questions on system integration and change	■ Operationally (action) oriented research projects vs. more scholarly, scientifically excellent research ■ Broader health system focus vs. flow management, "on the ground" models of service integration ■ Granting program vs. in-house and commissioned research ■ Think tank/policy forum vs. knowledge creator and capacity builder ■ Independence vs. interdependence with OHA

Source: Company records.

---

[9]Company records.

The Change Foundation had experience in health system integration, with several studies exploring international models of regionalization that could be transferred to the Ontario situation. Any potential research would be required to meet the following priority research themes: relevance, future orientation, multidisciplinary, potential for leveraging partnerships and potential to influence policy.[10]

Key goals and implementation strategies for priority 1 are outlined in Exhibit 7.

EXHIBIT 6   MISSION, VISION, VALUES

Vision	Mission	Values
A sustainable, high-performing and accessible health system for Ontario.	The mission of The Change Foundation is to inform and guide effective policy and practice that will contribute to building a high quality, integrated health system in Ontario. The Change Foundation carries out this mandate by promoting independent analysis and informed debate of known and emerging health issues, supporting outstanding research and facilitating knowledge transfer.	In fulfilling its vision and mission, The Change Foundation embraces the following core values: ■ Innovation & Excellence ■ Partnership & Collaboration ■ Transparency & Objectivity ■ Relevance & Timeliness ■ Trust & Respect

Source: Company records.

EXHIBIT 7   KEY GOALS AND IMPLEMENTATION STRATEGIES FOR PRIORITY 1

Goals	Implementation strategies
Establish an expert understanding of the health system integration and share that knowledge.	■ Collect and organize intelligence and insights around system integration from national and international sources. ■ Translate learning from other jurisdictions to the Ontario context. ■ Partner with other foundations in Ontario, Canada, the United States and Europe to learn from the experience of others on an ongoing basis.
Identify, promote and share best practices in health system integration.	■ Produce case and field studies showcasing innovative practices in health system integration. ■ Create the "tool kits" to help organizations achieve integration and to work with partners to disseminate knowledge. ■ Establish innovative models for improved care delivery from around the world and foster cross-national research and collaboration. ■ Use small grants to target action projects that apply an innovative idea, with a view to evaluating the project. ■ Sponsor a Future Ideas Conference in partnership with the OHA, MOHLTC, LHINs (explore partnership with CITY TV Ideas conference).

Source: Company records.

[10]Ibid.

Priority 2: Serve as a catalyst for multi-sectoral and informed public policy debate. The Change Foundation would operate as a "research broker" connecting people, evidence and action together. To achieve this strategic priority, The Change Foundation would begin by proactively seeking the pressing issues with which policy makers would be dealing within the next 12 to 18 months. The foundation would then connect research teams, policy makers and health leaders to conduct and support research collectively. Finally, The Change Foundation would leverage the integrated research approach through the dissemination of research results to the influential policy makers leading action.

Key goals and implementation strategies for priority 2 are outlined in Exhibit 8.

Priority 3: Foster leadership capacity building. The Change Foundation recognized that there had been insufficient support and resources directed at the next generation of health leaders. Many other organizations also recognized this, and the health leadership training industry was becoming saturated – including by the OHA, which was looking to expand its leadership development programming. Therefore, The Change Foundation would discontinue leadership training and become a catalyst

to support it. The foundation had experience working with international partners who provided innovative models of education such as visiting scholar, fellowship and cross-training programs that were not present in Canada. There was a unique opportunity to adapt these programs to the Ontario context and evaluate their effectiveness.

Key goals and implementation strategies for priority 3 are outlined in Exhibit 9.

Priority 4: Promote organizational excellence. The changes in the strategic direction towards a think tank model required a new set of employee competencies, either in The Change Foundation's existing employees or new ones. The required competencies would be assessed and the optimal approach to acquiring these skills would be evaluated. During the strategic planning process, The Change Foundation was being led by an interim CEO; therefore, a new permanent CEO would need to be hired to lead the new organization.

The Change Foundation did not receive adequate recognition for many of the successful and well-known research projects that it funded. The Ottawa Model for Smoking Cessation, for example, was a celebrated model for health promotion in over 140 sites across Canada. Very few knew, however,

EXHIBIT 8 KEY GOALS AND IMPLEMENTATION STRATEGIES FOR PRIORITY 2

Goals	Implementation strategies
Conduct action-oriented analyses of pressing or emerging policy issues.	■ Survey and report on national and international trends in policy, funding and delivery of integrated health systems. ■ Conduct an ongoing scan of the policy landscape and health delivery issues.
Connect research, policy and practice.	■ Convene meetings with local, national and international researchers, policy makers, academic experts and health leaders. ■ Establish a Multi-sectoral Advisory Board to identify key issues and research questions that need to be addressed. ■ Participate in the international network of policy-oriented health care researchers and foundations.
Communicate results to influential audiences.	■ Target knowledge transfer to specific target audiences' needs and interests; package information to attract target audiences. ■ Develop publishing and distribution strategies geared to the needs of influential audiences for easy to use information.

Source: Company records.

EXHIBIT 9   KEY GOALS AND IMPLEMENTATION STRATEGIES FOR PRIORITY 3

Goals	Implementation strategies
Collaborate with others in designing a High Performing Leadership Program for Ontario.	■ Collaborate with provincial health associations, government, academic and other training institutions to maintain a focus on the leadership challenge and solutions. ■ Partner with others to develop innovative solutions to fill gaps in leadership development and support.
Support the development of talented leaders.	■ Partner with other foundations in developing fellowships in health care policy. ■ Create fellowships and visiting scholars programs to selectively support The Change Foundation's priorities for leadership development.

Source: Company records.

EXHIBIT 10   KEY GOALS AND IMPLEMENTATION STRATEGIES FOR PRIORITY 4

Goals	Implementation strategies
Implement a board renewal strategy	■ Establish a Board Governance Committee to implement a board renewal strategy that is consistent with the foundation's role and strategies.
Enhance staff competencies to support changing role of the foundation.	■ Assess the skills and competency requirements for the CEO position and retain a permanent leader for the renewed organization. ■ Ensure a strong and supported professional staff to add value to the work of grantees.
Forge partnerships at the local, national and international level.	■ Collaborate with organizations that advance the vision, mission and strategic priorities of The Change Foundation. ■ Partner with policy makers and decision makers to inform and advance health policy and health system change.
Enhance the reach and profile of The Change Foundation.	■ Develop a communications strategy, including infrastructure requirements such as an enhanced website. ■ Develop signature products that are associated with The Change Foundation and promote them broadly.

Source: Company records.

that The Change Foundation was linked to the study. There was no model for monitoring outcomes and communicating them to the necessary stakeholders. The Change Foundation would focus on building its provincial and national reputation by profiling its successes to secure itself as a reputable research hub.

Key goals and implementation strategies for priority 4 are outlined in Exhibit 10.

Priority 5: Implement a sustainable future plan for the OHAfrica project.   The Change Foundation would continue its commitment to the OHAfrica Project and support its sustainability after three years by the creation of a new charitable organization focused on the existing work in Lesotho.

Key goals and implementation strategies for priority 5 are outlined in Exhibit 11.

EXHIBIT 11 KEY GOALS AND IMPLEMENTATION STRATEGIES FOR PRIORITY 5

Goals	Implementation strategies
Implement OHAfrica as a special purpose corporation that is self-sufficient within three years.	▪ Create a new charitable organization with a specific focus on sustaining the work underway in Lesotho by OHAfrica. ▪ Develop and implement a three-year transition plan for financial and operational independence of the new organization from the OHA and the Change Foundation.

Source: Company records.

New leadership at The Change Foundation

The Change Foundation board and the OHA approved the strategic plan in September 2006. Donner explained:

> The board was a transitional board, some from the previous and some newly recruited board members. I think the newly recruited members were quite determined to see it change, but getting some external review and also holding this large think tank really helped people understand that the timing was right for us to morph into something more valuable to the system.

The first step of the strategy was hiring a new full-time CEO. The board sought Cathy Fooks, executive director of the Health Council of Canada where she had responsibility for reporting about health care renewal to Canadians.

Fooks joined The Change Foundation in January 2007 after the draft strategic plan had been developed. She had previous experience with the foundation as a member of a project committee that examined the quality of the work being funded and how to implement it to a system level. She very quickly noticed several problems with the committee and the way it was run – most notably that it consisted of members who were leading the very projects the foundation was funding – and decided to leave it. In 2006, when she was approached by a headhunter with the proposition to lead The Change Foundation in a new direction, with full board support, she became very interested: "[It was] an opportunity to really start afresh and that is what I love to do." She elaborated:

> The attraction for me was the tabula rasa – this notion that I could go into an organization that was financially stable . . . which is really unusual for a foundation. I had a complete green light from the hiring committee. . . I had the authority and the ability to rethink from the beginning. In some ways, it was like coming into a new organization without having to do the infrastructure and financial build.

However, Fooks also knew that there would be several challenges if she were to accept the CEO position. First, she knew there would be a lot of ambiguity in her first year as the organization went in a new direction. Major changes would be happening: staff would have to be moved out, strategic priorities would be changing and operations and projects would have to be closed. Second, the position would require her to lead transformational change, which required a unique skill set. Third, there was some uncertainty about the relationship that The Change Foundation had with the OHA. Fooks knew that there was a chance, however small, that the foundation could spend an entire year developing a new strategic plan that the OHA would not approve.

During her interview with several of The Change Foundation's board members, Fooks was presented with the draft strategic plan for the organization and was asked what suggestions or changes she had to make. She immediately knew that significant changes had to be made to the draft plan and considered her options.

Rebuilding the strategic plan: A new direction

Fooks recalled,

My impression was that the organization had small effects at a very local level. They had done a lot of smaller grants – hundreds of them – without a lot of rigorous evaluation . . . the problem was, when you roll it up to a system level, there wasn't an impact. So we're called The Change Foundation, but what did we change?

The board and staff at The Change Foundation realized that they were not reaching the system-level impact with which they had been tasked, that is, to be a major contributor to the strategic planning process. However, Fooks noted that there seemed to be a common view within the organization that the way to achieve system-level impact was to promote and advertise the research projects more; she thought it was much more involved than that.

When The Change Foundation was founded in 1996, it was one of the major health research funding agencies in Ontario. Fast forward to 2006, and the market was much more crowded, with much larger agencies such as the Canadian Institutes of Health Research (CIHR) and the Canadian Health Services Research Foundation (CHSRF), which had endowment funds upwards of $200 million in comparison to The Change Foundation's $50 million. In addition to the financial barriers, Fooks thought that, in comparison to some of the larger organizations, The Change Foundation did not have the in-house talent to be able to manage all of its projects. The foundation had just seven full-time staff in comparison to hundreds at CIHR. She wondered if the new strategic plan would be able to meet the foundation's mandate of "promoting, supporting and improving health and the delivery of health care."

Options

Fooks knew that there were five main strategic directions that the foundation could take going forward. She carefully weighed which direction or combination of directions the organization should take:

1. Merger with the OHA.   The OHA could bring The Change Foundation in-house and manage its mandate internally. The Change Foundation would act as the research/policy department of the OHA. The foundation's CEO would also hold a vice president position in the OHA. Fooks made it very clear in her interview that she was not interested in this option.

2. Close the change foundation.   The Change Foundation had a large endowment that would remain in effect as long as necessary. It was not taking in any active donations, so there were no donors who needed to be satisfied. The foundation could be closed for a period of time until a new opportunity presented itself.

3. Merger with another foundation.   Several similar organizations such as the Wellesley Institute or the Atkinson Foundation were similar in size to The Change Foundation and had similar mandates. By entering into conversations with these organizations, a larger foundation could be created to lead even greater system-level change in Ontario health care.

4. Focus The change foundation as a granting organization.   It was clear the foundation was trying to do too much and was very unfocused. However, with some refinement, the grants program could be made more efficient, more high-profile and more focused. This option would also require a detailed funding plan. Decisions would be required outlining what types of projects would be funded, what research areas should be prioritized and what were the existing research gaps. Since the foundation's resources were limited, a decision was also required to determine whether it should choose a variety of smaller projects or one key area that no one was talking about now, but would be in two to three years, to address a key gap.

5. Change the foundation model.   The Change Foundation could cease its granting practices and transition to another health research organization type. Potential models could include leadership capacity building (supporting/educating health leaders), think tank (policy influencing), brokering best practices (evaluating clinical or managerial practices) or many others. However, despite strong management and research departments, The Change Foundation lacked many of the skill sets necessary for alternate models (e.g., policy experts, stakeholder engagement experts, communications team, etc.).

Regardless of the decision made, Fooks knew that each option carried with it a set of consequences that would have to be considered and overcome. For example, if The Change Foundation chose to focus on one target research area, its risk would increase as there was no fallback if the research did not go as planned. Therefore, integrated quality assurance would be an essential priority. If The Change Foundation chose a new health research organization type, staffing levels would have to change to reflect the new needs of the new model. Seemingly simple decisions could lead to significant organizational changes.

Summary

With multiple target audiences and strategic priorities, inconsistent project involvement and a vague mandate, mission, vision and values, Fooks had reservations about this plan. As she sat down in her new CEO office, she began to write her proposal to the board.

CASE

8

Federated Co-Operatives Limited: Change management

By Dionne Pohler

Scott Banda, chief executive officer (CEO) of Federated Co-Operatives Limited (FCL), sat down at his desk in June 2013 to read through the results of the second employee engagement survey conducted by FCL's human resources department. Since Banda took over the CEO position at FCL in February 2010, the company had undertaken massive, system-wide changes intended to address major areas of weakness. FCL's information technology (IT), marketing, and people-management processes were described by both insiders and outsiders as being outdated, and the organizational culture that Banda inherited was described as hierarchical and controlling.

Banda returned from a meeting with FCL's senior leadership team (SLT) where there was a discussion about the progress that had been made and the obstacles that were overcome to date. The SLT also held a frank conversation about where progress was still lacking and the challenges that were ongoing. There was still a long way left to go in updating FCL's IT and marketing, and improving its people-management processes. Given that the vast majority of organizational changes fail, Banda knew there was still a lot to be done for success.[1]

The pace and magnitude of change felt overwhelming to him (and to his SLT) at times and based on the comments he was reading in the engagement survey, many employees felt the same way. The next day, Banda was scheduled to address FCL's home office employees in the city of Saskatoon in Saskatchewan, Canada, at a Q&A session. Banda scheduled this kind of session once each quarter because he believed that direct and open two-way communication with FCL's employees was integral to changing the deeply embedded command-and-control

culture. The recent introduction of engagement surveys was another way to ensure employees would feel comfortable about voicing their concerns to the senior leadership team.

As Banda ruminated over the employee engagement survey comments and the concerns the SLT raised that morning, a number of questions surfaced. Had FCL taken on more than it could manage? Should they slow down the changes being made to processes and systems? What major obstacles could derail the process in both the short and long-term? Had the SLT developed a vision for what success would ultimately look like? How would they implement all of this change while at the same time avoiding employee burnout and still keep the business running smoothly? Would it even be possible to change such an embedded culture? There were no easy answers to these questions.

Federated Co-Operatives Limited

The origins of FCL could be traced back to the early 20th century when farmers established purchasing associations. By 1970, several provincial wholesale co-operatives amalgamated to serve a network of retail co-operatives across Western Canada, with a home office located in Saskatoon.[2] FCL provided central wholesaling, manufacturing, marketing, and administrative and technical services to its retail member-owners. FCL was a second-tier co-operative because it was owned by 210 retail consumer co-operatives spanning Manitoba, Saskatchewan, Alberta, and British Columbia, which in turn were owned by individual member-owners who purchased the goods and services supplied by these local retail

Version: 2016-04-29

[1]John Kotter, "Leading Change: Why Transformation Efforts Fail," Harvard Business Review 85 (2007): 59–67. Available from Ivey Publishing, product no. R0701J.

[2]Brett Fairbairn, *Building a Dream: The Co-operative Retailing System in Western Canada, 1928–1988* (Saskatoon: Western Producer Prairie Books, 1989).

outlets. FCL and these 210 co-operatives made up what was known as the Co-operative Retailing System (CRS).

As a second-tier co-operative business, FCL had a different ownership and governance structure than its investor-owned competitors. In co-operatives, the owners used the services or purchased the goods that the co-operative business supplied. Selection of board members at FCL was done through a democratic election process, where retail members were allocated votes based on the amount they purchased from FCL. The democratic election of board members made it difficult to ensure consistent levels of board members' experience and expertise. The democratic governance structure also made decision-making processes cumbersome. As a result, attempts at system-wide change proved difficult. According to Banda:

> *Our members own us. . . . We're not a head office; we are a home office for all the various retail co-ops. . . . It's not a top-down decision-making structure. . . . Trying to get all the retails to move in the same direction all at once is incredibly challenging.*

The vice-president of corporate affairs, Vic Huard, stated:

> *The way the governance model works and the expectations around democratic elections of board members . . . offer a fascinating peek into the "you get what you get" version of governance.*

In addition to the challenges associated with co-operative governance, FCL was a complex business. It had operations across multiple industries including energy, food, home and building supplies as well as feed and crop protection. FCL also owned and operated a large petroleum refinery complex, including an upgrading component, in Regina, Saskatchewan. FCL's complexity increased with the geographic scope of its operations and the vast difference in the size of its retail members. (FCL members included retail co-operatives in Calgary and Saskatoon as well as in smaller towns and rural areas.) Part of the complexity also included the large array of centralized technical services FCL offered to its retail members in the areas

of logistics, technology, marketing, and human resources. Huard elaborated:

> *We're not in one particular business line and we're not an integrated company. . . . We have to balance the competing interests of the various sizes of retails, geographic scope, and democratic governance processes. . . . Making decisions and implementing programs is challenging.*

Notwithstanding these challenges, FCL was successful. In 2013, FCL was named the largest company in Saskatchewan (with sales of $9.4 billion), and was consistently listed among the largest 50 companies in Canada.[3] Though it may have been tempting to become complacent with this level of financial success, FCL competed with large organizations across a variety of industries in both the wholesale and retail sectors, including, but not limited to, companies such as Wal-mart, Sobeys-Safeway, Loblaws, Costco, Esso, Shell, Rona, Home Hardware, and Cargill. And the competition was intensifying. Banda said, "We have to compete with major organizations . . . and so if we aren't generating the profit at the end of the day from our business model, we wouldn't be here."

However, a major difference between a for-profit co-operative and an investor-owned firm was what happened with the profits. Vice-President Treasurer, Randy Boyer, described the difference:

> *For our large private and publicly traded competitors, profits are returned to the shareholders who have a much different reason for investing in those entities: it's primarily for economic gain. In our case, those profits are returned to our retail co-op shareholders, who also happen to be our customers, for investment in their local retail co-operatives, or for further distribution to their own individual member-owners across Western Canada.*

Co-operatives also historically developed in locations where other private organizations would not invest, or would divest. FCL was deeply embedded in geographic communities and often served broader social objectives in addition to meeting the economic objectives of its members. According to

---

[3] All currency amounts are in CA$ unless otherwise specified. CA$1.00 = US$0.7146 on January 6, 2016.

Banda: "Our owners are our members, so they're vested in the business. They live in the communities in which our co-ops operate. They buy the goods and services we provide."

A company falling behind

Even with increasing competition, FCL was doing well, at least when measured by its financial position. This resulted in a lack of urgency for change. The adage "If it isn't broke, why fix it?" became the philosophy of many who did not feel change was necessary. FCL's strategy had been focused on providing value by returning the largest possible patronage refunds to its members, often at the expense of investing in innovation, employees, or social responsibility. As a result, FCL's processes and systems were outdated (senior executives didn't even have computers or personal email until the mid-2000s), and the sustainability of the status quo was being called into question. Banda was often quoted as saying that one of the major threats facing any organization is irrelevance. A change in culture was seen as necessary to move the organization forward.

Faramarz Farahani, vice-president of information technology, who was hired from outside the organization by Banda, commented, "When I joined, there was a very dormant culture. There had been a very homogenous senior leadership team that was very comfortable with where they were."

The director of organization development, Teresa Quilty, added:

People describe the old culture to me as being one that I've called a "culture of followership." There were a few senior leaders that really held most of the decision-making authority and the rest of the organization followed. Even people in management roles really were followers. They were following orders and they were just getting things done.

Banda was promoted from vice-president of corporate and legal affairs to CEO in February 2010. Though Banda had been raised around the co-operative movement and had been with FCL since 2002, the internal support for Banda's appointment was not unanimous. In his interview with the FCL Board of Directors for the CEO position, Banda commented that although what FCL was doing had worked for them in the past, the competitive landscape was quickly changing. He was worried about

the future sustainability of the company and identified a need for change. Banda bluntly stated to the Board at the time, "If you are looking for the status quo, then I'm not your guy."

Areas of change

Although Banda self-admittedly did not have a master plan, immediately upon being instated as CEO, he initiated change in three major areas: talent management, branding, and IT. A complete overhaul of FCL's talent management processes included changes to the organization's structure, talent acquisition, and board and leadership development. Not everyone agreed with the direction Banda wanted to take the company, and there was initially some turnover at the highest levels. Reflecting on this, Banda said:

The first step was with senior management. One of the changes we made was changing our team from a senior management team to a senior leadership team because within our company, we were very tactical. It was an evolution to get the leaders of the organization to really lead the teams. . . . God knows I didn't have all the answers and I knew we had to empower our people.

Banda hired Quilty as the new Director of Organizational Development, who in the short-term reported directly to Banda. A major task for Quilty was to develop a framework that identified the different levels of leaders in the organization. For Quilty, leadership was critical:

We don't create competitive advantage through things like products. Things like culture and brand are much more difficult to imitate. . . . It's really about building capacity. . . . The area to focus on was with leaders because leaders have a disproportionate impact on the organization. If you can make small changes in the leadership and help them be effective, that has a huge ripple effect.

At the same time, the challenges in upgrading FCL's IT systems were staggering. Farahani, said:

Our IT was very outdated. To be honest with you, when I came, I never thought that I would run into so many issues. There are many other organizations out there that have run into or are currently facing one of these issues, but not an organization that has all of them at the same time."

One of the first major IT projects was to migrate off the mainframe legacy application system. This was made all the more difficult because the change would inevitably result in job losses, which could derail the change early in the process. However, instead of laying off these employees, FCL struck an outsourcing deal with a company that took on almost all of the outsourced, unionized employees and kept them in Saskatoon as part of the contract.

Finally, both internal and external marketing communications were vastly outdated. Paper-based communication was still used to inform the retail outlets and employees about changes. Vic Huard, vice-president of corporate affairs – and in charge of FCL's marketing and communications – noted that because so much was happening all at once, internal messages were often reactive rather than proactive, and there were often too many messages coming out at the same time. To address this, FCL developed a strategic communications calendar so that important messages were not lost or ignored.

Externally, FCL conducted an online and telephone survey of 1,600 randomly selected individuals across Western Canada to determine how well the primary co-operative visual mark – known in the CRS as "The Shield" – was recognized and what feelings it evoked. This marketing research showed that the co-operatives's visual brand was highly recognizable and elicited positive emotional responses. However, there was an inconsistency in visual branding, identity, and messaging within FCL's various commodities and across the different retail co-operatives. There was also, initially, a sense among some of the retail outlets that promoting their image as a co-operative was not all that important. "There was always a sense of pride, but it was kind of ignored. People felt that it's not really that important to be proud of being a co-op. . . . We saw ourselves as a business. We didn't tell our story very well," explained Huard.

FCL worked on a completely new marketing and branding strategy to be rolled out over the next couple of years. Although IT and branding were obviously priorities, Banda also saw the need for a deeper culture change at FCL. He believed that this would ultimately determine whether changes in other areas would be successful. Banda stated:

People who don't want to change are a major risk to a successful change process. We're over

23,000 employees [in the CRS] and we're going to try and change a culture. It's one thing to change an IT or talent management system, but we were fundamentally changing a culture, trying to empower our people, to provide leaders with the ability to lead their organization, to really reframe our brand as that local alternative, and to celebrate our business model.

According to Huard, change across each of these areas was made more difficult by the co-operative structure:

The challenge is that you don't direct anything. You lead by example, you lead by influence, you lead by persuasion, by demonstrating excellence, but you can't make it happen because, put bluntly, they own us – "they" being the retails. The concept of a system-wide approach to anything is much more challenging here than it is in an integrated company.

Notwithstanding these challenges, the co-operative model also offered advantages over other types of organizations with regard to the ability to plan for the long-term. There was a commitment and loyalty among co-operative member-owners and employees that did not always exist elsewhere. Banda elaborated:

We have a stable shareholder network. These member-owners are committed and are invested very deeply in our organization, and that gives us the ability to plan. . . . It's a function of the [co-operative] model. . . . We have a very strong economic, philosophical, emotional attachment that exists in our members that makes them very loyal. . . . To contrast that with a publicly traded company where the shareholders and the capital base [are] constantly moving and evolving – that puts a lot of pressure to drive to those quarterly results. In our organization, to initiate a major brand re-introduction which is a three- to five-year, maybe a ten-year process, you've got to have some capacity to have the vision, but you also have to have an organizational model that allows you to do that.

Quilty said:

We have so many people in the organization that are really truly dedicated, that live the values and really believe in our values – they're very meaningful to them. People here really care and want to make a difference. I've seen that here more than [in] any other organization I've worked in.

Because the co-operative was local and rooted in communities, and board delegates and members were elected from local communities across Western Canada, FCL also had information that may not otherwise be as easily accessible to other types of organizations. "Another advantage of our model and structure is that we're local. . . . We have the best local intelligence network of any other organization. Our network can feed us information a lot quicker than anyone else can if we utilize it," Banda explained.

The major challenges

Given that the company had fallen so far behind, the magnitude of change appeared daunting to Banda:

I underestimated the size of the task. It was one thing to say we [needed] to evolve our technology but I honestly didn't know what that meant . . . the size and the scale and the scope of what had to be done there and how fast I thought we could evolve some of these processes. We pushed hard. In hindsight, I think I'd back up and just slow that down a little bit.

Quilty noted, "Just the cumulative volume and pace of change [is] what [is] probably most challenging for us right now. We certainly bit off a lot and I think many of us say that we're trying to do 30 years of change in about three years."

Farahani explained, "We have 36 active projects in IT. Out of those, seven of them are considered multi-million dollar, multi-year foundational projects which impact how we operate. When you put those numbers together you realize that you really have to be focused because it is challenging."

Banda believed employee involvement early in the change process was critical to its ultimate success. He involved employees early in everything from changing the dress code (to a less formal guideline) to the selection of the organizational values. "We let the employees pick the values of the organization because they're the ones that have to live with them. I believe in excellence, integrity, and responsibility; but we decided on and locked down the values in a way that they're not mine; they're ours."

Employees appeared to be excited. There was a feeling that something big was happening with this once sleepy, landmark company. Yet many also felt overwhelmed, as Quilty acknowledged:

It's a challenging time that we're in right now. People are very excited about the change; they know that it's good. Even intuitively they just go, "Yeah this feels good; it's exciting; we like where we're going." But it's hard. There's a lot happening and we don't always know how to do it. I think for many employees who have been here a long time – and we have lots of long-term employees – we're now asking things of them that have never been asked of them before.

The vice-president of human resources, Gary Mearns, added:

Probably 20 per cent of your employee group immediately adopt these changes and love them because they just like change generally. You've got a big cohort in the middle that are saying, "Well I kind of see the change as being something that's valued, but prove it to me first and then I'll jump on-board." And then there's a certain group that will resist change no matter what just because it is a change. We've seen examples of all of that in our management ranks where there's been the greatest amount of change. . . . And there's no question: the pace of change has been phenomenal the last two or three years and it's been challenging for everybody because of that.

Furthermore, there wasn't always a clear roadmap for how to undertake a change of this scope and magnitude. As Quilty put it:

This is true for any organization: senior leaders set a direction and they set some challenging goals – stretch goals – and that's where we want to get to. That's their job and that's hard to do, to know where we should go to. But then the task becomes, how do we execute that? "How do we execute?" is a whole competency set that is not in wide supply and people often don't know how to execute change well. Most change literature says something like 70 per cent of change efforts fail. . . . They either fail to be on time or to meet the scope that they had set out, to get the result they really wanted, to have the impact that they had hoped as an organization, or to be on cost. The odds are stacked against us: achieving everything on time, on budget, and the way we want.

These problems were amplified by the fact that the organization was engaged in a lot of hiring. According to Mearns, "A total of three-quarters of our HR home office team had been in their roles less than two years. When you get that many people that are new, it's challenging. They are learning as they go about their jobs, but we're also expecting them to be involved in the changes."

Responding to these concerns, Banda was becoming known for adopting an approach that emphasized learning, which reduced employee fears about making mistakes. Quilty described Banda:

Our CEO has sent the message loud and clear to give permission for all of us to learn and figure things out and make mistakes. I think this is very wise and has been great leadership on his part. He's not saying, "Hey, we're going to go and try anything and make lots of mistakes," but [he] recognizes that people are trying to do the right thing. Often people get concerned that they have to come up with the right answers now. That's a natural behaviour that people have. By him giving us a little bit of space to acknowledge that the fact is we are just learning, the fact is we don't know all the answers – it's realistic.

The growth in management and increase in staff at FCL raised a concern about hiring a number of people who may not understand the unique nature of the co-operative business model, and how this would impact the operation of the company. There was a fear that losing touch with what it meant to be a co-operative could undermine many of the strengths that came from the model itself, which differentiated FCL and its retail member co-operatives from their competitors. Banda appreciated this so focused on hiring values-based people from outside the co-operative sector who could quickly learn how to work within, promote, and defend the co-operative model.

Indicators of success

Although the senior leaders agreed that the change process would be ongoing and would take at least another three to five years before it could slow down, they began to articulate what future success would look like in three key areas.

Talent management

"A key measure will be that we are not only attracting and retaining [high performers], but that we're promoting those people as well – the people who are high performers and high-potentials and that are contributing the most to the way we need to be in the future. . . . Those potential leaders are the ones who actually become our future leaders," said Quilty.

Branding

On branding, Huard explained:

Are we selling more product? Are we gaining more market share? Are we effectively working at building relationships on a one-on-one basis with customers at the store level and getting a bigger share of their wallet? That's really important. There's a lot of wallet-share growth that can happen if we do things better. Are we seeing membership numbers at the individual co-op retails go up at an accelerated pace? Are we seeing more young people getting involved as members of their co-ops and getting interested in serving on their local co-op boards? Are we getting the message through to young people that there's a good reason to join [a] co-op and shop there? Those are hard metrics around brand and really important ones.

Alignment

With regard to alignment, Banda said:

One of the biggest potential threats to our organization is lack of unity. A major indicator of success will probably be the degree of alignment in the [CRS]. When we have the various business units that we have and a retail sector that's as big as it is all pushing our brand in the same direction, all pushing technology and supporting technology initiatives in the same direction, all working on the same talent management structure, and using the ability of our business model to plan for the future . . . then we'll be in pretty good shape.

It was also identified as critically important that throughout these changes, FCL remain true to being a co-operative, which meant also rediscovering internally what that meant. As Huard put it, repeating Peter Couchman, CEO of the Plunkett Foundation, a co-operative development organization based in the United Kingdom, "You can choose to be a business that happens to be a co-operative, or you can choose to be a co-operative business. We're choosing to be a co-operative business."

Co-operatives around the world often differentiated themselves from other organizations based on a common set of values, which included self-help, self-responsibility, democracy, equality, equity, and solidarity. Inspired by the Rochdale Pioneers, the founders of the modern-day co-operative movement, co-operatives often also chose to uphold ethical values of honesty, openness, social responsibility, and caring for others.[4] FCL created an operational balanced scorecard to continuously remind them of these values, and a co-operative's multiple objectives. The new scorecard placed an emphasis on the long-term sustainability of the second-tier co-operative, and on its broader social responsibilities. According to Quilty:

> Our balanced scorecard is based on five pillars in our organization. Our five pillars have to do with not only financial success, but also people, market performance and growth, operational efficiency and effectiveness, and social responsibility. Those pillars are our way of saying we need to pay attention to all five areas for us to be sustainable as on organization and to be successful over the long term.

And for Banda, a continued focus on checking in with employees was critical:

> An employee once asked me, "How do you know when you'll have gotten there?" I had no idea how to answer that question at the time, but I said, "I'm going to sit in the lobby of this building and watch the employees walk in. When you walk in with a smile on your face because you know you're valued at FCL, you know you can contribute everything

you can contribute, and you know we're going to recognize that contribution and make this place feel like home for you, then I would have done it." This was an off-the-cuff answer three years ago, but that's really the answer. Our success will ultimately come down to the culture change and engagement of our people.

The road ahead

While Banda was convinced FCL was headed in the right direction, he was concerned about employee burnout, and his SLT was showing signs of fatigue. The organization was starting to introduce certain elements of change to the unionized employee groups, bringing with it a new set of challenges. And there was the constant need to keep the retail member-owners engaged with the process by showing them how they would benefit from the changes being undertaken at FCL. Banda often questioned whether they should slow down the pace of change a little bit. However, there had been a number of early wins and Banda didn't want to lose momentum.

Banda knew the importance of trying to outline a roadmap for employees to show not only where they were headed, but also how to get there. However, given the scope, scale, and pace of change, the situation was constantly evolving. Banda thought that, at best, he might be able to lay out some guiding principles to aid decision-making. He attempted to achieve this through constantly orienting FCL's senior leadership and employees to the greater purpose and values of the co-operative business (see Exhibit 1).

Finally, Banda pondered the potential impact of the large number of new employees at FCL. Although some of the turnover in management had helped the culture change, there was a shortage of talent, not only with the relevant business knowledge and skills in key areas, but also with a deep understanding of the co-operative business model. This could pose a major threat to FCL's ability to sustain and leverage its unique advantages in an increasingly competitive environment.

[4]"What Is a Co-op? Co-operative Identity, Values, and Principles," International Co-operative Alliance, accessed July 18, 2015, http://ica.coop/en/whats-co-op/co-operative-identity-values-principles.

EXHIBIT 1   FCL'S VISION, MISSION, VALUES

FCL'S VISION

Federated Co-operatives Limited will set the world standard in consumer co-operative excellence.

FCL'S MISSION

To provide responsible, innovative leadership and support to the co-operative retailing system, for the benefit of members, employees, and Canadian communities.

FCL'S VALUES

- Excellence: Strive to be the best.
- Integrity: Be honest and trustworthy.
- Responsibility: Accountability matters.

FCL'S ASPIRATIONAL STATEMENT

Strong co-operative governance is the foundation upon which we pursue a common purpose with our retail owners. Working together, we sustain a vibrant Federation by creating shared value.

We leverage our financial strength to steward the sustainable growth of our Co-operative Retailing System. At Co-op, our members/customers feel at home, because we are part of the fabric of the communities we serve. We foster meaningful careers and inspire our employees to bring our brand to life every day. We model and celebrate a culture of teamwork, learning and innovation.

Source: Company documents.

With all of this in the back of his mind, Banda carefully considered what to say to FCL's home office employees the following day at the Q&A session.

Based on some of their responses to the engagement survey, many were obviously worried about similar issues.

The authors acknowledge and thank the Centre for the Study of Co-Operatives at the University of Saskatchewan for providing funding to support the development of this case.

CASE

9

Alibaba Group's Taobao: From intermediary to ecosystem enabler

By Professor Peter Williamson with Ms Michelle Wang Jingji

The Alibaba Group's senior executive team sat down to review progress of Taobao marketplace and its sister business-to-consumer (B2C) site, Tmall.com. They could not help but be pleased with the latest figures. Together, Taobao and Tmall. com had set a new record for highest single-day transaction volume during a special promotion. During China's "Single's Day" on November 11, 2013 (named after the date 11/11 because of the frequency of "1s") the equivalent of America's Cyber Monday, Taobao marketplace and Tmall.com had facilitated sales of goods totalling more than RMB 35 billion (US$5.7 billion) in just 24 hours. This represented a further step forward for the two marketplaces, which in the year ended March 31, 2013 had already achieved combined gross merchandise volume (GMV) of over RMB1 trillion (US$164 billion). However, the executive team knew there was no room for complacency in the fast-evolving world of e-commerce. How should Taobao and Tmall.com develop from here? What lessons for the future could Alibaba draw from its experience in moving from the role of an intermediary and platform provider to an enabler of one of the fastest growing e-business ecosystems[1] on the globe?

Crocodile in the Yangtze

Alibaba Group was founded by 18 friends, led by Ma Yun (also known as Jack Ma), in 1999. Ma had grown up in Hangzhou where the company is still headquartered. At the age of 12 he had become interested in learning English, so would ride 40 minutes to a hotel near the famous West Lake that attracted international tourists, and practised his English by offering to guide foreigners on free tours of the local sights. After being accepted into teacher training at university, he became an English teacher.

Ma left his low-paying teaching job and joined a Chinese delegation as interpreter in the US. It was in Seattle in 1995 that he first experienced the Internet. He purportedly typed the words "China + beer" into a search engine and found no results. On returning to China he set up China Pages, an online directory of Chinese companies wishing to sell abroad. He helped his clients create English language websites and list them on China Pages.

In 1998, Ma was asked by a company sponsored by the Ministry of Foreign Trade and Economic Cooperation (MOFTEC) to assist Chinese companies in becoming involved in "electronic commerce" based on private networks to facilitate electronic data interchange. However, Ma believed that the real potential lay in open networks enabled by the Internet, so he gathered 18 people in his apartment and outlined his vision in a discourse lasting two hours. The group was so inspired that they clubbed together US$60,000 to launch "Alibaba" – a name they felt embodied the idea of "open sesame to treasures of the world". The company began in 1999 with the website Alibaba.com, a business-to-business (B2B) portal to connect Chinese manufacturers with overseas buyers. The idea was to make the Internet accessible, trustworthy and beneficial for everyone.

Those noble aspirations, however, were not enough to ensure that the new venture was financially sound. Alibaba.com had a rocky time in its early years: most of its growth in user base had come from offering free services and by 2001 it was burning through the US$25 million funding it had raised from investors including Japan's Softbank, Goldman Sachs and Fidelity from the USA, at US$2 million per month, with less than US$10 million in the bank.

In response, Alibaba made a number of radical changes. First, it introduced fees-based membership packages that offered those who signed up priority

[1]Following James Moore, a "business ecosystem" may be defined as: a "network of organisations and individuals that co-evolve their capabilities and roles and align their investments so as to create additional value and/or improve efficiency" (J.H. Moore, Moore, "Predators and Prey: A New Ecology of Competition", *Harvard Business Review,* 1993, Vol. 71(3), May/June, pp 75–86.

placement in online directories and search rankings. Second, Alibaba offered extra promotion on its site for an additional fee. Third, it contracted leading credit-rating companies in China to provide data for what were called "Trustpass" profiles. The Trustpass profiles displayed credit worthiness information about vendors along with information from past customers who had used Alibaba. With these changes the company passed break-even profitability in 2002.

In 2003, Alibaba decided to enter the consumer-to-consumer (C2C) sector of the e-commerce business. Its first C2C marketplace, Taobao ("exploring treasures" in Chinese), was launched that same year. Here it faced direct competition with eBay, a company with much more experience and financial resources that had recently announced that it would invest US$100 million to conquer the Chinese market. eBay had also recently acquired EachNet, then the leading online auction site in China. Jack Ma and the Alibaba team were not deterred. Ma stated at the time: "eBay may be a shark in the ocean, but I am a crocodile in the Yangtze River. If we fight in the ocean we lose – but if we fight in the river, we win".

Growth and change at Taobao

Alibaba began by designing a "look and feel" for Taobao that it believed was more suited to Chinese consumer tastes and expectations than that offered by eBay; better customer service and, unlike eBay, a willingness to offer basic services for free. Perhaps the most decisive feature of Taobao in its battle with eBay, however, was the capability for buyers and sellers to "talk" with each other directly in real time before they agreed a deal, through a service called Wangwang launched in May 2004. eBay had insisted that any communication between prospective buyer and seller had to be via that cumbersome process of posting messages through its website. By reducing the uncertainties and suspicion with which customers in China approached online transactions and allowing direct negotiation, Wangwang proved a hit[2].

With China's credit card system still immature, customers also worried about the security of online payments or the delays involved in arranging payments by alternative means. Recognising this impediment, Alibaba Group introduced Alipay in late 2004. Alipay was a system under which, after agreeing a purchase, the customer would transfer their payment to Alipay where it would be held in an "escrow" account, only to be released to the seller once the customer had notified Alipay that they had received the goods and were satisfied. To achieve this Alipay formed partnerships with 40 Chinese banks. It also entered into an agreement with China Post that enabled customers to re-charge their Alipay accounts using cash, cheque or a debit card at any of China Post's 66,000 locations. Alibaba also agreed to work with China Post to facilitate parcel delivery, as well as with other leading courier and logistics companies in China. These deals reinforced a growing recognition in the company that it could not achieve its objectives working alone: it would need a great deal of help from partners.

By the end of 2005 Taobao had become the undisputed leader in C2C e-commence in China with a 59 per cent market share (up from 8 per cent in 2003). eBay China's share plunged from 79 per cent to 36 per cent over the same period. Continued losses and lack of progress in the market finally led eBay to shut down its own site in China in 2006.

In April 2008, Taobao introduced a dedicated business-to-consumer (B2C) platform, Taobao Mall, to complement its C2C marketplace. Taobao Mall carried brand name goods for Chinese consumers. Taobao Mall achieved good growth over the next two and a half years, but Alibaba's management felt that it could be improved to make it easier for customers to compare alternative offerings of similar products (product verticals) and to enhance the shopping experience. These improvements came with the launch of an independent web domain, Tmall.com, within Taobao in November 2010. This became an independent business in June 2011 and changed its Chinese name to Tian Mao (Tmall.com) in January 2012. By October 2013 it was the eighth most visited website in China. Some 402 million unique visitors used Tmall.com on the 11th November 2013 making purchases from 20,000 merchants.

Starting in October 2010, Taobao had also launched eTao as an independent search engine for online shopping. eTao provided product and merchant information from a number of major consumer e-commerce websites in China and so allowed shoppers to compare prices from different sellers. eTao offered products from Amazon China, Dangdang, Gome, Yihaodian, Nike China and Vancl, as well as Taobao and Tmall.com. In 2012, Taobao

[2] Within 2 years Taobao had far outstripped eBay's market share in China and by 2010 eBay's market share was down to 7 per cent compared with Taobao's 85 per cent. http://www.chinadecoded.com/2010/10/27/shark-in-a-river-how-taobao-beat-ebay-in-china/.

began to accept international Visa and MasterCard credit cards, augmenting the service from domestic banks supported by AliPay.

On April 29, 2013, Alibaba announced an investment of US$586 million in China's largest social media company, Sina Weibo with the aim of driving additional web traffic to Taobao Marketplace and Tmall.com. This led, starting on August 1, 2013 to a service called "Weibo for Taobao" that allows users to link their Sina Weibo accounts with Taobao accounts.

The emergence of ecosystem thinking

Behind these developments at Taobao and Tmall. com, the underlying business model and the role of Alibaba in these marketplaces was also changing. Looking back, Alibaba's senior management discerned three broad stages in the development of its business model towards an ecosystem. The first stage began after its difficulties with cash drain in 2001. At this time Alibaba had shifted from a pure platform to become a service provider charging membership fees to users. It had already recognised that reaping economies of scale was critical to spread fixed costs and hence drive down unit costs. But it would never be able to achieve a massive scale in e-business if it acted as principal (buyer or seller on its own right). To gain scale would require harnessing the power of a huge number of partners. That, in turn, meant making space for partners to develop their own businesses by limiting Alibaba's own activities.

The launch of Taobao heralded a second stage in developing an ecosystem: Taobao was conceived as a marketplace that encouraged others to serve customers. Alibaba would concentrate on providing the "platform" through which e-commerce could flow and take a commission for connecting buyer and seller. To gain scale economies, the platform would need to be standardised as much as possible. Then, partners needed to be able to differentiate themselves on top of the infrastructure platform. To achieve this mix of standardisation and differentiation, limiting the boundaries of the platform would be key.

"Our objective was to develop a platform of infrastructure that can attract a wide range of partners and boost growth and scale" explained Alibaba Group's Chief Technology Officer, Wang Jian. He went on to explain that Taobao had also spawned a myriad of diverse partner businesses: not only companies that designed sophisticated shop-fronts

for vendors and creators of advertising, but specialist companies that, for example, recruited models for photo shoots used to create online marketing materials to promote products in the Taobao marketplace. Wang Jian also drew attention to Alibaba's policy of nurturing small partners noting, for example that "Small customers can become big customers, so the technology for both should be the same. Alibaba wants to make sure small customers have a future."

Even at this stage, however, Taobao was acting as a kind of intermediary or "middleman" between buyers and sellers. As Ming Zeng, the Group Strategy Officer put it: "we realised our ability was so limited compared to both the potential of the market and the task facing us." As Taobao developed it "learned a lot of painful lessons by trying to over-control and becoming the bottleneck" said Zeng.

This led to a third stage in the emergence of ecosystem thinking at Alibaba: that it needed to become an "ecosystem enabler" – trying to back off and focus on becoming a provider of e-commerce infrastructure services for all e-commerce market participants. This would allow Taobao to gain the "network advantages" associated with large numbers of buyers and sellers. If Alibaba could position Taobao as "the place to go" for consumer e-commerce it could trigger a positive spiral whereby the larger it became, the more attractive it would become for buyers and sellers. By 2008 this thinking led to the adoption of the "Big Taobao" strategy that aimed to encourage a large number of diverse potential participants to join in, solve problems and develop and grasp new opportunities.

In order to make the transition from intermediary to ecosystem enabler, Taobao would need to reduce its role as the controller of activities around the platform. Instead it would encourage the shop owners to take more initiative in working with other participants in the ecosystem, including other sellers, providers of complementary services and the online shoppers themselves. For example, Taobao encouraged shop owners to organise more joint marketing activities, and also work more directly with providers of other services that could make their offering more attractive.

This shift of focus to becoming an enabler for the development of a broader and deeper ecosystem around Taobao and Tmall.com would also require Alibaba to change its revenue model. In 2009, 85 per cent of total revenues from Taobao and Tmall.com came from various types of advertising, including paid items appearing prominently in search results and additional fees for prime advertising positions on the sites. In order to enable growth of the ecosystem and improve value and service to customers, Taobao would need to reduce its reliance on these advertising and transactions fees. Growth in Alibaba's revenue and profit from Taobao and Tmall.com would need to come by opening up new revenue streams and sources of value from which Alibaba could capture a share. As Ming Zeng put it: "because you are no longer taking a cut as a middleman, an ecosystem enabler has to be continually finding innovative ways to create new and unique value added from which it can take a profit. Revenue growth will come from taking a small cut on an ever-expanding volume of interactions of many types."

Making space for partners

To become an ecosystem enabler, Alibaba had to learn to stop doing things, in some cases even those that had become sizeable activities. Zhang Yu, president of Taobao, explained: "Taobao used to organise a lot of small-scale, thematic promotional events to try to drive sales – even down to things like a special spring-festival promotion for red sweaters. Over time the number of these new promotions grew so that new ones were launched 3–4 times per day. When Taobao was smaller, this part of the business used to count for 30 per cent of the overall revenue. As Taobao total turnover increased, however, these promotional events initiated in-house had become redundant, accounting for only 0.8 per cent or 0.5 per cent of the total gross value flowing through the marketplace. They were enormously time consuming and complex to set up because the Taobao team needed to find the relevant products one by one and negotiate participation in the promotion with each seller individually. All this complexity was absorbing 80 per cent of the time of Taobao's marketing staff. We had to stop these promotions not least because we were becoming the bottleneck. To do so, however, we had to understand that less is exponentially more."

Some of these decisions were relatively easy, observed Wang Jian. "It is very clear that Alibaba should not sell product, but the boundaries of the ecosystem are not easy to determine. Take software services – in principle Alibaba knows it should leave them to partners, but in the short term partners may not be willing or equipped and so it would be easier for Alibaba to provide this service. But that would

lead to unsustainable complexity and fragmentation. The solution has been for Alibaba to provide the basic building blocks (such as the exchange platform and a very rudimentary CRM system for every shop owner on Taobao). Alibaba is clear that it will not provide anything that is only useful for a single seller or even a small group of sellers – only things to be used by large numbers of participants."

To maintain the health of the ecosystem Alibaba also found that it was critical to resist the temptation to encroach unnecessarily on its partners' domains. Brian Li, VP of strategy, explained: "someone in Alibaba will, perfectly reasonably, say: 'we see a new application (App.) is becoming popular, why don't we build an App. to do this? But a good ecosystem leader needs to say 'no'; we should instead encourage partners to build this type of App., so that we draw in the capabilities of partners and drive improvement and learning. By taking this approach users now have a choice of multiple Apps. within our ecosystem."

Making space for partners was very much in Alibaba's self-interest viewed from the perspective of ecosystem thinking. Ming Zeng explained: "If there are problems, for example, failures in logistics, Alibaba is usually the last to be able to help. It is much better to rely on third parties to see the opportunity to profit by providing an improved service. Just like the government trying to manage the market is a disaster, if Alibaba tries to be smart and fix a problem it usually messes up the system."

Zhang Yu gave another example of how Alibaba needed to focus on the role of a catalyst and enabler for partners to enhance the performance of the ecosystem: "With a more and more diverse set of businesses using Taobao and Tmall.com and increasing transactions volumes, new needs for more specialised services continually emerge. In the case of software for printing logistics information, for example, our simple, standard support service cannot cater for all users' needs. So many new service providers have come to fill the gap. But these service providers did so by calling each individual seller to obtain information about the relevant protocols, causing inconvenience and complicating their decision-making. Acting as an enabler, Alibaba decided to open up its Application Programming Interface to these software developers. To ensure quality, however, it introduced a new system to regulate the trade between its partners. This included criteria for selecting better service providers opening up the interface only to those service providers who made the grade.

Developing new revenue models

There were clearly benefits of leaving more and more of the activities, investments, and innovations in the ecosystem to partners. But this also created a new dilemma: how would Alibaba earn revenue within the ecosystem? Alibaba usually started a new ecosystem with the basic service given for free. Once the ecosystem began to gain traction it began to charge for value-added service add-ons. In doing so, however, it generally tried to align its revenue model with the success of the ecosystem so that it favoured revenue sharing models rather than fixed pricing. Revenue sharing provided both a way to share the risk and to benefit from the upside if things took off in to a phase of rapid growth.

In some areas this revenue-sharing model was difficult to implement. In these cases Alibaba sought to generate revenue by leveraging the increasing desire for sellers in their marketplaces to get ahead of their competitors. Revenue generated through advertising was an obvious example. In designing its revenue models, however, Alibaba also looked for ways to add value for buyers as well. By offering services to sellers such as "adwords", for example, Alibaba also benefitted buyers by making their searches more efficient.

Fundamental to Alibaba's thinking was the belief that if it could create value for the end customer then it would find a way to earn money for itself. This meant focusing first on creating end-customer value and then thinking how to capture and share a portion of that value. The Wangwang instant messaging facility on Taobao, for example, was of great value to buyers and sellers by helping to build trust in the Chinese context. Alibaba had also understood that many Chinese buyers wanted to see the physical address of the seller on the website in order to feel confident. Taobao provided this facility even though many others argued that it was unnecessary in a world of electronic commerce. Likewise Alipay ensured the net proceeds of each sale was transferred to sellers as soon as the delivery had been acknowledged and accepted by a buyer in contrast to competitors such as 360buy who typically kept the money for a month after the sale as "float" to enhance their own cash flow.

Ming Zeng explained how this fits into the broader ecosystem thinking: "Alibaba is a hub – so it is a switch that everything needs to go through. Conceptually that enables you to charge a "toll" for passing through which is our revenue. The more the flow through, the more the revenue." A good example was the creation of "Taobao Ke" a traffic aggregation system developed by Aibaba's staff that won a CEO Innovation Award from Jack Ma. Taobao Ke aggregated and analysed user data from more than 500,000 websites receiving billions of page views per day. It began by Alibaba agreeing with owners of the sites in question to carry a link that would direct potential customers to a Taobao store. The owner of the shop on Taobao contracted to pay commission of around 10 per cent of the gross sales value achieved when a lead came through that website. The website owner would receive 90 per cent of this commission and Taobao would retain 10 per cent of the commission (or 1 per cent of the gross sales value achieved).

This kind of commission arrangement was common across the global Internet, but Taobao Ke developed techniques to add a great deal of value from analysing and using the data it produced to improve the match between a Taobao store and the websites to which it was linked. To achieve this required technology-heavy capacity to automatically analyse the content of a site and work out which of more than 1 million Taobao stores were most likely to be of interest to its users. Alibaba would then propose optimal links to both Taobao storeowners and websites. This clearly improved the value and efficiency of the arrangement for each of the parties. Alibaba could then add even more value by making the system dynamic so that it could use the mass of data accessed through Taobao Ke to continually learn and improve the matching between linked websites and Taobao stores.

Taobao Ke was, therefore, an example of the kind of co-learning opportunities that ecosystem thinking could create: storeowners would learn more and more about what kind of websites were useful shop windows to attract businesses (and this could even be varied by time of day or location); while a wide variety of websites (including non-commercial information and community sites) could better understand how to create a new revenue stream from "click-through". Improving revenue streams would be shared, providing a win–win for all parties. Among them, Alibaba itself generated a substantial revenue stream from between 500 million and 1 billion user-flows that moved through Taobao Ke every day.

Improving interfaces

To attract new partners and participants to its ecosystems Alibaba needed to keep the entry barriers as low as possible. To do this, it was important to make the interfaces between parties in the ecosystem as simple and efficient as possible. To achieve this, Alibaba established standard data exchange interfaces so that when, for example, an order is placed on Taobao, data is immediately shared with the seller and logistics provider. The buyer can access more limited information on the status of the order. Alibaba also aimed to make it as easy as possible for new sellers to open a Taobao store by providing software tools to get up and running quickly, all for free.

But low entry barriers alone were not sufficient to win users. To be successful, an ecosystem also needed to be more efficient than the alternatives. One of the most important determinants of the efficiency of any ecosystem is the total cost of transactions involved in the interactions between parties. In order to reduce transactions cost required a strong focus on improving the information flows. As Brian Li observed this made: "Database management and search engine efficiency fundamental, even if it is 'very dirty detailed work'. Databases had to be flexible enough to allow everyone to put in and get out information. They also had to work smoothly when faced with high volumes of traffic. In the case of Taobao this meant creating a built-in search engine to ensure the free flow of data between millions of participants."

Leading the ecosystem

While Alibaba obviously could not completely control its ecosystem, it could play a leadership role by acting as an enabler and catalyst for its development. As a pivotal player in the ecosystem it was able to strongly influence and shape its future evolution. On the other hand, there was also a downside of being the "central switch" because, as Ming Zeng put it: "every problem comes at you". However, he also pointed out this burden had a corresponding upside: "You are also sitting at the hub of a system that generates lots of new knowledge – so you can continuously learn from experience, problem solving, 'learning by doing', and contact with the front line." This meant that they could learn and innovate based on feedback from the customer: "know the customer, know the challenges" and proactively: "watch what is happening and learn from and with partners and other participants in the ecosystem".

However, to get the benefit from this potentially rich learning environment, Ming Zeng cautions that

leaders, managers and staff also "needed to learn to enjoy this kind of work" rather than gaining satisfaction, power and prestige from management and control, as was likely to be the case in a traditional corporate organisation. This also meant that knowledge flow across the Alibaba Group itself was very important. This demanded strong internal networking which, in turn, required new mindsets and competences among staff, and new approaches to leadership that emphasised "influence without authority", collaboration, and stakeholder management.

In order to successfully shift from being intermediary between buyer and seller and adopt the role of ecosystem enabler, Alibaba's leadership would need to accept considerable loss of control and a certain amount of chaos. Instead of being the "manager" of an ecosystem it would need to lead by acting as a catalyst for development. Brian Li of the Alibaba Group strategy team pointed to considerable progress in putting this thinking into practice noting that: "more and more, Alibaba encourages the ecosystem and then backs off". But Ming Zeng also pointed out that the shift in mentality to "influence and support rather than control" was one of the most difficult aspects of implementing a strategy for gaining ecosystem advantage; "It is still difficult to fight the 'control' mentality in parts of Alibaba Group to this day" he said. It was also necessary to recognise that innovation and a significant amount of "trial and error" experimentation would be required to propel the ecosystem forward. On the other hand, there were significant benefits to accepting less control: "giving more room to everyone encourages more experimentation and flexibility, resulting in more co-learning and innovation in the ecosystem" added Zeng.

Alibaba had also recognised that knowledge creation in the ecosystem was about much more than its own learning – even as the "lead" firm. Lots of learning also occurred between partners within the ecosystem. This could improve performance and strengthen the ecosystem even when it did not involve Alibaba directly. Sometimes Alibaba needed to control or tap into the cross-communication and learning taking place between partners, while at others times this was unnecessary. The social networking sites (SNSs) around Taobao were a good example of why Alibaba, as the lead firm in the ecosystem, had to continually reassess what role it should play: when to act as a catalyst, when to step back and allow the ecosystem to evolve autonomously, and when to try and exert a more direct influence over the structure and processes in the ecosystem. Alibaba originally set up a SNS called Tao Jianghu within Taobao with the aim of connecting younger users and creating a "buzz" among this group around the site. Over time, many similar SNSs started to emerge around Taobao, but none of these reached a scale sufficient to energize and support the Taobao ecosystem as a whole. Instead, the proliferation of small SNS platforms also created internal competition and confusion within the Taobao ecosystem. As a result, Alibaba had to regain the initiative and catalyse the growth of a single, vibrant SNS that would also match the Taobao's identity and support its business model.

It was also critical for the lead firm in an ecosystem to act as an arbitrator and "police officer" where necessary. Zhang Yu gave the example of product categorisation on Taobao. In order to help buyers find what they were looking for and to compare alternative offers, it was important that products and services were assigned to relevant categories. One of Taobao's roles was to define product categories within its marketplace so that each seller has a suitable category into which products can be listed. However, categorisation was not always straightforward: Should multi-coloured mobile phone cases, for example, be listed under "electronics" or "fashion accessories"?

How a product or service was categorised was very dependent on the quality of decisions made by relatively junior, front-line Taobao staff. In Taobao's early days there wasn't any process for correcting categorisation anomalies that might arise, so frustration and confusion among sellers built up. This issue was aggravated by misrepresentation by some sellers, who intentionally classified their products into the wrong category in an attempt to get more exposure. A seller of a computer mouse, for example, might list it in a high traffic category such as women's dresses in an attempt to gain more visibility and increase sales. Alibaba needed a way of correcting errors and preventing sellers from gaming the system. Zhang Yu explained: "The difficulty in managing an ecosystem is everyone in the ecosystem is trying to maximize their own interest, sometimes at the cost of others, which then damages the principle of a healthy ecosystem (co-create and share). Therefore, there is always a need for police in the ecosystem to fight for public interest."

Instead of attempting to deal with these problems directly, Alibaba decided to leverage the potential of the ecosystem by recruiting new partners to help. So it introduced a categorisation feedback and dispute resolution process where a "Market Judgement Committee" made up of 3rd parties makes categorisation decisions. Members of the committee are selected from qualified representatives of both buyers and sellers. Decisions are made through voting. By choosing this approach, Alibaba was able to enhance the effectiveness of each party in the Taobao ecosystem and help it become self-sustaining and more robust.

Kick-starting new ecosystems

Once a particular ecosystem has become established, and particularly when it has emerged as the dominant player such as Taobao, its formula for success often looks deceptively simple. The reality is that kick-starting a new ecosystem is difficult: at the outset a new platform lacks critical mass, the capabilities of potential partners are often weak and their willingness to invest in something unproven is low.

The logistics network – an essential ingredient required to enable the success of the Taobao ecosystem, is a good example. Back in 2003, when the marketplace was launched, the capabilities of most logistics and delivery companies in China were weak, their service unreliable and their coverage patchy. Jack Ma was on record as saying that "terrible" logistics are slowing the growth of Internet retailing in China.

To overcome these problems Alibaba had to identify the right "seed" partners and work with them, starting to build trust and encourage them to invest and embark on a journey of co-learning. Alibaba started working with a number of partners but became so frustrated that it considered setting up its own, in-house delivery system. Despite these difficulties it realised that it could never invest the resources required for the nationwide system necessary to support Taobao. So it persevered. Through experience it identified a small group of partners it could cooperate with to improve the logistics capabilities of the ecosystem. This would, however, required sustained effort. In 2013 Alibaba said it would join with banks, delivery companies and industry competitors to invest US$16 billion to strengthen China's logistics network over the coming decade. This would include a comprehensive, real-time data system for logistics.

In December 2013, Alibaba announced that it would invest US$364 million in Haier Electronics Group Co, China's largest maker of appliances (with over 27 per cent of the domestic market). The companies said the agreement was aimed at creating a logistics and service network across China that will deliver and assemble household appliances and other large items. To establish the joint venture, Alibaba said it would invest US$240 million in Haier Electronics' Goodaymart unit, taking a 9.9 per cent stake. Alibaba will also acquire a 2 per cent stake in Haier Electronics for US$124 million.

Alibaba found a similar pattern in other areas where it was necessary to catalyse the development of new or strengthened capabilities in order for the ecosystem to deliver increased value to consumers. It would try to identify, relatively quickly, three or four partners in a particular area that were capable and willing to take risk and invest alongside Alibaba to upgrade the ecosystem's performance. Ming Zeng noted that Alibaba "worked almost day and night with these seed partners to get a prototype up and running as soon as possible; once it is operating then learning and competence can be accumulated". Contrary to early expectations, Alibaba found that the best initial partners weren't usually the industry leaders – they were too wedded to their traditional models and maybe complacent. Instead Alibaba needed to find new, up and coming firms who believed in the future of e-business and could see the upside of the ecosystem. Existing Taobao sellers who needed cloud capacity and trusted Alibaba, for example, were recruited as early adopters for AliCloud (Alibaba's platform for sharing data and providing cloud computing services), rather than large, existing IT users.

None the less, getting a new ecosystem off the ground was almost never easy. To overcome the barriers it was critical to have a leader with, as Ming Zeng put it: "The vision and guts to hold things together and a firm belief in the power of the ecosystem model."

Extending the model – where next?

By their very nature ecosystems are dynamic organisms where the future direction is far from fully controllable – especially in the fast evolving area of e-commerce. Among the new developments within the Taobao ecosystem was the rapid rise of "mobile shopping". In the first minute after midnight heralding the start of Single's Day on November 11, 2013, for example, some 2 million users clicked through to Taobao and Tmall.com using mobile devices. Just over an hour later US$163 million of mobile commerce had been transacted – more than the total for the entire day in November 2012. It was clear that mobile technologies would play a major role determining the future of Taobao and Tmall.com. Failure to keep up with these developments might threaten their future entirely, yet that would require creating relationships with many new potential partners from makers of mobile devices, through to the suppliers of operating systems and security software. The location of new customers joining Taobao and Tmall.com was also shifting. New customers were also increasingly coming from smaller, fifth- or six-tier cities rather than the China's developed mega-cities. Meanwhile, the consumer profiles were changing. The fastest growing buying segments were under 25 year olds (as might have been expected), but more surprisingly also those aged over 55. It wasn't so easy to discern how the ecosystem would need to respond to these changes. What new partners and capabilities would be required? What should Alibaba do to lead the Taobao ecosystem forward? How would Alibaba capture a share of future growth and potential revenue streams as Taobao and Tmall.com evolved?

As the Alibaba Group senior executive team sat down to review progress of Taobao and Tmall.com they wondered whether the lessons of ecosystem thinking (often learned through a process of trial and error) had sufficiently permeated the organisation? The average age of Alibaba's staff was just 29 years. Would its young leadership and management team understand what it takes to become an ecosystem enabler, especially when much of their education had emphasised "competing to win" and instilled a belief that man's determination can conquer nature? Most fundamentally, where would Taobao and Tmall.com go next?

Tesla Motors' business model configuration

By Dipl. Kfm. Erwin Hettich and Prof. Dr. Günter Müller-Stewens

Case study

"You'll be able to travel for free, forever, on pure sunlight."

Elon Musk, CEO and chief product architect of Tesla Motors

"The present is theirs; the future, for which I really worked, is mine."

Nikola Tesla

When Elon Musk drove to work with his Model S electric car on February 24, 2014, he knew that he was also steering a revolution in the automobile industry. It took Tesla Motors, Inc. only 10 years and 30 000 vehicles to pass the market valuation of car-making giant Fiat and reach half of the value of General Motors – a company that had manufactured 450 million cars over its more than 100 years of existence. Riding on significant tailwinds from bullish analyst reports on Tesla's visionary business model and its most recent announcements to connect the car to the Internet and build the world's largest "Gigafactory" for batteries, Tesla's market capitalization rose to $30 billion. The analyst Adam Jonas from Morgan Stanley recently attested that "Tesla may be in position to disrupt industries well beyond the realm of traditional auto manufacturing," and noted that "it's not just cars."[1] Tesla's once boldly formulated vision to "create the most compelling car company of the 21st century by driving the world's transition to electric vehicles"[2] (EVs) may these days not even be bold enough anymore.

So far, Tesla's journey to become one of most admired pioneers in the electric mobility domain has been a jolty one accompanied by liquidity issues, supply uncertainty, and ongoing skepticism about its long-term viability in an immature market and the looming competition of powerful incumbents. In his first company blog post in August 2006, Tesla Chairman Elon Musk revealed the "secret" master plan underlying the firm's ambitious endeavor: enter at the high end of the market, where customers are prepared to pay a premium, and then drive down the market as fast as possible to achieve higher unit volume and lower prices with each successive model. Beyond that, Musk revealed that Tesla aims to provide zero-emission power-generation options.[3] Since its inception until today, Tesla has taken groundbreaking decisions that deviate from traditional business models in the automobile industry. Thus far, however, profits have been marginal. With the path taken and many decisions lying ahead, Tesla's business concept may turn out to be a revolution or a big bust. While Tesla's short history has largely been a story of success, many issues that must be resolved still remain. Musk and his team face serious challenges and have to answer pressing questions, such as 'How to configure a viable business model that would defend against powerful incumbents?' and 'How to reap arising opportunities in a radically changing business landscape and position the business for future growth?' These are important questions that require answers.

Background on Tesla

The early years

Tesla Motors was founded in Silicon Valley by Martin Eberhard and Marc Tarpenning in 2003. They were soon joined and funded by Elon Musk, who has served as chairman since 2004. Musk was well-exposed to entrepreneurial endeavors, notably as a co-founder of PayPal, SpaceX, and SolarCity. The company's initial goal was to produce fully electric sports cars not for ultimate cost, but rather for performance, aesthetics, and sex appeal.[4] Early on, Musk

Authors: Dipl. Kfm. Erwin Hettich, Institute of Management University of St. Gallen and Prof. Dr. Günter Müller-Stewens, Institute of Management University of St. Gallen.

took a decisive role in designing and developing the first prototypes of Tesla's Roadster, which were introduced to the public in July 2006 and achieved an unprecedented range of 245 miles (394 km) on a single charge in company tests.

The market launch was accompanied by intense media attention and backed by celebrities such as Leonardo DiCaprio, Jay Leno, and George Clooney, who paid $109 000 in advance to receive one of the first 100 Roadsters, which were scheduled to be delivered in 2007; however, the first Roadster was not delivered until February 2008.[5] An internal audit revealed that the cost of building the car had climbed to $140 000, vastly overrunning the projected cost of $65 000. Tesla lost money before a single unit was delivered, and the company faced financial trouble. The board of directors unanimously decided to dismiss Eberhard. Tarpenning, who was vice president of electrical engineering, supervising the development of electronic and software systems for the Roadster, also left the company in 2008. Musk took over as CEO in October 2008.

When Musk took over responsibility, Tesla was selling fewer than 200 Roadsters and filling a niche in an industry that churns out millions of vehicles per year. The parts for the Roadsters were sourced separately and largely assembled one by one, in a garage behind a showroom in Menlo Park, California, based on the Lotus Elise template. The Roadster, however, was simply the launchpad for Musk's next step to build the more sophisticated Tesla Model S, a stylish four-door sedan. In the summer of 2008, he hired Mazda's lead North American designer, Franz von Holzhausen, and told him that he wanted a four-door car that seated seven (offering seating for five adults and two children). "That's an SUV, not a sedan," von Holzhausen responded, while Musk pointed to an opportunity to design something new.[6]

On the brink of bankruptcy

When the economic crisis hit in 2008, and financial markets dried up, Tesla's cash reserves reached a critical level. Despite the continuous improvement of financial figures due to increased production efficiencies and renegotiated supplier contracts, the company was facing "near-death experiences."[7] Musk was constrained by his second venture, SpaceX, which consumed a large amount of resources, and he could little afford any further investments. At the last possible hour, on Christmas Eve in 2008, Tesla managed to secure financing to keep the business going.

Prospects increased dramatically in 2009. Musk's strategy to sell battery packs to finance Tesla's operations paid off when Herbert Kohler, Daimler's head of advanced engineering signaled interest to come and see what Musk had to offer. In less than six weeks, Jeffrey Straubel, Tesla's chief technical officer, managed to convert Daimler's Smart into an electrically powered vehicle. Convinced of the compatibility of the battery packs, Daimler signed a deal buying 1 000 battery sets worth more than $40 million. In March 2009, von Holzhausen unveiled the prototype of the Model S, which allayed all concerns of Daimler and led to the company's acquisition of a 9 per cent stake for $50 million. Besides gathering the urgently needed fresh capital, this deal made Tesla worth more than $500 million and gave credibility to what was until then just a bold experiment. It also helped to stage a successful initial public offering, paving the way for Tesla's subsequent expansion.

Three months after the unveiling of the Model S, the federal government granted Tesla an alternative vehicle loan of $465 million to market the model, which brought the company another step closer to mass production. However, the payout was restricted by the precondition that sufficient production capacities existed. Fortune was on Musk's side, when just in time Akio Toyoda, president of Toyota, offered up his manufacturing plant in Fremont, California, for sale, after its crisis-shaken partner General Motors withdrew from joint operation. Musk seized the moment, bought these facilities dimensioned for 500 000 vehicles a year,[8] and shifted production from Lotus sites in England to Fremont in 2010. Unlike the Roadster, the Model S was developed as a flexible platform allowing multiple variations comparable to most advanced systems such as Volkswagen's modular production.[9]

From rich man's toy to mass market

In January 2010, Tesla Motors announced its filing of a registration statement with the Securities and Exchange Commission for an initial public offering (IPO) – the first American automaker going public since Ford in 1956. Around the same time, Tesla and Toyota formalized an agreement to jointly develop an electric version of the Toyota RAV4. Toyota also announced the purchase of $50 million worth of Tesla stock at the forthcoming IPO.

Six months later, Tesla placed its shares well above the expected range at $17 (Ticker: TSLA); even so, shares surged 41 per cent on the first day of the IPO and closed at $23.89. Despite having accumulated a loss of more than $300 million since its founding, Tesla was valued at $2 billion and managed to raise nearly $230 million of fresh capital. The company continued to run losses that peaked in 2012 when it was $396 million in the red due to massive investments in the factory ramp-up, building new stores across the country, and training workers. In June 2012, Tesla delivered its first Model S after three years of development. The first quarterly profit of $11.2 million was reported in 2013. In total, 4,750 deliveries of Model S were booked in the first quarter of US sales – more than any of the similarly priced gasoline-powered cars from the top three German luxury brands: Mercedes-Benz S-Class, BMW 7 Series, and Audi A8.

Early in 2012, Tesla unveiled an early prototype, the Model X crossover, produced on the Model S platform in 2015. The carmaker also announced it would soon begin to add lower-priced vehicles, which according to Musk "should be quite affordable ... on the order of $35 000."[10] With a stabilized financial situation, enthusiastic capital markets and customers, and a promising launch of its core product, a multitude of paths and challenges opened up for Tesla's future business model configuration. Tesla's impressive growth, however, has not yet translated into significant profits (Figure 1).

The Model S

In 2013, Tesla sold 22,477 units of its Model S, thus outperforming all forecasts. The Model S comes with a variety of battery-pack options – 40 kWh, 60 kWh and 85 kWh, with base prices (before tax credit) of $52 400, $62 400, and $72 400, respectively.[11] With ranges above 265 miles, the Model S more than doubles the next-best market offer – BMW's i3 five-door urban car, which allows the driver to cover a distance of 90 miles. The reach of the Model S far exceeds what is demanded by customers, who in 80 per cent of cases have to cover less than 50 miles daily.[12] To complement range capabilities for long-distance travel, Tesla offers fast-charging technology at its Supercharger facilities. The fast-charge capability allows Model S owners to replenish 50 per cent of the battery pack in as little as 30 minutes. Moreover, the Model S incorporates a modular battery pack at the floor of the vehicle, which enables it to make use of the battery-swapping technology – to exchange a discharged battery for a fully charged one instead of charging the vehicle's battery – at swapping facilities that will reportedly be installed in the future.

According to Tesla's 10-K reporting, the Model S provides a lower cost of ownership as compared with other vehicles in its class, when purchase price, cost of fuel and the cost of maintenance over a six year ownership period are taken into consideration.[13] This calculation assumes the residual values, warranties, insurance costs and promotions, and customer incentives of other cars in the luxury sedan-class. At current conditions of 11.2 cents per kilowatt-hour and $3.32 per gallon (average prices for electricity and gasoline across US, see Figure 4), the cost of fuel for the Model S is expected to be approximately $1 800 per year less than would be the case for a comparable premium internal combustion engine sedan.[14] Fewer

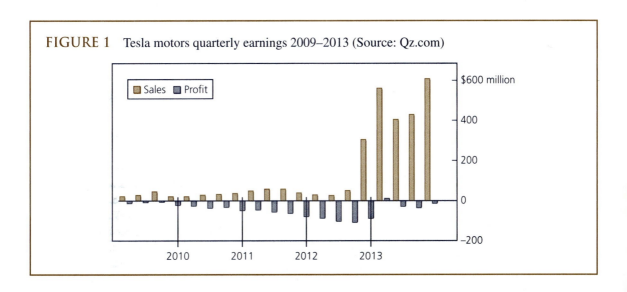

FIGURE 1   Tesla motors quarterly earnings 2009–2013 (Source: Qz.com)

moving parts and the absence of certain components, such as oil, oil filters, spark plugs and engine valves, mean lower maintenance expenses than comparable premium conventional internal combustion engines (ICEs).

The Model S is designed on the basis of an adaptable platform architecture and common electric powertrain that is intended to be leveraged by creating more electric vehicle models in the future. The powertrain and battery pack have a modular design, which will make it possible for future generations of electric vehicles to incorporate a significant amount of this technology. The upcoming Model X is designed as a crossover to fill the niche between the roominess of a minivan and the style of an SUV, powered by an all-wheel drive system. Tesla also plans to launch the Model E (Gen 3), a compact car with a range of perhaps 400 miles that would cost just $35 000.[15]

The electric vehicle market

The market for EVs is split into three segments:

- Hybrid electric vehicles (HEVs): Vehicles that generate all their electric energy onboard the vehicle. HEVs include all varieties of hybrids that use electric motors for traction, including series hybrids, parallel hybrids, through-the-road hybrids, and mild hybrids.

- Plug-in hybrid electric vehicles (PHEVs): Vehicles that are propelled by an electric motor that receives power from the grid but also have an ICE to extend the range of the vehicle.

- Battery electric vehicles (BEVs): Vehicles that use energy sourced from the grid. They get all their power from battery packs and thus have no internal combustion engine.

Hybrids (HEVs) have emerged as a viable alternative to ICEs since the introduction of the first commercially available hybrid-electric vehicle, the Toyota Prius, in 1997. The sedan had the lowest consumption in its category (3.6l/100km). After the company captured the Japanese niche market, it launched its Prius II in California in 2000. At present, more than 1 million HEVs are sold each year, however, at lower rates than in previous years.[16]

The market for plug-in electric vehicles (PEVs) comprises both plug-in hybrid electric vehicles (PHEVs) and battery-electric vehicles (BEVs). With 180 000 PEVs sold worldwide in 2012, this market is still in its infancy, accounting for only 0.02 per cent of the global passenger car market.[17] Unlike HEVs, which are charged through energy recuperation while driving (for example, a brake system), PEV diffusion is strongly dependent on the availability of charging infrastructure at home, at work, or other public places. Until now, the reason for this has largely been insufficiently developed charging infrastructure, which hinders battery-only propulsion technologies (i.e., BEVs) from competing with ICE vehicles, and thus the markets remain small, limited, and niche in scope. One of the biggest hurdles to BEV adoption is "range anxiety": Owners worry about being stranded by the side of the road with a fully discharged battery.[18]

The global market

Particularly over the past 10 years, the world has seen a significant rise in vehicle electrification driven by volatile oil prices, massive decline of urban air quality, and public attempts to decarbonize transportation. The BEV sales are expected to reach 6 million units by the end of 2020, and more than 10 million by 2025 (Figure 2). These figures imply

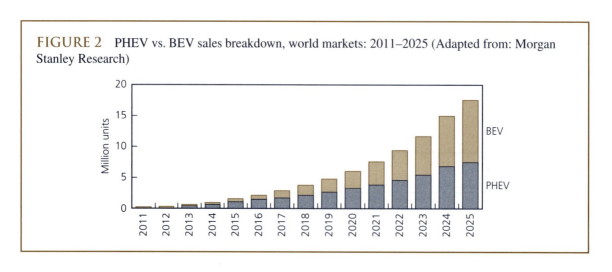

FIGURE 2   PHEV vs. BEV sales breakdown, world markets: 2011–2025 (Adapted from: Morgan Stanley Research)

growth at a compound annual growth rate (CAGR) of approximately 31.5 per cent from 2013 to 2020, almost tenfold as compared with the ICE market, which has an anticipated CAGR of 3.7 per cent throughout the same period.[19] BEVs are expected to generate even greater sales by 2023 and expand their share at the expense of PHEVs in subsequent years. These forecasts indicate that PHEVs could act as a bridging technology between conventional power trains (ICEs) and PEVs. Overall, the global market for PEVs is projected to surpass $415 billion in 2020 and $636 billion in 2030,[20] accounting for 5.5 per cent of global car sales by 2020 and 15 per cent by 2025.[21] Owing to technological, economic, and regulatory uncertainty, however, studies vary widely about PEVs' future share of new vehicles, with figures ranging from 1 per cent to 33 per cent over the 2020–2030 timeframe.

At present, four main regions crystallize as the lead markets with, on aggregate, roughly two-thirds of all PEVs registered worldwide: The United States, China, Japan, and Western Europe (Figure 3), which is also where the major PEV production is expected to shift.[22] In fact, the most likely customers for electric vehicles were found to be in India and China, where between 50 per cent and 60 per cent of car owners were willing to buy PEVs, forming a stark contrast to other countries, such as Japan (4 per cent), France (5 per cent), Germany (9 per cent), and the United States (12 per cent).[23] PEVs are particularly popular in dense urban areas with above-average wealth, limited commuting distances, developed charging infrastructure, and a high fleet penetration. Currently, a large amount of sales is attributed to fleets, such as electric taxis (for example, in Shenzhen and Hangzhou in China) or car-sharing schemes (such as Autolib in France or Car2Go in Germany).

Batteries make up more than one-third of the overall vehicle price of around $12 000–$15 000. Therefore, the market for PEV batteries including materials required for production, plays a particularly crucial role for PEV manufacturers. In the best-case scenario, this market was expected to grow to between $9 billion and $10 billion in 2015 and to $50 billion by 2020. Market consolidation is ongoing, since R&D expenses are high, and production capacities today are estimated to be twice the demand. Five frontrunners are set to control 70 per cent of the Lithium-ion (Li-ion) world market: AESC, LG Chem, Panasonic/Sanyo, A123 and SB LiMotive.[24] While markets for PEV battery are predominantly located in Europe, the United States, and Japan, we might see an increasing shift toward China in the future, where rare earths and critical raw materials are found.

The US market

According to Pluginamerica.com, 183 620 PEVs were sent onto US roads from December 2010

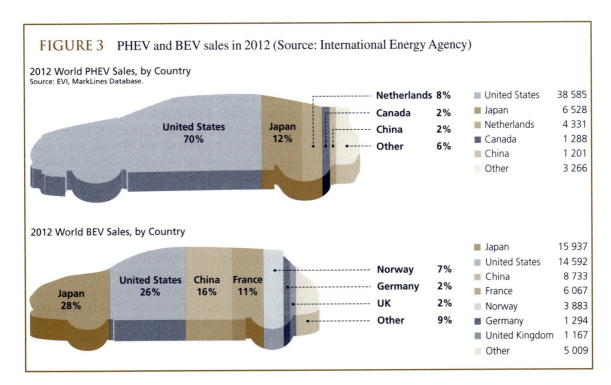

FIGURE 3   PHEV and BEV sales in 2012 (Source: International Energy Agency)

2012 World PHEV Sales, by Country
Source: EVI, MarkLines Database.

Netherlands 8%
Canada 2%
China 2%
Other 6%

United States 70%
Japan 12%

United States	38 585
Japan	6 528
Netherlands	4 331
Canada	1 288
China	1 201
Other	3 266

2012 World BEV Sales, by Country

Norway 7%
Germany 2%
UK 2%
Other 9%

Japan 28%
United States 26%
China 16%
France 11%

Japan	15 937
United States	14 592
China	8 733
France	6 067
Norway	3 883
Germany	1 294
United Kingdom	1 167
Other	5 009

FIGURE 4   US EV projected competitiveness with conventional vehicles (Adapted from: Carnegieendowment.org)

through the end of February 2014. More than half of these PEVs were sold in 2013, doubling sales from 2012.[25] As of 2013, EVs account for less than 1 per cent of cars sold in the United States, which means there is "a huge amount of untapped demand," as Musk notes in a company report.[26] The market for PEVs is highly concentrated in five cities buying more than half of all PEVs sold in the United States: Atlanta, Los Angeles, New York City, San Francisco, and Seattle. With a well-established charging infrastructure, tax cuts, and exclusive parking and traffic lane access, the incentive in these cities to go electric is very appealing. A study on electric mobility found that current EV buyers or leasers are more than twice as wealthy as most Americans (national median income $51 914), male (79 per cent), highly educated, and on average 46 years old. Those that are interested in buying EVs are younger, less wealthy, less idealistic about environmental issues and have high expectations concerning the quality and performance of EVs.[27]

Recent growth has been fueled by significant price cuts for electric cars, as automakers race for economic scale effects and falling battery prices. For instance, BMW announced it will charge $41 350 for its new i3 (before tax credits), while Ford and Nissan reduced prices on their Focus and Leaf models by $4 000 and $6 400, respectively, for 2014. With an additional $7 500 in tax credits for several PEV

models (including the Tesla Model S), the total cost of ownership (TCO), which comprises the costs over the whole lifecycle of vehicles, is significantly lowered, allowing electric vehicles to exceed the pricing thresholds that are acceptable for mass markets. Besides governmental incentives and infrastructure, the oil price and technological advancements, and particularly battery expenses, which account for a substantial portion of PEV costs, are critical for PEV versus ICE buying decisions (Figure 4).

The best-selling BEV model today is the Chevy Volt, with over 48 000 vehicles now on US roads competing with 15 other light-duty models of PEVs that are currently on the market. With the exception of the Cadillac ELR (six sold in 2013, starting at $76 000) and the Porsche Panamera S-E (86 sold in 2013, starting at $99 000), the BEV market is dominated by economy and compact-class cars (Figure 5).

Including all gasoline hybrids and fuel-cell EVs, consumers can choose among more than 56 models of electrically powered vehicles.[28] The scheduled introductions of several PEVs suggest that Tesla is about to face more headwinds, as major carmakers are moving into the electric luxury segment after Tesla had largely had this segment to itself since the launch of its Model S in 2012. In an attempt to counter the loss of trendsetting and affluent customers, several deep-pocketed rivals have announced PEV launches, such as the BMW i8 ($135 000), Audi R8

FIGURE 5   2013 monthly sales chart for the major BEV automakers (Source: http://insideevs.com/final-2013-plug-in-sales-rankings-for-the-us-are-in-who-did-well-who-did-not-infographic/)

2013	JAN	FEB	MAR	APR	MAY	JUN	JUL	AUG	SEP	OCT	NOV	DEC	Total
Chevrolet Volt	1 140	1 626	1 478	1 306	1 607	2 698	1 788	3 351	1 766	2 022	1 920	2 392	23 094
Nissan LEAF	650	653	2 236	1 937	2 138	2 225	1 864	2 420	1 953	2 002	2 003	2 529	22 610
Tesla Model S	1 200	1 400	2 300	2 100	1 700	1 350	1 800	1 300	1 000	800	1 200	1 500	17 650
Toyota Prius PHV	874	693	786	599	678	584	817	1 791	1 152	2 095	1 100	919	12 088
Ford C-Max Energi	338	334	494	411	450	455	433	621	758	1 092	941	827	7 154
Ford Fusion Energi	0	119	295	364	416	390	407	600	750	1 087	870	791	6 089
Ford Focus Electric	81	158	180	147	157	177	150	175	110	115	130	158	1 738
Toyota RAV4 EV	25	52	133	70	84	44	109	231	167	91	62	28	1 096
Mitsubishi i-MiEV	257	337	31	127	91	39	46	30	20	28	12	11	1 029
smart ED	2*	0	0	0	60	53	58	182	137	111	153	167	923
Fiat 500e*	0	0	0	0	0	0	150	160	50	40	125	120	645
Honda Fit EV	8	15	23	22	15	208	63	66	35	40	23	51	569
Chevrolet Spark EV	0	0	0	0	0	27	103	102	78	66	87	76	539
Honda Accord PHV	2	17	26	55	58	42	54	44	51	71	68	38	526
Porsche PanameraS-E	0	0	0	0	0	0	0	0	0	35	4	47	86
Cadillac ELR	0	0	0	0	0	0	0	0	0	0	0	6	6
Inside EVs	4 577	5 404	7 982	7 138	7 454	8 292	7 842	11 073	8 027	9 695	8 698	9 660	95 842

e-tron ($150 000), Volkswagen XL1 ($146 000), Porsche 918 Spyder ($845 000), and the Mercedes-Benz SLS AMG Electric Drive ($544 000), among many other smaller-sized models, such as the Mercedes B-Class (less than $40 000). Recently, Rudolf Krebs, the VW Group executive in charge of electric vehicle programs, revealed VW's plan to roll out 40 different PEVs over the next several years.[29] The future is not looking rosy for every manufacturer, however. By the end of 2013, Fisker Automotive, Tesla's main rival located next-door in Anaheim, California, filed for bankruptcy after suffering from safety recalls, the insolvency of a battery supplier, and severe losses of shipments during 2012's Hurricane Sandy.[30]

The role of government

The global market for electric mobility is promoted through various governmental policies and programs incentivizing sales and facilitating technological transition. Several governments support their national markets through subsidies to purchase costs, production facilities, research and development, and charging infrastructure development, but also through the purchase of fleets for public organizations and

favorable regulation (for example, special lanes, taxation, and parking). In terms of incentivizing vehicle adoption, the United States clearly takes the lead with more than $30 billion of overall funding from 2010 to 2017, far exceeding the second-largest program that is in place in China ($5.4 billion from 2006 to 2016).[31]

Governments also released ambitious roadmaps designed to increase widespread acceptance of electric mobility by targeting individual customers, commercial, and public fleets (Figure 6). Disincentives on ICEs, such as emission-based taxation and fuel economy regulation, have also been put in place and tilted economies toward electric vehicles. For instance, in Europe, CO_2 emission limits were set at an average of 130g/km and will be phased in between 2012 and 2015. The European Commission intends to tighten this limit to 95g/km by 2020. In China, new fuel-efficiency standards have been announced, changing prospects for electric cars there for the better.

In addition, public organizations work alongside private ones to address a lack of standardization in areas such as charging infrastructure, billing, and software, which inhibits customer acceptance and higher sales. Government-backed demonstration

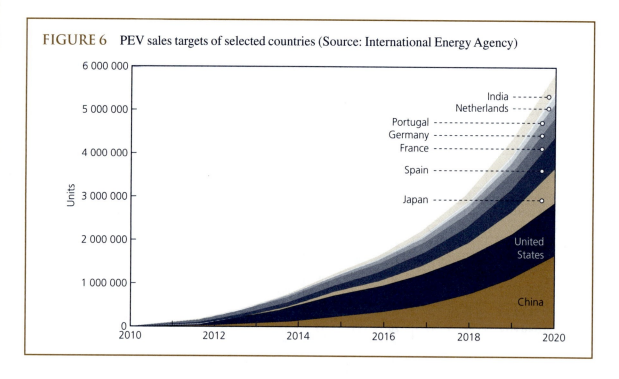

FIGURE 6   PEV sales targets of selected countries (Source: International Energy Agency)

and commercialization programs have been established to provide a testing ground and spur the uptake of electric mobility technology. Thus far, government action at all levels has greatly influenced PEV sales and the integration of these new vehicles into the electrical grid.

Tesla's business model

Key resources

Battery technology.   Tesla considers its core competencies to be the engineering of electric power-trains, including the battery pack, power electronics, motor, gearbox and the control software that enables the components to operate as a system. The battery pack system has been designed to allow for interchangeability of battery cell chemistry of independent manufacturers. Tesla aims to capitalize on substantial battery cell investments and advancements to quickly drive down the cost of batteries. The company itself compares and tests available lithium-ion cells on energy storage capacity, longevity, and power delivery to choose among the suppliers and chemistry types with the best value and performance for its battery packs.[32]

Battery technology plays a particularly important role: It constitutes a central competitive lever in the EV market because of its high share of the overall cost and its significance for customer acceptance, as it reduces "range anxiety," charging time, and concerns about security. While battery costs are declining at a rapid pace, they are expected to make up a major cost factor in the future (Figure 7). Prices dropped more than 50 per cent in the past four years from $1 000 per kWh in 2010 to less than $400 per kWh in 2014 (Figure 4). Based on the assumption of a 10 per cent learning rate per year and continuously improving economies of scale, most recent analyses see further price cuts until at least 2020.[33]

Software technology.   The Model S is equipped with the largest automotive touch screen in the world and the ability to add new features and capabilities using over-the-air software. This software also permits innovative car repair and performance updates. The ability to send updated software wirelessly to vehicles helped Tesla to instantly fix 29 222 Model S's that posed a fire risk because of overheating charger plugs. In other cases, Tesla created updates following customer requests, such as changing the suspension settings, which give the car more traction at high speeds, or a re-installed "creep" function that some customer were used to in ICEs, which slowly moves cars forward when the brake pedal is released. Commenting on wireless repairs,

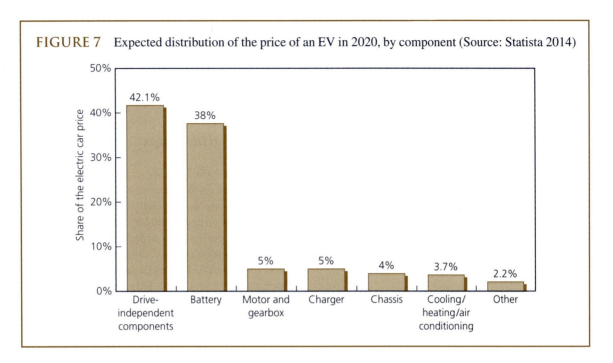

FIGURE 7   Expected distribution of the price of an EV in 2020, by component (Source: Statista 2014)

Musk tweeted that no vehicles were "physically recalled," and that in fact "the word 'recall' needs to be recalled."[34] Tesla also introduced apps that allow car owners to manage the charging process, track their movements on a map, analyze their driving behavior, and heat or cool the interior before driving.

Charging infrastructure.   Since 2012, Tesla has implemented company-owned Supercharger stations that rapidly recharge batteries in high-traffic corridors across North America, Europe, and Asia. Tesla's current charging network allows coast-to-coast travelling across the United States. European customers, Musk announced, "will be able to travel almost anywhere in Europe using only Superchargers" by the end of 2014. Supercharger technology provides a charge of between 90 kWh and 120 kWh, enough power for three hours of driving with only 20 minutes of charging, which means stops are frequent as on any road trip, as Musk said.[35] While investments of $100 000 to $175 000 per Supercharger station seem high, Tesla actually racks up more than it invests through the credits it earns for each zero-emission vehicle (ZEV) sold in California.[36] It is estimated that Tesla may earn up to $250 million in ZEV credits in 2014, thanks to its Model S. These revenues far exceed the funding required for the 237 Supercharger stations the company plans for the United States and Canada in the coming years.[37] Most charging, however, occurs at home through a standard plug (92 hours for a full charge) or a high-power wall connector (10 hours for a full charge), which may also be extended with a twin charger (five hours for a full charge) doubling the charging capacity.

Tesla, however, not only relies on charging technology but also experiments with battery swapping as an option alongside its Supercharger network. The switching station concept pioneered by Better Place, the now-bankrupt electric vehicle company, would provide an alternative to charging. Unlike Better Place, Tesla announced it would install battery swap stations in addition and next to its existing Supercharger locations, enabling the customer to choose between two options: charging batteries for free (30 minutes), or swapping batteries (90 seconds) for a service fee amounting to roughly $60 to $80, the equivalent of 15 gallons of gas at current rates. Car owners may then opt to return for the older pack to the station, have them delivered for a fee, or keep the replacement pack with Tesla charging the value difference of the battery pack based on its age. Tesla estimates the cost per battery swap station to be around $500 000.[38]

Energy management and storage.   While the production and storage of energy and solar power in particular do not form an explicit business segment, Tesla has teamed up with partner SolarCity (SCTY) to distribute solar panels through the website to complement its product portfolio. Both firms are collaborating to develop a smart energy storage system by using stored electricity to reduce peak demand – the highest amount of electricity used within the billing period. The business approach is to balance the generation and consumption of electricity by producing it through solar panels or retrieving it from the grid during daytime in order to store and discharge it into the EV (for example, Model S) at night. Besides offering grid-independent backup power in case of outages, both the demand and prices for energy are lowered. Tesla provides battery systems to store the electricity and promotes solar-power systems among its customers, and SolarCity installs the hardware and contributes its software to optimize utility charge savings for customers.

Human resources. Musk considers human capital to be of the highest importance, and he has a hands-on role in personally interviewing and hiring many of the job candidates.[39] The company's value, to a large degree, is made up of the quality of the talent and intellectual property (IP) it has generated over the years. According to Musk, working for Tesla is like "you are choosing to be the equivalent of Special Forces," as employees are expected to work at least 50 hours a week. Employees are asked to challenge the status quo and allocate sufficient time for innovation. The firm's culture rather resembles that of a technology startup than of a traditional car manufacturer. Tesla's engineering team is about 80 per cent smaller than the average team of a car manufacturer as the company tries to compensate for quantity with quality by hiring only the best engineers. In 2013, Tesla was listed ninth among the "most innovative companies" in a global innovation study.[40]

To draw on best practices from diverse fields of business, Musk hired an experienced top executive team with exceptional skills, including Franz von Holzhausen (Design: VW, Mazda, GM), George Blankenship (Sales: Apple, GAP), Chris Porritt (Engineering: Aston Martin), Doug Field (Product Design: Apple), Gilbert Passin and Rich Heley (Manufacturing: Toyota, Apple), Kristin Paget (IT: Apple, Microsoft), and Simon Sproule (PR: Renault-Nissan). Arnnon Geshuri, Tesla's HR director, who came from Google in 2009, assembled a highly talented team and created a culture geared toward interdisciplinary collaboration. Most of Tesla's facilities are located in California, allowing the firm to capitalize on the pool of highly qualified employees graduating

from top universities and some of the world's most innovative firms. Today, the company employs approximately 6 000 employees, nearly twice as many as in 2013. To meet its aggressive expansion targets, Tesla is expected to grow at the same pace in the future.

Strategic partnerships

Daimler. In 2009, Daimler acquired a stake in Tesla and took a seat on the company's board of directors. Today, both firms are intensely connected and leverage their joint strengths through Tesla's agility and Daimler's experience in order to drive the global commercialization of EVs. Over time, this collaboration increased to become a strategic partnership, which today covers knowledge exchange in various fields, such as engineering, production and supply chain. Musk noted that, in retrospect, Daimler's investment was most decisive for the firm's survival injecting capital when Tesla faced illiquidity. Today, both firms maintain strong ties and Bodo Uebber, Daimler's chief financial officer, recently said that Daimler is still looking "for more cooperation"[41] with Tesla.

Toyota Motor. The alliance between Tesla Motors and Toyota Motor Corporation was established in 2010 to cooperate on the development of EVs, parts, manufacturing system, and engineering support. Toyota intends to close the gap with other automobile firms that went ahead with pure EVs in the market. Moreover, Toyota wants to learn from the Tesla's challenging spirit, quick decision-making, and flexibility. In 2013, this partnership produced what was described by the press as the "cheapest Tesla on the market," the RAV4 EV – a small Toyota SUV outfitted with a Tesla-built battery and an all-electric drivetrain.

Panasonic. In 2009, Tesla entered into a partnership with Panasonic Corporation to secure battery-cell supply and insulate itself from lithium-ion supply market uncertainty. The following year, both firms intensified their partnership, and Panasonic became a shareholder when it invested $30 million in Tesla Motors. In late 2013, both parties updated an earlier agreement to expand Panasonic's supply to nearly 2 billion cells over four years. Owing to fierce competition and declining battery prices – partly caused by an oversupply of key raw materials – the lithium-ion battery business added to Panasonic's near-record net loss in the past year. Nevertheless, the company views the battery business as a key source of its turnaround strategy and future growth assuring it will increase production capacity of battery cells to serve Tesla's growing demand as it ramps up EV output.[42]

SolarCity.   Tesla maintains strong ties to SolarCity, a corporation based in San Mateo, California, and chaired by Musk, that designs, installs, and sells solar energy systems. The bulk of SolarCity's business comes from the leasing business, where SolarCity provides a system for free in exchange for a 20-year lease contract without the usually high upfront costs for customers. Partnering with SolarCity, Tesla aims to deploy its battery know-how to create a complete off-the-grid kit for home solar-power storage. This partnership is somewhat of a family affair, since Musk is the cousin of SolarCity co-founder and COO Peter Rive.

Early on, Rive revealed his plan to design systems for powering homes and cars. SolarCity's first foray into electric car-charging stations followed in 2009, when the company collaborated with Tesla to install solar-powered charging equipment on US Route 101 in California between San Francisco and Los Angeles.[43] Musk indicated the partnership could be intensified by pairing solar-power systems and grid storage components with the Supercharger stations to reduce marginal energy costs caused by "demand charge" – fees for demand during large spikes. Implementing solar power, however, would double the capital cost of Supercharger stations, excluding grid storage systems.[44]

AT&T, TeliaSonera, Telefonica.   In the past few months, Tesla announced several partnerships with mobile communications operators. The company collaborates with AT&T in the United States, and TeliaSonera and Telefonica in Europe to wirelessly enable and connect its vehicles for safety diagnostics, remote monitoring, and repair via machine-to-machine (M2M) interconnection.

Key value-creation activities

Design, engineering & production.   The design and engineering activities for external clients, such as battery packs, drive units, gearboxes and software, account for roughly 10 per cent of the company's revenue with a decreasing tendency. Tesla designs, tests and manufactures fully electric powertrain systems for other automakers, such as for its strategic partners

Toyota (RAV4) and Daimler (Mercedes-Benz and Smart). Automotive production contributes about 75 per cent to the firm's income. This last segment includes vehicles and related sales (vehicle options, accessories, and vehicle service). Another revenue stream is the sales of regulatory credits, such as ZEV emission credits or reimbursements received as part of the federal efficiency program (15–20 per cent). Since the production of the Roadster was phased out, the Model S is the only vehicle in Tesla's product portfolio, although there is an option to reserve the upcoming Model X crossover. As cars are built to order, there is no storage and very little inventory involved in the Tesla production system.

Sales, servicing and charging.   To sell its cars, Tesla relies on a non-traditional direct sales approach aiming to create an "experience" via company-owned stores, galleries, and service networks – and less on traditional advertising concepts as the media. Stores are designed to be informative and enjoyable without inventory on site, in contrast to traditional dealerships that maintain a large fleet of cars. The company employs "product specialists" rather than dealers, who are trained to explain Tesla's products and answer questions about EVs in general – without any ulterior motives (commission) or authority to sell the company's products. Jim Chen, Tesla's vice president for regulatory affairs, points out that the direct-distribution approach, including incentives for dealers to push EVs, is rather weak because of the small car volumes and servicing profits generated by Tesla's products as compared with combustion engine vehicles.

Orders may only be placed over the Internet, thus cutting out sales representatives and the apparatus that goes with them. Since many of the sales are processed online, Tesla developed a highly interactive and comprehensive homepage that features several configurators that meticulously calculate reach, charging time, and savings, among many other things, before visitors proceed to virtually assemble their desired vehicle in the "design studio." The company's homepage is also an important marketing instrument featuring "customer stories" that advertise Tesla's model through real-life experiences. Stores are positioned in visible and high foot-traffic retail locations, like shopping malls, to inform potential customers before car-buying decisions are made. Tesla's approach is to interact with future customers and "educate" them about the benefits of going electric early on. In this context, its buoyant blogs constitute a critical channel of customer feedback and are an invaluable source for product improvement and innovation. In addition, Musk blogs and makes frequent use of social media to communicate the firm's advancements, reach out to the Tesla community, and generally create awareness for the firm.

Service is a top priority for Tesla. Its goal is not only to fix things but to make them better than they were throughout the product lifecycle (for example, through software updates). To address concerns about owning and driving EVs, 24-hour roadside assistance (ranger service), remote diagnostics, and system monitoring were introduced. Tesla Service Centers are planned to be erected across North America so that Tesla customers will have to travel less than 50 miles to reach a Tesla Service Center. Technicians, concerned with repair and maintenance around the world, are tightly connected to the research and development facilities located in Silicon Valley and draw on this large pool of knowledge via online channels to quickly resolve any problems.

A central part of Tesla's service proposition is its widely accessible charging infrastructure, which has been aggressively expanded over the past few years. Activities around the charging process have not been designed to create additional revenue (profit centers), but rather to create some added value to boost its Model S sales. Customers pay a $2 000 access fee for the Supercharger network and thereby receive access to electricity "for free, for life." Beyond that, Tesla distributes additional home-charging devices that enabling faster charging processes.

Major challenges

Infrastructural patchwork. Publicly available electric vehicle supply equipment (EVSE) has been deployed across different locations, such as residential, office, retail, and street. EVSE expands quickly, particularly in the United States and Japan, with each maintaining approximately 20,000 non-residential charging stations, followed by China with roughly half the amount (Figure 8). Countries that currently hold over 90 per cent of world EV stock announced cumulative targets of more than 2.4 million chargers by 2020. Access to most non-residential charging stations is still restricted because of subscriptions and roaming charges, or limited to certain EV models. Moreover, various charging standards, such as the CHAdeMO (Nissan, Mitsubishi) or the SAE plug (GM, BMW) were established by the market players, hampering access. Officials said Tesla is already working on an adapter that is compatible with SAE Combo Chargers and is also willing to license its Supercharger technology if conditions are right. "We're not trying to create a closed system," Musk clarified. "We just need to solve the problem of long-distance travel, and we can't wait for others to agree with our strategy."[45]

Regulatory guesswork. The EV sector has received substantial backing from governments around the world in an attempt to stay ahead of the technology race, lessen dependence on oil and damaging pollution. Public money for tax incentives, subsidies, as well as favorable regulatory conditions, spurred innovation and the diffusion of EV technology over the past few years. Tesla has considerably benefited from revenues through ZEV credits in the past ($119 million in 2013 only). Recent developments show that regulatory conditions may quickly change and have serious implications for Tesla's business model.

Several states, such as New Jersey, Texas, Virginia, Maryland and Arizona, prohibited or restricted car manufacturers from selling vehicles directly to consumers, while others, such as New York, Minnesota, and Georgia, are about to follow the ban. Pushed by a strong ICE lobby, this decision threatens to shake Tesla's direct-sales model in favor of incumbent dealerships. The argument is that franchise laws were put in place to prevent a manufacturer from unfairly opening stores in direct competition with an existing franchise dealer and that a franchise middleman keeps carmakers from ripping off consumers and protects price competition. "I'd rather fight one federal battle," Musk said, who is preparing to go to Washington soon.

Technological risks. Tesla has been a technological pacesetter over the past few years. In contrast to its large incumbent rivals, Tesla faces a twofold challenge: scaling up production and its proprietary infrastructure, and keeping pace with technological advances. Both tasks demand high capital and human resource investments. Tesla's research and development budget ($270 million in 2012; $250 million in 2013) makes up only a fraction of what is available to competing incumbents (Figure 9). For instance, an already massive research effort is underway to explore autonomously driving (or self-driving) cars by firms like Google, BMW, and Volvo. A recent tweet by Musk, which called for applications of engineers interested in autonomous driving, indicates that Tesla is taking this challenge very serious.[46]

FIGURE 8   Non-residential EVSE stock in selected countries, by fast and slow chargers in 2012 (Source: International Energy Agency)

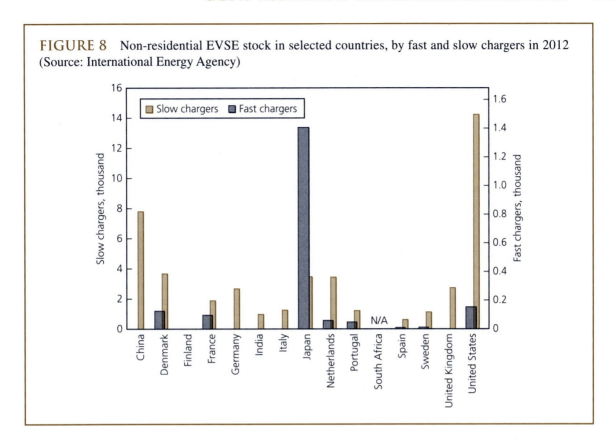

FIGURE 9   Estimated R&D spending (global and US) by selected automakers for 2013 (in billions of dollars). (Sources: Wards 2011; IRI 2013a; and Center for Automotive Research 2013)

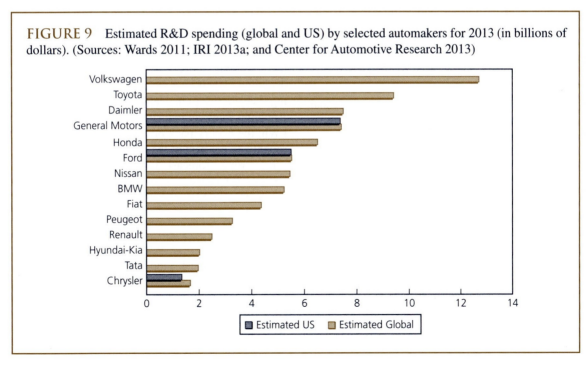

An unsophisticated production process, relatively loose supplier relationships, and little experience with assembled parts contribute to Tesla's exposure to multiple risks of delivery failure (such as quality defects or supply shortages). Moreover, there is some real concern about the safety of Tesla's battery technology after its Model S repeatedly caught fire. Most of Tesla's technology is new and has not had comprehensive market testing. While many problems can be fixed through software updates, some hardware issues remain. In a recent case, a Model S blazed while parked in a garage, prompting the company to send the owners new charging adapters and software upgrades to prevent overheating. To pre-empt damage to the company's reputation, Musk announced to amend the current warranty policy to cover damage due to fire. Today, Tesla faces recalls and even a federal inquiry into the security of its cars, which might call its quality and safety into serious question after it received record scores for being the "safest car in America" (National Highway Traffic Safety Administration) and the "best car in history" (Consumer Reports – 99 out of 100 points). The benchmark against which Tesla's quality is measured is high.

Market challenges. On several occasions, Musk has emphasized the importance of the battery supply as the bottleneck of the company. Particularly, the supply of lithium and cobalt as the most crucial raw materials carry significant risk for Tesla's business. A large portion of the global supply of cobalt originates in the unstable Democratic Republic of Congo. While interruptions in delivery could cause rapid price increases, producers are able to swap out cobalt for other materials, like manganese. This is different for lithium, which is an indispensable ingredient of Tesla's current battery technology, posing a serious threat to Tesla's battery supply chains.[47] While an oversupply of lithium exists today, the situation might change in the future as an increasing share of supply flows into competing demand for smart phones, tablets and other computing devices. Musk expressed his concerns about the company's supply base and its ability to keep up with Tesla's fast-paced growth.[48]

But there could be more problems ahead for Tesla. With new models introduced from high-end competition (such as BMW, Audi, and Mercedes), and a large amount of models already available in the mid-market segment (for example, Nissan, Chevrolet, and Toyota), Tesla risks being squeezed into a niche position. To respond to this threat, it seems crucial for Tesla to expand its capacity and operational

efficiency to lift economies of scale and distribute production cost on a larger output volume. However, with roughly around 25 000 cars produced, Tesla has a long way to go to receive supply conditions comparable to those of its far larger competitors.

Above all, the question remains whether market demand will allow further scaling or lock Musk's firm in a luxury niche. Tesla's business model has been configured, and its operation has been developed to serve the mass market. At some point, Tesla will sell automobiles with a sticker price for less than $40 000. However, scaling is crucial not only to reduce production costs and lower sales prices for mass commercialization but also to reach the profitable operation of many other activities included in Tesla's business model – most importantly, to achieve an increased utilization of battery charging and swapping infrastructure, and to fully exploit the potential of its sales network.

Product risks. Analysts expressed doubts about the viability of Tesla's current business model for potentially high costs of ownership involved due to the uncertainty of Model S value retention. To eliminate these doubts and lower upfront payment hurdles, Tesla announced an alternative financing option offered in cooperation with US Bank and Wells Fargo. A lease/ownership hybrid is available, where customers get 10 per cent off the car with funding from banks and then pay a monthly fee, and includes an option to sell the car back to Tesla at a minimum of 50 per cent of its original cost after three years of use. However, current predictions see battery cost declining by half over the next three years, thus posing a severe risk to the delicate resale-value promise. Applying a current industry average of around $400/kWh, the battery pack on its own is worth $34 000, roughly 46 per cent of the total cost of the vehicle. If prices drop as forecasted, Tesla's value will deteriorate faster than expected, causing guarantees to come at significantly higher costs to the company.

Looking ahead

Most recently, Musk announced to build a $5 billion US factory by 2020 and claims it will make more lithium-ion batteries than all other plants on earth combined. A press release stated that Tesla aims to leverage demand for lithium-ion batteries to reduce costs faster by achieving economies of scale and minimizing costs through innovative manufacturing. The target is to reduce battery costs by 30 per cent by 2017. The battery factory is planned in cooperation with strategic battery manufacturing partners (for example, Panasonic) to share the risk, optimize co-located processes, and reduce overhead costs.

Analysts are also confident that Tesla's Silicon Valley location will give it a head start in autonomous driving technology. The iPad-like control panel of the Model S and a recent meeting with Apple's head of M&A set off speculation that the two firms might soon join forces for deeper iOS integration in battery technology. Musk remained silent about concrete plans, however, only leaking that any scenario of a partnership or acquisition would need to bring Tesla closer to its pronounced goal of becoming a mass-market car manufacturer.

Musk has also revealed that he has been in talks with Google to bring driverless technology to Tesla's vehicles. Musk says he believes autonomous driving is the next logical step in the evolution of cars but thinks Google's technology (which uses sensors instead of an optical system) is too costly. "I think Tesla will most likely develop its own autopilot system for the car, as I think it should be camera-based," Musk said and added, "However, it is also possible that we do something jointly with Google."[49]

Tesla seems to be headed toward a more digitally interconnected business model. In April 2014, Telefonica made official that it will support the wireless connectivity for Tesla cars across the United Kingdom, Germany, the Netherlands and Spain. Telefonica will provide Internet connectivity for various in-car "infotainment" and telematics services (driver habits and usage), including navigation, streamed music, Internet browsing, and remote vehicle diagnostics. It follows similar carrier deals Tesla recently signed with AT&T in the United States, and TeliaSonera for Sweden, Denmark, Finland, Estonia, and Latvia. Generating data from car drivers has become a strategic issue for Tesla to convert cars from mere metal to mindful companions.

On 24 February 2014, Tesla raised almost $2 billon on the market to help fund a giant battery factory. Tesla now holds more cash than it ever had in the brief history of the company. Cash and cash equivalents at first quarter end of 2014 increased to almost $2.6 billion – a considerable sum for future investments.

References

1. http://qz.com/179318/teslas-most-disruptive-product-may-not-be-its-cars/.
2. http://ir.teslamotors.com/events.cfm.
3. http://www.teslamotors.com/blog/secret-tesla-motors-master-plan-just-between-you-and-me.
4. http://www.teslamotors.com/de_CH/node/3915.
5. http://www.autoblog.com/2008/02/05/elon-musk-takes-delivery-of-first-production-tesla-roadster/.
6. http://www.wired.com/magazine/2010/09/ff_tesla/4/.
7. http://blog.sfgate.com/energy/2014/02/28/tesla-from-the-brink-of-bankruptcy-to-auto-pilot-cars/.
8. http://www.teslamotors.com/about/press/releases/tesla-motors-announces-factory-northern-california.
9. http://www.volkswagen.co.uk/about-us/news/384.
10. http://www.bloomberg.com/news/2013-05-31/musk-says-fourth-tesla-vehicle-to-be-small-electric-suv.html.
11. A Model S performance version is offered at $87 400..
12. http://www.deloitte.com/view/en_US/us/Industries/Automotive-Manufacturing/f769ebb8bf4b2310VgnVC-M1000001a56f00aRCRD.htm#..
13. http://www.sec.gov/Archives/edgar/data/1318605/000119312513096241./d452995d10k.htm.
14. http://www.teslamotors.com/charging#/calculator.
15. http://www.mormngstar.com/earmngs/PrintTranscript.aspx?id=60430204.
16. http://www.smartgridobserver.com/n7-3-12-1.htm.
17. www.iea.org/publications/globaleveoutlook_2013.pdf.
18. http://www.autonews.com/article/20131015/OEM05/131019939/electric-car-rentals-hampered-by-range-anxiety.
19. http://www.navigantresearch.com/wp-assets/uploads/2013/06/EVMF-13-Executive-Summary.pdf.
20. McKinsey, Handelsblatt, February 7, 2011, page 27.
21. Morgan Stanley Research, "Tesla Motors Inc. America's Fourth Automaker", March 2011.
22. http://www.researchandmarkets.com/research/c67mxb/global_electric.
23. http://www.deloitte.com/view/en_US/us/Industries/Automotive-Manufacturing/f769ebb8bf4b2310VgnVCM1000001a56f00aRCRD.htm#.
24. http://www.rolandberger.com/press_releases/512-press_archive2012_sc_content/Update_to_study_on_Li_ion_battery_market.html.
25. http://insideevs.com/monthly-plug-in-sales-scorecard/.
26. http://www.mormngstar.com/eammgs/PrintTranscript.aspx?id=60430204.
27. http://www.businessinsider.com/electric-car-owners-are-richer-and-smarter-2012-11#ixzz2xirzxEP6.
28. http://innovation.luskin.ucla.edu/content/market-dynamics.
29. http://online.wsj.com/news/articles/SB10001424052702303653004579210053345661982.
30. http://www.bloomberg.com/news/2013-11-22/fisker-files-for-bankruptcy-with-plan-to-sell-assets.html.
31. Statista 2014, Business Insider "Level of funding into electromobility in selected countries" (as of 2012).
32. http://www.sec.gov/Archives/edgar/data/1318605/000119312513096241/d452995d10k.htm.
33. www.iea.org/publications/freepublications/publication/name,37024,en.html.
34. http://www.technologyreview.com/view/523621/tesla-motors-over-the-air-repairs-are-the-way-forward/.
35. http://www.teslamotors.com/supercharger.
36. The Zero Emission Vehicle (ZEV) Program is designed to achieve the state's long-term emission reduction goals by requiring manufacturers to offer for sale specific numbers of the cleanest car technologies available, which include: battery electric, fuel cell, and plug-in hybrid electric vehicles.

37. http://insideevs.com/model-s-could-earn-tesla-up-to-250-million-in-carb-zev-credits/.
38. http://www.forbes.com/sites/pikeresearch/2013/06/27/tesla-tries-out-battery-swapping/.
39. http://theamericanceo.com/2013/02/04/how-ceos-hire-elon-musk-on-interviewing-every-candidate/.
40. http://www.booz.com/global/home/what-we-think/global-innovation-1000.
41. http://www.reuters.com/article/2013/10/31/autos-daimler-tesla-idUSL1N0IL11N20131031.
42. http://www.teslamotors.com/de_CH/about/press/releases/panasonic-and-tesla-reach-agreement-expand-supply-automotivegrade-battery-cells.
43. http://www.greentechmedia.com/articles/read/solarcity-installs-electric-car-chargers-along-cal-highway/SolarCity.

44. http://www.plugincars.com/solar-powered-electric-car-charging-business-model-127710.html.
45. http://cars.chicagotribune.com/fuel-efficient/news/chi-tesla-connects-midwest-to-transcontinental-supercharging-network-20130530.
46. https://twitter.com/elonmusk/status/380454034659753984.
47. http://www.cnbc.com/id/101505280.
48. http://online.wsj.com/news/articles/SB20001424052702303636404579393391643110198.
49. http://www.bloomberg.com/news/2013-05-07/tesla-ceo-talking-with-google-about-autopilot-systems.html.

Ricardo Semler: A revolutionary model of leadership

By Professor William W. Maddux with Roderick I. Swaab, Betania Tanure and Elin Williams

The present: 2014

Ricardo Semler lets out a sigh of frustration. Leaning over his favourite Les Paul guitar in the basement of his house in the mountains near São Paulo, surrounded by a pile of musical equipment that would be the envy of any rock star – drum sets and keyboards and sound mixers, Fenders and Gibsons lined up like soldiers at attention in racks around the room. He frowns as he works through the Led Zeppelin song for the tenth or twentieth or hundredth time. How does Jimmy Page make the music sound so effortless, so powerful, so true? he wonders. But then he smiles to himself, because the kind of skill and passion that he hears in the rock legend's guitar work is exactly what Ricardo Semler has been getting from the thousands of colleagues and employees he has worked with over the years. And despite the naysayers who have always scoffed at his trying to run a business like a rock band, he has ended up succeeding more often than not.

Ricardo smiles because he's come so far and yet has ended up exactly where he started: in his basement playing his guitar. Today it is 2014, and his home country Brazil is busy preparing for its long-awaited time on the world stage: the World Cup in a few months and the (summer) Olympics in 2016. The Brazilian economy, cooling a bit after years of torrid growth, is still the envy of much of the rest of the world. In Brazil, things are happening. The world is arriving soon.

And even though Ricardo Semler is tucked away in his own little world, trying to unlock the mysteries of an enigmatic guitar genius, you could say that he, too, is working, working in much the same way he has been doing for decades at the head of some of the world's most innovative and profitable organizations: a multinational company called Semco that he reluctantly took over from his father, a hugely profitable NGO, a Brazilian business association, a luxury eco-resort, and a set of successful charter schools.

The one thing common to all these organizations is that they are run using Ricardo's overarching leadership philosophy, a philosophy that has ignited controversy and acclaim in a roughly equal measure – but one that has proven successful by any standard, whenever and wherever he has tried it. The philosophy could be summed up as follows: that leadership is often most effective when the boss is hunched over his guitar on a Wednesday afternoon; or feeding the ducks with his kids during the visit of an important client; or hiking in the mountains in Africa during a shareholders' meeting; or off somewhere else that is nowhere near the office, nowhere near his employees, not doing any special thinking about contracts or investments or strategic planning or the future of global business. In a word – gone.

The past: The origins of Semco

Antonio Curt Semler left Austria just before World War II to make a new life in South America. He took advantage of Brazil's first 'economic miracle' in the 1950s and 60s to build his company, a major supplier of marine pumps for the shipping industry. But he wanted to do more. He wanted to build a family business, a lasting legacy.

2016 - Winner of The Case Centre Awards in the category "Human Resource Management/Organisational Behaviour"

02/2016-5982

This case was written by William W. Maddux, Associate Professor of Organisational Behaviour at INSEAD, and Roderick I. Swaab, Assistant Professor of Organisational Behaviour at INSEAD, in conjunction with Betania Tanure, Professor of Organisational Behaviour at PUC/BTA, and case writer Elin Williams. It is intended to be used as a basis for class discussion rather than to illustrate either effective or ineffective handling of an administrative situation.

Financial support from INSEAD Alumni Fund is gratefully acknowledged.

Additional material about INSEAD case studies (e.g., videos, spreadsheets, links) can be accessed at cases.insead.edu.

His young son Ricardo was not, however, a natural successor. He did not do well in school and preferred strumming his guitar to poring over his books (though he did manage to wind up as class president and captain of the track team.) But he started to show some entrepreneurial flair in high school, where he took on the responsibility of running the school's snack shop. By altering the existing price structure, extending operating hours, and re-negotiating supplier contracts, he increased profits and invested them in the stock market, eventually earning enough to fly his entire class to a resort for the weekend.

A few years on, at São Paulo's prestigious law school (and centre of a political movement against the military dictatorship), Ricardo's grades were still mediocre. However, once he realized his guitar skills were similarly undistinguished, he decided to give the family business a shot.

Things did not start well. The father did not like the son's habits of sleeping late, putting his feet on the desk or working from home. And the son did not like the father's overly rigid schedule, excessive punctuality and tendency to barge in on his client meetings. To make matters worse, by 1980, the Brazilian miracle had gone into reverse and the shipbuilding industry that Semco supplied with its marine pumps was particularly a hard hit. Twenty-year-old Ricardo was convinced that diversification was the only solution; 68-year-old Antonio was adamant that Semco's specialist focus was its best asset.

Eventually, Antonio realized that father and son could no longer co-exist in the same company and made a leap of faith. He simply handed over the entire operation to his son and walked away: "Better make your mistakes while I'm still alive," he said somewhat ominously to his son.

Ricardo wasted no time in setting out to transform Semco. One Friday afternoon in 1980, he cleaned house, firing 60 per cent of his father's top executives. He hired his own people and began modernizing the company, making it more efficient and productive. Ricardo recalled:

(We) installed dozens of new procedures and invented new forms almost daily. ... persuaded salespeople to fill out customer-visit reports and keep statistics on orders closed versus quotes offered. Files were rigorously organized all over the company. ... Everyone was issued a plastic ID card and compelled to wear it. Production schedules were displayed on boards in our new planning and control department.

Members of our new time and methods department were dispatched around the plant, searching for ways to speed our workers up.

By 1982, Ricardo and the other new blood had turned the company around. They were manufacturing a wider range of products and secured some major contracts and new acquisitions. They had nearly doubled the workforce and tripled the number of plants, where they set about applying the new systems and financial controls.

However, there was a great deal of tension just below the surface about to make itself felt. "I knew our new tough-minded, statistical approach, along with our acquisitions and all the new employees, had created a lot of stress," he admits. "Semco appeared highly organized and disciplined, but we still could not get our people to perform as well as we wanted." People were working long hours and families were complaining. Deliveries were always late.

Most of our managers were proponents of classic authoritarian solutions such as rigid controls and long, gruelling hours. But a few of us were starting to doubt the effectiveness of this approach. I was particularly distressed by the malaise that was all too apparent in our factories. Workers just didn't seem to care.

Then, at the annual corporate retreat, things came to a head. During a lunch break, someone snuck into the conference room and drew a cartoonish Grim Reaper on one of the flip charts, holding a scythe and surrounded by bleeding stick figures. The message was clear: Ricardo's autocratic leadership style was wreaking havoc on his employees and the company. Ricardo hastily convened a group session which cleared the air but also revealed that two very different philosophical camps had formed: those who felt the controlling culture was necessary to get people to do their work; and those who found Semco's environment suffocating.

The final straw was Ricardo's realization that Semco's malaise was also having an effect on him physically. During a visit to a pump factory in the US, he collapsed on the factory floor. He went to the Mayo Clinic where doctors put him through a battery of tests, all of which came back negative. The final diagnosis? "The most advanced case of stress I have ever seen in a person of 25." As one doctor put it, "Either you continue your current life, in which case you will be back with us, or else you change." Ricardo asked for advice. "That's not for me to say," the doctor answered. "All I will say is that everything about your life has to change."

Botanique Hotel: 2014

The man lies on a massage table, face down, a towel around his waist, eyes closed, the sun streaming in the floor-to-ceiling windows, warming his tired body. As the masseuse works over his shoulders and back muscles, he feels the tension built up from years of 12-hour days at the office begin to drain out of him. He hasn't allowed himself time away from work in a long time. In fact, he wouldn't even be here had his doctor not insisted he take a vacation and start looking after his health. And so he's here, miles away from the office and the noise and the stress and all the decisions that he needs to be making. Right now.

Out in the hotel lobby, Ricardo stands with his wife Fernanda, smiling and greeting guests, talking to employees, looking around with a critical but satisfied eye. Botanique Hotel, a new luxury eco-resort two hours outside Sao Paulo, and Fernanda's and Ricardo's brainchild, opened just a few months prior. Although on the surface it looks just like a classic luxury resort, closer inspection reveals that this is a different sort of operation altogether.

Ricardo explains:

The hotel has no departments and no fixed positions... All employees are skilled waiters, many are barmen, all know how to operate the high-end cappuccino machine, all make beds fast, some play tennis, others play the piano and many are hikers, wildlife monitors or capoeira (Brazilian martial art of sorts) masters. Guests' smartphones receive an app and they can touch one icon to talk to their "Anchor" who solves everything.

Staff have a low fixed salary, but receive some 50 per cent added remuneration at 30 per cent occupancy. No tips are allowed, and this permits the hotel to function at 18.5 per cent breakeven, a level that no hotel has seen (average breakeven in hotels is 39 per cent occupancy). Everyone's fortunes vary together, with 200 per cent more profit distribution after breakeven than the average hotel. At three, five, and seven years in the job, there are important cash-outs in a

phantom-stock plan so that long-term fidelity can bring turnover from the average of 28 per cent in this industry to a target of 7 per cent.

According to Fernanda, the hotel provides a "post-luxury" experience that includes the best that Brazil has to offer. But Botanique is not only the most expensive hotel in Brazil, but also the first hotel based on a highly democratic philosophy where employees make all the hiring decisions themselves. For those who helped building the hotel, a position was created to match their talent as long as they were willing to be flexible as well. For example, Leandro, a capoeira teacher in his free time, helped cleaning during the construction of the hotel and now organizes capoeira classes for guests. But just like the drivers, waiters, and the hotel pianist, he also needs to clean the rooms. Botanique seeks to maximize the flexibility and freedom of its employees, giving them a level of control that encourages them to take initiative and craft their jobs in a way that best leverages their own individual abilities and interests.

Decision-making at Botanique is fully democratic and requires the input of all staff members who, in turn, need to be fully informed about occupancy rates, expenses and ongoing activities at all times. For example, everyone is involved in interviewing potential colleagues and bosses and new people cannot join without the input of all staff members first. Ricardo and Fernanda say that it is precisely because of these policies that Botanique has been a success story so far, having won numerous industry awards in its short time in operation. As Ricardo notes:

Starting from scratch made this implementation easier. But we still had to undo preconceptions from people in the sector. In the hotel it was easier, because 60 per cent of the staff came from outside the hotel business. But it also made it possible for Fernanda and me to change everything we hate about hotels: Botanique has no check-in or check-out times, does not charge for the mini-bar, laundry services, high-speed internet or even reasonable phone calls, and has a no tipping policy.

However, Ricardo didn't have the luxury of starting from scratch when he wanted to transform the culture and management practices at Semco. But he knew things had to change. His employees were stressed and unhappy, and his own health problems were a testament to the deleterious effects of such management practices on both followers and leaders.

So Ricardo did something different. He decided to take his own leap of faith.

Semco's radical makeover: 1984

Moving an organization or business ahead means giving up control, and allowing employees to manage themselves. It means trusting workers implicitly, sharing power and information, encouraging dissent, and celebrating true democracy. Few things are harder for managers, executives, shareholders, and owners to embrace.

Ricardo first set about changing himself. He started leaving the office at 19:00 and stopped working on weekends. Finding few concrete answers in management books, he started to read fiction and philosophy instead. He stopped wearing a watch and started spending time on activities outside of work. Ricardo explains the reason for the myriad changes to come at Semco itself:

I had no grand plan. Just a sense that there was a lifelessness, a lack of enthusiasm, a malaise at Semco, and that I had to change it. People weren't gratified by their jobs and often seemed oppressed by them. The traditional attitude about workers was that you couldn't trust them. You needed systems to control them. I wanted to know if it was possible to liberate people and free them from the elements of life that make it a drag by creating an entirely new kind of organization.

To help him manage the changes he wanted at Semco, Ricardo teamed up with a new Human Resources director, Clovis Bojikian, a former schoolteacher, whose idealism and progressive methods had got him into trouble with Brazil's former military government. Ricardo and Clovis began slowly at first; but in the end, little was left untouched.

The beginning-and-end-of-shift surveillance of workers was the first to go. Ricardo was worried about the message of distrust these checks sent to employees. So he replaced the guards with a sign that simply read: "Please make sure as you leave that you are not inadvertently taking anything with you that does not belong to you."

The dress code was next. Semco employees were told they could start coming to work dressed however they liked. Suits and ties gradually gave way to jeans and t-shirts and shorts for those who liked to dress more casually, though some (like Clovis) continued to show up in a suit and tie every day. (Interestingly enough, the smart clothes spontaneously returned whenever important clients came to visit.)

The car park was one of the most visible changes. Ricardo abolished the reserved spaces and then divided up the parking lot by department – in proportion to its size. Things like expense reports were then eliminated – employees would monitor their own spending when away from the office. And a non-territorial, open office plan was created with plants and flowers separating communal desk spaces that were used on a first-come-first-served basis.

The changes were not accepted overnight and many pushed back. The workers union itself objected to the abolition of home-time security checks, especially when two drilling machines disappeared from a plant one day. "Our people want the searches. They want everyone to know that they're not the ones taking the tools," said one shop steward. But Ricardo and Clovis refused. "I would rather have a few thefts once in a while than condemn everyone to a system based on mistrust," Ricardo explained. Similar objections were heard about the elimination of expense reports, which Ricardo had decided were "insulting." "If we're afraid to let people decide in which sections of the plane to sit, or how many stars their hotel should have, we shouldn't be sending them abroad to do business in our name, should we?"

Business magazines were amazed. They ran articles headed, "These Guys Run their Boss's Plant!" But Ricardo carried on. Did the thefts or time-card cheating decrease? "I don't know and I don't care," he says. "It's not worth it to me to have a company at which you don't trust the people with whom you work."

The biggest critics were the middle managers. "You have to let us control our people," said one. "They're beginning to think they don't have to obey us because they can come and go as they like and they know we won't fire them," said one. "All this touchy-feely stuff is bullshit," said another. Initially, Ricardo and Clovis tried to appease the middle managers by re-writing the new rules into the company manual. Then they decided the easiest thing was to toss out the manual altogether. Joao Vendramim, a Semco director, explained: "We want people to be bosses due to their knowledge and leadership qualities, not due to their titles."

The company that runs itself

Working at Semco means self-managing as much as possible. It isn't nearly as frightening as it sounds. In the end, it's self-interest at work. It requires conceding that managers don't – and can't – know the best way to do everything. People who are motivated by self-interest will find solutions that no one else can envision. They see the world in their own unique way – a way that others often overlook.

Ricardo moved on from dress codes and expense accounts to bigger matters. When a new factory was needed, a search committee of workers was created to research and make the decisions themselves. Workers were subsequently given control over how the plant itself was set up and run. Perhaps the most interesting was the employee-suggested system of "manufacturing cells": small clusters of workers, each responsible for creating batches of the entire product. Although each team would be entirely responsible for product quality, they would also have the satisfaction of learning how to operate all the machines involved and of completing a task from start to finish. As the accountability of the teams increased, the need for quality control decreased – and whole departments were abolished.

One of the departments that went on the chopping block was the Human Resources department, which was reduced from 90 people to two. In its place, a new worker-led hiring system sprang up. Workers started to recruit new members for their own teams – and fire those who did not measure up. And a new job rotation plan meant that employees were encouraged and even expected to change departments regularly.

Flexible working hours were introduced on the manufacturing shop floor so that employees could work the hours that were most convenient for them. Again, the naysayers pushed back, warned of chaos, and the policy was initially put into place on an experimental basis only, with a committee planning to meet daily to monitor and discuss problems. But the committee never met. The teams simply got together during the evenings to ensure that the next day they all arrived and left at times that allowed everyone to get their work done.

Around that time, Clovis received a call from a worker's wife who asked him what on earth he'd done to her tough, autocratic husband. For the first time in his life, she explained, he was listening to his children and taking their feelings into account before making decisions. Ricardo concludes, "The man was simply reproducing at home what he experienced at work. He knew it was a better system."

I'm often asked: How do you control a system like this? I don't. I let the system control itself.

In 1987 profits reached 20 per cent to 30 per cent of revenues – and Ricardo decided to give everyone a share. Only half a dozen or so Brazilian companies had ever experimented with profit-sharing, but Semco went one step further and asked the workers themselves to design and control the new system. In the end, every Semco unit decided to share profits equally across every worker in the company, with managers getting the same bonuses as lower level staff.

Semco then implemented a system whereby subordinates played a key role in directly evaluating their bosses. Every employee completed the form twice a year with anonymity guaranteed. However, the manager's overall score (average 80–85; 70 minimum to remain in good standing) was posted for the entire company to see, putting those with low scores (less than 70) "under intense pressure to change," as Ricardo put it. The system not only helped mangers improve their skill and increased communication; it helped insure bad managers could not hide for long. One manager who had previously had several promotions and was leading a large department received a score of 40 on his initial evaluation. After some investigating, it was clear that the evaluation was accurate; his team was succeeding in spite of him, rather than because of him. But although he was a terrible manager, he was a great salesperson, and he ended up thriving when moved into a position as a one-person sales staff.

With so many other radical changes in place, Ricardo couldn't help but let employees start setting their own salaries. Employees were asked to consider their length of service, level of decision making, and time spent with customers as they decided on a figure to request for themselves. And because Semco was becoming more transparent about the financials of the company and the different departments, workers were better able to understand what would be considered a reasonable pay package, and what was not. Could people be trusted to set even their own salaries? "Except for half a dozen people, everyone set salaries that were in line with our expectations," said Ricardo. "Only one set an outlandishly high sum – about 30 per cent more than he had been making, in the hope of immediate promotion to Partner. When challenged, he revealed that he'd been offered a sales director post elsewhere and left to take it up." The scheme was deemed a success and extended broadly throughout the company. Ricardo explained why his faith was rewarded:

> "Anyone who requests too large a salary or too big a raise runs the risk of being rejected by their colleagues. So self-interest almost always prevents them from asking for bigger pay checks."

By 1989, Semco had one of the highest growth rates in the country. It won a national award for labour relations. Sales had risen from around $4 million, when Ricardo took over, to $35 million. Where once it was a company with only one factory and 100 employees, it now had six factories and 830 employees. It was the first or second place company in all of its markets. Auro Alves summed up the result of the changes: "People are happier. And when they're happier, they produce more." It was certainly beginning to look like a happy ending.

The final transformation: The 1990s

In 1990, Brazil's economy crashed. Industrial output fell by 9 per cent and GDP was back to what it had been in the 1970s. By 1992 there were nearly 1.5 million unemployed in São Paulo alone. Between 1989 and 1991, Semco's sales fell by 40 per cent. Cost-cutting measures had to follow and layoffs seemed inevitable.

In response, some radical ideas were tried. In the Santa Amaro plant, where big industrial dishwashers were manufactured (and orders had dropped from 40 a month to just five), Ricardo agreed to a temporary experiment in "co-management" with the workers, who all took a 30 per cent pay cut and gave up most of their benefits. The twist was that they also took over all the services that had been provided by external contractors and third parties – from cleaning toilets to running the cafeteria. And all business decisions were agreed jointly with the management. The managers, for their part, agreed to an even greater pay cut. Ricardo explained:

> After just one month, we could hardly believe the results. The workers had saved so much that ... profit-sharing ... helped compensate for the reduced salaries. The second month was even better. By the end of third month, salaries had been restored to their old levels.

In an economic crisis that saw an average of 800 Brazilian companies going broke every month, Semco survived and managed to break even in the very worst years – but it was almost unrecognizable as the company founded by Antonio Semler. Productivity had soared to six and a half times the level of 1980 by 1994 and was four times the national average. Sales had recovered to around $20 million. Semco had become an industry stalwart and magnet for companies around the world as a model for how a modern-day organization could be run, in good times and in bad.

But Ricardo wasn't done. After some much-deserved time off, he set about pushing the boundaries of his leadership philosophy to the limits. He wanted to see if the Semco philosophy could work anywhere, with anyone, in any situation.

Lumiar school, 2014

> The child runs the two kilometres from the tiny house that she shares with a half dozen family members all the way to her fourth grade classroom. She is early today, but excited. It is the first day that all her classes are centred around the World Cup. And soccer is her favourite sport, the sport that all the kids in Brazil play, the sport that will bring the whole world to Brazil this year. She knows that today, like most days, she will savour each hour she gets to spend learning about the amazing world she lives in.

Ricardo was perhaps not the first person to realize that the model of traditional education was strikingly similar to that of traditional management: teachers tell students what to learn, and students absorb and regurgitate what the teachers tell them. A cynic might say it is the best way to prepare students to function in a typical corporate environment. So Ricardo took another leap of faith to find out if the same things that were working at Semco could also be applied to education. With some help from the Gates Foundation and the Harvard Graduate School of Education, he set up three schools in Brazil, the Lumiar schools, where the underlying pedagogical philosophy was to make students rather than teachers the centre of the learning experience. Ricardo explained:

> Children choose their own subjects so that they are more motivated to acquire relevant language, math, and social skills. But the focus on

the individual also takes place in the context of joint development. They vote collectively on their group activities and the majority decides.

In this system, the teacher is replaced by a "Tutor" and multiple "Masters." The Tutor is responsible for mapping out the future of each child's learning, with episodic consultation of parents. The Master is someone who must possess two qualities: expertise in some subject and passion. The expertise of these Masters can be math, even though the Master is trained as a violinist, for example.

The subjects are grouped under current interests of the students. At the time of a World Cup, a semester might be divided into Field, Wives, Cramps, and Flags, for example. Field would include students re-designing the soccer field, trying out squares as a field, or circles as a goalie's area – and then testing in practice to see if the rectangle is the best solution. Wives would cover why 40 per cent of the Dutch or French team might be composed of black players, and whether their wives would have a right to universal, free, medical assistance in Amsterdam and then, why Holland has a 2.7 per cent rate of caesarean sections, compared to Brazil's 26.5 per cent. Cramps would try to explain what happens in a body that makes even full-time professional athletes writhe in pain on the field, and what other biological functions are in place in exercise. Flags could make for an easy study of what diversity means, and why wars, blood and toil are the legacies of human history.

Although Ricardo is proud of the Lumiar schools which Fernanda has been running for seven years, he often wonders what fates await these students when they enter the workforce years from now. Sometimes he worries that he may be setting them up for disappointment and unrealistic expectations about what they will encounter in the real world. But more often he hopes that these students will be the ones who end up changing the world for the better, who refuse to take traditional management models at face value and insist on finding a better way to making work both more productive and more rewarding.

The new Semco model in place

Ricardo is the first to admit that his success at Semco was somewhat serendipitous:

I would have loved to have seen the big picture or a framework to start off with. Instead, it was a haphazard format of learning as we went along. As a result, the process was highly experimental and chockfull of highs and lows. The one constant was believing that people were much more resourceful and constructive than the photograph that classic management had taken.

A big part of the philosophy is finding the right fit between job and person. Ricardo explains why Semco wants people to move around a lot within the company: "We rarely fire anyone. This is not from altruistic motives. It's purely selfish. Unless we click with a worker, unless he latches on to something he is passionate about, our productivity won't be high."

The voluntary job rotation plan has been hugely popular over the years at Semco, with 20–25 per cent of managers shifting departments in a given year. Ricardo gushed about the benefits:

It obliges people to learn new skills, which makes life interesting for them and makes them more valuable. It discourages 'empire building' ... It gives people a much broader view of a company ... It encourages the spread of diverse personalities, outlooks, backgrounds and techniques, injecting new blood and fresh vision throughout the company.

Employees still hire and evaluate their bosses; something that is still extremely rare in other companies:

This review builds on one of Semco's great strengths: our transparency. People can always say what's on their minds, even to their bosses— even when it's about their bosses. It is instilled in our corporate culture that everyone should be willing to listen and admit when they're wrong.

The non-territorial, open office plan is also still in existence and is a model that is being more widely employed in many other companies in the 21st century:

Nothing ever came of the dire predictions that it would be impossible to work without confidentiality. I've conducted two very difficult negotiations while sitting two feet from employees that I'd never met. I've met with bank directors at the coffee tables by the espresso machine.

Meetings are another area where the Semco culture can still shock the unprepared. Anyone, including lower level workers, is welcome to attend almost any meeting, read any reports and memos. Everyone is allowed to attend the budget meetings where targets and quotas are decided. Two spots are reserved for anyone to sign up and attend board meetings but nobody is obligated to attend meetings either, and people come and go as they like. Because most employees are allowed to participate if and when they are interested, the decision-making process can seem fairly cumbersome at Semco:

> To be sure, organizations like Semco that welcome – or better, invite – dissent are more complex to manage. Without direct instructions, managers and employees end up engaging in a lot of back and forth. Traditional mangers will argue that this slows the company down, and is therefore a competitive no-no. What they don't consider is that decisions arising from debate are implemented much more quickly because explanations, alternatives, objections and uncertainties have already been aired. Because of democracy, employees have had their say, and projects or ideas have been analysed from every point of view.

Ricardo tells the story of a time when he was convinced that one of Semco's manufacturing plants needed to be closed. However, most of the rest of the company, including this senior leadership team, disagreed. Although Ricardo called several meetings to discuss the plan, few people showed up and he eventually dropped the idea. A year later, the same group of executives reconvened, eventually agreeing to close the factory and putting in place a similar plan to that Ricardo had initially proposed:

> You will say that the company would have been better off if I had insisted on my way and saved Semco 12 months of expenses by closing the plants. But the plan was refined greatly in everyone's mind during that one year, and the end solution was better than mine. Also, by now a lot of people were confident of the direction that we needed to take, so they were infinitely more convincing when dealing with the employees, clients and unions.

Ricardo remains an optimist, but also a realist. He acknowledges that the culture at Semco, however well it has helped the company thrive, is still not for everyone:

> Sure, a minority doesn't adapt to Semco because they need more direction, because they feel better when everyone arrives at the same

> time and abides by the same rules. There are also a lot of people who are not impressed or in any way moved by the Semco system because for them, a job is just a job. Participation imposes a weight they'd rather not carry... Although many people have left Semco over the years because they couldn't condone the 'excessive' freedom and lack of control, it's telling that most of them were managers.

Ricardo is sometimes asked about exporting this leadership style to other companies, other countries and other cultures. Sceptics say his success could only happen in certain innovative industries or in certain countries like free-wheeling Brazil or individualistic America, where employees are likely to be educated and socialized to adapt well to and thrive with such freedom. Ricardo understands the scepticism, but believes that he taps into something deeper and more fundamental that has the ability to transcend industries and cultural boundaries:

> Our story is about how people work together – nothing more. Humankind is no different anywhere on the globe, and cultural strictures are temporary, even if a thousand years old. In the case of work, a few years are usually enough for the benefits of freedom of experience, drive and reward to overcome collective legacies. I haven't run across any cultures that are inherently prohibitive.

> I will say, however, that I was amused when, after a talk to Arab leaders, I spoke backstage to an Emir who said that he loved what he had heard. I asked whether he planned to make use of any of it, and he quickly replied, "Absolutely not."

The present: 2014

"I am at my best when I am doing the least."

Ricardo Semler is no longer the CEO of Semco, and hasn't been since stepping down in 1999. But then, consistent with its democratic structure, the company often doesn't have a fixed CEO. Tellingly, Semco seems to be doing fine. In fact, Ricardo admits that if anything, the company is doing better than when he was in charge:

> Semco has grown on average 27 per cent a year for almost 30 years, and the pace has not changed in the last decade. It proves that

macro-economic scenarios are not very relevant in companies that are nimble. Semco has changed significantly in terms of business and gross revenues per industry, but the overall rate of growth and profits has been relatively unaffected through boom and bust. The 30 years encompass waves of hyperinflation and GNP deficits, but also these booming years of double digit growth in some of our industries. In our business, with strong unions and huge, tidal, shifts in economy, Semco has had some 2 per cent turnover over 20 years, and no lay-offs or strikes in the same two decades.

He is still the main shareholder but only loosely involved (a few days a month and a few emails a week). He has written two best-selling books and for some time was something of an evangelist for workplace democracy – giving speeches all over the world and being the subject of several documentaries and TV programmes. These days, however, he is moving away from the limelight a bit, at least partly the result of a recent serious car accident, which he admits he is lucky to have survived.

He is taking more time off, and focusing his energy on his life with Fernanda and their five children, while also looking for other interesting challenges: not only schools and hotels, but also investment funds, and possibly someday an entire village run on democratic principles:

Since stepping down from Semco I have been applying the Semco concepts to other worlds. I've done this with a business association (Federation of Industries of São Paulo), an NGO (SOS Mata Atlantica, Brazil's foremost environmental organisation), schools (including one owned by the state) and our new hotel, which has multiple shareholders. Other organizations have grown from within Semco, such as the Tarpon fund, now a public company with thousands of shareholders, such as hedge funds, foundations and university endowments. It manages US$4 billion, is worth US$700 million in market capitalization and still runs according to the Semco philosophy.

But he is still a firm believer not only in what he has accomplished, but how he has accomplished it, the power of his underlying philosophy:

I believe in workplace democracy more than ever. The principles I've used in education and hotels could only be identical to those used at Semco, because they relate to the manner in which people interact to make an organization move forward – money and profit are just two of many ancillary factors.

Irrespective of this leadership philosophy, it is hard to argue with the results. Semco currently employs thousands of people across three countries in manufacturing, professional services and high-tech software. It is now a loose federation of around 10 different companies, including the original industrial machine unit, where it all began with Ricardo Semler's late father Antonio, a young engineer from Austria who emigrated to South America, dreaming of building a business of his own and leaving a legacy for his son. The son who, incidentally, can still be found hunched over a Les Paul in the basement, still trying to conjure a certain perfect sound, succeeding on certain attempts and failing on others. But always with the faith that by doing things his way, the results will eventually follow.

CASE	# Huayi Brothers: Strategic transformation
12	*By Professors Jie Li and Jean-Louis Schaan*

In March 2015, Huayi Brothers Media Corporation (Huayi) was China's most influential entertainment company with 2014 revenues of close to ¥2.4 billion.[1] Founded in 1994 by brothers Dennis, (chairman and chief executive officer (CEO)) and James (president) Wang, the company's historic roots were in movie production as the owner, producer and distributor of some of China's most popular film and television (TV) productions, including "Cell Phone," "Assembly" and "Aftershock." In recent years, in an effort to leverage its movie content and copyrights, Huayi had also expanded into developing and distributing mobile games and building entertainment theme parks in Asia.

Huayi considered forging a partnership with Hollywood's STX Entertainment to jointly invest in and co-produce 18 films and distribute them worldwide by December 31, 2017. Huayi would share in the global revenue from the cooperatively produced films and have distribution rights for Greater China (mainland China, Hong Kong, Macau, Taiwan and Singapore). The impending move would represent a significant step in its growth towards internationalization and leveraging its proprietary content globally across all areas of the entertainment sector – visual entertainment, the Internet and gaming. However, some in the industry were skeptical that Huayi could succeed after three previous failed attempts with other US companies. The past failures were attributed to Chairman Dennis Wang's overly cautious nature and desire to have controlling interest.

The Huayi chairman wondered how to best grow his film and entertainment company internationally.

Should the company enter into partnership with STX or not? If yes, what was the best strategy to move forward with the impending partnership and grow internationally outside of China?

The film and entertainment industry in China

The Chinese film and entertainment industry had come a long way since 2004 from a full state monopoly to a small number of large, highly visible private media conglomerates with the size, strength and commercial success to rival Hollywood. It primarily consisted of producers and distributors of a range of entertainment formats, such as movies and music. The industry had experienced sustainable growth over the 2004 to 2014 period and continued to show strong upside potential in the medium term. In 2014, the industry posted revenues of $4 878.3 million, representing a compound annual growth rate (CAGR) of 30.3 per cent between 2010 and 2014. This number was forecast to decelerate to 18.6 per cent over 2014 to 2019, to a value of $11 449.7 million by the end of 2019.[2]

The media industry in China as a whole, which included advertising, broadcasting and cable TV, publishing, movies and entertainment, grew by 7.3 per cent with $90.4 billion in revenues and was expected to reach $162.1 billion by the end of 2019, or an anticipated CAGR of 18.6 per cent over 2014 to 2019.[3] The film, Internet and mobile gaming segments represented the most lucrative segments of the

Professors Jie Li (Antai College of Economics & Management, Shanghai Jiao Tong University) and Jean-Louis Schaan wrote this case solely to provide material for class discussion. The authors do not intend to illustrate either effective or ineffective handling of a managerial situation. The authors may have disguised certain names and other identifying information to protect confidentiality.

[1]¥ = yuan renminbi. All currency in US dollars unless specified otherwise. US$1 = ¥6.26, March 15, 2015, www.xe.com/currencytables/?from= CNY&date=2015-03-15 (accessed March 15, 2015).

[2]"Movies & Entertainment in China," *Marketline*, April 2015, www.reportlinker.com/p02906359-summary/Movies-Entertainment-in-China.html (accessed December 8, 2015).

[3]"Media in China," *Marketline*, October 2015, http://advantage.marketline.com/Product?pid=MLIP1741-0005 (accessed December 8, 2015).

Chinese entertainment industry. The film sector alone accounted for 94.6 per cent of the market's overall value. China's box office was roughly 10 per cent of global box office revenues.[4] The value of China's box office was expected to surpass that of the United States by 2019.[5]

Key growth drivers

The explosive growth in China's film and entertainment market was driven by three key factors: growing disposable income per capita, which reached ¥28,844 in 2014[6] from ¥11,759.5 in 2006;[7] broad-based government support in the form of training and financial subsidies; and the expanded wireless broadband access, which facilitated new media adoption. The immense size and diversity of the Chinese market also created substantial room for differentiation in terms of genre and content. Entertainment companies had been more inclined to focus on more mature markets in China's high tier coastal cities due to their higher rates of technology adoption and stronger receptiveness to foreign culture. However, many were seeking new ways to reach lower tier cities in the more inland regions where entertainment spending was growing most rapidly. Despite the Chinese government's quotas, imported foreign films, with box office revenues exceeding ¥13.2 billion in 2014, up by 51.9 per cent from 2013, accounted for a significant fraction of overall demand. In order to alleviate domestic competitive pressures, Chinese companies sought to diversify their customer base by exporting movies (2.7 per cent of total industry revenue in 2014, or $156.9 million).[8]

Industry characteristics

The Chinese film and entertainment industry was fraught with high risks and uncertainty, with competing yet complementary relationships between a small number of state and privately run media conglomerates. There was intense rivalry between private players, particularly large companies. In 2015, China Film Group Corporation (government-owned), Bona Film Group, Huayi and Beijing Enlight Group accounted for 47.7 per cent of total industry revenue.[9] They operated under similar business models while competing across broad swaths of the media sector including movies, music, the Internet and TV.

Companies competed aggressively in the distribution of creative content and constantly sought to strengthen their commercial horsepower to reach a wider set of audiences. Due to the importance of commercialization in the industry, film production in China was widely construed as a component of the overall commercial production chain rather than a creative endeavour in its own right. In most cases, box office receipts only accounted for a moderate fraction of total income, with the remainder coming from commercial spinoffs such as advertising and merchandising. The drive towards maximizing the reach and impact through novel and profitable distribution channels pushed large industry players towards vertical and horizontal integration. The industry began merging film production and distribution and intensifying its access to various commercial channels including TV production, TV channel management, audio/video (especially DVD) production, talent management and advertising. There was significant competition in the pre-production phase for financial capital and talent (particularly for renowned film directors and movie actors, important sources of differentiation).

The concentration of profits to just the few largest players was attributed to the high capital requirements of commercial big budget films, which still remained the most profitable type of film project. Only the largest players with deep experience in the industry were able to amass the requisite level of capital, use their brand reputation to attract top-notch talent and adapt to the rapid pace of technological change. In contrast,

[4]"China Film Industry Report 2014-2015 (In Brief)," Entgroup, http://english.entgroup.cn/uploads/reports/China%20Film%20Industry%20Report%202014-2015%EF%BC%88in%20brief%EF%BC%89.pdf (accessed December 8, 2015).

[5]"Spotlight on China: Building a Roadmap for Success in Media & Entertainment," Ernst & Young, 2012, www.ey.com/GL/en/Industries/Media---Entertainment/Spotlight-on-China---media-and-entertainment (accessed December 8, 2015).

[6]"China Statistical Yearbook: 2014," National Bureau of Statistics of China, 2014, www.stats.gov.cn/TJSJ/ndsj/2014/indexeh.htm (accessed December 8, 2015).

[7]"China Statistical Yearbook: 2006," National Bureau of Statistics of China, 2006, www.stats.gov.cn/TJSJ/ndsj/2006/indexeh.htm (accessed December 8, 2015).

[8]Entgroup, op. cit..

[9]"Movie Production in China: Market Research Report," *IBISWorld*, 2015, www.ibisworld.com/industry/china/movie-production.html (accessed December 8, 2015).

small to medium-sized firms, which composed the majority of industry players, lacked the advantages of scale and were limited to producing one to two budget films a year. Despite the promises of technological advancements and mobile platforms, which would encourage new entrants into the industry, the industry concentration was expected to intensify as major companies continued to gain in scale to feed larger production budgets and produce higher quality movies to cater to an international audience.

Major industry trends

Intra- and international growth.

The Chinese entertainment industry was positioned to trend in two directions. On the one hand, the presence of companies in Hong Kong, Taiwan and (South) Korea that were already in the co-production business with China were expected to continue to support a booming regional film market. On the other hand, the industry was becoming a major recipient and source of foreign direct investment. This was evidenced by the fact that several notable US companies such as Warner Bros. Entertainment and DreamWorks Animation had recently forged joint ventures (JVs) with major Chinese media companies to distribute and produce content in China.[10] Foreign filmmakers benefited from co-producing as opposed to importing films as it allowed them to retain a much larger share of box office profits.

The deals were also increasingly going in the other direction. The formation of co-production agreements with US companies had been popular with the Chinese as it facilitated the transmission of film production expertise and market knowhow from their more experienced US counterparts and supported the broader objective of raising China's cultural profile internationally. In 2012, Wanda Group bought AMC (a US theatre chain);[11] in 2014, Tencent entered an exclusive partnership with HBO[12] for China distribution and Hony Capital invested in STX;[13] and in 2015, Hunan TV partnered with Lions Gate Entertainment,[14] DMG Entertainment partnered with Valiant Comics[15] and Fosun partnered with Studio 8.[16]

Rise of mobility.

The convergence of mobile and media in China was rapidly accelerating. The Chinese market had grown immensely in both scale and technological sophistication. Despite low Internet penetration by developed country standards, the Chinese were avid digital consumers and led the world in many areas of technology adoption, mobile device usage and percentage of homes with smart TVs.[17] On-demand streaming video was a proven and robust distribution model in the country – according to China Internet Network Information Center, more than 461 million people in China streamed videos online.[18]

Many entertainment companies were entering the mobile space as it not only provided a lucrative distribution channel for content, but also enabled the delivery of a wider range of entertainment formats, such as online gaming, social networks and learning. As the shift of media consumption to online accelerated, TV and film companies that lacked a digital distribution platform could run a substantial risk of being edged out by mobile substitutes. Many large Internet companies such as Alibaba, Baidu and Tencent had taken advantage of shifting trends towards online media consumption by establishing film and production departments and making strategic acquisitions. These companies had relied on advertising as their main source of revenue but

[10]D. Barboza, "China Escalates Hollywood Partnerships, Aiming to Compete One Day," *New York Times,* April 5, 2015, http://www.nytimes.com/2015/04/06/business/media/china-escalates-hollywood-partnerships-aiming-to-compete-one-day.html?_r=0 (accessed December 8, 2015).

[11]Z. Mider, "China's Wanda to Buy AMC Cinema Chain for $2.6 Billion," *Bloomberg BusinessWeek*, May 21, 2012, www.bloomberg.com/news/articles/2012-05-21/china-s-wanda-group-to-buy-amc-cinema-chain-for-2-6-billion (accessed December 8, 2015).

[12]J. Osawa, "Tencent to Distribute HBO Dramas, Movies Online in China," *Wall Street Journal*, November 25, 2014, www.wsj.com/articles/tencent-partners-with-hbo-to-distribute-tv-dramas-movies-online-in-china-1416902891 (accessed December 8, 2015).

[13]R. Faughnder and R. Verrier, "China's Huayi Bros. to Partner with Robert Simonds' STX Entertainment," *Los Angeles Times*, March 17, 2015, www.latimes.com/entertainment/envelope/cotown/la-et-ct-huayi-bros-partner-with-robert-simonds-stx-entertainment-20150317-story.html (accessed December 8, 2015).

[14]L. Burkitt and B. Fritz, "Lions Gate Sees Marketing Advantages From Hunan TV Deal," *Wall Street Journal*, March 17, 2015, www.wsj.com/articles/lions-gate-sees-marketing-advantages-from-hunan-tv-deal-1426644758 (accessed December 8, 2015).

[15]D. Betancourt and M. Cavna, "As China Seeks American Fare, Valiant Buoyed by Deal for a Universe of Films," *Washington Post*, March 19, 2015, www.washingtonpost.com/news/comic-riffs/wp/2015/03/19/as-china-seeks-american-fare-valiant-says-dmg-film-deal-reflects-love-for-its-characters/ (accessed December 8 2015).

[16]E. Curran and B. Fritz, "China's Fosun to Invest in Robinov's Studio 8," *Wall Street Journal*, June 23, 2014, www.wsj.com/articles/chinas-fosun-to-invest-in-robinovs-studio-8-1403485547 (accessed December 8, 2015).

[17]Marketline, "Movies & Entertainment in China," op. cit..

[18]L.Y. Chen, "Alibaba Offers $4.6 Billion for Rest of Youku Video Site," *Bloomberg Businessweek*, October 16, 2015, www.bloomberg.com/news/articles/2015-10-16/alibaba-offers-to-buy-rest-of-youku-tudou-for-26-60-a-share (accessed December 8, 2015).

were pursuing new monetization models to offer differentiated value.

Two main factors drove the continual rise of mobility in the entertainment industry. First was the sizable number of young, affluent and well-educated consumers as a share of all Chinese media consumers. In 2014, 87 per cent of China's film audiences were between the ages of 19 and 40, and 50 per cent were aged from 19 to 30.[19] The lower costs of distribution through online platforms also encouraged the entry of new content creators. This was particularly true of producers of independent niche films, an increasingly popular film genre among young moviegoers. Another important catalyst of this trend was the improvement of China's network infrastructure towards a wider reach, expanded capabilities and faster speed. The government's plan to modernize its infrastructure entailed the merger of telecom, broadcast and Internet on a single platform to deliver voice, data and video content. According to one estimate, this was slated to create $250 billion in demand for entertainment content such as TV Internet subscription, video on demand and interactive services.[20]

Public private partnerships.

While the Chinese entertainment industry looked vastly different than what it had been under state monopoly just a few decades earlier, the government continued to wield control through several policy levers. Consequently, private companies still found it beneficial to retain political and social capital in the government, particularly when navigating stringent Chinese censorship laws. Recognizing their common interest in leveraging media to maximize China's global influence, the state and private sector had reshaped their interaction from one that had been top-down in structure to mutually beneficial partnerships. For instance, the state had committed to improve access to financing through its state-run banks, created private equity funds dedicated to the cultural sector and even loosened restrictions on foreign capital inflows into the entertainment industry.[21] Wanda Dalian, the world's largest owner of theatre chains, recently partnered with a municipal government to construct a production facility that aspired to be the "Hollywood of China."[22]

Huayi's strategic evolution and diversification

Huayi was created by brothers Wang Zhongjun (Dennis Wang) and Wang Zhonglei (James Wang) in 1994 when they founded the Huayi Advertising Company in Beijing. Within four years, the brothers had developed a successful advertising business and were intrigued by the prospects offered by the emerging Chinese film industry. The firm was one of the early entrants in the industry when in 1998 it produced a TV series that it sold through an innovative mechanism. Because China's TV stations were state-owned enterprises, they were not allowed to negotiate cash payment for the series. Payment was made in the form of advertising that Huayi sold to its clients, the proceeds of which helped finance its next productions.

Building on successful box office productions, in 2000 Huayi formed a 50-50 JV with Taihe Film Investment Co. (Taihe). Over time, this arrangement showed strains in decision making, so Huayi bought enough of Taihe's shares to take a majority stake in the JV. With greater control, Huayi was able to engage in film co-production with Columbia Pictures Corp. Through this collaboration and the ensuing opportunity for brand marketing, Huayi became a bona fide film production company in China. But by 2004, disagreements among the partners about distribution of benefits ended the collaboration.

Huayi continued on its successful trajectory with hits such as "A World of Thieves" and continued to attract investors. TOM Group helped the Wang brothers buy back the 45 per cent of the equity still owned by Taihe, bringing the Huayi brothers' ownership to 70 per cent. In 2005, Dennis Wang sold 15 per cent of Huayi to Jack Ma, chairman of Alibaba, and bought back 20 per cent of TOM's shares.

The year 2005 was a defining one for the company, as it did not release any movies. One of the reasons was that Huayi's star director, Feng Xiaogang, was shooting "The Banquet," a blockbuster that required more than a year to complete. Confronted with the financial risk inherent to the industry, management decided to expand its Visual Entertainment division into TV drama production and talent management.

---

[19]Entgroup, op. cit..

[20]Ernst & Young, op. cit..

[21]"Market Overview: The Entertainment Industry in China," *China Briefing*, March 6, 2015, www.china-briefing.com/news/2015/03/06/market-overview-entertainment-industry-china.html (accessed December 8, 2015).

[22]L. Burkitt, "Wang Jianlin Aims to Create Hollywood, China," *Wall Street Journal*, September 22, 2013, www.wsj.com/articles/SB100014240527 02304213904579090803470556012 (accessed December 8, 2015).

Huayi also diversified further by moving in two new directions – one was the tourist and entertainment property business, the other was exploring the Internet for distribution and games. Huayi was no longer satisfied to be just a creative studio. It was the first time the company thought about developing a future growth strategy to look for crossover opportunities. Said Chief Financial Officer (CFO) Brenda Hu:

We wanted to bring together different fields which used to be separated and try to integrate them. For example, we are trying to bring a film marketing company together with mobile app developers. Put these two teams together so they can do more film distribution on the Internet. For us, it is not innovation, it is not high technology. We are trying to bring together people who used to be separated, couldn't understand each other, and encourage them to create working platform across products and channels.

Generations born in the 1990s, now in their 20s, who had grown up on mobile devices, were not big consumers of newspapers, magazines or even TV. The convergence between movies, games and talent on the Internet – and how to best capture revenue from the interaction between these products – was the company's biggest challenge. Huayi started exploring and developing different celebrity promotional products to build a social networking presence over the next five to 10 years. An online ticketing company was also started to capture revenue from consumer transactions. However, pinpointing which new venture deserved the company's greatest attention was unclear. Said Dennis Wang:

There are lots of uncertainties in China's entertainment industry. You can think five years ahead, but it would be hard to predict [what the future will look like in] 10 years as there may be transformative changes in this industry. In the past five years, we've focused on our core business – Visual Entertainment. However, I would like Huayi to go international in the future.

Huayi became China's first official "movie stock" when it went public on October 30, 2009 on the Growth Enterprise Market of the Shenzhen Stock Exchange. The company made world news when its stock closing price of ¥70.81 more than doubled its initial public offering (IPO) opening price. Huayi raised ¥1.2 billion. Dennis Wang's 26 per cent share in the company put him on Forbes China's "Rich List" – he was ranked at 142 in 2013, with an estimated wealth of $1.1 billion.[23]

With a stronger financial position and facing increasing competition and risks, Dennis Wang and his team explored a number of potential business models including Warner Brothers and Disney. Profit-hungry investors had recently begun to swarm film and TV production, where large Internet companies such as Baidu, Alibaba and Tencent had set up film and production departments. In 2005, about 100 movie investors were in operation, whereas in 2015 there were more than 1,500.[24] With increasing competition on the content side of the entertainment business in China, Huayi looked for an opportunity to expand on the channel side in order to monetize its content. By 2015, the company was invested in three major businesses: Visual Entertainment, which represented 50 per cent of revenues; Live Entertainment, 20 per cent; and Internet Entertainment, 30 per cent The three businesses contributed almost equally to profits. Each is further summarized below.

Visual entertainment

This business included: films, TV shows, talent management, music, cinemas and entertainment marketing. Huayi was the owner, producer and distributor of some of China's most popular film and TV productions. It had established its brand for high-quality commercial entertainment. Many of its films were recognized at prestigious events such as the Hong Kong Film Awards, the Golden Horseshoe Awards, the Huabiao Awards, the Golden Rooster and Hundred Flowers Awards. The company's primary focus on content generation differentiated it as China's most original TV and film industry brand, with the nation's largest and most varied entertainment portfolio. Its business vision was to become Asia's largest integrated entertainment group and generate greater global respect for China through film.

Visual Entertainment, including film, TV drama, music, cinemas, a talent agency brokerage and other related businesses, had been the company's major source of operations revenue and profit since its

[23]"Why Huayi Brothers Wants to Become the Disney of China," *Knowledge at Wharton*, April 9, 2014, http://knowledge.wharton.upenn.edu/article/huayi-brothers-wants-become-disney-china (accessed December 10, 2015).

[24]Tang Yuankai, "The IP Boom," *Beijing Review*, September 3, 2015, www.bjreview.com.cn/nation/txt/2015-09/01/content_702281.htm (accessed December 10, 2015).

launch in 1998. In 2012, box office receipts exceeded ¥100 million and had combined revenue of approximately ¥2.1 billion, setting a record that year for privately owned film production. By 2013, box office revenues were in excess of ¥$3 billion and by 2015 accounted for 15 per cent of the domestic market share and 25 to 30 per cent of the market share for Chinese-made films. At the beginning of 2015, Huayi had produced 75 films with total box office receipts of ¥9.2 billion. Plans for 2014/15 were to produce 32 films, with a box office target of ¥10 billion.

Huayi's move towards diversification began in 2000. The company launched an entertainment talent brokerage and quickly grew to represent 300 artists, 100 of whom were considered "A list" emerging stars in movies, TV and music, making it China's leading talent agency. A music division followed in 2004, covering artist packaging, album production, music videos, concerts and live performance events. In 2005, Huayi started its TV division. Within the first 10 years, it grew to second in terms of national market share, generating revenues of ¥518 million in 2013. Its TV shows totaled 700 episodes, amounting to 600 hours of on-air programming each year, with such titles as "My Son is Wonderful," "Husband and Wife" and "Without Thieves." By the end of 2011, the company had developed a sophisticated production studio network of 12 studios. The company also built and operated 15 cinemas in major urban centres such as Beijing, Shanghai and Shenzhen.

Live entertainment

The second business included: film towns, cultural parks and movie theme parks. In 2011, Huayi announced plans to develop nearly 20 small live entertainment film towns (themed real estate) nationwide by the end of the decade. Modeled after Disney, the towns were designed to "bring memories and the silver screen to life" through recreating familiar scenes from the company's most popular movies as a backdrop for commercial shops, restaurants and hotels. The company's location-based entertainment (LBE) business model was to work with developers who bore the financial responsibility for planning and constructing the properties. Huayi then shared in the profits by collecting licensing fees. Said Dennis Wang: "Right now, all big cities in China look very much alike. But if we can build a movie commune near Beijing, or recreate a small town of 100 years ago, young people will love it."

The first of three, which opened in 2013, was the "Huayi Brothers Culture City," a ¥$1 billion ($152 million) fully functional indoor studio complex in Shanghai, incorporating studio tours and rides. It was followed by "Huayi Brothers Movie World," a major theme park initiative focusing exclusively on Huayi film content. The third "Huayi Brothers Film Studio" opened in the Shanghai suburb of Suzhou in June 2014. It featured backdrops from the movies "Back to 1942," "Aftershock" and "If You Are the One" and received more than 10 000 visitors on its first day. The fourth, "Feng Xiaogang's Movie Commune," named after Huayi's famous director, opened in spring 2015 in Haikou, the capital city of Hainan Province. Said Hu:

It works out very well. Tourists and consumers like sound stages because it makes them feel very close to the movie industry and to celebrities. We can attract both tourists and also retailers. And also, the construction is very quick. It's not the same kind of theme park as Disneyland or Universal Studios, but I think it will work out better here in China. We can expand very quickly.

Internet entertainment

The third business included games, new media, fan economy and online distribution. In an effort to break down the boundaries between film and other potential media revenue streams, Huayi became the first company in the industry to venture into the mobile games business. Many Chinese people accessed entertainment content via their cell phones or tablets, and the company recognized the need to expand its presence in mobile. Visual Entertainment was still the company's main source of content and revenue, but games were similar to films in terms of content creation and generating integration potential. The vision was to turn mobile games into films, and vice versa.

In 2010, the company invested ¥149 million to purchase 22 per cent of the shares of mobile game company Ourpalm, becoming its second largest shareholder. In May 2012, Ourpalm went public as the first listed company in mobile gaming, and stock held by Huayi reached the value of ¥1.5 billion. In the same year, in order to expand its presence in the gaming sector, Huayi invested ¥70 million to purchase 51 per cent of the stock of Giant Interactive Group and set up Huayi Giant Company to step into client-end gaming. However, the acquisition turned out to be unsuccessful as the new company failed to meet its profit goal.

In 2013, Huayi spent ¥670 million on the purchase of 50.88 per cent of the stock of Yinhan Technology (Yinhan), becoming its controlling shareholder. The two companies' corporate cultures were a good match, and they worked together to coordinate on celebrity endorsements, movie marketing and other businesses. Yinhan's "Space Hunter" was the first domestic mobile game with monthly turnover of over ¥100 million, while another game, "Shenmo," launched in November 2013, reached a monthly turnover of ¥50 million. Within just the first half of 2014, Yinhan games had achieved a turnover of ¥800 million. These numbers surpassed Chairman Wang's most optimistic expectations.

In the first quarter of 2015, Huayi's Internet Entertainment generated more than ¥410 million, accounting for 66.65 per cent of total revenue. The division accounted for the biggest portion of the company's first-quarter revenue and was also the fastest growing. Revenue from Internet Entertainment in the first half of 2015 was expected to be close to that of Visual Entertainment.

Internationalization

During the first three quarters of 2014, the rapid growth of Huayi's Internet Entertainment revenues helped cushion a steep drop in the company's Visual Entertainment revenues by 75 per cent. During that year, Huayi released only six films and did not have a major blockbuster. It was the first time the company's core revenue stream had declined considerably in almost 10 years. Such was not the case, however, with the health of China's overall film industry. While film revenues inched up globally by only 1 per cent in 2014, in China they increased 34 per cent, to $4.8 billion, a global box office record, according to the Motion Picture Association of America. In 2013 alone, China added more movie screens than the total for France.[25]

There was indeed promising box office potential at home, but it still relied heavily on acquiring much needed and missing talent – not just movie stars, but experienced directors, producers and distributors. After many years of state ownership, China's independent film industry was still relatively in

its infancy, only 10 to 15 years old. Huayi needed to look further afield and leverage the much more experienced, mature US talent pool in Hollywood to make its movie magic.

Dennis Wang began to search for international investment opportunities, particularly in Hollywood but also Europe, to collaborate on the financing, production and distribution of movies on a global scale. The aim was primarily to find solid US partners with strong production capabilities who were looking to establish a foothold to distribute films in the growing Chinese market. Huayi would invest and participate in co-producing US films and handle marketing and distribution in China. Said Dennis Wang: "I think the basic philosophy we had in going to Hollywood and Europe is that we wanted to [access] their product, their technology or their know-how and pull it in to China. We're not trying to sell in those foreign markets, because we feel it's not realistic. That takes time."

Huayi started its Hollywood journey by co-financing movies. However, the move towards greater internationalization was not without its challenges and false starts. A first attempt at partnering with Legendary Entertainment fell through in 2013. In 2014, the company pulled out of talks with Lions Gate Entertainment when it announced that it had agreed to invest as much as $150 million in Studio 8, the production company launched by former Warner Brothers executive Jeff Robinov. But the partnership never materialized because Dennis Wang decided at the eleventh hour to terminate negotiations. In all three cases, termination was motivated by a cautious approach to investment. The Shanghai-based conglomerate Fosun International later signed a deal to invest in Robinov's company, while Lions Gate entered into a partnership with Hunan TV.[26]

In 2014, the company changed its approach and invested $130 million to establish a wholly owned US subsidiary to produce and distribute movies and TV shows. Said Dennis Wang: "I think in the future, if we find the right target . . . we would like to have a controlling stake. We would control the operation, and we would prefer to have the management team have a minority interest in the business." That same year he found a new possibility: Hollywood's recent upstart, STX Entertainment (STX).

[25]Charles Clover, "China's Huayi Brothers Deepens Hollywood Ties," *Financial Times*, March 18, 2015, www.ft.com/intl/cms/s/0/41e24a14-cd47-11e4-a15a-00144feab7de.html#axzz3tw4PG6Nh (accessed December 10, 2015).

[26]Richard Verrier, "China's Huayi Bros. Media Closes Film Slate Deal With STX Entertainment," *Los Angeles Times*, April 2, 2015, www.latimes.com/entertainment/envelope/cotown/la-et-ct-china-huayi-stx-deal-20150402-story.html (accessed December 10, 2015).

The STX deal

Founded in spring 2014, Burbank-based STX was a fully integrated film and TV company specializing in producing, marketing and distributing film, TV and digital content. The company was financially backed by private investment firm TPG Capital, which managed $65 billion in assets and produced films with low- to mid-level budgets of $20 million to $60 million. Other investors included Chinese private equity company Hony Capital, hedge fund SeerCapital, Gigi Pritzker, JPMorgan Chase and Bank of America, Merrill Lynch.[27] Recent movie credits included such well-known titles as "The Wedding Singer" and "Happy Gilmore." Its output was limited to eight to 10 films per year. Led by Bob Simonds, STX rapidly attracted a wealth of elite talent from Disney, Warner Brothers, Sony, Universal, Fox, Metro-Goldwyn-Mayer, Dream Works, Paramount and DreamWorks Animation. It was dedicated to creating high-quality mainstream commercial films (low and medium budget) for global audiences. The goal of the company was to become a major studio and compete with Sony and Universal. Simonds was convinced that if he wanted to succeed in this regard he needed to have a China strategy.

STX had avoided the traditional distribution process and signed direct long-term distribution agreements with the four largest theatre chains in the United States, i.e., Regal Cinemas, AMC, Cinemark and Carmike. In January 2015, the company also signed an exclusive agreement with Showtime Networks, under which it was allowed to exclusively exhibit all films distributed in theatre chains on channels including Showtime, Flix and The Movie Channel. The company was also rapidly expanding into digital production, distribution and the mobile game business and was the first mainstream film and TV company in Hollywood to have such a broad presence in nearly 20 years.

If Huayi and STX proceeded with the proposed partnership, both parties would jointly invest in, shoot and distribute no fewer than 18 cooperative films internationally over the next three years. This was the first time that a Chinese company would participate in all activities in the value chain from production to marketing and distribution. Although the specific financial terms of the deal were not made public, the new arrangement would enable STX to spend approximately $1 billion each year producing and distributing its films through 2017 and give the company a foothold in China's rapidly growing film market.

In return, the deal would help Huayi promote its brand globally, obtain access to the Hollywood film industry and participate in all segments from film financing to production and distribution. Huayi would partner on nearly every title STX studios produced and be granted first rights to distribute STX films in China where the Wang brothers' reach and connectivity was far greater than the US studio's. Not all films were expected to be appropriate for the Chinese market, but they would qualify as co-productions and therefore have easier access to the market through the government quotas than 100 per cent foreign films. The impending partnership would leverage each company's strengths to expand their combined global reach.

The idea for the STX partnership came from Donald Tang who had close and long-standing relationships in the entertainment business in both China and the United States, in particular with Simonds and the Wang brothers whom he had known for over 20 years. He also was a personal friend of Dominic Ng, CEO of East West Bank, which was lined up to finance the transaction.

Huayi could not expand into the US entertainment market without bringing the right people to the table and tapping into their expertise. Said Hu: "(In China), we know those people . . . who is good and who is not. When we enter into a new market, a new world, we have no connections. We don't know how to judge people; it's very confusing." Whether or not those individuals could be recruited and developed within Huayi or needed to be acquired through mergers and acquisitions was uncertain.

The company's new wholly owned US subsidiary was a starting point to retain its own creative people and develop Hollywood productions. Huayi had already signed a co-production agreement with QED International to work together on the World War II film "Fury" starring Brad Pitt and Shia Leboeuf, which it would distribute in China. This agreement would provide challenging, creative work in the short term to help retain the company's top talent and grow organically while Huayi continued looking for the right US targets to invest in or acquire. In the United States, there were two other types of businesses

[27]"Huayi Brothers Media Corporation Closes a Funds Major Three-Year Film Slate Deal With Motion Picture And Television Studio STX Entertainment," *PR Newswire*, April 1, 2015, www.prnewswire.com/news-releases/huayi-brothers-media-corporation-closes-and-funds-major-three-year-film-slate-deal-with-motion-picture-and-television-studio-stx-entertainment-300059398.html (accessed December 10, 2015).

besides movie production that looked attractive for acquisition: talent agencies and social networking start-ups that the company could leverage to support the convergence between its core divisions' products.

Financial performance and growth

In April 2015, Huayi was worth an estimated ¥30 billion ($7.9 billion). The Wang brothers personally held a 30 per cent stake in the company. Other major shareholders included Tencent (4.86 per cent), Jack Ma (Alibaba, 4.03 per cent), Yu Feng (1.76 per cent) and Lu Weiding (1.42 per cent). For further details

about the balance sheets and income statement see Exhibits 1 and 2.

In September 2014, the reported operating income and net profit for Huayi was ¥958 million and ¥455 million, respectively. The company registered a 10.4 per cent rise in net earnings in the first nine months of the year. This followed a period of substantial growth during the previous year when income from the company's main business recorded a year-over-year increase of 43.7 per cent, of which ¥1.08 billion was from films and spin-offs. TV shows and associated business income totaled ¥517 million, a year-over-year increase of 36.13 per cent.

The company's growth was also evidenced in recent mergers and acquisitions, as in 2013 it merged

EXHIBIT 1 BALANCE SHEET (IN ¥ MILLION)					
	2014	2013	2012	2011	2010
Current assets					
Cash and cash equivalents	1 829	1 137	642	531	847
Notes receivable	6	–	–	–	–
Accounts receivable	1 612	1 147	1 001	410	458
Payment in advance	921	462	386	399	106
Interest receivable	–	–	–	0	1
Other receivable	50	67	53	7	20
Inventory	816	575	701	543	226
Non-current assets within one year	4	–	–	–	–
Other current assets	11	4	12	12	4
Subtotal – current assets	**5 250**	**3 393**	**2 794**	**1 902**	**1 662**
Non-current assets					
Available for sale	1 695	2 189	588	–	–
Long-term receivables	67	41	32	14	10
Long-term investment	784	878	386	319	184
Fixed assets	354	317	273	117	69
Intangible assets	74	2	–	20	–
Goodwill	1 486	354	33	77	77
Long-term deferred expenses	20	4	4	4	7
Deferred tax assets	89	35	28	10	15
Subtotal – non-current assets	4 569	3 819	1 344	561	360
Total assets	**9 819**	**7 212**	**4 138**	**2 464**	**2 022**
Current liabilities					
Short-term loans	785	668	593	–	–
Accounts payable	311	501	496	195	254
Receipt in advance	305	77	88	138	82
Accrued payroll	24	5	4	3	3
Tax payable	425	256	93	70	41

	2014	2013	2012	2011	2010
Interest payable	18	27	23	3	–
Other payable	303	110	23	48	72
Non-current liabilities within one year	142	–	–	–	–
Other current liabilities	600	600	300	300	–
Subtotal – current liabilities	**2 913**	**2 243**	**1 621**	**756**	**452**
Non-current liabilities					
Long-term loan	849	502	300	–	–
Long-term payable	0	–	–	–	–
Deferred tax liabilities	364	506	93	–	–
Other non-current liabilities	–	2	–	–	–
Subtotal – non-current liabilities	1 225	1 011	393	–	–
Total liabilities	**4 139**	**3 254**	**2 013**	**756**	**452**
Shareholders' equity					
Share capital	1 242	1 210	605	605	336
Capital surplus	830	1 632	989	710	979
Surplus reserve	247	137	68	40	32
Accumulated profits	1 836	964	458	333	205
Shareholders' equity attributable to parent company	5 037	3 942	2 120	1 687	1 552
Non-controlling interests	643	16	5	21	18
Total shareholders' equity	5 680	3 958	2 125	1 708	1 570
Total liabilities and shareholders' equity	**9 819**	**7 212**	**4 138**	**2 464**	**2 022**

Source: Company documents.

EXHIBIT 2   INCOME STATEMENT (IN ¥ MILLION)

	2014	2013	2012	2011	2010
Total operating revenue	2 389	2 014	1 386	892	1 072
Operating revenue	2 389	2 014	1 386	892	1 072
Total operating cost	1 636	1 565	1 188	654	890
Operating cost	934	910	685	377	566
Business tax and surcharges	14	20	40	41	34
Selling expense	330	383	281	154	232
G&A expense	230	95	79	78	58
Financial expenses	99	73	61	–8	–12
Asset impairment loss	30	84	43	12	13
Investment income	426	374	56	6	1
Operating profits	1 179	823	254	245	183
Non-operating income	103	82	68	33	15
Non-operating losses	3	7	1	4	7
Non-current assets disposal loss	0	2	0	0	0
Gross profit	1 279	898	321	273	190
Income taxes	245	225	80	68	40
Net profit	1 034	673	241	205	150

	2014	2013	2012	2011	2010
Net profit attributable to parent company	897	665	244	203	149
Non-controlling interests	138	8	–4	3	1
EPS					
Basic EPS	0.73	0.55	0.40	0.34	0.44
Diluted EPS	0.73	0.55	0.40	0.34	0.44
Other comprehensive income	–413	1 242	–	–	–
Comprehensive income	621	1 915	241	205	150
Comprehensive income attributable to parent company	483	1 907	244	203	149
Comprehensive income attributable to non-controlling shareholders	138	8	–4	3	1

Notes: G&A expenses: general and administrative expenses; EPS: earnings per share.

Source: Company documents.

with Yinhan and purchased TV producer Zhejiang Changsheng and Internet entertainment company Maizuo.com. Said Dennis Wang:

> *Financial performance for us is very easy to measure. Other indicators we use are box office revenues and the new directors we have signed up. If, for example, we sign up two or three new directors each year, we would think it is a success. Of course we use accounting metrics, like profit. But also, we have other key performance indicators such as number of visitors for Internet entertainment sectors, and in live entertainment it is how many sites are under construction.*

Organization and culture

In 2015, Huayi employed 1 500 staff across its three divisions, including its recent US subsidiary based in Hollywood. The senior management team was very small and was led by board chair and CEO Dennis Wang, President James Wang and CFO Brenda Hu.

Dennis Wang was responsible for the company's overall strategic planning and financial management and oversaw the company's Live Entertainment division. James Wang was responsible for the company's overall operations and Visual Entertainment division. Hu, who joined Huayi in 2005 and led the company's IPO in 2009, was CFO and in charge of the company's Internet Entertainment division.

Huayi's financial forecasting and strategic planning was very short term due to the constantly changing nature of the entertainment business in China.

With movies, in particular, it was still largely impossible to predict the right formula for box office success. Newly emerging Internet companies appearing on the scene were also trying to expand into producing movies and crowding the marketplace. While the management team looked ahead as far as three to five years trying to determine how to best diversify and grow, its focus was on executing a one-year strategy and adjusting quarter by quarter. Said Hu:

> *We have some principles of how we do business, but it's really difficult to do even a three-year business plan. We focus on a one-year period. We have our plan – but we don't have a budget. It is very short, two to three pages high level, with some targets. Not a formal document. It just changes so, so fast. We have to move very fast, as a management team, sitting around the table to discuss that document, or what goes in that document or not? We do it once a year, with all the management team. But we have daily communication.*

From a business standpoint, Dennis Wang focused on personally managing mergers and acquisitions, relying heavily on the company's professional managers to run the day-to-day operations. His educational background was a major in mass media and art studies from New York State University, so self-admittedly finance was not his strong suit. He was a passionate art collector, with his own personal gallery. His strength was to be hands-on in the recruitment of movie directors and devoting his energy to "future visioning." In spite of his title, he had no fixed role or responsibility and only visited his office a half dozen times a year at most, preferring instead to spend his time with film artists to get ideas and inspiration. He said:

> I bring romance and joy to the table, visioning the future of the company. I love my team; Huayi is more like a happy family. . . . My leadership style is more random, like painting. I don't plan my day. For example, I spent this morning with director Xiaogang Feng, chatting about his future and his new movies. I had a good time but also figured out where Huayi is moving towards.

Although it was over 20 years old, Huayi's corporate culture resembled that of a young start-up enterprise: very small, efficient and active. Its management hierarchy was flat, with very few formal roles and functions. The company used stick incentives to stimulate innovation and attract top talent. For example, when the equity structure of the Internet Entertainment division was revisited, 50 per cent of the stock went to the team. A key concern among the top management team was to retain talent, so deliberate steps were taken to nurture internal "intrapreneurs" and encourage them to start their own companies within the Huayi umbrella.

The company prided itself on its track record for innovation in the industry, proclaiming in its promotional materials to be "taking the road others didn't dare to tread." It claimed ownership of a number of industry firsts, including first to participate in all film development stages from investment to shooting to distribution. Huayi was also the first privately owned TV company to attract external capital, finance films through banks and go public with its IPO.

Next steps

Looking ahead, Dennis Wang wondered from where his company's future growth would come and what action would be needed. Huayi needed to establish a brand presence in North America if it were going to attract future investment on a global scale. He wanted to have controlling interest in whatever lay ahead – something he had not been able to achieve after one year of difficult negotiations with Robinov in the failed Studio 8 deal. This time, he was also looking for a more "roll up the sleeves," hands-on partner – someone who wanted to be more actively engaged in the entire process from film conception to release. In China, JVs were more collaborative. Producers and directors took an active role acquiring actors and developing the project early in the process. Dennis Wang discovered by comparison that Hollywood was not as eager to work together until all of the financial and legal negotiations had been finalized. And even then, in the movie business there were no guarantees the personal chemistry that was so important to him would be right. He said:

> I think finding a business partner depends to some extent on luck and fate. Huayi wasn't able to become a controlling shareholder of Studio 8 as I had hoped. The ideal partner for me would be someone who does both movie production and distribution. I sensed a stronger chemistry with STX . . . [but] I haven't stopped looking at other American film companies; I think China has a great chance to enter the US market.

STX was different than other US film companies in the sense that it was founded by a number of new entrepreneurs. And it was, in fact, doing both movie production and distribution – only a few of the large US companies did both. Dennis Wang wondered if this would bode well for a successful JV. Why had no foreign film company ever been successful in Hollywood? Could Huayi break this pattern?

INDEX